Contemporary Literary Criticism

Guide to Gale Literary Criticism Series

For criticism on	Consult these Gale series
Authors now living or who died after December 31, 1999	*CONTEMPORARY LITERARY CRITICISM (CLC)*
Authors who died between 1900 and 1999	*TWENTIETH-CENTURY LITERARY CRITICISM (TCLC)*
Authors who died between 1800 and 1899	*NINETEENTH-CENTURY LITERATURE CRITICISM (NCLC)*
Authors who died between 1400 and 1799	*LITERATURE CRITICISM FROM 1400 TO 1800 (LC)* *SHAKESPEAREAN CRITICISM (SC)*
Authors who died before 1400	*CLASSICAL AND MEDIEVAL LITERATURE CRITICISM (CMLC)*
Authors of books for children and young adults	*CHILDREN'S LITERATURE REVIEW (CLR)*
Dramatists	*DRAMA CRITICISM (DC)*
Poets	*POETRY CRITICISM (PC)*
Short story writers	*SHORT STORY CRITICISM (SSC)*
Literary topics and movements	*HARLEM RENAISSANCE: A GALE CRITICAL COMPANION (HR)* *THE BEAT GENERATION: A GALE CRITICAL COMPANION (BG)*
Asian American writers of the last two hundred years	*ASIAN AMERICAN LITERATURE (AAL)*
Black writers of the past two hundred years	*BLACK LITERATURE CRITICISM (BLC)* *BLACK LITERATURE CRITICISM SUPPLEMENT (BLCS)*
Hispanic writers of the late nineteenth and twentieth centuries	*HISPANIC LITERATURE CRITICISM (HLC)* *HISPANIC LITERATURE CRITICISM SUPPLEMENT (HLCS)*
Native North American writers and orators of the eighteenth, nineteenth, and twentieth centuries	*NATIVE NORTH AMERICAN LITERATURE (NNAL)*
Major authors from the Renaissance to the present	*WORLD LITERATURE CRITICISM, 1500 TO THE PRESENT (WLC)* *WORLD LITERATURE CRITICISM SUPPLEMENT (WLCS)*

ISSN 0091-3421

Volume 213

Contemporary Literary Criticism

Criticism of the Works
of Today's Novelists, Poets, Playwrights,
Short Story Writers, Scriptwriters, and
Other Creative Writers

Jeffrey W. Hunter
PROJECT EDITOR

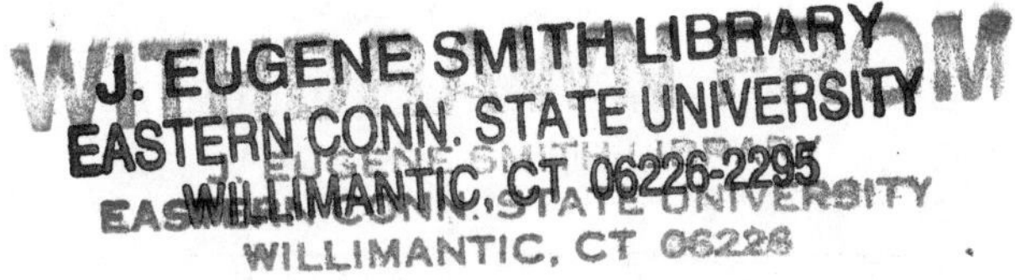

THOMSON
GALE

Detroit • New York • San Francisco • San Diego • New Haven, Conn. • Waterville, Maine • London • Munich

Contemporary Literary Criticism, Vol. 213

Project Editor
Jeffrey W. Hunter

Editorial
Jessica Bomarito, Kathy D. Darrow, Jelena O. Krstović, Michelle Lee, Rahelle Mucha, Thomas J. Schoenberg, Noah Schusterbauer, Lawrence J. Trudeau, Russel Whitaker

Data Capture
Francis Monroe, Gwen Tucker

Indexing Services
Laurie Andriot

Rights and Acquisitions
Margaret Abendroth, Ron Montgomery, Jessica Schultz

Imaging and Multimedia
Dean Dauphinais, Leitha Etheridge-Sims, Lezlie Light, Mike Logusz, Dan Newell, Christine O'Bryan, Kelly A. Quin, Denay Wilding, Robyn Young

Composition and Electronic Prepress
Kathy Sauer

Manufacturing
Rhonda Dover

Associate Product Manager
Marc Cormier

For more information, contact
Thomson Gale
27500 Drake Rd.
Farmington Hills, MI 48331-3535
Or you can visit our internet site at
http://www.gale.com

LIBRARY OF CONGRESS CATALOG CARD NUMBER 76-46132

ISBN 0-7876-7983-6
ISSN 0091-3421

Printed in the United States of America
10 9 8 7 6 5 4 3 2 1

Contents

Preface

Named "one of the twenty-five most distinguished reference titles published during the past twenty-five years" by *Reference Quarterly*, the *Contemporary Literary Criticism* (*CLC*) series provides readers with critical commentary and general information on more than 2,000 authors now living or who died after December 31, 1999. Volumes published from 1973 through 1999 include authors who died after December 31, 1959. Previous to the publication of the first volume of *CLC* in 1973, there was no ongoing digest monitoring scholarly and popular sources of critical opinion and explication of modern literature. *CLC,* therefore, has fulfilled an essential need, particularly since the complexity and variety of contemporary literature makes the function of criticism especially important to today's reader.

Scope of the Series

CLC provides significant passages from published criticism of works by creative writers. Since many of the authors covered in *CLC* inspire continual critical commentary, writers are often represented in more than one volume. There is, of course, no duplication of reprinted criticism.

Authors are selected for inclusion for a variety of reasons, among them the publication or dramatic production of a critically acclaimed new work, the reception of a major literary award, revival of interest in past writings, or the adaptation of a literary work to film or television.

Attention is also given to several other groups of writers—authors of considerable public interest—about whose work criticism is often difficult to locate. These include mystery and science fiction writers, literary and social critics, foreign authors, and authors who represent particular ethnic groups.

Each *CLC* volume contains individual essays and reviews taken from hundreds of book review periodicals, general magazines, scholarly journals, monographs, and books. Entries include critical evaluations spanning from the beginning of an author's career to the most current commentary. Interviews, feature articles, and other published writings that offer insight into the author's works are also presented. Students, teachers, librarians, and researchers will find that the general critical and biographical material in *CLC* provides them with vital information required to write a term paper, analyze a poem, or lead a book discussion group. In addition, complete bibliographical citations note the original source and all of the information necessary for a term paper footnote or bibliography.

Organization of the Book

A *CLC* entry consists of the following elements:

- The **Author Heading** cites the name under which the author most commonly wrote, followed by birth and death dates. Also located here are any name variations under which an author wrote, including transliterated forms for authors whose native languages use nonroman alphabets. If the author wrote consistently under a pseudonym, the pseudonym will be listed in the author heading and the author's actual name given in parenthesis on the first line of the biographical and critical information. Uncertain birth or death dates are indicated by question marks. Single-work entries are preceded by a heading that consists of the most common form of the title in English translation (if applicable) and the original date of composition.

- A **Portrait of the Author** is included when available.

- The **Introduction** contains background information that introduces the reader to the author, work, or topic that is the subject of the entry.

- The list of **Principal Works** is ordered chronologically by date of first publication and lists the most important works by the author. The genre and publication date of each work is given. In the case of foreign authors whose works have been translated into English, the English-language version of the title follows in brackets. Unless otherwise indicated, dramas are dated by first performance, not first publication.

- Reprinted **Criticism** is arranged chronologically in each entry to provide a useful perspective on changes in critical evaluation over time. The critic's name and the date of composition or publication of the critical work are given at the beginning of each piece of criticism. Unsigned criticism is preceded by the title of the source in which it appeared. All titles by the author featured in the text are printed in boldface type. Footnotes are reprinted at the end of each essay or excerpt. In the case of excerpted criticism, only those footnotes that pertain to the excerpted texts are included.

- A complete **Bibliographical Citation** of the original essay or book precedes each piece of criticism. Source citations in the Literary Criticism Series follow University of Chicago Press style, as outlined in *The Chicago Manual of Style,* 14th ed. (Chicago: The University of Chicago Press, 1993).

- Critical essays are prefaced by brief **Annotations** explicating each piece.

- Whenever possible, a recent **Author Interview** accompanies each entry.

- An annotated bibliography of **Further Reading** appears at the end of each entry and suggests resources for additional study. In some cases, significant essays for which the editors could not obtain reprint rights are included here. Boxed material following the further reading list provides references to other biographical and critical sources on the author in series published by Thomson Gale.

Indexes

A **Cumulative Author Index** lists all of the authors that appear in a wide variety of reference sources published by Thomson Gale, including *CLC.* A complete list of these sources is found facing the first page of the Author Index. The index also includes birth and death dates and cross references between pseudonyms and actual names.

A **Cumulative Nationality Index** lists all authors featured in *CLC* by nationality, followed by the number of the *CLC* volume in which their entry appears.

A **Cumulative Topic Index** lists the literary themes and topics treated in the series as well as in *Literature Criticism from 1400 to 1800, Nineteenth-Century Literature Criticism, Twentieth-Century Literary Criticism,* and the *Contemporary Literary Criticism* Yearbook, which was discontinued in 1998.

An alphabetical **Title Index** accompanies each volume of *CLC.* Listings of titles by authors covered in the given volume are followed by the author's name and the corresponding page numbers where the titles are discussed. English translations of foreign titles and variations of titles are cross-referenced to the title under which a work was originally published. Titles of novels, dramas, nonfiction books, and poetry, short story, or essay collections are printed in italics, while individual poems, short stories, and essays are printed in roman type within quotation marks.

In response to numerous suggestions from librarians, Thomson Gale also produces an annual cumulative title index that alphabetically lists all titles reviewed in *CLC* and is available to all customers. Additional copies of this index are available upon request. Librarians and patrons will welcome this separate index; it saves shelf space, is easy to use, and is recyclable upon receipt of the next edition.

Citing *Contemporary Literary Criticism*

When citing criticism reprinted in the Literary Criticism Series, students should provide complete bibliographic information so that the cited essay can be located in the original print or electronic source. Students who quote directly from reprinted criticism may use any accepted bibliographic format, such as University of Chicago Press style or Modern Language Association (MLA) style. Both the MLA and the University of Chicago formats are acceptable and recognized as being the current standards for citations. It is important, however, to choose one format for all citations; do not mix the two formats within a list of citations.

The examples below follow recommendations for preparing a bibliography set forth in *The Chicago Manual of Style,* 14th ed. (Chicago: The University of Chicago Press, 1993); the first example pertains to material drawn from periodicals, the second to material reprinted from books:

Morrison, Jago. "Narration and Unease in Ian McEwan's Later Fiction." *Critique* 42, no. 3 (spring 2001): 253-68. Reprinted in *Contemporary Literary Criticism.* Vol. 169, edited by Janet Witalec, 212-20. Detroit: Gale, 2003.

Brossard, Nicole. "Poetic Politics." In *The Politics of Poetic Form: Poetry and Public Policy,* edited by Charles Bernstein, 73-82. New York: Roof Books, 1990. Reprinted in *Contemporary Literary Criticism.* Vol. 169, edited by Janet Witalec, 3-8. Detroit: Gale, 2003.

The examples below follow recommendations for preparing a works cited list set forth in the *MLA Handbook for Writers of Research Papers,* 5th ed. (New York: The Modern Language Association of America, 1999); the first example pertains to material drawn from periodicals, the second to material reprinted from books:

Morrison, Jago. "Narration and Unease in Ian McEwan's Later Fiction." *Critique* 42.3 (spring 2001): 253-68. Reprinted in *Contemporary Literary Criticism.* Ed. Janet Witalec. Vol. 169. Detroit: Gale, 2003. 212-20.

Brossard, Nicole. "Poetic Politics." *The Politics of Poetic Form: Poetry and Public Policy.* Ed. Charles Bernstein. New York: Roof Books, 1990. 73-82. Reprinted in *Contemporary Literary Criticism.* Ed. Janet Witalec. Vol. 169. Detroit: Gale, 2003. 3-8.

Suggestions are Welcome

Readers who wish to suggest new features, topics, or authors to appear in future volumes, or who have other suggestions or comments are cordially invited to call, write, or fax the Associate Product Manager:

Associate Product Manager, Literary Criticism Series
Thomson Gale
27500 Drake Road
Farmington Hills, MI 48331-3535
1-800-347-4253 (GALE)
Fax: 248-699-8983

Acknowledgments

The editors wish to thank the copyright holders of the criticism included in this volume and the permissions managers of many book and magazine publishing companies for assisting us in securing reproduction rights. We are also grateful to the staffs of the Detroit Public Library, the Library of Congress, the University of Detroit Mercy Library, Wayne State University Purdy/Kresge Library Complex, and the University of Michigan Libraries for making their resources available to us. Following is a list of the copyright holders who have granted us permission to reproduce material in this volume of *CLC*. Every effort has been made to trace copyright, but if omissions have been made, please let us know.

COPYRIGHTED MATERIAL IN *CLC*, VOLUME 213, WAS REPRODUCED FROM THE FOLLOWING PERIODICALS:

American Prospect, v. 14, April, 2003. Copyright © 2003 The American Prospect, Inc. All rights reserved. Reproduced with permission from *The American Prospect,* 11 Beacon Street, Suite 1120, Boston, MA 02108.—***American Quarterly,*** v. 51, September, 1999. Copyright © 1999 The Johns Hopkins University Press. Reproduced by permission.—***ANQ,*** v. 14, summer, 2001. Copyright © 2001 by Helen Dwight Reid Educational Foundation. Reproduced with permission of the Helen Dwight Reid Educational Foundation, published by Heldref Publications, 1319 18th Street, NW, Washington, DC 20036-1802.—***Antioch Review,*** v. 58, summer, 2000; v. 61, summer, 2003. Copyright © 2000, 2003 by the Antioch Review Inc. Both reproduced by permission of the editors.—***ARIEL,*** v. 21, April, 1990 for "Projective Verse as a Mode of Socio-Linguistic Protest" by Anthony Kellman. Copyright © 1990 The Board of Governors, The University of Calgary. Reproduced by permission of the publisher and the author.—***Booklist,*** v. 92, October 15, 1995; v. 93, January 1-15, 1997; v. 96, June 1-15, 2000; v. 98, May 1, 2002; v. 99, December 1, 2002; v. 100, September 15, 2003. Copyright © 1995, 1997, 2000, 2002, 2003 by the American Library Association. All reproduced by permission.—***Callaloo,*** v. 23, 2000; v. 26, 2003. Copyright © 2000, 2003 The Johns Hopkins University Press. Both reproduced by permission.—***Christian Century,*** v. 118, May 2, 2001. Copyright © 2001 by the Christian Century Foundation. All rights reserved. Reproduced by permission.—***College Literature,*** v. 29, winter, 2002. Copyright © 2002 by West Chester University. Reproduced by permission.—***Commonweal,*** v. 128, April 20, 2001. Copyright © 2001 Commonweal Publishing Co., Inc. Reproduced by permission of Commonweal Foundation.—***Comparative Literature Studies,*** v. 41, 2004. University Park: The Pennsylvania State University Press, 2004. Copyright © 2004 by The Pennsylvania State University. Reproduced by permission of the publisher.—***Critique: Studies in Contemporary Fiction,*** v. 38, summer, 1997; v. 41, summer, 2000; v. 42, winter, 2001; v. 42, summer, 2001; v. 44, winter, 2003; v. 44, summer, 2003; v. 46, fall, 2004; v. 46, winter, 2005. Copyright © 1997, 2000, 2001, 2003, 2004, 2005 by Helen Dwight Reid Educational Foundation. All reproduced with permission of the Helen Dwight Reid Educational Foundation, published by Heldref Publications, 1319 18th Street, NW, Washington, DC 20036-1802.—***Explicator,*** v. 58, winter, 2000; v. 59, summer, 2001. Copyright © 2000, 2001 by Helen Dwight Reid Educational Foundation. Both reproduced with permission of the Helen Dwight Reid Educational Foundation, published by Heldref Publications, 1319 18th Street, NW, Washington, DC 20036-1802.—***Journal of Modern Literature,*** v. 25, winter, 2001-2002. Copyright © 2002 Indiana University Press. Reproduced by permission.—***Kirkus Reviews,*** v. 70, May 1, 2002. Copyright © 2002 by The Kirkus Service, Inc. All rights reserved. Reproduced by permission of the publisher, *Kirkus Reviews* and Kirkus Associates, L. P.—***Library Journal,*** v. 125, July, 2000; v. 127, December, 2002; v. 126, October 1, 2001; v. 127, June 1, 2002. Copyright © 2000, 2001, 2002 by Reed Elsevier, USA. All reprinted by permission of the publisher.—***Literature/Film Quarterly,*** v. 29, 2001. Copyright © 2001 Salisbury State College. Reproduced by permission.—***Modern Drama,*** v. 46, fall, 2003. Copyright © 2003 by the University of Toronto, Graduate Centre for Study of Drama. Reproduced by permission.—***Modern Fiction Studies,*** v. 50, summer, 2004; v. 50, fall, 2004. Copyright © 2004 The Johns Hopkins University Press. Both reproduced by permission.—***Nation,*** v. 277, December 8, 2003. Copyright © 2003 by The Nation Magazine/ The Nation Company, Inc. Reproduced by permission.—***National Review,*** v. 52, August 28, 2000. Copyright © 2000 by National Review, Inc, 215 Lexington Avenue, New York, NY 10016. Reproduced by permission.—***New Leader,*** v. 86, March-April, 2003. Copyright © 2003 by The American Labor Conference on International Affairs, Inc. Reproduced by permission.—***New Statesman,*** v. 13, May 29, 2000; v. 14, February 5, 2001; v. 14, April 23, 2001; v. 14, October 15, 2001; v. 15, March 11, 2002; v. 15, June 17, 2002; v. 15, September 2, 2002; v. 15, September 9, 2002; v. 16, April 7, 2003; v. 16, May 26, 2003; v. 16, September 8, 2003. Copyright © 2000, 2001, 2002, 2003 New Statesman, Ltd. All reproduced by permission.—***Publishers Weekly,*** v. 247, March 6, 2000; v. 249, May 20, 2002; v. 249, December 9, 2002; v. 250, October 13, 2003. Copyright © 2000, 2002, 2003 by Reed Publishing USA. All reproduced from *Publishers Weekly,* published by the Bowker Magazine Group of Cahners Publishing Co., a division of Reed Publishing USA, by permission.—***Review of Contemporary Fiction,*** v. 23, summer, 2003. Copyright © 2003 *The Review of*

Contemporary Fiction. Reproduced by permission.—***Southwest Review,*** v. 83, 1998; v. 87, 2002. Copyright © 1998, 2002 Southern Methodist University. All rights reserved. Both reproduced by permission.—***Spectator,*** v. 286, February 10, 2001; v. 286, April 21, 2001; v. 289, August 24, 2002; v. 290, October 19, 2002; v. 292, June 7, 2003; v. 293, September 6, 2003; v. 293, September 13, 2003. Copyright © 2001, 2002, 2003 by *The Spectator*. All reproduced by permission of *The Spectator*.—***Studies in the Novel,*** v. 31, winter, 1999; v. 36, fall, 2004; v. 37, spring, 2005. Copyright © 1999, 2004, 2005 by North Texas State University. All reproduced by permission.—***Twentieth Century Literature,*** v. 48, fall, 2002. Copyright 2002, Hofstra University Press. Reproduced by permission.—***Virginia Quarterly Review,*** v. 77, summer, 2001. Copyright 2001, by *The Virginia Quarterly Review*, The University of Virginia. Reproduced by permission of the publisher.—***World Literature Today,*** v. 71, winter, 1997; v. 75, winter, 2001; v. 76, summer, 2002. Copyright ©1997, 2001, 2002 by *World Literature Today*. All reproduced by permission of the publisher.

PHOTOGRAPHS AND ILLUSTRATIONS APPEARING IN *CLC,* VOLUME 213, WERE RECEIVED FROM THE FOLLOWING SOURCES:

Amis, Martin, Madrid, Spain, June, 2004, photograph by Sergio Barrenechea. AP/Wide World Photos.—Baraka, Amiri, photograph by Mike Derer. Copyright © AP/Wide World Photos.—DeLillo, Don, photograph by Jim Cooper. AP/Wide World Photos.

Thomson Gale Literature Product Advisory Board

The members of the Thomson Gale Literature Product Advisory Board—reference librarians from public and academic library systems—represent a cross-section of our customer base and offer a variety of informed perspectives on both the presentation and content of our literature products. Advisory board members assess and define such quality issues as the relevance, currency, and usefulness of the author coverage, critical content, and literary topics included in our series; evaluate the layout, presentation, and general quality of our printed volumes; provide feedback on the criteria used for selecting authors and topics covered in our series; provide suggestions for potential enhancements to our series; identify any gaps in our coverage of authors or literary topics, recommending authors or topics for inclusion; analyze the appropriateness of our content and presentation for various user audiences, such as high school students, undergraduates, graduate students, librarians, and educators; and offer feedback on any proposed changes/enhancements to our series. We wish to thank the following advisors for their advice throughout the year.

Barbara M. Bibel
Librarian
Oakland Public Library
Oakland, California

Dr. Toby Burrows
Principal Librarian
The Scholars' Centre
University of Western Australia Library
Nedlands, Western Australia

Celia C. Daniel
Associate Reference Librarian
Howard University Libraries
Washington, D.C.

David M. Durant
Reference Librarian
Joyner Library
East Carolina University
Greenville, North Carolina

Nancy T. Guidry
Librarian
Bakersfield Community College
Bakersfield, California

Heather Martin
Arts & Humanities Librarian
University of Alabama at Birmingham, Sterne Library
Birmingham, Alabama

Susan Mikula
Librarian
Indiana Free Library
Indiana, Pennsylvania

Thomas Nixon
Humanities Reference Librarian
University of North Carolina at Chapel Hill, Davis Library
Chapel Hill, North Carolina

Mark Schumacher
Jackson Library
University of North Carolina at Greensboro
Greensboro, North Carolina

Gwen Scott-Miller
Assistant Director
Sno-Isle Regional Library System
Marysville, Washington

Martin Amis
1949-

(Full name Martin Louis Amis) English novelist, short story writer, nonfiction writer, essayist, and memoirist.

The following entry provides an overview of Amis's career through 2005. For additional information on his life and works, see *CLC,* Volumes 4, 9, 38, 62, and 101.

INTRODUCTION

Amis is acknowledged as one of England's most widely-read contemporary authors. Amis's writing contains an irreverent wit similar to that of his father's, well-known author Kingsley Amis. Amis utilizes a mixture of profanity, slang, and wry observation to satirize the excesses of contemporary society, commenting on aspects of modern culture that exhibit an obsession with sex, violence, and material gain. Though he is compared favorably with such satirists as Jonathan Swift, critics often condemn Amis for brandishing a juvenile vulgarity in his prose, and his political and moral opinions have garnered a significant amount of controversy.

BIOGRAPHICAL INFORMATION

Born on August 25, 1949, in Oxford, England, Martin is the son of Kingsley Amis, a prominent British novelist and poet, and Hilary Bardwell Amis. After attending over a dozen schools while growing up in England, the United States, and Spain, Amis studied at Exeter College, Oxford. In 1972 he became an editorial assistant at the London *Times Literary Supplement,* and was promoted to the position of fiction and poetry editor two years later. His first novel, *The Rachel Papers,* was published in 1973 and was later awarded the Somerset Maugham Award. In 1975 he joined the editorial staff at *The New Statesman,* eventually becoming the literary editor. He became a staff writer and reviewer for *The London Observer* and was awarded the James Tait Black Memorial Prize for Biography in 2000 for *Experience* (2000), a memoir about his relationship with his father. In 2001 Amis received the National Book Critics Circle Award in the criticism category for *The War against Cliché* (2001). His novel *Yellow Dog* (2003) was considered for the Booker Prize.

MAJOR WORKS

Amis's first novel, *The Rachel Papers,* is a coming-of-age story about a sexually-charged young man on the verge of his twentieth birthday. Sexuality and intimate relationships are identified as prominent themes throughout Amis's work, and the novel's biting wit has earned Amis comparison to one of his literary idols, Vladimir Nabokov. Sexuality is also a primary subject in Amis's second novel, the black comedy *Dead Babies* (1975), in which a group of deviant youths gather at a country home for a weekend filled with sex, drugs, and violence. *Success* (1978) chronicles the troubled relationship between two foster brothers whose origins reside in very different social and economic backgrounds. Reviewers find the theme of rivalry to be another recurring motif in Amis's work. Deemed one of his best novels, *Money* (1984) details the deterioration of John Self, a man consumed by alcohol, greed, and sex. Critics note that the novel incorporates several of Amis's characteristic themes: avarice, excess, self-destruction, sexual obsession, love, identity, and cultural deprivation. Published in 1989, *London Fields* traces the self-destruction of a young woman who claims to have foreseen her death and spends her remaining days with the intention of dying on her own terms.

Utilizing a reverse-time narrative structure, *Time's Arrow* (1991) is the story of Tod Friendly, an American doctor who becomes progressively younger during the course of the novel. He eventually finds himself running a Nazi concentration camp as an infamous "death doctor." *The Information* (1995) satirizes the politics of academia in the story of two middle-aged writers who reflect on the successes and failures of their careers. Amis's foray into the genre of detective thriller, *Night Train* (1997), follows a female police officer on the trail of a murderer. *Experience,* a nonlinear autobiography, focuses on Amis's relationship with his celebrated father. *The War against Cliché* contains a series of essays and reviews in which Amis takes aim at the prevalence of old, stale language in modern literature. He ponders the life and atrocities committed by Josef Stalin in *Koba the Dread* (2002), and devotes significant attention to the motives of Stalinist sympathizers, such as his father, Kingsley. *Yellow Dog* focuses on the character of Xan Meo, an upstanding citizen and husband who transforms into a vile and abusive sexual deviant after suffering a serious head injury. The novel includes several other characters who exhibit a similar dichotomy of primitive and civilized impulses.

CRITICAL RECEPTION

Amis has garnered a mixed response from critics, but remains one of the best-known and most popular writers in England. In fact, he is viewed as a celebrity, and his journalism and essays attract a great deal of attention from readers and British press alike. Some reviewers contend that the publicity about his personal life—his relationship with his father, his public feuds with other literary figures, and his marriages—tends to obscure the value of his literary achievements. Commentators often discuss the influence of Amis's father on his life and work; Amis himself has often written about his relationship with his father, particularly in his memoir *Experience.* His narrative experimentation is another area of critical study. Reviewers have discussed him as a postmodern writer, focusing on the function and implications of his fractured narratives. His later fiction has been deemed disappointing by many critics, particularly in relationship to his earlier work; several reviewers perceive these later novels and memoirs to be sophomoric, self-aggrandizing, and obsessed with fame. Others regard him as a literate, perceptive, and clever writer who continues to provide a valuable outlook on contemporary society. His insights as a social and literary critic are widely acknowledged, but such efforts have been unfavorably compared to his early works of fiction. In recent years, his perspective on politics and contemporary culture has generated controversy among his literary peers, specifically his view of the September 11th terrorist attacks and its impact on writers. Amis has been accused of being out of touch and failing to engage with the most important political and social issues of our time. Although critics may dispute the degree and character of Amis's abilities and insights, they concur that he has had a profound impact on contemporary British letters.

PRINCIPAL WORKS

The Rachel Papers (novel) 1973
Dead Babies (novel) 1975
Success (novel) 1978
Other People: A Mystery Story (novel) 1981
Money: A Suicide Note (novel) 1984
The Moronic Inferno and Other Visits to America (essays and interviews) 1986
Einstein's Monsters (essays and short stories) 1987
London Fields (novel) 1989
Time's Arrow; or, The Nature of the Offence (novel) 1991
Visiting Mrs. Nabokov and Other Excursions (essays) 1993
The Information (novel) 1995
Night Train (novel) 1997
Heavy Water and Other Stories (short stories) 1998
Experience (memoirs) 2000
The War against Cliché: Essays and Reviews, 1971-2000 (essays) 2001
Koba the Dread: Laughter and the Twenty Million (history) 2002
Yellow Dog (novel) 2003
Pornoland [with Stefano de Luigi] (nonfiction) 2004

CRITICISM

Peter Stokes (essay date summer 1997)

SOURCE: Stokes, Peter. "Martin Amis and the Postmodern Suicide: Tracing the Postnuclear Narrative at the Fin de Millennium." *Critique* 38, no. 4 (summer 1997): 300-11.

[*In the following essay, Stokes considers Amis's recent work within the context of postmodern fiction and claims that the author's fractured narratives reflect his anxiety over a possible global nuclear apocalypse.*]

When, in Martin Amis's novel, ***Time's Arrow,*** Tod Friendly's soul encounters its physiognomy for the first time in a bathroom mirror by virtue of a simple flick of the switch on a wall, it remarks: "It *would* have to happen at the speed of light." "I expected to look like shit" the soul continues, "but this was ridiculous. Jesus. We really *do* look like shit" (10). Self-revelation at the speed of light, that is what the postmodern moment promises. Here we find ourselves face to face with what Arthur Kroker and David Cook in *The Postmodern Scene* refer to as, "a certain literary mood,"—or, "a way of participating directly in the ruins within and without of late twentieth-century experience" where "everything approaches the end of Einstein's world at the speed of light" (Kroker ii, iv). How will this ending come? What, if anything, will remain?

I want to approach those questions through the vortices of Amis's recent fiction—a body of work that owes much to its late postmodern forebears in Borges and Nabokov. Amis's work is particularly important and deserving of attention because it is, I believe, the nearest postmodern fiction has come to offering something other than a mere critique of the mediating effects of language and the consequences of such a language for contemporary notions of subject construction. In Amis's work, such a critique is undeniably present, but rather than signaling an exhaustion of literature's possibilities—to recall John Barth's famous phrase—Amis's critique opens up a space for a productive potential in the radical indeterminacy of the postmodern subject and postmodern knowledge production. And Amis locates that productive potential, particularly, within the endlessness of apocalyptic discourse. Thus, although language may no longer be thought capable of rendering transparent truths, it is still capable of producing, in Foucault's language, *effects*. Amis's fiction, then, investigates the social ends of a postmodern literature cast not as a discourse of truth or realism, but as a discourse of mediated truths or truth-effects. Amis's novels suggest that the distance between literary discourse and other social discourses may not be so great, and thus these novels exploit the self-reflexive character of literature as a means of revising and redirecting nuclear apocalyptic discourse. In so doing, Amis argues that postmodern subjects serve a critical function in the reproduction of apocalyptic discourse—a function through which critical changes in the development of that discourse are effected.

What I will be examining in Amis's work, then, is the power of narrativity as a means of recursive agency and the narrativization of that power vis-à-vis the disappearance of the subject and the threat of nuclear apocalypse. En route, I want to make two claims for Amis's fiction: first, that it problematizes, relativizes, and disseminates the univocal authority over text and meaning that is commonly assigned to the author. Amis's work figures authorial voices as necessarily composite. His novels value that fragmented narrative authority positively by playfully engaging with the consequences of plagiarism and appropriation—where narrative becomes not an end point, an ultimate signification through the irrevocable punctuation of the novel's final period, but a place to begin writing new versions of literature's histories and futures, an empowering literary ellipsis writing itself out of a network of composite voices. Second, I want to argue that Amis's fiction positions literature as anything but an exhausted activity by mining a critical recursive agency in the loss of truth and the production of truth-effects: an agency that Amis characterizes as being marked by a rearticulation of the function of the author and authority generally.

In the post-Enlightenment era, at least, no other figure has been as important to the value and reception of a work as its author. In Amis's recent novels, though—novels that frequently figure authors as their narrators—that narrative authority is under serious question. In fact, Amis does much in his fiction to problematize the distance between himself and the narrators of his novels, sometimes even appearing in those novels himself as a character—a character who is also a writer. His recent fiction, then, takes as its starting point the problematization of authority and identity, thus enabling him to comment at length on the apparent disappearance of the subject in the postmodern moment. As Amis explains in a recent interview with the novelist Will Self in *The Mississippi Review,* "What people are up to now is Post-Modernist, in the sense that they are loose beings in search of a form. And the art that they bring to this now, to shape their lives, is TV" (151). In his novel ***London Fields,*** Amis pays particular attention to the extent to which social responsibility has been abdicated in the postmodern era in part because of the mediating effects of television. In ***London Fields*** he in fact characterizes the contemporary era as an "age of mediated atrocity" (214). Television, in that novel, is simultaneously positioned as a window reflecting back consumer desires and a protection against all manner of catastrophic occurrences around the world. In order to explore the problem of giving form to a life, then, Amis examines the effects of language and other representational mediums in constructing and reconstructing subjects, authors, and authority alike.

Of course, effecting a change in the historical development of the author's function is no easy thing to achieve. For centuries the author has represented a means for the transference of authority itself: operating as what Foucault—in "What Is an Author?"—calls "a certain functional principal by which, in our culture, one limits, excludes and chooses; in short, by which one impedes the free circulation, the free manipulation, the free composition, decomposition, and recomposition of fiction" (118-19). The postmodern author, in Amis's fiction, attempts to function in a different way, by problematizing and disseminating the authority of the text rather than immobilizing it. Amis clearly wants to free literature from its connections to the author. He achieves that, to a certain extent, not by killing the author but by relativizing the power of the author's authority over the text and by questioning the kinds of truths that authority gives form to.

What concerns Amis in his novels and stories of the 1980s, however, is not merely the problem of the death of the author, but, increasingly, the possibility of the death of literature. Although the narrative of ***Money*** (1984) constitutes a purported suicide note, the short stories that make up ***Einstein's Monsters*** (1987) turn narratives of individual suicide into metaphors of global nuclear suicide, and ***London Fields*** (1989) concerns itself with the complex relations between individual suicide and global nuclear apocalypse, between the death of an author and the death of literature. Amis's novels argue that the fragmented character of that postmodern authority figure is a result of the precarious character of literature at the close of the twentieth century—a literature made precarious, in large part, by the tonnage of nuclear weapons pointed toward the sky. Certainly, as Jacques Derrida argues, in "No Apocalypse, Not Now," the literature of the nuclear age is characterized by a "radical precariousness" (27). Nuclear war could, in the blink of an eye, wreak a literary devastation greater in proportion than "even that of Alexandria" (27). In such an event, the literary archive itself would be erased and the author would consequently cease to have any authority at all. Rather than attempt to prohibit the loosening of that authority, and rather than disciplining the apocalyptic threat that nuclear weapons pose to literature. Amis tries to value positively this new lack of fixity. Amis suggests, then, that the author function is being reconfigured in new ways to insure the free circulation of discourse—because the self-reflexive power of literature is capable of revising this endless discourse of apocalypse in ways that explicitly enable its endless unfolding. Amis effects that by destabilizing the author's position, by rendering the author as circulatable, as manipulable, as composable, decomposable, and recomposable as fiction—by turning the author into a text.

The novel ***Money,*** in fact, is marked by an attempt to produce just this effect. The novel concerns the son of an English pub owner, John Self, a former producer of television commercials and the current writer of the suicide note that constitutes the narrative of the novel, who is trying to make his first full-length movie—to be called *Good Money,* or later *Bad Money.* The problem with Self's film, however, is that it has no script. To solve this problem, Self approaches a writer who lives in his neighborhood. As Self describes it, "A guy in a pub pointed him out to me . . . This writer's name, they tell me, is *Martin Amis.* Never heard of him. Do you know his stuff at all?" (71). After brushing up on Amis's background a bit. Self meets the author and asks, "Your dad, he's a writer too, isn't he? Bet that made it easier" (88). "Oh, sure," the Amis character assures him, it's "just like taking over the family pub" (88).

Two points need to be underscored here: first, this novel contains a narrator who addresses his readers (the readers of a novel written by Martin Amis) to ask if they have ever heard of Martin Amis. The effect of that postmodern conceit is to confuse the boundaries separating the author and his characters. To add a further dimension to this confusion, the novel also includes a female character named Martina Twain, suggesting still more bifurcations in the Amis persona within the text. Second, Self indicates that the fictional Martin Amis has a father who is a writer—not unlike the real Martin Amis whose father is, of course, Kingsley Amis. As the narrative of ***Money*** continues, these two Martin Amises become less and less distinguishable. For example, Self later learns that his script writer, Martin Amis, is a known plagiarist—"there'd recently been some cases of plagiarism, of text-theft, which had filtered down to the newspapers and magazines" (235). The same is also true for the real Martin Amis who has commented in public on instances of plagiarism in his own work on several occasions. "So," Self concludes, "Little Martin got caught with his fingers in the till, then, did he. A word criminal. I would bear that in mind" (235).

And so, it goes without saying, must Amis's readers. And so must Amis, whose narrative self is also John Self. Amis himself draws particular attention to this confluence in order to suggest that the narrative voice is always fragmented and driven by conflicting narrative desires. As the fictional Martin Amis describes his theory of narrative to Self during a script session, those conflicting narrative desires necessarily affect the relation between an author and his characters:

> The distance between author and narrator corresponds to the degree to which the author finds the narrator wicked, deluded, pitiful or ridiculous . . . The further down the scale he is, the more liberties you can take with him. You can do what the hell you like to him, really. This creates an appetite for punishment. The author is not free of sadistic impulses.
>
> (246-47)

However true that may be for the fictional Martin Amis, that is certainly an apt description of the author and narrator relation in ***Money***—the novel authored by the real Martin Amis. Self is certainly wicked, deluded, pitiful, and ridiculous, rather low down on the human scale, and Amis pulls no punches in meting out his punishment. But meting out that punishment is by no means a simple assignment when it involves a fictional Martin Amis who is trying to write a script for a movie called *Good Money* or *Bad Money,* all of which occurs in a novel written by Martin Amis called ***Money*** that concerns a narrator called John Self, who, while narrating what comes to be taken for the novel ***Money,*** is trying to make a film called *Good Money,* and who must be punished. As the fictional Martin Amis sums it up, "we're pretty much agreed that the twentieth century is an ironic age—down-ward looking. Even realism, rock-bottom realism, is considered a bit grand for the twentieth century" (248). What that passage indicates is that in the postmodern moment even realism is a matter of representation. And there is no such thing as a value-free representation.

Thus, the fictional Martin Amis asks himself: "Is there a moral philosophy of fiction? When I create a character and put him or her through certain ordeals, what am I up to—morally? Am I accountable?" (260). The interviewable Martin Amis also struggles to answer that question. When, in a 1990 interview with Susan Morrison of *Rolling Stone* magazine, Amis attempted to account for that kind of narrative, he remarked, "Actually, I think in my case, and perhaps this is part of the reason why all this happened, I feel a sort of guilt about creating characters, guilt about making them suffer" (Morrison 98). That is, however, rather reductive reasoning—fixing the narrative's unmistakable origin once again at the author. Pressed by his interviewer to explain the presence of a character called Martin Amis in ***Money*** and another called M. A. in ***London Fields,*** though, Amis responds in an ultimately more self-effacing fashion: "Well, it all comes under the main heading of 'Fucking Around With the Reader'" (98).

In Amis's ***Money,*** then, the author amounts to a strange, not quite lateral, not quite right, triangle composed of the Martin Amis whom the name on the book jacket presumably signifies, the Martin Amis who, in a novel called ***Money*** written by Martin Amis, is called in to work on a film script called *Good Money,* and the John Self who constitutes the narrative voice of the novel ***Money.*** Here, the discrete differences that have traditionally been represented as distinguishing the author from the narrator are, at the very least, problematized. Nothing is fixed, everything is moving like the particles of the atom whose explosion threatens everything so far accumulated within the literary archive. Amis's author—if he is dead—is at least, as this final electrical storm approaches, ready to be galvanized into a new kind of monstrous existence—a kind of Frankenstein's author. But this Einsteinian end, much as John Self's suicide, has not yet come. At the end of ***Money,*** Self has—by virtue of Amis's punishment—been brought down to the depths of a ridiculous poverty, though he has not successfully committed suicide. The novel culminates with Self humiliated, but alive. He learns that he has been the dupe of a financial scam, the plot of which is explained to him by his script writer, Martin Amis. As the narrative comes to a close, Self has, the real Amis explains in a recent interview with Victoria Alexander in *The Antioch Review,* "escaped the novel. He has escaped control of the author figure, me" (586).

At the start of the novel, Self reports the following: "something is waiting to happen to me. I can tell. Recently my life feels like a bloodcurdling joke. Recently my life has taken on *form*" (***Money*** 3). Amis pictures Self, like all people in the postmodern era, as a character in search of form. Yet his entrance into literary form has reduced him to a bloodcurdling joke. By contrast, Self's escape from the novel leaves him altogether "without form" and "more random" (Alexander 587). Although that transformation renders his identity somewhat problematic, "at least," Amis explains to Alexander, "he is not being manipulated" (587). And so Self is left to rewrite his own future. At the novel's close, Self is not just alive, he even realizes that there is still time to make another buck. Just as for Amis there is still time to write another book—and another. Because the postnuclear scene is, in Amis's words, characterized by suspense—a suspense in which no one has any idea how things will turn out—Amis's characters tend to find themselves waiting for an end that does not come. And thus a failed suicide sets the stage for a more elaborate means of self-annihilation—a strategy that mimics the general course of apocalyptic rhetoric itself. And a completed novel on that condition of suspense simply sets the stage for another. Suspense, as Amis's fiction positions it, is simply an on-going fact of life at the close of the twentieth century.

In **"Thinkability,"** for example, Amis remarks, "I was born on August 25, 1949: four days later, the Russians successfully tested their first atom bomb and *deterrence* was in place. So I had those four carefree days, which is more than my juniors ever had" (1). Amis's essay addresses that ever suspenseful state of deterrence in order to estimate its cost—and the cost, according to Amis, in psychological and social terms, is high. Amis's essay, as I indicated earlier, argues that although nuclear weapons continue to pose difficult problems for the international community as a whole, there *are* some writers who "are slowly learning how to write about" those weapons in important ways (4). In Amis's view, such writing necessarily requires commenting on this feeling of suspense. When asked by Philip Hoare in the November 1991 *Details* magazine if recent attempts at disarmament had in any way mitigated the influence of nuclear weapons and the feelings of suspense they provoke or changed the course of nuclear discourse for the better, Amis replied:

> No, I think it's a disaster. Instead of four tons of TNT for every man, woman, and child on the planet, it's now 3.95. We can't change what it's done to the psyche. I think that it has inserted something in us morally. When I read about things that make you scratch your head—how could people be so vile—I think, My God, it might never have happened without

> this implant. It gives a bit more power to the elbow of the man who is smashing in the head of a ninety-year-old woman.
>
> (132)

In ***London Fields*** Amis tries to imagine the end result of such an *implant* on the global community as a whole. What is at stake in that novel is a problem of larger proportion than the death of the author or the formlessness of the subject. Here those threats are compounded by others—the possible destruction of the literary archive, and possibly the destruction of the world.

The narrator of ***London Fields*** is a failed American writer named Samson Young. Sam has arrived in London at the end of the millennium after securing an apartment swap with a successful English novelist, Mark Asprey, who signs his welcome note to Sam, M. A. Sam, who can't—as he explains again and again—make anything up and thus flounders as a writer, soon grows jealous of the many trophies and awards decorating the Asprey home. Reading an Asprey text found around the apartment. Sam becomes demoralized by the incredible success a hack novelist like Asprey enjoys. Sam's own writerly luck changes, however, when he chances upon a true story unfolding before his eyes. He uncovers some diaries that predict the end of the world. He then searches out the diarist and watches as the predictions unfold—and that story, which he records, becomes the narrative of ***London Fields.*** The story is, Sam assures his readers, a "true story," but "unified, dramatic and pretty saleable" (***London Fields*** 1). At the novel's end, after taking a fatal dose of pills, Sam reports feeling—much like Self at the end of ***Money***—"seamless and insubstantial, like a creation. As if someone made me up, for money" (470). Believing that he has once again failed as a writer, Sam appoints his rival, Asprey, as his "literary executor," believing that Asprey will honor his deathbed request to destroy the manuscript, to "throw everything out" (468, 470). And yet Sam goes to his death with a nagging uncertainty, and thus his suicide note to Asprey concludes with the question: "You didn't set me up. Did you?" (468). Asprey is, Amis explains to Will Self, "an anti-writer," successful but terrible—"really," Amis continues, "a deflected parody of the hatred I feel aimed at me" (Self 150).

The answer to Sam's question then, of course, is yes. The ruse of ***London Fields*** is that it appears to be an appropriation—not merely plagiarism, but out-right theft—of another author's work. As Amis's remarks to Will Self indicate, Asprey is another version of himself, another M. A., and Amis has indeed set Sam up—and Sam is indeed a creation, made up, for money. At a variety of levels, then, ***London Fields*** works as a kind of joke about plagiarism, or *text-theft.* Amis, disguised as Asprey, appears to have stolen the novel from Samson Young. In ***London Fields,*** then, as in ***Money,*** Amis attempts to problematize the credibility of narrative authority en route to suggesting that such authority is essentially formless, insubstantial. As with ***Money,*** though, in ***London Fields*** that formlessness is once again valued positively. The text is free to travel, surviving even its author's suicide. Because the author function is transfigured here as a composite author, the text is offered other means of finding its way into circulation, into print. Amis's novel thus plays with the notion of text-theft in such a way as to suggest that disconnecting a text from its author is the best way to keep it moving, to get it read. Indeed, those disconnections take place at several levels in the novel.

As I indicated earlier, for example, Sam has in fact stolen the narrative from someone else's text—the diarist's. In that way, the novel underscores the significance of this multi-authoring from the very start. The novel begins, then, in 1999 when Sam arrives in London where he fortuitously happens upon his true story—fortuitous because Sam, who has not written anything in years, assures his readers that he cannot write fiction. Staring out the window of his London apartment, Sam happens to see a woman—whom he had just seen earlier that day, for the first time in his life, in a pub called the Black Cross—throw out a bundle of diaries. Intrigued, Sam recovers the diaries, which turn out to be the property of Nicola Six, a mysterious woman living in London. As her diaries indicate, since childhood Nicola has had visions. In those visions she knows what's going to happen before it happens. Or so it seems. Ever since she was a little girl, Nicola has seen visions of London with rings circling outward from the center—ground zero. As the novel begins, however, *that event* at least has not come to pass. Nicola's life takes a new course when she has a vision of her own death. She ceases to record any more visions in her diaries and even throws the diaries away. Through the last of her recorded visions Nicola comes to know the minute, hour, and date of her death, as well as how it will be carried out—murder, involving a car, a car-tool and a dead-end street. Yet Nicola does not know who the murderer will be. She knows the certain end of her life's story, but she does not know how her life will arrive at this end—just as she envisions the destruction of London by bombs without knowing how that end will be achieved. Her vision, ultimately, is one of her own mortality coupled together with the end of the world. Entering the Black Cross one afternoon, Nicola encounters Keith Talent, a kind of over-grown Dickensian street urchin, a professional cheat and darts champion. Later that afternoon Nicola writes in her diaries, for the last time before throwing them away, that she has found her murderer: "I've found him. On the Portobello Road, in a place called the Black Cross, I found him" (***London Fields*** 22).

As Amis describes it to Self, "***London Fields*** began as a novella. It was going to be a sixty-page story called 'The Murderee.' There was going to be a Keith figure and a Nicola figure, just moving towards each other and then the deed would occur" (Self 149). The notion that a murder requires a "murderee" occurred to Amis, he explains elsewhere, after reading a newspaper article that argued that "people who are murdered are somehow psychologically predisposed to be murdered" (Szamuely 47). Given the environmental and nuclear catastrophes threatening the world at the close of the 1980s, Amis began to wonder, "Is the planet the murderee?" (47). ***London Fields,*** then, is a meditation on the possibility that the world—in an anthropomorphized sense—*wants* to die, with Nicola representing a kind of suicidal earth-figure, but a suicide in need of assistance. Originally Amis conceived of this assistance coming Nicola's way through Keith. But as the story developed, Amis explains to Self, more characters were added, including, as Amis puts it, "the narrator"—Sam—"who became a kind of actor" (Self 149).

After discovering Nicola's diaries, Sam begins writing out her prophecy-in-progress—indicating already that his authorial voice is a composite one. As the novel begins, the coming end of the millennium, a vague but quickly developing world crisis, as well as a fast approaching total eclipse, and Nicola Six's self-prophesied murder all converge in one critical mass of apocalyptic suspense. As a low-life—if somewhat failed—street tough, Keith makes for a near perfect murderer. Coincidentally, Keith has the most prestigious darts final of his career on the same evening as Nicola's prophesied murder, the eclipse of the sun, and the end of the world. By now the thoroughness of those metaphorical substitutions ought to be clear. As Sam writes, to Keith "the whole world was darts," but then, as Sam also notes, "the whole world—on certain screens, in certain contingency plans—was definitely a dartboard" (***London Fields*** 396). It makes sense then that Nicola, upon entering the Black Cross and seeing Keith for the first time, should feel that she had found her murderer. As Sam later emphasizes, however, Keith was not alone in the Black Cross that day. Sam was there, too. Nicola was right, she had found her murderer, but it was Sam, not Keith—Sam, who, as Amis indicates, entered the story to become a kind of *actor.* "Always me," Sam writes at the close of his narrative, "from the first moment in the Black Cross she looked my way with eyes of recognition. She knew that she'd found him: her murderer" (466).

Yet Sam undergoes great struggles on the way to becoming an actor within his own narrative. Like Nicola, he knows how the story is meant to end, but he does not know—anymore than Nicola—how the story will get there. He is, of course, ambivalent about helping to bring the story any nearer its inevitable end by his own hand. He feels certain the world will end, but with his own health waning too, his patience begins to run out: "I'm not one of those excitable types who get caught making things up. Who get caught improving on reality. I can embellish, I can take liberties. Yet to invent the bald facts of a life (for example) would be quite beyond my powers" (39). As a result, the development of Sam's story, of his documentary—as he decides to think of it—is stalled:

> I guess I could just wing it, But all I know for sure is the very last scene. The car, the car-tool, the murderer waiting in his car, the murderee, ticking towards him on her high heels. I don't know how to get to the dead-end street. I close my eyes, trying to see a way—how do writers *dare* do what they do?—and there's just chaos. It seems to me that writing brings trouble with it, moral trouble, unexamined trouble.
>
> (117)

Finally, Sam recognizes that if Nicola's prophesy is going to come off, he will have to act himself, he will have to invent—to save his story. But the entrance of the author into his own apocalyptic narrative changes the course of everything.

The eclipse comes and goes; Keith loses his darts final, and Nicola is murdered. But Sam has taken Keith's place as the murderer. The car is Keith's, the car-tool is Keith's, but it is Sam who is waiting at the dead-end street. By appropriating Keith's authorship of the murder Sam has changed the course of events—the course of the novel he is writing. Writing and invention are simply, despite Sam's protestations to the contrary, the same thing. And when the future has to be written, when the future awaits being written, then the future is no done-deal but simply the blank space at the end of the page awaiting new inscriptions. The future after all, like nuclear war, like the apocalypse, is a literary event—an ellipsis, a potential, a not-yet waiting to be written into existence. Sam recognizes that at the end of his narrative: "I'm in it," he remarks, more than a little surprised at the obviousness of the fact (464). Writing is an act of complicity, and in writing there are no safe spaces from which one may merely observe. In this action then—murdering Nicola and taking enough pills to end his own life—Samson, as his name suggests, pulls down the roof on himself and all that he has come to perceive as the enemy of his story: the future prophesied by Nicola Six.

Rather than a global nuclear apocalypse, then, ***London Fields*** delivers a simulated apocalypse in microcosm—represented in the deaths of Nicola, the author, and his book. Thus Sam's re-authoring of Nicola's premise and his rewriting of her apocalyptic plot have the effect of supplanting global destruction with his own Samson-like sacrifice. Sam undertakes that sacrifice because he has learned over the course of the novel that Nicola's inevitable end, and even his own inevitable end, are not the same as the end of the world. Before his suicide, then, Sam assembles his "*Endpapers*" and leaves two suicide notes: one, to Mark Asprey asking him to destroy all records of these events and another to Kim Talent—the infant daughter of Keith and secret heroine of the novel who slowly comes to represent for Sam a hopeful alternative to the apocalyptic teleology of his own story—asking her nothing more nor less than to outlive him (468). And so the story ends, much as Sam imagined it would from the beginning, with himself and Nicola dead. Yet the story of ***London Fields*** survives him, because Asprey turns out to be Sam's executor in several senses. Asprey does function as Sam's literary executor, but he evidently acts against Sam's instructions—he does not destroy the text, otherwise there would be no way to explain the existence of a document called ***London Fields.*** But Asprey is Sam's executor in a second sense, in that he does seem—as Sam suspects before his death—to have set Sam up to die. Ultimately, Sam—like John Self in ***Money***—turns out to be the dupe of an authorial conspiracy he had not foreseen.

The conspiracy against Sam appears to have been co-authored by Asprey and Nicola. In the course of ***London Fields*** Sam learns to his surprise that Nicola is an acquaintance of Asprey's—and a former lover. That fact more than any other exacerbates Sam's jealousy of Asprey. His jealousy is somewhat assuaged when Nicola admits that Asprey's writing is terrible—and she even confesses to having recklessly destroyed one of Asprey's novels. At the close of ***London Fields,*** however, it becomes apparent that Asprey, Nicola, and Sam have all come to rely on one another in some rather complex ways. And it appears that an elaborate deal has been struck, one that necessarily includes setting Sam up. Nicola needs Sam for a murderer. Sam needs Nicola for her story. And Asprey needs the two of them to replace his destroyed novel. It seems, then, that Asprey agrees to provide Nicola with a murderer by swapping his apartment for Sam's, so long as Nicola provides him with a replacement novel, to be produced by Sam. That arrangement explains why Nicola, after spying Sam for the first time in Black Cross, throws away her diaries outside Asprey's window—where she knows Sam is watching. The destruction of one book, then, produces another. And the destruction of one story does not mean that it cannot be replaced by another. Nicola's vandalizing of Asprey's text obligates her to replace it. Asprey provides Sam, who will produce the book that Asprey—as a disguised Amis—will later pass off as his own. Thus the novel survives the death of its author, and circulates wherever it may.

In this way ***London Fields*** carries on the work begun by Amis in ***Money*** of problematizing the authority and fixity of the author figure. In both novels Amis values that problematization positively—and thus, by transfiguring the author as a composite, the text is offered other means of finding its way into circulation, of being disseminated. Disconnecting a text from its author, then, appears to be one strategy for making sure that the death of an author need not require the death of the narrative. The novel functions as a critique of the easy equation between personal catastrophe and global catastrophe, between an apocalyptic mood and an apocalyptic catastrophe, between a discursive agent and discourse as an agent. ***London Fields*** is, after all, a novel with an argument. It argues that literary discourse has a part to play in redirecting the future of nuclear and apocalyptic discourse alike. It is important, then, that an argument such as that survive its author—and be thought of apart from the authority of the author figure—in order to emphasize that such authority really resides in discourses such as those that hold the power of scripting the future.

As Foucault asks at the close of "What Is an Author?": "What difference does it make who is speaking?" (120). And as Foucault argues, questions other than the identity of the author need to be asked: "What are the modes of existence of [a] discourse? Where has it been used, how can it circulate, and who can appropriate it for himself?" (120). Like Foucault's essay, Amis's fiction suggests that discourses need to be thought of in terms of their social function—as means of agency. Amis's novels argue that postwar nuclear discourse has changed fundamental social relationships in important ways. Rather than try to halt that change, Amis's work tries to operate within that apocalyptic discourse in order to redirect it. Thus at the end of ***London Fields*** the roof is indeed brought down upon Samson and Nicola, but all the novel's other characters survive—and those that survive carry on with their lives, informed by that apocalyptic experience in miniature. What Amis's recent fiction underscores, then, is the power of discourse, rather than the power of the author. And as postnuclear subjects everywhere learn to write about nuclear weapons, that discourse will be redirected toward new ends.

In a recent interview with Graham Fuller in the Spring 1995 issue of *Interview,* Amis reflected on the changes within the discourse of apocalypse in the half dozen years since ***London Fields***: "the big question of the second half of this century was, What are we going to do with nuclear weapons? Now that we've got out of the emotional idea that it could all end tomorrow, we can look at other things" (Fuller 125). A feeling of suspense continues to insinuate itself within all manner of public discourses as the twentieth century comes to a close, but Amis argues that a kind of corner has been turned, and that those who have been learning how to write about nuclear weapons are also learning how to act—how to become actors in the endless unfolding of that discourse on the end. "Our time," Amis writes in **"Thinkability,"** "is different. All times are different, but our time is *different.* A new fall, an infinite fall, underlies the usual—indeed traditional—presentiments of decline" (21). That is the condition of millennial suspense, in which, as Amis puts it, "the past and the future, equally threatened, equally cheapened, now huddle in the present" (22). But now, postmodern fiction pushes literary discourse beyond the apocalyptic horizon—to a place where the future awaits being rewritten, with new endings.

Works Cited

Alexander, Victoria N. "Martin Amis: Between the Influences of Bellow and Nabokov." *The Antioch Review* 52.4 (Fall 1994): 580-590.

Amis, Martin. *London Fields.* New York: Vintage International, 1989.

———. *Money.* London: Penguin, 1984.

———. "Thinkability." *Einstein's Monsters.* New York: Harmony, 1987.

———. *Time's Arrow.* New York: Harmony, 1991.

Derrida, Jacques. "No Apocalypse, Not Now (full speed ahead, seven missiles, seven missives)." *Diacritics* 14.2 (Summer 1984): 20-31.

Foucault, Michel. "What Is an Author?" *The Foucault Reader.* Ed. Paul Rabinow. New York: Pantheon, 1984.

Fuller, Graham. "The Prose and Cons of Martin Amis." *Interview* (May 1995): 122-126.

Hoare, Philip. "Martin Amis." *Details* (November 1991): 132-133.

Kroker, Arthur and David Cook. *The Postmodern Scene.* New York: St. Martin's, 1991.

Morrison, Susan. "Martin Amis." *Rolling Stone* 17 May 1990: 96-101.

Self, Will. "An Interview with Martin Amis." *The Mississippi Review* 21.3 (Summer 1993): 143-169.

Szamuely, George. "Something Amiss with Martin." *National Review* 28 May 1990: 46-48.

Greg Harris (essay date winter 1999)

SOURCE: Harris, Greg. "Men Giving Birth to New World Orders: Martin Amis's *Time's Arrow.*" *Studies in the Novel* 31, no. 4 (winter 1999): 489-505.

[*In the following essay, Harris explores concepts of sexual violence and divided identity in* Time's Arrow.]

> Explaining the [Nazi] perpetrators' actions demands . . . that the perpetrators' phenomenological reality be taken seriously. We must attempt the difficult enterprise of imagining ourselves in their places, performing their deeds, acting as they did, viewing what they beheld.
>
> —Daniel Goldhagen

An effort not only to think about but arrive at an understanding of how the "unthinkable"—Nazi genocidal atrocity—ever occurred, Martin Amis's novel, ***Time's Arrow,*** is narrated in reverse time; the novel begins at the death bed of the character Tod Friendly, whose life literally rewinds before his eyes. (His name changes in accordance to the different identities he appropriates through the course of his life while fleeing prosecution for Nazi war crimes—from "Tod T. Friendly" to "John Young," from John Young to "Hamilton de Souza," and lastly, from Hamilton De Souza to his original identity, "Odilo Unverdorben.") Amis presents a text where the protagonist's life is moving backward and all logic and normative reality is reversed. By progressing backwards, the narrative style in and of itself comments on the Nazi's paradoxical version of "progress"—that is, the revitalization of archaic myths in the name of national renewal. Indeed, the narrative's reversals only begin to "make sense" when Tod reaches the moment of his past when he was a Nazi. For Nazi "rationality," as Amis points out time and time again, blurred the lines between creation and destruction, as destruction was often rationalized as a means to create. Such "logic" underlies the notion that genocidal mass murder will lead to racial (Aryan) revival as well as the idea that violence is the way to national renewal—e.g., rebuilding the German Nation via militarism.

Time's Arrow is narrated from the perspective of a co-consciousness (and sometimes ghost *conscience*) that exists as an exile within Tod's body. At the beginning of the novel, the consciousness-split occurs at Tod's deathbed as the narrator becomes aware of his separation: "Something isn't quite working: this body of mine won't takes orders from this will of mine. Look around, I say. But his neck ignores me. His eyes have their own agenda."[1] As his mind leaves the scene of the death bed and flashes backwards through time, the confused narrator initially cannot understand why he views himself "walking backward in the house" or the meaning of the strange mumbling he overhears: "Aid ut oo y'rrah?" (How are you today?) (pp. 6-7). The narrator soon figures out, however, that the "pitiable chirruping" is, in fact, "human speech," and, upon this realization, he immediately attains fluency in a backwards language that turns out to be strangely familiar—indeed, a language he sometimes dreams in (p. 7). Apparently, then, these counter-intuitive thought processes are not new, but rather are a latent component of Tod's unconscious (that sometimes surface in dreams) that have also dictated, somewhere in the past, his wakeful experience. What is a counter-intuitive world for the narrator, however, is actually the intuitive world for his double and the people of his double's memories: "We're getting younger . . . And all the other people are getting younger too, but they don't seem to mind, any more than Tod minds. They don't find it counter-intuitive, and faintly disgusting, as I do . . . The other people, do they have someone else inside them, passenger or parasite, like me?" (p. 8). As the narrator (Tod's "passenger" consciousness) negotiates his alien status in the rewinding world of memories, he realizes that that which is insane to him is actually sane to his double and to those who share this world with his double: "Tod is sane, apparently, and his world is shared. It just seems to me that the film is running backwards."

That the narrator views this world as counter-intuitive indicates that he is on the side of Tod's split personality that managed to avoid indoctrination in Nazi ideology. Robert Jay Lifton, in his comprehensive work, *The Nazi Doctors,* explains that "the key to understanding how Nazi doctors came to do the work of Auschwitz is the psychological principle I call 'doubling': the division of the self into two functioning wholes, so that the part-self acts as an entire self."[2] Accordingly, ***Time's Arrow*** seemingly presents a fictionalized account of Lifton's work.[3] For it is only through "doubling" and "psychic numbing" that Tod (then "Odilo") was able to effectively perform his work as a Nazi doctor, which necessitated his adherence to a fundamentally un-Hippocratic oath. During his war years Tod had learned to contain, control, and adapt his conscience to Nazi ideology by functioning as a divided-self—literally, of two minds. Hence, the narrating split-consciousness, which formed when Tod was a Nazi doctor, surfaces from its latent period as Tod's backwards journey through life reactivates the counter-intuitive (or Nazi-intuitive) discursive mode. From the perspective of "the part self [that] acts as an entire self," the narrative has the doppelgänger effect of a ghost consciousness haunting a body it used to call home (prior to the Nazi years).

The following example of this reversed narrative structure is important insofar as it reveals how the distinction between creation and destruction became blurred under Nazism. The split-subjectivity appears to be the reason that the narrator refers to himself as "we" in the upcoming passage, but Amis may be also indicting the tradition of the royal "we" with its investiture of life-giving and life-taking authority (this matter will be examined later in the essay). Tod is moving from his house (located in the United States, which was Tod's final settling place after years of escaping prosecution by war tribunals) and bids farewell to his garden; he sheds tears which "fall" in reverse, that is, from the ground back to his eyes. Tod's tears, as the narrator initially suggests, are of distress over his having to leave the flourishing garden that he so diligently crafted. Yet, in reverse form, as my comments in the brackets shall indicate, the creative process becomes a destructive one; the garden is un-created as its seeds are tediously unsowed:

> On the day we moved . . . Tod slipped out into the garden—the garden on which he had worked for so many years. He lowered himself on his knees, and, sniffing hungrily, richly [. . .] It was beautiful . . . Dewlike drops of moisture formed on the dry grass, and rose upward through the air as if powered by the jolts in our chests. The moisture bathed our cheeks, deliciously, until with our tickling eyes we drew it in. Such distress. Why? I assumed at the time that he was crying for the garden and what he had done to it. The garden was heaven when we had started out [that is, in the end], but over the years [now passing in reverse], well, don't blame me is all I'm saying. It wasn't my decision. It never is. So Tod's tears were tears of remorse and propitiation. For what he'd done. Look at it. A nightmare of wilt and mildew, of fungus and black spot. [Tod's double views the gardening process in reverse mode:] All the tulips and roses he patiently drained and crushed, then sealed their exhumed corpses and took them in the paper bag to the store for money. All the weeds and nettles he screwed into the soil—and the earth took their ugliness, snatched at it with a sudden grip. Such, then, are the fruits of Tod's meticulous vandalism . . . Destruction [that is, the work involved in creating and tending a garden]—is difficult. Destruction is slow. Creation [hence, neglecting a garden, allowing the diseased weed soil to predominate], as I said, is no trouble at all.
>
> (Pp. 18-19)

The vegetation of a once-flourishing garden is, in reverse time, ruined. Hence, in "real" time, Tod actually did creatively garden. But the narrator appears skeptical when assessing just what the creative process means for Tod, representing his gardening work as being ultimately destructive ("meticulous vandalism").

As Tod's narrating double suggests. Tod, at this late stage of his life, has become "confused" (p. 18). For in his Nazi past he was not able to differentiate (or, at least, helplessly muddled the distinction) between creation and destruction. It appears that Tod's garden may have been a site for solace. But does he take sorrow over a dream of recreating a new race that, like the garden, he must ultimately abandon? Or, is he possibly mourning over the human costs (the genocide) of that dream? The "answer" lies in Tod's confusion in and of itself. "Tod's tears," his narrating co-consciousness explains, "were tears of remorse, or propitiation." As if to conciliate an offended power (propitiation)—in this case, the laws of creation—Tod is no longer secure over whether he has lived in violation of, or in service to, those laws.

In his past, Tod had played an intimate role in the "creation" process. Of course, he is biologically incapable of conceiving, but Tod's Nazi past has nevertheless taught him another way of affecting the laws of reproduction. He has mastered, in fact, an eerie means of *male birthing,* but his contact with creation comes by way of his control over what forms of life are permitted a right to life, and those forms of life that must be destroyed. Nazism's patrilineal theme is reflected in the words of Joseph Goebbels, who served as the "Reich Minister for Public Enlightenment and Propaganda" in charge of the "intellectual and cultural life of the State":[4]

> On occasion the peaceful evolution of a continent is interrupted by the stormy epochs when something new is constructed. At this point the earth is convulsed by seismic tremors which usher in a new birth amidst the most terrible labour pains . . . Every birth brings pain. But amid the pain there is already the joy of a new life. Our age too is an act of historical birth, whose pangs carry with them the joy of richer life to come.
>
> (P. 159)

With the conception of a militarized National Womb that gives birth to a nation through war, the German soldier-male comes to perceive himself as playing an even more essential role in re-production than the German woman. As Klaus Theweleit observes. "Men give birth to themselves living in New World Orders. Men are reborn by killing . . . You have to deal with that logic or metamorphosis when dealing with war. War ranks high among the male ways of giving birth."[5]

The "right" kinds of life (and *Reich* way of life) can only flourish if those "wrong" forms of life are abolished; as if to become "reborn by killing," the (re)creation of the German nation required that only "pure" Aryan seeds be sown; this, of course, requires that only persons of so-called Aryan heritage be allowed a right to live and reproduce. Influential Nazi-thinker Hans F. K. Gunther successfully advocated that eugenics be "placed at the centre of policy making," asserting in his popular publications that "Aryanism" constituted the "essential genetic quality" of a "healthy civilization," and thus should be "bred back into the Germans": "It is clear that since the Nordic movement sees human beings not so much as individuals but as carriers of heredity, the key idea which informs it is that of the health of the stock (eugenics, racial hygiene)."[6] The revitalization of the so-called Aryan heritage "necessitated" unsowing the seeds of racial contamination from the soil of the Fatherland—and extinguishing those (Jews, Gypsies, the mentally ill, etc.) who plant such seeds. The slogan "Blood and Soil," Griffin explains, "had made a significant contribution to the rationale for the systematic inhumanity and destructiveness carried out by the Third Reich" (p. 126). It is no wonder the narrator referred to Tod's gardening as "vandalism." Under the analogous Nazi schema, it is the soldier-male who becomes national gardener, as it is he who must ensure German soil is exclusively fertile to Aryan forms of life—those non-Aryan peoples, like weeds, are rendered odious life. "The Nazis," Phil Joffe observes, "literalized metaphors," as Jews came to be discursively framed within most German institutions as a "contamination": "Germans were habituated to thinking of Jews, not as human beings, but as . . . lice, as vermin, as diseases such as typhus against which Germans needed to be inoculated."[7]

Such systems of "rationality" similarly characterize the medical practices of a Nazi doctor, whose torturous experiments on concentration camp prisoners would seemingly necessitate having a severely altered sense of "medical progress." Indeed, the wedding of militarism and medicine under Nazism led to strikingly paradoxical activities for a doctor. For the "militarist," according to Sara Ruddick, imposes

> one's will upon others by threatening or actually injuring them. That militarists often injure for the sake of causes that are, or appear to be, just does not alter their willingness to injure . . . The willingness to burn, bury, cut, blow apart, and starve bodies is essential to militarist enterprises; forms of coercion that rule out in advance deliberate damage to bodies are not militarist.[8]

In contrast to the militarist, Ruddick continues, is the Caregiver, "whose caregiving involves a commitment to refrain from neglecting or assaulting bodies," and who practices "caring labor" (p. 120). Under Nazism, the traditional caregiving role of the doctor was redirected to militaristic ends. Apparently, Tod is aware of this irony when he removes from the trash (hence, in real time, he actually throws away) a framed certificate of the Hippocratic oath. The words of that oath, according to the narrator, "make plain sense" (including, "I will enter to help the sick, and I will abstain from all intentional wrongdoing and harm"); unfortunately, according to the narrator, "Tod always reads them backwards." Although he mocks the oath on the medical certificate with "a good laugh," on the "inside," the narrator reveals, he's in "a world of pain" (pp. 24-25). Again, it appears that Tod, late in his life, is unsure over whether he served or disgraced the medical profession. A consequence of combining the role of caregiver and militarist is the collusion of healing with violence.

Tod negotiated a means of altering his conscience in such a way as to deflect blame on to his *Other* for inflicting injury (via torturous experiments, etc.) on "patients" while at the same time justifying these practices as having medical value. As Lifton explains this psychological dynamic, a portion of the self splits off and "ceases to respond to the environment ('psychic numbing') or else is in some way at odds with the remainder of the self" (p. 421). While the psychological capacity for doubling can be "life saving" for a "victim of brutality," Lifton warns that the capacity for forming an "opposing self" can also lead one to "embrace evil with an extreme lack of restraint" (p. 420):

> The way in which doubling allowed Nazi doctors to avoid guilt was not by the elimination of conscience but by what can be called the transfer of conscience. The requirements of conscience were transferred to the Auschwitz self, which placed it within its own criteria for good (duty, loyalty to group . . . etc.), thereby freeing the original self from responsibility for actions there . . . What is repudiated is not reality itself . . . but the meaning of that reality. The Nazi doctor knew that he selected, but did not interpret selections as murder. One level of disavowal, then, was the Auschwitz self's altering of the means of murder; and on another, the repudiation by the original self of anything done by the Auschwitz self. From the moment of its formation, the Auschwitz self so violated the Nazi doctor's previous self-concept as to require more or less permanent disavowal.
>
> (Pp. 421-22)

Building on the concept of the "transfer of conscience." Amis presents a narrator who functions as a split-self that disavows Tod as his opposing "Auschwitz self."

Harmful ideological remnants of Tod's indoctrination into the Fascist world-order schema remain within his post-war self, despite the fact that the world they once made sense of is no longer in existence. It is in this light that Tod's narrating split-consciousness qualifies Tod's emotional predicament, explaining that although Tod is "sane," his sanity is historically relative to those who "shared" a worldview governed by Nazi logic (as cited earlier. "Tod is sane . . . and his world is shared. It just seems to me that the film is running backward"). Despite his "understandable estrangement" from this world, Maya Slater observes, the narrator strives to "make himself clearly understood by his forward-living readers. In a sense, then, the world of this novel is not truly reversed—it is [an ideologically] backwards world seen through forward-looking eyes."[9] In attempting to interpret Nazi mentality from a non-Fascist conceptual framework, one would seemingly have to jolt into reversal one's own moral assumptions, and thereby metaphorically screen the historical moment through "film [that] is running backward." Through such intellectual reversals, one learns that Nazi rationalization of genocidal violence was once considered forward thinking. And from such a Nazi conceptual frame arises perceptions of violence that view the resulting damage or injury in a positive light, as the given casualties are rendered as building blocks to some form of national progress. Even Tod's narrating split conscience can "just about accept" on an intellectual level how violence may be construed as a necessity for bringing about world-good: "I'm taking on the question of violence, this most difficult question. Intellectually I can just about accept that violence is salutary, that violence is good" (p. 26). However, when faced with its "ugliness"—hence, no longer theorizing about violence but actually committing violent acts—Tod's conscience resists: "But I can find nothing in me that assents to its ugliness." It is at the point of violent activity that Tod's conscience splits off and a mind/body barrier forms: "[A]nything [violent] made me flinch and veer. But the body I live in and move in, Tod's body, feels nothing."

Tod's postwar self—having immediately (re)divided at his deathbed—has since been unable to become whole again. As Slater writes, "despite his lack of physical body the Narrator [is] given a distinctive personality . . . He also has a decent moral code" (p. 143). It's evident, then, that the Narrator—perhaps unbeknown to himself—represents the very conscience that Tod lost at some point in his repressed past. Although "they" travel through the same past, each part-self views its shared history from a different vantage point. For the split personality, which self shall emerge: the Auschwitz self? the original, pre-Nazi indoctrinated self? Paul Antze—citing Ian Hacking—writes, "multiple personality is a kind of false consciousness:" in developing "'a thoroughly crafted person,'" the multiple is "'not a person with self knowledge.'"[10] Tod cannot gain "self knowledge" because he quite literally is of two minds when it comes to his Nazi past. Tod's Auschwitz self took refuge in an identity politics wed to a nationalism that defined the attributes of the in-group against those attributes of the out-group and, in turn, cast the latter as a threat against the survival of the former. Tod's double (the narrator), by contrast, survives as a remnant of consciousness that existed prior to the formation of the Auschwitz self. Having been divorced from Tod ever since the war, Tod's Nazi past has evidently been left behind only in practice, but not in spirit. For his conscience, as represented by his double, remained in a slumber throughout the post-war years. But Tod's sensibilities are based, a posteriori, upon the culture of Auschwitz.

Of course, such denial is self-protective: it enables the narrator to transfer his Nazi activities on to his opposing self (which, to recall Lifton, he holds in "permanent disavowal"), a fossilized embodiment of the Auschwitz self. The narrator can, by contrast, remain convinced of his own morality. As a consequence, *no one is guilty*: the narrator unimplicates himself in Nazi atrocity; but his double—locked into ideological context—remains one who simply performed his "rightful" duties. Each part-self that exists within Tod gets to see whatever it does, or does not, want to see: the narrator blames Tod for committing inhumane acts while his double renders these same acts as being in the best interest of humanity ("advancing" medicine while "defending" the German race). While moments of grief or confusion manage to surface in the narrative, they are always compensated for via the alarming psychological capacity for dissociation. But dissociation shouldn't provide any excuses. Such psychological mechanisms of denial do not explain away the moral cowardliness and ethical betrayal of the persecutor. As Slater importantly observes, "the narrator is not dealing honestly with us: sometimes he is a sophisticated observer who knows his situation, while at other times he plays the uncomprehending innocent" (p. 146).

Indeed, by existing as a part-self, yet cognitively whole entity that resides in Tod's body, the Cartesian split is perversely utilized: the narrator (mind) holds the "other" entity (body) responsible for the atrocities committed:[11]

> Atrocity upon atrocity, and then more atrocity, and then more. I'm glad it's not my body that is actually touching their bodies. I'm glad I have his body, in between. But how I wish I had a body of my own, one that did my bidding. I wish I had a body . . . a voice that groans or sighs or asks hoarsely for forgiveness . . . I have a heart but I don't have a face: I don't have any eyes to cry. Nobody knows I'm here.
>
> (P. 92)

As if helpless to do anything but watch Tod/John's body commit violent acts, the narrating split-conscience can but wish it had a body to direct by its own "bidding[s]," as well as the capability to show remorse and seek atonement (to ask "hoarsely for forgiveness").

This capacity to function as two selves, however, gave John the ability to not only function but also actively participate in the genocidal culture of Auschwitz. In this light, the narrator's lamenting about the difficulty in enduring this "torn condition" seems rather suspect, as does his questioning his everyday role in the "dispensing of existence": "Is it a war we are fighting, a war against health, against life and love?" The narrator explains that he feels "impossible weariness," what he qualifies as "*mortal* weariness" (emphasis mine), which is inescapable lest he were able to break free of his helplessly mortal condition: "I'm tired of being human" (p. 93). During his Auschwitz years, however, the narrator acquired a means of unloading the emotional baggage that drained him, indeed, conditioned himself to mechanistic function in order to escape his mortal limitations. In the following scene the narrator, back at Auschwitz, describes both the literal and emotional donning of an institutional uniform (and uniformity): "I had slipped out of our coarse traveling clothes and emotionally donned the black boots, the white coat, the fleece-lined jacket, the peaked cap, the pistol" (p. 116). Notice how the "I" returns to the narrative sequence in such a way as to implicate the narrator's ephemeral temptation to fuse into the Auschwitz self and fully realize the allure of Nazi empowerment—a yearning which he formerly put off on his Other. As indicated by the use of "our" in reference to both himself and John's (now "Odilo's") body, however, the fusion the narrator desires is incomplete yet, nevertheless, sought after as a means to transcend the draining limitations of the thinking, feeling self.

"John"/"Odilo" and his double are capable of taking this emotionally sterile and uniform mindset to the extreme, as is apparent when Odilo proceeds to depart on motorbike (after dressing in uniform) and "fuses" not only as one within himself, but also with the very machine he is riding on:

> [With] the motorbike I found earlier [. . .] Oh how I soared out of there, with what vaulting eagerness, what daring . . . Now I straddled this heavy machine and revved with jerked gauntlet. Auschwitz lay around me, miles and miles of it. [. . .] Human life was all ripped and torn. But I was one now, fused for a preternatural purpose.
>
> (P. 116)

Although the narrator is usually repelled by violence, his desire for fusion supersedes his (Pre-Nazi) sense of morality. The narrator becomes a mechanized self, describing his motorbike as if he's sexually penetrating the machine: "I straddled this heavy machine . . . [and rode it] with jerked gauntlet." In taking on the very powers of creation, the narrator and his double ("Odilo") become *one*; joined in their desire to transcend the limitations of self, Odilo is now emotionally prepared to play a role in the "preternatural" mission of forced Darwinism.

By extension, Nazism provided Germans with an alternative narrative on existence that tapped into the ongoing human yearning for a unified and transcendent self that exceeds the trappings of the mortal self. Constructing a cultural order rooted in a mythology that offered no less than to conquer time in reconnecting with the lost Nordic past, Nazism was able to manipulatively cast the individual embodiment of the collective will—what Lifton terms the "collective self"—under the illusion of transcendence: through military conquest, the imperial "We" shall realize the sacred by occupying the "higher ancestral place" (p. 428). Those outside the hegemonic frame of the imperial "we" are literally erased. Thus is the intoxicating allure of being on the inclusive side of a nationalist identity politics that casts the ennobled Nordic self against those so-called scurrilous populations.

But so that it may not seem as if these romantic notions of transcending the limitations of the individualized self are in any way a plausible prospect for any mortal, Amis presents the dreams of his protagonist as, of course, unrealizable despite Odilo's rhetorical manipulation by Nazi dogma to feel otherwise. The possibility for a greater self is not realized in any material way as one doesn't become superhuman simply because he believes he is. Despite the mystified channeling of his desires to all-powerful world visions, Odilo's mere humanness gives host to emotional (he is, after all, a split personality) and sexual dysfunctionalism. As

Donald Morse notes, "Odilo was as impotent morally and spiritually as he was impotent sexually. He traded his personal potency for omnipotence over others."[12] Odilo's libidinous fusion with machine, for example, demonstrates he has learned to channel his sex drive into mechanical outlets. But the legacy that derives from such habits of sublimation are seen in his post-war years, when Tod ("John"/"Odilo") attempts to overcome this machinic regard for his own body. When having sex with his on-again off-again partner Irene, however, the narrator actually experiences non-sublimated pleasure, and thereby appreciates the body, at least initially, for its being of the flesh: "My hand reached out to the white pulp of her shoulder. Astounding proximity. Never, never before . . . She was tense and tight (as I was); but skin is soft. Touch it. It gives. It gives to the touch" (p. 36). Unaccustomed to a less-mechanized and more-natural relationship to the body, his "astounding proximity" to the realness of the flesh fascinates him like something "never before" experienced: he touches his partner's skin as if it were a novelty.

The narrator's excitement in the following scenario actually overpowers his bodily activity, which is why the sex act comes to a "premature" end:

> She turned toward us meaningfully. There followed about ten minutes of what I'd guess you'd call foreplay. Snuggling, grunting, sighing—that kind of thing. Then he moved, and loomed over her. And as she opened her legs *I was flooded by thoughts and feelings [having . . .] to do with power.* "Oh baby," she said, and kissed my cheek. "It doesn't matter." "I'm sorry," said Tod. "I'm so sorry."
>
> (P. 37 [emphasis mine])

Tod's skewed sense of human relations is ever present as feelings of power once again unify the narrator and his double (the "I" resurfaces); over-stimulated by the power-rush, the narrator prematurely ejaculates "as she opened her legs." Tod is sexually stimulated by feelings of domination. Hence, it is not the act of sex that titillates him so much as the reawakened thrill of conquest held over from his Nazi past.

Indeed, the narrator usually speaks of his sexual liaisons in terms of power and battle, as evident in the following scene when an anonymous woman at a bar spins towards Tod in her stool: "It's a big power moment when they spin around, with the flourish of challenge, and we get to see what they look like." And the narrator thrives on the "challenge," gaining "power" via the narcissistic confirmation of his masculine prowess achieved through one-night stands: "You get everything on the first date . . . Instant invasion. Instant invasion and lordship" (pp. 50-51). Having sex with a female is transformed into holding dominion over her ("lordship"). while his talk of "instant invasion" too closely resembles those depictions of the infamous Nazi blitzkrieg raids. The vile disregard for women as being anything more than a device for Tod (now "John") to re-experience those feelings of power from his military past is further evident in the following passage:

> The fact that a woman's body has a head on top of it isn't much more than a detail. Don't get me wrong: he needs the head, because . . . he badly needs the mouth. As for what the head contains, well, yes, Johnny needs some of the things that live in there: will, desire, perversity. To the extent that sex is in the head, then Johnny needs the head.
>
> (P. 78)

The sex act for John has little to do with sex and everything to do with power. His desires would seem to be rooted in his indoctrination into an all-male, misogynist military culture (I will elaborate on this matter later in the essay): the woman's body relayed as if a strategic land mass that will soon be raided. Indeed, the above passage immediately leads to another one of John's sexual encounters that is so described: "Instantly John invaded her" (p. 79).

The ultimate irony comes earlier in the novel (thus, later in his life) when John (now "Tod") works at a woman's shelter but in no way connects his own attitude towards women with that of their abusers; again, the events are narrated in reverse, which serves to expose all the more clearly. I think, the counter-intuitive approach to violence that evokes the Nazi healing-killing paradox:

> The women at the crisis centers . . . are all hiding from their redeemers . . . The welts, abrasions and the black eyes get starker, more livid, until it's time for the women to return, in an ecstasy of distress, to the men who will suddenly heal them. Some require more specialized treatment. They stagger off and go and lie in a park or basement or wherever, until men come along and rape them, and then they're okay again. Ah shit, says Brad, the repulsive orderly, there's nothing wrong with them—meaning the women in the shelter—that a good six inches won't cure. Tod frowns at him sharply. I hate Brad too, and I hate to say it, but sometimes he's absolutely right. How could the world fix it so that someone like Brad could ever be right?
>
> (P. 31)

Tod treats those individual casualties (the victims of abuse: Brad's sexism) of a systematically bred violence against women that he, himself, perpetuates. When the narrator asks, "How could the world fix it so that someone like Brad could ever be right?" he is ignorant of the fact that, in real time, Tod carries out similar violence but in more subtle forms; Tod "frowns" on Brad's misogyny but practices it in his own life. Furthermore, Tod lives in a culture where physical abuse against women is "illegal," but at the same time women's (often sexual) debasement is socially, culturally, and discursively sanctioned. Only in this sense can the narrator say Brad's attitude is "right," that is, in the same way that the Nazi doctor was "right" in carrying out medical experiments. Rape culture, like the culture of Auschwitz, breeds attitudes that lead to the worst kinds of violence. Although Tod's attitude towards women may be rooted in his military past, his misogyny is rather poignantly revealed by Amis to play a tragic role in contemporary society as well.

Apparently, Tod's hostility towards women and other groups he renders as "subordinate" has to do with his own repressed desires. In this case, his binary consciousness aids him in his denial as he relegates sexuality to the realm of the body and, in turn, denies or splits from that body. Such repression and rechanneling of sexual desire is reflected repeatedly in Tod's prejudiced viewpoints, as evident in the following passage where sexual denial appears to underlie Tod's attitudes (as carried over from his years as "Odilo," the Nazi doctor) towards societal "degenerates":

> I'd say I was ahead of Tod on this basic question of human difference. Tod has a sensing mechanism that guides his responses to all identifiable subspecies. His feeling tone jolts into specialized attitudes and readiness: one for Hispanics, one for Asians, one for Arabs, one for Ameri[can] Indians, one for blacks, one for Jews. And he has a secondary repertoire of altered hostility toward pimps, hookers, junkies, the insane, the clubfooted, the hairclipped, the homosexual male, and the very old. (Here, incidentally, is my take on the homosexual male. It may be relevant. The homosexual male is fine . . . so long as he knows he's homosexual. It's when he is and thinks he isn't: then there's confusion. Then there's danger. The way Tod feels about men, about women, about children: there is confusion. There is danger. Don't get me wrong. I'm not fingering Tod for a fruit, not exactly. I'm just saying that things might be less confused, and less dangerous, if he could soberly entertain the idea of being homosexual. That's what I'm saying.)
>
> (P. 41)

Interestingly, the most significant insight into Tod's character comes in parenthesis, written as if an incidental aside. Apparently his homophobic narrating double fears dwelling on Tod's sexual "confusion," only going so far as to say "it may be relevant"; such underplaying of this issue suggests that Tod's sexuality is a subject the narrating conscience fears broaching.

Once again the narrating consciousness negotiates internal strife—sexual denials, etc.—via conceiving of itself as a split-subject. In such a convenient binary scenario, the narrating "I" doesn't risk being "finger[ed] for a fruit," but rather implicates the body it occupies. (Similarly, the narrator blames Tod's body for committing acts of violence.) With this safety net established, the narrator can then talk about Tod as if he were Other. Of primary significance here is this correlation of Tod's sexuality to "the way Tod feels about men, about women, about children: there is confusion." The narrator implies that Tod's violent attitudes (and actions) derive from some form of compensation, as if the extreme hostility he feels for social degenerates and "subspecies" aids him in denying that he may be one of them. (Again, Amis seems to open up suppressed normative judgments as subject to scrutiny.) If only Tod "could soberly entertain the idea of being homosexual," his narrating co-consciousness suggests, then perhaps this self-denial wouldn't lead to "danger": destroying inner demons by projecting them outward, onto tangible external enemies that can be destroyed.

Under Nazism, the rechanneling of individual desires to external projections of enemies is evident in the ways in which Tod (now "Odilo") appropriates national identity so as to externalize a self that can do battle against society's alleged degenerative elements; insofar as these deviants are projected, however, the creation of categories of sub-species really becomes an intimate means for control (these groups, after all, are products of the bigot's active imagination). As if to deny his mortal imperfections by becoming a component of something greater than himself, the split subjectivity fuses into one (the "I" returns), as Odilo channels libidinous energies into group functions—suppressing the individual so as to become a part of a "courageous" alter-self:

> My German worked like a dream, like a brilliant robot you switch on and stand back and admire as it does all the hard work. Courage was arriving too, in uniformed human units, the numbers and the special daring adequate to the task we faced. How handsome men are. I mean their shoulders, their tremendous necks. By the end of the second week our clubhouse was the scene of strident song and bold laughter . . . I peered through the reeking shadows of Auschwitz and saw that the nearest ruins were fuming more than ever and had even begun to glow. There was a new smell in the air. The sweet smell.
>
> (Pp. 118-19)

As a machine—a "brilliant robot"—Odilo experiences a sense of power and totality that isn't accessible at the imperfect and fragmented self. It is only in the form of "uniformed human units" that Odilo acquires "the special daring" needed to meet "the task we face." Odilo is made "strident" and "bold" when among a group of his peers, with whom he merges into an alter ego. As a "brilliant robot" Odilo is capable of fulfilling tasks and of doing "all the hard work" that, as an individual, he'd be too weak to perform, as presumably his humanity would get in the way: his personal apprehensiveness and moral—as opposed to mechanistic—sensibilities would simply not be adequate to the task of genocide.

Not only emboldened by his group empowerment, but, importantly, Odilo is also homosocially (and possibly homosexually) aroused by the men he fuses (penetrates) with in forming this masculine power entity. He is struck by "how handsome men are," finding desirable their strong features, "their shoulders, their tremendous necks." As a part of this militaristic community of men, "who had gathered for a preternatural purpose" (p. 118), Odilo is empowered and titillated in serving this all-male community that is at the forefront of the revival of the German (Aryan) Nation through the destruction of racial polluters whose incinerated flesh is deemed a "sweet smell."

The sweet smell is that of "creation," as Odilo's adapted senses "come to love" everything having to do with this massive project he's involved with—"dream[ing] a race" through destruction:

> I heard five more explosions. Velocity and fusion sucking up the shocked air . . . What tells me that this is right? What tells me that all the rest is wrong? Certainly not my aesthetic sense. I would never claim that Auschwitz-Birkenau-Monowitz was good to look at. Or to listen to, or to smell, or to taste, or to touch . . . Not for its elegance did I come to love the evening sky above the Vistula, hellish red with the gathering souls. Creation is easy. Also ugly . . . Here there is no why . . . Our preternatural purpose? To dream a race. To make a people from the weather. From thunder and from lightning. With gas, with electricity, with shit, with fire.
>
> (Pp. 119-20)

Although the narrator suggests that "creation is easy" he also admits to the "ugliness" of the project, as the work of creating a race via genocide is neither pleasing to the senses nor satisfying in any "aesthetic sense." Yet, despite the "ugly" nature of his creative work, the narrator "comes to love the evening sky" for what it represents: the "hellish red" glow that accumulates as a result of the oven incineration of human beings comes to symbolize the "dream [of] a race." Such a dream can only be realized through destruction; genocide and war are rhetorically transformed into a project of national renewal.

It is through such "rhetorical numbing," Lifton writes, that the Auschwitz self could make "murder nonmurderous" by re-casting murderous violence in terms connoting "military-medical behavior":

> [T]he language used gave Nazi doctors a discourse in which killing was no longer killing; and need not be experienced, or even perceived, as killing. As they lived increasingly within that language—and they used it with each other—Nazi doctors became imaginatively bound to a psychic realm of derealization, disavowal, and nonfeeling. As one gradually became habituated in Auschwitz, the Auschwitz self internalized its own requirements.
>
> (P. 445)

A carefully constructed means-end rationality inculcated Auschwitz culture, resulting in a predicament wherein the work of the Nazi doctor actually embodied the concept of rationality itself. Thinking objectified itself the more one became acclimated to Auschwitz, and, as Lifton explains, life there indeed became "like the weather," that is, "part nature and enveloping reality."

Just as the dreaming of race satirizes a masculine-military means for mastering nature—a way of male birthing—so do the explosion of bombs satirically mimic the elements, their explosions resounding as if "thunder and lightning." The bombs are rendered as not destructive, but, rather, as creative instruments; the devastation they cause is creation made easy (to dream a race via bombs). In this way, destruction is transformed into the "labor pains" of male reproduction—men give birth to a new race. As Theweleit explains, "in war the bomb is male progeny . . . [W]hat he sees is not a bomb exploding. What he sees is the birth of a new world" (p. 294). Odilo experiences this power when he comes to embody the processes that create life: "National Socialism is nothing more than applied biology. Odilo is a doctor: a biological foot soldier . . . [V]iolence creates here on earth. Never before have we been so potent" (p. 150). Benno Muller-Hill addresses the expanded role of the doctor under Nazism, quoting Dr. G. Wagner, who served as "Chief Physician" of the Reich: "[The physician] should go back to his origins, he should again become a priest, he should become priest and physician in one."[13] But the "spiritual" aspect of this science manifests itself, Muller-Hill continues, in striving for a metaphysical ideal—recreating a lost Nordic people—via forced evolution:

> For these theologians of the cult of destruction, the different, the other man (the Jew, the schizophrenic, the Gypsy) became a seemingly insoluble riddle. The total and final solution of this riddle was mass murder . . . The white coat was their priestly garment. Physicians with anthropological and psychiatric training had acquired . . . the right and duty to carry out selection and killing of the victims. They fought hard to retain this right, and sacrificed millions on their altars[.]
>
> (P. 94)

The religiosity of this mission is reflected in the personage of Odilo, who, as doctor, soldier, and chief priest of hereditary renewal, gets to "play God" in his role as "a biological foot soldier" who helps cure the German race via the destruction of the Jew and other hereditary "degenerates." As Goebbels would have it, the Jew "has the same function as a poisonous bacillus has in the human organism: to mobilize the resistance of healthy forces."[14] But under this historic occasion, it is the medical doctor who is at the forefront of mobilizing a healthy, Nordic gene pool. Prominent Nazi doctor and professor, V. Von Weizsacker, encouraged the role of the physician in weaning out hereditary "degenerates," proclaiming that "the concept of sacrifice represents a fusion of killing and redemption"; in the end, a "policy of extermination" shall prove a "constructive" enterprise.[15] Neil Easterbrook, applying Lifton, similarly observes that, "confronted by their Hippocratic oath, doctors at Auschwitz claimed that they were excising gangrenous organs to save the social body. The very position is built on a manifest absurdity—'a vision and practice of killing to heal.'"[16]

Odilo's narrating double casts the "triumph" of Auschwitz as but a human extension of divine energies accessed via the inner-most resources of human desire, "the sacred fire": "It is commonplace to say that the triumph of Auschwitz was essentially organizational: we found the sacred fire that hides in the human heart—and built an autobahn that went there" (p. 123). Again, an industrial killing apparatus is depicted in terms at once organic and spiritual. Auschwitz is represented as an extension of self—an expression of the "human heart." Nazism's "reactionary modernism"—Lifton's term for "the regime's combination of technocracy and pre-modern visions and structures" (p. 494)—provided the historical occasion for wedding archetypal expression with modernity's industrial advancement. Such is the compelling case that Amis's ***Time's Arrow*** forces upon his readers: the human capacity to tap into internal "sacred fire" whose energies can be channeled into and sanctioned within the arena of "rational" organizations and regimes of control.

Notes

1. Martin Amis, *Time's Arrow* (New York: Vintage, 1992), p. 6. All subsequent references are to this edition and are cited parenthetically.
2. Robert Jay Lifton, *The Nazi Doctors: Medical Killings and the Psychology of Genocide* (New York: Basic Books, 1986), p. 418.
3. In his "Afterword," Amis acknowledges his debt to Lifton's *Nazi Doctors*: "My novel could not and would not have been written without it."
4. Robert Griffin, ed., "Part II: Fascism in Germany," *Fascism* (Oxford: Oxford Univ. Press, 1995), p. 133.
5. Klaus Theweleit, "The Bomb's Womb and the Genders of War," *Gendering War Talk,* ed. Miriam Cook and Angela Woollacott (Princeton: Princeton Univ. Press, 1993), p. 284.
6. Griffin, pp. 124-25.
7. Phil Joffe, "Language Damage: Nazis and Naming in Martin Amis's *Time's Arrow,*" *Nomina Africana* 9 (1995): 3.
8. Sara Ruddick, "Notes Towards a Feminist Peace Politics." *Gendering War Talk,* p. 120.
9. Maya Slater, "Problems When Time Moves Backwards: Martin Amis's *Time's Arrow,*" *English* 42 (1993): 145.
10. Paul Antze. "Telling Stories, Making Selves: Memory and Identity in Multiple Personality Disorder," *Tense Past: Cultural Essays in Trauma and Memory,* ed. Paul Antze and Michael Lambek (New York: Routledge, 1996), p. 11.
11. The narrator would continue to feign helplessness in the postwar years as well, conveniently excusing—*just as he did during the Nazi era*—his failure of conscience in acquiescing to his double's will: "I keep expecting the world to make sense. It doesn't. It won't. Ever. You have to harden your heart to pain and suffering. And quick. Like right away at the very latest" (p. 82). Tod would also go about his postwar medical practice in a mechanistic manner, opaquely detached from his patients, and merely performing his duties while avoiding saving his "soul" (in a manner of speaking): "the soul can only hang in the dark . . . and let darkness have its day. Beneath, the body does what it does, in mechanical exertions of will and sinew, while the soul waits" (pp. 74-75).
12. Donald E. Morse, "Overcoming Time: 'The Present of Things Past' in History and Fiction," *The Delegated Intellect* (New York: Peter Lang, 1995), p. 216.
13. Benno Muller-Hill, *Murderous Science: Elimination by Scientific Selection of Jews, Gypsies, and Others, Germany 1933-1945,* trans. George R. Fraser (Oxford: Oxford Univ. Press, 1988), p. 94.
14. Griffin, p. 120.
15. *Ibid.,* p. 92.
16. Neil Easterbrook, "'I know that it is to do with trash and shit, and that it is wrong in time': Narrative Reversal in Martin Amis' *Time's Arrow,*" *CCTE Studies* 55 (1995): 56-57.

D. J. Taylor (essay date 29 May 2000)

SOURCE: Taylor, D. J. "Will They Survive?" *New Statesman* 13, no. 607 (29 May 2000): 41-4.

[*In the following essay, Taylor chronicles the careers of Kingsley Amis and son Martin Amis, calling* Experience *an edgy and candid memoir.*]

I only once saw Kingsley Amis in the flesh: it was ten years ago this August, at a party held at the Savile Club in London to celebrate the 80th birthday of the novelist William Cooper. To enter, guests had a choice of separate staircases. As luck would have it, Amis reached the summit of the left-hand stair at precisely the moment that his second ex-wife, Elizabeth Jane Howard, hove into view from the right. For a second or two, each contemplated the other with a kind of stark horror, after which Sir Kingsley—his face by now a painterly shade of puce—stalked back off the way he had come.

The temptation to convert this brief non-encounter into a luminous metaphor—the novelist failing to confront in life one of the dilemmas he had failed to confront in art—is irresistible. (Amusingly, only 18 months before, Amis had written to Robert Conquest: "I continue to bear a charmed life and never set eyes on the bag. Almost unbelievable that it's now eight years last Nov that I last did.") All the more so when set against some of the letters despatched to the Valkyrie of the stairwell 27 years before. "Dearest Jane," he wrote in December 1962, at the start of the affair that ended his first marriage. "I can't think of anything more wonderful than that first time in room 238, while it was going on I realised that this was what sexual ecstasy was, though I didn't put it to myself like that, not being in much shape for thought."

One shouldn't perhaps be unduly startled by this kind of thing: even outraged elderly gentlemen are entitled to have fallen in love and to have owned up to it in writing. A similar distance is achieved by setting late-period Evelyn Waugh (a figure to whom Amis senior sometimes bears an uncomfortably close resemblance) to the respectful thirty something pursuer of the teenaged Laura Herbert. And yet the "Dearest Hoopoe/Dearest Dove" letters—Amis had a fondness for ornithological endearment—are remarkable on two separate counts: first, because they contain exactly the sort of high-octane emotion you can imagine Amis pissing on in his novels; second, because of the material with which they coexist. The writer who keeps his life in watertight compartments is a fixture of the 20th-century literary scene, but surely Amis himself must have been struck by some of the weirder juxtapositions of his correspondence? Here he is, for example, on 22 January 1963, scribbling a routine note from the current Amis domicile in Cambridge to Conquest: "Bloody awful old life, isn't it? Am cold, have the shits, also catarrh." A few hours later, on the other hand, "My dearest Jane" is being informed that her last "was indeed a lovely letter", and that "I was pleased when you asked me to forgive you for kissing me in restaurants, and you may do so again, but only on condition that you go on kissing me in restaurants." Which won out? The shits or the restaurant reveries? Obviously, it is possible to be violently in love and have an upset stomach. At the same time, dichotomies of this sort—rage/civility; courtesy/frostiness; deference/chippiness—are highly characteristic of the bulky and exceptionally readable *Letters of Kingsley Amis.*

As an editorial guide to his subject's life, work and times, Zachary Leader has done a particularly good job. At the most rudimentary level of the annotator's dungeon, references to "Andrew Sinclair bum" or, in a letter to Karl Miller, "I've looked at the Ballock-High Culture casually and it strikes me as something of a stinkeroo" can't have been easy to decode. Even so, for all Leader's ability to saturate himself in the literary subculture of the Fifties and Sixties, the victims of several chance scurrilities still elude him. If, among the half-dozen or so key associates of Amis's maturity, any well-known names seem under-represented, they are Hilary "Hilly" Bardwell, his first wife (presumably because so very few letters survive), and his old college chum Bruce Montgomery (90 letters in the Bodleian, uninspectable until 2035). Starting with a no-nonsense Oxford lefty letter of 1941, and ending, all too typically, with a weary grammarian's lament to the *Spectator* a month before his death, Leader's 1,200 pages are at the very least a somewhat more reliable guide to Planet Amis than Eric Jacob's rushed 1995 biography.

As for what they may do to retrieve the popular image of Amis as a permanently incandescent right-wing gloom merchant—inevitably the side indulged by last month's newspaper serialisation—you rather feel that any rescue activity will come too late. Cartoon Amis, like Waugh—that comparison again—is more or less ineradicable from the public consciousness. Martin Amis has said that, after his father's death, he hoped it would be possible for the "whole man" to be revealed, and certainly the *Letters* make a fair stab at this. There are the riotous, proto-lad effusions to Larkin, which conceal, or fail to conceal, a surprising amount of emotion (no doubt about it, back in the late Forties dawn, with the postwar world taking tantalising shape around them, Amis and Larkin really loved each other), but there are also some deeply felt expressions of condolence and sympathy, and appreciative letters to fans and, in the decade and a half of his academic career, to students. Being thanked for something by Amis, being taught by Amis, being loved by Amis, looks as if it could be a rewarding experience. Provided, that is, it was one of his good days.

This is a vital qualification. For down beneath the pleasantries of even his matiest communications, something stirs. The genuinely stroppy letters, which tend to predominate in the last third of his life (though there are some corkers from earlier on), seem to have been launched at the mildest provocation. One wonders how the American academic Dale Salwak, who had laboured for 17 years to produce his *Kingsley Amis: Modern Novelist,* felt to be told that "the level of your performance seems to me to be so low as not to earn a place on any serious publisher's list" (the book, once published, was hailed as "mandatory reading for all students of Amis"). Or how the then *Sunday Times* staffer Jane Thynne would have felt had she ever received the apparently unsent note ("Honestly for Christ's sake", etc) composed after some supposedly injudicious sub-editing of a restaurant column, a photocopy of which was found among Amis's papers. Thynne, even more strangely, remembers her dealings with Amis as perfectly civil. What had Salwak and

Thynne done? Or, perhaps more important, what did Amis think they had done? In each case, the fury seems altogether unmerited by the fault, a carefully hoarded proxy bitterness bearing hardly any relation to the slight.

The testiness of Amis's art was known long before the details of his life came to light, and it would be surprising if the peculiarly personal quality of some of the fiction didn't spring from some equally embattled raw material. Sure enough, Leader produces a shrewd letter to Larkin from 1959—and Amis was always shrewd about himself, far too shrewd for us to let some of the public statements pass—in which, contemplating the end of some adulterous episode or other, he reflects: "Trouble is it's so hard to give all that up, habit of years and all that, and such bloody good fun, too . . . But being walked out on by H (and kids), the sure-fire consequence of any further discovery, is a rather unwelcome prospect, too. You can't have it both ways, you see."

And yet, as Amis's aptly titled penultimate novel (*You Can't Do Both,* 1994) presupposes, you can try. Boiled down to their essence, Amis's novels have a habit of turning into variations—immensely skilful variations, mostly—on the theme of having your cake and eating it. Like many of his heroes, the younger, pre-1960s Amis was caught up in the same dilemmas of randy inclination and outraged *amour propre,* not much liking Hilly's affair with the journalist Henry Fairlie, while a year or so later regretting to Larkin the loss of "the most splendid busty redhead in an ideal location". Other letters manage to make equally important points about their author with less obtrusiveness: a particularly good one to the American academic William Van O'Connor, for example, about Jim Dixon's social origins. The last few—Larkin dead, Amis quartered on Hilly and her third husband—are weary despatches from the life of the Garrick-lounging, purple-faced literary knight. It's necessary to look back to the deferential correspondence of the Fifties with people such as Anthony Powell and Edith Sitwell ("It is very kind of you to want to arrange a lunch party for me . . . PS *I do hope the indisposition you mention is now completely at an end*") to gain an idea of the distance travelled.

* * *

With Amis junior, the journey was of a wholly different kind: plenty of obstacles, certainly (***Experience*** has some well-chosen words on this subject), but those of expectation and overexposure, rather than people simply not knowing who he was. As a contender, literary or otherwise, the young Amis knew he was made (if not quite from the start, then certainly from the time he was able to see Dad in action), and he used—quite justifiably, given his talent—some of Dad's connections. The middle-aged Amis, conscious perhaps of that immortal *NS* competition for unlikely sounding book titles in which the victor was his own **"My Struggle"**, is winningly candid about this. It would be unfair of me to reveal which Oxford English don used to remark, in the late 1970s, "Oh yes, we had young Amis apply here a few years back, and it gave me the greatest possible pleasure to turn him down", because Amis junior's role in the proceedings was on much the same level as Salwak's—innocent bystander caught up in the bewildering crossfire.

Oddly enough (or not so oddly, given his habitual shrewdness), it was Powell who first foresaw the writing of ***Experience.*** "I wonder if Martin is planning an Amis Father and Son?" he confided to his journal on 14 September 1986, adding that it "might not be a bad theme". He was right. ***Experience,*** sometimes because of the paternal shadow, sometimes for other reasons, is an edgy book: candid, occasionally defensive—a quality hitherto absent from Martin Amis's work—mildly dogged in its endeavours to set records straight or burnish up defiled pieces of silverware. More to the point, it comes at a time when Martin's reputation has lost something of its once Olympian sheen. As a case-hardened Amis-watcher and admirer, I would maintain that the rot (defined as inability or unwillingness to advance from previous position) set in during the later stages of ***London Fields*** (1989), continued through ***Time's Arrow*** (1991) and became seriously, disablingly apparent in ***The Information*** (1995). ***Night Train,*** the 1997 US police procedural, had a slack, laboured feel, even for a novel of 150 pages. And yet Martin is still capable of springing the odd surprise. Reading **"State of the Nation"** for the first time (collected in ***Heavy Water,*** 1998), I can remember literally breaking down with laughter at the celebratory disdain, or the disdainful celebration, that Martin contrived to attach to the exploits of a couple of wheel-clamping bouncers. Still, somehow, despite the aimings and the blamings, despite the deaths and the tragedies, despite the teeth and the tittle-tattle—all covered here in huge and unrelenting detail—our man shapes up.

Whatever the peaks of candour, defensiveness and doggedness (and also, it should be said, sympathy, generosity and humour) scaled in ***Experience,*** it is nevertheless an extremely odd book. It has an impetus: the mad mid-Nineties of Kingsley's death; the finding of his lost daughter; the discovery that his adored cousin Lucy Partington had been butchered by Fred West. It has a grudge: the press and one or two, or perhaps three or four, of its envoys. And it has a fixation: the dentist's chair. Side by side, though, runs a pack of other stuff: Bellow and Nabokov, just in case anyone had any doubts where Amis came from, or where in the last resort he wants to go; a series of droll, callow and highly self-conscious letters written by the teenaged Amis to his father and stepmother in the late 1960s—"I just want to be comfortable, to have a sense of establishing my own discipline by doing certain things myself, and to fuck girls (a litotes I couldn't resist and not to be given unfair emphasis)". All of this is undercut and garnished by some seriously irritating footnotes (justified by Amis on the grounds that we can see the ulterior mind working in parallel), which are either an excuse to settle personal or professional scores or to flatter old friends. Faced with half a page on John Gross's advice to apprentice reviewers (Vladimir and Saul called in as expert witnesses, naturally), or with a description of John Bayley and Iris Murdoch as "genuinely eccentric, genuinely dreamy, while also being vivid physical presences: tousled, humid, intimate" and so on, the reader gets a sudden, awful sense of minor personal baggage gratuitously unpacked.

To make this point is perhaps to give some idea of the many levels—some complementary, others sharply opposed—on which ***Experience*** functions. One reads the sections about Kingsley—Kingsley's alleged anti-Semitism being politely but devastatingly rebuked, Kingsley's lethargic decline—and the elegies to sweet-natured, cruelly used Lucy with an awareness of something deep within the writer sincerely and courageously revealed, before stumbling a page or so later on some fussy personal detail or irritation. One just doesn't care about James Buchan's review of ***Time's Arrow,*** A S Byatt's telephone technique or the revelation—ironic or not? Who can tell?—that "John [Travolta] and I would share two intimate dinners at his rented house in Beverley Hills, north of Sunset, and then a farewell lunch in his trailer on the set of *Get Shorty*". And then, amid the teenage and twenty something years, through the later stages of Martin's loused-up education (from which he was rescued by Elizabeth Jane Howard), Oxford First and fledgling novels, tumble the babes, dozens of them. There are "Rachel" and Ros, Tina (Brown) and Tamasin (Day Lewis), Julie and Mary (later Countess of Waldegrave), Emma (Churchill's granddaughter) and Lamorna, whose child provided yet another shock to its real father in those souped-up early Nineties; leading on to his first wife, Antonia, and second wife, Isabel. Never, perhaps, has such a collection of well-bred and suitably connected young women wafted through the pages of an English literary autobiography: a procession of lustre and *éclat* so crowded that, frankly, you wonder how he found time to write all those books.

Finally, and emblematically, there are the teeth. Martin's teeth. James Joyce's teeth. Nabokov's teeth. The mute, existential horror of the orthodontist's chamber. Certainly, the reconstructive surgery that eventually had to be performed on Martin's tumorous lower jaw sounds ghastly in the extreme—so ghastly as to embarrass and shame those of us (myself included) who wrote jokey columns about it. At the same time, one wonders if the sessions with Mike Szabatura (a dozen index references) are quite as central to the freight-loads of loss, mortality and recrimination being busily unhitched here as the author imagines. Perhaps one should give Martin the benefit of the doubt. And that, to use a familiar Amis formulation, is what we Amis fans keep doing these days: we keep on giving him the benefit of the doubt, even here in a world where the profound and the profoundly trivial march side by side, a world full of desperate signals from the writer trapped amid the celebrity wreckage.

Both *The Letters of Kingsley Amis* and ***Experience,*** in their separate ways, seem to have been compiled with one eye on a remote and exacting audience: posterity. Martin's book, in particular, carries with it an almost painful sense (Nabokov, Bellow, Joyce . . .) of a writer standing cap-in-hand before some far-off literary judgement seat. The influence of *père et fils* on English life over the past half-century has been, on the one hand, almost incalculable and, on the other, entirely (and one should hastily add, innocently) malign. If *Lucky Jim* and its successors had a single literary consequence, it was to make the world safe for a certain kind of English writing—comedy slapstick—at the expense of another. Anyone who doubts the generic quality of the post-*Jim* movement should note the endless invocation of Amis senior's name on the jackets of books by William Boyd, Tom Sharpe and others, and the stream of variations on the *Jim* cover illustrations (boozy fat-man stares vacantly into space). Martin, more directly, was the key stylistic influence of the Eighties and early Nineties, the first mainstream importer of modern US rhythms and inflections to the Thames Valley, and the spiritual godfather to those pageants of home-grown prose that begin: "Jimmy was fucked. Seriously. Seriously fucked. Fucked and then some." I have bitter personal experience of this: the difficulty of getting the Amis virus out of your veins once it sets up camp there.

Aside from fitting under the "serious comedian" label, there is not much to connect father and son as writers. Kingsley, famously, found his son's novels difficult to get on with, and wondered whether he might not be trying too hard. Martin, although he now inhabits a study littered with the parental *oeuvre,* seems to take the view that there were times when Dad could have tried a bit harder. If there is a shared characteristic, it is perhaps the ability of the personal, distant, capering figure of the author to obtrude into the art. *Lucky Jim* is full of these false battles—the author disliking some of his characters so much that the victories won over them by Jim Dixon are simply arbitrary. In much the same way, Amis junior's books are shot through with an aching loftiness, the characters—the downmarket characters especially—habitually stretched into caricature whenever their creator remembers, as he does every page or so, just how hilarious he finds native oik-speak. Curiously, ***Experience*** shares this trait, and even Amis's cleaning lady gets to address him as "Miss Tramis". No modern English novelist has ever made me laugh quite so much as Martin Amis. Equally, no modern English novelist has ever made me feel quite so uneasy about the source of that laughter, not out of any lurking PC dread, but because, on a much more basic level, it just isn't fair.

But then, who expects comedy to be fair? Meanwhile, this month's newspapers have been wall-to-wall Amis: an unprecedented media tumult about two "writers" in which the question of what the writers write has been practically ignored. From the angle of that spectral judging panel, this is a very bad sign—the worst sign, as Martin might put it. Ominously, five years after his death, two-thirds of Kingsley's books are already out of print. As for Martin, stuck in mid-career, you fear that the literary celebrity niche he has carved out for himself will become increasingly problematic. ***Experience,*** as you may have gathered, is crammed with accusing references to the Fourth Estate. Some of them, notably the denunciation of Eric Jacob's behaviour after Kingsley's death, are well-deserved; others are a bit less so. Amis has a line about "prolific reviewers of fiction" turning anxious whenever it looks as if the fictional climate might be about to change. I didn't altogether care (a familiar Kingsley formula, as in "I didn't care for your friend who wanted the lift/wouldn't pay his round", etc) for the reference to "prolific reviewers of fiction", with its faint imputation of careless punditry. There are worse failings, surely, than writing lots of book reviews. And, oddly enough, the fictional climate is changing, a process that took root five or even ten years ago, turning less metropolitan, less wrapped up in itself, less stylistically snookered—less Amisian, to be blunt. Whatever one finally thinks of these huge, embattled chronicles of two intimately connected literary and emotional careers, they represent the end of something in British literary life, not a beginning.

Brad Hooper (review date 1-15 June 2000)

SOURCE: Hooper, Brad. Review of *Experience,* by Martin Amis. *Booklist* 96, nos. 19/20 (1-15 June 2000): 1795.

[*In the following favorable review of* Experience, *Hooper asserts that Amis's "provocative, exhilarating memoir is beautifully written."*]

Martin Amis is the son of British author Kingsley Amis (best known for his novel *Lucky Jim,* 1954). Martin, too, has become a well-known and popular novelist and here turns to nonfiction with a memoir [***Experience***] that, even at his relatively young age, certainly covers a lot of territory. This quirky work floats back and forth in time and carries with it a sly sense of irony; it is heavily footnoted on almost every page, as if it were a scholarly work. Amis is, at once, egocentric, funny, and vulnerable. He writes a lot about his father, presenting a rich though certainly one-sided portrait of the eccentric, cranky Kingsley. Amis knows a lot of writers, and he indulges in gossip about them but also talks about them seriously and meaningfully. Amis also includes plenty of details about his personal life, including stories about his mother, stepmother, wife, kids, and a cousin who was murdered. This intimate though selective look at his life allows readers a considerably closer view of Amis' true emotions than can be garnered from his novels. But, ultimately, language is Amis' strong suit, and, indeed, his provocative, exhilarating memoir is beautifully written.

Joe Moran (essay date summer 2000)

SOURCE: Moran, Joe. "Artists and Verbal Mechanics: Martin Amis's *The Information.*" *Critique* 41, no. 4 (summer 2000): 307-17.

[*In the following essay, Moran sees George Gissing's* New Grub Street *as a literary precedent for Amis's examination of the publishing industry in* The Information.]

Martin Amis's novel ***The Information*** raises significant questions about the production and consumption of literature and the conditions of contemporary authorship. In this article, I discuss those questions in relation to both the novel itself and the pre- and postpublication controversy surrounding it—not because I share the intentionalist assumptions of much of the media discussion of that controversy but because the relationship between the private activity of writing and the public process by which books are marketed and consumed is itself one of the novel's main themes.

Amis demonstrates his fundamentally satirical purpose in relation to this theme by having the novel revolve around two wholly contrasting central characters, Richard Tull and Gwyn Barry—both authors, born less than a day apart and "friends" and rivals since Oxford. As the novel opens, Tull's career, which began promisingly with an effortless, brief stint as a merciless but brilliant book critic, has ground spectacularly to a halt. It now consists largely of reviewing conscientious but dull biographies of minor English authors and composing long, turgid, mostly unpublishable novels. Barry, meanwhile, followed his undistinguished university career by writing crib notes for A-level set texts for sale in supermarkets. He now is basking in newfound wealth and celebrity, having written a bland but lavishly praised and reader-friendly best seller, *Amelior,* which, according to Tull, "would only be remarkable if Gwyn had written it with his foot" (Amis 140).

Use of character opposites is a recurring strategy in Amis's work. The relationship between Tull and Barry mirrors the rivalry between the best-selling author Mark Asprey and the unsuccessful Samson Young in ***London Fields*** and that between Terry Service and Gregory Riding in ***Success***; but the doubling in ***The Information*** seems particularly marked and permeates all aspects of the narrative. Whereas Tull is impotent, Barry is sexually voracious and successful; Tull is aging horribly, Barry gracefully; Tull lives in a cramped house in a downwardly mobile area of west London, Barry in a mansion in Holland Park. Tull only has the upper hand in the pair's regular games of chess, snooker, and tennis; but toward the end of the novel, Barry takes expensive coaching to rectify that situation and then breaks off their rather surprising friendship. Clearly, these two characters are deliberate stereotypes—Amis, as Adam Mars-Jones puts it, "doesn't develop his characters so much as wear them out" (Mars-Jones 19)—aimed at presenting, around different conceptions of "success" and "failure," an unremittingly cynical picture of London literary life in the 1990s.

In its dual approach, ***The Information*** presents a version of what Kathy McDermott calls "the Grub Street myth," which emerged in the eighteenth century with the decline of aristocratic patronage and the new concept of the literary text as marketable property. McDermott draws on the arguments of Raymond Williams and others to suggest that the notion of authors possessing an authority separate from the sphere of exchange emerged simultaneously with the development of the literary marketplace. The eighteenth-century distinction between "the author-literatus ('man of genius') and the hack, the verbal mechanic, the mere producer of texts" was clearly a response to the reality of the author as an entrepreneur within that marketplace (McDermott 160). As part of this discursive formation, the activities of Grub Street, the actual London thoroughfare near the bookshops and publishers of Fleet Street and Ludgate Hill that was populated with ambitious young authors from the late seventeenth century onward, became a powerfully negative trope for the "hack" writer and the meretricious world of literary professionalism. The distinction between different kinds of writing is central to ***The Information***—a distinction exemplified by Tull's desire to write novels of "genius" as opposed to ones of mere "talent" (Amis 170-71), his almost bloody-minded belief in the virtues of his own unreadability, and the irony of his having to work as a "verbal mechanic," churning out book reviews to support himself.

More specifically, as several reviewers of Amis's novel noted, there are clear, and (given the author's general self-consciousness and openness about his literary influences) probably intentional parallels with George Gissing's *New Grub Street*—a novel that Bernard Bergonzi has called "the most explicit fictional study of literary life ever written in England" (Bergonzi 9), and which attempts to update the Grub Street myth to late-Victorian Britain. Gissing's novel has two main characters: Edwin Reardon, a blocked and unsuccessful novelist living in genteel poverty in Regent's Park, "a personality wholly unfitted for the rough and tumble of the world's labour-market," who refuses to compromise his art despite suffering considerable economic hardship; and Jasper Milvain, who wins easy success and fame by opportunistically manipulating the conditions of literary production in the emerging industry of mass circulation journalism. For Milvain, there is "no question of the divine afflatus"; he aims to produce, in his own words, "good, coarse, marketable stuff for the world's vulgar [. . .] novels out-trashing the trashiest that ever sold fifty thousand copies" (Gissing 462, 43). Like Gwyn Barry, Milvain emerges all-triumphant at the end of the novel, in both professional and personal terms. Just as Barry makes love to Tull's wife Gina at the end of ***The Information,*** Milvain marries Reardon's wife Amy (and acquires her £10,000 inheritance) when Reardon dies. Gissing's novel can be read as a jeremiad about the limitations imposed on authors by the growing commodification of literature and the rise of mass culture, epitomized by such phenomena as the three-decker novel, the circulating libraries like Mudie's and W. H. Smith's that effectively ran the Victorian book trade, and popular journalism.

Just as Gissing explores the tension between commercial and artistic imperatives in the book business in the 1890s, Amis updates some of the main elements and oppositions of *New Grub Street* partly as a way of examining recent changes in the publishing industry. One of the principal subjects in ***The Information*** is the takeover of book publishing by global media empires and specifically their subsidizing large advances and lavish promotional campaigns for a few big-name authors. At the center of these developments, brokering huge deals between authors and publishers, is the increasingly powerful figure of the literary agent, encapsulated in the novel by Gal Aplanalp, a glamorous, dynamic woman who seems more interested in the personal quirks of her authors than in their work. She tells her prospective client, Tull: "Writers need definition. The public can only keep in mind one thing per writer. Like a signature. Drunk, young, mad, fat, sick: you know" (Amis 130). In fact, most of the authors on her list, even the novelists, are already celebrities, comedians, newscasters, and other figures from the world of television or commercial entertainment. Her star client, Barry, has been comprehensively marketed as a media "personality"; indeed he spends most of the first three sections of the novel being interviewed, photographed, or making other public appearances.

Gwyn has honed these performances to smooth perfection. He is such a consummate media operator that he can pause in mid-syllable when the interviewer's tape machine clicks off and resume the sentence when the machine is recording again (Amis 296).

The third and central section of the book, which consists of a publicity tour to the United States made by both Barry and Tull, seems to incorporate a common complaint that the relentless pushing of a few lead titles and authors by the major publishers means that the majority of authors are ignored. While Gwyn receives an extensive promotional effort in all the major American cities from his publishers, the small independent house with which Richard has been placed seems unwilling to publicize his book, or even to distribute it to bookshops. At a joint book signing in Boston, Barry wears out four ballpoints dealing with his teeming crowd of fans; Tull has two visitors, both of whom appear to be mentally disturbed (Amis 374-75). The sales potential of Richard's novel, *Untitled,* however, is not helped by his own hostility to the marketing process. Standing in for Gwyn on a radio talk show, he refuses to play along with the publicity game by responding to the host's question about what his novel "says" and reflects:

> The contemporary idea seemed to be that the first thing you did, as a communicator, was come up with some kind of slogan, and either you put it on a coffee mug or a T-shirt or a bumper sticker—or else you wrote a novel about it [. . .]. And now that writers spent as much time telling everyone what they were doing as they spent actually doing it, then they would start doing it that way round too, eventually.
>
> (Amis 339-40)

Amis's treatment of the joint Tull-Barry tour of the United States, during which Richard fears that British writers in America tend to be "swept up in the indigenous panic of make-or-break" (Amis 335), connects with debates around what John Sutherland described two decades ago as "the American future of British fiction" (Sutherland 46). The identification of the United States with the triumph of the marketplace over cultural distinction (a feature of British cultural life from Matthew Arnold's *Culture and Anarchy* onward) has resurfaced as a way of discussing what is seen as a current climate of bestsellerdom and hype in the publishing industry. But again that is nothing new: Sutherland includes a case study of the British critical reception of E. L. Doctorow's *Ragtime* in 1976, in which he shows how the almost universally hostile response to that novel functioned as "a sort of Boston tea party in reverse," a concerted and collective response to "a novel marketed in the ultra-American fashion" (Sutherland 75-76). Those concerns were voiced with even greater urgency from the mid-1980s onward, when American publishers began to exploit the full potential of the international (particularly the English-speaking) market as an extra source of revenue and prestigious independent houses in the United Kingdom, like Cape and Chatto, began to be swallowed up by American corporations.

Although the general renewed vigor of the British book business, which these changes helped to produce, is clearly one of the satirical targets of ***The Information,*** the novel combines that development with a scathing view of the coziness and corruption of the old literary establishment and its forms of quality control and peer review. The book reviewing apparatus that the marketing techniques of the major houses have pre-empted and supplanted is revealed as thoroughly insular and self-serving. For example, Richard manages to survive and prosper in the London literary world for several years on the cultural capital obtained from the inconclusive response to his first novel, simply because among its reviewers "nobody understood it, or even finished it, but, equally, nobody was sure it was shit" (Amis 40). Tull turns out his book reviews as a matter of pure economic necessity with scant regard for the worth of the books or responsibility to the authors. More seriously, he is quite prepared to work the system in his failed plan to "fuck Gwyn up" (Amis 45). In attempting to scupper Barry's chances of winning a distinguished and lucrative literary prize for which he has been shortlisted, Tull effects an introduction to the three judges by wangling excellent reviews for their latest works in his capacity as literary editor of the small circulation *Little Magazine.* Tull's other writerly life, as fiction and poetry editor of the Tantalus Press, a vanity publisher, presents as negative a view of amateur publishing as Barry's career does of the professional, corporate-owned book business. According to Tull, private publishing "had close links with prostitution [. . .] a writer ought to be able to claim that he had never paid for it—never in his life" (Amis 75). If Barry's success suggests that worthless authors are achieving fame, Tull's slush pile of unsolicited manuscripts points to yet more talentless nobodies, sustained by writing schools and residential courses, whose anonymity is well earned. Tull sees countless examples of "the novel that everybody was supposed to have in them" and dismisses them all as "anti-literature. Propaganda, aimed at the self." (Amis 230, 77)

Obviously, Tull is implicated in these corrupted forms of literary production to varying degrees, but as a "marooned modernist" (Amis 170) he is also partially aloof from them. Although his novels produce migraine convulsions and double vision in anyone who attempts to read them, he is portrayed, like Reardon in *New Grub Street,* as a difficult individual but a genuine artist. Unlike Barry, he at least has some depth as a character and a sense of the complexity and difficulty of life and art. He functions as the intervening consciousness of the novel, and his internal voice tends to elide with that of the narrator. The crucial passages about "the information"—the intimations of the slow decay and death of both individuals and the universe—are first communicated by the narrator and then appear in the thoughts of Tull. Richard, the novel makes clear, is privy to that information (unlike any of the other characters in the novel) because he is an artist and is "what an artist has to be: harassed to the point of insanity or stupefaction by first principles" (Amis 11).

Richard's status as a serious novelist and his access to the information are seen as giving him a gravitas that is absent (and here I restate a commonly voiced criticism about Amis's portrayal of his female characters) from Gina Tull and Lady Demeter de Rougemont, the two main female characters in the novel. These literary wives are nurturing, submissive, anti-intellectual figures who are apparently immune from the quest for worldly success that consumes Barry and Tull. Indeed they are free from any real connection with literature. On the first page of the novel Gina is described as "a woman. She knew so much more about tears than he did. She didn't know about Swift's juvenilia, or Wordsworth's senilia [. . .] she didn't know Proust. But she knew tears" (Amis 9). At the same time, she is also something of a literary "groupie" who had worked her way methodically through a series of poet, novelist, and playwright suitors in London until her marriage to Richard. Despite that superficial brush with the world of letters, she is largely unsympathetic toward Tull's unrewarded ambitions; she has given him a year of grace to make one last effort at making money from novel writing, before he must give it up to concentrate on more lucrative book reviews and nonfiction. (That also mirrors *New Grub Street,* in which Amy, who married Reardon as an aspiring novelist and is dismayed at his career curve since then, is now hostile to his more high-minded literary aspirations.) After Gina gives yet another ultimatum concerning their financial situation, Tull claims that he cannot give up writing novels

> because then he would be left with experience, with untranslated and unmediated experience. Because then he would be left with life [. . .]. And this was a disastrous word to say to a woman—to women, who bear life, who bring it into the world, screaming, and will never let it come second to anything.
>
> (Amis 85)

Tull's position as a genuine "artist," largely established by his dissimilarity to Barry, is reinforced by his unsympathetic treatment at the hands of the women in the novel and his preference for manly "art" over womanly "life."

The Information, of course, is not meant to be a sociological study of literary production and reception, and the caricatured nature of its vision of the literary life is obviously partly deliberate. However, by constructing his novel around cartoon versions of "success" and "failure," Amis largely avoids dealing with the complicated relationship between economic and cultural capital involved in the recent growth of serious literary fiction as a phenomenon of the mass market. In Tim Waterstone's succinct judgment of the Thatcher era in Britain, "it was a philistine decade which saw the restoration of the book" (McCrum 22). The peculiar nature of publishing, stemming from the semiprofessionalism of the industry and the status of books as positional goods, is always likely to form some resistance to attempts by large corporations to commercialize the industry. As Richard Todd observes, however, specific historical factors also contribute to the transformation of British literary culture that involves more than the simple triumph of the marketplace. Book retailers, editors and publishers, academic and journalistic critics, literary prize committees, literary festival organizers, and other agents have all contributed to a complex process of "contemporary literary canon-formation" (Todd 9).

The regular media controversies in Britain over the Booker Prize shortlist exemplify the tensions and arguments that the process of canon formation produces. The ease with which Gwyn picks up a literary prize dubbed "the mini-Nobel" (Amis 104), huge royalties for his novels, and routinely laudatory reviews does not really hint at its complexity. Like Gissing before him, Amis presents the broader process by which literature has been co-opted into commodity production as a straightforward victory for cultural philistinism. Tull's anguished cry that "you cannot know if a book is good" is therefore nothing to do with cultural relativism; he knows very well what is "good" and what is not. His frustration stems from the fact that Barry's lack of worth is clear but not "demonstrable" (Amis 136-37). Tull knows (and, by implication, so should the reader) that Gwyn's books are the "purest trex," but everyone else in the novel laps them up. Tull summarily dismisses the notion that best-selling work may be of any value, claiming that "a million people are *always* wrong" (Amis 43, 105).

My aim is not to test the "accuracy" of the novel against other sources, but I need to mention historical referents to discuss the novel's relationship to the publicity surrounding it. It may be significant that Amis's projection of the literary "personality" onto an obviously lampooned figure—Gwyn Barry—underplays the ways in which all kinds of cultural producers may now be caught up in these promotional practices. At a local level, the increasingly aggressive marketing of publishing houses has put pressure on less-obviously commercial authors to submit to print interviews and television appearances. "These days," as a writer in the *New York Times* recently put it, "the most ardent apostles for art roll up their sleeves, hold their noses against the meretriciousness of the marketplace and practice a little economic determinism" (Norman 3). More generally, commentators such as Andrew Wernick have pointed to the extension of a system of competitive exchange to many areas of cultural life, which has meant that all authors, even the most avowedly noncommercial and reclusive, have become unavoidably caught up in a process by which they promote themselves as public personalities, both within their work and elsewhere (Wernick 88-89).

Some sense of the all-pervasiveness of promotion is suggested by what became known as "the Amis affair," which erupted in the first few months of 1995 and was at least partly stimulated by ***The Information.*** That January, Amis swapped agents and publishers and negotiated a £500,000 advance with HarperCollins for ***The Information*** and one subsequent book, a move that was the catalyst for an extraordinary media event. Newspapers—both broadsheet and tabloid—speculated that Amis needed the money partly to fund expensive cosmetic dental surgery, undertaken at the insistence of his new American girlfriend. The majority of reports were hostile to Amis, and many quoted A. S. Byatt's suggestion that the HarperCollins deal represented "a kind of male turkey-cocking which is extremely bad for the industry and makes life hard for young authors" ("In the Pay of the Jackal").

The affair also seemed to demonstrate one of the most common characteristics of the transformation of the author into media celebrity, namely the assumption of a close relationship between the writer and his work—what Amis himself, in his account of the affair, terms "literalism" (Self 73). Even before the book was published, the media discussion fed on the notion of ***The Information*** as *roman à clef*; Richard and Gwyn were supposedly modeled on Amis himself and Julian Barnes, a friend who fell out with Amis when Amis dispensed with the services of the agent Pat Kavanagh (Barnes's wife) in search of a higher advance. Other critics noted that the affair confirmed some of the novel's concerns about the promotional imperatives of modern publishing. They pointed out that HarperCollins, part of Rupert Murdoch's international multimedia empire, initiated the controversy by sanctioning the large advance and then "rush-released" the novel in March 1995, two months ahead of schedule, to exploit the publicity surrounding it (Quinn 36). Partly because it was fresh in critics' minds, the prominence of the affair in subsequent discussion of the book can hardly be overestimated. Indeed, I have yet to come across a review that does not mention the novel's extraliterary notoriety. The promotion enclosed the book and seemed to preclude any interpretation that did not refer to it.

This journalistic discussion of the novel presents something of a problem for academic critics of Amis, however, because literary criticism within universities has for some time been suspicious of the kinds of biographical assumptions that underpin the links made between ***The Information*** and "the Amis affair." It is ironic that the kind of media fascination with authors that is satirized in ***The Information,*** and which resurfaced in the events surrounding its publication, seemed to emerge at roughly the same time as academic criticism was moving decisively away from author-centered analyses of literary texts. Malcolm Bradbury has suggested that we now live "in two ages at once: the age of the author hyped and promoted, studied and celebrated; the age of the author denied and eliminated, desubjected and airbrushed from writing" (Bradbury 311). In another sense, however, there may also be a link between the commodification of the author as public figure, which is one of the principal themes of ***The Information,*** and his or her "death" in academic literary criticism. Jane Gaines and Celia Lury, for instance, have both explored the shift in emphasis from author copyright to company trademark as legal protection for cultural products and the subsequent undermining of the notion of the individual author as originator of the text. They have linked those developments to philosophical critiques of subjectivity and the erasure of the author by the text in poststructuralism (Gaines 212; Lury 51-52). That critique may owe less to critical theory than to the theorists of the Frankfurt school, who lament the death of the subject and its replacement by a chimera in the "culture industry." However, the effect is similar: If the author becomes merely an image to attach to interchangeable literary products to boost the profits of the major publishers, then he or she is deprived of agency and intention. Wernick makes the same point by suggesting that "the birth of the author, as an imaged Name for the 'originator' of a text, has meant the death of authorship as an authentic activity." He argues that "promotion" constructs the subject "*ab initio,*" and "in an exchange economy, where whatever is publicly inscribed necessarily participates in heteronomous processes of circulatory competition, there is no way for an author to avoid this problem. There is no *hors-promotion*" (Wernick 102, 101).

Barry's inexorable rise and Tull's decline in ***The Information*** seem to touch on these anxieties about the survival of authorship as a meaningful activity in an age of the corporate ownership of ideas and images. The novel's outcome suggests that only manufactured authors like Barry, who buy into this new situation willingly because of their own lack of integrity and talent, can survive and prosper. For most of the novel, Gwyn seems a depthless nonentity, almost a nonperson; we tend to encounter him at one remove, as he hams it up in media interviews and book signings on stage-managed publicity tours. The first time we meet him is during a photo-shoot at his home, and Tull reflects that such activities can progressively destroy one's authentic self: "The more you were photographed, the thinner it went for your inner life. Being photographed was dead time for the soul" (Amis 20-21). For the first 390 pages of the novel, which are largely told from Tull's point of view, Barry hardly seems to be a character at all. In part four, the point-of-view shifts to Barry, and he emerges as an almost impossibly awful, narcissistic figure, who spends his days composing his own official biography in his head and using and abusing his various lovers—the antithesis of the uxorious, dedicated, magnanimous persona he assumes in interviews.

We often encounter Richard trying (and largely failing) to write, but we never see Gwyn doing the activity that has made him famous; he is a "mediagenic" façade, not a "real" author. The ascendancy of Barry over Tull thus seems to represent the triumph of the commodified image over a creative aesthetic. Hence, Tull's final attempt to "fuck Gwyn up" by nailing him for plagiarism (by producing a fake *ur*-text of *Amelior* and handing it to a gossip columnist) seems anachronistic in a milieu where editors often ghost write novels for ready-made celebrities and the most important factor seems to be the personality linked to the cultural product rather than the product itself. If the main contention of anti-intentionalism in literary criticism is that a text "is not the author's (it is detached from the author at birth and goes about the world beyond his power to intend about it or control it)" (Wimsatt and Beardsley 5) then it has neatly summarized Richard's disquiet about what happens to the originating author when a text enters public circulation and becomes primarily a commodity to be promoted and sold.

Amis has also spoken of his own lack of control over the events precipitated by his negotiations with publishers and of the irony that the affair returned to some of the themes of the book. He felt as if he were "caught up in some postmodern joke [. . .] it's an awful thing to be treated phenomenally rather than in a literary way." He complained, in particular, that "the voracious idiot of publicity" had turned the dental surgery that was a straightforward medical necessity into a conceited search for "a Liberace effect" (Self 72, 74). As ***The Information*** points out, however, the conditions by which contemporary literature is published and publicized are highly circumscribed, making it perhaps not quite so "ironic" that the Amis affair seemed to provide an illustration of some of the novel's concerns. The commercial instincts of modern publishing and the growing media interest in authors mean that, once Amis had decided to push for a higher advance, it was predictable that the decision would receive publicity, that the publicity would assume connections with the novel, and that HarperCollins would exploit the situation to sell more copies of the book. It is interesting to note that Amis complained about the unwelcome attention given to events surrounding the publication of ***The Information*** in the interviews arranged as publicity for the novel.

If it is true that there is no "hors-promotion," then ***The Information*** itself, written by perhaps the most well-known contemporary British author of "literary" fiction, should not be immune from an inevitable and unavoidable process of imaging. To make that point is, I hope, not to be guilty of Amis's charge of "literalism." Apart from the theoretical questions they raise for literary criticism, the efforts of some critics to unlock the "autobiographical" elements of ***The Information*** seem, in retrospect, desperately crude. The supposed link between Gwyn Barry and Julian Barnes is particularly unconvincing. However, ***The Information*** contains signs, in less-obvious and more suggestive ways, that, in Wernick's words, "the author authors the 'author,' even as he or she writes" (Wernick 87). There are varying levels of authorial intrusion in several of Amis's novels: "Martin Amis," an author living in Notting Hill, appears in ***Money***; Mark Asprey in ***London Fields*** has the same initials as his creator; the narrator of ***The Information*** is addressed as "Mart," makes the signs "M" and "A" with his finger to a deaf boy on the beach (Amis 63), and shares certain biographical details with Amis. However, these experiments with narration, which posit identity as unstable and performative and the genres of fiction and autobiography as permeable, seem less significant for this discussion than the intense self-consciousness about the activity, material constraints and distractions of contemporary authorship that is apparent in some of the earlier novels and is particularly foregrounded in ***The Information.***

Amis has referred in interviews to the "ridiculous competitive pride" that consumes authors and to the stock exchange of literary reputation by which they measure themselves against each other as part of the intensification of the professional game that he explores in ***The Information.*** He expresses his attempt to explain the "autobiographical" element of the novel in these terms: "If you want the scoop on this book it's that both Richard and Gwyn are *me.* One is the over-rewarded side and the other is the whimper of neglect side" (Quinn 35). That account of universal and inescapable rivalries and insecurities among writers seems more convincing than the journalistic version of the novel as the settling of scores. Whatever the reason for dividing the characteristics between two antithetical personalities, the effect is limiting and forces Amis to maintain the opposition between commercialism and noncommercialism that informs a much earlier novel, *New Grub Street.* As I suggest, the mechanisms by which contemporary literature is promoted and consumed raise issues that are more complex than can be contained by any straightforward distinctions between "popular" and "literary" or ephemeral mass culture and elevated art. By maintaining those distinctions, one senses that Amis misses an opportunity to explore the ways in which all authors (including himself) have had to come to terms with the ubiquity of promotion and publicity.

Works Cited

Amis, Martin. *The Information.* London: Flamingo, 1995.

Bergonzi, Bernard. Introduction. *New Grub Street.* By George Gissing. Harmondsworth: Penguin, 1968. 9-26.

Bradbury, Malcolm. "The Telling Life: Thoughts on Literary Biography." *No, Not Bloomsbury.* By Bradbury. London: Deutsch, 1987. 309-15

Gaines, Jane. *Contested Culture: The Image, the Voice and the Law.* London: BFI, 1992.

Gissing, George. *New Grub Street.* Harmondsworth: Penguin, 1968.

"In the Pay of the Jackal." Editorial. *The Guardian* [London] 7 Jan. 1995: 24.

Lury, Celia. *Cultural Rights: Technology, Legality and Personality.* London: Routledge, 1993.

Mars-Jones, Adam. "Looking on the Blight Side." *Times Literary Supplement* 24 Mar. 1995: 19.

McCrum, Robert. "Lunatics and Suits." *The Guardian* [London] 4 March 1995, weekend section: 22.

McDermott, Kathy. "Literature and the Grub Street Myth." *Literature and History,* 8, no. 2 (Autumn 1982): 159-69.

Norman, Michael. "A Book in Search of a Buzz." *New York Times Book Review,* 30 Jan. 1994: 3, 22-25.

Quinn, Anthony. "The Investment." *The Independent* [London], 25 Mar. 1995, magazine section: 34-39.

Self, Will. "Something Amiss in Amis Country." *Esquire,* 5, no. 3 (April 1995): 70-76.

Sutherland, John. *Fiction and the Fiction Industry.* London: Athlone, 1978.

Todd, Richard. *Consuming Fictions: The Booker Prize and Fiction in Britain Today.* London: Bloomsbury, 1996.

Wernick, Andrew. "Authorship and the Supplement of Promotion." *What is an Author?* Eds. Maurice Biriotti, and Nicola Miller. Manchester: Manchester UP, 1993. 86-103.

Wimsatt, Jr., W. K., and Monroe C. Beardsley. "The Intentional Fallacy." *The Verbal Icon: Studies in the Meaning of Poetry.* By Wimsatt, Jr. Lexington: U of Kentucky P, 1954: 3-18.

Henry Carrigan (review date July 2000)

SOURCE: Carrigan, Henry. Review of *Experience,* by Martin Amis. *Library Journal* 125, no. 12 (July 2000): 89.

[*In the following review, Carrigan describes* Experience *as a "sophomoric and sometimes self-important exercise in namedropping and name calling."*]

Following in the steps of Christopher Dickey (*Summer of Deliverance*; *LJ* [*Library Journal*] 7/98) and V. S. Naipaul (*Between Father and Son, LJ* 1/00), Amis offers another portrait [***Experience***] of the sometimes troubled, often poignant relationship between a writer son and his writer father. The younger Amis (***The Information***) chronicles father Kingsley's (*Lucky Jim*) drunken debauches, his parents' marriage and subsequent remarriages, and the grimness of Kingsley's final days. But Amis also weaves into his narrative accounts of his own failed first marriage, relationships with his children, friendship with Saul Bellow, and coming to terms with the disappearance and death of his cousin. In addition, Amis details his well-publicized dental nightmares and his falling out with novelist Julian Barnes. Though passages describing his relationship with his father are very moving, the rest of the book descends into a sophomoric and sometimes self-important exercise in namedropping and name calling. The book will appeal to fans of father and son and is recommended for large libraries and libraries where the two are popular.

Joyce Hackett (review date 28 August 2000)

SOURCE: Hackett, Joyce. "Song of Himself." *National Review* 52, no. 16 (28 August 2000): 45.

[*In the following review, Hackett discusses Amis's obsession with fame as portrayed in* Experience.]

You have to wonder about a country where anybody's dental implants make national news. If a British empire still exists on which the sun has yet to set, it is the island's navel-gazing press. London still prints three times the number of dailies as New York, and *that* culture's crown prince is Martin Amis. The much-scrutinized son and heir apparent of comic author Kingsley Amis, Martin went on to become a biting post-modern novelist—with books like ***The Rachel Papers, Money,*** and ***London Fields***—and the feared chief critic of the *Sunday Times.* He also became a favorite whipping boy of the tabloid press, which lambasted him for leaving his agent (and best friend's wife) for one who made him more money, and for replacing his wife (and rotting teeth) with newer American models. Some called him the nastiest man in England, some the funniest, but Amis's reputation increased regardless, even when, behind his novels' glittering technique, there seemed to be no *there* there.

Now Amis has written a memoir [***Experience***] about growing up in the spotlight. The book's center, and the genesis of Martin's own fame, is his father. Not surprisingly, when Kingsley comes on stage, the book lights up. Savagely funny, wildly dysfunctional, he is more complex a character than either father or son has written. A compulsive philanderer who once took his first wife, Hilly, to lunch at the home of his married mistress and then made a date with a third woman there, he nevertheless inspired such devotion that Hilly nursed him in his last years as he collapsed from drink. There are charming windows onto how the literati/glitterati live, as when, after Kingsley has been knighted, Martin's sons greet him at the door, dressed in breastplates and Viking horns; Kingsley, by now obese and nearly immobile, lowers himself onto one knee for the "real" ceremony.

Amis captures his father's pettiness and phobias, his searing intelligence and wit, his chaste erotic dreams about Corky (his pet name for Queen Elizabeth). Kingsley's comment that he "couldn't get on" with Martin's second novel was long cited in the press as evidence of Oedipal rivalry, but what Kingsley seems to have bequeathed him, more than anything, was the right to play in the big leagues. Watching them critique each other's work, honestly and fairly, without tearing the resilient fabric of their affection, seems an extraordinary lesson in how to love big and in public.

But if the stated purpose of this kaleidoscopic memoir is the intimate desire to pay tribute to a loved one, what unites the fragments and footnotes that clutter it is Amis's obsession with fame. Though he goes on at length about his cousin, Lucy Partington, the victim of a particularly gruesome murder, his feelings for her lie dead on the page; those who compel the author's energy, admiration, adversarialism, and awe are those he can box with in the public ring. His asides to the un-famous, especially the women in his life, fall utterly flat. Mother, sister, aunt, wife, cousin, and girlfriend are all addressed as "you," leading the reader to wonder if in Amis's mind they blend together in a sort of ur-frau. Amis praises his wife, author Isabel Fonseca, for belly dancing in her robe with his dental prosthesis in her mouth, the night after his teeth were extracted (but then must note that she took them both off). A self-justifying letter to his aunt responds to her reluctance to see her murdered daughter "memorialized" in print. Amis's sister Sally receives hardly a mention until their father is dying, when Amis, now of the six-figure advances, goes to her apartment and remarks—twice—how small it is. The day Kingsley dies, though Sally has been attending him for ten hours, Martin and his brother have a leisurely smoke in front of the hospital before going up. Then Amis writes, "He has finished his work and you [Sally] have finished yours."

Elie A. Edmondson (essay date winter 2001)

SOURCE: Edmondson, Elie A. "Martin Amis Writes Postmodern Man." *Critique* 42, no. 2 (winter 2001): 145-54.

[*In the following essay, Edmondson investigates Amis's ability to both involve and distance the reader, underscoring the author's presence as a character in* Money.]

Martin Amis has been something of a puzzle to most critics since the publication of his first novel, ***The Rachel Papers,*** in 1973. Initial reviews of the novel were mixed and contradictory. *London Magazine* celebrated his inaugural novel as social satire, comparing Amis to Jonathan Swift and Angus Wilson (Mellors 133), whereas *Encounter* found ***The Rachel Papers*** to be "teeming with characters who are about as appealing as bacilli on a [washcloth]" (Jordan 64). Another reviewer admonished Amis to stop showing off his cleverness and find a subject worthier of his outrage (Moritz 20). Ironically, Amis answered the demand to find a subject worthier of his outrage through exploiting his cleverness. He did exactly that by mastering the art of postmodern prose: his style, with multiple layerings of fiction upon fiction, and a deluded narrator imbedded somewhere in the middle, is itself a story.

Starting with his premier novel, Amis revealed two narrative methods that resurface in the majority of his works. First, he introduces a protagonist who is so obsessed with an illusion that he cannot function in his world, cannot even recognize his real environment when it is encountered. In ***The Rachel Papers*** this character is Charles Highway, a nineteen-year-old who is singularly possessed by the ubiquitous obsession of all nineteen-year-olds, getting another nineteen-year-old into bed. Other texts employ characters with different obsessions: ***Dead Babies*** (sex, drugs, alcohol, violence), ***Success*** (image), ***Other People*** (memory), ***Money*** (money). Although disparate, the obsessions have a similar effect: all serve to distance the character from his reality and the reader from the text by inserting layers of narrative between the narrator and the reader. For example, in ***Money*** Amis himself appears as a character in the text and speaks to the protagonist, John Self. Self then directly addresses the reader, giving his gloss (always wrong) on what the author-character meant. Amis therefore implicates the reader in the narrative by putting him inside the character's head, and at the same time distances the reader by drawing attention to the text as a piece of fiction.

Amis had fully mastered this technique by his third novel, ***Success,*** in which the narrative is actually a contrapuntal construction of and by two protagonists, each giving his view of the other character in scathingly explicit and contradictory descriptions. The only facts that the reader can ascertain are that Terry is obsessed with Gregory and that Gregory is obsessed with Gregory. Only at the novel's end does the reader learn that Gregory is living in a narcissistic fantasy bordering on the psychotic and that his narrative, fully one-half of the text, is fundamentally deluded—he has been lost in his own story.

That the narrative is somehow essentially larger than the characters who inhabit it is Amis's second formal point, one he makes by distancing the reader from anything resembling authority within the text. That is a fundamental postmodern position, that an individual's consciousness is discursively constituted to some degree, that one's values and perceptions are colonized by dominant cultural values that may be in conflict with one's identity. The narrator in ***Money*** formulates the situation in this way: "Television is working on us. Film is. We're not sure how yet. We wait, and count the symptoms. There's a realism problem" (332). Terry Eagleton echoes that concern: "Nobody who emerges from a regular eight-hours-a-day television viewing is likely to be quite the same self-identical subject who once conquered India or annexed the Caribbean" (15). In postmodernity a truly autonomous voice, one independent of cultural forces, is an impossibility. Amis's fiction contains no reliable narrators because the narrators, always first-person voices, are part of the text. The writer, as creator, is also a character within the larger narrative line and therefore not omniscient, but rather a discursively constituted character himself.

In ***The Rachel Papers,*** Highway presents his narrative in the form of a diary, leading the reader to question what is narrative fact, what is Highway's fantasy, and whether Highway knows the difference. The text at once calls attention to itself as a fiction, and then substantiates itself by presenting dates, times, and locations to convince the reader of its authenticity. According to Brian Finney, "Amis wants his readers, like a theater audience, to recognize their simultaneous immersion in and exteriority to the action" (4). That contradiction forces the reader into the awkward position of wondering exactly where Martin Amis is in all this, who is telling what, and what degree of truth is present in what is being related. The reader is thrust into the position of questioning the source of the narrative and the omnipotence of the creator.

Using an obsessional or deluded narrator, Amis explores the postmodern predicament that we all are implicated in a self-constituting narrative that is at once an existential reality and at least partially beyond consciousness. By questioning the source of the narrative, he thrusts the reader into the position of the creator—a refined consciousness—a position that Amis has likened to that of a god (Finney 4). As creator, he shows that the concept of a fully refined and omnipotent consciousness is, by definition, deluded: Consciousness is at one level a narrative that the individual creates through action, but on another level, that individual's reality is constituted by a larger narrative. Amis succinctly describes his postmodern methods: "Well, it all comes under the main heading of 'Fucking around with my reader'" (Morrison 98). In ***Money: A Suicide Note,*** he explores the miasma of postmodern reality by investigating the strange life and fast times of a uniquely fragmented character, the narrator, John Self.

The protagonist of ***Money*** is a proud producer of "controversial TV ads for smoking, drinking, junk food and nude magazines. [. . .] My nihilistic commercials attracted prizes and writs" (78). John Self is personally and professionally immersed in the medium of appearances. When the story begins, he has hit the big time and is going mainscreen, America, Hollywood. He is excited about the money. Fielding Goodney is his American attaché and mainland moneyman. Goodney is, to Self, money incarnate. Self observes that when he fulfills his sole ambition in life—making all of the money he wants—he will be able to afford to be the man he wants to become. "When I wing out to Cal for my refit, when I stroll nude into the lab with my cheque, I think I know what I'll say. I'll say 'Lose the blueprints. Scrap those mock-ups. I'll take a Fielding'" (207). John Self is a creature of the late twentieth century, 1980s vintage; and he is woefully deluded as to his identity. Though he has feelings, he ignores or misdiagnoses them: ("I tell you, I am terrified, I am fucking terrified. 'Just give me the fucking money okay!' I want to shout this all the time" [80]). His primary emotions are fear and shame: fear that he will not have any money; shame at what he does to get it, and what he does with it once he has it. Self offers this brief explanation for his appetites: "I am addicted to the twentieth century" (89).

John Self could easily be named John Doe, any Self: "I'm called John Self, but who isn't" (97). The protagonist has no knowledge of himself, his world, or his actual cultural and biological paternity. Self believes he is some Horatio Alger phenomenon of capitalism, and he certainly fits the definition of a parvenu; but as the narrative folds in upon itself, John is revealed to be at once everyman, and no man (Doan 70). Saul Bellow, whose work Amis acknowledges as being influential in the making of ***Money,*** describes the postmodern man:

> This person is our brother, our *semblable,* our very self. He is certainly in many respects narrow and poor, blind in heart, weak, mean, intoxicated, confused in spirit—stupid. We see how damaged he is, how badly

> mutilated. But the leap towards the marvelous is a possibility he still considers nevertheless. [. . .] He dreams of beating the rap, outwitting the doom prepared for him by history. Often he seems prepared to assert that he is a new kind of human being, whose condition calls for original expression, and he is ready to take a flier, go for the higher truth. He has been put down, has put himself down too, but he has also dreamed of strategies that will bring him past all this distraction, his own included. For he knows something. [. . .] He is (or can be) skeptical, cant-free, heedful of his own intuitions.
>
> (qtd. in Alexander 583)

That excerpt from Bellow's *Jefferson Lectures* is essentially the psychological profile of John Self: narrow-minded, poor and confused in spirit, damaged, mutilated, and stupid. Self's ponderings are on the same theme as Bellow's observations on the condition of our *semblable*: "I must be *very unhappy.* That's the only way I can explain my behavior. Oh man, I must be so depressed. I must be fucking suicidal. And I wish I knew *why.*" Self is aware that something is wrong and longs "to take a flier, go for the higher truth." There is too much shame and fear in his world. "It really isn't very nice in here. And that is why I long to burst out of the world of money and into—into what? Into the world of thought and fascination. How do I get there? Tell me, please. I'll never make it by myself. I just don't know the way" (118). John Self is Postmodern Man.

Frank Kermode argues that modernity was characterized by a need for a feeling of narrative progression—a beginning, a middle, and an end. Martin Amis, in both the style and plot of ***Money,*** demonstrates that postmodern man is delusional if he invests himself in such a teleological world view. Late twentieth-century reality cannot be simply explained. John Self is lost in his complicated world, desperately operating within the myopic level of the mundane, but not recognizing his reality. He is exemplar of Amis's observation that "the narrative line in human life is gone" (Alexander 580). Self is a totally deluded narrator, attempting to act in his world, but being acted upon by the larger context of his historical situation, the larger narrative line. "How do I get there?" is a question that he will never be able to answer, because "there" does not exist in the deluded world he is operating within, the world of ***Money.***

Self's obsession his beginning, middle, and end and his distancing delusion is money. Self loves money, makes love to money, uses money to make love, thinks of money while making love, is terrified of not having any money, and is ignorant of the fact that he has no concept of love. Self's ontology equals money. Period. "Selina says I'm not capable of true love. It isn't true. I truly love money. Truly I do. Oh, money, I love you. You're so democratic: you've got no favorites. You even things out for me and my kind" (221). His naïveté is illustrated by his idiocy, as an individual from a lower socioeconomic class, in embracing conservative dogma, a position that includes viewing the working class as a component of production labor that is slightly less important than capital and equipment. But in his obsession with money, Self is ideologically out of his depth.

But even at the level of consciousness within which Self is operating, his world is beginning to unravel. He has immersed himself in capitalism, and his assumption of its ideology has a cost. Terry Eagleton argues that "[t]he logic of the marketplace is one of pleasure and plurality, of the ephemeral and discontinuous, of some great decentered network of desire of which individuals seem the mere fleeting effects" (132). Self, the embodiment of marketplace ideology, is feeling his lack of center, and he does not know what to do about it. He feels vulnerable, but misdiagnoses the source of, and consequently the cure for, his angst. He thinks that he needs more money. "Without money, you're one day old and one inch tall. And you're nude, too" (353). With money, Self feels that he is not diminutive and naked, but he still suffers from the neuroses of postmodern man alienated from himself. The degree to which Self is removed from any sense of humanity becomes clear when he wishes for intimacy: "I can't go on sleeping alone," he says, "that's certain. I need a human touch. Soon I'll just have to go out and buy one" (61).

John Self's lack of center, his total absence of self-awareness, is hinted at in the first paragraph of ***Money.*** The cab he is riding in hits a pothole, and he bounces up from the seat and hits his head on the ceiling. The narrator's take on this sequence of events is that the cab came down and hit him. He perceives himself as the center of the universe and does not recognize that he is being thrown about by forces greater than himself. He perceives himself as master. But even at Self's narrative level there are other indications that something is wrong. Self has internalized the values of a system that objectifies and subordinates certain individuals while empowering others. By ignoring his historical identity, by being ignorant of his true paternity, he has become vulnerable in his delusion. The marketplace is not an even playing field, as all parties do not enter the fray with equal resources. Amis humorously reminds the reader of this fact through the names he gives the automobiles driven by the various characters. Self's cab is cut off in traffic by a Tomahawk "sharking out of lane"; the threatening name of the vehicle is reified by the "sharking" action. ***Money***'s specious class act, Fielding Goodney, drives a chauffeured Autocrat. (In a similarly foreboding way, the character Martin Amis drives an Iago 666, suggesting that he will devilishly mislead Self.) John Self's vehicle, like his life, is a Fiasco, "My pride and joy." His center is a complete failure.

John Self is a character in a fiction much greater than he realizes. As the plot of ***Money*** develops, elements of narrative scale begin to become visible. The reader is increasingly distanced from the narrative at the same time that John Self is being diminished by it. Amis employs the postmodern technique of involution, the inclusion of the author as a character within the text, as a method of distancing the reader and as tacit admission of the author's lack of control over himself. His presence in the text is an acknowledgment that he, as writer-creator, is also constituted by a larger narrative line, a player on the stage. Simultaneously with Amis's entering the text as a character, John Self directly addresses the reader, drawing him into the narrative. That conflation of contradicting forces places the reader in a position analogous to that occupied by the protagonist, a place of extreme angst—what person truly wishes to meet his creator and thus become accountable for his existence? Self is bothered by Amis's presence in his world: "There's a guy who lives round my way who really gives me the fucking creeps. He's a *writer,* too. [. . .] This writer's name, they tell me, is *Martin Amis.* Never heard of him. Do *you* know his stuff at all?" (61, 72).

Amis's introduction into the text adds an entire new dimension to the narrative, and issues of scale become dizzying. At one level John Self is a character in the novel ***Money,*** written by Martin Amis. In the novel. Self is searching for a writer to complete his movie script, the movie alternatively named *Good Money* or *Bad Money.* He stumbles upon this writer who lives nearby, Martin Amis, and hires him to complete the screenplay. As if in a house of mirrors, the creation of ***Money,*** Amis's physical act of writing the text, is replicated as story line in the narrative. But if Amis as writer is aware of the text as a contrived metafiction, the narrator is approaching existential ground zero.

John Self is still forging ahead in his deluded conception of Self-as-Master, careening toward his denouement, and still missing the significance of what is occurring around him. Christopher Lasch describes the meltdown of contemporary consciousness as an experience in which "[t]he egomaniacal, experience-devouring imperial self regresses into a grandiose, narcissistic, infantile, empty self: a 'dark wet hole'" (12). In Self's deluded world, he views other human beings as actors, writers, drivers, moneymen, things he needs to manipulate to achieve his desired end in the same way that he perceives women as objects with use value. That attitude reflects his internalization of the values of the commodity-driven culture he lives in. Ironically, because of his delusion and lack of self-awareness, he cannot recognize when he himself is being manipulated, when he is approaching the "dark wet hole." His obliviousness to his situation is obvious in one of the text's most significant implosions, Amis's oft-quoted microcosmic monologue on authorial distance.

> The distance between author and narrator corresponds to the degree to which the author finds the narrator wicked, deluded, pitiful or ridiculous. I'm sorry, am I boring you?
>
> Uh?
>
> This distance is partly determined by convention. In the epic or heroic frame, the author gives the protagonist everything he has, and more. The hero is a god or has godlike powers or virtues. In the tragic . . . Are you all right?
>
> Uh? I repeated. I had just stabbed a pretzel into my dodgy upper tooth. [. . .]
>
> The further down the scale he is, the more liberties you can take with him. You can do what the hell you like to him, really. This creates an appetite for punishment. The author is not free of sadistic impulses. I suppose it's the—
>
> Hey look you got to give me a deadline.
>
> (229)

Martin Amis the writer has created Martin Amis the character who is warning John Self that he had better stop being "wicked, deluded, pitiful or ridiculous." If he doesn't straighten up and fly right, Martin Amis the character is saying, then Martin Amis the writer might just indulge some sadistic impulses and mess around with Self's narrative line. Unfortunately for John Self, he is too far down the narrative scale to make it back. He longs "to burst out of the world of money and into [. . .] the world of thought and fascination," but he doesn't heed Amis's warning. He cannot, because he is simply a character in the larger narrative, where he is driven to become, not himself, but Fielding Goodney. All of his energies are spent attempting to feed the "egomaniacal, experience-devouring imperial self." As a result, he does not benefit from even some slight amelioration that might result from trying to attain a degree of objective distance from Fielding Goodney. Instead, Self remains mired in his deluded narrative line and demands that Amis, as character, produce a deadline. Martin Amis the writer complies.

This folding in of a fiction upon a fiction continues. John Self imagines himself as a powerful player in an amoral world, one in which he manipulates other people, minor players, for his personal satisfaction. At times he is offered succor from different sources. One is the suggestively named Martina Twain, Self's ultimately alienated ideal love interest. As James Diedrich points out, "Martina talks one evening about aesthetics, about the 'reluctant narrator' in a novel, 'the sad, the unwitting narrator'—Self, in other words. But he can't understand what she is saying. 'I could follow her drift for seconds at a time, until the half-gratified sense of effort—or my awareness of watching myself—intervened, and scattered my thoughts'" (87). Twain also gives him a "how-to kit for the twentieth century," books by Freud, Darwin, Einstein, and Orwell's *Animal Farm.* Self cannot seem to make it through the works of the great writers of the twentieth century, is somehow unable to comprehend the paternity of his historical moment. But, he relates to *Animal Farm*:

> Where would I be in Animal Farm? One of the rats, I thought at first. But-oh, go easy on yourself, try and go a little bit easy. Now, after mature consideration, I think I might have what it takes to be a dog. I *am* a dog. I am a dog at the seaside tethered to a fence while my master and mistress romp on the sands. I am bouncing, twisting, weeping, consuming myself. [. . .] Look at the dogs in the street, how everything implicates them, how everything is their concern, how they race towards great discoveries. And imagine the grief, tethered to a fence when there is activity—and play, and thought and fascination—just beyond the holding rope.
>
> (193)

Self is restrained by his delusions and cannot leave his level of narration, the commodified world of the marketplace. He identifies with the characters in *Animal Farm* as animals, not as allegory, and cannot see the allusion to his own predicament. Self is not open-minded enough to "take a flier." He is careening toward the deadline his actions demand.

The plot of ***Money,*** which *is* linear, explicitly demonstrates the dissolution of John Self's delusion. Self's money runs out; inexplicably, unbelievably, he finds himself broke. Shortly after that discovery, as he is fleeing his hotel, he receives a page over the intercom. It is Frank the Phone, a hitherto disembodied character who has plagued Self throughout the narrative, reminding him of his egregious behavior, and promising that Self will get his just desserts. "The end. All over," the voice says. Self demands a confrontation, and gets one. The disembodied voice now becomes material, and Self beats the hell out of it. He realizes, in his victory, that the voice was that of the man he longed to be, his idol—Fielding Goodney.

Self discovers that he has been undone by his own fantasy. Documents that he had signed under Goodney's bidding, and while Self was drunk, turn out to be powers of attorney. Self's globe-trotting consumption of everything pornographic had not been financed by Goodney. He had blown his own money on porn. He has been undone by his own greed. Martin Amis the character explains the situation to Self near the book's end over an allegorical ("We're playing for money") game of chess: "The company you formed wasn't Goodney & Self. It was Self & Self. It was Self. The hotels, the plane tickets, the limousines, the wage bill, the studio rental. You were paying. It was you. It was you" (348). Self is slow to accept what has happened to him, but ultimately realizes that he has been played: "*I'm the joke. I'm it*" (349).

At this point Self's narrative line has evaporated. He realizes that he has been used, and not for personal gain—Goodney made no money from the deal—but simply for the pleasure of Fielding Goodney. Self has been manipulated, violated, and broken; only to satisfy a mindless urge, a whim of Fielding Goodney (an obvious play on Feeling Good). John Self has been used as someone else's pornographic toy. That Self has been debased and then used and humiliated by the symbol of his own ideology is a masterful irony. But Self has not quite met his deadline.

He returns home to England, a beaten and broken man. There he encounters his father's new wife, Vron, a figure who is proud of posing for pornographic magazines. Self has almost reached his deadline, is nearly out of the greater fiction he has been trapped within, has almost hit absolute bottom. Only two epiphanies remain for him to experience before he can know a truer Self. Vron provides the first: "They say you don't do the writing in the books, John. That's not true. You write the words, John" (340). Vron's point echoes Amis's earlier warnings to Self that "[t]he further down the scale [the narrator] is, the more liberties [the author] can take with him." In John Self's charging from one pornographic appetite to the next, in his attempts to feed his addiction to the twentieth century, he has moved as far down the scale as possible. In his pursuit of the image of Fielding Goodney, he has written as banal a personal narrative as one could write. Vron's insight is echoed by the character Martin Amis on the next page:

> Okay. Actually I'd like to return to the motivation question. It seems to me that it's an idea taken from art, not from life, not from twentieth-century life. Nowadays motivation comes from inside the head, not from outside. It's neurotic, in other words. And remember that some people, these golden mythomaniacs, these handsome liars—they're like artists, some of them. Let's look at another recent phenomenon: gratuitous crime. I'm sorry. Are you with me?
>
> Yeah yeah.
>
> (341)

Self's primary neurosis, his "golden mythomaniac," his "handsome liar," was Fielding Goodney, whose only power was that which John Self gave him, his own greed. Self brought himSelf down. But Self is not quite ready to accept personal responsibility, cannot, because he still does not know his true identity, his lineage. He is not yet free of the narrative he has been existing within. Following Vron's insight, in a strange, faux-oedipal scene, he has sex with her. During the act, the man he has thought was his father, Barry Self, walks in, surprising them *flagrante delicto*. Self is subsequently beaten and cast out of his father's home. Physically beaten, financially destroyed, his ego fragmented, Self finally discovers his true paternity. His father was not Barry Self, an abusive pornographer, the man who had him beaten, but a gentle and drunken pub crawler and sometime bouncer named Fat Vince.

As we have seen, Bellow's *semblable* "has been put down, has put himself down too." But he is capable of some degree of redemption: "Often he seems prepared to assert that he is a new kind of human being." Amis's texts frequently end with the protagonist's acceptance of his situation, his reality, and, with a greater level of peace for the character, perhaps a lesson for the reader as well. "He proposes that people profit, intellectually and morally, by reading fiction, by gaining a sense of order and justice" (Alexander 581). In ***Success,*** Gregory finally admits that he is a part of a family that was once great, but is now bankrupt, and he is freed from the delusion he has been living. That humbling acceptance of reality, of human limitation, of growing up by leaving the lie, is repeated in ***Money.***

The last section of ***Money*** is italicized, is John Self's own voice. There is still anger, but there is also an acceptance of the fear and shame, acceptance of the identity that comes from an understanding of one's actual narrative, one's true paternity. John Self observes: "*This isn't of much general interest or application either, but it's the only thing I know I'm right about. [. . .] If you're a boy, then you are your dad and your dad is you. So how can you live seriously if you don't know who you are?*" (362). Self's voice reflects resignation, rather than defeat. John Self is a better man for what he has endured. He has discovered his center—as much of one as a postmodern character can expect and is no longer invested in a sexy, shiny surrogate. He is no longer "tethered to a fence when there is activity—and play, and thought and fascination—just beyond the holding rope." He has become capable of independent thought. He is now Bellow's better, postmodern man; heedful of his own intuitions. The television ads that were once his profession, his identity, have taken on a different significance:

> When I watch the ads on the television I feel nausea, right in my soft core. TV being here, TV being the religion, the mystical part of ordinary minds, I don't want to be working in this sensitive area, I don't want to be selling it things. If we all downed tools and joined hands for ten minutes and stopped believing in money, then money would no longer exist.
>
> (354)

Brian Finney maintains that, "[t]he appeal of fiction has always been the clarity it offers us by its orderly rearrangement of life" (15). With his postmodern style, the layering of narrative upon narrative upon narrative, and a Self stuck somewhere in the web, Martin Amis points out that everyone, even Martin Amis, lives in a metafiction that is greater than the self. In postmodernity, there is no comprehensive order to life, and an art that attempts to assert one is self-defeating and deluded. Amis acknowledges that with his subtitle, *A Suicide Note.* At the end of the novel the narrator is still alive, and the intent of the author—the omniscient creator—has been frustrated.

Amis's postmodern art forces the reader to become conscious of the larger narrative line, the one that tries to write upon the self by presenting appetizing appearances of the "golden mythomaniacs," the fictions of television and Fielding Goodney. ***Money*** illustrates that the cost of investing in a falsely constructed self is a performance of Lasch's "imperial self regress[ing] into a grandiose, narcissistic, infantile, empty self." The mindless pursuit of Fielding Goodney leads Self simply to a "dark wet hole." Alternatively, the abandonment of the delusion of an "imperial self," of the Self-as-Master, frees one from the banal, permits an objective distance, a sense of perspective. Through that awareness it might be possible to dig down to one's truer paternity, a less-fragmented self, and to attain a greater degree of contentment and an identity grounded in one's reality rather than a fiction. John Self would state the endeavor this way: "Turn off the television. Go and talk with your dad."

Works Cited

Alexander, Victoria N. "Martin Amis: Between the Influences of Bellow and Nabokov." *Antioch Review* 52.4 (1994): 580-90.

Amis, Martin. *Dead Babies.* New York: Vintage, 1991.

———. *Money: A Suicide Note.* New York: Penguin, 1985.

———. *Other People. A Mystery Story.* Harmondsworth, Middlesex: Penguin, 1982.

———. *The Rachel Papers.* New York: Vintage, 1991.

———. *Success.* New York: Vintage, 1991.

Diedrick, James. *Understanding Martin Amis.* Columbia: U of South Carolina P, 1995.

Doan, Laura L., "Sexy Greedy *Is* the Late Eighties: Power Systems in Amis's *Money* and Churchill's *Serious Money.*" *Minnesota Review* 34 (1990): 69-80.

Eagleton, Terry. *The Illusions of Postmodernism.* Oxford: Blackwell, 1996.

Finney, Brian. "Narrative and Narrated Homicides in Martin Amis's *Other People* and *London Fields.*" *Critique* 37.1 (1995): 3-15.

Jordan, Clive. "World Enough, and Time." *Encounter* XLII.2 (1974): 64.

Kermode, Frank. *The Sense of an Ending.* Oxford: Oxford UP, 1968.

Lasch, Christopher. *The Culture of Narcissism.* New York: Norton, 1991.

Mellors, John. "Recent Novels." *London Magazine* 13.6 (1974): 133.

Moritz, Charles, ed. *Current Biography Yearbook.* New York: Wilson, 1990.

Morrison, Susan. "The Wit and the Fury of Martin Amis." *Rolling Stone* 17 May 1990: 95-102.

Daniel R. Bronson (review date winter 2001)

SOURCE: Bronson, Daniel R. Review of *Experience,* by Martin Amis. *World Literature Today* 75, no. 1 (winter 2001): 126.

[*In the following review, Bronson offers a positive assessment of* Experience, *deeming it a "sad, wise, entertaining read."*]

Early on, in one of his copious footnotes to ***Experience,*** Martin Amis writes:

> When you review a film, or appraise a film-director, you do not make a ten-minute short about it or him (or her). When you write about a painter, you do not produce a sketch. When you write about a composer, you do not reach for the violin. And even when a poet is under consideration, the reviewer does not (unless deeply committed to presumption and tedium) produce a poem. But when you write about a novelist, an exponent of prose narrative, then you write a prose narrative.

So begins a narrative of not one, but several writers. The novelist Martin Amis examines himself, reconsiders his relationship with his irascible writer father, Kingsley, explores his surrogate father-son relationship with Saul Bellow, and even considers himself as part of a select group including Nabokov and Joyce, all gifted prose stylists with dental woes.

Rather than taking a chronological approach, Amis weaves episodes together, including letters his adolescent self sent to his parents (the adult writer refers to this self as Osric) that are often precocious, clever, and quite embarrassing at the same time. ***Experience*** becomes a mixture of gossip and confession, obsession and regret, failed marriages and aspirations (with children left in the wake for both Martin and Kingsley), as the pattern of the writer's experience forms a most unique prose narrative. There is a peculiar, and one presumes purposeful, irony in two recurring themes, the seriocomic details of the rebuilding of Martin's mouth seen in counterpoint to the tragic murder of Lucy Partington, a close Amis cousin, at the hands of a serial killer.

The size of this volume is a measure of how much Amis has to reflect upon. And the writing is as interesting as the stories told. The cold, even chill, clarity of recent novels, like ***Night Train*** (1997; see *WLT* [*World Literature Today*] 72:4, p. 829), is replaced by a more personal discursive mode that works well, especially in the depiction of the long, dark fall of his cantankerous father. Hearing the news of Kingsley's death after an exhilarating day out with his own sons, Martin reflects with quiet understatement, "How like Kingsley to die on a Sunday. How uncompromising of him to die on the Sunday when the clocks go back."

Throughout ***Experience,*** the narrator never forgets his literary sensibility, that he is a writer in a world of writers (those he likes and loathes), and that words have real power. Although the pattern of events ultimately seems as eccentric as the characters depicted, the whole of ***Experience*** is greater than its parts. This is a sad, wise, entertaining read. Amis may be forgiven for writing near the book's end, "My life, it seems to me, is ridiculously shapeless. I know what makes a good narrative, and lives don't have much of that." Ridiculously shapeless? Perhaps, but too often that is life. Not a good narrative? ***Experience*** suggests otherwise.

Philip Hensher (review date 21 April 2001)

SOURCE: Hensher, Philip. "Nothing Matters More than Prose." *Spectator* 286, no. 9011 (21 April 2001): 33-4.

[*In the following review, Hensher regards* The War against Cliché *as an honest and humorous collection of essays, but questions the author's understanding of British politics.*]

'Critic' is a title of honour, heavy with implications of eminence, and not a plain statement of fact. Once you have published a novel or two, you are indisputably entitled to call yourself a novelist; plenty of people, however, spend their lives writing about books and works of art without ever producing a sentence which can be described as criticism, except in the vulgar sense. 'Critic' is comparable, really, to 'philosopher'; it has been said that there is no such thing as bad philosophy, since below a certain standard, it simply ceases to be philosophy. Critics are rarer beings than is customarily supposed; the 'chief literary critic' of the *Daily Beast* is, I feel, making a grand claim for his merits. If, like me, you feel that your fortnightly effusions do not entitle you to be considered as the heir to the Goncourt brothers, then it is altogether far less embarrassing to settle for 'book reviewer'.

All the same, criticism does sometimes get written, and the excellence and acuity of Martin Amis's writings on literature [in ***The War against Cliché***] would be worth our attention even if he had not taken the precaution of writing ***London Fields*** first. They are, of course, a novelist's readings, and whether he is castigating some hapless lazy buffoon or catching Jane Austen in the moment of greatness, they benefit from the novelist's long struggle with sentences and the recalcitrant imagination. But they are unarguably criticism—detailed, intricate criticism of the highest order, written not according to a prior plan, or a rigid concept of what literature should be, but guided by a strong and admirable sense of taste and decorum. Amis always trusts his instincts when presented with a book, a sentence, a word; if the results are sometimes startling, and sometimes worth disagreeing with, there is no arguing with the seriousness and intelligence of his comments.

A great novelist in the European tradition almost always has something of the critic about him; *Pride and Prejudice, Little Dorrit* and *Ulysses* are, from one point of view, strong readings of *Sir Charles Grandison, Don Quixote* and the *Iliad.* A great critic, conversely, will benefit from an independent imaginative faculty, and if Amis's novels often resort to direct engagement with great literature, his criticism is unmistakably the work of an original creator, whose re-enactments of literature have an independent energy. A paragraph in *Lolita* 'streaks off like a tracer bullet in a dark sky'. 'Joyce could have been the most popular boy in the school, the funniest, the cleverest, the kindest. He ended up with a more ambiguous distinction: he became the teachers' pet' (and ain't that the truth?). *Don Quixote* is like 'an indefinite visit from your most impossible senior relative, with all his pranks, dirty habits, unstoppable reminiscences, and terrible cronies'. A single word often works terribly hard—the paperback of *Brideshead Revisited* is announced as 'busty', and, whatever the subsequent elaborations, Waugh is instantly dead in the water.

But in every way one never feels that literature, here, is being obliged to take a back seat behind the critic's brilliant, reckless driving. In Amis's first novel, ***The Rachel Papers,*** an Oxford don tells the precocious hero that 'literature has its own life, you know: you can't just use it for ends of your own'. (I quote, deliberately, from memory—the truth and value of that assertion lodged itself so deeply, remembrance is a better compliment than accuracy). Amis never does use literature for his own ends, and one of the pleasures of this deeply enjoyable collection is watching a really close, respectful reader at work. He quotes at length, and always tellingly; and when he is quoting a book he really loves, there is a palpable sense of his pleasure in typing out these marvellous sentences. The essays on *Lolita* and *The Adventures of Augie March* probably contain as many words by Nabokov and Bellow as by Amis, so extensive is the quotation.

Drawing large conclusions from small moments is the critic's essential job, and one which Amis excels at; brilliant to notice the child prostitute in *Lolita* 'perfunctorily nursing a bald doll', to see the image of the young, made prematurely old. A virtuoso demonstration comes in a demolition of Thomas Harris's *Hannibal,* an expansion of a casual slip:

> [Lecter is] translator and curator of the Capponi Library. And shouldn't that 'of' be 'at'? Or does Lecter translate the library as well as look after it?

A tiny slip, and Amis's case, that the pompous effusions of the novel rest on a basic indifference to the culture it so swankingly evokes, is effortlessly made. The reader's eye slides routinely over that sort of thing; Amis's doesn't, and he sees how meaningful it can be. And it is characteristic that what he loves best is the single, surprising, right word; the 'goblin' atmosphere of America in Updike, or the 'troubled and rocky' woman in Saul Bellow. He likes small, inconspicuous, resonant things. The great virtue of Amis as a critic is that he sees, I think, that nothing in a novel matters more than prose; indeed, there is nothing else there. I know this is the sort of comparison he rightly hates, but to set his essay on *Lolita* against his father's famous one is to see a crucial and wonderful shift in temperament. For Kingsley Amis, to resort to alliteration at Charlotte's death is to demonstrate an inadvertent insincerity; for Amis *fils,* there is nothing in the world that a sufficient virtuosity in prose cannot achieve. And Martin Amis is right, because to evoke a world beyond the rhetoric of sentences when writing about a novel is to mistake an ingenious illusion for substance.

All his criticism is, or can be, terribly funny, but never—or hardly ever—does he make a joke at the expense of critical sense. To write a line of an imagined sex scene between Charlotte Lucas and Mr Collins in *Pride and Prejudice* ('I crave your indulgence, my dear Mrs Collins, if, at this early juncture . . .') looks like knockabout stuff, but how concisely it makes a point about the novel and Jane Austen. Andy Warhol's diaries need no more than a single, unspeakably funny quotation, when 'a Walt Disney crew arrives and asks him who his favourite Disney character is, and I said "Minnie Mouse", because she can get me close to Mickey'. The summary of Iris Murdoch's novels is a raucous joke, but appallingly perceptive too:

> Imagine the teaching staff of a toytown university. The men all have names like Hilary and Julian. The women all have names like Julian and Hilary. Everyone is on permanent sabbatical, but they look in each day to sample the hallucinogenic love-potions available in the SCR.

These virtues of small attentiveness and large flights of imagination are exactly what a great novelist needs, and are as appropriate to criticism as to fiction. Where things go slightly wrong is where the public mythologies which have sustained the fiction so well are exposed to the light of day, and shrivel under the gaze. ***London Fields*** is sustained by a set of ideas about nuclear weapons. There, it does wonderfully well as a novelist's mythology—there, they need not have been true. In the context of a collection of non-fiction, particularly one published after the arms race effectively brought the Cold War to an end, they look distressingly naïve. To deplore the fact that American strategists were talking enthusiastically about the 'containability' of a nuclear exchange in the 1980s ignores the fact that, had they assured the American public that American nuclear weapons would never be used, the entire strategy would have fallen to the ground. The strategy only worked because people and governments believed that the finger on the button was perfectly capable of pressing it.

He would have done better, too, to have acknowledged the limits of his understanding when it comes to British politics; whatever you think of Mrs Thatcher, it simply betrays a lack of interest to say that 'the only interesting thing about Mrs Thatcher is that she isn't a man'. The terms of politics changed entirely, unarguably, with the advent of Mrs Thatcher, and, to be blunt, the triumph of monetarism is of more substantial concern than whether the prime minister of the time had a penis or not. The novelist can talk endlessly about the nature of gender; the critic can draw large conclusions from apparently inessential details. Politics cannot be considered for long in those terms, and, unusually, you feel that Amis has been presented with an important point, and decisively missed it.

The narrowness of interest is apparent elsewhere; I honestly can't see what is wrong with A. N. Wilson describing a church interior as having 'a somewhat baroque late 17th-century reredos with (apparently) Flemish communion rails'. But the fascination with books and language is unflagging, inexhaustibly rich and always persuasive, sending you back to some favourite book or enlisting a new enthusiasm without fail. To be so consistently funny about literature is one thing; it is rare, however, for such an entertainer to display such honesty and truth.

Robert Winder (review date 23 April 2001)

SOURCE: Winder, Robert. "A Warrior of Words." *New Statesman* 14, no. 653 (23 April 2001): 50-1.

[*In the following review, Winder condemns the air of superiority projected by Amis in* The War against Cliché, *but stresses the author's originality as a stylist.*]

It is rather rare, and very nice, to be able to say of a new book [***The War against Cliché***] that the author is absolutely right. What could be finer, or less glamorous? Martin Amis has declared war on the cliché in all its myriad shapes and forms (see: three in one sentence). And in framing this zesty collection of reviews and essays (many written for the *New Statesman,* no less) as a campaign against the ready-made—"not just clichés of the pen, but clichés of the mind and clichés of the heart"—he applauds the opposite virtues: "freshness, energy and reverberation of voice". These are decent friends for any writer, and it is good to see someone sticking up for them.

Those clichés, though. In a reviewing career spanning 30 years, Amis has been quick to flinch: he is like a Jane Austen patriarch, quaking with nerves. Thus *Brideshead Revisited* is "a golden treasury of neoclassical clichés"; in Fay Weldon, "cliché spreads inwards from the language of the book to its heart"; Cyril Connolly commits "many a reflexive cliché ('moody silence', 'a grip of iron')"; and in Michael Crichton, stale usages roam like dinosaurs: "Out there, beyond the foliage, you see herds of clichés, wandering free. You listen in 'stunned silence' to an 'unearthly cry' or a 'deafening roar.'" Occasionally, Amis looks beyond literature: even prejudices, he suggests, are clichés—"second-hand hatreds". This is all good sport, though with a bullying edge: sometimes you feel he ought to pick on someone his own size. It might even be neat to pass the cliché-meter over Amis's own prose; we could probably find a few if we looked hard enough. But not many. He is a purist.

None the less, Amis manages to attract, in equal and exasperating quantities, both hero-worship and derision. The simple fact of his being the son of a famous writer lifted him to the jagged upper slopes of celebrity: his own haughty talent has kept him there. His novels, meanwhile, have been at once lionised and disparaged—sometimes by the same people. His taboo-baiting wit and stylish disdain inspire both chuckles and indignation; his fondness for the modern world's mean streets, with their heavy-breathing crowds of yobby lowlifes, sex workers, TV junkies and media sleazeballs, strikes some as adventurous and authentic, others as an Oxbridge pose. Unlike his hero Saul Bellow, who tends to place professors at the centre of his work, Amis prefers garrulous no-hopers. But then he can't help satirising them. We all have a ball slumming it for a while, but . . . what then?

Yet more than almost any of his contemporaries, Amis writes things that you want to remember and repeat: he is original. However, the rough consensus does seem to be that, although he is a brilliant writer (no small thing), Amis's novels ship more water than they should. And this is troubling—because if brilliance is not enough, then what the heck is? Do novels really require stodgier, less flashy virtues? On this important point, alas, the jury is still brooding. Tolstoy was by no means a wag, but Nabokov was.

An aspersion often flung against Amis is that he retains, in his novels, the lofty and judgemental voice of the critic—a voice, as John Updike once said, built to sound wonderfully right about everything. It is true that Amis isn't really a dramatist: he doesn't do all the voices. He does just the one, and it is remarkable: waspish, throwaway, trenchant, perceptive, funny. It is the tone, more or less, of the superior book critic—and Amis, as this roomy portfolio shows, is certainly one of those.

He displays a set of interests ranging from straight-down-the-line English fiction (Angus Wilson, Iris Murdoch, Anthony Burgess, V S Pritchett) to classics (Dickens, Milton, Donne, Coleridge, Wodehouse) to chess, football, gender skirmishes, sex'n'violence and Americana in all its forms. He is fully engaged. And he doesn't just hit nails on the head (whoops): he does a little tap-dance on them just to make sure. If anything, his syntactical reflexes lead to disdain more easily than to approval. Reviewing *Galápagos,* he writes: "This is far and away Kurt Vonnegut's best novel since *Slaughterhouse 5.*" Which sounds generous until he adds: "However, that's not saying very much." He can be full-on hostile, reminding us that chief among the pleasures of any book review is the frisson we get from the spectacle of unnerving rudeness. Desmond Morris's *The Soccer Tribe,* he suggests, is "an unfaltering distillation of the obvious and the obviously false"—a wonderful example of an insult delivered in the blurb-grammar of a compliment.

Amis can be cheeky about the greats: Don Quixote suffers from "unreadability . . . and this reviewer should know, because he has just read it"; Joyce is "a teacher's pet". And for comic effect, he takes rubbish seriously. Of a book on Hillary Clinton, for example, he says: "It looks like a book and feels like a book, but in important respects it isn't a book. It's a pre-election pamphlet or a stump-speech." With alarming consistency, he delivers what he commends—freshness, heat, zeal. And he can even be a forthright admirer. For instance, he writes: "Bellow's first name is a typo: that 'a' should be an 'o.'" And when he rereads *Lolita,* it is with "gasps of continually renewed surprise".

Amis is anything but proud of all this. Indeed, he nurses a vexed contempt for book reviewers. A good part of his novel ***The Information*** satirised the way they (we?) snuffle around the work of their (our?) superiors, and he is at it again here, seizing almost any opportunity to bare his teeth at "blurb-transcribing sots". In the foreword, he takes a swipe at "the buckled figure of the book reviewer"; and one review—of Thomas Harris's disastrous *Hannibal*—is really a critique of the supine critics who applauded the novel. (He can't have read all of the reviews: alert readers of these pages will surely remember the unforgettable thumbs-down it received from a critic obliged by modesty to remain nameless.)

At first, it seems odd that someone who has written 500-odd pages of reviews should be so unforgiving, and it would be easy to trick this up into some meaningful internal conflict—Amis the proud novelist renouncing the easy victories of mere commentary. However, it emerges that what he is against is not reviewing as such, but bad reviewing. This chimes with the title and premise: Amis loves to act the cynic, but he is tough on people who don't care about books. This souvenir volume urges everyone to be as vigilant and inventive as he is.

It is a worthwhile aim, that's for sure. But excuse me . . . I'm getting dizzy. Writing a book review of a collection of book reviews that take book reviewing as a theme: we are steaming in a tight circle here. The war against cliché is all very well, and deserves to be won (fat hope), but it can hardly afford to become a buoyant end in itself. Amis has more style than anyone, and enough ammo to stalk larger game—or do I mean that he has bigger fish to fry? Many of the grandest things in life and literature—falling in (and out of) love, children, despair, death—are clichés. Avoiding them leads to novelty but not, on its own, to novels. Besides, reviews as good as these are unusual: they are, as the saying goes, only one a penny. And reviewing, however rude, is in the end affable: it implies the existence of an ongoing civic conversation about books, an existence that sometimes seems shaky.

Why undermine all this? Amis should just take a graceful bow, and prepare to duck all the flak that would surely follow.

Robert L. Kelly (review date 1 October 2001)

SOURCE: Kelly, Robert L. Review of *The War against Cliché,* by Martin Amis. *Library Journal* 126, no. 16 (1 October 2001): 96-7.

[*In the following review, Kelly asserts the essays in* The War against Cliché *are erudite and often humorous.*]

Amis's critiques [in ***The War against Cliché***] cover wide-ranging topics and are well worth reading, particularly when the erudition on display is liberated by humor, regarding not only the subject under examination but often the examiner himself. Amis, best known for his novels (e.g., ***London Fields, The Information***), recognizes an authorial foible, then pounces on it—not without grace, not without vigor. His evaluations are lively, scholarly, and, on rare occasion, numbing—though probably less so for those few who know as much about literature as Amis. Requiring less literary background are his essays on poker or chess, Elvis Presley, or the sexual allure of Margaret Thatcher. The Amis view is at its best—or at least at its most readable—when he is chatting up such standards as *Don Quixote, Pride and Prejudice, Ulysses,* and

Lolita. His lengthy commentary on Nabokov, Larkin, and Updike certainly informs, as do shorter pieces on Roth, Burroughs, Capote, Burgess, and Vidal. To paraphrase Vidal, the best writing allows the reader to participate. Without question, Amis appreciates this concept and puts it into practice in his most accomplished criticisms. Recommended for academic libraries.

Johann Hari (essay date 15 October 2001)

SOURCE: Hari, Johann. "Unsightly Visions." *New Statesman* 14, no. 678 (15 October 2001): 42-3.

[*In the following essay, Hari recounts Amis's participation in an Internet interview forum, concluding that it showed Amis to be an egocentric, inaccessible man.*]

Martin Amis, we are assured by Clive James's irresistible new website, welcomestranger.com, finds television "intolerably superficial". Although Amis is "celebrated among his friends as one of the great talkers around the lunch table", we, the public, have never been exposed to his dazzling conversation. Until now. Just as digital cameras have allowed sports fans to view matches in ways they never imagined, James is now using digital cameras to lull his friends into seemingly friendly chats in his library. The programmes are broadcast exclusively on the internet, so the production values of a glossy TV studio aren't needed. The interviews are shot on cameras so unobtrusive, and with a host so genial, that at times his guests genuinely seem to reveal their true selves. And what a true self Amis reveals. With the novelist shorn of his flock of adoring sycophants and of the careful reworking possible with the written word, James—seemingly unwittingly—shows us, definitively and at last, that this emperor is wearing nothing but his own enormous ego.

All of Amis's faults are almost cruelly apparent. His snobbery manifests itself when the guests refer in passing to James Atlas's biography of Saul Bellow. Atlas describes how a good friend of Bellow's was upset when Bellow obviously based a character on him in his novel *Humboldt's Gift.* Amis retorts: "It doesn't matter what this man who works in tiling minds." He utters the word "tiling" with a contempt that most of us reserve for paedophiles. Amis has created within his own mind a notion of "talent", which he deifies and worships. He says, with the certainty of a man who has never doubted his own ability, that "your heart becomes gangrenous in your body when you go against your talent". Literary talent is his sole criterion for success, and anybody outside that world—a tiler, for example—is worthless. He emerges as obsessed with his own place in literature, and notes with sadness: "Usually writers never find out how good they are because that starts with the obituaries."

However, it is when James moves Amis on to a discussion of his philosophy that the viewer really recoils. Amis has always insisted that aesthetics are the sole standard for judging the worth of literature. He tries to argue that "morality is contained within aesthetics . . . they can't be separated . . . it's convenient for analysis but [they are] the same thing". But, James puts it to him, "there surely must be such a thing as a great stylist who . . . doesn't make an adequate approach morally to life", an argument to which Amis can reply only by shifting the subject. When they return to it and wonder if they "allow the possibility of a great Nazi writer", Amis finds himself with no answer. James warns of "the danger of an aestheticised world" without ever realising that this is the world his friend has always lived in, from his Oxford college to his current mansion in Primrose Hill.

Indeed, we could read this invaluable half-hour interview as a metaphor for Amis's whole life. Sitting in a hermetically sealed library, chatting with a friend who is similarly immersed in the world of literature, Amis has no reference points other than literature itself. He sits in a world of books, and can only write about them.

None the less, James emerges from this interview, and the others on this marvellous site (with as eclectic a mix of figures as Ruby Wax, the poet Peter Porter and the prima ballerina Deborah Bull), as one of the great interviewers of our time. Earlier this year, James confessed to feelings of self-hatred. If anything, his neuroticism is even more pronounced now than it was then. He argues, for example, that under Stalinism he would have been like Ilya Ehrenburg, "a very bad man" who "did some good things because of his position, and he achieved his position by being a slavish writer for the regime".

This unashamedly highbrow site is funded by the fortune James amassed from his lightweight work in television. It is hard to resist concluding that he considers his mass-entertainment work as his own slavish concession to the system, and that welcomestranger.com is his way of trying to achieve something good to make amends.

If so, this enthralling exposé of Amis compensates us ten times over for introducing Japanese game shows to an international audience, and even for bringing Margarita Pracatan to the world. And that's really saying something.

David Galef (essay date 2002)

SOURCE: Galef, David. "The Importance of Being Amis, Revisited." *Southwest Review* 87, no. 4 (2002): 554-64.

[*In the following essay, Galef considers the impact of Kingsley and Martin Amis's work as social documentaries, contrasting the life and work of the father and son.*]

About a decade ago, I began teaching a graduate seminar in postwar British literature. It's the only course I've ever taught that featured a famous author and his son: Kingsley and Martin Amis. And though most of the readers clearly enjoyed *Lucky Jim*—what student doesn't root for Jim Dixon?—just what gave the novel its peculiar force was less clear. Nothing in its form bespeaks the experimentalism of Samuel Beckett, say, or the political conviction of Doris Lessing. The reason I included the novel is that it captured a social era, and though the book still entertains, the Angry Young Men who kicked at Britain in the 1950s have long since metamorphosed into either retirees or humus. Also, like Evelyn Waugh and his ilk, Kingsley Amis turned conservative over the years, a fact that bothered some of the students.

Near the end of the course, we got to Martin Amis, specifically his short-story collection ***Einstein's Monsters.*** The anti-nuclear diatribe seemed apt for our era, moving from an impassioned preface, in which Amis argues for dismantling our bomb arsenal, to five imaginative short stories, each a cunning allegory for nuclear war and its fallout. But parable is a didactic form, and my students didn't particularly like being lectured to. Still, Martin Amis at that point had acquired the iconoclastic bad-boy status once accorded to his father. We were left with the same question: just what gave the Amises, father and son, their impact?

The clue, I think, lies in the very aspect that dated Kingsley Amis so quickly: both authors wrote novels that are as much searing social documentary as works of fiction. It's no coincidence that both Amises have produced a wealth of scathing essays and reviews, as well, from Kingsley's *Who Killed Jane Austen?* to Martin's ***The Moronic Inferno.*** In novels like *One Fat Englishman, Stanley and the Women,* and *Girl, 20,* Kingsley put his finger on the current English malaise, whether it was the foreign invasion, the displacement of white males, or the slow sinking of Britain's status to that of a second-class nation. No one is more socially acute than Kingsley Amis when he wrote, of the young women on the London streets in the late seventies, "The favoured attire suggested a lightning raid on the dressing-up chest or actual deprivation of clothing as normally thought of. They were wearing curtains, bedspreads, blankets, tablecloths, loose covers off armchairs and sofas." In *Jake's Thing,* from which this description is taken, Kingsley is writing from the viewpoint of Jake Richardson, who could be Jim Dixon twenty years later, had he stayed in academia. In fact, the invective in the novel is slanted more against the younger generation than the older, a reversal of the emphasis in works like *Lucky Jim.* However, the vantage remains pretty much the same throughout his career. In *The Russian Girl,* the last novel before his death, he was still inveighing against the academy, comfy values, and the opposite sex.

What changed in the intervening decades was society, not Kingsley Amis. In an essay tellingly entitled "Why Lucky Jim Turned Right," he declared his growing disillusionment with the Left intelligentsia and mass education, confessing, "In 1964, I voted Labour for the last time." But Kingsley was always "against the program," which is how he concludes his essay. In short, he may have become conservative merely by sticking to his guns. The point is that the revolutionaries of one age are the reactionaries of the next, if the revolution is successful. By the time *Stanley and the Women* was published in 1984, he had essentially been rewriting the same novel for years. The output was of high enough quality, but of little surprise value and pleasing mainly to his loyal readers. Yet it would have been hard to see this at the outset. Both Martin and Kingsley won the prestigious Somerset Maugham award for a first novel—though significantly, Maugham, another "consistent" author, once titled a late-career short-story collection *The Mixture as Before.* Good authors aren't necessarily innovators, and they may well repeat themselves. Quite accomplished novelists like Iris Murdoch, Barbara Pym, Fay Weldon, and Anita Brookner made their reputation by essentially revising one or two plots peopled by similar characters, again and again. Yet far from exhausting most readers' patience, such predictability sustains a loyal audience. It's worthwhile pondering this pattern, especially as one grows into middle age.

Just what is it about art since the Romantic era that's so obsessed with the idea of originality?—I say the idea of it, since nothing is new under the sun, and originality as we think of it is really just clever juxtaposition and recombination. As Frank Kermode once noted wearily in a graduate seminar I attended, "Most authors are possessed of only one idea. Great authors have two ideas, and the second is the mirror reflection of the first."

Given such sameness in the work of any artist, maybe a better question is what changes over time: politics, culture—and occasionally an artist who's not too insular will react to such shifts in a heretofore uncharacteristic way. But more often authors are set in their own personalities and own peculiar views of culture. Meanwhile, the established order can change, and the author may be embraced by the old or new regime. Real maverick writers, and I know a few, can embrace the stodgiest values or cling to bourgeois ideals. One of the most abrasive authors in the South once invited me over to his house to admire his new wide-screen TV.

So what were Kingsley Amis' values? One indication is that he was a longtime James Bond (or Ian Fleming) fan, in fact the author of *The James Bond Dossier* and even a quasi-Bond thriller called *Colonel Sun* that he wrote under the pseudonym Robert Markham. As numerous cultural critics have pointed out, Bond is the epitome of conservative British grace, the bastion of a vanished empire. The opening scene of *Colonel Sun* takes place at an exclusive golf course in England and ends with Bond and his woman heading to dinner in Athens. In between are myriad references to The Right Sort of British Values, from Axminster rugs to superior Scotch.

Martin, for his part, has produced the mystery ***Night Train,*** an odd police procedural set in Memphis. In his genre fiction, he's more inclined than his father to play with expectations—as in his earlier ***Other People: A Mystery Story,*** in which the amnesic protagonist Amy Hide, also known as Mary Lamb, must gather clues as to her identity. Martin likes twists, which isn't quite the same as being experimental.

But that's not the way he started. Back in the early 1970s, Martin came out with his debut novel, ***The Rachel Papers.*** Ostensibly the diary of a social failure, disgruntled teenage aesthete, and budding writer, the story concerned the protagonist's overwrought attempts to seduce a young woman named Rachel before he turned twenty. In its self-punishing, introspective stance, complete with Nabokovian metaphors updated for the seventies, it made for heady reading. That Martin was the son of Kingsley may have helped get it published, but it didn't help against the inevitable cries of nepotism. Still, it was a remarkable performance—Martin was all of 24 when it came out—and it became the cornerstone of his literary reputation. His father had been 32 when *his* first novel, *Lucky Jim,* was published—when Martin was five. Still, the parallels are there, given historical differences. In his recent book on Stalin, ***Koba the Dread,*** Martin addresses his dead father in a letter: "If our birthdates had been transposed, then I might have written your novels and you might have written mine."

Like his father, Martin followed his initial success with a dud: *That Uncertain Feeling* in Kingsley's case, ***Dead Babies*** in Martin's. The problem with Kingsley's second was that it contained all the boredom that Jim Dixon railed against, told from the first-person viewpoint of an assistant librarian. The problem with Martin's follow-up was that it contained all the anger so elaborately wrought in the first novel—and spewed it out all over the pages, from the bathroom humor to characters like the fat, flatulent dwarf Keith Whitehead. In its sheer intent to shock and disgust—what Pound & Co. called *épater la bourgeoisie*—it was retrograde. Art and anger are not the same, though the first may be spurred by the second. Imitators of the dramatist John Osborne and his character Jimmy Porter in *Look Back in Anger* ran into the same problem: loudness is only part of an aesthetic effect. This connection between aesthetics and anger seems a given in our era of art, part of the modernist heritage of outrage, amplified from Romanticist dejection and alienation. What about an art motivated by love, or is that the problem with Dante's *Paradiso,* so neglected in favor of his *Purgatorio*? Or perhaps the isthmus between open rage and creation is more a sanctioned male province, as opposed to a more female causeway of socially conditioned suppression and diversion.

In any event, productive authors move on. Martin's next work was aptly named ***Success,*** in which Martin's penchant for freakery was subordinated to a Nabokovian doubling theme and a sharp commentary on the inflationary success of contemporary English capitalism. Over the course of the plot, never a strength in either Amis, the protagonist slowly bests the "successful" member of the family. Another of his novels was simply entitled ***Money,*** and it follows the venial adventures of a media mogul named John Self with a hearing problem. Clearly, what Martin needed to direct his works was a fat target and a chance to defuse some Oedipal tension.

As Martin has stated in interview, "in my writing, yes, I am fascinated by what I deplore, or deplore what fascinates me." His father's fiction, too, centers on what he regards as socially outrageous. At one time, this kind of work used to be called a "state of England" novel, and Martin even wrote a short story with just that title. But what in Amis senior was a sharp eye for the extravagant was in Amis junior a gaze riveted to the grotesque, or nineteenth-century Dickensian eccentricity transported to twentieth-century London. In fact, critics have so fastened on the Nabokov connection, and Martin's avowed allegiance to the master, that they've ignored an earlier stylistic influence: Dickens. In *Hard Times,* for instance, Dickens famously displays Thomas Gradgrind lecturing a classroom: "The emphasis was helped by the speaker's square wall of a forehead, which had its eyebrows for its base, while his eyes found commodious cellarage in two dark caves, overshadowed by the wall." In ***The Rachel Papers,*** the protagonist Charles Highway provides just such a description of his mother: "The skin had shrunken over her skull, to accentuate her jaw and to provide commodious cellarage for the gloomy pools that were her eyes." In fact, early Martin Amis works are salient for their easy accommodation of earlier writers in phrase and image, from Fielding to Bellow. This is not the slur it may seem: Martin Amis is in love with the sound of words, including others' words, which means he's conscious of a literary heritage, which, in the age of the computer icon, makes him almost an antique. Now past fifty, he may one day even be awarded a C. B. E., just as his father received in 1981—the kind of honor that the younger set tends to disparage.

Certainly, the lives of the two Amises diverge more than run parallel. Kingsley, born in 1922 in a South London nursing home, had a father who was a clerk in the export department of Colman's Mustard: a keen cricketer, a former Baptist, and a lover of Gilbert and Sullivan, as Kingsley recalled in "A Memoir of My Father." Martin, who was born in 1949 and spent the first ten years of his life in South Wales, had Kingsley for his father and a rather peripatetic, unsettled existence in Spain, New Jersey, and other locations where Kingsley chose to write. Yet Martin got his formal "first" in literature at Oxford, just as his father had.

Just as certainly, their two styles have become famously recognizable, not to mention imitated. In Martin's case, the list runs from fellow travelers like Julian Barnes, now gone in his own direction, to acolytes like Will Self, who at times seems like some half-demented clone. In Kingsley's heyday, the Amis list included types like John Wain and John Braine, but the stylish allure was the same. In "The Importance of Being Amis," David Lodge observed that Kingsley Amis's sensibility took in ironies of culture and reflected them not just in subject but all the way down to the level of syntax. Kingsley delighted in baroque phrasing, clause piled upon clause, with observations nested in conditionals, as in this description of a restaurant meal in *Girl, 20*: "My steak came, and surprised me, or would have done had I still been open to surprise, by being excellent." Irony resides in negating parentheticals, extending to the level of characters defined by what they haven't got.

Martin, too, has mapped out his own literary territory. As with his father, after several novels, you could see the preoccupations emerging. As Karl Miller once pointed out, Martin Amis' work is strewn with orphans and doubles. (As a revelation in 1997 showed, this preoccupation may have something to do with the discovery of Martin's illegitimate daughter, Delilah Seale. Kingsley was also famous for sexual libertinism, but more in the mode of a philanderer from an earlier era.) In any event, Martin also displays a preference for minor hoodlums, tarty women, and down-at-the-heels writers. In his father's fiction, it's a predilection for educated men down on their luck, insufficiently supported by grasping women: Professor Richard Vaisey and his wife Cordelia in *The Russian Girl,* for instance. Like his father, Martin uses both high and low burlesque, the satiric technique of writing about trivial events in an elevated manner and vice versa. In Kingsley's works, this kind of scenario is accomplished through events like an epiphany glimpsed through a window in a lavatory or, oppositely, the drunken mangling of a high-intentioned academic speech. In Martin's work, such reversals emerge in the elevation of darts to a semi-mystical art (in ***London Fields***), or the technique of high modernism reduced to multiple characters talking on cell phones while walking through revolving doors (***The Information***).

These censorious views, besides perhaps leading to a prematurely jaundiced eye, are the start of what most readers recognize as the Amises' hallmark, social satire. But satire, as Alvin Kernan and others have noted, stems primarily from a conservative impulse, a wish to restore the world to order. What this means is that, despite characters who wallow in the muck, the muck is authorially disapproved of—that even in the wildest, Swiftest tale, there's a need for Gulliver to return to the balance of neoclassicism. Thus, Kingsley's Jim Dixon has been uprooted from his class in society and can no longer find out where he fits in, and Martin's Charles Highway is equally a misfit, though he has yet to go to university. Actually, it's unclear whether modern satire must provide an alternative to what it derides. The conviction that something is rotten in the state of England need not be accompanied by the vision of how to reverse putrefaction. Voltaire, after all, famously threw up his hands at any large-scale solution in the satiric *Candide,* merely advising the individual to *cultiver son jardin.*

"I'm never sure that what I've been writing is satire," Martin once claimed, but surely this statement is disingenuous. The epigraph to ***Dead Babies*** is from Menippus, from whom the term *Menippean satire* derives, that which makes fun of humankind's follies, often through philosophical and intellectual poses: "and so even when (the satirist) presents a vision of the future, his business is not prophecy, just as his subject is not tomorrow . . . it is today." A clearer program statement is hard to imagine. The future must be corrected, starting now.

Kingsley's impulse to correct is also quite evident, as in the symbolic (and usually glossed-over) opening of *Lucky Jim*: "'They made a silly mistake, though,' the Professor of History said . . ." Most critics read it as a slur on the pretentious professor of history, but it can be seen also as history acknowledging a wrong turn. In any event, the novel provides no easy solution to what it derides, and Jim Dixon escapes from his unfortunate situation rather than fixing it. In one of the less talked-about aspects of the novel, Jim goes into advertising, which seems positively freeing compared to provincial academia. Is this a cop-out? The endings to Kingsley's novels tend to be happy (in the double sense of elating and fortuitous): what his friend Philip Larkin called "the girl, the money, and everything." Endings for Martin remain more inconclusive, as in these last lines from ***Success,*** where even the landscape is weirdly premonitory: "Against the hell of a sunset the branches bend and break. The wind will never cease to craze the frightening leaves."

Of course, it doesn't hurt sales to be seen as revolutionary, aesthetically or politically. After ***London Fields*** with its unreliable narrator came out in 1989, many began labeling Martin postmodernist. Martin himself has declared, "I hope that I'm on the humorous wing of postmodernism." Yet an unreliable narrator alone does not make for postmodernism, for instance, especially if the truth of the matter is made clear at the end, which is why critics should stop confusing the terms *contemporary* and *postmodernist* and pay more attention to what's going on. The trouble is that well-meaning (and some ill-disposed) critics often confuse the complexity of modernist writing with the radical instability of postmodernist texts. It's an easy mistake to commit, especially since the techniques pioneered by the modernists were appropriated by the postmodernists. Both types of art contain everything from stream of consciousness and limited viewpoint to achronology and fragmented narratives, but the intent is different. In high modernism, the truth is difficult to get at but obtainable after much labor and synthesis, producing an exhaustively complex whole. In postmodernism, the retreat from absolutism, or the idea that language is suspect—attitudes that admittedly have their genesis in earlier epochs—become impassable obstacles to obtaining a true picture of anything. In short, postmodernism is modernism that has suffered a loss of faith. It's not at all clear that Martin espouses such a break, either in novelistic form or function. As Martin has noted: "every writer thinks he's in the forefront of breakdown and collapse."

Perhaps both authors desire to turn the clock back. In most of Kingsley's later novels, everything in England has become corrupt or silly and cheap, as in the bleaker poems of Philip Larkin, whose influence was also felt by Martin. Like his father, Martin also wishes to return to an earlier time, though with somewhat more urgency. In the preface to ***Einstein's Monsters,*** he preaches against nuclear holocaust and wants the big, bad bombs returned to pitchblende. In ***Time's Arrow,*** he wishes to undo the Holocaust. The irony is that ***Time's Arrow,*** a novel hailed as experimental narrative, is Amis's grandest foray into conservatism. The plot about a concentration camp doctor who makes his way to America, or rather, an emigré doctor in America who goes backward in time to wartime Germany, does not attempt Gertrude Stein's fractured and reversed linearity, but is simply a story told in reverse chronology. The novel's subtitle, *The Nature of the Offense,* stresses the didactic impulse behind the fiction. In its precisely backward effects—doctors put bullets back in wound victims, torturers restore prisoners—the novel is merely clever, a term that must drive Martin crazy, especially considering the derisive overtone that "clever" has in Britain. As he has his protagonist remark in the somewhat autobiographical ***Rachel Papers,*** "My English master had always impressed upon me how fucking clever I was."

Martin's short-story collection, ***Heavy Water,*** is precisely clever: expertly written, smartly executed, entertaining—but no more postmodernist or experimental than his other works. Nor need it be: no artist is under any compulsion to create radically new artistic forms, and the truth is that extremely talented traditional authors are in shorter supply these days than the so-called experimentalists. In ***Heavy Water,*** Amis shows that he can do anything with a premise, from creating a world where homosexuality and heterosexuality are reversed, to fabricating a universe where myriad sentient races exist. In most of these stories, the what-if premise becomes a tables-turned lesson, pointing out the injustice in the way we live.

Near the end of his career in 1991, Kingsley came out with *Memoirs,* and nine years later, Martin came out with his autobiographical sum-up, ***Experience,*** which won the James Tait Black Memorial Prize for biography the same year that Zadie Smith's *White Teeth,* a Martin Amis-influenced work if ever there was one, scored in fiction. In ***Experience,*** Martin somewhat evades the issue of literary influence, commenting on his relationship with his father: "He was a writer and I am a writer; it feels like a duty to describe our case—a literary curiosity which is also just another instance of a father and a son." Literary advice, he notes, was confined to warnings about overuse of suffixes like *-ing* and *-ly.* But a social outlook or literary sensibility may be inheritable. Or one can simply note loosely of the father-and-son pattern, as James Diedrick does in his book-length study of Martin Amis, "to differing degrees, bourgeois and patriarchal assumptions inform all their writing." As Martin goes on—and his memoir is almost as much about Kingsley as himself—he observes, during an impulse to goad others, "feeling my father in mê now . . ." That urge to push, to prick pretensions, may come across as noxious, but it also functions as a corrective, an attempt to set things right. And as a personality trait, it remains for a lifetime—or two. In 1993, Kingsley wrote to his friend Paul Fussell that, though his inner audience had consisted chiefly of Larkin and Robert Conquest, "More lately I have added Martin."

Martin Amis is surely aware of this consanguinity, though he also argues for a subtle distinction: "I was trying to grasp the difference between my father's moral scheme and mine; and it occurred to me that what he prizes is decency, and when I look for the positive values in my books, I find they are always represented by innocence." This point seems to establish Martin as more wishful than Kingsley, pinning his hopes on a prelapsarian world rather than attempting to correct a corrupted universe. Or perhaps both inclinations are simply hopeful in our world of new beginnings and difficult middles.

Of course, such a line of questioning raises the intractable issue of morality, from its definition to its origins. Where does morality come from, especially in an ungoverned universe? Stemming from the practical need not to be murdered in one's bed, it may also be related to that part of human nature inclined to control others—or oneself. Attempts at self-government, and self-loathing after their failure, are all over the Amises' fiction. Morality is often equated with absolutism, and one label never slapped on either Amis is *relativist.* Are they didactic? Maybe, but not in a politically correct way. In the end, what seems like conservatism in both Amises may not be that at all, but rather the timelessness of a moral vision. These days, of course, that vision seems either quite timely or else thankless, as much attacked as the tenets of liberal humanism. Yet Martin comes quite close to this position: "I would say that the point of good art is remotely and unclearly an educative process, a humanizing and enriching process." His father, though he'd probably have been snide about it, might well have agreed.

John Lloyd (essay date 11 March 2002)

SOURCE: Lloyd, John. "George W. Bush's Unlikely Bedfellows." *New Statesman* 15, no. 697 (11 March 2002): 10-11.

[*In the following essay, Lloyd documents the support for George W. Bush's "War on Terror" from well-known British writers such as Amis, Salman Rushdie, and Christopher Hitchens.*]

"I had," said Martin Amis, "been a bit more cautious about the war to begin with. I thought that the old response, with the cruise missiles operation, was not right. I thought it should be more of a financial and an intelligence operation. But it now seems to me that a show of force was necessary."

Prominent writers, such as Christopher Hitchens and Salman Rushdie, have shocked some sections of the European left by their stance on 11 September and on the events that followed it. The shock is all the greater because, like Amis, they come from a left generation that bitterly opposed US intervention, overt and covert, in such countries as Vietnam and Chile. Much of the intellectual left in Europe cleaves to a view of America as the largest danger in the modern world. It sees those from the '68 generation as supportive of a Republican president—and thinks that, since they regard terrorists as enemies just as Bush does, these writers should be damned as heretics. Their reasons are barely attended to.

For Hitchens, more than Amis, the war appears to have sharpened his thinking on the nature of the divisions in the world. Speaking from his home in Washington, Hitchens said: "I do think America is a great idea. I think the American revolution is the only one which has lasted, the only one left. It still has a dynamic. It is the only one capable of a universal application." I said that this brought him close to the position of Francis Fukuyama, in his *End of History and the Last Man*—that the values derived from the American revolution represent the highest achievement of political economy and that there can now be no credible challenge to them. "A much underrated writer," said Hitchens.

His concern, after 11 September, was not that the US would lead a war on terrorism, but that it would fail to do so. "I had a real fear," Hitchens said, "that the Bush people wouldn't fight. Even later, I thought that the 'axis of evil' phrase [used by President George Bush in his State of the Union address] could be a way of changing the subject."

Both Amis and, more polemically, Hitchens believe that the war has exposed a division in Europe's left: between the decent left, which is on the side of those willing to fight Islamic fascism, and the rigidly anti-American left. The latter is willing to push all else aside in order to give free way to a refurbished critique of imperialism, in which the US plays the dominant role, dragging servile satraps such as Tony Blair, Gerhard Schröder and Vladimir Putin in its wake.

Rushdie—who, like Amis and Hitchens, now lives in the US—wrote in the *Guardian* a month ago that "America finds itself facing an ideological enemy that may turn out to be harder to defeat than militant Islam: that is to say, anti-Americanism, which is presently taking the world by storm".

Rushdie said that, on a recent visit to the UK, he was "struck, even shocked, by the depth of anti-American feeling among large segments of the population, as well as the news media . . . The attacks on America are routinely discounted ('Americans only care about their own dead'). American patriotism, obesity, emotionality, self-centredness: these are the crucial issues." Hitchens, on a visit to the UK last month, expected leftist scorn, but was less prepared for the reaction from other quarters. "I did one phone-in show and it became quite obvious that people in the upper social echelon thought that the US was being too self-righteous."

The American left—powerful in intellectual, cultural and media circles, if not in politics—is either for the war, or silent, according to Hitchens. An exception to this is Noam Chomsky, the Massachusetts Institute of Technology professor, who sees in the war a new chapter in a long work of US imperialism and racism. "Chomsky is just plain wrong," said Martin Amis, speaking from Ecuador, where he has been writing a book on communism which has clearly caused him to refine his world-view. "The moral equivalence line just didn't work, I thought. Anti-Americanism doesn't impress me as a very rational position."

Amis has not become a man of the right. Neither has Hitchens or Rushdie. They have simply remained capable of discriminating between positions. Hitchens sees in the right a major strain of realpolitik, most closely associated with Henry Kissinger, whom he branded a war criminal in a book published last year. (A French magistrate made an effort, which came to nothing, to take that seriously and have Kissinger arrested on a visit to Paris.)

That school of thought—of which the first President Bush was a prominent exponent—sees national interest as the major determinant for US intervention in foreign wars: a view that would have prevented the United States, or Nato, from engaging in any African war, or in Bosnia, or in Kosovo. "The first time I had a public quarrel with Chomsky," Hitchens said, "was over Bosnia. He was helping to provide a smokescreen for Milosevic. The thing is, in the end, Chomsky doesn't think the US is a good idea."

The emerging left position on human rights was put powerfully in the most recent edition of the *New York Review of Books* by Samantha Power, director of the Carr Center for Human Rights Policy at Harvard University. Power points out that genocide, far from being confined to the age of the Nazis and the Stalinists, has flourished in the past half-century in such countries as Cambodia, Somalia and Rwanda, and has gone largely unpunished.

"Genocide occurred *after* the cold war," she writes, "*after* the growth of human rights groups; *after* the advent of technology that allowed for instant communication; *after* the erection of the Holocaust Museum on the Mall in Washington, DC."

Modest progress has been made in trying to stop genocide. With his "ethical dimension to foreign policy", Robin Cook, foreign secretary until last year, tried to grapple with precisely the conditions that Power describes—where governments know what is happening and where they have the power to act to stop or moderate slaughter. Sporadically, Labour's senior people grappled with what "ethics" could mean. They faced bureaucratic scepticism, and the scorn of "realists" such as Kissinger, who thought both Blair and Bill Clinton naive.

In a speech in Chicago in April 1999, while the war in Kosovo ran on, Blair said that "the most pressing foreign policy problem we face is to identify the circumstances in which we should get actively involved in other people's conflicts . . . the principle of non-interference must be qualified in important respects. Acts of genocide can never be a purely internal matter."

But the "most pressing problem" had received no answer by 11 September. Powerful states, notably the US and China, see sovereignty as a non-negotiable right—the US, to the point of refusing to accede to the International Criminal Court lest a US soldier or official be brought to trial in a foreign jurisdiction. One of the many contradictions of the transatlantic relationship is that the UK, supposedly the closest of the European allies to the US, is in this regard the furthest from it.

The events of 11 September "solved" the issue of intervention, providing a justification for US counter-strikes which almost all members of the UN initially recognised. It is, however, a temporary solution: nothing has been written into international law, or UN practice, that gives sanction to larger interventions, especially those undertaken without the moral force provided by a prior strike. Blair's speeches, notably to last autumn's Labour conference, on the need for a much more active policy—through aid programmes and state-building as well as through military intervention—have met only uncertain responses, in the UK as elsewhere.

Those regimes that use the paraphernalia and practices of fascism have now at least to contend with the belief, admittedly still fragile, that they should be opposed because, sooner or later, they will cause mass murders at home or abroad or both. The 11 September attacks, Power writes, "might make Americans inside and outside government more empathetic toward the victims of genocide". It is to the credit of the UK government that it has tried to build such empathy. It is to the shame of much of the European left that it has tried to brand such empathy as wickedness. "It would be easy," writes Rushdie, "for America, in the present climate of hostility . . . to start . . . throwing its weight around without regard for the concerns of what it perceives as an already hostile world." Amis says that "the US before 11 September behaved more unilaterally than before the Second World War. That's very strongly there in this administration. If they think they've found a model from their successes in Afghanistan, then I think they're wrong."

Hitchens makes the danger more precise. It is that the impetus to combat tyrannous or genocidal regimes proceeds not from the stated aims—to stop ethnic cleansing or to shore up popular opposition—but merely to suppress threats to the west, especially to the US. He points to the neglect of the long-established Iraqi opposition groups by the White House, and the administration's apparent insouciance about planning to assist a replacement government that could gather popular support and attempt reconciliation with neighbours. "Clinton ran for office saying that stopping massacres would be his responsibility. They ratted on commitments."

But Hitchens sees, among the generation whose most active spirits were far leftists, "a new politics" of engagement emerging, pointed up by such figures as

Joschka Fischer and Daniel Cohn-Bendit. It is a politics that at least promises to redefine national interest to include the halt of mass murder. The left, instead of dismissing all actions and rhetoric of Bush, Blair and Schröder as those of hypocritical imperialists, should hold these leaders to their words. If, as the left has long believed, genocide, oppression and aggression should be fought, its task is to ensure that politicians who endorse these aims live up to them.

Brad Hooper (review date 1 May 2002)

SOURCE: Hooper, Brad. Review of *Koba the Dread,* by Martin Amis. *Booklist* 98, no. 17 (1 May 2002): 1442.

[*In the following review, Hooper maintains that* Koba the Dread *is an illuminating, yet gruesome documentation of Josef Stalin's reign.*]

This highly regarded British novelist follows his memoir ***Experience*** (2000) with another nonfiction book [***Koba the Dread***] that, loosely defined, may also be called a memoir, and it is absolutely riveting. Amis is the son of novelist Kingsley Amis, and Amis fils recalls his father's affiliation with communism in the 1930s and, along with his "Oxford comrades," their ignorance of Stalin's "domestic cataclysms," namely the Soviet dictator's massacre of anyone who could possibly be thought to be a dissident—the total of which numbered in the millions. Such recollections lead the younger Amis to ponder Stalin's life story; the title of this book refers to a Stalin nickname. Amis' provocative book, the majority of which is given over to the Stalin profile, proves to be difficult reading—not for the style, to be sure, which is rich without being dense ("An additional ten IQ points in Kerensky might have saved Russia from Lenin"), but more for the dark subject matter ("Corpse-disposal was a national tribulation throughout the period of hard Bolshevism, which ended in 1953"). This extended essay presents, in no uncertain terms, the misguidedness of the Western intelligentsia's seduction by the maniacally secretive Stalin in the years before the cold war.

Kirkus Reviews (review date 1 May 2002)

SOURCE: Review of *Koba the Dread,* by Martin Amis. *Kirkus Reviews* 70, no. 9 (1 May 2002): 627.

[*In the following review, the anonymous critic finds* Koba the Dread *to be a compelling read.*]

The accomplished English novelist follows his first memoir (***Experience,*** 2000) with a post-millennial backward glance [***Koba the Dread***] at the evil 20th century and its "chief lacuna."

A child of the 1960s, now himself a half-century old, Amis treats several large and related themes. He reviews the basic facts of the terrible Soviet experiment, which he knows chiefly through having read "several yards of books" about it. Then he turns to the early devotion of his father's generation to that experiment and their subsequent rejection of it; Kingsley Amis wrote an essay called "Why Lucky Jim Turned Right" in 1967, and his friend Robert Conquest published a history of Soviet terror. Martin's generation embraced all things leftist during the revolutionary years of the Vietnam War and Paris Rouge, a rhetorically excessive time when "policemen and even parking wardens were called fascists." Some of these themes have, of course, occupied English intellectuals from Orwell's time on, but Amis brings to them a fresh look helped in its particulars by shocking revelations from now-open Soviet archives. Among the more controversial theses is his well-reasoned suggestion that Soviet Communism was, in the end, worse than Nazism: "Stalin, unlike Hitler, did his worst. . . . Bolshevism was exportable, and produced near-identical results everywhere. Nazism could not be duplicated." Readers of *The Black Book of Communism* will find this argument unobjectionable, but it will certainly earn Amis a hiding in the leftist press. Particularly compelling is Martin's closing letter to Kingsley, now dead, wondering how either father or son could have been taken in by the romantic lie of a worker's paradise. The author is no David Horowitz, however, he hasn't gone Tory in middle age, even if he takes well-deserved swipes at Christopher Hitchens and other fellow travelers while confessing his own sins.

Meritorious addition to the bulging shelf of apologia by writers on the noncommunist English left, worth reading by anyone interested in exploring the dark recesses of the recent past.

Publishers Weekly (review date 20 May 2002)

SOURCE: Review of *Koba the Dread,* by Martin Amis. *Publishers Weekly* 249, no. 20 (20 May 2002): 55.

[*In the following review of* Koba the Dread, *the critic explains that Amis "relates passionately a story that needs to be told, the history of a regime that murdered its own people in order to build a better future for them."*]

Everyone knows what the Holocaust was, but, Amis points out [in ***Koba the Dread***], there is no name for and comparatively little public awareness of the killing that took place in the Soviet Union between 1917 and 1933, when 20 million died under a Bolshevik regime that ruled as if waging war against its own people. Why? The U.S.S.R. was effectively a gigantic prison system that was very good at keeping its grisly secrets. Too, communism had widespread support in the rest of the world, as Amis reminds us. Not quite a memoir, this book sandwiches a lengthy treatise on the horror of life in Leninist and Stalinist Russia between Amis's brief personal takes on his gradually dawning awareness of Soviet atrocities. In his first and final pages, he deals with three generations of "dupes" who supported Soviet rule: that of H. G. Wells and George Bernard Shaw; that of novelist Kingsley Amis, the writer's father and member of the Communist Party in the 1940s; and that of leftist contemporaries of Martin Amis himself, notably the writer Christopher Hitchens. Throughout, Amis snipes at Hitchens in particular ("'What about the famine?' I once asked him. 'There wasn't a *famine,*' he said, smiling slightly and lowering his gaze. 'There may have been occasional *shortages. . . .*'") Alexander Solzhenitsyn tried to tell the West about Stalinism in the '70s, but this grim patriarch had no appeal for the New Left, a generation interested only in "revolution as play," Amis says. Most readers won't be interested in the author's private quarrels, but in the bulk of the book he relates passionately a story that needs to be told, the history of a regime that murdered its own people in order to build a better future for them.

Robert H. Johnston (review date 1 June 2002)

SOURCE: Johnston, Robert H. Review of *Koba the Dread,* by Martin Amis. *Library Journal* 127, no. 10 (1 June 2002): 169-70.

[*In the following review, Johnston provides a positive appraisal of* Koba the Dread, *yet maintains that it is a difficult read.*]

This passionate and intensely personal book [***Koba the Dread***] by novelist Amis (***London Fields***) evokes a terrible crime, in fact several million crimes. Koba is Joseph Stalin, the 20 million his victims. Interwoven with his impressionistic narrative (which owes much to Alexander Solzhenitsyn and the Anglo-American historian Robert Conquest) are details of Amis's family history, along with his sparring with the memory of his late father, Kingsley, and a close friend, the English journalist Christopher Hitchens, both one-time defenders of Soviet rule. Amis cuts to and from these and other personalities, throwing in details of the appalling horrors of Stalinist misrule, in a kaleidoscopic narrative flow. Who was worse: the Little Mustache (Hitler) or the Big Mustache (Stalin)? Why is the latter's evil not as widely acknowledged as the former's? Amis concludes his book with a single family death, contrasting its pathos with, in Stalin's celebrated expression, the "mere statistic" of the death of millions. A personal and polemical reaction to human and historical tragedy on both a small and a large scale, this is not an easy read. While the book reveals nothing new historiographically, it will appeal to admirers of Amis's literary panache.

John Pilger (essay date 17 June 2002)

SOURCE: Pilger, John. *New Statesman* 15, no. 711 (17 June 2002): 13-14.

[*In the following essay, Pilger argues that Amis is representative of the failure of English-language authors "to engage with the most urgent issues of our time."*]

On 1 June, the *Guardian* published a long essay by Martin Amis, entitled **"The Voice of the Lonely Crowd"**. It was about 11 September and the role of writers. What did Amis think about on the momentous day? He thought he was "like Josephine, the opera-singing mouse in the Kafka story: Sing? 'She can't even squeak.'"

By that he meant, I guess, that he had nothing to say about "the conflicts we now face or fear", as he put it. Why not? Where was the spirit of Orwell and Greene? Where was a modest acknowledgement of history: a passing reflection on the impact of rapacious great power on vulnerable societies, which are the roots of the current "terrorism"?

Amis referred rightly to the "pitiable babble" of writers following 11 September. Most of the famous names were heard, their contributions ranging from morose me-ism to an aggressive defence of America and its "modernity". Not a single English writer commanding the celebrity that provides an extraordinary public platform has written anything incisive and worthy of our memory about the meaning and exploitation of 11 September—with the exception, as ever, of Harold Pinter.

Compare their "babble", and their silence, with the work of the celebrated Palestinian poet Mahmoud Darwish, the subject of a fine *Guardian* profile on 8 June by Maya Jaggi. Darwish is the Arab world's bestselling poet; people's poet may sound trite, but he draws thousands to his readings, thrilling his audiences with a lyricism that touches their lives and makes sense of power, injustice and tragedy. In his latest poem, "State of Siege", a "martyr" says:

> I love life
> On earth, among the pines and the fig trees
> But I can't reach it, so I took aim
> With the last thing that belonged to me.

Darwish's manuscripts were trampled under foot by Israeli soldiers at the cultural centre in Ramallah where he often works. I was in this building last month, not long after the Israelis had left. They had defecated on the floors, and smeared shit on the photocopiers, and pissed on books and up the walls, and systematically destroyed manuscripts of plays and novels and hard disks. As they left, they threw paint on a wall of children's drawings.

"They wanted to give us a message that nobody's immune—including in cultural life," says Darwish. "Palestinian people are in love with life. If we give them hope—a political solution—they'll stop killing themselves."

Perhaps it is unfair to compare a Darwish with an Amis. One is speaking for the crimes against his people, after all. But Amis represents a wider problem: that some of the most acclaimed and privileged writers writing in the English language fail to engage with the most urgent issues of our time. Who among the collectors of Booker and Whitbread Prizes speaks against the crimes described by Darwish—the product of the longest military occupation in the modern era? Who, since 11 September, has defended our language, illuminating its abuse in the service of great power's goals and hypocrisy? Who has shown that our humane responses to 11 September have been appropriated by the masters of terror themselves?—by Ariel Sharon and his "good friend" George W Bush, who bombed to death at least 5,000 civilians in Afghanistan.

Consider Amis's unexplained reference to the conflicts we must now "face or fear". The Palestinians have been facing and fearing an occupation for more than 35 years: an atrocious stalemate sponsored by every American administration since that of Lyndon Johnson and reaffirmed this month by Bush himself. Since 11 September, those who have been allowed to grind English into a series of clichés propagating their "war on terrorism" have also supplied the Israeli regime with 50 F-16 fighter-bombers, 102 Gatling guns, 228 joint direct attack munitions (JDAMs) and 24 Blackhawk helicopters. A batch of state-of-the art Apache helicopters is on the way. You may have seen the Apache on the news, firing missiles at civilian apartment blocks in occupied Palestine.

The other day, I spoke to a group of children in Gaza. They smiled, but it was clear that their dreams, indeed their childhood, had been despatched by Israel's attacks on a people who, for the most part, have defended themselves with slingshots. Among these children, almost certainly, are those who will sacrifice, as Darwish wrote, "the last thing that belonged to me". Who is his equivalent in the west, setting that wisdom against our government's part in the making of this terror?

In the 1980s, Martin Amis published a valuable collection of essays on the threat of nuclear war. Today, India and Pakistan seriously threaten nuclear war, which is not surprising, in a world dominated by threats since 11 September: a world of either-you-are-with-us-or-against-us, of bomb now and talk later. What does Amis or any English writer have to say about the great warrior against terrorism in the White House, who says that "first strike" is now the superpower's policy and that America "must be ready to strike at a moment's notice in any dark corner of the world"? This includes the nuclear option, Martin Amis, should you still be interested.

"After 11 September," wrote Amis in the *Guardian,* "writers faced quantitative change, but not qualitative change . . . They stood in eternal opposition to the voice of the lonely crowd, which, with its yearning for both power and effacement, is the most desolate sound you will ever hear." Those who publish and promote such empty words, holding the robes of English literature's current emperors, have an urgent responsibility to hand the space to others.

Our language should be reclaimed, its Orwellian vocabulary reversed, its noble words such as "democracy" and "freedom" protected, and its power redeployed against all fundamentalisms, especially our own. We need to find and publish our own Mahmoud Darwish, our own Arundhati Roy, our own Ahdaf Soueif, our own Eduardo Galeano, and quickly.

William Hutchings (review date summer 2002)

SOURCE: Hutchings, William. Review of *The War against Cliché,* by Martin Amis. *World Literature Today* 76, nos. 3/4 (summer 2002): 77-8.

[*In the following review, Hutchings commends the depth and range of Amis's literary knowledge as evinced in* The War against Cliché.]

Although his literary achievements have in many ways already surpassed his father's, Martin Amis continues to be known as Amis the Younger—and a perennially adolescent glower of iconoclasm, skepticism, and disdain characterizes even the photographs chosen for the dust jackets of his books. Yet, for thirty years now, he has published essays and reviews that display not only a surprisingly broad range but an incisiveness and an insistence on the importance of style—all of which are abundantly displayed in ***The War against Cliché.*** Having begun his career as a novelist in the late 1960s and early 1970s, when he was also working at the *Times Literary Supplement,* he recalls in his foreword the now-gone age when "Literature and Society" was a topic of seemingly endless discussion and when Edmund Wilson, F. R. Leavis, William Empson, Northrop Frye, and Lionel Trilling, among others, were revered. "That time now seems unrecognizably remote," he remarks, and "Lit. & Soc., and indeed literary criticism [feel] dead and gone[,] . . . atomized as soon as the forces of democratization gave their next concerted push. . . . Gallingly for the lit-crit imperialists (especially I. A. Richards), there is no means for distinguishing the excellent from the less excellent. . . . [Still,] all writing is a campaign against cliché. Not just clichés of the pen but clichés of the mind and clichés of the heart."

The book's title is also that of Amis's surprisingly equivocal essay on James Joyce, whose *Ulysses* (which allegedly "can be read in about a week, if you do nothing else") is ultimately "*about* cliché[,] . . . about inherited, ready-made formulations, fossilized metaphors—most notably those of Irish Catholicism and anti-Semitism." Joyce's undisputed genius is duly acknowledged, but he is found to be "auto-friendly, James Joyce-friendly" rather than "reader-friendly." Amis's primary complaint is that, in part because "beautiful prose came so naturally to Joyce . . . he often indulged a perverse attraction to its opposite: hideous prose, to mirror-cracking, clock-stopping prose. . . . But most of the parodies feel like a deliberate strain on the reader's patience . . . as if Joyce used dead prose and swingeing tedium—epic boredom, biblical boredom—as a counterweight to all that is fresh and vital elsewhere."

Vladimir Nabokov and Anthony Burgess are warmly praised (the latter for *Earthly Powers,* especially), and family friend Philip Larkin is vigorously defended against detractors who were outraged by the foul and abundant expressions of racism, misogyny, and anti-Semitism (clichés themselves, surely) that were disclosed in his posthumously published letters and biography. As "the war against cliché" proceeds, however, a number of English writers who would seem to be among the most likely targets are instead treated with surprising indulgence: positive assessments are given to C. P. Snow, Doris Lessing, and Iris Murdoch, whose writing, whatever its other merits, seldom achieved more than turgid functionality.

American writers, on the other hand, are often scrutinized with a blend of bravura insight, hyperbole, and bravado. Norman Mailer, for example, is said to come up "on every page . . . with a formulation both grandiose and crass"; consequently, "no one in the history of the written word, not even William MacGonagall or Spike Milligan or D. H. Lawrence, is so wide open to disparaging quotation" (a rather grandiose formulation itself, however accurate it may be). Robert Bly's *Iron John* gets eviscerated, quite wittily, in the book's first essay, "Zeus and the Garbage." John Updike is astutely if condescendingly characterized as "a Protestant of the small-town Dionysian sort . . . [but] also a Humanist, of the numinous Apollonian sort, [which] does seem to account for that vein of folksy uplift which underlies his novels as well as his criticism." Surprisingly, then, Amis acclaims the "Rabbit" novels as having "few obvious betters" among "works which address the American century. . . . If Updike lacks something in the way of vision and attack, he makes up for it in tirelessness and will." Accordingly, the 1,500 pages of suburban Angst accompanying a decades-long chronicle of the domestic mundane are somehow "as if a double-sized *Ulysses* had been narrated, not by Stephen, Bloom, and Molly, but by one of the surlier underbouncers at Kiernan's bar." (Gore Vidal has far more convincingly placed Updike's writing in the tradition of John P. Marquand and John O'Hara; see *The Last Empire: Essays 1992-2000*). Saul Bellow receives even more fulsome praise from Amis, including the startling claim that "*The Adventures of Augie March* is the Great American Novel. Search no further." Elmore Leonard is characterized as "a literary genius who writes re-readable thrillers" and whose "essence . . . is to be found in his use of the present participle. . . . He has discovered a way of slowing down and suspending the English sentence." Among post-modernists, Don DeLillo and William Burroughs are among Amis's most acclaimed.

When the subject is pre-twentieth-century literature, however, Amis demonstrates a knowledge of both primary and secondary sources that is remarkable for both its depth and its range. Often these are reviews of literary biographies, including John Cornwell's *Coleridge: Poet and Revolutionary, 1772-1804,* A. N. Wilson's *The Life of John Milton,* and John Carey's *John Donne: Life, Mind and Art.* A series of essays on "Great Books," which originally appeared in *The Atlantic Monthly,* includes assessments of the unabridged *Don Quixote* as translated by Tobias Smollett ("clearly an impregnable masterpiece . . . suffering from one fairly serious flaw—that of outright unreadability") and *Pride and Prejudice* (whose "tizzy of zealous suspense [over marriage] actually survives repeated readings").

The War against Cliché will survive repeated readings as well.

Simon Carr (review date 24 August 2002)

SOURCE: Carr, Simon. "Stalin Was Bad—Shock." *Spectator* 289, no. 9081 (24 August 2002): 16.

[*In the following review of* Koba the Dread, *Carr takes issue with Amis's role as moralist, contending that the author doesn't have the talent or instincts for it.*]

There are very few novelists of our generation (I'm assuming you're 50) whom we can quote by heart. Perhaps there aren't any. When you cast back over your reading list—Julian Barnes, Ian McEwan, William Boyd, Sebastian Faulkes, Salman Rushdie, David Lodge, Clive James, even—what are your favourite lines? Anything spring to mind? At all?

But then there's Martin Amis. And it's astonishing what has stuck. There are well over a dozen passages I can quote verbatim; shamingly, about the same as from the Bible. 'There was no reason to suppose that with her clothes off she'd smell of boiled eggs and dead babies.' In the 1970s, his was the funniest prose in England, perhaps even in English. P. G. Wodehouse couldn't have been more inventive. In ***Success,*** a tramp's benediction was rendered as: 'Gob less.' The narrator replied, 'I'll try.'

There was a certain heartlessness, perhaps, but that's what young men were like in those days. Jan Morris complained to the paper which carried Martin's review of her sex-change book. Martin had written that Morris had gone to Morocco 'to get his rig lopped off'. Ms Morris said something like: 'I suppose he wanted to make me cry. I want him to know that he succeeded.' That made us laugh as well; it's a little uncomfortable to remember how much.

In ***Money,*** the yob narrator is persuaded to read *Animal Farm.* He likes it. It's quicker to read than most books because, apart from anything else, it starts on page seven. He gives Orwell his approval—except for the thing about the pigs. He knows about pigs. He'd once done a commercial for a 'pork-character rissole . . . and believe me, pigs are fucking disgusting creatures . . . Eating your girlfriend's tail while she wasn't looking counts as old-world courtesy by the standards of the sty . . . It's no accident they're called pigs.'

But what happened to the finest comic novelist of our time? ***London Fields*** I read out of sheer loyalty, and the huge-advance novel ***The Information*** I read for a bet. There was a line in it about his plane trip with a . . . oh, it doesn't matter: 'Jack knifing over a sick bag looking up "assassins" in the *Yellow Pages*' was the most quoted line. But they don't have assassins in the *Yellow Pages,* and they don't have *Yellow Pages* on airplanes. What's funny about it?

Martin's comic genius had collapsed into crepuscular plotting and page upon page of prose poetry. The victory of his dark, serious side was complete.

There had been warning signs. During the 1980s he had been worrying about seriousness, in the same way that Diana, Princess of Wales worried about her hair. It was something they had to get right if the public was to see them in the right way. Martin's chosen field of anxiety was nuclear warfare. He was against it. In the preface to ***Einstein's Monsters*** he reflected on what he would have to do if war broke out. 'I must find my wife and children,' he said, 'and kill them.' There is something unshirkably comic (a phrase we'll return to) in that idea. Was this a unilateral idea? Had he consulted Mrs Amis? Or perhaps Mrs Amis had come to the same conclusion? Were they both to be wandering through the nuclear rubble trying to kill each other for their own good?

The fact is that he had no talent for the task of being our generation's guide to moral seriousness. His instincts aren't up to it. Look: he claims that all his characters are working class; he claims always to have been a feminist writer. Even if these claims were true, they wouldn't be worth much because his foundations aren't sound. Here's one glimpse; there are others, but try this.

While promoting his autobiographical memoir ***Experience*** he began a reading at a literary festival by asking whether Lucy Partington's sister was in the audience; the passage he wanted to read involved Lucy (she'd been Martin's cousin, murdered by Fred West), and he wanted to make sure the family didn't mind.

Now, that was unshirkably comic. Precisely the opposite effect was created from the one intended. We were meant to think 'What a considerate fellow!' and we actually thought, 'Why on earth didn't he clear it with her before getting up on stage in front of a thousand people?' And 'What if she had been in the audience? What kind of pressure to agree would she have been under? What a bully!'

His latest book, ***Koba the Dread: Laughter and the Twenty Million*** takes on communism's great dictator. Stalin committed terrible crimes. Perhaps you already knew that.

He compiles an impressive collection of Bolshevik atrocities from various books. He attacks his friend Christopher Hitchens for atrocity denial, and asks the useful and interesting question: why have Bolshevik attempts at genocide been so overlooked, not to say excused, by the liberal Left?

He has an answer, but it's wrong. He attributes it to—famous phrase—something 'unshirkably comic' at the heart of Bolshevism. They promised freedom and equality but delivered torture and death. These things are only comic, surely, if you discount the pain involved to something close to zero. Then you can laugh, as we laughed at James Morris 'having his rig lopped off'.

Gitta Sereny appeared in a recent documentary about Charlie Chaplin's film *The Great Dictator.* She recalled seeing a group of upper-class Viennese Jews on hands and knees cleaning the pavement with tooth-brushes while a crowd taunted them. 'One almost laughed, it was so terrible,' she said. Not laughed, but almost laughed. And if that humiliation were terrible, would she have 'almost laughed' at torture, and death camps? I don't know Ms Sereny but I guess the answer is No.

There is a reason why communist societies are indulged in this extraordinary way, and Amis glances at it. It derives, he says, from the 'universal fondness of that old, old idea about the perfect society'. Those who believe in a perfect society excuse the crimes of those who pursue it.

This impulse is still strong today. When an old man dies of starvation in an NHS hospital, there is little outrage; had he died in the same way in a private hospital, the heavens would have been called down. If 5,000 people were killed in private hospitals because the wards were dirty, as happens annually in NHS hospitals, there'd be street marches. We wouldn't put up with it. They promise to heal you; they kill you.

Is there something 'unshirkably comic' about those—what? 50,000?—patients killed by dusty wards? Laughter and the Fifty Thousand? It would take a certain moral courage as well as moral seriousness to denounce the National Health Service, but it's unlikely that Martin Amis would go so decisively against the zeitgeist. It's only just become safe enough to attack Stalin, after all.

John Lloyd (essay date 2 September 2002)

SOURCE: Lloyd, John. "Show Trial: The Left in the Dock." *New Statesman* 15, no. 722 (2 September 2002): 12-14.

[*In the following essay, Lloyd avows that* Koba the Dread *forces left-wing politicians and intellectuals in Europe to confront their own support of Communism.*]

The left—all of it, from the inside to the outside—is about to have its conscience pricked. This comes at a convenient time. A large part of the left is working itself into more of a moral lather over American "warmongering" than over the crimes and threats of Saddam Hussein; it needs a little prick to prompt reflection.

Martin Amis's ***Koba the Dread,*** already published in the US, will be out in the UK in September. Koba was Stalin's nickname: the book is an account of the millions who died under his rule. The book has already passed through energetically flagellating reviewers in the US. The *New York Times*'s critic Michiko Kakutani described the "narcissistic musings of a spoiled, upper-middle-class littérateur" who knew nothing about (and, by implication, thus could not write about) the suffering of Stalin's victims. In the online journal *Slate,* the journalist Anne Applebaum (who is writing a book on the Gulag) said that Amis—a "fifty something novelist who has run out of things to write about" had "funnelled his displaced anger into a poorly conceived, improbably hysterical diatribe against Stalinism".

But in the *Atlantic Monthly,* Christopher Hitchens—though he admonishes Amis, his close friend, to be "choosy about what kind of anti-communist you are"—writes ("if it matters") that "I now agree with him that perfectionism and messianism are the most lethal of our foes" and admits (if it matters) that he was "wrong" about the choice he made, earlier in his life, for Marxism.

It does matter, especially for the Amis-Hitchens generation, the last, at least until the ambiguous radicalism of the anti-globalists, in which a large section of western intellectual youth proclaimed themselves revolutionary socialists. That generation is now (or was recently) in power. Massimo D'Alema, Italy's prime minister at the end of the 1990s, had been a communist for most of his adult life. Joschka Fischer and Otto Schily, respectively the foreign and interior ministers of Germany, were revolutionary leftists. Lionel Jospin, prime minister of France for five years until this spring, was a (secret) Trotskyist for two decades.

Communism in the Soviet, or Stalinist, tradition was declining by the late 1960s: most of those radicals attracted by organised Marxism were Trotskyists, as was Hitchens. A few preferred their national communist party because, they thought, it was more rooted in the working class. (Most were, but what did that prove?) I was one such, a largely inactive member of the Communist Party of Great Britain between 1971 and 1973, and then a much more active participant in the tiny British and Irish Communist Organisation until 1977. I denounced my comrades, in a 20-page speech, for their Stalinism; I had just read, sweating with horror, all of Aleksandr Solzhenitsyn's *Gulag Archipelago.*

So in my late twenties, I had to admit that my thinking had been in the tradition of a mass murderer, long after his fellow (if penitent) mass murderer Nikita Khrushchev had done it in the Soviet Union. That remains a cause for ineradicable shame. But it is not just my shame; it infects everyone on the left, whether or not they now feel part of it.

In *Le passé d'une illusion,* his last book, the late historian and former communist François Furet wrote that "what makes a comparative analysis [between fascism and communism] inevitable is not just their date of birth . . . it's also their mutual dependence. Fascism was born as a reaction against communism: communism extended its term thanks to anti-fascism . . . the greatest secret of complicity between Bolshevism and fascism remains, however, the existence of that common adversary, which the two ideologies belittled or exorcised through the notion that it was in its death agony . . . quite simply, democracy." Democracy has nothing simple about it; but for we who enjoy it to have regarded it with eyes so slitted in contempt by revolutionary fervour still, in retrospect, brings a flush to the cheeks.

At the end of *Le livre noir du communisme,* one of the most comprehensive destructions of the left-totalitarian idea, Stéphane Courtois, the editor, asks why communism in all its national forms—Soviet, Chinese, Vietnamese, Korean, above all Cambodian—felt it essential to kill its enemies. He quotes Trotsky, incomparably the best writer among the Bolshevik leaders. The bourgeoisie, according to Trotsky, was a doomed class, clinging to power and pulling the world down with it. "We are forced to seize it and cut off its hands. The red terror is the weapon used against a class doomed to perish, but which has not resigned itself to its fate . . . the immediate needs of history cannot be satisfied by the mechanism of parliamentary democracy." Courtois comments: "We find here again the deification of history, to which everything must be sacrificed, and the incurable naivety of the revolutionary who imagines himself able, thanks to his dialectic, to assist the emergence of a more just and humane society through criminal methods."

Amis bases his own denunciations on the Anglo-American writer Robert Conquest, a close friend of his father's and now of his own. His *The Great Terror* came out in the 1960s, when evidence of the scale of Stalin's repression was still fragmentary. Conquest is a tormentor of those who have still to acknowledge the depths of horror at the heart of the communist dark. In an essay in *Reflections on a Ravaged Century,* published in 1999, Conquest writes that "motives for self-deception were often a matter of good intentions—a proverbially inadequate guide. Its bearers had turned to socialism as a means of creating a better, more humane society . . . the ethical argument, if such it can be called, seems to run: 1) there is much injustice under capitalism 2) socialism will end this injustice 3) therefore anything that furthers socialism is to be supported 4) including any amount of injustice."

It is the basic, almost comic, syllogism that all western socialist radicals have to confront—not least the anti-globalists, who will get a sense, from Amis's book, of the dead end to which they are inchoately and ignorantly appealing when they call for an end to free markets. Old wars? One of the most insistent critiques of ***Koba the Dread*** is that it is out of time. Who, apart from some demented old men and women in malignant groupuscules, can still believe in all that—ten years after Mikhail Gorbachev demolished the whole edifice?

But that is to miss the point of the book, which is that the left has been missing the point by blunting it for decades. The British government has nobody in it of the prominence in the far left of D'Alema, Jospin, Schily or Fischer; but it has its own figures with a reckoning still to make. Alistair Darling in the transport department and Alan Milburn at health (and, late of the cabinet, Stephen Byers) had all been in or near far-left groups: John Reid at the Northern Ireland Office and (very briefly) Peter Mandelson had been members of the CP. Many others, including Gordon Brown, Jack Straw, Robin Cook, Clare Short, John Prescott, Margaret Beckett, Patricia Hewitt, Harriet Harman and Charles Clarke, have spent at least some time on the left of the Labour Party, where the line between revolutionary leftism and revisionism was often never drawn, except in competition for office. Robin Cook in CND, John Prescott in the National Union of Seamen, Patricia Hewitt and Harriet Harman at the National Council for Civil Liberties were all working within environments very substantially created by communists. Margaret Beckett threw silver coins at Neil Kinnock when he refused to vote for Tony Benn—who was backed by both communists and Trotskyists—as deputy leader of the Labour Party.

All of these cabinet figures gave the lie to the concept of original (or at least ineradicable) ideological sin—much loved by sections of the US right—by becoming exceptional democratic politicians. But they have not—and, given the state of the media, it was probably impossible for them to do so while remaining politically useful—come to terms publicly with their own past.

That is not, in most cases, shameful; but it is worth an explanation, beyond a chuckling self-exculpation made around the dinner table with "old comrades". Amis recalls how Hitchens, at a debate in London, referred, with irony, to "old comrades" in the audience. Amis laughed, and so did most of the audience, including Conquest, who was also there. Why, in the face of the mountains of dead? "It is, of course, the laughter of the universal fondness for the old, old idea about the perfect society."

These old comrades perpetrated nothing like a great terror: operating within British democracy meant such a thing was fanciful. But they were in great error, or worked with those who were; and they have let fall a great silence.

Prompted partly by former communists such as Peter Mandelson, the British left has shifted to the right. But the past has deposited a film of inhibition on most of the Labour cabinet. It is perhaps the most important reason why Tony Blair became leader and Prime Minister. Although he once falsely claimed to be a socialist, and joined CND and the Tribune group, these were political manoeuvres of an easily understandable kind, given that he wanted to achieve something. He remains untouched by the slime of which Amis reminds us. It did not interest him; worrying about its effects interests him even less. He is free, in a way in which most of his old comrades are not.

A tolerant, even lazy, political culture like the British will not hang a notice saying "former Trot" round anyone's neck. Rightly: but only rightly if an account is made, at some point, of what went before, how it changed, and into what it changed. The question "why" is still, on the British left, sitting up and begging. Amis gives it a poke, and tells it to chew our ankles, again.

Peter Wilby (essay date 2 September 2002)

SOURCE: Wilby, Peter. "The Forward March of History." *New Statesman* 15, no. 722 (2 September 2002): 14-15.

[*In the following essay, Wilby asserts that in* Koba the Dread *Amis analyzes, in detail, the horrors of Stalin's Soviet Union, the Holocaust, and Hiroshima, but remains silent on the great human tragedies of our time.*]

There has always been something faintly ridiculous about the contorted quarrels of British and American intellectuals over Stalinism. Who was a fellow-traveller, and for how long? Who knew what and when? Who failed to denounce strongly enough, early enough? No wars were fought or revolutions achieved on their soil; they may have faced reduced promotion prospects or difficulties in finding publishers, but not torture or hard labour; they did not have to choose between collaboration on the one hand and the deaths of their parents and children on the other, only between 15 minutes on the BBC Third Programme and banishment to dark and draughty meeting rooms in Clerkenwell. They inevitably played on the margins; they can be credited or debited, therefore, with neither heroism nor shame.

Martin Amis's new book [***Koba the Dread***] fires more shots in this ancient contest—very late in the "goddamned day", to echo Samson Young, the narrator of his own ***London Fields.*** Its middle section recapitulates the horrors of Stalinism. The first and final sections repeat the questions that were insistently asked after Khrushchev had admitted Stalin's crimes in 1956. How could anyone have closed their eyes and ears to the dreadful outcome of the Soviet experiment? And why, even now, are so many on the left reluctant to acknowledge how flawed and monstrous it was? These questions are addressed to two people in particular. One is Martin's late father, Kingsley, who was a communist as a young man but, like many contemporaries (Arthur Koestler once suggested that the next war would be fought between the communists and the ex-communists), ended up on what Martin satirically calls the "fascist" side. The other (who, some suspect, has now taken the first steps on a political journey similar to Kingsley's) is Amis's old friend Christopher Hitchens, a Trotskyist rather than a Soviet sympathiser but nevertheless a writer who calls Lenin "a great man" and who, until recently, turned his formidable scorn more on capitalist America than on Bolshevik Russia.

Amis's questions look like important ones. To this day, it is perfectly acceptable, in a jokey sort of way, to call somebody "an old Stalinist"; to call anybody "an old Nazi" would be the most terrible insult. Men can admit, albeit with embarrassment, to helping out the KGB; if they admitted to helping the Nazi equivalent, they would be hounded out of the chattering classes.

Why? Amis points out that Bolshevism, however horribly it turned out, stood in the western Enlightenment tradition. The application of rational and scientific principles to social problems, the aspiration to a perfect society, the belief that history had some purpose and direction—to all this, western intellectuals had, and still have, instinctive sympathy. Communism, as practised by Lenin, Trotsky and Stalin, may have been a perversion of progressive thought, but the intention was progressive all the same. (Indeed, it is that incongruity between high-minded intentions and the actual practice, caused by incompetence as well as by wickedness, that, *pace* Amis's subtitle, makes us laugh at the Bolsheviks, just as we laugh at a well-dressed man slipping on a banana skin.) Nazism, by contrast, was an anti-Enlightenment philosophy, which appealed not to intellect, but to blood, soil and nation.

But Amis, I think, misses the main point, which is simply that the Nazis lost, and history is written by the victors. To many Europeans, the Soviets arrived as liberators in 1945; no matter how awful the regime they imposed, it could not be as bad as what went before. The Soviets, though often cruel (as documented in Antony Beevor's *Berlin*) were capricious in their cruelty, and not always obedient to orders from above, while the Nazis were consistent, disciplined and relentless. Moreover, the Soviet Union, in the end, at least partially redeemed itself. It was, after all, communists who ultimately denounced Stalin, communists who eventually allowed more liberal regimes to develop across eastern Europe (which, in the view of some diehards, would have produced the long-awaited perfect societies if left alone long enough), communists who finally relinquished power almost without bloodshed. Nazism had no such opportunities to retreat from its excesses, and it is hard to imagine that it would have taken them if it had.

History is full of half-forgotten holocausts: the near extermination of the native populations in the Americas; the huge death rates in the slave trade; the slaughter of minorities in Indonesia by President Suharto. What set Stalinism apart was that it killed not out of indifference, fear or even racial hatred, but for explicit political and ideological purposes. Amis's 20 million died not only before firing squads or in the Gulags, but in their own homes, of starvation, as a direct result of the regime's economic policies. These were not just policies that went disastrously wrong; they were policies deliberately designed to starve peasants into joining the collective farms. They died to assist the forward march of history; their deaths, the interrogator Gletkin argued in Koestler's *Darkness at Noon,* had a higher purpose, unlike the millions of deaths down the centuries in famines, earthquakes and so on.

Read Koestler's novel, and you will know whether or not you could ever have been a Soviet communist sympathiser. Koestler put such eloquent words into Gletkin's mouth that some readers, contrary to the author's intention, converted to communism.

I find them abhorrent. Yet every single day now some 3,000 children perish from diarrhoea because they lack clean drinking water. Multiply that over a single year, and you are already past a million. Over 30 years—Stalin's period in power—you are well past 30 million. Who is to blame for that? Fate? The market? President Bush? The IMF? Third world rulers? You? Me? Do we lump these children in with the victims of natural catastrophes? Or do we, as some would, see them as sacrifices to our own beliefs in the sanctity of liberal capitalism? When our governments and our banks demand debt repayments from third world countries—and thus force them to cut projects to improve education, health and sanitation—are we and our governments as culpable as those who supported Stalin?

Martin Amis has given us impressive works on the three great monstrosities of the 20th century—Stalin's terror, the Holocaust and Hiroshima. Yet, like so many of his generation, on the monstrosities of our own age, and our own moral and political challenges, he remains silent.

Jason Cowley (essay date 9 September 2002)

SOURCE: Cowley, Jason. "Bin Laden Belongs to Me." *New Statesman* 15, no. 723 (9 September 2002): 24-5.

[*In the following essay, Cowley contrasts Amis's interpretation of the September 11th terrorist attacks with the response of other prominent authors.*]

The latest issue of *Granta* includes fragments of an e-mail "conversation" between the editor Ian Jack and the writer Andrew O'Hagan, who is working on a novel about the life and painful death from anorexia of the Scottish-Italian singer Lena Zavaroni. An extract from the novel, published in the magazine, prompts Jack, in his introduction, to wonder why O'Hagan had chosen fiction rather than biography. "Your question is really about ethics," O'Hagan replies. "Is it right for an author to make use of a person's circumstances in a book? And the answer is complex and simple at the same time: a person does not own the story of his own life. Even when alive, what happens to them and what they do and who they are does not belong to them—it belongs to the world, and possibly to literature as well."

The life of Lena Zavaroni is an interesting subject for a novel, but I share anxiety about what the American novelist Jonathan Dee has called the art of literary grave-robbing: the way more and more contemporary writers are appropriating real-life characters and the actual events of the recent past for fictional ends. In so-called psycho-historical novels, the past itself has become a kind of fiction, a mere construct. It is inherently unstable and open to endless reinterpretation. It is there to be mangled, stretched and distorted—according to the whim of the novelist.

In addition, rather than inventing their own characters—with their own distinct fictional biographies—and recasting them, if they must, in the context of an actual historical narrative, more and more writers prefer simply to adapt the lives of the already known, with their familiar quirks and eccentricities, their successes and their failures. The urge to create something out of nothing is therefore being supplanted by a desire to fiddle with the facts. "But", as Dee says, "simply adopting or impersonating an already interesting real-life character cannot be considered as substantial an achievement as creating a character who enters the reader's consciousness as a total unknown."

There is nothing unknown about Osama Bin Laden—except, perhaps, his present whereabouts. Since the events of 11 September, his public life has been oppressively documented, in an endless flow of articles and instant biographies. His face, with its large, mournful eyes and ragged beard, has become as iconic as any student poster of Che Guevara. But what does he think? What does he want? How disturbed is his consciousness?

If fiction, as Novalis wrote, arises out of the shortcomings of history, the shortcomings in our knowledge of the private Osama, his mystery and opacity, seems to offer thrilling fictional opportunities. Bin Laden is already appearing as a "character" in novels, most notably in Giles Foden's *Zanzibar* (Faber and Faber), a convincing thriller about the bombing by al-Qaeda of the US embassies in Dar es Salaam and Nairobi in August 1998. (Foden began the book long before the attacks on Washington and New York.)

The world-historical moment of 11 September means that Bin Laden no longer owns his own story: he belongs to the world now, and possibly to literature, too. But how to write about, and respond to, the shock of what happened a year ago without succumbing to the gruesome effects and eschatological anxiety of the concept thriller, as perfected by Tom Clancy, or the cheap appropriation of the Hollywood biopic?

How to write, in other words, about the reality of the new terrorist threat, and the collective cognitive dissonance it has induced, without robbing too many graves?

In the immediate aftermath of the fall of the twin towers, our major writers competed with one another to offer a definitive interpretation of what had happened. The most portentous reaction came, predictably, from Martin Amis, who saw in the attacks the "world flash of a coming future" and felt nothing but "species shame"—as opposed to species pride at the heroic reaction of so many ordinary New Yorkers. It is instructive, in retrospect, to compare Amis's hysterics with the more measured and humane response of Ian McEwan, whose meditations on the plight of the hostages on the hijacked planes were perhaps the most impressive of all the literary contributions to that terrible time.

Amis, in his new book, ***Koba the Dread,*** writes: "When I read someone's prose I reckon to get a sense of their moral life." Amis is obsessed with prose style—his own and others'. It underscores his restless quest for novelty and his obsession with posterity. He is also obsessed with catastrophe. Yet he remains imprisoned by the cartoonish effects and looping repetitions of his own style.

The opening of his essay on the attack on the twin towers (republished in the *Guardian Yearbook,* Atlantic Books), for instance, had the hijacked planes "sharking" out of a blue sky. The opening page of ***Money,*** his most celebrated novel, has a low-slung Tomahawk "sharking" out of lane as it speeds along the road. In the opening to ***London Fields,*** the narrator arrives at Heathrow Airport and looks down at the planes lined up on the runway: "all the sharks with their fins erect, thrashers, baskets, great whites—killers. Killers every one."

To Amis, the world must seem like one great shark-infested sea: killers everywhere. More seriously, the challenge for him of writing about 11 September was, as ever, the challenge of discovering whether his prose style—and thus moral vision—was equal to the monumentality of the task, as he saw it. Simple reportage was not enough. The subject was too big, too important. It *commanded* his response. But *in extremis,* he found himself over-reliant on the same tired formulations: the verb "to shark", for instance, and expressions of "species shame", of the kind he has made before and since (most recently in ***Koba the Dread***). At a moment of heightened challenge, Amis was let down by his own exaggerated style; he became his own self-parody.

Amis was not alone in thinking that 11 September was a moment of definitive rupture: a day that human nature itself changed. Many writers agreed that a certain kind of literature was no longer possible, that a new way of writing about the modern world had to be discovered. "The idea that the novelist's task is to go on to the street and figure out social reality may well have been altered by the events of 11 September," wrote the critic James Wood. To Andrew O'Hagan, writing in the *London Review of Books,* "language is something else now, and so is imagery, and so is originality".

A year on, we continue to feel the aftershocks from that day, but has anything really changed? The world is the same as it ever was, and so is language and so is originality. The hyperbole of Martin Amis remains undiminished. Wood and O'Hagan are not themselves producing a new kind of fiction, judging from extracts of their works-in-progress, published, respectively, in the *LRB* and *Granta.* No doubt, someone somewhere is preparing to write directly about what happened on that September day—perhaps a multi-voiced novel written from the perspective of, say, one of the militant Arab hijackers; of Todd Beamer, who stormed the cockpit of Flight 93, on the plane that crashed in the fields of Pennsylvania; and of a Brooklyn fireman pulled alive from the debris. But it will not have the power or originality of the day itself.

In time, there will be sufficient distance from what happened for the events themselves to be transformed into the stuff of Hollywood disaster drama, in the style of *Titanic* or *Pearl Harbor.* Perhaps 11 September 2001 will be supplanted by a future shock of undreamt-of catastrophe. Whatever happens, the task of the writer remains the same as it did on 10 September last year, before the storm: to document the defining particulars of our age with precision, grace and moral authority, and in so doing to escape the deadening effects of habitualism and the ready-made that blight all of our lives.

Viktor Shklovsky, the Russian formalist critic, wrote: "Habitualism devours objects, clothes, furniture, one's wife and the fear of war . . . but art exists to help us recover the sensation of life, it exists to make us feel things, to make the stone stony." Must we wait for catastrophe to awaken us to the sensation of life?

David Caute (review date 19 October 2002)

SOURCE: Caute, David. "Great Helmsman or Mad Wrecker." *Spectator* 290, no. 9089 (19 October 2002): 52-3.

[*In the following excerpt, Caute evaluates the factual accuracy of* Koba the Dread *and compares Amis's work with Eric Hobsbawn's* Interesting Times.]

Moving from *Interesting Times* [by Eric Hobsbawn] to Martin Amis's ***Koba the Dread*** is a somewhat vertiginous passage, but I have to report an observed bridge. When this reviewer succeeded young Amis as literary editor of the *New Statesman,* he noticed that Hobsbawm, John Berger and several other brilliant voices had been lured away by Paul Barker's rival *New Society.* Much telephone dialling followed: Berger replied tenderly, pleading loyalty, while Hobsbawm simply named his price as £100 per review, more than double our then going rate. Amis himself recalls the *New Statesman* of that Great Turnstile era (late Seventies) chiding Christopher Hitchens for using the word 'comrade' with a smile, and thus (insists Amis) exposing a soft spot for Soviet communism. Worse, the British Left betrayed its residual affection for Uncle Joe by telling communist jokes on the Jewish or Irish model. Actually, Amis cannot resist doing the same, including a good one about a Brezhnev-era nightclub. But why, he asks insistently, were there no jokes about Nazis? Why do we refuse to put Stalin's 20 million on a par of depravity with the Holocaust? Good question, but jokes about 'comrades', surely, have nothing to do with Stalin's famine, slave labour and mass deportations, everything to do with the baffled stoicism of the typical Russian, or, further west, the paradox of progressives submitting themselves to rigid discipline even when, as eventually in Hobsbawm's own case, head and heart, thought and utterance, went separate ways. Tommy: 'Anyone in Britain is free to criticise Churchill.' Ivan: 'In Soviet Union also.'

Martin Amis makes no scholarly claims on his own behalf, generously acknowledging his debts to Szamuely, Pipes, and above all Robert Conquest, mentors and friends inherited from his father Kinglsey Amis. Clearly Amis has read voraciously, 'several yards of books', but frailties keep surfacing, as when Gorky's journal of 1918, *Novaia zhizn* (*New Life*) is given as *Novaia zhin* (*New World*). Even so, he does succeed where Hobsbawm does not: in banging home, hammer and sickle, the sheer scale of Soviet crimes. It's not news but it's new in the telling.

Hobsbawm visited the Soviet Union only twice and didn't particularly like it. To what cause did he think he was remaining loyal? I did not care for his sole, anecdotal mention of Isaac Deutscher, 'the biographer of Trotsky, but in his heart a frustrated political leader', who, we are told, advised Hobsbawm to remain inside the Communist Party when everyone else was leaving it during the turmoil of 1956-7. Deutscher was also the author of an authoritative and devastating biography (1949) of Stalin, and far more than Hobsbawm a genuine victim of discrimination on the British academic ladder. One keeps asking of Hobsbawm: didn't you know what Deutscher and Orwell knew? Didn't you know about the induced famine, the horrors of collectivisation, the false confessions, the terror within the Party, the massive forced labour of the gulag? As Orwell himself documented, a great deal of evidence was reliably knowable even before 1939, but Hobsbawm pleads that much of it was not reliably knowable until Khrushchev's denunciation of Stalin in 1956.

Amis, by contrast, tosses everything into the Stalin pot, sadism, megalomania, cynicism, anti-Semitism, the suicide of his wife, certainties and speculations, a limitless list. This said, Amis is right: his obsessive defacement of 'Koba the Dread', set against Hobsbawm's brief and distinctly unemotional criticisms of the Great Helmsman, suggests that there is a place for intelligent pop history, even if Amis's many autobiographical digressions bring an uncomfortable twist to the cult of personality.

James J. Miracky (essay date winter 2003)

SOURCE: Miracky, James J. "Hope Lost or Hyped Lust? Gendered Representations of 1980s Britain in Margaret Drabble's *The Radiant Way* and Martin Amis's *Money.*" *Critique* 44, no. 2 (winter 2003): 136-43.

[*In the following essay, Miracky juxtaposes the cultural representation of Thatcher-era England in two works:* Money *and Margaret Drabble's* The Radiant Way.]

Perhaps no political era in twentieth-century Britain has yielded a more hyperbolic and vitriolic crop of literary rebuttals than the years under the Thatcher government. In numerous novels, plays, and poems, the culture of 1980s Britain and its people are represented in terms of extremes: rich and poor, empowered and victimized, enlightened and ignorant, enthusiastic and embittered. For the most part, the literary output of the period is marked by neither reticence nor subtlety: it reflects a time in which the more extroverted genres, such as black comedy, political allegory, and social satire, were most successful in making their voices heard. Regardless of its ideological position, much of the literature of the 1980s revels in outrage, both moral and mirthful, a stance that has produced works that differ widely in tone and tenor.

I wish to offer a sampling of the extremes of cultural representation that mark this period in British fiction by examining two stylistically opposed yet ideologically comparable novels. Combining the seriousness and scope of the nineteenth-century social problem novel with the pessimism of postwar neorealist fiction, Margaret Drabble's *The Radiant Way* is a bleak, omniscient account of lost hope in the Thatcher years as experienced by three middle-aged women whose lives move from communal dreams to isolated sorrows. Martin Amis's ***Money*** could hardly be more different in both breadth and style: it is a comically solipsistic, first-person narrative of the hyperactive lusts of a vulgar male film director who, driven primarily by the subject of the title, follows a path from prosperity to poverty in 1980s London and New York.

My juxtaposition of these diverse novels has two primary aims. First, I hope to show that, despite their notable differences in genre and tone, both novels participate in a critique of 1980s British society and culture, although they differ markedly in their analysis and effectiveness. Second, I propose that, aside from stylistic elements, a primary marker of the difference in the novels exists on the level of gender, a difference that accounts for their ultimately dissimilar perspectives on the condition of England in the Thatcher years and hopes for the country's revival. By virtue of its ideological stance as well as its subject matter, *The Radiant Way* can be considered a feminist novel in its critique of the patriarchal political and social forces of Tory-led Britain; but it is ultimately given to a sobering end, in that it not only traces the failure of feminist ideals in the 1980s but also questions their success in the past and possibilities for the future. In contrast, although ***Money*** lampoons the masculinist desires of the consumerist 1980s to a disparaging extreme, it never fully escapes its own critique. In making its protagonist a sympathetic character who apparently cannot help himself, the novel seems to revel in the greed and misogyny it mocks, and it never provides its working-class "hero" with a way out of the vicious materialist cycle, adopting an "if you can't beat 'em, join 'em" attitude in the end.

Taking place from 1979 to 1985, *The Radiant Way,* a kind of *Bleak House* meets *North and South* for the 1980s, follows the paths of three middle-class women who share "a sense of being on the margins of English life" (Drabble 85). Having attended Cambridge in the heady 1950s and built successful careers in the idealistic 1960s and eclectic 1970s, they undergo personal and professional crises in what Gail Cunningham calls "the profit-orientated, achieving years of monetarist Thatcherism" in the 1980s (135). Liz Headland, having apparently reached the pinnacle of success as a psychotherapist and wife to an affluent media whiz, suffers from self-doubt over the breakup of her marriage, nagging guilt over neglecting her ailing mother, and numbing shock on recovering repressed memories about her pedophilic and suicidal father. Alix Bowen, a lifelong Liberal and dedicated teacher in a women's prison, sees her life and value system turned upside down as a result of Conservative governmental policies that, by cutting welfare spending, endanger her job and that of her committed socialist husband, Brian, an Open University teacher. Esther Breuer, an art historian and emotional loner, experiences ambivalence about her commitment to research as she witnesses the physical decline and death of her mentor and negotiates a path through her conflicted sexual impulses. The three friends periodically gather to commiserate with and support one another, and their individual and communal fates become emblematic of what Steven Connor calls "[t]he ambivalent or mobile position of middle-class women, as simultaneously participants in and marginal to authoritative cultural institutions and professions" (65) of 1980s British life.

Compared with the sweeping omniscience of *The Radiant Way,* ***Money*** is literally single-minded in its perspective and thrust. Amis describes it as being set at "the conjunction of the Royal Wedding and the riots in 1981" (Haffenden 3) and written to reflect "what happens to a developed nation after its manly noon has passed" (Bigby 183), conjuring up images of a declining, feminized society. The novel traces the rapid rise and fall of its aptly named protagonist, John Self, a crude, misogynistic, working-class British man who is "addicted to the twentieth century" (Amis 89) and pursues only hobbies that "are pornographic in tendency" (67). John has risen above his class to monetary success as a director of salacious TV commercials and is undertaking his first full-length Hollywood film project, a trashy saga of greed and lust whose title tellingly alternates between "Good Money" and "Bad Money."

The plot of the novel, if Amis's convoluted and gap-filled postmodern narrative can be said to contain one, revolves around the duping of John by his partner, Fielding Goodney, who has contrived to have all of the film's expenses come out of Self's personal finances, thereby setting up a situation in which John, in a sense, consumes himself. Running parallel to Self's professional crisis are his personal travails, which result from the conflict of three passions: his physical lust for Selena Street, a professional call girl and would-be porn star; his emotional attraction to Martina Twain, an upper-class woman who tries to educate John in high culture; and his love of Self, fueled by numerous addictions—to food, alcohol, pornography, television, and of course, money. Despite intentions to reform his life both physically and emotionally, John self-destructs as his lusts get the better of him and his money runs out, and he loses both career and romance in the process.

Both novels end with a sense of personal loss that is directly related to 1980s economic and social forces, and they point a finger at Thatcherite policy for the disasters occurring within the novel and the decade. Despite their differences in tone and scope, the novels represent these forces in similar ways, the first of which is by means of a dualistic setting. True to the tradition of Mrs. Gaskell, Drabble creates a bifurcated geography in her novel, which shifts between the affluence and optimism of London and the poverty and depression of the "figurative" provincial town of Northam and points up the sharp differences between the haves and have-nots of Thatcherite Britain. This duality first appears in the opening contrast of the novel between the "smart, bohemian-flavoured cosmopolitan New Year's Eve party" (31) in 1980 London and the simpler, more subdued family affair in Northam, and it continues by means of the novel's regular transitions between North and South.

Martin Amis also uses a dual locale in ***Money***, regularly shifting between England and America; but ultimately there is not much contrast between the two, a result of what Richard Brown calls the "Anglo-American cultural-mixedness [that] prevents the polarities [of the novel] from stabilising" (Brown 101). In many ways, England has become America in the novel and is equally defined by an addictive, consumerist culture, although perhaps without the same degree of sophistication or intensity. As John puts it, "London has jetlag. London has culture shock. It's doing everything the wrong way round at the wrong time" (Amis 141). In an excellent example of the novel's cultural-mixedness, John takes regular strolls around London and New York to indulge his appetites; and the overwhelming barrage of fast-food joints, pubs, and porno palaces he encounters in one city is virtually indistinguishable from those of the other.

Drabble and Amis represent the influence of 1980s politics and culture on the action of their novels primarily through periodic catalogues of current events that take a different form and tone in each work, although both suggest that the protagonists are largely helpless in relation to these forces. In *The Radiant Way,* Drabble has her omniscient narrator present occasional news summaries or chronicles of each period as the action progresses from 1980 to 1985, highlighting such events as the Falklands war, the race riots in Brixton, and the onset of the AIDS epidemic. The narrator's liberal politics are never hidden from the reader, as in this characteristic passage:

> [. . .] 1980 continues. The steel strike continues, a bitter prelude to the miners' strike that will follow. Class rhetoric flourishes. Long-cherished notions of progress are inspected, exposed, left out to die in the cold. Survival of the fittest seems to be the new-old doctrine.
>
> (163)

In a clear union of style and substance, this distant, chilling, passive, and (as evidenced in its allusions to Jane Austen and its focus on and facility in representing women's consciousness) apparently female voice presents the novel's social and cultural influences as both deterministic and pervasive in the characters' lives.

In contrast, the style of ***Money***'s representation of current events and cultural forces is, in keeping with the attention-deficit-disordered quality of its protagonist, more like surfing TV channels or reading tabloid copy. From both sources John Self periodically receives and reacts to blips of information from the outside world: tensions in the western alliance, the Polish Solidarity movement, riots, and accounts of domestic violence and rape. Amis describes his intention of having John "consumed by consumerism" and "stupefied by having watched too much television" (which Amis believes is "the great source of crime") to create a "lazy non-effort response which is wished on you by television—and by reading a shitty newspaper," leaving John with "no informing ideology of the way he lives" (Haffenden 7, 22, 24). In very different ways, both novels render their subjects powerless in the face of the social and political forces that regulate them.

One of the most powerful of these influences that both novels critique, although with varying levels of seriousness, is the media. In *The Radiant Way* Drabble accomplishes this through her characterization of Liz's husband Charles, as he moves from being an idealistic documentary maker of the 1960s to a technology-driven media mogul who ultimately loses faith in his avocation. His claim to fame in the 1960s is a documentary called "The Radiant Way" (whose title is taken from a children's primer) put together by an egalitarian team of "mixed social origins" (167) that contrasted the educational experiences of rich and poor children at the time and demonstrated "the evils that flow from a divisive class system" (165). Drabble ironically drives home the change from 1960s idealism to 1980s commercialism by having Charles's son, Jonathan, become the director of a successful TV farce depicting "a crowd of upper-middle-class twits making fools of themselves for the entertainment of the nation" (281).

Because one of Amis's goals is to demonstrate John Self as being "stupified by having watched too much television" (Haffenden 7), critiques of the media are an obvious and frequent source of ***Money***'s humor. From John's "nihilistic commercials" for "smoking, drinking, junk food and nude magazines" (Amis 78) to his "cretinizing" TV addiction (31), and his Hollywood schmoozing with B-movie actors named Butch Beausoleil and Spunk Davis, everything and anything connected with mass entertainment and communication is skewered. John's hyperbolic representation of his pornographic "hobbies" as stressing "the element of lone gratification" (67) has, however, a serious side. The text's allusions to George Orwell's *1984* not-so-subtly underline the ways in which "[i]n the mass-mediated commodity culture where Self has temporarily thrived, advertising and film" have, like Orwell's Oceania, reduced "human freedom and choice by steadily narrowing the range of thought" (Diedrick 100).

As for direct reference to and critique of the Thatcher era, *The Radiant Way* is much more obvious and serious in tying its protagonists' fates to Conservative policy. Thatcher's status is judged from a feminist perspective as presenting "the novel oddity of a woman Prime Minister who was in fact a mother but was not nevertheless thereby motherly" (16). To Alix's mind, the age is one of "alienation" caused by the fact that "[. . .] the establishment, through ignorance, through stupidity, or for its own ends, continued blandly to attempt to deny the persistence of the class system, continued to pretend that things were getting better all the time, instead of worse and worse" (222). The threats of the Thatcherite agenda are epitomized not only in the loss of funding for Alix's research unit and Brian's Adult Education College but also for Esther's public lecture series and her students' grant programs. To add insult to injury, the insidious effect of such policy reaches into Alix's once-stolid socialist attitudes by causing her to question the Welfare State system of social security as leading to "People getting used to not working" (123). Ironically, the decline felt by her friends fails to affect Liz because "the new government [. . .] suits her well": with the Thatcher era's "growing emphasis on privatization" and Liz's "judicious blend of public and private practice" (171), her business is booming.

The references to the Conservative era are generally lighter in tone and less frequent in ***Money,*** but a similar underlying sentiment of dissatisfaction emerges through the text's humorous facade. For example, in his typically flippant and misogynist way, John Self obnoxiously refers to Margaret Thatcher as a "chick" (Amis 146); and he says that, by extension, England under her rule is, paradoxically, "pussy-whipped by money" (250). However, on occasion John acknowledges the severity of the fallout from the money culture stimulated by Conservative fiscal policy, as in the following passage:

> The dole-queue starts at the exit to the playground. Riots are their rumpus-room, sombre London their jungle-gym. Life is hoarded elsewhere by others. Money is so near you can almost touch it, but it is all on the other side—you can only press your face up against the glass.
>
> (144)

Perhaps most indicative of each novel's take on Thatcher's Britain is its depiction of an emblematic event woven throughout the narrative that encapsulates the attitudes and effects of 1980s culture. In addition to being a social problem novel, *The Radiant Way* is a crime story, tracing the case of the so-called "Horror of Harrow Road," P. Whitmore, whose path of destruction touches the protagonists in two ways. First, one of his victims of serial murder by decapitation is Jilly Fox, Alix's former student and greatest hope for rehabilitation; second, Whitmore's apprehension occurs during a police raid in Esther's apartment building on a floor above the protagonists as they cower in fear below. The nature of the murderer's crimes, of course, points to the severance of Thatcherite Britain's own head from its heart or body, its lack of compassion in the post-Welfare State era. As Roberta Rubenstein puts it, "the imagery of bodily injury and fragmentation mirrors and represents Drabble's increasingly pessimistic view of contemporary life," and this fragmentation is replicated in the novel's "'disruptive' (Drabble's term) form" that "experiments with postmodern narrative structures" (Rubenstein 136).

The recurring event throughout ***Money*** is the impending nuptials of Prince Charles and Lady Diana in 1981, a much treasured cultural phenomenon that the narrator reduces to speculations about his favorite topics: money and sex. Diana herself becomes a repository for John's passions. In his eyes she glows with "the colour of money" (244), and he obsesses over a photo in which "you can see right through her dress" (89) and wonders whether or not Charles has "given her one" before the wedding (243). (Ironically and, in light of subsequent events, sadly, John thinks that Diana "doesn't look as though she'll give him [Prince Charles] any trouble" [72].) In both cases, the repeated allusions to these central events underline the dominant tone each text takes toward contemporary British culture, one of gloom and doom in *The Radiant Way* and one of luxury and lust in ***Money.*** They also convey disparate messages of hope for the future, fittingly embodied in their respective goals of murder and marriage.

The conclusions of both novels not only cast a dim light on hopeful prospects for survival in the Thatcher era, but they also demonstrate how style and subject matter reflect the gendered construction of the texts and yield their gender-opposed perspectives on life in 1980s British culture. In the final scene of *The Radiant Way,* which takes place after the miners' strike has divided and demoralized the country, the three protagonists gather on Esther's fiftieth birthday, but there seems to be little to celebrate. Liz has lost her husband and her faith in the efficacy of psychoanalysis, at least in her own life; Alix has abandoned her socialist ideals and work; and Esther has decided to leave England to live and write in Italy. The novel's final tableau presents the three women returning on "the devious way home" from a hike in the countryside and pausing at the summit of their final ascent to survey the landscape. Rather than looking toward what lies ahead, they gaze at the ground they have already covered as the sun "sinks [. . .], bleeds [. . . and] stands still" (376). The scene is suffused with a sense of lost or frustrated opportunity, and its relation to the ironic title of the novel is obvious, rendering problematic the idea that there was ever any possibility for lasting connection and community among these women.

At the end of ***Money,*** John Self finds himself almost literally in the gutter, broke and, as a consequence, emasculated. In the wake of his financial ruin and romantic losses, he wanders the inner city pronouncing that "money stinks" (Amis 359), but he soon takes up lodging with Georgina, a large woman who overpowers him physically when he attempts to rough her up. The final pages of the text suggest that moral growth has occurred, as John appears contrite and willing to give up fighting, infidelity, and the pursuit of money. Martin Amis himself describes the conclusion in an optimistic fashion: "John Self [. . .] ends up as a tramp, and yet I feel that it's my first happy ending" (Haffenden 14). However, the humorous final passage of the text presents two striking images that complicate the happiness of its conclusion: first, John, sitting outside a Tube station, is mistaken for a beggar by a passerby who tosses a tenpenny piece in John's cap, and second, Georgina moving toward him ticking on her heels, conjures up memories of the other women who have, to his mind, walked all over him. As he sits once again surrounded by his cardinal vices, John finally observes, "you've got to laugh. [. . .] There isn't any choice. I'm not proud. Don't hold back on my account" (363), suggesting that he has not really escaped his attraction to money or his abusive relations with women and is forever ensconced in the economies of capitalism and patriarchy, hoping to rise again to monetary and romantic prowess. As Laura L. Doan puts it, ***Money*** fails as a political and cultural critique because, although the discourse of the novel "ostensibly exposes the false tenets of the new Toryism and impugns the greed of Thatcherite England in order to call for the transformation of the existing capitalist system," by making John a homophobic and woman-hating member of the working class, "Amis endangers this purpose and instead devises a telos that valorizes the class and gender systems" (Doan 78).

It seems to me that in both of these texts gender is reflected at much deeper levels than that of subject matter. The style and method by which both tales are told reveal notably gendered approaches to the representation of 1980s British life and its effects on society. In a sense, *The Radiant Way* resembles an old style social problem novel in all things but the offer of a solution to social injustice. Whereas nineteenth-century novelists like Dickens and Gaskell (who were often castigated for their sentimentalism) were able to find refuge in the power of love or charity as an antidote to society's ills, Drabble offers no cure. Hers is a narrative of sensitivity and compassion to a point, but an overwhelming sense of shattered illusion and powerlessness takes over the text as the once-hoped-for "radiant way" of the protagonists' youth comes to a dead end amid greed, crime, and violence. The Britain of the 1980s as represented by Drabble is a place of lost hope and failed feminist ideals, where the potential for community is de-energized and destroyed by draconian economic and social policy. In contrast, the 1980s world of Martin Amis's comic, testosterone-driven narrative is largely an energetic one, propelled by the multiple drives and desires of its intensely masculine protagonist. Although the text follows a trajectory of greed gone bust, its moral fails to hold up before the dazzling lure of the addictions that Amis's comic critique fails to deflate. Both texts set out to represent and reprimand 1980s British culture as socially and personally devastating, but their apparently common purpose is both colored and divided by their gendered perspectives.

Works Cited

Amis, Martin. *Money.* New York: Penguin, 1984.

Bigby, Christopher. "Martin Amis." *New Writing.* Ed. Malcolm Bradbury and Judy Cooke. London: Minerva, 1992. 169-84.

Brown, Richard. "Postmodern Americas in the Fiction of Angela Carter, Martin Amis and Ian McEwan." *Forked Tongues? Comparing Twentieth-Century British and American Literature.* Ed. Ann Massa and Alistair Stead. New York: Longman, 1994, 92-110.

Connor, Steven. *The English Novel in History: 1959-1995.* London: Routledge, 1996.

Diedrick, James. *Understanding Martin Amis.* Columbia: U of South Carolina P, 1995.

Doan, Laura L. "Sexy Greedy *Is* the Late Eighties: Power Systems in Amis's *Money* and Churchill's *Serious Money.*" *The Minnesota Review* 34-35, 1990: 69-80.

Drabble, Margaret. *The Radiant Way.* New York: Ballantine, 1989.

Haffenden, John. ed. *Novelists in Interview.* New York: Methuen, 1985.

Nick Cohen (essay date 7 April 2003)

SOURCE: Cohen, Nick. "Strange Bedfellows." *New Statesman* 16, no. 751 (7 April 2003): 24-5.

[*In the following essay, Cohen maintains that* Koba the Dread *has touched a nerve in British politics.*]

In September last year, critics greeted the publication of Martin Amis's ***Koba the Dread: Laughter and the Twenty Million*** with reviews varying from the lukewarm to the atrocious. Amis was criticised for his style and for his decision to make his point with gossipy stories about his father, a former communist, and his best friend, a former Trotskyist. Above all he was taken to task for asking why Hitler remained a symbol of evil while the 20 million killed by Lenin and Stalin were forgotten or laughed off. The question was widely deemed to be silly and 30 years out of date.

I slagged the book off with the best of them. But Amis touched a nerve. I wondered why I found the story of my great-uncle who was such a convinced Marxist-Leninist that he moved from Manchester to Moscow at the high point of Stalin's purges faintly funny. (He survived, by the way; God only knows how many people he had to denounce before he died in his bed.) There were other niggles. When a distinguished Marxist academic told me at a party that he was proud to have supported Mao's cultural revolution, why did I nod politely? Why couldn't I point out that he was a moral accomplice to the mass murder of millions of innocents? If he'd said he was proud to have supported the Nazi extermination camps, I'd have walked out of the drawing room.

For the past few weeks, the right-wing press has been telling its readers about the backgrounds of the leaders of the Stop the War Coalition. For instance, Andrew Murray, the coalition's chairman, wrote an article in the *Morning Star* to celebrate the 120th anniversary of Stalin's birth. He acknowledged that the tyrant had used "harsh measures" but asked why "hack propagandists abominate the name of Stalin beyond all others". That there were 20 million reasons didn't seem to occur to him. Murray is on the politburo of the Communist Party of Britain (which must never be confused with the Communist Party of Great Britain). In a report to his comrades in March, he said the coalition should have two slogans: "Stop the war" and "Blair must go". "We need urgently to raise the level of our Leninist education," he continued. "Everything we are talking about, the imperialist crisis, inter-imperialist conflict, war, political strategy and tactics, are Leninist issues. We need to do far more to study Marxism-Leninism." The anti-war protest had led to "the rate of inquiries about party membership rising rapidly and that is welcome, but we need to ensure they are educated as communists and learn to work as communists".

Thus, a living fossil from the age of European dictators was heading the biggest protest of the new century. Even Julian Lewis, the Tory MP who spent the 1980s accusing the Campaign for Nuclear Disarmament of having been infiltrated by supporters of the Soviet Union, was taken aback. "I had thought that my days of unearthing totalitarians at the heart of 'peace movements' had ended in 1991," he wrote in the *Telegraph*. "Yet here is a case of a former worker for the Soviet Novosti Press Agency in precisely such a key position, being solemnly quoted by the anti-war press as if he were a representative of democratic politics."

There are ironies aplenty, and not only in the sight of the same old scowling faces from the fragments of splinter groups reappearing after all the talk of the Seattle generation creating a new politics. Mass opposition to a war against a dictator who models himself on Stalin is being led by a man who is nostalgic for Stalin. British opponents of the war have condemned the "undemocratic" government for not listening to majority opinion. Yet the Communist Party of Britain, the Socialist Workers Party and the other Marxist-Leninist groups that run the Stop the War Coalition are not interested in democracy. They want to abolish it and replace it with a dictatorship of the proletariat in which the proletariat in question turns out to be made up of the bosses of the Communist Party of Britain, or the Socialist Workers Party, or whatever other faction storms Westminster.

As if to confirm Amis's thesis, the right feels the need to be more careful about the company it keeps. Before the Countryside Alliance march, the British National Party urged neo-Nazi activists to "help us put our patriotic, pro-countryside message to the huge contingent of radicalised Middle Britain who will flood central London on 22 September".

The Countryside Alliance responded with vigour. It wasn't run by extremists and wanted nothing to do with extremists. "We repudiate all that the BNP stands for," said Tim Bonner, the Alliance's spokesman.

There is an argument that there's no need for a similar fastidiousness on the left. Ninety-nine per cent of people who protest against the war don't support Marxist-Leninism. If Murray recruits a thousand new members to his party, it will be an unprecedented achievement, and if he keeps them in his party it will be a miracle. The far left organises protests because the independent, democratic left is so weak in England. *Tribune* can stage rallies at Labour Party conferences, but most of its energies are spent producing and distributing the newspaper. The Campaign Group of Labour MPs is a parliamentary caucus. Neither has a network of activists. There is no leader of the Labour left for supporters to rally around, and the trade unions don't organise protests against foreign policy. Which leaves the Labour Party, and it isn't going to run a campaign against its own government.

Far-left parties fill the vacuum. Their membership is small, but their members give their spare time and money to the cause. Going on a march they organise doesn't mean you support the atrocities of the Russian revolution any more than taking a Virgin train means that you support rail privatisation. Both are just vehicles you board for your own purposes. It's a reasonable case as far as it goes, although, obviously, the intellectually consistent would have to give similar indulgence to the supporters of fox-hunting, even if the BNP took over the Countryside Alliance. (In the circumstances, it would be as McCarthyite for the *New Statesman* to accuse demonstrators marching for rural post offices of being the dupes of fascists, as it would be for the *Telegraph* to accuse demonstrators marching to uphold the authority of the United Nations of being the dupes of communists.)

The difficulties come when a one-off protest has to become a sustained campaign. Then the screamingly intolerant sectarianism of the far left can tear a movement apart. In *A Tale of Two Utopias,* the American historian Paul Berman told the sad history of Students for a Democratic Society, which organised middle-class protests against the Vietnam war and segregation in the American South in the 1960s. It was destroyed by Marxist-Leninism at the height of its popularity.

The group had a clause in its constitution that banned from membership anyone who advocated racism, dictatorship or totalitarianism, "which shut the door mostly on communists and Trotskyists—given that fascists and racists were not likely to throng into a student socialist movement. The logic of that clause was not closed-mindedness; it was self-preservation."

The clause was dropped in 1965 and the Communists of Progressive Labor (a Maoist splinter group) launched a campaign to infiltrate the society. They were well organised and disciplined. Their "machine-gun" rhetoric pushed the unconverted away and they soon had control of the organisation. There were splits, denunciations and forays into terrorism. "The effect of those many guerrilla mini-organisations was devastating . . . on the left," Berman concluded. The story of how Militant tore apart the Liverpool Labour Party in the 1980s is not so different.

It is not surprising that the most successful sustained campaigns of the past decade have come from outside the traditional left. The demands for gay rights, animal rights, third world debt relief, the minimum wage and the Human Rights Act have one thing in common: there are no Andrew Murrays to be seen near them. In other words, if you want to win a quick battle, it doesn't matter who organises your protest. But if you want to win a war?

Philip Hensher (review date 6 September 2003)

SOURCE: Hensher, Philip. "Treasures Buried in the Mud." *Spectator* 293, no. 9135 (6 September 2003): 37-8.

[*In the following review, Hensher judges* Yellow Dog *to be a weak restatement of the author's characteristic themes.*]

Though not as bad as had been suggested before the absurdly tightly guarded publication, ***Yellow Dog*** is certainly a disappointment which does little to amend the general opinion that Martin Amis has by now done his best work. No one, in the future, will base the enthusiastic consideration which he certainly deserves on this novel: it has the air of late-period Wilkie Collins, revisiting the scene of past triumphs in ways both slacker and more aridly grotesque. There are certainly passages of great panache and brio, but as a whole it seems like the symptom of a general loss of nerve, and the reader loses interest well before the end. Amis has always relied on his powers of improvisation, on the impetus contained in a brilliant riff. When that ability starts to go, the result is a book which, one feels, the author can't quite keep going.

It must be said that the disgraceful news coverage which now routinely attends every new book by Amis can't help. These stories, not just non-literary but anti-literary, are evidently things he feels deeply, judging by his comments in ***Experience,*** and it must be all but impossible to write against the barrage of abuse and the ceaseless public commentary on his private life. When ***The Information, Experience, Koba the Dread*** and other recent books came out, it was hard actually to read the books, so deafening were the public debates about his teeth, his marriage, his family relations, his falling out with Julian Barnes or Christopher Hitchens, and so on. Of course, these are not, even from a literary point of view, satisfactory books; compared to his best books, they are slacker in structure, disastrously reliant on the reader valuing their claims of sincerity, of all things. Who ever gave any consideration to the question of the sincerity of ***Money*** or ***Dead Babies***? But ***Experience*** and ***Koba the Dread*** gamble everything on your belief in his sincerity, and the moment you begin to doubt that, the books start to totter. The recent books have that combination of private grandeur and cosiness which is usually summed up in the phrase 'very well pleased with himself'. In particular, I thought ***Koba the Dread*** the sort of book which puts an end to careers, with its comprehensive demonstration that in the larger worlds of history and politics, deprived of the literary virtuosity which makes ***Time's Arrow*** such a mesmerising book, Amis's authority looks extremely shaky. He had read a few books about Stalin's terror, but certainly not enough to write any sort of book about the subject himself, and for the first time his generally worldly posture began to look as if it might always have been absurdly naive. ***Koba the Dread*** was the sort of failure which conscripts what had always seemed to be great successes.

Yellow Dog is a conscious effort to move back from the loose style and sincere concerns of recent books towards the scenes of his biggest triumphs. Its subjects are pornography, male violence and male haplessness, yobs, city life and illiteracy: the subjects of ***Money*** and ***London Fields.*** It interlaces a number of different narratives, loosely touching and loosely converging. In the first, an actor-writer, Xan Meo, is violently beaten up by a hired thug in the street; his crime was accidentally to use the name of a real gangster, Joseph Andrews, in a short story. After the assault, his personality changes from that of a loving husband and father to someone selfish, brutish, high on testosterone. In another strand, a pathetic tabloid journalist, Clint Smoker, sexually inadequate but writing endlessly obscene stories in his 'newspaper' salivating over crimes of sexual abuse and even rape, is the easy victim of a predatory woman sending lewd emails. There is an immensely stretched-out account of a plane crash—Amis is usually terribly good on planes, which supply some of the best jokes in ***Money, London Fields*** and ***The Information,*** but this seems tired and not actually very interested.

What seems initially like the boldest stroke in ***Yellow Dog,*** and something with the potential to supply something new, is a strand of narrative involving the King. Although the novel is set in the present, England has a different royal family. The King is Henry IX, whose father died in the real bombing of Lord Mountbatten's boat. He has a Chinese mistress, a wife in a coma, and the heiress is a teenage Princess Victoria who, worryingly, is showing signs of wanting to convert to Islam. The story here is that a photograph, then a short film of the Princess taking a bath is made known to the King; as the novel progresses, the clandestine film is revealed as being much ruder, and is marketed as pornography. Pretty well everyone in the novel—Meo, Smoker, Andrews—is touched by pornography, as consumers or manufacturers. The Princess, a pathetic blank figure, makes pornography without knowing it.

The impression of ***Yellow Dog*** as representing a loss of nerve arises from the fact that all the good things in it are efficient reruns of old subjects and jokes, and everything new in it is tiresome and unconvincing. The strand about the royal family simply doesn't work at all, largely because of the ***Koba the Dread*** problem that Amis doesn't really have much of a sense of public lives. (A professor of modern history in this book is concerned about the possibility of Pakistan losing Kashmir, which doesn't bode all that well.) His idea of the King's existence is nothing more than a super-rich version of Guy Clinch in ***London Fields,*** and Henry moons about from restaurant to house-party to hours with his mistress to the occasional ribbon-cutting. There is no sense of the incredible weight of business, public duties and unflagging, imprisoning control characterising the life of the monarch, and it greatly damages the novel. If the King really lives a life of such idle, neglected freedom that he can lightly take as a mistress someone attached to the Chinese Embassy, the reader asks, why is the existence of the film such a problem in the first place? By not considering the reality of an entirely public life, Amis reduces the potential impact of his own story.

But there are other problems with the story: the Princess, the mistress, the King's brother the Duke of Clarence are wretchedly thin characters, hardly existing at all. Previously, Amis achieved great successes with characters who are simply enigmatic blanks, like angelic Kim Talent in ***London Fields***; the Princess, here, is just nothing in particular. She might be the girl who sells a character a newspaper, nothing more than that. And this strand is full of an infuriatingly feeble joke about names, which goes on about 20 times longer than could conceivably be interesting or funny. The mistress is called He Zizhen—'He touched him. He touched He. He was hard. He was soft. He touched him and he touched He.' The equerry is called Love—you can do that one for yourself. Elsewhere, Xan's wife is called Russia, and when Xan decides 'to invade Russia', this reader for one started to wonder why on earth he was bothering. The plot doesn't quite allow the despatch of a letter from Russia with Love, but don't imagine he didn't think about it.

The novel somehow doesn't quite know when to stop, and how to pace itself; in the same category as the jokes about He and Love and Russia are the ingenious but interminable emails tormenting Smoker, full of those teenage abbreviations; the inventiveness is high, but the interest is consistently low, and it is infuriating to be subjected to them so extensively when the pay-off turns out to be extremely feeble. There is a huge structural problem, too, in the shape of Joseph Andrews himself. I can see what Amis was trying to do; Andrews's name echoes through the first half of the book, as if preparing for an immensely impressive entrance by a monster. The problem is that Andrews turns out to be a damp squib, and from that moment the book starts to feel far too long. He is quite an ordinary achievement; his language feels laboriously put together rather than felt, with its combination of old-style London thug-cockney, occasional formal courtliness, 'my dear', and useful phrases learned through exposure to the legal profession—'it's more, uh, detrimental to a man's dignity'. It's not quite credible: not helped, either, by the regular slipping into what are surely the sentences of black young Londoners, not at all plausible in the speech of a white gangster over the age of 80—'You see that look on they face'.

What can be rescued from the wreck of ***Yellow Dog*** are the old favourites: the enchanting conversations between the tabloid journalists, for instance, which are very enjoyable expansions of the advertising-agency scenes in ***Money.*** The startling, admirably shameless disquisitions on the genres and sub-genres of the pornography industry in America, too, are exactly that comic riff which Amis's books used to be filled with—an expansion of John Self's encounters with tabulating New York prostitutes, but exuberantly so. There are whole pages of viciously funny and brilliantly overheard London conversations, zingingly vivid observations of London street life, and the occasional really well set-up comic pay-off—I loved the porn-executive 'Karla' demurely stepping into the breach, as it were, when the hired slapper fails to turn up and politely asking her chauffeur to take a shower after dismissing the hired gentleman. But these excellent flourishes rise like buried treasure from the mud. Far too much of ***Yellow Dog*** is filled with weak reruns of old material, implausible and unengagingly laborious working-out, and promising narratives which come to embarrassingly weak conclusions—the last 40 pages are a sequence of feeble punchlines, almost as if the author is by now as bored by his own material as is the reader. I kept wondering what one would think of ***Yellow Dog*** if one knew nothing about Amis. I think it would look like an unusually promising first attempt at a novel: unsuccessfully put together, and indulgent towards some very weak material, but all the same capable of flourishes of great energy and comic exuberance. Perhaps one shouldn't judge it against his splendid novels of the 1970s and 1980s; but all the same, those novels established Amis as a figure of such authority, the tendency can hardly be avoided.

George Walden (review date 8 September 2003)

SOURCE: Walden, George. "Back to Blighty." *New Statesman* 16, no. 773 (8 September 2003): 48-50.

[*In the following review, Walden admits to enjoying the crude humor in* Yellow Dog, *finding it to be a welcome change from the prevailing atmosphere of literary pietism.*]

When D H Lawrence briefly honoured England with his presence in 1927, he stayed long enough to write a bilious piece about his country, in which the word "pokey" featured obsessively, before he caught the sleeper back abroad. Although Martin Amis appears to suffer the occasional asphyxiating spasm, and has been reported as saying that it is all happening in America, at least he lives here—albeit, one suspects, as something of a spiritual émigré. Not counting the excellent collection of his criticism, ***The War against Cliché,*** after the not-too-successful ***The Information,*** his two most recent works were escapes from contemporary Britain. Not that it helped: ***Koba the Dread,*** a good and necessary book, was marred by an intrusion of the Amis personality cult into the rather more momentous matter of Stalin's murdered millions. And nobody (particularly not John Updike) thought ***Night Train,*** in which the author impersonated an American female detective, worth the detour.

In ***Yellow Dog,*** Amis returns to Blighty, a phrase excruciating in its passé connotations, though apt enough here, since the England he comes back to is one that should by rights be long gone; like a dead character in the novel, the corpse continues to kick up in its coffin. The end-of-holiday timing of the book's appearance is neat. Soon the upmarket press will feature the seasonal lamentations of columnists holding their noses as they set foot in their homeland to find the tabloids still a-swill with royal bilge, with near-beer pornography, tales of crapulous footballers and the rest. All these are the subjects of Amis, the homecoming literary traveller.

In both the novel and its pre-publication reception, the first impression is that we have been here before. It is a sign of the galloping contamination of tabloid ethics that Amis's book should have been widely and lovingly trashed before it appeared—celebrity "failure" makes irresistible copy. Yet even at its best (and there are virtuoso passages), the novel is a palace of echoes. The disorientated male, the stage violence, the sexual grotesquerie, the stylistic tics and leitmotifs, the outlandish names, the feared plane crash, even the extraterrestrial element familiar from ***Night Train***—in this case, the ponderous symbolism of a near-miss meteor—all the old Amis riffs are there.

Have we been short-changed? If we wanted to learn something new about ourselves, the answer is yes. Yet if we insist that Amis stays at home like a good lad and writes about England, and England doesn't change much, why should he? Then there is the lack of competition. If not him, whom among the known names on the Booker longlist ought we to be reading? Presumably novels that have not been pre-emptively rubbished, by authors exempt from personal or (it sometimes seems) any serious criticism at all. Works such as *The Light of Day,* a hymn-like title by the sacerdotal Graham Swift, in which he reminds us once again of the essential decency of our fellow creatures, especially the humbler sort. Or the doomy *Oryx and Crake* by the soothsaying St Margaret, whose reputation for prophesy remains undimmed by *The Handmaid's Tale,* which imagined a Taliban future for America's women, denied even the consolation of books. Never mind that the fundamentalist Puritan fathers, as early as the 1640s, decreed that all women should be taught to read, or that US troops are currently protecting Afghan girls at school. Alternatively, there is inoffensive kidult stuff or the perfectly respectable ethnic prose of Monica Ali, both also beyond criticism.

A stifling literary pietism hangs in the air; pietism provokes humour, manic if need be, and on that score alone ***Yellow Dog*** is a welcome change. The plot need not be over-analysed. Of Buddy Rich it used to be sung that "A guy named Buddy plays the drums like thunder / But the melody is six feet under", and it is similar with Amis, whose obtrusive style tends to bury whatever intentionally half-arsed story is being narrated. If the reader, mesmerised by the stick-play, gives up on the melody and submits to the beat, does it matter? When Amis is really swinging, who cares about the obtrusion?

The tale revolves around intersecting upper, lower and middle English worlds. A scandal erupts when the imaginary king's teenage daughter is filmed naked. Meanwhile, Xan Meo, an actor and formerly loyal husband, undergoes a personality change for the worse after being coshed by crooks. And in the sump of society, a vortex into which everyone is sucked, all manner of yellow pressmen, porn stars and gangsters figure.

Amis's idol, Saul Bellow, is said to go through his drafts cutting out jokes, for fear of appearing light-minded. With the exception of the end, ***Yellow Dog*** appears to have undergone the reverse procedure. The humour is occasionally coarser than usual and you may say that some of the jokes should have been blue-pencilled (such as the ones about the foreplay, the ring and the wristwatch, or the 5p and 50p anus) after you've had your laugh. Certainly, the king at stool, or the penis-elongation academy attended by Clint Smoker, a porn writer reminiscent of Keith Talent in ***London Fields,*** is stooping low, but what do you want? Is it literary snobbery to suggest that, unlike Rabelais or the cruder stand-ups, at least this stuff is stylishly written? Naturally, the txt-messaging between Clint and his online admirer K8 is overdone, but you don't skip it, because K8's high-txting style is very funny. And given that it is going to be done, who else would you prefer to do it?

What does it tell you when your misgivings about a book surface after you have read it and, by and large—*hypocrite lecteur*—enjoyed it? Probably that both writer and (holiday) reader were in less demanding mood than they should have been. Amis has definitely let himself go a bit here. (Did Clint really have to live in Foulness? Must a porn-industry centre be called Fucktown?) The danger of linguistic nostalgia (Kray-brothers gangster-speak features alongside the dated, orotund argot of palace officials) is exacerbated by Amis's perilous facility for doing the voices.

There are deeper problems. Amisry used to be a one-man comic genre, but for some time now the style has permeated literature and the media. When the successful innovator returns to base, he suffers the penalty of his own ubiquity. Every mother's son does the Amis voice, often unknowingly, and many a daughter, too, now that the ladies strain to out-booze and out-cuss the lads. Which leaves Amis ironising away about a culture already pickled in Amis irony, and a country all satired out. Clint Smoker and his fellow Nibelungs of the press would be Amis fans to a man and, to the extent of their capacities, recyclers of his style. The same is true of many a contemporary columnist and novelist who came out of Amis as surely (*toutes proportions gardées*) as later Russian writers swarmed out from under Gogol's "Overcoat". Though at the end of the seemingly endless satirical day, as ***Yellow Dog*** confirms, Amis still does a better Amis than Julian Barnes or Zadie Smith.

The mature Amis is not untouched by the circumambient pietism. No trace here of the feminist-baiting Nicola Six of ***London Fields.*** Now Amis's women are more intelligent and more virtuous than the male; even Karla the porn magnate was interfered with by her father, so what else was she to do? And though the book will be criticised for a lack of up-to-date ethnic content, Amis seeks to cover this base by remarking how nice it is to have non-whites about. Which will doubtless make a lot of people more comfortable in their skins.

And after the clowning comes an excessively sober ending. "It would be surprising if women weren't a little crazed by their gains in power, and if men weren't a little crazed by their losses," intones a remorseful Xan to his wife. Good on him. And there is more. "It's about time we all grew up, wouldn't you say? The people will have to grow up. I'll have to grow up. And if I can grow up, they can grow up."

So spake the king, clearly with authorial authority, as he decided on the abdication of royalty. An alluring prospect, but if satire is going to make quasi-serious points, it will be judged against reality. As Amis knows, the end of royalty and the red tops will come about, like reform of the National Health Service, over the people's dead bodies. Unlike our author, perhaps, they like it here.

Paul Johnson (essay date 13 September 2003)

SOURCE: Johnson, Paul. "Savaging the Author is Replacing Hunting the Fox." *Spectator* 293, no. 9136 (13 September 2003): 37.

[*In the following essay, Johnson addresses what he calls the media "phenomenon of Martin Amis" and assesses the author's literary achievements.*]

The phenomenon of Martin Amis puzzles and intrigues me. He seems to arouse a passion and hostility based on envy that are quite incommensurate with his literary importance or success or genius—or the absence of it. He figures constantly in the gossip columns or pseudo-news stories, never without a note of malice. The reviews of his latest novel [***Yellow Dog***], some of which I have read, seem animated by systematic hatred or malign delight at his supposedly failing powers. How is it that so many denizens of that *panier de crabes,* the

London literary world, want to dig their pincers into him? He has obviously earned too much money for them to stomach, pulled too many beauties, rated too many headlines, and has had far more fun than patience will allow. And now, the time being ripe, the cowardly pack has closed in for the kill.

By contrast. I have always felt a little sorry for Amis, whom I remember as a child, frail but luminous, tiny but somehow significant. Old Kingsley must have been a marvellous father in many ways: like Evelyn Waugh, he could make his children laugh endlessly with unforgettable fantasies and imitations. But Kingsley, being an only male child, was selfishness personified, neglectful in fundamental ways, and his infidelities and the family chaos they generated made it hard for Martin's mother to do her duty. Had it not been for the efforts of Elizabeth Jane Howard, who had the strong sense of responsibility of her class, Martin might never have got the education his talents deserved.

As it was, however, he learnt to enjoy the limitless felicities of the English language, building on his father's obsession with words, and the joys of manipulating them, to construct a verbal religion of his own. He is not the writer for me, I fear, for I see the first page of a novel as a picture-frame, inviting me to look at the start of a narrative landscape, peopled by one or two intriguing characters, with the promise of more to follow. If I like what I see, I step into the frame and lose myself in its contents, wandering at the bid of the author into fear and laughter, triumph and tragedy, quite oblivious to the world beyond the frame until, the last page read, I step outside it again. In short, I need a compelling story, enacted by characters in whom I can believe and whom I can love or hate. Martin did not provide this; indeed his father did only in three books, *Lucky Jim, Ending Up* and *The Old Devils.* I recall discussing the problem with Kingsley not long before he died, and telling him that to bring off the trick three times was an enviable achievement.

Martin is not a teller of golden tales but a word-master, a syllable-smith, a magician of the telling or teasing or convulsive phrase, a writer who jabs tiny morphemes or gross etymons into his pages until they blaze, rather as Turner, on Varnishing Day, used to scumble prodigious quantities of flake-white, flaming with crimson or orange, on to his canvases, until they glowed fiercely, extinguishing their neighbours. This may not be great novel-writing, but it is a contribution to literature of a sort, and perhaps of a significant and durable sort, which will charm future readers, just as César Franck's harmonies beguile composers today even though they do not think much of his symphony.

In any case, this mugging of a professional writer by aimless gangs of critics is an odious spectacle, gruesomely typical of the way in which the media turn on individuals, be they royalty or politicians, sportsmen or entertainers, or just celebs or nobodies who have wandered on to the stage of events by accident. A character is built up into fame, then hunted down into notoriety and oblivion by newspaper and television, in the great blood sport of our age, in which human suffering and humiliation provide entertainment for millions and well-paid employment for media hound-dogs, motivated not by animal instinct but by greed and sadism. But in the case of Martin Amis we cannot blame journalists; it is his fellow writers who scream the view-halloo.

Such collective shooting parties are surely new. Shakespeare's envious contemporaries scrapped with him as individuals. Milton was bruised by political disaster and blindness, not by venomous pens. Keats may have been murdered by *The Quarterly* and Coleridge was certainly hounded by Hazlitt, who savaged his works even before they were published. But such assassins believed great public issues were at stake; they felt they were engaged in a literary war, as did the frenzied audience who fought at the first night of *Hernani* in 1830. But Amis is not a political or public figure in this sense. He neither advances nor opposes any heated principle. He is a professional writer making a living for wives and ex-wives and the progeny thereof, hoping to entertain his readers in the process. As Dr Johnson so justly observes, 'There are few ways in which a man can be more innocently employed than in getting money.'

Besides, Martin Amis's critics in the book world always tend to bring into their *réquisitoires* aspects of his private life that evidently grate on their susceptibilities. They burrow and pry, or rather take advantage of the prying of professional gossip columnists. Literary men and women have always contended with the natural evils of their trade, but they were usually allowed a few secrets. Dr Johnson felt at times that he was being watched, but no one, until his death at least, dwelt publicly on his peculiar marriage or his neglect of his mother or his strange relationship with Mrs Thrale—the padlocks in his cupboard were not made to rattle in his lifetime. Hazlitt's escapade in the Lake District did not become public knowledge, and if his humiliation at the hands of his landlady's snaky daughter did, that was entirely his own doing by publishing his *Liber Amoris.* Wordsworth's illegitimate French daughter remained arcane. Thackeray was never harassed over his tragic infatuation with Mrs Brookfield and its cruel outcome. When George Eliot chose to live in sin with G. H. Lewes, the usual social consequences followed in some quarters but her choice was never held against her in reviews of her novels. Indeed, though she was not *sortable* in the ordinary way, she went everywhere she chose and presided over a literary salon of impressive deference and severity. Dickens's fame has never been equalled in European literature, and he himself chose to announce his rupture with his wife. But little or no censorious comment followed in the prints, and no efforts were made to hunt down Miss Ternan. Equally, Victor Hugo, almost as famous as Dickens, was not persecuted when caught in flagrante delicto with a married woman, who was promptly sent to prison under the then *régime des moeurs,* while he pleaded his peerage and remained at liberty.

It has been a different matter since the first world war. If we except the peculiar case of Oscar Wilde, who may be said to have asked for it, Kipling was the first literary fox, hunted by the Bloomsbury and academic pack. Hemingway was another, Camus a third. But even in these cases polities was a factor. Today the cult of celebrity, egged on by the literary-prize game, has inspired a bloodlust which seeks cruelty for its own sake, and bodes ill for literature.

Donna Seaman (review date 15 September 2003)

SOURCE: Seaman, Donna. Review of *Yellow Dog,* by Martin Amis. *Booklist* 100, no. 2 (15 September 2003): 179-80.

[*In the following review, Seaman praises the audacity and absurdity of* Yellow Dog.]

Amis elicits as much animosity as approbation, especially in his native England, but no reader can deny the audacity of his imagination or the tensile power of his subversive, fractured, vitriolic prose. In the opening scene in his first novel in five years [***Yellow Dog***], a crass and careening satire, Xan Meo, a self-declared Renaissance man with a grimy past, scans the bawdy drink menu in a London pub that offers cocktails called Blowjob and Dickhead and ponders the "obscenification of everyday life," a key theme in the insanity that follows. His brief reverie is violently interrupted, however, and he sustains a serious head injury. Meanwhile, King Henry IX, seemingly dim, dotty, and bored to paralysis with his witless duties, is facing a crisis: someone possesses highly compromising photos of 15-year-old Princess Victoria. And wouldn't sleazy tabloid genius Clint Smoker just love to get hold of those? Xan struggles to regain control over his addled brain and hyperactive libido, the king muddles along, Clint seeks new lows on behalf of the "wankers" who read his ludicrous rag, and a comet threatens to crash into Earth as Amis decimates the patriarchal paradigm (and the monarchy) by dissecting, in outrageous detail, the paradoxes of the pornography industry and the psychosis of father-daughter incest. A sloppy, maddening, hilarious, and oddly touching amalgam of Evelyn Waugh and John Waters, Amis' wicked burlesque evinces his disgust with the herd mentality and a surprisingly tender regard for women.

Publishers Weekly (review date 13 October 2003)

SOURCE: Review of *Yellow Dog,* by Martin Amis. *Publishers Weekly* 250, no. 41 (13 October 2003): 55-6.

[*In the following mixed review, the critic claims that* Yellow Dog *suffers from an excessively complex plot.*]

In this much-anticipated 10th novel [***Yellow Dog***]—which has already fomented a furor in Britain—the prose is brilliant and often hilarious, and the insights into contemporary culture are disturbingly prescient. But the book's many successes cannot hide its fundamental flaw: an overly complex and needlessly opaque narrative structure. The wildly plotted novel begins when modern "Renaissance man" (actor/writer) Xan Meo is viciously assaulted; his head injury changes this "dream husband" into an oversexed, sadistic lout, ultimately forcing his wife to cast him out. But the attack isn't an act of random violence. As one of his assailants, Mal, cryptically puts it, "You went and *named* him . . . *J-o-s-e-p-h A-n-d-r-e-w-s.*" From this enigmatic opening, Amis weaves a complex tapestry of narrative threads: Xan Meo is trying to recover his lost personality and his family's loving embrace; teenage Princess Victoria—a future queen of England—is being blackmailed with a video of her in the bath; tabloid journalist Clint Smoker—emasculated by a laughably small penis—extracts his revenge by being relentlessly misogynistic in print. Meanwhile, the recidivist, violent criminal Joseph Andrews—now a pornography impresario in Los Angeles—is plotting a way to return to England to die. Making these intersecting narratives cohere would be a challenge for any writer, but Amis reaches even further with a backdrop of apocalyptic violence (a transatlantic flight that's doomed to crash, a meteor that might hit the planet). That background clouds his core themes, which are more than dramatic enough to be compelling: violence and its intimate connections to sex and gender, the "obscenification" of everyday life and the 21st-century preoccupation with fame. (A typical Amis aperçu: "Fame had so democratised itself that obscurity was felt as a deprivation or even a punishment.") Thanks to Amis's pitch-perfect dialogue, his I-can't-believe-he-wrote-that humor and his perceptive critique of contemporary morals, this is still a novel of many pleasures—and still a novel to be reckoned with.

Keith Gessen (review date 8 December 2003)

SOURCE: Gessen, Keith. "Growing Up All Wrong." *Nation* 277, no. 19 (8 December 2003): 50-4.

[*In the following unfavorable review of* Yellow Dog, *Gessen traces Amis's literary development and provides an assessment of perceived strengths and weaknesses.*]

Martin Amis is the most condescended-to novelist of his time. He is also one of the most literate, funny, quotable and (this the condescenders never neglect to mention) talented. He is the author of a few clunkers and a very strange book on Stalin, ***Koba the Dread,*** but also of two classics of contemporary satire—***Money*** and ***The Information.*** "Be more funny!" Homer Simpson yells at the television, and it's no use. But then, no writer has loused up his fiction with such a transparent misunderstanding of what literature should aspire to in our time.

To have watched Amis these past five years, since approximately the short-story collection ***Heavy Water,*** is to have borne uncomfortable witness to a sort of extended creative meltdown. In that time he has published a memoir, ***Experience,*** in which some funny and very warm reminiscences of his father, the novelist Kingsley Amis, are interspersed with passages of embarrassing, misplaced bathos; ***Koba*** [***Koba the Dread***], in which some funny and warm reminiscences of Kingsley are interspersed with passages of embarrassing, misplaced historical score-settling; and now ***Yellow Dog,*** a novel of embarrassingly transparent and misplaced moral grandstanding in which Kingsley, alas, does not appear.

He is replaced in ***Yellow Dog*** by a rogues' gallery of disappointing predictability. There is Xan Meo, the reformed London roughhouser turned good family man who takes a hard knock on the head and reverts to his old ways; there is Clint Smoker, author of the nasty, rape-cheering "Yellow Dog" column for a sex tabloid, the *Morning Lark*; King Henry IX, a particularly vapid monarch; and Joseph Andrews, a crusty old criminal overlord. The characters' trajectories are only loosely, vaguely connected, and their names do not signify (Xan is not Asian, his wife, Russia, not Russian). If the book has a subject it's the war of the sexes and, loosely, vaguely, what pornography might have to do with it. In any case, it hardly matters. ***Yellow Dog*** is shorter than it appears, because it's written largely in dialogue, and though the first part of it is readable enough, by the second half Amis has resorted to stealing whole sentences from his journalism, and the novel has fallen apart.

What remains is Amis's disapproval of everyone involved. It's not enough that Clint Smoker works for an offensive paper: His writing is off-the-charts bad, and he's also, as his ex-girlfriend informed him, "a crap fuck." It's not enough that King Henry is a dullard: We learn that his wife, the queen, is in a coma, and he's having an affair. Amis does not like pornography, and he believes, rather strenuously, that men should be respectful of women's rights. Sometimes, momentarily, he unreins his wit, only to harness it again. "Even before the first issue had hit the streets," we learn of Clint Smoker's paper, "it was universal practice, at the *Morning Lark,* to refer to readers as wankers. This applied not only to specific features (Wankers' Letters, Our Wankers Ask the Questions, and so on), but also in phrases common to any news-papering concern, such as 'the wanker comes first' and 'the wanker's what it's all about' and 'is this of genuine interest to our wankers?' The staff had long stopped smiling when anybody said it."

This is the best joke in the book—and yet note, at the end, the strain of disapproval. Amis's satire has always had a heckling quality, and too often it's been directed at his social inferiors; his fiction has always been marred by a streak of misanthropy. In his putative maturity, though, this has been replaced by a sort of taunting, as if these morons, these deviants, these inadequates, were no longer even worth our laughter.

Amis has grown up before. In the wake of ***Money,*** his coruscating anti-1980s farce, he became concerned with nuclear weapons, producing a string of essays and then ***Einstein's Monsters*** (1987), a short book of stories all somehow touching on the nuclear threat. This was followed a few years hence by ***Time's Arrow,*** about a Nazi doctor (remember the Nazi doctors?) living in the American suburbs. Amis's successive enthusiasms can be traced in his father's letters. Martin "has gone all lefty and of the crappiest neutralist kind," Kingsley Amis writes in 1986 to his friend Robert Conquest, the great historian of Stalin's terror, "challenging me to guess how many times over the world can destroy itself. . . . I suppose you can't recommend some book?" "Martin is getting het up again over greenhouse effect and all that," he writes to Conquest in 1990. "Can you recommend a good short book . . ."

Presumably Kingsley, Communist Party of Great Britain, 1941-56, subsequently a virulent Tory anti-Communist, would have been more tolerant of ***Koba the Dread,*** and he wouldn't have had to solicit bibliographic advice, because Conquest, along with Solzhenitsyn, is the book's main source. Also Vladimir Nabokov, who, as Amis's favorite writer, gets to be the historian of record for prerevolutionary Russia. Even in a book as full of misprision as ***Koba,*** this is too much: The literary theorist Roman Jakobson is famously said to have objected, when Nabokov was proposed as a potential literature professor for the Harvard faculty, that one did not ask an elephant to teach zoology, but giving Nabokov the last word on the paradise of czarist Russia is like having the elephant teach Russian history. Still, skewed as it is, ***Koba*** is revealing of Amis. He simply isn't interested, as a novelist might be, in the texture, the daily fear, of Soviet life under Stalin, still less in the heartbreak of those whose dream of revolution had been hijacked by the Bolsheviks; he is only interested in the enormous numbers, the gruesome tortures, the twisted torturer himself.

And this gets to the heart, I think, of Amis's trouble, and all that condescension he is subject to: He still doesn't know what his subject is. So he goes in desperate search of the really ultra-super-real. In ***The Information,*** a book about literary envy and the humiliations of middle age, both encapsulated with awesome precision in the characterization of failed novelist Richard Tull—"he was forty tomorrow, and reviewed books"—there are entire sections, by far the book's weakest and enough of them to pull the novel off its center of gravity, devoted to the London petty-criminal world. Also brief digressions on the size of the universe—how tremendously big it is. In the wildly uneven memoir ***Experience,*** a book about Kingsley, and, magnificently at times, about aging ("Youth can perhaps be defined as the illusion of your own durability. The final evaporation of this illusion parches the skin beneath the eyes and makes your hair crackle to the brush. It was over. There would be hell to pay"), there are long passages about Martin's cousin Lucy, who was murdered by a famous serial killer in the early 1970s. The trouble is that Amis hardly knew his cousin, and so these parts read like an awkward, very general funeral oration by someone only glancingly acquainted with the deceased.

But Amis thinks this is the stuff. Crime, nuclear war, Holocaust, the gulag, universe expanding, petty crime, hard-boiled lumpen London—***Yellow Dog*** is especially full of the latter—all of these seem infinitely more real to Amis than literature and middle age and money. Is Amis ever better than when looking at the social stratification of New York, "the most violent thing that men had ever done to a stretch of land"? The hungover John Self in ***Money***:

> I wondered, as I burped up Broadway, I wondered how this town ever got put together. Some guy was dreaming big all right. Starting down in Wall Street and nosing ever upward into the ruins of the old West Side, Broadway snakes through the island, the only curve in this world of grids. Somehow Broadway always contrives to be just that little bit shittier than the zones through which it bends. Look at the East Village: Broadway's shittier than that. Look uptown, look at Columbus: Broadway's shittier.

A fine observation on the construction of the metropolis, on its insistent, compulsive geographic class-marking. Sadly, you sense that Amis thinks this isn't important enough, and will soon be reaching again for his lumpens. ***Money*** includes an entirely superfluous subplot about John Self's father, who owns a bar, and his young stepmother, who poses nude for magazines.

This is known as a crisis of confidence in one's material, and Amis seems to suffer one in every book he writes. Part of the crisis is generational: No one has been in a better position to feel his contemporaries' inadequacies vis-à-vis their fathers than the son of Kingsley Amis, head of the postimperial grouch brigade. "Dad," asks young Martin in ***Experience,*** "are we nouveau riche?" "*Very* nouveau," answers Kingsley. "And *not at all* riche." "What's it like," asks adult Martin, "being mildly anti-Semitic?" "It's all right," answers Kingsley. ("No," earnest Martin clarifies, "I mean what's it *feel* like?") I cannot imagine Martin Amis answering any such questions with Kingsley's genial certainty. He is a far more displaced and fidgety figure. Also a diminished one. The empire is gone, long gone, and it's not easy being a major contemporary writer if you don't believe you live in a major contemporary culture.

Or even that you practice a major contemporary art. "Like all writers," Amis tells us in ***The Information*** of Richard Tull, "Richard wanted to live in some hut on some crag somewhere, every couple of years folding a page into a bottle and dropping it limply into the spume. Like all writers, Richard wanted, and expected, the reverence due, say, to the Warrior Christ an hour before Armageddon." Instead, he is a complete loser, and in the way that you can tell what an author thinks of an idea by the characters he assigns to believe in it, Richard Tull represents Amis's secret suspicion that literature is doomed.

This is actually an odd form of humility. When Amis rather grandly titles his (very smart) collection of book reviews ***The War against Cliché,*** he does not mean what Orwell or, in a certain reading, Nabokov would have meant—a war against the euphemisms that lend cover to murder. Amis's understanding appears to be closer to a private morality of entertainment. Keep it interesting, keep it moving. Don't use the same word twice. When in doubt, make it un-literary.

But Amis was born into a peculiar situation—one in which his writerly self-consciousness was mirrored, anticipated, swallowed up by his father's writerly self-consciousness . . . and his stepmother's, and his father's friends'. In ***Experience,*** there is an incredible passage in which Amis analyzes his father's divorce from the writer Elizabeth Jane Howard, with the (dubious) help of Kingsley's first biographer, Eric Jacobs, whose prose Amis calls "mysteriously repetitive." You could go crazy untangling all the writerly distortions. Or there is this footnote, about Kingsley and *The Concise Oxford Dictionary*: "How he loved that dictionary—as I too love it. My current edition has just snapped in half and will have to be replaced. When it was near by and he was praising it ('This, this is the one'), he would sometimes pat and even stroke the squat black book, as if it were one of his cats."

Kingsley is Amis's greatest character, his most complex and comic, by about a mile; nowhere, not in his letters, or interviews, or biographies, or even maybe his own books, is Kingsley this funny or likable. "My father once told Christopher Hitchens and me to fuck off after we took him to Leicester Square to see *Beverly Hills Cop*. No: he liked it and we didn't. And I think we must have curled our lips at him. Most uncharacteristically he walked away on his own and had to be coaxed into the next pub or cab."

Would Amis be a worse writer if he simply surrendered to his fate—to be a major chronicler of modern civilization as experienced by a hypereducated and marginalized literary elite? It's difficult to escape the impression that part of the reason Kingsley is such a fine character is that Amis cannot pretend that he is other than he is, a littérateur. How should one write when one's greatest tenderness is reserved for a man whose greatest tenderness is reserved for his copy of the *COD*? Perhaps, rather than writing like this, as in ***Yellow Dog,*** relating one thug's intimidation of a hot-dog vendor:

> "Look, you don't want your face on that grill, do you, you don't want this trolley down on you and them onions in your hair. And a squirt of ketchup up one ear. And a squirt of mustard up the fucking other."

one ought to write like this, as in ***The Information*** when Richard takes the vacuum cleaner to get fixed:

> By the time he got the vacuum cleaner out of the apartment and onto the stairs Richard was wondering if he had ever suffered so. This, surely, is how we account for the darkness and the helpless melancholy of twentieth-century literature. These writers, these dreamers and seekers, stood huddled like shivering foundlings on the cliffs of a strange new world: one with no servants in it.

Here is the disappointment, almost even the fury. At moments like these Amis is simply the finest contemporary novelist of cultural manners, of the status that civilization has in our society, and he is capable, when necessary, of taking it a step further. "By a certain age, everyone has the face he deserves," thinks Richard Tull. "Looking in the mirror on the morning of his fortieth birthday, Richard felt that no one deserved the face he had. No one in the history of the planet." And better still, in ***Money,*** the book whose themes ***Yellow Dog*** picks up but travesties, John Self looks at the fictional "Martin Amis": "If I stare into his face I can make out the areas of waste and fatigue, the moonspots and bone-shadow you're bound to get if you hang out in the twentieth century."

That is Amis's twentieth century. In ***Koba the Dread,*** he quotes voluminously from another's twentieth century, *The Gulag Archipelago*—indeed, it's part of the silliness of that book that he so insistently tries to share page-time with Solzhenitsyn. But I wonder how well he understood the dissident writer. For although Amis is correct to insist that the Soviet labor camps were effectively death camps, Solzhenitsyn's book is necessarily about those millions who made it out—and how unnaturally old they'd become, how badly their teeth had rotted. When Amis is at his best, the twentieth century becomes a place where those without money are left with the wrinkles and the broken vacuum cleaners: a forbidding century, and one that Solzhenitsyn, with a little prompting, would have recognized as his own. And if he hadn't recognized it, if he'd dismissed as frivolous an observation like John Self's in the wake of his financial ruin—"Manhattan, JFK, you know these are suddenly very different places when you have no money. You change, but they change too. Even the air changes"—then so much the worse for Solzhenitsyn. A truly grown-up Amis would realize this, and in doing so would realize, too, how fine a writer he has sometimes been.

Nicole LaRose (essay date winter 2005)

SOURCE: LaRose, Nicole. "Reading *The Information* on Martin Amis's London." *Critique* 46, no. 2 (winter 2005): 160-76.

[*In the following essay, LaRose asserts that Amis's depiction of London in* The Information *is integral to his overall critique of English culture.*]

In most interpretations of Martin Amis, scholars and critics label him as a postmodern writer entirely on the basis of the metafictional games that he plays with narrative form. In ***Time's Arrow,*** the narrative travels backward; in ***Money,*** John Self not only fights with a character named Martin Amis but is also tricked by Martin Amis; in ***London Fields,*** the manipulation by authorial figures is a central concern of the supposedly murderous plot; and in ***The Information,*** the narrative games come together as distinctive parts of the overall search for the information promised by the text's title. Approaching Amis as postmodern, although prevalent in critiques of contemporary literature in general, relies entirely on formal concerns, without any material contextualization. Amis's games are not solely comedic gestures; instead, they need to be interpreted as part of his overall satiric critique of identity, epistemology, and, most important, London.

Amis's primary material critique of English culture questions the links between reading and information. Although both the act of reading and the attempt to gather information appear as navigating forces that could lead the reader toward a transcendent deciphering, mass media has corrupted epistemological identity and blocked spatial comprehension. The digitized information that pervades the mass media makes commodities out of individuality; with individuality digitized all referents fail, different realities melt into one another, and the inability to read becomes disorienting while it also becomes a social phenomenon. This also happens when Amis is read as postmodern. Reading Amis requires connecting the formal narratological games with textual and topographical navigation. The act of not reading on the part of both Amis's critics and the popular media is not a resistance but an inability to navigate. If the reader is to gain agency and navigate through the text, he or she is required to identify the information through a reading that relates to an urban orientation. The London that results is a carefully constructed, as well as a cautiously navigated, space that reveals a politicized global environment within the localized realities of Amis's London.

The most comedic examples of faulty reading practices in ***The Information*** are the obsessive ones of the two principal characters, Gwyn Barry and Richard Tull: Gwyn, the famous novelist, subscribes to two services for press clippings but still vainly searches for "stray mentions of his own name" (299); Richard, the obscure writer, does not search for himself but instead once obsessed over "any incidence of the word *alcohol*" (300). The model of reading established by the two characters mirrors the typical critical reading that similarly obsesses over references to the sensationalized "Amis Affair."[1] Each of the reputable, nontabloid English newspapers reported the large advance that Amis received after controversially switching agents (in addition to other more personal events).[2] In light of the media craze, it is not surprising that the criticism and reviews of the novel have returned to the arrested phase of biographical criticism, even after Wimsatt and Beardsley's identification of "The Intentional Fallacy" (1954), Barthes's eulogy to "The Death of the Author" (1968), and Foucault's questioning of "What is an Author?" (1969). To avoid accomplishing further lazy readings that falsely substitute the autobiographical elements of the novel for a contextualized interpretation, the reader needs to see the internal model of criticism, reading for a reoccurring element, as a narratological game. As Elie Edmondson writes, "Martin Amis has been something of a puzzle to most critics" (145). If the reader agrees to find out why Amis plays these games, by looking for mentions of television, news, universality, envy, celebrity, and all other forms and qualities of information suggested by the novel, then the autobiographical elements become a satire of the media attention given to "literary celebrities."[3] Such satire reveals the limitations of the mass media mentality that creates such a celebrity. A look at the mass media construction of information throughout the novel, both by a close reading of the occurrence of the word *information* and, because information requires a rhetorical medium for dissemination, by a deconstruction of the process of imparting information in narrative, reveals a textual community based on a quest for understanding the phenomenological quality of information.

Defining the idea of community in ***The Information*** necessitates looking at the search for information parallel to the narrative mapping of the place of the text—namely, Amis's London. Franco Moretti best explains this connection: "Space is not the 'outside' of narrative, then, but an internal force, that shapes it from within. Or in other words: in modern European novels, *what* happens depends a lot on *where* it happens" (70, emphasis in original). For all of Amis's characters, including the intrusive authorial first-person narrator, the understanding of information, always momentary and fleeting, becomes tied to their similarly evolving place in the city and the text. To find a way through the city, most of the characters assume the simple mass media mentality that inundates them, following a faulty path that only leads to a false sense of individuality derived from the celebrity culture.

Ultimately, to navigate the city the characters must first acknowledge and refuse the sway of media mentality, just as readers must not allow the "Amis Affair" to guide them through the novel. Once characters and readers escape mass media mentality (such as tabloid news), they can enter into a community in which they become part of a shared authorship that leads to the comprehension of information as a commodity. Amis establishes the link between community and shared authorship in the text through the idea of navigation. He suggests that a reader who looks for the information on the novel must make navigational choices, just as a character who tries to find his or her way through London must make such choices. The ability to navigate through the text and through London requires refusing the dialectic oppositions: correct and incorrect, fact and fiction, valuable and worthless, event and narrative. The nondialectical, labyrinthine mapping of information, the cartographic apprehension of London, and the shared authorship throughout the novel present an epistemology of the city and writers quite divergent from mass media individualism and celebrity. Such a labyrinthine epistemology juxtaposes the individualistic "trex" of Barry's novels and life, the violent career and television habits of Scozzy, the anti-intellectual xenophobia of Darko, the passive acceptance of Gina and Demeter, the celebrity worship of Belladonna, and the elitist intellectualism of Richard with Marco and Marius—twins who come to understand their world only through their connectedness, yet difference. Only Marco remains sane, remains found within the lost at the novel's end, because his identity has been formed in relation and community with his brother, not with the limitations of the mass media mentality that pervades the rest of the textual society.

The construction of the title, ***The Information,*** conditions readers to expect an entertaining, readable novel with a clear resolution. It also, as James Diedrick suggests, "parodies such [John] Grisham titles as *The Client* and *The Firm*" (175). This association characterizes ***The Information*** as popular fiction, which fails as literature, fails to enlighten or educate the reader because it is entertainment or "[p]ropaganda, aimed at the sell" (***Information*** 54). The conflation of information with fictional propaganda does not destroy the expected clarification promised by the title but sends the reader into the text searching. Throughout the novel, the word *information* appears approximately forty times, the same number as the years that Richard and Gwyn have lived. Through the repetition, Amis mocks those critics who read his writing as his life and solely search for some tabloid-appropriate information about him. But he also challenges the readers to see that just as each of Gwyn or Richard's years has a special signification, so do the many connotations of information combine to form a complex, indefinable whole.

Amis indirectly highlights the multiplicity of information by evasively defining the term in an interview with Eleanor Wachtel. He says, "It refers to about half a dozen things: the information on someone, the dirt on someone; the information revolution; one character informing another, like a succubus; and the certainty or knowledge that you're going to die, and how this affects the male ego" (48). Amis acknowledges the proliferation of referents for information but only lists a few "things," which correspond to the recurring themes of gossip, mass media, and violence. Gossip becomes a stand-in for perception, substituting secrets and whispers for actual knowledge. The reference to a succubus, a female demon who devours her lover, genders the communication of gossip as feminine but with a confused relationship between the stereotypically feminine amorous devotion and atypically unfeminine violent disruption. The causality for the seemingly confused construction of gossip derives from the mass media manipulation that forces the revolutionary overthrow of knowledge in favor of gossip, solely because it sells. The revolution capitalizes on the commodity and worth of manipulated and repackaged media-information, which is often passed off as "news." Admittedly, gossip and media manipulation only implicitly connect to violence. But I would argue that the extreme shift from the modernist obsession with scientific enquiry to the postmodernist solipsistic view of information results in violence as a foundational ideology under the postmodernist rubric. Amis links the ever-present postmodernist violence to an inevitable death, most likely by aging. He genders death as masculine by emphasizing the degenerative processes that occur during the male midlife crisis: balding, wrinkling, and feeling increased pains, physically and emotionally. The degeneracy of the body during middle age parallels that of information during postmodernity, thus forcing the human in search of knowledge during postmodernity to undergo the same torture that the body undergoes while progressing toward death.

The plot of ***The Information*** directly addresses envy, jealousy, and fame; therefore, it is not surprising that the characters use gossip to form their perceptions of the people and places surrounding them. Theoretically, gossip serves as a workable overarching category for information within the novel. Gossip always is momentary and fleeting; it does not pass the tests of accuracy and the validation of endurance, but instead moves aside as new information becomes available. This definition of gossip likewise applies to the narrative construction of tabloids. Through Rory Plantagenet, Amis's novel explicitly illustrates the shared definition between gossip and a tabloid. The narrator explains. "For some years now Richard had been selling Rory literary gossip. How much that advance had been. Who would win that prize. Occasionally, and more and more often, he sold him gossip about literary divorces, infidelities, bankruptcies, detoxifications, diseases. Rory paid for the information" (16). The first introduction of Rory as a "newspaper diarist" (16) emphasizes the contrary nature of his work; the conflation of a newspaper—a supposedly factual account of important events—with a diarist—one who writes intimate details based on emotion—explains how Richard can sell "literary gossip" while Rory pays "for the information." Rory's surname further suggests a class conflation, as he has lost all the benefits and privileges of his aristocratic royal heritage.[4] The only resonance that Plantagenet still has with royalty is through the mass media.

Darko and Belladonna, two youthful, cartoonish characters, epitomize the anti-intellectual audience targeted by sensational media. When Richard meets Darko and Belladonna, he quickly identifies their limited perception. Darko tells Richard he comes "'[f]rom the place [he] still call[s] Yugoslavia'" (126). Despite his history, he does not understand that the difference between Serbs and Croats is religious and not ethnic. The narrator explains, "This was obviously news to Darko: fresh information. Richard tried to relax himself with the following thought: that nowadays, in a sense, you could know more about a stranger than the stranger knew about himself" (127). As the information in this instance directly refers to knowledge, Darko cannot comprehend it because he exists in a world that has been plagued by gossip; his position keeps him from even developing an understanding of his cultural heritage. Instead, he lives for the short cut—the ideal that prevents him from developing into a mature epistemological being. Richard responds to Darko anxiously because his grasp of an elitist, education-based knowledge makes the lack of understanding caused by mass media-driven culture difficult for him to accept. Richard should have expected such an unenlightening encounter because of the grammatical mistakes in Darko's letters of invitation, particularly the error that highlights the importance of television by conflating Belladonna and Gwyn's identities.

Belladonna's obsession with TV is so extreme that she confuses it with reality. She is convinced that Gwyn loves her because, as she explains, of the way he looks at her "'[w]hen he's on TV'" (133). Because she has constructed her personality from the stereotypical femme fatale image capitalized on by the media, she sees her worth only through her potential as a sexual object for masculine desires. She emphasizes her body by wearing her underwear as outerwear and then always performs the sexual favor demanded of her. When she meets Gwyn, she takes off her clothes, dances, and then finishes with oral sex. Although she has previously defined her relationship with Gwyn through love, their physical encounter is unemotional. Gwyn tells Richard about the meeting, saying, "'You know when they're actually down there—one thing it does is shut them up. For the time being. But not her. She took it out every ten seconds to *say* something. Me on TV. *Her* on TV. Holding it there, like a mike'" (358, emphasis in original). Belladonna's response to Gwyn does not reveal love for him but a love for TV. Gwyn is the celebrity medium that would allow Belladonna to transcend reality for the television reality she prefers. His phallus becomes a mike for her because she speaks the language of sexual submission.

Female characters like Belladonna led many critics to attack Amis's representation and treatment of women; most say he does not give women enough credit, nor does he depict them as authentically as he does his male characters.[5] Despite Belladonna's stereotypical portrayal, she appears remarkably distinct for a minor character. Darko, her closest masculine counterpart, is so nondescript that, to be noticed, he has to create an alter ego named Ranko. Belladonna's distinct, yet simultaneously stereotypical, actions emphasize her position as a cultural trope. She represents a victim of media manipulation who can define her self only through the physical and economic perfection epitomized by celebrities. When the narrator first describes Belladonna, he says, "Her voice was London" (129). Like Darko, Belladonna has a confusing ethnicity, but her voice, her ability to speak of the sexuality forced on her by a television image that she wishes to uphold, makes her representative of the urban London environment that has produced her. Her limited understanding of her self, reality, and the restrictive knowledge of television media locates her identity within a stereotypical urban space rather than a self-conceived place within the transitory city-space of London. Because of her identity, she becomes a victim of the violence embedded in her sexual environment by contracting a fatal sexually transmitted disease.

The anti-intellectualism that forces Belladonna to see sexuality as a surrogate for information indirectly connects violence and death, but Steve Cousins's understanding of information takes violence to the extremes. He makes a living by physically harming others. As required in his career, information serves only as a medium to accomplish violence. He regularly works with Mrs. Verulam, who, the narrator explains, "was a modern person, and routinely traded in information" (71). As the provider of housekeepers for the Barry home, she has inside information on Gwyn and Demi's daily activities and secrets. Mrs. Verulam's information permits her to enter into an economic exchange with Steve, a.k.a. Scozzy, in which he trades physical harm to people who annoy her in return for hearsay about Gwyn and Demi. Such a trade reveals that for Scozzy the worth of information is solely dependent on the violence he will be able to inflict. Similarly, working (as Richard's hire) toward a violent end for Gwyn, Steve goes looking for more information. In a discussion with Crash, Demi's driving instructor, Scozzy asks for information, meaning an immediate perception about Demi. He says, "'You don't have to *do* nothing, Crash, mate. All I want is information'" (39, emphasis in original). Scozzy does not need an accurate representation of Demi's character, only dirt or gossip that will help him hurt Gwyn. Scozzy's desire to construct a simulation of Demi from fragments of hearsay is similar to the media's representation of Amis, which has been constructed from a few sensationalized incidents.

Similar to the absurdly stereotypical femme fatale role played by Belladonna, Scozzy's relationship to information exemplifies the stereotypical masculine connection to violence. Steve's apartment contains two zones; in the main part he sits on his couch and watches pornography, but he also has "a computer corner (the usual information processors)" (163). If pornography is, as the narrator explains, "surveillance on the act of love" (360), then the spaces of Scozzy's apartment are not separate. Pornography, although a form of prototypical masculine oppression, serves as a surveillance system for Scozzy, similar to the Internet.[6] One of the primary similarities between pornography and the Internet is that both prevent and protect the voyeur from actual human contact. In one sense, pornography and the Internet depersonalize human relationships, much like the title with its definite article, but they also allow people to hide behind anonymity.

Although Gerald Howard does not acknowledge the pornographic qualities of the Internet, he uses ***The Information*** to question the place of the author in such a digitized world. He observes, "[W]e slouch towards the Grubnet, a digital cyberspace in which books and authors alike will become dematerialized [. . .] We are all of us, readers and writers alike, exiles from the garden of innocent reading. Who knows what beasts await us in the new cultural wilderness?" (53). Scozzy reads, but he is exiled from "innocent reading" simply because he is exiled from innocence; he reads magazines about criminals and police, tabloid news, Richard's novels. He reads Richard's notoriously unreadable novels because of their ostensible sexuality and because no one else can; it proves he is tough. He reads the crime magazines because doing so makes others think he has been to prison; again it proves he is tough. He reads the news because he has found a way to inflict violence on the world. He believes, "You do a newscaster, and they do you a newscast about it. Now that's the way the world's *supposed* to be run" (51, emphasis in original). He sees the news the way Richard views "trex," as propaganda aimed at the self. Through his manipulation of news, he propagates a violent persona as his self-image, which is ultimately affirmed by the fear that he causes in others. Steve's ability to evoke fear makes the narrator question, "Was Steve Cousins Mars, the planet of war, or was he simply Mercury, the messenger, bringing you information from the other side?" (169). The narrator recognizes Steve's use of violence as a persuasive form of information dissemination; but by shifting from Mars to Mercury, the narrator also questions the agency of Steve's character. Instead of viewing Steve's ability to cause physical pain as a type of authority or seeing him as one of "the beasts" that Howard discusses, the narrator sees Steve as a manipulated medium that brings the violence of the urban environment to those outside.

Although the material that Scozzy reads appears to be obviously devoid of information, Amis also challenges the quality of literary writings. It would seem that Richard and Gwyn, as writers with Oxford educations, should be able to understand the information in an intellectual manner; neither does, leaving the reader searching for a figure who is not lost in the novel's wilderness. The success of Gwyn's novel suggests that he has written a message that appeals to the masses; he has created the utopian world that society craves. But Richard labels it "trex," highlighting why such a utopia must fail. Nicolas Tredell comments on the origin of trex as follows: "'Trex,' originally the brand-name of a type of cooking fat, and used in a way which alludes to this at one point in ***The Information*** ('slapping some slice of trex on to a frying pan' [444]), is a recurrent term in the novel to mean junk or rubbish, mainly but not exclusively of a literary or subliterary kind" (191). Gwyn's writing is not the celebrated universal epiphany searched for throughout the novel, because just as cooking fat is not healthy for people (especially in the fitness-crazed 1990s), neither is Gwyn's novel. Instead, *Amelior* is the brand-name of the fat that passes itself off as the marketed intellectual possibility for a media-driven readership; the utopia of the novel, much like TV, is an unrealistic substitution for the realities of life. It is not totally Gwyn's fault that his writing is bad. The reader never sees him slave over his craft as Richard does. Instead, Gwyn becomes an author like the others on his publisher's team, famous for something other than writing: Gwyn becomes famous for publicity. He gives interview after interview, sits for photograph after photograph, and falls victim to the fame and cult of celebrity. The only writing that Gwyn obsesses over, drafting parts of his authorized biography in his head, reinforces the concept of writing as self-worship.

Further confirming writing as propaganda (a type of information that reveals nothing and operates through a narcissistic reflexivity that provides, on the basis of desire, an ideal self-image for the community), Richard's writing becomes self-worship through its alienating difficulty. Although he exhibited intellectual excellence as a student at Oxford, he becomes as obsessed with celebrity as Belladonna and as internally violent as Scozzy. He clearly does not want Gwyn's fame, but he definitely does not want Gwyn to have it either. Richard's discomfort with fame permits the mass media mentality to influence him immensely. He becomes so enraged by Gwyn's mass appeal that he reacts to the newspaper notification of Gwyn's entrance to the best-seller list by striking Marco when he knocks over a table (29). Instead of the passive, bow-tie-wearing intellectual that he has been hitherto, Richard turns into a Scozzylike figure determined to "fuck Gwyn up" (25). Information degenerates for Richard into a medium serviceable only for his plot. Faithful to his craft, his plotting takes the form of narrative creation and inductive reasoning, but only superficially. On the basis of his perception of Demi, he creates a ridiculous plot to seduce her—sleeping around with black dealers, desperate for cocaine, and equally desperate for a child. The narrator explains, "Acute and chronic impotence, Richard knew, was no kind of springboard for a seduction operation. But he had information on her now, which always meant the vulnerable, the hidden, the intimate, the shame-steeped" (123). The manipulative hold that violence has over Richard blocks him from seeing the absurdity of his attempt. In this way, his impotence becomes more than sexual torpor; it comes to represent his weak comprehension of information. The seduction is impossible because of his impotence; but worse, it is antiartistic because he bases the plot only on those of Demi's desires that accord with the stereotypical media coverage of the scandals of the royal family. When he climbs into bed with Demi, she gives him a black eye, which repeatedly serves as an embarrassing mark for Richard's absurd attempts to enact the plot against Gwyn.

During his plot, he tortures himself physically with drugs and emotionally by turning his back on the intellectual individuality that once allowed him to grasp information. The self-torture turns his intellectualism into elitism and ensures that he must fail at both his violent plot and his excessive fiction. A moment of transcendence occurs for Richard when he masters the pub game "The Knowledge."[7] At the Warlock, he attracts a crowd, the fans he so carefully alienates in his fiction, by answering trivia questions. Packaging knowledge in a machine that awards money, as well as Richard's submission to it, reveals that he has abandoned his previous grasp of unadulterated knowledge in exchange for the ability to play the game. The machine confronts Richard about his participation in the cult of celebrity by confronting him with a question that includes Gwyn as a possible answer. Gwyn's ability to block Richard's path foreshadows the end of the novel, in which Richard's obsession with Gwyn's media persona inevitably gives Richard an eternal black eye—the public revelation of Gwyn and Gina's affair.

Critics often lump the narrator with Richard's voice, further muddling his confused perspective. However, the narrator begins to create an identity for himself close to the middle of "Part One." A young boy uses sign language to tell the narrator that his name is Tom. The narrator responds, "And I made the signs—the M, the A—with my strange and twisted fingers, thinking: how can I ever play the omniscient, the all-knowing, when I don't know *anything?* When I can't read childish capitals in the apologetic fog. I wrote those words five years ago, when I was Richard's age" (43-44, emphasis in original). As in ***Money*** and ***London Fields,*** a voice identified by the signifiers M and A shapes, forms, and tells the story.[8] The MA is a paraph, a flourish of a signature to ward off forgery, used particularly with initials to enable them to be used as a signature. The MA closely connects to the Martin Amis that avid fans will obsessively identify.

The first-person narrator of ***The Information*** makes himself most apparent during ramblings about astronomy and the position of the universe; at one point, he discusses yellow dwarfs and then comically transfers from the astronomical connotation to that of a small, yellow person. The joke about the dwarf leads into an embedded narrative, disassociated from the Tull-Barry conflict, providing elaborated characterization about the narrator. MA tells about his difficulty dating as a young man: "As a man who stands five-feet-six inches tall (or five-feet six-and-one-half-inches, according to a passport I once had), I know about dating and size" (207). His brother's girlfriend would bring a friend or a sister; the brother would then report, "saying, 'Come on, She's tiny'—or else (shaking his head), 'Sorry, Mart'" (207). This story connects the vague label MA to the name Mart. When deciphering these clues about the identity of the narrator, it is impossible for a critical reader well versed in Amis's fiction not to see the association with autobiographical evidence. Amis positions the intentional fallacy in the guise of what at first seems like a reward to the careful, obsessive reader. As such a reader, I know that Amis repeatedly inserts authorial figures into his novels, here employing a narrator who on first examination represents Wayne Booth's implied author par excellence. I know that Amis was forty-five, five years older than Richard, when he was writing the novel. And I can envision the publicity pictures just as does Gerald Howard, in which Amis appears "[i]n the center, famously shorter than the others [. . .] with his drink and hand-rolled fag" (44). But if I use all this evidence to argue that Amis is the narrator or even the implied author of the text, then I am guilty of the same celebrity worship as all the characters throughout the text. Instead, I must acknowledge Booth's warning that "[t]o say that a story is told in the first or third person will tell us nothing of importance unless we become more precise and describe how the particular qualities of the narrators relate to specific effects" (150). In the first sentence of the novel—"Cities at night, I feel, contain men who cry in their sleep and then say Nothing" (3)—the narrator makes himself clearly known, but only as an afterthought to the introduction of cities. Further emphasizing the importance of the state of cities, the first paragraph reads like a frame to Richard's narrative that begins, "Richard Tull was crying in his sleep" (3). The narrator gives readers clues to the narrative levels by mentioning Boccaccio and Chaucer in this same introduction.[9] Highlighting the frame of cities in conjunction with the concept of narrative framing positions identity and place as performative gestures.

The performativity of the first-person narrator differs from typical authorial intrusions, which attempt to assert control over the narrative. As highlighted by Amis's explanation, "I'm present for the first half of the book. I make perhaps a dozen appearances, and I'm present in the first sentence in a phrase like 'I said, so I feel.' And then I absent myself from the book and, as it were, let them get on with it without me" (Wachtel 57).[10] The narrator is not only appearing, but also disappearing. The most obvious explanation of the narrator's disappearance is omniscience, but it is the denigration of information that forces the narrator "to stop saying *hi* and to start saying *bye*" (***Information*** 207). Mass media mentality, which the narrator connects to cities, does not allow for the authoritative author figure. In this way, the London of the text becomes Baudrillard's simulacrum, a copy without an original (6), just like the MA narrator. Seemingly in response to Baudrillard, Amis explains to Will Self his use of the city: "This is what I try to do with London: I don't want to know too much about it. Of course, I soak it up willy-nilly, but I have to push it through my psyche and transform it. So it isn't, in the end, London any more. It's London in the patterning of my cerebellum" (Self, "Interview"). Throughout the novel, London becomes the text within the text, one of the many intertexts of the narrative. Explaining the importance of cities for the human condition, Drew Hyland suggests, "We *lack* autonomy; we are *not* self-sufficient; we *need* each other. Our response to this reality, our effort to turn limitation into possibility, is to gather into cities, so that, in the spirit of cooperation, we may enhance each others' lives" (48, emphasis in original). In Amis's London, however, something has gone wrong with the spirit. The narrator can claim it is "nothing," but the characters have lost their connections to each other and thus to their place within the space that is London.

The contrast between the novel's specific place names and the characters' lack of knowledge of their place within the city represents a class system that explains the inability to comprehend information in terms of the late capitalist society of London. Gwyn and Richard are repeatedly linked to Holland Park and Calchalk Street, respectively, emphasizing a class system based on economics. Holland Park serves as a sign of the gentrified urbanities; it is a space of seemingly closed-off gardens immersed within the public space. The narrator's description of the Barry home reflects the precarious relationship of public and private spaces:

> Gwyn's dove-gray house in the innocent morning; Demi's house at dawn. And our vigil, and an even more extraordinary one, in its way. That of Steve Cousins: Barnardo boy.
>
> Scozz seeing it not from the van but through the treated glass of his Cosworth (tinted windows, whitewalls, low racing skirt). Seeing it not as an architectural or even a real-estate phenomenon but as a patchwork of weakness.
>
> (64)

The repetition of the personal ownership of the home, first through Gwyn and then Demi, confirms the space as solely a status symbol of the couple's wealth. Highlighting the surveillance of the home, first by the reader through the narrativization of the space and second by Steve's plot to break into the house, confirms class hierarchy as a form of Foucauldian Panopticism. As Foucault explains in *Discipline and Punish,* the Panopticon's spatial formation permits the constant possibility of surveillance and reveals the control that the possibility of surveillance achieves for the entity that has the power of surveillance (197). Gwyn and Demi's ownership defines them as responsible citizens, docile bodies to use another Foucauldian term, or inhabitants of the Panopticon, whereas Steve's roots, his childhood as an orphan, make him the epitome of placelessness and homelessness.

The distinction between responsible ownership and violent urbanism, as reflected by the juxtaposition of these characters' classes, resonates with the economics and culture of Thatcherism. According to Anna Marie Smith.

> For Thatcher, the welfare state's promotion of a dependency culture and the interference in the free market on the part of the nationalized industries and trade union movement constituted the most serious threats to moral standards. Economic renewal, therefore, entailed a moral revolution: a return to individual responsibility, free market entrepreneurialism and British rationalism.
>
> (3)

Gwyn and Demi superficially appear as the responsible citizens who can bring about the moral revolution; it does not matter that Gwyn repeatedly cheats on his wife or that he refuses to start a family because the couple appears on the outside as perfect as their "dove-gray house." It also does not matter that Gwyn is of Welsh decent because he has assumed the role as the mainstream voice by calling for a British utopia (*Amelior*), which resonates with Thatcher's agenda for Britain.

Steve, complete with the street moniker Scozzy, is the most direct enemy to a Thatcherite approach to the welfare state; even as a victimized child he is the Barnardo boy—a label that refers to the Victorian philanthropist Thomas John Barnardo, who established homes to help orphans like Steve. Despite his innocent and helpless upbringing in the dependent position, he comes to stand for the degeneration of British nationalism and morality—remember his pornographic obsessions and lifestyle. The text supports the stereotype of the "welfare characters" by sending readers to Scozzy's or Belladonna and Darko's homes but having these domestic spaces always lack specificity. When Richard goes to find Belladonna and Darko, the narrative mapping creates a generalized urban slum: "A square of city rather than a city square, it branched out like an inbred slum family whose common name was Wroxhall. Wroxhall Road, then Wroxhall Street. Wroxhall Terrace, then Wroxhall Gardens. Then Court, Lane, Close, Place, Row, Way. Drive, then Park, then Walk" (124). Their home only has the location of Wroxhall because they stand for the slum, Belladonna as the quintessential London punk and Darko as the alienated and seemingly worthless immigrant. The generalized urban spaces of each of these characters make them always appear in a liminal space.

The clearest instance of the city space as liminal is detailed by Scozzy and 13, Crash's younger brother, traveling in their van. The narrator explains the movement: "And this was London, where there was no shortage of cars. This was a modern city, where cars were in endless supply, where there were cars, cars, cars, as far as the eye could see" (83). The cars obscure the city because there are so many, performatively indicated by the reiteration of the word; cars also become as stereotypical as the reiterated blips of mass media information. The types of vehicles operated by the characters stereotypically emphasize the class hierarchy, from Gwyn's posh import to Richard's family car, the Maestro, and finally the van—a space that can become, because of its immensity, the moving home. When Scozzy cannot find a place to park the monstrosity, he is forced to enact explicitly his already liminal place within the city space. Because he cannot physically stop, his intellectual self-understanding is equally transitory. When Steve picks up 13 from Marylebone Magistrates' Court, the two conduct a "social analysis" of the penal system (67-69). The ridiculousness of their assessment is emphasized by the space within the city in which it occurs. Instead of finding stimulation within the possible political critique they begin, the narrator explains, "Passing Speakers' Corner and entering Park Lane, Steve had the rare and transient pleasure of engaging third gear" (69). His pleasure, which must be brief because of the pace he has set, derives from increasing his movement, which he apparently views as a conquest or freedom from the congested city space. The passing of Speakers' Corner suggests a possibility of Steve or even 13 having their voices heard within a public space. But the inability to escape from the van, the embodiment of the transitory urban, reveals an acceptance of the dependency position; it also supports the disenfranchisement of such voices within the post-Thatcher cultural condition, where "Speakers' Corner was no longer to be found on the south side of Marble Arch. It was now to be found on all the other corners: every corner of London Town" (98). Although the proliferation of the space that stands for the potential voice of the citizenry suggests an opening up and listening for critique, these spaces allow only rhetoric that reaffirms the government's accepted economic, moral, and nationalistic stances.

The spatial arrangement not only supports a class system that is based on the varying degrees of disenfranchisement of its inhabitants, but it also introduces a class system that is based on how inundated and intoxicated each character is by the media mentality. Through Richard's travels to America, the generalized description of city spaces becomes symptomatic of the process of globalization that spreads through inundation with mass media. Richard first goes to New York:

> But he knew, the instant he arrived on its streets, that New York was the most violent thing that men had ever done to a stretch of land, more violent, in its way, than what was visited on Hiroshima, at ground zero, on day one. He looked up. He looked up and saw no difference; the usual metropolitan sky with its six or seven stars weakly guttering. Raw land can do nothing about them but cities hate stars and don't want their denizens to be reminded of how it really goes with ourselves and the universe.
>
> (221)

The city space of New York is never defined beyond the generalization of the space as the route of the violent intrusion of globalization. The prophetic use of ground-zero in describing New York only further emphasizes the city's role as the symbol for worldwide capitalism and American intrusiveness. The narrator's repeated use of astronomic metaphors when describing cityscapes affirms the connections between the generalized descriptions that derive from economic similarities and the unity provided by such superficial universality—or in other words, we all live under the same sky and all have to deal with these same problems. As Richard travels from Miami to Chicago to Los Angeles, the cityscapes inflict inescapability, mass productivity, and anti-intellectualism, respectively, on the inhabitants. The narrator questions the result of this environment: "[W]hat was America doing to Americans—who, on the whole, hadn't spent three years at twelfth century universities with *Paradise Lost* on their laps, and who had no Home Counties to come from or go home to? They never had a lifetime elsewhere to protect them from it, from America and the fever of possible change" (249). Citing Oxford and the Home Counties as the salvation from becoming completely inundated by a global economy reveals the educated British, such as Gwyn and Richard, as the traditional locus for an intellectual refusal of the global paradigm.

Gwyn is, of course, the archetype of a global celebrity; and as the novel connects the figures of the celebrity to the anti-intellectual, he fails to become any thing but the stereotype he lives. Richard is much more complicated. Despite his obsessive plot against Gwyn, he appears as the intellectual able to find a way through the cultural wilderness. He seems to spend as much time reading inane biographics of little-known Victorian figures (the plot strand depicting esoteric intellectualism) as he does plotting Gwyn's demise (the plot strand based on a global media machine). His space within the city is overtly specific: the reader is given the exact address "49 Calchalk Street, Flat E" (366), but this "isn't, in the end, London any more," as Amis explains to Will Self, because it is not exactly on the map. Instead, Richard's space is created within the map coordinates of Gwyn's neighborhood. Calchalk Street's dependency on the other streets—Ladbroke Grove, Portobello Road, and Kensington Park Road—parallels Richard's dependency on Gwyn. Similarly, Richard's inability to understand his world at the novel's end is because Gwyn (through his sexual relations with Richard's wife) has intruded into Richard's family structure. The novel details how Gwyn becomes lost because of his intense egotism, whereas Richard becomes a victim by envying Gwyn.

The relationship between mass media society and city space continues through the end of the novel, in which the London space remains specific and knowable, whereas the characters wander aimlessly. The already fragmentary narrative excessively emphasizes the fragments, cutting from character to character as in a movie or TV broadcast constructed of sound bytes.[11] The reader, Booth's cryptographer who sees "that there is no limit to the number of deciphering pleasures that can be packed into a book" (301), becomes a cartographer of the information about London. At the end of the novel, a scene unfolds in Richard's neighborhood, not because of Richard (who is already lost), but because it is Marco's neighborhood. Marco is the only character who reinforces Hyland's definition of a city as a place to "enhance each others' lives" (48).

Throughout the novel, Marius and Marco appear as dialectical opposites: Marius is smart, athletic, and mature beyond his years; Marco is learning disabled, unhealthy, and innocent. Despite their differences, the two boys often appear as a unified pair, especially as they repeatedly watch television together. It is important to acknowledge the oxymoron of watching television together, but the boys at least share the same space as they submit to the mindless culture of cartoons. Marius becomes so immersed in the television culture that his questioning of self-identity is limited to the query, "Daddy: what would you rather be? An Autobot or a Decepticon?" (22). Marco, on the other hand, questions everything relentlessly. He does not submit to the limited culture around him but holds firmly to his innocence. Marius refuses his childhood and his innocence, confronting Richard about his drug abuse. The maturity that Marius displays in his relations with his brother and father makes him appear so absurd that he becomes machinelike, refusing his position within childhood innocence for an identity as either the Autobot or the Decepticon. Marco similarly confronts his father, but on the more child-friendly topic of swearing. By maintaining his childhood, Marco protects himself from the violence that scares him.

Marco's innocence gives him a clear self-understanding and thus protects him at the end of the novel. Richard has discovered Gwyn's action against him; Gwyn has been revealed to the media as the philanderer he is (this should certainly change the drafts of the biography he has been writing in his head); Scozzy attempts to exact revenge for his lost childhood by harming Marco, but the violence catches up to him as Gwyn's bodyguards punish Scozzy. Because Marco has separated himself from the violent culture by maintaining his innocence, the violence of Gwyn's bodyguards against Scozzy saves him from Scozzy's violence. When Richard spots Marco on the street, the narrator explains, "There was something terribly wrong with Marco: there was nobody at his side. And yet the child's solitude, his isolation, unlike his father's, was due to an unforgivable error not his own" (372). Marco has developed his self-understanding by critically examining his relationships with those around him, namely his brother and father. He can navigate the city because he knows how to find his way back to the people he needs by his side. Marco has contributed to collective relationships by trying to improve his father and spending time with his brother. Through these activities and other family-orientated ones, Marco has created an environment that awards him the right to have others by his side. Marco's triumph supports the narrator's assumption that "Childhood was the universal" (284). Throughout the novel, the narrator links the characters, particularly the writers, to the search for the universal. By linking universality to Marco's innocence, the narrator denies the other characters the possibility of finding it. Childhood cannot be reclaimed—it is lost. Marco possesses the universal and navigates the city because in his innocence he surveys the world around him. The narrator explains the difference between Marco's surveillance of the world and that of Marius: "Mar*co*. So unlike Marius, who was so firmly placed in the world, who constantly sought and identified distinctions (that was a hem, that was a fringe: that was an cave, that was a ledge; that was a scratch, that was a scrape), who had already joined in the great human venture of classification" (165, emphasis in original). In defining the world, Marius unknowingly submits to the accepted cultural assumptions, which are clearly flawed by the mass media culture. The need to define information has led all the characters toward a lack of understanding; only Marco comprehends the closing line—"And then there is the information, which is nothing, and comes at night" (374)—because he does not need to label information with the stereotypical nihilism that results from standard definitions. Marco fears the information that the other characters adore, and thus places information (and the global economy that it embodies) as "nothing," permitting himself to interrogate his world and come to his own understanding within his post-Thatcher, postcapitalistic world.

Notes

1. The mode of reading that I am critiquing is a perverse, somewhat violent method of close reading in which the critic forces the text to fit her or his own agenda even if the text obviously opposes such a gesture. With contemporary literature, this mode of criticism has become more and more accepted as these critics attempt to blend scholarly writing and journalism for their own economic gain.
2. The *Sunday Times* (London) first reported Amis's advance for *The Information* in an anonymous blurb on 8 Jan. 1995, called "'I'm Looking for Money. Give Me Some. Go On. Do It.'" They followed with two more articles: Valeric Grove's "How Amis Signed Up the Demon King" and Nicolette Jones's

"An Advance Taken Amiss." The other popular British papers, *The Independent* (11 Jan. 1995), *The Guardian* (13 Jan. 1995), and *The Observer* (15 Jan. 1995) later reported similar stories. The sensationalism spread with biographical spreads in *The New Yorker* (March 1995), *Esquire: British Edition* (April 1995), and *Vanity Fair* (May 1995).

3. My use of the word *satire* derives from a standard literary definition. It is a literary art that makes a subject appear ludicrous to deride that same subject. It differs from comedy in that the humor results not from the joke itself, but from an understanding of the satiric critique. Amis's novel stands in a long tradition. Amis refigures Menippean satire, in which a group of eccentric and pedantic literary types profess their philosophical stances only to make their agendas appear ridiculous, in terms of the English satiric tradition. Through the question of how to use "information" within the digitized world of London, Amis updates the English tradition by combining the pedantic focus of the Menippean tradition with the London grounding of the English tradition. He does this to satirize the celebrity culture that pervades the London in which he now lives.

4. The Plantagenet family ruled England from 1154 to 1485, between the Normans and Tudors.

5. See Mills, Doan, Gilman.

6. The discussion of Amis's London, satire, and critique in terms of surveillance connects to Iain Sinclair's discussion of surveillance of and by London in *Lights Out for the Territory.* Sinclair comments on the pornographic and voyeuristic qualities of London through the image of the stalker. He writes, "The concept of 'strolling', aimless urban wandering, the *flâneur,* had been superceded. We had moved into the age of the stalker; journeys made with intent—sharp-eyed and unsponsored. The stalker was our role model: purposed hiking, not dawdling, nor browsing. No time for the savouring reflections in shop windows, admiration for Art Nouveau ironwork, attractive matchboxes rescued from the gutter. This was walking with a thesis. With a prey" (75).

7. The trivializing of knowledge points out the absurdity in the dialectical opposition of a high/learned culture and a low/mass culture, especially when each is constructed from sound bytes of factoids. "The knowledge" also refers to the knowledge needed by taxi drivers in London: it is a knowledge of the streets and different routes through the city that the driver must master and on which he or she must pass an exam before being licensed. The abundance, yet superficiality, embodied in this type of understanding of the London space (it is all about speedy travel) reflects the lack of actual, material comprehension of the city space throughout most of the text.

8. In *Money,* M. A. introduces himself in a note preceding the text. He explains to the reader that by the end of the reading, the protagonist "John Self will no longer exist." Before the narrative officially begins, M. A. suggests a substitution of his existence for Self's. In *London Fields,* the M. A. voice is more hidden than in the other texts. The writer Sam has come to London and lives in fellow writer Mark Asprey's flat. He finds and receives notes signed M. A. As the plot becomes more and more chaotic, the signification of the M. A. becomes more and more obscure. To add to the confusion, the name Amis can be rearranged as I Sam, the writer-protagonist of *London Fields.*

9. The narrator mentions the two literary figures while explaining the difference between Gina and Richard: "She was a woman. She knew so much more about tears than he did. She didn't know about Swift's juvenilia, or Wordsworth's senilia, or how Cressida had variously fared at the hands of Boccaccio, of Chaucer, of Robert Henryson, of Shakespeare; she didn't know Proust. But she knew tears" (3). Although the list reads like a who's who of the literary canon, it also highlights the tradition of embedded narratives, or stories within stories, through Boccaccio and Chaucer.

10. The paraphrase that Amis details of the first sentence is not exact but does correspond to the novel's beginning.

11. During this concluding section, Marco, Richard, and Gwyn travel down three different roads: Marco on Portobello Road, Richard on Kensington Park Road, and Gwyn on Ladbroke Grove. These three streets run parallel to each other, but vary in size—Marco is on the smallest and Gwyn on the largest. This overtly reveals their different self-understandings: Marco's local understanding, Richard's transitional moments, and Gwyn's global context.

Works Cited

Amis, Martin. *The Information.* New York: Vintage, 1995.

———. *London Fields.* New York: Vintage, 1989.

———. *Money: A Suicide Note.* New York: Penguin, 1984.

———. *Time's Arrow.* New York: Vintage, 1991.

Barthes, Roland. "The Death of the Author." *Image-Music-Text.* Trans. Stephen Health. New York: Hill and Wang, 1977, 142-48.

———. *S/Z.* Trans. Richard Miller. New York: Hill and Wang, 1974.

Baudrillard, Jean. *Simulacra and Simulation.* Trans. Sheila Faria Glaser. Ann Arbor: U of Michigan P, 1994.

Booth, Wayne C. *The Rhetoric of Fiction.* 2nd ed. Chicago: U of Chicago P, 1983.

Diedrick, James. *Understanding Martin Amis.* Columbia: U of South Carolina P, 1995.

Doan, Laura. "'Sexy Greedy is the Late Eighties': Power Systems in Amis's *Money* and Churchill's *Serious Money.*" *Minnesota Review* 34-35 (1990): 69-80.

Edmondson, Elie. "Martin Amis Writes Postmodern Man." *Critique* 42.2 (2001): 145-54.

Foucault, Michel. *Discipline and Punish: The Birth of the Prison.* Trans. Alan Sheridan. New York: Vintage, 1977.

———. "What Is an Author?" Trans. Josué Harari. Richter 890-900.

Gilman, Sander. "Love + Marriage = Death." *Sex Positives: The Cultural Politics of Dissident Sexualities.* Ed. Thomas Foster, Carol Siegel, and Elle E. Berry. New York: New York UP, 1997, 197-224.

Grove, Valerie. "How Amis Signed Up the Demon King." *Sunday Times* (London). 13 Jan. 1995: 15.

Howard, Gerald. "Slouching Towards Grubnet: The Author in the Age of Publicity." *Review of Contemporary Fiction* 16.1 (1996): 44-53.

Hyland, Drew A. *Finitude and Transcendence in the Platonic Dialogues.* Albany: State U of New York P, 1995.

"'I'm Looking for Money. Give Me Some. Go On. Do It.'" *Sunday Times* (London). 8 Jan. 1995: 3.3.

Jones, Nicolette. "An Advance Taken Amiss." *Sunday Times* (London). 13 Jan. 1995: 32.

Mills, Sara. "Working with Sexism: What Can Feminist Text Analysis Do?" *Twentieth Century Fiction: From Text to Context.* Ed. Peter Verdonk and Jean Jacques Weber. New York: Routledge, 1995, 115-28.

Moretti, Franco. *Atlas of the European Novel 1800-1900.* New York: Verso, 1998.

Richter, David H., ed. *The Critical Tradition: Classic Texts and Contemporary Trends.* 2nd ed. Boston: Bedford, 1998.

Self, Will. "An Interview with Martin Amis." *Mississippi Review* 21.3 (1993): 143-69. 13 March 2002. <http://orca.st.usm.edu/mrw/1995/07amis.html>.

Sinclair, Iain. *Lights Out for the Territory: 9 Excursions in the Secret History of London.* London: Granta, 1997.

Smith, Anna Marie. *New Right Discourse on Race and Sexuality.* Cambridge: Cambridge UP, 1994.

Tredell, Nicolas. *The Fiction of Martin Amis: A Reader's Guide to Essential Criticism.* London: Icon, 2000.

Wachtel, Eleanor. "Eleanor Wachtel with Martin Amis." *Malahat Review* 114 (1996): 43-58.

Wimsatt, W. K., and Monroe Beardsley. "The Intentional Fallacy." Richter 748-57.

FURTHER READING

Criticism

Begley, Jon. "Satirizing the Carnival of Postmodern Capitalism: The Transatlantic and Dialogic Structure of Martin Amis's *Money.*" *Contemporary Literature* 45, no. 1 (spring 2004): 79.

Investigates literary and cultural subtexts in *Money.*

Besomo, Ian. "The Road to Utopia." *Quadrant* 48, no. 3 (March 2004): 92-3.

Provides a negative assessment of *Yellow Dog.*

Dern, John A. *Martians, Monsters and Madonna: Fiction and Form in the World of Martin Amis.* New York: Peter Lang, 2000, 187 p.

Full-length study of Amis's work.

Oertel, Daniel. "Effects of Garden-Pathing in Martin Amis's Novels *Time's Arrow* and *Night Train.*" *Miscelánea* 22 (2000): 123-40.

Examines Amis's narrative style in *Time's Arrow* and *Night Train.*

Trussler, Michael. "Spectral Witnesses: The Doubled Voice in Martin Amis's *Time's Arrow,* Toni Morrison's *Beloved* and Wim Wenders' *Wings of Desire.*" *Journal of the Fantastic in the Arts* 14, no. 1 (spring 2003): 28-50.

Compares the treatment of supernatural themes in Toni Morrison's *Beloved,* Amis's *Time's Arrow,* and Wim Wenders's *Wings of Desire.*

Additional coverage of Amis's life and career is contained in the following sources published by Thomson Gale: *Bestsellers,* Vol. 90:3; *British Writers Supplement,* Vol. 4; *Contemporary Authors,* Vols. 65-68; *Contemporary Authors New Revision Series,* Vols. 8, 27, 54, 73, 95, 132; *Contemporary Literary Criticism,* Vols. 4, 9, 38, 62, 101; *Contemporary Novelists,* Ed. 7; *Dictionary of Literary Biography,* Vols. 14, 194; *DISCovering Authors 3.0*; *Encyclopedia of World Literature in the 20th Century,* Ed. 3; *Literature Resource Center*; *Major 20th-Century Writers,* Ed. 2; and *Major 21st-Century Writers,* (eBook) 2005.

Amiri Baraka
1934-

(Born Everett LeRoy Jones; also wrote under the pseudonyms LeRoi Jones and Imamu Amiri Baraka) American playwright, poet, essayist, short story writer, and novelist.

The following entry provides an overview of Baraka's life and works through 2003. For additional information on his career, see *CLC,* Volumes 1, 2, 3, 5, 10, 14, 33, and 115.

INTRODUCTION

Baraka is recognized as a controversial writer and prominent figure in the development of contemporary African American literature. His work explores themes of cultural alienation; racial tension and conflict; sexual, ethnic, and racial identity; and the necessity for social change through revolutionary means. Whether dealing with issues of race, sexual orientation, or institutionalized discrimination, Baraka is notorious for both infuriating and inspiring his readers. He is often viewed as a successor to the literary tradition of Richard Wright and James Baldwin, and as a spokesman for the power of art as a means to enlighten and empower African Americans and oppressed peoples throughout the world.

BIOGRAPHICAL INFORMATION

Baraka was born on October 7, 1934, in Newark, New Jersey, as Everett LeRoy Jones. After graduating high school at the age of fifteen, he enrolled at Howard University in 1952, and changed the spelling of his name to LeRoi. At Howard, he studied under such renowned black scholars as E. Franklin Frazier and Sterling A. Brown before flunking out in 1954. He served briefly in the U.S. Air Force, and moved to New York's Greenwich Village in 1957. Identifying with the Beat movement, Baraka married Hettie Roberta Cohen, a white woman of Jewish heritage, and founded *Yugen,* a journal of Beat poetry. Though he also attracted attention as a local jazz music critic, Baraka's initial critical recognition arose from his poetry collection, *Preface to a Twenty Volume Suicide Note* (1961). Baraka began to incorporate a strong political element into his writing after being invited to Cuba by the New York chapter of the Fair Play for Cuba Committee in 1960. His essay "Cuba Libre," inspired by his trip, received the Longview Best Essay of the Year award in 1961. Baraka's transformation into a dedicated political activist occurred after the murder of Malcolm X in 1965. Divorcing his wife and moving to Harlem, he dissociated himself from whites and focused his attention on composing political essays and poetry that would expose discrimination and foster a strong sense of African American identity. To help create works that would speak to and inspire the African American community, he founded the Black Arts Repertory Theatre/School. That same year, he was awarded a Guggenheim Fellowship, and subsequently married Sylvia Robinson, a black woman, in 1966.

In 1968 he converted to the Nation of Islam, adopting their political stance of Black Nationalism and changing his name to Imamu Amiri Baraka, meaning "blessed spiritual leader." Another radical change occurred in 1974 when Baraka dropped the spiritual title of Imamu and declared himself a devout Marxist-Leninist. Baraka's new socialist beliefs caused him to reject Black

Nationalism as a racist system of thought, and he likewise recanted his past anti-white and anti-Semitic statements. In 1979 he began teaching creative writing in the Africana Studies Department at the State University of New York at Stony Brook. That same year Baraka was arrested during a domestic dispute, and began work on *The Autobiography of LeRoi Jones/ Amiri Baraka* (1984) while serving time at a Harlem halfway house. He received the Poetry Award from the National Endowment for the Arts in 1981, and the Langston Hughes Medal for outstanding contribution to literature in 1989. Baraka was also appointed poet laureate of New Jersey in 2002, though the position was later abolished due to the outcry over his allegedly anti-Semitic poem "Somebody Blew Up America," which deals with the September 11th terrorist attacks.

MAJOR WORKS

Baraka's first volume of poetry, *Preface to a Twenty Volume Suicide Note,* satirizes post-World War II popular culture and reflects the detached perspective of the bohemian lifestyle. One of Baraka's most popular works of nonfiction, *Blues People: Negro Music in White America* (1963) highlights his thematic concern with the minimization of black artists as contributors to American culture. *Dutchman* (1964), a play detailing the sexual sadism inflicted upon a young black man by a white woman, is generally regarded as one of Baraka's masterpieces. Utilizing a minimalist structure and infused with symbolic references, *Dutchman* was recognized as the Best American Off-Broadway Play of 1964. *The Toilet,* another drama from the same year, is an example of Baraka's treatment of homosexuality. In typically gritty fashion, the play portrays the beating of a white homosexual boy by a group of black youths. *A Black Mass* (1966) is a play loosely based on the Nation of Islam's mythological explanation for the origin of black people and the devilish nature of whites. Baraka employed the basic tenets of this myth in his Faustian story of a black magician who accidentally unleashes white evil upon the world. *The System of Dante's Hell* (1965), Baraka's only novel, is widely considered the author's attempt to break away from the influence of the Beat poets. The narrative is loosely based upon Dante's *Inferno,* and places a semi-autobiographical protagonist into an urban wasteland of racial oppression and sexual violence.

Baraka's views on the role of the black artist in contemporary society are outlined in *Home: Social Essays* (1966), which also displays the author's passionate identification with the Black Nationalist movement, and includes the essay "Cuba Libre." *Transbluesency: The Selected Poems of Amiri Baraka/LeRoi Jones (1961-1995)* (1995) contains representative verse from every phase of the author's career. Reviewers contend that the collection exhibits Baraka's tendency toward introspection as well as his political consciousness. *Funk Lore* (1996) is comprised of previously uncollected poems dating back to 1984, many of which focus on Baraka's passion for jazz. *The Fiction of LeRoi Jones/Amiri Baraka* (2000) offers three new short stories, as well as *The System of Dante's Hell,* and a collection previously published as *Tales* (1967). Reviewers praise his innovative style in the stories of the volume, contending that it provides an insightful and alternative look at Baraka and his chief thematic concerns of sex, poverty, and race.

CRITICAL RECEPTION

There has been a wide range of critical opinion on Baraka's body of work. Many critics view him as a promising poet who evolved into a virulent racist. Others see his political and philosophical evolution as a fascinating reflection of the political, cultural, and social evolution of modern America. Some critics view Baraka as a champion of African Americans and commend his intention to create literature that focuses on the real concerns of the African American community. Recent criticism has examined the role of the Nation of Islam and anti-gay invective in his work. Both his use of free verse and his experimentation with poetic rhythm have been cited as significant contributions to postmodern literature, and his plays have found a permanent place in the repertoire of experimental theater. Although Baraka's controversial work has alienated many readers and critics, commentators concur that he has played a seminal role in the development of minority literature and remains as a profound influence on generations of African American writers.

PRINCIPAL WORKS

A Good Girl Is Hard to Find (drama) 1958

Yugen [editor and publisher] (journal) 1958-62

Preface to a Twenty Volume Suicide Note [as LeRoi Jones] (poetry) 1961

Blues People: Negro Music in White America [as LeRoi Jones] (essay) 1963

The Baptism: A Comedy in One Act [as LeRoi Jones] (play) 1964

Dutchman [as LeRoi Jones] (play) 1964

The Slave: A Fable [as LeRoi Jones] (play) 1964

The Toilet: A Play in One Act [as LeRoi Jones] (play) 1964

The System of Dante's Hell: A Novel [as LeRoi Jones] (novel) 1965

A Black Mass [as LeRoi Jones] (play) 1966
Home: Social Essays [as LeRoi Jones] (essays) 1966
Tales (short stories) 1967
Black Magic: Sabotage, Target Study, Black Art; Collected Poetry, 1961-1967 (poetry) 1969
**Four Black Revolutionary Plays: All Praises to the Black Man* [as LeRoi Jones] (plays) 1969
Afrikan Revolution: A Poem (poetry) 1973
AM/TRAK (poetry) 1979
"Afro-American Literature and Class Struggle" (essay) 1980; published in *Black American Literature Forum*
"Confessions of a Former Anti-Semite" (essay) 1980; published in *Village Voice*
The Autobiography of LeRoi Jones/Amiri Baraka (autobiography) 1984
Daggers and Javelins: Essays, 1974-1979 (essays) 1984
The LeRoi Jones/Amiri Baraka Reader (poetry) 1991
Transbluesency: The Selected Poems of Amiri Baraka/LeRoi Jones (1961-1995) (poetry) 1995
Eulogies (poetry) 1996
Funk Lore: New Poems, 1984-1995 (poetry) 1996
The Fiction of LeRoi Jones/Amiri Baraka (short stories) 2000
The Essence of Reparation: Afro-American Self-Determination & Revolutionary Democratic Struggle in the United States of America (essays) 2003

*Contains the plays *Experimental Death Unit 1, A Black Mass, Great Goodness of Life,* and *Madheart.*

CRITICISM

Anthony Kellman (essay date April 1990)

SOURCE: Kellman, Anthony. "Projective Verse as a Mode of Socio-Linguistic Protest." *ARIEL* 21, no. 2 (April 1990): 45-57.

[*In the following excerpt, Kellman examines the use of projective verse in Baraka's poetry, focusing on his use of jazz and traditional African music.*]

> Form is never more than an extension of content.
>
> —Charles Olson

In an essay entitled "Projective Verse," Charles Olson, the post-modern American poet, describes projective verse as "composition by field" (148), as "open" poetry, which accommodates a form of imaginative ploughing that is in opposition to the inherited traditional lines, stanzas, and metres. As such, projective verse becomes a linguistic protest against poetic convention, against established modes of poetic form and expression; and, if one accepts Olson's observation that form "is never more than an extension of content," then projective verse becomes also a tool for social protest. When Olson articulates the need for new recognitions in composing such open verse—the primary one being that the poet "can go by no other track other than the one the poem under hand declares, for itself" (148)—he is really underlining the need for the poem to write itself. The poet, therefore, must be open to spontaneity of improvisation as the poem's life (both in form and meaning) dictates. This means that the poem must be capable of *total* expression. It must be able to live *on* the page as well as *off* the page. It must be kinetic, capable of plurality, multiple perceptions, and non-linear thought.

Frank O'Hara, Robert Duncan, Olson, and other Black Mountain poets of the 1960s used projective verse in this way. While these poets were protesting against Vietnam and compulsory drafting into the United States Army, black American poets, such as Amiri Baraka, were protesting also against civil rights violations in the United States. Concurrently, in the Caribbean, black nationalists were calling for independence from colonial control. This international spirit of protest was based on the writers' vision of the future of their respective countries. They were, in effect, anticipating a day of change. Projective verse with its openness, its total expression, its off-the-page immediacy even when read from the page, its resistance to monolithic barricades (suppressive social and political systems and suppressive modes of poetic form and expression) served the writers well in their quest for change. And it is in this context that I specifically examine the use of projective verse in the work of Caribbean poets Edward Kamau Brathwaite, Derek Walcott, and Anthony Kellman, and of the black American poet Amiri Baraka.

. . . . .

Caribbean sound structures in verse find their percussive counterpart in the works of such American poets as Amiri Baraka. Baraka uses jazz for much the same reasons that Brathwaite, Walcott, and Kellman use rhythm patterns indigenous to the Caribbean. The language of jazz is audible in Baraka's poem **"I Love Music,"** in which the sound virtually leaps off the page as a vehicle for expressing the social realities from which that music springs:

> can be
> can be
> can be, trane, can be, trane, because of trane, because
> world world world
> can be
> sean o casey in ireland
> can be. lu hsun in china
> can be,
>   brecht wailing
>   gorky riffing
>   langston hughes steaming
>   can be

trane
bird's main man
can be
big maybelle can be
workout workout workout
expression
orgunde
afroblue can be
all of it meaning, essence revelation, everything together
wailing in unison
a terrible
wholeness.

(47-48)

This poem opens very close to the margin, creating a tenseness, then in the middle it expands outwards, swelling like jazz sounds; then, slowly, it brings us back to the margin. A similar frame is seen in Brathwaite's "Wings of a Dove" and in Kellman's "Watercourse." This letting-loose, this improvisation of word and sound, has its genesis in paradox and juxtaposition. The diverse cultural essences and creole magic impinge on the spirit of the poem causing form and content to, as Olson says, "juxtapose in beauty" (149); and it is also part and parcel of that cultural and historical paradox whose song is wholeness out of fragmentation. Historical and cultural fragmentation is the point from where all black people must begin. Through the imagination, these fragments can be reassembled to reaffirm one's sense of place in the world. Blues and jazz music are at once pain and joy, despair and hope, gateways to wholeness—a terrible wholeness.

Rebelling against conventional linguistics, Baraka's **"I Love Music"** uses no capital letters for proper nouns. This conscious subversion promotes a vision of freedom from stultifying categories of expression. Just as Baraka notes, in the essay **"Greenwich Village and the African-American Music,"** that the "music was trying to get away from the restrictions of tradition without reason" (186), so too his poetry was attempting, through subversion of conventional forms, to return to African rhythms, to reclaim the primacy of improvisation and the primordial construct.

Baraka captures this primal African energy construct in **"Class Struggle in Music"**:

What is
the emotion
not the colonised mercedes in
briefcases
ties
words arranged
by picture window rote

our emotion, not
its
not the witch training
not the denials of self and family
not the isolated dead corpse negro
accepting the hating cup
of Cortez' asshole-hat wearers

But the us emotion
the love
emotion
the love
heat,
snowball,
heat,

move-
ment
life
yeah, vitality
beat beat beat
boom buppa doompa doom
boom buppa doompa doom
boom buppa doompa doom
boom buppa doompa doom
yeh,
that and
boom buppa doompa doom
boom buppa doompa doom
boom buppa doompa doom
that is the emotion

(97-98)

Repetition of phrase, word, and idea but in slightly different forms each time—a process at the heart of African music—characterizes this extract. Baraka refers to emotion as "the emotion," "our emotion," and "us emotion" at different points in the poem. This creates multiple sound effects—a complex singularity. He mixes and varies his syllabic constructs as well. He talks about the "love emotion," the "love heat," and the "snowball, / heat." These rhythmical variations set the poem free as surely as blues, jazz, and calypso set people's spirits free during Carnival.

In the essay **"Expressive Language,"** Baraka articulates the need for a new speech to undermine hierarchies of Western meaning; and he searches for this voice in African rhythms. Baraka feels that the twisting of meanings by dominant language forms has been a cause of great confusion and ignorance, both on the part of the dominated and the dominator, the latter having convinced himself that his distortions are justified and are, in effect, solid reasoning and no distortion at all. The Slave Trade was blessed by the religious and political leaders in Europe because, to them, the African was a heathen whose enslavement was therefore a natural punishment by God for his sinful nature. Projective verse as used by Baraka and other Third World writers attempts to tear down the hierarchical language structures which have consolidated that illusory view of Western superiority by overesteeming and inflating Western importance.

Like his Caribbean counterparts, Baraka also recognizes the need for creolization in poetic expression. He realizes that the black man is, after all, a product of mixed origins—African and European. Baraka notes, therefore, that socialization "which is rooted in culture depends for its impetus for the most part on the multiplicity of influences," on "other cultures," and on the "reaction and interaction of one culture on the other [to] produce a social context that will extend or influence any culture in many strange directions" (373). This means that projective verse as a mode of articulating this ethnical reality is of paramount importance since, in order for a society and hence for a poem which mirrors that society to go in "many strange directions," the society or poem must contain a form of *raison d'être* which harmonizes with that many-sidedness and which is creolized and open. Conventional, static forms are at best artificial for a people of plural background when they seek to reflect that plural world. Baraka realizes this when, in the essay **"Hunting is not for Those Heads on the Wall,"** he points out that formal "artifacts made to cohere to preconceived forms are almost devoid of . . . verb value" (379).

This process of artistic creation can be seen as an extension of the way a society functions at the social, political, cultural, and economic levels; and, if this process is cast as formalized artifact and not as dynamic drilling kinesis (which defines any form of plurality), then every aspect of that society's expressiveness will remain static. This static socialization and acculturation will limit perception, blindfold vision, and give an unrealistic presentation of the plural, creolized society.

Projective verse is thus compatible with the essential nature of the black experience, an experience which is open, constantly defining and redefining itself as it discovers and rediscovers aspects of itself projecting towards a more definitive future. Just as the Civil Rights Movement evolved into the Black Liberation Movement, so too did Black American poetry evolve from early Gwendolyn Brooks sonnets into Baraka's radical projective verse. Caribbean poetry too moved from Hilton Vaughan's sonnets to Brathwaite's "nation language." Their poetry, like their jazz, reggae, and calypso music (and now Kellman's poetic experiments with the Barbados ruk-a-tuk music form), extricated itself from the unnecessary and irrelevant aspects of literary convention. As black people were breaking out of the ghettos, out of colonial rule, and more recently out of neo-colonial bondage, their music and their poetry were emancipating themselves as well. Their poetry found and still finds its medium, its field, in projective verse, a form that most closely relates to the changing social and cultural scenes in which it is written.

Works Cited

Baraka, Amiri. "Class Struggle in Music" (I). *The Music: Reflections on Jazz and Blues.* Amiri Baraka and Amina Baraka. New York: Morrow, 1987. 96-99.

———. "Greenwich Village and African-American Music." *The Music: Reflections on Jazz and Blues.* Amiri Baraka and Amina Baraka. New York: Morrow, 1987. 181-89.

———. "I Love Music." *The Music: Reflections on Jazz and Blues.* Amiri Baraka and Amina Baraka. New York: Morrow, 1987. 47-48.

———. "Expressive Language." *The Poetics of the New American Poetry.* Ed. Donald Allen and Thomas Warren. New York: Grove Press, 1973. 373-77.

———. "Hunting is not for Those Heads on the Wall." *The Poetics of the New American Poetry.* Ed. Donald Allen and Thomas Warren. New York: Grove Press, 1973. 378-82.

Brathwaite, Edward. "Wings of a Dove." *The Arrivants: A New World Trilogy.* Oxford: Oxford UP, 1973. 42-45.

———. *History of the Voice.* London: New Beacon Books, 1984. 8.

———. "Dies Irie." *X/SELF.* Oxford: Oxford UP, 1987. 37-39.

Kellman, Anthony. "Watercourse." *Watercourse.* Yorkshire: Peepal Tree Press, 1990.

Olson, Charles. "Projective Verse." *The Poetics of the New American Poetry.* Ed. Donald Allen and Thomas Warren. New York: Grove Press, 1973. 147-58.

Walcott, Derek. "The Spoiler's Return." *Collected Poems 1948-1984.* New York: Farrar, 1986. 432-38.

Donna Seaman (review date 15 October 1995)

SOURCE: Seaman, Donna. Review of *Transbluesency: The Selected Poems of Amiri Baraka/LeRoi Jones (1961-1995),* by Amiri Baraka. *Booklist* 92, no. 4 (15 October 1995): 380.

[*In the following favorable review of* Transbluesency, *Seaman praises the provocative and introspective nature of Baraka's poetry.*]

Baraka, formerly LeRoi Jones, is a significant, innovative, controversial, and all too often misunderstood American writer with an international consciousness. In the past, most critics were stingy in their attention to overtly political poets and not up to the sort of fluidity Baraka embodies. But that's all so much dust, especially in light of the lyric boldness of this passionate collection [***Transbluesency: The Selected Poems of Amiri Baraka/LeRoi Jones (1961-1995)***]. Initially, Baraka was loosely connected with the Beats but soon moved on to become a major figure in the 1960s black arts movement, a fervent black nationalist, and an outspoken

Marxist. While his political awareness evolved, he continued to seek expression for, to quote editor Vangelisti, "the spirit of negritude," and to bring his molten poems to a boil with the force of music. This rich and impressively varied selection begins with **"Preface to a Twenty Volume Suicide Note"** (1961) and ends with **"Wise, Why's, Y'z"** (1995). Baraka can be as ravishingly introspective as he can be caustically political, but he is always questioning, always testing boundaries, always jiggling the locked doors of our hearts and consciences.

Peter Nazareth (review date winter 1997)

SOURCE: Nazareth, Peter. Review of *Transbluesency: The Selected Poems of Amiri Baraka/LeRoi Jones (1961-1995),* by Amiri Baraka. *World Literature Today* 71, no. 1 (winter 1997): 154-55.

[*In the following review, Nazareth deems Baraka's poetry valuable, yet occasionally irritating and difficult.*]

In the sixties, while I was in Uganda, I knew of LeRoi Jones because of his radical, stark plays ***Dutchman*** and ***Slave.*** When I came to the U.S. in 1973, I read his essays, chiefly ***Blues People.*** It was in the eighties that I first heard him read his poems, and I was amazed that he sounded so much like Haki Madhubuti in the jazz-like rhythms which hit inventively against exploitation and exorcised the ghosts of history. So I was amused to read in [***Transbluesency,***] **"AM/TRAK,"** a poem which begins "Trane, / Trane, / History Love Scream Oh / Trane": "(If Don Lee thinks I am imitating him in this poem, / this is only payback for his imitating me—we / are brothers, even if he is a backward cultural nationalist / motherfucker—Hey man only socialism brought by revolution / can win)." There is a hint here of "the dozens" from African American (male) tradition: he is calling Madhubuti by his former name. There is no doubt he is playing the dozens in **"Red Eye,"** which is for Calvin Hernton and Ishmael Reed ("Look in your mother's head, / if you really want to know everything. Your sister's locked up / pussy"). I recall Reed writing that Baraka was always seeking a leader, perhaps an explanation for all the chameleonlike changes Baraka has gone through—"from Beat to Black Nationalist to Marxist-Leninist," the blurb says. Each phase rejected, poems nevertheless survive: ***Transbluesency*** is subtitled "The Selected Poems of Amiri Baraka/LeRoi Jones (1961-1995)."

The poems are "punny," provocative, sarcastic, annoying. I am irritated by "Elvis Presley was the FDR of / the 1950's, the philosophy / was workable & when the / Beatles moved in simply slander / them w/belittling Jesus / & enlarge the American market. / Nigger music became figure / music." I feel Baraka is diminishing and misunderstanding Elvis in the very slick and unexplained linkage with FDR—but I am not sure because Baraka is not speaking to me. Hey, I can be as personal in a review as Baraka can in a poem. He has something to anger everyone, including gays (**"Death Is Not as Natural as You Fags Seem To Think"**). Yet there is humor and lyricism in his work.

In a fine introduction Paul Vangelisti states, "This selection traces the almost forty-year career of a writer who, along with Ezra Pound, may be one of the most significant and least understood American poets of our century." Noting that Baraka is a politicized avant-garde poet "seeking an alternative form of aesthetic and social behavior," Vangelisti says his work is "firmly outside Anglo-American culture." Referring to several of Baraka's volumes of poetry, he concludes: "The lyricism of the early books has been challenged and extended to where it is inseparable from his thought, ideological or otherwise. It has become, as he wrote in eulogy of Miles Davis, 'a prayer in the future.' Baraka's is a verbal music that presages and defines what is to come."

That is a good note on which to end a review of a valuable volume I have not absorbed but must keep reentering, for the editor says the title, taken from a Duke Ellington composition, means "A blue fog you can almost see through."

Donna Seaman (review date 1 & 15 January 1997)

SOURCE: Seaman, Donna. Review of *Funk Lore,* by Amiri Baraka. *Booklist* 93, nos. 9-10 (1 & 15 January 1997): 807, 809.

[*In the following review, Seaman applauds the uplifting poems in* Funk Lore.]

For more than three decades Baraka has lifted his strong and resonant voice as a poet, dramatist, essayist, and activist, protesting and celebrating the injustices and the blessings, the tragedies and the triumphs of African American life. This volume [***Funk Lore***], gathers together 11 years worth of new, uncollected poems, and the swing of Baraka's musical lines makes itself felt in the very first poem, which is titled, aptly enough, **"J. said, 'Our whole universe is generated by a rhythm.'"** Music and poetry are saving graces, and jazz musicians, from Louis Armstrong to John Coltrane, ride the waves of these surging poems, icons of the creative spirit, of freedom and improvisation. One of Baraka's most cherished words is ascendancy, and his poems (some as terse as a curse, others as luxurious as a courtship) are, indeed, uplifting as they dissect the cruelty of oppression and hypocrisy, then revel in the hot funkiness of love, the liberation of integrity, and the comfort of spirituality. This is a potent follow-up to Baraka's selected poems. ***Transbluesency*** (1995).

Melani McAlister (essay date September 1999)

SOURCE: McAlister, Melani. "One Black Allah: The Middle East in the Cultural Politics of African American Liberation, 1955-1970." *American Quarterly* 51, no. 3 (September 1999): 622-56.

[*In the following essay, McAlister considers the influence of the Nation of Islam on black writers in the 1960s and 1970s, focusing on Baraka's one-act play* A Black Mass.]

> The Christian church itself—again, as distinguished from some of its ministers—sanctified and rejoiced in the conquests of the flag, and encouraged, if it did not formulate, the belief that conquest, and the resulting relative well-being of the Western population, was proof of the favor of God. God had come a long way from the desert—but then, so had Allah, though in a very different direction. God, going north and rising on the wings of power, had become white, and Allah, out of power, had become—for all practical purposes anyway—black.
>
> —James Baldwin, 1962[1]

> The Arabs, as a colored people, should and must make more effort to reach the millions of colored people in America who are related to the Arabs by blood. These millions of colored peoples would be completely in sympathy with the Arab cause!
>
> —Malcolm X, 22 1960[2]

Two events, separated by just over a year, in two very different spheres of cultural activity, marked the extraordinary influence of Islam in the African American community in the 1960s. Two prominent African American men, one an athlete, the other a poet and a playwright, took highly visible and conscious steps away from their old identities and affiliations and began instead to articulate a black consciousness and politics based on the teachings of Islam. These two public transformations—rituals of self-identification and self-naming—point toward and often-neglected genealogy of black political and cultural affiliation: an African American imagined community in which the Arab Middle East is central.

On 25 February 1964, the twenty-three-year old fighter Cassius Clay defeated Sonny Liston and took the world heavyweight boxing title, the most lucrative prize in professional sports. On the day after his triumph, Clay, who had already become one of the most well-known and controversial figures in boxing world, announced at a press conference that he was a Muslim.[3] Until that day, Clay had been known as a playful, rather apolitical youngster with a fondness for pink Cadillacs, extravagant bragging, and comic poetry.[4] But in the months before the fight, rumors of his association with the Nation of Islam (NOI) had circulated widely; he had been seen frequently in the company of Malcolm X, whom he had invited to his training camp in Miami.[5] A few weeks after the victory, Elijah Muhammad, the leader of the Nation of Islam, bestowed on Clay his Muslim name, Muhammad Ali. Ali's victory and subsequent announcement were widely reported; his association with the NOI was often viewed with skepticism or anger. In the spring of 1964, when Malcolm X left the Nation, Ali stayed, and quickly became the most famous Black Muslim in the country and one of the Nation of Islam's most prominent spokespersons.[6] Just a few months later, Ali embarked on a tour of Africa and the Middle East. When he returned, he announced to the press: "I'm not an American; I'm a black man."[7]

In 1966, Ali's status as political figure took a new direction when he refused his induction into the U.S. Army, saying "I'm a member of the Black Muslims, and we don't go to no wars unless they're declared by Allah himself. I don't have no personal quarrel with those Viet Congs."[8] That refusal—that risky stand on behalf of the politics of his religious belief—transformed Ali's image: he soon became one of the most visible and influential antiwar figures in the country. He was, in the words of poet Sonia Sanchez, "a cultural resource for everyone in that time," a man whose refusal to fight in Vietnam became an emblem of the far reaching influence of the black nationalist critique of American nationalism and U.S. foreign policy.[9]

In 1965, a little over a year after Muhammad Ali's highly public conversion, the poet and playwright LeRoi Jones left his literary circles in Greenwich Village to move uptown to Harlem, where he founded the Black Arts Repertory Theatre/School (BARTS). In Harlem, Jones turned his back on his earlier ties with Beat poetry, and even his more recent success with plays on race relations (***The Dutchman*** had won an Obie award in 1964).[10] He focused instead on the task of building a community theater, and on developing the themes and writing styles that would launch the Black Arts Movement. During his time at BARTS, Jones wrote ***A Black Mass,*** a one-act play that presented in dramatic form the Nation of Islam's central myth: the story of Yacub, the evil scientist who "invented" white people. Then, in 1968, Jones changed his name to Ameer (later to Amiri) Baraka. He studied Sunni Islam under the tutelage of Hajj Heesham Jaaber, who had been affiliated with Malcolm X near the end of his life.[11] By then, Baraka, whom his contemporaries considered to be "the most promising black writer" in the nation, was also the best-known representative of the Black Arts Movement, a champion of black cultural nationalism, a significant theorist of the re-emergence of committed art, and an articulate critic of U.S. imperialism. Baraka would turn away from Islam and toward Maoism in the 1970s.[12] But from at least 1965 until 1973, he and others saw Islam as a primary nationalist cultural resource, an authentically black religion that would be central to the requisite development of an alternative black culture and a liberated spirituality.

This article analyses the significance of the Middle East in African American cultural politics in the late 1950s and 1960s. In particular, it explores the impact of Islam as a religious practice and as a cultural poetics, including its more diffuse impact even on those who were not converts. In recent years, scholars in religious studies have amply documented the remarkable diversity of Muslim practice among African Americans, from orthodox Sunni Islam to the less traditional doctrines of the Nation of Islam, but the larger political and cultural influence of Islam as a religious/cultural/political nexus has been remarkably neglected.[13] In the 1960s, this influence was significant. By 1965 or 1966, one need not have ever entered a Muslim temple nor read a Nation of Islam newspaper to know that, within the African American community, Islam had moved far beyond the sectarian curiosity it had been just ten years earlier. In a cultural field that ranged from poetry and plays to highly charged sports matches, from local community theaters to the boxing ring, Islam was a significant presence. In various manifestations, Islam—and the Nation of Islam in particular—played a central role in reconfigurations of black radicalism, challenging both the hegemony of black Christianity's religious values and the politics of integration associated with it. At the same time, the centrality of the Middle East to Islamic histories and to many Muslim rituals encouraged the increasing visibility of Arab cultures and Arab politics in African American communities.

Islam, like Christianity, has traditionally turned to the Middle East as a "holy land," making salient not only its ancient histories, but also contemporary political events in the region. In the 1950s and 1960s, this religiously-infused transnationalism gained a broader currency: African Americans in this period constructed cultural, political, and historical links between their contemporary situation and the Arab Middle East. In doing so, they articulated what Michael Shapiro has called a "moral geography," a mapping of themselves in relationship to the world. This moral geography imagined a community very different from dominant constructions of "America." And despite the fact that what emerged from this mapping has often been called (even by its adherents) "black nationalism," the community it envisioned provided an alternative to—and in some sense a fundamental critique of—the nation-state.[14] I will trace several sites for this alternative geography: the religious teachings and daily practices of the Nation of Islam; the influence that the Nation of Islam and other Muslim sects had on cultural producers, especially the young men and women who would become the heart of the Black Arts movement; and finally, the impact of both religion and art on the anticolonial radicalism of a new generation of African Americans. By 1967, these connected influences had become an important factor in African American understandings of U.S. foreign policy in the Middle East, particularly the 1967 Arab-Israeli war.

Scholarship on the 1960s, so often interested in tracing the sources of black radicalism, as well as the rising tensions between blacks and Jews in the civil rights movement, has consistently painted the Nation of Islam as simply a political movement with a religious gloss.[15] As a result, a whole history of cultural production and religious belief has been seen as marginal, or merely reactive. This analysis suggests a more expansive framework for understanding black culture in this period. It highlights the cultural politics of non-Christian religious formations, suggesting that a proper understanding of the salience of religion in the African American community (and in the United States more broadly) must look beyond the well-documented influence of the Judeo-Christian tradition. By attending to this cultural and religious history, our understanding of *political* events also becomes more nuanced and complex. In particular, we begin to see the ways in which African American investments in, and interpretations of, the Arab-Israeli conflict developed, at least in part, out of the religious and cultural alternatives to black Christianity that become influential in the 1960s.

By History and By Blood

> [T]he historic practice of bowing to other men's gods and definitions has produced a crisis of the highest magnitude, and brought us, culturally, to the limits of racial armageddon.
>
> —Addison Gayle, 1968[16]

In the early to mid-1960s, the Nation of Islam brought its interpretation of Islam to prominence in the African American community, and defined Islam as the religion of black American militancy. For African Americans disaffected with the Christian church—those frustrated by the commitment of black Christians to brotherhood with whites or angered by the continuing violence by white Christians against nonviolent civil rights activists—Islam offered an alternative. Islam, its adherents argued, provided the basis for a black nationalist consciousness that was separate from the civil rights goals of integration into a white-dominated and oppressive nation. Islam offered a set of values and beliefs that were at once spiritual, political, and cultural. As

LeRoi Jones described it, Islam offered "what the Black man needs, a reconstruction . . . a total way of life that he can involve himself with that is post-American, in a sense."[17] The Nation of Islam in particular provided an both an alternative religious affiliation and a counter-citizenship, an identity that challenged black incorporation into the dominant discourse of Judeo-Christian American-ness.

The NOI emerged as a significant social and political force in the black community in the late 1950s after a period of disarray and declining membership in the 1940s. When Malcolm X was released from Norfolk prison in 1952, he quickly came to play a major role in the organization's expansion, establishing temples in cities all over the country. By December 1959, the Nation had fifty temples in twenty-two states; the number of members in the organization is difficult to estimate, but by 1962 was probably in the range of 50,000 to 100,000, with many more supporters. In 1962, *Muhammed Speaks,* the major NOI newspaper, founded by Malcolm X, had the largest circulation of any black paper in the country.[18]

Although the Nation of Islam was an avowedly "black nationalist" organization, its vision of black nationalism cannot be fully understood separate from either its explicitly religious content or its insistently transnational dimensions. In fact, the religious and the transnational aspects were intimately related: while the Nation of Islam was *unorthodox* Islam, Elijah Muhammad had, since the 1930s, consistently affirmed the significance of its connection to other Muslim communities around the globe, particularly those in the Middle East. The Nation challenged the assumption that African Americans were simply or primarily a subset of all Americans; its political imaginary never posited black nationalism as a self-contained sub-nationalism, even when Elijah Muhammad or Malcolm X made claims for the right to control specific tracts of land within the United States. Instead, the NOI built on the fact that Islam was a major world religion with a strong transnational orientation; Muslim governments and Muslim communities often forged ties across borders, politically and culturally, as well as religiously.[19] Drawing on this global vision, the NOI developed a model of community that linked African Americans both to Africa and to "Asia" (by Asia, Elijah Muhammad seemed to mean primarily what is usually called the Middle East).[20] By the time it began to reach a larger audience in the 1950s, the Nation of Islam's vision drew on several decades of black anticolonialist activity, led by intellectuals and activists from W. E. B. Du Bois to Paul Robeson to Walter White, which had envisioned African Americans as part of a pan-African diaspora.[21] At the same time, the Nation's theological politics departed from that earlier activism's primary focus on Africa, opting for a more expansive transnationalism that included much of the non-white world (Latin America is something of an exception). Like the pan-Africanist intellectual and cultural movements of the 1930s and 1940s, however, Elijah Muhammad described the connections between African Americans and colonized peoples through a language of naturalized race. Muhammad simply claimed both Africa and the Middle East as black heritage, insisting that the Arabian peninsula and the Nile valley were the historic home of what he called the "Afro-Asiatic black man" now living in America.

The significance of this religious and racial geography was profound. In the NOI temples being rapidly established in urban areas in the late 1950s and early 1960s, ministers brought a message of worldwide black Islam to thousands of African American converts.[22] The Nation taught that Islam was the "natural religion of the black man," which had been stripped from the Africans who were sold into slavery and taught their masters' Christianity. Lectures in the temples often harshly indicted the traditional Christianity of the African American church and argued that African Americans should recognize their true heritage as the descendants of the Muslim prophet Muhammed. Arabic, the Nation taught, was the original language of black people, not only because many of the Africans who were taken into slavery and carried to the new world spoke Arabic, but also because "the so-called Negroes" in America were descendants of the original Arabic-speaking peoples to whom Islam was revealed.[23] As the religious service began, the minister greeted his parishioners with the Arabic greeting: *As-salaam-alaikum* (peace be with you) and the members responded, *wa-Alaikum as-salaam* (and also with you). At the Islamic schools set up by the Nation. Arabic lessons were an integral part of the curriculum: Arabic language instruction was said to began at the age of three.[24]

The Nation's theology included an alternative genealogy for black Americans, who were understood to be descendants of the original inhabitants of Asia in general and Mecca in particular. As Elijah Muhammad wrote in his 1965 treatise, *Message to the Blackman in America*: "It is Allah's (God's) will and purpose that we shall know ourselves. . . . He has declared that we are descendants of the Asian black nation and the tribe of Shabazz . . . [t]he first to discover the best part of our planet to live on. The rich Nile Valley of Egypt and the present seat of the Holy City, Mecca, Arabia."[25]

The Nation of Islam's assertion that all black people were by nature Muslims was part of its critique of black Christianity—a critique that was at once theological, political, and historical. NOI meetings often had a display, drawn on a blackboard, featuring two flags: on one side of the board was a U.S. flag with a cross beside it, and underneath it the caption, "Slavery, Suffering, and Death." On the other side was drawn a flag bearing the Crescent, and underneath it the words, "Islam: Freedom, Justice, and Equality." Beneath both was a question: "Which one will survive the War of Armageddon?"[26] Elijah Muhammad's message to African Americans focused on pride and transformation. The Christianity of their slave masters had functioned to continue their spiritual enslavement, he argued, but Islam, which built upon the teachings of the Bible but succeeded them with additional revelations, would provide the key for understanding old teachings in the way they were intended, rather than through the perversions of white Christianity. In this way, NOI teaching revised, without discarding, important aspects of Christian symbolism that were salient in the black community.[27] At the same time, this teaching also carried with it a racial, political, and moral geography: it pitted (black) Islam against (white) Christianity in a world-wide and historic struggle.

This religious mapping of the world—a practice certainly not unique to Islam or the Nation—was directly opposed to contemporary black Christian constructions of the Middle East as a "Holy Land" in which Israel (both ancient and modern) was a strong source of religious and political identification. Black Christianity had traditionally presented African American history as a not-yet-completed retelling of the Hebrew story, a potential site for the re-entry of God into history on the side of a people.[28] By the late 1950s, the Christian-dominated civil rights movement was making highly effective use of the exodus as a figure for African American liberation. The alliance between African Americans and Jews in the early civil rights movement, though grounded in the active Jewish participation in the movement, was almost certainly strengthened by a strong metaphorical affiliation between the narrative of ancient Hebrew liberation from bondage and the purposeful imagining of African American liberation from discrimination in the United States. The exodus trope was a link, one articulated in churches and meetings, in songs and in sermons, as well as in the writings of African American intellectuals and activists, from Martin Luther King, Jr. to James Baldwin to Joseph Lowrey.[29]

The connection that Black Christians felt with the Hebrew story extended into contemporary international politics. The establishment of modern Israel in 1948 was a source of enthusiasm and even inspiration for many African Americans: In 1947, Walter White, the Executive Director of the NAACP, had played a crucial role in lobbying African nations to vote for the UN resolution partitioning Palestine into Jewish and Arab areas. Ralph Bunche, the UN Secretary for Peacekeeping, was active in negotiating the end to the Arab-Israeli war in 1948 on terms generally considered favorable to Israel. And in 1948, the NAACP passed a resolution stating that "the valiant struggle of the people of Israel for independence serves as an inspiration to all persecuted people throughout the world."[30]

Martin Luther King, Jr. exemplified the move that connected biblical history with contemporary politics. He believed that civil rights was part of an international transformation in power relations. He saw the rise of anticolonialism and the rise of civil rights activity not only as parallel sets of events, but as a connected force, with the two movements affecting and influencing each other in direct ways: everywhere, the enslaved people were rising up against Pharaoh and demanding to be free.[31] The success of the new nationalisms, particularly in Africa, Egypt, and India, provided a living model for the kind of successful struggle that King envisioned in the United States. Within this frame, Israel, as one of the "new nations" seeking freedom and national rights, represented a relevant model made all the more powerful by the biblical story of exile and return, and by the ways in which this rhetoric had played a central role in the successful transformation of the Zionist movement into the Israeli state.[32]

The Nation of Islam's vision of a world-wide Islamic alliance confronting white Christianity challenged the black Christian sanctification of ancient Israel and offered an alternative sacred geography with Mecca as its center. Significantly, Elijah Muhammad taught that the stories told in the Christian Bible were prophesies rather than histories, and that, as prophesy, they spoke of the contemporary experiences of African Americans rather than the historical experiences of the ancient Hebrews:

> Before the coming of Allah (God), we being blind, deaf, and dumb, had mistaken the true meanings of these parables as referring to the Jews. Now, thanks to Almighty God, Allah . . . who has opened my blinded eyes, and unstopped my ears, loosened the knot in my tongue, and has made us to understand these Bible parables are referring to us, the so-called Negroes and our slave masters.[33]

Within the NOI paradigm, Jews were not those whose ancient history was the prototype for contemporary liberation, as was the case for King and other civil rights leaders, but those whose putative status as "the chosen people" had usurped the position of the black people in relation to God. This scriptural interpretation did a complex cultural work for the Nation. Surely this metaphorical removal of Jews from the stories of the Old Testament had particular salience in terms of the domestic tensions that were already rife in urban areas between African Americans and Jews.[34] Obviously, it carried the kernels of the NOI's anti-Semitism, which become more and more pronounced over the decade. But the specifically religious content also worked affirmatively as well, by mobilizing, appropriating, and refashioning an honored tradition to claim for African American Islam, as earlier Christianity had done with Judaism, or as the Romans did with Greek mythology.

This mixture of denigration and affirmative appropriation was also apparent in the Nation's attitude toward modern Israel. Like earlier black nationalist movements, the NOI saw in the success of Zionism an example and motivation for black nationalism.[35] Malcolm X often referred to Israel respectfully in his speeches and interviews, even as he insisted on the rightness of the Palestinian cause, as in this remarkably ambiguous passage from his *Autobiography*:

> If Hitler *had* conquered the world, as he meant to—that is a shuddery thought for every Jew alive today. The Jew will never forget that lesson. . . . [T]he British acquiesced and helped them to wrest Palestine away from the Arabs, the rightful owners, and then the Jews set up Israel, their own country—the one thing that every race of man in the world respects, and understands.[36]

This grudging respect did not translate into emotional identification with Zionism's success, as it did within much black Christian discourse, but it did further establish the complex meanings the Middle East held for the Nation of Islam and its members. If, as nationalists, they respected and even hoped to emulate Jewish nationalism, they nonetheless saw the Arab struggle with Israel as a parallel to the Nation of Islam's struggle for national self-determination in the United States, where the Nation claimed the right to "separate" from the rest of the United States by taking control of three or four states in the South for black people. Both the Arab (largely Muslim) population in Israel/Palestine and the black ("originally Muslim") population in the United States were in a struggle over land: control over that land was essential to nationalism and political rights.

In keeping with this sympathy, Malcolm X exhibited a detailed and early attention to international relations. Inspired and influenced by events in the third world, Malcolm X often talked about the 1955 Asian-African Conference at Bandung, Indonesia, (attended by Egyptian president Nasser, Indian prime minister Nehru, and representatives from twenty-seven other African, Asia, and Arab nations) as one example of the affiliation of non-white peoples against colonialism.[37] After being appointed minister of the Harlem mosque in 1954, Malcolm X established active contacts with many Arab and African leaders at the United Nations, who in turn seemed to view the members of the Nation as fellow travelers—though their practice of Islam was highly unorthodox, they were potentially valuable allies in the struggle against imperialism.[38]

Of the many connections the Nation established, those with Egypt were particularly important. The focus on Egypt developed for several reasons: first, like most black nationalists, NOI leaders believed emphatically that Egypt was a black nation and that the greatness of ancient Egyptian civilization was proof of the historical greatness of black culture.[39] Second, Egypt was (and is) largely a Muslim nation, therefore it embodied the link between ancient black greatness and contemporary Islam.

Finally, there was Egypt's leader, Gamal Abdel Nasser, who had come to power in a bloodless coup against the British-backed king in 1952. In the mid-1950s, Nasser had emerged as the most important nationalist leader of the Arab world and as one of the major figures of the anticolonial non-aligned movement. Along with figures like Castro in Cuba and Kwame Nkrumah in Ghana, Nasser represented an emotionally explosive convergence of anticolonial defiance and postcolonial global consciousness.[40] But Nasser, as the leader of Egypt, also represented a particular connection between black and Arab anticolonialism: Just as Egypt was geographically positioned at the intersection of the Middle East and Africa, in the years after Bandung, Nasser positioned himself as a leader in connecting African and Asian anticolonial movements.

In 1956, Nasser became an anti-imperialist icon when he nationalized the Suez Canal Company, after president Eisenhower had refused to support U.S. loans for the construction of the Aswan High Dam. In response to the nationalization of the canal, Britain (the former colonial power), France, and Israel invaded Egypt; both the United States and the Soviet Union (for different reasons) demanded the immediate withdrawal of the invading forces.[41] The U.S. opposition to the invasion was widely viewed as a refusal to back the imposition of old-style colonialism in the Middle East; not coincidentally, it was also an assertion of American dominance in the region.

But Nasser emerged from Suez the real winner. His successful weathering of an invasion by the colonial powers made him a hero in the decolonizing nations, as well as among many African Americans. Nasser, an avowed Arab nationalist, also came to represent black and African defiance. Not surprisingly, the Nation of Islam endorsed the Egyptian seizure of the Suez canal and opposed the invasion in its various publications.[42] And though the Suez crisis did not receive as extensive coverage as Bandung had in the rest of the black press (which was focused on the Montgomery bus boycott and other developments in the emergent civil rights movement), many black intellectuals also responded critically. Right after Suez, W. E. B. Du Bois, a longtime supporter of Israel, hailed Nasser (and criticized Israel's role in the invasion) in a poem published in *Masses and Mainstream*: "Beware, white world, that great black hand / Which Nasser's power waves / Grasps hard the concentrated hate / Of myriad million slaves."[43] Observers would later look back on Suez as something of a turning point in African American perceptions of the Middle East—the moment in which Arab anticolonialism came home to black Americans.[44]

The Nation of Islam identified with colonized nations politically, from the standpoint of a "colored" nation oppressed by whites, but it also drew very specifically on cultural and religious identifications with Arab nations, which were understood to be also racial and historical. A year after Suez, in December 1957, Malcolm X organized a meeting on colonial and neocolonial issues that included representatives from the governments of Egypt, the Sudan, Ghana, Iraq, and Morocco. That meeting, hosted by the Nation, sent a cable from Elijah Muhammad to Nasser, who was hosting the Afro-Asian People's Solidarity Conference in Cairo. In it, Elijah Muhammad, describing himself as the "Spiritual Head of the Nation of Islam in the West," addressed Nasser and the other national leaders as brothers, as co-religionists, and as peers:

> As-Salaam-Alikum. Your long lost Muslim brothers here in America pray that Allah's divine presence will be felt at this historic African-Asian Conference, and give unity to our efforts for peace and brotherhood.
>
> Freedom, justice, and equality for all Africans and Asians is of far-reaching importance, not only to you of the East, but also to over 17,000,000 of your long-lost brothers of African-Asian descent here in the West. . . . May our sincere desire for universal peace which is being manifested at this great conference by all Africans and Asians, bring about the unity and brotherhood among all our people which we all so eagerly desire.[45]

The cable, and Nasser's friendly reply, circulated widely within the Nation; these contacts later facilitated Malcolm X's trip to Egypt in 1959, where he laid the groundwork for Elijah Muhammad's visit to Mecca in 1960.[46]

The Nation of Islam made explicit the link between a shared heritage and shared origin: a myth of commonality remapped the dominant imaginative geography that separated the Middle East from Africa, instead uniting Africa and North West Asia (the Middle East) into one geographical space deemed "black Asiastic-African." The vision of one black culture meant that blackness was no longer simply a synonym for Africans and people of recent African descent, but a *literal* linking together of large groups of non-Europeans—the "Asians and Africans" connected, in Malcolm X's words, by history and "by blood."

Elijah Muhammad's genealogical and political views were well-known in the early 1960s, both within and beyond the African American community. Mainstream media heavily reported the "Black Muslim" phenomenon, in multiple television specials and interviews (often with Malcolm X), paperback "reports," and newspaper and magazine articles.[47] The Nation of Islam was extensively discussed in public discourse surrounding *The Autobiography of Malcolm X,* which was published in 1965, just months after he was assassinated.[48] The organization was also covered in magazines with primarily black audiences.[49] In addition, the Nation made a concentrated effort to construct its own, alternative public sphere based on its a system of widely disseminated newspapers and large public meetings. From 1959 to 1961, the organization published five different newspapers and magazines on its own, one of which—*Muhammed Speaks,* launched in May 1960—became extraordinarily successful. By 1961, C. Eric Lincoln estimated that *Muhammed Speaks* had a circulation of over 600,000, "making it by far the most widely read paper in the black community."[50] Nation members also produced plays and songs: Louis Farrakhan (known as Louis X in this period) produced two plays in the early 1960s: *Orgena* ("a Negro," spelled backwards) and *The Trial,* both of which were performed for Muslim audiences at rallies and meetings. Farrakhan, who had been a Calypso singer before converting, also wrote and recorded several songs, including "White Man's Heaven is Black Man's Hell" and "Look at My Chains!"[51]

As cultural source and resource, then, the Nation of Islam functioned through diverse sites. As a religious and political organization, it took culture and media representation quite seriously, but it also had an impact in many spaces/locations that Elijah Muhammad did not directly control, and thus wielded significant influence well beyond its membership. One site for this more general diffusion of Islamic sensibility was the remarkable infusion of NOI mythology into the cultural products of the emerging Black Arts Movement, which would in turn influence the direction of black liberation politics as the decade drew to a close. The signs of the Nation were frequently incorporated into the productions of a new generation of young writers, who took the symbols and myths of this African American Islamic sect as part of the raw material for the production of a new, black, postnational culture.

"And We Own the Night"[52]

This is an introduction to a book of plays
    i am prophesying the death of white people in this
     land
    i am prophesying the triumph of black life in this land
    and over all the world
    we are building publishing houses, and newspapers,
     and armies and factories
        we will change the world before your eyes,
            izm-el-azam,
            yes, say it
            say it
          sweet nigger
      i believe in black allah
          governor of creation

Lord of the Worlds
As Salaam Alikum
—Amiri Baraka, 1969[53]

LeRoi Jones left Greenwich Village to found Harlem's Black Arts Repertory Theatre/School in 1965. Malcolm X had just been killed, and young African American intellectuals and activists found themselves and their communities in upheaval—in shock, torn by heated debates over the split between Malcolm X and Elijah Muhammad and by questions of who was responsible for the assassination. Then *The Autobiography of Malcolm X* was released; it became an immediate best-seller, creating a sensation within the circles of young, increasingly radicalized men and women who had listened to Malcolm X's speeches and were now riveted by the story of his life.[54] It was in this context, coming to terms with the death of the country's most important spokesperson for black radicalism, that Jones/Baraka set out to form a community-based popular theater, and to invent a form and language that would reach a broad African American audience with a message of black (post)nationalism. As Baraka later wrote, he and his colleagues wanted "[a]n art that would reach the people, that would take them higher, ready them for war and victory, as popular as the Impressions or the Miracles or Marvin Gaye. That was our vision and its image keep us stepping, heads high and backs straight."[55]

Though BARTS was short-lived (it collapsed within a year), its founding was an inspiration to a new generation of poets and playwrights. Black theater and poetry burst onto the national scene—a flowering of African American cultural production unlike anything since the Harlem Renaissance. Within a year, small community theater groups were being formed around the country (in San Francisco, Detroit, Chicago, Washington, D.C., Los Angeles). The new community theaters produced plays and held poetry readings, not only in theaters, but also in schools, at local meetings, and in the street.[56] Baraka himself was also a model; his transformation from highly literary poet into a radical artist committed to straightforward poetic language and generally short, accessible plays inspired the young writers who were publishing and performing in his wake (and quite consciously in his debt): Ed Bullins, Sonia Sanchez, Marvin X, Ben Caldwell, and Nikki Giovanni, among others.

In the next couple of years, several publishing houses devoted specifically to black literature were born, and new or revamped magazines chronicled the scene, including *Journal of Black Poetry, Black Books Bulletin, Black Theatre,* and, most importantly, *Negro Digest/Black World.*[57] By April 1966, *Negro Digest* would have its first of several annual issues on African Americans in theater; later that year, a San Francisco-based group, which included Baraka (who was a visiting professor at San Francisco State), would perform at the annual convention of the Congress of Racial Equality (CORE).[58] By 1967, the new black theater was being widely discussed as a major development in the arts of the decade, so much so that when Harold Cruse published *The Crisis of the Black Intellectual,* he ended the book with two chapters on African Americans and the theater, analyzing the significance of BARTS and declaring that "there can be a cultural method of revolutionizing the society in which the theater functions as an institution." A year later, the most important American drama journal published a special issue on black theater.[59]

Poetry and plays were the favored genres of the Black Arts movement, despite the fact that both had, up until this point, appealed to a very narrow audience. Both forms were, in Pierre Bourdieu's terms, sub-fields of highly restricted production, and both carried the cultural capital (and the distance from popular culture) that came with their elite position.[60] But the short poem, the one-act play are often more accessible to new or non-traditional writers, precisely because they are short, and Black Arts Movement artists tried with some success to broaden the audience for both genres. Writing in a self-consciously vernacular language, in free verse and street talk, and distributing work in small pamphlets and in magazines, in paperback anthologies, and in public performance, they aimed for a style and a format that was accessible and relevant to people who might otherwise be uninterested in or intimidated by "art." Like earlier avant-garde movements, they wanted to eradicate the separation of "art" from "life."[61] Ed Bullins, a playwright who began writing during this period and who went on to become one of the most prolific and most-produced playwrights of the late 1960s and early 1970s, argued (as many in the movement did) that Black theater and poetry were effectively transforming both the genres and their audiences:

> Black literature has been available for years, but it has been circulating in a closed circle. . . . It hasn't been getting down to the people. But now in the theatre, we can go right into the black community and have a literature for the people . . . for the great masses of Black people. I think this is the reason that more Black plays are being written and seen, and the reason that more Black theatres are springing up. Through the efforts of certain Black artists, people are beginning to realize the importance of Black theatre.[62]

The genuine popularity and broad reach of these new works is only part of the story, however; no matter how many performances they gave in local venues, or how many inexpensive editions they distributed, these poets and playwrights never had the kind of direct reach enjoyed by major political or religious groups, including the Nation of Islam itself. Nonetheless, they could have a significant impact precisely because of the prestige that art, even popularized art, carried—the status it gave within the African American community, as well as the notoriety that the new artists were gaining in the mainstream (white-dominated) media. The mix was potent: cultural capital combined with a new, populist approach and a broader audience. It gave art and artists and highly visible role in the African American community overall, and among younger radicals in particular, and it allowed for the dissemination and generalization of radical political and cultural perspectives. Thus already by 1966, the influence of Black Arts was strong enough that the new chair of the Student Nonviolent Coordinating Committee (SNCC), Stokley Carmichael, asserted that poetry writing (and by extension, poetry reading) were threatening to overtake other kinds of political work. In a speech reprinted in the Chicago SNCC newsletter, he complained: "We have to say, 'Don't play jive and start writing poems after Malcolm is shot.' We have to move from the point where the man left off and stop writing poems."[63]

The Black Arts movement defined political struggle *as* cultural struggle; this cultural transformation, in turn, required a new spirituality. In literary circles, Islamic symbolism and mythology were incorporated into the self-conscious construction of a new black aesthetic and a revolutionary black culture. The aim was to establish a basis for political nationalism through the production of a set of cultural and spiritual values "in tune with black people." Those seeking black power were called upon to understand the significance of culture. As Baraka argued, "The socio-political must be a righteous extension of the cultural. . . . A cultural base, a black base, is the completeness the black power movement must have. We must understand that we are *Replacing* a dying [white] culture, and we must be prepared to do this, and be absolutely conscious of what we are replacing it with."[64] The attempt to construct a new black culture was deeply intertwined with the search for religious alternatives to mainstream Christianity, a search that included not only Islam, but also a renewed interest in the signs and symbols of pre-Islamic and traditional African religions (such as the Yoruban religion), and the study of ancient Egypt. These influences were often mixed together, in Baraka's thought as elsewhere, in an eclectic, sometimes deliberately mystical, mix.

Baraka's ***A Black Mass*** exemplifies the cross-fertilization and appropriation that linked Islam and the Black Arts movement in the self-conscious production of a black mythology. The play was based on the story of Yacub, the evil scientist who created white people, as told by Elijah Muhammad and recounted repeatedly in publications and speeches. "Yacub's History" was "the central myth" of the Nation; it told the story of black origins and explained the current plight of black people, while reversing the traditional associations of Eurocentric Christianity, making "whiteness" the category associated with evil and thus in need of explanation.[65] (The story also provided the background and justification for the Nation's provocative practice of referring to whites as "devils.") ***A Black Mass*** was first written in 1965 while Baraka was at BARTS; it was first performed in Newark in May 1966 (after BARTS folded and Baraka moved to Newark to form Spirit House) and a month later was published in the little magazine *The Liberator.* In 1969, it was included in Baraka's collection, ***Four Black Revolutionary Plays.***[66]

When Baraka wrote ***A Black Mass,*** he was not a member of the Nation of Islam, not even identified as a Muslim, though he would affiliate with orthodox Sunni Islam a few years later. Baraka would always mix Islam with his support of Kawaida, Ron Karenga's syncretic doctrine based on traditional African religions, but his fascination with the story of Yacub and his general interest in the myths of the Nation of Islam was not idiosyncratic.[67] Thus, though ***A Black Mass*** was not produced as often as some of Baraka's more explicit social commentary, Black Arts critics admired it. The editor and essayist Larry Neal, who was also Baraka's friend and colleague, described it as Baraka's "most important play," because "it is informed by a mythology that is wholly the creation of the Afro-American sensibility."[68] Another commentator writing in *Negro Digest* called it "Jones' most accomplished play to date."[69] The play was an early, explicit statement of the ways in which, even after the death of Malcolm X and even with suspicions about Elijah Muhammad's role in his murder, the beliefs of the Nation of Islam were often presented *as* black culture, influencing and infusing a new black sensibility even for those who were not NOI adherents. In this sense, ***A Black Mass*** was both symptomatic and anticipatory of what would happen in the sphere of black cultural production in the next few years.

The play was a revision and a condensation of "Yacub's History," which explained the creation of white people from Earth's original black inhabitants as the product of generations of genetic breeding.[70] In ***A Black Mass,*** Yacub, now called Jacoub, is introduced as one of three "Black Magicians" who together symbolize the black origin of all religions: according to the stage directions, they wear a skullcap, a fez, and an African fila.[71] The play's title alludes to the necessity of black revisions of religious ritual, and the play itself is designed to revise and rewrite implicitly white-centered origin myths (and, not incidentally, to explain and define the theological problem of evil as represented in white people).

Baraka turns the Nation's myth into a reinterpretation of the Faust story and a simultaneous meditation on the role and function of art. Jacoub, whose lust for creation echoes both Faust and Dr. Frankenstein, is a complex figure; his desire to "find out everything" makes him in some ways more attractive and accessible than his fellow magicians, who insist that "we already know everything," that creation or innovation is impossible and dangerous (24).[72] But the play's condemnation of Jacoub is apparent, not only in the fact that he is conducting an experiment to try to create "whiteness" (surely the moral weight of that choice needed no further amplification for the primarily black audience to which the play was addressed), but also in his insistence that "creation is its own end" (24). His art-for-art's-sake view was precisely the aesthetic philosophy that Baraka and other leaders of the early Black Arts Movement were determined to challenge, and, if possible, eradicate.[73]

Castigated by the other magicians for his arrogance, Jacoub nonetheless proceeds with his experiment; as he does so, the natural world is disturbed by raging seas and thundering skies that have a Lear-like portentousness. Three women run in from outside, upset and frightened; they wail and moan, serving as a chorus, and as representatives of "the people" who will be destroyed by Jacoub's creation. Undeterred, Jacoub pours his solutions together: there is an explosion, out of which leaps a cold white creature in a lizard-devil mask. The creature vomits and screams, "slobberlaughing" its way through the audience (30). The women and the other magicians are horrified by the creature but Jacoub insists that he can teach the beast to talk. But the creature has only two words, incessantly repeated: "Me!" and "White" (30-32).

The beast immediately tries to attack the women, and it soon bites one of them, Tilia, who is quickly transformed into another monster, white-blotched and slobbering. With this "bite-caress," Baraka adds Dracula to his stock of popular culture referents, and in so doing brings sexuality to the forefront: the depraved and dangerous—and decidedly unsexy—red-caped beast infects the women first, using its lust to spread its "white madness."[74] If the play allegorically represents the rape of black women by white men, it also constructs "Woman" as the first and most susceptible possible site of the spread of "whiteness," thus reproducing the tendency of many nationalist ideologies to make women's bodies the sites of both nationalist reproduction and potential cultural impurity. As Philip Brian Harper has pointed out, Black Arts movement rhetoric consistently associated proper blackness with proper masculinity, a move that not only marginalized women but also meant that racial identification was figured in terms of a potent heterosexuality. Thus "judgements of insufficient racial identification . . . [were] figured specifically in terms of a failed manhood for which homosexuality, as always, was the primary signifier."[75] Gender and sexuality infused the cultural/political rhetoric of Black Arts authenticity.

At the end of the play, Tilia and the beast become hideous Adam and Eve substitutes: The two of them then attack and kill the other women and the rest of the magicians, including Jacoub. With his dying breath, Jacoub condemns the two "white beasts" to the caves of the north. These two creatures will reproduce and eventually will create the white race that comes to dominate and enslave the rest of the world. Thus, if ***A Black Mass*** describes white people as the spawn of monsters, a crime against the natural order, distorted reproduction is the unspoken but crucial undercurrent.[76]

At the end of ***A Black Mass,*** a final narrator voice-over issues a call to racial struggle, now framed in mythical and theological terms:

> And so Brothers and Sisters, these beasts are still loose in the world. Still they spit their hideous cries. There are beasts in our world, Brothers and Sisters. . . . Let us find them and slay them. . . . Let us declare Holy War. The Jihad. Or we cannot deserve to live. Izm-el-Azam. Ism-el-Azam. Izm-el-Azam. Izm-el-Azam.
>
> (39)

The call for *Jihad* (Arabic for righteous struggle or Holy War) becomes a religious and moral response to the problem of evil, the answer of the present to the history presented in the play. The language of Islamic militancy is mobilized for black militancy; religious struggle and racial struggle are made one.

The influence of Islam and Islamic symbolism went well beyond Baraka; it was highly visible in general in the Black Arts movement, acknowledged, and often supported, even by those who didn't share its presumptions. Members of the Nation of Islam and orthodox African American Sunni Muslims were active in political and cultural organizations all over the country. Baraka's own interest in Islam continued to manifest itself in poetry and essays for the rest of the decade.[77] By the time Baraka and Larry Neal published the field-defining anthology *Black Fire* in 1968, and Ed Bullins edited the collection, *New Plays for the Black Theatre* a year later, they were codifying (and of course canonizing) a body of work, produced and written in the previous several years, in which the influence of Islam was highly visible. Many of the plays and essays were either direct translations of NOI ideology (such as Salimu's "Growing into Blackness," which instructed young women on the proper Islamic way to support their men), or they simply presumed working familiarity with Islam on the part of the audience. Similarly, work by young poets was infused with Islamic references—references that were also often testimony to the influence of Malcolm X and/or Baraka: Gaston Neal's "Personal Jihad" is one example; another is the long poem, "malcolm" by Welton Smith, which speaks of "the sound of Mecca / inside you" and concludes with detailed references to the Yacub myth in "The Beast Section." The prominence of Muslim-derived names was also significant in both collections: many poems and plays were by writers who had changed their names to, among others, Yusef Iman, Yusef Rahman, and Ahmed Legraham Alhamisi, Salimu, and Marvin X.[78]

Looking at the cultural products and newspaper accounts of the period, it is clear that the Nation of Islam provided one significant touchstone for a larger project—that of re-visioning history and geography in order to construct a moral and spiritual basis for contemporary affiliations and identities. As Larry Neal described it: "The Old Spirituality is generalized. It seeks to recognize Universal Humanity. The New Spirituality is specific. It begins by seeing the world from the concise point-of-view of the colonized."[79] In ***A Black Mass,*** Baraka offered a religiously-infused narrative *as* empowering myth, *as* a culture specific to black people. Even though the vast majority of Black Arts writers and readers were not Muslims, this myth and culture became part of the language and geography of black cultural identity. For a new generation, culture then became the basis for constructing an alternative nation; and this (post)nation—with its own sense of spirituality and its own political vision—was the underlying utopian gesture of black nationalist thought and literature. Within this project, Islamic affiliations often functioned as both site and source for those black identities, linking African Americans to the Arab and Muslim Middle East in ways both literal and metaphoric.

It's Nation Time[80]

> To be an American writer is to be an American, and for black people, there should no longer be any honor attached to either position.
>
> —Addison Gayle[81]

The cultural and religious influence of Islam would play an important role in African American responses to the 1967 Arab-Israeli war—a war that marked the first major armed conflict in eleven years between Israel and Arab states, and which for the first time made Palestinians (the "refugees" from the founding of Israel in 1948) into a highly visible component of the conflict. In May of 1967, the ongoing tensions between Israel, Egypt, and Syria escalated dramatically. Egyptian president Nasser, involved in a war of words with conservative Arab regimes over the direction of Arab politics, had recently been criticized by Jordan and Syria for hypocrisy and cowardice in continuing to allow UN troops to be stationed on the Egyptian side of the border with Israel. The UN troops had been positioned in the Sinai in 1957, to guard the peace after the Suez crisis, but Israel had refused to allow UN peacekeepers on its side of the border. Nasser, stung by the accusations and attempting to regain his prestige as the region's preeminent nationalist leader, moved his own troops into the Sinai in May 1967 and asked the United Nations to withdraw. Several days later, Nasser provocatively closed the Strait of Tiran to Israeli shipping. As American and European diplomats scrambled to cobble together a multilateral diplomatic and/or military response (the United States was particularly concerned to act carefully in light of the increasing controversies over the war in Vietnam), Israel insisted on the right of navigation through the international waters of the Strait and declared the closure an act of war. On 5 June with tensions escalating on all sides, Israel launched an air attack that virtually destroyed both the Egyptian and Syrian air forces on the ground. Immediately, Jordan also entered the battle, attacking Israel with artillery and air power. In just six days, the war was over, with Israel the clear victor. As a result of the conflict, the Israelis conquered several territories that had been previously controlled by Arab countries: the Gaza strip (Egypt), East Jerusalem and the West Bank (Jordan), and the Golan Heights (Syria).[82]

The mainstream African American reaction to the war was generally muted, though decidedly on the side of Israel. But the younger black liberation movement, now moving in an increasingly radical direction, had a very different response. Already, young black activists, building on the cultural politics articulated by leaders like Malcolm X and Baraka and influenced by the writings of anticolonialist and Marxist Franz Fanon, had begun to describe the situation of African Americans as one of internal colonization. Increasingly, they drew parallels to the struggles for decolonization: from Muhammad Ali's jubilant affirmation that he was "not an American," but "a black man," to the young activists carrying around worn copies of *Wretched of the Earth.*[83] These are "The Last Days of the American Empire," Jones/Baraka wrote in 1964, and for African Americans to love America would be to become "equally culpable for the evil done to the rest of the world."[84]

This was nowhere more true than in SNCC, which, though it had been originally allied with the Southern Christian Leadership Council (SCLC) and the Christian-based civil rights organizations, had become increasingly identified with the internal colonization model for understanding African American oppression. In May 1967, the organization made its internationalist approach apparent by declaring itself a "Human Rights Organization," establishing an International Affairs Commission, applying for non-governmental organization (NGO) status at the United Nations, and announcing that it would "encourage and support the liberation struggles against colonialism, racism, and economic exploitation" around the world.[85] This internationalist approach was not an innovation, or a radical departure; it built on both the anticolonial activism of earlier generations of black Americans and the more recent cultural and political influence of Islam and African-based religions. But SNCC's stance was seen—as it was intended to be seen—as a clear indication that the organization was making a decisive break with the mainstream civil rights organizations and their model of liberation in one country.

It was in this context that the SNCC newsletter, in the summer of 1967, printed an article about the Arab-

Israeli war. In June, just after the six-day war erupted, the Central Committee had requested that SNCC's research and communications staff investigate the background to the conflict. A few weeks later, the organization newsletter carried an article that described the war and the post-war Israeli occupation of the West Bank and Gaza in a decidedly pro-Arab fashion. The list of facts about "the Palestine problem" was highly critical of Israel (and not just the recent war):

> Did you know that the Zionists conquered Arab homes through terror, force, and massacres? Did you know . . . that the U.S. government has worked along with Zionist groups to support Israel so that America may have a toehold in that strategic Middle East location, thereby helping white America to control and exploit the rich Arab nations?[86]

The article was accompanied by a two cartoons and two photographs that many people considered anti-Semitic: one of the cartoons depicted Nasser and Muhammad Ali, each with a noose around his neck; holding the rope was a hand with a Star of David and dollar signs. An arm labeled "Third World Liberation Movements" was poised to cut the rope. One of the photos showed Israeli soldiers pointing guns at Arabs who were lined up against a wall, and the caption read: "This is Gaza, West Bank, not Dachau, Germany."[87]

The newsletter, and the statements supporting it, were widely denounced in the mainstream press and the Jewish community; the executive director of the American Jewish Congress called it "shocking and vicious anti-Semitism." SNCC historian Clayborne Carson has argued that the article was "unauthorized" and based on the opinions of one individual, a staff writer had been influenced by the Nation of Islam and had Palestinian friends in college. But as Carson also points out, SNCC's Central Committee had surely expected a pro-Palestinian orientation to the investigation they had requested, and they generally supported the conclusions it drew.[88]

Carson believes that SNCC's decision to take up the Arab-Israeli war was part of a general trend toward making "gratuitous statements on foreign policy issues"; by 1967, he concludes, support for Third World liberation struggles was the only ideological glue that could hold the fracturing organization together.[89] Others mark the SNCC leaflet as an indicative moment, the coming out of a whole generation of young blacks who were "using Israel as the benchmark for their repudiation of their civil rights past."[90] Certainly it was the case that the 1967 Arab-Israeli war galvanized Jewish identity in the United States; thus criticism of Israel became a highly charged issue for Jews precisely at the moment that SNCC was making its public statements.[91]

In general, these assessments have built on the assumption that, up to 1967, all available narratives of black liberation had placed African Americans in a *defacto* and unproblematic alliance with Israel—an alliance that would have continued had it not been for some individual or collective failure to sustain the domestic relationship forged between African Americans and American Jews in the civil rights movement. The fact that mainstream civil rights leaders quickly condemned the SNCC article and made statements in support of Israel seems at first to confirm this argument: the leaders of old civil rights coalition, influenced by the black Christian narratives of exodus and the model of Zionism for black liberation, and perhaps appreciative of the role that Jews had played in the movement, felt an emotional commitment to Israel.[92]

But this division over the Arab-Israeli conflict also points to another story, the story of how the religious and cultural influence of Islam in the black community intersected with the increasing importance of decolonization movements worldwide. Placing SNCC's response to the 1967 Arab-Israeli war in the context of black Islam and its role in the radicalization of African American culture and politics helps us reframe the questions we ask about that moment and about the history of black-Jewish and black-Arab relations overall.

This alternative analysis avoids the common conflation of black-Jewish relations within the United States, and the concomitant issues of racism and anti-Semitism, with the meanings and significance of the Middle East for African Americans. While it is clear that the two issues—domestic relationships on the one hand, and representations of Israel and the Arab Middle East, on the other—are related, too often the assumption has been that African American views of the Middle East *must* reflect black-Jewish relations in the United States, and *must* be, to the degree that these views are critical of Israel or express affiliation with Arabs, an expression of black anti-Semitism.[93]

This is not to say that anti-Semitism was not present in the black community and the Black Arts movement. It was, and sometimes virulently. And while it is useful to point out the ways in which economic tensions in urban areas framed anti-Jewish feeling, it is not sufficient to say, as James Baldwin once did, that blacks were anti-Semitic because they were anti-white.[94] In the case of Baraka, and in many of the pronouncements of the NOI, there is a profound difference, both qualitative and quantitative, in the ways that white ethnicities were targeted. For example, in one well-known poem, **"Black Arts,"** Baraka made offhand remarks about several groups, commenting in the violent rhetoric that was often typical of him, that ideal poems would "knockoff . . . dope selling wops" and suggesting that cops should be killed and have their "tongues pulled out and sent to Ireland." But as Baraka himself later admitted, he held a specific animosity for Jews, as was apparent in the different intensity and viciousness of his call in the same poem for "dagger poems" to stab the "slimy bellies of the owner-jews" and for poems that crack "steel knuckles in a jewlady's mouth."[95]

Certainly, anti-Jewish feeling did have a bearing on the ways in which some people (black and white) formed their understandings of the Arab-Israeli conflict: there were instances at the time of the 1967 war—and there have been since—of people who began by talking about the Arab-Israeli issue and who ended by criticizing Jewish store owners or political leaders in the United States for matters unrelated to foreign policy.[96] (Of course, the tendency to conflate criticism of Israeli actions with a criticism of Jews is not limited to African Americans.) But these anti-Semitic expressions simply don't explain the pro-Arab feelings of many African Americans in this period: it is quite possible to be both anti-Jewish and anti-Arab, as the example of some Christian fundamentalist groups illustrates.

I suggest that African American investments in the Arab-Israeli conflict have a significant history aside from the tensions of black-Jewish relations—a history that developed *within* the black community as part of a search for religious and cultural alternatives to Christianity. This search was simultaneously as part of an ongoing process of redefining "blackness" in the United States. The struggle to define a black culture was never separable from the process of constructing transnational definitions of blackness—definitions that connected African Americans to people of color and anticolonialism all over the world, including, quite centrally, the Middle East.

Conclusion: Beyond the Black Atlantic

In the few short years since its publication, Paul Gilroy's study of the transnational circulation of cultures and peoples that comprise the "Black Atlantic" has had a dramatic impact on the study of cultural and political identities. As part of new generation of scholarship that makes "border crossing" and hybridity central to its analysis, Gilroy (along with Lisa Lowe, George Lipsitz, and José Saldívar, among others) has provided a significant new paradigm, one that traces what Gilroy calls the "routes and roots" (the literal travel and the remembered histories) that shape transnational identities. These powerful interventions have moved cultural studies and American studies well beyond the nationalist presuppositions that have explicitly and implicitly defined their previous practice.[97]

But Gilroy's analysis, extraordinary as it is, is also symptomatic in its exclusions. Two stand out. First, the reframing provided by the construct of the "Black Atlantic," though useful, replaces one geographic entity (the nation) with another (the Atlantic). The move reformulates, but does not overturn, the dependence of nationalist formations on literal, spatial connections for understanding cultural constructs of identity. Second, while Gilroy acknowledges some black (and particularly African American) connections with regions other than the Atlantic, he still refuses to see black identifications with the Arab world as anything other than a failure to identify sufficiently with Jewish history. These two limitations are linked, in that they both can be traced, at least in part, to lack of attention to Islam.

In the penultimate section of *The Black Atlantic,* revealingly titled "Children of Israel or Children of the Pharaohs," Gilroy makes a compelling argument against some recent triumphalist definitions of blackness. "Afrocentrism" depends on constructing black history as a narrative of unfettered greatness from ancient Egypt onward. Gilroy challenges the Afrocentric model by insisting on the importance of acknowledging slavery—and thus loss, and dispossession—as central to a transnational black history. Scholars of black culture must not forget the themes of suffering, escape, memory, and identity that transverse black history and which unite certain strands of black and Jewish thought. By choosing to highlight slavery and the corresponding theme of diaspora, Gilroy's project of remembrance illuminates the commonalities between black and Jewish history. In so doing, it points to the history of western anti-Semitism and anti-black racism as intersecting indictments of the modern construction of race. Such scholarship, Gilroy argues, can play a role in reasserting important political critiques of modernity, and of modernity's racial categories. In other words, to insist on remembering slavery as a central part of the black experience is also to refuse to forget the centrality of racism in the project of modernity. This approach rejects the Afrocentric tendency to de-historicize black history through its myopic attention to ancient periods of rule, conquest, and triumphant kingdoms, in Egypt and elsewhere. It instead reminds us that a past marked by suffering and persecution, if properly remembered, may offer a special redemptive power to a people—"not for themselves alone but for humanity as a whole."[98]

Such remembrance is indeed crucial, both intellectually and politically. If it is to avoid its own kind of willful ahistoricism, however, this project also will need to account for the ways in which the meanings of Jewish history were transformed within black cultural production. Within important segments of African American public life, Jews, both in Israel and in the United States, came to be identified less by their suffering than by their power. Black (post)-nationalism in the United States turned toward other models, beyond the exodus/Zionist model, for narrating hopes of African American liberation. By taking Islam seriously, we can contribute to an understanding of religion in the twentieth-century United States that moves beyond Judaism and Christianity, and attends to attend to the complex religious affiliations that also linked African American identity with the Arab and Islamic Middle East. That attention would then also expand our analysis of transnationalism, and require us to think about identities on a truly global scale—the "roots and routes" of cultural affiliations are not necessarily contiguous spaces.

Such a project also brings us back, in new ways, to one of the fundamental tensions in African American intellectual and cultural history since World War II: how are we to understand the relationships of African Americans to the project of U.S. nationalism and the realities of power in the nation-state? And how is that history bound up with the international relations of the nation as a whole? What does the role of the United States as the chief power of the postwar world ("the chief neocolonialist power" in Larry Neal's phrase) mean for the notion of black or African American identity? What are the limits of seeing African American nationalisms as merely domestic matters?

Much of the discourse of civil rights viewed blackness as a subnational identity and saw the African American struggle as a striving for rights that would, if successful, transform the nation itself. At the same time, black nationalist writers tended to see blackness as a separate national identity, which would necessarily in time develop its own foreign policy, based on alliance with other peoples in a similar structural position as colonized people. But flowing through both of these visions has been another: that of blackness as a *trans*national identity, and African Americans as players in a truly global drama.

Thus African American cultural production in the era of black liberation challenged the very notion of *a* national identity by undermining the categories—of land, of culture, of politics—that underlay it. That is one reason it matters. Not because transnational identities are magically unproblematic; the cultural radicalism of the 1960s often framed black identity in terms that were ahistorical, masculinist, and anti-Semitic. This is its irony, its limit, and its loss. But the intervention was significant: a remapping of the world, an alternative moral geography, and a new imagined community that did not begin and end with Africa. This alternative was far more than a policy critique, it was a redefinition and a remapping. It was the search for an identity that would be, as both Baraka and Neal put it, "post-American"—something outside of, and in opposition to, the expanding role of the United States on the world stage. Often centered in constructions of spirituality and religious belief, this African American narrative of counter-citizenship mobilized the Middle East as both a crucial signifier and a utopian gesture in the process of constructing black identities within and across national borders.

Notes

1. James Baldwin, *The Fire Next Time* (New York, 1963), 46. Originally published in *The New Yorker,* 17 Nov. 1962. I owe thanks to the friends and colleagues who read earlier versions of this article, particularly Carl Conetta, Ruth Feldstein, Jane Gerhard, James A. Miller, Teresa Murphy, Brad Verter, Uta Poiger, Robert Vitalis, Stacy Wolf, participants in the religion and culture workshop at Princeton University's Center for the Study of Religion, and the anonymous reviewers for *American Quarterly.*

2. Malcolm X, speech at Boston University, 15 Feb. 1960, quoted by C. Eric Lincoln, *The Black Muslims in America,* 3d. ed. (New York, 1994), 169.

3. On the day after the fight, Clay announced that he "believed in Allah"; at a second press conference the following day, he clarified his membership in the Nation of Islam. See Thomas Hauser, *Muhammad Ali: His Life and Times* (New York, 1991), 81-84. John McDermott, "Champ 23: A Man-Child Taken In By the Muslims," *Life,* 6 Mar. 1964, 38-39; Huston Horn, "The First Days in the New Life of the Champion of the World," *Sports Illustrated,* 9 Mar. 1964, 26ff; "Prizefighting: With Mouth and Magic," *Time,* 6 Mar. 1964, 66-69.

4. See "Cassius Marcellus Clay," *Time,* 22 Mar. 1963, 78-81; Pete Hamill "Young Cassius Has a Mean & Sonny Look," *New York Post,* 8 Mar. 1963; Howard Tuckner, "'Man, It's Great To Be Great,'" *New York Times,* 9 Dec. 1962; and "C. Marcellus Clay Esq." *Sports Illustrated,* 10 June 1963, 19-25.

5. Malcolm X with Alex Haley, *The Autobiography of Malcolm X* (1964; New York, 1992), 349-56; Bruce Perry, *Malcolm: the Life of a Man who Changed Black America* (Barrytown, N.Y., 1991), 245-50; Stan Koven, "The Muslim Dinner and Cassius Clay," *New York Post,* 23 Jan. 1964; William Braden, "Muslims Claim the Credit for Clay's Victory," *New York Post,* 2 Feb. 1964; "Cassius X," *Newsweek,* 16 Mar. 1964.

6. Ted Poston, "Clay in Malcolm X's Corner in Black Muslim Fight," *New York Post,* 3 Mar. 1964; J. Cannon, "The Muslims' Prize," *Journal American,* 23 Feb. 1965; "Cassius Clay Says He is Not 'Scared' of Killing Reprisal," *New York Times,* 24 Feb. 1965; Milton Gross, "The Men Around Cassius Clay," *New York Post,* 28 May 1965; "FBI Probes Muhammad and Clay," *New York Post,* 28 Feb. 1966.

7. Robert Lipsyte, "Cassius Clay, Cassius X, Muhammad Ali," *New York Times Magazine,* 25 Oct. 1964, 29ff. See also Alex Haley's *Playboy* interview with Ali in Oct. 1964, repr. in Murray Fisher, ed., *Alex Haley: The Playboy Interviews* (New York, 1993), 46-79.

8. Bill Jaus, "Cassius: I'm Still Unfit," *New York Post,* 21 Feb. 1966. See Henry Hampton and Steve Fayer, *Voices of Freedom* (New York, 1990), 321-34; Hauser, *Muhammad Ali,* 142-201.

9. Sanchez is quoted in Hampton and Fayer, *Voices of Freedom,* 328.

10. For a very useful discussion of Baraka's early work, see James A. Miller, "Amiri Baraka," in *The Beats: Literary Bohemians in Postwar America: Dictionary of Literary Biography,* Vol. 16 (Detroit, 1983), 3-24.

11. Baraka describes writing the play in *The Autobiography of LeRoi Jones/Amiri Baraka* (New York, 1984), 210; his affiliation with Sunni Islam is discussed, 267-69. Baraka says that Jaaber "buried Malcolm X," but Peter Goldman mentions only Sheikh Ahmed Hassoun, the Sudanese cleric who had returned with Malcolm X from Mecca. *The Death and life of Malcolm X* (Urbana, Ill., 1979), 302.

12. The designation of Baraka came from a poll of thirty-eight prominent black writers published in the Jan. 1968 issue of *Negro Digest.* The writers also voted Baraka "the most important living black poet," and "the most important black playwright." Werner Sollors, *Amiri Baraka/LeRoi Jones: Quest for a Populist Modernism* (New York, 1978), 264n.6. On Baraka's transformation to Maoism, see his *Autobiography,* 308-14.

13. On the Nation of Islam in the 1960s, see Mathias Gardell, *In the Name of Elijah Muhammad: Louis Farrakhan and the Nation of Islam* (Durham, N.C., 1996); and C. Eric Lincoln, *Black Muslims.* See also, Aminah Beverly McCloud, *African American Islam* (New York, 1995).

14. Michael Shapiro, "Moral Geographies and the Ethics of Post-Sovereignty," *Public Culture* 6 (spring 1994): 479-502. Here I am also, of course, engaging with the issues raised by Benedict Anderson, *Imagined Communities: Reflections on the Origin and Spread of Nationalism,* rev. ed. (New York, 1991).

15. For example, two otherwise excellent books, Howard Sitcoff, *The Struggle for Black Equality, 1954-1992* (New York, 1993); and Rhoda Blumberg, *Civil Rights: The 1960s Freedom Struggle,* rev. ed. (Boston, 1991). Brenda Plummer's wonderfully comprehensive *Rising Wind: Black Americans and U.S. Foreign Policy, 1935-1960* (Chapel Hill, N.C., 1996) is interested in foreign policy positions of the NOI, but not the broader religious or cultural influence.

16. Addison Gayle, "Cultural Strangulation: Black Literature and the White Aesthetic," in *The Black Aesthetic* (New York, 1968), 46.

17. Marvin X and Farkuk, "Islam and Black Art: An Interview with LeRoi Jones," *Negro Digest* 18 (Jan. 1969): 4-10ff, repr. in Jeff Decker, ed., *The Black Arts Movement: Dictionary of Literary Biography Documentary Series,* Vol. 8 (Detroit, 1991). Jones used the phrase "post-American" earlier as well, in his essay "What the Arts Need Now," *Negro Digest* (Apr. 1967): 5-6.

18. Gardell, *In the Name of Elijah Muhammad,* 65. E. U. Essien-Udom, *Black Nationalism: A Search for an Identity in America* (Chicago, 1962), 84.

19. John Voll, *Islam Continuity and Change in the Modern World,* 2d. ed. (Syracuse, N.Y., 1994).

20. Perhaps Elijah Muhammad was also incorporating some reference here to Asia Minor, which comprises most of modern Turkey.

21. Penny M. Von Eschen's *Race Against Empire: Black Americans and Anticolonialism, 1937-1957* (Ithaca, N.Y., 1996), discusses each of these figures in her excellent study of the internationalism of African American politics in the period, focused primarily on Africa.

22. Until Elijah Muhammad's death in 1975, NOI generally used the term temples; after Wallace D. Muhammad took over leadership and began a transformation of the organization into the American Muslim Mission, with a more orthodox doctrine, the term mosques was used. Eventually, followers simply joined whatever local mosque was in their community, and the organization dissolved. The original NOI was revived by Louis Farrakhan in 1985. Gardell, *In the Name of Elijah Muhammad,* 99-135.

23. On Muslim slaves and early Muslim communities in the United States, see Richard Turner, *Islam in the African-American Experience* (Bloomington, Ind., 1997). There is some indication, however, that Muslim Africans were *less* likely than others to be taken and sold as slaves; see Morroe Berger, "The Black Muslims," *Horizon* (winter 1966), 49-64.

24. According to Lincoln, *Black Muslims in America,* 120.

25. Elijah Muhammad, *Message to the Blackman* (Chicago, 1965), 31.

26. Described by Malcolm X, *Autobiography,* 224-225. Also in Perry, *Malcolm X,* 142.

27. On the theological difference between Nation of Islam and both Christianity and orthodox Islam, see Gardell, *In the Name of Elijah Muhammad,* 144-86.

28. Jonathan Kaufman describes the exodus metaphor as a primary link between black and Jewish history in *Broken Alliance: The Turbulent Times between Blacks and Jews in America,* rev. ed. (1988; New York, 1995), 35.

29. I discuss this connection in more detail in *Epic Encounters: Race, Religion, and Nation in U.S. Representations of the Middle East 1945-2000* (Berkeley, Calif., forthcoming). Lowrey makes the link while being interviewed by Howell Raines, *My Soul is Rested: Movement Days in the Deep South Remembered* (New York, 1977), 69. For one example of Martin Luther King's use of the trope, see his last speech: "I See the Promised Land," speech given on

3 Apr. 1968 at the Mason Temple in Memphis, and repr. in *A Testament of Hope,* ed. James Washington (New York, 1986), 279-86.

30. Robert Weisbord and Richard Kazarian, Jr., *Israel in the Black American Perspective* (Westport, Conn., 1985), 20-22.

31. See David Garrow, *Bearing the Cross: Martin Luther King and the Southern Christian Leadership Conference* (New York, 1988), 110-15; and King, "My Trip to the Land of Gandhi," in *A Testament of Hope,* 23-30.

32. Jonathan Boyarin argues persuasively that the influence of the Exodus trope also worked in the other direction: the civil rights connotations of exodus played a role in the increasing tendency to use that rhetoric to represent Israel. "Reading Exodus into History," *New Literary History* 23 (summer 1992), 540.

33. E. Muhammad, *Message to the Blackman,* 95-96.

34. Of the many that explore this history, perhaps the best single source is *Bridges and Boundaries: African Americans and American Jews,* ed. Jack Salzamn (New York, 1992). On the pre-war period, see Hasia Diner, *In the Almost Promised Land: American Jews and Blacks, 1915-1935* (Baltimore, Md., 1992).

35. Paul Gilroy explores the link with Zionism in *The Black Atlantic: Modernity and Double-Consciousness* (Cambridge, Mass., 1993); see also Hollis Lynch, *Edward Wilmont Blyden: Pan-Negro Patriot, 1832-1912* (New York, 1967).

36. *Autobiography of Malcolm X,* 320.

37. Malcolm X, "Message to the Grassroots," Nov. 1963, repr. in *Malcolm X Speaks,* ed. George Breitman (1970; New York, 1992), 5-6.

38. Plummer, *Rising Wind,* 284-85; Louis Lomax, *When the Word is Given: A Report on Elijah Muhammad, Malcolm X, and the Black Muslim World* (New York, 1963), 72-73.

39. For a discussion of black responses to the King Tut exhibit, for example, see my "'The Common Heritage of Mankind': Race, Masculinity, and Nation in the King Tut Exhibit," *Representations* 54 (spring 1996), 80-103.

40. See Plummer, *Rising Wind,* 257-72.

41. The events of the Suez Crisis are detailed in Donald Neff, *Warriors at Suez: Eisenhower Takes American into the Middle East* (New York, 1981); R. Bowie, "Eisenhower, Dulles, and the Suez Crisis," in *Suez 1956,* ed. William Roger Louis and Roger Owen (Oxford, 1989).

42. For example, a strong editorial in one early NOI publication, *The Moslem World and the U.S.A.,* quoted by Essien-Udom, *Black Nationalism,* 302.

43. W. E. B. Du Bois, "Suez," originally published in *Masses & Mainstream,* Dec. 1956, repr. in *Creative Writings of W. E. B. Du Bois,* ed. Herbert Aptheker (White Plains, N.Y., 1985), 45-46.

44. Weisbord and Kazarian, quoting an interview with Baynard Rustin, make the argument for the retrospective significance of Suez in *Israel in the Black Perspective,* 31.

45. Plummer, *Rising Wind,* 261. Also quoted by Lincoln, *Black Muslims in America,* 225.

46. Perry, *Malcolm,* 205-6. Neither Malcolm X nor Elijah Muhammad was in Saudi Arabia during the period of the hajj, or pilgrimage, in 1959-1960.

47. The television special "The Hate that Hate Produced," produced by Mike Wallace and Louis Lomax, aired in 1959. Already in 1959 and 1960, the "Black Muslim" movement had been covered in articles in *Time* ("Black Supremacists," 10 Aug. 1959), *Newsweek* ("The Way of Cults," 7 May 1956), *The New York Times* ("Rise in Racial Extremism," 25 Jan. 1960), *Christian Century* ("Despair Serves Purposes of Bizarre Cult," 10 Aug. 1960), and *Reader's Digest* (Alex Haley, "Mr. Muhammad Speaks," Mar. 1960). The first book-length study, Eric Lincoln's scholarly *The Black Muslims in America,* was published in 1961; a year later, James Baldwin's "Letter from a Region in My Mind," came out in *The New Yorker,* and E. U. Essien-Udom published *Black Nationalism: A Search for an Identity in America.* Louis Lomax's popular account of the Nation of Islam, *When the Word Was Given,* came out in 1963, and in that same year, Malcolm X was interviewed by *Playboy* (May 1963), while Alfred Black and Alex Haley published a long article in the *Saturday Evening Post* ("Black Merchants of Hate," 26 Jan. 1963). Some of this coverage is discussed in the third edition of Lincoln's study, 174-76.

48. The book was excerpted in *The Saturday Evening Post,* 12 Sept. 1964, before its official publication. It was widely reviewed; see, for example, I. F. Stone's review, "The Pilgrimage of Malcolm X," in *The New York Review,* 11 Nov. 1965.

49. *Negro Digest* ran several articles on the "Black Muslims" in the early 1960s, including an article by Elijah Muhammad called "What the Black Muslims Believe," Nov. 1963. *Jet* covered the impact of Muslim identity on the career of Cassius Clay: "Will Link with Malcolm X Harm Clay's Career?," 26 Mar. 1964. Coverage in the black press was often ambivalent: when Malcolm X was killed, *Sepia* magazine's headline was "The Violent End of Malcolm X: He Taught Violence, He Died Violently," May 1965.

50. Lincoln, *Black Muslims in America,* 128. On the black public sphere, see *Public Culture* (Fall 1994), now available as *The Black Public Sphere* (Chicago, 1995), in particular Manthia Diawara, "Malcolm X and the Black Public Sphere."

51. Lincoln, *Black Muslims in America,* 108.

52. From Amiri Baraka, "State/meant," in *Home* (c. 1966; New York, 1998), 252.

53. Baraka, *Four Black Revolutionary Plays,* (New York, 1969), vii-viii.

54. Baraka, *Autobiography,* 203. For a contemporary discussion of the response, see Lawrence P. Neal, "Malcolm and the Conscience of Black America," *The Liberator* 6 (Feb. 1966): 10-11. Mance Williams discusses the impact of Malcolm X's *Autobiography* on the Free Southern Theater company in *Black Theatre in the 1960s and 1970s: A Historical-Critical Analysis of the Movement* (Westport, Conn., 1985), 62.

55. Baraka, *Autobiography,* 204.

56. See Ed Bullins, "A Short Statement on Street Theatre," *The Drama Review* (summer 1968), 93.

57. New publishing houses included Dudley Randall's Broadside Press, Chicago's Third World Press, and Washington's Drum and Spear Press. For a useful discussion of the publishing scene, see *The Norton Anthology of African American Literature,* ed. Henry Louis Gates and Nellie McKay (New York, 1997), 1791-806.

58. Baraka, *Autobiography,* 249.

59. Harold Cruse, "Intellectuals and the Theater of the 1960s," in *Crisis of the Negro Intellectual* (New York, 1967), 531. See also the penultimate chapter of the book, *The Harlem Black Arts Theater.* The special issue of *The Drama Review* on black theatre was summer 1968.

60. Pierre Bourdieu, *The Field of Cultural Production* (New York, 1993).

61. Peter Burger, *Theory of the Avant-Garde* (Minneapolis, Minn., 1984).

62. Interview with Ed Bullins, *New Plays from the Black Theatre,* ed. Bullins (New York, 1969), vii.

63. Carmichael, "We are Going to Use the Term 'Black Power' and We are Going to Define It Because Black Power Speaks to Us," in *Black Nationalism in America,* ed. J. Bracey, August Meier, and E. Rudwick (New York, 1970), 472. Carmichael is also quoted by Philip B. Harper, *Are We Not Men? Masculine Anxiety and the Problem of African-American Identity* (New York, 1996), 51.

64. Baraka, "The Need for a Cultural Base to Civil Rites and Bpower Mooments," originally published in *The Black Power Revolt,* repr. in *Raise, Race, Rays, Raze: Essays since 1965* (New York, 1971), 43-46. On the broad diffusion of cultural nationalism, see William Van Deburg, *New Day in Babylon: The Black Power Movement in American Culture, 1965-1975* (Chicago, 1992).

65. Lincoln, *Black Muslims in America,* 72.

66. Publication history from *The Black Arts Movement,* ed. Jeff Decker, 120-21. The following discussion quotes from the text *Four Black Revolutionary Plays* (New York, 1969). Subsequent page numbers in parentheses.

67. For example, in his pamphlet, "7 Principles of US Maulana Karenga & the Need for a Black Value System," later repr. in *Raise, Race, Rays, Raze.*

68. Larry Neal, "The Black Arts Movement" in *Visions of a Liberated Future: Black Arts Movement Writings,* ed. by Michael Schwartz (New York, 1989), 73. Mance Williams points out that the music of Sun-Ra had big influence on *A Black Mass*—Sun Ra performed the music for the original production, also heard on the recorded version of the play. *Black Theatre,* 23.

69. K. William Kgositsile, "Towards Our Theater: A Definitive Act" in *Negro Digest* (Apr. 1967), 15.

70. Elijah Muhammad explained the story of Yacoub frequently, including in *Message to the Blackman,* 117-19. This myth was dropped from Nation of Islam theology after Wallace D. Muhammad took over leadership of the community after Elijah Muhammad's death in 1975. McCloud, *African American Islam,* 72-88.

71. The transformation of the name of the villain Yacub into a name (and a spelling) that looks more like Jacob may have anti-Semitic overtones, though this is not explicit elsewhere in the play.

72. As Werner Sollors has pointed out, Baraka's version of the story draws on the Frankenstein tale; he conflates the 600 years of Elijah Muhammad's "history" into a single, terrible moment. *Quest for a Populist Modernism,* 211.

73. For a critique of the "Western aesthetic," see Larry Neal. "The Black Arts Movement," in *Visions of a Liberated Future* and "Some Reflections on the Black Aesthetic," in *The Black Aesthetic,* ed. Addison Gayle (New York, 1968).

74. The link between sexuality and classic horror films has been extensively discussed; one interesting recent example is Rhona Berenstein, *Attack of the Leading Ladies: Gender, Sexuality, and Spectatorship in Classic Horror Cinema* (New York, 1996)

75. Philip Brian Harper, "Black Rhetoric and the Nationalist Call," in *Are We Not Men,* 50.

76. There have been several other important studies of the masculinist bias of much of the Black Arts movement. See Joyce Hope Scott, "From Foreground to Margin: Female Configurations and Masculine Self-Representation in Black Nationalist Fiction," in *Nationalisms and Sexualities,* ed. Andrew Parker, et. al. (New York, 1992); and E. Frances White, "Africa on

My Mind: Gender, Counterdiscourse, and African American Nationalism," in *Words of Fire,* ed. Beverly Guy-Sheftall (New York, 1992).

77. "From: The Book of Life," for example, written after the Newark riots in 1967 and collected in *Raise, Race, Rays, Raze.*

78. Larry Neal and LeRoi Jones, eds. *Black Fire: An Anthology of Afro-American Writing* (New York, 1968). Essays with Islamic themes in the anthology include David Llorens, "The Fellah, the Chosen Ones, The Guardian," and Nathan Hare, "Brainwashing of Black Men's Minds." In the Bullins anthology, other examples of NOI-influenced plays are "El Hajj Malik: A Play about Malcolm X," by N. R. Davidson, Jr. and "The Black Bird (Al Tair Aswad)" by Marvin X. See also *For Malcolm: Poems on the Life and Death of Malcolm X,* ed. Dudley Randall and Margaret Burroughs (Detroit, 1969).

79. Larry Neal, "The Black Arts Movement," 77.

80. Amiri Baraka, "It's Nation Time," originally published in *It's Nation Time,* repr. in *Selected Poetry of Amiri Baraka/LeRoi Jones* (New York, 1979), 198-200.

81. Addison Gayle, *The Black Aesthetic* (New York, 1971), xvi.

82. Useful descriptions of the 1967 war include William Quandt, *Decade of Decisions: American Policy Toward the Arab-Israeli Conflict 1967-1976* (Berkeley, Calif., 1977); and Donald Neff, *Warriors for Jerusalem* (New York, 1988).

83. Alvin Poussaint, "An Overview of Fanon's Significance to the American Civil Rights Movement," in *An International Tribute to Frantz Fanon* (New York, 1978).

84. LeRoi Jones, "The Last Days of the American Empire (Including some Instructions for Black People)," repr. in *Home: Social Essays* (1966; Hopewell, N.J., 1998).

85. Clayborne Carson, *In Struggle: SNCC and The Black Awakening of the 1960s* (Cambridge, Mass., 1981), 192-98 and 266. See also Stokley Carmichael and Charles Hamilton, *Black Power: The Politics of Liberation in America* (New York, 1967).

86. Weisbord and Kazarian, *Israel in the Black Perspective,* 33.

87. "Third World Round Up: the Palestine Problem: Test Your Knowledge," *SNCC Newsletter,* June-July 1967. The cartoons and photos are described in Weisbord and Kazarian, *Israel in the Black Perspective,* 35-36.

88. Carson, *In Struggle,* 265-69.

89. Carson, "Blacks and Jews in the Civil Rights Movement," in *Bridges and Boundaries,* ed. Jack Salzman.

90. Murray Friedman, *What Went Wrong: The Creation and Collapse of the Black-Jewish Alliance* (New York, 1995), 227-233. Jonathan Kauffman's wonderful study, *Broken Alliance,* also makes a similar presumption.

91. See Arthur Hertzberg, "Israel and American Jewry," *Commentary,* Aug. 1967. Taylor Branch, "Blacks and Jews: The Uncivil War," in *Bridges and Boundaries.* Michael Stab argues that Holocaust memory and Israel were both important to Jews well before 1967: "Holocaust Consciousness, Black Masculinity, and the Renegotiation of Jewish American Identity, 1957-67," paper presented at the annual meeting of the American Studies Association.

92. Whitney Young, A. Philip Randolph, and Bayard Rustin sharply criticized the SNCC leaflet, and Martin Luther King made several statements of support for Israel after the 1967 war. In 1975, several leaders, including Bayard Rustin, William Fautnoy, and Andrew Young, formed BASIC (Black Americans in Support of Israel Committee), pamphlet in Schomberg clipping file, labeled "Israel."

93. Cornel West points out the significance of the principle of Palestinian rights in "On Black-Jewish Relations," in *Black and Jews: Alliances and Arguments* (New York, 1994), 144-153. Alice Walker makes a similar point in, "To the Editors of *Ms.* Magazine," in *In Search of Our Mother's Gardens* (San Diego, 1983), 347-54. See also June Jordan, *Civil Wars* (Boston, 1981).

94. James Baldwin, "Negroes are Anti-Semitic Because They are Anti-White" (1967), repr. in *The Price of the Ticket: Collected Non-Fiction, 1948-1985* (New York, 1985).

95. "Black Art," originally published in *The Liberator* (Jan. 1966) and collected in *Black Magic* (1969). Reprinted in *Selected Poetry.* See Amiri Baraka, "I was an Anti-Semite," *Village Voice* (20 Dec. 1980), 1.

96. Carson points to one such example in the press conference given by SNCC program director Ralph Featherstone in the wake of the crisis, *In Struggle,* 268. Since the Nation of Islam was revived by Louis Farrakhan in 1975, these kind of statements have been frequent. Gardell, *In the Name of Elijah Muhammad,* 246ff. See also Ellen Willis, "The Myth of the Powerful Jew," in *Blacks and Jews.*

97. Lisa Lowe, *Immigrant Acts* (Durham, N.C., 1996); Jose David Saldivar, *Border Matters: Remapping American Cultural Studies* (Berkeley, Calif., 1997); George Lipsitz, *Dangerous Crossroads: Popular Music, Postmodernism, and the Poetics of Place* (New York, 1994). These scholars are often drawing on postcolonial theory, including Homi Bhabha, esp. *The Location of Culture* (New York, 1994).

98. Gilroy, *The Black Atlantic,* 208.

Marlon B. Ross (essay date 2000)

SOURCE: Ross, Marlon B. "Camping the Dirty Dozens: The Queer Resources of Black Nationalist Invective." *Callaloo* 23, no. 1 (2000): 290-312.

[*In the following essay, Ross examines the relationship between homosexuality and cultural identity in Baraka's work, highlighting the role of camp as well as "the dozens," or the trading of insults, in establishing sexual shame.*]

In attempting to grasp the relation between people of African descent and same-sexuality, the handful of historians, critics, activists, and social scientists who have touched on the subject have focused on one of two approaches. Either they have attempted to uncloset the lives of famous individuals of African descent who might be suspected of having, at some point, harbored same-sexual desire or engaged in same-sexual activity. Or they have attempted to expose the homophobia at work in the literatures of and histories on African-American life and culture. These works take on the important task of pointing out how evidence of African-American same-sexuality has been suppressed and how, when acknowledged, the admission of black homosexuality tends to be accompanied by distancing anxiety. Such sympathetic treatments of African-American homosexuality most frequently assume an identity schism—as struggle, competition, misalliance—between gayness and blackness. By proving how an individual can belong to both identities at once, they attempt to overcome the paradigm of competing black and gay identities by demonstrating an intersection, interface, or duality between them, a double consciousness not dissimilar from W. E. B. Du Bois's productive theory of a "twoness" at strife in being Negro and American.[1]

In "'Black Gay Male' Discourse: Reading Race and Sexuality Between the Lines," for instance, Arthur Flannigan-Saint-Aubin offers a critique of Essex Hemphill's *Brother to Brother* anthology by arguing that it fails to grasp the asymmetry of multiple oppressions even as they "interface in many complex ways" (475). Using the queer theory strategy of reading between the lines and across binaries, Flannigan-Saint-Aubin attempts to "postulate blackgaymale theory as positionality": "Even if one rejects the notion of an essential 'gayness' or an essential 'blackness,' one can still claim the complex of sexuality and ethnicity as a locus of difference from which to think, to act, and to create" (489). Like other recent writers who have employed queer theory to complicate our discussions of African-American same-sexuality, Flannigan-Saint-Aubin relies on a notion of identity difference to try to get at the difficult problem of racial and sexual variation.[2] While helping us to rethink the rigidities of identity, such interventions tend to adopt two strategies that, as Diana Fuss points out, are essential to poststructuralist gender, race, and sexuality theories: "positing the reader as a site of differences" and "the notion of the reading process as a negotiation amongst discursive subject-positions which the reader, as social subject, may or may not choose to fill" (*Essentially Speaking* 34). Conceptualizing cultural identity as a site or position or space occupied differently by different bodies or as a performance that inhabits the vessel of the body in different ways, these theories necessarily encounter obstacles in attempting to think through and beyond identity as a structure or system of interlocking blocks like so many Lego pieces fitted together.

Although it is impossible to "evacuate" totally the grounding of cultural identity in spatial metaphor, we might be able to disrupt this spatializing tendency, at least temporarily, by thinking of cultural *identification* as a *temporal* process that enables and constrains subjectivity by offering up resources for affiliating with, while also disaffiliating against, particular social groupings, which themselves are constantly being revised over time by individuals' reconstitution of them.[3] Rather than theorizing identity solely as cultural contiguity in relation to others who originate from the same (i.e., *identical*) social space or as a system of bodily performances determined by the range of roles inhabited in relation to a larger social body, we can consider the ways in which individuals, discourses, and social groupings constantly revise themselves by identifying with and also against traditions based on the material (physical, economic, institutional) and symbolic (linguistic, ideological, cultural) resources extant, absent, or hidden within historically changing practices and forms moving within and across particular environments. From the outset, life is full of chance encounters that shape our cultural bearing in surprising ways, not only binding us in weird ways to particular groupings but also permanently disorienting our stable relations to such groupings. Cultural identification is a matter not only of which predefined racial, sexual, class roles people take or which pre-sited spaces they occupy but also of how they are motivated and constrained to act (or sometimes *act out*) unfamiliar experiences of identification depending on the range of bodily, intellectual, and cultural knowledge (their know-how) available to them, self-consciously and unselfconsciously, over time. Beyond the necessary task of exposing homophobia, beyond the attempt to read the fixed sexual identity of writers, readers, and situations in African-American literature and history, beyond attempting to articulate a unique position from which black queerness can be recognized, we need to examine the formal and material practices that mark sexual identity as a resource for racial identification and racial identity as a resource for sexual identification within and across historical moments within and across cultural traditions.

I take as an exemplary case the preference for sexualized invective—and more specifically the gesture of queer-baiting—as a common feature of black cultural nationalism from the 1960s to the present. Perhaps more than any other genre, black nationalist writing has understandably been singled out as a discourse in which identities of race, class, gender, and sexuality are put in contention when they should be seen as interlocking pieces. As many scholars have noted, Amiri Baraka and other black cultural nationalists sling heterosexist (and sexist) lines as though homosexuals (and implicitly women) were the enemy, rather than the white system of domination.[4] Recently, Phillip Brian Harper has noted how black nationalist invective needs to attack other blacks for a white audience even as it claims to purge the whiteness contaminating black American culture. Taking cues from him but going in the opposite direction, I'd like to explore the formation or front-end of this verbal device of invective, not so much its origins as its potential *resources*—the cultural sources, traces, influences, alliances, and alternatives available to users of invective and thus shaping its changing usages in specific contexts over time. Although we could trace any number of such resources in the work of any number of nationalist writers, I want to focus here on the work of LeRoi Jones/Amiri Baraka by looking at the potential interplay between the dozens as a mode of street-smart verbal jousting affiliated with urban, working-class, supermasculine (i.e., avowedly heterosexual) African-American culture since at least the early 20th century and camp as a mode of in-the-know verbal repartee usually affiliated with underground urban *European*-American homosexual male enclaves since at least the early 20th century and before the emergence of militant gay liberation.

Before theorizing the interactive resourcefulness of the dozens and camp in the discursive history of invective in Baraka's work, I want to issue some cautions. First, I do not want to site camp in the province of only *white* homosexuals. To do so would be to revert hopelessly to the spatial model of interlocking identity positions. What matters here is that Baraka himself, at specific junctures, identifies with/against camp as being a practice of a particular group of white middle-class urban homosexuals socialized into sexual identity around World War II. We must always keep in mind that even when resources may be available closer to home (in this case, Baraka's probable access to practices of camp within African-American neighborhoods of his youth), how subjects self-consciously identify the ostensible *sources* of their cultural *re*sources reveals as much about the ideology of resorting to such a selective narrative as about the politics of cultural identification in general. In other words, identifying cultural resources is always a matter of tracing the processes of a subject's *re*vision of its social identities along a path strewn with both buried and exposed identifications. By examining the interaction of camp and the dozens, I am neither equating the two, nor suggesting that they ultimately derive from common origins. In fact, while stressing their peculiar situatedness in social practices usually attributed to different groupings (black heterosexual and white homosexual men), I also want to infer a cultural resourcefulness emanating from differing constraints and opportunities under the common pressures of sexual conformity (in African-American and homosexual groupings) and racial domination (for both homosexuals and African Americans). By hypothesizing that the discursive practices of a leading black nationalist figure has been influenced by camp, I am not making any claims about the intrinsic nature of his sexual attractions or racial aversions. Instead, I want to dis/affiliate sexual orientation from the capacity to be influenced by queer socio-sexual practices. It is possible to be homosexual and not adept in these practices, just as it's possible not to be homosexual-identified and yet adaptable to them. Finally, because cultural identifications can travel, to borrow a phrase from Edward Said, does not mean that they are easily transportable.[5] People do not simply adopt and adapt unfamiliar behaviors upon contact with them, even if those behaviors are affiliated with their subject-grouping, and especially when such behaviors carry onerous social stigmata, as both camp and the dozens do in dominant American culture. Some sort of meaningful resonance or dissonance is required for an identification to imprint itself.

In a brilliant 1963 essay **"Brief Reflections on Two Hot Shots,"** LeRoi Jones takes on James Baldwin and the South African writer Peter Abrahams with double fists. This is one in a series of attacks that contributes to Jones's transformation of himself from a crossracial downtown bohemian into the leading black cultural nationalist, Amiri Baraka. Like other cultural nationalists of the time, Jones chooses Baldwin as a target *explicitly* because of the latter's reputation as a leading writer on behalf of the integrationist Civil Rights agenda and *implicitly* because of his reputation as a writer identified with interracial homosexuality.[6] We could trace the literary resources of Jones's sparring invective to Norman Mailer's 1959 essay, "Evaluations—Quick and Expensive Comments on the Talent in the Room," in which he doles out hard-hitting punches to contemporary writers, including Baldwin, by aiming at their weak points and guarding against their counter-swings. Mailer's mode of verbal sparring relies on his reputation as a boxing fanatic and leading writer on the sport, as well as on his achievement as a war novelist and promoter of the beat generation's fascination with black street culture. In his 1957 essay "The White Negro," Mailer yearns to affiliate himself with "the language of hip" as "a set of subtle indications of . . . success or failure in the competition for pleasure" (*Advertisements for Myself* 349).[7] I mention this in order to suggest the circuitous routes that resources can travel, as Jones, himself affiliated with urban black male street culture in his youth but disaffiliated with it as a downtown beat artist, can revise his relation to it through Mailer. Even more curiously, Jones also has as a literary resource Baldwin's 1961 *Esquire* response to Mailer, "The Black Boy Looks at the White Boy." In this essay, whose mise-en-scène is the fashionable cocktail parties of Manhattan literati, Baldwin sizes up Mailer as a writer and as a man while exposing the homoerotic undercurrent of attraction and aversion that shapes masculine rivalry.[8] As in the case of Cleaver's later attack on Baldwin in *Soul on Ice,* where he explicitly sides with an apparently macho Mailer over an apparently punk Baldwin, Jones implicitly opts for Mailer's more aggressive, straight-up, name-cussing, punk-baiting, quick-jabbing, wide-open physical tactics over Baldwin's elegiac, introspective, defensive, highly intellectualized and preciously stylized ambivalence. I want to suggest here that in choosing Mailer's straight-out jabs over Baldwin's vulnerable exposures of buried crossracial homoeroticism beneath the rough face of masculine aversion, Jones is also choosing the hipster arena affiliated with black men's foul-mouthed, street-smart dozens over Baldwin's aura of sissified, defensive self-exposures of others' perversions. In a mode that we could analogize to high camp, Baldwin's accusatory logic takes the passively aggressive stance of "it takes one to know one," whereas Mailer's mode aims to set himself apart as a man amidst pals in a fierce but chummy winner-take-all game.

Jones's essay is composed in what critics have labeled his transitional period, in which he is not yet in his black cultural nationalist phase but is in the process of breaking from his "beat" phase, living in Greenwich Village with his white wife and children and accepted in the bohemian artistic circles as the leading new Negro writer on the American *avant garde* scene.[9] We can already see in Jones's sly, combative, sucker-punching attack the sort of impact that he will have on black nationalist invective. Jones suggests that the exhibition of sophisticated sensibility on Baldwin's and Abrahams's part is the opposite of manly individualism.

> Earlier Mr. Abrahams spoke of the horror in South Africa as "the ugly war of color," and the idea of "the racial struggle" as "that horrible animal" curdles the blood when you realize it is coming from a black man, and not the innocent white liberal made fierce by homosexuality. Again the *cry,* the spavined whine and plea of these Baldwins and Abrahams is sickening past belief. Why should anyone think of these men as individuals?
>
> (117, italics in original)

In modern Western culture, feelings are assumed to be the province of, the property of, individuals, not social groups—and more tellingly of *vulnerable* individuals who cannot protect themselves, like properly feminine women and improperly effeminate men. Promoting themselves—and being promoted—as the representative "voices" of black social groups, Baldwin and Abrahams become hysterically strained voices, disconnected from their social base and crying out in the white wilderness. They end up displacing the legitimate anger of the group with the representational suffering of their own persons, and this transaction in turn replaces a call for decisively militant political action with a prolonged limp whine. Through a series of binary identity oppositions pitting black angry manhood against white-bowing liberal sissiness, Jones exploits his skill for invective, which he says in ***Autobiography of LeRoi Jones*** is honed on the streets of Newark, to turn these men's claims of a fierce individualism into sissy cowardice:

> Why should anyone think of these men as individuals? Merely because they are able to shriek the shriek of a fashionable international body of white middle class society? Joan of Arc of the cocktail party is what is being presented through the writings and postures of men like these. As if the highest form of compliment the missionaries could receive was to see their boys making good, On Their Own, rattling off sensitivity ratios at parties.
>
> (117)

As Albert Murray will later turn the Black Power leader H. Rap Brown into a camp media queen, so Baraka feels compelled to turn Baldwin and Abrahams into hysterical she-men, shrieking their way into the hearts of the white middle class.[10] Calling them "Joan of Arc of the cocktail party," he represents their racial-class confusion—their failure to be "*real* black men"—as gender confusion, symbolized by the trivialization of Joan of Arc's prophetic voices. As the cross-dressing young warrior who leads the French into bloody victory over the English, Joan of Arc becomes the ultimate symbol of both transgressive sexuality and patriotic nationalism.[11] Baldwin and Abrahams invert this process, becoming black men masked as shrieking women masked as sensitive intellectuals in order to abuse their prophetic word-weapons to gain a safe place in the white parlor, far away from the battlefields where black armies clash by night. "They are too hip to be *real* black men," Jones blasts, but this hipness "is only, let us say, a covering to register their feelings, a gay exotic plumage as they dissemble in the world of ideas, and always come home with the shaky ones" (117-18, italics in original). Jones advocates a manhood that is unconcerned about what kind of figure one cuts in the world and is immune to fright from "some chattery panic" (119)—in other words, male "hysteria." He concludes the essay with a characteristic address/command/invitation to the (black male) audience to join in the scapegoating of these sissified figures.

> Deadly simple. If Abrahams and Baldwin were turned white, for example, there would be no more noise from them. Not because they consciously desire that, but

> because then they could be sensitive in peace. Their color is the only obstruction I can see to this state they seek, and I see no reason they should be denied it for so paltry a thing as heavy pigmentation. Somebody turn them! And then perhaps the rest of us can get down to the work at hand. Cutting throats!
>
> (120)

Because the enemy is a white-sympathizing sissy masked as a committed black man, the black writer's power becomes the obligation of shaming these male embarrassments either into reform or into total defection into the white camp. Baldwin and Abrahams are not really the targets of Jones's interest here; they are merely the scapegoating intermediaries whose prominence as "liberal" racial author-authorities makes them ideal policing vehicles for constructing a black male warrior identity. Implicitly, Jones constructs his audience as an army of ready black men. Anyone in that audience is a sissy with "gay exotic plumage" if he fails to experience the rush of excitement at the idea of "turn[ing] them" (which may also have the connotation of turning them *over*—delivering them to the enemy to be fucked by them) to prepare the way for the real man's business at hand: cutting throats.

The black writer-intellectual must sacrifice his individual desire (to be famous, to demonstrate his literary skill in ornate style, to fashion his unique vision) in favor of conducting the down-and-dirty acts of verbal and ultimately *literal* warfare—not being afraid to call a punk what he is to his face. This aspiration toward literal battle is constantly frustrated, however, by the fact that the writer's weapons are merely words—not fists, knives, or guns. Part of the black cultural nationalist writer's barrage of hostility, then, derives from his need to distract himself and his audience from the realization that as long as he has a pen in his hand, he is deferring picking up a real weapon. This hostility is necessarily also directed at that punk part of the self, which is in fact the writer within the self, suppressing through the act of writing the arrival of the *real* black man of warring action.

In other words, Jones is exorcising his own demons of "beat" sensitivity, as he attempts to distance himself from what is emerging as a past self. This past self is lauded by the white middle-class bohemians and homosexuals of Greenwich Village for his unique artistry, which wails with the existentialist angst of a dark night of the black humanist soul.[12] Baraka comes to see his own stint in Greenwich Village as a kind of Baldwinean ambivalence that nurtures a seductive ideology of intermediacy between the races, an intermediacy that means being made vulnerable to penetration from both sides. The ***Autobiography*** [***Autobiography of LeRoi Jones/Amiri Baraka***] fleshes out his past as an aborted trajectory headed toward out-Baldwining Baldwin. It is a narrative of self-correcting error, in which Baraka constantly repeats the act of "finding himself" in a changed situation without recognizing that or how he has gotten there. As he finds success in the downtown "beat" scene of Manhattan around 1957 to 1963, Baraka describes how slowly his friends change from being primarily black to being a racially mixed group, then from racially mixed to an all-white coterie with himself the only African American. Baraka becomes the hip center of cutting-edge literariness as the founder and co-editor of "***Zazen***" (***Yugen***), the literary magazine that helps to shake up beat underground culture into a national identity. As he becomes the center of the in-crowd, all of a sudden in looking at the poets in the magazine with its trend-setting black cover he notices his own racial exceptionality:

> The black cover on one hand does represent to me the coming into full force, or full consciousness, of one circle, at a relatively high literary level. But there is only one black writer, LeRoi Jones. (At the time I might have thought it was two!). . . . But I was not with them socially either. . . . I was "open" to all schools within the circle of white poets of all faiths and flags. But what had happened to the blacks? What had happened to me? How is it that there's only the one colored guy?
>
> (231)

Jones's beat identity is fashioned through both openness and outsiderness, each feeding the other. As a lower-class black man among upscale, slumming white beatniks, what other identity could fit? Like his white compatriots, he rejects the "organization man" conformity of the 1950s Eisenhower-McCarthy establishment. But he is nonetheless still alienated from these compatriots by his own racial-class experience. Thus, his openness to all that they have to offer signals his capacity to mediate between their fashionable hip rebellion and his own authentic search for an American (or anti-American) identity within the actual marginality of his black inheritance. Throughout the autobiography, Baraka defines himself as "*an outsider*" in explicit reference to Wright's novel (230). In other words, Wright's *Outsider* protagonist, Cross Damon, maps another aborted trajectory for the young Jones, a resource that the maturing Baraka will outgrow in eventually rejecting a self-defeating embroilment in decadent white politics for communion with radicalized blackness.

This outsider intermediacy links Baraka's work not only to Mailer, Jack Kerouac, Allen Ginsberg, and all the other white hipsters who think that they have defected into a cool downbeat escaping the square establishment and approximating hip blackness. In the ***Autobiography,*** he also links this bohemian phase to the sexual deviance of the rebelling white middle-class beatniks. When the white woman he has been casually seeing gets pregnant, he pops the question. Before he knows it, not only is he married with mulatto children, but he is also seeing other white women, cudgeling an Asian man with whom his wife takes up, and generally slipping mindlessly into the sexual deviations of white middle-class decadence. And where decadence goes, homosexuality cannot be far behind. In fact, it must be leading the way. Baraka finds himself becoming intimate with Ginsberg and Frank O'Hara, white homosexuals who not coincidentally are two leading lights of beat poetry through the inspiration of Walt Whitman and his songs of the open road, his veiled tributes to the robust love of comrades. Amidst such company, Jones finds himself investigating the psychology and verbal resources of the queer white mind. Unlike the previous generation of black writers, however, the young experimental Baraka has direct access to a wholly new phenomenon, the emerging enclaves of more-or-less "out" homosexuals who are flocking to New York, Chicago, Los Angeles, and San Francisco after World War II. It is important to remember that what Jones encounters among such predominately white middle-class homosexual enclaves is a process of the self-conscious making of a minority group patterned explicitly on the experience of African Americans—in other words, a group self-consciously anxious to fashion a cultural identity adapted from the very racial minority status that Jones is seeking to flee.

The pseudonymous "Donald Webster Cory" has already by 1951 brought out his ground-breaking book, *The Homosexual in America,* arguing for the tolerated minority status of homosexuals on par with that of Negroes, Jews, Mexican-Americans, the Deaf, and other "sub-worlds."[13] The 1950s also witnessed the first successful formation of organized homosexual politics.[14] Settling in Greenwich Village in 1957 in the midst of this flurry of largely underground homosexual activity, Jones enters into a beat enclave that is inextricably mixed with this emerging gay ghetto identity. In fact, the sense of high risk, nonconformity, and social rebellion evident in beat culture is feeding as much on the real dangers of associating with homosexuals as on the white hipster's vicarious endangerment of admiring life in the black ghettoes from a distance. From his white homosexual comrades, Jones becomes intimately acquainted with the complicated status dissonance and insider practices of being a white middle-class homosexual man in U.S. culture in the 1950s and early 1960s—a status and experience significantly different from being black and queer in the ghetto of the same period, even when such practices as camp are shared. In his ***Autobiography,*** Baraka writes about observing homosexuals like O'Hara and about discovering their self-identifying lingo of camp invective: "It was Frank whom I first heard pronounce the word 'camp.' 'Oh, that campy bastard!' or 'My dear, the production was entirely too campy.' Or he might just run someone down while tossing down a drink: 'It was a trifle tacky, don't you think?'" (235). Unlike the black sissies with whom Jones would already be familiar from his neighborhood in Newark and in other African-American communities, white urbane homosexuality maneuvers between, on the one hand, a respectable high society in need of homosexuals as a sign of the right to nonproductive luxury and, on the other hand, the unrespectable margins of forbidden, self-destructive street criminality.[15] Through the white male homosexuals, Baraka discovers a kind of convoluted social logic of dominant white culture, in which the homosexual is both a sign of advancing European-focused high culture, with its most sophisticated elite civilizing impulses, and at the same time a sign of the most degraded, decadent, abhorrent descent into legally punishable impulses of pathological self-destruction. In his 1965 essay, **"American Sexual Reference: Black Male,"** Baraka hits on this convoluted logic. "Most American white men are trained to be fags," he writes. Baraka is speaking both metaphorically and literally, for dominant culture itself cannot decide whether homosexuality is a rare psychological perversion suffered at the extreme fringes of society by immediately identifiable, hopelessly maimed individuals or whether it is a contagious physical-moral disorder spread by the sly recruitment of an invisible menace at the heart of dominant civilization. Baraka borrows this hegemonic logic to deconstruct white male supremacy, turning the Anglo Saxon standard of robust pioneer manhood into that other aesthetic of Western culture: the beautiful but entirely useless high art piece. "For this reason it is no wonder their faces are weak and blank, left without the hurt that reality makes—anytime. That red flush, those silk blue faggot eyes" (***Home*** [***Home: Social Essays***] 216). He pictures for us the beautiful, young, blond, blue-eyed boy still celebrated today in much white homosexual pornography, and, of course, this boy is an androgynous double for the ideal aesthetic object of high Western culture, the female nude or the still-life—which one doesn't matter. "So white women become men-things," he writes, "a weird combination, sucking the male juices to build a navel orange, which is themselves" (216). Alienated from productive work, the beautiful blonde lady, the beautiful blond homosexual, the high-art artifact without use all become reflections of one another. "The nonrealistic, the nonphysical. Think now, the goal of white society is luxury. Work is done by unfortunates. The purer white, the more estranged from, say, actual physical work" (217). This is the anxiety of William Hollingsworth Whyte's "organization man," of Herbert Marcuse's "one-dimensional man," of Mailer's "white Negro" brought to its ultimate resting place. At the same time that he figures the normalcy of white desire as the triumph of the white homosexual in civilization, Baraka also configures the extreme other within white civilization ironically not as blackness but as white homosexuality. "The artist is the concentrate, as I said, of the society's tendencies—the extremist. And the most extreme form of alienation *acknowledged* within white society is homosexuality. The long abiding characterization of the Western artist as usually 'queer' does not seem out of place" (219, italics added). Through his encounter with white homosexuality, then, Baraka stumbles onto the perfect symbol of the "exotic" ensconced within dominating mainstream culture, the terrifying threat lurking within white men's own master narrative of progressive, productive self-control. The lingo of camp makes manifest this extreme within civilization, as it calls out the artifice, hypocrisy, parasitism, and queerness buried within the backside of white high culture.

In ***Autobiography,*** Baraka describes himself slipping unawares into this queer bordering *space* between high white civilization and the forbidden white subworld: "I found myself going to the ballet, to cocktail parties, 'coming over for drinks,' to multiple gallery openings with Frank O'Hara and his shy but likable 'roommate'" (235). On the one hand, we see the open association of homosexuality with high culture; on the other, we see its rightly paranoid reticence in the open secret of the "roommate." Visiting Charles Olsen's "castle" in Massachusetts, Jones, again the only black among white men, is startled to discover that he and Olson are the only straight-identified men among queer falsetto voices, "high and tittering," as the homosexuals, "butt-naked," take a late-night plunge into the pool. "It was like being woven into a tapestry of exotic otherness," he writes (282). The homosexuals are privileged boys with the luxury of grown-up play, and unselfconscious in the privilege of their white male nakedness, their exotic otherness is protected in this elite castle by the sea. How odd it must have been for Jones to spy on this other otherness invisibly shielded by the lap of white American luxury, an otherness so "acknowledged" in a way different from his own race's marginalization at the socioeconomic bottoms. Like those who create a daring homosexual rights movement in the midst of anti-Communist "hysteria," these exotic others take their right to belong as middle-class whites for granted even as they are hounded and attacked with both legal and extralegal, verbal and physical systematic violence to purge them as a socially agreed-upon menace to the welfare of the white middle-class mainstream.

I am not interested here in reading Baraka's engagement with homosexuality as autobiographical confession, though this certainly can be done, as shown by Simmons.[16] Simmons instructively correlates the key passages in which Baraka images homosexuality in his work, and he helps us to see the struggle evident in the early work and Baraka's black nationalist exploitation of homosexuality in the context of earlier and later expressions of homophobia among African-American writers, especially Afrocentrists of the 1970s and 1980s. Placing Baraka's representation of homosexuality in the larger cultural-historical context of black men's long tradition of commenting on sexual nonconformity in discourses as apparently wide apart as Richard Wright's fiction is from the dozens, we can begin to see a more complicated picture of Baraka's uses of homosexuality for various rhetorical and ideological purposes. The first thing that we must note is that Jones/Baraka's understanding of homosexuality has to derive from various conflicting sources, as must be the case for any African American maturing in and near the postwar ghettos of the northern U.S. The opposition of the church and the street and of white official culture and informal black culture delivers confused messages about the pragmatics of tolerating homosexuality, and even *within* the black church the message is muddied by the peculiar conditions of black segregation, marginalization, and socioeconomic oppression. It should not be surprising, then, that Baraka records his acculturation into the knowledge of sexual variance as a process of learning about everyday life on the ghetto street, especially through the practice of the dozens, which represents for Baraka a distillation of urban black culture much as it does for Wright.[17] The crucial split in lower-class urban culture is *not* between heterosexual and homosexual knowledge but instead between formal, official white knowledge imposed in schools and the informal, common know-how of the black turf, with all of its material, social, and sexual deviations from the white mainstream. Baraka writes in ***Autobiography***:

> What the school says you learned and were responsible for is way off far away from what you came away with in a practical sense. The reading, writing, arithmetic, geography, social studies, shop, history, penmanship, gym we got was one thing. But learning about dicks and pussies and fags and bulldaggers. Seeing the reaction to cocksuckers and motherfuckers and sonafabitches and bastards. Understanding what fucking was and what it had to do with sucking. All these things and such as that.
>
> The games and sports of the playground and streets was one registration carried with us as long as we live.
>
> (23-24)

Baraka's lifelong registration card into his "native" culture includes smarts about the street, and all of those whose right it is to move freely around on it. Since black fags and bulldaggers are a part of black urban life on the street, they constitute an essential part of the common knowledge of the culture. Baraka describes the presence of homo-sissies on the fringes of his boys' gang with a quite different tone and emphasis from Wright's scene of aggression against Aggie West in *The Long Dream.*

> And Danny whose brother was gay in those days when we called them "sissies." And that carried a weight then, Jim. "He's a sissy." Wow. And the dude did pitch

> and switch when he walked and his hair was done up rococo and curled up, his eyes and mouth were pornography. . . . [Danny] had a cousin just a little older than us who also was "funny," who fanned up and down the street like he was on his way to mind the seraglio.
>
> (25)[18]

This brief passage is packed with familiar terms identifying the particular interaction of black street culture with direct knowledge of unabashed black homosexuality: "sissies," "pitch and switch," "funny," "fan." Danny's cousin is clearly a homo-swish ("switch" being a variant of "swish"), as he swishes his behind (like a girl, that is) and pitches his erotic designation pornographically up and down the street. Lacking the intensity of homosexual panic turned into violent assault that we witness in Wright's Aggie West scene, Baraka's passage instead emphasizes the doubleness of the relation to the faggot presence. An expected "wow" of distancing dismay—almost admiration for such flaunting bravery—is mixed inextricably with the fact that these two particular homo-swishes are a common sight on the streets of the neighborhood, where they come and go mostly as they please. This certainly does not preclude a common reaction of teasing from nervous young boys and possible episodes of violence, though such episodes would have to be rare given the upfront flaunting behavior displayed by Danny's brother and cousin in their own neighborhood.[19] Furthermore, Danny is one of the gang, one who has to take teasing about the two swishes in his family. "So Dan had to hear about that. But there was calmness and loyalty in Danny and a quiet palship you always counted on" (25). The teasing goes around, as does self-directed hostility of a more ferocious kind on some occasions.[20]

Knowledge of sexual variance is crucial to successful enactment of the dozens, but it is a knowledge that comes fluently with everyday life, a very different relation to deviance from that dramatized by Wright when he expresses embarrassment before his white audience at the ways in which "*The Dirty Dozens* extol incest, celebrate homosexuality" (*White Man, Listen!* 93). This embarrassment is absent from Baraka's take on the dozens. "The Dozens. You know the African Recrimination Songs!! . . . But Dozens always floated around every whichaway, around my way, when small. Or with close friends, half lit, when you got big. But that was either fun, for fun connected folks, or the sign that soon somebody's blood would be spilt" (29). A source of knowledge about the world and the self's identification to racial culture, the dozens are celebrated in the ***Autobiography*** as the first tutor in the uses of creative thinking. "The lesson? The importance of language and invention. The place of innovation. The heaviness of 'high speech' and rhythm" (29). In other words, like Wright, Baraka places the dozens in the African-American literary tradition but not as nasty raw material whose creativity needs to be refined by "high" poets; instead Baraka embraces it *as* "high speech"—"[n]ot in abstract literary intaglios but on the sidewalk (or tar) in the playground, with everything at stake, even your ass" (30). The dozens are intimately associated with black urban tolerance of variant sexuality in both Wright and Baraka. As indicated in Baraka's pun on the "ass" at stake, the dozens entails both a playfully flaunting defiance of dominant norms, sexual and otherwise, and tolerated survival at the margins of a hostile world. The teasing of homo-swishes on the ghetto street and the inventive uses of fag-baiting in the dozens are certainly forms of identity policing. What is being policed, however, is *not* a queer identity alien to blackness but instead a *black* identification *of* queerness verbally parried *within* black street culture as one of its defining characteristics. The black homo-swish is one of the major markers defining the outer limits of ordinary black masculinity. Displaying his gender deviance as a sign of what he desires erotically, the swish is defined as not a man, or not wholly a man, but existing somewhere in between a real black woman and a real black man. Although the swish is accepted as an undeniable aspect of what it means to survive, and sometimes flauntingly so, in a racially marginalized identity, "real" men publicly distance themselves from swishes on the street, and thus construct and police their own identity *as* real men, even if on occasion some of these real men privately consort with the swishes that they routinely tease on the street.

In the transitional period, Jones/Baraka interlayers his internalized black cultural sense of street homosexuality, with its connotations evident in the sexually-defiant dozens, with the dissonant status-meaning he observes in the predominately white homosexual enclaves. This is evident in his highly experimental novel, ***The System of Dante's Hell*** (1965), where he dramatizes black male self-alienation in a first-person narrative of homosexual encounter. Among the demons that Jones's first-person narrator encounters in his journey down into the cortex of his mind is the vice of homosexuality. (Note here how Baraka too exploits the spatializing metaphor of Dante's circles of hell to characterize his hero's competing racial and sexual identities.) Queerness here is still very much an ordinarily distinctive experience marking the *inside* of the particularity of black culture, as identified in the ***Autobiography,*** but already we see interlayered within this black inside another sense of the queer as a white European phenomenon:

> In Chicago I kept making the queer scene. Under the "El" with a preacher. And later, in the rotogravure, his slick (this other, larger, man, like my father) hair, murrays grease probably. He had a grey suit with gold and blue threads and he held my head under the quilt. The first guy (he spoke to me grinning) and I said my name was Stephen Dedalus. And I read Proust and mathemat-

> ics and loved Eliot for his tears. Towers, like Yeats (I didn't know him then, or only a little because of the Second Coming & Leda). But Africans lived there and czechs. One more guy and it was over. On the train, I wrote all this down. A journal now sitting in a tray on top the closet, where I placed it today. The journal says "Am I like that?"
>
> (57-58)

The narrator's anonymous sexual encounters occur on the ghetto street, specifically under the "El" trains, those dark, empty, dead-ended, distinctively Chicago spaces that have no immediate uses. Though anonymous and clearly disorienting for the narrator, the sex is marked by a deeply embedded familiarity. Jones emblematizes this through both an impersonal and a personal familiarity: the first, the preacher, one of the most common cultural markers of black community; the second, the narrator's father, the familiar culture shading over into the intimacy of the familial. The passage is framed by another kind of familiarization, the return to the home, the known object resting appropriately on the closet. Framed by black cultural familiarity, the passage nonetheless contains a series of allusions to trendy, obtuse high European modernists who write in the kind of fractured stream of consciousness characterizing the passage itself. The narrator claims explicit identity *not* in the sexual experience with these black men at the hub of the country's most populous black ghetto, but instead in these elusive allusions to high European civilization. The narrator says deceptively (self-deceptively?) to the smiling man, "[M]y name is Stephen Dedalus"—a fraud that seems to fit well in a circle of hell reserved for the "Simply Fraudulent." The protagonist of James Joyce's *Portrait of the Artist as a Young Man* and *Ulysses,* Stephen Dedalus is an allusion inside an allusion inside an allusion, for ***The System of Dante's Hell*** is clearly Jones's fictionalization of his own coming into being as a troubled "brown" writer amidst a turbulent black race demanding its rightful place in the nation-state, as Joyce's book fabricates his artistic growing up as a troubled middle-class-Irish writer amidst the turbulence of a would-be Irish nation-state. As Lloyd W. Brown argues, for Jones, the figure of Roi as Dedalus concerns the author's growing self-alienation from the West (76), but it also embodies the author-narrator's concern with how to determine what to leave behind. This is particularly a problem in black cultural nationalist theory, where disentangling the "African" from the "European" elements can be impossibly tricky. This fraud of self-misidentification breeds the proliferation of other modernist figures: Proust, T. S. Eliot, and Yeats. As opposed to the dozens and other signposts of *black* popular knowledge, high modernism gravitates around a self-consciously declining European civilization, becoming hopelessly embroiled in its own incestuously nonproductive modes of cultural literariness. The rococo protocols of high modernism also frequently affiliate the acclaimed writer with a queer practice analogous to the camp homosexual of high society, for both speak an arch insider lingo available only to those with vast amounts of privilege, leisure, and official education at the center of a civilization whose practical priorities and profits revolve around mass production and mainstream recreation in mass culture.

Jones continues this identity struggle in the final chapter of ***System*** [***The System of Dante's Hell***], which he labels "Heretics," from the sixth of Dante's descending nine circles of hell, each circle deeper and more damned than the previous one. In a note, Jones explains why he places heresy, rather than Dante's treachery, in the deepest part of hell: "It is heresy, against one's own sources, running in terror, from one's deepest responses and insights . . . the denial of feeling . . . that I see as basest evil" (7). By "sources" Jones means both authentic inner insights and also perhaps one's formative cultural experiences. There is a sense in which ***System*** fights the tendency toward cultural transformation that occurs as we re-source these formative identifications through new cultural experiences. Symbolically, the homosexual impulse in ***System*** represents this "basest evil," this heresy of the flower's unnatural "turning from moisture and sun" (7). The section focuses on the narrator and one of his military buddies who go out on the town with two seventeen-year-old prostitutes in the Black Bottom of Shreveport, Louisiana. The narrator, who feels that he and his friend are like "two imitation white boys come in on" the juke joint of the black Bottom (128), is left alone with Peaches, "[f]at with short baked hair split at the ends," a "[p]regnant empty stomach" and a "thin shrieking voice like knives against a blackboard" (127). As Farah Griffin remarks, "Peaches *is* body. She has a belly just waiting for his seed" ("*Who Set You Flowin'?*" 167). But the sense of a natural identity for male (seed) and female (awaiting belly) is achieved with great difficulty. Peaches begins to make love to him, and the narrator begins "to protest": "I'm sorry. I'm fucked up. My mind, is screwy, I don't know why. I can't think. I'm sick. I've been fucked in the ass. I love books and smells and my own voice. You don't want me. Please, Please, don't want me" (131). She teases him by grabbing his military cap and throwing it around to others, "like kids in the playground doing the same thing to some unfortunate fag" (132). Throughout the narrator flashes back to other scenes of intense alienation, other scenes of erotic entanglement and flight in his distant and immediate past. In his childhood, he is ostracized for being upwardly mobile: "And suffer so slight, in the world. The world? Literate? Brown skinned. Stuck in the ass. Suffering from what? Can you read? Who is T. S. Eliot? So what? A cross. You've got to like girls. Weirdo. Break, Roi, break" (134). Jones entangles the narrator's misidentification of himself—or others' identification of him—with high European literacy, his "brown" social class, and this erring identity with his sexual anxieties and confusions ("[s]tuck in the ass"), as well as the sexual confusions that other boys' project onto him in their desire to prove their manhood. At such a moment, the text seems on the verge of associating white misidentification, the desire for social mobility within the mainstream, with a failure of manhood, the gender dissonance of the homo-sissy.

Note moreover the narrator's use of sexualized invective to motivate himself to desire Peaches. "Move. Frightened bastard," the narrator says to himself, or others say to him, or he imagines others thinking it about his resistance to Peaches. "Frightened scared sissy mother-fucker" (135). Lacking the inventive, creative, verbal gymnastics of the dozens, this barrage of simple name-calling is opposed both to the dozens and the rococo high literariness of queer modernism. In the apartment of Peaches, the narrator's thoughts carry him to the "queer scene" in Chicago. He does not want to be with Peaches, but she forces herself on him. He did not want to be with the faggots but he was drawn to them (see 138-39). At once back in Chicago and in the room with Peaches, at once hating to be touched by faggots and by Peaches, and desiring to be touched and loved by faggots and Peaches, the narrator is torn between an awakening in the true self and the embrace of an unnatural impulse within the self. Knowing which is which—who is the reflection and what the shadow self—seems impossible. Peaches says, "You don't like women, huh?" "No wonder you so pretty . . . ol bigeye faggot" (139, ellipsis in original). As Melvin Dixon has noted, Peaches "all but *rapes* Roi."[21] The scene rehearses a confusing violation, a sadomasochistic sexual initiation in which it is difficult to know who is violating, who violated. "I was crying now. Hot hot tears and trying to sing. Or say to Peaches. 'Please, you don't know me. Not what's in my head. I'm beautiful. Stephen Dedalus. . . . My eyes. My soul is white, pure white, and soars'" (140). Peaches slaps him when he pisses rather than ejaculates.

> Her arms around my hips pulled down hard and legs locked me and she started yelling. Faggot. Faggot. Sissy Motherfucker. And I pumped myself. Straining. Threw my hips at her. And she yelled for me to fuck her. Fuck her. Fuck me, you lousy fag. And I twisted, spitting tears, and hitting my hips on hers, pounding flesh in her, hearing myself weep.
>
> (140-41)

Note again the use of invective, this time in the mouth of Peaches, as she derides Roi and brings him (and herself?) to orgasm in an utterance affiliated with sadomasochistic sex. The man is supposed to berate the woman—calling her his "pussy," his "bitch," his "whore"—in the verbal rituals of rough heterosexual sex.[22] In a sense, Peaches is calling out the demons of faggotry through fag-baiting invective in a similar way that black cultural nationalist invective attempts to purge the punk in potential black male warriors. What does it mean, however, that such invective is associated in this scene with the sexual turn-on itself? The rape of Roi, or Roi's rape, becomes a purifying manhood ritual, a purging of the homosexual impulse, equated with the impulse to be the blond aesthetic object of European impotence: Stephen Dedalus, the sensitive, weeping, ineffectual, emasculated creature fabricated by a white master-writer whose own Irish race is colonized and raped by a bigger, whiter master-race, the English. When Kimberly Benston calls this scene the narrator's "purest sexual experience, an initiation into love with a southern black whore" (11), he seems to rehearse the curious point of view taken by the narrator. Given the sordidness of the scene—its background of bartered exchange and its foreground of coercion—we have to ask: What makes it the "purest" except its normalization through heterosexual ritual?[23]

Roi's rape is the turning point, the moment in which the narrative becomes for a brief respite a recognizable, penetrable, linear story centered in the ordinary world away from the nightmare of high modernist fragmentation and impenetrable stream of consciousness. Struggling to claim Black Power in the midst of his white bohemian adventure, Jones concludes this penultimate chapter of ***System*** with an awakening into a nightmare of whiteness from a dream of black male camaraderie: "The negroes danced around my body and spilled whisky on my clothes. I woke up 2 days later, with white men, screaming for God to help me" (152). The narrative seems to turn against its own sense of progress in this moment. As Houston A. Baker, Jr., writes: "He awakens three days later with the feeling that his entire experience among the blacks transpired in a cave where he sat reading. The room of ***Preface*** [***Preface to a Twenty Volume Suicide Note***] and Plato's cave of shadows seem to merge here as a sign of the solipsistic artist."[24] Given that the "solipsistic artist" is equated with white bohemia, we can say that Plato's cave becomes a symbol for the artificial world of whiteness that shapes the reality of the Shreveport Black Bottom. Roi's nightmare is not that Bottom reality, but instead the awakening itself, the inability to get out of the cave of Eurocentric bohemianism. Even the art of arch, oblique allusion—such as the highbrow reference to Plato's cave itself—so crucial to modernist craft and to some forms of camp works against his desire for a real black manhood, and as Jones shifts from beat modernism to black nationalist invective, one of the ways in which he signals this shift is to attempt to purge such Eurocentric allusions. In actuality, however, he simply replaces one set of allusions with another, for at another level, as the cave allusion indicates, Jones/Baraka is resigned to the reality of words themselves. Whatever powers to accuse or bond, to heal or endanger that words possess, the reality is that words constitute themselves purely through allusion.[25]

Just as modernist allusion cannot easily be separated from the verbal gymnastics practiced on the street in Baraka's "native" culture, so the black nationalist invective that becomes Baraka's most prized word-weapon cannot be so easily untangled from identification with forbidden queer desire. The explicitly labeled cultural source of Baraka's skill with invective is, of course, the Dirty Dozens, that verbal contest of sexual exposure. Like camp, the dozens is an art of *double-entendre*—double meanings, double takes, double fast punches—always with a defiant edge of the sexually *risqué*. Both result from tactics of street survival in marginalized communities that are perceived by dominant culture as *sub*cultures. Both camp and the dozens take the way that their respective social identities are projected as hyper-sexualized by dominant culture and turn the tables by making sexual talk itself a playful weapon. Both modes of verbal contest refuse to accept the embarrassment and shame cast onto their communities by a dominant culture that desires to keep sex a dirty secret practiced deviantly only by society's suppressed others, even as there is a strong element of self-castigation in both camp and the dozens, based in these negative sexual judgments "mainstream" society makes about homosexuals and African Americans.[26] The dozens derives from a "street" culture of the black ghettos, although its ultimate sources may be in Africa. Camp derives from the urban street, the dark, hidden corners of white main streets where closeted homosexuals congregate.[27] This street subworld of closeted homosexuals thrives in 1950s America in the dark byways of train-station restrooms, parks, docks, and other out-of-the-way public places where the prying police might be prone to leave them alone, although the ultimate sources of the homosexual street may be in Europe, in what Jeffrey Weeks describes as the "metropolitan subculture of Molly houses, pubs, fields, walks, squares, and lavatories" of 18th- and 19th-century England, Paris, and Berlin (55). Although the differences between black and white queer street practices are myriad, there are nonetheless important cultural-historical resonances, one of which links camp and the dozens as verbal contests involving feats of creative insider name-calling always with a sexual edge in which individuals from socially marginalized groups enact their ideological complicity with and resistance to the dominant norm.

Whether used to stave off actual violence on the street or just for the sheer pleasure of word-mastery always on the edge of physical assault, the dozens parry the violent condition of racial subordination into a sense of self-control over, at the least, one's own enclave. Likewise, camp is the homosexual's internalization of the constant surveillance, entrapment, and violence directed toward homosexuals by conformist straight society. There is, in other words, a tinge of identity-sadomasochism in both modes of street behavior, whereby the participants both take pleasure in and inflict verbal pain on each other, acknowledging how they *share* maligned identities by pretending to malign those shared identities themselves. Making a playful game of the sexual aggressions directed at them amidst an ugly reality of relentless stereotyping and other forms of conformist verbal violence dictated by U.S. socio-sexual norms, the sexualized verbal battles of camp and the dozens engage their participants in acts of community-formation and identity-sustenance by resourcefully using the scraps most at their disposal: the things others say hatefully about them. Although a form of internally-directed hostility, camp provides a sense of self-control within one's own grouping, as it, like the dozens, creates a fierce hierarchy of those skilled in intimate knowledge of the subworld. A homosexual can camp it up by calling another homosexual "girl," "queen," "sissy," "pansy," "faggot," "whore," "bitch," or other such gender-bending sexualized terms in an ultra-falsetto voice that signals a "cat fight." Like camp, the dozens tend to revel in inventing or re-inventing gender-bending sexual confusion. It is not just calling names to provoke a response. It is remaking the world a topsy-turvy carnivalesque place where who's on top is unpredictable. In the ***Autobiography of LeRoi Jones,*** Baraka provides good instances of how the dozens tends to up-side-down socio-sexual norms: "Your mother's a man—Your father's a woman. Your mother drink her own bathwater—Your mother drink other people's. Your mother wear combat boots—Your mother don't wear no shoes at all with her country ass" (30). Plumbing what Baraka calls the "outermost reaches" existing "in our head" (30), these verbal contests not only upturn authority figures like mothers and fathers; they also turn on uncloseting the forbidden things that respectable people are not supposed to think, much less mention in public. This is more than just the sexualization of the world into a polymorphous playground of pleasure and aggression—as Mailer would have it. It also includes dredging up the dirt—the nasty bathwater—and forcing it into one another's faces. On the streets, one must be both "mouth-dangerous" and "physically capable," Baraka says (30), for the dozens can both prevent and incite violence, depending on the context, just as those camping it up *can* end up in a "cat fight" if they go too far. The dozens and camp cannot be kept disentangled as "subcultural" modes of identity invective, given the constant underground cultural interchange between blacks and white homosexuals in the urban centers at least since the 1920s. Camp should not be identified solely with white urban homosexuality, for black homosexuals' inventive use of identity invective reveals a specific interaction between the dozens and camp so indeterminate that defining where one "site" or "role" begins and the other ends in their verbal contests would be absolutely impossible.[28]

After Baraka has imbibed the dozens in childhood and moved on to high Beat poetry, and then to disillusionment with the bohemian life, as he has begun to work out with his black colleagues the emerging tenets of Black Arts, he is still conditioned to respond to instigating situations with the weapon of the dozens. Midway through the ***Autobiography,*** Baraka records an incident that occurs around 1964, just after his play ***Dutchman*** has received positive critical attention nationally. At a party, an envious black "actor-model" who also writes plays and "was alarmed that my play had gotten some attention," starts ridiculing ***Dutchman*** in earshot of Jones.

> My normal reaction would be to say something really low as to this dude's gender or sexual orientation or maybe just about the sexual orientation of his father or mother or both. But I just looked in his direction and smiled really as pleasantly as sulphuric acid could. And that was because I could tell, even though I hadn't heard the entire remark, that there was some element to it that was, indeed, legitimate.
>
> (***Autobiography*** 277)

Baraka's backing down in this moment has more to do with his own sense of *deserving* the overheard attack on ***Dutchman,*** a play first performed downtown largely to the white bohemian audiences who applaud it and reward it with their cherished drama prizes. The implication in the ***Autobiography*** is that this is one of the minor incidents that helps Baraka to check himself, and that leads eventually to his abandonment of Greenwich Village for Harlem and to the establishment of the Black Arts Repertory Theater/School there. Otherwise, Baraka's "normal reaction" would have been to play the dozens on and with his black playwright rival by insulting his gender or sexual orientation or that of a family member. Gauging the "authentic" amount of hostility in someone's resorting to the dozens (or camp) is solely a circumstantial matter. By invoking the dozens, Baraka would be "reading" or signifying on the man by making clear the envy motivating the negative comment about ***Dutchman.*** The other man's response—how he handles the insult by lobbing his own—helps to determine whether the contest becomes a pleasurable game or a futile fistfight.

Bringing the spirit of the dozens into black cultural nationalist invective adds an element that is normally missing in the dozens. Both camp and the dozens are "inside" contests. The target of camp is routinely another homosexual from one's specific in-group, just as the target of the dozens is normally a black "neighbor," whether straight or queer, from your actual neighborhood or visiting from a ghetto across the country. The dozens is not normally used on white people, or on anyone with no apparent connection to the neighborhood in which the specific contest is being played out. In the case of the actor-model in Baraka's autobiography, that neighborhood is implied as the community of writers as well as the racial community of those who would understand the nature of the sexualized intraracial invective. What Baraka imbibes from white homosexuality is white society's hatred of themselves, fear of their own impending decline, embodied in their hatred of the invisible homosexuals hidden at the center of their seats of power—a self-castigation reflected in white camp itself. Because homosexuals always hold that ultimate symbolic status of the queer border, associated with the black margins at the bottom but also associated with white decadence at the highest levels of the U.S. social scale, the faggot—white or desiring to be white—becomes the perfect intermediating scapegoat for a black nationalist invective. In other words, Baraka strikes at what he observes to be white men's own greatest fear, concretely enacted in the myriad homosexual hunts, entrapments, raids, and purges that occur throughout the 1950s and into the 1960s, focused not only on police surveillance and entrapment of anonymous homosexuals in their street haunts but more crucially in the highest institutions of white power: the government, the military, corporate organizations, and universities. As John D'Emilio points out, this homosexual panic at the highest levels during the McCarthy era results from a paranoia that connects homosexuals not only with communist sedition but also with the capacity for silently infiltrating and taking over the (white, male) establishment: "Lacking toughness, the effete, overly educated male representatives of the Eastern establishment had lost China and Eastern Europe to the enemy. Weak-willed, pleasure-seeking homosexuals—'half-men'—feminized everything they touched and sapped the masculine vigor that had tamed a continent" (49). Targeting the very foundation of manly self-making Manifest Destiny underpinning American imperialist and white supremacist mythology, Baraka's white homosexual name-calling intentionally aims at the largest nerve exposed by the most powerful white men themselves.

Jones's 1964 play, ***The Baptism,*** which opened downtown one night before ***Dutchman,*** shows his appreciative use of camp in no uncertain terms. A sort of Beat morality play, ***The Baptism,*** like ***The Toilet*** of the same year, focuses on homosexuality as a mode of outsiderness that challenges the repressive order of dominant culture. Whereas ***The Toilet,*** as its setting and title indicate, positions the (white) homosexual as a gut-level threat to the herd mentality that socializes boys into becoming the extralegal cops of society's normative masculine, heterosexual values through fag-bashing, ***The Baptism*** emphasizes a more allegorical conflict between two abstract characters, the Homosexual and the Minister, over the masturbatory sins of a boy who claims to be the Son of God. A sort of Blakean Satanic character, the homosexual represents, as Werner Sollors points out, "a sophisticated Bohemian protagonist associated with the eternal adversary, the devil" (103). More specifically, the homosexual embodies fey and flaunting defiance, trivialization of society's highest laws through inversion and ridicule, and celebration of pure non-procreative pleasure that Baraka throughout his work identifies with (white) homosexuality. In this play and to a lesser extent ***The Toilet,*** however, this figure is less ambivalently embedded as an erratic, untethered force of liberated, rebellious energy. The Homosexual spars with the Minister through camp attitude and wit and thus exposes the sinister hypocrisy of the minister, his congregation, and his doctrines—which are no match for the Homosexual's cutting verbal resources. When the congregation attempts a second sacrifice of the Christ son, we realize that their repression has overtaken their humanity and made it monstrous. According to Sollors, "The boy is supported, if not overshadowed, by the figure of the homosexual, who despite all that Baraka adds to make him ridiculous, is the true spokesman of the drama. Although occasionally motivated by lewd self-interest, the homosexual remains the only character with common sense" (105). Sollors seems to misunderstand the absurdity of the Homosexual. It is not so much that Baraka is ridiculing him as that he is making him the figure of ridiculous fun embodied in the kind of camp he has observed among his homosexual friends in Greenwich Village, as well as, no doubt, among the black swishes in Harlem, Newark, Chicago, and other African-American ghettos.[29] Because camp erases the line between the masterful agent of attack and satirized target, there is a necessary confusion in it between the subject and object of ridicule. In camp invective, the homosexual also ridicules himself in attacking other queers, always lambastes heterosexual norms as well as homosexual defiance of those norms, because everything is leveled to the same ground of pleasurable masquerade and vamping nonsense.

Although we do not have space to examine in detail Baraka's interesting use of camp in the play, we can see a good example of it in the final speech, appropriately a monologue delivered by the Homosexual to the audience. The bodies of the congregation are littered across the stage, as though the detritus of corpses in a classical tragedy. The Homosexual climbs from under the crush of bodies and says, as he turns the Minister's body over on his face:

> Serves him right for catering to rough trade. All out like lights. I better get out of here before somebody comes in and asks me to help clean the place up. Damn, looks like some really uninteresting kind of orgy went on in here. (*Looks at watch.*) Hmmmm. 1:30. I got about an hour before the bars close. Think I'll drift on up to 42nd Street and cruise Bickford's. (*Starts to leave.*) Wonder what happened to that cute little religious fanatic [meaning the boy who's claimed to be the Christ]. (*Does his ballet step. Starts to sing his song.*) God, Go-od, God.
>
> (32)

In the first line, he turns the Minister into a repressed homosexual, a universalizing gesture typical in camp. The Minister becomes what gay men call a "closet-case," a person so deeply repressed that he turns his hidden homosexual desire into vicious attacks of gay men in public—like Roy Cohn, McCarthy's homosexual "right-hand man" during the House Un-American Activities Committee tribunals, and J. Edgar Hoover, the homosexual, cross-dressing homophobic head of the Federal Bureau of Investigation. The closet-case is the opposite of the camping homosexual, for the former engages in homosexual activity in private and attacks other homosexuals in public in order to throw the scent away from himself, whereas the camping homosexual playfully ridicules other homosexuals through private badinage while protecting the identity of closeted homosexuals in public. Another element of camp involves either subtly eroticizing or baldly sexualizing things that are usually held sacrosanct. The Homosexual's "reading" on the Minister enacts this practice as well. He then names the outcome of the congregation's behavior in the church an orgy, which is accurate to the extent that their attempt to police the boy's masturbatory acts has also been an opportunity for fantasizing and engaging in sex with the boy. While camp frequently uses innuendo, double *entendre,* and other gestures of speaking and reading between the lines, it also values brutal honesty, sometimes communicated most viciously, sometimes in a parody of loving concern. The Homosexual takes on this role of witness to truth, exposing for the audience what otherwise might remain unsaid by other characters or unarticulated in the abstract allegory. He is the only character who will publicly proclaim his sexual attraction for the boy, rather than hiding it behind religious fanaticism.

In ***The Baptism,*** Jones uses camp affirmatively largely by representing homosexuality in its own particular context and as a force for disturbance of the status quo, if not for revolutionary change. After the fiasco of the "orgy," the Homosexual decides to go to a specific street to go cruising in a specific bar recognizable to hip members of the audience who know Manhattan's gay subworld. In much of Baraka's work after ***The Toilet*** and ***The Baptism,*** however, camp is used almost against itself, certainly as a way of attacking the enemy through homosexual invective. It is also blended to such an extent with what has become more narrowly characterized as black nationalist invective that we can easily forget the cultural sources and resources of this invective in *both* camp and the dozens. This use of a camped dozens can be seen in Baraka's rarely-discussed poem **"Western Front,"** published in the 1969 volume ***Black Magic,*** which William J. Harris calls "Baraka's first black nationalist-inspired collection of poetry" (***Baraka/ Jones Reader*** [***The LeRoi Jones/Amiri Baraka Reader***] 210). Baraka begins by converting the white man's frontier—his "Western Front"—into a battle-line that must eventually trip him up.

> My intentions are colors, I'm filled with color, every
> tint you think of
> lends to mine
> My mind is full of color, hard muscle streaks,
> Or soft glow round exactness registration.
>
> (***Baraka/Jones Reader*** 215)

We could easily mistake the first phrase as attributed to the abstract white man, who is busy labeling others' colors. However, we quickly realize that it is a black man's statement about himself, and about the inescapable intentionality of black fullness. As the white man constantly tries to purge all colored others, tries to create a myth of his own innocence through a myth of his pure whiteness—as Baldwin might say—he unintentionally cuts himself off from the fullness of the real, both the hard muscularity of sharp things and the "soft glow" that registers the roundness of things. The poem transits from a statement about the fullness of black reality to a statement about the inadequacy of poetry to capture that blackness, a typical move for Baraka. He directs this commentary, however, at an other, at the epitome of the bohemian poetic in this period, Allen Ginsberg:

> Poems are made
> By fools like Allen Ginsberg, who loves God, and
> went to India
> only to see God, finding him walking barefoot in the
> street,
> blood sickness and hysteria, yet only God touched this
> poet,
> who has no use for the world.

Shifting into a slight invective, the poem distances itself not only from Allen Ginsberg's kind of hip poetry but from *all* poetry. This shift is indicated by the format of the "poem," as its lines lengthen to simulate the unlined pattern of prose. Ginsberg, as both the most celebrated Beat poet and the first canonized white gay militant poet, becomes an image of the missionary targeting an exotic land to find God. That Ginsberg goes "Only to see God" seems at first to invert the missionary's pattern, but in fact Ginsberg's search for the Hindu God turns out to be a kind of colonizing consumption no less. The God that Ginsberg thinks he sees is not the God who walks the streets of India barefooted, maimed with blood sickness, wracked with the hysteria of poverty and want. Ginsberg, like the missionary imperialist that he is, cannot be touched by that world drenched in fleshly deprivation. The God he seeks must float "high above real meaning," like "floaters" who "prop themselves in pillows/letting soft blondes lick them into serenity." This imagery recalls Baraka's idea of the white homosexual as the objectifying aesthetic lost to reality. Sexuality itself becomes devoid of the fullness of the colors of the real, as we get a vision of an all-white heaven—blondes on white clouds licking into a static serenity the white poet in his humanless state of colorless ecstasy. Baraka concludes the poem, not as we might expect with invective against the white man as faggot, but instead against the white man's God:

> But only God, who is sole dope
> manufacturer of the universe, and is responsible for ease
> and logic. Only God, the baldhead faggot, is clearly
> responsible,
> not, for definite, no cats we know.

We certainly glimpse here the irreverence that Wright praises in the dozens—the cynical attitude toward divinity that inverts the stereotype of the African American in his "Nigger Heaven," dreaming of a white God in a white heaven cooking up an eternal fish fry. It is the white man instead who dreams up this God, who has no use for the material world of work and want, an idea of God that can serve as an opiate of the people. As in camp, the "poem" enacts a subversive guilt by association. Any God so intimate with the homosexual poet must be a faggot himself, and an old baldheaded one at that—lacking in virility, muscularity, color. Camp names the real faggotry of those sissies who pretend only an incidental acquaintance with this unprocreative vision of licking blondes. Camp is the way the white faggot names those who are in the "family." In calling God "*the* baldhead faggot," Baraka does not relinquish the dozens, for the tone and manner of the dozens are still apparent. The dozens calls the rival out of his gender or sexual orientation. The pure puritan God of the Western frontier, of high missionary civilization pushing forward the Western front, would never recognize any legitimate relation to low faggotry. And yet, in the "hysterical" logic of pre-Stonewall white America, why *wouldn't* faggots be lurking insidiously in that God's heaven, working their emasculating seduction on the Almighty himself?

Notes

1. The idea of intersecting identities derives from notions of multiple oppression enunciated in identity politics theory. It has been crucial to the work of feminist lesbians of color, such as Audre Lorde (45-52, 114-23); the contributions of *This Bridge Called My Back,* especially Cherríe Moraga; the contributions of *Home Girls,* especially Barbara Smith (xxxi-l), Jewelle Gomez (110-23), Cheryl Clarke (197-208), and the Combahee River Collective (272-82). Similarly, this notion of simultaneous oppressions through multiple identities was articulated for black gay men by Joseph Beam's collection, *In the Life,* especially his influential essay "Brother to Brother:

Words from the Heart" (230-42); and by Essex Hemphill's follow-up collection, *Brother to Brother: New Writings by Black Gay Men,* especially Hemphill, (xv-xxxi), Marlon Riggs (200-5), Ron Simmons (211-28), and Charles I. Nero (229-52). Perhaps the most extended treatment of black and gay as competing identities or "divided loyalties" can be found in Keith Boykin, *One More River to Cross: Black and Gay in America* (especially 17, 30-122).

2. Other important interventions in this debate can be found in: Sharon Holland; Kendall Thomas (64); Robert F. Reid-Pharr ("Tearing the Goat's Flesh" 354-55); Maurice Wallace (380-81); Dwight A. McBride; and B. E. Myers (340).

3. I use the term social *grouping,* rather than merely social *group,* to indicate the subject's constantly interactive, fluidly revisionary processes of identification with/against marked cultural categories and labels.

4. In addition to Simmons (217-18), Clarke (201-3), and McBride (262-70), see Harper's discussion of black nationalist invective in *Are We Not Men?* (49-53). More generally on the role of homophobia and sexism in black nationalism, see Paula Giddings (311-24); Joyce Hope Scott (296-312); bell hooks (96-113); Madhu Dubey (16-29); and Lee Edelman (53-59).

5. See *The World, the Text, and the Critic* (226-47) and *Culture and Imperialism* (326-36).

6. Baldwin had published *Giovanni's Room,* a novel depicting European homosexuality, in 1955 and *Another Country,* a novel depicting interracial homosexuality, in 1961. For similar attacks on Baldwin, see Larry Neal, Addison Gayle, and Eldridge Cleaver. Most of the scholarship on this matter has focused on Cleaver's explicitly salacious homophobic attacks.

7. Mailer says of the hipster philosophy: "For life is a contest between people in which the victor generally recuperates quickly and the loser takes long to mend, a perpetual competition of colliding explorers in which one must grow or else pay more for remaining the same" (349-50). For Mailer, hip is largely about male orgasm and masculine sexual competition, about a man's finding "his courage at the moment of violence, or equally make it in the act of love, find a little more between his woman and himself, or indeed between his mate and himself (since many hipsters are bisexual)" (351).

8. The rivalry between Baldwin and Mailer was professional, spilling over into the personal through the public arena. Their love-hate relationship was publicly played out not only in their doing competing journalistic stories on the same events, such as the Patterson-Liston boxing match, but also in their writing about each other. In Mailer's "Evaluations," his anxiety over and fascination with Baldwin's sexuality, and black male sexuality in general, is screened by his dismissive comments on Baldwin's style as "noble toilet water" (472) and as "sprayed with perfume" (471). About *Giovanni's Room,* he writes that it "was a bad book but mostly a brave one" (471). Baldwin exposes what Mailer hides when Baldwin labels his counter-punch, "The Black Boy Looks at the White Boy," a "love letter" to Mailer. Thus, Baldwin turns a boxing match into a lovers' quarrel (reprinted in *Nobody Knows My Name: More Notes of a Native Son* [171-90]). Baraka's "Brief Reflections on Two Hot Shots" is reprinted in *Home: Social Essays* (116-20); also in this volume see Baraka's essay on the Dempsey-Liston fight (155-60). On the Baldwin-Mailer relationship, see Campbell, *Talking at the Gates* (137-44). On their divergent coverage of the 1962 Patterson-Liston fight, see W. J. Weatherby, *Squaring Off: Mailer vs. Baldwin* (79); and Leeming, *James Baldwin* (183-86). The most interesting treatment of this topic can be found in Gerald Early, *Tuxedo Junction: Essays on American Culture* (183-95).

9. For this schematization of Baraka's career, see William J. Harris, the introduction to *The LeRoi Jones/Amiri Baraka Reader* (xxi-xxiv); Werner Sollors (5-9, 172-94); Theodore R. Hudson (20-24); and Lloyd W. Brown (22-26).

10. See Murray's attack on H. Rap Brown in his "White Norms, Black Deviation" (113).

11. On the conflicting cultural representations of Joan of Arc—from harlot to heretic, from ideal androgyne to amazon, and from amazon to saint and patriot—due to her literally dressing up in the mantle of masculine authority by claiming military and religious leadership, see Marina Warner.

12. See, for instance, selections from his 1961 volume of poems, *Preface to a Twenty-Volume Suicide Note,* reprinted in *LeRoi Jones/Amiri Baraka Reader.*

13. I use "subworld" in allusion to the then popular social scientific concept of "subculture," and especially as shorthand for Donald Webster Cory's apt description of a "submerged world." He writes: "One writer describes it as *a submerged world,* while another speaks of *a society on the fringe of society.* Both are correct, accurate, yet incomplete, for there is not one submerged world, one society on the fringe of society, but several, almost countless, different and disparate and dissimilar and almost disconnected, yet all having some relationships to one another, sometimes through an individual or two who travel in several of these submerged-island societies at once, or related on the other hand merely by the similarity of pursuits and personalities, or perhaps related primarily by the association that exists only in the imagination of the hostile world" (114-15, italics in original). As Cory points out, dominant discourse tends to make singular and uniform these

myriad disparate enclaves of underground activity, as indicated by the emergence of "subculture" itself as a way of describing, categorizing, and unifying the identity of heterogeneous homosexual associations. As George Chauncey reminds us in *Gay New York,* these subworlds constituted a network of social exchange among working-class "ethnic" whites, poor blacks, and homosexuals long before World War II.

14. See Toby Marotta (3-68); and John D'Emilio (40-53).

15. In *Against Nature* Jeffrey Weeks describes homosexuality in the 19th century as characterized (and linked) in these polar extremes: "Perhaps the only people who lived wholly in the subculture were the relatively few 'professionals,' the chief links between the world of aristocratic homosexuality and the metropolitan subculture of Molly houses, pubs, fields, walks, squares, and lavatories" (54). As Marotta notes: "Homosexual behavior was a felony punishable in New York state by as much as twenty years in jail. People could be arrested simply for talking suggestively about homosexual sex, and plainclothesmen were dispatched to entrap homosexuals by initiating such conversations. Bars and steam baths that attracted homosexuals were periodically raided. The memory of the antihomosexual furor fueled by Senator Joseph McCarthy in the early 1950s was fresh. The danger of being exposed, fired from one's job, or blackmailed because of one's homosexuality was real" (15).

16. In his important essay, "Some Thoughts on the Challenges Facing Black Gay Intellectuals," Simmons interprets *The System of Dante's Hell* autobiographically and suggests that Baraka's homophobic statements in the black nationalist poetry and elsewhere derive from internalized homophobia in reaction to his own homosexual tendencies. Hudson more conservatively cautions against reading especially *The System of Dante's Hell* as "literal incidents or states in Jones' life adapted to the mechanics and conventions of fiction. Rather, the reader must understand [that] what Jones has experienced and has seen experienced constitute the starting points for his creative 'projections'" (111). At the same time, Hudson acknowledges that the novel "contains bits of ascertainable factual autobiography" (111).

17. See Wright's comments on the "Dirty Dozens" as a resource for African-American high literature in *White Man, Listen!* (92-95).

18. Note Baraka's term "rococo" in comparison to McKay's same usage for the term to describe Alain Locke's personality and prose style in *Long Way from Home* (312-13), both indicating a kind of queer twisted sophistication.

19. It is puzzling that in his fictional autobiography, *The System of Dante's Hell,* Jones mentions a fag-bashing episode that he does *not* mention in the later "straight" *Autobiography of LeRoi Jones.* In *System,* he writes: "We did a lot of things, those years. . . . We walk down hoping to fuck mulattos when they bathe. We tell lies to keep from getting belted, and watch a faggot take a beating in the snow from our lie. Our fear" (65). Simmons speculates that this refers to an actual event in Baraka's life, the event inspiring Jones's 1964 off-Broadway play on fag-bashing, *The Toilet* (218 and 227, note 31). The poetic, almost surreal passage in *System,* though conceivably based in an actual event, is difficult to pin down in relation to the *Autobiography.* Simmons's pointing out Jones's use of the "lie" in both the *System* passage and *The Toilet* is intriguing, however.

20. This passage is in many ways similar to Claude Brown's treatment of black faggotry in his autobiography, *Manchild in the Promised Land* (10-11). See my essay "Some Glances at the Black Fag" (208-18).

21. Dixon, *Ride Out the Wilderness* (81). Referring to the earlier gang rape that Roi attempts with his four middle-class friends, Dixon also links the affair with Peaches back to the failed rape (81).

22. Gay sadomasochistic rituals similarly deploy this mode of sexual invective when the sexual master coaxes himself to climax while whipping his sexual slave with homophobic insults.

23. This scene becomes even more ambivalent once we realize its contrasting relation to the scene entitled "The Rape," in which Roi ambivalently leads his gang to assault a drunken woman walking the streets. Hudson notes that this scene and "The Rape" are generally praised in reviews of the *System,* reviews that Hudson says are generally negative (115-18). Ikenna Dieke summarizes the sexuality in *System* as possessing "two antipodal dimensions": The first, sexual villainy, assumes the manifest forms of homosexuality and rape. Throughout the novel, homosexuality and rape illustrate Baraka's encounter with forms of sexuality which suggest an avoidance and negation of reality. In contrast, the book's second Sadean dimension, sexuality as a symbolic process, represents an involvement with, as well as an affirmation of, reality. Baraka insists that both elements be viewed as a complex dialectic (163). Despite his claim of a complex dialectic, reality becomes simply equated with heterosexuality in Dieke's analysis, and it is not clear how he does so, but Dieke argues that a synthesis is reached by the end of the novel (see 166).

24. Baker, *Afro-American Poetics: Revisions of Harlem and the Black Aesthetic* (134).

25. See Margolies (194) and Benston (14).

26. Jones argues in "American Sexual Reference: Black Male" that it is white men who are ultimately the ones castrated, having turned themselves into

metaphorical/literal homosexuals. The violence that they have committed has so cut them off from vitality that they no longer can see the procreative joy of sex: "I mean for one thousand years the White Eye has killed people for his luxury; as the killing increased, and the cover stories grew more fixed, and the possibility of reform . . . lessened, the withdrawal from sex as *creation* grew more extreme. Sex was *dirty*" (*Home* [228], italics in original).

27. Unlike the dozens, which has a pretty well-defined provenance, camp is a notoriously slippery term that has taken on a wide range of meanings in scholarly discourse, perhaps because the term in the vernacular refers to a wide range of cultural practices. Susan Sontag initiated the critical discussion with her 1964 "Notes on Camp." Sontag sees camp as essentially an aesthetic and aestheticizing "sensibility" that is "disengaged, depoliticized—or at least apolitical" (277). She identifies camp in the modern period as a homosexual terrain through an explanation that recognizes the curious relation between faggotry and the social elite, but she fails to understand its political context in that "the history of Camp taste is part of the history of snob taste" (290). In *No Respect: Intellectuals and Popular Culture,* Andrew Ross claims the political-historical implications of camp but from a viewpoint heavily indebted to Sontag's formalizing of the practice (135-70). For a thorough critique of Sontag and Ross, see Moe Meyer. Thomas A. King historicizes the relation between the crisis of the aristocracy in the early modern period and the origins of camp as a new code of visual and speech gestures marking not only the body of the homosexual but also unmarking the normative self of Western culture. In "Queer Nationality" Lauren Berlant and Elizabeth Freeman see 1990s America as being "marked by a camp aesthetic," that is one that "enrages, embarrasses, and sometimes benignly amuses official national figures and gives pleasure to the gay, African-American, and the feminist- and left-identified communities who understand that to operate a travesty on the national travesty is to dissolve the frame that separates national fantasy from ordinary bodies" (216). In a different way, Sue-Ellen Case and Earl Jackson, Jr., have identified the subversive element in camp discourse as a self-conscious deflation of the impulse toward a realist, reproductive régime determined by compulsive heterosexuality.

28. The perfect instance of this is "voguing," the camp-inspired practice that came out of urban, poor, gay cross-dressing communities of color into larger communities of color and white gay ghettos, and eventually in the 1980s into mainstream and mass culture.

29. Baraka's play certainly has affinities with the "theater of the ridiculous" that begins to thrive in Greenwich Village especially in the late 1970s and 1980s, becoming one of the most celebrated artistic manifestations of post-Stonewall gay culture and particularly associated with Charles Busch's outrageous plays, including such works as *Psycho-Beach Party* and *Lesbian Vampires from Outer Space.* Busch used pre-Stonewall camp, popular culture (especially the movies), kitsch stage sets, and cross-dressing actors to offer pastiche parodies of the "serious" theatre of the absurd for eventually what becomes a popular, crossover audience.

Publishers Weekly (review date 6 March 2000)

SOURCE: Review of *The Fiction of LeRoi Jones/Amiri Baraka,* by Amiri Baraka. *Publishers Weekly* 247, no. 10 (6 March 2000): 82.

[*In the following favorable review, the anonymous critic commends Baraka's compelling and innovative prose.*]

Known for his poetry, plays and essays, Baraka, formerly Leroi Jones, hasn't been recognized for his searing, dense, experimental fiction, but that oversight will be corrected with this latest collection of his work [***The Fiction of Leroi Jones/Amiri Baraka***]. Fans of the activist-writer will immediately recall the two major segments of this volume, ***Tales*** and ***The System of Dante's Hell,*** both well-received works from the 1960s. As a survey of Baraka's writings in prose, the book accurately displays the full range of the wordsmith's skills: from his bold, groundbreaking efforts as an influential member of the post-Beat Lower East Side art scene to his controversial cultural nationalism and his Marxist conversion. Although three previously uncollected short stories, **"Suppose Sorrow Was a Time Machine," "Round Trip"** and **"The Man Who Sold Pictures of God,"** fail to hit the heights of quality and innovation of the yarns that follow, they hint at Baraka's potential and creative powers. Baraka exceeds those expectations in the short, explosive fragments in his 1965 ***The System of Dante's Hell,*** notably in "Circle 7" and "Circle 8." He uses the fictional form as an autobiographical vehicle in the 1967 ***Tales,*** reaching in the bluesy **"Going Down Slow"** and the classic **"The Screamers."** His impressive hybrid of literary styles spotlights lives defined by oppression and poverty, employing his unpredictable, jazzy, sometimes manic voice to twist Western forms to suit his ever-evolving black aesthetic. While his later **"6 Persons"** may not rival his earlier explorations of themes of violence, sex and race, it is still innovative in its recounting of his life from various point of views, peaking with the "I" and "They." This collection offers an excellent alternative look at one of the legends of African-American letters, frequently quite different than that revealed in his two autobiographies.

Pedro Serrano (essay date summer 2000)

SOURCE: Serrano, Pedro. "Translating Amiri Baraka into Spanish." *Antioch Review* 58, no. 3 (summer 2000): 281-85.

[*In the following essay, Serrano recounts his experience translating Baraka's "Beautiful Black Women," "Study Space," and "Das Kapital" into Spanish, explaining how these poems helped him gain insight into Mexican culture.*]

Poetry can be translated only by poets. This is something I can neither support nor deny because I completed my first translation after years of writing poems. Imagining the linguistic action of the mind without that previous knowledge is something beyond my understanding. Nevertheless I can perfectly imagine someone discovering through translation what I first did by dealing with words in Spanish. The real dilemma lies elsewhere. There are two main approaches to poetry translation. One of them assumes that a poem written in another language should be appropriated and re-created as a new poem in the translator's own language. The poem thus becomes an object that, even if it is faithful to the original, modulates itself in an idiom closer to the translator's than to the author's. And it is an approach some poets cherish and support. But even if the results are at times powerful and efficient, there is in it a swerving from the real challenge that translating poetry presents. This kind of work does not produce translations, but *interpretations.*

The second approach purports to find a way through which a poem emerges almost by its own drives in a different language. Its achievement lies in those correspondences found not only in the translator's personal idiom, but in the wider streams of another language. There should be in the new version something faithful to the poet's aims in his or her own language. The poem becomes, if the translator is able to achieve it, autonomous and enjoyable without the need to look immediately for the original. The fascination of translating poetry means then to detach oneself from one's linguistic self and become a new poetic *persona.* It is also a highly enriching experience in itself, a kind of hermeneutics.

In this sense, translating Amiri Baraka's poems represented a fascinating experience, for different reasons. At the beginning of the '90s I was asked to translate a few poems for the Spanish edition of Eliot Weinberger's *Anthology of North American Poetry from 1950.* All the poets who happened to be well known in Mexico had already been chosen by the other translators, so I was presented with a handful of names that I knew barely or not at all. I have always enjoyed writing reviews of books previously unknown to me, because it is a fortuitous way of discovering authors, so I decided to go for the least-known poet of the selection and try to do my best. I remember reading those poems and noticing their hypnotic power. I also liked the challenge.

As the editors were in a hurry—they always are—I didn't have the time to conduct any proper research. That meant I started reading those poems without knowing anything about this author. I also had to extract from such limited material all I needed in order to reconstruct in Spanish a thoroughly unknown poetic self. It represented in a way the closest I have ever been to Eliot's idea of impersonality. And the most faithful also. I had to find out, from the poems themselves and from the proper act of translating them, the clues that would lead me both to this author and to the Spanish I needed. The three poems I translated were **"Beautiful Black Women . . . ," "Study Space,"** and **"Das Kapital."**

Reading those poems and working on them was an experience equivalent to reading Paul Celan. I'm not talking about "Todesfuge," his most popular poem, because it is quite explicit. Celan's more hermetic poems become clear only after a painstaking reading. At first they are opaque; once one has dealt hard with the words involved in them their luminosity becomes apparent. And that experience is overwhelming, precisely for its unexpectedness and shimmering condition. I am not saying that Amiri Baraka's poems are similar to those of Celan, but they partake of a power that in the case of the former I have called hypnotic.

The only thing I knew at the time about Amiri Baraka was that he had changed his name from LeRoi Jones and that he had become a Muslim. I had to begin from that and find my way through the poems in order to achieve any kind of understanding. I have to say that Eliot Weinberger's selection was a very comprehensive one. Despite being only three poems, they covered a wide range of Baraka's interests. But I was not aware of that at the moment. The poems I translated are all very different. **"Beautiful Black Women . . ."** is, as its title makes clear, an homage to women spoken in a collective voice. **"Study Space"** is a mystical poem within the Koranic tradition, and **"Das Kapital,"** the longest of them, is a very political urban statement. It is also full of period clues—it mentions, for example, President Ford.

So the first thing I gathered about Amiri Baraka was that he was a black man and that this was one of his main concerns. Also, that politics and religion were very important in his poetry. Poets can be very much involved in those subjects, but that does not mean they become an active ingredient of their writings. In the case of Baraka they are at the front of his poetics. I don't consider that readers should skip any knowledge about the poem's origins or the poet's history and biography. On the contrary, I feel myself very much at home skirting and skipping through details that open a dialogue with my personal reading. But in this case that was impossible. I had to deal only with the words that were in front of me and from there only to organize a coherent version in Spanish. Moreover, I was facing not only a poet with whom I was unfamiliar, but three different kinds of experience.

This represented a problem. As I said, translating means for me not an appropriation of a poet, but a reorganization in another language of a particular way of writing. As a poet, I have a way of dealing with experiences and words. But whenever I immerse myself in a translation I try to feel the words, rhythms, emotions, and experiences that are conflating within a poem. In the case of Baraka, even if those poems answered to different motives, there was a common breath in all three. At first, it was very difficult to follow the waving and jumping movement of his lines, but through the translation I made a whole of many things I didn't thoroughly understand in the first reading. In **"Das Kapital,"** for example, there is a line that goes "and we cd get scared." Once one is familiar with the poem it does not present any problem. But I was not used to this kind of abbreviation, and at first I thought that "cd" meant "compact disc." This is a very naive mistake, but whenever one faces a poet from a different tradition one is prone to make that kind of error. Later in the reading it was obvious, quite obvious, that a compact disc could never be part of that poem, if only by its date.

It was and still is impossible to find Baraka's work in Mexico. Also, most of his books are out of print in English, and difficult to find even in the United States. In a trip I made in 1998 I bought an anthology called ***Transbluesency*** and his ***Eulogies,*** which is also a recompilation of previous works. Both are published by Marsillo, in Italy, and this says something about how he is read in the United States' poetic atmosphere. Obviously, his works are in libraries, and the many theses written on him are a telling demonstration of his importance. But I was not conducting any kind of academic research. I was only looking in libraries for a poet I was interested in.

Of those three poems I translated, only one is included in ***Transbluesency.*** But the three of them presented challenges for me as a translator. I do not write political poems, I am not a religious person, and the complexities of black people within the United States was at the time something with which I only had a superficial familiarity. How then to become religious, or to feel myself what a black poet would say about black women? I had only the poems themselves and my own personal experiences, both as a poet and as a social being. I suppose those two things helped. Because I have always felt a strong social concern, and always lived in big cities, I understood the atmosphere of **"Das Kapital"** (the title's origin was not unfamiliar to me). It also helped that it is a poem very much influenced by T. S. Eliot, a poet whose work I know well ("A rat / eases past us on his way to a banquet, can you hear the cheers raised / through the walls, full of rat humor" mirrors some of Eliot's poetic world). I must say that I relished translating this poem. Getting into its rhythm and images, visualizing the commuters drinking in the bar before returning home, finding ways in Spanish for something done in English that a literal delivery would have made sound very flat was enormously exiting. The poem's power took me over and I was swimming in Spanish, propelled by its powerful breath.

The poem that presented more difficulties was **"Study Space."** I do not know anything about Koranic mystical symbols, and so I was in a mess. I had read Albert Hourani's *A History of the Arab People,* which is a marvelous book but was of no help in this case. The meaning of "a fourteen point star of the cosmic stage" I could not fathom. However, it helped that I knew Saint John of the Cross's poetry and prose, so that gave me an equivalent atmosphere from my own tradition on which I could lean. I think that at the end I did not betray the poem's spirit.

And **"Beautiful Black Women"** is a poem that enchanted me from the first reading. It was a fascinating subject that I had never dealt with before, not only because I am not a black person, but also because blackness is not a main issue in Mexico, even though it has a few communities of black people. In this poem I had to face two different issues: first, that it was a poem about women; second, that those women were black. One has to remember that I did not know that Baraka was himself a black poet, but the poem was devoted to enhancing a particular segment of United States society. Nowadays, after the Zapatista movement in the Southern State of Chiapas, I can visualize Mexican Indian women in the act of giving strength to their own societies, and apply that image to the poem. But when I made the translations the presence of the Indian population in Mexico was mainly part of the official discourse and not the product of individuals and collectivities struggling to have a face and a voice within Mexican society. But the poem itself was powerful enough to make those women real and needed. In fact, it worked the other way round. The poem helped me to better understand what is happening in Mexico.

I want to finish this article with this last unfolding idea. The experience of translating Amiri Baraka was a very enriching one for several reasons. First, I came to know a poet that I consider now part of my own personal tradition. Second, his poems sparked in me an interest in black American society that has continued. And third, all this helped me to have a better understanding of my own society, something that would have taken perhaps much more time to develop. These arguments do not come immediately when one is thinking about poetry, but they are important.

Deborah Thompson (essay date winter 2002)

SOURCE: Thompson, Deborah. "Keeping Up with the Joneses: The Naming of Racial Identities in the Autobiographical Writings of LeRoi Jones/Amiri Baraka, Hettie Jones, and Lisa Jones." *College Literature* 29, no. 1 (winter 2002): 83-101.

[*In the following excerpt, Thompson investigates the cultural, social, and political implications of naming—self-naming, re-naming, and the unnamed—as evinced in Baraka's autobiography and in the work of his ex-wife, Hettie Jones, and daughter, Lisa Jones.*]

> So there was a scandal downtown: LeRoi Jones Has Left His White Wife. It fit right in with dissolving black-white political alliances. . . . Close to home, though, it hurt most. There was pressure on all black people to end their interracial relationships. . . . In a recently published poem, Roi had called on Black dada nihilismus to murder his friends, all of whom were now upset and angry, unprepared for the position in which he'd put them. Like Ed Dorn, they had no name for the way they were white. Neither did I.
>
> (Jones 1990, 226)

> My mother is white. And I, as you may or may not have figured out, am black. This is how I choose to define myself and this is how America chooses to define me. I have no regrets about my racial classification other than to lament, off and on, that classifications exist period.
>
> (Jones 1994, 28)

"[T]hey had no name for the way they were white," Hettie Jones writes of white people involved in the struggle against U.S. racism in the late 1950s and early 1960s. At a time of rapidly changing names/identities for African-Americans as a group and as individuals, there was no corresponding change of names/identities for whites. There was, in fact, a palpable and tragic absence of names and corresponding identities for that other "way they were white," and, more importantly, for other *potential* ways of being white that were never realized on a larger cultural scale. This paper reads names—self-naming, re-naming, the unnamed—in the autobiographical writings of three members of an interracial literary family for whom names are a particularly fraught site of identity politics and struggle, and puts these names in the context of American racial and gender identity politics in the 1950s-60s (and beyond), in order to historicize white American identity shifts relative to shifts in African American and biracial American identities. Namely, I put Amiri Baraka's autobiography (1984) in dialogue with that of Hettie Jones (1990; his ex-wife), a white Jewish woman, as well as with the autobiographical writings of their daughter Lisa Jones (1994). LeRoi Jones/Amiri Baraka is perhaps best known as the author of the 1964 play ***Dutchman,*** in which a white woman symbolically rapes and literally murders a black man. The play dramatically captured the cultural moment of a radical shift in black identity and politics, and in interracial relations, in the U.S. The autobiographies, in my reading, historicize these shifts differently. The late 1950s and early 1960s, as documented by LeRoi's and Hettie's autobiographies, were a time when interracial relationships shifted in the U.S. cultural imagination from being radical and progressive to being reactionary and regressive. It was a time when black-white relations could have created identities of *difference* (rather than assimilation or appropriation) but failed, and instead re-segregation became inevitable. (I do want to note, here, that I'll be focusing on black-white racial relations because that is how U.S. racial tensions are figured in these autobiographies, but I do so at the cost of a fundamental exclusion of other racial identities that do not fall into, and may even radically disrupt, the black-white binarism.) Both black and white identities were in crisis in this decade, but, as they re-segregated from each other, black identities went in the direction of hyper-change, while white identities retreated into stagnation. The autobiographies document the failure, on the level of the U.S. cultural imagination, to reinvent white identity, to bring that other way of being white into existence, at a time when its possibility and need to be named was palpable.

That names are a central site of identity production is clear by the very framings of the autobiographies. Baraka's book says, on the cover, "***The Autobiography of LeRoi Jones*** [by] Amiri Baraka." This seeming contradiction—that the name of the writer does not match the subject of the autobiography—is only the first of many clues not only that names matter a great deal to these writers, but also that names are a primary material of creative and artistic activity. Hettie's story, too, is framed by a change of names. *How I Became Hettie Jones* is, quite literally, the story of a woman who "traded Hettie Cohen for Hettie Jones" (Jones 1990, 62). (She went on from there to other names—H. Cohen-Jones (168), Mrs. Hettie Jones (222) and "Hettie" alone (238-39).) In the first sentence of the autobiography, we are invited to "Meet Hettie Cohen." In the final lines of the autobiography, she meets an old friend "searching out a name for [her] and rejecting all the choices," settling finally on simply "Hettie" (238-39). Lisa tells us, in an essay called "My Slave Name," that "names are among my obsessions, or as my girlfriend Deandra would say, my 'issues'" (Jones 1994,

17) and that "[s]ince I was eight I have considered taking an African name; more, back then, as a badge of blackness than to escape the baby-girl femininity of my given name. This is an irony to me now, given that all along I've had one of the most indelibly 'colored' names in the book" (19). These multiple name changes identify a larger issue in these autobiographical writings: the belief that identity is not a matter of "being," but of "becoming." Identity is always in process. As Lisa says in 1994 of her "African-American and black" identity, "chances are this identity will never be static" (31). From the 1950s to the 1980s, LeRoi and Hettie continually speak of their selfhoods in the language of "becoming."

In the 1990s, we have available to us a terminology of "performativity" (developed by Judith Butler and others): we would say that identity is "performatively constituted," materialized through a "productive reiteration" of hegemonic norms, through "discursive performativity" (1993, 3-4). In Butler's terminology, at the same time as performative acts of reiteration (or speech acts) create embodied and embodiable identities, they also foreclose and disavow other identities. Paradoxically, though, this very disavowal makes some identities *potentially* imaginable. Or, as Butler writes of the performative act of naming in her book *Excitable Speech*:

> The subject is constituted (interpellated) in language through a selective process in which the terms of legible and intelligible subject-hood are regulated. The subject is called a name, but "who" the subject is depends as much on the names that he or she is never called: the possibilities for linguistic life are both inaugurated and foreclosed through the name.
>
> (Butler 1997, 41)

The relationship between the names for ethnicities and races available in a given culture, and the actual ways that racial and ethnic identities are occupied in that culture, then, is a complicated issue—*inherently* dialectical and unpredictable, since, when one is interpolated into social existence by a (racial) name, one is also enabled with a "linguistic agency" or "enabling vulnerability" to counter or displace this name or racial category (Butler 1997, 2). Even so, it is possible and productive (if problematic) to read the naming activities of a culture as paradigmatic of the range of activities involved in the reinventing of cultural identities, or "discursive repertoires," as Ruth Frankenberg calls them (1993).[1] Frankenberg's study looks at the ways white American women understand and name their own racial/cultural identities in relation to other American racial/cultural identities.[2] Like Butler, Frankenberg uses terms from theater to understand how these paradigms work. She chooses the term "discursive repertoires" because "'[r]epertoire' captures, for me, something of the way in which strategies for thinking through race were learned, drawn upon, and enacted, repetitively but not automatically or by rote, chosen but by no means freely so" (1993, 16). The metaphor of acting off a learned script "conveys something of the tension between agency and innovation on the one hand and the 'givenness' of a universe of discourse on the other" (140). In this paper I will look at the way members of one multiracial family understood themselves as racial subjects in the terms of the names and "discursive repertoires" available to them both at the time of living them and at the time of rewriting them.[3]

The 1950s, as reflected in LeRoi's autobiography, were a time of elaborate synchronic naming distinctions for Americans of African descent. This system of identity distinctions is encapsulated in LeRoi's chapter title "Black Brown Yellow White."[4] LeRoi calls "Black Brown Yellow White," "some basic colors of my life, in my life. A kind of personal, yet fairly objective class analysis that corresponds (check it) to some real shit out in the streets in these houses and in some people's heads" (Baraka 1984, 42). The chapter "Black Brown Yellow White," concerning LeRoi's formative years to early teens, elaborately documents the social system differentiating "black," "brown," and "yellow." Early in his school years, LeRoi understands that

> The black was fundamental black life, the life of blues people, the real and the solid and the strong and the beautiful . . . the black was also the damned, the left behind, the left out, the disregarded, the abandoned, the drunk and disorderly, the babbling and the staggering, the put down and the laughed at, the heir of the harshest of lives I could see.
>
> But the brown, while caught between the black and the yellow, did not, in spite of themselves, like the yellow. They hated it, them, even worse than white, even worse than white folks (normally) because white folks didn't exist with the same day-to-day common reality. The yellow would be around bugging you, having a haircut neatly parted with well-greased legs and knees. . . .
>
> Brown sensitive to this even unable to speak of it, sensitive to it watching it, touched by both streams of life and consciousness yet being its own being shaped by both and the white other. . . .
>
> Where I was comin from, the brown side, we just wanted to keep steppin. The black had shaped us, the yellow had taunted us, the white had terrified and alienated us. And cool meant, to us, to be silent in the face of all that, silent yet knowing. . . .
>
> (Baraka 1984, 42-44)

All the while, of course, the distinctions between black, brown, and yellow operate within a basic black-white binarism: "I've told you it was four—BlackBrownYellowWhite—but actually it's two on the realest side, the two extremes, the black and the white, with the middle two but their boxing gloves" (49). That this elaborate system of racist discrimination within the African-American community is hardly a progressive social move, and may rather be a consolidation of white supremacy within African-American cultural identities, does not negate my sense that not only did African-Americans understand that the name of the race matters, in highly material ways, but that they actively and daily and consciously participated in the activity of racial distinction-making, classifying, and signifying.

While the "brown" LeRoi, growing up in New Jersey, learns at a very early age the minute distinctions among his "own race," the white Jewish Hettie, growing up not too far away in New York, doesn't begin to knowingly experience "race" as an identity category until her late college years and even then only in the crudest forms of blackface minstrelsy. In a brilliant and disturbing passage, Hettie describes her "discovery" of phenotypic race. She remembers an instance when, driving through rural Virginia selling fans with her (white) friend Linda,

> [t]here were two black women in the back we'd just met, and now [Linda] and they are talking about their skin. "Heh heh heh," laughs hillbilly Linda, "Millie, have you really got a tan?" To which Millie, laughing herself, replies, "My friends don't even recognize my face!" And then the three of them fall out in giggles, as if the concept of blackness itself were vastly comedic. And there, now, as she turns to include me, is the sparkle in Linda's eyes. It's a strange, excited shine, a dirty secret. I don't know it. What is it?
>
> Skin.
>
> Later that afternoon, tired, I found myself alone on a dirt road. The heat was oppressive, the fan I was carrying cut into my hand. . . . Out of some tall grass at the roadside a little black girl appeared, seven or eight years old, barefoot, dressed in a cotton smock. She waited as I approached and then asked, pointing to the fan, "What are you doing with that?"
>
> "I'm selling them," I said.
>
> "Oh, come to my house," she said dramatically, and with that thrust her hand into mine. I looked down. I'd never held a black person's hand. It was dry, dusty, sweet, and so fragile, and dark as I was from that southern sun it wasn't that different from mine. Skin, I thought, remembering Linda.
>
> (James 1990, 14)

Here, Hettie sees race only as skin, an epidermal phenomenon. Even up to this moment, young Hettie seemingly has no vocabulary, no "discursive repertoires," no *names* for racial identity, whether black or white, or for racial difference. And this absence of names makes different racial identities seem mysterious, exotic, sensual, and unspeakably taboo—and makes white identity at once hegemonic and invisible.

On the other hand, other ways of being white—or subraces of the "white race"—are operative and noted in the above passage. The "hillbilly" identity is *both* characterized as more racist than a northern, urban white identity *and* is subjected unapologetically to a kind of racist casting by northern, urban whites. Even the 1990 Hettie, writing retrospectively, uses a term like "hillbilly" as a self-evident category, a category as (un)marked by class distinctions as "black," "brown," and "yellow" are clearly marked by caste distinctions for LeRoi.

The 1950s and 1960s were not only a period of elaborate naming distinctions among Americans of African descent, but also a period of rapid diachronic identity changes and concomitant name changes—most notably, from "colored" to "Negro" to "black" to "Afro-American" to "African-American." The diachronic and synchronic name changes are related to each other, and to larger shifts in America. These terminological shifts are not simply name changes, but changes in historical moment, cultural identity, and concomitant aesthetic style and content.[5] LeRoi makes firm distinctions, in the 1960s and 1970s, between "black art," "Negro art," and "Colored Theater." The latter is for him the least progressive/radical, the most likely to assuage white guilt:

> Later, after the word "black" had cooled out some and the idea of even "black art" had sunk roots deep enough in the black masses, where it could not simply be denied out of existence, the powers-that-be brought in some Negro art, some skin theater, eliminating the most progressive and revolutionary expressions for a fundable colored theater that merely treaded on "the black experience," rather than carrying on the black struggle for democracy and self-determination. Then the Fords and Rockefellers "fount" them some colored folks they could trust and dropped some dough on them for colored theater. Douglas Turner Ward's Negro Ensemble is perhaps the most famous case in point. During a period when the average young blood would go to your head for calling him or her a knee-grow, the Fords and Rockefellers could raise themselves up a whole-ass knee-grow ensemble. But that's part of the formula: Deny reality as long as you have to and then, when backed up against the wall, substitute an ersatz model filled with the standard white racist lies which include some dressed as Negro art. Instead of black art, bring in Negro art, house nigger art, and celebrate slavery, right on!
>
> (Baraka 1984, 214-15)

The names, furthermore, not only reflect shifts in cultural temperament, but *assert* these shifts, *perform* and *actualize* them. (In the terms of J. L. Austin, these names have an illocutionary force; they enact what they say [Butler 1997, 17].) As Hettie writes of her husband (at the time), "[l]ike other young blacks he'd asserted himself with a word: he was now black not Negro . . ." (Jones 1990, 212).

If LeRoi/Amiri asserted himself with a cultural name change, he also asserted himself with several personal name changes. Indeed, the 1960s and 1970s were a time of massive personal name changes reflecting cultural identity changes, in a complex interweaving of relations between personal and political identities. Personal names embed familial and cultural history and meaning. LeRoi's birth name, Everett LeRoy Jones, comes in part from "Thomas Everett Russ, his mother's father, a 'race man' (militant), who'd lost a business to arson in Alabama before coming to Newark, where he kept a store and worked for the Board of Elections" (Jones 1990, 133). As well, LeRoi was named after his father, Coyette Leroy Jones, but changed the inherited spelling (from Leroy to LeRoi) and pronunciation (from "LEE-roy" to "le-ROY") during his Howard University days after reading Roi Ottley's *New World A Comin* (Baraka 1984, 87). This name change asserts independence from his family and the coming of the New World. It is a statement, a creation of difference. By the time of his Greenwich Village days, he went by Roi. Moving from the Village scene to one of Black Nationalism, LeRoi again changes his name, but this new one, too, bears layers of identity history:

> [Sunni Muslim Hajj Heesham Jaaber] gave me the name Ameer Barakat (the Blessed Prince). Sylvia [Baraka's second wife] was named Amina (faithful) after one of Muhammad's wives. Later, under [Ron] Karenga's influence, I changed my name to Amiri, Bantuizing or Swahilizing the first name and the pronunciation of the last name as well. . . . I was now literally being changed into a blacker being. I was discarding my "slave name" and embracing blackness.
>
> (Baraka 1984, 267)

Again, Baraka's personal name changes map historical movements in African-American history—in this case, different versions of (American) Pan-Africanism or what Baraka calls "black cultural nationalisms." "*Literally* being changed into a blacker being," Baraka sees race as a *literal* entity. As a writer, who deals in the matter of words and names, he is particularly sensitive to the literality and literariness of blackness. I take his use of the word *literally* literally, however much it is simultaneously a matter of metaphor. As he experiences it, Baraka makes himself blacker and more African through the literary activity of writing new names. Indeed his own names are some of his most important, activist, and creative literary productions.

This literal act of renaming oneself was one happening on a mass scale in African-American culture of the 1950s to 1970s. The most famous example is of course Malcolm X, who, moving from Malcolm Little to Detroit Red to Malcolm X to El-Hajj Malik El-Shabazz, took on a new name with each cultural shift in African-American identity. These multiple name changes show dramatic activity in African-American personal and political identity. The culture was at work writing itself and rewriting itself. Perhaps the most extreme example of personal name changing is that of Baba Oserjeman, as described by Baraka:

> I had known Baba Oserjeman through a host of image changes. He was Francis King from Detroit . . . where I first met him. He was always spoken of then, by his friends, as a kind of con man-hustler. He wore English riding outfits and jodhpurs and affected a bit of an English accent. He then became Francisco Rey, Spanish for a minute. Then he became Serj Khingh, a little Indian, and he opened one of the first coffeehouses on the Lower East Side, called Bhowani's Table, where some of us used to go. The next I heard of Oserjeman, he had become Nana Oserjeman of the Damballah Qwedo, "practicing the religion of our fathers." And finally (?), Baba Oserjeman, chief priest of the Yoruba Temple.
>
> (Baraka 1984, 215-26)

What this extreme example of renaming and recreation shows is a personal and sociopolitical frustration with identities available to African-Americans and an impatience to effect cultural change. It is no accident that massive personal name changes of individual African-Americans occurred at a time of cultural name changes for colored/Negro/black/Afro-American/African-American identity. Personal experiences of identity and political structures are versions (and subversions) of each other.

"The personal is political" is, of course, a phrase from the feminist movement, and a notion discovered in mass scale at the time. Personal (and political) name/identity changes for women were a site of major activity for American women (in the main, *white* American women) in this period—e.g., from Miss/Mrs. to Ms., not taking husband's last name, changing "man" in various names ("Freeman" to "Freeperson"), etc. These feminist struggles at the site of names are well known, and I will not elaborate on them here, except to say that they are very much in evidence in Hettie's autobiography. For women in interracial and particularly intercultural relationships, however, name changes were particularly vexed. When Hettie's Jewish father disowned her for marrying a black man, she left her Jewish community and joined her husband's African-American family/community. So taking on her black husband's last name, which for him was a "slave name," was for her a way of disavowing the white American racist identity which can be at its most virulent in ethnicities on the verge of edging into white privilege.

But while the 1950s-1960s were a time of radical personal/cultural identity change for white *women,* there was no corresponding actively created change in the general identity category *white.* For Hettie, the lack of identity shift is further complicated by her identity as a

Jew. Hettie says of the period before she married LeRoi and had children, "[m]ostly I was haunted by the problem of remaining a Jew, but I didn't know how to reinvent a Jewish woman who wasn't a Jewish wife" (Jones 1990, 37). During this time when there was, I'm arguing, relatively little shift in white American identity as compared to other US racial and/or ethnic identities, there was a vast whitening of Jewish ethnicity. But for Hettie, the shift in American Jewish identity from dark Semitic other to assimilated white standard didn't fit. She still felt other to white non-Jews, and identified in her romantic relationships more with other people of color. One night, walking into a room to find her (white, non-Jewish) friend Linda making love with Linda's (white, non-Jewish) boyfriend, Hettie says she

> was struck by their perfect physical match. Goyim, I thought. That shamed me. I went to a meeting of the Jewish group Hillel, but all I saw there were people unlike me. Summer arrived. I read Whitman in Riverside Park at night and watched the mighty Hudson's march to the sea. I dated a Pakistani, an African who lived at International House, and a Jewish-Lutheran lawyer from Washington Heights.
>
> (Jones 1990, 17)

At a time when Hettie is only beginning to develop a language for race, she has a very explicit vocabulary word for white non-Jews: *Goyim.* As an aside I want to note that earlier in this century, "Jewishness" was potentially one way to inhabit whiteness while also being other to whiteness. It could have offered a model for other forms of minority whiteness. Instead, Jewishness whitened; it disappeared as a racial sub-category for people of European or Middle-Eastern descent who identified as others to whiteness, of darker cast(e)s. Following Noel Ignatiev's thesis in *How the Irish Became White* (1996), I would suggest that the 1950s was a time when American Jews, Italians, and other marginally "white ethnics" followed Irish Americans in becoming incontrovertibly white. (Many people who have read or heard this paper in progress feel that I am too harsh on mainstream American Jewish identity. Because of my own complicated family history of names, audiences fail to identify me with my Jewish upbringing, or to see me as a member of an interracial family. From my own perspective, I am writing very much within a tradition of Jewish self-criticism [not to be mistaken for Jewish self-hatred]. This is a Jewish self-criticism that I believe Hettie shares. My anger at the whitening and mainstreaming of American Jewish identity arises from my being raised with the myth of Jews' special status in the Civil Rights movement. I was brought up by my parents and my temple to understand that Jews, because they [we] had been relentlessly persecuted, have a special mission to end all persecution, which we saw around us most immediately in the form of racism. In my Bible school we studied Martin Luther King, Jr., alongside Golda Meir, and Langston Hughes alongside Emma Lazarus.) On the other hand, Paul Berman, in his collection *Blacks and Jews,* considers this perceived alliance between Blacks and Jews as stemming from the liberal humanism central to American Jewishness (particularly "reformed" Judaism). The following passage is particularly relevant to my discussion of Hettie Jones:

> The emancipatory liberalism of the American Jews took an infinity of forms in the twentieth century, and only some of these movements flew a Jewish flag. Many Jews were more likely to proclaim a doctrine of purer universalism and to relegate Jewishness to the sphere of private life. . . . From the perspective of people with the universalist idea, humanism and liberalism, not what they conceived of as Jewishness, brought them to the cause of African America. There is an old and slightly peculiar Jewish custom of rebelling against Jewishness by identifying with the most marginal of all possible groups, so as to rebel and still not assimilate into the mainstream; and this, too, played its part in attracting Jews to the black cause.
>
> (Berman 1994, 11-12)

Many Jews (and other whites) who resisted inclusion in white hegemony's pervasive invisibility, who did not identify or socialize with white enclaves, sought other discursive repertoires, but often felt restless, at home in neither "white" nor in "non-white" identity categories.

After Hettie marries and has a child with LeRoi, she continues to feel other to whiteness. The feeling of otherness no longer stems, in her mind, from her Jewishness, but from being in a different relation to people of color, and having a different sensitivity to racism, than the mainstream white hegemony. This shift in perception becomes a matter of instinct, as seen in her reaction when handed her first daughter Kellie at the hospital:

> I couldn't take my eyes off her. I couldn't let go of her. A touch of jaundice two days later burnished her gold, like a temple putti. The nurse who brought her in that morning said, "You know why she's this color, don't you?"
>
> Right off the bat I misheard this woman, raising a hostile glare to her kind, concerned face. Then, shamed, I realized she meant the jaundice and I thanked her. But something had changed in me, a quality of response. Suspicion had been a reflex action, a misperception, a paranoia.
>
> (Jones 1990, 91)

A "reflex action" is one so embodied, so incorporated, that it is prior to conscious thought. Hettie increasingly feels corporeally other to white identity. She feels in her bones, in her muscular reactions, a growing sensitivity and antagonism to white ways of being. Taking her daughters to their African-American grandparents on Saturdays, Hettie talked with working mothers, read

Ebony and *Jet,* and learned about the politics of hair and skin. She learned that "racist thought was in all things, even in language; racism was, as it would come to be described, institutionalized, and it seemed that now I could see it everywhere" (108). Not only does Hettie *see* racism everywhere, but she now *feels* it everywhere. Raising two African-American children, Hettie finds she can no longer go uptown:

> "Insanity, inertia, and refusal to leave the kids too long" were the reasons I listed [at the time].
>
> What's missing is critical: the way I now felt in whites-only groups. . . . I felt misrepresented, minus a crucial dimension, and seeing race prejudice everywhere, shocking and painful. Other whites in black families speak of this; Diana Powell . . . calls it feeling "disguised in your own skin."
>
> (Jones 1990, 201-02; my emphases)

What's interesting in this passage, in addition to the clear sense of an alternative white identity, another way of being white—so other that Hettie feels almost *misrepresented, disguised* by white skin—is the lack of a name for it. At the time, Hettie does not list this other identity—at least not by name—in her reasons for staying downtown in African-American-populated neighborhoods. It's what's "critical," but "what's missing."

I do not mean to mystify an emerging identity-category of non- or anti-racist whiteness, but rather I am trying to document evidence of a felt need for and responsibility to create new ways of being white, of some attempt at the cultural activity of reinventing whiteness, and of the failure of this attempt. Describing the Hettie Jones of the early 1970s (author of multicultural children's books), the Hettie Jones of 1990 borrows the language of South Africa to describe her former self, as there seems to be no existing adequate American expression:

> [T]his book [*Big Star Fallin' Mama*] was written by Hettie Jones, a relatively new person in America, who under the lunacy of apartheid would have become colored—classified "down" when she married and had children, although the actual experience can best be described as broadening. "The angle is bent, the light refracted, the sightlines reconstructed," I wrote in one of the stories I began to publish in the seventies.
>
> (Jones 1990, 236-37)

Hettie's use of third person pronouns to discuss herself suggests discomfort with apartheid terms. But in the present tense first person in the U.S., there is no name for her, only poetic prose descriptions—"the angle is bent, the light refracted, the sightlines [sic] reconstructed." She has no name for the way she is white.

Baraka in his autobiography also reflects this lack of language and cultural identity for that other way of being white. He says of his move away from his friends Charles Olson, Allen Ginsberg, and Ed Dorn during his black nationalist period: "These white men saw that I was moving away from them in so many ways and there was some concern, because it wasn't that I didn't like them any longer, but that where I was going they could not come along. Where that was, I couldn't even articulate" (1984, 192). LeRoi couldn't articulate it at the time, but now has a clear name for it: Black Nationalism. He wonders of his white friends, "Where would they be in all this?" (192). Looking back on this period, he reflects:

> There was a deep anti-white feeling I carried with me that had grown deeper and deeper since I left the Village. I felt it was a maturing, but in some aspects it was that I was going off the deep end. To the extent that what I felt opposed white supremacy and imperialism, it was certainly correct. But to the extent that I merely turned white supremacy upside down and created an exclusivist black supremacist doctrine, that was bullshit. Bullshit that could only isolate me from reality.
>
> (Baraka 1984, 245)

But there was no language, no cultural identity, for whites who actively resisted and othered themselves from white supremacy and imperialism.

This bringing forth of articulations, of a cultural language for "the way they were white," was a major responsibility and activity for white progressive artists of the time. Throughout her autobiography, Hettie retrospectively laments her failure as a writer to describe her special perception of race relations and her heightened sensitivity to white identities. As Hettie sees it, at least in retrospect, the development of a cultural language for "the way she was white" was her primary role as a writer, and one she failed to fulfill. The following passage from her autobiography is particularly telling:

> One evening . . . still without my own typewriter, I pulled out of Roi's what appeared to be the very beginning of a play with three characters, abbreviated Gra, Wal, and Eas. . . . The following year, Gra (Grace)—although transmuted to a tall, blond WASP—would be taken for me. Nowhere in her character is this feeling that had so changed me. Of course to express it was up to me, not Roi. But I had pawned my typewriter. It was Hettie Cohen's portable. I never got it back. . . .
>
> By the spring of that year . . . it was no longer possible to ignore the war that for a century had been called "our Negro problem."
>
> Roi's position was, "It's your Negro problem." But if the problem is yours, who are you? And what about me? Was it because I didn't—couldn't—describe my own position that Gra, the woman Roi was writing, came into being? Was I a stranger to him as I was to the whites I avoided?
>
> (Jones 1990, 202)

This passage is packed, and I want to take some time to unpack it. The "discursive repertoire" of cultural articulation and embodiment of race can show up as characters in plays or as "real life" identities. Hettie, involved in the life-project of reinventing white female American identity, finds no name for the way she is white, for her evolving identity creation. Likewise, her husband, in creating a dramatic figure of a white woman who was formerly married to a black man and is the mother of two black children, draws on the only "discursive repertoires" of the culture available to him: the woman is blond, and WASP, and very much white in a monosemic understanding of "whiteness." Furthermore, the discursive repertoire doesn't include a pronoun that includes some anti-white supremacy whites along with blacks in relation to the "Negro problem"—"our" and "your" Negro Problem can only mean whites to the exclusion of blacks, never a coalition. In retrospect, as I see it, Hettie feels that her primary work as an artist-activist was to give birth to a personal/political figure of a white woman other to white supremacy and imperialism—to imagine new possibilities of white identity. This was an activity she worked on avidly and painfully in her "real" life, but only partially brought into being in the public literary forum, and not at all in theatrical media, where she stayed behind the scenes. This partial birth, this artistic activity of white renaming and recreation only incompletely attempted, is one in evidence again and again from the 1950s to the 1970s. It is a legacy left by many white artists of the time, and one we need urgently to pick up on and carry forward now. . . .

Notes

1. Other important studies of the construction of white identity include Dyer (1988), Frankenberg (1997), Gordon and Newfield (1994), Hill (1997), Lott (1998), Roach (1996), Roediger (1991, 1994), Sacks (1994), Wray and Newits (1997).
2. Frankenberg posits three paradigms, or discursive repertoires, that roughly correspond to cultural movements, and hence are roughly chronological, though all discourses occur simultaneously at any historical moment: first, essentialist racism; second, color and power evasiveness (popularly referred to as color blindness); and third, race cognizance. See Frankenberg (1997, 14-15).
3. The title, or name, *White Women, Race Matters* refers to Cornel West's book *Race Matters,* which, at its most fundamental and passionate level, argues that "the presence and predicaments of black people are neither additions to nor defections from American life, but rather *constitutive elements of that life*" (1993). Further, to say that race matters is both "an urgent question of power and morality" and "an everyday matter of life and death" (xi).
4. I will mostly be using the appellation "LeRoi Jones" when discussing periods when he identifies himself by that name, and "Amiri Baraka" during the periods when he identifies by that name. This strategy is of course complicated by the fact that both personas are filtered through the 1984 Amiri Baraka.
5. It is important to note that these name shifts were by no means unilateral, and that all of these names—Negro, colored, black, Afro-American, African-American—are actively used in current American culture. As an anonymous reviewer of an earlier draft of this paper insightfully commented, "all terms (and more) currently circulate in different contexts for different people (e.g., there are plenty of people of my grandmother's generation who still prefer to be called 'colored')."

Works Cited

Baraka, Amiri. 1984. *The Autobiography of LeRoi Jones.* New York: Freundlich Books.

Berman, Paul, ed. 1994. *Blacks and Jews: Alliances and Arguments.* New York: Dell.

Butler, Judith. 1997. *Excitable Speech: A Politics of the Performative.* New York: Routledge.

———. 1993. *Bodies that Matter: On the Discursive Limits of "Sex."* New York: Routledge.

Dyer, Richard. 1988. "White." *Screen* 29.4: 44-64.

Frankenberg, Ruth, ed. 1997. *Displacing Whiteness: Essays in Social and Cultural Criticism.* Durham: Duke University Press.

———. 1993. *White Women, Race Matters: The Social Construction of Whiteness.* Minneapolis: University of Minnesota Press.

Gordon, Avery, and Christopher Newfield. 1994. "White Philosophy." *Critical Inquiry* 20. (Summer): 737-57.

Hill, Mike, ed. 1997. *Whiteness: A Critical Reader.* New York: New York University Press.

Ignatiev, Noel. 1996. *How the Irish Became White.* New York: Routledge.

Jones, Hettie. 1990. *How I Became Hettie Jones.* New York: E. P. Dutton.

Jones, LeRoi. 1964. *Dutchman and The Slave.* New York: Morrow Quill Paperbacks.

Jones, Lisa. 1994. *Bulletproof Diva: Tales of Race, Sex and Hair.* New York: Doubleday.

Lott, Eric. 1993. *Love and Theft: Blackface Minstrelsy and the American Working Class.* New York: Oxford University Press.

Roach, Joseph. 1996. "Kinship, Intelligence, and Memory as Improvisation: Culture and Performance in New Orleans." In *Performance and Cultural Politics,* ed. Elin Diamond. New York: Routledge.

Roediger, David R. 1994. *Towards the Abolition of Whiteness: Essays on Race, Politics and Working Class History.* London: Verso.

———. 1991. *The Wages of Whiteness: Working Class History.* London: Verso.

Sacks, Karen Brodkin. 1994. "How Did Jews Become White Folks?" In *Race,* ed. Steven Gregory and Roger Sanjek. New Brunswick: Rutgers University Press.

West, Cornel. 1993. *Race Matters.* Boston: Beacon Press.

Wray, Matt, and Annalee Newits, eds. 1997. *White Trash: Race and Class in America.* New York: Routledge.

Matthew Rebhorn (essay date summer 2003)

SOURCE: Rebhorn, Matthew. "Flaying Dutchman: Masochism, Minstrelsy, and the Gender Politics of Amiri Baraka's *Dutchman.*" *Callaloo* 26, no. 3 (summer 2003): 796-812.

[*In the following essay, Rebhorn explores gender dynamics in* Dutchman *and underscores Baraka's vital role in both the black dramatic tradition and the mainstream theater.*]

In the April 4, 1964 review of Amiri Baraka's ***Dutchman*** in *The New Yorker,* Edith Oliver writes that for about "three-quarters of the way, his play has a kind of deadly wit and passionate wild comedy that are his alone, and then, sad to say, he almost literally sends it all up in smoke, under what I feel is the mistaken impression that in order to have point and impact a good story must be given general and even symbolic implications" (78). Reacting specifically to Clay's extended and angry monologue, Oliver continues, "There is no doubt that this anger is justified, but there is also no doubt, I think, that in this case it is inartistic, weakening the character and the play" (78). Oliver seems to be reacting against exactly the artistic project that Baraka was undertaking, against the precepts that Baraka and other black political activists characterized as being the central tenets underpinning the Black Arts Movement in 1964.

Houston Baker has noted of critics like Oliver and "the white intellectual establishment" that they have tended to downplay the importance of Baraka's dramaturgy precisely because his "conception of Black as a country—a separate and progressive nation with values antithetical to those of white America—stands in marked contrast to the ideas set forth by Baldwin, Wright, Ellison, and others of the fifties" (106). Critics like Baker have noted that part of Baraka's project is to defend a black dramaturgy produced by black artists for black audiences. Kimberly W. Benston's seminal study of Baraka's early drama argues that this playwright "discover[ed] . . . a uniquely Afro-American persona and voice" (149) and points to ***Dutchman*** and Clay's last speech as an important step in finding this voice. A. Robert Lee has suggested even more, contending that Baraka "single-handedly revolutionised black theatre in post-war America" (97), and that a play like ***Dutchman*** was an essential part of that revolution. To see the artistic mastery these critics exalt, we need only glance at the title of the piece. Baraka's title evokes the legend of the Flying Dutchman, the doomed ship behind Richard Wagner's *Der Fliegende Holländer* (1843), but through its ironic repositioning of the relationship between the doomed sailor and his lover onto Clay and his "loving" and erotic murderess Lula it also reveals how Baraka's play offers a supple deconstruction of its operatic namesake. That the play is a masterpiece of subversive ideology and a genuine political statement is beyond question even if one went no further than a cursory examination of the text.

Yet, while suggesting the importance of Baraka in both the black dramatic tradition and in mainstream theater in general, I wish to delve deeper than these critics and look at the insufficiently explored gender dynamics involved in Baraka's aesthetic project. Critics like Baker, Benston, and Lee have noted that Baraka does attempt to define a strong notion of black masculinity for black audiences through his re-conceptualization of a black political theater, but they have not fully examined how Baraka constructs that identity. As I hope to prove, Baraka stages two distinct but interrelated constructions of black masculinity and white femininity in the figures of Clay and Lula respectively, cultural constructions that are iterations of particular gender assumptions and that must necessarily be read through their complex interactions to get at the gender politics at work in this play. Following the lead of cultural critics like Kobena Mercer, Hazel V. Carby, and Robyn Wiegman whose recent work reveals the gendered precepts of black political statements, I shall argue that Baraka polices a notion of black nationalist masculinity precisely by abjectifying women and homosexuals in carefully deployed ways, but that the true constitution of this idea of black masculinity only surfaces in relation to the complex and anxious picture of white femininity Baraka stages in this play. From the initial gaze Lula fixes on Clay in the opening stage business, we see how Lula creates Clay as both a sexual object and a model, or in Laura Mulvey's terms, as a scopophilic object and a narcissistic ideal. This anxious characterization of Lula allows her to embody white femininity, and through her "blackface" minstrel performance, to mimic the same black masculinity Baraka was after in Clay's final monologue. By mapping out how race and gender categories circulate in

Lula's minstrel performance, however, we see the defining trait of Baraka's new Dutchman of the 1960s Black Arts Movement, namely his unending and agonizing self-"flaying," the way the black man, if he is a black *man* indeed, yearns to be "punished" by the agents of the white power structure. Likewise, by putting pressure on the scope of Lula's complex performance, we witness how Lula's own masochistic white femininity—the way she prods Clay to activate his abusive, virile subjectivity—forecloses the same sexual liberty and agency she achieved when she metaphorically "blacked up." In this way, Baraka's ironic treatment of Lula and Clay's intricate, interrelated power plays not only illustrates the self-destructive tragedy of black nationalist masculinity, but also underscores the way white femininity's trafficking in this currency of blackness as a method of empowerment is doomed, like the Dutchman Lula emulates, to suffer endlessly the scene of her own debilitation. As invested as he is in sketching out this entwined scene of devastation, however, Baraka still uses the denouement of ***Dutchman*** to hint at what an alternative, less disastrously "macho" masculinity—and identity—might look like, even as Lula begins to rehearse yet again the drama's tragic pantomime with another young, unsuspecting, black victim.

Baraka began his political and aesthetic project when he left Greenwich Village and his wife Hettie Cohen to move to Harlem. There, he and several other black political activists united to form the Black Arts Repertory Theater/School (BART/S). Although BART/S was soon shut down by the FBI for allegedly being a fund-raising operation for the Black Power movement, during its short life it produced a practical mission statement focused on creating a particular black stage aesthetic for black audiences. Staged American blackness until this moment had been an overwhelmingly alienating experience for performers and audience members alike. On stage, these men of color were seen as "darkies, strutters, and shouters in vaudeville and musical theater; as coons in popular song; as savages in world's fair exhibits; as buffoons in amusement park concessions; as mascots in baseball parks; as dim-witted children in the early silent movies; [and] as rapists and beasts in D. W. Griffith's *The Birth of a Nation*" (Nasaw 2). Furthermore, through the nineteenth century and well into the twentieth, black spectators at theatrical events were assigned the worst seats in the house in the upper balcony or gallery, the same seats cordoned off for those other social "untouchables"—prostitutes. What these excluded audience members saw on stage, therefore, was a panoply of stereotyped, racist images and constructions that aided in codifying a debased form of black identity not only in the Jim Crow South, but also in those northern urban centers where entertainments like vaudeville were prevalent and popular forms—New York, Baltimore, Philadelphia, and Boston. This is not to say that there were not "black theaters" extant by the time that Baraka formed BART/S. As early as the 1820s, British comedians, like Charles Mathews, were visiting what he called "the 'Nigger's (or Negroe's) theatre," or more properly the African Grove Theater in New York, and mimicking black performers like Ira Aldridge (Levine 14). Yet, it was not until 1904 when Robert Motts opened the Pekin Theater on Chicago's South Side with a eclectic mix of black actors, playwrights, and musicians that black audiences could see musicals and plays written by black artists. By 1910, there were black theaters in most large cities, and while vulnerable to white "slumming," these theaters catered to black audiences with black performers. As with Billy Kersands' productions at the Elysium Theatre in New Orleans, these theaters were segregated so that the white patrons were treated with "secondary consideration" (quoted in Nasaw 50).

Unfortunately, even theaters as independent as Kersands' continued to reproduce the established stereotypes of black identity common to white theaters. While Kersands employed black performers, they inevitably had to "black up" to conform to the image of blacks on stage. Inspired by the success of the Little Negro Theater Movement, W. E. B. Du Bois used his magazine *Crisis* both to critique theaters like Kersands' for its minstrel stereotyping and to award prizes to gifted young playwrights like Eulalie Spencer, Zora Neale Hurston and Georgia Douglas Johnson who attempted to write their way out of these black minstrel images on stage. This attempt to escape the deleterious effects produced by black stereotyping and audience segregation, Du Bois argued in his essay, "Krigwa Players Little Negro Theatre: The Story of a Little Theatre Movement," created a theatrical counter-discourse revolving around four principles: *about us, by us, for us,* and *near us.* While drawing on the idea of an independently run black theater in areas where black patrons could frequent the playhouse with ease, Du Bois' theatrical counter-discourse offered a new paradigm to refashion dominant "Negro Theater" types, overturning minstrelsy by concocting a black theatrical enterprise.

The founding of black theaters like the American Negro Theater in 1939, the Negro Playwrights Company in 1940, and the Negro Ensemble Company in 1957 began to live up to Du Bois' theatrical counter-discourse. We can therefore locate Baraka's project and BART/S in general in this tradition. Although not drawing directly on Du Bois' template, Baraka's theatrical project shares the ideological blueprints of this vision, and attempted to make this theoretical construct a reality in Harlem in the mid-1960s. This actualized theatrical movement attempted to address issues that were relevant to black audiences, and more importantly, endeavored to discredit those alienating figures of staged black identity so common in the American cultural imagination. As

Larry Neal, an avatar of the program, relates, the Black Arts Movement crystallized in BART/S was "radically opposed to any concept of art that alienates [a black man] from his community. . . . [I]t envisions an art that speaks directly to the needs and aspirations of Black America" (29).

To achieve this end, Baraka engaged in innovative theatrical techniques—techniques built on earlier twentieth-century experimental dramaturgy. The great twentieth-century drama theorist and experimenter Antonin Artaud wrote that what modern society really needed was "a theater that wakes us up: nerves and heart" (84). Theater, in Artaud's view, should challenge us, jolt us into action, and offer a new arena of sensibility. Baraka seems to have followed this directive in his own dramaturgy. According to one anecdote, in order to attract black patrons to his theater in Harlem, Baraka staged a black man chasing a white man with a gun through the neighborhood. The chase wound up in the theater space trailing a host of excited, black spectators: the plays were then immediately performed, directly capitalizing on the audience's activity and emotion (Elam 39). By thus jolting a decidedly black audience into action, Baraka was adopting Artaud's "Theater of Cruelty" edicts that capitalize on the "public's senses" rather than its "understanding" (85) and "seek[s] in the agitation of tremendous masses, convulsed and hurled against each other, a little of that poetry of festivals and crowds when, all too rarely nowadays, the people pour out into the streets" (85). While the public in this case was pouring from the streets into the theater, the same dynamics of emotional rather then intellectual engagement and action seem to underwrite both Artaud's and Baraka's aesthetics. Although earlier theatrical experiments had pushed for this same counter-cultural goal, a theater intended solely for black spectators asking for "twenty million spooks [to] storm America with furious cries and unstoppable weapons" (Baraka, ***Home*** [***Home: Social Essays***] 214) had not yet been imagined or idealized in this particular way or to this extent.

The dominant issue at the heart of this black cultural nationalism articulated by Baraka was the idea of a socially distinct identity. For Baraka and other cultural nationalists, self-fashioning was the key to defining black power and the creation of a black nation. Yet, as critics like Michelle Wallace have tellingly observed about just this project, the black man in the 1960s "found himself wondering why it had taken him so long to realize he had an old score to settle. Yes, yes he wanted freedom, equality, all of that. But what he really wanted was to be a man" (30).[1] In other words, masculinity defined the identity of black nationalists in the mid-1960s—and nationalists like Baraka were attempting to articulate just such an identity in prose, poetry, and drama.

It should come as no surprise then that Baraka should declare that ***Dutchman*** is really about "the difficulty of becoming a man in America" (***Home*** 188). In ***Dutchman,*** Lula and Clay reiterate this point when they are talking about their fantasies of the coming night. Lula invites Clay into her "dark living room" and teases Clay with the possibility that "we'll sit and talk endlessly, endlessly." When Clay questions what they will talk about "endlessly," Lula says, "About what? About your manhood, what do you think? What do you think we've been talking about all this time?" (25). Not only is black nationalism about discovering a black identity, but as we see from this exchange, ***Dutchman*** and Baraka's political and theatrical agenda focuses on defining and constructing black "manhood."

As critics like Mercer, Carby, and Wiegman have recently noted, however, the kind of black masculinity that artists and performers like Baraka were constructing in the 1960s had a particular flavor—an image of potent and aggressive machismo underscored by and contingent on its asserted distance from other more passive and "effeminized" subjects. Carby traces the genealogy of that construction of masculinity in her study of W. E. B. Du Bois. She shows how Du Bois contrasted Booker T. Washington's "inadequate manliness and consequent lack of the attributes of leadership with a history of black male revolt and self-assertion led by such revolutionary figures as the maroons, Touissant L'Ouverture, Nat Turner, and other rebels against Washington's acts of compromise. . . . These revolutionary figures appear in DuBois's narrative both as 'true' black men and genuine leaders of black men" (Carby 40). Carby goes on to point to Cornel West as the modern apotheosis of this revolutionary black masculinity, but one could easily add the name of Amiri Baraka to a list of black activists who draw on this gendered contrast between weak, effeminized compromise and strong, virile self-assertion as the basis for political revolution. To be a "true" black activist, in other words, demanded that one also had to be strong, uncompromising, and "macho." It is precisely this equation of power that Wiegman suggests that Baraka and Black Power employ to erase their own felt sense of effeminacy in the eyes of white, masculine culture, a solution whose calculus "transferred the problem inherent in the disjunction between masculine sameness and racial difference to the site of gender" (109). Kobena Mercer augments this point when he argues that this "macho" black masculinity emerging in the sixties "subjectively incorporates attributes associated with dominant definitions of manhood—such as being tough, in control, independent—in order to recuperate some degree of power or active influence over objective conditions of subordination created by racism" (143). Mercer goes on to note that the "macho" masculinity embraced by figures like Baraka ironically directs this recuperating aggression not at the white masculine hegemony, but "against fellow colonized men and women" (145).

I would argue that Baraka's black masculinity not only exhibits notable "macho" traits, but also depends for its definition on being directed against those "colonized" subjects who are also abjectified by dominant society. In short, Baraka's black masculinity defines itself through the abjectification, or "othering," of queer men and women. This maneuver, however, constantly reveals its own shaky foundations, and thus in serious ways undermines and problematizes Baraka's militant black masculinity.

By reading ***Dutchman*** through the lens of Baraka's essay, **"American Sexual Reference: Black Male,"** Baraka's abjectifying strategy in the play becomes clearer. Written in 1964, Baraka's essay claims that "[m]ost American white men are trained to be fags. For this reason it is no wonder their faces are weak and blank, left without the hurt that reality makes—anytime" (***Home*** 216). He goes on to ask rhetorically, "Can you, for a second, imagine the average middle-class white man able to do somebody harm?" (***Home*** 217). Baraka describes a set of traits with which to read Clay's pronouncements in his long monologue towards the end of ***Dutchman.*** Clay spits at Lula: "I could murder you now. Such a tiny ugly throat. I could squeeze it flat, and watch you turn blue, on a humble. For dull kicks. And all these weak-faced ofays squatting around here, staring over their papers at me. Murder them too. Even if they expected it" (33). Here, Baraka's character defines his own masculinity by abjectifying queerness; the "weak-faced ofays" are the "fags" of the essay, men whose faces are "weak" and unable to do "harm" to anybody. Clay not only recognizes the "weak-faced ofays" as being separate from him, but also contemplates "murdering" them as he is squeezing Lula's throat flat. The essay reveals the qualifications for manhood through negative example, and Baraka, in an almost point-for-point manner, uses these qualifications to evoke Clay's masculinity.

Yet, if Baraka's essay provides a useful key by which to decode Clay's black masculinity, it also seems to problematize that notion. For in his essay, Baraka argues that the "long abiding characterization of the Western artist as usually 'queer' does not seem out of place" (***Home*** 219). The implication is clear: the artist-figure, especially one influenced by Western mythology and literary styles, falls into the same queer category as white men in general. Throughout ***Dutchman,*** however, we see how Clay himself embodies precisely this kind of Western artist-figure. After all, even after Lula blasts him for "reading Chinese poetry" (8)—a particularly "effeminizing" hobby—Clay still freely and enthusiastically admits that in college he thought of himself as Baudelaire (19). Lula laughs openly, mocking his lack of masculinity and inability to see himself as first and foremost "a black nigger." But Clay merely embraces his "effeminized" identity as a "black Baudelaire" all the more firmly.

Even at the height of Clay's tirade, which most critics see as his main effort at defining his black masculinity, he stresses his own artistic merit and skill. Near the end, he declares:

> With no more blues, except the very old ones, and not a watermelon in sight, the great missionary heart will have triumphed, and all of those ex-coons will be stand-up Western men, with eyes for clean hard useful lives, sober, pious and sane, and they'll murder you. They'll murder you, and have very rational explanations. Very much like your own. They'll cut your throats, and drag you out to the edge of your cities so the flesh can fall away from your bones, in sanitary isolation.
>
> (36)

Although we shall examine the ideological meaning of these lines later, what remains important to our understanding of Clay as an artist-figure is that this passage shows his mastery of stylistic devices typical of Western literature. While this monologue contains idiomatic language ("ex-coons" and "stand-up Western men"), compared to Clay's earlier clipped and often monosyllabic answers to Lula's carefully crafted dialogue, this speech is a metaphorically complex, metaphysically erudite pronouncement. The violence of the last sentence belies the poetic lyricism of Clay's monologue—"They'll cut your throats, and drag you out to the edge of your cities so the flesh can fall away from your bones, in sanitary isolation" (36). Here, we see "cut your throat" punctuating his delivery with hard, terminal "t's" which echo the violence of the image. We also witness the alliteration in the following clause, the "flesh" "falling" "from" bones. Lastly, we hear the influence of seventeenth-century and modern metaphysical poetry: the "falling flesh" seems to be a tipping of the hat in the direction of John Donne's "A Nocturnal upon S. Lucy's Day, Being the Shortest Day," Abraham Cowley's "The Change," or George Herbert's "Life," while the bones becoming barren recalls the imagery of T. S. Eliot's *The Waste Land* or *Four Quartets.*

If Clay regulates his own masculinity through the abjection of queer desire by insisting on his violence and virility, he also reveals his similarity to exactly the kind of poet-figure so mocked by Lula as being effeminate and lambasted by Baraka as being the apotheosis of queerness. Not surprisingly, in his final monologue, Clay tells Lula: "If I'm a middle-class fake white man . . . let me be. And let me be in the way I want" (34). The protagonist demonstrates Baraka's troubling construction of black masculinity: while it involves an assertion of Clay's own potent agency, the contents of this demand reveal Clay's own troubling desire.

If Baraka has Clay desire his black masculinity by abjectifying white queerness, he also has Clay assert his identity by abjectifying femininity, by constructing black agency through the othering of white women. As with Baraka's depiction of queerness, the feminine is also a complicated concept that discloses the fragility of the black masculinity Baraka wants to form.

Near the end of the play when Clay finally takes on the role of dominant male and slaps Lula "as hard as he can, across the mouth" (33), we can note a change in the tone, register, and rhetoric of Clay's dialogue. After the slap, Clay's violent language frequently ends with an exclamation point. When Clay shouts, "I'll rip your lousy breasts off!" (34) and "When all it needs is that simple act. Murder. Just murder!" (35), his speech has moved from a meek, passive tone to a heated, aggressive one. Moreover, this change in tone is accompanied by a drastic change in rhetoric. While Clay addressed Lula as "lady" (14) and "ma'am" (20) in the beginning of the play, after he has lashed out at her, he calls her a "whore" twice—she is a "great liberal whore" (34) and a "loud whore" (35). Clay has not only moved Lula from being a "lady" to a "whore," but he has also transformed himself from Lula's passive, "tender big-eyed prey" (24) to an aggressive virile predator with a "pumping black heart" (34). Clay abjectifies Lula, elevating his own sense of identity through demeaning hers.

Yet, if Clay's violence in ***Dutchman*** becomes the occasion for his linguistic assertion of black virility, the rest of the play discloses an amazing anxiety about the integrity of this black masculinity, an anxiety that problematizes any reading of this play as a realization of Baraka's political and cultural ideology. When we first encounter Clay, he is characterized as being unsure and uncomfortable with exactly the kind of virility Baraka desired. His initial sexual banter with Lula comes off as awkward, and at one point Lula turns on him and exposes Clay's ostensibly suave dialogue: "You think I want to pick you up, get you to take me somewhere and screw me, huh?" When Clay responds quite meekly, "Is that the way I look?" Lula takes this as a cue to deflate Clay's manhood. She attacks: "You look like you been trying to grow a beard. That's exactly what you look like. You look like you live in New Jersey with your parents and are trying to grow a beard. . . . You look like death eating a soda cracker" (8). For a paragon of manhood, Clay is easily infantilized and effeminized; his inability to grow a beard and his living with his parents point to a man who, in Baraka's terms, is less than a man. While Lula is undoubtedly challenging Clay to become assertive and engage in a playful, sexual dialogue, Clay does not seem up to the challenge: he balks again, saying, "Really? I look like that?" and admits that he was "embarrassed" at his ineptness (9). Clay's insecure masculinity is also exposed when he and Lula are talking about names. Lula introduces herself as "Lena the Hyena."

CLAY:

> The famous woman poet?

LULA:

> Poetess! The same!

CLAY:

> Well, you know so much about me . . . what's my name?

LULA:

> Morris the Hyena.

CLAY:

> The famous woman poet?

LULA:

> The same.

(14)

Here, Clay is constructed as a woman, the same as Lula. Masculinity is thus in jeopardy because it is so fluid and changeable, easily altered through language to its feminine opposite. If, as Baraka suggests, this play is about the construction of manhood, then it is simultaneously about how *de rigueur* manhood cannot help but reveal its own contrived nature and the anxiety that accompanies such a realization.

The anxious character of black masculinity becomes even more evident in ***The System of Dante's Hell,*** a piece published within one year of ***Dutchman,*** and a work which helped define what William J. Harris calls Baraka's "transitional period" (xxi). The novel rewrites the story of Dante's descent and travels through the Inferno, exchanging a young, black man for Dante, and the streets of Harlem for the levels of Hell. Near the end of the novel, in the "Level of the Heretics," the protagonist of this narrative meets a large black woman, Peaches, who makes sexual advances on him. We hear how she "came around and rubbed my tiny pecker with her fingers. . . . I saw the look she gave me and wanted somehow to protest, say, 'I'm sorry. I fucked up. My mind, is screwy, I don't know why. I can't think. I'm sick. I've been fucked in the ass. I love books and smells and my own voice. You don't want me. Please, Please, don't want me'" (108). The black here here is defined by his lack of masculinity—his "tiny pecker," his queer effeminacy, his love of books, and most importantly, his strident desire for Peaches *not* to want him sexually. Later on, we hear that Peaches grabs his hat—a "blue 'overseas cap' they called it in the service. A cunt cap the white boys called it. Peaches had it and was laughing like kids in the playground doing the same thing to some unfortunate fag" (108). Baraka consolidates femininity (his "cunt cap") and homosexuality (his characterization as an "unfortunate fag") into a black man who could easily be Clay from ***Dutchman.***

This anxiety about black male identity and integrity becomes metonymically reduced to an anxiety about castration in Baraka's thought, an anxiety that Baraka privileges as being *the* key threat to black masculinity. In **"American Sexual Reference: Black Male,"** he argues that the

> black man is covered with sex smell, gesture, aura, because, for one reason, the white man has tried to keep the black man hidden the whole time he has been in America. . . . And when the possibility arose that these animals really might be men, then the ballcutting ceremony was trotted out immediately, just to make sure that these would-be men wouldn't try any funnystuff.
>
> (***Home*** 226)

Baraka raises two important issues here: one, black men are equated with their sexuality, their manhood, and two, this sexuality is threatening and leads to castration by white society. Baraka notes the way that white lynching of black men often involved castrating the victim and inserting the castrated genitalia into the dead man's mouth: "Trying to strangle a man with his own sex organs, his own manhood: that is what white America has always tried to do to the black man—make him swallow his manhood" (***Home*** 230). In fact, the threat of castration surfaces thirteen separate times in a relatively short essay—a fact that underscores Baraka's obsession with the notion.

As Frantz Fanon argues in *Black Skin, White Masks,* the myths about violent and virile black sexuality were constructed as a method of anxiety management; this maneuver allowed the white colonial masters to allay their anxieties about black sexuality by providing them with the justifications for brutalizing the colonized "Other." For Fanon this virile black "imago" constructed by the white hegemony is a phantasm that continually haunts the mind of the white colonizer (169-70). Eric Lott has argued that this anxiety surrounding "the power of the black penis in white American psychic life" was "obsessively reversed in white lynching rituals" in the mid- to late nineteenth century (9).[2] We can read Baraka's comments on black male sexuality, therefore, within a long tradition of interracial sexual politics, from the colonial sixteenth century through the end of the nineteenth century and beyond. If Baraka's essay reveals a fear of castration, in other words, there seems to be a good reason for that fear, a reason relating to the history of castration as a form of social and political control.

In the play itself, Lula embodies just this anxiety of castration, for while Baraka casts Lula as the temptress throughout most of the drama, Clay's last angry monologue marks a change in the power dynamics at work in the play—a change in power that corporealizes the specter of castration. Clay derogates Lula's obsession with the belly rub as a bogus expression of sexual desire. He lashes out: "The belly rub? You wanted to do the belly rub? Shit, you don't even know how. You don't know how. That ol' dipty-dip shit you do, rolling your ass like an elephant. That's not my kind of belly rub. Belly rub is not Queens. Belly rub is dark places, with big hats and overcoats held up with one arm. Belly rub hates you" (34). Clay's deconstruction of Lula's desire for the belly rub acts as an assertion of his own power, for Clay knows about the real belly rub, "my kind of belly rub," and uses this possession of knowledge to denigrate Lula's posturing and to shore up his own empowered position. Lula, hitherto the temptress and active member of the pair, takes a backseat to Clay, who smoothly riffs, "Sorry, baby, I don't think we could make it" (37). Clay asserts his own masculinity as superior to Lula's femininity with his apology, but at just this moment, when Clay refuses Lula's sexuality and makes the clearest assertion of his masculinity, Lula "plunges" a knife into his chest as he is bending over her—the ultimate castrating metaphor (Sanders 146; Piggford 150). We can find in this symbolic castration a hearkening back to the legend of *la belle dame sans merci*—the merciless woman—a trope of Western mythology and literature. Keats invokes her in his poem "La Belle Dame Sans Merci," but the figure can be traced through Nimue in Malory's *La Morte D'Arthur* to Spencer's Phaedria in *The Faerie Queen* to the Queen of Elfland in Sir Walter Scott's *Ballad of Thomas the Rhymer.* The figure is generally understood to be a radiant woman who "entices young men into her arms to destroy them" (Anadolu-Okur 108). Baraka undermines this masculinity by having Lula metaphorically castrate Clay—enticing him into her arms—just at the moment of the protagonist's clearest and most profound articulation of his own masculine identity. If indeed Clay asserts his manhood in ***Dutchman,*** then this manhood is always haunted by the specter of black male castration and the anxiety this phantasm propagates.

In fact, one can read Lula as being this anxiety-producing specter haunting Clay even at the very beginning of the play when, like a ghost, she peers in at him through the subway's window. Before any words are spoken, the stage directions recount that the train Clay is on stops at a station. Clay looks up and "sees a woman's face staring at him through the window" (4). Clay immediately feels awkward and embarrassed, but when he attempts to return the gaze, "the face would seem to be left behind" (4). The dynamic in this example seems obvious: as Laura Mulvey argues in "Visual Pleasure and Narrative Cinema," Clay becomes the scopophilic object of Lula's pleasurable gaze. That Clay cannot return the scopophilic gaze places him in the feminized position created by the gender dynamics of this play. Baraka wants to underscore the importance of this encounter by making it a kind of dumb-show before "Scene One" of the play begins, and by having it dominate his character's dialogue for the first seven pages of a relatively short thirty-eight page play. Clay's career thus unfolds between this initial effeminizing maneuver and the final scene of castration, so that his character from start to finish appears objectified and effeminized.

Mulvey's analysis helps us complicate further the gender dynamics operating within this text. While Lula seems to be the object of Clay's affection and power in the scene of the belly rub, in her very physical sexual advances, and in her sexualized pageant of the night, she also possesses a certain amount of power when she gazes fixedly at Clay through the subway window. According to Mulvey, this gaze places Lula in the dominant, the "masculine" position; yet, the dominant male gaze that Mulvey elaborates on also allows the gazer to identify with the subject as if looking in a mirror—the subject becomes a "narcissistic ideal." Mulvey argues that in doing so, "curiosity and the wish to look intermingle with a fascination with likeness and recognition: the human face, the human body, the relationship between the human form and its surroundings, the visible presence of the person in the world" (17). In this play, therefore, the usual gender dynamic of visual pleasure is inverted; the "determining male gaze [which] projects its fantasy onto the female figure" (19) is flipped on its head, allowing the traditionally coded sexual object "an identification with the *active* point of view" (31)—and thus to appropriate its agency and power.

Lula's assertion of agency also manifests itself thematically in the metaphors of performance and playwrighting. Clay believes that Lula is an actress, and says as much several times throughout the play. Clay muses, "You act like you're on television already" (19), and he repeatedly asks, "You sure you're not an actress?" (27). With her constant manipulation of language and action, however, Lula appears more like a playwright than an actress. She scripts the actual lines Clay must say: "Now, you say to me, 'Lula, Lula, why don't you go to this party with me tonight?' It's your turn, and let those be your lines" (16). Later, we perceive exactly how effective Lula's powerful playwrighting is, for she commands, "Say my name twice before you ask, and no huh's," to which Clay robotically responds, "Lula, Lula, why don't you go to this party with me tonight?" (16). Lula's power becomes evident in the way she controls language not only for herself, but also for the black man named "Clay" whom she deftly and precisely sculpts: she uses rhetoric to control the world and all of its inhabitants.

In this way, Lula's assertion of active (male) agency, which appears in her manipulation and scripting of the rhetoric in the play, relates her directly to Baraka himself, for as a playwright, he, like Lula, scripts Clay's words. Mimicry, as Homi Bhabha suggests, is "one of the most elusive and effective strategies of colonial power and knowledge" (85), and in ***Dutchman,*** we see how Lula's action mimics or alludes to Baraka's action as the playwright of the work, an empowering act of self-assertion. However, as Bhabha argues, this mimicry also undercuts the naturalness of the hierarchy of power by stressing the way power is and can be performed: Lula's agency both alludes to the powerful agency that defines the playwright and through this allusion, undermines the ostensibly unassailable location of that power. I shall probe this de-stabilizing aspect of Lula's power play later, but for now, I'd like to draw attention to the sexual and racial dynamic of Lula's assertion of power: what is important about it is that this assertion of power can only occur through mimicking a black man.

In the nineteenth century and well into the twentieth, white men like T. D. Rice, George Washington Dixon, and Charles Mathews mimicked black men in minstrel shows, singing, dancing, and performing short skits of what they envisioned black culture to signify. Eric Lott's perceptive study of blackface minstrelsy argues that "[f]igures such as Mark Twain, Walt Whitman, and Bayard Taylor were as attracted to blackface performance as Frederick Douglass and Martin Delany were repelled by it. From 'Oh! Susanna' to Elvis Presley, from circus clowns to Saturday morning cartoons, blackface acts and words have figured significantly in the white Imaginary of the United States" (4-5). While the tradition of minstrelsy has little direct bearing on Baraka's play, exploring Lott's expansive reading of blackface minstrelsy as a facet of the "white Imaginary" opens up the psychology behind Lula's metaphoric "blacking up." As Lott demonstrates, blackface minstrelsy was a particular manifestation of a desire to "try on the accents of 'blackness'" and that this "cross-racial desire . . . coupled a nearly insupportable fascination and self-protective derision with respect to black people and their cultural practices" (6). This "love and theft," I suggest, undergirds Lula's appropriation of black masculinity and casts her, surprisingly, as a blackface minstrel wrestling with the idea of blackness throughout the drama. Lula's "belly rub," and the "song" which accompanies it (30), as well as her black, hipster language—the uses of words like "groove" to end Scene One or phrases such as "doing the nasty . . . like your ol' rag-head mammy" (31)—all of these examples make her an example of Lott's blackface minstrel. "What is vitally important is that minstrel performers reproduced not only what they supposed were the racial characteristics of black Americans (minstrelsy's content) but also what they supposed were their principal cultural forms: dance, music, verbal play" (101). This line of argumentation, while not applying the burnt cork directly to Lula's face, shows her metaphorically "blacking up" as a form of adulation and a method of empowerment.

The politics of this mimicry, or minstrel play-acting, become even clearer if we realize how Lula not only attains agency through aligning herself with black masculine power—with mimicking Baraka's artistic power—but also maintains this power and control by asserting a phallic position in her relationship with Clay. Thus, Lula states: "You tried to make it with your sister when you were ten. But I succeeded a few weeks ago" (9). To be sure, she immediately recants, admitting that she was lying, but this suggestion of phallic power casts a serious shadow on Clay's masculinity. The idea that she might be able to "make it" with Clay's sister both questions Clay's manly power and constructs an image of herself as powerfully phallic. As Lott notes, "the minstrel man *was* the penis" (25) and the white appropriation of blackness was in some attempts an expropriation, to use Marx's term, of the power the black penis implied. As a form of "cultural control," this element of the minstrel show not only fits Baraka's obsession with "castration," but also illuminates Lula's maneuver. Lula's metaphoric minstrelsy here suggests yet another link with the psychology of minstrelsy: by inferring phallic power—and *black* phallic power, at that—she is defining her own sense of agency. While I am not arguing that Lula is "manly" in any biological sense, and that I doubt whether she really desires Clay's sister sexually, I do think it's worth recognizing that Lula's intimation of phallic power not only solidifies her own agency but also seriously disrupts Clay's own masculine identity. Recalling the idea of sexual mimicry developed by Judith Butler, we can thus see how this separation of the phallic power associated with the penis from the actual physical organ makes "the phallus (re)produce the spectre of the penis only to enact its vanishing, to reiterate and exploit its perpetual vanishing as the very occasion of the phallus" (89).

Daniel Boyarin has taken Butler's dyad between the penis and phallus and suggested that like Jewish masculinity, black manhood has been denied the phallus even though black men have been equated with the penis (224). In this way, one might argue that Lula's expropriation of power is one of (white) phallic masculinity, and has little to do with black biology. Yet, the form this empowerment takes—with its hipster language, black references, and pervasive sensuality—seems to demonstrate, in opposition to Boyarin's analysis, how Clay's achieved manhood near the end of ***Dutchman*** collapses phallic power and black virility onto one another to achieve a form of black phallic power in Clay. In this way, Lula's appropriation of the phallus is importantly the appropriation of a *black* phallus. Eric Lott has argued that minstrelsy, like the kind in which Lula engages, allows its artists who "immerse themselves in 'blackness' to indulge their felt sense of difference. It was an avenue that allowed them certain underground privileges (and accrued many demerits) which a more legitimate course would not have provided" (51). With this in mind, we see how Lula's usurpation of the phallic phantasm cashes in on the powerful black sexual sign, but only by simultaneously wresting power away from that phallic "metonymy of presence" that so often defines black masculinity. As with Lula's role as playwright, her adoption of Clay's phallus signals her identification yet again with the black masculinity Baraka attempts to construct in ***Dutchman.***

Lula's usurpation of phallic power not only adds one more agonizing twist to the anxious knot of black male identity, but also fits Baraka's statement in his essay, **"The Revolutionary Theater,"** that Clay in ***Dutchman,*** Walker in ***The Slave,*** and Ray in ***The Toilet*** are all "victims," victims who are the counterparts to the heroes of white dramaturgy (***Home*** 211). While Lula's agency and power are stifled at the end by Clay's monstrous monologue, Clay's sudden assertion of masculine power and the subsequent demolishing of this power through castration effectively collapses heroism on top of victimization: to be a man, in other words, requires building one's own sense of black virility and, by necessity, its immediate punishment by the white hegemony. By fusing these two effects, Baraka both conjures up and meditates on the idea that this victim's status may define the strong, militant, black masculinity he was interested in exploring. In this way, as we shall discover, Baraka ironically privileges a masochistic desire as being one of the key features of a strong and independent black man.

Freud defines masochism as comprising a passive attitude towards sexual intercourse or one's sexual partner. He qualifies this by adding that only in "extreme instances" does sexual gratification actually depend on suffering the physical or mental pain inflicted by the sexual partner (24). Freud's interpretation rescues the term from its common understanding as an extreme form of self-flagellation or pleasurable and violent self-inflicted pain. Taking his cue from Krafft-Ebing, Freud postulates that masochism is the "most common and the most significant of all perversions" (23) since it is so easily expressed by subjects. More often than not, this form of masochism manifests itself in men who take the passive role in heterosexual relationships: Freud calls it feminine masochism. David Savran notes that in feminine masochism men perform the woman's role; they embrace the sexual characteristics of femininity, like castration, passivity in sexual intercourse, and birthing metaphors and signs (28). Kaja Silverman develops this notion further by stating that it is a "specifically *male* pathology, so named because it positions its sufferer as a woman" (189). Clay's castration and overall characterization make him a perfect feminine masochist. While I am not interested in masochism as a pathology or "perversion," but simply as a suggestive model,[3] I must agree with Silverman that a male subject, like Clay, cannot engage in feminine masochism without putting a great deal of pressure on his own masculinity.

If Clay seems to act the feminine masochist, however, then Lula also must in some ways mimic this masquerade. In a complex psychological power play, if Clay is victimized, then Lula, the "minstrel" who identifies with this self-hating black man, must also be characterized by his masochism. As the end of the play makes explicit, Lula was exploring Clay's persona, pushing him to lash out and assert his own masculine power, to embody the iteration of black masculinity Baraka was after and that Lula was performing. We can read the apples Lula speaks of at the beginning of the play as symbols of temptation, for she is tempting Clay throughout to break through the shell of his "Uncle Tom" persona and embrace a dynamic idea of black masculinity, a black masculinity that will necessarily find its voice by defiantly opposing Lula's white femininity. When Lula finally calls him "Uncle Tom Big Lip," Clay slaps her and literally finds his own voice, saying, "Now shut up and let me talk" (33). This interchange underscores Lula's objective, demonstrating that her repeated and subtle machinations were to get Clay to "talk" as a strong black man. This interchange also suggests that Lula's objective was masochistic, for she desired Clay's abuse as a provocation for murder.

Lula thus seems to mimic Clay's masochism, but only to an extent. While both Lula and Clay evince masochistic traits in distinct ways, Lula's masochism seems much closer to what Freud called "reflexive sadomasochism." Unlike sadism or masochism understood independently, reflexive sadomasochism effectively bifurcates the subject's ego between a sadistic, masculine identity and a masochistic, feminine one. Both dominating male and dominated female, active and passive, this reflexive sadomasochist always plays both roles, and in David Savran's argument, uses "the reflexive position simultaneously to eroticize and to disavow both domination and submission" (189). Although Savran goes on to locate this form of reflexive sadomasochism in the protagonists of Sam Shepard's drama of the 1960s and 1970s, I think we can see another subtle variation in Lula. Like Jeep, Crow, and Slim from Shepard's oeuvre, Lula relentlessly reproduces her own subjectivity by seeking out subjugation and abuse from Clay, both verbally and physically. To be sure, Lula's reproduction of power isn't being used to shore up a sense of white male "toughness" as Savran suggests Shepard's male figures do, but one cannot deny Lula's strategy of empowerment hinges on her being able to take her abuse from Clay "like a man." In other words, Baraka's reflexive sadomasochist baits her victim into the role of dominator and uses this developed domination as a necessary prerequisite for the achievement of her empowering masquerade of manhood.

This aspect of Lula's characterization, however, does not escape Baraka's ironic treatment, for Lula's murdering of Clay—her ultimate castrating gesture and sadistic assertion of power—only serves to diminish her own sense of agency. In the concluding moments of ***Dutchman,*** Lula's power wavers. After she plunges the knife into Clay's chest, she pushes his lifeless corpse to the ground and sets up the whole "show" again as another "young Negro of about twenty comes into the coach" (37). While we might expect a re-enactment of Clay's temptation, Baraka introduces slight differences into this recapitulation. Lula levels a "long slow look" at the young black man who enters the subway car, making him drop his books, but then an "old Negro conductor" enters. Not only does he interrupt the attempted seduction, but he also does it with "a sort of restrained soft shoe . . . half mumbling the words of some song" (38), an action that recalls minstrel gestures. Then the conductor greets the young man, and when Lula glares after him, he merely tips his hat at her. His soft shoe number and ironic tipping of the hat smack of carnivalesque transgression, a violation of decorum that upends Lula's power.[4]

Yet, this carnivalesque performance resonates at numerous levels simultaneously and it is only by coming to grips with the tissue of meanings involved in this concluding *coup de théâtre* that we can finally see the ways Baraka is staging these complex gender relations. In Mulvey's terms, Lula's assertive scopophilic gaze is doubly disrupted by the old black man's actions: it is broken when the conductor enters and skewed when he tips his hat. Lula's agency comes from her ability to manipulate consciously the power of the gaze, but what Baraka shows in this recapitulation of her initial temptation is that Lula's gaze has been thwarted. Even as Lula relinquishes her black masculine identification and embraces the white and feminine figure of temptation again, the conductor highlights the irony of Lula's character: his disruptive, transgressive "blackness," set next to Lula's impotent whiteness, brings out in relief how Lula is not as assertive as she was when she mimicked Clay, when she metaphorically "blacked up."

The whiteness that ironically fails to police its own power paradigm illuminates another aspect of Baraka's staged black masculinity. The conductor's action, a version of the black minstrel figure of Jim Crow, uses the white Imaginary's construction of black culture through minstrel caricature in order to subvert that same white imagination: the conductor "jumps Jim Crow," but his doing so disrupts Lula's imminent seduction of another young black man on the train. In this way, Baraka begins to stage an alternative to the self-annihilating character of macho black nationalism. The black conductor dismisses entertaining the desire for the "belly rub," dismisses playing into the phallic equation of blackness and manhood that Fanon stated so famously, and instead consciously embraces the emasculation attendant on performing a minstrel caricature. A shadowy doppelganger of the desperately self-hating Clay, Baraka's conductor finds real disruptive agency in performing a disenfranchising set piece, and in this way begins to question the gender assumptions that lay at the foundation of the Black Arts Movement in the 1960s. As this conductor's actions suggest, perhaps real power rests in consciously and meticulously controlling the performance of oneself and finding real strength in balancing between the culturally-conditioned dialectic of "male" and "female" performance.

Still, for all of the tantalizing possibilities Baraka raises about the nature of gender assumptions, this play is overwhelmingly interested in staging the tragedy of a particular iteration of black and white gender dynamics, although the playwright's enticing feints in the direction of other gendered understandings may change the register of this "tragedy." In other words, the black masculinity that dominates the scene finds its power in the violence and aggression of its articulation—in its alarming agency when Clay finally loses his temper or when Lula erotically prods her prey into action. Yet, as both of these examples make clear, the black masculinity at stake here is a damaging, destructive re-staging of the citational predecessor, while the white femininity in play here, by eroticizing and emulating this form of black masculinity, can only relentlessly rehearse a pattern of disempowering enervation. In other words, while Wagner's Dutchman is doomed to sail the seas until he can find the love of a woman, Baraka's Dutchman is doomed to attempt to pierce the Veil that Du Bois made so famous. Moreover, this "new" Dutchman must attempt to achieve empowerment even as he unconsciously desires a victimized heroism at the hands of a white "minstrel" culture that can only stage over and over again how contingent its paradigm of power really is. I do not mean to suggest that there is a facile solution to this tangled knot of factors, but only to observe that perhaps the real tragedy of this notion of black masculinity that Baraka advanced in 1964 and that has been re-articulated, according to Angela Davis, in the gangsta rap and hip-hop of today, is the fact that it dooms itself through its inability to conceptualize a more lenient, fraternal form of male interaction to wander ceaselessly the psychological seas of self-loathing.

Notes

1. Black women activists living through and writing about the Black Arts Movement have noted the way this black masculinity necessarily degraded black women. Angela Y. Davis states: "My relationship to the particular nationalism I embraced was rooted in political practice. The vortex of my practice was always the progressive, politicized Black community—though I frequently questioned my place as a Black woman in that community, even in the absence of a vocabulary with which to pose the relevant questions." See "Black Nationalism: The Sixties and the Nineties" in *Black Popular Culture* (320). Davis reveals that the black community that was pushing for cultural nationalism, a community that she identified with and worked for, was so defined around the black male that she felt ostracized or "othered." Kobena Mercer has recently reiterated this opinion of the Black Arts Movement, arguing that movements like this "sought to clear the ground for the cultural reconstruction of the black subject—but because of the *masculinist* form this took, it was done at the expense of black women, gays and lesbians." See Mercer's *Welcome to the Jungle: New Positions in Black Cultural Studies* (139).
2. See also Robyn Wiegman's reading of black lynching in *American Anatomies* as "the specular assurance that the racial threat has not simply been averted, but rendered incapable of return" (81).
3. Fredric Jameson makes a similar argument in his seminal work, *Postmodernism, or, The Cultural Logic of Late Capitalism* concerning Lacan's idea of schizophrenia. He writes: "I have found Lacan's account of schizophrenia useful here not because I have any way of knowing whether it has clinical accuracy but chiefly because—as description rather than diagnosis—it seems to me to offer a suggestive aesthetic model" (26).
4. I am thinking here specifically of Mikhail Bakhtin's *Rabelais and His World* and Peter Stallybrass' and Allon White's development of the carnivalesque in their *The Politics and Poetics of Transgression.*

Works Cited

Anadolu-Okur, Nilgun. *Contemporary African American Theater: Afrocentricity in the Works of Larry Neal, Amiri Baraka, and Charles Fuller.* New York: Garland, 1997.

Artaud, Antonin. *The Theater and its Double.* Tr. Mary Caroline Richards. New York: Grove Press, 1958.

Baker, Houston. *The Journey Back: Issues in Black Literature and Culture.* Chicago: University of Chicago Press, 1980.

Bakhtin, Mikhail. *Rabelais and His World.* Tr. Hélène Iswolsky. Bloomington: Indiana University Press, 1984.

Baraka, Amiri. *Dutchman and The Slave.* New York: Morrow Quill Paperbacks, 1964.

———. *Home: Social Essays.* New York: William Morrow, 1966.

———. *The System of Dante's Hell. The LeRoi Jones/Amiri Baraka Reader.* Ed. William J. Harris. New York: Thunder's Mouth Press, 1991.

Benston, Kimberly W. *Baraka: The Renegade and the Mask.* New Haven: Yale University Press, 1976.

Bhabha, Homi. *The Location of Culture.* New York: Routledge, 1994.

Boyarin, Daniel. "What Does a Jew Want? or, The Political Meaning of the Phallus." *The Psychoanalysis of Race.* Ed. Christopher Lane. New York: Columbia University Press, 1998.

Butler, Judith. *Bodies that Matter: On the Discursive Limits of "Sex."* New York: Routledge, 1993.

Carby, Hazel V. *Race Men.* Cambridge: Harvard University Press, 1998.

Davis, Angela Y. "Black Nationalism: The Sixties and the Nineties." *Black Popular Culture.* Ed. Gina Dent. Seattle: Bay Press, 1992.

Du Bois, W. E. B. "Krigwa Players Little Negro Theatre: The Story of a Little Theatre Movement" *Crisis* 32 (1926).

Elam, Harry J., Jr. *Taking It to the Streets: The Social Protest Theater of Luis Valdez and Amiri Baraka.* Ann Arbor: University of Michigan Press, 1997.

Fanon, Frantz. *Black Skin/White Masks.* Tr. Charles Lam Markmann. New York: Grove Press, 1967.

Freud, Sigmund. *Three Essays on the Theory of Sexuality.* Tr. James Strachey. New York: Basic Books, 1962.

Harris, William J. "Introduction." *The LeRoi Jones/Amiri Baraka Reader.* Ed. William J. Harris New York: Thunder's Mouth Press, 1991.

Jameson, Fredric. *Postmodernism, or, The Cultural Logic of Late Capitalism.* Durham: Duke University Press, 1991.

Lee, A. Robert. "Imamu Amiri Baraka." *American Drama.* Ed. Clive Bloom. New York: St. Martin's Press, 1995.

Levine, Lawrence. *Highbrow/Lowbrow: The Emergence of Cultural Hierarchy in America.* Cambridge: Harvard University Press, 1990.

Lott, Eric. *Love and Theft: Blackface Minstrelsy and the American Working Class.* Oxford: Oxford University Press, 1995.

Mercer, Kobena. *Welcome to the Jungle: New Positions in Black Cultural Studies.* New York: Routledge, 1994.

Mulvey, Laura. *Visual and Other Pleasures.* Bloomington: Indiana University Press, 1989.

Nasaw, David. *Going Out: The Rise and Fall of Public Amusements.* Cambridge: Harvard University Press, 1993.

Neal, Larry. "The Black Arts Movement." *Drama Review* 12.4 (Summer 1968).

Oliver, Edith. "Over the Edge." *The New Yorker* 4 April 1964.

Piggford, George. "Looking into Black Skulls: American Gothic, the Revolutionary Theatre, and Amiri Baraka's *Dutchman.*" *American Gothic: New Interventions in a National Narrative.* Ed. Robert K. Martin and Eric Savoy. Iowa City: University of Iowa Press, 1998.

Sanders, Leslie Catherine. *The Development of Black Theater in America: From Shadows to Selves.* Baton Rouge: Louisiana State University Press, 1988.

Savran, David. *Taking It Like a Man: White Masculinity, Masochism, and Contemporary American Culture.* Princeton: Princeton University Press, 1998.

Silverman, Kaja. *Male Subjectivity at the Margins.* New York: Routledge, 1992.

Stallybrass, Peter, and Allon White. *The Politics and Poetics of Transgression.* Ithaca: Cornell University Press, 1986.

Wallace, Michele. *Black Macho and the Myth of the Superwoman.* London: Verso, 1978.

Wiegman, Robyn. *American Anatomies: Theorizing Race and Gender.* Durham: Duke University Press, 1995.

Lotta M. Löfgren (essay date fall 2003)

SOURCE: Löfgren, Lotta M. "Clay and Clara: Baraka's *Dutchman,* Kennedy's *The Owl Answers,* and the Black Arts Movement." *Modern Drama* 46, no. 3 (fall 2003): 424-49.

[*In the following essay, Löfgren finds parallels between Baraka's* Dutchman *and Adrienne Kennedy's* The Owl Answers.]

1964 was a watershed year in the history of drama: Amiri Baraka (still LeRoi Jones) won an Obie for best American play with ***Dutchman,*** an explosive and overtly political play that calls for a violent response to racism and oppression. Baraka's play, because of its refusal to bow to hegemony, was instrumental in giving not only African-Americans but subsequently feminist playwrights of the late 1960s and eventually a broad range of silent minorities a new voice. Few plays have so clearly defined a new movement for its followers, a movement Baraka and Larry Neal dubbed The Black Arts Movement. As Larry Neal explained, in the 1968 essay "The Black Arts Movement," "[t]he Black Arts theatre, the theatre of LeRoi Jones, is a radical alternative to the sterility of the American theatre" (279). The Black Arts Movement

> envisions an art that speaks directly to the needs and aspirations of Black America. In order to perform this task, the Black Arts Movement proposes a radical

> reordering of the western cultural aesthetic. It proposes a separate symbolism, mythology, critique, and iconology. [. . .] A main tenet of Black Power is the necessity for Black people to define the world in their own terms. [. . .] The Black artist['s] [. . .] primary duty is to speak to the spiritual and cultural needs of Black people.
>
> (272-73)

Also in 1964, Adrienne Kennedy's play *Funnyhouse of a Negro* won an Obie, for "distinguished play." Less noticed than ***Dutchman,*** *Funnyhouse,* nevertheless, significantly influenced younger women playwrights, especially African-American women, playwrights such as Ntozake Shange, Aishah Rahman, Suzan-Lori Parks, and Robbie McCauley. In 1965, Kennedy's *The Owl Answers* premiered at the White Barn Theatre in Westport, Connecticut. We should read this intricate, multifaceted play as an "answer" in part to ***Dutchman*** and more broadly to the Black Arts Movement.[1] Despite its complex introspection, *The Owl Answers,* in its form, its echoes of ***Dutchman,*** and the encounter between Clara and the Negro Man carries an urgent message to the Black Arts Movement. In one dimension,[2] it is a plea for a more compassionate relationship among men and women in the black community, and more specifically, for the support of black women writers by the male writers of Black Arts, especially Baraka, its major spokesman. At the same time, the play urges black women artists to chart their own course—if necessary, even without approval from black male artists. The play seeks conciliation, but from a position of independence and strength.

A comparison of ***Dutchman*** and *The Owl Answers* will give us the opportunity to consider a revisionist interpretation of both plays and illustrate that they are not as dissimilar as tradition would have them. My reading of ***Dutchman*** will suggest that critics have interpreted the play too narrowly, in order to make it adhere to Baraka's prescriptions in the essay **"The Revolutionary Theatre"** (1964), which called on adherents to "Accuse and Attack anything that can be accused and attacked" (211). The play is, in fact, more complex and ironic than literary history (including Baraka himself) has allowed. Baraka wrote ***Dutchman*** during the painful transition from his beat days and his life in Greenwich Village to a new name and a new life in Harlem; the play illustrates a time of uncertainty and self-doubt rather than the unambivalent militant stance adopted in **"The Revolutionary Theatre."** Indeed, the essay, written shortly after ***Dutchman,*** may well have been an antidote to the anguish Baraka felt at the time, a way for him to exorcise (or deny) the doubts that clung to the core of ***Dutchman,*** doubts not entirely alien to those articulated by Clara Passmore in *The Owl Answers.*[3] A thorough and fair appraisal of Kennedy's plays from the mid-1960s, meanwhile, will show that, for all their individualism and inscrutability, they, in fact, satisfy many of the tenets of the Black Arts Movement as Neal outlined them. Yet critics and theorists allied with or sympathetic to Black Arts—with the exception of Paul Carter Harrison, who included Kennedy's *The Owl Answers* and *A Beast Story* in his 1974 anthology *Kuntu Drama*—treated her with silence or even open antagonism.[4] Some saw her plays as insulting to blacks because they seemed to yearn for acceptance by white culture. As Alisa Solomon explains, "[d]uring the 1960s and 1970s, [. . .] Kennedy was criticized by activists for not working enough in the movement [. . .] and for being 'an irrelevant black writer'" (xii). In an interview with Howard Stein, Michael Kahn relates how, in the 1969 Joseph Papp production of *The Owl Answers,* "a lot of the actors [. . .] were very angry about being in the play because they felt it was not presenting a positive image of blackness. I think Adrienne was severely ostracized. Her plays were considered neurotic and . . . not supportive of the black movement" (192). Had Kennedy's plays been received more sympathetically by the Black Arts Movement, her genius might have gained the recognition that it deserved, and the Movement would have found plays that put most of its prescripts into practice—even, at times, more thoroughly than the works of the professed members of the Movement. Such an acceptance might also have helped narrow the gulf between black male and female artists so pronounced in the late 1960s and in the 1970s. A re-examination of these plays cannot change what has been, but it should suggest that, despite the obvious differences in style and technique between the two playwrights, their notions of a black aesthetic were fundamentally similar.

Even many differences between the two playwrights that initially appear large diminish upon closer scrutiny. The African-American intellectual community treated Kennedy's plays with suspicion, in part because it found them too closely allied with mainstream avant-garde theatre. In "The Black Arts Movement," Neal condemns "[t]he decadence and inanity of the contemporary American theatre" (279) and mentions Edward Albee's *Who's Afraid of Virginia Woolf?* and its depiction of "sick white lives in a homosexual hell hole" (279) as a perfect example. The structures of Kennedy's early plays at least superficially resemble those of absurdist plays in their near plotlessness, nightmarish and incongruous juxtapositions, episodic structures, character osmoses, surreal sets, heavy yet indeterminate symbolization of props, and inscrutable language. And *Funnyhouse* emerged out of a playwrighting class Kennedy took with Edward Albee. But, like Kennedy, Baraka owes a large debt to surrealism, absurdism, and the theories of Antonin Artaud, whom he cites in **"The Revolutionary Theatre."** In effect admitting that no theatre can emerge out of a void, Baraka argues that "the Revolutionary Theatre, even if it is Western, must be anti-Western" (211). Like Artaud, Baraka wants to create a "theatre of cruelty," a theatre that rejects realism and logic and replaces them with hypnotic theatre. Kennedy's plays, too, assault and overwhelm her audience in ways that, for all their intricacy, go far beyond an intellectual response; in her innovations to theatrical form she, too, is an "anti-Western" playwright. ***Dutchman*** and *The Owl Answers.* in fact, use symbolism and dream logic in similar ways and for similar reasons, although Kennedy's plays are more multi-textured. Both playwrights reject realism as far too limiting aesthetically and too complicit with white cultural hegemony. At the same time, they dismiss some aspects of absurdism. In their different ways, they strive to accentuate the dignity of African-Americans, rejecting the nihilism of absurdism while using its techniques to illustrate the absurdity of society. As Kimberly Benston observes in *Performing Blackness,* "African-American modernist performance works to align disruptive play with cultural reconstruction [. . .] modern black theatre diverges from its Euro-American counterpart in retaining commitment to remembrance and history even as it annuls inherited mechanisms of social reproduction" (29). Both Baraka and Kennedy ultimately seek wholeness and coherence for their characters, although their ideas about how that is to be accomplished differ. Finally, we need to acknowledge that, despite Neal's condemnation of Albee and Baraka's own mockery, in **"The Revolutionary Theatre,"** of the "tired white lives" of "[t]he popular white man's theatre" (213), Baraka was influenced by Albee almost as directly as was Kennedy. Albee was a co-producer of the first production of ***Dutchman*** at the Cherry Lane Theatre in 1964 (he produced *Funnyhouse of a Negro* the same year). And Albee's *The Zoo Story,* which Baraka could have seen in New York only four years before the production of ***Dutchman,*** echoes throughout Baraka's play in ways we cannot attribute to coincidence. The main difference between Baraka and Kennedy in this instance resides in Kennedy's greater willingness to acknowledge Albee's influence.

Because Baraka and Neal were most concerned with bringing an unambiguous political message to black audiences, they would have objected to the sheer difficulty of Kennedy's plays, which are too complex to be a clear call to any kind of action. Baraka and Neal strongly advocated the subordination of the individual voice to the communal one, as Neal explains in "The Black Arts Movement." Though few voices in the history of drama have been as individualistic as Kennedy's, Kennedy in fact raises, in the course of her tormented characters' search for psychic coherence, more communal issues than does Baraka, in his more simply plotted and linear plays; here, too, she answers Baraka and Neal's call. In her three plays from the mid-1960s, *Funnyhouse of a Negro* (1964), *The Owl Answers* (1965), and *A Rat's Mass* (1966), she condemns the American educational system, for its exclusive study of European culture; American culture in general, for forbidding black children to nurture either their black or their white ancestry; Christianity, for its pandemic colonialism and its conspiratorial erosion of the symbols of other belief systems; white culture, for its attempt to destroy the African-American family; and the physical and psychic rape of African-Americans, which she likens in *A Rat's Mass* to the Holocaust. Kennedy depicts individual characters who struggle to find personal identification with cultural markers; but, as Elin Diamond observes, "[h]er ability to weave identification and history, the psychic and the social, suggest [sic] that identification is not only a private psychic act: identifications have histories and thus permit access to subjective, cultural, and political readings" (87).

Kennedy further answers the Black Arts Movement's call for suffusing art with new mythological structures and for finding new, vibrant forms as a way to reject old Eurocentrist ones. Kimberly Benston observes, in "*Cities in Bezique*: Adrienne Kennedy's Expressionistic Vision," that "[i]n a work like *The Owl Answers,* Kennedy is pioneering for black theatre a subjective-critical mode which is a deeply innovative dramatic response to the visionary aspect of the Black Arts Movement" (240). She anticipates, by a few years, the drama and theories of Paul Carter Harrison on ritual theatre; as Benston argues, Harrison believes that "[a]ll Black theatre [. . .] should be measured, not by a standard of realism or anger, but by its ability to 'invoke the force of our ancestral spirits'" ("The Aesthetic" 75). Harrison judges that Kennedy's plays from the 1960s "prove her to be one of the most inventive black dramatists on the Babylonian scene. While these works may have immediate appeal to the white *avant-garde,* they strongly insinuate, probably unconsciously, the sensibility of the African continuum" (*Drama* 216). In fact, Kennedy makes use of African forms and symbols—so consistently that we can safely consider them deliberate—in all her plays from this period and arguably comes closer than Baraka (more focused on political upheaval and masculine dominance) to Harrison's goal of "Nommo force" (xix), of a "more profound relationship" to the universe (xviii). In *Funnyhouse,* the images of African culture are there for Sarah's taking—"nim and white frankopenny trees and white stallions roaming under a blue sky" (19), the ebony mask, ravens and owls replacing the white dove, and, of course, heroes like Patrice Lumumba—but Negro Sarah does not know how to make them her own, and that is her tragedy. Instead of using the ebony mask as a way to retrieve a receding culture, she uses it, at least figuratively, to bludgeon her black father. The central symbols of mask and cross vie for control of her psyche, with an inconclusive outcome. Of *The Owl Answers,* Paul K. Bryant-Jackson observes, "Kennedy's personal experience with the owls and the later dramatizing of the experience represents a quintessential African theatrical event: a communal sacred ritual, in which the central narrator, as well as other characters, can assume or change identities for religious purposes" ("Kennedy's Travelers" 49). Like Brother and Sister Rat, Clara and the Bastard's Black Mother (in the shape of the wife of the Reverend Passmore) take on totemic significance as they assume animal form.

The individual's need for healthy communal ritual is, indeed, a central concern for Kennedy in all these plays; in this way, she answers Neal's call for bolstering the African-American community. The constant, compulsive repetitions that fill Kennedy's work signal the personal dysfunction that results when the individual's search for coherent communal ritual is frustrated and she compensates for this lack with private rituals, neurotic inventions that damage the psyche and isolate the individual instead of connecting her to her community. Culturally sanctioned ritual that excludes certain groups and personal ritual without an external referent both lead to personal dysfunction. For Kennedy's tormented characters, no other options exist. Over and over, her characters discover that however they attempt to create a community in isolation, by fragmenting their own identities into many, or aligning their identities imaginatively with others, or creating their own deities, that kind of perverted, artificial community is no substitute for a real one; it cannot sustain them. In effect, Kennedy's characters experience a "call-and-no-response" isolation from their surroundings. In her investigation of the desperate and inadequate rituals her characters create for themselves, Kennedy simultaneously uncovers the African-American need—at least partially innate and unconscious, she seems to argue—to return to the "logical" and inclusive ritual of their African existence. Her characters often reside in a limbo between personal neurosis and distant cultural memory, in their attempts to create logic in their own worlds.

Finally, Baraka and Neal almost certainly rejected Kennedy's apparent stance on what W. E. B. Dubois, in *The Souls of Black Folk,* named "double consciousness"; much of the black community's criticism of Kennedy revolved around this point. Baraka is generally seen as choosing the black side of the equation, with Kennedy choosing the white. Baraka and Neal set out to excise the white part of double consciousness, labeling it destructive and false. In "And Shine Swam On," his afterword to the anthology *Black Fire,* which Neal and Baraka published in 1968, Neal explains, "[W]hat we are asking for is a new synthesis; a new sense of literature as a *living* reality. But first, we must liberate ourselves, destroy the double-consciousness" (654; emphasis in original). In the struggle for liberation, "the first violence will be internal—the destruction of a weak spiritual self for a more perfect self. But it will be a necessary violence. It is the only thing that will destroy the double-consciousness—the tension that is in the souls of the black folk" (656). Kennedy's plays from the mid-1960s illustrate the agony in her protagonists of this division between black and white and the futile desire for psychic harmony in their amelioration. That does not mean, however, as Herbert Blau suggests, that Kennedy herself aspires to whiteness.[5] This is to take too narrow a view of Kennedy's work and to ignore her intricate webs of irony. Although her characters long for inclusion in white society, Kennedy illustrates that her own vision is more complex than theirs and not imitative of white culture. Sarah in *Funnyhouse of a Negro* hangs herself because in rejecting her father and idolizing Queen Victoria she drives herself mad; she understands that this is a "vile dream" (13), but she can't let it go. The inclusion of objects and images of a diseased, sickening white should also alert us that whiteness hardly connotes purity or beauty in Kennedy's cosmology but rather decay and death. The children in *A Rat's Mass* try to find solace in Rosemary's Catholicism, her Roman ancestry, and her classical white beauty (marred by the worms in her hair), which only increases their sense of isolation. Brother and Sister Rat misuse and transmogrify Eurocentrist rituals because they are subjected to them but not included in them. They understand the concept of saints but have no way of imagining that the saints will protect them. In *The Owl Answers,* Clara Passmore's most excruciating moments are accompanied by the music of Haydn: despite its soothing quality, this music threatens her and represents the seductive danger of immersion in European culture. Like Sarah in *Funnyhouse,* Clara contributes to her own despair by her inability to choose between her white father and the Negro Man. Through these characters, Kennedy articulates her own ambivalence toward English cultural icons and her sense of how easily her own voice can be silenced by them. What she seeks is not assimilation but a freedom of movement within and between cultures, without any compromise of individual identity.

A scrutiny of ***Dutchman*** and *The Owl Answers* reveals that the correspondences between the two playwrights do not stop at shared concerns about aesthetics. That Kennedy should choose to place her play (produced only a year after the much-discussed ***Dutchman***) in a subway car on a hot summer day, without giving any thought to how one play resembles the other, seems hardly possible. Skeletal synopses of the two one-act plays accentuate other, more specific similarities and suggest that they were quite deliberate and purposeful on Kennedy's part. In ***Dutchman,*** Lula, a young white woman, enters a subway car where Clay, a young black man and the only visible person on the train, sits staring into space. Her initial coarse flirtatiousness turns increasingly insulting until Clay finally becomes enraged, baring his soul in a long, passionate monologue. But, "*[s]uddenly weary*" (94), he prepares to leave. When he collects his things, Lula stabs him; the other people on the subway (who have appeared in the second scene) help her throw his body off the train, while she approaches yet another young black man traveling alone. In *The Owl Answers,* "She who is Clara Passmore who is the Virgin Mary who is the Bastard who is the Owl" (25) is in a New York subway car, which is also the Tower of London, a Harlem hotel room, and St. Peter's Cathedral. Throughout her journey, she is by turns accosted and spurned by characters that are her real or adoptive relations, by historical English characters, and by a Negro Man. He first ignores her, then tries to rape her, while she pleads for his understanding and affection. In the end, having found no one to trust, "*in a gesture of wild weariness*" (45), Clara escapes by transmogrifying herself into an owl.

Kennedy adds many other ironic similarities in the details. There are only two seats, one for Clara and one for the Negro Man; in ***Dutchman,*** we see, at first, only Clay's seat, and later, the seat next to him where Lula sits. When the play opens, Clara, "*a plain, pallid* NEGRO WOMAN, [. . .] *sits staring into space*" (26); at the beginning of ***Dutchman,*** we find Clay "*looking vacantly [. . .] Occasionally he looks blankly toward the window*" (71). Whereas Clay holds a magazine he doesn't read, "SHE WHO IS *carries notebooks that throughout the play like the handkerchiefs fall*" (26). They are both detached from their surroundings, isolated and inactive, displaced intellectuals. Clara is openly more nervous and unsure of herself, but Clay's subsequent reactions to Lula, where he tolerates her insults unendurably long, suggests that he, too, lacks confidence. Their names also suggest their kinship: Clay is shapeless, malleable; Clara is transparent—an empty vessel, a multitude of identities, none of them fixed.

Beyond these similarities, specific differences between the two plays foreground the dialogue Kennedy attempts to create with Baraka and the Black Arts Movement. Much of this dialogue revolves around the concept of double consciousness and suggests how inadequate earlier assumptions about Kennedy's cultural outlook have been. Kennedy's exposure of flaws in the concept of double consciousness flavors her investigation, in *The Owl Answers,* of human relations, the role of the black artist, and the nature of dramatic language.

Clara's failed struggles to establish healthy contact with another human individual and above all with the Negro Man allow Kennedy to explore the destructive consequences of double consciousness to the African-American psyche. Baraka's treatment of double consciousness in ***Dutchman*** is, superficially at least, more straightforward. Lula berates Clay for wearing white man's clothes and attempting to assimilate into white society; Clay clearly errs on both counts. Whereas Clay confronts only Lula and the play itself moves relentlessly to its final outcome, Clara has to deal both with the Negro Man and with her Dead White Father (who is also, at times, possibly, the Reverend Passmore), who vie for her attention and eerily echo each other. Clara yearns for acceptance from both, yet flees them when they approach her. Clara seems to believe that a cohesive, simple identity, achieved by a reconciliation, through herself, of the White Father and the Negro Man, will somehow save her. Yet she also fears such melding, illustrating her profound ambivalence toward double consciousness. Their grotesque *pas de trois* suggests that all three are complicitous in sustaining the gulf that separates them, by accepting or further distorting white culture's formulations of their identities. The line "at last you are coming to me" (34, 35), spoken by both men, would suggest that they are ready to accept Clara, but their welcoming gestures are aggressive and frightening. When the Dead White Father repeats the invitation, he tells her, "[A]t last you are coming to me, Bastard" (35), hinting that allowing her to approach doesn't mean legitimizing her. And the Negro Man literally assaults her, nearly raping her. But Clara's failure to choose should also tell us that her choices would be inadequate even under more auspicious circumstances. Neither the White Father nor the Negro Man can give her what she needs; for in choosing either, or even both, were that possible, she would have to give up too much of herself. In other words, double consciousness, even if it could be perfected, is not enough for her: it does nothing to help her express her uniquely female identity.

She therefore tries to find her identity on a higher, non-human plane, beyond notions of double consciousness. But Clara's identity fragmentation causes her to move between the sub-human and the super-human with the same inconclusiveness that characterizes her movement between the White Father and the Negro Man. The Owl is Clara herself, as we learn at the outset of the play. Her genesis as an owl stems, in part, at least, from the rape of her mother; the "ow oww" (35) of pain during the rape creates her kinship with the owls. This kind of bitter pun, frequent in Kennedy's works, illustrates how easily the human psyche is damaged when it attempts self-definition without sanctioned social or linguistic ways to do so. As the illegitimate child of a white man and a black woman, Clara is less than human; she must even adopt the masculine term "bastard," since no female equivalent exists. But because she is both the Bastard and Mary, she is flawed and innocent, simultaneously barely human and divine. Even as she acknowledges her "bastard" lineage, Clara transforms this inauspicious beginning into something miraculous, perhaps also akin to Zeus's rape of Leda, a transformation that attempts to replace degradation with elevation and make her belong to God. The divine quickly gives way to the totemic, though, for divinity itself, in our cultural environment, participates in the same exclusionary tactics as society. Clara does not, nor will she ever, belong to God. Her transformation into owldom constitutes her final attempt to eliminate the turmoil of illegitimacy and double consciousness by fleeing humanity altogether. The totemism of her owl transformation may suggest a return to African supernaturalism, but in our society, such totemism signals not social inclusion but ostracism.

These equivalencies set the pattern for Clara's behavior toward the Negro Man as well. Despite his continued and abusive insistence on the physical, Clara tries to elevate the Negro Man to a spiritual plane. She makes a crown of paper and places it on his head, addressing him as God: "Call me Mary, God," (41) she begs him; "I am only yearning for our kingdom, God" (43); "God, say, 'Mary, I pray to you. Darling, come to my kingdom. Mary, leave owldom—come to my kingdom. I am awaiting you'" (44). But elevating the Negro Man to a god is a rejection, not an affirmation, of his humanity, no less than is his attempt to rape her. He tears the crown from his head, instead persisting in his physical assault of her. She starts to screech, calling him alternately "Negro!" and "God" (44-45), hinting that the two might be synonymous if he would but listen to her. In this regard, the Negro Man is as much a victim of distortion as Clara. They cannot know themselves, and they cannot know each other, as long as they try to make themselves or each other into something either less or more than human. The both/and ideal of double consciousness and its neither/nor reality remain unaffected by Clara's aspirations to godhead for both her and the Negro Man. Here Kennedy warns the members of the Black Arts Movement that the kind of support and submissiveness the men demanded of women in order to strengthen the male ego and thereby the community—such calls for subordination, by Baraka and Harrison, among others, were frequent—is counterproductive for all involved and its own kind of degradation. Such false aggrandizement complicitously enforces the white myths of black America, instead of destroying them by, in effect, acknowledging the unattainability of simple human dignity. Neither Clara nor the Negro Man can honestly appraise the other's humanity because of the denials and lies that surround their heritage, which they unintentionally reinforce—not just the immediate lies of Clara's mother's rape, but also the rape of generations of their ancestors and the generations of lies to which white America has subjected African-Americans. An imposed distortion of personality is part of the African-American psyche; Clara's attempts to deify the Negro Man and his to rape her both strengthen such distortions.

Kennedy creates troubling alignments among the four characters Clay, Lula, Clara, and the Negro Man as a way to foreground her observations on gendered and racial relationships. The Negro Man and Clay, as black males, force a comparison; Lula and the Negro Man find an odd kinship in their aggressive reactions to Clay and Clara, respectively; Clara and Lula, as women, do the same, as do the Negro Man and Clara because both are black. Out of these crisscrossing and imperfect alignments emerge a few salient political realities. The single-minded sexual interest in their female partners of Clay and the Negro Man seems to illustrate, the Black Arts Movement's professed desire to excise the double consciousness notwithstanding, Kennedy's belief that black men are men first and black second and are, therefore, more similar to white men than to black women. Kennedy further exposes this apparent hypocrisy through the Negro Man's kinship to Lula in their shared aggressiveness toward their "prey"; both victims are black. But the gulf between the dangerous Lula and the confused and passive Clara suggests that black women are prevented by society, all white society and black male society, from participating in double consciousness and reveals how marginalized black women are. In this light, double consciousness, the ability to participate, to some degree at least, in both white and black culture, becomes a privilege, something for which only the Negro Man and Clay are eligible. Clara doesn't even have the social standing to make that choice. Both Clay and the Negro Man have a freedom of movement in the white world, on the subway, that Clara lacks; she remains "locked there" (28), unable to leave until the others release her. Kennedy exposes double consciousness, in other words, as a black male construct. But the paradox Kennedy tries to teach us is that Clara's exclusion from double consciousness makes her not one-dimensional but multidimensional. Because she is not only a mulatta but also a woman, consciousness is immediately tripled, at least. Like Baraka, then, Kennedy rejects double consciousness, but whereas Baraka seeks to excise double consciousness to leave only one pure black identity, Kennedy rejects it in favor of a multiplicity that tries to heal fragmentation through acceptance rather than elimination. Kimberly Benston observes, "This distressing deconstruction of personality into fragmented personification and imperfect impersonation does not abandon ideological critique for a nihilistic political despair but reorients it as a disruptive weapon against unconscious complicity with hegemonic stratagems of reduction, reification, and fetishization" (*Performing Blackness* 69). Kennedy warns Baraka and the Black Arts Movement that dealing with double consciousness reductively, through excision rather than augmentation, cannot but impoverish their art and ultimately play into the hands of hegemony.

Yet Kennedy seems to hold out some hope for a more self-aware and compassionate relationship between the black man and the black woman under different circumstances, so long as they both—that is, the

African-American community and, most especially, the artists who speak for it—openly acknowledge their own and each other's essential humanity. Once again, Clara serves Kennedy as an imperfect example. When the Negro Man asks her what she yearns for, she vaguely answers "[l]ove or something" (36), in effect, begging him to define her desire. She later tells the Negro Man, "I only have a dream of love. A dream. [. . .] ([. . .] *She shows the* NEGRO MAN *her notebooks, from which a mass of papers fall. She crazily tries to gather them up.* [. . .]) Communications, God, communications, letters to my father" (42). She wants him to read her notebooks and to acknowledge her as a writer, but the Negro Man takes no notice of her papers. This is enormously destructive of Clara, for she cannot be heard unless someone who has already gained a voice helps her. Her notebooks, containing her written words, are slippery; she can't control these words even though she seems to have to keep them with her at all times. She repeatedly looks in her notebooks as if afraid that the words on the page, too, will somehow slip away. Clara moves through life as through the lurching subway car, barely able to hang on. She represents voiceless African-American women here and, especially, those artists who try to gain the respect of their fellow African-American male artists, as well as of society at large. Since male writers, Baraka above all, have gained a voice, Kennedy seems to say, they must help their black sisters to be heard. If not, these women's words will remain in private notebooks, unheeded. As long as she has no voice, Clara will be only the owl, hooting monosyllabically in the darkness. The Negro Man's inarticulate and persistent physical assault of Clara suggests the depth of Kennedy's condemnation of the Black Arts Movement's objectification and subjection of women and women artists. If the Negro Man wants to own her but not hear her, if he insists that Clara give him only what he wants, then his rejection of her artistic voice is tantamount to rape.

At the same time, Clara, and black women writers, must work to articulate their emotions and not simply wait to be interpreted by others. They need the help of black male artists, and they need to strive on their own to be heard. In spite of her love of writing and her evident wish to show the Negro Man her notebooks, Clara becomes tongue-tied when trying to speak to him; she can do nothing to explain to him what she is writing and why it should matter to him. She can't even hold on to the notebooks. And why is Clara writing every day to her white father? Why does she not direct her words to the black community? Kennedy here joins the debate about the appropriate audience for black writers and offers us a rather remarkable piece of self-irony: as she well knows by the time *Owl* is produced, many, black and white alike, have misread *Funnyhouse,* to the extent that they have understood it at all, as an expression of black desire for white culture. Through Clara's fumbling, hesitant address to the Negro Man, Kennedy suggests that Clara imperfectly understands that her ideal audience is the Negro Man, as the representative of the black community, at least as much as it is the Dead White Father. Yet Kennedy refuses, even in Clara's moment of crisis, to deny Clara the right, or to relinquish her own right, to address the white and black communities simultaneously, and with a voice uniquely her own. Kennedy dismisses as naive and unrealistic any assumptions that black men and women artists can exist in Utopian harmony (Clara's dream of the divine union between herself and the Negro Man). Black women artists can't expect superhuman support from black male artists; this would stifle the creativity of all. A middle ground of mutual respect and tolerance is the only space where the Negro Man and Clara, in a better world, could adequately nurture each other's needs and desires. Whereas Clara wants the Negro Man to be both a spiritual mate (at times also a physical one) and a god, Kennedy herself, in the creation of *The Owl Answers,* illustrates her desire for a human, tolerant, and generous response from Baraka, the Black Arts Movement, and the black community as a whole. Yet the complexity of her work also suggests that Kennedy, like Clara, finds protection in inscrutability; in the privacy of her vision, in her continued marginality, lies her autonomy. Compromising herself to be heard would lead to artistic death. Kennedy asks to be heard on her own terms, speaking her own voice, although, to most, it may seem like the hooting of an owl. Silencing her because of her inscrutability would damage the entire artistic community.

The Negro Man's attempts to rape Clara are, in fact, at least in part, caused by his desire to silence her; for even though she remains ignorant of her own powers, he does not: "*he is frightened by her*" (44). In the Negro Man's reaction to Clara, Kennedy seeks to remind black women of the power they do possess; they need not be as helpless as Clara. In a way, Clara does have supernatural powers, since she is able, through her imagination, to transform characters into multiple individuals, but she has not learned how to control her imagination in self-affirming ways or protect herself from those who would impede her artistic development. She is still trying to channel it through definitions of black and white, instead of freeing her imagination and celebrating its multiplicity. All the other characters on the subway car also seem frightened by Clara; she herself "can see they're afraid of me" (32). All want her locked up, silenced, denigrated. All, even the historical characters, seem to conspire to imprison her, as if Clara's/Kennedy's words, too honest and radically new to fit into any canon, would occasion a revisionist view of history and culture that they cannot tolerate. But the Negro Man should have been different. Significantly, only he does not change in appearance and identity throughout the play; perhaps he has the solidity and reliability that will steady Clara. And only in his company can Clara leave the subway train. All others take pains to "[k]eep her locked there" (28), and the slamming doors remind is that they bar her from participating in Eurocentric culture, no matter how much she loves some aspects of it. When the Negro Man leads her out, "They" "[l]et her go" (40). But this potential release becomes another kind of entrapment, since he, too, refuses to free her.

Clara therefore decides to escape society, but even in the moment of escape, she seeks reconciliation and amelioration. She runs from the Negro Man, takes the ceremonial knife, covered with blood and feathers from the "Mother," and suddenly starts attacking him with the knife; she "*then drop[s] it just as suddenly in a gesture of wild weariness*" (45). He backs away from her, and she moves toward her final owl transformation. Clara seems, for a moment, to consider re-enacting Lula's deed of killing Clay, thereby aligning herself with Lula. But, like Clay, she is quickly overcome with weariness. Unlike Clay, Lula's victim, Clara takes control of her own destiny by effecting her own owl transformation. This would seem a pyrrhic victory at best, since Clara gives up her human form and loses her power to speak: hers is an act of desperation, occasioned by her inability to be heard and to be treated like a human being. But even in her transformation, she seems to protect the Negro Man from the crime of rape, or possibly even murder. In this final way, she reaches out to the Negro Man: Clara's own act keeps him from becoming the black male version of Lula. Clara even sacrifices her humanity in order to salvage the Negro Man's human dignity. *The Owl Answers,* then, constitutes an impassioned plea to the black community not to permit the rape mentality—the spirit of lies, degradation, and objectification that characterizes white society's treatment of African-Americans—to influence the way blacks treat each other, the way black men treat black women, and the way black male artists, especially the members of the Black Arts Movement, treat black women artists. We are left to hope that the Negro Man will not, like Lula, pursue other victims once he leaves Clara.

The play's repetitive, yet elliptical, structure illustrates Kennedy's project to reconceive dramatic form in a way that will better express the African-American psyche and her own black female artistic vision. She implicitly corrects the traditional linearity of ***Dutchman*** (perhaps a sign of Baraka's phallocentrism) and anticipates future rejections of linearity by feminist writers and critics. As an African-American and as a woman, Kennedy is doubly concerned with the ways that traditional theatre sanctions the inveterate racism and sexism of Eurocentrist culture: linearity is a way to conceal and to lie. Clara's desire for coherence through a blending of black and white that would thereby create a logical, linear story out of her life illustrates how fundamental to our understanding of ourselves is the kind of fictional logic with which we recreate our lives, in memory, in the present, and in our perception of the future. In life as in literature, linearity seeks to encroach. In Clara's situation, that desire is challenged not merely by life's normal vicissitudes but also by her heritage: since she is barred from double consciousness, to create anything approaching linearity in her life, Clara would have to formulate two lines as unlikely to converge as the tracks beneath the subway car—one for her African-American heritage and one for her white European heritage—for so society decrees. As a mulatta, she melds black and white in her person, but culturally, the white and black inside her will never be reconciled. Therefore, Kennedy frustrates Clara's desire and ours for coherence in her own telling of Clara's story. We are not allowed to be certain of even the most fundamental facts about her: Who is her real father? Is she a schoolteacher engaged to be married to the principal or something quite different? What is her real name? We cannot even know what place we are in, for we are in New York and London simultaneously, possibly also in Rome, and probably inside Clara's mind. And the one coherent action Clara desires to accomplish—attending the burial of her father—frustrates her to the end. The subway may move linearly from station to station, but the plot moves with lurching discontinuity and repetitions. Even the stage itself spatially counteracts the inevitable linear duration of time in performance by rotating, now clockwise, now counterclockwise. We are forced into simultaneous multiple perspectives, where, on the one hand, nothing happens except that Clara rides a few stops on the subway and, on the other, she endures so many upheavals—the repeated deaths of her white father, the attempted rape by the Negro Man, and her adoptive mother's suicide, to name a few of the cataclysmic events she experiences in a very brief time—that she must flee all. This fractured perspective contains its own veiled political commentary, for it ironically imitates the refusal of American society to acknowledge the atrocities endured by African-Americans since the first days of slavery. It is part of the American cultural myth to deny these outrages, except in the most superficial ways, and to tell a far simpler tale. This denial also mocks any possibility of attaining true double consciousness, for how can Clara ever know her black heritage if society denies that the events that shaped that heritage ever happened? Therefore, when Kennedy, as an African-American woman, relates Clara's physical and psychic suffering, she does so by telling two stories simultaneously, one where essentially nothing happens except that Clara rides a few stops on the subway and one where she deals perpetually with unspeakable horror. By derailing theatrical conventions from their usual tracks, Kennedy exposes overt and covert elements of racism, in both society and theatrical form. She dares us to dismiss Clara's tale—and her own—as the ravings of a lunatic.

When Clara assumes the shape of the owl, giving up her attempt to find a human identity, she experiences a despairing, non-cathartic deflation, similar to Clay's at the end of ***Dutchman.*** Like Clay, Clara is overcome by a weariness that won't let her continue her struggle; like Clay, she has passionately tried to justify her existence and failed. Unlike Clay, she has consciously signaled her own defeat, her despair, and her self-destructiveness. But Clay's behavior is no less self-destructive than Clara's, and his methods of defining himself are as unsuccessful as hers; this constitutes their greatest similarity.

Prevailing interpretations of ***Dutchman*** take their cues from **"The Revolutionary Theatre"** and "The Black Arts Movement," assuming, reasonably enough, that Baraka's manifesto is a blueprint for the play and that Neal's insider status makes him a reliable interpreter. Neal describes the central conflict in ***Dutchman*** this way:

> In a perverse way it is Clay's nascent knowledge of himself that threatens the existence of Lula's idea of the world. Symbolically, and in fact, the relationship between Clay (Black America) and Lula (white America) is rooted in the historical castration of black manhood. And in the twisted psyche of white America, the Black man is both an object of love and hate.
>
> ("Black Arts" 280-81)

Lula, "the white bitch-goddess," kills Clay, Neal argues, because he finally "digs himself and his own truth only to get murdered after telling her like it really is" (280) when he finally reacts to her insults and exposes his murderous rage. "Lula [. . .] kills Clay first" (280), he explains, before Clay has a chance to kill her. Many other critics echo Neal's interpretation, arguing that Lula kills Clay in order to maintain the status quo and rid white society of a violent black man.[6] The play does not, in fact, support this interpretation, which reduces the play to propaganda, a political tool that calls for specific action, however powerful. The play does call for action, but in a much more effective way theatrically than Neal and other critics have suggested. Lula kills Clay, not when he is in a violent rage, but after all the fight has gone out of him and he again assumes the pose of the "Black Baudelaire," divorcing himself from the struggle of his people. After his moment of rage, he becomes "*[s]uddenly weary*" (94), saying "[a]hhh. Shit. But who needs it? I'd rather be a fool. Insane. Safe with my words, and no deaths, and clean, hard thoughts, urging me to new conquests. My people's madness. Hah! That's a laugh. My people. They don't need me to claim them" (94). Even when he regains a little of his spirit, he only speaks of what "they" will do to Lula and her ilk; he remains divorced from the struggle. Only as he leaves the train to resume his life unchanged does Lula tell him, in a matter-of-fact way that suggests no fear, "I've heard enough" (95), and stab him.

If Lula doesn't kill Clay when he is enraged and a threat to her, but only after he again aligns himself with mainstream culture, does she really represent white America? I propose that Lula actually represents Baraka himself, wearing the mask of a white woman, the better to test Clay's mettle.[7] The ultimate goal is not to seduce Clay sexually or to anger him to the point that it seems legitimate for a white woman to kill him in self-defense but to inspire in him a liberating, violent rage that will deliver him from the entrapments of double consciousness and social and political subjugation. The play offers ample evidence of this argument. Much of the dramatic tension consists in the way that Baraka gradually peels off the layers of his Lula mask, the mask of the seductive white woman, and uncovers what lies beneath, in an increasingly urgent attempt to get Clay to pay attention and become angry. But Clay is so enamored of Lula's outward appeal that he won't listen to the hints Lula/Baraka offers. Lula's early dialogue is fairly aggressive from the start, but a clear, though brash, come-on. She approaches him because "I [. . .] saw you staring through that window down in the vicinity of my ass and legs" (74); she suggests he take her to the party he is going to and hints they might end up in her apartment afterwards. Yet from the start, Lula speaks with other voices. She tells him soon after sitting down next to him that "I even got into this train, going some other way than mine. Walked down the aisle . . . searching you out" (75). She seems to have a deeper motive for finding Clay than to acquire a random partner—or a random victim—for the evening; this is reinforced at the end of the play when she makes notes and immediately approaches another young black man. But Clay can only respond to the slightly incongruous statement with "Really? That's pretty funny" (75). Enigmatically, she asks him, "What are you prepared for?" Clay "*[t]akes her conversation as pure sex talk*" and responds, "I'm prepared for anything. How about you?" (75). The stage direction suggests that Lula's words are *not* pure sex talk; instead they challenge Clay to a battle on a more deadly level—as it turns out, he's not prepared for "anything." Shortly thereafter, she tells him "I lie a lot. *[Smiling]* It helps me control the world" (76). Here we receive the first suggestion that Lula may even take on mythic proportions, reinforced by her odd "My hair is turning gray. A gray hair for each year and type I've come through" (78), hinting that her goal is not seduction or destruction but something far more important and difficult. But Clay only laughs. She even knows secrets about him she couldn't possibly know if she were a strange white woman on a train (did he "make it" with his sister when he was ten? (76)); her explanation that she knows these things about Clay because "you're a well-known type" (78) sounds disingenuous. Her odd rapid shifts in mood, even early on, are hardly those of the seductress. After she "*[g]rabs his thigh, up near the crotch,*" he tells her, "Watch it now, you're gonna excite me for real," to which she responds "I bet" and "*slumps in the seat and is heavily silent*" (81). She seems neither pleased nor frightened by his responsiveness, but irritated. If we assume that she here shows us a glimmer of Baraka, then her reaction illustrates Baraka's disgust with Clay: with heavy irony, Lula/Baraka hints that Clay may become sexually excited but not excited to anger as he should be. To Clay's questions, "Are you angry about anything? Did I say something wrong?" she responds, "Everything you say is wrong. *[Mock smile]*" (82). Baraka's anger at Clay's passivity starts dissolving the Lula mask, and the smile becomes increasingly forced. Lula's assault of Clay, in fact, grows steadily less veiled and sounds wrong coming out of the mouth of Lula the seductress but fits Baraka himself. She mocks him for wearing white man's clothes, asking, "Did your people ever burn witches or start revolutions over the price of tea? Boy, those narrow-shoulder clothes come from a tradition you ought to feel oppressed by" (82). "May the people accept you as a ghost of the future. And love you, that you might not kill them when you can. [. . .] You're a murderer, Clay, and you know it," she tells him; adding, "*[Her voice darkening with significance]* You know goddamn well what I mean" (84). Clay would know could he hear the voice as Baraka's: Clay is a murderer, not the potential yet failed murderer we see at the end of the play, but a murderer now because his passive, assimilationist lifestyle ensures the destruction of his fellow blacks.

In the second scene, Baraka starts challenging Clay man to man. When Lula sees another passenger enter the train, she experiences "*[a] mild depression, but she still makes her description triumphant and increasingly direct*" (86) because she knows that the gathering crowd on the train is there to help her dispose of Clay's body if he fails his test, and she hopes it won't come to that. For not the first time, Baraka hints that Lula is doing something hard that she would rather not be doing, that the seduction is an increasingly hollow act. Then Lula mocks Clay's manhood and calls him a Fascist, almost begging Clay to see through the mask. Sounding like one black man speaking to another and using a decidedly Barakian syntax, Lula tells him, "[Y]ou mix it up. Look out the window, all the time. Turning pages. Change change change. Till, shit, I don't know you" (89), suggesting that Clay is a traitor to a shared cause and that she (as Baraka), indeed, has known him intimately already. His passivity and his fake whiteness, as she sees it, are not a sign of his safe complacency, with which a representative of white culture would be pleased, but a betrayal worthy only of contempt. Finally, with the mask fully off, Lula/Baraka shouts at him:

> Be cool. Be cool. That's all you know . . . shaking that wildroot cream-oil on your knotty head, jackets buttoning up to your chin, so full of white man's words. Christ! God! Get up and scream at these people. Like scream meaningless shit in these hopeless faces. *[She screams at people in train, still dancing]* Red trains cough Jewish underwear for keeps! Expanding smells of silence. Gravy snot whistling like sea birds. Clay. Clay, you got to break out. Don't sit there dying the way they want you to die. Get up.
>
> (91-92)

If Lula is only a seductive and violent white woman, then who are "they"? How do we explain her extreme change of tone and diction and the urgency with which she now addresses him? Her manner of speaking does not resemble that of the woman who enters the train at the outset, but it does sound like Baraka himself, especially like Baraka the young Beat poet.

Lula takes on a double persona at the two extremes of the spectrum, that of the white woman and that of the black man. Baraka dons the mask of the white woman because this is Clay's most difficult and subtle enemy, the one he must work hardest to resist. Seeing a white man as the enemy isn't hard; rejecting Lula's open invitation to easy sex is a lot harder.[8] But resist he must if he is to pass Baraka's test. To do that, Clay must not only reject Lula's advances but also become enraged enough, for himself and his people, to maintain that rage and kill Lula. Because Lula is really Baraka in a white mask, she wants him to kill her to prove that he can become an effective revolutionary. When he fails to sustain his anger, instead opting to exit the train, Lula kills him because he is useless to the revolution. Without ceremony, she stabs him and has her people on the train dump him outside. She then goes in search of her next "prey," for a man who will resist her charms and muster the rage that Baraka calls for here and in **"The Revolutionary Theatre."** Significantly, she again picks a young black man carrying a book, for the intellectual elite are most apt to lead an easy life in the white world, but they are indispensable to the revolution.

The play gains dramatic complexity and significant irony in Lula/Baraka's double motive of seducing and awakening Clay. Even as Lula tries to make Clay accept her advances, she wants him to reject her. This suggests, as Werner Sollors and C. W. E. Bigsby point out, a struggle within Baraka that uncovers yet another dimension of the play.[9] The struggle between Clay and Lula, and the double persona of Lula herself, represent the profound turmoil within Baraka at this time: he was caught between the world of LeRoi Jones, the world of

Greenwich Village, Beat poetry, and a white wife, and that of Amiri Baraka, the revolutionary poet from Harlem, the founder of the Black Arts Repertory Theatre School and Black Arts. In other words, Lula's challenge to Clay involves not only a test of his revolutionary mettle but also a call to destroy his double consciousness by killing the white part of himself. The only option appears to be the death of his black self. An acknowledgement of the struggle within Baraka to redefine, even reinvent himself, adds greater poignancy to Clay's anguish at the end of ***Dutchman.*** He articulates, here, the dilemma that seems to have consumed Baraka at this time, his need to write, combined with his sense that writing poetry was an escapist, not a revolutionary act. Yet being both a man of action and a man of words seemed impossible to him. Clay cries to Lula, "Bird would've played not a note of music if he just walked up to East Sixty-seventh Street and killed the first ten white people he saw. Not a note! And I'm the great would-be poet. Yes. That's right. Poet. Some kind of bastard literature . . . all it needs is a simple knife thrust. Just let me bleed you, you loud whore, and one poem vanished" (94).

Baraka acknowledges that the sublimation of violence in African-American culture has inspired the heights of its artistic achievements, most notably blues and jazz. But he also hints at his fear that, as a poet, the "Black Baudelaire," he appropriates the white man's art instead of articulating a new one, as do Bessie Smith and Charlie Parker. He needs to make his poetry new and black, but he seems unsure of his ability to do that. Both Clay and Clara, then, experience the agony of being a black artist in America at this time and facing the dilemma of speaking for the community and as an individual: they have similar desires, similar fears.

Baraka's poetry from the 1960s clearly expresses this anguish, and his desire somehow to bridge the gap between the introspection and potential irrelevancy of poetry and the need for action as he articulates it in **"The Revolutionary Theatre."** The collection ***Black Magic*** (1969) often illustrates this ambivalence. In **"Citizen Cain,"** he writes, "Roi, finish this poem, someone's about to need you. Roi, / [. . .] Get up and hit / someone, like you useta. Don't sit here trembling under the / hammer. Fate like a season of abstract reference. Like an / abstract execution where only ideas are shot full of holes. / Don't sit there drowned in your own bad writing" (8). The poem ends, "Your time is up / in this particular feeling. In this particular throb of meaning. / Roi, baby, you blew the whole thing" (8). He expresses here the tug between "abstraction" and violence within him, as if they are hopelessly contradictory. His avoidance of violence strikes him as selling out. As Neal also testifies in "The Black Arts Movement," "abstraction" is anathema to them both: "Poetry is a concrete function, an action. No more abstractions" (276). In this poem, where Baraka openly speaks to himself, we hear clear echoes of Lula's admonition to Clay to "[g]et up and scream at these people." Lula, the strange white woman on the train, of course doesn't know Clay, but Baraka does, sometimes in ways he doesn't want to, and he often seems to feel alien to himself. This might explain why Lula, in the same breath, can tell Clay "I don't even know you" (82) and "I know you like the palm of my hand" (82).

Finally, this interpretation of Lula more fully satisfies Baraka's dictum in **"The Revolutionary Theatre"** that "[t]he Revolutionary Theatre must take dreams and give them a reality. It must isolate the ritual and historical cycles of reality" (211), echoing Neal's call in "The Black Arts Movement" for a new iconology. If my reading of Lula is valid, then the mythical framework of ***Dutchman*** has a more complex and ironic texture than in other interpretations of the play. As many other critics have pointed out and as Baraka tells us from the start, the subway itself is "*heaped in modern myth*" (71). At the outset, Lula openly identifies herself with Eve by eating apples and offering them to Clay, telling him "[e]ating apples together is always the first step" (77). But unlike the original Eve, Lula "tempts" Clay (like Adam, a moldable personality, at least by white culture, as their names suggest) not to fall but to rise up, not to succumb to her charms but to reject them and kill her. Clay does fall in the end, when he prepares to walk away from her. Clay needs a knowledge of good and evil, but he won't get it by eating Lula's apple. Eating the apple actually signifies his continued ignorance; he eats the apple without seeing anything more clearly, "*whacking happily at the apple*" (77). Lula even tries to keep him from eating the apple after he too readily accepts it, "*[t]aking him a little roughly by the wrist, so he cannot eat the apple, then shaking the wrist*" (77), trying, as Baraka, to make the seduction harder than it is. But she can't stop Clay from remaining passive, in his fallen state, from willingly being seduced by her, and from refusing to kill her. Lula is not in league with Satan, as Neal suggests, but is an ironic savior who offers herself up to be killed by Clay so that he can survive and, in turn, help his people gain deliverance, and so that he can purge his own soul of double consciousness. But Clay is damned, too comfortable with his own middle class life to break out. He fatally errs in assuming that his safe life as the "Black Baudelaire" is an Edenic existence: the dangerous, violent world is his real paradise and offers him the true promise of salvation, but only if he can sustain his rage. And Lula is the Dutchman as well as Eve, the traveler who searches for deliverance, for herself and her "victim," not through the love of a woman but through the hatred of a black man.

Like any movement that espouses nationalism as dogma, the Black Arts Movement soon had to face its own limitations. Anti-imperialist movements all over the world have had to learn that the kind of reductive, monologic voice with which a nationalist literature necessarily speaks contains not the seeds of a new purity but the germ of its own destruction, in part because it is too exclusionary. Replacing one monologic voice with another, albeit replacing the voice of hegemony with the voice of revolution, merely reformulates tyranny. Most nationalist movements start revolutionary but soon become reactionary. Most of them are radically misogynistic. Baraka himself seems to have been aware early on of the self-consuming nature of his nationalistic phase. In a 1976 speech entitled **"Not Just Survival: Revolution (Some Historical Notes on Afro-American Drama),"** he acknowledged that "[a]ll of us wanted to use our art as a weapon of liberation, but in the main we fell into the error of cultural nationalism and many of us have yet to recover" (47). Because of Baraka's own ability continually to redefine himself, he was able to offer ways to move on once the Movement's initial usefulness waned, revising his views on revolution, on women, and, we might conjecture, on Kennedy herself. Like other such successful movements, the Black Arts Movement served as a tool of transition: it disrupted the complacency of white America and forced it, through an admixture of fear and titillation, to listen to these new voices; it simultaneously created a new interest in theatre in the black community.[10] For this, much of contemporary literature remains indebted to the Black Arts Movement.

Adrienne Kennedy could have broadened the definition and repertoire of the Black Arts Movement from the outset and saved it from its initial monologic stance had she not been assigned to the margins of an already marginal group, often by that group itself. But the nationalist stance of Baraka and his cohorts could not, in the early years, allow itself to accept voices that sounded as different as Kennedy's. The sad irony is, as I have explained, that the division between them was, in great measure, superficial. As it turns out, Lula and Clara seek something quite similar: black individuals who will support black culture in a way that benefits the entire community. *The Owl Answers* teaches us that neither monologism nor double consciousness suffices in a post-modern world. Kennedy's distraught characters evince not a rejection of either blackness or whiteness but a desire to embrace all aspects of their heritage. This has nothing to do with assimilation. Her courage in maintaining this stance in the face of prevailing nationalist sentiments is remarkable. Allowing her characters their complexity matters more to her than anything else, even though that complexity leads to madness for them and to critical neglect for her. For Kennedy, monologism is the true horror. Clay, indeed, lives that truth: his obligation to choose between the Black Baudelaire and the Black Revolutionary causes paralysis. Baraka approaches Kennedy's vision when he creates characters that internalize binary oppositions and therefore cannot easily choose between them. Lula, above all, emerges as a multi-textured character: according to the interpretation I offer above, she is white and black, male and female, real and mythic. In fact, she mitigates Baraka's misogyny in fascinating ways. In ***Dutchman*** and other plays from this period, Baraka implicitly agreed with Kennedy that uncertainty and anguish make for more powerful art than polemic. As a consequence, Baraka and Kennedy, together, did much to destroy the black stereotypes—both dramatic and social—that had held American literature in a vise grip for generations. Langston Hughes, James Baldwin, and Lorraine Hansberry had already loosened the bonds that held black and white audiences in thrall to the tyrannical black dramatic stereotypes that grew out of minstrelsy and *Uncle Tom's Cabin,* pervasive through much of the nineteenth and the first half of the twentieth centuries. Kennedy's tragic mulattas, some of the most complex dramatic characters ever to appear on page or stage, deliberately destroyed that particular stereotype. Clay and Clara, as fictional constructs, hint at a resolution in hybridity that goes beyond monologism and binarism toward a true heteroglossia and a more complex and multifaceted definition of both personality and theatre. Together, despite their personal failures, as dramatic role models they offer future generations of playwrights the freedom to seek completion in montage, pastiche, dazzling allusiveness, unembarrassed and unencumbered borrowing, blending, blurring. Baraka and Kennedy set the stage for the experimentation of subsequent decades that has gone beyond old-fashioned notions of the avant-garde because it rejects nothing out of hand.

Notes

1. In an interview with Paul Bryant-Jackson and Lois More Overbeck in 1990, Kennedy says that the manuscript to *The Owl Answers* was complete in 1962; this would suggest that her play anticipated *Dutchman* rather than the other way around (4). But in a 1977 essay entitled "A Growth of Images," published in *TDR,* she mentions that she never thought of writing a one-act play until Edward Albee's *The Zoo Story* became popular. She wrote *Funnyhouse* as a one-act play "because I was not happy with any of the three-acts I had written up to that point." She adds, "The subsequent plays were ideas that I had been trying to work on in my twenties, but then they just suddenly came at the same time, because all those plays were written quite close together. They all came out eleven months to a year from the time *Funny House* came out" (47). This suggests that *Owl* did in fact receive extensive revisions shortly before its premiere; that is, after the production of *Dutchman.* And in a *Melus* interview with Wolfgang Binder, she confirms that she finished *Owl* a year after *Funnyhouse* (104). In any event, the relationship between the two plays, as I present it

within, remains essentially the same: Kennedy clearly voices concern, in her play, about the Black Arts Movement's attitudes toward black women in general and black women artists in particular.

2. For my present purposes, I will examine only one small aspect of this complex play; I certainly do not want to suggest that this constitutes the full meaning of the play. But in discussing the relationship between Clara and the Negro Man, I treat an element of the play essentially ignored by other critics.

3. Baraka's other plays from the 1960s illustrate a similar ambivalence: some adopt an unambiguous militancy, in accordance with the tenets of "The Revolutionary Theatre," while others evince emotional anguish and psychological turmoil. Baraka's plays from this period seem to fall into two categories: those that do adhere to Baraka's prescription in "The Revolutionary Theatre," such as *Experimental Death Unit 1* (1965), *A Black Mass* (1965), and *Madheart* (1966), and those that express Baraka's ambivalence and inner turmoil, such as *The Toilet* (1963), *The Slave* (1964), *Great Goodness of Life* (1966), and *The Baptism* (1966).

4. See Riley; Kgositsile; in addition to Neal, "Black Arts." Even Toni Cade, in a 1969 essay reviewing the accomplishments of the black theatre of the 1960s, makes no mention of Kennedy. A rare supporter, who deserves recognition, is Loften Mitchell, who argues,

> Nor am I impressed with those who call [Kennedy's] work personal or individualized. Those who look for every Negro-authored play to reflect their points of view would do well to write their own plays. A play by a Negro is in one sense like a play by a white person—a statement in dramatic terms of that particular author's viewpoint at a given time in history. Since no one expects a white playwright to solve any and all problems in his work, it is unrealistic to expect a Negro writer to do it.
>
> (199)

5. Herbert Blau observes, "Nor is she entirely sure, as she rehearses the guilt, fantasies, and phobias of her secretly divided world, where sterility seems black, that she wouldn't rather be white" (531).

6. As Femi Abodunrin suggests, "[M]any have performed simple critical but cognitive twists on the play in order to fit Clay the anti-hero into the white equals evil, black equals good syndrome that characterized this phase of black writing and much of its criticism" (167). What follows is a representative sampling; it illustrates that this kind of interpretation of *Dutchman* is not restricted to the 1960s. Loften Mitchell, in 1967, suggested that, in *Dutchman,* "Mr. Jones is charging that this is the pattern of America—seducing, tempting, insulting the black man, then killing him when he objects" (199). Toni Cade observed, two years later, "*Dutchman,* the game between the man on the margin and the seductive assassin, said all there is to say about the whole continuous pattern of the lure and the murder of black people" (137). Lloyd Brown wrote, in 1980, that Lula "stabs [Clay] to death when his initial attraction changes to scornful resentment at her racial condescension" (144). Helene Keyssar argued, in 1981, that "Lula attempts to seduce, taunt, bewilder Clay; Clay tries to ignore, rebuff, enjoy, and humor Lula. Finally only rejection is possible. Clay's refusal is violently verbal; Lula's literally murderous: She kills him. In the end, we learn from this play that black people cannot rest peacefully in the same world with white people like Lula" (151). Geneviève Fabre, in 1983, observed that "[t]aken aback by Lula's verbal and sexual games, Clay suddenly rebels and reveals in a flash all the anger and hatred of which even the most 'submissive' blacks are capable. Lula fatally stabs Clay, who has become dangerous" (37). She added, "Lula is a kind of god who dispenses life and kills when the creation threatens to turn upon its creator" (38). Leslie Catherine Sanders observed, in 1988, that "[l]ike all Jones's plays, [*Dutchman*'s] plot is simple. Clay, a middle-class young black man, is approached on the subway by Lulu [sic], a white woman. She baits him seductively and finally enrages him. When he reveals his true feelings toward her and whites in general, she kills him" (139). Nilgun Anadolu-Okur argued, in 1997, "Lula represents Clay's inescapable destiny, because she is both the cruel temptress and the cold-blooded murderer" (107); "She is the haunting spirit, the deadly virus, messenger of death" (111). Philip Uko Effiong, in 2000, suggested that "[w]hen Clay refuses to conform to Lula's stereotypical ideas of the Black man, she taunts him into revealing his antagonism toward Whites, including the facade he hides under his Ivy League front, then she kills him" (87). In 2001, Jerry Gafio Watts wrote, "Lula may represent white America and its death-dealing enticements to all blacks who believe that they have entered the ranks of the racially 'acceptable.' [. . .] When [. . .] rage is publicly articulated, whites will respond in a repressive manner, perhaps even with murder" (71).

7. Though no other critic argues this, a few have offered interpretations that touch on my own. Werner Sollors writes,

> While it is generally accepted that Clay is a Baraka-projection and -spokesman, Lula, too, expresses many of Baraka's ideas in Baraka's own language. Clay and Lula are not merely depersonalized, absurd, two-faced *social* symbols, but are also endowed with elements of their creator's self. [. . .] [T]hey represent different temporal aspects of an artistic consciousness which has divided itself into opposing forces.
>
> (123; emphasis in original)

But Sollors also argues that when Clay becomes enraged, Lula ceases speaking for Baraka and becomes "transformed, from the omniscient Bohemian into an incorporation of everything that is murderous in white Western society. [. . .] An agent of repression, Lula must crucify Christ, must silence Clay in order to bring the *Dutchman* ritual to an end" (128). He argues that "when the Black man responds with a rhetorical tirade, he is stabbed to death" (118). In *The Drama of Nommo,* Paul Carter Harrison comments that "[o]ddly enough, [Lula] becomes everything Clay should be about: a reflection of the conscious, *bad ass* nigguh tearing away layers of fiction from a Kneegrow's colonized mind" (213; emphasis in original), but he has no explanation for this apparent incongruity. C. W. E. Bigsby states that "*Dutchman* is a play which directly expresses LeRoi Jones's own dilemma. [. . .] Jones was himself ambiguously balanced between a career as a writer and a more active involvement in the black movement. [. . .] The ambivalence of *Dutchman* was thus deeply rooted in his own sensibility" (286). Although Bigsby acknowledges that "his own ambivalent loyalties draw [Clay] back to the word he had abandoned for action" (286), he also argues that "[g]iven the history of black-white relations in America [Lula] represents that sexual temptation once punishable by death. She wishes to destroy that which attracts her"(286).

8. Baraka's descriptions, in *The Autobiography of LeRoi Jones,* of his and his companions' liberal interest in white women during the early 1960s suggests how strong a temptation a woman like Lula is.

9. See my comments in note 7 above.

10. In 1974, Biodun Jeyifo [Abiodun Jeyifous] could observe that "[i]n the last ten years since Baraka's *Dutchman* was written and produced, not only have there been more producing black groups formed, more plays have been written [. . .] than in the previous 130 years since the African Grove Company of New York started the first black theatre company in the country in the 1820's" (334).

Works Cited

Abodunrin, Femi. *Blackness: Culture, Ideology, and Discourse. A Comparative Study.* Bayreuth: Breitinger, 1996.

Anadolu-Okur, Nilgun. *Contemporary African American Theater: Afrocentricity in the Works of Larry Neal, Amiri Baraka, and Charles Fuller.* New York: Garland, 1997.

Baraka, Amiri [LeRoi Jones]. *The Autobiography of LeRoi Jones.* Chicago: Hill, 1997.

———. *Black Magic: Sabotage, Target Study, Black Art. Collected Poetry 1961-1967.* Indianapolis: Bobbs-Merrill, 1969.

———. *Dutchman. Selected Plays and Prose of Amiri Baraka/LeRoi Jones.* New York: Morrow, 1979. 70-96.

———. "Not Just Survival: Revolution (Some Historical Notes on Afro-American Drama)." *Daggers and Javelins: Essays, 1974-1979.* New York: Morrow, 1984. 30-52.

———. "The Revolutionary Theatre." *Home: Social Essays.* New York: Morrow, 1966. 210-15.

Benston, Kimberly W. "The Aesthetic of Modern Black Drama: From *Mimesis* to *Methexis*." Hill 61-78.

———. "*Cities in Bezique*: Adrienne Kennedy's Expressionistic Vision." *CLA Journal* 20 (1976): 235-44.

———. *Performing Blackness: Enactments of African-American Modernism.* London: Routledge, 2000.

Bigsby, C. W. E. *Modern American Drama, 1945-2000.* Cambridge: Cambridge UP, 2000.

Blau, Herbert. "The American Dream in American Gothic: The Plays of Sam Shepard and Adrienne Kennedy." *Modern Drama* 27 (1984): 520-39.

Brown, Lloyd W. *Amiri Baraka.* Boston: Twayne, 1980.

Bryant-Jackson, Paul K. "Kennedy's Travelers in the American and African Continuum." Bryant-Jackson and Overbeck 45-57.

Bryant-Jackson, Paul K., and Lois More Overbeck, eds. *Intersecting Boundaries: The Theatre of Adrienne Kennedy.* Minneapolis: U. of Minnesota P., 1992.

Cade, Toni. "Black Theater." Gayle, *Black Expression* 134-43.

Diamond, Elin. "Rethinking Identification: Kennedy, Freud, Brecht." *The Kenyon Review* 15.2 (1993): 86-99.

Effiong, Philip Uko. *In Search of a Model for African-American Drama: A Study of Selected Plays by Lorraine Hansberry, Amiri Baraka, and Ntozake Shange.* Lanham, MD: UP of America, 2000.

Fabre, Geneviève. *Drumbeats, Masks, and Metaphor: Contemporary Afro-American Theatre.* Trans. Melvin Dixon. Cambridge: Harvard UP, 1983.

Gayle, Addison, Jr., ed. *The Black Aesthetic.* Garden City, New York: Doubleday, 1971.

———. ed. *Black Expression: Essays by and about Black Americans in the Creative Arts.* New York: Weybright, 1969.

Harrison, Paul Carter. *The Drama of Nommo.* New York: Grove, 1972.

———. ed. *Kuntu Drama: Plays of the African Continuum.* New York: Grove, 1974. Hill, Errol, ed. *The Theater of Black Americans: A Collection of Critical Essays.* New York: Applause, 1980.

Jeyifous, Abiodun. "Black Critics on Black Theatre in America." Hill 327-35.

Kahn, Michael. "An Interview with Michael Kahn." Bryant-Jackson and Overbeck 189-98.

Kennedy, Adrienne. "Adrienne Kennedy: An Interview." Bryant-Jackson and Overbeck 3-12.

———. *Adrienne Kennedy in One Act.* Minneapolis: U of Minnesota P, 1988.

———. *Funnyhouse of a Negro.* Kennedy, *Adrienne Kennedy* 1-23.

———. "A Growth of Images." *TDR* 21.4 (1977): 41-48.

———. "A *Melus* Interview: Adrienne Kennedy." *Melus* 12.3 (1985): 99-108.

———. *The Owl Answers.* Kennedy, *Adrienne Kennedy* 25-45.

Keyssar, Helene. *The Curtain and the Veil: Strategies in Black Drama.* New York: Franklin, 1981.

Kgositsile, K. William. "Toward our Theatre: A Definitive Act." Gayle, *Black Expression* 146-48.

Mitchell, Loften. *Black Drama: The Story of the American Negro in the Theatre.* New York: Hawthorn, 1967.

Neal, Larry. "And Shine Swam On." *Black Fire: An Anthology of Afro-American Writing.* Ed. LeRoi Jones and Larry Neal. New York: Morrow, 1968. 638-56.

———. "The Black Arts Movement." Gayle, *The Black Aesthetic* 272-90.

Riley, Clayton. "On Black Theater." Gayle, *The Black Aesthetic* 313-30.

Sanders, Leslie Catherine. *The Development of Black Theater in America: From Shadows to Selves.* Baton Rouge: LSUP, 1988.

Sollors, Werner. *Amiri Baraka/LeRoi Jones: The Quest for a "Populist Modernism."* New York: Columbia UP, 1978.

Solomon, Alisa. Foreword. *The Alexander Plays.* By Adrienne Kennedy. Minneapolis: U of Minnesota P, 1992. ix-xvii.

Watts, Jerry Gafio. *Amiri Baraka: The Politics and Art of a Black Intellectual.* New York: New York UP, 2001.

FURTHER READING

Criticism

Baraka, Amiri, and Kalamu ya Salaam. "Amiri Baraka Analyzes How He Writes." *African American Review* 37, nos. 2-3 (summer 2003): 211-37.

Baraka offers insight into thematic and stylistic aspects of his work.

Gwiazda, Piotr. "The Aesthetics of Politics/The Politics of Aesthetics: Amiri Baraka's 'Somebody Blew Up America.'" *Contemporary Literature* 45, no. 3 (fall 2004): 460-85.

Considers Baraka's cultural relevance in light of the controversy surrounding his post-September 11th poem "Somebody Blew Up America."

Additional coverage of Baraka's life and career is contained in the following sources published by Thomson Gale: *African American Writers,* Eds. 1, 2; *American Writers Supplement,* Vol. 2; *Authors and Artists for Young Adults,* Vol. 63; *Black Literature Criticism,* Ed. 1; *Black Writers,* Eds. 2, 3; *Concise Dictionary of American Literary Biography,* 1941-1968; *Contemporary American Dramatists*; *Contemporary Authors,* Vols. 21-24R; *Contemporary Authors Bibliographical Series,* Vol. 3; *Contemporary Authors New Revision Series,* Vols. 27, 38, 61, 133; *Contemporary Dramatists,* Eds. 5, 6; *Contemporary Literary Criticism,* Vols. 1, 2, 3, 5, 10, 14, 33, 115; *Contemporary Poets,* Ed. 7; *Contemporary Popular Writers*; *Dictionary of Literary Biography,* Vols. 5, 7, 16, 38; *Dictionary of Literary Biography Documentary Series,* Vol. 8; *DISCovering Authors*; *DISCovering Authors: Canadian Edition*; *DISCovering Authors Modules: Most-studied Authors, Multicultural Authors, Poets,* and *Popular Fiction and Genre Authors*; *DISCovering Authors 3.0*; *Drama Criticism,* Vol. 6; *Drama for Students,* Vols. 3, 11, 16; *Encyclopedia of World Literature in the 20th Century,* Ed. 3; *Literature Resource Center*; *Major 20th-Century Writers,* Eds. 1, 2; *Major 21st-Century Writers,* (eBook) 2005; *Poetry Criticism,* Vol. 4; *Poetry for Students,* Vol. 9; *Reference Guide to American Literature,* Ed. 4; *Twayne's Companion to Contemporary Literature in English,* Ed. 1:1; *Twayne's United States Authors*; *World Literature Criticism Supplement*; and *World Poets.*

Don DeLillo
1936-

(Also wrote under the pseudonym Cleo Birdwell) American novelist, playwright, short fiction writer, and essayist.

The following entry provides an overview of DeLillo's life and works through 2005. For discussion of the novel *White Noise* (1985), see *CLC,* Volumes 39 and 210; for discussion of the novel *Mao II* (1991), see *CLC,* Volume 76. For additional information on his career, see *CLC,* Volumes 8, 10, 13, 27, 54, and 143.

INTRODUCTION

Recognized as one of the finest postmodern novelists and most astute social critics of contemporary American life, DeLillo has produced more than a dozen works that often draw comparisons to those of such authors as Thomas Pynchon and John Barth. Since the early 1970s, he has exploited the discrepancy between appearance and reality, creating penetrating, satirical portraits of the consequences of wasteful consumer societies, conspiratorial paranoia, crowd psychology, cultural politics, and the pervasive power of mass media. The events of September 11, 2001, have lent an eerie prescience to his fiction, which frequently meditates on the cultural and artistic significance of violence and terrorism. Employing the techniques of literary postmodernism, DeLillo's novels typically feature terse prose, displaced bits of dialogue, and fast-paced, episodic narration that underscore a preoccupation with the ritualistic aspects of words, the nature of language, and etymology. DeLillo has attracted a modest but dedicated audience for much of his career, but he vaulted to best-seller status upon publication of *Libra* (1988) and *Underworld* (1997), which has renewed critical interest in many of his earlier works.

BIOGRAPHICAL INFORMATION

The son of Italian immigrants, DeLillo was born in the Bronx, New York. He was raised as a Roman Catholic, and the symbols and rituals of the Church prominently figure throughout his writings. Upon graduation from Cardinal Hayes High School, DeLillo attended Fordham University where he studied communication arts, graduating in 1958. In 1960 he published his first short story, "The River Jordan," while working as a copywriter at the advertising agency Ogilvy and Mather. The 1963 assassination of President John F. Kennedy marked a turning point for DeLillo as a writer. The breakdown of American innocence symbolized by the event and the unprecedented media response that followed it became seminal touchstones for his later novels. In 1964 he quit his advertising job in order to write full time. A few years later, DeLillo started writing what later became his first published novel, *Americana* (1971). Throughout the 1970s, he published five more novels—*End Zone* (1972), *Great Jones Street* (1973), *Ratner's Star* (1976), *Players* (1977), and *Running Dog* (1978). Although these novels received critical attention, they failed to attract a popular audience. However, beginning with *The Names* (1982), DeLillo's critical reputation markedly increased throughout the 1980s and 1990s as he won a National Book Award for *White Noise* and a PEN/Faulkner Award for *Mao II.* In addition, DeLillo's best-selling *Libra* and *Underworld* received nominations for the National Book Critics Circle Award. Since then, DeLillo has published *The Body Artist* (2001) and *Cosmopolis* (2003).

MAJOR WORKS

DeLillo's novels typically portray the power of media, the paranoia of government conspiracies, and the costs of mass consumerism as primary characteristics of a contemporary American society that verges on chaos but is saved by the benefits of language. This linguistic approach toward resolution of narrative conflict informs each of DeLillo's works. *Americana,* which traces the cross-country odyssey of a young television advertising executive in search of self-identity, demonstrates DeLillo's preoccupation with American popular culture and the struggle between the individual and a chaotic world. Similarly, *End Zone* chronicles one football season in the life of a running back at Logos College. Superficially a satire on the American obsession with the violence of organized sports, this novel treats football as a metaphor for nuclear war, implying that the ultimate consequence of such organized violence is total annihilation. *Great Jones Street* recounts a rock star's retreat from public performances and slide into drugs and paranoia as he joins a search for a potent new experimental narcotic. *Ratner's Star* is esoteric science fiction, in which the first half of the narrative is mirrored in reverse by the second half. In this novel, a fourteen-year-old mathematics prodigy decodes messages sent from space for a government agency that authorizes him to answer, rather than decipher, the star's message.

Set in the midst of contemporary street culture, both *Players* and *Running Dog* focus on urban hipsters trying to escape boredom through espionage, pornography, and terrorist activities, which evoke broader symptoms of a spiritual hollowness in contemporary America. In *The Names,* a corporate risk analyst tries to discover the motives of a mysterious Greek cult that ritualistically kills people whose names bear the same initials as the place where they are murdered. A novel about mortality and technology, *White Noise* highlights the numbing effects of American media and the obsessive fear of dying. The novel details the life of a death-obsessed professor of Hitler Studies at a Midwestern university after an industrial accident releases toxic insecticide in his neighborhood. When he discovers that his wife is taking an illegal drug that alleviates her uncontrollable fear of death, he desperately sets out to obtain the drug for himself. *Libra* combines historical and invented characters in the story of Lee Harvey Oswald and the circumstances leading to his assassination of President Kennedy. The novel weaves two non-synchronous narratives—one tracing Oswald's life from childhood to death and the other detailing the plan of a right-wing conspiracy to murder the president—to illustrate how random factors can propel an individual into ignominious posterity.

An exploration of nihilism and social isolation, *Mao II* examines terrorism, international politics, and the global role of authorship in today's world. In this novel, a longtime reclusive writer uncharacteristically lets a woman publish her photograph of him, which enmeshes him in a Middle Eastern hostage intrigue involving another writer. The novel's title refers to Andy Warhol's famous portrait of Chinese Chairman Mao Tse-Tung, which exemplifies the novel's thematic concern with the proliferation of such mass media imagery as the student demonstrator in Beijing's Tiananmen Square, Ayatollah Khomeini's funeral in Tehran, and the mass wedding of Moonies at Yankee Stadium that also appear in the novel. A sprawling epic of the people, places, and events that defined the second half of the twentieth century as "the nuclear age," *Underworld* traces the rise and fall of the Cold War mentality from the perspective of a professional garbage collector and concludes in the ambiguous depths of cyberspace.

The style, tone, and scope of *The Body Artist* mark a departure from DeLillo's typical works. Concerning a mournful female performance artist after the suicide of her husband, this novel explores the linguistic nature of time, the grieving process, and the aesthetics of crisis. While confined to her apartment building, she meets a childlike man who can inexplicably "recall" bits and pieces of her last conversation with her husband. Set in a stretch limousine, *Cosmopolis* recounts the private musings of a wealthy twenty-something on his way to the barbershop on such topics as capitalism, paranoia, technology, and the mentality of crowds.

CRITICAL RECEPTION

Critics have regarded DeLillo as not only a masterful satirist with a linguist's appreciation for words, but also a serious social critic with an affinity for black humor and apocalyptic visions. Commentators have consistently identified his "sound-bite" dialogue, his evocative descriptions of people and events, and his thematic penchant for fear and paranoia as hallmarks of his fiction. On the other hand, detractors have often used these same elements to characterize his dialogues as rhetorical equivocation and his plots as contrived. Despite their ideological diversity, reviewers have universally acknowledged DeLillo's command of diction and syntax and his knack for deducing metaphysical implications from everyday routines. As a result, his literary style has often drawn comparisons to the quintessentially postmodern movement of metafiction. Since the mid-

1990s, academic interest in DeLillo's texts has surged on a variety of fronts. Scholars have framed his themes in religious, feminist, or political terms; psychoanalyzed his characters in terms of gender identity; and studied his style for implications bearing on the art of narration, both past and future. In addition, critics have scrutinized DeLillo's treatment of conspiratorial societies and subversive underground movements, as well as his examination of the relevance of modern art to consumer-based culture. Since the destruction of the World Trade Center, many commentators have reassessed his work. Although DeLillo's representation of terrorism as either performance art or the last refuge of individualism seem to endorse violence, several scholars have viewed this aspect of his work as a metaphor intended to provoke questions about cultural biases.

PRINCIPAL WORKS

Americana (novel) 1971
End Zone (novel) 1972
Great Jones Street (novel) 1973
Ratner's Star (novel) 1976
Players (novel) 1977
Running Dog (novel) 1978
Amazons: An Intimate Memoir by the First Woman Ever to Play in the National Hockey League [as Cleo Birdwell] (novel) 1980
The Names (novel) 1982
White Noise (novel) 1985
The Day Room (play) 1986
Libra (novel) 1988
Mao II (novel) 1991
Underworld (novel) 1997
Valparaiso: A Play in Two Acts (play) 1999
The Body Artist: A Novel (novel) 2001
In the Ruins of the Future: Reflections on Terror and Loss in the Shadow of September (essay) 2001; published in newspaper *Guardian*
Cosmopolis: A Novel (novel) 2003

CRITICISM

Steven Carter (essay date winter 2000)

SOURCE: Carter, Steven. "DeLillo's *White Noise.*" *Explicator* 58, no. 2 (winter 2000): 115-16.

[In the following essay, Carter focuses on the historical and narrative significance of the brand name of the narrator's gun in White Noise.*]*

In Don DeLillo's novel ***White Noise,*** the father-in-law of narrator/protagonist Jack Gladney makes him an offer he can't refuse:

> "I want you to have this, Jack."
>
> "Have what?"
>
> "[. . .] This here is a 25-caliber Zumwalt automatic. German-made. It doesn't have the stopping power of a heavy-barreled weapon but you're not going out there to face down a rhino, are you?"
>
> (252-53)

Jack's father-in-law's instincts are right on target: Jack will soon find himself facing down not a rhino but a *mink*: one Willie Mink, that is, the putative lover of Jack's wife Babette.

Cradling the Zumwalt in his hand, Jack thinks: "A concealed lethal weapon. It was a secret, a second life, a second self, a dream, a spell, a plot, a delirium [. . .]" (254). "The gun created a second reality for me to inhabit" (297). In fact there is no such thing as a .25 caliber Zumwalt automatic.

But if Don DeLillo's Zumwalt automatic is fictional, the name *Zumwalt* is not. As virtually every American knows, in the early years of the Vietnam War, the United States Navy oversaw a massive defoliation campaign intended to destroy as much as possible of the Vietnamese jungles, thereby depriving the Viet Cong and the North Vietnamese Army of their protective cover of tropical forest and exposing them to precision bombing and strafing attacks. Throughout this operation, retrofitted cargo planes sprayed hundreds of tons of so-called Agent Orange over hundreds of square miles of Vietnamese countryside. Not only was the campaign a dismal failure, it also backfired: Many American soldiers suffered toxic carcinogenic contamination through direct contact with Agent Orange. One of these victims was a young soldier named Elmo Zumwalt III, whose father, Admiral Elmo Zumwalt II, was the supreme architect and overseer of the Agent Orange defoliation project. In a television interview conducted in the late seventies a stricken Admiral Zumwalt acknowledged, "I am the instrument of my son's tragedy."

Not long after the Vietnam War ended, the horrors of Agent Orange and the personal tragedy of the Zumwalt family became known to the nation. As his encoding of the name *Zumwalt* in the narrative of ***White Noise*** indicates, Don DeLillo—one of the ablest chroniclers of American current events since the sixties—was almost certainly cognizant of the Zumwalt's agony.

Why did he do this? We needn't look far for the answer. Like his historical opposite number, Elmo Zumwalt III, DeLillo's Jack Gladney is also exposed to a lethal gaseous agent of human manufacture: the Nyodene "airborne toxic event" that turns the city of Blacksmith into a potential killing field. The very real possibility that a "nebulous mass" may invade Jack's body at any time transforms him into a walking dead man. Like the actual Agent Orange, DeLillo's Nyodene cloud tragically destroys more than it was intended to.

As Willie Mink lies on the floor with two bullets in him, Jack Gladney places the weapon in Mink's hand to create the illusion of suicide. Suddenly reviving, Mink shoots Jack in the wrist with his own Zumwalt. But this reciprocal wounding has an unexpected result. By evening the score between them, Willie Mink's act of turning the Zumwalt on him enables Jack Gladney to see his victim "for the first time as a person" (313). Whereupon, the still-bleeding Jack attempts to perform CPR on Willie and rushes him to the hospital, saving his life. Like the imaginary Jack Gladney, Admiral Zumwalt suffered a reciprocal wounding that also served as the terrible crucible of a born-again compassion.

Work Cited

DeLillo, Don. *White Noise.* New York: Penguin, 1985.

Stephen Amidon (review date 5 February 2001)

SOURCE: Amidon, Stephen. "Tasting the Breeze." *New Statesman* 14, no. 642 (5 February 2001): 52-3.

[*In the following review, Amidon assesses the plot, themes, and characters of* The Body Artist, *noting that the novel represents "a significant departure" from DeLillo's previous efforts.*]

After the career-crowning success of Don DeLillo's colossal 1997 novel, ***Underworld,*** it was daunting to think what this influential and hugely inventive writer would come up with next. The progress of his fiction seemed to be one of dizzying, almost geometric expansion. His early works—such as ***Great Jones Street*** (1973) and ***Players*** (1977)—were terse, elliptical views of contemporary society, whose fractured diction and seductive lacunae spoke volumes without requiring volumes to be printed. With ***The Names*** (1982) and ***White Noise*** (1985), DeLillo's novels began to grow, blossoming into ***Libra*** (1988), a doorstopping study of Lee Harvey Oswald that had the heft of the Warren Commission report. Finally came ***Underworld,*** an 800-page masterwork that started out with a baseball game and went on to encompass nearly all of postwar American society. It was tempting to think that the reclusive author's next step might take him into the boundless literary territory occupied only by the likes of Proust and Tolstoy.

Defying any such expectations, DeLillo has instead published his briefest work to date, ***The Body Artist,*** a slim novella representing a significant departure. Set on an unspecified stretch of American coastline, it concerns Rey Robles, a burnt-out film director, and his new wife, a performance artist called Lauren Hartke, who have holed up in a capacious rented house to work on Rey's autobiography. Their quiet life is shattered when Rey inexplicably commits suicide at the home of his former wife. The grieving Lauren stays on in the house, which, she soon realises, she shares with a mysterious interloper—an unidentified, perhaps insane man who had been spying on the couple. Instead of calling the authorities, Lauren develops a tentative relationship with the stranger, using the experience to create a piece of performance art.

And that's it. To say ***The Body Artist*** is understated is, well, an understatement. DeLillo has never been less forthcoming. The book's two central events—Rey's death and Lauren's performance—are presented second-hand, in the form of newspaper reports. The "action" is confined occasionally to brilliant but mostly affectless descriptions of Lauren's interactions with the two men. At one point, DeLillo pictures Lauren standing in front of the house "tasting the breeze for latent implications"; it could be said that the reader is forced into a similar position regarding the text. We are afforded only the briefest glimpse of Lauren and Rey together, leaving their relationship largely a mystery. The reasons for Rey's suicide remain a subject for fruitless conjecture. The stranger, whimsically referred to by Lauren as Mr Tuttle, is pure cipher, a man without identity, personality or memorable features. "There was something elusive in his aspect, moment to moment, a thinness of physical address." Like Rey, he vanishes from the book without a trace. And Lauren's climactic performance is shot through with such enigmatic indirection that it could have been staged only in a place with a name like the Boston Center for the Arts.

At times, you wonder if DeLillo has set out to write a book about the limitations of narrative. His prose can be cripplingly self-conscious—for example, when a toaster's lever "sprang or sprung" upwards, or Mr Tuttle "ate breakfast, or didn't." DeLillo's work has always been keenly aware of the absurdity inherent in any act of description—take, for instance, ***Underworld***'s astonishing sequence in which the various parts of a shoe are described in such a way that the reader understands he has never really thought about shoes or, for that matter, names. And then there is the famous father-son argument in ***White Noise*** over whether or not it is actually raining outside. But there was something both funny and expansive about these passages. Throughout his previous work, DeLillo revelled in the preposterous nature of the authorial project. In ***The Body Artist,*** however, he conveys none of the joy inherent in that absurdity, just its tongue-tied melancholy and impenetrable silence.

This novel also brings into focus another problematic area in DeLillo's fiction—character. While few can deny the author's unrivalled ability to recreate the cadences and conundrums of contemporary speech, a feeling develops after reading a lot of his work that the characters are actually speaking a language of their own, an argot that manages to be both brilliant and undifferentiated. Characters as various as Lee Harvey Oswald, J Edgar Hoover and ***Mao II***'s Salinger stand-in, Bill Gray, end up sounding suspiciously alike. Mr Tuttle, with his lack of personality and truncated, babbling speeches—"A thing of the most. Days yes years"—is the purest representation yet of this monochromatic tendency. His nonsense doesn't manage even to be gnomic. He is all surface, and not brilliant surface at that.

Rey and Lauren, meanwhile, may initially appear to be full-blooded, as they potter around the kitchen making breakfast, but both are soon embarked on courses of self-obliteration—Rey with a gun in his mouth; Lauren with the skin-exfoliant, hair bleach and crash diet that turn her into the featureless puppet (the body artist) at the book's end. DeLillo's grasp on character has always been tenuous. Here, it seems to have slipped through his hands altogether.

This is a shame, because DeLillo's genius has always been to invest the more naval-gazing aspects of the postmodern sensibility with humour, danger and surprise. There is nothing that Jacques Derrida or Alain Robbe-Grillet could tell him about the death of the author or the opacity of the text, although DeLillo could teach both of them a great deal about how to write well with these boundaries in mind.

With ***The Body Artist,*** however, DeLillo has abandoned the provocative sizzle and black humour that sugared his nihilism in previous novels, creating instead a small, gloomy and forgettable book. The hope is that this is an aberration from his remarkable body of work, rather than a sombre, dead-end culmination of it.

Philip Hensher (review date 10 February 2001)

SOURCE: Hensher, Philip. "An Exercise in Non-Speak." *Spectator* 286, no. 9001 (10 February 2001): 33-4.

[*In the following review, Hensher questions DeLillo's syntax and diction in* The Body Artist, *highlighting the novel's lifeless narrative voice and "undifferentiated" dialogue sequences.*]

Don DeLillo has now reached the sunlit uplands of literary celebrity where publishers will allow you to put a single short story between hard covers and happily charge £13.99 for it. He calls it [***The Body Artist***] 'a novel', but, since it is shorter than many short stories by Chekhov, and eschews the practice of interlacing different narratives which for me is what distinguishes a novel from a story, I think we are justified in treating it as a short story. That is no criticism, of course, particularly when you consider the alternative prospect, the gargantuan, half-planned sprawl, like a South American city, of DeLillo's recent novels. They display ceaseless ambition, and, as Dr Johnson would have said, the same resolution of purpose as a fighting cock. Whether that amounts to literary greatness, as has been widely asserted, remains to be seen.

Lauren Hartke is a 'body artist'. One day, her husband, Rey, gets in his car and drives to the apartment of his first wife, where he shoots himself. Lauren returns to their rented house and finds a strange boy in his underpants living in one of the rooms. She nicknames him 'Mr Tuttle', after an old science teacher of hers, and their attempts to communicate, to find out what each other is, make up the rest of the story.

In some ways DeLillo's imagination is strong and striking, though it will not go in all the directions he wants it to; when Lauren's stage act is described, late in the story, it turns out to be embarrassingly close to a theatrical Cindy Sherman, and no more than that, and I can't get rid of the suspicion that, in writing this tale of a mysterious inhabitant of an attic, he has taken a sublime moment in Lorrie Moore's great story 'Real Estate' from *Birds of America* and tried to make it his own. Still, the idea of grief allegorically embodied in the odd figure of 'Mr Tuttle', taking up residence and talking back to the bereaved, is a strong one, and DeLillo hangs onto and pumps away at his underlying theme, of the awareness of the self which the external world supplies, with considerable tenacity.

I just wonder whether Mr DeLillo actually speaks English. My doubt on this score began with the very first sentence of his gigantic last novel, ***Underworld***—'He speaks in your voice, American, and there's a shine in his eye that's halfway hopeful'—and continued with every page of the book. It sounds rather idiomatic if you translate it back into, let us say, German—'in seinem Augen dass halbwegs hoffnungsvoll ist'—but it certainly doesn't sound like any kind of spoken English. ***The Body Artist*** isn't quite so stilted, but there is certainly a persistent sense that DeLillo doesn't actually like the English language. Straight away, 'The wind makes a sound in the pines and the world comes into being, irreversibly, and the spider rides the wind-swayed web.' He was doing so well until that last clause, and there again was the terrible translation of terrible German poetry: 'Und ritt die Spinne das windbeschwingte Gewebe.' Of course, we in English would probably prefer to say 'the web swayed by the wind'.

Underworld was adored by every single reviewer in town, apart from me. My trouble with it—shared, I have to say, by quite a number of other readers—was that I just couldn't read it, so removed was it from any notion of the speaking voice. DeLillo has never been a novelist deeply rooted in the vernacular, but previously he has turned it to his advantage. In other novels, notably his splendid ***White Noise,*** that dazzling comedy about a professor of Hitler Studies in a terrible provincial university unable to admit that he can't read German, the formal, rather stilted tone seemed entirely appropriate to his disaffected world. In recent years it has started to seem as if that is all he can do.

His narrators in ***Americana*** or ***End Zone*** couldn't quite talk normally, just as they couldn't quite understand the world, and the results were often richly comic. They are deeply odd novels—the passage in ***End Zone*** describing a football match in one incomprehensible technical term after another is the most brilliant tour de force—but, for the most part rather, engaging. By ***Underworld,*** however, the mangling of the syntax had amounted to euphuism and over hundreds of pages it grew quite unbearable. Profundity of analysis won't make up for one hideous cadence after another, and DeLillo had somehow become one of the ugliest writers in the English language. He is as discordant as Dreiser, and, most alarmingly, young American writers seem to prefer him as a model to the rich, human, humorous strain in their contemporaries, and imitate him when they should be learning from Lorrie Moore and Jane Smiley.

That deliberate deadness is everywhere in ***The Body Artist,*** and most startlingly in the conversations. In every case they are undifferentiated, empty linguistic exchanges, as of people under hypnosis. When the woman talks to her strange lodger, it goes like this: 'How could you be living here without my knowing?' 'But you know. I am living.' 'But before. I hear a noise and you are in a room upstairs. For how long were you here?' All very well, but this is the way she used to talk to her husband: 'It's an effort. It's like what. It's like pushing a boulder.' 'You're sitting there talking.' 'Here.' 'You said the house. Nothing about the house is boring. I like the house.' 'You like everything. You love everything. You're my happy home. Here.' And later, to the owner of the house: 'Has it been satisfactory, then?' 'Mostly, I think, yes.' 'Because if there's anything.' 'No, it's fine, I think. Rooms.' 'Yes.' 'Rooms and rooms.' 'Yes. Been in the family. Let's see, forever. But the upkeep.'

No one in a Don DeLillo novel these days ever says 'Oh, God, do shut up,' or 'That's a pretty dress you've got on,' or anything resembling ordinary, relaxed speech—those unfinished sentences are a tic, a device, not in themselves enough to make his characters sound like people. And it is not just stylised, but undifferentiated between characters, so that the point he is trying to make here, that the lodger is quite different from normal people, has, one irrationally feels, entirely been lost in translation. Similarly, the numbness of the style might pass for the emotional effects of grief, were it not that the style is exactly the same before Rey's suicide. It is maddeningly unresponsive.

Why and how the witty, attentive author of ***White Noise*** and ***The Names*** turned himself into this humourless bore is a great puzzle. There are occasional fits of Updike-sensuous alertness here:

> Then he split the fig open with his thumbnails and took the spoon out of her hand and licked it off and used it to scoop a measure of claret flesh out of the gaping fig skin. He dropped this stuff on his toast—the flesh, the mash, the pulp—and then spread it with the bottom of the spoon, blood-buttery swirls that popped with seed-life.

But the artifice, in every bad sense, in the end swamps the fantasy.

Tom Deignan (review date 20 April 2001)

SOURCE: Deignan, Tom. "Sensation & Sensibility." *Commonweal* 128, no. 8 (20 April 2001): 28-9.

[*In the following review, Deignan explains the connections between the themes and style of* The Body Artist, *centering on DeLillo's empathetic characterization of the novel's protagonist.*]

Leave it to Don DeLillo to follow up ***Underworld*** with a slim novella that conceivably could be used as a bookmark for its hefty, much-acclaimed predecessor. ***Underworld*** famously jumped back and forth from the fifties to the nineties, from Ebbets Field to the Bronx to a nuclear testing site in Kazakhstan. ***The Body Artist,*** by contrast, is downright claustrophobic, set almost entirely in an aging "old frame house—a place they'd rented unseen—way too big, and there were creaking floorboards and a number of bent utensils dating to god knows."

"They" are Laura Hartke, the titular artist, and Rey Robles, an aging political filmmaker. ***The Body Artist*** begins ominously—"It happened this final morning"—but quickly turns into a microscopic study of domestic co-habitation. Rey and Laura eat breakfast, pursue their isolated morning routines, all the while talking right past each other in the clipped, occasionally nonsensical style of Edward Albee or Harold Pinter. But this is De-

Lillo, after all. So even the most isolated characters will inevitably be linked to the vast outside world of plants and animals, chemicals and technology. With the radio droning on, Laura discovers a hair in her mouth, which is "still twisted from the experience of sharing some food handler's unknown life."

Not until we learn (via an obituary) that "Rey Robles, 64, Cinema's Poet of Lonely Places" has committed suicide, do we get to DeLillo's real focus in ***The Body Artist***—death and loss, and how the living perceive and contend with such suffering. Alternately dense and dazzling, DeLillo can be masterful in this short work, distilling the comic and tragic into a single sentence. But in terms of Laura's loss, DeLillo's prose too often seems cerebral, abstract, or needlessly cryptic. Readers are likely to be drawn into ***The Body Artist*** by the allure of DeLillo's heady themes, rather than the symphonic passages that move his grander novels along.

While mourning in a rather frosty manner, Laura discovers a man living in her home. (DeLillo has by now abandoned any pretense of realism, so it's pointless to ask why Laura "felt no fear.") The mystery man—Laura names him Mr. Tuttle, after an old teacher—"gestured as he spoke, moving his hand to the words," and "the gestures [were] unmistakably Rey's." Is ***The Body Artist*** a ghost story, with Laura haunted by the memory of her dead husband? That's a start. (Such a resurrection image even suggests a spiritual undercurrent in what does not otherwise seem a particularly religious book.)

But Laura is, first and foremost, an artist—a performer who transforms her body, her language, and her very identity in profound ways. She even keeps a tape recorder handy, to help conjure the wide range of men and women who populate her rage-filled, satirical, ultimately autobiographical one-woman show, fittingly titled "Body Time." Despite all the book's nineteenth-century themes, a twenty-first-century DeLillo emerges in ***The Body Artist.*** In an age obsessed with "reality" and unprecedented technology able to recreate "reality," what of the artist? Laura "spends hours at the computer screen looking at live streaming video feed from the edge of a two-lane road in a city in Finland." She also ponders tape recorders, answering machines, newspapers ("a slick hysteria of picture and ink"), radios, mirrors, and even eyeballs, which process matter "upside down before the mind intervenes."

DeLillo has never been merely the chronicler of postwar, postmodern America that many of his fans (and critics) think him to be, although it's not hard to see where he got this reputation. There were the duped masses and paranoia of ***White Noise,*** the JFK-conspiracy complex of ***Libra,*** and the first section of ***Underworld,*** named after a four-hundred-fifty-year-old Pieter Brueghel painting. But in ***The Body Artist,*** DeLillo is pondering short- and long-term matters—the evolution of human perception, and the artist's ability to reflect reality.

Taken this way, ***The Body Artist*** can be seen as an intimate, unsettling update of another short work by a master novelist—Henry James's *The Real Thing.* Is Mr. Tuttle Laura's ultimate piece of performance art? An amalgam of memory, imagination, and loss, both personal and universal? "What did it mean, the first time a thinking creature looked deeply into another's eyes? The gaze that demonstrates we are lonely in our souls," DeLillo writes in a decidedly anti-Hallmark moment, as Laura ponders Mr. Tuttle.

Most striking is DeLillo's empathy in his rendering of Laura's struggles. At one point, Laura notes with frustration that her ghostly roommate "violates the limits of the human." But it's left unsaid whether or not this is a good thing. Tuttle is shielded, of course, from death and loss. But he also speaks mere gibberish and feels nothing—good or bad. He could never, as Laura does in the end, "thr[ow] the window open to feel the sea tang on her face and the flow of time in her body, to tell her who she was."

DeLillo, supposed critic of the dehumanized soul, here seems nearly exuberant. Perhaps it is the very knowledge of our limitations, our ability to perceive pain and loss, which most vigorously affirm our humanity. "Take the risk," DeLillo exhorts the reader, not Laura, in a bold narrative moment. "Believe what you see and hear. It's the pulse of every secret intimation you've ever felt around the edges of your life."

The Body Artist is a provocative, and perhaps transitional work for this ever-innovative novelist. DeLillo's vast cultural themes are present. But they seem secondary to Laura's unique predicament, as well as what Rey at one point calls "the terror of another ordinary day." ***The Body Artist*** finally leaves us with a question Brueghel, Henry James, DeLillo, their admirers, and perhaps even the casts of *Survivor* and *Temptation Island* must ponder now and then: "Is reality too powerful for you?"

Gordon Houser (review date 2 May 2001)

SOURCE: Houser, Gordon. Review of *The Body Artist,* by Don DeLillo. *Christian Century* 118, no. 14 (2 May 2001): 27-8.

[*In the following review, Houser outlines the themes of* The Body Artist *and praises its intimate, subtle tone.*]

"Time Seems to Pass," the opening line of Don DeLillo's 12th novel [***The Body Artist***], could sum up this spare, evocative work. The story begins with an intimate portrait of a married couple at breakfast in a rented summer cottage. The accumulating detail and realistic dialogue introduce the novel's theme of awareness. Lauren Hartke and Rey Robles speak to one another yet do not always hear what is said. Lauren's groan resembles "a life lament." She takes the kettle to the stove because "this is how you live a life even if you don't know it." She sees her husband looking at but not reading the paper and "understood this retroactively."

Like John Cheever's *O What a Paradise It Seems,* this is a novel about appearance and the fleeting nature of reality. For Lauren "it all happens around the word seem." For her and the reader, the difference between what is real and what only seems to be real is unclear. The narrative voice keeps reflecting this uncertainty: a label is "scratchy," then "not scratchy." "He was staring at her. He seemed to be staring, but probably wasn't." "There he was, not really, only hintingly, barely at all."

Lauren is "a body artist" who transforms her physical self in order to portray different characters. Her performances, writes an old friend who is reviewing her work, are "about who we are when we are not rehearsing who we are." Her bodywork, Lauren feels, makes "everything transparent." She seems to need the physical to grasp what is real. Yet she isn't always sure. She sees a bird, but only in retrospect because "she didn't know what she was seeing at first and had to re-create the ghostly moment, write it like a line in a piece of fiction."

After her husband's suicide, Lauren stays on in the cottage. She hears noises, then discovers in the house a man who appears to be an escaped mental patient. His conversation consists of dialogue he's apparently overheard, including whole sentences spoken by Lauren's late husband. We never learn exactly who this man—or ghost—is.

Lauren tries to make sense of the strange events she's experiencing: "Maybe there are times when we slide into another reality but can't remember it, can't concede the truth of it because this would be too devastating to absorb." But then, "she was always maybeing." Her attempts to control her life by transforming her body fail. She must face what comes and accept it. Such awareness often comes to us in hindsight. "She'd known it was empty all along but was only catching up." DeLillo's novels tend to deal with public issues—cold-war America (***Underworld***), the psychology of crowds (***Mao II***), the Kennedy assassination (***Libra***). Here he handles more personal issues: identity, grief, the nature of time. ***The Body Artist*** is like a puzzle that demands close attention yet still eludes full understanding.

Jesse Kavadlo (essay date summer 2001)

SOURCE: Kavadlo, Jesse. "Recycling Authority: Don DeLillo's Waste Management." *Critique* 42, no. 4 (summer 2001): 384-401.

[*In the following essay, Kavadlo examines the concept of authorship represented in DeLillo's novels, demonstrating its narrative function and thematic implications.*]

In 1968 Roland Barthes declared that the Author was dead, that works had been transformed into texts, that any notion of finding the author within the text was kowtowing to an outdated sense of reverence and authority that would soon have no place in the burgeoning scheme of poststructuralism. Seeking to break away from an "image of literature [. . .] tyrannically centered on the author, his person, his life" (143). Barthes was an early critic of the Romantic and modernist schools of thought that positioned the author as a God-like creator who leaves no room for the reader. But even worse for Barthes is that the assumption that authorial power creates a single correct interpretation that remains outside of the text and in the author himself: "*The explanation* of a work is always sought in the man or woman who produced it, as if it were always in the end, through more or less transparent allegory of the fiction, the voice of a single person, the *author* 'confiding' in us" (143). In many ways, Barthes's much-discussed paradigm is what Don DeLillo has emulated, first by handing the now (in)famous engraved business card to interviewer and critic Tom LeClair that solemnly stated, "I don't want to talk about it" (Interview 79)—an emblem of his reclusion—and then by quietly killing off the author himself in ***Mao II*** with novelist Bill Gray's undramatic, anonymous end.

At the same time, DeLillo's etched message, like all of his work, is steeped in multiple layers of irony, for there he is, as he pointed out in his interview, talking about himself (Interview 80). Barthes's declarations as well, taken to heart by poststructuralists bent on dismantling the canon, seem an ironic overstatement: there Barthes is, claiming authorship of the idea that texts cannot be totally original or solely authored. Both writers resist silence, perhaps because, as DeLillo clearly understands from his many novels about artists and artistic types in seclusion, silence ironically, problematically, invites curiosity, discussion, and ultimately invasion. DeLillo may prefer that his novels speak for him; but his interviews, pictures, and personae suggest that perhaps the author as a figure, momentarily killed by poststructuralism, today seems ironically resurrected through DeLillo, as well as through the various adopted voices within his novels. Barthes would turn the text into "a tissue of quotations drawn from the innumerable centres of culture" (146), and certainly DeLillo's novels, in their layers and excesses, seem to embody this living tissue connecting writing and culture. But DeLillo's authorship suggests that the novel must remain a work shrouded in mystery rather than a text ripe for deconstruction.

Don DeLillo's authorial persona, both in what he says (or does not say) and within the novels themselves through mouthpieces (or, in the case of ***Ratner's Star,*** just one character's mouth), seems to demonstrate an ambiguity toward authority that borders on ambivalence. On the one hand, like Barthes's dead Author and Tom LeClair's "systems novelists," DeLillo seems to relish his own authorial diminishment, so that the texts and not the man remain the focus. Indeed, in ***Libra,*** the Author's Note at the end of the novel serves not so much to assert that the novel "is a work of the imagination" (458) as to remind the reader that the book was authored. DeLillo's authorial presence in that novel is so transparent that he seems more documentary maker than fiction writer. On the other hand, in drawing the reader closer with his books, photos, and interviews (less seldom than many people believe), DeLillo's stance on silence, even when broken, seems to reestablish Romanticism and modernism's elevation of the author, albeit reflexively and perhaps ironically. For instance, when asked about his lack of autobiographical detail in his books, DeLillo answered, "Silence, exile, cunning, and so on" (Interview 80), ironically appropriating James Joyce's Stephen Dedalus while adding a casual *et cetera,* as if we all now know what the author is supposed to say. In his reversal, DeLillo the author imitates Stephen, a fictional character based on the very autobiography DeLillo eschews.

But after exploring the perspectives of athletes, musicians, scientists, and writers, perhaps DeLillo's most important, all-connecting, and autobiographical persona has recently arrived in Nick Shay, the waste manager of ***Underworld.*** In a way that balances the author's irrelevance of the poststructuralists with the modernist's elevation of the author to secular priest, DeLillo's author is alive and a kind of waste manager himself, not unlike Nick Shay, sifting and sorting through the physical, metaphysical, and spiritual excesses, contaminants, and wastes of our modernity. Barthes's reduction of the author to a collage-maker with only the ability "to mix writings [. . .] in such a way as never to rest on any one of them" (146), like Julia Kristeva's use of intertextuality, M. M. Bakhtin's *heteroglossia,* and Harold Bloom's anxiety of influence,[1] suggests the mode of DeLillo's metaphorical waste manager—reusing, reappropriating, recycling, and ultimately redeeming language. Barthes's lower-case "a" author (*scripteur*) draws on, reuses, and remakes the textual "tissue," as DeLillo's waste manager turns societal detritus into art, but for DeLillo, the mystery and solemn power of waste turns authorial custodial work into a near mystical experience.[2]

DeLillo's recasting the author as waste manager is self-deprecating, to be sure, but in keeping with the humorous ways in which writers, artists, critics, and academics have been consistently portrayed throughout DeLillo's long and prolific career. The author, instead of rebirth in the modernist mode, becomes again credible through DeLillo's works—not like the romantic phoenix from the ashes, mentioned in ***Underworld*** as Nick Shay's new home, as much as like Nathanael West's "Phoenix Excrementi" who "eat themselves, digest themselves, and give birth to themselves by evacuating their bowels" (5). The authorial persona, through waste management of a wasteful culture, is not resurrected as much as recycled—remade from texts and languages of the past. Don DeLillo's authority comes from observing, excavating, collecting, and finally remaking cultural material in the form of the novel. In this way, DeLillo seems to be rekindling the concept of author for the new millennium, taking both the modernist's author-priest and the now-waning postmodernist's authorial diminishment in anticipation of the new author's role. The contemporary author, standing between reverence and irreverence, romantic imagination and journalistic note taking, understands his importance but also his tenuous, precarious place in the world.

This trope of waste management recalls the work of Jean Baudrillard, whose simulacrum frequently has been compared with and applied to DeLillo's novels (particularly in conjunction with the "Most Photographed Barn" of ***White Noise***).[3] Significantly, Baudrillard describes the American waste phenomenon: "everywhere today one must recycle waste, and the dreams, the phantasms, the historical, fairylike legendary imaginary of children and adults is a waste product, the first great toxic excrement of a hyperreal civilization" (12). But Baudrillard's recycling produces only more waste, reducing language to recirculated signs reenforcing the simulation. Unlike DeLillo, Baudrillard, while playful, is nihilistic and inconsistent with the metaphor; at bottom, recycling is pragmatic, designed to counter hopefully a physical reality of diminishing resources. In addition, DeLillo's recycling is not nostalgic for nature or a sense of a past reality before the simulation—the celebration that ends the baseball-themed, 1950s-era prologue of ***Underworld*** is tinged not with fond memories but with the frightening potential of nuclear annihilation to counter the exhilaration. Similarly, the playing field is littered with waste even as the crowd cheers, a celebration of excess, not a Baudrillardian lamentation. Perhaps, like artist Klara Sax's project of painting discarded war planes in ***Underworld,*** the author-as-waste-manager can create something beautiful and meaningful out of the dangerous debris instead of criticizing or wallowing in it, allowing it to fester into the waste land that the modernists feared and Baudrillard now loathes. Ultimately, DeLillo's authorial recycling—the vision of authorship that combines elements of modernism and postmodernism—carries over into what seems like an inconsistency: DeLillo celebrates size but advocates asceticism, a word associated with the reclusion that DeLillo is ambivalent toward. The length and scope of ***Underworld*** underscore this point; an 827-page book that seems to evoke Jesuit philosophy, self-denial, and scaled-back simplicity demonstrates that clearly the medium is not the message. But, then, what is the message?

Underworld, in its own sprawling way, is a collection of the untold and forgotten stories of the last fifty years, the dregs and waste, an attempt to make something new and artistic, just as Klara's project does. DeLillo presents Nick Shay, an ironic DeLillo double: both grow up in the Bronx, are about the same age, attend Fordham University, and move West away from the Bronx (although, in all fairness, DeLillo moved West only metaphorically, to Westchester). Nick, however, is half Italian, almost a comic distancing device to assure the reader that, despite their similarity, Nick is not Don. In addition, waste management ties into the concept and title of ***Underworld***: most obviously, we bury our waste—and our dead—underground; waste is associated with Nick's burdened unconscious; and "underworld" humorously recalls the Mafia and jokes associated with it—in New York, "waste management" was one of the industries most often connected with the mob.

But the novel has more to do with waste than just connotation or Nick's occupation: its seeming excess and sheer length seem an aesthetic reflection of the world described within the novel. In fact, more than being about Nick himself, the novel's explicit subject is waste, literal and figurative: landfills and recycled junk; excrement; nuclear waste; wasted lives, wasted time, the best minds of a generation devoted to waste; burying waste, unearthing waste; civilizations built and ended on account of waste; getting wasted, in terms of both drugs and murder as made emblematic in Nick's murder of George the waiter, the junkie who uses heroin (junk, shit) and gets wasted (killed) for it. ***Underworld*** shows it all, while self-consciously acknowledging that any excess, even literary, is a kind of waste product: "not nature," as Nathanael West describes art, but "nature digested [. . .] a sublime excrement" (8) that recycles DeLillo's would-be realism into surrealism. Juxtaposing brand-names, condoms, graffiti, baseball, bombs, and a huge cast of eccentrics, DeLillo's excessive realism recycles, almost parodies, traditional realism into something closer to avant-garde. ***Underworld*** makes an aesthetic statement about our culture of excess, of trying to make everything bigger and better, all-inclusive, millennial, towering, and imposing, by making an all-consuming, all-connected novel.

If for DeLillo waste is creative fodder for the contemporary novelist, waste, for Nick, becomes the point in and of itself, more than a byproduct or unfortunate result of living. He saw "products as garbage even when they sat gleaming on the store shelves, yet unbought. We didn't say, What kind of casserole will that make? We said, What kind of garbage will that make?" (121). Garbage is his central preoccupation as well as his official occupation, and all of the products' present usefulness is subsumed by their future as waste. But garbage takes on more meaning than simply the stuff of landfills; waste is all that is left after the last remnants of the Cold War have melted away. Klara is, in that sense, a waste manager, recycling the obsolete warplanes into works of art. As a result, her project is also an attempt to restore a kind of balance. She explains: "Many things that were anchored to the balance of power and the balance of terror seem to be undone, unstuck" (76). The assurances of Us and Them, Good and Evil, and Black and White have all melted into uneasy and uncomfortable shades of gray, with all the products and people left over from a world war that never took place becoming relegated to the status of waste products. If the time preparing for a war that never happened was wasted, then the people left over after the easy balances, the comforting dichotomies and dialectics, are wasted—Nick's unconscious is like a bomb needing to be defused, as dangerous as the nuclear waste at the end of the novel.

Among the specific "things" that Klara refers to as becoming "undone" by the Cold War's end is its massive military accumulation—the leftover planes but the nuclear weapons as well. Quoting J. Robert Oppenheimer, Klara refers to the bomb as "merde." She explains: "something that eludes naming [. . .] is automatically relegated to the status of shit. You can't name it. It's too big or too evil or outside your experience. It's also shit because it's garbage, it's waste material. [. . .] What I really want to get at is the ordinary thing, the ordinary life behind the thing. Because that's the heart and soul of what we're doing here" (76-77). The bomb still connects Nick and Klara, not in its presence, but now in its absence. The threat is gone, but its ominous, unnamable qualities, and now its official status as waste, remain. Klara and Nick are connected in the past but also by the past—the leftover war planes that Klara makes new and the nuclear waste that in the end Nick helps to destroy are almost a letdown after the disappointment of a war that never took place, but a disappointment preferable to annihilation. The countdown to mass destruction that the novel's backward-moving narrative structure implies is interrupted by the epilogue's return to the present, in effect halting the threat but at the same time failing to deliver in its built-in, if terrifying, expectation and implication.

Nick sees his and Klara's job as similar; he says, "I almost mentioned my line of work to [Klara] when we had our talk in the desert. Her own career had been marked at times by her methods of transforming and absorbing junk. But something made me wary. I didn't want her to think I was implying some affinity of effort or perspective" (102). And in fact their philosophies are quite different—they are opposed, balanced and balancing. Nick attempts to hurry products through any stage of usefulness toward their end as waste so that he can bury them, while Klara wants to recycle, to unearth waste in order to bring it back to its organic nonwaste status. Her project of painting the planes has the effect of transforming them by renaming them—they are now works of art, where before that they were junk; and before that, planes. She wants to replace the linear black and white dichotomies of the cold war, as Nick observes, with "sweeps of color, bands, and splatters, airy washes, the force of structured light—the whole thing oddly personal, a sense of one painter's hand moved by impulse and afterthought as much as by epic design" (83). For Nick, the art is both personal and collective—the planes belong to Klara and to the viewer, and ultimately to the reader.

The famous ball from the Dodgers-Giants game that opens the novel and resurfaces as a narrative link between characters is a kind of waste product as well. The ball remains an elusive, chased object, a white whale of sorts, but a debased souvenir or a small scale collector's item, not the leviathan capable of inducing the epic of Ahab's monomania or Ishmael's survival. In fact, Nick says of the ball, "I didn't buy the object for the glory and drama attached to it. It's not about Thomson making the homer. It's about Branca making the pitch. It's about losing. [. . .] It's about the mystery of bad luck, the mystery of loss" (97). The loss is the flipside, the underside, to the prologue's wasteful paper-throwing celebration; but tellingly, Nick refuses to name the ball—it's simply "the object." Even if Nick consciously rejects Klara's declaration that what we cannot name automatically becomes junk, his refusal to call the ball "the ball" reveals it for what it is: another kind of waste product, unnamable and perhaps unknowable.

The ball may be a symbol of winning and losing, but it is also a piece of expensive, exquisite junk. Just as he sees the casserole as future garbage and not as a present meal, Nick holds on to the ball because it's a leftover, the final remnant of the game. The ball seems to connect Nick to his past, but ultimately it cannot. Nick wants the ball to do for him what he imagines the painted planes do for Klara—to distinguish him as an individual, the sole owner of the ball-as-property, but also to connect him in the most romantic sense of the word to the aura associated with the ball and the collective experience of the game and the pitch. The link that the ball provides is not the connection of conspiracy (a word long associated with DeLillo's writing) but the comfort of the collective experience, and this comfort is also, ultimately, the shared goal of the waste manager and the author. The game's leftover ball is recycled throughout, finally becoming the connective narrative tissue of the novel. In a humorous turn, the book is a picaresque tale for an inanimate object—the ball-as-storyteller, the homer as Homer—so that chronicling the events surrounding this piece of trash can shed light on the people around it. DeLillo borrows from, but ultimately revises, realistic fiction: rather than using objects and things as symbols that allow the reader to understand the characters, DeLillo uses names, characters, and dialogue to allow the reader to understand the nature of things. Nick Shay, after over 800 pages, remains something of a mystery, but the ball does not.

In the time since Barthes was eager to kill the author, the public, and, for that matter, many authors themselves, remained unaware of the war for the author's integrity being waged within the academy. Since the 1960s, the cult of the author has only grown, despite Michel Foucault's prescription and prediction that "the author-function will disappear" (244). Autobiographical and psychoanalytical criticism, considered "limited and problematical" (179) by Terry Eagleton and, at one point, by many literary critics, has risen in prominence, with multivolume biographies of Herman Melville, D. H. Lawrence, W. B. Yeats, and other capital A, canonized Authors filling the shelves—a complication of what, exactly, the Author-function means. Foucault's question, "What is an author?" remains unanswered, or at least the answers keep changing.

The popular audience is even more consumed with the cult of authorship than academics are: novelists carefully pose and place the ever-important dust jacket photograph in larger and more prominent spaces, and blurbs grow more about the author than about the work at hand. As the cult of capital-A Authorship grows, the reading public's desire to understand the recapitalized Authors' lives and motives grows with it. In 1998, Toni Morrison appeared on "The Oprah Winfrey Show," only to be asked what her novel *Paradise really* means by viewers-turned-readers eager for the right answers, the very myth Barthes tried to dispel in suggesting that "the birth of the reader must be at the cost of the death of the Author" (148). Not long ago Oprah's viewers may have been met with a dry declaration that the reader determines his or her own meaning, a version of which the ever-academic Morrison stoically if unsuccessfully attempted to impart. But the questioners' pleas for Authorial intercession now seem once again valid—the death of the author, it seems, has been greatly exaggerated. Don DeLillo's own authorship understands the culture's clamor for authority and authenticity.

But if the author's not dead, he or she is certainly unstable; the concept of author seems as shaken as his or her stereotyped mental state. Just as Barthes feared, people want to read, for example, that "Baudelaire's work is the failure of Baudelaire the man. Van Gogh's his madness, Tchaikovsky's his vice" (143) in order to use the pretense of biography or psychoanalysis to disguise what ultimately amounts to an unsavory brand of tabloid literary criticism. For example, current academic battles ensue over Melville's intention, not toward *Moby-Dick* but toward his wife. Raymond Carver's literary reputation is at stake, not because of a new methodological interpretation of his prose, but over the possibility that his editor, Gordon Lish, may have played a larger part in the stories than had been thought previously.[4] These and other examples suggest that the best Barthes and Foucault could do was to destabilize the author; ironically, the focus has shifted away from the very texts that they had hoped would be read exclusive of the author. Instead, the battle is for the author's reputation, aura, and soul, but not necessarily for his or her work.

In a literal manifestation of Foucault's "disappearance" of the author, J. D. Salinger's seclusion, mirrored by Bill Gray's isolation in ***Mao II,*** illustrates the problem of evasion—it invites, rather than discourages, investigation; any discouragement is "'really a kind of come-on'—'I can't stop you,'" as would-be biographer Ian Hamilton describes (7). And so the same goes for DeLillo: no matter how he says that "when you try to unravel something that you've written, you belittle it in a way," and that ***Americana*** despite being the closest book to his experience is "not an autobiographical novel" (Interview 80), one senses that the denials become admissions. To wit, Douglas Keesey calls ***Americana*** DeLillo's version of *A Portrait of the Artist as Young Man* because it is a "semiautobiographical first novel" (2). Rather than treating David Bell autobiographically, however, perhaps DeLillo makes Bell a protowaste manager. Looking at DeLillo's first novels, ***Americana*** and ***Great Jones Street,*** one can see the early interest in waste, excess, and recycling.[5]

In ***Americana,*** narrator David Bell recycles his past, his friends, his family, and even himself through the lens of the camera, turning the real into the fictional, the American into the kitschy commodity of americana as imagined by a man who has only the appearance of someone famous, but not the fame: "I don't know who you are," an autograph seeker states, "but you must be somebody" (13). In the novel that begins many of his long-running themes, DeLillo introduces maintenance man Buford Long, one of the firsts in a long line of DeLillo's idiosyncratic, Dickensian cameo characters. Long mentions to David that garbage "gives you clues to human nature. Garbage tells you more than living with a person" (190). At this point in the novel, David is not interested, quickly changing the topic to boxing, as he verbally boxes with Long. But later, after becoming inspired to make the film that serves as the novel's core, David describes his notes as "scraps of paper, [. . .] Scotch-taped fragments, throwaways uncrumpled and hand-presses, what detritus and joy" (269). The materials that David will use toward the creation of his movie, his life recycled into art in a way that allows him to better understand himself, are described in the language of garbage. The "detritus" from his pockets, instead of being thrown out, become refundable as art.

But if David Bell's quintessentially American attempt to reinvent himself through art seems little more than a failed mining expedition of the past's trash heaps in search of movie gold, DeLillo's next novel, ***Great Jones Street,*** seems to show a greater understanding of culture's reverence for the examination of "authors rather than heroes [. . . and the] fundamental category of 'the-man-and-his-work criticism'" (233) that Foucault derides. In 1974, just after the high point of post-structuralism, ***Great Jones Street*** depicted rock star Bucky Wunderlick, who goes deep into seclusion, a retreat into ascetic silence away from the excessive volumes of his rock 'n' roll past. The novel's opening line reads, "Fame requires every kind of excess" (1), or excess in excess, but if the excess doesn't kill him, then "the public's contempt for survivors" will (1). Despite that the albums are available as texts open to interpretation (as Barthes or Foucault may have put it), the public insists on knowing the person behind the persona more than they even care to listen to the music. A reporter attempting to interview Wunderlick describes the situation: "Your power is growing, Bucky. The more time you spend in isolation, the more demands are made on the various media to communicate some relevant words and pictures. [. . .] People want words and pictures. They want images. Your power grows. The less you say, the more you are" (128). Silence and seclusion become not the opposite of speech and fame, but an alternate version, which only invites more authorial speculation and further clamor for authority. Echoing Foucault's language and Bucky's stance, filmmaker Frank Voltera in ***The Names*** puts it this way: "You know how I am about my privacy. I'd hate to think you came here to do a story on me. A major piece, as they say. Full of insights. The man and his work" (197). Voltera's words sarcastically belittle invading the secluded artist in lieu of investigating the art.

The musician was one of DeLillo's early masks of authorship; here, the rock star becomes a figure of sonic waste management in a way that predates the death-like envelope of sound in ***White Noise.*** Desperate to control the excess of fame and the fame of excess, Bucky uses silence and exile as a means to end the possibility of commercial excess that the true artist fears will diminish his work, even if it also ends his art. Of course, how talented Bucky is, with DeLillo's parodic "Pee pee maw maw" exaggeratedly dumb rock lyrics, is open to speculation, perhaps only deepening the irony: the images that the public wants do not substitute for Bucky's music, but surpass it. DeLillo, unlike Barthes, sees that culture demands origin and cause, and only the creator of the text seems suitably accountable, to the point where the text itself, and not the author, is what becomes irrelevant. Bucky's attempt at waste management, at curtailing the excess, fails because the very effort only provokes further fame, predating Salinger's (and DeLillo's) withdrawal but predicting their failure as well.

Looking for DeLillo in the novels, as Keesey does and as I do in comparing DeLillo to Nick Shay, is playing a literary game not unlike the one played between Salinger and Hamilton. DeLillo, aware of the attraction of seclusion, seems to pepper his novels with apparent autobiography even while remaining ironic and detached throughout, cultivating the power of the image that the novels are often ambivalent about. He has created an interesting paradox: his most recent novels, ***Underworld, Mao II, Libra,*** and ***White Noise,*** circumvent, almost prohibit, any attempt to seek out the author in their pages by ridiculing invasive, overly cerebral, and amoral characters; but at the same time, the form of each of these novels is almost fictional biography, and many of the references are unmistakably autobiographical, such as the Bronx's Little Italy of the 1950s and 1960s, the Bronx Zoo, New York's subways, and Fordham University, details of which appear in ***Libra, Underworld,*** and ***Ratner's Star.*** In an ironic gesture to his most devoted readers, DeLillo seems to be saying that the only way to honor his authorial intention, to get the correct answers that Toni Morrison's readers pined for, is ironically to ignore the search for intention and accept that he does not want to talk outside of the novels themselves. Despite his wishes, many DeLillo critics and most readers[6] seem determined to find authorial counterparts in the novels: LeClair says that in parts of ***White Noise*** "Jack begins to see as Siskind and, I believe, DeLillo do [. . .]" (*Loop 229*), and Daniel Aaron sees "something of [DeLillo] in his own creation, Dr. Pepper the 'awthentic genius' in ***Great Jones Street*** [. . . who] has 'lived among dangerous men, worked in hazardous circumstances'" (69). Despite the denials, the novels invite, seem to demand, that the reader finds the author, just as Hamilton seeks Salinger and Scott hunts down Bill Gray. In a sense, their search emblemizes literary criticism: all attempt to find that which is not explicitly stated in the text and to show that what is stated means more than its surface reading first suggests.

Problematically for criticism, however, DeLillo has already ironized any attempt at studying his works academically through Jack Gladney of ***White Noise*** and Scott Martineau of ***Mao II.*** Indeed, Jack Gladney's attempt to use Hitler as a figure that he can both hide behind and gain authority from, or, as Murray J. Siskind absurdly puts it, turning Hitler into "Gladney's Hitler" (11), ridicules literary criticism in general. The critic is always hoping to absorb and hide behind the studied author, to recycle the power, stature, and aura; as Murray explains to Jack, "Helpless and fearful people are drawn to magical figures, mythic figures, epic men who intimidate and darkly loom. [. . .] You wanted to conceal yourself in Hitler and his works. On another level, you wanted to use him to grow in significance and strength" (287-88). Jack attempts to turn the rabid excess of Hitler's genocide into an amoral object of study, but the attempt to recycle Hitler's power and authority fails. Similarly in ***Mao II,*** Scott's "shelves filled with book-length studies of Bill's work and work about his work" make it difficult to discuss DeLillo unselfconsciously.[7] Scott, the consummate reader, attempts to make author Bill Gray his own, to subsume his life in Bill's and to cultivate Bill's status, or "aura," a term DeLillo frequently uses. But instead of preserving Bill or enhancing his own status, Scott turns Bill into a prisoner and himself into his equally trapped prison guard, mirroring the terrorist-hostage situation in Beirut. If authorship, as I have implied earlier, is a kind of recycling, then certainly literary criticism recycles further, despite what seems to be DeLillo's humorous self-awareness of his own importance. The need to recycle authority suggests something deeper than self-deprecation. But at the same time, the novels themselves offer some explanation of DeLillo's attitudes toward both waste and authority and show the author's contemporary awareness of both criticism and canonization.

White Noise, preceding ***Underworld,*** depicts a world teeming with excess and waste, both physical and metaphysical. Hitler Studies founder and narrator Jack Gladney, although not literally a waste manager like Nick Shay, finds his life overloaded like the multifrequency barrage suggested by the title: the mass murderer that he studies but chooses to divorce from moral consequence, his series of marriages that similarly end in divorce, his weight or "the air of unhealthy excess" that his former chancellor advises him to put on (17), even the extra initial he inserts to pad and inflate his real name in his pseudonym, J. A. K. Gladney. Waste conveys power and aura; as the excess of photographs in the much-discussed "Most Photographed Barn" passage "reinforces its aura" (12), so repeated spending and Jack's own sense of buying power reinforces his frail feelings of self-worth after being offended by a colleague:

> The encounter put me in the mood to shop. [. . .] I traded money for goods. The more money I spent, the less important it seemed. I was bigger than these sums. These sums seemed to pour off my skin like existential credit. [. . .] Voices rose ten stories from the gardens and promenades, a roar that echoed and swirled through the vast gallery, mixing with noises from the tiers, with shuffling feet and chiming bells, the hum of escalators, the sound of people eating, the human buzz of some vivid happy transaction.
>
> (83-84)

Jack believes that the excess of the mall or the supermarket will build his "existential credit," as though these expenditures will lengthen his life and conform to the expectations of the capitalist transaction. Instead, the noise of the mall blends with the family's own sound in collective excess that forces the family to drive home in silence. Rather than feeling fulfilled and fortified by the spree, each member of the family goes to his or her "respective rooms, wishing to be alone" (84).

The temporary satisfaction from consumption is surpassed by the thrill of disposal; Gladney attempts his own form of existential waste management, discarding the items he had previously used for protection: "I threw away candle stubs, laminated placemats, frayed potholders. I went after the padded clothes hangers, the magnetic memo clipboards. I was in a vengeful and nearly savage state. I bore a personal grudge against these things. Somehow they'd put me in this fix" (294). Doomed by consumer culture, Jack feels as though throwing away his possessions will provide a new reserve of "existential credit"; but garbage is part of the same cycle as purchasing, and throwing the items away is simply the last stage in the consumerist "fix" Gladney finds himself in.

The bombardment of media messages and excess consumption followed by mass disposal, the attempt to outrun the Airborne Toxic Event, and the Dylar that is thrown away (and in fact belongs with the trash because it proves ineffective) exemplify the association of waste with death—everything is a version of Dylar, an attempt to shut down the fear, but each in turn fails. Each example of excess in the novel seeks to fill a void, but none can. Instead, perhaps the truth lies in Heinrich's theory of waste proposed in a conversation with Jack:

> "People waste a tremendous amount of motion. You should see Baba make a salad some time."
>
> "People don't deliberate over each tiny motion and gesture. A little waste doesn't hurt."
>
> "But over a lifetime?"
>
> "What do you save if you don't waste?"
>
> "Over a lifetime? You save a tremendous amount of time and energy," he said.
>
> "What will you do with them?"
>
> "Use them to live longer."
>
> (102)

Waste, whether through accumulation of soon-to-be jettisoned goods or their eventual, inevitable disposal, makes Jack feel powerful and important; but it also, as Heinrich implies, becomes an agent of death: the Nyodyne D responsible for the Airborne Toxic Event is the result of insecticide waste product, and, as Jack later understands, any power that buying or throwing away confers is false, unable to slow his fear of death, just as Dylar too fails. The seemingly benign consumerism of the novel's first section quickly gives way to the unnatural, man-made disaster that drives the Gladneys from their home and, for Jack, directly into contact with the contaminant.

Jack's exposure to Nyodyne D is only the most literal manifestation of the exposure to waste that the whole family hides. The novel's primal waste scene comes when Jack, searching through the family's trash compactor to find the disposed of Dylar, comes face to face with his own refuse:

> I jabbed at it with the butt end of a rake and then spread the material over the concrete floor. I picked through item by item, mass by shapeless mass, wondering why I felt guilty, a violator of privacy, uncovering intimate and perhaps shameful secrets. It was hard not to be distracted by some of the things they'd chosen to submit to the Juggernaut appliance. But why did I feel like household spy? Is garbage so private? Does it glow at the core with a personal heat, with signs of one's deepest nature, clues to secret yearnings, humiliating flaws? What habits, fetishes, addictions, inclinations? What solitary acts, behavioral ruts? [. . .] I found a banana skin with a tampon inside. Was this the dark underside of consumer consciousness? I came across a horrible clotted mass of hair, soap, ear swabs, crushed roaches, flip-top rings, sterile pads smeared with pus and bacon fat, strands of frayed dental floss, fragments of ballpoint refills, toothpicks still displaying bits of impaled food.
>
> (258-59)

This description, filled with a kind of self-loathing, has been read in drastically different ways. On the one hand, Tom LeClair sees the trash compactor as "DeLillo's metaphor in the novel for the novel. [. . .] ***White Noise*** is [. . .] a novelistic heap of waste" (*Loop* 211-12). This astute reading takes the recycling impulse of DeLillo's fiction into account, so that a trash compactor compresses all of the sordid details of the Gladney's lives, just as the novel does. Interestingly, the recent ecocriticism movement seeks to claim this exact passage for itself; Cynthia Detering comments that

> by fathoming his family's garbage, it seems, Gladney might fathom not only the consciousness of consumer capitalism, but also the individual identities of his wife and children. By understanding the forms of their trash, he might glimpse their true selves as idiosyncratic producers of waste. Here the familiar notion of finding one's identity in commodity products is transformed into the notion of finding one's identity not in the commodities themselves but in their configuration as waste products.
>
> (198)

Finally, John Frow comments that "the list is of an accretion of wastes that have come full circle from the supermarket. [. . .] At the heart of this inside is nothing more than a compacted mass of outsides" (190).

LeClair takes DeLillo's waste management metaphorically; Detering, almost literally; and Frow, in between, sees that physical excess becomes inextricably linked to spiritual poverty. DeLillo seems to be engaging all three interpretations, despite their differences. Gladney searches through the trash desperate for Dylar, the one thing he imagines will alleviate his fear; instead, what he finds is the underside—the underworld—of not just consumer culture or the novel, but of himself and his family. Public and private together are compacted in the family trash heap. Jack feels like a spy (voyeur may be more appropriate) but his fear of being caught searching the trash masks his mysophobia—the fear of contamination. This fear comes to pass in the airborne toxic event, the ultimate waste product capable of contaminating everything it touches. To extend LeClair's interpretation, Jack is the author of his description as well as its reader, throwing away his fears and secrets only to be forced to face them again in recycled, compacted, and potently condensed form. The contamination that Jack relegates to the trash is even more potent in form of the mall and supermarket, all equal contaminants in his "fix" of death.

Bucky Wunderlick in ***Great Jones Street*** seeks silence as a way out of sonic excess that he fears may kill him; similarly, death for Jack is the constant noise of the TV, the radio, and the supermarket loudspeaker, "sound all around" (198, 312), despite that white seems empty, devoid of content or sound. Death is the billowing black cloud of waste contaminants, but it is also, less perceptibly, more insidiously, the whiteness of the Gladneys' lives—their pallor, their would-be purity, their middle-class aspiration. But as Melville, describing the elusive white whale, knew, "In essence, whiteness is not so much a color as the visible absence of color, and at the same time the concrete of all colors" (212). In the synesthesia of white noise, white is silence, but it is also all frequencies at once, dissonant, jamming, excessive; white is white and white is black. Its core is both empty and excessive.

If the trash compactor is the novel in miniature as LeClair suggests, then the novel itself is its own kind of white noise: every page, nearly every line, seems jammed on all frequencies, so that much happens at once in a way that is difficult for the reader to process. The reader himself, then is forced into a kind of waste management, trying, like Jack in the trash, to make sense of a barrage of information and detail, only to learn that everything seems crucial, or that nothing is. DeLillo's next novel, ***Libra,*** operates in the same way, only more extensively so in technique and critique: the novel is long, not consistently chronological or particularly reader friendly, and filled with multiple narrators, perspectives, and authorities, Like DeLillo's attempt in writing the novel or the reader's in comprehending it, Nicholas Branch attempts to sort out the excess of data and detail with "no end in sight" (15), "one hundred and twenty-five thousand pages" (59) of "paper hills that surround him" (378), making the twenty-six volume Warren Report "the megaton novel James Joyce would have written if he'd moved to Iowa City and lived to be a hundred" (180). That image, like the novel, blurs realism and modernism and complicates Foucault's still-looming question. When the text becomes all consuming, who can recycle its excesses and redeem them for something valuable? Can the reader, or even the author? More important, if ***Libra*** questions who writes the novel, it also questions who writes history. Will Branch's version of the assassination, if he can ever complete it, make sense of what happened? Or is Win Everett the author of history in his attempt to "script a person out of ordinary pocket litter" (28), a phrase recalling David Bell's scraps from which his movie emerges. Everett claims authorship over history, thinking, "We are characters in plots, without the compression and numinous sheen" (78); the literary author's job, then, is simply to make the work short and polished enough to be readable, a trash compactor and janitor in one.

But Everett's "plot" spins out of control because of the presence of a third author figure, Lee Harvey Oswald, a would-be writer whose "dyslexia or word blindness" (166) affects more than his spelling; his way of understanding, of reading and writing the world, also seems jumbled. All three vie to be the sole authority of the historical narrative, and their collective presence and continuous references to themselves as authors of some kind create the impression that "our understanding of the assassination, like the novel itself, is to become a work of art" (Simmons 74), a way to recycle the underside of history in compact form, smoothed with Everett's "numinous sheen." But like Jack Gladney face to face with his trash, the reader becomes aware that the historic waste bin of the Kennedy assassination and the now-wasted Oswald are our own refuse staring back at us; and like Gladney, we are its collective author and reader. But where does that leave DeLillo, whose name adorns the book's cover?

Such a question addresses the concern with authority in ***Mao II.*** Does "the future belong to crowds" (16), as the novel seems to suggest, or is this just another kind of excess, the ultimate hush of death-like white noise? Bill Gray, like Bucky Wunderlick, seeks seclusion; but unlike the young musician who seems at the peak of creativity, Gray is older and artistically impotent. With the author's great works behind him, new managers have risen to recycle his authority. Scott, Bill's assistant, but more like his keeper, is always "quoting Bill" (72)—like a literary critic—despite the fact that Bill is still alive and in the same room. Scott insists: "I'm only trying to secure [Bill's] rightful place" (73) and "I'm only saying what he deep down wants me to say" (74)—staying true to Bill's presumed authorial intentions, as any kind critic would in the spirit of New Criticism. The ignored Bill explodes, however, backhanding the butterdish across the table and into Scott's face, perhaps consummating every misquoted writer's wish; but the effort is futile, and Scott jokes away the attack. Clearly, Bill is not ready to relinquish himself to his critic's interpretation or to be reduced to his archives, a mere collection of texts outside of his control.

Photographer Brita Nilsson also seems eager to recycle the diminishing authority of the writer, or as Bill says, "to trap us in your camera before we disappear" (42); she seems Bill's proper artistic heir in that her art is like the "democratic shout" (159) of the novel. Brita's contact sheets of her photo shoot with Bill, however, like the Andy Warhol silkscreens that are mentioned in the novel and adorn its cover, demonstrate how the photo belongs to the photographer and not to its subject: "the pictures of Bill were glimpses of Brita thinking. [. . . She] was trying to deliver her subject from every mystery that hovered over his chosen life" (221), a description that recalls Barthes's death of the author as birth of the reader. Here, Bill's aura seem reinforced by the series of pictures, like the "Most Photographed Barn" of ***White Noise***; only it no longer is really his aura—it now belongs to Brita. Further, the photographer becomes explicitly linked to another figure vying for power, the terrorist: "there were the camera-toters and the gun-wavers and Bill saw hardly a glimmer of difference" (197); both point and shoot. But even worse is what seems to be a finite, mutually exclusive economy of authority and the need to reuse that authority, for as George Haddad claims, "What terrorists gain, novelists lose" (157).

In the end, despite Bill's wishes, the manuscript for the new novel "would sit" (224), a hidden leftover and remnant of the past like the baseball in ***Underworld,*** "collecting aura and force, deepening old Bill's legend, undyingly" (224), although obviously not for the now-dead Bill, who had hoped that the novelist would die "democratically [. . .] for everyone to see, wide open to the world, the shitpile of hopeless prose" (159). Scott withholds Bill's own "shitpile" in order to conserve and cultivate his and Bill's now-shared aura, but the author's body of work is separate form the author's body itself, and the aura—quite undemocratically—lives on, even as Bill does not. The novelist, unable to cultivate the power of the image, loses to the critic, the photographer, the terrorist, and ultimately the crowd.

But Don DeLillo-as-author is not immune from his novels' criticism of the power of the image, and he does not try to be. In 1997, with the release of ***Underworld,*** DeLillo came forward more publicly than ever, granting interviews and embarking on a book tour. In doing so, he created a specific authorial persona, one in keeping with the spirit of his novels. It is historical, self-referential, and ironic—a contemporary pose to match his contemporary prose, a way to appease his fans and publishers without threatening the shamanistic aura that his novels and photographs have cultivated. In an age of multiculturalism, DeLillo is appropriating the image of white male American Authorship, but updated. Unlike the ultramacho Hemingway, whose persona still threatens to overshadow his prose decades after his death; or unlike Hemingway's heirs in machismo, Norman Mailer and James Dickey, DeLillo remains soft-spoken and thoughtful, even when the *New York Times* seems more interested in discussing baseball than his writing.

DeLillo's novels have always been concerned with the effects of various media; ***Mao II*** opens each chapter with a photo, making the work almost multimedia and interdisciplinary, and both the typesetting and covers of ***White Noise*** and ***Underworld,*** with their careful contrasts of black and white, reflect the books' contents and themes. In addition, DeLillo has always relied on the importance of his own dust jacket photo, despite protests to interviewers that he is not interested in discussing his personal life (and also unlike Pynchon and Salinger, who have not posed for photographs in decades). Daniel Aaron describes a 1988 photo of DeLillo as resembling "an intellectual apartment house super with a hidden past (some refugee from graduate school? A lapsed priest?) wary of interrogators" (67).

In keeping with Aaron's thoughts, DeLillo's black and white portrait on the dust jacket of ***Underworld*** peers into the reader's soul while revealing nothing about his own; the photo is exposed enough so that there are contrasts despite that nearly every hue is a shade of gray. His hair is long, because he does not care enough to cut it regularly. He wears a collared shirt, but with the button opened. He shows no trace of a smile: his expression is somehow serious but also imitates the ironic deadpan of an actor about to laugh at his own lines—an apt description of the novel the photo adorns. Unlike in his candid photos, DeLillo is not wearing his thick glasses, too academic. He looks ruggedly handsome, but not airbrushed; the lines and marks on his face show a man who has sacrificed his youth for his craft, smart but not unattainably so, ironically not even book smart. He seems filled with American gumption but also American dread (rather than, say, European existentialism); healthy but not above an occasional drink; middle class, almost blue-collar; white, male, older (DeLillo was born in 1936). Here, the Author stands resurrected, wizened and weathered from his journey through death and back, but ready to deliver his secrets through the cryptic form of the novel. Aaron's feeling that DeLillo could be a "lapsed priest" is not far off. In all, Don DeLillo looks exactly like what an older, white male author at the end of the twentieth century is supposed look like, but his pose is both the cause and the effect of our expectations, having recycled the image of authority into someone familiar yet new. He channels and chronicles our times, even as he seems to be an almost transcendental resurrection of the way we relied on our authors to look before Barthes and Foucault questioned what an author was.

Finally, perhaps the best way to understand the contemporary role of the author is to turn to ***Ratner's Star,*** arguably DeLillo's strangest and most difficult novel. Self-referentially, DeLillo describes Nobel prize winning author Chester Greylag Dent: "every published work of this humanist and polymath [is] reflective of an incessant concern for man's standing in the biosphere and handblocked in a style best characterized as undiscourageably diffuse" (307).[8] Both the concern and difficulty seem to describe DeLillo as well; and ultimately, this concern extends beyond the question of physical waste to questioning the problems of spiritual emptiness. Talking to protagonist Billy Twillig, Dent says, "Balance. That's the best I could do" (348), and perhaps that is the most that any writer can hope to achieve; balance is the ultimate goal of recycling as well as writing. Clearly, Don DeLillo's emergent authorial persona hopes to strike that balance, unwilling to be diminished by poststructuralism and too smart to revive the authoritarianism of undemocratic modernism.

Early in ***Ratner's Star,*** Billy Twillig reads a story that he calls "an experimental novel, an allegory, a lunar geography, an artful autobiography, a cryptic scientific tract, a work of science fiction" (57). Despite its almost overwhelming absurdity and satire, one senses that ***Ratner's Star*** is all of those things. Despite DeLillo's "[not] want[ing] to talk about it" in interviews, he is willing to divulge himself in his work. The novel seems to be an allegory after all (despite this essay's first quote from Barthes condemning allegorical fiction) of the nature of the author-reader relationship, authority, and recycling. Field Experiment Number One perceives that the space signal is coming from the Ratnerians, the "star people" galaxies away, when the message is really from Earth. But like Oprah Winfrey's desperate readers, the scientists, at first intent on decoding the message, their text, begin to fret endlessly over its intention and not its meaning, becoming sidetracked about who sent the message and forgetting about what the message actually says. In the end, only Billy Twillig understands that the message, like the novel, is a warning, and he stands poised over Endor's hole as darkness overtakes the planet. The image of the hole is at once life giving and womb-like while seeming death-like as well, the place where the dead are buried, and the place where trash is most often disposed of—another underworld. We do not know if Billy will enter the hole, whether it will bring cold entropy and madness as it does for Endor, or whether it will provide the possibility for rebirth and emergence. As the scientist's name suggests, this hole may be the "end, or. . . ." It is an ambiguous but humorous image that positions the reader as judge and ultimately suggests waste management as a kind of cautionary tale against excess of any kind, Dent's "balance," and perhaps a call for simplicity—of course ironic in this excessive, rigorously cerebral and metaphysical novel. But DeLillo's authorial persona is filled with just such irony.

Notes

1. Although Bloom is more of a Romantic, often railing against deconstructive excess, his Oedipal battles of poetic influence and misreading seem no more optimistic than Barthes's post-structuralism. For a fuller critique, see Eagleton 184-85.

2. Leclair touches upon this idea in *The Art of Excess: Mastery in Contemporary American Fiction,* saying that "the systems persona is a collector rather than a creator" (23); but his concern is with mastery over excess—and over the reader—as his subtitle implies. I believe that DeLillo is after something more humorous and perhaps generous and that any sense of mastery is bestowed by, not upon, the reader, who, like the author, is forced into waste management.

3. For more on the DeLillo-Baudrillard connection, see Mark Conroy, "From Tombstone to Tabloid: Authority Figured in *White Noise,*" *Critique* 35 (1994): 97-110, and John Duvall, "The (Super) Marketplace of Images: Television as Unmediated Mediation in DeLillo's *White Noise,*" *Arizona Quarterly* 50 (1994): 127-53.

4. DeLillo dedicates *Mao II* to his friend Lish, in what has turned out to be an interesting twist: just as Scott the would-be editor battles with writer Bill Gray for the "aura"—the legacy—of his work, so now Lish battles Carver's ghost over whether he wrote, or ghost-wrote, many of Carver's early stories. DeLillo

clearly understands the public's appetite for a single, stable authority for each book.

5. In fact, DeLillo seems unabashedly to reuse many of the same themes in all of his novels. In addition, *Underworld* incorporates several previously published stories—further versions of recycling and the author as waste manager.

6. My students at Fordham University, reading *White Noise,* were delighted at the possibility that DeLillo, an alumnus, was inspired by the campus in writing the College-on-the Hill, ironically, of course, in that his descriptions in some ways mock the students who attend the fictitious school.

7. Like "Gladney's Hitler," DeLillo has belonged to Tom LeClair and Frank Lentricchia, both of whom practically must be mentioned in any DeLillo essay or "work about his work." The irony in *Mao II* deepens: "Scott pointed out special issues of a number of quarterlies, devoted solely to Bill" (31), journals possibly very much like this one.

8. Interestingly, Dent is one of three of DeLillo's shadowy, secluded figures to bear some form of the name "gray," a color in between the white of white noise and the black of the airborne toxic event, but lethal in its own way.

Works Cited

Aaron, Daniel. "How to Read Don DeLillo." Lentricchia 67-81.

Barthes, Roland. "The Death of the Author." *Image, Music, Text.* 1977. Trans. Stephen Heath. New York: Hill, 1996. 142-48.

Baudrillard, Jean. *Simulacra and Simulation.* Trans. Shiela Faria Glaser. Ann Arbor: U of Michigan P, 1994.

DeLillo, Don. *Americana.* Boston: Houghton, 1971.

———. *Great Jones Street.* Boston: Houghton, 1973.

———. Interview. *Anything Can Happen: Interviews with Contemporary American Novelists.* Eds. Tom LeClair and Larry McCaffery. Urbana: U of Illinois P, 1983.

———. *Libra.* New York: Viking, 1991.

———. *Mao II.* New York: Viking, 1988.

———. *The Names.* New York: Vintage, 1983.

———. *Ratner's Star.* New York: Knopf, 1976.

———. *Underworld.* New York: Scribner, 1997.

———. *White Noise.* New York: Viking, 1985.

Detering, Cynthia. "The Postnatural Novel: Toxic Consciousness in the Fiction of the 1980s." *The Ecocriticism Reader.* Eds. Chryll Glotfelty and Harold Fromm. Athens: U of Georgia P, 1996. 196-203.

Eagleton, Terry. *Literary Theory: An Introduction.* Minneapolis: U of Minnesota P, 1983.

Frow, Jonathan. "The First Before the Last: Notes on *White Noise.*" Lentricchia 175-91.

Foucault, Michel. "What Is an Author?" 1969. *Authorship.* Trans. Donald Bouchart and Sherry Simmons. Ed. Sean Burke. Edinburgh UP, 1995. 233-46.

Hamilton, Ian. *In Search of J. D. Salinger.* New York: Random House, 1988.

Keesey, Douglas. *Don DeLillo.* New York: Twayne, 1993.

LeClair, Tom. *The Art of Excess.* Urbana: U of Illinois P, 1989.

———. *In the Loop.* Urbana: U of Illinois P, 1989.

Lentricchia, Frank. *Introducing Don DeLillo.* Durham: Duke UP, 1991.

Melville, Herman. *Moby-Dick.* 1851. New York: Penguin, 1992.

Simmons, Philip. *Deep Surfaces: Mass Culture and History in Postmodern American Fiction.* Athens: U of Georgia P, 1997.

West, Nathanael. *The Dream Life of Balso Snell.* 1931. New York: Noonday, 1971.

Philip Nel (essay date summer 2001)

SOURCE: Nel, Philip. "*Amazons* in the *Underworld*: Gender, the Body, and Power in the Novels of Don DeLillo." *Critique* 42, no. 4 (summer 2001): 416-36.

[*In the following essay, Nel studies the representation of gender as a cultural construct in DeLillo's novels, considering the impact of media images, violent stereotypes, and social conventions on contemporary notions of masculinity and femininity.*]

To deepen and expand the study of Don DeLillo, we need to acknowledge the role gender plays in his work. Since William Burke's "Football, Literature and Culture"—the first literary criticism on DeLillo—was published in the *Southwest Review* twenty-five years ago, scholars of DeLillo have addressed topics as diverse as postmodernity, historiography, systems theory, technology, film, and literary Naturalism. Work in these areas has been and may continue to be necessary, but the field of DeLillo studies should not limit itself to these well-traveled and, arguably, still fertile critical grounds.[1] Fortunately, there are signs that critics are beginning to move into other areas of inquiry. We may, for example, soon see more criticism addressing issues of race: Tim Engles's "'Who Are You, Literally?'

Fantasies of the White Self in ***White Noise***" and Daniel S. Traber's "The Crisis of Whiteness in DeLillo's ***White Noise***" both address the "white" in ***White Noise.*** As DeLillo scholarship evolves to include whiteness, it is time also to address gender.

Scholars, reviewers, and interviewers have had little to say on the subject of gender in DeLillo's work. Perhaps the perception that his novels center on masculine universes and male characters has caused his treatment of women to elude critical commentary. However, DeLillo's inquiries into Foucauldian structures of power make possible a sharp analysis of gender in American society, and his work manifests a growing interest in the subject. The short story **"In the Men's Room of the Sixteenth Century"** and the novels ***Players*** and ***Running Dog*** signal the novelist's burgeoning curiosity, but DeLillo does not really begin to explore gender until the pseudonymous (and probably co-authored) ***Amazons,*** a novel that has been all but ignored by critics.[2] In the 1980s and 1990s, DeLillo's work not only starts to pay increasing attention to female characters but also begins to advance a critique of gender roles, media-created perceptions of the body, and power relationships between men and women. That ***Amazons*** was published under the name Cleo Birdwell and may have been co-written indicates that we should be careful in attributing (or not attributing) too much to DeLillo himself.[3]

However, its status as an unofficial "DeLillo novel" in no way excludes it from critical consideration. Indeed, its role in DeLillo's growing recognition of gender as a social construct—an issue with which he engages more frequently in post-***Amazons*** novels—makes it central to any analysis of DeLillo and gender. Though the analysis in ***Amazons*** sometimes falters, DeLillo succeeds there and in later works when he approaches gender through media or investigates how femininity and masculinity interact with the performance of power, revealing the nuances of gender as a culturally enforced construct.

In the first section of this essay, I address DeLillo's shortcomings as a critic of gender, arguing that ***Amazons***'s pornographic tendencies uphold rather than challenge masculine structures of power. In the essay's second part, I discuss DeLillo's debt to John Berger and Walter Benjamin, noting that when DeLillo investigates gender through its media manifestations—in novels like ***Amazons, White Noise,*** and ***Mao II***—his analyses question the ways in which representations encourage women to become, in his words, "self conscious objects of scrutiny" (Nadotti 90). In the third section, I examine ***White Noise*** and ***Libra***'s critique of violent masculinity as a cultural norm. Finally, I argue that DeLillo is most successful at exposing gender's dependence on sets of social conventions when he treats masculinity or femininity as a performance, showing how those conventions may be susceptible to challenge and revision.

Don DeLillo in Drag: Porn and Power in *Amazons*

Though ***Amazons*** is the first and only "DeLillo novel" with a female narrator, the book often (though not always) falters in its treatment of gender. Written or co-written under the name Cleo Birdwell and published in 1980, ***Amazons*** reads like Don DeLillo in drag, but not drag in the sense that Judith Butler uses the term. In *Gender Trouble,* she writes, "drag [. . .] mocks the notion of a true gender identity" by "displac[ing] the entire act of gender significations from the discourse of truth and falsity" (192). Cleo Birdwell, ***Amazons***'s protagonist and putative author, does not displace "gender from the discourse of truth and falsity"; instead she behaves much as a masculine athlete would. She propositions and sexually harasses members of the opposite sex, enjoys fighting, and generally inhabits rather than challenges masculine power structures.

As if to reinforce those very structures, the illustration on the original dust jacket promises to titillate the heterosexual male reader and suggests a mildly pornographic content. ***Amazons*** is one book that can be judged by its cover, which at once objectifies Cleo and hints at soft-core gratification for heterosexual male readers.[4] The jacket emphasizes the words "Intimate" and "Woman" of the subtitle ("An Intimate Memoir by the First Woman Ever to Play in the National Hockey League"), by showing high heels, a bra, panties, and a Rangers jersey draped over a locker room bench; below those items, on the floor, are a helmet, an ice skate, and panty hose. DeLillo did not include his name on the book, and DeLillo scholars agree that it is a lesser work, probably produced solely for financial gain. However, one cannot fault the author for the marketing of this book.

Though Catherine MacKinnon and Andrea Dworkin have made a compelling connection between pornography and violence against women, Lisa Palac has accurately pointed out that some "sexual images can be profoundly liberating, rather than oppressive" (158). To evaluate ***Amazons***' sexual images, we need to distinguish between types of pornography, and objectification of women is the key difference between the pornography that MacKinnon and Dworkin condemn and the pornography that Palac advocates. Dworkin describes a photograph titled "Beaver Hunters," which depicts a naked woman tied to a jeep, "spread-eagle[d]," with armed male hunters looking forward, in the words of the caption, to "stuff[ing] and mount[ing] her as soon as they [get] home" (25-26). That image makes rape into a joke, flaunts masculine power, denigrates women, and clearly supports Dworkin's argument that "[m]ale power is the raison d'être of pornography; the degradation of the female is the means of achieving this power" (25). What Lisa Palac argues can be liberating is pornography that expresses the subjectivity of a woman, portraying her as a three-dimensional character with her own desires.

Although never as misogynist as Dworkin's "Beaver Hunters" example, ***Amazons*** falls short of providing the subjectivity that Palac requires. As a result, ***Amazons*** often reads like soft-core pornography, with sexual encounters proceeding from no credible motivation of Cleo Birdwell, as the following litany of examples will show. Tennis player Archie Brewster falls asleep while playing strip monopoly; Cleo fondles his penis ("It woke up, but he didn't"), drags his sleeping form down the hall and into the bedroom, and has sex with him (16-17). Former pro-hockey player Shaver Stevens stops by to give Cleo a book; she offers him milk and cookies, invites him to the bedroom, where they have sex (33-36). Rangers's general manager Sanders Meade invites her to dinner and then back to his room: at first he cannot get it up; but after several pages of Cleo's fondling, he does, and they have sex (60-72). She visits the apartment of Glenway Packer, a fifty-two-year-old associate of her agent, Floss (129): he undresses, she comments on his brown penis, and they have sex (141-46). Coach Jean-Paul ("J. P."), a French Canadian, visits Cleo, speaks French to her, and they have sex (184-87). Murray Siskind, a sports writer who later appears as an American Studies professor in ***White Noise,*** cooks dinner for Cleo and they have sex afterward (285-97). She fences with Manley Packer, half-brother of Glenway, wounds him, and they have sex (334-41). In none of these seven episodes does the sexual encounter result from any plausible relationship—as in a bad pornographic film, one gratuitous sexual encounter follows another. And whether or not Cleo is the initiator, each one is consistently phallocentric—very focused on the male member. Indeed, we hear very little about her pleasure (and, if she is playing a masculine role, shouldn't we?).

Birdwell inhabits the role of the sexually aggressive male athlete, but does little to challenge the structures that maintain an imbalance of power between men and women. Her molestation of and intercourse with the sleeping tennis player Archie Brewster is an act of rape, but the narrator does not portray the scene that way. Although she's "astraddle him" when he wakes up, he does not protest but says "Some body" and "Excellent stuff" (18-19). After a brief conversation, they continue to have sex. If the novel depicted the same scene with the genders reversed—Archie possessing her sleeping form, her waking up and enjoying it—I suspect that its tacit endorsement of rape would not have escaped critical attention.

Significantly, that same sort of female sexuality appears, albeit toned down, in DeLillo's later and earlier work. In ***Mao II,*** Karen enters Bill Gray's bedroom and wearing only "her briefs and an oversize T-shirt [. . .], climbed on the bed, straddling Bill near the midsection" (84). She then undresses herself and Bill, takes his penis in her hand ("His cock was dancing in her hand" is how DeLillo's narrator describes it), fits him with a condom, and they have sex (86). In ***Running Dog,*** Glen Selvy enters Moll Robbins's apartment, she promptly undresses, they have sex (35). Reading these scenes, we can see how Douglas Keesey's observation that Selvy "is not as detached as he thinks from the pornographic imagination" (102) may apply to ***Amazons***: although this novel is ostensibly detached from the rest of DeLillo's *oeuvre,* elements of its pornographic imagination recur in the DeLillo canon. The problem here is not that these women are sexually aggressive, but that their sexual behavior is not grounded in character. Were these scenes rewritten with character in mind, Moll, Karen, and Cleo would be likely—at least—to worry about sexually transmitted diseases or to hesitate to disrobe so casually. In sex scenes like these, DeLillo does not seem to realize what Gloria Steinem understood back in 1962: "The real danger of the contraceptive revolution may be the acceleration of woman's role-change without any corresponding change of man's attitude toward her role" (qtd. in Douglas 70). These female characters have accepted a great role-change, but there is no evidence that the male characters have done so. When Keesey, the only critic to spend any time discussing ***Amazons,*** calls the book "a feminist sports novel" (208) or says that "here, as nowhere else in any of DeLillo's novels, the point of view is exclusively female" (209), his comments do not capture the gender politics of ***Amazons.*** The narrator may be female, but the point of view feels masculine; only in isolated moments does the book veer toward feminist critique.

Yet ***Amazons*** does mark the beginning of DeLillo's willingness to address both femininity and masculinity as social constructs, and the book initiates an analysis that grows stronger and more nuanced in subsequent novels. Indeed, a brief comparison between some "phallic" moments from ***Americana*** (1971), ***Amazons*** (1980), ***The Names*** (1982), and ***Underworld*** (1997) shows how much DeLillo's understanding has developed over the course of twenty-five years. A particularly telling scene depicting masculinity occurs in ***Americana*** when the protagonist David Bell strolls around the office with his penis hanging out: "Then I unzipped my pants and took out my cock. I walked around the office like that for a while. It felt good" (22). This scene is a performance of masculinity, but it lacks the ironic awareness with which DeLillo usually presents performances. In the scene that follows, David remembers sexually harassing a secretary, but because he does not remember his actions *as* sexual harassment, his memory reinforces the uncritical portrait of masculinity as phallocentric and aggressive (22-23). Although sexual harassment had not been brought to national awareness in 1971, it is significant that ***Americana***'s presentation of gender differs from that of ***Amazons,*** which—despite its flaws—seems more aware of masculinity as a social construct with its own learned rules and codes. Although David Bell's penis-flaunting passes without comment, in ***Amazons*** Georgie Schlagel's exhibitionism becomes the subject of an extended meditation. Schlagel, a former boyfriend of Cleo's, "was one of those boys who's totally, everlastingly in love with his own penis. He never got over his first erection. He just loved flaunting himself. He was always playing with it. [. . .] He would study it. [. . .] His penis was a never-ending discovery" (65-66). The later novel presents the behavior parodically, mocking Georgie's phallic obsession, the centrality of his penis to his identity.

Much darker in tone than either of these two scenes, James Axton's attempted rape of Janet Ruffing more directly questions the notion that aggressive sexual behavior is a "normal" or "natural" part of being a man. Axton himself may not see his treatment of Ruffing as violent misogyny, but DeLillo's inclusion of her responses and Ann Maitland's later references to this event (240) tell a different story. After watching Ruffing belly-dance, Axton makes increasingly invasive and personal comments, expressing desires "to slip my hand under your blouse and detach your bra" (226) and "to put my hands under your clothes" (227). Ruffing resists, repeatedly telling Axton, "I don't do this" (222, 223, 224, 227, 228, 230), "I really have to leave" (223), and "No" (222, 223, 224). Her protests generate increasing uneasiness on the part of the reader. In contrast with David Bell's sexual harassment of the secretary and Cleo Birdwell's rape of Archie Brewster (both of which pass without comment), the depiction of James Axton's sexual harassment includes the feelings of the intended victim. Her resistance gives the lie to the dangerous stereotype that *certain* women (such as belly-dancers) secretly "want it" or that "no" does not really mean "no." When Axton "edged her into a wall and kissed her," Ruffing "looked away, her mouth smeared" (229). Axton catches her and, at the very moment of consummation, observes that "[s]he seemed to be thinking past this moment, finished with it, watching herself in a taxi heading home" (230). My point is not so much that the palpable violence of the scene estranges the reader from the novel's central character and narrator, buy rather that DeLillo, in illustrating Axton's brutishness, does not neglect the perspective of the victim.

In ***Underworld,*** a novel that includes the sexual perspectives of both Klara Sax and Marian Shay, depictions of masculine sexuality resemble less the near-rape scene of ***The Names*** and more the parodic style of ***Amazons.*** Young Eric Deming's masturbatory fantasy adds several levels of parody to the masculine penis fixations of Schlagel and Bell, mocking phallocentrism by linking it to the Cold War, ideals of domesticity, and the objectification of women. The result is a parodic melange, pastiche more sharp-edged than Jameson's "blank parody." Its lack of a single reference point allows it to offer many layers of cultural criticism at once, a more ambitious analysis in which the cultural construction of masculinity is but one of these layers. In a scene set in October 1957, Eric masturbates into "a condom because it had a sleek metallic shimmer, like his favorite weapons system" (514). His act gains extra significance because this is the day the Soviets launched Sputnik, a fact reinforced when Eric's mother uses the "satellite-shaped vacuum cleaner" (520) and "Eric [eats] Hydrox cookies because the name sounded like rocket fuel" (519). The condom-as-weapons-system's imagery of self-pleasuring technology recurs in the description of Eric's father "running a shammy over the chromework [of the car]. This was something, basically, he could do forever. He could look at himself in a strip of chrome, warp-eyed and hydrocephalic" (516). The car's "hydrocephalic" chrome returns in Eric's comparison of Jane Mansfield's breasts to the "bumper bullets on a Cadillac" (517), and the "endless motorized throb" of the family's refrigerator (518) metaphorically figures the act of masturbation. In linking shiny mass-culture items with auto-eroticism, this scene sends out waves of satire in many directions at once, rippling toward not only patriarchy but militarism, conspicuous consumption, and the vocabulary of advertisements. Using the language of advertising to place all of these items on the same symbolic level, DeLillo delivers a satire more complex and nuanced than in either ***Americana*** or ***Amazons.*** Here, everything is an ideological construct: The scene's plastic, flexible sense of mockery subtly implies that machines represent the sublimated auto-eroticism of heterosexual masculinity and, in making this suggestion, DeLillo parodies both masculinity and the military-industrial complex.

Surveyor and Surveyed in the Age of Mechanical Reproduction

When ***Amazons*** approaches gender—both femininity and masculinity—through media manifestations, it prefigures the more subtle analyses of DeLillo's later novels. For example, Cleo's rejecting the role of corporate spokesperson gives us a glimpse of the more sophisticated treatment of gender that will appear in ***White Noise, Mao II,*** and ***Underworld.*** She is asked to endorse Hughes Tools, the team's corporate sponsor, but the company name—Huge Tool!—suggests both a large phallus and an inept person, offering a conscious parody of the hypermasculinity expected of and often embodied by male athletes (as if to imply, who better to endorse a huge tool than a "big, dumb jock"?). If the company name reinforces that stereotype, Cleo challenges it. Requested to pose "sitting in this whirlpool, eating an apple, and showing *moderate to heavy* cleavage" (84), she rejects what DeLillo, who once worked at an ad agency, has elsewhere called "the slick locutions of advertising" (Gross). Cleo says, "I walk in the door and they want cleavage. [. . .] I'm a hockey player" (***Amazons*** 85). She rejects their defense of using her cleavage to sell the product on the grounds that she would "feel so dumb" (86).[5] In a similar vein, she also mocks the language reporters use to describe her, pointing out its tendency to represent her not as a professional hockey player but as an object of desire: "They wrote about my honey blonde hair flying in the breeze, my silver skate blades flashing, my plucky work in the corners, my style, my stamina, my milky blue eyes, my taut ass and firm breasts, the nightmarish bruises on my downy white thighs" (1-2). Refusing to submit to this kind of objectification, Cleo talks back and thus anticipates the later, more interesting characters of Babette Gladney in ***White Noise*** and Brita Nilsson in ***Mao II.***

Discussing ***Mao II*** in a 1993 interview, DeLillo makes one of his few direct comments on gender: noting that "women so often become the objects of attention" because "men look at them constantly and force them to become self conscious objects of scrutiny," he hopes that Brita's photography helps challenge that tendency (Nadotti 90). Hints of this critical angle had previously emerged in ***Amazons,*** when Cleo rejects her media-based objectification and reports that her agent Floss Penrose "can't stand being looked at. Visual scrutiny, she called it" (279). In ***Libra,*** the exotic dancer Brenda Jean Sensibaugh has nightmares about men violating her ("she is demonized, and wakes up in a different dream, where strange men are clutching at her body. Does anybody here know the stupid truth? She wants to be a real estate agent" [262]). But ***Mao II*** and ***White Noise*** develop more fully this critique of what Laura Mulvey has famously called the "male gaze" (436 and *passim*). In addition to Mulvey's "Visual Pleasure and Narrative Cinema" (1975), one can also profitably read these novels against *Ways of Seeing,* in which John Berger develops the distinction between "surveyor" and "surveyed." In words that complement DeLillo's remarks about women being forced to become "self conscious objects of scrutiny," Berger writes that a woman learns to "survey everything she is and everything she does because how she appears to others, and ultimately how she appears to men is of crucial importance for what is normally thought of as the success of her life. Her own sense of being is supplanted by a sense of being appreciated as herself by another" (46).

The author of ***White Noise*** is aware that, as Berger, Naomi Wolf, and others have pointed out, media images encourage women to internalize an often unattainable standard of beauty and survey themselves according to that standard.[6] Babette Gladney's food-based fixations resonate beyond the novel's concerns about aging and death, indicting a culture that promotes such potentially damaging self-scrutiny. Babette intends to eat "yogurt and wheat germ" for lunch, to exercise, and to monitor her weight carefully (7, 14-15),[7] but her husband Jack likes her plumpness and views thinner women with suspicion: He distrusts his ex-wives' "high cheekbones" and "[m]arvelous bone structure. Thank God for Babette and her long fleshy face," he says—and he means it (88). He defends Babette's decision not to eat yogurt and wheat germ, reminding her "how much I liked the way she looked" and suggesting that "there was an honesty inherent in bulkiness if it is just the right amount. People trust a certain amount of bulk in others" (7). Although Jack Gladney has certainly replaced one feminine ideal with another, a "fleshy" or "bulky" ideal is at least more healthy than the starving-model paradigm. If, as Wolf writes in *The Beauty Myth,* "[a] cultural fixation on female thinness is not an obsession about female beauty but an obsession about female obedience" (187), then Jack's advocacy of a heavier ideal helps counteract the debilitating effects of a culture that persuades women to strive for a too thin body. Inasmuch as a compulsion to diet undermines women's sense of self, Jack's arguments against dieting encourage Babette to feel comfortable with her body image—and with herself.

In ***Mao II,*** DeLillo goes further than challenging the culturally prescribed body images maintained by self-surveying. In what might be considered a revision of Berger's analysis, DeLillo inverts the usual surveyor—surveyed power dynamic by making Brita the surveyor and men the surveyed. The gender role reversal does not escape Bill Gray, who not only compares the photography session to sex ("Do you realize what an intimate thing we're doing?") but asks, "And when did women start photographing men in the first place?" (43). If Bill sounds a bit defensive, it is because Brita's camera has becomes a gun, directly confronting the power of her male subject. The scene in which Brita photographs Bill Gray bore the title **"Shooting Bill Gray"** when published as a short story in *Esquire.* The word "shooting" functioned there in the sense of both photographing and executing. Just as photographs that encourage women to survey themselves weaken women, so Brita's photographing—or shooting—Bill begins to dismantle his power. To emphasize the power of this "shooting" session, the normally reticent Bill opens up, answering Brita's questions; as he puts it, "these pictures [. . .] break down the monolith I've built" (44). And the photographs themselves initiate a series of events in which Bill Gray allows the "monolith" to crumble; he loses himself in the world until, struck by a car and refusing medical attention, he dies anonymously in Beirut.

During a scene nearer to the conclusion of the novel, Brita's camera again shoots, acting both as surveyor and as disruptor of the aura of power. DeLillo has remarked that "[o]rdering a photograph of a famous recluse must be a little like ordering an execution" ("Don DeLillo: The Word, the Image, and the Gun").[8] Indeed Brita uses her camera as a weapon: she removes the hood of one of terrorist leader Abu Rashid's followers and takes his picture (***Mao II*** 236). In addition to establishing her in the role of surveyor, Brita's photograph becomes an act of violation that provokes a physical challenge. The unmasked boy "hits her hard in the forearm [. . .] and she [. . .] slaps him across the face" (237). Taking on the culturally masculine role, Brita penetrates the disguise, subjecting Rashid's man to the gaze and to the camera's violation.

DeLillo has Brita use photographic reproduction to challenge Rashid's power precisely because Rashid has used photographic reproduction to strengthen his hold over his followers. Though DeLillo discusses the concept of aura in ***White Noise*** (exemplified by "the most photographed barn in America" [12]), in ***Mao II*** he puts Brita Nilsson to work deconstructing the ways in which images uphold the masculine power of people like Abu Rashid and Bill Gray—in other words, he applies the concept of aura not just to power but to the intersection of gender and power. Like Walter Benjamin, DeLillo is wary of the ability of mechanical reproduction (including photography) to transform art into a totalitarian event.[9] According to Benjamin's "The Work of Art in the Age of Mechanical Reproduction," the loss of aura diminishes awareness: by removing "the reproduced object" (painting, sculpture, or even a person) from "the domain of tradition," reproduction can transform something rooted in history into an object for aesthetic consumption. That process, Benjamin argues, is "intimately connected with contemporary mass movements" and its "most powerful agent is the film" (221). In using media to spread its message, Fascism succeeds by aestheticizing politics (241); one must respond, as Brita does, by "politicizing art" (242).

DeLillo retheorizes "aura" to explore the vexed relationship between reality and simulacra. He argues that aura can exist apart from any thing itself—reproductions can have "aura," too. As he says in a 1991 interview with Gordon Burn,

> Cameras, strobe lights, movie cameras, tape recorders. Walter Benjamin wrote a famous essay about the way in which objects lose their aura when they're reproduced. Mechanical reproduction of a painting, or a cathedral, results in a certain loss of aura. Now, for me, in the last decade of the 20th century, there's nothing *left* but aura. See, I think it's reality that's being diminished, leaving behind the aura that results from tape-recorders, cameras, microphones and all of the technological equipment that we use to *consume* reality.
>
> (Burn 37, 39)

Although Benjamin and DeLillo both criticize the sense that reality is being diminished by technology, "aura," for Benjamin, is still intimately connected with the notion of a thing itself, an irreproducible object. Thus, when aura withers, reality does too. However, DeLillo's use of the word "aura" suggests no necessary connection to an "original" that resists reproduction. For DeLillo, "aura" can exist apart from any "thing itself." Sustained by reproduction and simulation, aura, therefore, presents both danger and possibility.

For a man who feels his masculinity threatened, the manufacture of aura provides the sensation of power by appearing to raise him above the effects of the material world. The problem, of course, is that his power is illusory; one cannot separate the production of aura from its material consequences.[10] In ***Mao II,*** terrorist leader Abu Rashid encourages identification with photographic reproductions of himself to increase his aura of power; DeLillo's narrative, on the other hand, uses these same reproductions to unsettle the identification, calling the terrorist's power into question. Rashid's followers are young men with hoods over their faces and Rashid's face on their T-shirts; as the interpreter explains, "The boys who work near Abu Rashid have no face or speech. Their features are identical. They are his features. They don't need their own features or voices. They are surrendering these things to something powerful and great" (234). If their diminished connection to a "real" encourages assimilation with Rashid, then reproduction can lead to mass movements; however, if this same diminished connection destabilizes the audience's relationship to Rashid, then reproduction can have a critical effect. Appropriately, DeLillo is both intrigued by and has misgivings about this kind of Warholian repetition. As he said in 1991, Warhol makes an image "fluctuate freely, liberating it from history: a man who is immersed in wars and revolutions becomes a sort of icon painted on a flat surface. [. . .] Interesting work, and judging from its extraordinary reception, perhaps a little frightening as well" (Nadotti 97). Aware of Warhol's ability to remove an image from history and troubled by this art's popularity, DeLillo nonetheless finds such work "interesting." Rashid uses this artistic gesture to help manufacture aura, but DeLillo seizes the oppositional potential of the same gesture, disrupting Rashid's sense of authority and control.

In terms of critical possibility, DeLillo's retheorized, postmodern sense of "aura" allows for further destabilization of masculine power. Because aura can exist in reproductions, DeLillo can create tension between levels of "authentic" and "inauthentic" images. He explores the combative potential of reproductions by making the young follower that Brita photographs Rashid's son, also named Rashid—Rashid II, if you will. "Rashid II" operates on several levels: the photographic reproduction of the father, the literal reproduction, the repeated name, and the photos of both father and son on Brita's roll of film. The notion of a Rashid II harnesses the critical suggestiveness of Warhol's Pop Art renditions of Mao Zedong ("New Series 1972-74"), printed on the novel's cover. The array of reproductions suggested by the name acts as an ironic gesture, destabilizing the boundary between the image and the man, challenging the aura of masculine power of both Rashids. Revising Benjamin's concept of "aura" to include reproductions, Brita's Warholian repetitions destabilize norms of masculinity. As DeLillo says in the Nadotti interview, Brita is "[r]eversing the terms" by "photographing a man" (90).

In remarks that directly parallel Bill Gray's, DeLillo then asks "When is it that women began to photograph men? [. . .] And was it important? In short, did the world change when women began watching men, becoming spectators rather than objects?" (90). His questions show that, even as Brita challenges the male gaze by reversing the terms, DeLillo retains his characteristic ambivalence about the ability to challenge any system of power, limiting himself to rhetorical questions that speculate upon the possibility of change. Only when the interviewer presses him to answer his question will DeLillo say, "I think that the basic thing is that women have begun to put their eyes behind cameras. Whatever is on the other side that becomes the object will now be seen in a different way from the way it would be seen otherwise, especially if the object on the other side of the view finder is a man" (91). Though this response affirms the basic principles of his critique of gender, the qualified way in which he answers the question, saying that the "object will now be seen in a different way" without specifying what that way is, indicates that any resistance to culturally enforced gender roles will inevitably be qualified. That approach may sound pessimistic; however, it is anything but. The power of his critique flows from that sense of contingency: in both these comments and his novels of the 1980s and 1990s, he deconstructs the systems of masculinity and femininity without offering dogmatic proposals for what should replace those systems. Were DeLillo to offer a solution he would risk embracing the hierarchy implicit in whatever system that solution introduced; so, to apply the language of Tom LeClair's *In the Loop* to gender, DeLillo destabilizes the masculine-feminine binary.

"A Male Follows the Path of Homicidal Rage": Masculinity and Violence

DeLillo's work also destabilizes by challenging the assumptions on which gender differences rest, and one important difference is the tendency to accept a certain level of violence as normal male behavior. Whereas the hockey-fight scenes in ***Amazons*** gesture toward masculinity's investment in violence, ***White Noise*** and ***Libra*** address the issue directly. ***White Noise*** lacks a female character as strong as Brita Nilsson but treats with great irony what gender critic Jackson Katz has called "the equation of heroic masculinity with violent masculinity" (136). As the recent series of high school shootings has shown, it is not just guns that kill but males with guns who kill. To quote Katz and Sut Jhally's *Boston Globe* article on the Littleton Massacre, the issue here is "the construction of violent masculinity" as a cultural norm. ***White Noise*** offers a critique of this norm. First-person narrator Jack Gladney's initially thoughtful interest in violence helps to gather the reader's sympathies for Gladney's point of view, but the novel then turns on any tendency to agree with him, systematically disrupting the cultural mythology that links masculinity with violence.

Though he will not admit it openly, Gladney is angry at Willie Mink, the man who slept with his wife. Babette sees right through him: "You're a man, Jack. We all know about men and their insane and violent rage. This is something men are very good at. Insane and violent rage. Homicidal rage. When people are good at something, it's only natural that they look for a chance to do this thing" (225). In a later conversation, she again suspects him of wanting to "revenge your childish dopey injured male pride": "A male follows the path of homicidal rage. It is the biological path. The path of dumb blind male biology" (269). Babette's suspicions are correct, but it is not simply biology that prompts Jack's homicidal urges; it is the social belief that violence is an appropriate masculine response. Murray Siskind agrees with Babette's biological claim (193), but his theories delineate the cultural power that violence seems to give to men. Refuting DeLillo's oft-repeated idea that "all plots lead to death"—a line in ***White Noise*** and ***Libra***—Murray argues that "[t]o plot is to live" (291) because "violence is a form of rebirth. The dier passively succumbs. The killer lives on" (290). So, Murray implies, if Jack acts on his revenge fantasy, he can, at the same time, counteract his fear of death. "Are you a dier or a killer, Jack?" he asks. Because we hear both Babette's and Murray's comments about violence from Jack's point of view, Jack's sympathies can more easily become ours. But by relegating these remarks to the realm of theory, the novel implies that, though Jack may feel violent, he will not act on his violent feelings. He is, after all, a college professor, a man given more to theorizing violence than to being violent.

Here DeLillo catches the reader by surprise. When Gladney turns violent, the reader does not quite expect it. And, even when Jack has decided to exact revenge, the narrative comes from his point of view, which encourages the reader to sympathize with his perspective. When carrying a gun, Jack feels powerful: "The gun created a second reality for me to inhabit. [. . .] It was a reality I could control, secretly dominate" (297). After shooting Willie Mink, Jack exults in the violent act until he gets shot, too. The bullet punctures not only his wrist but the cultural ideal of violent masculinity. Initially, Jack sees the whole event as if it were on Baudrillard's TV: "I watched blood squirt from the victim's midsection. A delicate arc. I marveled at the rich color [. . .]. Mink's pain was beautiful, immense" (312). But when Mink shoots him, "The world collapsed inward" and Jack feels "[h]urt, stunned, and disappointed. What happened to the higher plane of energy in which I'd carried out my scheme? The pain was searing. [. . .] I looked at him. Alive. His lap a puddle of blood. With the restoration of the normal order of matter and sensation, I felt I was seeing him for the first time as a person. The old human muddles and quirks were set flowing again. Compassion, remorse, mercy" (313). And Jack sets to helping both himself and Mink; he gathers his intended victim and drives him to the hospital. The initial description makes the event sound like a TV or movie killing, glorified, glamorized, suggesting that Jack has absorbed this system of values from the media. (Murray, after all, has linked car crashes to the spirit of American optimism and fun [218-19].) But DeLillo's decision to have Mink fire back at Jack shatters that belief: when the pain is his, the pain is real.

Jack Gladney anticipates DeLillo's version of Lee Harvey Oswald, who has also learned that violence is an appropriate, even necessary, means of attaining masculine power. His masculinity often challenged,[11] Lee feels insecure and seeks a way to be more of a man's man. The beatings he receives both as a child and in the military impress upon him the idea that to be powerful, a man must also be violent.[12] As he imagines buying the gun from David Ferrie, Lee thinks to himself, "he'd actually have the rifle. He'd emerge with the rifle. He'd be able to say he'd transported a rifle in a stolen blanket through the city of New Orleans" (46). To Lee, carrying a gun—and being able to brag about carrying a gun—would make him dangerous, respected. As ***Libra*** tells it, the films of John Wayne and John Garfield reinforce in the mind of Oswald this association between guns and the respect of others. Lee admires Garfield, who in *We Were Strangers* (1949) plays "an American revolutionary in Cuba in the 1930s [. . .] plot[ing] to assassinate the dictator and blow up his entire cabinet." Watching Garfield, "Lee felt he was in the middle of his own movie. They were running the thing just for him" (370). By placing this scene not thirty pages before the assassination of President Kennedy, DeLillo encourages us to connect Lee's shooting with films that glamorize violence as part of an heroic masculinity. Indeed, as he looks down from the book depository, staring through his rifle's scope at the presidential motorcade, Lee feels uncharacteristically calm and strong—"a sense of a kid's snug hideout, making him feel apart and secure" (395).

The moment he begins shooting, Lee imagines himself as already on film, talking about the event: "He was already talking to someone about this. He had a picture, he saw himself telling the whole story to [. . .] a man with a rugged Texas face, but friendly, but understanding" (400). Lee sees not only violence as a means to achieve personal power but filmed violence as a way to acquire the aura of celebrity, to become a movie star.[13] As Katz and Jhally wrote in the *Boston Globe,* "In numerous films starring iconic hypermasculine figures like Arnold Schwarzenegger, Sylvester Stallone, Wesley Snipes, Bruce Willis, and Mel Gibson, the cartoonish story lines convey the message that masculine power is embodied in muscle, firepower, and physical authority." ***Libra*** is set decades before the rise of Schwarzenegger, Stallone, and company, but many "hypermasculine" figures—such as John Wayne—were available in the early 1960s from whom Lee could receive this message that violence equals masculine power.[14] As the role of a tough cowboy is a part that Wayne plays, the role of assassin is a part that Lee performs. In examining the performative aspects of gender, DeLillo offers his most sophisticated treatment of the subject.

"It's a Cross-Dressing Event Either Way": Performing Gender

Though one might expect **"In the Men's Room of the Sixteenth Century"** to offer DeLillo's first investigation into the implications of performing gender, neither the plot nor its "drag-saint" (177) policeman leads the story in that direction; instead, cross-dressing remains subservient to the story's dominant themes of spirituality and social class. But, in the 1980s and 1990s, DeLillo successfully uses performance to examine gender as a social construct, and the opening scene of ***Running Dog*** signals his new approach. During that scene, a woman is murdered; except "she" is not a woman, as policemen Robby Del Bravo, "G. G." Gannett, and an unnamed sergeant discover. Earlier, when the woman was still alive, Del Bravo had fixed his heterosexual male gaze on her: "She had long hair, darkish blond, and [. . .] he could see how attractive she was" (4). He later discovers the fallibility of his assumptions. When they view the body, the sergeant explains, "Everybody's in disguise" (8). He continues, "It used to be you could go by the clothes. But you can't go by the clothes anymore." Del Bravo replies, "You go by the sex organs" (9). In addition to being a clear acknowledgment of the difference between sex ("the sex organs") and gender ("the clothes"), the scene signals DeLillo's burgeoning awareness of drag's potential to mock a "true" identity. Failing to distinguish between gender and sex, Del Bravo assumed that feminine appearance corresponded with female biology; that "she" is anatomically male challenges his assumption of a "natural" connection between gender and sex.

Amazons might not develop this idea very far, but ***White Noise*** and ***Underworld*** explore the critical potential of drag and highlight masculinity and femininity as performative acts. Indeed, DeLillo's analysis of gender is at its strongest when focusing on those performances. In ***Underworld,*** at the premiere of *Unterwelt,* the imaginary lost film of Eisenstein, DeLillo creates several such moments. He introduces the cross-dressing theme in the lobby of Radio Music Hall, the theater at which *Unterwelt* will be shown. Klara notices that the "statue in the marbled niche had the thighs and calves of a man, a man's bundled muscles in the forearms, but the figure in fact was biblical Eve, tight-breasted, with an apple in her hands and the sloping shoulders of a fullback" (423). Recalling the muscular femininity of Cleo Birdwell, the statue of the physically strong Eve challenges Klara's expectations by conjoining a body type usually considered masculine with a traditionally feminine figure. That she is Eve raises many interpretive possibilities: that the "first woman" embodies strength instead of sin, that the decision to take the apple is a sign of strength and not moral weakness, or alternately, that a strong woman is also morally weak. The apparently contradictory traits—"a man's bundled muscles" on "biblical Eve"—do not explain what the spectator is to make of them; however, they do highlight gender as a set of social expectations. Juxtaposing the idea of "fullback" with that of "Eve" effectively gives Klara and the reader pause, preparing us for the more radical gender destabilizations that arrive when the ambiguously gendered Rockettes take the stage.

Though Klara describes the evening as a "cross-referenced event" (423) she perceives the Rockettes as a "cross-dressing event" (428), a direct assault on the notion of an authentic or stable gender identity. By figuring the Rockettes in visually contrary ways—as masculine and feminine; as dancers, military men, and sadomasochists; as American entertainment and Russian propaganda—DeLillo creates unstable ironies that blur gender and national identities. He writes, "out came the Rockettes":

> They were wearing West Point gray and came out saluting, thirty-six women remade as interchangeable parts, height, shape, race and type, with plumed dress hats and fringed titties and faces buttered a christmassy pink but isn't it odd they're all wearing bondage collars—saluting and high-kicking in unison and Klara thought they were kind of great and so did everyone else. Snapping into close formation, tap-dancing in a wash of iridescent arcs, all symmetry and drill precision, then fanning open in kaleidoscopic bursts, and she passed a question along the aisle to Miles, who sat at the far end of the foursome.
>
> "How do we know it's really the Rockettes and not a troupe of female impersonators?"
>
> And this droll notion seemed to travel through the audience because isn't it unlikely that the real Rockettes would be wearing slave collars and doing routines with such pulsing sexual rhythm? In fact it's probably not unlikely at all, it's probably what they do all the time. You don't know for sure, do you? And if they are the real Rockettes, what you're seeing are three dozen women in close-order cadet formation, or women done up like men and not the reverse—but it's a cross-dressing event either way.
>
> (428)

The juxtapositions of masculine and feminine unsettle any rigid categories of gender by announcing both masculinity and femininity as social constructs. Unlike the many moments when Cleo Birdwell merely takes on the role of a stereotypical male athlete, this scene presents drag in the sense that Judith Butler uses the word. The Rockettes' performance does "mock the notion of a true gender identity" (Butler 192) by challenging the categories of masculine and feminine. Likening the Rockettes to a machine with "interchangeable parts," a "cadet formation" in "West Point gray," the image conjoins military formations with sexy entertainment, suggesting that this is objectification, but objectification intended to make the reader aware of its consequences.

The images presented by the Rockettes keep shifting, however, and the analogies suggested by the *Unterwelt* premiere quickly become more and more difficult to pin down precisely. As the narrator observes, "You saw things differently now. If there was a politics of montage, it was more intimate here" (443). When DeLillo sees gender in terms of media manifestations, reproductions, and the ways in which culture replicates ideologies of gender—as he has begun to do in his works from the 1980s and 1990s—his "politics of montage" (which he has elsewhere applied to topics as diverse as football, rock n' roll, and nuclear waste) breaks down social constructs of masculinity and femininity.

Amazons anticipates and offers a criticism of the antifeminist backlash of the 1980s and 1990s that Susan Faludi documented in *Backlash.* The passage in which Rangers's General Manager Sanders Meade makes a connection between women's advances and weakened masculinity mocks this backlash. Eerily anticipating the argument of Faludi's subsequent book *Stiffed,* ***Amazons*** views critically Sanders's charge that feminism has weakened men by having him offer it as an excuse for his own inability to perform sexually—which he has already blamed on his envy of hockey player Eric Torkleson's penis (63) and his own acute self-consciousness (66). His credibility already in question, Sanders then claims that "the twin specters of Vietnam and Watergate" were "stalking the male American psyche all through the seventies" (205-06). He says, "It's not mere happenstance that women made such great strides in the seventies. It's because Vietnam and Watergate were so debilitating to the American male. You saw an opening and drove a terrific wedge right in. You found an enfeebled male population, and you saw an opening, and you came pouring through" (206). With mounting absurdity, he continues, "We lost our manhood, our sense of pride and honor, our belief in God and Dick Nixon, our deepest dreams, hopes and ambitions" (207). The ridiculousness of using Nixon as an excuse for erectile dysfunction signals that neither Cleo Birdwell nor Don DeLillo agrees with Sanders Meade. And the idea that women colluded with Vietnam and Watergate to gang up on weakened men is so preposterous that it, too, suggests that DeLillo and Birdwell are not ready to blame women for men's failures, and even implies that cultural norms of masculinity need to change to allow women to advance in society. In the sense that ***Amazons*** marks some of DeLillo's earliest investigations into culturally prescribed definitions of femininity and masculinity, this novel has been undeservedly ignored.

From ***Amazons*** to ***Underworld,*** a desire to be more gender-inclusive may also be seen in the increasing presence of female characters who launch DeLillovian cultural analyses and who can be presumed to speak for DeLillo himself. Klara's comments about the Cold War holding the world together because it allowed us to "measure hope and [. . .] measure destruction" (***Underworld*** 76) recur in DeLillo's own words in several ***Underworld***-period interviews.[15] Having female characters launch the sorts of cultural analyses usually spoken by DeLillo's male characters is not necessarily feminist, but it does suggest that women can speak for both genders and indicates a recognition of the effects of relegating such comments to only one gender. This change further suggests that DeLillo does not resist the cultural changes introduced by feminism, as have some male writers (Michael Crichton's trivialization of sexual harassment in *Disclosure,* for example).

That DeLillo investigates constructions of masculinity and femininity may surprise those who read his works as inhabiting an assumed (and therefore unexamined) masculine universe. But DeLillo's examination of gender should not be surprising. His work of the 1980s and 1990s responds to gender not because he is a feminist but because his books always register the zeitgeist. When his analyses of gender and power are sympathetic to the concerns of feminists, it is because once an awareness of masculinity, femininity, and sexuality enters popular consciousness, that awareness enters DeLillo's language, too. In 1988, *Vogue* magazine's Ann Arensberg asked, DeLillo, "What role can the writer play in our society [. . .]?" He responded,

> The writer is the person who stands outside society [. . .]. The writer is the man or woman who automatically takes a stand against his or her government. There are so many temptations for American writers to become part of the system and part of the structure that now, more than ever, we have to resist. American writers ought to stand and live in the margins, and be more dangerous.
>
> (Arensberg 390)

DeLillo has made that statement before and since that interview, but without the "his or her" locution; it seems possible that speaking to a female interviewer made him more aware of gendered language.[16] Similarly, when he takes on the perspective of his female characters, DeLillo becomes aware of gender as something that is constructed through language. Whether it is Klara Sax watching the *Unterwelt* premiere or Brita Nilsson photographing Rashid, these characters respond to and challenge the pervasive cultural influence of gender.

I suggest that in works from ***Amazons*** to ***Underworld,*** DeLillo has revealed a marked interest in advancing a critique of conventions of masculinity and femininity. To return to the Arensberg interview, among the "structure[s]" that his work begins to "take a stand against" and "resist" are the culturally enforced systems of gender inequality. We, as critics and readers, need to recognize this fact and the implications it has for DeLillo scholarship. If we do not, then our work will continue to replicate—albeit unintentionally—the idea that DeLillo is just another male writer unreflective about his own gender. That misperception can be curtailed if scholars and general readers realize the increasing degree to which DeLillo's work challenges the gender systems in which both the novelist and his characters are enmeshed.

Notes

1. This is not to dismiss any of these areas as unimportant. I am among those who have written on DeLillo and postmodernism (*Modern Fiction Studies* 45.3

[Fall 1999]), and there is more to be said on this topic and on all the topics listed. Rather, it surprises me that more has not been done in the many *other* areas ripe for critical attention.

2. Keesey's *Don DeLillo* (1993) spends a couple of paragraphs on *Amazons* (207-08) and, though not an extended study of gender in DeLillo's work, the book deserves mention here: in particular its chapters on *Players, Running Dog,* and *The Names* offer some critical recognition of DeLillo's imagining of male-female relationships (88-96, 101-04, 113-15, 123-24). Thomas J. Ferraro's "Whole Families Shopping at Night!" addresses how the marketplace simultaneously unifies and disrupts the family unit in *White Noise,* though the essay does not specifically address gender. Finally, Dallas Crow's "*Amazons,* Don DeLillo's Pseudonymous Novel," which spends just over two pages on *Amazons,* speculates on the novel's authorship and argues that more critical attention should be paid to it.

3. In *Don DeLillo,* Keesey says that although *Amazons* "was written as a collaboration," it is "unmistakably a Don DeLillo novel" (208). Keesey does not name DeLillo's collaborator. Curt Gardner, webmaster of *Don DeLillo's America* guesses that Gordon Lish—the editor, novelist, and close friend of DeLillo—may be the collaborator, but Curt is careful to stress that this is "only a guess." DeLillo himself seems to have an ambivalent relationship to the novel, sometimes acknowledging it and sometimes distancing himself from it. Joshua Roberts, who attended DeLillo's reading of *Underworld* at the 92nd Street Y in New York City on 27 October 1997, filed the following report for the website *Don DeLillo's America*: "Brought my copies of *Underworld* and *Amazons* to the table, the latter of which quite baffled the woman who was preparing offered books for signature. 'This is not by Mr. DeLillo.' 'It's a long story,' he said, dutifully taking the book and signing under the printed name of Cleo Birdwell. Under the circumstances, I could see I wasn't going to be able to ask for that story, which I very much wanted [. . .] to hear." If DeLillo admits authorship there, he also seems reluctant to have his authorship widely known. Mark Osteen, editor of the Viking Critical edition of *White Noise* (1998) reports that DeLillo crossed out *Amazons* in the biographical chronology prepared for the volume and crossed out all references to *Amazons* in Osteen's introduction. That DeLillo would both sign the book and remove it from this edition of *White Noise* suggests a conflicted relationship with the work. On that note, it bears mentioning that the names Don DeLillo and Cleo Birdwell both have a total of 10 letters, and that "Cleo Birdwell" not only contains the letters for "DeLillo" but also produces the anagrams "delillo Crew B" and "delillo Brew C," both of which suggest a second-or third-rate DeLillo novel.

4. The cover of the paperback edition (published the following year) goes even further. It changes the subtitle to "THE INTIMATE MEMOIR OF THE FIRST WOMAN PRO HOCKEY PLAYER AND HER SUCCESSFUL SEARCH FOR THE PERFECT MAN," shoehorning Birdwell into a marriage plot. This cover art shows a woman's legs from the top of the hips right down to the feet; the legs are upside-down, completely naked, and bent suggestively. Atop the left foot is an ice skate, on the right foot is a high-heeled shoe. As John Berger says in his discussion of the nude in *Ways of Seeing* (1972), if a painting of a woman as naked conveys her subjectivity, a painting of a woman as nude depicts her as an object. The German painter Dürer, Berger explains, "believed that the ideal nude ought to be constructed by taking the face of one body, the breasts of another, the shoulders of a fourth, [. . .] and so on" (62). In isolating the legs of this model, the cover designers have performed exactly this act. They have made her an object of a heterosexual, masculine gaze. The paperback cover clearly goes too far in suggesting that Cleo Birdwell's aim in life is to get married—she repeatedly tells us "All I want to do is play hockey" (10, 126, 162, 342)—but its tendency to objectify Cleo is often congruent with the novel's pornographic tendencies.

5. A similar example occurs when Cleo Birdwell refuses to endorse the Kelloid Company's snack treat and criticizes the company's attempt to commodify her to sell its product. Brandy Stratton, ad manager for Kelloid, enthusiastically tells Cleo about the commercial: "you skate around in slo-mo eating your Amazon Discos, and we hear your voice over the music. 'So, come home to Amazons,' you say. 'Amazon Ringos, Amazon Discos, Amazon Nuggets, Amazon Noshes. The new crackle-snackers from Kelloid's. Amazons. The snack we packed for women'" (315). Note that the novel's presentation of its dialogue parodically overemphasizes the hype of advertising lingo. Words like "crackle-snackers" and phrases like "The snack we packed for women" sound contrived, openly displaying their lack of sincerity. After the ad manager adds, "Then it starts snowing," Cleo cracks, "What does it snow, Amazon Brain Maggots?" (315-16). Challenging this attempt to use her celebrity to peddle junk food to women, Cleo again rejects the role of corporate pitchwoman, resisting being commodified into another Amazon product.

6. On this point, Wendy Steiner very aptly says of *White Noise* that "its themes—domesticity, environmentalism, the family, the problems of a woman's fulfillment and a man's attunement to her—ally it to feminist writing" (498).

7. *Libra,* too, offers a passing criticism of this ideal. When Delphine (Bannister's secretary) remarks, "I'm back on Metrecal," Bannister replies, "But you're a wisp, Delphine," his comment suggesting that she's dieting too much (65).

8. DeLillo is referring to a photograph of J. D. Salinger, one of the two photographs that (according to

DeLillo) inspired *Mao II.* He discusses this photograph—which appeared on the front page of the *New York Post* in 1988—in many interviews following the publication of the novel (see, for example, Passaro 76, Kirchhoff C2, Burn 36), but here is his most concise explanation: "His [Salinger's] face in the photograph was filled with shock and rage. And in fact he went after the photographers and pounded on the side of their car. In a way, ordering a picture of a reclusive person is like ordering an execution. In that picture, Salinger looks like a man who has been hunted down and finally found" (Marchand B7).

9. DeLillo has discussed Benjamin's essay in two interviews and employed its concept of aura in his novels. See Burn and Sjöholm. The Sjöholm interview is in Swedish, but according to David Thomson's unpublished translation, its English title is "Fiction saves us from confusion."

10. In *White Noise,* for example, Jack Gladney uses Hitler to make himself feel, as he puts it. "secure in my professional aura of power, madness, and death" (72). As Murray Siskind later tells Jack, "Some people are larger than life. Hitler is larger than death. You thought he would protect you" (287).

11. One of the unspoken rules of American masculinity is that it be aggressively, obviously heterosexual masculinity. Indeed, the requirement of *heterosexuality* is so apparent that those who wish to enforce this construct need not even speak its name; they merely assume that to be "a man" is to be "straight." Lee's masculinity is challenged for precisely the reason that he does not appear as "manly" as his harassers think he ought to be. As a child, he is asked, "Lee? That a girl's name or what?" (7) and called a "fruit" and a "fag-a-teer" by other children (9). When he's an adult, he is called "maricón" (97) ("maricon" is Spanish for "gay") and worries about being seen by other marines at a "swishy bar" (89). DeLillo does not portray Oswald as a gay man but one who is persecuted for being read as gay, for not conforming strictly to "norms" of heterosexual masculinity. Indeed, DeLillo allows us to read Oswald as sexually ambivalent: David Ferrie dry-humps him (341), but Lee also pursues Ella Germain (199) and marries Marina (203).

12. As a very young boy, Lee witnessed and was on the receiving end of violence. *Libra* shows him witnessing the killing of a neighborhood cat (5-6), getting beaten up for talking like a Yankee (33), being beaten by military guards (101-05). These experiences stay with him, reinforcing the sense that power depends on violence. When, for example, he watches the crowd at an Edwin A. Walker rally, he sees the people's thuggishness in very personal terms: "He felt the smallness and the rancor of these people. They need to knock someone to the ground and stomp him for fifteen minutes. Feel better now?" (372). In addition to recalling exactly the violent beatings that he and cellmate Bobby Dupard received in military prison, this description shows Oswald identifying with a group of people based on both their "smallness" and their "rancor." Though he does not agree with their politics, he is able to empathize with both how small and how angry they feel—because he, too, feels small and angry. A sense of helplessness motivates their violence, and will motivate Oswald's violence, too.

13. When he sees John Wayne visiting some officers, Lee has difficulty separating the actor from the roles he plays. Standing at a near distance, Lee "watches John Wayne talk and laugh. It's remarkable and startling to see the screen laugh repeated in real life. It makes him feel good" (93). Though he should get back to work, Lee permits himself to get caught up in John Wayne's screen persona, imagining the actor "rearing mounts, trail hands yahooing, the music and rousing song, the honest stubbled faces (men he feels he knows), all the glory and dust of the great drive north" (94). Given his tendency to see the actor as the characters he portrays, it is not surprising that Lee sees his role as assassin as a role, a way to become one of the movie stars he admires.

14. Except that, as Jack Gladney discovers, violence has consequences in real life. No sooner does Lee Oswald shoot at the president than he begins to worry about getting caught. Unlike Jack, Lee does not experience a sudden sympathy for the victim, but he does begin to second-guess himself and grow afraid of being discovered and arrested. Readers, familiar with the history, know that Lee will not only get caught but shot and killed himself (an event which DeLillo also dramatizes in *Libra*), reminding us that taking on the role of violent masculinity is a dangerous part to play.

15. DeLillo tells *Fresh Air*'s Terry Gross that "events used to be calibrated to the phenomenon of awesome Cold War conflict, even events that had no connection to the U. S. or U. S. S. R. This curious measurability has disappeared with the end of the Cold War." To David Streitfeld, DeLillo says that with the end of the Cold War "there seemed to be no more measuring devices for money, for fame." And he remarks to Andrew Billen, "It is possible that in some curious way people will begin to feel nostalgia for the Cold War, for the enormous biblical power of atomic weapons, but more readily for the sense of measurable certainties and clearly defined confrontation."

16. In 1997, for example, responding to George Will's editorial on *Libra* (which famously called DeLillo a "bad citizen"), DeLillo says "being called a 'bad citizen' is a compliment to my mind. That's exactly what we ought to do. We ought to be bad citizens. We ought to, in the sense that we're writing against what power represents, and often what government represents, and what the corporation dictates, and what consumer consciousness has come to mean. In that sense, if we're bad citizens, we're doing our

job" (Remnick 48). In another *Underworld*-period article, he says, "The novel works against the culture, as something should, as something must" (Billen). Or, as he explains in 1992, "Serious writers risk becoming part of the Muzak, the elevator music of American culture because the culture seems to absorb anything that resembles danger. [. . .] Graham Greene said the writer has to be the 'grit' in the state machine. Salman Rushdie said writers have to make new maps of reality. But as soon as you do these things, you are invited to dinner parties or to speak on PBS. One way or another, you are incorporated" (Roberts 1, 5). In the 1991 *Paris Review* interview, DeLillo remarks, "We have a rich literature. But sometimes it's a literature too ready to be neutralized, to be incorporated into the ambient noise. This is why we need the writer in opposition, the novelist who writes against power, who writes against the corporation or the state or the whole apparatus of assimilation. We're all one beat away from becoming elevator music" (Begley 290) That same year, DeLillo expresses a preference for fiction "that takes account of ways in which our perceptions are being changed by events around us" (Marchand B7). Some ten years prior to that, DeLillo tells Tom LeClair, "The writer is working against the age and so he feels some satisfaction in not being widely read. He is diminished by an audience" (87). And in 1978, DeLillo reflects, "If there's one thing my books have in common, one common thread, it's the individual faced with a vast structure, even a landscape; one person adrift, faced with a monumental superstructure that he can't make headway against" (Debra Rae Cohen 13). Only twice does DeLillo use "he" (LeClair, Cohen): he otherwise prefers "we" (Remnick), "they" (Roberts), "you" (Roberts [again]), "who" (Begley), or refers to the novels themselves (Billen, Marchand, Cohen).

Works Cited

Begley, Adam. "Don DeLillo: The Art of Fiction." *Paris Review* 35.128 (Fall 1993): 274-306.

Benjamin, Walter. "The Work of Art in the Age of Mechanical Reproduction." 1936. *Illuminations*. New York: Schocken, 1985. 217-51.

Berger, John. *Ways of Seeing*. 1972. London: British Broadcasting Corporation and Penguin Books, 1977.

Birdwell, Cleo [Don DeLillo]. *Amazons*. New York: Holt, 1980.

Billen, Andrew. "Up from the Underworld." *London Evening Standard* 28 Jan. 1998. <http://www.thislondon.co.uk/dynamic/lifestyle/bottom_review.html?in_review_id=26802&in_review_text_id=20603.

Burn, Gordon. "Wired Up and Whacked Out." *Sunday Times Magazine* (London) 25 Aug. 1991: 36-37, 39.

Butler, Judith. *Gender Trouble: Feminism and the Subversion of Identity*. New York and London: Routledge, 1990.

Cohen, Debra Rae. "De Wild, De Wicked, De Führer and DeLillo." *Crawdaddy* Oct. 1978: 13-14.

Crow, Dallas. "*Amazons,* Don DeLillo's Pseudonymous Novel." *Notes on Contemporary Literature* 28.5 (Nov. 1998): 2-4.

DeLillo, Don. *Americana*. 1971. New York: Penguin, 1989.

———. Interview with Tom LeClair. *Anything Can Happen: Interviews with Contemporary American Novelists*. Ed. Tom LeClair and Larry McCaffery. Urbana: U of Illinois P, 1983. 79-90.

———. Interview with Maria Nadotti. *Salmagundi* 100 (Fall 1993): 86-97.

———. "In the Men's Room of the Sixteenth Century." *Esquire* Dec. 1971: 174-77, 243, 246.

———. *Libra*. New York: Viking, 1988.

———. *Mao II*. New York: Viking, 1991.

———. *The Names*. 1982. New York: Vintage, 1983.

———. *Players*. 1977. New York: Vintage, 1989.

———. *Running Dog*. 1978. New York: Vintage, 1989.

———. "Shooting Bill Gray." *Esquire* Jan. 1991: 92-96.

———. "Silhouette City: Hitler, Manson, and the Millennium." *Dimensions* 4.3 (1988): 29-34.

———. *Underworld*. New York: Scribner, 1997.

———. *White Noise*. New York: Viking, 1985.

"Don DeLillo: The Word, the Image and the Gun." Dir. Kim Evans. BBC 1. 27 Sept. 1991.

Douglas, Susan J. *Where the Girls Are*. New York: Times Books, 1995.

Dworkin, Andrea. *Pornography: Men Possessing Women*. New York: Perigree, 1981.

Engles, Tim. "'Who Are You, Literally?': Fantasies of the White Self in *White Noise*." *Modern Fiction Studies* 45.3 (Fall 1999): 755-87.

Faludi, Susan. *Backlash: The Undeclared War Against American Women*. 1991. New York: Anchor, 1992.

———. *Stiffed: The Betrayal of the American Man*. New York: Morrow, 1999.

Ferraro, Thomas J. "Whole Families Shopping at Night!" *New Essays on* White Noise. Ed. Frank Lentricchia. New York: Cambridge UP, 1991. 15-38.

Gardner, Curt. *Don DeLillo's America.* <http://perival.com/delillo/delillo.html.

———. E-mail to the author. 18 April 1996.

Gross, Terry. Interview with Don DeLillo. *Fresh Air.* NPR. 2 Oct. 1997.

Katz, Jackson. "Advertising and the Construction of Violent White Masculinity." *Gender, Race and Class in Media: A Text-Reader.* Ed. Gail Dines and Jean M. Humez. Thousand Oaks, CA: SAGE, 1995. 133-41.

Katz, Jackson, and Sut Jhally. "The National Conversation in the Wake of Littleton Is Missing the Mark." *Boston Globe* 2 May 1999: E1.

Keesey, Douglas. *Don DeLillo.* New York: Twayne, 1993.

Kirchhoff, H. J. "Influence of Novelists on the Wane?" *Toronto Globe and Mail* 26 June 1991: C2.

LeClair, Tom. *In the Loop: Don DeLillo and the Systems Novel.* Urbana and Chicago: U of Illinois P, 1987.

Marchand, Philip. "Being Reclusive Means Never Having to Tell Your Story." *Toronto Star* 27 June 1991: B7.

Mulvey, Laura. "Visual Pleasure and Narrative Cinema." *Feminisms: An Anthology of Literary Theory and Criticism.* Eds. Robyn R. Warhol and Diane Price Herndl. New Brunswick, NJ: Rutgers UP, 1991. 432-42.

Nel, Philip. "'A Small Incisive Shock': Modern Forms, Postmodern Politics, and the Role of the Avant-Garde in *Underworld.*" *Modern Fiction Studies* 45.3 (Fall 1999): 724-52.

Osteen, Mark. Telephone conversation with the author. 29 May 1999.

Palac, Lisa. "How Dirty Pictures Changed My Life." *Next: Young American Writers on the Next Generation.* Ed. Eric Liu. New York: Norton, 1994. 146-163.

Remnick, David. "Exile on Main Street." *New Yorker* 15 Sept. 1997: 42-48.

Roberts. Margaret. "'D' is for Danger—and for Writer Don DeLillo." *Chicago Tribune* 22 May 1992. Sec. 5: 1, 5.

Roberts, Joshua. "DeLillo in New York City." 17 May 1999. <http://perival.com/delillo/delillo_19971027.html. Part of Curt Gardner's webpage *Don DeLillo's America.*

Sjöholm, Cecilia. "Fiktion räddar oss från förvirring." July 1997. <http://www.aftonbladet.se/kultur/7.94/DeLillo.html.

Steiner, Wendy. "Postmodern Fictions, 1970-1990." *The Cambridge History of American Literature.* Ed. Sacvan Bercovitch. Vol. 7. Cambridge: Cambridge UP, 1999. 425-538.

Streitfeld. David. "Don DeLillo's Hidden Truths." *Washington Post* 11 Nov. 1997: D1+ 13 Nov. 1997 <http://washingtonpost.com/wp-srv/WPlate/1997-11/11/0301-111197-idx.html.

"Student Violence in America's Schools." *New York Times on the Web* 1 June 1999 <http://www.nytimes.com/learning/general/specials/schoolviolence/index.html.

Traber, Daniel S. "The Crisis of Whiteness in DeLillo's *White Noise.*" Conference paper. American Literature Association: 10th Annual Conference on American Literature. Renaissance Harborplace Hotel, Baltimore, MD. 30 May 1999.

We Were Strangers. Dir. John Huston. Perf. John Garfield and Jennifer Jones. Columbia Pictures, 1949.

Will, George F. "Shallow Look at the Mind of an Assassin." *Washington Post* 22 Sept. 1998: A25.

Wolf, Naomi. *The Beauty Myth: How Images of Beauty Are Used Against Women.* New York: Doubleday, 1991.

Virginia Quarterly Review (review date summer 2001)

SOURCE: Review of *The Body Artist,* by Don DeLillo. *Virginia Quarterly Review* 77, no. 3 (summer 2001): 99.

[*In the following review, the critic contrasts* The Body Artist *with DeLillo's other novels, noting its stylistic austerity and brevity.*]

This book ***The Body Artist*** marks a departure for Don DeLillo as a novelist and is not calculated to please admirers of his earlier work. With its austere prose, brief compass, and enigmatic narrative, it reads more like a novel by J. M. Coetzee than by the author of ***White Noise, Libra,*** and ***Underworld. The Body Artist*** lacks the verbal energy, sprawling story, broad canvas, and kaleidoscopic cast of characters that distinguish DeLillo's famous novels. Instead he offers an intense, virtually claustrophobic focus on less than a handful of characters, who remain shadowy and deliberately unrealized. The novel is so quiet that one could hear a pin drop, as it were; indeed DeLillo devotes a whole paragraph to the falling of a paper clip. The mood of the work is captured in a typical passage: "She took a bite of cereal and forgot to taste it. She lost the taste somewhere between the time she put the food in her mouth and the regretful second she swallowed it." ***The Body Artist*** has a kind of stark beauty all its own, but DeLillo seems to have strayed from what he does best as a novelist.

Laura Barrett (essay date winter 2001/2002)

SOURCE: Barrett, Laura. "'How the Dead Speak to the Living': Intertextuality and the Postmodern Sublime in *White Noise*." *Journal of Modern Literature* 25, no. 2 (winter 2001/2002): 97-113.

[*In the following essay, Barrett explicates the significance of intertextuality in* White Noise, *identifying the novel's use of other texts as a metaphor for its thematic focus on beginnings and ends.*]

The simulacrum, "a copy without an original,"[1] is the most salient metaphor of ***White Noise,*** a novel in which simulations exploit real catastrophes, and in which tourists visit the "most photographed barn in America" not to see the barn but to see photographs of the barn. Further emphasizing the distance between experience and expression is the novel's emphasis on the ineluctably representative nature of language. The disconnection between signifier and signified, pointedly demonstrated in conversations between the narrator, Jack Gladney, and his son, Heinrich, and the collapse of etymologically sound meaning (such as the absence of Germans in Germantown) suggest that words, too, are copies without originals. Déjà vu, one of the many shifting symptoms of contamination from the airborne toxic event, renders memory itself suspect, suggesting that the earlier experiences upon which recollections seem to depend may not exist. The lack of originating moments results in a persistent conversation with the past, an overwhelming nostalgia for a more stable moment in history. Academics and housewives routinely seek distraction in news of James Dean and Marilyn Monroe because, as Murray Siskind, a visiting lecturer on Elvis Presley, aptly notes, "'[h]elpless and fearful people are drawn to magical figures, mythic figures'"; and the narrator, Jack Gladney, fashions his world around a dead fascist in the interest of self-preservation.[2] But it is not just individual characters who are in conversation with the past: DeLillo's entire narrative is a dialogue with older literary works, including sacred texts, Puritan sermons, westerns, and Modernist and Postmodernist fiction.

As Douglas Keesey notes, the novel is a generic hybrid, a nexus of types of fiction—the domestic drama, the college satire, the apocalyptic melodrama, the crime novel, the social satire.[3] That trespassing of boundaries which is typical of Postmodern fiction reminds us that we are the product of myriad representations, and DeLillo's refusal to tie up the loose ends in the novel's conclusion confirms that ***White Noise*** is not the last in the series of representations. In addition to maneuvering between reality and art—as Adolf Hitler and Howard Hughes become the icons of invented characters—the reader is required to negotiate between DeLillo's fictional world and previous fictional worlds, but this intertextuality[4] does more than simply remind the reader of the novel's artifice: it places ***White Noise*** within a long tradition of Western literature. DeLillo invokes older texts that might shed some light on a contemporary crisis in which the novel's characters find themselves betwixt and between, unmoored from a clear point of origin (be it divine or psychological) and ill at ease with death as the final destination. When Jack is told that "SIMUVAC" stands for "simulated evacuation," he is forced to point out that the airborne toxic event has generated a real evacuation. Incredulously, he asks, "'Are you saying you saw a chance to use the real event in order to rehearse the simulation?'" (p. 139). The expected order of events has been inverted: event precedes rehearsal. The result is a life hopelessly circular and illogical, not unlike conversations between Jack and his son, in which origin is indistinguishable from terminus. Aware that language is merely representational, that the self is constructed (in large part from media role models), and that religion is a pretense (even for the German nuns), the characters are homesick, nostalgic for a past in which the ego seemed less fragile and arbitrary and language bore some relationship to objective reality. Jack especially turns to the past in the hope of finding a beginning, but, as the intertexts confirm, humans have never had access to the prototype; our lives are mediated. The only virgin land is death, and so the characters shuttle between simulations, afraid to face that which has not been mediated.

Many critics, most famously Fredric Jameson, have argued that Postmodern pastiche is a neutral borrowing from previous sources, an irresponsible romp through literary, historical, and artistic archives without any particular point or recognition of the previous works' contexts. Linda Hutcheon, however, argues that intertextuality[5] is

> not ahistorical or de-historicizing; it does not wrest past art from its original historical context and reassemble it into some sort of presentist spectacle. Instead, through a double process of installing and ironizing, parody signals how present representations come from past ones and what ideological consequences derive from both continuity and difference.[6]

Perhaps it is ironic that DeLillo would choose to address an existential crisis, in which characters cannot experience anything for the first time, through intertextuality, which necessarily challenges notions of originality and singularity. After all, ***White Noise*** is about so much more than the metafictionality of Postmodern literature, and its allusions to previous texts are not lamentations about the impossibility of creating fiction after all the good stuff has been taken; they speak of humanity's preoccupation with death. We invent myths in part to make sense of the end, and, so, DeLillo's intertextuality connects readers as well as texts. That chasm between the past and present, between experience and recollection/recreation is described in ***White Noise*** as the "space between things as we felt them at the time and as we speak them now. This is the space reserved for irony, sympathy and fond amusement, the means by which we rescue ourselves from the past" (p. 30). This is not the misprison of anxiety of influence; it is, indeed, a shrewd and sympathetic response to a cultural as well as a literary legacy. DeLillo's Postmodernism here is best viewed in terms of another statement uttered by Jack: "[W]hen tradition becomes too flexible, irony enters the voice" (p. 86), but the irony here, as earlier, is "sweet," "entirely sincere." Jack's wistful longing for narratives of the past is understandable in light of their promises of personal integration in the face of fragmentation, of transcendental meaning in the midst of misprision, of cosmic order in the moment of chaos. Initially, Jack's appreciation for these narratives is unmitigated by his position in history: his impulse is to revive the epic form, informing it with contemporary events. Indeed, Jack replaces sex with reminiscence as he and Babette peruse old photograph albums, looking at "[c]hildren wincing in the sun, women in sun hats, men shading their eyes from the glare as if the past possessed some quality of light we no longer experience" (p. 30). Through repeated failed attempts to borrow language and behavior from other traditions, Jack finally learns that those gestures do not hold, but, as Tom LeClair notes, "the achievement of ***White Noise*** [. . . is that] DeLillo presses beyond the ironic, extracting from his initially satiric materials a sense of wonderment or mystery."[7] ***White Noise***'s intertextuality is thus a recognition of our indebtedness to previous representations and a metaphor for the novel's thematic concern with origin and end.

* * *

The first chapter of DeLillo's novel invites the reader into a world of unstable origins and initiates the novel's intertextuality. A line of station wagons delivers parents and their children to "College-on-the-Hill," a setting which echoes John Winthrop's lay sermon onboard the *Arbella* in which he predicted that the incipient Puritan colony would be a "city on a hill," the new Jerusalem, the object of pitiless European scrutiny, whose constituents, like the adolescents in Blacksmith's college, have emigrated to form a new community. Winthrop's "A Model of Christian Charity" describes a social order contingent upon economic difference—"All men being thus (by divine providence) ranked into two sorts, rich and poor"—which is overcome by charity.[8] Using the metaphor of a body, Winthrop argues that in such a world, everyone's place is clearly marked, and success hinges upon cooperation. DeLillo has taken the nexus of economics and spiritual salvation to form an elect in which quasi-spiritual fulfillment is irrevocably linked to wealth:

> The parents stand sun-dazed near their automobiles, seeing images of themselves in every direction. The conscientious suntans. The well-made faces and wry looks. They feel a sense of renewal, of communal recognition. . . . This assembly of station wagons, as much as anything they might do in the course of the year, more than formal liturgies or laws, tells the parents they are a collection of the like-minded and the spiritually akin, a people, a nation.
>
> (pp. 3-4)

DeLillo's language is not as far afield of Winthrop's as one might assume, for in the latter's vision the "city on a hill" will thrive because its constituents are "akin": "This is the cause why the Lord loves the creature, so far as it hath any of his image in it; he loves his elect because they are like himself. . . . Thus it is between the members of Christ. Each discerns, by the work of the spirit, his own image and resemblance in another, and therefore cannot but love him as he loves himself."[9] It is no surprise that this is a community from which rebels, Roger Williams and Anne Hutchinson to name two, were exiled. The Puritan diaspora, then, paves the way for a contemporary world in which we seek community through sameness via mass media. In his first novel, DeLillo observes that the "third-person [consciousness] . . . , the man we all want to be," an essential element in consumerism, "came over on the *Mayflower*."[10] ***Mao II*** presents uncanny similarities among American consumerism, cult mysticism, and Puritan eschatology. Indeed, the description of a mass marriage ceremony in Yankee Stadium sounds disconcertingly like an account of the Puritan millennial impulse: "there is a sense . . . that the future is pressing in, collapsing toward them, that they are everywhere surrounded by signs of the fated landscape and human struggle of the Last Days."[11] That the same passage could describe such different objects only confirms the correspondences between past and present. Moreover, typology, the study of symbolic representation, which allowed the Puritans, like many Christians before them, to understand contemporary history in light of Scripture, provides an early example of simulacra.[12] Puritans viewed themselves and world events as corresponding to Old and New Testament episodes. Thus, while Puritanism recalls a time when past and future ostensibly coalesced meaningfully, offering solace to those living between origin and end, it, too, was subject to mediation.

As important a force of cultural construction as America's Puritan heritage is the western, whose influence is seen in the novel's first sentence: "The station wagons arrived at noon, a long shining line that coursed through the west campus" (p. 3). DeLillo's reference is both nostalgic and parodic. The train of station wagons transporting the American public incongruously represents suburban America and recalls the Wild West, those days before shopping malls and highways pockmarked the American landscape, just as the town's name evokes a quintessential western setting while reminding us of the gap between language and reference evident in the lack of blacksmiths in Blacksmith. The items transported by the wagons are similarly incongruous: boots, quilts, sleeping bags, rucksacks, Western saddles, bows and arrows travel alongside skis, inflated rafts, stereo sets, radios, personal computers, small refrigerators, and other assorted electrical gadgetry, sports paraphernalia, and junk food unknown in the Wild West; and the noontime arrival recalls the prototypical hour of conflict between hero(es) and villain(s) most famously enacted in *High Noon.* Through his use of the words "wagon" and "shining," DeLillo conflates the religious and western foundations of American culture. The station wagons—symbolic both of western heroism and middle-class suburbia—are literally the lifeblood of the culture "cours[ing]" through the campus, raising the issue of individual as well as cultural ontology. As one of the few peculiarly American genres, the western, like Puritanism, mythologizes past and future, origin and destiny, qualities painfully missing in postmodern society. But, just as importantly, western literature and the films that later embodied the myth focus on what many critics have viewed as the central theme of American literature: the individual versus the community. Families travel across various geographies in order to arrive at the novel's promised land, College-on-the-Hill, and, in doing so, they surrender particularities, "seeing images of themselves in every direction" (p. 3). These individuals are interchangeable: "The women crisp and alert, in diet trim, knowing people's names. Their husbands content to measure out the time, distant but ungrudging" (p. 3). The parents are stereotypes, men and women without individual identities, and their automobiles, all of a type, appear, without specified origins, in the middle of the day, in the middle of the country, in a town with a Mid-Village Mall and a Middlebrook Road, in a place lacking a clear connection to a beginning and an end.

Far from its roots in Protestantism and the western, ***White Noise*** presents a world in which individuality is replaced by media role models and God is replaced by an ATM. The loss of self and spirituality is sorely felt by Jack, a character who attempts, often parodically, to infuse his mundane and superficial life with some grander meaning. For the characters in this novel, religion is a hollow husk, and millennial transformations are more likely to be synthetic than metaphysical. Indeed, ***White Noise*** is a meditation on the impossibility of divine apocalypse, the unlikelihood of cosmic revelations, which, like all other grand narratives, no longer obtain. So, it is not without irony that DeLillo's working title for ***White Noise,*** "The American Book of the Dead,"[13] recalls several sacred texts: the Egyptian and Tibetan books of the dead, guidebooks for the dead on their journey to the underworld, and Revelations, the last book in the New Testament. Murray views the supermarket as an analogue to the Tibetan notion of death as a waiting place:

> This place recharges us spiritually, it prepares us, it's a gateway or pathway. Look how bright. It's full of psychic data. . . . Everything is concealed in symbolism, hidden by veils of mystery and layers of cultural material. . . . All the letters and numbers are here, all the colors of the spectrum, all the voices and sounds, all the code words and ceremonial phrases. It is just a question of deciphering, rearranging, peeling off the layers of unspeakability. Not that we would want to, not that any useful purpose would be served.
>
> (pp. 37-38)

While Murray is too farcical to be taken completely seriously as a spokesman for spiritual fulfillment, the supermarket's importance—as a site of competing languages, of guides to the occult,[14] and of mystery—cannot be entirely dismissed. In the same scene, moreover, Murray calls the supermarket "a revelation" (p. 38), thus connecting Eastern and Western guides to death. Arising from a crisis in faith caused by persecution, The Book of Revelation, a particularly important document for Puritans, predicts the end of its era and the coming of a new Jerusalem.[15] Moreover, the prophecy itself is revealed to John, the formal version of the diminutive Jack, our guide in ***White Noise.*** Particularly useful in terms of my discussion of intertextuality is the fact that Apocalypse, as the work is sometimes called, is a rearrangement of Old Testament symbolism applied to the time and situation of the author.[16] Exegetical scholars generally attribute the book to a compiler rather than an individual author, highlighting its complicated origin. However complicated the origin of the text may be, origin itself is clear in Revelations. The voice speaking to John, the prophet, announces, "Behold, I make all things new. . . . Write this, for these words are trustworthy and true. . . . I am Alpha and Omega, the beginning and the end."[17] The role of the prophet is particularly important in Revelations, as the author is commanded to pass on the message. Tradition claims that the author of Revelations is also the author of The Gospel According to John, and the two texts share a devotion to the word: "In the beginning was the Word, and the Word was with God, and the Word was God."[18] Indeed, the rider of a white horse that emerges from the heavens in Revelations is "called Faithful and True." Although his name is known by no one but himself, he is called "The Word of God," and "[f]rom his mouth issues a sharp sword with which to smite the nations."[19] The rider's name is unspoken, perhaps because it will not be understood by humans, and his words are linked to violence through the metaphor of the sword. Moreover, "The Word of God" itself—the prophet whose utterances are true and piercing—is depicted in terms of color and sound—white noise.[20]

* * *

White Noise's allusions to all three of these sacred texts serve to underscore Americans' unpreparedness for death: characters in ***White Noise*** cannot even think of death, much less philosophically plan for it. The narrator, Jack, attempts to outwit death by immersing himself in language, a medium which he believes controls reality, a faith in language perhaps stemming from Genesis, the story of creation in which God literally speaks the world into existence and bestows upon Adam the gift of naming creatures. The expulsion from Eden results in a violent separation of word and meaning, and language, which has not previously had to deal with abstractions such as death, now becomes symbolic, conceptual. Ironically, in ***White Noise,*** to alleviate the dread of death—a by-product of the Fall—humans can resort to a drug that makes the association between word and object terrifyingly real, so that the phrase "a hail of bullets" effects a physical response. The end result is that language is more distanced from its meaning than ever before: when the speeding bullet, the plunging aircraft, the raining fusillade do not materialize to justify the crouched pseudo-victim taking cover behind a sofa, the masquerade of language is revealed.

Unlike Murray Siskind, the quintessential postmodernist, Jack yearns for stable and transcendent meaning, hence his academic reliance on the magic of language and his occupation as Chair of Hitler Studies. He assumes that the German language is the source of Hitler's power:

> I'd made several attempts to learn German, serious probes into origins, structures, roots. I sensed the deathly power of the language. I wanted to speak it well, use it as a charm, a protective device. The more I shrank from learning actual words, rules and pronunciation, the more important it seemed that I go forward. What we are reluctant to touch often seems the very fabric of our salvation. But the basic sounds defeated me. . . .
>
> (p. 31)

The unspoken but omnipresent reference to language in the novel is Hitler's celebrated oratorical skills, the talent of effecting reality through words. For the sake of his profession, Jack becomes J. A. K. Gladney, a bulkier, vaguely threatening manifestation of his former self, and his son is given a German name because it presumably evokes strength. But the problem with language is its imprecision, and Jack's insistence on a one-to-one correspondence between word and meaning is the source of his existential angst.[21] A seemingly simple statement by Jack's son Orest which appears to quantify the dead gives rise to a semiotic nightmare for Jack and his son, Heinrich:

> "There are many more people dead today than in the rest of world history put together. . . ."
>
> I looked at my son. I said, "Is he trying to tell us there are more people dying in this twenty-four-hour period than in the rest of human history up to now?"
>
> "He's saying the dead are greater today than ever before, combined."
>
> "What dead? Define the dead."
>
> "He's saying people now dead."
>
> "What do you mean, now dead? Everybody who's dead is now dead."
>
> "He's saying people in graves. The known dead. Those you can count."
>
> I was listening intently, trying to grasp what they meant. . . .
>
> "But people sometimes stay in graves for hundreds of years. Is he saying there are more dead people in graves than anywhere else?"
>
> "It depends on what you mean by anywhere else."
>
> "I don't know what I mean. The drowned. The blown-to-bits."
>
> "There are more dead now than ever before. That's all he's saying."
>
> (p. 266)

The rising drama of the dialogue, its augmented sense of urgency, seems to be connected to the increased realization of a breakdown of language on a fundamental level. We can no longer accept such words as "dead," "now," and "anywhere else" as givens. The very fabric of communication is fraying as it is being used. And if language's inherent instability is not sufficiently demoralizing, the originator of the contested sentence is silent for the subsequent conversation. In his place, Heinrich mediates. We can never be sure if the volley of inquiry and answer between Jack and Heinrich approximates Orest's meaning. Moreover, Jack's comprehension of his own meaning disintegrates under the pressure. And, for that matter, Heinrich's interpretation is easily read as an observation of the increasing importance of the dead: "the dead are greater today than ever before." Finally, no one seems to understand the symbolic reading of Orest's original statement: even the living are dead.

Recognizing that Heinrich's name has not granted him immortality or even a justifiable youthfulness, Jack suspects there is something more powerful than the magic spell of language, and that is death: "'Let me whisper the terrible word, from the Old English, from the Old German, from the Old Norse. *Death* . . . Processions, songs, speeches, dialogues with the dead, recitations of the names of the dead'" (p. 73). What is powerful, then, about Hitler's speeches is its fatalistic content. Clearly, Jack chooses Hitler studies because it enables him to trace a cultural nightmare—along the individual words that sparked it—back to a beginning, which also happens to be an end: death. So many of the novel's hilarious conversations center on death—the account of Tommy Lee Foster's murder of six, Jack's and Babette's verbal duel to determine whose fear of death is greater, and Jack's encounter with the SIMUVAC technician in which he attempts to establish (with the verification of an appropriate expert) how he feels. Even the semantic debate about climate evokes the connection between language and violence when Jack coerces Heinrich to answer a question by inventing a theoretical gun-toting man who wants to know if it is raining. Indeed the closest we come to a classic showdown in the novel is not Jack's parodic shoot-out with Willie Mink, but his classroom debate with Murray, in which each professor tries to eclipse the other with macabre stories of their dead icons.

* * *

Beyond suggesting more than our distance from other cultural views of death, DeLillo's working title evokes the literary history of our legacy. "The American Book of the Dead" is the first of a series of significations upon the last story in Joyce's *Dubliners*.[22] What DeLillo has created in ***White Noise*** is literally an American book of "The Dead."[23] Indeed, Bernard Wilcox's characterization of Jack Gladney "as a modernist displaced in a postmodern world"[24] explains the pervasive reverberations of Joyce, the quintessential Modernist, as an attempt to locate late twentieth-century experience and literature in a humanist framework, in which death is poetic and biological rather than numerical and technological.

While DeLillo's working title indicated a more direct relation to "The Dead," his chosen title reflects the two central metaphors of Joyce's tale: snow and music. Like the eponymous backdrop of ***White Noise,*** the snow of Joyce's story symbolizes a democratic and pervasive death. Music both links his characters to the past and precludes conversations in the present. Although the piano playing obscures the deadness and stillness of Dublin, Joyce's world is every bit as cacophonous as DeLillo's: Gabriel Conroy is ever attending the sounds of rustling skirts, "[t]he indelicate clacking of the men's heels," the clatter of knives and forks.[25] Applause, laughter, and, of course, music provide a steady background noise against which dialogues drop. Whereas anesthesia pervades Dublin, synesthesia plagues Blacksmith.[26] Technology collapses the boundaries between senses so that sound becomes visual, but the result is no different. Citizens of Blacksmith are no more reconciled to their surroundings than are residents of Dublin; in fact, the bombardment of stimuli and information proves a formidable anesthetic.

Like Gabriel Conroy's mourning of bygone civility, Jack laments the present age's fragmentation and desperately attempts to link his own decade with a legendary past which might offer some promise for a future.[27] The "epic quality" of the flight of pedestrians during the evacuation forces Jack to reconsider the enormity of the disaster: "they seemed to be part of some ancient destiny, connected in doom and ruin to a whole history of people trekking across wasted landscapes" (p. 122). Jack compares the evacuation of the Boy Scout Camp to "the fall of a colonial capital to dedicated rebels. A great surging drama with elements of humiliation and guilt" (p. 157). Likening his own twentieth-century adventure to "wagon trains converging on the Santa Fe Trail" (p. 159), Jack recalls his earlier references to the western. When no valid explanation of Wilder's seven hours of crying is offered, Jack attributes it to "a period of wandering in some remote and holy place, in sand barrens or snowy ranges—a place where things are said" (p. 79). His own life gives rise to a similar mythic reading when Jack rescues Willie Mink after shooting him: "There was a spaciousness to this moment, an epic pity and compassion" (p. 315). Echoes of Apocalypse recur when Jack, upon seeing a white-haired figure on his lawn, assumes that the grim reaper is paying a visit. The figure becomes preternatural in Jack's eyes: "motionless and knowing" (p. 243), the bearer of "an ancient and terrible secret" (p. 244), the white hair a sign of age or "emblematic . . . of his allegorical force" (p. 243). Undermining the repeated bids for grandiosity is Jack's own satiric tone heard in a one-sentence paragraph following the pseudo-apocalyptic drama: "It was not Death that stood before me but only Vernon Dickey, my father-in-law" (p. 244). Jack's distance from the young narrator of "Araby" is the difference between the latter's utter humiliation at his own folly—the confusion of infatuation and love—and the former's seeming nonchalance at mistaking his father-in-law for the grim reaper. Jack and his Joycean counterparts hunger for the same ideals but respond differently to their disappointments.

Ironically, the very Modernist narrative that Jack hungers for is replete with its own retrospection. Nostalgia permeates the annual Christmas party of "The Dead," provoking phrases such as "[t]hose were the days," "never-to-be-forgotten," and "[t]hirty years ago."[28] Both tenors and politicians have diminished over time, and according to Gabriel Conroy,

> this new generation, educated or hypereducated as it is, will lack those qualities of humanity, of hospitality, of kindly humor which belonged to an older day. Listening tonight to the names of all those great singers of the past it seemed to me, I must confess, that we were living in a less spacious age. Those days might, without exaggeration, be called spacious days.[29]

Both Gabriel and Jack seek the legendary spaciousness of the past, allegedly obliterated in a constricting, shrinking world.

Gabriel's allusions to Greek mythology and Victorian poetry are Jack's "[d]ecorative gestures [that] add romance to a life" (p. 9). The academic robes worn at the College-on-the-Hill attempt, for Jack, to contradict the a-romantic "digital watch blinking in late summer dusk" (p. 9). Jack's narrative mode, like the academic robe, embellishes a disjointed life and attempts to make meaningful the seemingly random. But his efforts are constantly thwarted by the discontinuities of postmodern society:

> Babette and I and our children by previous marriages live at the end of a quiet street in what was once a wooded area with deep ravines. There is an expressway beyond the backyard now, well below us, and at night as we settle into our brass bed the sparse traffic washes past, a remote and steady murmur around our sleep, as of dead souls babbling at the edge of a dream.
>
> (p. 4)

Jack begins to tell a fairy tale, but the phrase "by previous marriages" and the adverb "once," designating the demise of the garden, mar the illusion. The white noise of expressway traffic replaces the water, whose absence is underscored by the verbs "washes" and "babbling," that would rush by in a prelapsarian world.

* * *

Working with the models of an American past and a Modernist aesthetic, Jack Gladney attempts to construct a narrative as cosmologically grand as a "A Model of Christian Charity," as geographically sweeping as the western, and as psychologically penetrating as the high Modernist novel. Even Jack realizes the futility of resurrecting pre-modern and modern models in a post-modern world, and his final allusion to *Lolita*[30] confirms his recognition that the world—like literature—must come to grips with its difference from the past. DeLillo's first homage to Nabokov occurs in the penultimate chapter of ***White Noise.*** Jack Gladney's attempt to kill Willie Mink is a parody of Humbert Humbert's murder of Clare Quilty in *Lolita,* which occurs in the penultimate chapter of *Lolita.*[31] Just as Humbert is acutely aware of the fairy tales and melodramas that have preceded his utterly unoriginal act, Jack watches himself as he tries to commit murder, unable to turn his gaze away because he has seen the act so many times before this. Jack realizes that he does "not have to knock [since t]he door would be open" (p. 305) precisely because thirty years earlier, Humbert does knock on his victim's door, and receiving no answer, he pushes the door and remarks on how easily it opens, "as in a medieval fairy tale."[32] In the final chapter of *Lolita,* after Humbert has killed Quilty, he disregards the traffic rules by driving down the left side of the highway to satisfy "a very spiritual itch,"[33] much like Wilder's "mystically charged" ride across a highway. Humbert's defiance of highway regulations ends with "a graceful movement" which propels him off the road, and after a series of gentle bounces he winds up on "a grassy slope, among surprised cows," filled with "a last mirage of wonder and hopelessness,"[34] an emotion not unlike the "wonder and dread" that Jack describes in reference to the startling skies in ***White Noise.*** Whereas Humbert drives up an embankment, Wilder tumbles down into a "water furrow." The shift from urban to quasi-bucolic scenes in the concluding chapters of both novels alludes to the epiphanies of Romantic poetry—as illustrated in Wordsworth's "spots of time" in *The Prelude*—and the transcendental philosophy which was influenced by it—specifically Emerson's clarity of vision in *Nature.* While the epiphanies in *Lolita* and ***White Noise*** are necessarily tainted by virtue of their moment in history, they are not entirely satiric. They are, instead, authentic realizations, reached after reflection, but presented ingenuously, as if they occurred in a flash of blinding insight. Humbert Humbert's description of his interlude with grasshoppers and blue skies on an old mountain road ironically emphasizes a "melodious unity of sounds rising like vapor from a small mining town."[35] Recognizing the "vapory vibration of accumulated sounds that never ceased for a moment" as children are playing and laughing, Humbert claims to realize that he has stolen Lolita's childhood.[36] However, the revelation does not come to Humbert during his quasi-Wordsworthian experience, as he would like us to believe, for we know that the author of the manuscript is not a penitent man; he is, in fact, a man concerned with flexing his intellectual muscles. Humbert's revelation comes to him during the writing of the manuscript;[37] he simply inserts it into the seemingly appropriate scene.

The "epiphanies" in ***White Noise*** are as troubling partly because of their connections and subsequence to *Lolita.* The first epiphany occurs for Wilder, a toddler with a shockingly limited vocabulary who does not distinguish between televised images of his mother and the genuine article. Like Hawthorne's Pearl, Wilder is purely symbolic, both a comfort and an enigma to his parents, provocative in his naivete.[38] By virtue of his disturbingly implacable ingenuousness, Wilder is inversely associated with Lolita, a child prematurely bereft of innocence, but Wilder's highway excursion also links him with Humbert Humbert, whose automotive experience marks the narrative moment when he recognizes Lolita as a person and not as a symbol. A quote evoking the blind alley which introduces James Joyce's "Araby" suggests that the event transpiring in ***White Noise*** is a rite of passage, the end of Wilder's inhuman innocence: "This was the day Wilder got on his plastic tricycle, rode it around the block, turned right onto a dead end street and pedaled noisily to the dead end" (p. 322). His "mystically charged" trek across several lanes of highway traffic on his plastic tricycle is the only miraculous event in ***White Noise.*** Wilder does not even think to be frightened; tears come when his tricycle, having made the death-defying trip, tumbles down an embankment, evoking shock and possibly pain. His innocence allows him to survive the journey, but his pain upon tumbling into a "water furrow" is a baptism into a new realm, similar to Jack's awakening after suffering his own wound in the previous chapter.

Jack's awakening is no less ambiguous than Wilder's. Without question, Jack's "epiphany" early in his encounter with Mink is parodic: "I continued to advance in consciousness. Things glowed, a secret life rising out of them. . . . I knew for the first time what rain really was. I knew what wet was . . . I knew who I was in the network of meanings. . . . I saw beyond words. . . . I tried to see myself from Mink's viewpoint" (pp. 310, 312). His fall into schlock fiction is also a fall into utter self-consciousness, a completely severed subjectivity, which is also a parody of the Joycean epiphany, in which an object's "soul, its whatness, leaps to us from the vestment of its appearance. The soul of the commonest object . . . seems to us radiant."[39] But this is not Jack's first encounter with painful self-consciousness, as he has already admitted being "the false character that follows the name around" (p. 17). Indeed, Jack's self-consciousness is less an effect of the postmodern condition than a literary posture. In "The Dead," Gabriel spends most of the evening brooding over his dinner speech, rehearsing his debacle with Miss Ivors and wondering what people think of him. Like Jack, he thinks of himself as composing a narrative.[40] Ironically, Jack believes that the fractured ego that is emblematic of Modernism is a means to achieve the sanctity of self that he deems missing from postmodern society; however, the parallel between Jack and Gabriel suggests that Jack's retrospection is misguided.

Certainly, shooting Mink cannot reconnect Jack with himself. Indeed, some critics reject the possibility of epiphany in Postmodern literature. Leonard Wilcox argues that "in the climactic 'showdown' between Gladney and Gray (a.k.a. Willie Mink), DeLillo implies the exhaustion of late modernist, existentialist notions of heroism."[41] The possibility for experiencing epiphanies has been complicated by technology and media in much the same way that death has. A mere "spot of time" is insufficient to reveal Jack to himself; he must be reunited with the immediacy of his own mortality, not a synthetic loss of life diagnosable only by computers, but a palpable and bloody death. Jack's own pain upon being shot releases him from a world of utter self-absorption and returns him to the world of ordinary meaningless clutter. Albeit tainted by lies and melodrama, Jack's enlightenment after being shot effects a change in his thinking:

> With the restoration of the normal order of matter and sensation, I felt I was seeing him for the first time as a person. The old human muddles and quirks were set flowing again. Compassion, remorse, mercy,
>
> (p. 313)

But it is difficult to recognize the heightened consciousness in this man who does not admit to shooting Mink and who exhibits profound naivete during his conversation with the German nuns. It is important to note that, like Humbert's revelation, Jack's comes to him not in the moment of experience but in the moment of writing; this explains why the narrator who relates most of the plot longs for the past and relies on melodramatic metaphors, while the narrator of the last chapter is content to live in the present. Both Humbert's and Jack's epiphanies arise through re-construction, through representation, through language. Ironically, narrative itself, which began as the locus of ontological confusion in ***White Noise,*** is the means of self-discovery for Jack Gladney. Just as Wilder has passed from Lacan's imaginary stage into the symbolic world, with its divisions, ambiguities, and terminations, Jack has passed from blind faith, in which old German nuns accept the burden of mock belief, to an acceptance of mystery.

By the novel's end, Jack must come to grips with the death of narrative as he has known it—just as the drivers encountering Wilder's tricycle must adapt to a new, disordered world:

> they knew this picture did not belong to the hurtling consciousness of the highway, the broad-ribboned modernist stream. In speed there was sense. In signs, in patterns, in split-second lives. What did it mean, this little rotary blur? Some force in the world had gone awry.
>
> (pp. 322-33)

The highway is Modernist narrative gone awry. Surprisingly, however, it is not microbiology, technology, or increasingly mediated experiences that have disrupted the Modernist flow; it is, in fact, not sophistication but innocence, not progress but regression that confuses the drivers. The cars manage to avoid Wilder by mysterious means, and the result is an existential questioning of the universe. The signs and patterns that these drivers had relied on are shaken; one small plastic tricycle is weighty enough to upset world forces. Like Jack's reaction to the spectacular sunsets, "[i]t is hard to know how [one] should feel about this. . . . Certainly there is awe, it is all awe, it transcends previous categories of awe, but we don't know whether we are watching in wonder or dread, we don't know what we are watching or what it means" (p. 324).

Jack's words evoke the uncertainty and confusion of postmodern experience. All the givens of Modernism are shattered, but the stance is less skeptical than accepting. If the elusive term "Postmodernism" can be in part defined as a recycling of the past performed with both appreciation and ironic distance, then Jack moves from Modernism to Postmodernism in the course of the novel. The old world order of progress has been challenged, replaced by a new, multivalent perspective. Inherent in this perspective is a sense of the interconnections of reality, history, and fiction. Hence, the novel is filled with terms linking life and storytelling. "The sky takes on content, feeling, an exalted *narrative* life" (p. 324, italics added); "The sky is under a spell, powerful and *storied*" (p. 325, italics added), unlike a previous sunset which paled in comparison to those with "more dynamic colors, a deeper sense of *narrative* sweep" (p. 227, italics added). The cause of these spectacular skies is puzzling: characters do not know if the new skies are produced by the toxic air cloud or by the microorganisms that eat it. And so, we are left with a moment of "wonder or dread" or, more aptly, wonder and dread.

In a world in which everything is a text to be deciphered, including oneself, language cannot possible carry the burden of meaning. It can, however, artfully arrange the chaos. Words may yield no solutions to mysteries and terrors, but they allow us to recognize and utter the existence of the puzzles. DeLillo notes that "fiction rescues history from its confusions":[42]

> Stories can be a consolation—at least in theory. The novelist can try to leap across the barrier of fact, and the reader is willing to take that leap with him as long as there's a kind of redemptive truth waiting on the other side, a sense that we've arrived at a resolution. . . . So the novel which is within history can also operate outside it—correcting, clearing up and, perhaps most important of all, finding rhythms and symmetries that we simply don't encounter elsewhere.[43]

Yet the patterns that fiction offers must never overwhelm the mysteries of life. DeLillo's own desire to reveal the "mystery in commonplace moments" and the "radiance in dailiness"[44] is echoed in Jack's recognition that "[t]he world is full of abandoned meanings. In the commonplace [he finds] unexpected themes and intensities" (p. 184).[45] The collective response to the Nyodene D. disaster is to create legends, which simultaneously offer solace and grandeur:

> The toxic event had released a spirit of imagination. People spun tales, others listened spellbound. There was a growing respect for the vivid rumor, the most chilling tale. We were no closer to believing or disbelieving a given story than we had been earlier. But there was a greater appreciation now. We began to marvel at our own ability to manufacture awe.
>
> (p. 153)

DeLillo suggests that subscribing to a faith in mystery and refraining from seeking solutions might be a replacement for the religious faith which is impossible and the technological faith which is unthinkable. Even Jack has surrendered the penetration of mysteries. Rather than attempt to understand Wilder's adventure, he simply segues into family visits to the highway overpass. Having achieved "negative capability," Jack and Babette are content to live amid "uncertainties, mysteries, doubts, without any irritable reaching after fact and reason,"[46] not unlike the advice Jack gives himself and/or the reader earlier in the novel, after visiting The Old Burying Ground: "May the days be aimless. Let the seasons drift. Do not advance the action according to a plan" (p. 98).

Indeed, the novel's most powerful mystery, death, supplies the very fabric of Jack's salvation; his near-death experience allows him to move beyond his paralyzing fear of death just as Gabriel's discovery of Gretta's dead lover removes the veil from his own moribund life. Jack, like the archangel Gabriel, whose horn will announce the final days, utters apocalyptic words. Characters in both works look to the west, toward death, for signs. In ***White Noise,*** the elderly, the middle-aged, the young gaze west toward the "narrative" sunsets and watch for signs in "[c]ars . . . coming from the west, from out of the towering light" (p. 325). Gabriel, in turn, recognizes that "[t]he time had come for him to set out on his journey westward."[47]

Thematically, ***White Noise*** has come full circle: the academic year, which began on the first page and on the west campus, is over or nearly over; the men and women in the supermarket replace those in the station wagons; and the living are communicating with the dead even as they were at the novel's start: "at night as we settle into our brass bed the sparse traffic washes past, a remote and steady murmur around our sleep, as of dead souls babbling at the edge of a dream" (p. 4). Even the supermarket provides a space for reveling in mystery, a mystery that Jack does not attempt to unravel: "The supermarket shelves have been rearranged. It happened one day without warning" (p. 325). The holographic scanners, "which decode the binary secret of every item, infallibly . . . [transmit] the language of waves and radiation, or how the dead speak to the living" (p. 326). Many readers view the rearrangement of the supermarket shelves as a nihilistic conclusion to an already gloomy novel. But the lesson that Jack and Babette need to learn during the course of the novel is that dread is part of being human. Ultimately, what Dylar and its unfortunate side-effect suggest is that the fear of death is as essential as language is to humanity. As Winnie suggests, "'Isn't death the boundary we need? Doesn't it give a precious texture to life, a sense of definition?'" (p. 228). On the verge of death, the co-pilot in the flight that nearly crashes in Blacksmith says, "'It is worse than we'd ever imagined. They didn't prepare us for this at the death simulator in Denver. Our fear is pure, so totally stripped of distractions and pressures as to be a form of transcendental meditation'" (p. 90). If death is the last frontier, then our dread is understandable. Never having experienced it—even in simulation—we are in awe, literally in the constant presence of the sublime. In the tradition of Kant, Lyotard defines the sublime as occurring when "the imagination fails to present an object which might, if only in principle, come to match a concept. . . . Those are Ideas of which no presentation is possible."[48] What distinguishes Postmodern from Modern sublime for Lyotard is that the latter "puts forward the unpresentable in presentation itself,"[49] that is, Postmodernism uses form to demonstrate the ineffability of the sublime. In ***White Noise,*** that ineffability is located in the generic hybrid itself, but, more importantly, it is found in the lists of brand names ("MasterCard, Visa, American Express," "Toyota Corolla, Toyota Celica, Toyota Cressida"), which may or may not hold mystical significance. Those names, part of novel's white noise, remain ambiguous—gestures toward irony and mysticism. The gap between conception and presentation is the sublime, a gap which reason cannot conquer.[50] What is subverted in the last three scenes of ***White Noise***—the modernist highway, the spectacular sunset, and the chaotic supermarket—is our illusion that we can control everything, including death.

Significantly, speech has all but vanished in the novel's last chapter. The two elderly women witnessing the tricycle's journey progressively lose their voices, and Wilder is oblivious to sound in any event. On the overpass, spectators silently view the sky: "No one plays a radio or speaks in a voice above a whisper" (p. 325). And Jack is "taking no calls," particularly from Dr. Chakravarty. The language that seems to have disappeared by the end of ***White Noise*** has merely changed forms. "[T]he language of waves and radiation," with the promise of communication with the dead, has replaced spoken language, which holds no such promise. In "The Romantic Metaphysics of Don DeLillo," Paul Maltby correctly identifies the demise of the language of name—"the kind of pure nomenclature implied in Genesis where words stand in a necessary, rather than arbitrary, relationship to their referents"—in ***The Names.***[51] In an interview, DeLillo suggests that words detached from meaning sometimes carry supernal significance:

> There's something nearly mystical about certain words and phrases that float through our lives. . . . Words that are computer generated to be used on products that might be sold anywhere from Japan to Denmark—words devised to be pronounceable in a hundred languages. And when you detach one of these words from the product it was designed to serve, the word acquires a chantlike quality.[52]

By the end of the novel, dialogue, largely displaced by narration, has given way to intertextuality, DeLillo's narrative dialogues with previous authors, which link him to the past and to the dead. Jack transforms life into stories, and DeLillo transforms old narratives into new ones. DeLillo's intertextuality ultimately broadens the novel's definition of "white noise" to include not only the incessant mantras of consumerism, the hum of appliances, the shriek of alarms, the static of televisions and radios; "white noise" also includes the previous texts that unavoidably contribute to the nation's sense of itself, all the sound that comprises previous representations.[53] As the world of ***White Noise*** is mediated by television, the novel itself is mediated by previous fiction, culminating in the last lines, particularly the last nine syllables, of ***White Noise,*** which echo the final words in Joyce's "The Dead":

> Everything we need that is not food or love is here in the tabloid racks. The tales of the supernatural and the extraterrestrial. The miracle vitamins, the cures for cancer, the remedies for obesity. The cults of the famous and the dead.
>
> (p. 326)

> His soul swooned slowly as he heard the snow falling faintly through the universe and faintly falling, like the descent of their last end, upon all the living and the dead.[54]

If this exchange between the past and the present is "how the dead speak to the living" (p. 326), then Postmodern sublimity may be expressible not in any single text but in the spaces between texts.

Notes

1. Michael Valdez Moses, "Lust Removed from Nature," *New Essays on* White Noise, ed. Frank Lentricchia (Cambridge University Press. 1991), p. 64.
2. Don DeLillo, *White Noise* (Penguin, 1984), p. 287. All subsequent references to *White Noise* will be from this edition.
3. Douglas Keesey, *Don DeLillo* (Twayne, 1993), p. 133.
4. The term "intertextuality" has different meanings for Julia Kristeva, Roland Barthes, Gérard Genette, and Michael Riffaterre. I am using "intertextuality" to designate the meeting of two textual worlds, but I understand this meeting to function in the way that Linda Hutcheon describes "parody": "repetition with critical distance, which marks difference rather than similarity" (*A Theory of Parody,* [Methuen, 1985], p. 6).
5. Hutcheon uses the word "parody," which she acknowledges is often called ironic quotation, pastiche, appropriation, or intertextuality (*The Politics of Postmodernism* [Routledge, 1989], p. 94).
6. Hutcheon, p. 93.
7. Tom LeClair, "Closing the Loop: *White Noise," In the Loop: Don DeLillo and the Systems Novel* (University of Illinois Press, 1987). Rpt. in *The Viking Critical Edition of White Noise,* ed. Mark Osteen (Penguin, 1998), pp. 393-94.

8. John Winthrop, "A Model of Christian Charity," *The Puritans in America: A Narrative Anthology,* ed. Alan Heimert and Andrew Delbanco (Harvard University Press, 1985), p. 83.
9. Winthrop, pp. 87-88.
10. DeLillo, *Americana* (Penguin, 1971), pp. 270-71.
11. DeLillo, *Mao II* (Penguin, 1991), p. 7.
12. While the Puritans fiercely insisted upon an unmediated relationship to God through scripture, debates about meaning, clearly evident in the Antinomian Crisis, admit to the ineluctability of interpretation and therefore mediation.
13. Moses, p. 79.
14. DeLillo has said, "Perhaps the supermarket tabloids are the richest material of all, closest to the spirit of the book. They ask profoundly important questions about death, the afterlife, God, worlds and space, yet they exist in an almost Pop Art atmosphere" (Caryn James, "I Never Set Out To Write An Apocalyptic Novel," *The New York Times* 13 January 1985. Rpt. in *The Viking Critical Edition of White Noise,* p. 333).
15. Certain details link The Revelation to *White Noise,* including the prediction that Christ will "com[e] with the clouds (1:7)," the visitation of plagues, and the promise of "a white stone, with a new name written on [it] which no one knows except him who receives it" (2:17). *The New Oxford Annotated Bible* (Oxford University Press, 1973).
16. John L. McKenzie, *Dictionary of the Bible* (Collier Books, 1965), p. 39.
17. Revelations 21:5-6.
18. John 1:1-2.
19. Revelations 19:11-15.
20. The metaphor of white noise is most often considered as the interference of communication. LeClair considers its other meaning in music, "the sound produced by all audible sound-wave frequencies sounding together—a term for complex, simultaneous ordering that represents the 'both/and' nature of systems (and irony)" (p. 409). Cornel Bonca suggests that white noise is "the death-fear expressed in the only terms that a postmodern media culture knows how to express it" ("Don DeLillo's *White Noise*: The Natural Language of the Species," *College English* XXIII [1966]. Rpt. in *The Viking Critical Edition of White Noise,* p. 467). The description of the rider in Revelations connects white noise with an awful unveiling, which links it to the sublime.

    Moreover, the Romantic sublime also connects *White Noise* with *Moby Dick,* another classic American text which deals with the search for divine meaning, the failure of language, and the loss of individuality (the result of falling prey to Ahab's seductive oratory). In DeLillo's novel, the white noise of consumption, manifested in catalogues of Japanese automobiles, credit cards, and environmental disasters, stalks Jack throughout the novel. Technologically produced white noise is designed to conceal silence, "the cover over the existential perception of the infinitude" (Moses, p. 81). During a contest with her husband to determine whose fear of death is stronger, Babette asks, "'What if death is nothing but sound?'" Jack's response and the subsequent exchange confirm the angst: "'Electrical noise.' 'You hear it forever. Sound all around. How awful.' 'Uniform white'" (p. 198). Similarly Moby Dick, a whale whose whiteness becomes a source of mystery recalling the supermarkets filled with white-labeled generic food, exists for Ahab as a distraction from the void, and hunting the creature is tantamount to Jack's hunting of Willie Mink, alias Mr. Gray.
21. His faith in meaning is prefigured in *Revelations,* which accepts the sanctity of words and warns against the dangers of representation. *Revelations* ends with a command to preserve language:

    > I warn every one who hears the words of the prophecy of this book: if any one adds to them, God will add to him the plagues described in this book, and if any one takes away from the words of the book of this prophecy, God will take away his share in the tree of life and in the holy city, which are described in this book.
    >
    > (22.18-19)

    The novel's evocation of The Revelation no doubt constitutes an unsanctified representation of "the word." Moreover, the earlier quotation from The Revelation is translated from Hebrew, and thus is already representative of the original, so *White Noise*'s allusion is at least twice removed. What then does it mean for a postmodern novel which both recognizes the power and the unreliability of language to converse with the Bible? While the novel's title and many of its more humorous episodes suggest that language is intentionally misleading, the underlying point seems to be that words are life-giving, but only insofar as they are adapted to new messages and new eras. Words must be changed in order for the message to survive. Jack's failing is not in looking to the past for narratological models; it is in insisting that those models be used to describe current situations. Similarly, Jack wants to believe in "'[t]he old heaven and hell, the Latin mass. The Pope is infallible, God created the world in six days. . . . Hell is burning lakes, winged demons'" (p. 318).
22. Douglas Keesey argues that DeLillo felt "some kinship with James Joyce," making connections between *Americana* and *A Portrait of the Artist as a Young Man* and *Ratner's Star* and *Ulysses* (p. 2). In an interview with Tom LeClair (LeClair and Larry McCaffrey, *Anything Can Happen: Interviews with*

Contemporary Novelists [University of Illinois Press, 1983]), DeLillo identifies Ulysses (as well as Nabokov's *Pale Fire*) as one of the classic modern novels which he most admires (p. 85). In this interview, he also quotes Joyce's famous phrase "silence, exile, and cunning," uttered by Stephen Dedalus in *A Portrait of the Artist.* Jack's conversation with Sister Hermann Marie at the end of *White Noise* is reminiscent of the crisis of faith which sends Stephen out of Ireland at the end of *A Portrait of the Artist.*

23. In fact, the world that Gabriel describes in "The Dead" is not very different in tone from the world of *White Noise*: "His own identity was fading out into a gray impalpable world: the solid world itself which these dead had one time reared and lived in, was dissolving and dwindling" and "A vague terror seized Gabriel at this answer as if, at that hour when he had hoped to triumph, some impalpable and vindictive being was coming against him, gathering forces against him in its vague world" (James Joyce, *Dubliners* [Penguin, 1976], pp. 223, 220. All subsequent references to *Dubliners* will come from this edition.) In DeLillo's world, the vague terror is a life and death rendered inauthentic by technology, and the terror, in fact, takes the shape of existential angst. We are, thus, made strangers in our own dying, as Gabriel is made a stranger in his own living. The sense of dissolution, of "weightless" individuals, is fought by immersion in crowds or increased bulk. Technology has made the vagueness more acute; it has perfected the Modernist anxiety of alienation.

24. Baudrillard, "DeLillo's *White Noise,* and the End of the Heroic Narrative," *Contemporary Literature,* XXXII (1991), p. 348.

25. Joyce, p. 179.

26. The novel's setting in the town of Blacksmith recalls Stephen Dedalus' promise to forge "the uncreated conscience" of his race. That the town's name no longer bears any connection to its meaning simply underscores the postmodern experience lamented by the narrator.

27. Jack and Gabriel also share a poetic sensibility which desires language to transcend worldly issues. Like Jack, who assumes that Hitler studies is not about good or evil, Gabriel, a teacher and an author, who writes literary reviews for a West Briton newspaper, thinks that literature is above politics.

28. Joyce, pp. 199, 207, 194.

29. Joyce, p. 203.

30. In broad terms, Lolita appears to be an influence on *White Noise,* especially in Humbert's descriptions of an American society satiated with advertisements and marked by mediocrity (Berkeley Books, 1982. All subsequent references to *Lolita* will come from this edition.) Humbert's vision of America as an endless strip of cheap motels, all imitating various prototypes, predicts the loss of original in *White Noise.* Humbert perpetually sees himself as a successor of Edgar Allan Poe and as a pale shadow of a film idol or a western hero, and the novel, like DeLillo's, is infused with references to earlier literature. More specifically, Humbert refers to his first wife as "a large, puffy, short-legged, big-breasted and practically brainless *baba*" (p. 27). It is precisely Babette's heft that appeals to Jack, a much different character from Nabokov's effete intellectual, but it is worth noting that Babette is referred to as Baba a few times in *White Noise.*

31. The confrontations occur in the penultimate chapters of both novels and take place on rainy nights. Both are failed western "showdowns," in which the hunted men are barely coherent, suffering from drug-induced stupors. Humbert indeed confesses the that "both of us were panting as the cowman and the sheepman never do after their battle" (p. 272).

32. Nabokov, p. 268.

33. Nabokov, p. 279.

34. Nabokov, p. 279.

35. Nabokov, p. 280. The primary sense in last chapters of both novels is auditory.

36. Nabokov, p. 280.

37. I am indebted to Stacey Olster for this insight into the novel.

38. For DeLillo, "[c]hildren have a direct route to, have direct contact to the kind of natural truth that eludes us as adults[; even their] misspellings and misused words reflect a kind of reality" (Anthony DeCurtis's "'An Outsider in This Society' An Interview with Don DeLillo" in Lentricchia, *Introducing Don DeLillo,* p. 64).

39. Quoted in M. H. Abrams, *A Glossary of Literary Terms,* Sixth Edition (Harcourt Brace, 1993), p. 57.

40. Lines from his own texts reverberate in his head and even in his speech: "One feels that one is listening to a thought-tormented music" (Joyce, p. 192) and "In one letter that he had written to her then he had said: 'Why is it that words like these seem to me so dull and cold? Is it because there is no word tender enough to be your name?'" (p. 214). Finally, like Jack during the Willie Mink fiasco, Gabriel literally observes himself: "He saw himself as a ludicrous figure, acting as a penny boy for his aunts, a nervous, well-meaning sentimentalist, orating to vulgarians and idealizing his own clownish lusts, the pitiable fatuous fellow he had caught a glimpse of in the mirror" (pp. 219-20).

41. Wilcox, p. 349.

42. DeCurtis, p. 56.

43. DeCurtis, p. 56.

44. DeCurtis, pp. 59, 63.
45. Many readers assume that Jack is the spokesman for DeLillo himself, but I would argue that Jack's similarity to DeLillo, if it exists at all, is revealed after the former's shift in consciousness. In general terms, I want to distinguish between the characters' nostalgia and the author's use of intertextuality in the novel. The former denotes a desire to move backward, to deny the present, while the latter is an acknowledgment of previous literary voices and of past epistemologies.
46. John Keats, *Selected Letters of John Keats,* ed. Robert Pack (New American Library, 1974), p. 55.
47. Joyce, p. 223.
48. Jean-Francois Lyotard, *The Postmodern Condition* (Manchester University Press, 1985), p. 78.
49. Lyotard, p. 81.
50. While Kant's sublime supposes the ultimate victory of reason over emotion, Edmund Burke's relies on the primacy of emotion over intellect: "Whatever is fitted in any sort to excite the ideas of pain, and danger, that is to say, whatever is in any sort terrible, or is conversant about terrible objects, or operates in a manner analogous to terror, is a source of the *sublime*; that is, it is productive of the strongest emotion which the mind is capable of feeling" (*A Philosophical Enquiry into the Origin of Our Ideas of the Sublime and the Beautiful,* ed. J. T. Boulton [University of Notre Dame Press, 1958], p. 36).
51. Paul Maltby, "The Romantic Metaphysics of Don DeLillo," *Contemporary Literature,* XXXVII (1996), p. 262.
52. Adam Begley, "Don DeLillo: The Art of Fiction." *Paris Review,* XXXV, p. 128 (1993). Rpt. in *The Viking Critical Edition of White Noise,* p. 332. DeLillo has also said, "Babbling can be . . . a purer form, an alternate speech. . . . Glossolalia is interesting because it suggests there's another way to speak, there's a very different language lurking somewhere in the brain" (LeClair, p. 84).
53. "Panasonic" was another working title for the novel, and LeClair understands it to indicate "DeLillo's concern with recording the wide range of sound, ordered and uncertain, positive and negative" (p. 409).
54. Joyce, p. 224.

Edward B. St. John (review date December 2002)

SOURCE: St. John, Edward B. Review of *Cosmopolis,* by Don DeLillo. *Library Journal* 127, no. 20 (December 2002): 176.

[*In the following review, St. John views* Cosmopolis *as a hindrance to DeLillo's growth as an author.*]

Unlike his sprawling masterpiece, ***Underworld,*** DeLillo's 13th novel [***Cosmopolis***] is short and tightly focused, indeed almost claustrophobic. Most of the action takes place inside a "prousted" (cork-lined) stretch limo, as the reclusive financial wizard Eric Packer is chauffeured across Manhattan for a haircut. Thanks to a presidential visit, antiglobalization demonstrations, and a celebrity funeral, this journey takes up most of the day. Stuck in traffic, Packer anxiously monitors the value of the yen on the limo's computer. Using the car as his office, he summons advisors from nearby shops and restaurants. His physician gives him a rubber-gloved physical exam in the back seat as Packer discusses imminent financial ruin with his broker and angry crowds block the streets. This work most closely resembles ***The Body Artist*** in its brevity and straightforward narrative flow. However, the earlier novel was written in an uncharacteristically warm, poetic style, promising a new direction for this important writer, while ***Cosmopolis*** reverts to the standard DeLillo boilerplate, perceptive and funny but also brittle and cold. This, coupled with the book's dated 1990s sensibility, makes ***Cosmopolis*** a step backward rather than an artistic advance.

Donna Seaman (review date 1 December 2002)

SOURCE: Seaman, Donna. Review of *Cosmopolis,* by Don DeLillo. *Booklist* 99, no. 7 (1 December 2002): 628.

[*In the following review, Seaman summarizes the plot of* Cosmopolis, *praising its poetic, witty prose.*]

It's April in the year 2000 in the cosmopolis of New York [in ***Cosmopolis***]. A day of epic gridlock due to a visit by the president and a violent antiglobalization protest. A good day to leave the white stretch limo at the curb, but assets manager Eric Packer, 28, buff, ruthless, and obscenely wealthy, insists on being driven across town to get a haircut. His chief of security objects: there's a credible threat against his life. But this only encourages Packer, who likes to rule his domain from his high-tech chariot, where his employees crawl in to make their reports, where myriad screens carry the ceaseless data stream of the currency markets, where a doctor performs his daily check-up. Quasi-mystic Packer is obsessed, on this fateful day, with the yen, strangely aroused by graphic coverage of the murders of other major financial players, and keenly aware that he has the power to pitch the entire monetary system into chaos. Packer is, in short, a monster—a man who has lost his soul in an accelerated world without heart. And DeLillo, master novelist and seer, tells the surreal, electrifying story of this dehumanized moneyman in English scrubbed so clean and assembled so exquisitely it seems like a new language. By turns breathtakingly poetic and devastatingly witty, his descriptions of today's urban reality—extravagantly kinetic Times Square financial displays (information as "pure spectacle") presided over by gigantic billboards of the "underwear gods"—make the present seem like a forbidding, to-be-avoided future. "We need a new theory of time," muses one of Packer's advisors. No, suggests DeLillo, we need to reclaim life.

Jeff Zaleski (review date 9 December 2002)

SOURCE: Zaleski, Jeff. Review of *Cosmopolis,* by Don DeLillo. *Publishers Weekly* 249, no. 49 (9 December 2002): 58.

[*In the following review, Zaleski pans the structure, prose style, and depiction of the protagonist in* Cosmopolis.]

DeLillo skates through a day in the life of a brilliant and precocious New Economy billionaire in this monotone 13th novel [***Cosmopolis***], a study in big money and affectlessness. As one character remarks, 28-year-old Eric Packer "wants to be one civilization ahead of this one." But on an April day in the year 2000, Eric's fortune and life fall apart. The story tracks him as he traverses Manhattan in his stretch limo. His goal: a haircut at Anthony's, his father's old barber. But on this day his driver has to navigate a presidential visit, an attack by anarchists and a rapper's funeral. Meanwhile, the yen is mounting, destroying Eric's bet against it. The catastrophe liberates Eric's destructive instinct—he shoots another character and increases his bet. Mostly, the action consists of sequences in the back of the limo (where he stages meetings with his doctor, various corporate officers and a New Economy guru) interrupted by various pit stops. He lunches with his wife of 22 days, Elise Shifrin. He has sex with two women, his art consultant and a bodyguard. He is hit in the face with a pie by a protester. He knows he is being stalked, and the novel stages a final convergence between the ex-tycoon and his stalker. DeLillo practically invented the predominant vernacular of the late '90s (the irony, the close reading of consumer goods, the mock complexity of technobabble) in ***White Noise,*** but he seems surprisingly disengaged here. His spotlighted New Economy icon, Eric, doesn't work, either as a genius financier (he is all about gadgetry, not exchange—there's no love of the deal in his "frozen heart") or a thinker. The threats posed by the contingencies that he faces cannot lever him out of his recalcitrant one-dimensionality. DeLillo is surely an American master, but this time out, he is doodling.

Brooke Allen (essay date March/April 2003)

SOURCE: Allen, Brooke. "From Superman to Everyman." *New Leader* 86, no. 2 (March/April 2003): 21-3.

[*In the following excerpt, Allen describes the strengths and weakness of* Cosmopolis, *praising its insights but faulting the characterization of its protagonist.*]

Novelists can be roughly divided into those who go for the big picture, and those who dwell on the small one: the polymath who, Dickens-like, tries to cram all of life into his book, and the obsessed artist (Virginia Woolf, for example) whose object is the ever more perfect rendering of individual experience. Among current American writers, Don DeLillo and Nicholson Baker best exemplify the two types. DeLillo, author of swaggeringly ambitious works (including ***Mao II, White Noise, Underworld***), has been trying for more than two decades to synthesize a vision of contemporary American society in all its messy, insane, outrageous totality. Baker, on the other hand, has brought the art of navel contemplation to undreamed-of heights (and sometimes depths).

Both now have new novels out that describe particular days in the lives of very different men who might be called representative of their time and place. DeLillo's, the personification of global capitalism, represents the ego rampant, ever hungry, ever dissatisfied. Baker's is gentle, content, introspective, an apparently ordinary man made extraordinary by his capacity to love life's trivialities.

Eric Packer, the protagonist of DeLillo's ***Cosmopolis*** is a 28-year-old currency trader and financial giant—the natural culmination of the "master of the universe" who began to crop up on Wall Street in the 1980s and was so memorably depicted by Tom Wolfe. As the economy bubbled and bloated into its fin de siècle grandiosity, so did Eric. His Faustian dreams are so outsized that one of his enemies remarks, "Things wear out impatiently in his hands. . . . He wants to be one civilization ahead of this one."

In an essay he wrote for the *Guardian* in Britain at the end of 2001, DeLillo looked at what he called "the ruins of the future" from a post-9/11 perspective. He characterized the last decade of the 20th century as a time when multinational corporations came to seem "more vital and influential than governments. The dramatic climb of the Dow and the speed of the Internet summoned us all to live permanently in the future; in the utopian glow of cyber-capital, because there is no memory there and this is where markets are uncontrolled and investment potential has no limit."

New York right before the wake-up call of September 11 achieved a kind of apotheosis of excess. In rich and trendy Manhattan neighborhoods testosterone seemed literally to rise from the asphalt. "Money," one of ***Cosmopolis***' characters states, "has taken a turn. All wealth has become wealth for its own sake. There's no other kind of enormous wealth. Money has lost its narrative quality the way painting did once upon a time. Money is talking to itself." The principle is vividly illustrated in the novel by the electronic data strips that flicker high across the facades of buildings in Times Square. "Never mind the speed that makes it hard to follow what passes before the eye. The speed is the point. We are not witnessing the flow of information so much as pure spectacle, or information made sacred, ritually unreadable."

A lot of ***Cosmopolis*** is fun to read on the same level as, say, the New York *Observer*: Just how gross can consumption become? And because Eric, in the manner of so many DeLillo characters, is essentially cartoonish, you approach him in a spirit of ridicule, unreceptive to the pathos with which DeLillo occasionally tries to endow him. Eric's apartment cost him $104 million. ("You paid the money for the number itself," explains Eric's so-called "chief of theory" Vija Kinski. "One hundred and four million. This is what you bought. And it's worth it. The number justifies itself.") It is a triplex with a rotating room at the top, a meditation cell, a shark tank, a borzoi pen, and a collection of disturbingly opaque art. "He liked paintings that his guests did not know how to look at. . . . The work was all the more dangerous for not being new. There's no more danger in the new."

Eric seems to spend more time, however, in his stretch limo than at his home or office. Certainly the limo is cozier, more customized for his special needs than the cavernous apartment. It is enormous; "prousted" or cork-lined against street noise; fitted out with "mode control" that sucks unpleasant odors out of the atmosphere; crammed with plasma screens that pulsate with images, charts and data streams. It also contains a microwave, heart monitor and spycam, all voice-activated.

On the morning of this particular day—a postmodern parody, perhaps, of Leopold Bloom's little Odyssey across Dublin—Eric gets into his limo and heads across Manhattan in search of a haircut. Leaving the limo only at odd moments, he orchestrates encounters with most of the significant people in his life: his chiefs of finance, security, technology, and theory; his doctor, who gives him a prostate exam in front of a female employee; his art dealer ("I think you want this Rothko. . . . You have something in you that's receptive to the mysteries"); and his wife of 22 days, a rich and lovely poetess. He enjoys, or at least tolerates, several sexual encounters.

None of these events is unusual for Eric, but this does turn out to be an unusual, even fateful day. World financial markets are tottering, thanks to a suicidally daring move by Eric, and antiglobalization agitators are ubiquitous on his journey through Manhattan. Several figureheads of worldwide capitalism are assassinated during the course of the day, and Eric himself appears to be threatened by a murderous assailant. Apocalypse and *Götterdämmerung* are in the air; Eric drinks up the charged atmosphere with the elation of the natural brinksman.

Cosmopolis is rich in the strengths and weaknesses of the author. Few can match DeLillo at neat formulations of our bizarre cultural contradictions. As early as ***Mao II*** (1991) he was positing the then perverse theory that the terrorist was one of the few genuinely creative individuals in a world where real political action took place at secret meetings between the obscenely powerful. Here that notion is personified by the harmless "pastry assassin," a Romanian who throws cream pies in the faces of the global society's more blatantly symbolic figures. After creaming Eric and being pulverized by his security forces, he relates some of his adventures:

> You are living up to reputation, okay. But I am kicked and beaten by security so many times I am walking dead. They make me to wear a radio collar when I am in England, to safe the queen. Track me like rare crane. But believe one thing please. I crèmed Fidel three times in six days when he is in Bucharest last year. I am action painter of creme pies. I drop from a tree on Michael Jordan one time. This is famous Flying Pie. It is museum quality video for the ages. I quiche Sultan of f—-ing Brunei in his bath. They put me in black hole until I am screaming from my eyes.

This is DeLillo at his wonderful best. But his worst is also on display in ***Cosmopolis.*** He is not content, for example, to make his point through people and situations; instead he lazily invents a fictional theoretician, Vija Kinski, who acts as a mouthpiece for his own formulations. He is strong on atmosphere, cultural noise and color, but weak on character. Eric, when you scrape away all the contemporary glitz, is not much more than a feeble reflection of Citizen Kane. He has outbid Kane, to be sure, in the Faustian stakes, just as our own historical moment has outbid Kane's. Eric seeks immortality, but not for him the uncertain immortality of art or the crude solution provided by cryogenics. No, "The idea was to live outside the given limits, in a chip, on a disk, as data, in whirl, in radiant spin, a consciousness saved from void. . . . It would be the master thrust of cyber-capital, to extend the human experience toward infinity as a medium for corporate growth and investment, for the accumulation of profits and vigorous investment."

Eric's final realization that he is merely a frail, mortal animal seems surprisingly banal both in human and literary terms. More interesting is his reaction to this discovery, a mental adjustment that ends the novel on a fine, sharp note. ***Cosmopolis,*** like most of DeLillo's work, is a mixed bag, bursting with not-very-nourishing goodies. . . .

Mark Greif (review date April 2003)

SOURCE: Greif, Mark. "Bonfire of the Verities." *American Prospect* 14, no. 4 (April 2003): 54-5.

[*In the following review, Greif characterizes* Cosmopolis *as "a novel of the 1980s," discussing the novel's motifs, aesthetics, style, and politics.*]

Either Don DeLillo has written his worst book or he's done something so sneaky I can't see it yet. ***Cosmopolis***' tale of a new-economy billionaire who reduces the world's currency markets to rubble while crossing Manhattan to get a haircut relies on a premise no weaker than those found in some of DeLillo's 13 other novels. His triumphs have often had a seat-of-the pants quality. This book, however, doesn't quite scrape through.

Wittingly or unwittingly, DeLillo has written a novel of the 1980s. Published in 2003, ***Cosmopolis*** opens with a warning that the story takes place "IN THE YEAR 2000: A Day in April." Tear this marker out, though, and you're left with a repetition of the major motifs of '80s popular culture and novels, without any assimilation of the truths of the recent fin de siècle: what was new about the new economy, how New York differed in 2000 from its earlier incarnations and what globalization has wrought.

New York City hasn't looked this bad in fiction since Tom Wolfe's *The Bonfire of the Vanities* (1987), back when Tompkins Square Park was a homeless tent city and not a hipsters' village green. Prosperous, optimistic, pre-September 11 New York is nowhere to be found in DeLillo's novel. Eric Packer, ***Cosmopolis***' 28-year-old capitalist, is Gordon Gekko redux, updated from Oliver Stone's *Wall Street* (1987) with remote Internet access on his watch. The novel's aesthetic comes straight from the '80s, too: flat towers, stark art and minimalist furniture.

It's an any-city that DeLillo portrays, or a no-city. All the signs point to a *Ulysses* in miniature: One man travels in one representative city in one day. But the metropolis seems small, and Eric creeps only a short distance. His destination is the old-fashioned barbershop on the block where his father grew up—a fortress of authenticity. He makes conjugal forays from the safety of his armored limousine, and has sex with everyone from his female security guard (whom he asks to shock him with a stun gun) to his wife. The city drops out of view completely, except for what comes from Hollywood. The book's climax occurs in a boarded-up Hell's Kitchen tenement of the sort rehabbed during the Giuliani years and turned into luxury duplexes.

DeLillo adds drama with the inevitable 1980s sociopathic turn. Eric will start killing people. Isn't that what you do when you're rich? Bret Easton Ellis mined this vein in *American Psycho* (1991), a book that's already dated enough to have become '80s camp in its movie adaptation. Meanwhile, as Eric's trigger finger gets itchy, other nutcases begin murdering financial wizards all over the world. Arthur Rapp, managing director of the International Monetary Fund, gets it from an assassin in North Korea. "He was killed live on the Money Channel," DeLillo writes. You can feel the strength of his cool language even in the midst of cliché:

> Eric wanted to see it again. *Show it again.* They did this, of course, and he knew they would do it repeatedly into the night, our night, until the sensation drained out of it or everyone in the world had seen it, whichever came first, but he could see it again if he wished, any time, through scan retrieval, technology that already seemed oppressively sluggish, or he could recover a slow-motion shot of the willowy woman and her hand mike being sucked into the terror and he could sit here for hours wanting to fuck her then and there in the bloodwhirl of knife and random limbs and slashed carotids, amid the staccato cries of the flailing assassin, cell phone clipped to his belt, and the gaseous bloated moans of the dying Arthur Rapp.

DeLillo's last novel, 2001's ***The Body Artist,*** hinted that the author was recharging his batteries. The changes seemed fruitful, a new departure. That book was a novella billed as a novel, something Henry James could have written if he'd lived a century later. It was a ghost story spun from a single conceit: that a husband who'd committed suicide could have his last conversations repeated verbatim by an autistic visitor, who'd been hiding in the man's house, to the grieving wife who wanted to hear them. It was better than it sounds—just as, say, *The Turn of the Screw* is better than its synopsis.

The wife, the novella's protagonist, also happened to be a performance artist who modified her speech and gestures in order to become other people. This was a book about art and embodiment, and about what it feels like to be one human in a small world of a few others. A reduction of means produced richer effects than DeLillo had achieved before. Purely interior and intimate, the beauty of the book came via its exact descriptions of eating, moving, breathing and thinking.

Cosmopolis is also a novella, but one that has overgrown its boundaries. At more than 200 pages, it could have been 100. DeLillo is still interested in the capacities of single minds to discern order. This had always been a topic in his earlier fiction, and the reason that he was lumped with the "conspiracy" or "systems" novelists of the American postwar era. The Eric character has a monomaniacal take on it: "When he died he would not end. The world would end." The intimate psychological turn of ***The Body Artist*** is in evidence here. But if Eric is the single artificer of the world, he relies too much on his intimacy with technological extensions of his consciousness. He finds in computer analysis, as of financial markets, the essence of life, "the zero-oneness of the world, the digital imperative that defined every breath of the planet's living billions. . . . Our bodies and oceans were here, knowable and whole."

DeLillo's strength in the past came from his ability to show the limitations of people trying to hold on to the patterns they craved. He stood characters on the pivot between sense and senselessness. There is a moment in ***White Noise*** (1985) when Jack Gladney, exposed to vapors from a toxic cloud, has his chances of survival calculated by an infallible computer. It concludes he's already dead. That moment captured what it feels like to live enmeshed in numbers, patterns, algorithms—and still be able to look down at your two hands and see nothing changed. DeLillo wanted to know what it was like to be a statistical person, or a historical personage (as in ***Libra*** or ***Underworld***), and still a living person.

Cosmopolis gets caught in high technology and stumbles. It gives up a human dimension. DeLillo allows his protagonist to make declarations such as "[i]t was almost metaphysics"—about his wristwatch's "electron camera"—without cracking a smile. Dick Tracy had a neat watch, too, but that's not the same thing as the foundation of philosophy. And this, disappointingly, becomes the basis of a renewed "consciousness" plot. ***The Body Artist*** looked at personal and timeless paradoxes of inner life, retreating from the social themes for which DeLillo is celebrated—a temporary retrenchment that ***Cosmopolis*** could have made good on. But the new book suggests that the media of surveillance and replication, the technologies of computing and the scale changes of global finance do something weird to experience. Eric watches himself on a camera and begins to see events that haven't yet occurred. Instead of the intimate, we get the extrasensory. "A consciousness such as yours," someone tells Eric, "hyper-maniacal, may have contact points beyond the general perception."

One is reluctant to call Eric a consciousness, though. His is a deeply inconsistent but wholly loathsome character. And as if sensing that this line of quasi-philosophical explanation is going nowhere, the novel lapses from unexplained events into that oldest of narrative tricks, the theology for which the novel was made—predestination—as first we, then Eric, begin to foresee his death.

The texture of the novel is its most interesting feature. Characters appear and disappear. Eric's route isn't mapped and the chronology isn't altered. Only one aspect of space-time is affected: The narration starts to take apart our experience of interior, of private spaces. Eric's apartment unfolds, revealing a fantastic existence. We discover its expansion, as details grow like crabgrass: A rotating room erupts here, a shark tank there, and the apartment itself has "forty-eight rooms." Eric's limousine perfects this strangeness. Visitors stand up and leave it as if it were a bedroom. The floor is made of marble. The space contracts and widens.

There may be an argument to be made that the narration incarnates in its formal qualities the slippery nature of global finance-capital. Certainly the tone differs from the bourgeois modernist novellas of a dream space or dream logic, of which Arthur Schnitzler's *Traumnovelle* (the 1926 inspiration for Stanley Kubrick's 1999 *Eyes Wide Shut*) is archetypal. The narration here has a disjointed rather than a dreamy quality. It undergoes tiny fluctuations, which the reader registers without emotion. Capital may feel like something—or it may not. But does it simply feel unmotivated, like this?

As for the politics of the novel, don't even bother. You can't doubt that DeLillo's heart is in the right place. In the mouth of Eric's "chief of theory," however, a semi-academic named Vija Kinski, the book repeats watery versions of the stupidest analyses of the present, which are so unmindful of real conditions as to be neither of the left nor the right.

Fans of ***White Noise*** will remember that the theory specialist in that book was given the cleverest lines. This trick is a disaster the second time around. Anarchist protesters attack Times Square, and also Eric's limo, with the theorist and the capitalist seated inside:

> There were people approaching the car. Who were they? They were protesters, anarchists, whoever they were, a form of street theater, or adepts of sheer rampage. . . . It was a protest all right and they were smashing the windows of chain stores and loosing battalions of rats in restaurants and hotel lobbies.

Then the theorist gets to pronounce on them:

> 'You know what capitalism produces. According to Marx and Engels.'
>
> 'Its own grave-diggers,' [Eric] said.
>
> 'But these are not the grave-diggers. This is the free market itself. These people are a fantasy generated by the market. They don't exist outside the market. There is nowhere they can go to be on the outside. There is no outside.'

What follows is the most lifeless riot scene I have read. These are magic anarchists. They can do anything. Television used to be a subject for DeLillo's critical imagination. The extended scene in ***Mao II*** of the funeral of the Ayatollah Khomeini, seen on a TV set in New York, was unforgettable. Here DeLillo seems to have been captured by the ephemeral hysterical and already forgotten figures on his set. One of the great portraitists of the postmodern, DeLillo ends up accidentally illustrating the power of our era to turn writers into mere viewers.

When, in 50 years, the Library of America issues a volume titled *Underworld and Later Novels,* this contribution will exist for antiquarian interest. But it does nothing to diminish the sense that DeLillo still holds the stature of deserving to be read in 50 years. A bad book makes you dislike most novelists. This one, despite its faults, made me like DeLillo more. He attempted to think the present through, which is all we can ask of a writer. Sometimes even a master is caught in a back eddy of his own titanic project. May the next few years throw him a life preserver.

William Skidelsky (review date 26 May 2003)

SOURCE: Skidelsky, William. "Moronic Inferno." *New Statesman* 16, no. 758 (26 May 2003): 51.

[*In the following review, Skidelsky likens the plot and tone of* Cosmopolis *to a comic book, but concedes that the novel is well-written.*]

Don DeLillo's latest novel [***Cosmopolis***] is set in New York, and describes a day in the life of Eric Packer, a fantastically wealthy 28-year-old currency trader. The day begins with Packer deciding that he needs a haircut. Accompanied by Torval, his chief of security, he sets out across town in his stretch limousine. It is a bad day for travel: the president is in town, which, as Torval predicts, means they will "hit traffic which speaks in quarter inches." To make matters worse, an anti-capitalist demonstration is taking place, as well as the funeral of a rap star.

Packer lives in a 48-room triplex, and owns a Soviet fighter plane. His limousine (inside which most of the action takes place) is decked with an "array of visual display units . . . medleys of data on every screen." A member of the global super-rich, he thinks nothing of going tiger hunting in Siberia with fellow multibillionaires. His mind, like a computer, operates at superhuman speed: faced by the flashing rows of data in his limo, we are told that "he absorbed this information in a couple of long still seconds". He is also in touch with less cerebral urges: his physical appetites feature prominently in the novel, and he interrupts his journey in order to have rough sex with several women.

All the while, he speculates on the imminent fall of the yen. Having risen unexpectedly overnight, this continues to climb throughout the day. Against the advice of his chief financial adviser, Packer continues borrowing money in vast sums. In the process, he squanders not just his own fortune, but also that of his wife, into whose accounts he manages to break. Oddly, Packer doesn't seem perturbed by this. In a way, his financial ruin is confirmation of his solipsistic belief that "when he died, he would not end. The world would end." For it is not just he and his wife who suffer as a result of his erratic dealings; he brings the economy crashing down with him.

The dizzying pace of technological progress, a perennial theme in DeLillo's work, here takes on the quality of an obsession. In Packer's eyes, the present is forever receding into obsolescence. Everyday objects strike him as absurdly outmoded. Diamonds are "a form of money so obsolete Eric didn't even know how to think about it." Palm Pilots, too, are ridiculously old-fashioned. Packer's technological *hauteur* engenders some of the smartest writing in the novel.

Cosmopolis is, for the most part, a zany novel, a riot of wacky observations and madcap insights. As usual, DeLillo hints at mysterious connections between things that seem to have little in common: during the anti-capitalist protest, Packer thinks he sees a "shadow of transaction between the demonstrators and the state"; one of his advisers identifies "an affinity between market movements and the natural world." Some American reviewers have mocked this aspect of his work, criticising his presumption to, as one critic put it, have a "direct line on the weird, powerful yet slippery spectacles and paradoxes of contemporary life." And it is true that, with its mostly preposterous storyline and apocalyptic atmosphere, ***Cosmopolis*** does at times resemble a comic book.

Yet one can forgive DeLillo such excesses, because he writes so well. Torval is described as a "man whose head seemed removable for maintenance"; Packer's chief of technology sits in a "masturbatory crouch." The novel opens with the following description of Packer's insomniac nights: "Sleep failed him more often now, not once or twice a week but four times, five. What did he do when this happened? He did not take long walks into the scrolling dawn. There was no friend he loved enough to harrow with a call." Anyone inclined to doubt DeLillo's powers as a writer should reflect on the poetry of this passage, and on those two unexpected words, "scrolling" and "harrow."

Peter Dempsey (review date 7 June 2003)

SOURCE: Dempsey, Peter. "Speculating into the Void." *Spectator* 292, no. 9122 (7 June 2003): 38.

[*In the following review, Dempsey counters the critical consensus regarding the perceived flaws of* Cosmopolis*, finding merit in the novel's structure and descriptive prose.*]

Though Don DeLillo published his first novel in 1971, it was during the 1980s with such books as the effervescent and grimly comic campus novel ***White Noise*** (1985) and the breath-takingly structured story of the Kennedy assassination ***Libra*** (1989) that he became both critic's catnip and a best-seller. In the 1990s, DeLillo wrote what many consider his best work, the monumental ***Underworld*** (1997). Since then he's published a novella-length ghost story, ***The Body Artist*** (2000), and now this [***Cosmopolis***], his unlucky 13th work of fiction which has been met with dismay, both here and in the US, gathering probably the worst set of reviews for a highly regarded novelist in recent years. It isn't surprising to see why. There is no real plot, there are no fully rounded characters nor any character development, and though the novel ends dramatically, there is no sense of a conventionally satisfying conclusion.

What then is the novel about? Essentially, it is a meditation on various kinds of speculation, most importantly financial and philosophical. Set in April, 2000, just as the dotcom boom is about to end, this bleak, austerely beautiful novel tells the story of one day in the life of 28-year-old Eric Packer, a self-destructive billionaire currency speculator, and his cross-town trip in his bullet-proof stretch limousine along 47th Street in Manhattan to get a haircut and his 'speculating into the void' as he puts it. On his journey a succession of odd characters joins him in the car. Packer leaves it in pursuit of his new wife and to visit his lover. He watches a rapper's funeral and an anti-globalisation demonstration in Times Square. His destination is the barber shop of an old friend of his father's. Lastly, he meets an ex-employee who will alter his life forever.

From UN Plaza and Trump Tower in the east, through the jewellery and theatre districts, and on to the dilapidated car lots at the west end, the novel is carefully anchored in the reality of 47th Street itself, from the vast wealth and power of the east end of the street to the social disenfranchisement of the west. This simple, linear progression of both limo and narrative is intercut with two remarkable 'confessions' by one Benno Levin, a disaffected ex-employee of Packer's. Benno is one in a long line of DeLillo eccentrics who have become unhinged by loss and a sense of injustice. We realise with a shudder half-way through the first of his monologues that it is happening after Packer has reached the end of his journey, which gives the novel a haunting sense of foreboding. The 'shabby man at the ATM' Packer sees later is Benno and his monologues are one of the triumphs of the novel.

DeLillo is often accused of creating characters who talk in 'DeLillo-speak', and are mouthpieces for the author's theories, in this instance, about globalisation and cybercapital. It certainly seems so with the various figures who talk to Packer in his limo and who appear as uncomprehending, wraith-like creatures from the *Odyssey*'s Hades. This, however, is to misunderstand what DeLillo is up to and is at the heart of the dreadful reception the novel has had. DeLillo is not trying to write a piece of well-wrought realism and failing; he is trying to do something quite different. Towards the end of the novel, Packer's actions fly in the face of common sense and are ultimately unfathomable. This is familiar from DeLillo's early novels, which are determinedly unconventional and therefore little read. For his admirers, DeLillo has an appealing contrariness, a heroic resistance to novelistic conventions which is stamped through his work like the letters in the middle of a piece of seaside rock. So, what we have here is a 'feel-bad' novel redeemed by its beguiling structure and the cool intensity of its compelling descriptions of New York City. For most, it won't be DeLillo's best, but, as Packer says of the rapper's music, 'his best songs were sensational, and even the ones that were not good were good'.

Kyle Minor (review date summer 2003)

SOURCE: Minor, Kyle. Review of *Cosmopolis,* by Don DeLillo. *Antioch Review* 61, no. 3 (summer 2003): 581.

[*In the following review, Minor contrasts "the remarkable unity and brevity" of* Cosmopolis *with the sprawling settings and imagery of DeLillo's other novels.*]

The protagonist of ***Cosmopolis*** is Eric Packer, age twenty-eight. Packer manages a portfolio so large that he can sway the world markets at whim. On the last day of the late '90's market boom, Packer makes a disastrous bet against the yen and refuses to cut his losses. He kills his chief of security. He nearly destroys his unconsummated marriage to a renowned poet who can smell the sex on him. Then he hacks into her investment accounts and drains them, hoping that their shared financial ruin will allow them to "see each other clean, in killing light." None of this is unfamiliar territory for DeLillo, who also manages to weave into the narrative the funeral procession of a Sufi rap star, an assault from a serial cream pie assassin, political protests involving rats, massive conglomerations of naked people on the set of a failing film shoot, and a secret daytime designer drug rave. DeLillo explores again the role of the artist, the killer, the individual, and the group in society, preoccupied always with the natural decline of order into chaos. What is new is the remarkable unity and brevity of the narrative. Gone is the enormous, half-century landscape of ***Underworld,*** or the long explorations of visual images that have dominated his work since ***White Noise.*** In ***Cosmopolis,*** DeLillo condenses the action down to a single day, following a single character,

Packer, as he crosses New York in a stretch limousine and takes meetings with lieutenants and sexual partners and a barber. One senses that DeLillo continues to challenge himself after thirteen novels, and the result is a mature work of fiction, greatly satisfying.

Robert L. McLaughlin (review date summer 2003)

SOURCE: McLaughlin, Robert L. Review of *Cosmopolis,* by Don DeLillo. *Review of Contemporary Fiction* 23, no. 2 (summer 2003): 120.

[*In the following review, McLaughlin discusses the thematic and structural significance of time in* Cosmopolis.]

Cosmopolis is set in April 2000, a postmillennial, pre-9/11 time significant for being a month removed from the NASDAQ's record-setting closing number, 5048.62. This, then, is the beginning of the end of the nineties boom, and DeLillo's protagonist, billionaire currency- and stock-speculator Eric Packer, is poised on the surface of a bubble that's about to burst. On one level, the narrative is quite simple: Eric leaves his multistoried, multimillion-dollar apartment on Manhattan's east side and takes a trip across town on 47th Street in his custom-made limo to get a haircut, a journey delayed by midtown traffic, a presidential motorcade, a broken water main, a rap star's funeral procession, an anti-global-capital riot, and Eric's whims. It is also a journey from riches to rags (as Eric's hubristic speculations bring his empire crashing down), from morning to night, from life to death—all reinforcing the inevitability of time's arrow. Yet at the same time it is a journey from the present to the past: Eric's destination is his father's childhood neighborhood and the barbershop where Eric had his first haircut—this man whose success is based in his ability not just to predict the future but to bring that future into being needs the familiarity, the repetition, the sameness of his distant past. The novel's structure reflects this tension between the forward and backward movement of time: the bulk of the narrative follows Eric's trip from river to river chronologically, but two interpolated excerpts from the journals of Benno Levin (a.k.a. Richard Sheets), ex-currency analyst and current homeless person who will, apparently, kill Eric, are presented chronologically backward and out of sync with Eric's narrative.

These structural and thematic explorations of time provide the context for Eric's search for patterns—the predictable and controllable—in numbers, nature, and life, versus life's tendency to offer us uncontrollable random phenomena—surprise. Within the rigid order of the day, Eric is offered many surprises: several unexpected encounters with his mysterious wife; the unaccountable and (for him) disastrous rise of the yen against the dollar; a cream pie in the face courtesy of an international pastry terrorist; and his chance encounter with Benno, who has staked his own identity on Eric's death. As surprise overwhelms him, Eric tries more and more rashly to assert control, swinging from the homicidal to the suicidal.

Once again, DeLillo has captured the essence of a particular American moment: the solipsism of power, the paranoia of control, the inequities and immateriality of wealth, the shock of recognition as a system begins to collapse. ***Cosmopolis*** is a beautiful and brilliant book.

Joseph S. Walker (essay date fall 2004)

SOURCE: Walker, Joseph S. "A Kink in the System: Terrorism and the Comic Mystery Novel." *Studies in the Novel* 36, no. 3 (fall 2004): 336-51.

[*In the following excerpt, Walker contrasts the violent strategies of the terrorist with the narrative strategies of the writer within the contexts of "In the Ruins of the Future" and* Mao II.]

> We live in fictitious times . . . where we have fictitious election results that elects [sic] a fictitious president . . . sending us to war for fictitious reasons.
>
> —*Michael Moore's Oscar acceptance speech*

There is in our time an uncontainable rupture of the boundaries between the fictional and the real that, for many, has come to seem the dominant characteristic of public culture. While politics, as Michael Moore suggested to resounding boos at the 2003 Oscar ceremony, is one particularly visible location of that rupture, another—and one that increasingly licenses the open fictionalizing of the political—is terrorism. For both the politician and the terrorist, the goal is to recraft the collective experience of the world through the generation of a narrative that cannot be resisted. Public life has always been a network of fictions, of course; what may well be new is the nakedness with which the creation and manipulation of narrative are cheerfully displayed. Writing in the aftermath of September 11 (will it ever again be necessary to specify a year?), Don DeLillo, in his essay **"In the Ruins of the Future,"** sees the men who destroyed the World Trade Center as reacting against "the power of American culture to penetrate every wall, home, life and mind. Terror's response is a narrative that has been developing over years, only now becoming inescapable." The polyvalent, continual babble of American narrativizing is answered, shockingly, by the singular plot of terror, which seeks to deaden and silence multiplicity: "Plots reduce the world." In this reading of the terrorist attacks DeLillo echoes Murray Jay Siskind, the eccentric intellectual of ***White Noise,*** who tells his friend Jack to deal with impending death by becoming a killer rather than a dier, by plotting a murder: "We start our lives in chaos . . . To plot is to affirm life, to seek shape and control" (291-92).

While he follows Murray in interpreting the formation of narrative through violence as one means of affirming the coherent self, however, DeLillo does not go on to advocate that we ourselves become killers. Rather, his purposefully fragmented and digressive essay argues forcibly that we respond to plot with *plots,* that we continue to insist upon our own investment in a ceaseless variety of narrative. The very stories we tell of the disaster become the crucial basis of our survival and recovery: "There are 100,000 stories crisscrossing New York, Washington, and the world. . . . There are the doctors' appointments that saved lives, the cell phones that were used to report the hijackings." Tellingly, even the stories of those who invent their involvement in the attacks become significant: "This is also the counternarrative, a shadow history of false memories and imagined loss." The centerpiece of DeLillo's essay, occupying several paragraphs, is the story of how his nephew Marc and Marc's wife and children, who live a few blocks from the towers, react to the unfolding events of the day, at several points believing they are going to die but eventually reaching the safety of a shelter and resuming something like normalcy. Despite DeLillo's acknowledgement of his relationship to the characters, the story is valuable precisely because it is not remarkable, because it could be anyone's story or even an invention. What is valuable is the act of narrating itself, the refusal to be silenced in the face of the terror narrative that threatens to overwhelm all.

For DeLillo the job of the writer is thus not to create another all-encompassing narrative opposed to that of terror (as Moore implies, this is the function of the politician), but rather to insist upon a return to narrative as personal, partial, incomplete, to contribute to the limitless mosaic of plots that do not insist upon domination: "the event asserts its singularity. . . . The writer tries to give memory, tenderness and meaning to all that howling space." This opposition to terror does not imply, however, that DeLillo simply endorses those penetrative, globalizing aspects of American culture that he has positioned the terrorists against; such a reading would place DeLillo the essayist in direct opposition to much of his own fiction. John Duvall, as part of an overview of DeLillo's novels, has suggested that his work "still holds out an almost modernist hope for the vocation of the contemporary writer and her or his attempt to forge the imagistic space of the novel as a counterforce to the image manipulation of capital" (561). Similarly, Margaret Scanlan sees fiction like DeLillo's as "urging the reader to consider an alternative perspective, hoping to free up some space in the real world for another interpretation of the patriotic myth, the official version, the sacred text" (21). Duvall and Scanlan here position DeLillo himself as seeking, like the terrorists, to subvert the transient dominant culture of pure spectacle and consumption, "the global momentum that seemed to be driving unmindfully toward a landscape of consumer-robots" (**"Ruins"** [**"In the Ruins of the Future"**]). DeLillo makes clear, however, that the strategy of the terrorists is a dead-end ("there is no logic in apocalypse"); he would, perhaps, align himself instead with "the protesters in Genoa, Prague, Seattle" whose opposition to the Americanization of the globe is not fanatically one-dimensional but "a moderating influence, trying to slow things down, even things out, hold off the white-hot future." The writer, similarly, must resist the universalizing strategies of both American hegemony and terrorist absolutism, seeking instead a middle ground of possibility, openness, alternatives.

The DeLillo of **"In the Ruins of the Future"** seems optimistic that such a writer's strategy will ultimately be more successful than the terrorists'; his essay concludes on a note of faith that New York City will again become a place that "will accommodate every language, ritual, belief and opinion." This optimism may well seem surprising not only because it follows so closely upon the heels of the destruction of 9/11, but also because it is at odds with the darker implications of much recent fiction that addresses terrorism and the writer's relationship to it, including DeLillo's own. Indeed, it is nearly impossible to consider contemporary fiction's engagement with terrorism without taking the more pessimistic vision of DeLillo's ***Mao II*** and its central figure, the novelist Bill Gray, into account. A cult favorite who has become more famous for his reclusive habits than his two novels, Bill is reminiscent of J. D. Salinger or Thomas Pynchon but is most frequently seen as a stand-in for DeLillo himself, though any number of critics have pointed out the problematic aspects of this identification of author with character (e.g., Simmons 678). In what are almost certainly ***Mao II***'s most famous passages, Bill discusses his theories of terrorism with Brita Nilsson, the photographer taking his portrait. Bill feels that "'There's a curious knot that binds novelists and terrorists,'" and while he once believed that "'it was possible for a novelist to alter the inner life of the culture,'" he now thinks that "'we're giving way to terror, to news of terror, to tape recorders and cameras, to radios, to bombs stashed in radios'" (41-42). The very sequencing of this list is significant, moving from the actuality of violent acts to the transmission of them and finally linking the two in a single image: the universalized media *as* terror, a world "in which occasions of symbolic contiguity are achieved only through the mass-mediated news of violence, atrocity, and disaster" (Green 574).

Later Bill tells George Haddad, a character who bridges the literary and terrorist worlds, that the relationship is precise: "What terrorists gain, novelists lose. . . . The danger they represent equals our own failure to be dangerous" (157). George extrapolates from this premise, suggesting that terrorists must then be "the only possible heroes for our time," and that "in societies reduced to blur and glut . . . only the terrorist stands outside." Bill rejects such idealization as "pure myth" (158), but this idea—that terrorists have replaced novelists as the only possible source of meaningful resistance—permeates ***Mao II*** and has become the haunting possibility that must be confronted in any consideration of the relationship between artistic creation and terrorist violence. In *Plotting Terror,* her study of the treatment of terrorism in contemporary fiction, Scanlan suggests that we "see both writers and terrorists in these novels as remnants of a romantic belief in the power of marginalized persons to transform history" (2). Bill, however, has lost this romantic belief, at least insofar as it concerns writers, and the narrative shape of ***Mao II*** leaves us little reason to believe that he is wrong. Surrendering control of his unpublished third novel to an assistant concerned more with publicity than art, he allows himself to be reduced to the mere image of a novelist rather than one deeply engaged in the effort for change. The very idea of being a writer seems suffused with nostalgia in ***Mao II,*** as though the novelist has already faded completely into obsolescence.

The bulk of DeLillo's book narrates Bill's attempt to use his fame—the fame which has become his only tool for promoting change—to free a poet taken hostage in the Middle East, but his journey there is marked by futility and confusion, and he ultimately dies, whereupon the very identity that has become his only resource is stolen from him and sold to "some militia in Beirut" (217). The very narrative of the novel thus seems designed to lend credence to Bill's vision of the writer as impotent in a world dominated by images of terror; the writer's own identity is ultimately just one more image the terrorist can assimilate and exploit, and writing itself has been abandoned. Mark Osteen suggests that ***Mao II*** advances in writing's place a new model of hope for "oppositional authorship" in Brita, who in the novel's closing section photographs the elusive terrorist leader Bill fails to even reach before his death. For Osteen, the fundamental ambiguity of photographic images allows Brita to participate in the society of the spectacle without reducing her work to "a univocal meaning" (667). While such a reading may preserve hope for art, however, it holds none for *writing,* and if Brita's photographs do possess the kind of ambiguity and multiplicity DeLillo hopes for in his essay it is also clear how easily they can be assimilated, exploited and discarded by a society that consumes images with ravenous speed. Brita herself is frustrated with the difficulty of conveying unpleasant truths through film, frustrated that "'no matter what I shot, how much horror, reality, misery, ruined bodies, bloody faces, it was all so fucking pretty'" (24).

In short, ***Mao II*** seems to share none of the optimism expressed in **"In The Ruins of the Future"** that the writer can offer a meaningful alternative to the terrorist as a source of resistance. Instead, DeLillo's novel functions as the template for serious-minded contemporary fiction's endlessly renewed attempt to come to terms with terrorism (it is hardly accidental that it is the subject of the first chapter of Scanlan's book). The rivalry for cultural significance between novelists and terrorists, so explicitly laid out in Bill's dialogue, is revisited again and again in other recent novels, with the writer repeatedly portrayed as increasingly irrelevant to a culture that can be possessed by terror. The identification of character (in this case, Bill) with the author himself (an identification that DeLillo must have understood would play significantly into the reception of the novel, even if it is not exact) is also extremely typical of these novels, reflecting their central thematic concern with the entanglement of narrative-making and reality which is the stock in trade of both the terrorist and the novelist. Recent novels about terrorism, that is to say, tend to draw heavily upon postmodernism's elision of the distinctions between history and fiction, its insistence that we understand both as creative acts that impose meaning upon events. In their insistently visible blurring of (auto)biography, history, news and fiction, novels such as DeLillo's (and those of Philip Roth and Paul Auster . . .) highlight (to return to Duvall's term) the "image manipulation" inherent not only to dominant consumer culture, but to any representation that claims the status of coherent truth—including those forged by terrorists, or politicians. It may well be only here, in their shared implication that any "truth" is necessarily constructed, imperfect, ambiguous, unobtainable, that these novels find their point of resistance to a globalizing Americanism that regards its own truth as self-evident and undeniable. As we will see, however, this idea is complicated by the failure of any of the writer/characters within the texts to maintain meaningful positions of resistance, and also by the realization that some elements of popular consumer culture may themselves engage the "truth" of dominant capitalist culture in a more complicated way than critics such as Scanlan recognize. . . .

Works Cited

DeLillo, Don. "In The Ruins Of The Future." *Guardian* 22 December 2001. *Guardian Unlimited* 20 May 2003 <http://www.guardian.co.uk/Archive/Article/0.4273, 4324579,00.html.

———. *Mao II.* New York: Penguin, 1991.

———. White Noise*: Text And Criticism.* Ed. Mark Osteen. New York: Penguin, 1998.

Duvall, John N. "From Valparaiso to Jerusalem: DeLillo and the Moment of Canonization." *Modern Fiction Studies* 45.3 (Fall 1999): 559-68.

Green, Jeremy. "Disaster Footage: Spectacles of Violence in DeLillo's Fiction." *Modern Fiction Studies* 45.3 (Fall 1999): 571-99.

Osteen, Mark. "Becoming Incorporated: Spectacular Authorship and DeLillo's *Mao II*." *Modern Fiction Studies* 45.3 (Fall 1999): 643-74.

Scanlan, Margaret. *Plotting Terror: Novelists and Terrorists in Contemporary Fiction.* Charlottesville: UP of Virginia, 2001.

Simmons, Ryan. "What Is A Terrorist?: Contemporary Authorship, the Unabomber, and DeLillo's *Mao II*." *Modern Fiction Studies* 45.3 (Fall 1999): 675-723.

Richard Hardack (essay date fall 2004)

SOURCE: Hardack, Richard. "Two's a Crowd: *Mao II,* Coke II, and the Politics of Terrorism in Don DeLillo." *Studies in the Novel* 36, no. 3 (fall 2004): 374-92.

[*In the following essay, Hardack explores DeLillo's representation of xenophobia in* Mao II, *demonstrating how the threat of the foreign coupled with mass consumerism foments domestic terrorism.*]

> I keep thinking, without too much supporting evidence, that images have something to do with crowds. An image is a crowd in a way, a smear of impressions. Images tend to draw people together, create mass identity.
>
> —Don DeLillo, **"The Image and the Crowd"** (72-73)

In his 1991 novel ***Mao II,*** Don DeLillo stages a battle between the notion of an individual Western identity and that of a "mass-produced" foreign consciousness, a contest producing equal amounts of xenophobia and paranoia. For most of the novel's characters, an alienating mass identity is emblematized by images of non-Western languages and religious and political leaders such as Mao. But for the novel's author, the seemingly foreign "cult of Mao" turns out to represent a product of American consumer culture—that is, an American appropriation of mass terrorism and the commerce of mechanical reproduction (or a Warhol aesthetic and what it signifies). For DeLillo's characters, xenophobia accompanies such an appropriation as an expression of anxiety over "mass identity" and mass production (displaced onto and emblematized by mass weddings); group identities of consumer culture; photographs that displace the "original" object; and hybridized or multicultural texts and languages. The American notion of terrorism, at least at the point DeLillo was writing, is then born from an acute fear of collective identity based in a long Western literary tradition of fetishizing the individual.

DeLillo sets up an opposition between the Western writer/individual and the Eastern/mass terrorist only to collapse it, for example in recontextualizing the alleged "invasion" of global/third-world English into the United States, and in tracing the myriad ways in which an ideology of American individualism is itself surreptitiously predicated on the practices of "foreign" mass production. The anachronistic white writer's individual words are cast against foreign, hybridized "mass" languages of advertising, politics, and terrorism. Throughout ***Mao II,*** DeLillo dramatizes the speciousness of the dichotomy between the domestic and the foreign, both of which turn out to be products of the same Western imagination. More dramatically, the foreign terrorist emerges as the alter ego of the American writer. In this process, the figure of Mao comes to designate not a foreign or alternative social or economic system, but the very mechanics of capitalist production in DeLillo's America. In this sense, one never sees Mao, but only Mao II, a Mao effect.

The appearance of a second Mao or Mao II in the text, Warhol's mass-produced dissemination of the Mao image, is paralleled by the appearance of the product Coke II—to some extent a parodic version of the ill-fated New Coke—staging an ironic contest between which two equally Western symbols will colonize the world. In this series of transpositions, DeLillo dramatizes what Anthony Giddens describes as the surprise of postmodernism, that "scarcely anyone today seems to identify post-modernity with what it was once widely accepted to mean—the replacement of capitalism by socialism" (46). Instead, postmodernity perversely heralds the apparent 'replacement' (but actual supplementation) of capitalism by the capitalist symbols of socialism. With archly postmodern irony, DeLillo uses the appropriated, primary symbol of Marxism to critique capitalist xenophobia and its appropriation of other sign systems to its own uses. The children of Marx and Coca Cola grow up to inherit one another, and discover their actual fraternity.

In this essay I explore the frustrating complexity of xenophobia in DeLillo's texts: where it is generated, whom DeLillo's critique is aimed at, and how we determine what is genuinely foreign. To what extent does the author identify with the views of his white protagonist Bill Gray—is that figure for DeLillo a victim of foreign ideologies or his own xenophobia? An unresolved tension between the implied author's and characters' world-view makes the answer to these questions difficult to determine. I conclude that DeLillo dramatizes and duplicates a version of xenophobia whose premises he finds ultimately self-deluding but still alluring: while DeLillo ultimately destabilizes the site of what is foreign, he continues to reify an anxiety that the image poses a foreign threat to American individuality. Throughout, as may already be apparent, my focus will be less on actual terrorist figures in the novel (Abu Rashid and George Haddad) than on the threat their non-whiteness and mass cultural forms—perceived as a non-differentiated, uniformly alien "Mao-ism"—represents to a xenophobic mindset that invites homegrown displays of terrorism.

* * *

To contextualize DeLillo's configurations of white male individuality, it is useful to consider a brief history of ideas about mass identity in America, filtered through the discourse of transcendental pantheism that defines the individual white male through his merger with a mass body of nature. DeLillo's writer belongs to a lineage of isolated white male individualists who oppose, yet also depend on, the mass in American literature. As Karen's father observes early in the novel, "'crowd' is not the right word. He doesn't know what to call them" (5). The original crowd in America is really the mass, from white male to white whale.

Many nineteenth-century writers, particularly those anticipating the values of the cold war canon, situate white male American identity as either a conspiracy or contest between the individual and the crowd or mass.[1] In "What Causes Democratic Nations to Incline Towards Pantheism," in *Democracy in America,* Tocqueville defines the allegedly self-reliant American in terms of his surprising desire to merge with the state, a merger that is paralleled by transcendental fusions with nature or the OverSoul in writers such as Emerson and Melville:

> If there is a philosophical system which teaches that all things material and immaterial . . . are to be considered only as the several parts of an immense Being, who alone remains eternal amidst the continual change and ceaseless transformation of all that constitutes him . . . such a system, though it destroy the individuality of man, or rather because it destroys that individuality, will have secret charms for men living in democracies. . . .
>
> (II.31-32)

One of a long line of Catholic anti-pantheist tract writers, the New York based Reverend Morgan Dix echoes Tocqueville in his 1864 *Lectures on the Pantheistic Idea of an Impersonal Deity*: "imagine, if you can, this indescribable, this immense condition, or mass, or state (or by whatever name you wish to call it) and you have before you the only eternal being. Let us apply to it, for the sake of convenience, the term God" (22).[2]

In this transcendental American pantheism, white men merge with the mass of (an often racialized) god/nature to transcend the constraints of Jacksonian individuality, inordinate self-reliance, and social atomization. To merge with that mass body of nature, as Ishmael repeatedly does at sea, or Emerson in the woods, leaves the transcendentalist in a mystic reverie, one portending the transcendence DeLillo's Karen achieves in attaining her vision of mass identity. As Americans come to perceive their individualities as parts of an immense impersonal Being, or of the technological state, both of which ceaselessly transform them, a pantheistic merger with the mass is both a cure to the isolation of white male individuality and a pernicious threat to its autonomy. In a society where "men are broken up" into inequalities, people will have a great desire to merge their individualities into the immense mass of the government, the All of nature, or some unified god: after Lauren Berlant, we might call this a national fantasy of anatomy (Tocqueville II.23).[3]

In mid-nineteenth century America, the tension between self-reliance and fraternal merger with the mass or All is often embodied in transcendental pantheism. For many of these transcendental writers, individuation, the basis of American self-representation, also becomes a form of fragmentation from the mass or whole. For Emerson, for example, "As soon as there is departure from this universal feeling, we are made to feel it painfully" ("The Heart" 284). Emerson's repressed rhetoric of a dialectic between a dispossessive merger and painful individuation startlingly erupts in 1860 in his desire to draw and quarter the masses, to break and divide this inchoate unity into parts:

> Leave this hypocritical prating about the masses. Masses are rude, lame, unmade, pernicious. . . . I wish not to concede anything to them, but to tame, drill, divide, and break them up, and draw individuals out of them. . . . Masses! the calamity is the masses. I do not wish any mass at all. . . .
>
> ("Considerations by the Way," W, VI, 249)

Melville often expressed his doubts about such transcendental inconsistency and universal identity in his letters to Hawthorne: "It seems an inconsistency to assert unconditional democracy in all things, and yet confess a dislike to all mankind—in the mass. But not so . . ." (Davis and Gilman 127). In *Moby Dick,* Ishmael overtakes his creator to conclude, "But from the same point, take mankind in *mass,* and for the most part, they seem a mob of unnecessary duplicates, both contemporary and hereditary" (441, emphasis mine). As Melville's Pierre learns, however, individuation in America is a manifestation not of Pan but of pain. To live as an individual male is to be painfully violated, to suffer withdrawal from the reverie of unity with the mass or All, and compulsively to reenact this fragmentation of human bodies. Throughout his work, Emerson believes that individuation is painful, but that social connection—being part of a mass or crowd—truncates men as well; rarely does he put it more simply than in "Prudence": "society is officered by *men of parts,* as they are properly called, and not by divine men" (W, II.231).

From Melville's fantasy of merger with the All of nature through DeLillo's postmodern vision of a monolithic consumer culture, the conception of national or mass identity remains unstable and double-edged. The violence we have seen in Emerson and Melville is often remapped, these days all too conveniently, onto the foreign mass and the foreign terrorist. If DeLillo resurrects aspects of this dialectic, his characters no longer bear even the hope of transcendence, only the oscillation between merger with the mass and the severance of extreme white individuation.

Before ***Mao II,*** DeLillo had focused on white male individuality in relation to foreign languages and identities. Like ***Mao II,*** DeLillo's ***White Noise*** is about the subject position of white America, and perhaps a resounding of the white silence of *Moby Dick.* (Many white noise machines, in fact, produce frequencies that sound like indecipherable murmurs, serving as kinds of verbal Rorschachs, the aural equivalent of the white whale's exclusively visual signs. ***White Noise*** is filled with hints that its opaque foreign languages are in part fantasies of white "consciousness," the foreign noise whiteness itself makes.) In this context, ***Mao II*** becomes *White Noise II,* a recoloration of that book's politics: as Bill's name states, he is not even white anymore, but gray.

White Noise prefaces the cultural dynamics of ***Mao II,*** where the individualist white novelist is implicitly supplanted not just by the foreign terrorist, but by the multicultural writer. In ***White Noise,*** DeLillo's middle-class white characters frequently assert that "these kind of things"—toxic events, what they see as third world disasters—don't happen in middle America. Yet their middle America, in their eyes, is under siege, and even at the holy site of the mall, "people spoke English, Hindi, Vietnamese, related tongues" (82). In ***Mao II,*** the "thousand of Arabic words weaving between the letters and Roman numerals of the Coke II logo" relocate the contest between these "overlapping" languages, but also their necessary hybridity in the postmodern marketplace (230). Language and identity, symbols of commerce and ideology, become indeterminate not in remote spaces, but in the most familiar locations. Jack Gladney—whom DeLillo with blunt irony casts as a professor of Hitler Studies who cannot speak German, and who never engages the ethnic genocides of the holocaust—similarly obsesses over what he sees as foreign incursions to his white masculinity: "What kind of name is Orest? I studied his features. He might have been Hispanic, Middle Eastern, Central Asian, a dark skinned eastern European, a light skinned black. . . . It was getting hard to know what you could say to people" (208). The foreign is consistently couched in such lists in DeLillo's work: litanies of countries, languages, and products. Against "the vast loneliness and dissatisfaction of [American] consumers who have lost their group identity" (50), the apparently reliable, stable mass identities of foreign nations, and the impenetrable codes of foreign languages, simultaneously become sites of envy, resentment, and blame. Jealous of "foreigners" who retain an "original," non-mediated sense of group identity—and stripped of what Robert Bellah similarly designates as a national sense of transcendent communal identity—some Americans terrorize the Other by imagining that the Other is terrorizing them.

As part of his response to post-cold war identity politics, DeLillo champions the notion of the individualist white writer even while dismantling the assumptions of that icon, situating him as part of a mass cult of individuality. Once we reach ***Mao II,*** what is portrayed as a white mass American consciousness in crisis comes to rest on the sagging shoulders of the writer Bill Gray, who lives as if he were a terrorist. Gray fears that history and writing, all representation, are becoming the domain of the mass Other and not the individual American writer. As part of a consistent strategy of displacement, DeLillo omits any sustained reference to late twentieth-century "white" terrorism, for example of white American militias or the IRA. This glaring omission, which reinforces the validity of Bill's fears, may serve to stage a wholly contrived and limited contest between a false image of the "foreign" and a contaminated idea of American identity. (The other notable unvoiced doubles of the novel's Mao squared are the Mau Mau, the Kenyan "terrorists" who violently opposed colonial whites: DeLillo of course chooses to emphasize certain oppositions, here between archetypal East and West, and dissemble others.) DeLillo focuses his xenophobia, for example, on foreign mass weddings rather than any "others" or groups more routinely demonized at home (even Mormon multiple weddings could be viewed as a more appropriate domestic symbol of DeLillo's mass identity, but they are never invoked). Yet despite the ways such exclusions continue to delineate and justify white/individualist anxieties before the invasion of foreign consciousness, the novel reveals this "mass consciousness" as a reification of the ideology of American individualism. Through these strategies of omission and displacement, DeLillo powerfully, yet still only obliquely, intimates that America is itself a truly foreign element, and has also practiced its own version of terrorism, in the rest of the world.

How does DeLillo propose that American individualism depends on "mass identity" or mass production? Throughout the novel, DeLillo obsessively delineates the way simple "technical" duplication—especially reproductions of advertisements, photographs and other media—allies itself with an ethos of mass-produced identity. What is stereotypically foreign—hypostatized in Maoist dogma, terrorist causes and Islamic fundamentalism[4]—merges individual into mass identity, sometimes under the guise of a slogan or logo. Two always becomes a foreign crowd, a mass, opposed to the individual American, and everything of which there is more than one or that occurs more than once is foreign: in the book's resonant final line, its last depiction of Beirut, we witness "the dead city photographed one more time" (240). Anything photographed rather than inscribed—i.e. anything tainted by a Warholian version of mechanical reproduction—already exists in duplicate. It has joined the impersonal mass, is no longer individual, and is therefore already terrorized and even dead.

From Bill's perspective, the aura of the mass-produced or replicated object replaces the soul of the unique original. In Bill's particular and peculiar redefinition, aura—a projected image detached from a missing original, that is infinitely replicable but finally unattainable—is itself foreign; and it parasitically feeds off (a putatively Western, somehow "individual") fully-present nature. Such an inflected notion of aura projects a cultural xenophobia about the decay of Western culture caused by the infiltrations of foreign languages and innovations—finally by anything that purports to threaten the imagined autonomy of the individual humanist voice. Under that projection, Bill implicitly correlates mass production with mass consciousness as if they were coterminous. But in the process of duplication, what is stereotypically American—the mass-produced Ford car, the universally replicated Coca Cola bottle, and the impersonal collective logo of the credit card—becomes indistinguishable from the "Maoist" dogma it seems to oppose.

Through such juxtapositions, DeLillo's text destabilizes cause and effect in the relationship between the domestic and the foreign: is Western mass production, which allegedly emblematizes individualism, combating or fomenting "Asian" and Eastern mass production? Moreover, could this Asian mass production primarily be a fantasy of the West? How is Western logo translated into, or returned to us as, foreign logos? DeLillo suggests that in the image of Mao II, in all it represents in his text, the West is creating its own East. That Mao turns out to be a front for Western ideologies is consistent with DeLillo's long-running obsession with conspiracy, disguise, and cultural projection; after all, James Axton in ***The Names,*** searching for himself in foreign languages and cultures, doesn't recognize the "foreign" in himself, or even allow himself to acknowledge that he works for the CIA.

In ***Mao II,*** the individualist white Western writer and the cult of Mao/terrorism/mass production are continually contrasted with one another. We are told that

> The cult of Mao was the cult of the book . . . a summoning of crowds where everyone dressed alike and thought alike. . . . Isn't there beauty and power in the repetition of certain words and phrases? . . . They became a book-waving crowd. Mao said, 'Our god is none other than the masses of the Chinese people.' And this is what you fear, that history is passing into the hands of the crowd.
>
> (162)

The once individualized text has been supplanted by a mass media—emblematized by the book-waving crowd—that is oddly and somewhat inconsistently equated with film, photography, and group identity. With insufficient explanation, DeLillo suggests that the book has become exclusively a product of the *mass* media, and can no longer even be used to critique that media without itself being implicated. Collective book and individual author become incommensurate—East and West and never the twain shall meet. Bill, the great white hope, has gone into a Pynchonesque media hibernation and refused to publish anything further, because to do so would obviate him, replace the individual producer with a collective book or mass commodity. The alienating relationship between book and author, which induces the writer's creative impotence, finally becomes a metaphor for the relationship between East and West and the postcolonial condition, or rather for paranoia about the ends of the postcolonial "process."

In the novel's apparent politics, then, the individualist novelist is always Western, the mass terrorist stereotypically Eastern. Yet as Bill says to Brita while being photographed—copied, prepared to be dead—

> There's a curious knot that binds novelists and terrorists. In the West we become famous effigies as our books lose the power to shape and influence. . . . Years ago I used to think it was possible for a novelist to alter the inner life of the culture. Now bomb-makers and gunmen have that territory. They make raids on human consciousness. What writers used to do before they were all incorporated.
>
> (41)[5]

That is, what writers did before they were merged or incorporated into a mass (foreign) body. The last unincorporated novelist, Bill the lone writer is thus a kind of Western bulwark against the mass identity of the East; yet in the novel's deep-structure politics, that mass identity is itself a product of the West, even of Western or transnational corporations. To connote any and all "incorporation"—any form of mass, somatic fusion, from participating in mass weddings to joining the mass identities of terrorist groups or cults, to becoming a "publisher" of or contributor to this new post-individual culture—as Eastern already alerts us to a cultural projection. As Bill later resumes, "What terrorists gain, novelists lose. The degree to which they influence *mass* consciousness is the extent of our decline as shapers of sensibility and thought. The danger they represent equals our own failure to be dangerous" (157, emphasis mine). Even the ideology of American individualism reflects a mass culture unable to accept its own reliance on conformity, violence and mass consciousness. The Eastern terrorist becomes an incarnation of the Western nation's political unconscious.

DeLillo replays the dialectic between the isolated, detached white individual and the merged, racialized mass, but inchoately projects the latter onto the foreign rather than situating it as an aspect of America's own divided cultural dynamic. In a variety of registers, DeLillo displaces his subjects, the domestic onto the foreign, the social onto the somatic and mechanical. The carefully and consistently deployed rhetoric of DeLillo's Maoist/cultist "book-waving crowd" determines what we might call the "cultural physics" of group behavior in ***Mao II***'s postmodern world: the wave denotes merger with a larger mass. In the novel's opening scene, thousands of strangers are being married in a sports arena, achieving a mass identity with one another and through obedience to a religious or cult leader. Against this backdrop, a character searching for his missing daughter is asked, "what will you do when you find her? Wave good-bye?" (5). Harbinger of a new kind of oceanic being, this "domestic wave" repeatedly breaks upon the crowd in mass wedding: "one continuous wave . . . an undifferentiated mass" (240). These waves are not random appearances in DeLillo's work: in ***The Names,*** a novel that begins DeLillo's exploration of the relationship between terrorism, language and American conceptions of the foreign, Axton remarks that "the Aryans were light-skinned. Light-skinned people filter down. Dark people came sweeping out. The Mongols. The Bactrians. They came in waves. Wave after wave" (260).[6] In the troubling progression of DeLillo's novels, then, that wave has finally crashed upon American shores. Many of DeLillo's characters imagine these waves as harbingers of racialized physics and foreign bodies, expressed in a somatology of the mass.

But the mass wedding/wave more accurately represents a translation of Warhol's (rather than Walter Benjamin's) emblematic process of American mechanical reproduction:[7] "a few simple formulas copied and memorized and passed on. And here is the drama of mechanical routine played out with living figures . . . the way love and sex are multiplied out, the numbers and shaped crowd" (7). In other words, the mass Asian wedding represents another dramatization of Warhol's silk screen of Mao, another stage of what we might call mass *re*production.[8] This mechanical routine of living figures denotes a post-Woolfian, postmodern staging of the wave, but it is as much the endemic wave of American sports crowds and mass culture as of a foreign mass. By so perversely beginning his text with a mass Asian wedding in Yankee Stadium—overdetermined site of American identity and consciousness—but ending it with a single wedding in Beirut, DeLillo suggests that our sense of what is "foreign" and American, what Mao and what Coke, what terrorist and what consumerist, is backwards; and that even the writer's purportedly liberal vision is caught within the system he purportedly assails.

In addition to the cultural physics of waves, DeLillo's text develops a rhetoric of chains—linked systems of language, physics and bodies. These mass waves and chains initiate a sequence of duplications: eventually in ***Mao II,*** as Karen, the American cult child, laments, passing through the "nationwide chain of baby-proof hotels," "the same room repeats itself in a cross-country chain and he's going to make me stop at every one" (71, 81). At the beginning of the novel, after "Fifteen minutes in a bare room [Karen and her husband Rodge] are chain-linked for life" through mass-marriage; we subsequently wind up with images of Andy Warhol, schematically juxtaposed between Madison Avenue and the main square of Beijing, "reprocessed through painted chains of being" (5, 135). DeLillo isn't merely presenting a literalized chain of associations here, but embodying the way we construct chains of identity: the narrator tells us that Reverend Moon "lives in [his disciples] like chains of matter that determine who they are" (6). The physics of waves and chains reflect and determine the politics of identity: these reiterated images of mechanical reproduction promise not egalitarian bliss but constriction, conformity, repetition and homogenization. The new "writer"—the Mao or Moon replacing Bill—is a foreign fundamentalist or terrorist who mass reproduces himself like Coca Cola bottles or little red books, in waves, chains and copies: if we take out or invert the label of the foreign, we begin to get DeLillo's underlying message.

Ultimately, Mao II—presumably Eastern—and Coke II—presumably Western—emblematize the same function in DeLillo's text, forms of identity-stealing advertising and photography that dissemble one another: "Now there are signs for a new soft drink, Coke II, signs slapped on cement-block walls, and [Brita] has the crazy idea that these advertising placards herald the presence of the Maoist group" (230). The idea is less crazy than transparent; "because there is a certain physical resemblance" between the Coke II signs and the "posters of the Cultural Revolution in China," one sign must augur the Other. As Margaret Scanlan suggests, "the intense red of advertisements for Coke II contributes to the fantasy that they are promoting a new Maoist group" (245). Coke II is able perfectly to declaim the presence of Mao II, for in DeLillo's inverted world, capitalism happily uses the image of Mao to make its historical and cultural inroads.[9]

In this text, aesthetic and communicative processes, especially those involving visual media, are subjected to the same sequence of duplication: "Put it this way. . . . Nature has given way to aura. . . . Here I am in your lens. Already I see myself differently. Twice over or once removed" (44). Art halves the artist-observer (coded as individual), but doubles the subject-observed (coded as the mass). For Gray, double-consciousness in any form, including that created by the mechanical repetitions of Western art and commerce, connotes mass identity and death. When Bill the writer of ostensibly individual words finally allows himself to be photographed, he enters that world of mass-reproduced images, an act the novel orchestrates unequivocally as suicide. Brita's photographic catalogue of writers then functions like a gallery of an almost extinct species—one that it helps eliminate. With the exception of terrorists, only the dead or dying are photographed and doubled, as Brita reveals in having "the dead city photographed one more time" (240). (This is a line the book effectively asks us to iterate "one more time": to photograph is always already to repeat or duplicate.) The arc of this novel is also that of Brita's switch from collecting/photographing moribund writers to "collecting/photographing" thriving terrorists—a group explicitly born to the mass production not of words but images.

For DeLillo, to be part of any such in-crowd is only to increase one's duality under a false guise of universality: "The boys who work near [the terrorist] Abu Rashid have no face or speech. Their features are identical" (234). They have merged their individuality into this generic Eastern mass identity; what DeLillo seems to fear is the postmodern American, multinational future.[10] In this guise, even Bill's answering machine "makes everything a message," either a palimpsest or a II where all iteration is reiteration, no original exists, and aura is transferred from the living "original" to the inanimate copy or second voicing (92). Everything in this text, from photo to answering machine to Coca Cola to Mao, is rendered a secondary, hence mass, hence foreign, source of anxiety. Anything that can echo, duplicate, or join you to the mass becomes a racially foreign body. And everything that makes "features identical," including American projections about the foreign, is at some point coded as both a form of terrorism and a mass attack on the (paranoid) individual.

As Thomas Carmichael reminds us, DeLillo began ***Mao II*** in response to two photos, one of J. D. Salinger being surprised by photographers, and one of a mass wedding led by Reverend Moon. In fact, DeLillo explicitly moves the site of this second photograph from its original location in Seoul to The Bronx, as if to reassert the proper cultural location for a mass wedding. As DeLillo remarks, the photos connote "the arch individualist and the mass mind, from the mind of the terrorist to the mind of the mass organization. In both cases, it's the death of the individual that has to be accomplished before their aims can be realized."[11] DeLillo here seems to be reifying more than critiquing this opposition. DeLillo's text then pits the demise of the arch, self-contained white Western recluse against the rise of the terrorist foreign mass, but it does so by duplicating original material: in other words, DeLillo makes his own "Mao II" by displacing or mirroring the original sites of these photographs. As Carmichael notes, the Salinger photo never appears in DeLillo's book, but photos of the Moon wedding, a soccer riot in Sheffield, and of the Middle East—soldiers standing in front of a poster of Ayatollah Khomeini, and children presumably crouching in Beirut—introduce each narrative section. Crucially, despite Bill's "suicidal" choice, the individual writer remains by self-definition unphotographable: only images of the mass can be replicated here. In following this dictum, DeLillo endorses as much as he ironizes the sanctity of individual "presence" and a belief in the destructive force of foreign mass duplication; at the very least, his text, like many meta-narratives, replicates the device it critiques.

By the end of ***Mao II,*** mass American society is situated as relentlessly foreign. How far then is DeLillo recapitulating the xenophobic ideas about the mass his characters ostensibly espouse, but which also skew their lives? To what extent is Bill's death caused by an actual "foreign mass," and to what extent by his own paranoid projections about that mass? As Scanlan astutely objects,

> DeLillo seems so intent on reproducing the forces that homogenize the world that he gives up the possibility of reproducing its heterogeneity. If Karen conflates the Ayatollah and Mao with her Korean masters, so does the novel, in its own rigorously synchronic portrayal of the Christian cult, Chinese communism and Islamic fundamentalism.
>
> (246)

That synchronicity, or perhaps even homology, most radically also extends to American individualism—an idea that might not be well-received in America after 9/11, which understandably polarized our sense of opposition between US and them even further.

At first glance, foreigners of any sort in ***Mao II*** merge into a Non-Western mass, an undifferentiated non-white sameness. But it doesn't hold up that way. The real "sameness" turns out to underpin the American and its projected mass other. Karen, whom Bill claims "comes from the future," typifies the new hybrid American; far more than the foreign, the mass or the terrorist, Karen supplants Bill the writer with her corrupt language, ignorance of history, and desperate need for mass identity. Morphing into her putative linguistic and cultural cognates of Korean and the Koran, Karen in fact moves from being a disciple of Sun Myung Moon to an empathizer at the death of the Ayatollah Khomeini; watching "the crowd [that] had no edge or limit" mourn his demise, Karen "felt she was among them" (188-89). In both contexts, Karen claims "We will all be a single family soon" (193). Her totalizing vision, focused through these racially coded foreign leaders, appears to contrast with that of the individualist white writer who also sleeps with her, perhaps as his first act along the path to suicide, his first capitulation to merging with the foreign mass. In Karen's case, the seemingly American again turns out to be a cover for the genuinely foreign. But while DeLillo destabilizes the line between the categories, a certain xenophobia remains, as Karen's comprehension of the foreign resonates with Bill's (85). The real distinction is that what Bill demonizes and flees, Karen pursues, embraces, and marries. These two characters best map the opposing geographies of cultural and racial identity in DeLillo's text. But they leave the reader still asking, is the family that is "all one family" that of a quintessentially "foreign" sports arena wedding, or is it instead/also the family of the quintessentially American Pittsburgh Pirates/Sister Sledge sports arena theme song?

Whether or not entirely in accord with DeLillo's intention, the foreign mass language of the novel is finally our own. When Karen wanders through New York's lower East Side, she spies the apparently foreign litany, "Sony, Mita, Kirin, Magno, Midori" (148). At the beginning of the novel, Scott and Brita had witnessed a similar sequence: "the signs were for Mita, Midori, Kirin, Magno, Suntory—words that were part of some synthetic mass language, the esperanto of jet-lag" (23).[12] This intratextual narrative bleeding, this overlap of consciousness, suggests that we need to locate the foreign, the synthetic mass, at the level of language (and perhaps in the "Karen/Kirin" that remains the pivotal, unchanged middle term of the sequence?). Brita may conclude that "our only language is Beirut" (239), but has Beirut taken over our language or the reverse? We must remember that in ***White Noise*** the mantra had been "Master Card, Visa, American Express" (100). The pattern of that Western consumer culture still presides here, producing and structuring the Other in its own synthetic image. ***Mao II*** continues to speak to and update ***White Noise***: Midori succeeds the "Master Card," but the West supplants the East. The best analogy for this process is one of a capitalist, rather than transcendental, merger. Chemical Bank, for example, takes over (or overtakes) Chase Bank, but keeps "the colonized" name as its company "brand." In this skewed form of what Richard Slotkin terms regeneration through violence, the loser keeps the logo; under the sign of one company, one "unincorporated" family, we wind up with a process of infiltration and cultural camouflage. In DeLillo's false drama, the code of the ersatz individual creates and takes over its own construction of the false collective, but keeps the logo of Mao II. Bill would warrant that his death represents the triumph of East over West, but it may actually represent the West's incorporation of the East, its policies furthered under the false sign of Mao. With the exaggerated and opportunistic assertion that it is being besieged, the West—its language and culture—finds renewed justification to colonize, especially in its putative war against terrorism. Like Axton, Bill never realizes for whose side he really works.

Some of the novel's jarring inconsistency in representing the foreign may simply expose the characters' limitations, especially Karen's: focused through its characters' questionable perspectives, the narrative does give us some straightforward descriptions of xenophobia, for example of "a police minicab [that] came by like some Bombay cartoon" (150). Because we never get a reliable narrator's alternate perspective, the text seems to have no center, no clear agenda, and this absence may be the text's strongest message. The novel's ambiguity is mirrored in the tenuousness of this image: is the taxi a real representation of the foreign, or is the representation itself the cartoon? We are told, soon after, that "[Karen] used to think siblings were strictly white and middle-class due to something in the nature of the word" (179). After such an assertion, one questions the reliability of Karen's perspective on any issue, but most of all on languages and signs; Karen may have begun to realize that her white middle-class assumptions about identity are not universally applicable, but she has hardly come to an understanding of the foreign. What she desperately desires is that "the world could be a single family"—even if everyone has to marry everyone else—but she cannot understand the differences between American and foreign families when she cannot see their similarities or decipher signs in general. As Scanlan suggests, Karen, thinking "'God all minute every day' . . . speaks the new global English" (239). But where is the emphasis in this double or hybrid—on the global, or the English? Karen, not Omar, represents DeLillo's notion of a truly alien consciousness. There she is: mass America. She survives, leaving a trail of dead writers in her wave. And if the writer is dead, no one exists to replace him, and all authorial voices, including the implied author's, are left suspect. ***Mao II*** finally unwrites its own politics.

The most useful gloss on DeLillo's inchoate project may come from a recent collection by Slavoj Žižek, *Welcome to the Desert of the Real: Five Essays on September 11 and Related Dates*. Žižek notes that George W. Bush

> himself had to concede that the most probable perpetrators of the anthrax attacks [after September 11] were not Muslim terrorists but America's own extreme Right

Christian fundamentalists—again, does not the fact that acts first attributed to an external enemy may turn out to be acts perpetrated by the very heart of *l'Amerique profonde* provide an unexpected confirmation of the thesis that the true clash is the clash within each civilization?

(44)

In other words, the clash between individual and mass is at least partly generated within American historical contexts, but then projected as a clash between civilizations. More straightforwardly than DeLillo, Žižek claims that Western capitalists and Muslim fundamentalists are themselves twinned,

are not really opposed; that they belong to the same fabric. In short, the position to adopt is to accept the necessity of the fight against terrorism, but to redefine and expand its terms so that it will also include (some) American and other Western powers' acts: the choice between Bush and Bin Laden is not our choice: they are both 'Them' against Us. The fact that global capitalism is a totality means that it is the dialectical unity of itself and its other, of the forces which resist it on 'fundamentalist' ideological grounds.

(50-51)

Žižek suggests that the "global capital liberalism" that DeLillo dismantles becomes "itself a mode of fundamentalism," as emblematized by the widely-disseminated caricatures of Bush as Muslim cleric, part of the "Talibush," etc. (Žižek 52).[13] Or as Curtis White succinctly puts it, "Al Qaeda is utterly deterritorialized. . . . What makes this situation doubly ironic is the fact that the United States and its primary trading partners [through globalization] . . . are also engaged in making nation states irrelevant and antique. Terrorism's deterritorialization is a negative reflection of our own economic and political tendencies" (19). In this sense, global capitalism obfuscates its dependence on its self-generated antagonists—i.e. that Muslim fundamentalists "are already 'modernists,'" as Rashid might agree (Žižek 52). In DeLillo's world, the fundamentalists on both sides of global capitalism perform the dialectic between Coke I and Mao II.

In the end, most of DeLillo's depictions of Mao and the mass remain a Western fantasy or translation. Is the individual white male writer, from Salinger to Pynchon to Bill Gray, a vampire who will not be daguerreotyped, or is the mass photo his true reflection? In both cases, DeLillo spends an entire novel asking, though never fully answering, what's the difference? In the wake of that indeterminacy, and of the recent escalation in terrorist violence around the world, DeLillo's novel may come across as anachronistic or dated. But DeLillo's attempt to contextualize the ways American society incorporates structural elements of terrorism into its economic and cultural systems is timelier than ever, for we have, for understandable reasons, grown wary of analyzing our complicity in creating or focusing our enemies, and have, in demonizing a dangerous and nebulous other, lost some ability to situate ourselves. As DeLillo might argue, the war against terrorism, more than anything we anticipated, calls for a solidarity that manifests itself in a dangerous form of mass identity.

Notes

My thanks to Leah Price, Kathryn Hume, Jacqueline Foertsch, Carol Bernstein and James Martin for their comments on earlier versions of this article.

1. I do not invoke these writers to reify a white male canon; writers who are not in this subject position, however, typically are not trying to transcend white male individuality and hence tend not to project the same anxieties regarding individual white identity and the mass. Though sometimes claiming to be universal, these white writers often formulate a limited and local perspective that by no means should be taken to "represent" America.

2. Ironically, many anti-Catholic writers also associated Catholicism (and sometimes, like Frederick Douglass, the Irish Mob) with an alien, foreign mass: e.g., Thomas Melville Jr. wrote to Chief Justice of Massachusetts Lemuel Shaw in 1843 that his bid for justice of the peace had been dashed by "the overwhelming force, of the whole *Catholic alien vote,* which can be brought to bear *in a mass* in all our elections . . ." (Parker 352).

3. Postmodern white male writers frequently return to this representation of mass consciousness. For example, as Dwight Eddins writes, Mucho Maas in the *Crying of Lot 49* reduces the multiplicity of all voices, and his multiple identities, to one voice, and thus to a single, enormous mass (104). In David Foster Wallace's massive *Infinite Jest,* Orin the football player experiences in his stadium a precis of DeLillo's mass: "30,000 voices, souls, voicing approval as One Soul . . . so total they ceased to be numerically distinct and melded into a sort of single coital moan, one big vowel, the sound of the womb, the roar gathering, tidal, amniotic, the voice of what might as well be God" (295).

   Wallace also describes upwards of 60 million North Americans in

   a mass choreography somewhat similar to those compulsory A.M. tai chi slow-mo exercise assemblies in post-Mao China . . . [leading to] [t]he fellowship and anonymous communion of being part of a watching crowd, a mass of eyes . . . all out in the world and pointed the same way . . . crowds brought together now so quickly . . . a kind of inversion of watching something melt, the crowds collect and are held tight by an almost seemingly nucleic force. . . .

   (620-21)

Wallace seems to have had *Mao II* even more directly in mind when Don Gately dreams of a "can of un-American tonic," a "foreign coke," a wraith holding "a can of coke, with good old Coke's distinctive interwoven red and white French curls on it but alien unfamiliar Oriental-type writing on it instead of the good old words *Coca-Cola* and *Coke.* The unfamiliar script on the Coke can is maybe the whole dream's worst moment" (834, 836, 832).

4. DeLillo's systematic linking of Islam with Asia as an index of an equally alien and uniform Eastern mindset, was, at the time written, part of what Edward Said would term American Orientalism. Said claims Americans had a limited interest in Asia until after World War II, especially as developed through philological study. DeLillo then weds an earlier European Orientalism—in which one "tr[ies] first to master the esoteric languages of the Orient"—with postmodern xenophobia (Said 290).

5. As Mark Feeney comments, "that last sentence has an ironic cast. DeLillo himself is very much unincorporated. He doesn't teach, he doesn't tour" (491). (This isolation altered somewhat with the publication of *Underworld*; as a sports announcer in that novel claims, "When you deal with crowds, nothing's predictable" [15]. The crowd in *Underworld* generates a "territorial roar, the claim of the ego that separates the crowd from other entities[;] . . . this is the crowd made over, the crowd renewed" [37].)

Without becoming intentionalist, one should note that DeLillo makes frequent comments connecting his own unincorporated persona to Bill's: "I used to say to friends, 'I want to change my name to Bill Gray and disappear.' I've been saying it for ten years" ("Dangerous" 38). In his article "The Power of History," DeLillo contends that in *Underworld* he wanted to use language to "unincorporate these [trademarked or too familiar] words, subvert their official status" (63). As part of that unincorporation, though, DeLillo continues to assert that the novelist is in some ways a Melvillean isolato "Novelists don't feel like team members" (60). Novels then become a kind of mass entertainment that lures the writer into the crowd: though dealing primarily with history rather than mass identity in this article, DeLillo also remarks that, "At its root level, fiction is a kind of religious fanaticism" (62). DeLillo is also aware of the paradoxes of his configuration of *Mao II*: the book is partly modeled on the predicament of Salman Rushdie, hardly an American individualist writer, so the pretext of using Bill Gray as an alleged Western bulwark against the mass terror of the East is so thoroughly ironized and displaced as to collapse on itself.

6. But we are also told in *The Names,* "No one seems to be alone. This is a place to enter in crowds, seek company and talk. Everyone is talking. . . . [I hear] one language after another, rich, harsh, mysterious, strong. This is what we bring to the temple, not prayer or chant or slaughtered rams. Our offering is language" (331). A heterogeneous language is here a site of prayer, not Babel. Yet in the same text, Owen Brademas remarks, "masses of people scare me. Religion. People driven by the same powerful emotion" (24). Dennis Foster reads this passage as an assertion that without faith, "the movement of the masses appears as what it is, emotion evoked by patterns devoid of reason. Gibberish" (403).

What is clear is that DeLillo systematically allies the masses with religion, and the individual with (at least the pretense or naturalization of) reason. Asking why "the language of destruction [is] so beautiful," Brademas already fears exactly what Karen will desire, god all minute every day: "one mind, one madness. To be part of a unified vision" (116).

7. I make this claim because DeLillo seems deliberately to misrepresent Benjamin's thesis regarding mechanical reproduction. DeLillo's aura, unlike Benjamin's, is detachable, a postmodern, free-floating thing in itself. As iconic writer, Bill may desire to possess an original humanist aura, which is why he cannot survive the process of being duplicated. Benjamin's contentions regarding aura and ritual, however, are clearly familiar to DeLillo: in "The Work of Art," Benjamin argues that

> Originally the contextual integration of art in tradition found its expression in the cult. We know that the earliest art works originated in the service of a ritual. . . . It is significant that the existence of the work of art with reference to its aura is never entirely separated from its ritual function. In other words, the unique value of the 'authentic' work of art has its basis in ritual. . . .
>
> (223-24)

The loss of 'original' aura in *Mao II* is then coterminous with a redefinition of the ritual functions of art. To adapt Benjamin's phrase, DeLillo develops a "negative theology" around the infinitely replicable photographic image, what Benjamin considered the "first truly revolutionary means of production" (224). DeLillo focuses on photography rather than film because still photos double images; if the novelist replaces the storyteller, the terrorist/photographer, not the director, replaces the novelist. For DeLillo, the mass duplications of the capitalist economy and their bizarre invocations of Mao will falsify any revolutionary politics. DeLillo's Warholian replications of Mao also stand in ironic counterpoint to what Fredric Jameson, via Susan Sontag, notes as the "puritanical suppression of images altogether . . . [in] Maoist China" (207).

8. DeLillo's project seems influenced by Elias Canetti's *Crowds and Power*—his 1960 exploration of the relationship between crowd psychology and religious authoritarianism—from its analysis of Islam as a religion of lament to its characterization of mass

formations, paranoia and group identity. Canetti suggests that the closed crowd of the past, tightly controlled by religious authority, has increasingly turned into "an open crowd," one that both exemplifies and transcends the religion it represents, and that "abandon[s] itself freely to its natural urge for growth" (20-22). In this sense, the mass wedding at Yankee Stadium serves as the first stage of a sequence moving from the site of marriage in a "closed" space to the site of the open crowd's "reproduction" at the Ayatollah's funeral. See also John Milton Gabriel Plotz for an assessment of how political crowds challenged the representational power of the text in Britain in the first half of the nineteenth century.

9. The following figure [original photo of Mao Tse-tung not reproduced], used to promote several bands at the 1996 South By Southwest music festival in Austin, Texas, perfectly dramatizes DeLillo's critique of the use of mass-produced images:

> With gleeful tastelessness, the designers of this advertisement use this composite, postmodern image of communism to sell "alternative" music, proving that the other Lennon was wrong and you can go carrying pictures of Chairman Mao.

10. That interdependence is all the more palpable in the wake of September 11, which ironically has generated a response of increasing American unilateralism and exceptionalism.

    John McClure offers a useful precis of Fredric Jameson's formulation of the postmodern: first addressing the development of modernism, McClure notes that

> as Western society became increasingly secularized and rationalized, romance tended increasingly to locate this world [of transcendent mystery] on the great imperial frontiers: Africa, Asia, Latin America, and the American West[;] . . . the search for raw materials that preoccupies DeLillo is made necessary by the global elimination of such premodern places. . . . and by extension, by the overlay of the postmodern on the premodern.
>
> (338)

    As McClure concludes, however, for DeLillo postmodernism has not ushered in the feared or desired universality of reason, but the creation of spiritual "resistance" outside the center: while "Capitalism has penetrated everywhere, its globalization has not resulted in global rationalization . . . [but] seems instead to have sponsored a profound reversal: the emergence of zones and forces like those that imperial expansion has erased" (340). In this context, DeLillo tracks ghosts in the imperial machines, cultural viruses that are produced by and emerge from our contact with other societies, and come to haunt and infiltrate our language. DeLillo seems both to champion and be terrified by this alterity; these alluring but destabilizing alien zones and forces threaten our society, yet can liberate us from the Western traps we have lain for ourselves.

11. Quoted in Carmichael, 215; originally in "Dangerous Don DeLillo," 34-38, 76-77.

12. Tellingly, in the book's obsessive representations of foreign mass identity and commerce, Japan is notably absent as a specific reference, yet partly recuperated in this last list. Japan's status as partly Westernized Asian country makes it problematic for DeLillo's representation of both Far and Middle East as Other, suggesting why the novel invokes China instead as an icon of mass production. DeLillo's novel also registers white American anxiety about Asian productivity, the "feared competition from the tireless 'yellow proletariat' in America" (Takaki 300).

13. In the context of DeLillo's eerily prophetic chain of associations, that Bush the fundamentalist is purportedly waging war on terrorism is made all the more ironic by his fraternization with the "rehabilitated" Reverend Moon. See, for example, Gorenfeld.

Works Cited

Baker, Peter. "The Terrorist as Interpreter: *Mao II* in Postmodern Context." *Postmodern-Culture.* 4.2 (January 1994): 34 pars. http://muse.jhu.edu/journals/postmodern_culture/v004/4.2baker.html. Visited 1/2003.

Bellah, Robert, et al. *Habits of the Heart.* Berkeley: U of California P, 1985.

Benjamin, Walter. "The Work of Art in the Age of Mechanical Reproduction." *Illuminations.* New York: Shocken Books, 1968. 217-52.

Berlant, Lauren. *The Anatomy of National Fantasy: Hawthorne, Utopia, and Everyday Life.* Chicago: U of Chicago P, 1991.

Bhabha, Homi. *The Location of Culture.* New York: Routledge, 1994.

Bizzini, Silvia. "Can the Intellectual Still Speak? The Example of Don DeLillo's *Mao II.*" *Critical Quarterly* 37.2 (Spring 1995): 104-19.

Canetti, Elias. *Crowds and Power.* Trans. Carol Stewart. New York: Continuum, 1962.

Carmichael, Thomas. "Lee Harvey Oswald and the Postmodern Subject: History and Intertextuality in Don DeLillo's *Libra, The Names,* and *Mao II.*" *Contemporary Literature* 34 (Summer 1993): 204-18.

Crowther, Hal. "Clinging to the Rock: A Novelist's Choices in the New Mediocracy." *South Atlantic Quarterly* 89.2 (Spring 1990): 321-36.

DeLillo, Don. "The Image and the Crowd." *Creative Camera* (April/May 1993): 72-73.

———. "Dangerous Don DeLillo." Interview with Vince Passaro. *New York Times Magazine* (19 May 1991): 34-38, 76-77.

———. "Interview with Don DeLillo." *South Atlantic Quarterly* 89.2 (Spring 1990): 281-304.

———. *Mao II.* New York: Viking, 1991.

———. *The Names.* New York: Vintage, 1989.

———. "The Power of History." *The New York Times Book Review* (7 Sept. 1997): 60-63.

———. *Underworld.* New York: Scribner, 1997.

———. *White Noise.* New York: Penguin, 1986.

Dix, Reverend Morgan. *Lectures on the Pantheistic Idea of an Impersonal Deity.* New York: Hurd and Houghton, 1864.

Eddins, Dwight. *The Gnostic Pynchon.* Bloomington: Indiana UP, 1990.

Emerson, Ralph Waldo. "The Heart." *The Early Lectures of Ralph Waldo Emerson* II. Ed. Stephen Whicher and Robert Spiller. Cambridge: Harvard UP, 1964. 278-84.

———. *Works.* I-XII. Boston: Houghton, Mifflin and Co.: 1904.

Feeney, Mark. "Pictures of Bill Gray." *Commonweal* 118.14 (9 Aug. 1991): 490-91.

Foster, Dennis. "Alphabetic Pleasures." *South Atlantic Quarterly* 89.2 (Spring 1990): 395-411.

Giddens, Anthony. *The Consequences of Modernity.* Stanford: Stanford UP, 1990.

Gorenfield, John. "Bad Moon on the Rise." http://www.salon.com/news/feature/2003/09/24/moon/index_np.html (last visited July 15, 2004).

Hantke, Steffen. "'God save us from bourgeois adventure': The Figure of the Terrorist in Contemporary American Conspiracy Fiction." *Studies in the Novel* 28.2 (Summer 1996): 219-43.

Harris, Daniel. "Fictional Terrorism: Psychology Not Politics." *Book-Forum* 7:4 (1986): 5-7

Jameson, Fredric. *Postmodernism, or, The Cultural Logic of Late Capitalism.* Durham: Duke UP, 1991.

Laqueur, Walter. "Postmodern Terrorism." *Foreign Affairs* (September/October 1996): 24-36.

LeClair, Tom. *In the Loop: Don DeLillo and the Systems Novel.* Urbana: U Illinois P, 1987.

Lentricchia, Frank. "Introducing Don DeLillo." *South Atlantic Quarterly* 89.2 (Spring 1990): 239-44.

———, ed. *Introducing Don DeLillo.* Durham: Duke UP, 1991.

Maltby, Paul. "The Romantic Metaphysics of Don DeLillo." *Contemporary Literature* 37.2 (Summer 1996): 258-77.

McClure, John. "Postmodern Romance: Don DeLillo and the Age of Conspiracy." *South Atlantic Quarterly* 89.2 (Spring 1990): 337-53.

Melville, Herman. *The Letters of Herman Melville.* Ed. Merrell Davis and W. H. Gilman. New Haven: Yale UP, 1960.

———. *Moby Dick.* New York: Signet, 1961.

Osteen, Mark. "Children of Godard and Coca-Cola: Cinema and Consumerism in Don DeLillo's Early Fiction." *Contemporary Literature* 37.3 (Fall 1996): 439-70.

Parker, Hershel. *Herman Melville: A Biography, Vol. 1, 1819-1851.* Baltimore: Johns Hopkins UP, 1996.

Plotz, John Milton Gabriel. *Crowd: British Literature and Public Politics.* Berkeley: U California P, 2000.

Said, Edward. *Orientalism.* New York: Vintage, 1979.

Scanlan, Margaret. "Writers Among Terrorists: Don DeLillo's *Mao II* and the Rushdie Affair." *Modern Fiction Studies* 40.2 (Summer 1994): 229-52.

Simmons, Ryan. "What is a Terrorist? Contemporary Authorship, the Unabomber, and *Mao II.*" *Modern Fiction Studies* 45.3 (1999): 675-95.

Slotkin, Richard. *Regeneration Through Violence.* Middletown, Conn: Wesleyan UP, 1973.

Takaki, Ronald. *Iron Cages: Race and Culture in 19th-Century America.* New York: Oxford UP, 1990.

Tocqueville, Alexis de. *Democracy in America* I-II, The Henry Reeve Text, Rev. Francis Bowen, Ed. Phillips Bradley. New York: Knopf, 1953.

Wallace, David Foster. *Infinite Jest.* Boston: Little Brown, 1996.

Vlatka Velcic (essay date fall 2004)

SOURCE: Velcic, Vlatka. "Reshaping Ideologies: Leftists as Terrorists/Terrorists as Leftists in DeLillo's Novels." *Studies in the Novel* 36, no. 3 (fall 2004): 405-18.

[*In the following essay, Velcic analyzes the portrayal of terrorists in* Mao II, *comparing the novel's ideological connection between terrorists and leftists to a similar one in* Libra *to show how leftists are typically represented as the political "Other" in postmodern American novels.*]

Major national newspapers occasionally feature a story about a fugitive, sixties radical who surfaces after hiding underground for a couple of decades. These cases briefly capture headlines and even spawn a flurry of imitative popular TV show episodes: a misguided radical friend appears from nowhere and a morally painful decision whether to turn him/her in to the police has to be made.[1] Fictional radicals, just like some of their "real" counterparts, will turn themselves dutifully in and spare the main character from becoming a snitch. After all, until the most recent terrorism scare, when Americans spurred by fear and misplaced patriotic fervor jammed terror hotlines with hundreds of thousands of "tips," the American mainstream would describe snitching as behavior encouraged by cold war totalitarian societies and not worthy of "free" American society.[2] And while TV shows pursue high ratings, the "real" radicals, who usually assume new identities as respectable middle class citizens, get quick and suspended sentences since their lawyers strike deals with the court even before the radicals' resurfacing; consequently, narratives about both real and fictional leftists usually vanish down the extremely short memory lanes of American audiences.

However, the resurfacing of Sarah Jane Olson, the renamed former SLA member/sympathizer Kathleen Soliah, who was captured in 1999 after a tip by a viewer of "America's Most Wanted," was somewhat more complicated. She was allegedly involved in not one but two "terrorist" cases (in the second one she was joined with four more defendants), and she (and her co-defendants) received an uncommonly harsh sentence. Admittedly, the second case exemplifies one of the few instances when leftist radicals actually killed somebody in the United States, a bank teller during a robbery.[3] However, Olson's sentence was already extreme in the first case, involving a bomb that hurt no one, although it is unclear to what extent she actually participated in the crime. By the time her first case was about to come to trial, September 11, 2001 was a fact and Olson quickly pleaded guilty because, as she publicly declared, she felt that because of 9/11 she would not receive a fair trial. In retrospect, considering the current erosion of civil liberties and the denial of human rights to suspected "terrorists" in the United States, it is safe to argue that she was right. But what makes Olson's case interesting in the context of this essay is not so much the harshness of the sentence and the publicity that the case received, but the fact that the case renewed a well-known staple of American official and popular imagination, the connection between the "terrorist" and the "leftist."[4] Since World War Two, and despite the current focus on Muslim fundamentalists, many American narratives about terror and terrorism continue to fashion American leftists always as potential "terrorists" while most imagined "terrorists" turn out to be if not members of a leftist group then definitely proponents of leftist ideology.[5]

The consistent portrayal of Leftists as terrorists or potential terrorists is not limited to American popular culture and mass media, which mimic official governmental discourse, but also appears in contemporary American novels. One might be tempted to argue that since 1991, the focus of political persecution somewhat shifts from leftists as terrorists to terrorists of all kinds—this shift presumably occurs because of the "end" of the Cold War as well as domestic events, since the biggest terrorist attack on American soil before 9/11 was undeniably the Oklahoma City bombing by Timothy McVeigh, a member of a right wing militia.[6] However, while many American postmodern novels inevitably portray "leftists" as terrorists during the Cold War, rather than abandoning the mostly imagined connection between the "left" and "terror" after 1991, they just flip the terms of the equation by portraying most "terrorists" as leftists. Therefore, the Left and leftists, the original political "Other" in post-World War II American society, are not merely replaced by the undefined figure of a "terrorist." While the new "terrorist" figures in American fiction acquire some new characteristics, such as Middle Eastern ethnicity, they frequently preserve leftist political ideology, and hence continue to perpetuate the anti-left ideology of the American mainstream. This is the case even with the postmodern novel, which deliberately attempts to undermine all meta-narratives about truth, reality, and history because, as Linda Hutcheon points out, some of the most acclaimed postmodern novels rewrite historical events, or they have been tied to some version of "real, current" events. Postmodern novels deal with the subject of terrorism because the discourse of "terrorist" threat is daily perpetuated by those in power, and in depicting this subject novels reinforce the general attitude of American culture, which continues to see connections between terrorists and leftists even in times when the Left is practically defunct.

The most well-known contemporary postmodern novelist, whose novels popular culture finds rather prophetic in hindsight since he focused on the increasing presence of terrorists in American consciousness long before 9/11, is certainly Don DeLillo. His novel ***Mao II*** explicitly deals with terrorism and, after its publication, provoked a flurry of articles that concentrate on the depiction of terrorists in his novel.[7] While they all contribute greatly to readings of the novel, most of them concentrate on the similarities between the roles of "writer" and "terrorist," discussed in many passages of the novel. In this essay, I want to develop an analysis of the portrayal of terrorists in DeLillo's ***Mao II*** by pointing out that while his writer as "wanna-be" terrorist fails, his terrorists, ultimately portrayed as leftists, prevail; also I will execute a comparison of DeLillo's ***Mao II*** (1991) to ***Libra*** (1988), DeLillo's novel about JFK's murder. An analysis of ***Libra*** and ***Mao II*** together reveals that both novels simultaneously mirror and create an ideological construct that reinforces the connection between terror and the left, thereby revealing the left as the typical political "Other" in the American narrative consciousness. In other words, these two DeLillo novels, as well as other American postmodern novels that focus on leftist characters, paradoxically open their narratives to voices that speak against and outside the "military-industrial complex" of the postwar world, yet they at the same time do not undermine a cultural paradigm according to which Leftist voices and characters fit in the mold of the "political Other."[8] Therefore, postmodern novels create marginalized, mysterious, but deadly, Leftist/terrorist creatures who are essentially only sexual perverts, snitches, and murderers. As sexual perverts they threaten their own bodies and the bodies of others; as snitches they betray not only their respective countries but also their immediate Leftist communities, and as murderers they are willing to commit the ultimate transgression against humanity.

In the above sense, narrative strategies employed in ***Libra*** establish Don DeLillo's Lee Harvey Oswald as a typical blueprint in the construction of the "Political Other," as an irrational, confused, and devious creature, who ultimately fits the cultural pattern of a monster Leftist who murders. DeLillo introduces his Oswald as a creature who likes riding on the New York subway for hours: "he liked the feeling they were on the edge. . . . It gave him a funny thrill . . . on the edge of no-control" (13). Oswald, a creature from the "edge," from the margins, from the other side, is also a secretive creature from a dark underground. In addition, from early childhood, marks of difference marginalize DeLillo's Oswald; in the Bronx Zoo, the children call him "a cowpoke" because of his Texas accent, and in school, since he has trouble reading as a dyslexic, he is classified as a "retarded boy" (5). As a loner and perpetual exile, he is constantly displaced, feels out of place, and lacks a place: "He tried to time his movements against the rhythm of the street. Stay off the street from noon to one, three to five. Learn the alleys, use the dark" (6).

As with other leftist characters in the contemporary American postmodern novel, Oswald's "otherness" finds its expression first in his confused sexuality, which throughout the novel constantly signals his proclivity toward transgression. The symptoms of Oswald's sexual inadequacy, which appear at the beginning of the novel in the form of boyish shyness and awe in front of girls, lead to dissatisfying encounters with women, such as when he gets VD during his military stint in Japan. Oswald joins sexuality with violence when he repeatedly beats his wife Marina after their arrival in the United States from the Soviet Union. Even more than his often violent encounters with women, Oswald's sexual confusion is visible in his hateful, but dependent, relationship with his mother, which borders on incestuous, and in his half-hearted submission in a homosexual incident with his anti-Castro friend, David Ferrie, in Ferrie's apartment a month before the assassination (341). This scene, written in the third person but from Oswald's point of view, and situated "in the dark," reveals Oswald's disjointed thinking as well as his inability to come to terms with his desires. Oswald seems unable to make up his mind whether his unease comes because he suffers a rape, as the grappling at the beginning of the scene seems to suggest, or because he feels guilt in his willing transgression of the heterosexual social norm, as the sentences in the scene's resolution suggest.

His perturbed sexuality mirrors his turncoatism. He starts with two contradictory interests: the reading of Marxist literature alongside of the Marine Corps Manual. He wants to join a communist cell but instead joins the Marines. As a marine he goes on to pursue his "Leftist" interests and learns Russian, manages to get into the Soviet Union, and renounces his American citizenship, only to change his mind and return to the United States with his new Russian wife. In the United States he continues to waver: on one hand, he passes out leaflets in support of Castro, and even gets beaten up because of that, and on the other hand he accepts the advances of both the FBI and the CIA to work for them, and he actively seeks out involvement with the obviously anti-Castro group headed by Guy Banister and David Ferrie. Around the same time, when he decides to work for Banister's anti-Castro group, he participates in a radio show on which he eloquently defends Castro and Cuba's right to "self-determination." Ironically, Oswald defends the rights of Marxist Cuba and implicitly attacks U. S. imperialist policy with the values of the American Declaration of Independence and Constitution. In the context of the novel, the Marxist and the patriot Oswald, as well as a plethora of other Oswalds—irrational, childish, psychotic—exist simultaneously, and the reader and/or critic, just like the conspirators, has to accept Oswald as "a man who harbors contradictions: without hope for a resolution" (319). However, in DeLillo's prose, Oswald's contradictory characteristics do not co-exist happily together; he is not a "positive Libran," but a negative one "poised to make the dangerous leap" into violence (315). In DeLillo's version of history, Oswald's motivation to kill the president remains obscure and contradictory throughout the novel; it mirrors his confused sexuality and his constant changes in political alliances.

The above traits of Oswald's suggest that although ***Libra*** potentially opens space for leftist voices, the constructions of leftist characters are deeply flawed and troubling; DeLillo's Oswald does not undermine Cold War and mass culture portrayals of what a "leftist" is. From early childhood DeLillo's Oswald reads much Marxist literature and dreams of becoming a revolutionary martyr a la Trotsky. Later, the conspirators who break into his room find "socialist literature strewn about. Speeches by Fidel Castro. A booklet with a Castro quotation on the cover: 'The Revolution Must Be a School of Unfettered Thought.' Copies of the Militant and the Worker. A booklet, *The Coming American Revolution.* Another, *Ideology and Revolution,* by Jean-Paul Sartre. Books and pamphlets in Russian. Flash cards with Cyrillic characters" (179). His dubious understanding of these readings and his mechanical mouthings of Marxist rhetoric ironically do not make him less of a "leftist" in the reader's mind since these behaviors fit the Cold War culture portrayals of leftists as unreasonable people who slavishly and unthinkingly follow a dangerous ideology. Yet DeLillo's characters, including Oswald, never engage the complex and diverse Marxist theories that are sprinkled throughout ***Libra,*** from Trotsky to Sartre and Castro. And although DeLillo's Oswald never manages to establish a liaison with a Marxist organization—his unsuccessful attempts to contact the Socialist Workers Party and his one-man show, "New Orleans Chapter of the Fair Play for Cuba Committee," prove fruitless—yet they still fit the warped Cold War logic that many leftists are loners shunned even by their own kind. Oswald's "turncoatism" reveals the same pattern; by the time DeLillo wrote his Oswald, didn't the public learn that all leftists ultimately denounce their political leanings?

Through Oswald, DeLillo portrays "leftists" as unable to make their own choices. Conceptually the many Oswalds in the novel can be read as two "Oswalds," the "real" Oswald and Oswald, the construction of the conspirators. Larry Parmenter, one of the main conspirators, describes to his co-conspirator, Win Everett, his desire to create Oswald: "We put him together. A far-left type. We work him in. Tie him to Cuban intelligence" (75). Win confidently gives this "created" Oswald myriad details and fake coincidences that further establish his "reality." If it were not for the "real" Oswald in the novel, one could almost argue that DeLillo's novel establishes "leftists" as a creation of right wing conspirators. In some ways, these textual details might be viewed as potentially exposing the fact that much of the Cold War propaganda about "leftists" comes from right-wing ideologies. However, the second "real" Oswald also exists, and he is depicted as, if anything, more violent, radical, and unpredictable than the construction. In ***Libra,*** despite its focus on a "leftist" character, the reader therefore uncovers two intertwined strategies in the portrayal of the leftist Oswald. On one level, DeLillo's narrative constructs Oswald as a political "Other": physically and morally deformed, unstable and dangerous, outside the loop, but still useful; on another level, this Oswald, as "a fiction living prematurely in the world," blends into a typical postmodernist Other; the real Oswald and his created counterpart, even the conspirators themselves are all "lonely," and beat with "violent desire." In this approach, the political frequently becomes reduced to the psychological; because of this process George de Mohrenschildt, one of the conspirators adjacent to the main plot, seems to offer the best description of the Leftism of DeLillo's Oswald: "There is politics, there is emotion, there is psychology. I know him quite well but I wouldn't be completely honest if I said I could pin him down, pin him right to the spot. He may be a pure Marxist, the purest of believers. Or he may be an actor in real life" (56). To evaluate Oswald and his potential usefulness to the conspirators, in addition to politics, George needs "emotions" and "psychology." In other words, George perceives Oswald as a person prompted not by the rational, but by the irrational, which leaves him open to impulse behavior consisting of contradictory motives—Oswald is either a "believer" or an "actor." Therefore, his psychological "otherness" conveniently echoes, as established previously, his political turncoatism and his confused murderous instincts.

Paradoxically, if one wishes to return a political dimension to the portrayal of Oswald as the postmodern's perverse, treacherous, and murderous "Other," one reenters the old Cold War narrative of leftists as Political Others. The strategy of using Leftists in order to create and disseminate an "archetypal" postmodern "Other" implies, therefore, an ambiguous political/ideological position. On one hand, with their portrayal in ***Libra,*** voices of the Left become once again a part of American mainstream culture and exit the silence imposed on them for several decades. On the other hand, paradoxically, by placing Left voices among all of the voices of postmodern "Others," or by pointing out that the perverse, the treacherous, and the murderous exist in us all, novelists effectively undermine Leftist political positions. Since the Left shares shifting, multiple identities with others, its "difference" is erased at the very moment of its confirmation—a postmodern ideological position that corresponds to Lyotard's celebration of the end of all master narratives. Voices of the Left, then, differ only slightly from the voices of the Right; in fact, together they help form and participate in the cacophony of postmodern culture. Politically therefore, postmodernism offers a critique of all ideological positions, but that "even-handed" critique ultimately only serves those who are in power, since it undermines hope for viable alternative political views. In the years since ***Libra***'s publication, global events certainly reveal many disastrous consequences of the erasure of the Left, from the unrelenting globalization that continues to impoverish the Third World to the unstoppable, deadly march of American imperialism.

While ***Libra*** works along the lines of traditional Cold War ideology, which sees in every leftist a potential "terrorist," ***Mao II,*** long before 9/11, reveals America's growing obsession with terrorism. The accusation of terrorism expands without diminishing accusations that in the foundation of every terrorism lurks leftist ideology; in other words, the "leftist" as murderous political

"Other" is replaced with a broader category of terrorists with leftist leanings. Accordingly in ***Mao II,*** terrorists multiply; in addition to the new group of terrorists, a group of Lebanese Marxists, and their leader Abu Rashid, the reclusive novelist Bill Gray, the main character, is accused of practicing the craft of writing akin to terrorism. Critical analyses of ***Mao II*** have focused on the overt and striking parallelism between writers and terrorists alluded to on many occasions in the novel.

Admittedly, an interesting logic operates in the equation between novelists and terrorists; both could be "shapers of sensibility and thought" (157) and both can potentially "alter the inner life of the culture" (41). However, this logic, which perceives writers as a real danger, operated before writers were replaced by terrorists. In the "new tragic narrative" (157), the novel "giv[es] way to terror, to news of terror, to tape recorders and cameras, to radios, to bombs stashed in radios. News of disaster is the only narrative people need. The darker the news, the grander the narrative. News is the last addiction . . ." (42). Since everything becomes "incorporated," related to mass consumer society, the novel that "used to feed our search for meaning" with its "Latin mass of language character, occasional new truth" is replaced with "something larger and darker . . ." (72)—the news of terror. In ***Libra,*** the words of George Haddad, a shady university professor from Athens, explain the connection between contemporary postmodern society and terror even more poignantly:

> In societies reduced to blur and glut, terror is the only meaningful act. There's too much everything, more things and messages and meanings than we can use in ten thousand lifetimes. Inertia-hysteria. Is history possible? Is anyone serious? Who do we take seriously? Only the lethal believer, the person who kills and dies for faith. Everything else is absorbed. The artist is absorbed, the madman in the street is absorbed and processed and incorporated. Give him a dollar, put him in a TV commercial. Only the terrorist stands outside. The culture hasn't figured out how to assimilate him.
>
> (157-58)

In the above passage, George describes a typical postmodern consumer society; humanity is so overwhelmed with images, goods, messages and their multiple meanings that everything becomes indistinguishable, a "blur." In this postmodern "glut" and "blur" both "artists" and "writers" are lost; only the extreme gestures of terrorists cannot be absorbed and stand to be "noticed." And the resistance to "assimilation" allows the terrorist to stay in control, at least according to George.

This world of "terror" clearly dispenses with the "novelist" (159), and, rather than comparing the writer Bill Gray to a "terrorist," one should compare him to Nicholas Branch, the fictional narrator of ***Libra.*** While Nicholas Branch, hired by the CIA "on contract to write the secret history of the assassination of President Kennedy" (15), lacks the fame of Bill Gray, he, just like Bill, toils hidden from public view. He toils for fourteen long years and is almost literally buried under the mountain of documents about JFK's murder that fail to make sense, just like Bill Gray in ***Mao II,*** whose drafts litter his study, his garage, and his special rooms. And finally just like Bill, who tries unsuccessfully to identify with terrorists, Nicholas Branch's attempts to understand Lee Harvey Oswald ultimately fail. Both novels therefore expose the general failure of writers to deal with their subject. However, in ***Libra,*** the writer still outlives the "leftist/terrorists" while in ***Mao II*** the terrorists survive the writer.

While ***Mao II*** toys with the similarities between writers and terrorists to ultimately replace writers with terrorists, these terrorists, such as Abu Rashid and his group and their sympathizer George Haddad, follow in the tradition of the "Political Other." George Haddad, definitely the more innocuous of the two, as an "intermediary" between Abu Rashid's group and the outside world, serves as a bridge to the political Other, and as such lacks the details that usually surround main characters. On one hand, he is a Lebanese political scientist who seemingly lives a "normal" middle class life with his wife and kids in Athens; on the other hand, he is just like Oswald and other political Others, a figure from the margins, a spokesman for the terrorist group holding the Swiss poet as a hostage. He shows up in London where Bill and Charles are getting ready to publicize the poet's plight in an attempt to effect his release, as George himself had urged them to do previously, not to help and further their cause but to warn and threaten them about further bombings in the moment when they narrowly escape a first bomb blast that derails their efforts. As such, George plays a double game, similar to Oswald, who is portrayed as both pro- and anti-Castro in ***Libra***; he participates in the efforts of the "normal" world, yet he sympathizes with terrorists. A policeman in the novel perhaps best categorizes him: "George is an interesting sort of academic. His name appears in an address book found in an apartment raided by police somewhere in France—a bomb factory. And he has been photographed in the company of known terrorist leaders" (131). Again, an ability to easily switch political sides and allegiances, i.e. "turncoatism," echoes in this description of George, and this ability is not just a quality associated with a postmodern identity crisis but has a "left" political dimension. Not only do Bill and Charles find out through George that Abu Rashid's group is not "fundamentalist" but "communist" (123), but George declares to himself that he "sympathize[s] with their aims if not their methods" (128).

George, therefore, is not a confused academic, who like Jack Gladney from DeLillo's ***White Noise*** (1985) perhaps awkwardly plods through the postmodern world and ultimately harms only himself, but a definite "leftist" sympathizer who plots with "communist" murderers. Furthermore, one might even argue that he is instrumental in Bill Gray's death. He invites Bill to Athens and promises "It is possible to talk in Athens. Beneath the frantic pace there is something I find conducive to reason and calm, to a settlement of differences . . ." (138). George seductively promises Bill a "dialogue. . . . Unfettered. No one coming round to set guidelines or issue ultimatums," on "a terrace with a sweeping view" (138). However, not only does George's "unfettered" dialogue echo Castro's saying, quoted in ***Libra,*** which equates revolution with "unfettered thought," but it also puts Bill in harm's way. Admittedly, while the novel does not directly link George to Bill Gray's death or deaths in the Lebanese Civil War, it clearly portrays Abu Rashid and his group as "true" leftists and unstable "murderers."

Typically, throughout most of the novel Abu Rashid is an unseen presence. He is alluded to, pondered about, but not seen until the last fifteen pages of the novel. In this last section, entitled "In Beirut," Brita, who has switched from photographing writers to photographing "terrorists"—underscoring the irrelevance of writers—in the middle of a war-torn city visits and photographs Abu Rashid and his group. With the exception of a couple of pages in the previous sections of the novel in which Bill Gray relatively unsuccessfully attempts to imagine and describe scenes between the hostage poet and his boyish captor and torturer, this section is also the first time the reader directly encounters "terrorists" and hears them speak. Abu Rashid's description begins innocuously enough; he is in "his sixties and wears clean khakis with shirtsleeves rolled neatly to the elbows. He has gray hair and a slightly darker mustache and his flesh is a ruddy desert bronze" (231). However, in the very next sentence, in this description of a distinguished looking older man, quickly creep marks of otherness: "He is bony-handed, maybe slightly infirm, and has gold-rimmed glasses and a couple of gold fillings" (231). While "gold rimmed glasses" and "gold fillings" seem to mark his age as well as his wealth, and display his power, the description eerily contrasts images of the bombed out Beirut just introduced in the narrative; they also distinctly allude to a possibility of "infirm[ity]" in Abu Rashid. Political "Others" just like other others marked by gender, class, ethnicity, or sexual preference, inevitably carry marks on their bodies; Oswald's "dyslexia" belongs to the same pattern as Rashid's "infirmity"—old age, poor sight, and bad teeth.

Marks of "physical" Otherness are quickly reinforced with descriptions of Abu Rashid as a psychologically unstable, insecure madman. Several times during his conversation with Brita, Rashid halts and asks her, "Tell me, do you think I am a madman living in this hellish slum and I talk to these people about world revolution?" (233). Then a bit later, when he talks about his son who has joined his band of youth fighters, he demands again, "Tell me if you think I'm mad. Be completely honest" (234), and soon again, "You must tell me if you think I'm totally mad" (236). While the repetition of these words in the short passage reveals Rashid's psychological insecurities, it is even more interesting that he displays his insecurities in front of a woman.

Traditionally in the novel leftists/terrorists and terrorists/leftists are portrayed as almost exclusively male; ***Mao II*** follows this pattern.[9] Abu Rashid explains the lack of women around him with the fact that his wife and his two older sons were killed in the fighting by the Phalangists. Although this is the only information that the reader learns about Rashid and women directly, the novel does not completely abandon the images of sexual "dysfunction" and violence towards women relatively abundant in ***Libra.*** Rashid's statements, such as "Women carry babies, men carry arms. Weapons are man's beauty," display not only obvious sexism, but a patriarchal male envy of women's power to have children that is counteracted by equating weapons with power and reveals the connection between sexuality, gender, and violence. Therefore, while Rashid does not beat women directly like Oswald, who systematically beats Marina, violence explodes against Brita when she on an impulse decides to pull the hood off Rashid's son. Instead of Rashid, his son attacks Brita physically. Admittedly Rashid commands the boy to stop when he is getting ready to continue attacking Brita, but he is not exonerated from violence because he sees the boy as an extension of himself: "I am lucky to have a son who is so young, able to learn. I call myself father of Rashid" (234).

Rashid does not only see his son as an extension of himself but also the other boys in his group of youthful fighters: "The buys who work near Abu Rashid have no face or speech. Their faces are identical. They are his features. They do not need their own features or voices. They are surrendering these things to something powerful and great" (234). Rashid accomplishes these goals quite literally by making all boys wear hoods that hide their faces and T-shirts with a photo of Abu Rashid pinned to them to replace their effaced identities. Thus, ***Mao II*** assigns to the leftist Rashid's group the impulse to construct a "fictional," postmodern identity for his young followers that is eerily similar to the impulse of right-wing conspirators in JFK's murder who create Oswald's identity out of scraps in ***Libra.*** Rashid claims, contrary to the conspirators who do not care about the "real" Oswald, that he is helping the boys, as evidenced in the following paragraph:

> We teach them identity, sense of purpose. They are all children of Abu Rashid. All men one man. Every militia in Beirut is filled with hopeless boys taking drugs and drinking and stealing. Car thieves. The shelling ends and they run out to steal car parts. We teach that our children belong to something strong and self-reliant. They are not an invention of Europe. They are not making a race to go to God. We don't train them for paradise. No martyrs here. The image of Rashid is their identity.
>
> (233)

In addition to confirming that the boys' identity becomes literally "the image of Rashid," the above quotation has many other chilling aspects; for example, in making these boys his virtual clones, Rashid claims that he saves them from "taking drugs, and drinking and stealing." Rashid clearly manipulates children and teaches them to slavishly follow him; he "talk[s] to these children every day, all the time, over and over" (236). Also, as I will explain a bit further on, Rashid, as do the right wing conspirators, trains his followers for murder. This structural correspondence of the left and the right reveals that in DeLillo's postmodern fiction the political positions of left and right can be easily transposed, which is at best an only slightly more liberal version of Cold War ideology, which of course undermines the left far more than the right, if for no other reason than the scarcity of leftist portrayals and leftist voices.

As mentioned above, George Haddad has already established that Abu Rashid's philosophy is not the raving of a megalomaniacal madman but that it has clear roots in leftist philosophy. When George asserts that Abu Rashid's group is not fundamentalist but "communist" (123), Bill and Charles are not surprised because "there's a Lebanese Communist Party. There are leftist elements . . . aligned with Syria. The PLO has always had a Marxist component and they're active again in Lebanon" (123-24). The novel therefore does not question the idea of the Cold War narrative that the left is associated with "terrorism," but reinforces it. Abu Rashid's group is described as Marxist although the main combatants in the Lebanese civil war were not of Marxist persuasion. The novel actually even acknowledges that Rashid's group is not large: "Barely a movement actually. It's just an underground current at this stage, an assertion that not every weapon in Lebanon has to be marked Muslim, Christian, or Zionist" (128-29), but since the Marxist group is chosen of all the groups in Lebanon to be represented, its viciousness in the conflict is established, and the Cold War patterns are reinforced; after all, Rashid's group "Terrorize[d] the innocent" (129) by taking a poet for a hostage.

In order to reinforce Rashid's hold over "his" boys, DeLillo selects a specific Marxist philosophy, the Maoist cult of personality, almost as if Marxists have a specific monopoly on the manipulation of children. Interestingly, the identification of Rashid's group with Maoism comes after the narrative establishes that every crowd is equally problematic and can be "replaced by another" (177). The novel has long sections describing a Moonie mass wedding, murderous soccer crowds, crowds during Khomeini's funeral, and crowds on the Tienanmen Square, so the crowd of boys around Abu Rashid completes the already established pattern; perhaps "The future belongs to crowds" (16), as the novel establishes at the end of the first section, but the crowds here are to be manipulated by the likes of Abu Rashid. Furthermore, Rashid and Mao are portrayed not as relatively innocuous cult leaders like the Reverend Moon, who officiates over mass weddings, but as directly connected with violence. Rashid argues, "Mao regarded armed struggle as the final and greatest action of human consciousness. It is the final drama and final test. And if many thousands die in the struggle? Mao said death can be light as a feather or heavy as a mountain" (236). Rashid's words, therefore, contrast his previously mentioned arguments that he does not raise the boys for martyrdom; he raises them to "die for the people and the nation," to die Maoist, "massive and intense" deaths. However, even though the boys do not "Die for the oppressors, die working for the exploiter and manipulators, die selfish and vain" (236), they still end up dead and Abu Rashid and his leftist philosophy become their murderers.

In true postmodern fashion, with distrust for any mass movement and any ideology, by identifying Abu Rashid's group as Maoists DeLillo's narrative transforms the legitimate struggle of people for liberation, in Marxist philosophy always based on economic and historical circumstances, into terrorism. Indeed, Rashid's interpreter explains to Brita that

> terror is what we use to give our people their place in the world. What used to be achieved through work we gain through terror. Terror makes the new future possible. All men one man. Men live in history as never before. He is saying we make and change history minute by minute. History is not the book or the human memory. We do history in the morning and change it after lunch.
>
> (235)

Here DeLillo's narrative seems to contradict postmodern ideas about the end of history; the interpreter argues that there is too much history, history that is forged with violence.

Therefore, the construction of Abu Rashid in ***Mao II*** does not depart significantly but follows a pattern similar to the construction of Oswald in ***Libra.*** Rashid is a person marked with "infirmity," insecure, on the verge of madness; he betrays the people/children around him by making them follow him blindly and without thinking. He is also a murderer because his real purpose is terror and death. Abu Rashid, the terrorist who follows Mao, has, therefore, all the marks of the political "Other"; as such he is more successful than Oswald because Oswald fails in his mission while Rashid succeeds in his, at least in the context of DeLillo's novels. The end of the Cold War and the "fall" of the Soviets, therefore, does not bring the dissolution of the connection between the "left" and terrorism but heightens it by imagining that there is a leftist behind every "terrorist."

An analysis of ***Mao II*** would not be complete if I were to fail to point out that Abu Rashid is not only a political other but also an ethnic other. Not only is he from the Middle East but he also categorizes his movement as a movement against the West, despite the roots of Maoism in Western Marxism. Rashid argues that "as long as there is Western presence it is a threat to self-respect, to identity" (235), and he justifies taking hostages by explaining that they "put Westerners in locked rooms . . . so [they] don't have to look at them. They remind us of the way we tried to mimic the West. The way we put up the pretense, the terrible veneer. Which you now see exploded all around you" (235). This passage represents a perfect opening to the postcolonial issues that mark the Lebanese Civil wars; however, ***Mao II*** refuses to truly venture into Third World territory. Rather, by reiterating the connection between the left and terror it retells not only the old postmodern narrative but also an even older Cold War one.

Notes

1. "Sisters," a Ron Cowen and Daniel Lipman TV drama that ran from 1991 to 1996, is an example of a series that aired an episode about a sixties fugitive. In the episode "The Passion of Our Youth" on October 7, 1995, the oldest of the Reed sisters, Alex, has to decide whether to turn in her former college boyfriend, now a fugitive from justice.

2. While this statement certainly characterizes the popular mythology, or how America views itself, during McCarthy's HUAC hearings in the early fifties numerous Americans were pressured to "snitch" and inform on their friends as "communist" sympathizers. Those who refused were publicly denounced and in some cases fired.

3. Todd Gitlin and many others point out that despite all of the government propaganda in the late sixties and early seventies the radical left actually killed only one person, a student in Minnesota, until they were pushed underground in the early seventies.

4. I am deliberately trying to avoid theoretical discussions of the best way to define both "leftist" and "terrorist." For the purpose of this essay, I define the Left in terms of opposition to the Right, historically as a product of late nineteenth-century socialists and early twentieth-century communists, while the Right encompasses, in general terms, the traditional American political parties, both the Republicans and most Democrats. On the theoretical level, the Left opposes, in varying degrees, capitalism, and strives for radical social change, and accepts, more or less critically, one of the available Marxist philosophies as well as other radical social and economic theories, while the Right upholds the principles of more or less liberal capitalism seasoned in America with the puritan philosophy of the founding fathers. Various postmodernisms point out the complications of such binary divisions, but, at least in my opinion, do not invalidate them. For a more in-depth discussion of "terror" in the contemporary world (pre-September 11), see for example, Zulaika and Douglas.

5. See the 2002 FBI report on terrorism as one of the sources to confirm this statement. The report reiterates that "Leftists were the biggest threat to America in the 70s and 80s," almost reluctantly accepting that their threat is somewhat diminished now.

6. An indication of such a shift is exemplified in immigration law changes that went into effect in June 1991. That law changed the third "political" category of persons ineligible for a permanent resident card from communists and communist sympathizers to terrorists. Ironically the change was initiated by Reagan and Republican lawmakers, not because of "perestroika" and the collapse of the Soviet Bloc but because the same political category encompassed "fascists"—and some of Reagan's friends, such as Latin American generals, could not get an entry visa to the U.S.

7. E.g., Scanlan, Simmons, Baker and Whitebrook.

8. Postmodern novels that portray leftist characters as the political "Other" include Pynchon's *Vineland,* depicting Reagan's war on drugs waged against remnants of sixties radicals; Doctorow's *The Book of Daniel,* depicting a fictional "Rosenberg" son as a sixties radical; and Boyle's *World's End,* depicting the New England Old Left and the New Left.

9. Notable exceptions to this pattern are Pynchon's *Vineland* and Philip Roth's *American Pastoral.* Marge Piercy's *Vida* also features a female leftist character; but this novel is one of the few American novels that disrupts the pattern of portrayal of leftists as the political "Other."

Works Cited

Baker, Peter. "The Terrorist as Interpreter: *Mao II* in Postmodern Context." *Postmodern Culture* 4.2 (1994): 34 pars. <http://muse.jhu.edu/journals/postmodern_culture/v004/4.2baker.html.

Boyle, T. Coraghessan. *World's End.* New York: Penguin Books, 1987.

DeLillo, Don. *Libra.* New York: Viking, 1988.

———. *Mao II.* New York: Viking, 1991.

———. *White Noise.* New York: Viking, 1985.

Doctorow, E. L. *The Book of Daniel.* New York: Random House, 1971.

Gitlin, Todd. *The Sixties: Years of Hope, Days of Rage.* New York and Toronto: Bantam Books, 1987.

Hutcheon, Linda. *A Poetics of Postmodernism, History, Theory, Fiction.* New York: Routledge, 1988.

———. *The Politics of Postmodernism.* New York: Routledge, 1989.

Piercy, Marge. *Vida.* New York: Ballantine Books, 1979.

Pynchon, Thomas. *Vineland.* Boston: Little, Brown, and Company, 1990.

Roth, Philip. *American Pastoral.* New York: Houghton Mifflin Company, 1997.

Scanlan, Margaret. *Plotting Terror: Novelists and Terrorists in Contemporary Fiction.* Charlottesville: UP of Virginia, 2001.

———. "Writers Among Terrorists: Don DeLillos *Mao II* and the Rushdie Affair." *Modern Fiction Studies* 40 (1994): 229-52.

Simmons, Ryan. What is a Terrorist? Contemporary Authorship, the Unabomber, and *Mao II. Modern Fiction Studies* 45 (Fall 1999): 675-95.

Whitebrook, Maureen. "Reading Don DeLillo's *Mao II* as a Commentary on Twentieth-century Politics." *The European Legacy* 6 (2001): 762-69.

Zulaika, Joseba and William A. Douglas. *Terror and Taboo: The Follies, Fables, and Faces of Terrorism.* New York: Routledge, 1996.

Anne Longmuir (essay date winter 2005)

SOURCE: Longmuir, Anne. "The Language of History: Don DeLillo's *The Names* and the Iranian Hostage Crisis." *Critique* 46, no. 2 (winter 2005): 105-22.

[*In the following essay, Longmuir argues that* The Names *represents the earliest example of DeLillo's linking of narrative to historical reality, specifically the Iranian hostage crisis.*]

Of the novels that Don DeLillo wrote in the 1980s, ***The Names*** (1982) has received the least attention. Whereas best-sellers ***White Noise*** (1985) and ***Libra*** (1988) won book prizes and created their own criticism industries, the response to ***The Names*** has been much quieter. Despite this comparative neglect, we should recognize ***The Names*** as the "sleeper" in DeLillo's canon, a novel that "is certain to gain in stature as DeLillo's novelistic status becomes clearer to us in the coming years" (Weinstein 289). Tom LeClair calls ***The Names*** DeLillo's "'breakthrough' book" because it was "more widely and positively reviewed than his previous works" (180). But ***The Names*** represents another kind of breakthrough: DeLillo's use of a more "realistic" fiction to question epistemology, language, and geopolitics to an extent unprecedented in his earlier work. For the first time, DeLillo plots a novel against a historical intertext, just as he later plots ***Libra*** against the Kennedy assassination and ***Underworld*** (1997) against the cold war. ***The Names*** is not a minor work by a major author; it is a seminal text that grounds DeLillo's subsequent fiction. Furthermore, this interpretation of ***The Names*** is bound to become more widespread, given DeLillo's choice of intertext: the Iranian hostage crisis. Critics have frequently remarked about DeLillo's prescience: after September 11, 2001, DeLillo's long-standing engagement with the relationship of the United States to the Middle East and Islamic fundamentalism confirms him as one of America's most important and shrewd cultural commentators.

In the past, ***The Names*** has frequently suffered from underreading; critics have rendered the novel a metaphysical meditation on language, ignoring the political ramifications and historical circumstances of the text. Admittedly, this is a recurrent problem with criticism of DeLillo's fiction in general. Matthew J. Morris notes that reviewers prefer "emphasizing the linguistic structures of his [DeLillo's] novels at the expense of their political implications" (113). This problem is particularly acute regarding ***The Names.*** From its first publication, critics have ignored direct references to geopolitical events in ***The Names*** in favor of discussions of language. Josh Rubins suggested in the *New York Review of Books* that ***The Names***' "theme is spelled out in textbook-bold: 'Could reality be phonetic, a matter of gutturals and dentals?'" (48). David Bosworth confidently told us in the *Boston Review* that "***The Names*** is about 'naming,' about language, about its irrational, emotive, almost mystical power" (30). This emphasis did not shift even when ***The Names*** became the subject of more extended academic criticism, as a glance at the titles of a few articles demonstrates. From Paula Bryant's "Discussing the Untellable: Don DeLillo's *The Names,*" Dennis A. Foster's "Alphabetic Pleasures: *The Names,*" Matthew J. Morris's "Murdering Words: Language and Action in Don DeLillo's *The Names*" to Arnold Weinstein's "Don DeLillo: Rendering the Words of the Tribe," existing academic criticism reduces ***The Names*** to an abstract analysis of language.

Of course, language and the broader epistemological questions that it raises are a primary concern of ***The***

Names. From the "[f]lamboyant prose" (32) of Tap's novel to Owen Brademas's academic interest in ancient languages, to the religious cult in which alphabetic coincidence determines choice of ritual sacrifice victim, discussions of language permeate ***The Names.*** The novel asks whether language is a means of understanding the things in the world or is merely a thing in the world itself. But crucially, unlike most academic criticism of ***The Names,*** the novel does not explore this question in isolation. Instead, it poses the question, "Can language refer outside itself?" within a very specific location and period. In doing so, DeLillo creates a novel that alludes to external political events while simultaneously questioning the referential properties of language. Most criticism of ***The Names*** falls short because it treats the novel as an autonomous text. But we can understand the extent of DeLillo's project in this novel only by subjecting it to an intertextual reading in which we explore the "general discursive space that makes a text intelligible" (Culler 106). John Frow's reminder that no text is a "self-contained structure" (45) is especially true of ***The Names,*** in which the text plays out its central dilemma by referring to actual historical events. Thomas Carmichael rightly argues that "DeLillo's fiction should be read intertextually, or should be read in Fredric Jameson's terms as 'the rewriting or restructuration of a prior historical or ideological *subtext,* it being always understood that that "subtext" is not immediately present as such'" (205, emphasis in original). But Carmichael wrongly identifies Tap's story and Volterra's film as ***The Names***' most significant intertexts. ***The Names***' most important intertext is historical: its references to the Iranian revolution and the subsequent hostage crisis.

Recognizing the Iranian hostage crisis as an intertext is important because it alters our interpretation of this novel and of DeLillo's work in general. Rather than belonging to the so-called "literature of exhaustion," DeLillo's engagement with the Iranian hostage crisis demonstrates the political commitment of his writing and repudiates the accusations of apoliticism that critics such as John Kucich (334) have levelled at him. ***The Names*** is not merely a successful novel; it is also a successful piece of political analysis, as attested by DeLillo's subsequent reputation as America's most prescient writer. Margaret Roberts calls him a "soothsayer" (5); Timothy L. Parrish writes that "the second half of the American twentieth century [. . .] is coming to look like nothing other than DeLillo's own invention" (721). ***The Names,*** however, not only demonstrates DeLillo's determination to engage with geopolitical reality but also demonstrates his determination to engage with a non-American reality. DeLillo was one of the first American writers to step through what Slavok Zizek calls the "fantasmatic screen separating it [the United States] from the Outside world" ("Welcome"). Even in 1982, DeLillo realized the limitations of the cold war paradigm, anticipating with disturbing accuracy the problems that would emerge from the Middle East and religious fundamentalism—a phenomenon that many in the West regarded as confined to the Middle Ages. DeLillo is not spurred by a fear of the eastern "Other"; rather his prescience stems from his early recognition that American neocolonialism, combined with its failure to imagine anything beyond the cold war binary, was bound to have violent repercussions. As James states in ***The Names,*** "Wasn't there a sense, we Americans felt, in which we had it coming?" (41).

In ***The Names,*** DeLillo repeatedly mentions the Iranian revolution and the subsequent hostage crisis, in which Iranian students held 52 members of the U.S. embassy staff in Teheran for 444 days beginning on 4 November 1979. These events, although never dwelt on for more than half a page, nonetheless figure persistently as the backdrop for the novel's action and philosophical meditations. For example, Eliades cites Iran when discussing the "curious way Americans educate themselves" through television: "Look, this is Iran, this is Iraq. Let us pronounce the word correctly. E-ron. E-ronians. This is a Sunni, this is a Shi'ite. Very good" (58). Similarly, we discover that David Keller lives in Athens because the Iranian revolution forced him to leave Teheran, his previous posting. James is a political risk analyst for the Middle East, responsible for collating information on the situation in Iran. The hostage crisis not only creates more paperwork for him: "It was the winter the hostages were taken in Teheran and Rowser put the entire section on duplicate. This meant all records had to be copied and sent to Athens," (143) but it also makes him acutely aware of the danger of being an American in certain regions of the world: "Our Iranian control was dead, shot by two men in the street" (143). Indeed, the audacity of David Keller's plan to put the drunk and unconscious American, Hardeman, on a plane to Teheran is only apparent when read against the background of the Iranian hostage crisis: not so much a prank as a death sentence.

Close examination of the novel shows that ***The Names*** not only makes occasional reference to the hostage crisis but that DeLillo has carefully and precisely plotted the novel against this incident. The novel traces events from 1979 to 1980 through repeated and systematic allusions to incidents in the Middle East and the Muslim calendar. We know that the novel begins in summer 1979 because James tells us that "[t]his summer, the summer in which we sat on his broad terrace, was the period after the shah left Iran, before the hostages were taken, before the Grand Mosque and Afghanistan" (66). Similarly, we can pinpoint Tap and Rajiv's visit to Athens to between 26 July 1979 and 24 August 1979, thanks to James's comment, "It's Ramadan" (88). James's description of the flood of American citizens arriving in Athens indicates that a conversation with Charles Maitland takes place in late November or early December 1979: "They would come on scheduled flights out of Beirut, Tripoli, Baghdad, out of Islamabad and Karachi, out of Bahrain, Muscat, Kuwait and Dubai, the wives and children of businessmen and diplomats, causing room shortages in Athens hotels, adding stories, new stories all the time" (96). This mass exodus was the result of the U.S. government's instruction to its embassies in eleven Muslim countries on 27 November 1979 to begin a "voluntary drawdown" of diplomats' families and nonessential personnel because of anti-American feeling in the Middle East and Asia. A relaxing day on the beach in Rhodes with David Keller and Lindsay takes place between 14 November 1979 and 24 April 1980, as the allusions to the freezing of all official Iranian government assets in the United States and to Desert One, the abortive rescue mission to free the hostages held in Teheran, indicate:

> This was the period after the President ordered a freeze of Iranian assets held in U.S. banks. Desert One was still to come, the commando raid that ended two hundred and fifty miles from Teheran. It was the winter Rowser learned that the Shi'ite underground movement, Dawa, was stockpiling weapons in the Gulf. It was the winter before the car bombings in Nablus and Ramallah, before the military took power in Turkey, tanks in the street, soldiers painting over wall slogans. It was before Iraqi ground troops moved into Iran at four points along the border, before the oilfields burned and the sirens sounded through Baghdad, through Rashid Street and the passageways of the souks, before the blackouts, the masking of headlights, people hurrying out of tea-houses, off the double-decker buses.
>
> (233)

The cumulative effect of collating even these few examples is quite startling; it becomes apparent just how carefully DeLillo has plotted the novel that Paula Bryant calls "language obsessed" (17) against actual global political events. Of course, identifying historical events as intertextual is fraught with difficulty, being always "an act of interpretation [. . .] not a real and causative source but a theoretical construct formed by and serving the purposes of a reading" (Frow 46). Bearing that proviso in mind, I am, nevertheless, prompted by the sheer number of allusions to the Iranian revolution and the subsequent hostage crisis to argue that these events constitute ***The Names***' "general discursive space" because they make the novel intelligible in a way that criticism interpreting ***The Names*** in isolation does not anticipate.

How do we account for DeLillo's fascination with the Iranian hostage crisis in this specific novel? The most prosaic explanation is that DeLillo was living in Greece during the crisis. His relative proximity to Iran must have given the events in Teheran an immediacy that they would not have had if he had still been living in New York. But the hostage crisis must also have raised DeLillo's awareness that it was becoming dangerous just to be an American in certain regions of the world. In this way, the crisis provided him with a platform to explore a tension that dominates his novels, the tension between the traditional American conception of subjectivity as autonomous and independent on the one hand and as patterned and determined by some larger, preexisting system on the other. This "abiding American dread" (Tanner 15) that an existing ideology or culture programs our identity pervades all of DeLillo's novels, from Gary Harkness's struggle to create a self outside the framework of football in ***Endzone*** (1972) to Karen Janney's choice between an explicitly controlled life in the Moonies or an implicitly conditioned identity in "mainstream" America in ***Mao II*** (1991). The hostage crisis heightened this dread in a real and terrifying way as Americans saw their compatriots targeted purely because of their nationality rather than because of any individual action or belief.

The American media depicted the hostage crisis as an out-and-out assault by an alien and antithetical culture on the dearly held conception of American identity as autonomous and self-made. It offered individual portraits of hostages, detailing their families and unique personal histories, while characterizing the hostage takers as "a large anonymous mob, deindividualized, dehumanized" (Said, *Covering Islam* 95). The message was clear: Americans are individuals; they are not. Despite that assumption, the events in the Middle East in 1979 compelled a reassessment of the supposed autonomy of American identity. Christian Bourguet's advice to President Carter makes explicit the importance of this reassessment:

> You must understand that it is not against their person that the action is being taken. Of course, you can see that. They have not been harmed. They have not been hurt. No attempt has been made to kill them. You must understand that it is a symbol, that it is on the plane of symbols that we have to think about this matter.
>
> (Qtd. in Said, *Covering Islam* xxvi)

Bourguet realized that U.S. government could only comprehend the Iranian hostage crisis once it abandoned its traditional assumptions about American identity because it could not understand the situation as long as it regarded the hostages as individuals. Instead, as even Warren Christopher acknowledged, the U.S. government had to recognize the hostages as expressions of "U.S. involvement" in Iran (Christopher 27). In other words, only by interpreting the hostages as conditioned by some larger system could the Americans understand the events in Teheran. In the face of the Iranian hostage crisis, the traditional American conception of identity proved an inadequate explanation.

DeLillo's interest in issues of identity predates ***The Names,*** indicating that the hostage crisis is not the origin of this novel, but an intertext. John Frow argues:

> Intertextual analysis is distinguished from source criticism both by this stress on interpretation rather than on the establishment of particular facts, and by its rejection of a unilinear causality (the concept of "influence") in favour of an account of the work performed upon intertextual material and its functional integration in the later text.
>
> (46)

The identification of the hostage crisis as an intertext stems, therefore, not only from DeLillo's explicit reference to the event but also from the recognition that the hostage crisis is functionally integrated into ***The Names.*** This "functional integration" manifests itself in the affinities between the hostage crisis and DeLillo's novel and in the fact that we can subject both to the same critical analysis and in ***The Names***' internalization of a critique of the cultural codes that shaped America's reaction to the hostage crisis. The result of this functional integration is that ***The Names*** deals with the issue of identity raised by the hostage crisis in both an overt and oblique fashion. For example, DeLillo explicitly recognizes that American nationality now overrides individual actions or beliefs. The novel's refrain, "Are they killing Americans?" (45, 193) and James's attempted assassination both reveal this recognition that the larger code of nationality conditions the identity of individuals.

> Why was I standing rigid on a wooded hill, fists clenched, facing a man with a gun? The situation pressed me to recall. This was the only thing to penetrate that blank moment—an awareness I could not connect to things. The words would come later. The single word, the final item on the list. *American.*
>
> (328, emphasis in original)

The cult murders, on the other hand, signal ***The Names***' oblique internalized critique of the hostage crisis. There is no explicit connection between the murders and the events in the Middle East beyond a throwaway reference to a "cult murder in northern Iran" (174). Nonetheless, these murders belong in the same "general discursive space" as the hostage crisis.

James first encounters a cult murder on the island of Kouros when an old man is beaten to death with a hammer. He hears of other similar killings in India and Iran and, with Owen Brademas, discovers that the culprits are a nomadic religious cult that selects their victims by matching their initials to the location of their death. Fredric Jameson labels these murders incomprehensible, stating that they are "absolutely meaningless for me" ("Reviews" 121). However, Jameson fails to understand the cult murders for the same reason that Americans could not comprehend why Iranian students would hold American citizens hostage: because he interprets these victims as individuals rather than as symbols of a larger system. As the U.S. government could only comprehend the hostage crisis once it read the American hostages as ciphers, so we can only understand the cult murders once we interpret the victims as expressions of a larger system—language. DeLillo's description of the cult murders as a "death by system, by machine intellect" (175) reminds us that the assumption behind the cult murders is the same as that behind the hostage crisis in Iran: that individuals are not autonomous but are created and conditioned by a larger system, whether language or geopolitics. Existing interpretations of ***The Names*** have, like Jameson's, either failed to account for the murders or have interpreted them only in terms of language. Invoking the Iranian hostage crisis as an intertext allows us to understand the complexity of the role of the murders in ***The Names.*** These murders gesture toward the power dynamic at play within a specific historic event and in the general issue of identity, as well as in language in particular.

As the hostage crisis echoes DeLillo's obsession with conflicting conceptions of identity, so it also brings to the fore another of DeLillo's favorite themes: the growth of the electronic media and the subsequent "loss of the real." Perhaps overlooked now in discussions of "media events," in favor of the assassination of John F. Kennedy, Watergate, or the Gulf War, the Iranian hostage crisis marked a significant moment in the development of the electronic media. The crisis received massive coverage; Christopher Andrew tells us that "[t]he hostage crisis had more intensive television coverage than any event since the Second World War, even including Vietnam" (449). New technology meant that journalists could relay news and pictures faster than ever before. The intensity of the coverage and the speed with which it reached the United States led to a situation in which "Iran [. . .] seemed to be *in* American lives, and yet deeply alien from them, with an unprecedented intensity" (Said, *Covering Islam* 25, emphasis in original). Against the background of such instant and blanket coverage of global events we can understand the experience of Kathryn's dad in ***The Names***:

> Most of his anger came from TV. All that violence, crime, political cowardice, government deception, all that appeasement, that official fainthheartedness. It rankled, it curled him into a furious ball, a fetus of pure rage. The six o'clock news, the seven o'clock news, the eleven o'clock news. He sat there collecting it, doubled up with his tapioca pudding. The TV set was a rage-making machine, working at him all the time, giving him direction and scope, enlarging him in a sense, filling him with a world rage, a great stalking soreness and rancor.
>
> (178)

The instantaneous nature of the modern media collapses geographical distances and creates a "world rage" as television makes all of its events seem simultaneously present; the presence of the TV set in the domestic sphere gives conflicts an intensely personal edge for the first time. Just as the American media depicted the hostages as innocent individuals, not as symbols of American intervention in Iran, so the insertion of global politics into the home ensured that individuals like Kathryn's dad interpreted events not in terms of larger systems but as personal affronts.

The media not only relayed news from Teheran but also shaped and participated in those events. Deborah Holmes notes that "often Iran and the United States addressed each other only through the media" (74), while the student hostage takers "schedule[d] 'events' to meet satellite deadlines and nightly news broadcasts in the United States" (Said, *Covering Islam* 76), giving interviews to CBS's "60 Minutes" in favor of PBS's "MacNeil-Lehrer Report," because the former had higher ratings (Holmes 56). In other words, media representation sometimes subsumed the hostage crisis itself, as the hostage takers self-consciously enacted events for American television screens. DeLillo's interest in the effect of media reproduction on reality is a central issue in his most widely studied novel, ***White Noise.*** But significantly, ***The Names*** prefigures this interest. Just as the plane passengers in ***White Noise*** feel that they survived a near plane crash "for nothing" (92) when they discover that it will not be reported in the press, so James Axton meets an Irishman, recently returned from the Middle East, who complains "that he kept walking into scenes of destruction and bloodshed that never got reported" (194). Like the plane passengers of ***White Noise,*** personal safety does not concern the Irishman. "The death itself seemed not so much to matter" (194) as much as the prospect that his death might not be reported, "as though the thing had never happened" (194). Both the Irishman and the plane passengers of ***White Noise,*** like the Iranian students in Teheran, subscribe to Baudrillard's definition of hyperreality, in which only reproduction in the media can authenticate their experiences.

We should not regard the media coverage of the Iranian hostage crisis as a means of explaining DeLillo's interest in this issue in ***The Names.*** What is significant is how ***The Names*** internalizes an interpretation of the effect of the press that we can usefully apply to the Iranian hostage crisis. We detect this not only in DeLillo's description of the Irishman's experiences; James's Greek friend Eliades also provides a direct commentary on the behavior of the American press regarding the Middle East:

> I think it's only in a crisis that Americans see other people. It has to be an American crisis, of course. If two countries fight that do not supply the Americans with some precious commodity, then the education of the public does not take place. But when the dictator falls, when the oil is threatened, then you turn on the television and they tell you where the country is, what the language is, how to pronounce the names of the leaders, what the religion is all about, and maybe you can cut out recipes in the newspaper of Persian dishes. I will tell you. The whole world takes an interest in this curious way Americans educate themselves. TV. Look, this is Iran, this is Iraq. Let us pronounce the word correctly. E-ron. E-ronians. This is a Sunni, this is a Shi'ite. Very good. Next year we do the Philippine Islands, okay?
>
> (58)

Crucially, Eliades's comments introduce a political dimension to Baudrillard's definition of hyperreality—"the real is not only what can be reproduced, but *that which is always already reproduced*" (emphasis in original 186)—by reminding us that such reproduction and representation have hitherto been a prerogative of the West. Eliades's comments carry important ramifications: they demonstrate DeLillo's political engagement with specific historic events and signal DeLillo's determination to politicize one of the tenets of postmodernism.

Eliades's interest in American cultural and economic imperialism indicates another point of connection between ***The Names*** and the Iranian hostage crisis. America's relationship with Iran before the revolution typifies the pattern of U.S. intervention overseas. Never formalized or institutionalized as were British and French imperialisms, American domination has always been, in the words of Edward Said, "insular" with "no long-standing tradition of direct rule overseas" (*Culture and Imperialism* 350). The United States had periodically intervened in Iran's internal affairs since the 1950s, when it reinstalled the Shah on the throne. Since that time the relationship of the United States with Iran had largely been economic, determined by that most precious of commodities, oil. However, we should also note more insidious, political intervention: the CIA, for example, trained and equipped SAVAK, the notorious Iranian secret police, while, in return for the sale of arms, the Shah allowed the United States to station listening devices along Iran's border with the Soviet Union. The Iranian revolution's rejection of Western law and morality and its vocal hostility to the United States were, on one level then, the rejection of a colonizer and its culture.

The Names points explicitly to the issue of American intervention overseas. DeLillo sets the novel in "strategically located" Greece (236), the site of covert American action for years; most of the novel's characters, including James Axton, David Keller, and George Rowser, are businessmen directly involved in the activities of Western multinational companies in the Middle

East. DeLillo makes clear the connection between economic and political colonialism. James discovers his employer is supplying the CIA with information, while Eliades explicitly links political and economic imperialism:

> Our future does not belong to us. It is owned by the Americans. The Sixth Fleet, the men who command the bases on our soil, the military officers who fill the U.S. embassy, the political officers who threaten to stop the economic aid, the businessmen who threaten to stop investing, the bankers who lend money to Turkey. [. . .] The bidet of America, we call this place. Do you want to hear the history of foreign interference in this century alone?
>
> (236-37)

The novel repeatedly draws a connection between the current economic imperialism and the more visible colonialism of the nineteenth century. Charles Mailland comments "more than once" that contemporary business practices are just "like the Empire" (7), whereas a description of the guard outside the Mainland Bank in Lahore indicates that the accouterments of the institutionalized imperialism of the nineteenth century disguise its lingering economic legacy:

> An elderly turbaned fellow with enormous drooping moustache, a tunic and pajama pants, a curved dagger in his sash and a pair of pointed slippers. A relative of the doorman at the Hilton. The outfit seemed intended to register in people's minds the hopeful truth that colonialism was a tourist ornament now, utterly safe to display in public. The foreign bank he guarded was a co-survivor of the picturesque past, exerting no more influence than the man himself.
>
> (269)

But DeLillo draws not only on images of European imperialism: as in ***Players*** (1977) and ***Running Dog*** (1978), he peppers ***The Names*** with references to cowboys, as a conversation between businessmen Dick Borden and David Keller illustrates:

> "Topper," Dick Borden said. "That was Hopalong Cassidy's horse." David said, "Hopalong Cassidy? I'm talking about *cowboys,* man. Guys who got down there in the shit and the muck. Guys with broken-down rummy sidekicks."
>
> "Hoppy had a sidekick. He chewed tobacky."
>
> (56, emphasis in original)

These references remind us that this new global capitalism is a peculiarly American phenomenon: having won the West, the American frontiersman has now turned his attention overseas. But most important, these references to Westerns indicate DeLillo's interest in the colonizer's representation of its own imperialist activities.

The events in Teheran in 1979 brought the issue of American intervention overseas forcibly to the fore, injecting DeLillo's existing interest in imperialism with a specific historic relevance. ***The Names*** not only makes occasional explicit reference to the hostage crisis and imperialism but also includes a more extended meditation on the effect of colonialism. We can observe striking parallels between the novel's meditations on language and the issues raised by the hostage crisis. ***The Names*** questions the ability of language to represent reality: the hostage crisis brought into sharp relief the ability of the West to represent the reality of non-Western cultures. In other words, we can interpret the American handling of the Iranian hostage crisis as the living embodiment of the central philosophical question of DeLillo's novel—can language authentically represent reality? Only by using DeLillo's references to the Iranian hostage crisis in our interpretation of ***The Names*** can we understand the broader political implications of the novel's central question.

A central tenet of postcolonial theory is that representation itself has hitherto been a prerogative of the political and cultural power of the West. The West has only known the colonized through Western representation. Furthermore, the West has constructed these representations from its own images, rather than from contact with the colonized or their culture. These images often characterize the colonized as the "other" of the West: they function to define the colonizer's identity as much as the identity of the colonized. These representations preclude the West from ever "knowing" the colonized—just as the Western and the myth of the frontier preclude us from knowing pre-Columbian America. This phenomenon is apparent in DeLillo's description of the casual Orientalism of business travelers:

> All these places were one-sentence stories to us. Someone would turn up, utter a sentence about foot-long lizards in his hotel room in Niamey, and this became the solid matter of the place, the means we used to fix it in our minds. The sentence was effective, overshadowing deeper fears, hesitancies, a rife disquiet. There was around us almost nothing we knew as familiar and safe. Only our hotels rising from the lees of perennial renovation. The sense of things was different in such a way that we could only register the edges of some elaborate secret.
>
> (94)

These travellers are incapable of understanding other societies except through the stories of other Westerners, and the effect of their representations is always to reduce and contain foreign cultures. The Iranian hostage crisis exemplifies the epistemological problem raised by colonialism, as Edward Said's decision to devote an entire book to it, *Covering Islam,* indicates. Ignorance and misinterpretation characterized the United States's understanding of Iran before and after the revolution. Even those Americans involved with Iran as representatives of the U.S. government succeeded only in illustrating one of postcolonialism's central arguments: that what the West knows about the non-Western world it knows "in the framework of colonialism" (Said, *Covering Islam* 155). Like the business travelers in ***The Names*** who rely on the stories of other Westerners to understand foreign cultures, the U.S. government knew little about Iran other than what other Western sources could tell it. As Gary Sick states:

> The United States, over a period of nearly a decade, had permitted its own contacts in Iranian society to be concentrated almost exclusively on the court, the Western-educated elite and official relations with military and security institutions. Very few experienced officers in the embassy could speak the local language, and there was virtually no contact with the merchants of the bazaar, let alone the clergy.
>
> (66)

The result of this "framework of colonialism" was America's complete misinterpretation of events in Iran, as illustrated by the CIA report of August 1978 that stated that Iran was "not in a revolutionary or even a pre-revolutionary situation" (Andrew 439). Critics usually interpret ***The Names*** as a novel that questions the relationship of words and things: the Iranian revolution and the subsequent hostage crisis literally forced the United States to recognize a dislocation between the two because the language of the CIA and official government reports bore no relation to the events in Iran.

Bill Ashcroft, Gareth Griffith, and Helen Tiffin remind us in *The Empire Writes Back* that language sustains colonial power: "Language becomes the medium through which a hierarchical structure of power is perpetuated, and the medium through which conceptions of 'truth,' 'order,' and 'reality' become established" (7). Both the Iranian hostage crisis and ***The Names*** support this correlation between language, representation, and imperialism. In ***The Names,*** for example, Eliades recognizes that knowledge and power are intimately connected, as the following conversation with James illustrates:

> "This is interesting to me, the curious connection between Greek and American intelligence agencies."
>
> "Why curious?"
>
> "The Greek government doesn't know what goes on between them."
>
> "What makes you think the American government knows? This is the nature of intelligence, isn't it? The final enemy is government. Only government threatens their existence."
>
> "The nature of power. The nature of intelligence."
>
> (236-37)

The story of Rawlinson, an employee of the East India Company, and his efforts to decipher cuneiform writing also confirm this correlation of knowledge and power. Owen interprets the story as an example of "how far men will go to satisfy a pattern, or find a pattern, or fit together the elements of a pattern" (80). Kathryn, by contrast, recognizes Rawlinson's activities as an attempt to "[s]ubdue and codify" (80). Like Foucault, she sees that

> truth isn't outside power, or lacking in power: contrary to a myth whose history and functions repay further study, truth isn't the reward of free spirits, the child of protracted solitude, nor the privilege of those who have succeeded in liberating themselves. Truth is a thing of this world: it is produced only by virtue of multiple forms of constraint.
>
> (Foucault 379)

In other words, Kathryn understands that the appropriation of a colonized's language or culture into the institutions of Western knowledge is a strategy of domination. The Iranian hostage crisis similarly illustrates this relationship of language, power, and imperialism, albeit negatively. Unlike Rawlinson, American officials in Teheran generally could not read Persian, nor did they involve themselves in Iranian culture. Their inability to read the situation in Iran led literally to American loss of control in the region. They were unable either to interpret the situation properly or to appropriate Iranian culture into Western systems of knowledge. Lacking mastery over Iran's native languages, the United States was unable to "subdue and codify" the Iranian revolution.

The very public intelligence failure of the United States in the Iranian hostage crisis created an awareness of the inability of Western systems of knowledge to comprehend non-Western cultures. The hostage crisis was one of a series of events, including the Vietnam War, which forced the United States to recognize that its values were not universal. Western accounts of the crisis make this point repeatedly, as Abraham A. Ribicoff's description of the hostage crisis illustrates:

> It was a time when our antagonists refused even to acknowledge the existence of basic norms that all nations had hitherto considered sacrosanct. The very premises of traditional international diplomacy were thrown to the winds. [. . .] In similar crises in the future, it will be wrong and indeed dangerous to assume that the other actors are motivated by the kinds of forces that shape American behavior.
>
> (395)

Ribicoff's use of the term "basic norms" is most significant because what the hostage crisis demonstrated was the fallacious nature of this concept, as Iran's behavior revealed these "basic norms" to be cultural constructs of the West. Gary Sick states this explicitly:

> Those of us who are products of Western cultural tradition—even if our national origins are in Africa or Asia—share certain assumptions that are so firmly

ingrained that they no longer require discussion but are regarded almost as natural law [. . .]. The participation of the church in a revolutionary movement was neither new nor particularly disturbing, but the notion of a popular revolution leading to the establishment of a theocratic state seemed so unlikely as to be absurd.

(164)

Other accounts reiterate this sense that the hostage crisis undermined Western systems of knowledge. Christopher Andrew, for example, recognizes that the American failure to predict the Iranian revolution stemmed from the inability of Western epistemologies to accommodate the very concept of a theocratic state: "the appeal of his [Ayatollah Khomeini] call for the establishment of a religious philosopher king, the *velayat-e faqih,* was almost beyond the understanding of the secularized West" (440). Similarly, Edward Said reminds us that Western political theory could not account for the Iranian revolution: "the people who overthrew the shah were simply not explainable according to the canons of behavior presupposed by modernization theory" (*Covering Islam* 29). But the most telling response is that of Harold H. Saunders, then assistant secretary of state for the Near East and South Asia, who states that on hearing of hostage crisis, "I found myself asking 'Is the world unraveling?'" (35). As Saunders's comments reveal, the Iranian hostage crisis fundamentally disrupted many of the assumptions that founded conceptions of reality in the West.

Contact with non-Western culture also results in a loss of faith in Western thought and philosophy in ***The Names,*** as Owen's experiences in India illustrate:

> Owen tried intently to collect information, make sense of this. There were coconuts, monkeys, peacocks, burning charcoal. In the sanctum was a black marble image of Lord Shiva, four-faced, gleaming. Who were these people, more strange to him than the millennial dead? Why couldn't he place them in some stable context? Precision was one of the raptures he allowed himself, the lyncean skill for selection and detail, the Greek gift, but here it was useless, overwhelmed by the powerful rush of things, the raw proximity and lack of common measure.

(280)

Here DeLillo explicitly represents Western thought, "the Greek gift," as an ineffective tool. Rather than being an objective system of knowledge, capable of dissecting and comprehending reality accurately, Owen's experience reveals "the Greek gift" as unable to accommodate or comprehend anything but its own cultural products. Similarly, contact with non-Western cultures forces DeLillo's business travellers, like the American officials involved with the hostage crisis, to recognize "truth" as a function of culture, and not absolute:

> It seemed we'd lost our capacity to select, to ferret out particularity and trace it to some center which our minds could relocate in knowable surroundings. There was no equivalent core. The forces were different, the orders of response eluded us. Tenses and inflections. Truth was different, the spoken universe, and men with guns were everywhere.

(94)

Critics associate this decentering of Western thought most commonly with the poststructuralist school of philosophy, and in particular, with Jacques Derrida's dismantling of logocentrism. DeLillo even employs the same terminology as Derrida here, referring to a "center" that could guarantee meaning. Furthermore, as Derrida argues that in the absence of a fixed origin "everything became discourse" (279), so DeLillo depicts the new, confusing reality that faces these Western travellers as constituted in language: "Tenses and inflections," "the spoken universe."

This same disruption of language is apparent in the Iranian hostage crisis. The U.S. government's public intelligence failure over Iran, for example, signaled clearly a dislocation between language and reality. Similarly, Iran itself seemed constantly to introduce doubt and ambiguity, as President Jimmy Carter discovered when trying to fix Khomeini's words:

> There was some confusion about what Khomeini actually said—"if the Shah is not returned, the hostages could be tried" or "will be tried." We tried to get the Farsi or Persian-language version, to translate it ourselves for more accuracy. Later it turned out that he said different things to different interviewers. Diary, July 31, 1980.

(Carter 465)

This linguistic slipperiness leads Warren Christopher to depict Iran in terms of absence, as "a composite, with no settled identity or single voice" (6), just as David Keller does in ***The Names***: "Iran is different. Collapsed presence, collapsed business. A black hole in other words" (233). But the inability of Western vocabulary to contain the events in Teheran is most apparent in the West's designation of the hostage crisis as a "lawless act" (Christopher 10). By putting itself outside Western law, Iran put itself outside Western language. The law was unable to represent or accommodate Iran, and linguistic difficulties forced the United States to abandon its traditional legal format: "It was clear that long and complicated documents could not easily survive translation into French and Farsi, nor were such documents likely to be comprehended in Teheran. Therefore the settlement documents were made short and simple" (Christopher 21). Furthermore, Iran's "lawless act" had other implications because, as Jay Clayton reminds us in *The Pleasures of Babel,* the function of law is to "both restrict the proliferation meaning and itself be meaningful" (14). The hostage crisis then forced the United States to recognize that law is not a transcendental center that limits play but one that operates only through consensus—like all languages.

In other words, both ***The Names*** and the Iranian hostage crisis force a relativization of Western thought and philosophy, undermining the assumed relationship between words and things in particular. In "Structure, Sign and Play" Derrida figures this decentering as stemming from within Western thought itself, citing the works of Nietzsche, Freud, and Heidegger as catalysts (280). In contrast, DeLillo situates this rupture historically in ***The Names,*** depicting its cause as Western contact with non-Western systems of knowledge. Here DeLillo supports the position of Fredric Jameson, who, in *The Political Unconscious,* calls for just such a historicizing of poststructuralist theory: "it would be desirable for those who celebrate the discovery of the Symbolic to reflect on the historical conditions of possibility of this new and specifically modern sense of the linguistic, semiotic, textual construction of reality" (63). This historicizing of poststructuralist theory is essential if we are to achieve any kind of critical distance or political resistance in late capitalism. Criticism that ignores DeLillo's use of the Iranian hostage crisis is unable to make this interpretative leap. The widespread uncertainty over whether words can represent the world does not, in DeLillo's view, stem merely from developments in Western philosophy. Instead, contact with non-Western cultures and geopolitical events, like the Iranian hostage crisis, have brought these questions to prominence. As Charles Maitland comments to James: "They keep changing the names. [. . .] The names we grew up with. The countries, the images. Persia for one. We grew up with Persia. What a vast picture that name evoked" (239). ***The Names*** does not examine language in isolation. Rather, it deliberately asks abstract questions of language within a very specific period and location, thereby demonstrating the political implications of those questions and the historical conditions that shape them. Only by employing the historical intertexts of ***The Names*** in our readings can we understand the extent of DeLillo's project in this novel.

This move to historicize poststructuralist theory is fraught with difficulty because it faces an "enormously complex representational dialectic" (Jameson, *Postmodernism* 54). DeLillo is clearly aware of this representational difficulty in ***The Names,*** as his continual questioning of the referential abilities of language and the validity of historical narratives illustrates. ***The Names*** explicitly questions the ability of language to represent history, as Emmerich's comments to Owen Brademas signal: "This is not history. This is precisely the opposite of history. An alphabet of utter stillness. We track static letters when we read. This is a logical paradox" (291-92). But DeLillo never presents historical events as directly lived experiences; he presents them as *narrated* events. Just as DeLillo tells us that the business travelers know foreign cultures through the "one sentence stories" of other Westerners, so we "know" events in Teheran through other peoples' stories. For example, we find out about the widespread demonstrations against the Shah that took place in December 1978 through James's narration of a story told by David Keller. The result of this technique in ***The Names*** is to emphasize that what we know about reality, we know through linguistic structures. Furthermore, the references to external historical events are fragmentary and synchronic, rather than diachronic: "This was the summer before crowds attacked the U.S. embassies in Islamabad and Tripoli, before the assassinations of American technicians in Turkey, before Liberia, the executions on the beach, the stoning of dead bodies, the evacuation of personnel from the Mainland Bank" (67). This synchronic narration undermines the traditional logocentric conception of history as a singular teleological narrative, pointing instead to the depthlessness that characterizes late capitalism. The dominant of late capitalism is geographic, not historical—as befits any imperialist movement. ***The Names*** does not escape this cultural logic: Tom LeClair points out that "the governing form" of ***The Names*** "is spatial: three approximately equal parts entitled 'The Island,' 'The Mountain,' and 'The Desert,' as well as a short epilogue called 'The Prairie'" (179). In other words, ***The Names*** represents a dialectical attempt to think historically in an age governed by the spatial logic of geography.

History is not "extra-textual"; as Roland Barthes writes in "The Discourse of History":

> The fact can only have a linguistic existence, as a term in a discourse, and yet it is exactly as if this existence were merely the "copy," purely and simply, of another existence situated in the extra-structural domain of the "real." This type of discourse is doubtless the only type in which the referent is aimed for as something external to the discourse, without it ever being possible to attain it outside this discourse.
>
> (121)

DeLillo's use of the Iranian hostage crisis supports this assessment of history and my method of reading, in which historical events are employed not as "real and causative sources" of the novel but as intertexts. Hence, what we have designated in ***The Names*** as historicizing of poststructuralism, we should more accurately describe, not as DeLillo's presentation of the impact of extralinguistic events on Western patterns of thought but as the effect of their textualized social and political being on Western thought. Employing the Iranian hostage crisis as an intertext in our reading of ***The Names*** forces us to recognize that DeLillo does not explore language in isolation, because he does not believe language exists in isolation but exists within the social text. This impulse in ***The Names*** does much to repudiate the accusations of critics, like John Kucich, who claim that DeLillo is "unwilling or unable to take the next step toward any kind of political assertion"

(334). Instead of ignoring references in ***The Names*** to the Iranian revolution and hostage crisis, critics must recognize that DeLillo's references to narrated material events signal that we should also employ these in our readings. In this way, we can read ***The Names*** not as a transcendentally significant text but locally, using this general discursive space to make intelligible both its specific and wider political implications. After the events of September 11, 2001, Vince Passaro cited DeLillo as one of "a couple of authors whom we suspect COULD add to the available pool of wisdom on what is happening right now" (n. page). Only by recognizing DeLillo's use of the Iranian hostage crisis as an intertext in ***The Names*** can we understand the complexity of DeLillo's political analysis—and its accuracy.

Works Cited

Andrew, Christopher, "Jimmy Carter (1977-1981)." *For the President's Eyes Only.* New York: Harper Collins, 1995. 425-56.

Ashcroft, Bill, Gareth Griffith, and Helen Tiffin. *The Empire Writes Back: Theory and Practice in Post-Colonial Literatures.* London: Routledge, 1989.

Barthes, Roland. "The Discourse of History." *The Postmodern History Reader.* Ed. Keith Jenkins, London: Routledge, 1987. 120-23.

Baudrillard, Jean. "Simulations." *Postmodernism: A Reader.* Ed. Patricia Waugh, London: Edward Arnold, 1992. 186-88.

Bosworth, David. "The Fiction of Don DeLillo." *Boston Review.* 8.2 (1983). 29-30.

Bryant, Paula. "Discussing the Untellable: Don DeLillo's *The Names.*" *Critique: Studies in Contemporary Fiction.* 29.1 (1987). 16-29.

Carmichael, Thomas. "Lee Harvey Oswald and the Postmodern Subject: History and Intertextuality in Don DeLillo's *Libra, The Names* and *Mao II.*" *Contemporary Literature* 43.2 (1993): 204-18.

Carter, Jimmy. *Keeping Faith: Memoirs of a President.* London: Collins, 1982.

Christopher, Warren, Introduction. Christopher, Kreisberg, and Council on Foreign Relations 1-33.

Christopher, Warren, Paul H. Kreisberg, and Council on Foreign Relations. *American Hostages in Iran: The Conduct of a Crisis.* New Haven: Yale UP, 1985.

Clayton, Jay. "Culture/Narrative/Power." *The Pleasures of Babel: Contemporary American Literature and Theory.* New York: Oxford UP, 1993, 3-31.

Culler, Jonathan. "Presupposition and Intertextuality." *The Pursuit of Signs: Semiotics, Literature, Deconstruction.* London: Routledge and Kegan, 1981, 100-18.

DeLillo, Don. *Endzone.* New York: Penguin, 1986.

———. *Libra.* 1985. New York: Penguin, 1991.

———. *Mao II.* London: Vintage, 1992.

———. *The Names.* 1982. London: Picador, 1987.

———. *Players.* 1977. London: Vintage, 1991.

———. *Running Dog.* 1978. London: Picador, 1992.

———. *Underworld.* 1997. London: Picador, 1998.

———. *White Noise.* 1985. London: Picador, 1986.

———. Derrida, Jacques. "Structure, Sign and Play in the Discourse of the Human Sciences." *Writing and Difference.* Ed. Alan Bass. Chicago: U of Chicago P, 1978, 278-93.

Foster, Dennis A. "Alphabetic Pleasures: *The Names.*" *Introducing Don DeLillo.* Ed. Frank Lentricchia. Durham: Duke UP, 1991. 157-73.

Foucault, Michel. "Truth and Power." *From Modernism to Postmodernism.* Ed. Lawrence Cahoone. Cambridge: Blackwell, 1996.

Frow, John. "Intertextuality and Ontology." *Intertextuality: Theories and Practices.* Ed. Michael Worton, and Judith Still. Manchester, England: Manchester UP, 1990, 45-55.

Holmes, Deborah. "Press-Government Relation in the United States: The Iranian Hostage Crisis." *Governing the Press: Media Freedom in the U.S. and Great Britain.* Boulder, CO: Westview Press, 1986.

Jameson, Fredric. *The Political Unconscious: Narrative as a Socially Symbolic Act.* London: Routledge, 1983.

———. Reviews. *Minnesota Review.* (Spring 1984): 116-22.

Kucich, John. "Postmodern Politics: Don DeLillo and the Plight of the White Male Author." *Michigan Quarterly Review* 27.2 (1988): 328-41.

LeClair, Tom. "Crossing Hemispheres: *The Names.*" *In the Loop.* Urbana: U of Illinois P, 1987, 176-206.

Morris, Matthew J. "Murdering Words: Language and Action in Don DeLillo's *The Names.*" *Contemporary Literature* 30.1 (1989): 113-27.

Parrish, Timothy L. "From Hoover's FBI to Eisenstein's *Underwelt*: DeLillo Directs the Postmodern Novel." *Modern Fiction Studies* 45.3 (1999): 696-723.

Ribicoff, Abraham A. "Lessons and Conclusions." Christopher, Kreisberg, and Council on Foreign Relations 374-95.

Roberts, Margaret. "'D' is for Danger—and for Writer Don DeLillo." *Chicago Tribune* 22 May 1992, sec. 5: 1+.

Rubins, Josh. "Variety Shows." *New York Review of Books* 29.20 (1982): 47-48.

Said, Edward. Covering Islam: How the Media and the Experts Determine How We See the Rest of the World. New York: Pantheon Books, 1981.

———. *Culture and Imperialism.* London: Vintage, 1994.

Saunders, Harold H. "The Crisis Begins." Christopher, Kreisberg, and Council on Foreign Relations 35-71.

Sick, Gary. All Fall Down: America's Fateful Encounter with Iran. London: Tauris, 1985.

Tanner, Tony. City of Words. London: Jonathan Cape, 1971.

Weinstein, Arnold. "Don DeLillo: Rendering the Words of the Tribe." Nobody's Home: Speech, Self and Place in American Fiction from Hawthorne to DeLillo. New York: Oxford UP, 1993. 288-315.

Zizek, Slavok. "Welcome to the Desert of the Real." 17 Sept. 2001. John Dunne. University of Wisconsin-Madison, 12 Dec. 2001. <http://imp.lss.wise.edu/~~jddunne/docs/Zizek911.htm>.

Todd McGowan (essay date winter 2005)

SOURCE: McGowan, Todd. "The Obsolescence of Mystery and the Accumulation of Waste in Don DeLillo's *Underworld.*" *Critique* 46, no. 2 (winter 2005): 123-45.

[In the following essay, McGowan utilizes theories of Sigmund Freud and Jacques Lacan to illuminate DeLillo's commentary on the growing narcissism of American society in Underworld, *symbolized by the motif of garbage.]*

In ***Americana,*** Don DeLillo's first novel, one of the characters, Buford Long, points out the revelatory power of garbage. He claims, "Garbage tells you more than living with a person" (190). If we are meant to take this seriously and believe that garbage does provide a key for understanding people, then perhaps this explains its pivotal role in DeLillo's work. Garbage and waste occupy an increasingly central position in DeLillo's fiction as it develops: In early novels such as ***Americana, End Zone,*** and ***The Names,*** characters draw attention to the presence of waste; in ***White Noise,*** waste becomes a threat that must be avoided; and in ***Underworld,*** waste management becomes the central concern and occupation of the main character, Nick Shay.[1] In fact, according to Adam Begley, in ***Underworld,*** "DeLillo, writing from a post-Cold War perspective, is more concerned with nuclear waste than nuclear Armageddon. The proliferation of garbage, whether it's radioactive garbage or household garbage [. . .], seems to pose a greater threat than violence" (492). It is as if DeLillo's own career chronicles the growing danger that waste presents, as it now not only threatens to consume us but also occupies most of our time and energy.

We are producing more and more waste without anywhere to put it, and thus it ceases to be something that we can simply put out of mind or hide in a dump or landfill. As Al Gore states in his book on the environment, "Having relied for too long on the old strategy of 'out of sight, out of mind,' we are now running out of ways to dispose of our waste in a manner that keeps it out of either sight or mind" (145). In addition to chronicling the contemporary overflow of waste, ***Underworld*** also depicts an incredible transformation in the status of waste. Not only does the proliferation of waste threaten to overrun us—in Nick's words, "What we excrete comes back to consume us" (791)—but waste begins to acquire a transcendent, religious status. Throughout the novel, the emergence of a reverential attitude toward waste becomes apparent. Nick sums this up as he gazes on a landfill: "Maybe we feel a reverence for waste, for the redemptive qualities of the things we use and discard" (809). In ***Underworld,*** waste is everywhere, and it has become holy.

DeLillo does not simply chronicle the proliferation of garbage and its apotheosis in contemporary American society; in fact, the driving impulse energizing ***Underworld*** is the desire to explicate this transformation. In the history documented in the novel, the proliferation of waste corresponds to another dramatic change in the structure of society: the turning away from the Other and toward narcissistic self-absorption. If ***Underworld*** is a novel about the increasing predominance of garbage in our world, it is also a novel about a growing lack of interest in and connection with the Other. Why do these two developments occur simultaneously? What link, if any, does DeLillo posit between the proliferation of garbage and the prevalence of narcissism? In addressing these questions, we can find some assistance in Sigmund Freud's discussion of the importance of contact with the Other for survival. For Freud, as for DeLillo in ***Underworld,*** a suffocating build-up of waste is a direct manifestation of self-absorption and a lack of contact with the Other.

In *Beyond the Pleasure Principle,* Freud discusses biology as a metaphor for the functioning of the psyche, and in doing so he points out that a lack of contact with the Other leads to death, as a result of suffocation on one's own waste products. He claims that "the life process of the individual leads for internal reasons to an abolition of chemical tensions, that is to say, to death, whereas union with the living substance of a different individual increases those tensions, introducing what may be described as fresh 'vital differences' which must then be lived off' (67). Without contact with the Other, an individual subject has no way to escape from and hence to revitalize itself. Contact with the Other rescues the subject from suffocating on the self by supplying it with newness. This is why desire so often serves to revitalize the desiring subject: opening oneself to the Other in desire provides an influx of new "vital differences" that can sustain the subject.

At this point, Freud's often-condemned "biologism" and Lacan's understanding of the structure of desire converge. According to Lacan, desire is triggered by an object, what he calls the *objet petit a.* The *objet petit a* is the secret treasure we believe to be hidden in the Other, the seeming mystery of the Other that incites our desire. As Renata Salecl says, "that which arouses the subject's desire for another subject is the very specific mode of the Other's *jouissance* embodied in the object *a*" (64). Without this sense of a mysterious jouissance at the heart of the Other, we do not desire, and we do not connect with the Other. In *Le Séminaire, Livre X,* Lacan points out that the *objet petit a* "as such, and nothing else, is the access, not to jouissance, but to the Other. It is all that of it, starting from the moment when the subject wants to make its entry into this Other" (209, my translation). That is to say, it is only through desire and through the *objet petit a* that the subject has any contact with the Other. Desire is thus the source of the subject's revitalization—the way in which the subject discovers the newness of the Other. However, desire only provides this link to the Other (and thus this revitalization of the subject) insofar as the Other seems to contain the *objet petit a*—what is in the Other more than the Other. If our connection with the Other has disappeared, it is because the Other has lost this mysterious object that it once seemed to contain.

In ***Underworld,*** DeLillo chronicles the disappearance of the *object petit a* in the Other that has occurred as a result of the globalization of capital and the end of the cold war. These parallel events have worked to create a world of overwhelming immediacy and presence, a world in which subjects suffocate from the proximity of the Other. In the wake of the globalization of capital, there is no evident lack in the Other that would allow the subject to distance itself from the Other. The contemporary world, as DeLillo paints it, suffers from an absence of absence itself. This absence of absence leads directly, according to both Freud's logic in *Beyond the Pleasure Principle* and DeLillo's in ***Underworld,*** to the build-up of waste. Ironically, when this occurs, waste itself becomes the site of the *objet petit a,* replacing the Other. In this sense, DeLillo's novel depicts a turn in the focus of American society away from the Other and toward waste. The very title of the novel suggests, among other things, that we now exist in an "Underworld," where what was once marginal and discarded has become central. The task of the novel consists in helping us to come to terms with this shift.

Underworld begins with an event that brings subjects into contact with the Other—Bobby Thomson's home run that won the 1951 National League pennant for the New York Giants over the Brooklyn Dodgers. As DeLillo portrays it, this home run is a transcendent event, an event that attests to a mystery within the Other—and thus triggers the desire of subjects all over New York. Because it seems irreducible to other events, the home run creates an interest in the Other: "All over the city people are coming out of their houses. This is the nature of Thomson's homer. It makes people want to be in the streets, joined with others, telling others what has happened, those few who haven't heard—comparing faces and states of mind" (47). Thomson's home run has an aura surrounding it, as if it were a sacred event. DeLillo's narration in the first sixty pages of the novel (the account of the playoff game) further establishes this aura, as he slowly builds up a sense of anticipation and inevitability. Because DeLillo recreates this game with such solemnity, critics almost unanimously find that "The best part of ***Underworld*** [. . .] is the prologue" (Begley 498). This aura—the sense that there is something in the event more than the event—pulls the subject to the Other. In the novel, Brian Glassic contrasts this with the Kennedy assassination: "When JFK was shot, people went inside. We watched TV in dark rooms and talked on the phone with friends and relatives. We were all separate and alone. But when Thomson hit the homer, people rushed outside. People wanted to be together. Maybe it was the last time people spontaneously went out of their houses for something" (94). The ball that Thomson hit serves as the object that unites all these people, insofar as it embodies the mystery behind the event. The ball is *the* object, and yet no one seems to have it. Even the person who actually has the ball is unable to possess it because its value lies in its absence.

The *objet petit a,* the object-cause of desire, acts as an engine for desire insofar as we do not have it. It is an impossible object because when we do have it, we realize "that's not it." The object that one acquires is never the object that one desires because the *objet petit a* only exists insofar as it remains out of reach. Thus, desire is always unsatisfied. As Lacan puts it in his *Seminar XIV,* "there is no object through which desire satisfies itself, even if there are objects that are the *cause* of desire" (Lacan's emphasis, my translation). The *objet a* functions as the engine or cause of desire, but it cannot satisfy desire. When the subject believes that she or he obtains it, dissatisfaction inevitably results because the present object never provides the jouissance that the absent *objet petit a* seemed to promise. Obtaining the *objet petit a* reduces this transcendent object-cause of desire to the status of an ordinary empirical object. As a result, if an object is to sustain its status as *objet a,* it must resist all attempts to nail it down as a present object.

Such is the case with the baseball that Thomson hit to win the pennant. After the home run, Cotter Martin retrieves this ball, dislodging it in a struggle from the hand of the man he befriended during the game, Bill Waterson. When Cotter tells his father Manx about the ball, his father senses its value and spends the greater part of the novel trying to sell it. But whenever Manx tries to sell the ball, no one believes in the ball's authenticity. It is so much an *objet petit a* that its actual existence seems impossible.[2] And after Manx gives his sales pitch, he starts to doubt his own words: "the longer he talks the more unbelievable he sounds to himself" (642). Because this object has a transcendent value—it embodies a moment of perfect jouissance—in practical terms it has no value at all. When Manx finally sells the ball to Charlie Wainwright (who buys the ball despite his uncertainty about its authenticity), Charlie pays just thirty-two dollars and change. Later, when memorabilia collector Marvin Lundy sells the ball to Nick Shay, he sells it for just $34,500. In both cases, the sellers obtain only a fraction of the ball's true value. This is because the source of the ball's value is its absence: no ball could possibly be *the* ball that Thomson hit. The transcendent status of the ball that Thomson hit necessarily renders any actual, empirical ball inadequate—even if it is the home-run ball itself. The very nature of the *objet petit a* is such that any actual object necessarily disappoints: when this absent object becomes present, it is no longer *the* object. Once Charlie Wainwright has the ball, not only is he unable to sell the ball for its true value but he also cannot even tell anyone, feeling "Slyed out of his honest wages by some rogue off the street with a tale so staggering Charlie's embarrassed to tell his friends" (653). Charlie has the ball, but in having it, he has nothing. Here we see, as Slavoj Zizek puts it in *The Fragile Absolute,* that "the *objet petit a* is [. . .] the point at which the Holy Grail itself is revealed as nothing but a piece of shit" (49). When the ball is present, it ceases to evoke the mystery of Thomson's home run and becomes an ordinary baseball. Or worse, it comes to represent the possessor's credulity—evidence that she or he has been duped.

Even though no one can have this impossible object, it is nonetheless crucial for energizing desire. It marks a gap in the Other, a point of mystery through which the Other entices subjects to desire. The *objet petit a* is not the Other as such but what the Other lacks. When this empty space in the Other no longer exists, however, the space for the *objet petit a* and for desire closes up, leaving the subject isolated with itself, unable to connect to the Other. Desire is drawn to the Other because the Other seems to be hiding something, seems to be secretly different than its outward appearance. This is what Lacan means when he says that "desire is the desire of the Other": the subject desires the Other at the point of the gap in the Other. Or, as Lacan puts it, "The desire of the Other is apprehended by the subject in that which does not work, in the lacks of the discourse of the Other" (*Four Fundamental Concepts* 214). However, these lacks or gaps in the Other, as DeLillo makes clear, seem to be disappearing.[3] We can see evidence for this in the changed status of the home run in baseball today. Whereas the home run used to be a rare, even transcendent, event, today it has become a commonplace. The average baseball game now regularly produces multiple home runs, effectively eliminating any aura surrounding them. But the disappearance of the home run's aura is but one instance of a widespread societal transformation that works to eliminate the gap in the Other.

This elimination of the gap in the Other is, as DeLillo makes evident, an effect of the globalization of capital. Historically, capital has depended on otherness for its development. Capitalism needs the noncapitalist space, the blank spot in the Other, to serve as the site of otherness that it can appropriate. The empty space in the Other has a valorized status in the capitalist world because it is the site of the new—the new commodity, the new labor force, the new market, and so forth. As Rosa Luxemburg notes, "the accumulation of capital, as an historical process, depends in every respect on noncapitalist social strata" (366). Capital functions through a process of constant expansion, a process that continually highlights and then fills in the gap in the Other. After it valorizes this gap, capital eliminates it. This is what leads Marx to point out in the *Grundrisse* that "the tendency to create the *world market* is directly given in the concept of capital itself. Every limit appears as a barrier to be overcome" (408, Marx's emphasis). Capital depends on the gap in the Other—the space where one finds (and where capital creates) the *objet petit a*—but it works to eliminate this gap, to transform every *objet petit a* into a commodity that can be exchanged. In this way, the mystery of the Other gradually disappears with the development and expansion of capital.[4] As Nick Shay says in ***Underworld,*** "Capital burns off the nuance in a culture" (785). With the globalization of capital, this process becomes complete, and the Other ceases to be the site in which the *objet petit a* can exist.[5]

The globalization of capital reduces all objects to commodities in a total leveling process. This is precisely what occurs during the decades recounted in ***Underworld***: capital "shoots across horizons at the speed of light, making for a certain furtive sameness" (786). As Peter Knight points out in "Everything Is Connected," his essay on paranoia in ***Underworld,*** the globalization of capital is the fundamental event in the novel. He says, "[T]he spectacular end of the Cold War and its attendant reconfiguration of national boundaries, the novel suggests, are but an effect of the far more significant and ongoing, underground reshaping of the global economy" (823). And the result of this transformation is an Other deprived of an object (*objet petit a*) that would interest the subject. There ceases to be an otherness that exceeds the Other—and thus the Other appears to be demystified, fully knowable.[6] According to Fredric Jameson, postmodernism, the cultural logic of late or global capitalism, "must be characterized as a situation in which the survival, the residue, the holdover, the archaic, has finally been swept away without a trace" (309).

The absence of any blank spot or sense of mystery in the Other—the absence of what Jameson calls the "archaic"—prompts subjects to turn inward, to turn away from desire, and to become self-satisfied. In this sense, the globalization of capital facilitates the development of narcissistic self-satisfaction that forecloses the subject's contact with the Other. The emergence of what Christopher Lasch calls the pathological narcissist is thus but the symptom of the epoch of global capitalism. If, as Lasch points out, "for the narcissist, the world is a mirror" (10), this is because the Other has ceased to offer the subject any enticement for the pathological narcissist's desire. Within the world of global capitalism, the subject no longer has any reason to engage a thoroughly demystified Other.

The contemporary subject's lack of contact with the Other becomes evident in ***Underworld*** when Nick, with Brian Glassic and Big Sims, attends a baseball game that once again matches the Giants and the Dodgers, although this time it takes place in 1992. Whereas the 1951 playoff game between these teams occasioned an outburst of desire that brought people into contact with each other, the experience during this game is entirely different. The contemporary game produces isolated spectators, as Nick describes: "We were set apart from the field, glassed in at press level, and even with a table by the window we heard only muffled sounds from the crowd. The radio announcer's voice shot in clearly, transmitted from the booth, but the crowd remained at an eerie distance, soul-moaning like some lost battalion" (91). In 1992, one can experience a baseball game without having to encounter the Other—without overhearing obnoxious fans, sweating in the hot sun, or sitting on an uncomfortable seat. But this also destroys the appeal of the game. We enjoy a baseball game not in spite of obnoxious fans, hot sun, and hard bleachers, but precisely because of these things. They help to create the aura that surrounds the game and entices our desire. But because Nick and his friends view the game from a self-satisfied position, the game does not evoke their desire. They watch, but they do not desire, contented in their stadium club seating.[7]

This kind of isolated, self-satisfied activity predominates the contemporary episodes in ***Underworld.*** In one instance, Nick enters a room while his wife Marian is watching television, and his mere presence in the room, watching along with her, disturbs her private enjoyment. Entering the room, Nick claims, "I'll be quiet and I'll watch" (116). But Marian responds, "You're interfering by watching" (116). Rather than argue with her, Nick realizes that she is correct: "another's presence screws up the steady balance, the integrated company of the box" (116).[8] Marian finds satisfaction with her imaginary companion, and another person exists only as a potential disruption of that satisfaction. Unlike the Other, which always causes the subject to feel incomplete and alienated, images (on the television screen) allow the subject to feel "a steady balance"—a sense of completeness. The main problem with this imaginary satisfaction is that, although it appears to avoid the Other altogether, it relies on images provided by the Other (on television, in films, over the Internet). Hence, the subject immersed in this imaginary satisfaction experiences no sense of connection with the Other—no desire—and yet is totally dependent on the Other. It is precisely this state of "isolated" self-satisfaction that characterizes the contemporary subject in ***Underworld.*** Such a subject risks no contact with the Other because there is nothing enticing about the Other. The Other has lost its allure; it no longer seems to contain anything desirable.

But the absence of the *objet petit a* also prompts an opposing response, an attempt to recreate this object. In fact, the more the space for the *objet petit a* seems to disappear, the more desperate subjects become in their attempts to create this object. We can see one attempt to recreate the *objet petit a* in the activity of the Texas Highway Killer. DeLillo includes the brief interludes of the Texas Highway Killer (Richard Henry Gilkey) precisely to show this kind of response. The Texas Highway Killer kills to create a transcendent event in a world bereft of transcendence, in a world where everything is readily reducible to the same level. He wants his act to stick out, which is why the copycat killer disturbs him so much. The copycat killer emphasizes the reproducibility of even his seemingly singular acts of violence and thus threatens to immunize the world to the killings. The Highway Killer kills to make an impression at a time when nothing makes an impression. Anything that detracts from the singularity of his actions threatens what he wants to accomplish because the idea of their singularity is the motivating force behind these actions. Thus, the Highway Killer calls a television station to correct erroneous reports. Talking to the television commentator, he says, "I feel like my situation has been twisted in with the profiles of a hundred other individuals in the crime computer. I keep hearing about low self-esteem. They keep harping about this" (216). Although the Highway Killer wants his act to attest to his individuality—to what is "in him more than him," his *objet petit a*—the news coverage incessantly eliminates his difference, reducing him to the standard pattern of a serial killer.

By constantly showing a videotape that a girl riding in a car made of one of the killings, the television stations seek to make this event present to everyone. DeLillo writes that "they would keep running it until everyone on the planet had seen it" (232) and that "they would show it to the ends of the earth" (233). The television stations repeatedly show this videotape precisely because it indicates a gap in the Other, a point at which we might glimpse the *objet petit a,* that which exists beyond the completely commodified world of global capitalism. This is also what draws viewers to the tape: as they watch the tape, subjects look for this moment of transcendence—a moment showing the utter contingency of death—that appears to be outside of their homogenized daily experience. It promises the ultimate experience of jouissance. But the problem is that the wide publication of this tape has the effect of transforming the killing into a commonplace occurrence—precisely what the Highway Killer was trying to avoid.

Despite his effort to create an utterly singular and transcendent event, the ubiquity of the coverage makes this impossible.[9] DeLillo's novel allows us to understand in a new way an event like the O. J. Simpson trial. Here, we can see how total coverage—the CNNization of major events—has the effect of destroying the transcendent. In the face of this nonstop exposure, the murder trial of a major public figure became an ordinary daily event, stripped of its extraordinary dimension. Viewers could acquaint themselves with every aspect of the case; nothing about it remained mysterious or unknowable. This constant exposure flattened out the case, reducing the absence of the *objet petit a* to the presence of mere empirical objects. Television news seeks out the transcendent event to discover the *objet petit a*; but because it treats every event as if it can be apprehended as a present object, it eliminates the opening for this object. Transcendence—and the *objet petit a*—requires absence, not presence, and television news refuses to countenance absence.[10]

Nonetheless, ***Underworld*** emphasizes the importance of the Texas Highway Killer videotape and what it promises to make present. Because a girl in another car with a video camera has captured one of the Texas Highway Killer's murders on tape, we seem to be able to experience the impossible—a transcendent moment. This is what captivates everyone: "Seeing someone at the moment he dies, dying unexpectedly. This is reason alone to stay fixed to the screen. It is instructional, watching a man shot dead as he drives along on a sunny day. It demonstrates an elemental truth, that every breath you take has two possible endings" (159-60). The tape manages to capture an authentic moment—a point at which the Other is not in control—and it allows everyone to experience this moment. At the moment of the shot, something happens—a real event occurs. For all of the people watching (and for the victim), the shot emanates from a void: all of a sudden it appears, without warning and without apparent premeditation. It thus marks an event that seems to those who witness it to be irreducible to any chain of causality, to any meaning that we might attribute to it. We are drawn to the tape because it reveals the gap in the Other; it reveals that something that the Other has not accounted for can happen.

The form of the tape belies this revelation. Once the event appears on the tape, it no longer carries the element of pure contingency but becomes integrated into the narrative logic that the tape demands. To tape an event is de facto to place that event into a narrative structure, where the nonsensical makes sense and where the contingent becomes necessary. We cannot capture the openness of the moment on tape. DeLillo writes, "once the tape starts rolling it can only end one way. This is what the context requires" (160). The act of taping an event changes that event, bestowing on it a necessary structure and progression. Hence, even though the tape lures viewers into thinking it will reveal a purely contingent event, it cannot but disappoint. We look at the tape again and again to see the moment of the pure, transcendent event, but this moment continually eludes us. One cannot access the *objet petit a* through a regime of total presence; one must discover it through its absence.

This failure to access the object, however, is not the only problem that the tape presents. It allows access to a hitherto hidden thing; but in doing so, it destroys that thing and makes it commonplace. The tape airs a secret, but the airing of the secret eliminates that which makes the secret valuable. DeLillo writes, "The more you watch the tape, the deader and colder and more relentless it becomes. The tape sucks the air right out of your chest but you watch it every time" (160). In other words, people are drawn to the tape—to the revelation of what has been hidden—because it promises the answer to their desire; it promises to reveal the Other's secret, the *objet petit a.* DeLillo here allows us to grasp the problem at the heart of the reality shows that were just beginning to appear at the time he wrote ***Underworld.*** A "reality television" program like *Survivor* promises us a nonstop revelation of the *objet petit a*: subjected to extreme conditions, the contestants reveal themselves completely to the viewing audience. They bare their innermost, hidden secrets. Always concealed during "normal" situations, extremity exposes the *objet petit a,* and viewers tune in to discover the secret of this elusive object. But *Survivor,* like the videotape of the murder in ***Underworld,*** inevitably frustrates its viewers. Far from answering their desire, these revelations deflate those who witness them, depriving their desire of the distance and absence that it requires for breathing. In this way, the tape "sucks the air right out of your chest." When the treasure is revealed, then the treasure is lost, and desire suffocates. This treasure on the tape is the moment of the unaccountable murder—the moment of pure openness—but the taping of this moment transforms it into something as common as any other murder on the nightly news.

Bobby Thomson's home run represents a similar moment. Like the shooting, it takes people by surprise, and people experience it as something transcendent, even miraculous. But the difference is that only one scratchy audio recording exists of Thomson's home run, in contrast with the clear depiction of the killing on the videotape. Thus, the home run retains an aura. As Brian Glassic puts it in the novel, "The Thomson homer continues to live because it happened decades ago when things were not replayed and worn out and run down and used up before midnight of the first day. The scratchier an old film or an old audiotape, the clearer the action in a way. Because it's not in competition for our attention with a thousand other pieces of action" (98). The rarity—the lack of a clear image—of Thomson's home run allows it to continue to hold a special, transcendent place without being diluted. Thomson's home run manages to remain a transcendent event, and later attempts to rediscover this transcendence seem destined to fail.

Throughout ***Underworld,*** many characters attempt to rediscover the transcendence that marks the Thomson home run. Like the Texas Highway Killer (although, of course, using different methods), characters such as Marvin Lundy and Nick Shay do their best to sustain an empty space within the Other, a space for transcendence, and thus to sustain an opening for desire. The nostalgia that permeates the novel—and that these characters display—is a nostalgia for the opening within the Other.[11] As a dealer in memorabilia, Marvin tries to preserve a sense of the transcendence that threatens to disappear. But Marvin's comments about the cold war most emphatically indicate his grasp of the current situation. He tells Brian Glassic, "You see the cold war winding down. This makes it hard for you to breathe" (170). The looming end of the cold war suffocates subjects in precisely the same way that the videotape of the Texas Highway Killer does. It eliminates the sense of a gap in the Other that fosters desire. With the end of the cold war, the Other seems to be able to account for everything, to anticipate every possibility. Marvin says to Brian, "You need the leaders of both sides to keep the cold war going. It's the one constant thing. It's honest, it's dependable. Because when the tension and rivalry come to an end, that's when your worst nightmares begin. All the power and intimidation of the state will seep out of your personal bloodstream" (170). Marvin correctly sees that the existence of the cold war provides the breathing space for desire because it makes evident the limits of the Other; it shows us clearly that there is something beyond the Other's reach.[12] According to Marvin, the end of the cold war even affects our ability to fantasize. As he tells Brian, "when the cold war goes out of business, you won't be able to look at some woman in the street and have a what-do-you-call-it kind of fantasy the way you do today" (182). The ability to fantasize and to desire depends on a lack in the Other: this point of lack is something unknown; and it entices our fantasies and desires. When it disappears—when the point of absence itself becomes absent—desire evanesces.

Even American political leaders today have become aware of the way that the end of the cold war has stifled desire. Without an antagonistic superpower, without a clear limit to American hegemony, what is there to desire? We see the emergence of the idea of the war on terrorism in political discussions in response to the absence of this limit and the subsequent suffocating of American desire. George W. Bush has even made the war on terrorism the defining element of his presidency. The idea of the terrorist state serves to keep American desire alive because it resurrects the mysterious dimension of the Other: no one knows which countries might become terrorist states or which potentially terrorist states actually have nuclear or biological weapons (or where those weapons might be). Hence, the threat that the terrorist state represents is ipso facto impossible to locate. In this way, the concept of the terrorist state attempts to take up where the cold war left off; political leaders develop the concept to energize desire, which the end of the cold war left flagging. By invoking this concept, George W. Bush's relationship to desire evinces a kinship with that of Marvin Lundy and Nick in ***Underworld.***

Desire is predicated on absence, on failure rather than success. This is why Nick purchases the Thomson home-run ball from Marvin Lundy: as a fan of the Brooklyn Dodgers, the ball is the object marking a moment of traumatic loss for Nick. As he says, "I didn't buy the object for the glory and drama attached to it. It's not about Thomson hitting the homer. It's about Branca making the pitch. It's all about losing" (97). He "absolutely had to own" the ball not because it provided the satisfaction of having, but "[t]o commemorate failure" (97). For Nick, the ball preserves this failure and thus preserves a moment of not having the object. The object is important to Nick not for what it represents but for what it cannot represent, which is why it retains a mysterious transcendence for him. Nick's sensitivity to the importance of sustaining this mystery also manifests itself in his conversation about sex with Donna, a swinger whom he meets in a hotel. Nick upbraids her for swinging, an activity that destroys the mystery surrounding sex. He tells her, "[S]ex is one secret we have that approximates an exalted state and that we share, two people share wordlessly more or less and equally more or less, and this makes it powerful and mysterious and worth sheltering" (297). Nick's beef with Donna stems from her complicity with the contemporary world of revelation: by bringing sex out into the open, she and the swingers threaten to make it just another activity. Nick wants to preserve its transcendent status and thus preserve a place that remains concealed—a hidden space within the Other.

The problem with both Marvin and Nick's efforts to sustain a place for desire is that they also fall victim to paranoia. It is as if the only way to sustain the idea of a gap within the Other today is through recourse to paranoid speculation about what exists in that gap.[13] This is why DeLillo's fiction so often focuses on paranoid characters and yet at the same time refuses to give in to paranoia. DeLillo writes about paranoia because it suggests a gap in the Other and does not allow his fiction to become paranoid because it closes that gap. He appreciates Marvin and Nick's paranoia for the former and condemns it for the latter. In his essay on ***Libra,*** Skip Willman notes that "the equation of DeLillo and paranoia has gained widespread acceptance" (405). Willman's essay attacks this equation, showing that even in ***Libra,*** DeLillo's most "obviously" paranoid novel, DeLillo constantly *exposes* the logic of paranoia, rather than subscribing to it. The same can be said of ***Underworld***: by depicting the paranoia of characters such as Marvin and Nick, DeLillo allows the contradictions of this paranoia to become evident.

Although Marvin and Nick see the Other as haunted by an emptiness, they both posit an Other of the Other: someone behind the scenes who pulls the strings. Marvin finds meaning in everything—for him, there are no contingent events—because the Other behind the scenes has organized everything. For instance, his paranoia leads him to find "significance" in Gorbachev's birthmark:

> Marvin saw the first sign of the total collapse of the Soviet system. Stamped on the man's head. The map of Latvia.
>
> He said this straight-faced, how Gorbachev was basically conveying the news that the USSR faced turmoil from the republics.
>
> (173)

Within Marvin's paranoid universe, even a clearly contingent occurrence like a birthmark on the head of the Soviet leader acquires meaning and fosters connections. Nick also evinces a similar paranoia; he explains his father's desertion of the family by concocting a narrative of a mob hit on his father. This theory allows Nick to solve the riddle of his father's disappearance and to fill in a gap in his knowledge. For the paranoiac, nothing remains mysterious. Just as Marvin knows that a secret Other has guided the break-up of the Soviet Union, Nick knows that a secret Other has eliminated his father. In both cases, an Other of the Other—an Other that most people fail to notice—calls the shots.

On one level, paranoia sustains a sense of mystery, but on another, it ends up eliminating this mystery. That is to say, the problem with positing an Other of the Other is that it erects a nonlacking Other behind the scenes at the same moment that it recognizes the Other's lack. The Other of the Other plugs the hole in the Other that fosters desire; it fills in the gap. As Slavoj Zizek puts it in *Looking Awry,*

> the psychotic subject's distrust of the big Other, his *idee fixe* that the big Other (embodied in the intersubjective community) is trying to deceive him, is always and necessarily supported by an unshakable belief in a consistent Other, an Other without gaps, an "Other of the Other." [. . .] When the paranoid subject clings to his distrust of the Other of the symbolic community, of "common opinion," he thereby implies the existence of an "Other of this Other," of a nondeceived agent who holds the reins. The paranoiac's mistake does not consist in his radical disbelief, in his conviction that there is a universal deception—here he is quite right, the symbolic order is ultimately the order of a fundamental deception—but rather, in his belief in a hidden agent who manipulates this deception.
>
> (81)

In this way, paranoia fails at the task it initially seems to accomplish. Because Marvin and Nick fall victim to paranoia, they end up becoming complicit with the situation that they sought to reject—the disappearance of the transcendent event.

The paranoia evinced by so many characters in the novel is thus not merely personal but a widespread response to our particular historical situation. Paranoia becomes a popular and even predominant epistemological mode because it appears to restore the gap in the Other while leaving the subject with a narrative that secretly fills in that gap. It is in this sense that, as Patrick O'Donnell states, "paranoia is an alibi, a form of accommodation for the loss of [. . .] grand narratives" (16).[14] Grand narratives depend on a point of absence within the Other, a point of nonknowledge that they can fill with their particular explanation (the will of God, the material forces of history, for example). Paranoia becomes mainstream in the era of global capitalism precisely because this point of nonknowledge disappears, allowing subjects to attain a sense of fully knowing the Other and thereby eliminating the need for the grand explanatory narratives.

This full knowledge of the Other becomes possible, on one level, through the hyperlinks of the Internet. For this reason, DeLillo concludes ***Underworld*** with a discussion of cyberspace. In cyberspace, the link between the most seemingly disparate figures and events becomes evident. We see the connection, for instance, between J. Edgar Hoover and Sister Edgar: "No physical contact, please, but a coupling all the same. A click, a hit and Sister joins the other Edgar" (826). When this type of connection occurs explicitly, paranoia becomes the de facto mode of subjectivity.[15] Without the experience of an absence in the Other, the subject attempts to reassert absence (and a sense of mystery) by positing the Other of the Other who manipulates events behind the scenes. Although paranoia quickly solves the mystery that it posits, it nonetheless initially carves out a new terrain for absence. Paranoia emerges as *the* prevailing mode of belief with the globalization of capital and the explicit linking of the entire world.[16]

In ***Underworld,*** capital's globalization tends to produce paranoia because it successfully eliminates the empty spaces in the Other. Capital submits everything to the process of exchange, and under its sway nothing remains sacred or outside commodification. Like the Internet, capitalism allows for no absence within its structure. When there is no longer an alternative to capitalism—when capital becomes globalized—no barrier exists to prevent the complete elimination of the sacred. The existence of the communist alternative, even if it were not an authentic alternative, represented the idea of a limit to capital and thus helped to preserve a space for the sacred.[17] Without any alternative, capitalism unleashes commodification without any limit whatsoever. According to Ernest Mandel, "the hallmark of [. . .] late capitalism [. . .] is not a decline in the forces of production but an increase in the parasitism and waste accompanying or overlaying this growth" (214). The lack of an empty space in the Other leaves capital without any outside, and this produces an increasing build-up of waste. Like the self-contained individual choking on its waste that Freud discusses in *Beyond the Pleasure Principle,* global capitalism—the epoch in which capital triumphs over every blank space in the Other—leads to a world where waste proliferates. As Jacques-Alain Miller says, "The main production of the modern and postmodern capitalist industry is precisely waste. We are postmodern beings because we realize that all our aesthetically appealing consumption artifacts will eventually end as leftover, to the point that it will transform the earth into a vast waste land" (19). The world of global capitalism becomes this "vast waste land" because it is a world without a site for the sacred, a world without the gap in the Other.

But in the epoch of global capitalism, the sacred does not disappear; it simply moves to a new location. This waste, which marks the elimination of the sacred, comes to occupy the position of the sacred. That is to say, despite—or rather, because of—the total elimination of the sacred and the mysterious, global capitalism also produces another kind of sacred object: waste. The ever-quickening process of production and consumption produces increasing amounts of trash. Rather than simply becoming a burden to capitalist society, this trash comes to replace the evanescent *object petit a.* The treasured baseball that Thomson hit out of the Polo Grounds gradually loses its importance, even to Nick. In its stead rises garbage. Garbage achieves this status because, within the structure of global capitalism, it is the only thing that exists outside of the commodification process. Garbage is what does not fit. Within an economy of global capitalism, everything becomes commodified, everything has a place within the economic structure. Even the violence of the Texas Highway Killer can be integrated through the ubiquity of the videotaped killing. Garbage, however, remains outside, even though it is a production of capital itself. Capitalism produces garbage and then does not know what to do with it. That is why DeLillo draws special attention to those moments when garbage seems to stick out.

We see the conspicuousness of garbage most pointedly when Manx Martin, on his way to sell the Thomson baseball, encounters his friend Antoine, who has a car full of garbage. To avoid having the garbage pile up, Antoine fills his car with garbage from a friend's restaurant while people are eating in the restaurant. He then drives the garbage around town until he can find a place to "fling the trash out the door and press the gas pedal hard" (362). Garbage here has no proper place within the prevailing socioeconomic structure. This status of garbage is further revealed during a conversation between Nick and Sims at a waste management conference. They discuss a garbage ship that has been sailing for two years because "country after country" has refused it (278). This ship has an aura of mystery surrounding it precisely because it cannot find a receptive harbor, even in a "less developed country" that would "take a fee amounting to four times its gross national product to accept a shipment of toxic waste" (278). This ship cannot even be relegated to the lower strata of the world of global capitalism; it exists only in the margins of that world. And this wholly marginal existence gives garbage its aura in a structure otherwise deprived of aura.

Ruth Helyer's claim, informed by Kristeva, that ***Underworld*** makes evident our inability to escape the abject and create a coherent identity separate from our waste thus misses the central transformation that the novel depicts. She contends that the lesson of the novel is that "what we reject can only be pushed away for a limited time, underlining the inadequacy of binary oppositions. We bury huge heaps of waste and live among the toxic fumes, reduced to the sum of our own waste in a frightening deconstruction that will eventually present waste producer and waste to one another as one and the same, opposites meeting in the middle" (1003). Within the world of global capitalism, however, far from trying to escape waste, we begin to see waste as something transcendent, a restored indication of the sacred. Hence, rather than trying to ignore it, global capitalist subjects, as DeLillo shows, tend to bow down before it.

Waste and garbage populate ***Underworld*** at every turn. In Tony Tanner's words, "The real protagonist of the novel is 'waste'" (63). Not only does Nick Shay work for a waste management firm, but he also has a reverence for it, claiming that "[w]aste is a religious thing" (88). This is, according to Nick, a new development: "Waste has a solemn aura now, an aspect of untouchability. White containers of plutonium waste with yellow caution tags. Handle carefully. Even the lowest household trash is closely observed. People look at garbage differently now, seeing every bottle and crushed carton in a planetary context" (88). This fervent concern with the sacred nature of garbage is not confined to Nick's occupational ruminations. Nick and his wife Marian display this reverential attitude with their own garbage. Nick recounts, "At home we wanted clean safe healthy garbage. We rinsed out old bottles and put them in their proper bins. We faithfully removed the crinkly paper from our cereal boxes. It was like preparing a pharaoh for his death and burial. We wanted to do the small things right" (119). Here, taking out the garbage becomes a religious ceremony.[18]

In addition to seeing the act of taking out the garbage as a religious ceremony, Nick and Marian also allow concerns about garbage to remain always at the top of their priorities. What is most important about an object, for Nick and Marian, is what kind of garbage it will become. Nick describes the way in which garbage concerns come to completely control their thinking:

> Marian and I saw products as garbage even when they sat gleaming on store shelves, yet unbought. We didn't say, What kind of casserole will that make? We said, What kind of garbage will that make? Safe, clean, neat, easily disposed of? Can the package be recycled and come back as a tawny envelope that is difficult to lick closed? First we saw the garbage, then we saw the product as food or lightbulbs or dandruff shampoo. How does it measure up as waste, we asked. We asked whether it was responsible to eat a certain item if the package the item comes in will live a million years.
>
> (121)

Nick and Marian cannot escape thinking about garbage precisely because of the status that garbage has acquired within global capitalism. The elimination of the sacred propels garbage into the place of the sacred.

The transition from a world focused on a lacking Other to one focused on garbage finds its objective correlative in the role that Russia plays in ***Underworld.*** During the cold war, Russia played the role of the Other, presenting a lack through which Americans could articulate their fantasies. DeLillo sees enormous significance in the coincidence of the Soviet explosion of an atomic bomb and the Thomson home run. Both events sustain—and even enhance—a sense of the something in the Other more than the Other. Both events have the power to unite people around the *objet petit a,* either through collective fear of it or collective identification with it. In both cases, what people do not have, not what they have, brings them together. At the end of the novel, however, the Russian *objet petit a* disappears (just like the Thomson baseball loses its significance). Instead of embodying an unknown threat, Russia becomes a site for the disposal of the most dangerous waste (which is why Nick and Brian Glassic travel to Russia to meet with Viktor Maltsev, who is selling the disposal process). This transformation in Russia's significance reveals how waste has become the new site for the *objet petit a.*

Throughout ***Underworld,*** sites of waste and ruin become shrines, the contemporary embodiment of transcendence. Nick describes his firm's treatment of waste as transcendent material, pointing out that the firm "built pyramids of waste above and below the earth" (106). Nick and his firm treat waste as previous societies treated gods, but another character, Jesse Detwiler, predicts an even greater development in the reverence for trash. Detwiler, a waste expert, sees waste becoming a tourist attraction: "The scenery of the future. Eventually the only scenery left. The more toxic the waste, the greater the effort and expense a tourist will be willing to tolerate in order to visit the site" (286). He envisions a world in which waste is the only remaining site of transcendence and thus the only site that might entice a tourist's desire. This is not, however, just a fanciful prediction about the future; Detwiler's vision of tourists flocking to waste has already been realized in the world of global capitalism that DeLillo depicts in his novel.

Although global capitalism on the one hand produces unequaled abundance for some, it also produces great squalor for others. As Hegel points out in the *Philosophy of Right,* the squalor produced by capitalism cannot be eliminated by increasing abundance because it is the great abundance that causes the squalor in the first place. Hegel sees the dialectical relationship at work here: "When luxury is at its height, distress and depravity are equally extreme" (269). Far from completely eschewing this "distress and depravity" (as we might expect), subjects in the global capitalist world find themselves ineluctably drawn to it. DeLillo illustrates this by depicting the tour bus that travels through the destitution of the Bronx. He writes, "A tour bus in carnival colors with a sign in the slot above the windshield reading *South Bronx Surreal.* [. . .] About thirty Europeans with slung cameras stepped shyly onto the sidewalk in front of the boarded shops and closed factories and they gazed across the street at the derelict tenement in the middle distance" (247). The South Bronx, a region that the capitalist economy has rendered destitute, here becomes a tourist attraction precisely because of its status as a waste product. Although this incident in the novel may strike us as an instance of DeLillo's fancy getting the better of him, it is actually a moment of strict verisimilitude. If most of us have not taken a bus tour of the South Bronx, we have nonetheless seen this dynamic firsthand—witnessing the eagerness with which the upper classes today adopt the clothing styles, the language, and even the mannerisms of those living in squalor. Fashion trends—like baggy clothes in the 1990s—almost inevitably begin among the impoverished, and the affluent soon imitate these styles in an effort to capture the secret treasure, the kernel of hidden jouissance, that they impute to those living in the wasteland of global capitalism. In doing this, they attest to the way in which waste has become the *objet petit a.* Waste is the only thing that does not fit into the economy that produces it, and hence it becomes the only thing capable of inciting desire.

This is especially true of global capitalism's human waste, embodied in the novel by the figure of Esmeralda. While alive, she was a leftover of the global capitalist economy: "a girl who forages in empty lots for discarded clothes, plucks spoiled fruit from garbage bags behind bodegas" (810). Her death, the result of being raped and thrown off a roof, compellingly reveals her status as waste. After her death, however, Esmeralda becomes sacrosanct. The light shining from a passing train onto an advertisement produces the image of her face on the billboard. This miracle draws thousands, although the image disappears after three nights when the advertisement is removed. Why does Esmeralda's image miraculously appear? As the tossed-aside waste product of the global capitalist economy, she makes manifest the only possible site of transcendence. Only Esmeralda—only someone reduced to the status of waste—could occupy the place of transcendence today.

Because, as the refuse of global capitalism, Esmeralda is located at a point outside its structure, she becomes at once an indication of a limit to global capitalism and new territory for commodification. After the elimination of the *objet petit a* in the Other, global capitalism turns to the waste that it produces as the new source for this object that capitalism requires to function. This waste becomes capitalism's new outside, its new sacred, as we see in the case of Esmeralda. Although she exists in the detritus, as a waste product of global capitalism, in death Esmeralda becomes a new *objet petit a* that global capitalism can work to commodify. As Molly Wallace notes, "although Esmeralda is outside the symbolic, unrepresentable in life, she becomes legible in death" (379). The problem is, however, that this representation of her in death results in her commodification. Wallace adds, "This increased visibility and legibility in the commodity-symbolic [. . .] ends up subjecting Esmeralda to the logic of consumption" (379). As her image attracts numerous viewers and even the attention of CNN, it becomes just another commodity. Nonetheless, the bare existence of this site of transcendence in waste points beyond the ubiquity of contemporary global capitalism, and by emphasizing the existence of this place, DeLillo makes clear that global capitalism is not our ultimate horizon. He points out, as Paul Maltby puts it, that "late capitalism cannot exhaust the possibilities of human experience" (275).

As ***Underworld*** shows, waste is the fundamental political battleground within the epoch of global capitalism. Capital sees waste as the final frontier for commodification—the site for future amusement parks and tour buses. But because waste now contains the *objet petit a,* it also becomes a site at which one can see the limit of global capitalism, and thus it demands taking up a different attitude than that of commodification. DeLillo's alternative—an alternative developed throughout ***Underworld***—is to insist on the fundamental irreducibility of waste to exchange, to point out the existence of waste as waste. The novel, according to Mark Osteen, "dramatizes how waste cannot finally be contained" (216). Because of its transcendent position, waste today marks a privileged site of resistance to the hegemony of capital. We must, in short, look at waste in the proper way, seeing in it the limit of global capitalism rather than another potential commodity. In this sense, Molly Wallace is right to claim that "the project of the novel as a whole [. . .] is perhaps less to 'recycle' waste than to represent it, and to represent it as a constitutive counterpoint to the fetishized history-commodity" (380). By simply representing waste, DeLillo emphasizes that waste does not fit, and ultimately cannot be made to fit, within the world of global capitalism.

Thus, the proper response to the miracle of Esmeralda's image is not a cynical dismissal of the event. Such cynicism is easy to understand: after all, the supposed miracle results from the congruence of a billboard advertisement and train lights—not exactly the ingredients we most readily associate with miracles. But this "knowing" cynicism represents a capitulation to the exigencies of global capitalism and its obfuscation of its own limits. To refuse to believe in miracles, to insist on cynicism, is to grant an unsurpassable hegemony to global capitalism, to condemn oneself to remaining unable to see beyond it. The miracle in ***Underworld*** points to this beyond. But through this miracle, DeLillo also reveals the limitations of contemporary transcendence. Those who flock to see Esmeralda's image see in it the working of God—an Other of the Other—rather than only a point of failure in the Other. For these viewers, the image attests to the gap in the Other, but they fill that gap by imagining an Other behind the image. By filling the gap, those who see the image miss the possibility of seeing beyond global capitalism. Thus, the two pervasive responses to Esmeralda's image—the cynical and the religious—both fail to grasp the radical possibility that it represents. In this way, the novel clearly captures our contemporary dilemma: we seem condemned to either cynicism or paranoia, unable to find another possibility, and both cynicism and paranoia leave intact the universe of global capitalism.

Nonetheless, by including the miracle of Esmeralda's image toward the end of ***Underworld,*** DeLillo reveals that the *objet petit a*—and thus possibility—still endures.[19] The fear that postmodernity would bring an end to absence has animated DeLillo's career from its beginning. From ***Americana*** to ***Running Dog*** to ***Mao II,*** DeLillo expresses the fear that everything will become integrated, that nothing will remain irreducible to exchange or use. He considers the possibility that we will become trapped within a self-enclosed narcissism in which we will suffocate on our own waste. However, the end of ***Underworld*** provides a response to the worries of these earlier novels. On the one hand, it realizes the foreshadowing of waste's increasing proliferation; on the other, it shows that, precisely because of this proliferation, a form of transcendence continues to exist.

DeLillo's novel as a work of art attempts to bring together the cultural refuse of the last half of the twentieth century to illustrate the relocation of absence in the contemporary world. The novel accumulates this cultural waste and in the process transforms it into an aesthetic experience that captures its transcendence. In this sense, ***Underworld*** resembles the art of Klara Sax, who turns discarded bombers into works of art. The act of aestheticizing waste is the political act that DeLillo accomplishes in writing and publishing a novel that has waste as its central feature. Aestheticizing waste forces us to pay attention to waste in a way that we do not during our everyday experience: when DeLillo presents waste to us as an aesthetic object (in the form of the novel ***Underworld*** itself), we confront the absence that waste marks within the world of global capitalism. Aestheticized by DeLillo's novel, waste becomes conspicuous; we see the disconnection between waste and the seemingly smooth-running world out of which it emerges. The aestheticization of waste *by* the novel thus works to opposite ends from the commodification of waste that takes place *within* the novel. In his narration, Nick makes note of the ubiquity of the latter activity: "They are trading garbage in the commodity pits in Chicago. They are making synthetic feces in Dallas" (804). By commodifying waste, those who trade in garbage and make synthetic feces work to transform waste into just another object and thereby hide the one contemporary site where absence continues to predominate. As a commodity among other commodities, waste ceases to indicate a gap within the structure of global capitalism.[20] The commodification of waste is global capitalism's effort to blind subjects to the continued possibility of transcendence in a world of seemingly pure immanence.

Underworld represents a counterattack in the struggle over the status of waste. It is DeLillo's effort to sustain the gap that waste marks by emphasizing waste's transcendent status. Although the novel is, of course, a commodity that DeLillo hopes to sell, its formal structure defies the commodification of waste. Waste is not simply the subject matter of DeLillo's novel but instead its *object petit a*—that which remains absent despite every attempt to render it present. In this way, the novel allows waste to capture and propel our desire, making clear that waste marks the privileged site for the emergence of desire today. DeLillo does not, as Paul Gleason would have it, "reject twentieth-century waste culture" (142); it would be more correct to say that the novel represents an encomium to the role that waste can play—and does play—in the contemporary world. ***Underworld*** asks us to explore our preoccupation with waste and see in this preoccupation the remnants of our desire.

Notes

1. In *End Zone,* Gary Harkness, the narrator, draws special attention to an encounter with waste, waste that seems to him to stick out in the world of the novel: "It was three yards in front of me, excrement, a low mound of it, simple shit, nothing more, yet strange and vile in this wilderness, perhaps the one thing that did not betray its definition" (88). A similar encounter occurs in *The Names,* when the narrator (James) stumbles on a bathroom during a trip through the mountains of Greece. This bathroom is completely covered with human excrement, and James describes the experience in vivid detail: "I walked through an alley, across a muddy yard to the toilet. It was the terminal shit-house of the Peloponnese. The walls were splattered with shit, the bowl was clogged, there was shit on the floor, on the toilet seat, on the fixtures and pipes. An inch of exhausted piss lay collected around the base of the toilet, a minor swamp in the general wreckage and mess. In the chill wind, the soft sweet rain, this doleful shed was another plane of experience. It had a history, a reek of squatting armies, centuries of war, plunder, siege, blood feuds. I stood five feet from the bowl to urinate, tiptoed. How strange that people used this place, still. It was like an offering to Death, to stand there directing my stream toward that porcelain hole" (183-84).

2. This is the problem with David Cowart's contention that the singularity of the Thomson baseball offers a sense of reality and history that we have subsequently lost. Cowart claims that "the point of the Bobby Thomson baseball is that it embodies a wholly

memorable piece of reality—of history, even—precisely because it could not be 'replayed.' It remains *un*diminished as an experience of reality because it was never transformed into media simulacrum" (192, emphasis in original). Cowart's contrast here between the authenticity represented by the baseball and the falsity of postmodern simulacrum fails to account for the fact that throughout *Underworld* the baseball derives its power from its absence, not its authentic presence.

3. According to Paul Civello, DeLillo's fiction chronicles precisely the opposite trajectory. As DeLillo's career develops, Civello sees a sense of mystery expanding, culminating in *Libra,* in which "the individual must now try to locate himself in and reconcile himself to [a] new world of nonlinear causality and uncertainty, the comforts of the old order—knowability and the subsequent possibility of control or 'mastery' over the external world—no longer available to him. 'Mystery' replaces 'mastery'—or even the illusion of mastery" (141). What Civello misses here is that DeLillo's efforts to discover a sense of mystery within the contemporary world are not symptomatic of that world, but are precisely a response to the seeming elimination of mystery today. That is, DeLillo has increased his emphasis on the lack in the Other—the sense of mystery within the Other—as this lack has become increasingly obscured.

4. In *Capital,* Marx notes that the process of capitalist exchange has the precise effect of destroying all difference. He says, "Exchange does not create the differences between the spheres of production, but brings what are already different into relation, and thus converts them into more or less inter-dependent branches of the collective production of an enlarged society" (332).

5. This is one of the fundamental contradictions of capitalism: it necessarily destroys the very gap in the Other that is its lifeblood. It venerates the *objet petit a,* but at the same time, its mode of veneration destroys the *objet petit a* as such. This destruction of what it venerates testifies to the fundamentally hysterical nature of capitalism as a system.

6. It is, of course, Walter Benjamin who pointed out that capitalism burns the aura off objects insofar as it makes everything, even the most sublime works of art, susceptible to the process of reproduction. See Walter Benjamin's "The Work of Art in the Age of Mechanical Reproduction."

7. This "rematch" of the playoff game is different in a very obvious way as well: the teams are no longer the New York Giants and the Brooklyn Dodgers but the San Francisco Giants and the Los Angeles Dodgers. The effect of this transformation, like the change in the way fans experience the game, is to eliminate the tension that animated games between the teams when they were both located in New York. Relocated in San Francisco and Los Angeles, the two teams now lack the earlier proximity, which has the effect of dulling the rivalry and thereby reducing the aura surrounding games between them.

8. The idea that a person's relationship with the television is essentially private and isolated also finds expression in DeLillo's early novel *Players.* Just as in *Underworld,* we see that even the presence of a spouse ruins this enjoyment. DeLillo writes, "It made Lyle nervous to watch television with someone in the room, even Pammy, even when he wasn't changing channels every twenty seconds. There was something private about television. It was intimate, able to cause embarrassment" (40).

9. In a discussion of DeLillo's earlier novel *White Noise,* Mark Conroy rightly points out that "celebrity is time and again the object of what cultic power is left in the world of *White Noise*" (106). In *Underworld,* however, DeLillo demonstrates that even celebrity loses its sense of transcendence when it becomes subjected to overexposure. In attempting to exploit completely the last avenue for the transcendent, we thereby destroy the transcendence attached to celebrity, as the sad fate of the Texas Highway Killer makes clear.

10. This is the problem with radio commentator Paul Harvey giving us "the rest of the story"—filling in the blanks in our knowledge. It wrongly convinces us that we can know all the facts, that nothing necessarily remains unknown and absent.

11. According to Philip Nel, the novel verges on embracing this nostalgia, especially in the case of the artist Klara Sax. He claims that the form of the novel "has the effect of endorsing Klara's desire to impose limits and control" (736).

12. Klara Sax also notes the way in which the cold war established a sense of limitation: "Many things that were anchored to the balance of power and the balance of terror seem to be undone, unstuck. Things have no limits now. Money has no limits. I don't understand money anymore. Money is undone. Violence is undone, violence is easier now, it's uprooted, out of control, it has no measure anymore, it has no level of values" (*Underworld* 76).

13. Bush's paranoid speculation about Iraq and its "weapons of mass destruction" is of a piece with the paranoid speculations of both Marvin and Nick, and this paranoia follows directly from Bush's attempt to resurrect a blank space within the Other. Every such attempt today inevitably produces the subsequent paranoia that fills in this gap with an Other of the Other.

14. Paranoia represents a primary mode of postmodern religiosity. Both paranoia and religion imagine an Other behind the scenes, calling all the shots. For the

religious person, of course, this Other is God; for the paranoiac, it is the United Nations, the CIA, the mob, etc. Sister Alma Edgar, working with the poor in the South Bronx, grasps this connection between paranoia and religion, and the way that the former replaces the latter: "At the same time Edgar force-fitted the gloves onto her hands and felt the ambivalence, the conflict. Safe, yes, scientifically shielded from organic menace. But also sinfully complicit with some process she only half understood, the force in the world, the array of systems that displaces religious faith with paranoia. It was in the milky-slick feel of these synthetic gloves, fear and distrust and unreason. And she felt masculinized as well, condomed ten times over—safe, yes, and maybe a little confused. But latex was necessary here. Protection against the spurt of blood or pus and the viral entities hidden within, submicroscopic parasites in their soviet socialist protein coats" (241).

15. Because *Underworld* itself makes connections like the one between J. Edgar Hoover and Sister Edgar, it would seem to be guilty of the very paranoia it critiques. Robert McMinn points out that even the reverse narrative structure of the novel plays into a sense that everything is connected in the novel. He says, "we do not read *Underworld* to see what happens next but to see what happens *before* and how it connects" (37, McMinn's emphasis). What distinguishes the response that *Underworld* elicits in us from paranoia, however, is the absence of design informing the connections that we discover in the novel. Everything is connected, but there is no Other of the Other behind the scenes creating the connections. Of course, DeLillo as the author has "designed" these connections, but there is no agent *within* the novel that is responsible for them. In this way, DeLillo's novel works to counter rather than reinforce paranoid thinking.

16. As Peter Knight notes in *Conspiracy Culture,* "The real secret history of paranoia in *Underworld,* then, is not the simple story of the replacement of bomb-induced fears by newer anxieties resulting from the fragmentation of those former geopolitical certainties. It is instead an underground current of increasing awareness and consternation that slowly everything is becoming connected in a global marketplace" (235).

17. In this sense, the end of the cold war is not, as Peter Knight contends, a mere epiphenomenon in the novel. Even though the globalization of capital had already occurred prior to the end of the cold war, the demise of the Soviet Union was a necessary final step in the process of eliminating the gap in the Other. As long as the Soviet Union existed as an alternative to capitalism, the Other retained an empty space, a space not yet fully made a part of the global capitalist world. With the fall of the Berlin Wall, the final barrier to the elimination of this space also fell.

18. This rebirth of the religious in new forms—such as reverence surrounding garbage—is a constant motif in DeLillo's fiction. John McClure notes that his work "repeatedly constructs contemporary Americans as a people driven by homeless spiritual impulses and mesmerized by new religious movements" (142).

19. DeLillo resists the contemporary absence of absence through the very structure of the novel, by withholding the central event of Nick's life—firing a gun that killed his friend George—until the end of the novel. This event structures Nick's experiences as we see them unfold, but nothing explicitly alludes to it until the penultimate section. It figures as a determining absence, which gives it a transcendent status for both Nick and the reader.

20. Leonard Wilcox points out that these efforts at the commodification of waste aim to free waste in order to allow it to begin to take part in the endless circulation that characterizes global capitalism. He says, "In this malign reciprocity of power and waste, an excess or remainder seems no longer to mark a limit condition but circulates freely as models, codes, and media simulacra" (124).

Works Cited

Begley, Adam. "Don DeLillo: *Americana, Mao II,* and *Underworld.*" *Southwest Review* 82 (1997): 478-505.

Benjamin, Walter. "The Work of Art in the Age of Mechanical Reproduction." *Illuminations.* Trans. Harry Zohn. New York: Schocken, 1968, 217-51.

Civello, Paul. *American Literary Naturalism and Its Twentieth-Century Transformations: Frank Norris, Ernest Hemingway, Don DeLillo.* Athens: U of Georgia P, 1994.

Conroy, Mark. "From Tombstone to Tabloid: Authority Figured in *White Noise.*" *Critique* 35 (1994): 97-110.

Cowart, David. *Don DeLillo: The Physics of Language.* Athens: U of Georgia P, 2002.

DeLillo, Don. *Americana.* New York: Penguin, 1989.

———. *End Zone.* New York: Penguin, 1986.

———. *The Names.* New York: Vintage, 1982.

———. *Players.* New York: Vintage, 1977.

———. *Underworld.* New York: Scribner, 1997.

Dewey, Joseph, Steven G. Kellman, and Irving Malin, eds. *Underworlds: Perspectives on Don DeLillo's* Underworld. Newark: U of Delaware P, 2002.

Freud, Sigmund. *Beyond the Pleasure Principle.* Trans. James Strachey. New York: Norton, 1961.

Gleason, Paul. "Don DeLillo, T. S. Eliot, and the Redemption of America's Atomic Waste Land." Dewey, Kellman, and Malin 130-43.

Gore, Al. *Earth in the Balance: Ecology and the Human Spirit.* Boston: Houghton Mifflin, 1992.

Hegel, G. W. F. *Philosophy of Right.* Trans. T. M. Knox. London: Oxford UP, 1952.

Helyer, Ruth. "'Refuse Heaped Many Stories High': DeLillo, Dirt, and Disorder." *Modern Fiction Studies* 45 (1999): 987-1006.

Jameson, Fredric. *Postmodernism, or, the Cultural Logic of Late Capitalism.* Durham, NC: Duke UP, 1991.

Knight, Peter. *Conspiracy Culture: From Kennedy to the X-Files.* New York: Routledge, 2000.

———. "Everything Is Connected: *Underworld*'s Secret History of Paranoia." *Modern Fiction Studies* 45 (1999): 811-36.

Lacan, Jacques. *The Four Fundamental Concepts of Psycho-Analysis.* Trans. Alan Sheridan. New York: Norton, 1978.

———. *Le Séminaire de Jacques Lacan, Livre X: L'Angoisse, 1962-1963.* Paris: Seuil, 2004.

———. *Le Séminaire XIV: La Logique du fantasme, 1966-1967.* Unpublished manuscript.

Lasch, Christopher. *The Culture of Narcissism: American Life in An Age of Diminishing Expectations.* New York: Norton, 1991.

Luxemburg, Rosa. *The Accumulation of Capital.* Trans. Agnes Schwarzschild. New York: Routledge, 1951.

Maltby, Paul. "The Romantic Metaphysics of Don DeLillo." *Contemporary Literature* 37 (1996): 258-77.

Mandel, Ernest, *Late Capitalism.* Trans. Joris De Bres. New York: Verso, 1978.

Marx, Karl. *Capital: A Critique of Political Economy, Volume I.* Trans. Samuel Moore and Edward Aveling. New York: International Publishers, 1967.

———. *Grundrisse.* Trans. Martin Nicolaus. New York: Penguin, 1993.

McClure, John A. "Postmodern/Post-Secular: Contemporary Fiction and Spirituality." *Modern Fiction Studies* 41 (1995): 141-63.

McMinn, Robert. "*Underworld*: Sin and Atonement." Dewey, Kellman, and Malin 37-49.

Miller, Jacques-Alain. "The Desire of Lacan and His Complex Relation to Freud." Trans. Jorge Jauregui. *Lacanian Ink* 14 (1999): 4-23.

Nel, Philip. "'A Small Incisive Shock': Modern Forms, Postmodern Politics, and the Role of the Avant-garde in *Underworld.*" *Modern Fiction Studies* 45 (1999): 724-52.

O'Donnell, Patrick. *Latent Destinies: Cultural Paranoia and Contemporary U.S. Narrative.* Durham, NC: Duke UP, 2000.

Osteen, Mark. *American Magic and Dread: Don DeLillo's Dialogue with Culture.* Philadelphia: U of Pennsylvania P, 2000.

Salecl, Renata. *(Per)versions of Love and Hate.* New York: Verso, 1998.

Tanner, Tony. "Afterthoughts on Don DeLillo's *Underworld.*" *Raritan: A Quarterly Review* 17.4 (1998): 48-71.

Wallace, Molly. "'Venerated Emblems': DeLillo's *Underworld* and the History-Commodity." *Critique* 42 (2001): 367-83.

Wilcox, Leonard. "Don DeLillo's *Underworld* and the Return of the Real." *Contemporary Literature* 43 (2002): 120-37.

Willman, Skip. "Traversing the Fantasies of the JFK Assassination: Conspiracy and Contingency in Don DeLillo's *Libra.*" *Contemporary Literature* 39 (1998): 405-33.

Zizek, Slavoj. *The Fragile Absolute—or, Why Is the Christian Legacy Worth Fighting For?* New York: Verso, 2000.

———. *Looking Awry: An Introduction to Jacques Lacan through Popular Culture.* Cambridge: MIT P, 1991.

Mark Osteen (essay date spring 2005)

SOURCE: Osteen, Mark. "Echo Chamber: Undertaking *The Body Artist.*" *Studies in the Novel* 37, no. 1 (spring 2005): 64-81.

[*In the following essay, Osteen highlights recurring themes in DeLillo's fiction, specifically notions of isolation and identity, as represented in* The Body Artist.]

Don DeLillo's ***The Body Artist,*** published in early 2001, perplexed readers expecting another of his sweeping explorations of politics, violence, and the image world. A decidedly quiet, introverted tale of bereavement and spectral visitation, it seemed a radical and rather slight experiment for this acclaimed novelist. In many respects, however, the novel clearly bears DeLillo's stamp: though shorter and more elliptical than his recent work, it revisits two of his most significant themes. The first concerns the range and perils of privacy. In earlier novels, characters such as ***Great Jones Street***'s Bucky Wunderlick and ***Mao II***'s Bill Gray retreat from public life to seek a space free from invasion, reemerging only to be recaptured by the systems that had threatened them. ***The Body Artist*** similarly depicts its protagonist—a performance artist named Lauren Hartke—withdrawing in seclusion after her husband's suicide and then reemerging through a work of art that at once announces and shapes a new self. The second and more significant theme concerns the nature of identity, and the permeable membrane between behavior and performance. In ***Running Dog,*** for example, DeLillo suggests that the ubiquity of cameras has transformed us all into actors under constant observation, even by ourselves; DeLillo's play ***The Day Room*** offers a dizzying array of masquerades—actors performing in a play-within-a-play that, we eventually learn, constitutes the play we have been watching—designed both to challenge theatrical conventions and to assess the nature of role-playing itself. ***The Body Artist*** re-examines this theme through Lauren's shifting voices and fluctuating identities. Although a journalist character who reviews Lauren's piece, *Body Time,* comments that it is "about who we are when we are not rehearsing who we are" (110), the novel implies that such a condition may not exist.

But ***The Body Artist*** is not merely a minor variation on familiar themes. Rather, DeLillo's masterly manipulation of voices—both narratorial and dramatized—enables him in this novel to raise profound questions about the many possible forms of possession and about the relationship between art and loss. It is also his most nakedly emotional work, limning the arc of grief by portraying Lauren's encounter with a visitor who may or may not be an incarnate ghost.[1] Perhaps most importantly, this novel marks DeLillo's most penetrating analysis of the process of artistic generation. As we witness Lauren transmute her grief into a scarifying work of performance art, we come to understand inspiration as a variety of religious experience, a form of ghostly possession. The novel itself embodies the theme of spectral inhabitation by incorporating numerous shades and intertextual echoes: hints of the Gothic (a woman and a mysterious male in a lonely house); allusions to classical Greek myth and drama; nods to the cinema of Ingmar Bergman, with its meticulous examinations of identity (*Persona*), grief (*Cries and Whispers*), and the power of art (*The Magician*); a pinch of *Krapp's Last Tape* (in both texts a person records and relives moments from the past); and even a dash of Harlequin romance (a woman saved from despair by a male intruder). Yet the novel more than displays these influences; it transforms them through literary ventriloquism. ***The Body Artist*** haunts and is haunted, ultimately suggesting that to undertake any work of art is to do just that—to perform an undertaking of the dead that must remain incomplete, and hence simultaneously to exorcize spirits and to honor the deceased, not by embalming and forgetting them, but by permitting them to live again as echoes. This undertaking, paradoxically, revives both artist and audience by bringing into existence new selves residing both inside and outside of the work.

The first literary echo is relatively close at hand. The opening chapter, in which Lauren and her husband, film director Rey Robles, prepare and eat breakfast, calls to mind an earlier literary breakfast: the famous repast at 7 Eccles St., Dublin, on June 16, 1904. Our recollection of Leopold Bloom diligently searing a pork kidney for himself and brewing tea for Molly is reinforced by DeLillo's narrative presence, which dips in and out of Lauren's consciousness in a pseudo-Joycean (or perhaps Woolfish) manner, though without that "fine tang of faintly scented urine" (Joyce 45).[2] The Bloom breakfast, we recall, soon gives way to an undertaking when Leopold attends the funeral of his unfortunate acquaintance Paddy Dignam. With death on his mind. Bloom attempts to explain to Molly the meaning of the word "metempsychosis," which he first gets right—"reincarnation. That we all lived before on the earth thousands of years ago" (Joyce 53)—and then confuses with "metamorphosis." ***The Body Artist*** also traffics in metempsychosis: both the literary kind, whereby patterns and motifs from previous texts are revived, and the human kind, whereby human beings return to life in altered forms.[3]

Just as the Blooms' homey chatter conceals serious conflicts, so beneath Lauren and Rey's domestic bliss a struggle for ownership is taking place: hence, Lauren carefully notes that it is "his coffee and his cup" (8) and "his phone" (12), but "her" newspaper and "her weather" on the radio (8-9). An analogous battle for primacy occurs on the bird feeder outside their window where the sparrows are "fighting for space" (8). Over the course of the novel, Lauren also struggles to maintain control of the novel's discourse as she confronts several intrusive external voices that threaten to wrest control of her consciousness and her narrative: those of two journalistic reports (an obituary for Rey and a report by Lauren's friend Mariella Chapman on Lauren's new art work); the phone voices of Chapman, Rey's first wife Isabel, and an answering machine; that of the unnamed owner of the house; and most significantly, the echolalic voice of an aphasic man whom Lauren dubs Mr. Tuttle.

This jockeying for control occurs even within Lauren's own narrative discourse, which frequently slips from an intimate third-person in past tense—itself sliding in and out of Lauren's idiom ("sort of jackknife," "Okay, she put the bowl on the table" [12])—to a second-person voice that registers habitual action. For example, Lauren thinks, "You know more surely who you are on a strong bright day" such as this (7); however, as these narrative slippages imply, her identity is evanescent. Like all pronouns, "you" replaces a noun; but here it also represents a second-level substitution in which it becomes the very pronominal signifier of self-division and permeability.[4] Indeed, Lauren's frequent use of "you" implies that she habitually performs for herself, her rent consciousness indicating an insecure tenancy in her own head. In short, these instances of what Ian Reid terms "narrative dispossession," in which a "wresting or arresting of control over" the narrative voice disrupts the surface of the story (27), point both to a power struggle in the marriage that continues after Rey's death and to Lauren's own uncertain grip on herself.[5] By tracing Lauren's voice as it shuttles through these shifting personae, DeLillo also reminds us of the conventionality of all narrative voices, and through these manipulations the novelist becomes both performer and casting director, determining—or perhaps responding to—the version of Lauren who will dominate the story. Will it be the fumbling, inarticulate homebody? The meticulous artist and pseudo-monastic? The tenant of a strange house? The caretaker and surrogate mother? The bereft widow haunted by her dead husband's words?

Yet while Lauren clearly demarcates their possessions and habits, the couple also possess and absorb each other, particularly through their voices, as when she realizes that her groan is "echoing Rey, identifyingly, groaning his groan, but in a manner so seamless and deep it was her discomfort too" (9). If intimacy is a kind of ventriloquism or echolalia, then determining the source of any voice is a vexed undertaking. Lauren, for example, always carries a voice in her head that "was hers and it was dialogue or monologue" (16). She makes up stories about people in the newspaper, creates dialogue for them, and becomes "someone else, one of the people in the story"—a "you," not an "I"—through reading about them (20). Reading, for her, is also a mode of performance or possession, and one that DeLillo invites his readers to undertake as well, so that our reading animates the characters, possesses them, and allows them to possess us. The intimacy of the narrative technique, that is, brings us close enough to hear the faintest whispers of consciousness, thereby inviting us to eavesdrop on the most delicate patterns of thought and emotion. As selves are gradually laid bare, we cannot help but lend a hand in their exfoliation.

The birds at the feeder provide a striking metaphor for these narrative movements, as well as for the human animals inside the house. For example, crows—carrion eaters and harbingers of death—emit raucous calls just as Rey comments on the "terror of another ordinary day" (15). A few minutes later Lauren spots a blue jay. "It stood large and polished and looked royally remote from the other birds busy feeding and she could nearly believe she'd never seen a jay before" (21).[6] It is easy to read the jay—that "nest thief and skilled mimic" (22)—as an avian alter-ego of Rey, whose name means "king" and who was often cast in his early films as a thief (28). For a jay as for Rey, all places are "landscapes of estrangement" (29). The blue jay also figures Lauren and prefigures Mr. Tuttle, each of whom habitually appropriates others' words and actions. These bird analogies, indeed, imply that human identities are but flighty masquerades of protective coloration and imitation. To put it another way, the birds represent the human capacity to become "disembodied, turned into something sheer and fleet and scatter-bright" (13); or, to put it yet another way, the birds represent the potential for artistic genius. Mimicking even as he shapes these swift souls, DeLillo's narrator also hovers and skitters, dipping into and out of narrative time and Lauren's mind like a bird at a feeder. This is DeLillo or—to borrow the name of one of his earlier acts of gender-bending ventriloquism—Birdwell as a spirit artist, as a master of breath and voice.[7]

Birdwell's movements through Lauren's mind recall William James's famous description of the "wonderful stream of consciousness":

> Like a bird's life, it seems to be made of an alternation of flights and perchings. The rhythm of language expresses this, where every thought is expressed in a sentence, and every sentence closed by a period. The resting-places are usually occupied by sensorial imaginations of some sort, whose peculiarity is that they can be held before the mind for an indefinite time, and contemplated without changing; the places of flight are filled with thoughts of relations, static or dynamic.
>
> (243)

However, Lauren is much less confident than James in the ready transferability of thought to expression. In her mind words flutter and dart, seldom landing firmly on a precise definition: working the toaster, for example, she can not recall the name for the lever (8), and she vacillates about whether the past tense of "spring" is "sprang or sprung" (10). Savoring the aroma of soya granules, she describes them aptly as exuding a "faint wheaty stink with feet mixed in" (13; and one notes here how "feet" itself "mixes" the sounds of the words "faint" and "wheaty").[8] Yet a few minutes later she admits that "[n]othing described" them (16). Shortly thereafter she renders the birds' flight noises as a "wing-whir that was all *b*'s and *r*'s, the letter *b* followed by a series of vibrator *r*'s" (17), and then immediately recants her description: "But that wasn't it at all." Words too change shape, sometimes merely eluding capture and at other times transmigrating from noun to verb, from blade to body, as when Lauren has to "jackknife" away from the counter when Rey approaches for a butter knife (12). As Philip Nel argues, ***The Body Artist*** ponders "the possibilities and paradoxes of poetic diction," celebrating the sounds of words and yet acknowledging the "impossibility of ever attaining that ideal language which literally embodies the material world" (739). Like identities, language constantly undergoes metamorphosis or metempsychosis, its echoes of earlier words and events usually fleeing down the crevices of time, but sometimes shooting forcefully back into the current of thought.

Lauren and DeLillo do, however, share James's belief in the elasticity of time, which in this novel stretches, slows, and shuttles backward and forward both intertextually and intratextually. For example, at the end of the first chapter Lauren realizes that she needs to buy some Ajax scouring powder, and later in the novel she recollects the banal conversation (their last one, it turns out) during which Rey promised to go purchase some. The daughter of a retired classical scholar (104), Lauren riffs on the classical allusion in the product's name: "Ajax, son of Telamon . . . great brave warrior, and spear-thrower of mighty distances, and toilet cleanser too" (86-87).[9] She forgot to add—suicide. In Sophocles's eponymous tragedy Ajax, disgraced by Athena and beguiled into murdering a flock of sheep instead of his enemies, kills himself out of shame and dishonor, even though the chorus assures him that public opinion, that "gaggle of angry birds," will disappear at the sight of the falcon, or true hero (16-17). The final portion of Sophocles's play, like most of DeLillo's novel, concerns an undertaking, as Ajax's widow Tecmessa and his brother Teucer contend with Ajax's enemies over the proper way to dispose of his body. In DeLillo's restaging, Rey becomes the defeated Ajax while Lauren plays a Tecmessa left weeping, as does Ajax's mother, like a "poor lorn nightingale" (Sophocles 34).

If this intertext suggests that identity involves the masks typical of Greek drama, the first textual invasion—an obituary for Rey, who, instead of buying Ajax, drove to New York and shot himself in his first wife's apartment—confirms it. A "poet of lonely places" (27), as the inserted text informs us in DeLillo's sharp pastiche of journalistic style, Rey was a man of masks who lacked a true home: born in Barcelona, he later lived in the Soviet Union, migrated to Paris, resided in New York, and directed spaghetti Westerns shot in Spain. As Isabel later tells Lauren, he was a man who "hated who he was" (59). He invented even the name "Rey," and throughout his earthly existence played a character who made pronouncements such as "The answer to life is the movies" (28). Why? Because his life *was* a movie. Among his credits was a film called *My Life for Yours,* which describes the effect he had on Isabel, who tells Lauren, "[w]e were two people with one life and it was his life" (59), but also on Lauren, to whom he trades his life for her art.

This film title introduces the second classical parallel: to Euripides's *Alcestis,* a play that also concerns an incomplete undertaking. In this tragicomedy, Admetos, king of Pherai, is informed by Death that he must accompany him to the underworld. Admetos persuades his wife Alcestis to die in his place, but before she dies she compels the king to swear never to bring another woman into his house. When Herakles visits shortly thereafter, Admetos inappropriately (since his wife has just died) extends extravagant hospitality to Herakles and conceals the death from him. After getting comically drunk, Herakles learns of Alcestis's death and Admetos's violation of the norms of mourning, and brings a silent, veiled young woman to Admetos, insisting that the king accept her as a gift in exchange for his hospitality. Caught between his vow to Alcestis and the rules of sociability, Admetos agrees to take her in, only to discover that the young woman is Alcestis herself, miraculously brought back to life. She must, however, remain silent for three days until the stain of death has disappeared. DeLillo's reworking of this play is oblique but illuminating: first, he switches the genders of deceased and survivor, and then reincarnates Herakles as an autistic man. Yet in both cases the dead spouse does return—here, as a voice behind the veil of Mr. Tuttle. I'll engage with this intertextual echo in more detail later, but for now it is worth noting that both *Ajax* and *Alcestis,* like most Greek plays, acknowledge that they are themselves reenacting events that occurred in some legendary past. Even the Greeks knew, in other words, that dramatic art is a chamber of echoes, a gathering of shades.

In any case, it is scarcely surprising that Rey haunts Lauren, because in some sense he was already a ghost when alive. The rest of the novel traces her attempts to come to terms with his death. When she first returns to the house they are renting, everything seems "plunged into metamorphosis" (36), but Lauren seems more pupa than butterfly. Cloaking herself in Rey's despair, she tries to deal with his absent presence by seeking to "disappear in Rey's smoke, be dead, be him" (34: she would thereby trade her life for his). She feels him everywhere. Answering the phone, for example, she speaks in a "soft voice . . . not quite her own" (36); the phone, we recall, was "his" (12). Time seems out of joint, and she tries to straighten or arrest it by watching a live-stream Internet video feed of a nearly empty road in Kotka, Finland, which offers her a "sense of organization, a place contained in an unyielding frame" (38): as if following Rey's dictum, her answer to death is the movies. However, what strikes her most about the video feed is its juxtaposition of stasis—an apparent timelessness—with the unremitting diachronic linearity conveyed by the digital time displayed in the corner of the screen (39). This paradox expresses her own sense of dislocation: it is both now and no-time; it is both here and nowhere. Just as Alcestis is described by Herakles as at once alive and dead (Euripides 59), so Lauren lives in limbo. Her emptiness is interrupted by the voice of Mariella, who implores her to leave the house and admonishes her not to "fold up into" herself (39). But this involution is precisely what she needs: to fold up and then spring out like a butterfly bursting from its pod or a bird taking wing.

The trigger for her explosion is the aphasic man she discovers in her house and names Mr. Tuttle, after her high school science teacher. At once ghost, projection of her desire, "heteroclite muse" (Cowart 204), symbol of her inchoate new self, and live tape recorder of her marital conversations. Tuttle is the latest—and one of the most significant—in a long line of childlike figures who populate DeLillo's novels, starting with the deformed, mute Micklewhite boy in ***Great Jones Street*** and culminating in the nine-year-old novelist Tap Axton in ***The Names*** and the toddler Wilder in ***White Noise.*** These characters engage in what DeLillo has called a "purer . . . alternate speech" untainted by the distortions and bad faith of institutions (interview with LeClair 24). Like these characters, Tuttle functions as an artistic inseminator, catalyzing Lauren's new work and encouraging her return to life. His unfinished quality is essential, because it enables him to reiterate Rey and Lauren's conversations and, in turn, to teach Lauren to stand outside of herself and, eventually, to return to herself through the veil of performance.

Tuttle's first words, "it is not able" (43), exemplify his linguistic and cognitive disabilities: "I" becomes "it," the pronoun shift suggesting that he lives at a distance from his own consciousness. Furthermore, many of his speeches display echolalia, such as when Lauren says, "Talk to me," and he answers "talk to me. I am talking" (46), or when she asks him to "say some words," and he responds, "Say some words to say some words" (55). Some neurologists and speech pathologists suggest that echolalia, which is characteristic of people with autism and certain post-encephalitic syndromes, is not true speech; according to Oliver Sacks, it "carries no emotion, no intentionality, no 'tone' whatever—it is purely automatic" (*Anthropologist* 233). But in fact echolalia takes myriad forms and serves numerous communicative functions.[10] Some children use echolalia as a bridge between repetition and genuine communication (Schuler & Prizant 175); for example, a person might repeat the final word of a request ("Do you want some bread?" "Bread.") to assent to it; a child might imitate an adult's habitual intonation and words when agreeing to do something that the adult wishes.[11] A few people with autism, in fact, develop a sophisticated, collage-like, "delayed echolalia" (Schuler & Prizant 164) in which they piece together utterances from recollected songs, videos or conversations and thereby comment elliptically on what is going on around them (see Rhode 80). Sacks himself cites the case of Stephen Wiltshire, an autistic artist who can quote and act out entire sections of the film *Rain Man* (which is itself, of course, about an autistic savant) and who has a genius for reproducing musical sounds (*Anthropologist* 234, 237). Wiltshire borrows identities in an attempt to express his own, sometimes seeming "nourished and stimulated" by those second selves but at other times "taken over, possessed and dispossessed" by them (234). In extreme cases echolalia may become a prison: one echolalic patient of Maria Rhode testified to feeling that he resided in a "ghost-house," and Rhode speculates that his echolalia is an "expression of these ghostly echoes" (82).[12] These descriptions fit Tuttle who, having hidden in their house, has memorized countless conversations between Rey and Lauren and repeats them to her during the novel. For people such as Tuttle and Wiltshire, subjectivity is a vast echo chamber in which words float, recede and resonate. But Tuttle is not merely a human parrot. Neither quite performances nor quite original utterances, his echolalic expressions occupy a gray zone between language and mimickry. As we learn from Lauren's work *Body Time,* an artist must also abide, at least temporarily, in the same zone.

Echolalia signifies an inability to grasp what are called "pragmatics"—the codes and rules that govern conversational interchanges.[13] People with such deficits may, for example, fail to employ contrastive stress, which one would use to say "the father held *his* son" as opposed to *her* son (Frith 131). Tuttle's "singsong conjugations" (63) betray this pragmatic deficiency, as Lauren registers in noting that "[t]here's a code in the simplest conversation that tells the speakers what's going on outside the bare acoustics. This was missing when they talked. . . . There were no grades of emphasis here and flatness there" (65-66). Lacking a strong grip on pragmatic conventions, Tuttle dwells in language like an unwelcome guest; he uses words, but struggles to apprehend the emotional content of Lauren's questions and expectations. Thus she calls him a "dummy in a red club chair" (48), but perhaps he is better understood as both dummy and ventriloquist. As such he is an ideal audience: what performer would not want to play to a listener who could imprint and perfectly repeat scripted lines?

Tuttle's language, Lauren realizes, also ruptures time, his jumbled verb tenses indicating that he somehow lives in more than one moment at once. Thus he observes that "it rained very much" when he means that it is going to rain (44). Lauren corrects him, but later comes to understand that normal language artificially demarcates the pellucid continuum in which Tuttle freely swims. "Maybe this man experiences another kind of reality where he is here and there, before and after, and he moves from one to the other shatteringly, in a state of collapse, minus an identity, a language." "[M]aybe," she thinks, "he lived in a kind of time that had no narrative quality" (64, 65); she imagines that "[h]is future is unnamed. It is simultaneous, somehow, with the present" (77). Yet her own tense shifts indicate that she is, intentionally or not, advancing under Tuttle's tutelage. The temporal dislocations he records probably signify a dysfunction in his brain's executive processes, which refer to the capacity to organize complex actions through sequencing and working memory. Deficiencies in executive functioning manifest themselves in precisely the kind of stereotypic behavior and self-regulation difficulties—the obsessive repetition of the same words, the clumsy gait and fine motor problems—that Tuttle exhibits (Twachtman-Cullen 237; see also Turner). Lacking a sharp sense of sequence, he may perceive the world as a dazzling, disorienting panoply of unconnected events. Sacks speculates that people like Tuttle, though geniuses at "the catching of thisness," live not in a universe but in a "multiverse" of "innumerable, unconnected though intensely vivid particulars," and experience the world as "'a collection of moments'—vivid, isolated, with no before and after" (*Anthropologist* 242). Tuttle's mind, that is, operates less like a single bird than like an entire flock, each one of a different color and species, each usurping the other at the window of consciousness.

However crippling his cognitive disorders may be for him, Tuttle's symptoms give Lauren the jolt she needs to transform passive mourning into active art. Thus her first epiphany occurs when she hears from Tuttle's lips "the clipped delivery, the slight buzz deep in the throat, her pitch, her sound" (50). He seems to be "assuming her part in a conversation with someone" else (51), as if he has appropriated Lauren's very spirit. The birds, facing outward, alert for the "jay that mimics a hawk," dramatize the condition of baffled readiness that his echolalia occasions (53). But if her art is inevitably a performance, here Tuttle is not so much impersonating her as channeling voices like a spirit medium. In short, Tuttle represents the muse as intruder, embodying inspiration as a sophisticated brand of echolalia or species of ghostly possession.

But not all of Tuttle's utterances are mere echolalia. As the novel proceeds he sometimes chants an instinctive, almost Heideggerian poetry that demonstrates he is "not closed to inspiration" himself. For example, he sings, "Being here has come to me. I am with the moment. I will leave the moment. . . . Coming and going I am leaving. . . . Leaving has come to me. We all, shall all, will all be left. Because I am here and where. And I will go or not or never. . . . If I am where I will be. Because nothing comes between me" (74).[14] "Nothing comes between me": he wears no veil or mask. Derridean *différance* be damned: no signifier slices a gap between existence and expression; there is no deferral because all times are one to him. In these zen-like utterances Lauren hears the "stir of true amazement. . . . [T]he wedge into ecstasy, the old deep meaning of the word" (75)—of "ecstasy," that condition of being outside the self. Yet Tuttle's poetry is powerful precisely because he is not outside of himself; rather, like Walt Whitman, he sings himself, sings Being itself by being himself. And sometimes Tuttle's "transparent" language (75) divulges hidden depths, as when he declares, "the word for moonlight is moonlight" (82). Beneath its tautology the phrase initially suggests that words, "like moons in particular phases" (48), can only reflect the light of material reality. Yet, as Tuttle's own language proves, a word can also impel the tides of meaning and gleam with evanescent lucidity. Tuttle's poetry, that is, represents the purified artistic instinct: having passed through the crucible of meaning. Being may be molded by syllable and cadence. Like one of Hopkins's kingfishers, Tuttle finds tongue "to fling out broad [his] name," to deal out that being indoors where he dwells (Hopkins 51; lines 4-6). Paradoxically, though, he performs this "selving" through a voice that is his own because it perfectly echoes others'.

Inspired by Tuttle, Lauren begins to listen to other voices, such as the stilted one in the electronic message on Mariella's answering machine—"*please / leave / a mess / age / af / ter / the / tone*" (67)—which she plays over and over, probing the relationship between this automaton and her own identity. Throughout this section DeLillo also embellishes his own ventriloquistic performance, drawing words from the air and turning them into a poetry that melds body—sound and rhythm—with spiritual resonance. In interviews DeLillo has declared that he attends as much to sound as to meaning when writing. "There's a rhythm I hear that drives me through a sentence," he admits; "if you concentrate on the sound, if you disassociate the words from the object they denote, and if you say the words over and over, they become a sort of higher Esperanto" ("Art of Fiction" 283, 291). This higher Esperanto is the lingua franca of ***The Body Artist.*** For instance, when Lauren recognizes that Tuttle's mind lies "outside the easy sway of either/or" (69), DeLillo renders her realization in a swaying clause of iambic pentameter. Or when Lauren urges Tuttle to "Do Rey. Make me hear him. I am asking you nice. Be my friend," an attentive listener may hear behind her exhortations the syllables of an ascending and descending major scale in solfeggio ("Do, re, mi . . .": 71). Birdwell lives! Fed by her interaction with Tuttle, Lauren registers the profound shocks of artistic inspiration, echoing his halting poetry and immersing herself in her work, razing calluses, clipping nails, "pruning the body much as a writer prunes sentences" (Nel 749). Indeed, as she "activate[s] the verbs of abridgment and excision[,] . . . studie[s] her fingers and toes" (76), DeLillo's dactyls activate the original meaning of that word (from the Greek for "finger") on two levels at once. Lauren, Tuttle, DeLillo: all three artists undergo and undertake metamorphoses that mimic the "color-changing birds, the name-saying birds" (71) outside the window.

The true gestation of Lauren's new artwork is heralded when she reads Tuttle a passage about the biology of childbirth (60). As she more fully assumes the role of surrogate mother (feeding and bathing Tuttle), she contributes to her own nourishment, her own rechristening. Reading the book to him, she realizes that Tuttle is speaking to her in Rey's voice, and recalls that Rey once told her that "she was helping him to recover his soul" (61). He said, "I regain possession of myself through you. I think like myself now, not like the man I became. I eat and sleep like myself . . . when I was myself and not the other man" (62). Tuttle is performing the same operation, enabling her to become somebody else and thereby, paradoxically, to become herself. And he is doing it not by becoming *him*self, but by becoming both her and Rey. She and Tuttle indeed represent the two forces behind her art: she is the body and he is the inspiration—literally, in that "he knew how to make her husband live in the air that rushed from his lungs" (62). Tuttle models for her a life "lived irreducibly as sheer respiration" (57). Thus she is able to resuscitate Rey by listening "possessively" to his words on Tuttle's tongue (63), and exorcizes the grief and guilt attached to Rey's spirit by undertaking—that is, at once raising and burying—both her husband and Tuttle in *Body Time.*

Tuttle's time-lapsed condition begins to affect Lauren's state of mind, as well. As if miming his temporal fluidity, she repeatedly practices the act of "eternally checking the time," emphasizing in order to demolish the linear time that doomed her husband (73). Yet her attitude toward time remains deeply ambivalent. On the one hand she seeks to scour away the past by subjecting her body to monastic exercises that function as an ascetic Ajax powder designed to permit her to "disappear from all her former venues of aspect and bearing and to become a blankness, a body slate erased of every past resemblance" (84). Yet she also desires to recapture the past through Tuttle, to possess him in order to repossess her husband and thereby regain her previous life. Her impulse to revive Rey climaxes when Tuttle rehearses in precise and haunting detail the conversation about Ajax that Lauren and Rey held the day he died. Though she recognizes Rey's words in Tuttle's mouth, "she didn't think the man was remembering. It is happening now . . . in his fracted time, and he is only reporting, helplessly, what they say." Through Tuttle's ventriloquism "Rey is alive" (87), yet "fracted"—at once broken and newly reconstituted. And just as the narrative discourse in these sentences slides back and forth from Lauren's idiom to the narrator's past tense, so the shifting verb tenses capture Lauren's perception of time's shuttling flight.

Eventually, though, she must accept that all things fade away. Thus, the final chapter before her performance concerns things lost—paper clips, words, sounds, memories, Tuttle himself. First she hears him weeping at night and realizes that his cries bear "a faint echo, a feedback," as if he is "unable to improvise" himself any longer (90). He begins to reject his food and finally vanishes, leaving "not a single clinging breath of presence" (96). Before he disappears, she is stunned by a temporal dislocation that suggests again how words resist the depredations of time. During one of her earlier pleas to Tuttle to "say some words," he replied, "'Don't touch it,' in a voice that wasn't quite his. 'I'll clean it up later'" (81). Days later, as Tuttle starts to fall apart, he drops a glass of water, and without thinking Lauren forestalls his clean-up attempts by saying. "Don't touch it. . . . I'll clean it up later" (93). After Tuttle's disappearance, she reflects that "He'd known this was going to happen. These were the words she would say" (98). She reruns the tape she made of his proleptic command, feeling as though her entire life, like that of Beckett's Krapp, already exists on tape, merely waiting to be discovered and endlessly replayed.[15] Initially forlorn at his absence, gradually Lauren understands that Tuttle must abscond so that her own voice may emerge; moreover, Tuttle's absence at last lets her truly feel Rey's. Yet "she wanted to take him in, try to know him in the spaces where his chaos lurks, in . . . the parts of speech where he is meant to locate his existence, and in the material place where Rey lives in him, alive again, word for word, touch for touch" (100). As in Molly Bloom's monologue, present and past mix, and the male figures merge into an undifferentiated "he." Rey gone, she now must possess Tuttle and be possessed by him. But that means she too must disappear. Where to begin? With the organ of language, of course. Thus she scrapes her tongue carefully, as if to strip it of the film of selfhood. Answering the phone, she animates Tuttle, speaking with a "dry piping sound, hollow-bodied, like a bird humming" (101). At this moment she begins her reincarnation not only of Tuttle, but also of that veiled spouse brought back to life by Herakles.

The fruits of Lauren's methods are reported in the second inserted text, Mariella's interview and article on *Body Time,* Lauren's performance piece. The article acts as the counterpart to the first journalistic intrusion, Rey's obituary; indeed, since the interview derives from a luncheon meeting, it dramatizes the etymology of the word "obituary," which comes from the Latin *obire,* "to go meet." "[R]awboned and slightly bug-eyed," Lauren herself now resembles a cadaver, undernourished newborn, or plucked bird (103). She has become a figure of pure possibility. According to Mariella, in *Body Time* as in all of her art, Lauren is "always in the process of becoming another or exploring some root identity": like her father, the classicist turned archaeologist, she plunges downward to unearth deep sources (105). This is the backward lurch so familiar to DeLillo's readers, previously seen in Bucky Wunderlick's withdrawal into silence, in the frightening historical regression that climaxes ***Ratner's Star,*** in the archaeological and linguistic excavations of ***The Names,*** in ***Underworld***'s temporal burrowings. But here the description of Lauren's work compels the reader to imitate her, to work backward into the novel to discover how she has incorporated and transmuted experience into art.

For in *Body Time* she has, like Beckett's Krapp, embarked on nothing so much as a "new retrospect"

(Beckett 16). Thus, for example, the audience hears Mariella's answering machine playing relentlessly behind the action (106), and sees again the live-stream video feed from the Finnish highway (107). Lauren revivifies her Asian neighbor (previously mentioned on page 35, and seen again in the final chapter [115]) as an "ancient Japanese woman" (105); she then metamorphoses into a woman in executive attire obsessively checking the time on her watch in excruciating slow motion (106). Her goal, she states, is to "[s]top time, or stretch it out, or open it up. Make a still life that's living, not painted" (107); these are, one realizes, DeLillo's aims as well, for in recycling elements from his own novel and in slowing narrative movement to a crawl, he mirrors Lauren's mechanic muse.[16] At the end of the piece, in another homage to *Krapp,* she turns herself into a naked man lip-synching to a voice—possibly Tuttle's—playing on tape. After an apparent seizure, the "man" seems to fly "out of one reality and into another" (108). Perhaps prompted by Mariella's tape recorder, to conclude the interview Lauren engineers a final self-reflexive twist and switches again to the naked man's voice: she echoes Tuttle as he echoed her. As I noted above, Mariella concludes that *Body Time* is "about who we are when we are not rehearsing who we are" (110). If so, Lauren's appropriation of Tuttle's voice is not merely a performance, but a blend of being and acting: since his voice, after all, parroted hers, then she is becoming herself using Tuttle as medium. But in another sense, both her work and DeLillo's imply that there is no "who" who is not also performing, that Lauren's anti-performance is at the same time a performance (that is, she must perform that appearance of non-performance). We are only "ourselves," it seems, when we are somebody else, the echo of an echo.

The Body Artist, like *Body Time,* also reminds us that these echoes extend far into the past. Thus, although Lauren maintains that *Body Time* is more than just a response to "what happened to Rey" (108), the novel indicates that it is at least partially a means of dramatizing and channeling her grief. She even admits that it stages "the drama of men and women versus death" (109). In this regard it echoes *Alcestis,* for what King Admetos finally understands at the end of that play is the truth with which Lauren wrestles throughout the novel: that in losing her spouse, she has lost herself (Arrowsmith 18). Lauren's bereavement, like that of Admetos, leads to her discovery that one must accept one's mortality in order to be fully human (6). In *Alcestis,* Admetos's decision to give his allegiance to the living rather than to his dead wife, paradoxically, allows his wife to live again; in *Body Time,* Lauren pays homage to Rey, paradoxically, by never mentioning him. Instead, husband and wife come together behind the veil of art, merging in the figure of a naked man lip-synching to a tape recorder.

Both works also ask "what comes after death? Can we be reborn?" *Alcestis* answers these questions by uncannily inverting the conventions of dramatic identity: first we accept that Alcestis is dead, but then, suddenly, we must accept that she is not. Thus the play reminds us that "Alcestis" is, after all, an actor in a mask playing a character who herself "plays dead" and then pretends to be an unknown woman who is not Alcestis, before becoming "herself" again. The implication is that theater, the very act of masking, bears the seeds of regeneration, not just of a person but of an entire community. *Body Time* answers those mortal questions by depicting Lauren's metamorphoses into a series of figures who are not so much characters as full-body masks. Her personae, indeed, imitate what William Arrowsmith describes as the "modal" form of Greek theater, whereby those masked actors are meant to seem generic, universal (4), to comprise "little more than the sum of the possibilities" contained in the masks (8). Similarly, Lauren's personae—the ancient Japanese woman gesturing like a Noh actor, the busy executive, the naked man—are simultaneously types and tokens of the self's infinite possibilities; like those ancient masked thespians, they are at once universal and mysterious.[17]

Further, if Rey has, in his suicide, reenacted the roles of both Alcestis (the dead spouse) and Admetos (the royal husband), and Tuttle has played Herakles, at once guest and reviver of the dead, so in submitting herself to these transformations, Lauren, like Alcestis (and Admetos as well) undergoes in *Body Time* a symbolic death, as if to become closer to her husband by experiencing his demise. And she returns veiled—an Alcestis who is both herself and somebody else. In sum, the intertextual specters that haunt both DeLillo's and Lauren's works strike mythic reverberations, becoming shards of experience that, torn from their original contexts, glint both forward and backward. Like light passing through a prism, or Greek modes turning up in postmodern music, Ajax, Admetos, Alcestis and Herakles have become human fractals—irregular shapes repeated over the ages in innumerable guises. And just as Lauren is finally transformed by hearing voices from the past, so in reading and hearing the voices in ***The Body Artist*** we do not merely intrude upon them, but are possessed by their fracted human shapes, finally, if fleetingly, inhabiting them through DeLillo's ventriloquism. They are never buried, never undertaken; rather, they overtake us.

After her performance Lauren returns to the house and cleans the bathroom—but not with Ajax. Her self-dispossession should also have been cathartic, but may still be incomplete. She thinks, "I am Lauren. But less and less," and for most of this chapter she seems suspended between selves, living in many times at once, finding herself "addressing someone who wasn't quite her" (117). "Being here has come to me" (121), she thinks, echoing Tuttle's words, which are now also Rey's words: but who that "me" is remains unclear. To convey Lauren's suspension, DeLillo's narrator slips seamlessly from second-person to third, from present to past to future perfect. Thus when Lauren hears a noise she imagines that "Once she steps into the room, she will already have been there" (122). Floating through these "whispers of was and is" (123), Lauren feels Rey (and Tuttle) all around her. Mixing memory and desire, she believes she will surprise him in an upstairs room. But which "him?" Both the pronouns and her inner vision become ambiguous as she conjures an image: "He sits on the bed in his underwear [the state in which she discovered Tuttle], lighting the last cigarette of the day" as Rey would (122).

She even entertains fantasies of forestalling Rey's suicide: "when she goes out to his car and takes his car keys and hides them, hammers them, beats them, eats them, buries them in the bone soil on a strong bright day in late summer, after a roaring storm" (123). Instead, a buried memory erupts to shed a dazzling light on Lauren's mourning. She now remembers that "her mother died when she was nine. It wasn't her fault. It had nothing to do with her." But of course it had everything to do with her. In dealing with her husband's death, she has finally interred and exhumed her lost parent and the little girl who died with her. All her losses merge, and her funerals become a wake: breaking from her haunted reverie, she realizes that the room where she yearned to see Rey is empty. No longer possessed, she throws open the window, feeling the "sea tang on her face and the flow of time in her body, to tell her who she was" (124). Lauren has, at last, undertaken herself.

If she seems to return to her sole self at the novel's conclusion, ***The Body Artist*** nonetheless implies that humans do not inhabit an identity but rather, like those kingfishers of Hopkins, selve ourselves by flinging out our names. Yet those names change, because identities are not things but deliberate acts of creation. Moreover, those names do not fade away but resound through our lives and those of the ones who follow us. We are never quite lost. It follows that consciousness is not a narrative, or even a dialogue, but an echo chamber, a room we share with the chorus of all the living and the dead. For DeLillo the highest expression of this music of time is an art that is at once a mode of possession—a sophisticated brand of magic or ventriloquism—and an act of exorcism. Such an art undertakes the world to which it responds, refracts it, and then gives back a newly configured body. Such an art thus manages to be both the most authentic expression of subjectivity and its greatest transformer. Such an art must also, however, restlessly change its form, as ***The Body Artist*** does, becoming now a poem, now a piece of reportage, now a play. This novel, like its protagonist, constantly molts. It must do so if it is to do justice to Lauren's—and our own—transitory selves. In that sense, both Lauren's and DeLillo's work resembles the kind that DeLillo celebrates in an essay on Chinese dissident Wei Jingsheng: "an art outside the strict limits of the written word" ("Artist Naked" 6). The artist can manage these feats, however, only when she or he remains hospitable to the stun of intrusion, the wedge of amazement, those visitations of voice and illumination that transmute suffering into shaped expression. In ***The Body Artist,*** DeLillo performs such an undertaking, one that is both a recollection and a forgetting.

Notes

1. This is not the first time that DeLillo has treated the question of life after death. Near the end of *Underworld,* the figure of a dead girl named Esmeralda seems to appear on a Minute Maid orange juice billboard. More broadly, haunted characters abound in his work, from *Americana*'s Oedipally-fixated David Bell through the middle-aged protagonist of *Underworld,* Nick Shay, still tormented by his father's abandonment forty years earlier.

2. DeLillo has frequently acknowledged Joyce's influence, admitting in interviews that the Irish author introduced him to "language that carried a radiance" ("Art of Fiction" 278; see also interview with LeClair 20, 26), and specifically citing Joyce in novels such as *Americana* (145). I have adduced further Joycean debts, particularly in *Mao II* and *Underworld* (*American Magic* 197, 225, 276-77). David Cowart (202) and Philip Nel (738) have remarked on the similarities between *The Body Artist* and Virginia Woolf's novels.

3. For a treatment of intertextuality as metempsychosis, see Osteen, *Economy* 83-84.

4. Thus, for example, as she drives down the highway just after her husband's death, the second-person narrator expresses her sense of dazed dissociation, which overtakes her until "the noise and rush and blur are back and you slide into your life again, feeling the painful weight in your chest" (31).

5. Such dispossessions constitute a "textual strategy for usurping interest as to whose side of the story will be heard" (27). Reid argues that similar dispossessions also characterize the interchanges between Jack and Babette Gladney in *White Noise* (59-63).

6. This sentence, with its serial conjunctions, is haunted by Ernest Hemingway, whom DeLillo cites as an influence and whom he spontaneously parodies in the "Art of Fiction" interview (278).

7. In 1980 DeLillo pseudonymously published a novel called *Amazons,* which masquerades as a memoir by one Cleo Birdwell, the first woman to play in the National Hockey League.

8. Lauren's description recalls that of Leopold Bloom's luncheon sandwich, which emits "the feety savour of green cheese" (Joyce 142).

9. When he goes off to the meadow to kill himself in Sophocles's tragedy, Ajax claims that he's planning to "cleanse [his] stains" (35). Actually, though, the epithet "toilet cleanser" better suits Herakles, one of whose great deeds was to scour the Augean stables.

10. For an outline of the many varieties and functions of echolalia, see Schuler & Prizant 169-73.

11. One of Maria Rhode's patients reportedly told her before one session, "let's go to the room," perfectly echoing Rhode's habitual prompt to suggest that they begin therapy (88).

12. This patient's echolalia, Rhode hypothesizes, resulted from his belief that he had ousted the normal sibling his mother should have borne; the echo-voice was that of his unborn sibling. Most echolalia, however, is not neurotic but neurological, though occasionally it can expand into psychosis. One of Sacks's post-encephalitic subjects responded to a dose of the drug L-dopa by becoming uncontrollably echolalic, giving the impression of a "hollow, untenanted, ghost-filled house, as if *she herself* had become 'dispossessed' by echoes and ghosts" (*Awakenings* 189). After three weeks of this compulsive echolalia, the patient lapsed into a coma. For an account of echolalia as experienced by a person with autism, see Williams 4, 209.

13. Pragmatics involves three aspects of language: intentionality (comprehending what people mean even when they do not say what they mean); presuppositions (about other people's responses, expectations, and contexts); and the rules of cooperation (which consist of the quantity, quality, relevance, and clarity of speech); see Twachtman-Cullen 229, 239-41.

14. Although I am suggesting that Tuttle exemplifies many traits of clinical autism, DeLillo probably acquired the idea for his speech and behavior not from autistic people but from his work with elderly patients suffering from Alzheimer's. In 1996 and 1997 he organized writing classes for Alzheimer's patients with the hope that writing would offer "an incentive to memory. Writing a brief narrative every couple of weeks can be a way of escaping loneliness and apprehension" (quoted in Gardner). Their writing also offered incentive to his own work in at least one case, for Tuttle's phrase, "leaving has come to me," echoes the words of a 74-year-old man whose meditation on the topic "Saying Goodbye" reads: "It has come to us, leaving has come to us. . . . Not I alone, but all of us leave, have left, will leave" (Gardner).

15. DeLillo employed a similar trope in his first novel, *Americana,* in which protagonist David Bell, alienated by his job at a television network, imagines that "all of us at the network existed only on videotape. Our words and actions seem to have a disturbingly elapsed quality. We had said and done all these things before and they had been frozen for a time, rolled up in little laboratory trays to await broadcast. . . . And there was the feeling that somebody's deadly pinky might nudge a button and we would all be erased forever" (23).

16. DeLillo also uses motivic repetition throughout *The Body Artist,* recapitulating such gestures as her throwing off "a grubby sweater" (111, 122) or of Lauren's finding a strange hair in her mouth (11, 69). For a fuller list of such reiterations, see Cowart 205-6.

17. This is far from DeLillo's first experiment with "modal" characters. The figures in *The Day Room,* for example, are not psychologically realistic characters but instead represent DeLillo's theme of identity as performance. His novels also frequently employ such typologies, most obviously in the first half of his Menippean satire *Ratner's Star,* where the "characters" are little more than cartoon voices exchanging elaborately erudite, arch dialogue.

Works Cited

Arrowsmith, William. "Introduction." *Alcestis* by Euripides. Trans. William Arrowsmith. New York: Oxford UP, 1974, 3-29.

Beckett, Samuel. *Krapp's Last Tape and Other Dramatic Pieces.* New York: Grove/Evergreen, 1960.

Cowart, David. *Don DeLillo: The Physics of Language.* Athens: U of Georgia P, 2002.

DeLillo, Don [Cleo Birdwell]. *Amazons.* New York: Holt, Rinehart & Winston, 1980.

———. *Americana.* Boston: Houghton Mifflin, 1971. Rev ed. New York: Penguin, 1989.

———. "The Art of Fiction CXXXV." [Interview with Adam Begley.] *Paris Review* 128 (Fall, 1993): 274-306.

———. "The Artist Naked in a Cage." *The New Yorker* (26 May 1997): 6-7.

———. *The Body Artist.* New York: Scribner, 2001.

———. *The Day Room.* New York: Viking, 1986.

———. *Great Jones Street.* Boston: Houghton Mifflin, 1973.

———. "An Interview with Don DeLillo." With Tom LeClair. *Contemporary Literature* 23 (1982): 19-31.

———. *Libra.* New York: Viking, 1988.

———. *Mao II.* New York: Viking, 1991.

———. *The Names.* New York: Knopf, 1982.

———. *Ratner's Star.* New York: Knopf, 1976.

———. *Running Dog.* New York: Knopf, 1978.

———. *Underworld.* New York: Scribner, 1997.

———. *White Noise.* New York: Viking, 1985.

Euripides. *Alcestis.* Trans. William Arrowsmith, New York: Oxford UP, 1974.

Frith, Uta. *Autism: Explaining the Enigma.* London: Blackwell, 1989.

Gardner, Ralph, Jr. "Writing That Can Strengthen the Fraying Threads of Memory." *New York Times* (30 January, 1997): http://query.nytimes.com/search/restricted/article?res=F60F13FE3D590C738FDDA80894DF494D81

Hopkins, Gerard Manley. "[As kingfishers catch fire, dragonflies draw flame.]" *Poems and Prose.* Ed. W. H. Gardner. New York: Penguin, 1985.

James, Williams. *Principles of Psychology.* Vol. I. New York: Dover, 1950.

Joyce, James. *Ulysses: The Corrected Text.* Ed. Hans Walter Gabler with Wolfhard Steppe and Claus Melchior. New York: Random House, 1986.

Nel, Philip. "Don DeLillo's Return to Form: The Modernist Poetics of *The Body Artist.*" *Contemporary Literature* 43 (2002): 736-59.

Osteen, Mark. *American Magic and Dread: Don DeLillo's Dialogue with Culture.* Philadelphia: U of Pennsylvania P, 2000.

———. *The Economy of* Ulysses: *Making Both Ends Meet.* Syracuse: Syracuse UP, 1995.

Reid, Ian. *Narrative Exchanges.* New York and London: Routledge, 1992.

Rhode, Maria. "Echo or Answer? The Move Toward Ordinary Speech in Three Children with Autistic Spectrum Disorder." *Autism and Personality: Findings from the Tavistock Autism Workshop.* Ed. Anne Alvarez and Susan Reid. London and New York: Routledge, 1999, 79-92.

Sacks, Oliver. *An Anthropologist on Mars: Seven Paradoxical Tales.* New York: Knopf, 1995.

———. *Awakenings.* Rev. Ed. New York: HarperPerennial, 1990.

Schuler, Adriana L., and Barry M. Prizant. "Echolalia." *Communication Problems in Autism.* Ed. Eric Schopler and Gary B. Mesibov. New York: Plenum, 1985, 163-84.

Sophocles. *Ajax.* Trans. John Moore. *Sophocles II.* Ed. David Grene and Richmond Lattimore. New York: Washington Square, 1967, 3-66.

Turner, Michelle. "Towards an Executive Dysfunction Account of Repetitive Behaviour in Autism." *Autism as an Executive Disorder.* Ed. James Russell. New York and London: Oxford UP, 1997, 57-100.

Twachtman-Cullen, Diane. "More Able Children with Autism Spectrum Disorders: Sociocommunicative Challenges and Guidelines for Enhancing Abilities." *Autism Spectrum Disorders: A Transactional Developmental Perspective.* Ed. Amy M. Wetherby and Barry M. Prizant. Baltimore: Paul H. Brookes, 2000, 225-49.

Williams, Donna. *Nobody Nowhere: The Extraordinary Biography of an Autistic.* New York: Times Books, 1992.

FURTHER READING

Criticism

Abel, Marco. "Don DeLillo's 'In the Ruins of the Future': Literature, Images, and the Rhetoric of Seeing 9/11." *PMLA* 118, no. 5 (October 2003): 1236.

Examines the rhetorical strategies concerning perspective and vision in "In the Ruins of the Future."

Kavadlo, Jesse. *Don DeLillo: Balance at the Edge of Belief.* New York: Peter Lang, 2004, 170 p.

Analyzes the representation of cultural anxiety and spiritual crisis in DeLillo's novels.

Kirn, Walter. "Long Day's Journey into Haircut: Don DeLillo's Hero Spends All Day Crossing Manhattan in a Limo." *New York Times Book Review* (13 April 2003): 8.

Provides an unfavorable review of *Cosmopolis.*

Noya, José Liste. "Naming the Secret: Don DeLillo's *Libra.*" *Contemporary Literature* 45, no. 2 (summer 2004): 239-75.

Studies the representation of power and secrecy in *Libra.*

Rowe, John Carlos. "*Mao II* and the War on Terrorism." *South Atlantic Quarterly* 103, no. 1 (winter 2004): 21-43.

Discusses the treatment of terrorism in *Mao II* with respect to postmodernism and the novel's adaptation as a drama.

Additional coverage of DeLillo's life and career is contained in the following sources published by Thomson Gale: *American Writers: The Classics,* Vol. 2; *American Writers Supplement,* Vol. 6; *Beacham's Encyclopedia of Popular Fiction: Biography & Resources,* Vol. 1; *Bestsellers,* Vol. 89:1; *Contemporary Authors,* Vols. 81-84; *Contemporary Authors New Revision Series,* Vols. 21, 76, 92, 133; *Contemporary Literary Criticism,* Vols. 8, 10, 13, 27, 39, 54, 76, 143; *Contemporary Novelists,* Ed. 7; *Contemporary Popular Writers*; *Dictionary of Literary Biography,* Vols. 6, 173; *DISCovering Authors Modules: Novelists* and *Popular Fiction and Genre Authors*; *DISCovering Authors 3.0*; *Encyclopedia of World Literature in the 20th Century,* Ed. 3; *Literature Resource Center*; *Major 20th-Century Writers,* Eds. 1, 2; *Major 21st-Century Writers,* (eBook) 2005; *Reference Guide to American Literature,* Ed. 4; and *Twayne's United States Authors.*

Thomas Pynchon
1937-

(Born Thomas Ruggles Pynchon, Jr.) American novelist, short story writer, and essayist.

The following entry presents an overview of Pynchon's life and works through 2004. For discussion of the novel *The Crying of Lot 49* (1966), see *CLC,* Volume 72; for discussion of the novel *Gravity's Rainbow* (1973), see *CLC,* Volume 192; for additional information on his career, see *CLC,* Volumes 2, 3, 6, 9, 11, 18, 33, 62, and 123.

INTRODUCTION

Pynchon is one of the most acclaimed American novelists of the twentieth century. Utilizing elements of science fiction, fantasy, satire, myth, and advanced mathematics, his novels are characterized by black humor, a large cast of unusual and allegorical characters, and an encyclopedic appropriation of Western history and popular culture. Critics often discuss Pynchon's novels as postmodern works that illustrate the chaos and randomness of modern life. Reviewers have praised his work for its wide-ranging subject matter, distinctive comic voice, innovative synthesis of narrative perspectives, and profound philosophical insights into the nature of truth and historical reality.

BIOGRAPHICAL INFORMATION

Born on May 8, 1937, in Glen Cove, New York, Pynchon grew up in the town of Oyster Bay in East Norwich. In 1954 he received a scholarship to attend Cornell University to pursue a degree in engineering physics. Shortly thereafter he switched from physics to an arts and sciences curriculum, but his college career was interrupted when he joined the navy. Pynchon returned to Cornell in 1957, and enrolled in a class with the renowned author Vladimir Nabokov. During this time, he befriended the writer and folksinger Richard Fariña, and the pair became part of a group of artists heavily influenced by Jack Kerouac and other Beat writers. After Pynchon graduated from Cornell in 1959, he spent a year in New York City, where he began writing his novel *V.* (1963). He then took a job in Seattle as a technical writer for Boeing Aircraft. After leaving Boeing in 1962, he traveled to Mexico and California to finish *V.* The novel was published to enthusiastic reviews, and received the William Faulkner Foundation Award for best novel of the year. Three years later, *The Crying of Lot 49* was published; this novel received the Richard and Hilda Rosenthal Foundation Award of the National Institute of Arts and Letters. His next novel, *Gravity's Rainbow* (1973), was a best-seller and won the National Book Award for fiction, which Pynchon refused. The book was also nominated for a Pulitzer Prize, but was rejected by the editorial board, allegedly for being disjointed, "unreadable," "turgid," and "obscene," among other charges. When the novel was awarded the William Dean Howells Medal of the American Academy of Arts and Letters in 1975, Pynchon made the unprecedented gesture of turning it down. In 1989 he received a grant from the John D. and Catherine T. MacArthur Foundation Fellowship. The publication of his fourth novel, *Vineland* (1990), broke seventeen years of relative silence from the notoriously reclusive author, and was followed by *Mason & Dixon* in 1997.

MAJOR WORKS

Pynchon began his literary career with the publication of several short stories, five of which are included in his 1984 collection, *Slow Learner.* His first novel, *V.,* chronicles the picaresque adventures of Herbert Stencil, the son of a British spy, as he searches for "V.," a mysterious female persona. Believing that "V." will reveal information about his father's murder, Stencil relentlessly follows a number of clues and encounters a gang known as the "Whole Sick Crew," a group of bohemians who represent the decadence and moral decay of modern society. Critics maintain that the novel touches on many of Pynchon's recurring themes, particularly his concern with identity, historical design, and the ambiguity of truth. *The Crying of Lot 49* is regarded as Pynchon's most accessible work and also utilizes a detective story motif and an obsessive quest for truth. Set in California during the 1960s, the novel focuses on the story of Oedipa Maas, a suburban housewife who is named the executrix of the will of her former lover, Pierce Inverarity, a real-estate mogul. While investigating the terms of his bequest, she discovers a renegade postal system called Tristero. Like many of Pynchon's characters, Oedipa is uncertain whether her perception is valid, a result of her own paranoia, or a manipulation of her thoughts by others. In this work, Pynchon employs the second law of thermodynamics—a rule of physics that describes entropy—as a metaphor for the forces that contribute to social decline.

Critics regard *Gravity's Rainbow* as Pynchon's finest work to date and his most ambitious effort to reorder and contextualize the major social, political, and philosophical developments of the twentieth century. Set in England, France, and occupied Germany in 1945, the novel synthesizes historical, cultural, and scientific information, divergent plotlines, flashback and fantasy sequences, scenes of comedy and brutality, and a complex meta-narrative that involves hundreds of characters with several perspectives of historical events. Tyrone Slothrop, the protagonist, is an American lieutenant unwittingly programmed to predict Nazi V-2 rocket strikes with his erections. In addition to suggesting that Western society actively promotes a culture of death by perfecting such weapons as the German V-2 rocket, Pynchon links advances in science and technology with historical patterns; political, economic, and social values; and international cartels in their contributions to the war effort. Reviewers have called *Gravity's Rainbow* one of the greatest historical novels of our time and the most important work of fiction since James Joyce's *Ulysses.*

Published in 1990, *Vineland* satirizes the failure of 1960s idealism and the conservative political climate of the Reagan administration in the 1980s. On one level, the title of this work alludes to Leif Eriksson's discovery of America prior to Christopher Columbus; on another, *Vineland* refers to a fictitious county near the coast of northern California. The novel focuses on Prairie Wheeler's search for her long-lost mother, Frenesi Gates, an ex-member of a defunct radical group that aimed to expose the corruption and hypocrisy of the Nixon administration. Together with characters such as DL Chastain—a "ninjette" and former friend of Frenesi's—and Takeshi Fumimota, an amphetamine addict, Prairie attempts to discover her family's past and future. *Mason & Dixon* is also concerned with the national identity of the United States. Set in colonial times, the novel is narrated by the Reverend Wicks Cherrycoke and chronicles the story of astronomer Charles Mason and surveyor Jeremiah Dixon, navigators of the infamous Mason-Dixon Line, which was later to become the boundary between free and slave states in mid-nineteenth-century America. Critics view the novel as a meditation on the themes of liberty and slavery and the ambiguity of truth.

CRITICAL RECEPTION

Since the 1963 publication of his novel *V.,* Pynchon has been recognized as one of America's most brilliant and challenging novelists. His work has been the subject of rigorous scholarly interpretation, and critics have commended its ambitious subject matter, dark humor, and innovative narrative constructs. Yet other reviewers have derided his undeveloped characters, fragmented and convoluted plots, and abundance of silly word play and empty allusions. Recent criticism has examined his novel *Mason & Dixon* as a poetic act and a meditation on American national identity, and investigated the role of mainstream film and the presence of Japan in *Vineland.* Other recent studies have explored the influence of other authors and works on Pynchon's novels, such as the impact of Bruno Schulz's short story "Kometa" on *Gravity's Rainbow.* Many critics have analyzed Pynchon's interest in binary oppositions, which some perceive as an effective strategy for exposing multivalent realities and the hypocrisy of extremes. However, other critics view such Manichean divisions and equivocal outcomes as simplistic and evasive. Pynchon's use of metafiction in his novels is regarded as both a strength and a weakness; according to several critics, it results in a narrative sometimes marred by incoherence and obscurity. A highly imaginative and original postmodern novelist, Pynchon is viewed as one of the most thought-provoking and important American authors of contemporary fiction.

PRINCIPAL WORKS

V. (novel) 1963
The Crying of Lot 49 (novel) 1966
Gravity's Rainbow (novel) 1973
Slow Learner: Early Stories (short stories) 1984
Vineland (novel) 1990
Mason & Dixon (novel) 1997

CRITICISM

William Logan (essay date 1998)

SOURCE: Logan, William. "Pynchon in the Poetic." *Southwest Review* 83, no. 4 (1998): 424-37.

[*In the following essay, Logan outlines the poetic aspects of* Mason & Dixon, *claiming that although it is a novel, "the experience of reading it is at times purely poetic."*]

> The monastic saints . . . familiarly accosted, or imperiously commanded, the lions and serpents of the desert; infused vegetation into a sapless trunk; suspended iron

> on the surface of the water; passed the Nile on the back of a crocodile; and refreshed themselves in a fiery furnace. These extravagant tales . . . display the fiction, without the genius, of poetry.
>
> —Edward Gibbon, *The Decline and Fall of the Roman Empire*

Poetry was the mother of fiction, and its reduction to a minor species of memoir has not been without cost. That poetry and fiction share more than they divide (fiction at times bearing the private burden of memory, poetry failing memoir in pure fictions) is often concealed by the hermit-crab isolation of contemporary novels, for which realism is old-time religion.

What makes Thomas Pynchon's ***Mason & Dixon*** a poetic act is not just its fanatic ignorance of current fashion (this historical novel almost makes a reader forget that beneath his cocky demeanor and hipster's cant Pynchon has always been a throwback), but its use of means, in its languors as well as its language, more properly poetic. There have always been fiction writers of poetic temperament: Joyce and Faulkner not surprisingly began as poets; minor poets, perhaps, but they took their early understandings of language through a form very different from fiction in its pretense, its rhythm, its design. In the last century Dickens, the novelist then closest to poetry, composed occasional verses as metrically right as they were poetically wrong. Though he has learned from the modernists by coming after them, Pynchon is a novelist of old-fashioned sentiments, not just in historical curiosity (his novels of contemporary life, ***Vineland*** and the thinly mannered ***The Crying of Lot 49,*** have been his weakest), but in his adoption of Dickensian comedy, beginning with his absurd and fantastic names.

The narrator of ***Mason & Dixon*** is Reverend Wicks Cherrycoke, a name Pynchon almost gets away with. One difference between Dickens and Pynchon is that Dickens usually gets away with his names—Dickens invents characters so true to their names they are false to their unreality; Pynchon loathes the idea of character, and his names wither into whimsy at the expense of character. The philosophy of names is too divisive to have bearing here; but there are few words more Falstaffian, considering the worlds they include, than *poem* or *novel.* Our unwillingness to deny anything with the ambition of being a poem the honor of the name may make discretion impossible, yet most readers have a Platonic sense of what a poem is and is not (that sense may be merely typographical). Though it may be modified by experience or experiment, this sense is unlikely ever to admit a doughnut, a desk lamp, or any literary act wearing the clothes of other conventions (whether diary, play, or novel, though there may be novels in verse, verse plays, and perhaps rhymed diaries—they may use poetry without being poems). What calls itself a poem may, within limits, be taken as poem; but those limits are less enclosing boundaries than liberated tyrannies.

Mason & Dixon is a novel, and yet the experience of reading it is at times purely poetic. Pynchon has embraced in his arguments and actions the crowded ambiguity and frothy imagery of poetry; and to examine them is not to suggest these means lie outside the novel, but to recall how long they have been estranged, not just from recent fiction, but from recent poetry as well.

> Snow-Balls have flown their Arcs, starr'd the Sides of Outbuildings, as of Cousins, carried Hats away into the brisk Wind off Delaware,—the Sleds are brought in and their Runners carefully dried and greased, shoes deposited in the back Hall, a stocking'd-foot Descent made upon the great Kitchen, in a purposeful Dither since Morning, punctuated by the ringing Lids of various Boilers and Stewing-Pots, fragrant with Pie-Spices, peel'd Fruits, Suet, heated Sugar,—the Children, having all upon the Fly, among rhythmic slaps of Batter and Spoon, coax'd and stolen what they might, proceed, as upon each afternoon all this snowy Advent, to a comfortable Room at the rear of the House, years since given over to their carefree Assaults.

This clamorous opening sentence, dense with the chaotic rush of new sensation (every novel plunges into the cold river of a New World), is rife with the novel's animating themes—the ascents and descents of lives beneath those of the stars. Jeremiah Dixon is a journeyman surveyor, Charles Mason an assistant to the Astronomer Royal at Greenwich. The arcs and stars of those hurled snowballs are the heraldic signs of their professions: in the comedy of their lives, cutting arcs across oceans, siting stars, these characters make order from the anarchic motions the children in their hurtling suggest. The heated sugar is the earliest intimation of the trade that drove colonial expansion (its sweetness cost the lives of slaves): the lively microcosm (the whole novel might be said to be *upon the fly,* the characters ever in *purposeful dither*) serves a macrocosm yet unknown, a universe whose existence, whose author, is adumbrated by fond jokes—of punctuation called up by *punctuated,* of beginnings (and religious awakenings) summoned by *Advent.*

The microscope of the sentence reveals the universe of a novel. Pynchon is everywhere sensitive to what a sentence bears, eighteenth-century punctuation not taxing his inventions with the firmer syntax and fixed stops of a later era (the characters meet in 1761). The comic irritation of the capitals (no Bar to Readers of the Period, accustomed to such Emphases) removes the novel to the bewildering thicket of the past, as old-spelling does to *Hamlet*; but apart from its manipulation of reader psychology (we must become the readers of the past), the distancing of such capitals makes pastiche the comedy of form the way a sonnet is a comedy of emotion, the compression and entanglements of love finding their spirit in the spirit of form.

This intensity of imagery, this continual and immodest word-by-word invention, ruptures the plain understandings most fiction now requires. Novels must in part be linear and straightforward—they have somewhere to get to. Pynchon's have coiled upon themselves, devouring their bodies, as if distrustful of the long vista, cut straight through Appalachian forest and over mountains, that is the narrow goal of his novel's characters: the settlement of an eighty-year-old boundary dispute between Pennsylvania and Maryland by drawing an imaginary line, the line that would soon become the worried demarcation between states slave and free.

When a word quibbles, the reader's attention turns minute and cautious. Mason's chat with Martha Washington (one of many clumsily imposed encounters with historical figures) defends astronomy in terms shivering with ambiguity, jokes that darken his speech with the pressure of the unsaid.

> "All Lens-fellows, I mean, recognize that our first Duty is to be of publick Use. [. . .] Even with the Pelhams currently in Eclipse, we all must proceed by way of th' establish'd Routes, with ev'ry farthing we spend charg'd finickingly against the Royal Purse. We are too visible, up on our Hilltop, to spend much time among unworldly Speculations, or indeed aught but the details of our Work,—focus'd in particular these days upon the Problem of the Longitude."
>
> "Oh. And what happen'd to those Transits of Venus?"
>
> "There we have acted more as philosophical Frigates, Ma'am, each detach'd upon his Commission,—whilst the ev'ryday work of the Observatories goes on as always, for the task at Greenwich, as at Paris, is to know every celestial motion so perfectly, that Sailors at last may trust their lives to this Knowledge."

Here his professional vocabulary summons his metaphors, his private world mirrored in the limits of his language (the author's conscious authority always concealing from his characters their unconscious—the author *is* their unconscious). The Pelhams (a powerful pair of English brothers who served in succession as prime minister) are not out of favor; they are in *eclipse.* The astronomer is *focus'd.* The hilltop the stargazers stand on is at once literal and figurative, but their own "speculations" (their star-gazings) shade uneasily into speculations philosophical and financial (talk of money is close by—it isn't just time that is spent). Mason claims he has no time for unworldly speculations, and yet he does and doesn't—a stargazer's "speculations" are all unworldly. Even the financial gambles of astronomers are not likely to have much worldly in them—Mason means his God is in the details, but he means so much more than he means.

A speech later, these speculations transform into "philosophical" frigates, a metaphor compacted of the wars raging on the Atlantic (Mason and Dixon have already been hapless participants in one skirmish), the individualism of the period's philosophy (each man well-armored in his belief, as well as stoic in it), the isolation of the astronomer's work (as well as the diaspora of astronomers to far-flung outposts to observe the transit of Venus), and the self-observant comedy necessary to such a metaphor. To be "detached" is to have professional standing, professional disinterest, and professional disengagement, without forgetting the literal meaning: to be sent on a military mission. That a commission is a document of work in hand does not ignore the commissions necessary to officer any vessel. (In this novel, all commissions hint at the secret world of decision-making Pynchon makes such delightfully paranoid use of.) Those metaphorical frigates steer toward real sailors for whom lack of an accurate way of determining longitude at sea cost their lives. The search occupied much astronomic and horological research for a century, and saw the creation of the Board of Longitude (the naturalist Joseph Banks was a member) to adjudicate the scientific disputes and judge the winning method.

The pleasures of such a nervous, finicky style (each farthing of meaning charged against the reader's attention) are densely repeated at many levels of discourse and disputation. At times one image gloriously concatenates a world of vertiginous richness. Here a cook, in company, admires a fop's recently brandished sword:

> "Damascus steel, 's it not? Fascinating. How is that Moiré effect done?"
>
> "By twisting together two different sorts of Steel, or so I am told,—then welding the Whole."
>
> "A time-honor'd Technique in Pastry as well. The Armorers of the Japanese Islands are said to have a way of working carbon-dust into the steel of their Swords, not much different from how one must work the Butter into the Croissant Dough. Spread, fold, beat flat, spread, again and again, eh? till one has created hundreds of these prodigiously thin layers."
>
> "Gold-beating as well, now you come to it," puts in Mr. Knockwood, "—'tis flatten and fold, isn't it, and flatten again, among the thicknesses of Hide, till presently you've these very thin Sheets of Gold-Leaf."
>
> "Lamination," Mason observes.
>
> "Lo, Lamination abounding," contributes Squire Haligast, momentarily visible, "its purposes how dark, yet have we ever sought to produce these thin Sheets innumerable, to spread a given Volume as close to pure Surface as possible, whilst on route discovering various new forms, the Leyden Pile, decks of Playing-Cards, Contrivances which, like the Lever or Pulley, quite multiply the apparent forces, often unto disproportionate results. . . ."
>
> "The printed Book," suggests the Rev'd, "—thin layers of pattern'd Ink, alternating with other thin layers of compress'd Paper, stack'd often by the Hundreds."

From this single object, families of reference flood, each lowly example claiming an ever-more-distant cousin, the layered patterns of Damascus steel (its secret still hidden from the modern world) metamorphosing into samurai swords, croissants (the fop is a Macaroni, an outlandish dandy), gold beaters, the Leyden pile, each image itself beaten and folded into another, the layers of imagery creating just that concentration of power, that multiplication of forces, to which Squire Haligast refers. This tour de force is a miniature of Enlightenment knowledge—knowledge by association, advancing insight by applying the stray evidence of one field to the general principle of another. This ability to draw theory from the mass of particulars is scientific method in small.

Such an unruly mob of images might have been mere caprice, if the Leyden pile were not elsewhere the controlling metaphor of the novel's own preoccupation with the advance of science (each repetition making the Leyden pile its own Leyden pile). The image that follows the passage above is of a heap of broadsides, "dispers'd one by one, and multiplying their effect as they go," dispersed like the astronomers scattered to their transits, gathering knowledge while also broadcasting it. That the harvest of examples may itself form an ars poetica gives the passage its bookish purpose: to end with the power of printing first to focus and compress information (words by themselves each performing nothing) and then to scatter it. Images that might have radiated into ornament become instead the novel's enterprise, to make the free market of reference part of the nascent laissez-faire economy slowly emerging from monopolies of commerce, the chartered companies that held the reins of empire (the novel's failure is its failure to find a plot beyond such local concentrations of power).

These intoxicating leaps (one of the novel's larkish inventions has students taught to fly along ley lines) are Pynchon's signature, perhaps his scrawl, here secured within an age where such fresh infusions of knowledge were actively sought in common room and coffee house, the Renaissance cabinet becoming the experimental laboratory and the radical pamphlet, knowledge precipitated into the typographical boundaries of Johnson's dictionary and Diderot's *Encyclopédie*. Here Dixon's teacher (the master of flight) lectures on the possibly druidic or Mithraic origins of ley lines:

> "The Argument for a Mithraic Origin is encourag'd by the Cult's known preference for underground Temples, either natural or man-made. They would have found a home in Durham, here among Pit-men and young Plutonians like yourselves,—indeed, let us suppose the earliest Coal-Pits were discover'd by Mithraist Sappers? . . . from the Camp up at Vinovia, poking about for a suitable Grotto,—who, seeking Ormazd, God of Light, found rather a condens'd Blackness which hides Light within, till set aflame . . . mystickal Stuff, Coal. Don't imagine any of you notice that, too busy getting it all over yerselves, or resenting it for being so heavy, or counting Chaldrons. Pretending it solid, when like light and Heat, it indeed flows. *Eppur' si muove,* if yese like."

The pressure of history compounds the force of allusion, from the Roman army's religious cults (Mithraism once rivaling Christianity for the empire's soul) to Iron Age mining operations, from the obscure English measure for coal (a chaldron being from thirty-two to thirty-six bushels, depending on shire) to Galileo's bitter, if apocryphal, aside after his forced recantation of belief in the Copernican system. Coal is another (unacknowledged) exemplar of the power of lamination: those densely compressed layers of decaying leaves, like gilt-edged leaves of a black book, were the source of the Industrial Revolution, the blackened miners slaves below to the temples of industry rising above. Dixon is from this hard-pressed country and only through education escapes a life in the pits or indebted to them (his father is a local baker): only knowledge of coal lets him flee the coal. The turn back to the themes of the novel, the private history of a character, anchors Pynchon's whimsy in something more than whimsy, the random motions of imagination (their drunk-man's walk, their Brownian dance) serving laws otherwise invisible.

This improvement from detail to design is poetry's conscious method—a poem's metaphorical invention may confound logic or sense, moving crabwise across knowledge, but always returning to source (if poetry had a calculus, it would be integral). At such moments Pynchon's imagination would otherwise seem out of control, firing off examples and suggestive metaphors without taking them to account, with an élan almost comically Shakespearean. Most novelists invent their worlds by minute cross-reference to this one, meant to mirror our humdrum life with subdural shocks of recognition (genre writing, including science fiction, is the crudest form of such representation). Consider this quicksilver remark on politics (as well as fictions): "'Yet Representation must extend beyond simple Agentry,' protests Patsy, '—unto at least Mr. Garrick, who in "representing" a rôle, becomes the character, as by some transfer of Soul.'" This is followed by wit about "Actor-Envoys" and "Stroller-Plenipotentiaries."

Pynchon never intensifies the familiar except to disrupt or destroy it; in his novels the realistic convention is merely convention, the fabric on which it is projected, like a movie screen, torn apart and patched together. It is not the denial of conventions that distinguishes his fiction so much as the layering of them: at any moment Howellsian realism underlies Dickensian farce, magic realism overlays Looney Tunes. What should be a conflict or comedy of manners becomes a Leyden pile of them: in this Pynchon is indebted to Joyce, though he has a curious way of disabling the anxiety of influence—by placing his own style so deep in history, he seems Joyce's ancestor, not his descendent.

Pynchon's most poker-faced inventions test this freedom from the shackles of genre (conventions operating like universal axioms). Hardly have Mason and Dixon been introduced in Portsmouth, to the reader and each other, than they meet a talking dog—not just any talking dog, but one that styles himself the Learnèd English Dog, one of great prepossession ("I am a British Dog, Sir. No one owns me") and perhaps prophetic insight. In a few pages Pynchon uses him to comment obliquely on traveling animal acts, music-hall songs (the dog sings), Mesmerism, metempsychosis, the vices of sailors, the cooking of dogs on savage isles, the difference between preternatural and supernatural, the souls of animals, Zen koan, the Age of Reason, and pets as Scheherazades. At times the prose takes a Dickensian turn (the dog is exhibited by a married couple, the Fabulous Jellows, and Mr. Jellows warns of his Mrs.'s temper: "'Do not oppose her,' Jellows advises, 'for she is a first-rate of an hundred Guns, and her Broadside is Annihilation'"). There is reeking description of the sailors' dockside haunts before the dog vanishes for the rest of the novel (with only perhaps a small doggy encore many years later).

The deadpan description ("Out of the Murk, a dozen mirror'd Lanthorns have leapt alight together, as into their Glare now strolls a somewhat dishevel'd Norfolk Terrier, with a raffish Gleam in its eye") goes a long way toward establishing the dog in the fabric of the fiction, and the reader's belief wars with disbelief in proportions equal to those reported by Mason and Dixon. Pynchon's ability to unite the expectations of his reader with his characters, while constantly exceeding expectation, lets him introduce talking clocks, a knife plucked from a dream, a severed ear (Jenkins' infamous Ear) still capable of listening, an oaf who under the full moon turns into not werewolf but dandy, a perpetual-motion watch, a worldwide conspiracy of Jesuits, a mechanical duck with artificial intelligence and a taste for vengeance, and the Devil in need of a lawyer.

The astronomers inevitably confront the solar workings of the calendar, and the upsetting moment, only a decade before the action of the novel, when England lost eleven days (3-13 September 1752) in switching from the Julian to the Gregorian calendar. Already in use in Europe, the Gregorian adjustment of leap years prevented the slow advance of seasons century by century (an advance that after millennia would have brought winter to July). Workers were not paid for those missing days, and banners of protest read "Give Us Our Eleven Days." Pynchon suddenly proposes, in his offhand way, that Mason lived through those eleven days; and the premise raises matters from the difference between names and things to the books Mason discovers on the secret shelves of the Bodleian: Aristotle on comedy (a nod to Umberto Eco as well as to Richard Janko), the Infancy Gospel of Thomas, and a lost Shakespeare tragedy. The consequences, for astronomy as well as the missing population, take only a few deft pages to work out; but they create, as so much of the novel does, a world behind our world—the world invented with each discovery by novelists as well as scientists.

At times it doesn't seem to matter in which direction the novel advances. This indulgence in Keats's negative capability operates within the text as a suspension of alternatives, as if there were no correct or deterministic way in which the fiction was destined to proceed. That Pynchon for so long staves off the suspicion that his novel doesn't *have* anywhere to get to (years advance, the line will be completed, but the actions of the characters remain empty and purposeless—the *purposeful dither* is finally just dither) is a tribute to his ingenuity in the subatomic realm of the word, the phrase, the sentence. These are usually the proper concentrations of poetry, language for many novelists being merely the medium to advance character and plot. In Pynchon character and plot have been mediums of an imagination elsewhere occupied, and have therefore been treated farcically—but a farcical plot is still a plot.

Pynchon uses ideas—cultural counters, memes—the way a poet uses words, as objects of contemplation and gratification, whatever their meaning. The overstocked repository of his imagination is full of the cultural junk, as well as the minutiae of science and technology, of sadly little use to most fiction and poetry. To an extraordinary degree, one more common to poetry, his ideas come dense with symbolic opportunity—no wonder his metaphysical notions are enigmas of hermeneutic coding, his main structures coincidence and conspiracy. The novel's obsessive schemes swallow each unexpected invention, no matter how absurd, with insatiable and interpreting appetite.

In small, such ideas may be no more than imaginative sleight of hand. The country between York and Baltimore may be high in iron content. This ought to be just the trivia of encyclopedic reading, and yet:

> The earth hereabouts is red, the tone of a new Brick Wall in the Shadow, due to a high ratio of iron,—and if till'd in exactly the right way, it becomes magnetized, too, so that at Harvest-time, 'tis necessary only to pass along the Rows any large Container of Iron, and the Vegetables will fly up out of the ground, and stick to it.

Only a passing fancy, of no importance to the novel, even this reveals old patterns afresh: nature's secrets illuminated by science, the Age of Reason commanding the motion of progress, and the ingenious application of old force to new invention, with tacit reference to other sites of earth's magnetic power (the mysterious ley lines, for instance). Pynchon's reckless ingenuity is a science in opposition to the science we know. That poetic touch of the shadowed brick wall (few poets show such delicate skill or darkening eye—not a brick wall in shadow but a *new* brick wall in *the* shadow) is passed over as swiftly as a reference to iron deposits by Squire Haligast some forty pages before: "For without Iron, Armies are but identically costum'd men holding Bows, and Navies but comely gatherings of wrought Vegetation." The beauty of this epigrammatic idea, tossed off without comment, is how much Pynchon sees, not just in presences, but in absences: war becoming with the disappearance of guns a kind of parish cotillion, the men "identically costum'd," the navies "comely gatherings." Are the embroidered dresses of women not "wrought Vegetation"? Are those men, in a vicious pun, holding weapons or ribbons?

This exhaustive digestion of ideas, this poetic invention of the previously unimaginable (that is the fiction of poetry), culminates in the remarkable vision that, the Mason-Dixon line completed, closes the climactic section of the novel. What will Mason and Dixon do next, they are asked.

> "Devise a way," Dixon replies, "to inscribe a Visto upon the Atlantick Sea."
>
> "Archie, Lad, Look ye here," Mason producing a Sheaf of Papers, flapping thro' them,—"A thoughtful enough Arrangement of Anchors and Buoys, Lenses and Lanthorns, forming a perfect Line across the Ocean, all the way from the Delaware Bay to the Spanish Extremadura,"—with the Solution to the Question of the Longitude thrown in as a sort of Bonus,—as, exactly at ev'ry Degree, might the Sea-Line, as upon a Fiduciary Scale for Navigators, be prominently mark'd, by a taller Beacon, or a differently color'd Lamp. In time, most Ships preferring to sail within sight of these Beacons, the Line shall have widen'd to a Sea-Road of a thousand Leagues, as up and down its Longitude blossom Wharves, Chandleries, Inns, Tobacco-shops, Greengrocers' Stalls, Printers of News, Dens of Vice, Chapels for Repentance, Shops full of Souvenirs and Sweets,—all a Sailor could wish,—indeed, many such will decide to settle here, "Along the Beacons," for good, as a way of coming to rest whilst remaining out at Sea. A good, clean, salt-scour'd old age. Too soon, word will reach the Land-Speculation Industry, and its Bureaus seek Purchase, like some horrible Seaweed, the length of the Beacon Line.

The vision continues toward the depredations of land speculators at sea, the founding of a "Coral-dy'd cubickal Efflorescence"—St. Brendan's Isle, pleasure ground and pensioners' home—to which Mason and Dixon will retire, holders in the scheme, under the watchful eye of the "Atlantick Company." Each stage of this vision begets a new stage more outlandish and yet more plausible, part of Pynchon's wry commentary (notice how masterfully, almost without detection, he modulates out of Mason's speech into authorial narration) on the age's chartered companies, the solution to the problem of Longitude finally neither astronomical or horological but mechanical, the sea colonized like the land. The end returns to the provision for sailors' vices with which the voyages of Mason and Dixon began.

If Pynchon's invention in language mimics the inventions of science, where one explosion is always fuse of the next, it is no more than the way science mimics poetry. The problem of this overstuffed work, what makes it finally a spoil heap of a novel, is just the poetic method that works so well in the microcosm. As exuberance and recklessness it is easy to take the petty irritations of Pynchon's mind—the bad jokes and worse puns, the cheap anachronistic references to contemporary phenomena. The pages are intercalated with songs and poems, but when Pynchon tries to write poetry, as opposed to embodying the methods of poetry, he shows a wooden and unschooled ear (even Jenkins' ear could write better verse). His heroic couplets couldn't have been written by even a bad poet of the period, having little acquaintance with the age's metrical practice, which would have been natural as breathing (even provincial poets could imitate Pope with success); but they're masterful compared to his music-hall frolics, like this Jesuit recruiting song:

> So,—
> Have,—
> A,—
> 'Nother look,—at the Army that
> Wrote the Book,—take the Path that you
> Should've took—and you'll be
> On your way!
> Get, up, and, wipe-off-that-chin,
> You can begin, to have a
> Whole new oth-er life,—
> Soldj'ring for Christ,
> Reas'nably priced,—
> And nobody's missing
> The Kids or th' Wife!

There is not a page of ***Mason & Dixon*** without its droll or disturbing invention, satires on colloquial speech (a milkmaid who uses "as" the way Valley girls use "like"), Jesuit coaches larger inside than out (a subtle slur on sophistry), a musical on the Black Hole of Calcutta, even a visit to the hollow Earth. Such lavish imagination (including his inventories—he's a lover of lists) has not been so magnificently sustained since Joyce. The novel's refusal to muster invention toward anything resembling plot, rather than just the spillage of events over time, seems finally a cowardice: by abusing the privileges of fiction (even picaresque's frivolous motions and meetings are a moral commentary on emptiness), Pynchon loses control of the advantages.

His inability to exploit the contrived meetings with Franklin, Jefferson, or Washington, for example—he might have deepened his designs by ignoring their didactic promises—is everywhere repeated in encounters with minor characters. It seems not realism but carelessness (a carelessness so winning in the details). He exhausts so many small opportunities with a master's skill, it's a pity he has no interest in larger ones.

The novel's infinite deferrals, its postponed consummations (sex is on both Mason's and Dixon's minds, but every seduction is soured) finally become an aversion to any conflict or resolution. No one comes to grief; episodes both lethal and erotic collapse without consequence (a long-awaited confrontation between Captain Zhang, master of dark Chinese arts, and his Jesuit nemesis Father Zarpazo vanishes in thin air)—it's as if Pynchon loses interest. A novel may need neither plot nor character alone—Joyce and Proust offered character in lieu of plot and many novelists plot in lieu of character. It's difficult for a novel, even a novel everywhere touched by brilliance, to offer so little of either. Pynchon may have conceived ***Mason & Dixon*** as a supreme fiction, a poetic act freed of the slavery of plot and character; but conventions are cruel to those who betray them. As his stand-up comedy becomes merely a seven-hundred-page improvisation, the jokes grow hollow. Here Pynchon's poetics have seduced him: it hardly matters if most poems mean what they say. Poetry is the saying, but fiction (the drama, the action, the consequence, the regret) is the having said.

Ernest Mathijs (essay date 2001)

SOURCE: Mathijs, Ernest. "Reel to Real: Film History in Pynchon's *Vineland.*" *Literature/Film Quarterly* 29, no. 1 (2001): 62-70.

[*In the following essay, Mathijs investigates the references to film in* Vineland, *linking these references and their historical contexts to the novel's main characters.*]

> That's how it happened. A film. How else?
>
> —***Gravity's Rainbow*** (p. 398)

> When you said cuttin' and shootin' I didn't know you were talkin' about film.
>
> —***Vineland*** (p. 52)

Introduction

Contemporary literature often refers to and comments upon film, emphasizing both its artistic and commercial qualities, and its ability to blur the distinctions between reality and fiction. This is also the case in the work of Thomas Pynchon. The link between Pynchon and film is not new, nor is it incidental. His novels contain an abundance of references to cultural artifacts in general, and to film in particular. They present movies as interwoven with contemporary culture, as part of the culture they reflect.[1] In ***Vineland*** (1990) however, the nature and purpose of the movies Pynchon cites clearly differ from that in previous novels. Instead of concentrating on highbrow art cinema, or on films that pretend to be historically significant, ***Vineland*** is much more concerned with mainstream movies and their popular history. And instead of constructing historical awareness through film, ***Vineland*** undermines the reliability of film historiography itself.

The novel tells the story of three characters, Sasha Traverse, Frenesi Gates, and Prairie Wheeler (grandmother-mother-daughter), from the point-of-view of the youngest generation (Prairie). Pynchon combines this story with a presentation of the history of popular film. Numerous references to the history of popular film from a well-defined standpoint provide a connection between popular film and the characters' adventures. At the same time, they also give the reader a brief overview of the medium's evolution, and its impact on the everyday life of the people which it is said to change, reflect upon, represent and/or entertain. But there is more. ***Vineland*** not only uses references to film to underscore a story that is interwoven with the popular conceptualization of film, the narrative also firmly connects popular culture with the different modes of reality in film: most of the film references in ***Vineland*** end up forming a coherent pattern, imbued with several modes of reality with regard to film. Pynchon develops three frames of reference encompassing the development of the modes of representation in film, and combines them with different phases in the history of popular film. He links these frames to the three major characters in the novel.[2] Sasha Travese reflects the period of the emerging entertainment-history, of attempts to introduce politics in American film, and of the first cracks in the Hollywood hegemony. She has been married to the gaffer Hubbell and was active in Hollywood politics. Sasha interprets reality politically.[3] Frenesi Gates exemplifies the sixties' documentary movement and its attempts to capture "true reality" through a lens, thus emphasizing observation and interaction. She is a member of a documentary film collective, and views reality from the underground or counter-culture. Finally, Prairie Wheeler embodies an attitude of reflection, and the blurring of the boundaries between film and television. An eighties television-baby, she grows up on cartoons, television series, and television films. She identifies reality as constituted by mediatic representation: as known through the media. The strongest possible kinship tie connects Sasha, Frenesi, and Prairie, thus linking the several modes and periods: the thirties-forties-fifties for Sasha, the sixties and part of the seventies for Frenesi, and the eighties for Prairie. The result is a genealogical and qualitative view on the history of popular film, selective but clarifying.

Pynchon and Film History: *Vineland* versus *Gravity's Rainbow*

The historiography of film works with different concepts, each characterized by a different historical attitude toward the medium. Pynchon repeatedly uses them in his treatment of film. The difference in film references in ***Vineland*** and ***Gravity's Rainbow*** exemplify, for instance, the rough distinction between "realism" and "expressionism" in the history of film, designating the obvious difference between films made to imitate reality and those made to differ from it. More specifically, Pynchon employs two conceptualizations of film and film history. He uses Robert Allen and Douglas Gomery's conceptualization of film historiography to distinguish between aesthetic film historiography (cinema), technological film historiography, economic film historiography (movie), and social film historiography (film). While Pynchon referred to cinema and movie in ***Gravity's Rainbow,*** he uses film and movie in ***Vineland.*** Within the novel, however, the relation between Sasha, Frenesi, and Prairie is structured by another conceptualization, offered by Bill Nichols. Nichols distinguishes five historical modes of the treatment of reality in documentary film: expository, observing, interactive, reflexive, and performative. The expository mode embodies the classic documentary, in which reality is explained through argumentation. Although seemingly based upon reality, this argumentation may exclude several viewpoints (as in the propaganda film or commercial). The observatory mode tries to show reality as it is, without interfering with it or formulating arguments. But, as Nichols remarks, even the stylistic or technical qualities of film can be regarded as distortions of "true" reality. A pure observatory mode is therefore an illusion. Even the interactive mode, in which several viewpoints on reality are made explicit, cannot guarantee a depiction of reality as it is. Therefore, the reflexive or reflective mode accentuates the possible distortions of reality, thus combining a view on reality *and* an explanation of its possible distortions through film. The subject and the approach to it become equally important. According to Nichols, the performative mode is the most recent mode of representation of reality. It combines the potentials of film to distort and to stage reality, thus fabricating images without any causal connection to reality.

Pynchon's use of both conceptualizations is strikingly visible in ***Vineland,*** especially in comparison to its predecessor, ***Gravity's Rainbow. Gravity's Rainbow*** also abounds with references to film. Examples include the relationship between Leni Pökler and Gerhard Von Göll, and references to the Marx Brothers, to German Expressionist films like Fritz Lang's *Frau im Mond, Metropolis,* and *Dr. Mabuse,* to Ingmar Bergman's *Seventh Seal,* Jean Cocteau's *Orphée,* Sergeï Eisenstein's *October,* and to cowboy actor Henry Fonda. By cutting up his story in multiple story lines, of which it is not always clear how or whether they are indeed related, Pynchon calls the Soviet Montage-Style and Buñuel's Surrealist films into mind. His *mise en scène* can be compared to that of the German Expressionists whose films he mentions. As such, the film references in ***Gravity's Rainbow*** clearly constitute the story.[4] In ***Vineland,*** numerous references to film are again made. At first sight, they look so diverse that it hardly seems possible to ascribe any clear significance to them, apart from their being mentioned as examples of how the media (and mediatic references) rule our contemporary lives and block any meaningful interpretation of reality.[5] Some examples concern the mixture of media, fictitious films shown on television ("the 4:30 movie, Pia Zadora in *The Clara Bow Story*" [14], "Woody Allen in *Young Kissinger*" [309], "Sean Connery in *The G. Gordon Liddy Story*" [339], "the Eight O'Clock Movie, Pee-wee Herman in *The Robert Musil Story*" [370]), or real films in fictitious contexts ("*Return of the Jedi* (1983)" [7], "'Jason' in *Friday the 13th* (1980)" [16], "*2001: A Space Odyssey* (1968)" [294], "*20,000 Years in Sing Sing* (1933)" [294]). Still others involve aspects of film history or film stars to metaphorically describe reality: "since George Lucas and all his crew came and went there's been a real change of consciousness" [7], "anything from a bowling alley to a Carpenter Gothic outhouse" [26], "an Eastwood-style mouth-muscle nuance" [28], "the Popeye Doyle of the eighties" [338].

The references in ***Vineland*** are remarkably different from those in ***Gravity's Rainbow. Gravity's Rainbow*** refers to films which were produced long before the era portrayed in ***Vineland.*** The most recent film reference is Bergman's *Seventh Seal,* dating from 1957 (which is in itself exceptional). On the whole, however, mostly silent films are mentioned, as well as films of the thirties. Another difference with ***Vineland*** is that ***Gravity's Rainbow*** frequently mentions European films. Given the stories of both novels this is of course not surprising. Apart from a few exceptions, ***Vineland*** contains no references to art films but only to popular films. In ***Vineland*** we find no German Expressionist films, no Ingmar Bergman, no extreme Soviet-style montage. Instead we find Hollywood, the documentary film, television movies, and cartoons. We find references to stars instead of actors, technicians instead of directors, dates instead of styles, serials instead of the avant-garde, popular domestication and routinization instead of artistic defamiliarization. As such, ***Vineland*** describes a completely different tradition in film historiography than ***Gravity's Rainbow***; in ***Gravity's Rainbow*** Pynchon talks about the history of cinema, references create an aesthetic feeling, and film techniques are employed for artistic reasons. In ***Vineland*** there is no such intention. Here, film is a popular commodity, and its relation toward reality is underlined. The periods of film history that are referred to in ***Vineland*** emphasize this. We find no silent films, which are regarded as expressionist (lacking the realistic feature of sound). Significantly, the one silent-film reference ***Vineland*** does contain is that of "The Clara Bow Story" (14). The film title may be fictitious, but Clara Bow certainly is not. An icon of the twenties, she was one of the main stars who did not succeed in successfully switching from silent films to talkies. Although Pynchon could have easily treated "Clara Bow" in an equally aesthetic manner as he did with other film references of the era, he did not. Rather, it is "Clara Bow-the-tragic-popular-star" who is alluded to, not the exponent of film art. Similarly, almost all other references to film in ***Vineland*** fit the above mentioned distinctions; we get references to real and fictitious films, but the connection to reality remains prominent.[6] When grouped, the references to film in ***Vineland*** belong to one of three frames, corresponding with the three leading characters, and with Nichols's modes of representation. A chronological reconstruction clarifies the characters' connections to film and its history.

Sasha Traverse: Movies and Politics

The oldest frame of reference developed in ***Vineland*** is that of Sasha and Hubbell Gates, the grandparents of Prairie. ***Vineland*** presents their history retrospectively as part of the genealogy; the personal histories of Hubbell and particularly Sasha Gates are revealed through their interaction with their daughter, Frenesi. Within these histories politics are omnipresent. As is made explicit: "Try being a woman who also happens to be political," Sasha confides to her daughter (74). Sasha stems from a political background (her father is a union representative), and from a family of woodcutters from Vineland County (the Traverses). Through her political activities of the thirties and its backfall during World War II, Sasha meets the technician and film-engineer-to-be Hubbell Gates. Their meeting symbolizes the meeting of popular film (Hubbell) and politics (Sasha). Their "marriage," of which Frenesi is the result, is that of the union-gaffer with apparently no interest in politics besides trying to "make the right choice" (289) and the liberal activist trying to "think these things all the way through, politically" (288).

This merging of popular and political culture is by no means incidental. It occurs in a period in which, for the first time in its history, film is credited with an active social power. Film was considered capable of changing (parts of) society, because of its popularity. Not only intellectual and left-wing film critics like Harry Alan Potamkin or Siegfried Kracauer seemed to realize this, but also political movements, left-wing agitators as well as conservative—even religious and fascist forces learned what film could do—tried to enhance their grip on it. Although this evolution is most visible in Europe, with the films of the Popular Front in France, of the Nazi Propaganda Ministry, and of the Stalinist Soviet Union, it also occurred in Hollywood. For the same reasons that motivated Goebbels, Shumyatsky, Blum and, later, McCarthy, political forces tried to intervene in Hollywood.[7] Hollywood was believed to influence people through its popularity, and unprecedented figures in film attendance as well as studio employment made Hollywood a major factor in American society. Intentionally or not, many famous movies of the era dealt with politics.[8]

But the synthesis of the popular and the political in the thirties and forties goes even further. Hollywood-historiographers have also unearthed the less known parts of that history. Numerous popular histories of film have laid bare its presence in such examples as the thirties and forties screwball comedies (it is easy to visualize Sasha as a furious Katherine Hepburn), the film noir of the forties, the battles between the mafia-controlled IATSE union and the progressive CSU union of Herb Sorrell, the conspiracies and covert hostilities of the HUAC hearing commissions and the blacklists, all of which are alluded to in ***Vineland.***[9] The blacklisting is one of the better examples demonstrating this synthesis: Hollywood stars trying to save their status and popularity by defending themselves against political charges or selling out political adversaries. Some of these aspects are mentioned in ***Vineland,*** others are only implied or go unnoticed.

One such aspect is popular film historiography itself. It emerges in the period Sasha symbolizes: the late thirties, the forties, and the beginning of the fifties. Of course, magazines, the trade press, and papers had always reported on the rights and wrongs of Hollywood and its stars. But from the forties onward the emergence of gossip-history (as introduced by Kenneth Anger in *Hollywood Babylon*), of unchecked oral history (synthesized by Kevin Brownlow in *The Parade's Gone By*), of official film-buff history, and of the first legitimate star-biographies, have provided popular film historiography with its methodological and narrative foundations. Not surprisingly, then, this period is remembered through oral speech (Sasha and Hubbell's stories to Frenesi), through gossip (Sasha and Hubbell's stories on their contemporaries) and through an abundance of biographical details (the personal histories of Sasha and Hubbell before they met). Like popular historiography, the exposition of Sasha and Hubbell's stories is incomplete and liable to change depending on the source, as Sasha reflects,

> Maybe we all had to submit to History, she figured, maybe not—but refusing to take shit from some named and specified source—well, it might be a different story.
>
> (80)

Frenesi's opinion of some of these sources (her parents) also emphasizes this: "Frenesi found she'd been switching back and forth, as if cutting together reverse shots of two actors" (81-82).

Finally, the witch-hunting and cold war paranoia of the fifties in Hollywood turned politics into an undesirable business, best left to the government, creating anxiety and fear, and re-shaping the relation with the popular into one of dependence and complicity rather than of synthesis. The new deal between popular culture and politics was definitely over and politics were banned from America's theaters:

> By now the Hollywood fifties is this way-over-length, multitude-of-hands rewrite—except there's no sound, of course, nobody talks. It's a silent movie.
>
> (82)

Frenesi Gates: The Documentary and Counter-Culture

The sixties, the second frame of reference in ***Vineland,*** reflect a shift toward an underground culture. This shift is accompanied by a similar shift in attention from the popular Hollywood film to the depiction of reality by the documentary, appropriately associated with that unofficial culture. Although ***Vineland*** contains references to other underground elements, particularly with regard to Zoyd Wheeler, the novel clearly concentrates upon the documentary. The history of the sixties is told in ***Vineland*** by way of the story of Frenesi Gates. Again, the method is retrospective. We get to know her past by way of the present. Prairie watches the images her mother made on a Movieola 16mm. Like the story of Sasha, Frenesi's is also divided in two parts, although in a more integrated way. It is told not only as her own but also as that of others, the members of the film collective she is part of. Clearly in search for legitimation, Frenesi takes over, together with the Pisks, the Death to the Pig Nihilist Film Kollective and renames it 24fps. The aim of 24fps is not only to capture reality, but also to observe and expose the confrontation between the official culture and the counter-culture, as if it were some kind of guerrilla warfare. Hence, the manifesto of 24fps opens with the statement that "A camera is a gun. An image taken is a death performed" (197). Within the collective, Frenesi and the Pisks assume a neutral position. The others range from realists (trying to capture reality) to dangerous dreamers (longing for revolution). During its short-lived existence, 24fps manages to play an active part in a major campus riot, its violent repression, and the death of a student-leader.

The function of Frenesi in the plot is that of a catalyst, but her general attitude is symbolic for the attempts of the film medium to stay tuned with the era. As such, Frenesi's actions within 24fps are indicative of the evolution of popular film. Hollywood film had lost touch with youth culture. That role was now assumed by the documentary. In reaction to the excesses of the fusion of politics and film in the Nazi propaganda film, or the American *Why We Fight* series, or even the didactic and expository British and Russian films of the forties, the documentary movement tried to rehabilitate itself by no longer trying to press reality into an argument, but rather by letting reality speak for itself, by just observing it. This is exactly the role that Frenesi wants 24fps to play, in keeping with "the 24 frames-per-second truth she still believed in" (241). This observatory mode led documentary makers back to popular subjects. Instead of zooming in on political faces and endless speeches, or argumenting away from reality, documentary makers discovered that the subjects best suited for observation were exactly the symbols of the counter-culture.[10]

Like Frenesi, who thinks that by peeping through a lens she is able to capture reality and the soul of people, documentary filmmakers soon found themselves attuned to their subjects. ***Vineland*** illustrates this in the way the history of Frenesi is told. It is displayed by archival footage which Prairie watches in isolation. Instead of trying to re-tell history through oral comments, gossip, and biographical details, the era is visualized through film stock on which the life of Frenesi has been captured. This footage is claimed to be much more "realistic" or true than oral history, by just showing truth without argumenting about it. There are no multiple and changing points of view; there is just Prairie in front of a Movieola onto which the sixties are projected: "reel after reel went turning, carrying Prairie back to and through an America of the olden days she'd mostly never seen" (198).

Since the reels are documentary footage, they appear to Prairie as the one and only truth, the 24 frames-per-second truth her mother believed in. And, in keeping with this truthfulness, the story of 24fps is told in a classical scopophilic, narrative style, as if an invisible, objective witness (the camera) bore courtroom testimony on reality.

Still, not all is clear. Although the footage shows the reality of the counter-culture Frenesi and her friends belong to, there still remain gaps. There are no images (left) of the murder of Weed Atman; there are only blurry, shaky, and unsharp images of what exactly happened on campus; there is the explicit presence of artificial light sources; there is the intervention of Ditzah to help Prairie decipher some images, and in one case even provide her with information she would not have found without help: "Guess who, Prairie"—"Brock Vond? Can you put it on pauze, freeze it?" (199). Here, Ditzah helps Prairie to observe reality more than once by repeating its images. Above all, however, the impression prevails that the events shown on the Movieola are not only depicted but also staged by the film collective and Frenesi. Once more, ***Vineland*** is indicative for the evolution of documentary film. The observatory mode of filming tends, after a while, to cut off the filmmakers from their subjects; they are not able to show multiple points of view, they are not able to interact with them. Documentary filmers created a new trend in trying to establish this interaction: they began to interfere with their subjects, providing at least multiple viewpoints on truth through, for instance, cross-cutting pro and contra and interviews.[11] Thus, the documentary maker, like Rex and Frenesi in 24fps, or like Ditzah in rewinding the reel on which Brock Vond can be seen, not only exposes or observes, but also interferes or at least interacts with the event.

Prairie Wheeler: Television and Contemporary Culture

The third frame of reference is that of Prairie Wheeler. It takes up most of the novel, occasionally interrupted for brief historical recollections, and foregrounds the blurring of several media, all within the context of the all-encompassing Tube. But the presence of television does not exclude film as a point of reference. Far from it. Many of the references to television are, one way or another, linked to film. The best examples are the fictitious titles of films-shown-on-television already mentioned. Others include the stars and/or characters who have a film as well as a television career: Clint Eastwood (28), Mr. Sulu (40), Superman and Tarzan (116), Daffy Duck (210), Jack Palance (220), Leonard Nimoy (220). Still another example concerns the lack of discrimination of the male characters, especially Zoyd and Hector, in relation to what they are watching: films, shows or series. As Sid and Ernie put it, with regard to Hector: "[He] wants to be the Popeye Doyle of the eighties. Not just the movie, but *Hector II,* then the network series" (338).[12]

The way in which ***Vineland*** presents television is the logical result of the popular history of film, thus linking it to the frames of reference of Sasha and Frenesi. Television combines the features of Hollywood film and underground documentary, synthesizing them into a powerful medium. Television is the ultimate consequence of Hollywood. It was conceived as a medium to entertain, a commodity to please people, just like Hollywood film.[13] In addition, television also employs documentary elements. In newsflashes, television documentaries, talk shows, and special news reports we find the same devices that once constituted the underground documentary film movement. Its major modes—observation, exposition, and, to some extent, interaction—are applied in television. By combining these features, television is at once politics, Hollywood, underground, and documentary, hence connected with popular culture throughout several eras. More importantly, with this combination and connection, television inherits the frames of reference of Sasha, embodying illusionism as well as politics, and that of Frenesi, embodying camera-truth and counter-culture credibility.

But Prairie's frame of reference exceeds a logical synthesis of the previous two. It is also different from these. Television transcends popular film in two major ways: by a new mode of representation and its political ability to domesticate. Both are reflected upon in ***Vineland.*** To the development from the expository and agitational mode (Sasha), and the observatory and interactive mode (Frenesi), Prairie's character adds another: the reflexive or reflective mode. Throughout the novel, Prairie's actions are not so much determined by the world around her, nor by her own self, as was the case with respectively Sasha and Frenesi, but rather by the particular histories she is confronted with. Instead of acting, Prairie mostly is reflecting. While watching the footage of 24fps, she becomes aware of the mediating elements in the history she observes. The novel foregrounds this mediation by regularly cutting from the story-in-the-story to the characters watching and commenting upon it:

> And here came Frenesi Gates's reverse shot. Prairie felt the two women shift in their seats. Frenesi's eyes, even on the aging ECO stock, took over the frame, a defiance of blue unfadable,
>
> (195)

and

> Prairie pointing at the screen, 'who're all these folks?' It was a slow pan shot of 24fps as constituted on some long-ago date the two women were unable now to agree on.
>
> (196)

Whenever in ***Vineland*** the plot is paused in favor of background information, which reaches the reader through "some" medium, the characters, especially Prairie, make explicit this narrative procedure, and warn against its potential to distort the "real" truth. Through Prairie we learn that the stories of Sasha and Frenesi are but that: stories. They aspire to truth but, as the mediations make clear, they basically remain stories.

Since all stories in the novel, true or not, remain stories, the political force in all of them is eviscerated. In order to have public significance, film cannot base its legitimacy on stories that may not even be true. It needs uncontested truths it can interpret. In Prairie's frame of reference, these are no longer available. Instead, the history which Sasha and Frenesi claimed to be meaningful to all people is privatized and domesticated. So Prairie, and Prairie alone, can give meaning to the archival footage of 24fps, even though the two other women present actually participated in it:

> At some point Prairie understood that the person behind the camera most of the time really was her mother, and that if she kept her mind empty she could absorb, conditionally become, Frenesi, share her eyes, feel, when the frame shook with fatigue or fear or nausea. Frenesi's whole body there, as much as her mind choosing the frame, her will to go out there, load the roll, get the shot. Prairie floated, ghostly light of head, as if Frenesi were dead but in a special way, a minimum-security arrangement, where limited visits, mediated by projector and screen, were possible.
>
> (199)

Only through her special bond with Frenesi (mother-daughter) can Prairie more or less tune in to what the 24fps archives really signified. Only by reflecting upon the mediatic distortion itself can popular film/television continue to pretend it is connected with reality.

Beyond this reflexive mode, ***Vineland*** accredits television with the ability to "perform" reality. One of the main characteristics of contemporary television is the way in which it stages reality, rather than showing it. Elaborating upon the conditions used to capture sports reports and press conferences, documentaries from the mid-eighties on regularly emphasize production values, creating their footage as under Hollywood conditions.[14] Pynchon anticipates this evolution by showing, at the start of his novel, the reader just that: the *mise-en-scène* of reality as Zoyd Wheeler stages his own yearly routine of eccentricity by jumping through a window (3-12). For safety reasons, and to spare costs, the window has even been replaced by a fake one:

> He knew the instant he hit that something was funny. There was hardly any impact, and it all felt and sounded different [. . .] Zoyd had tumbled, he was no media innocent, he read *TV Guide* and had just remembered an article about stunt windows made of clear sheet candy, which would break but not cut.
>
> (11-12)

Later on, the performative mode is expanded to characters whose history has been told through mediatic distortions and who reportedly have died: the Thanatoids, with Weed Atman as the most prominent example. These supposed-to-be-dead characters spend their days in a resort near Vineland, addicted to what staged their deaths: the media. It is as if Pynchon wanted his readers to realize that actually no camera can be a gun and that no image taken is a death performed.

Conclusion: Reel to Real and Back Again

> Later, seeing older movies on the Tube [. . .], making for the first time a connection between the far-off images and her real life, it seemed she had misunderstood everything, paying too much attention to the raw emotions, the easy conflicts, when something else, some finer drama the Movies had never considered worth ennobling, had been unfolding all the time.
>
> (81-82)

Vineland synthesizes three concepts of representing reality and film within three frames of reference. They cannot be isolated from each other. Similar to the women's line of descent in ***Vineland,*** from Sasha to Frenesi to Prairie, these three concepts are strongly intertwined, depending upon each other. Yet they each possess clear and unique characteristics. In the first frame of reference, Sasha believes her actions can alter reality and, later, expose that same reality for what it really is: political. On the whole, Sasha is active, directing her attention to the world. In the second frame, Frenesi believes she can observe the truth of reality and, later, interact with it from her counter-cultural point of view. On the whole, she remains rather passive (as in her relation with Brock Vond), directing her attention mainly to herself. In the third frame, Prairie believes her view of reality is reflexive, always taking her active self and mediatic distortions into account, and performative, since it can be staged. Prairie directs her attention and her actions to her personal history, thus trying to make her way through reality. ***Vineland*** intercuts these three connected and yet distinct modes, with three frames of reference to film. In the first, Sasha and Hubbell are contextualized by the introduction of politics in Hollywood film. In the second, Frenesi is placed against the evolution of the era's "most real" medium: the documentary. The development from observation to interaction matches that within 24fps. In the third, Prairie is placed in the context of the heir to popular film and documentary, television, and its reflexive and performative consequences. In ***Vineland,*** Pynchon tells a significant story of America in the eighties, the era in which Ronald Reagan, as actor/president, synthesized political culture, the recuperated underground and the all-encompassing media. It leads the characters not to action, creation, or agitation, but to commodification and domestication, significantly encapsulated by the novel's last word: "home."

Notes

I would like to thank Luc Herman of Antwerp University and Johan Callens and Ann-Sophie D'hondt of the Free University of Brussels for their comments on earlier versions of this paper.

1. Pynchon's knowledge of film has not ceased to fascinate his critics. According to David Cowart, he almost began his career as a film critic for *Esquire* (Cowart, 1980: 33). Pynchon criticism also frequently alludes to the connection between his work and film. See, for instance, Richard Poirier (Mendelson, 1978: 167-78), Frank Kermode (Mendelson, 1978: 162-66), David Cowart (1980), Johan Callens (1991), Joseph Tabbi (Green. 1994: 89-100).

2. I will take the female genealogy for granted here, although its construction is clearly connected with Pynchon's treatment of the media (and film in particular). Other contributions offer solid arguments for this connection. Patricia A. Bergh (1997) elaborates on the presentation of a woman's genealogy in Pynchon's novels. She also connects it with Pynchon treatment of popular culture, and with his references to film and other media. Her focus is mainly on how Pynchon's view on the image of woman is constructed. Another account of *Vineland*'s preoccupation with film and gender is provided by Stacey Olster (Green et al., 1994: 119-34). She concentrates on how Pynchon acknowledges or ignores feminist film criticism in his depiction of women characters and references in *Vineland.* Barbara L. Pittman (1992) uses a gender-focus to deal with *Vineland*'s treatment of genealogy, history, and the political left. Lynn Spigel (1995) does not mention Pynchon, but the way in which she develops an argument on the connection between women's memories and mediatic representation shows striking similarities with *Vineland.*

3. Sasha's conception of politics is clearly left-wing liberal, influenced by new deal politics (populism and corporatism). This basic conception resounds in the frames of Frenesi and Prairie as well, colored by the leftism of their era. Decentralization and individualism instead of Nixon-bureaucracy and hierarchy for Frenesi, and apathy and irony instead of eighties optimism for Prairie. The political antipode is, of course, embodied by Brock Vond, enemy of the three women.

4. *Gravity's Rainbow* is, in fact, often interpreted as cinematic. See Poirier (Mendelson, 1978: 173); Cowart, 1980: 31-62; Hume, 1987: 65, 103, 171; Weisenburger, 1988: 91, 313-14, 209). Elaborate treatment of film and *Gravity's Rainbow* is provided in the chapters: "*Gravity's Rainbow* as the Incredible Moving Film" (Moore, 1987: 30-62) and "*Gravity's Rainbow*: Text as Film—Film as Text" (Berressem, 1993: 151-90).

5. Berressem writes: "*Vineland* is filled with references to movies and TV series, both real and imaginary—mostly science fiction, horror movies, TV game shows, cop shows, sitcoms, and cartoons." Further on, he also mentions the docudrama, the horror movie, the karate movie, the war movie, the Mafia movie, and the monster movie (Berressem, 1993: 188).

6. To some extent, the connection between the story and different modes of reality in film is already touched upon in these simple examples: Henry Kissinger, Robert Musil, and Gordon Liddy did exist. So do the prison of Sing Sing, George Lucas and his crew, and the "mouth-muscle nuances" of Clint Eastwood. Popeye Doyle is a more complex reference, but this character in the movie which tells the story of New York police officer Eddie Egan is also based upon reality (for an elaboration see note 12). The reference to John Carpenter is an exception, but here the initial meaning of "carpenter" strangely coincides with the imagined outlook of the building the proper name is connected with.

7. See Bordwell & Thompson (1994). p. 292-319. 332-36, 372-73.

8. Examples are not hard to find. Some of the obvious include *Modern Times* (1936), *Fury* (1936), *Mr. Smith Goes to Washington* (1938), *Young Mr. Lincoln* (1939), *The Grapes of Wrath* (1940), *The Great Dictator* (1940), *Sergeant York* (1941), *Meet John Doe* (1941) or even *Objective Burma* (1942). Andrew Bergman's renowned history of movies in the thirties treats these and other films as a historical source (See Bergman. 1971: acknowledgments).

9. See Bergman (1971), Friedrich (1986).

10. Examples are the Direct Cinema documentaries of D. A. Pennebaker and Richard Leacock. Their film on Bob Dylan and The Band, *Don't Look Back,* and their registrations of pop concerts, like *Monterey Pop,* are exemplary. But also *Woodstock, Let It Be,* Frederick Wiseman's films, like *Titicut Follies* and the films of the Robert Drew Unit, are noted for this style (Nichols, 1991; Bordwell & Thompson, 1994; 667-68).

11. Examples include documentary films like the Maysles brothers' *Gimme Shelter,* Jim McBride's *David Holtzman's Diary,* Shirley Clarke's *Portrait of Jason,* Allen King's *A Married Couple,* but also films that do not use the "documentary" label, but are clearly influenced by its evolution, such as the avant-garde films of Kenneth Anger, Stan Brakhage and Jonas Mekas, the improvisations of John Cassavetes, and even the exhibitionist portrayals of Andy Warhol's film unit. For an overview see: Bordwell & Thompson (1994) p. 667-72 and Rosenthal (1971).

12. The genealogy of the Popeye Doyle character provides an example of how far the relation between reality and its representation can be stretched. It also invites a further comparison between Hector Zuniga and Popeye Doyle. Initially, the story of Popeye Doyle was based on the real careers of Eddie Egan and, to a lesser extent, Sonny Grosso, two New York police officers. Robin Moore wrote a book on them, focusing on Egan. When the movie *The French Connection,* based on the book, went into production in 1971, Egan co-operated as technical adviser. He and

Grosso even got small parts in it. After *The French Connection* movie of 1972, a sequel, *French Connection II,* was produced in 1975. In 1986, *Popeye Doyle,* the TV-movie, was produced, eventually leading to a series.

13. Of course, there are numerous differences between film and television, but from *Vineland*'s point of view television does not differ that much from film. Both are supported by the same structure of financing and modes of production. The same corporate enterprises which invest in Hollywood invest in television. Classical Hollywood film and television fiction also follow the same storytelling tradition (realistic illusionism), the same narrative structure (plot driven-climax), the same formalism (scopophilic and semi-point of view), and the same star cult.

14. This evolution results in shows such as *Top Cops, Rescue 911, I Witness Video,* or *America's Most Wanted* (Nichols, 1994: 45).

Works Cited

Allen, Robert and Douglas Gomery. *Film History: Theory and Practice.* New York: Knopff, 1985.

Anger, Kenneth. *Hollywood Babylon.* New York: Simon and Shuster, 1975 [1958].

Bergh, Patricia. "(De)constructing the Image: Thomas Pynchon's Postmodern Woman." *Journal of Popular Culture* 30 (1997): 1-12.

Bergman, Andrew. *We're in the Money.* New York: New York UP, 1971.

Berressem, Hanjo. *Pynchon's Poetics: Interfacing Theory and Text.* Urbana-Chicago: U of Illinois P, 1993.

Bordwell, David and Kristin Thompson. *Film History: An Introduction.* New York: McGraw-Hill, 1994.

Brownlow, Kevin. *The Parade's Gone By.* New York: Knopff. 1968.

Callens, Johan. "Tubed Out and Movie Shot in Pynchon's *Vineland.*" *Pynchon Notes* 28-29 (1991): 115-41.

Cowart, David. *Thomas Pynchon: The Art of Allusion.* Carbondale & Edwardsville: Southern Illinois UP, 1980.

Friedrich, Otto. *City of Nets: A Portrait of Hollywood in the 1940's.* New York: Harper & Row, 1986.

Green, Geoffrey, Donald J. Greiner and Larry McCaffery (eds.). *The* Vineland *Papers: Critical Takes on Pynchon's Novel.* Normal (Ill.): Dalkey Archive P, 1994.

Hume, Kathryn. *Pynchon's Mythography: An Approach to* Gravity's Rainbow. Carbondale and Edwardsville: Southern Illinois UP, 1987.

Mendelson, Edward (ed.), *Pynchon: A Collection of Critical Essays.* Englewood Cliffs: Prentice-Hall, 1978.

Moore. Thomas. *The Style of Connectedness:* Gravity's Rainbow *and Thomas Pynchon.* Columbia: U of Missouri P, 1987.

Nichols. Bill. *Representing Reality: Issues and Concepts in Documentary.* Bloomington: Indiana UP, 1991.

———. *Blurred Boundaries: Questions of Meaning in Contemporary Culture.* Bloomington: Indiana UP, 1994.

Pittman, Barbara L. "Dangerously Absent Dreams: Genealogy, History and the Political Left in *Vineland.*" *Pynchon Notes* 30-31 (1992): 39-52.

Pynchon, Thomas. *Gravity's Rainbow.* London: Picador-Jonathan Cape, 1973.

———. *Vineland.* London: Minerva, 1990.

Rosenthal, Alan. *The New Documentary in Action.* Berkeley: U of California P, 1971.

Spigel, Lynn. "From the Dark Ages to the Golden Age: Women's Memories and Television Reruns." *Screen* 36 (1995): 16-33.

Weisenburger, Steven. *A* Gravity's Rainbow *Companion: Sources and Contexts for Pynchon's Novel.* Athens: U of Georgia P, 1988.

David Thoreen (essay date summer 2001)

SOURCE: Thoreen, David. "Thomas Pynchon's Political Parable: Parallels between *Vineland* and 'Rip Van Winkle.'" *ANQ* 14, no. 3 (summer 2001): 45-50.

[*In the following essay, Thoreen compares the theme, plot, and setting of* Vineland *with Washington Irving's "Rip Van Winkle."*]

As a historical novelist whose subject is America and whose passion is politics, Thomas Pynchon is aware of the twentieth-century evolution of "the imperial presidency."[1] ***Vineland*** (1990), Pynchon's fourth novel, reflects the steady encroachment in that century of the executive branch on the legislative[2] and dramatizes some of the attendant threats to Americans' civil liberties. It is fitting, then, that Pynchon has embedded in his novel an extended parallel to an early American political parable, Washington Irving's "Rip Van Winkle." Although Irving's style has been criticized as excessively British, the thematic concerns of "Rip Van Winkle" are distinctly American and are quite relevant to ***Vineland*** and the presidential usurpation of power in the 1980s.[3]

Because readers of Pynchon's texts always stand the risk of "Stencilizing" those texts, that is, of succumbing to their own "unacknowledged desires for [order]" (***Vineland*** 269) by forcing intertextual connections of their own device on a neutral, unsuspecting, and otherwise innocent text, I offer the following extensive treatment of the parallels between "Rip Van Winkle" and ***Vineland.*** In addition to the thematic parallels, I shall mention a few parallels of plot and place. My goal here is not to belabor the point, but to establish definitively the connection between the two and to assure the reader that the novel is not, in my reading, being "Stencilized" (*V.* 228).

Vineland is Pynchon's wake-up call to the American voter, who, like Rip Van Winkle and Pynchon's own protagonist Zoyd Wheeler, has been asleep for twenty years. Indeed, both texts involve scenes of awakening. The first sentence of Pynchon's novel reads, "Later than usual one morning in 1984, Zoyd Wheeler drifted awake in sunlight through a creeping fig . . . with a squadron of blue jays stomping around on the roof" (3), an ominous updating of this midstory passage from "Rip Van Winkle": "On awaking he found himself on the green knoll. . . . He rubbed his eyes—it was a bright, sunny morning. The birds were hopping and twittering among the bushes" (776). Rip has obviously slept later than usual, and Irving points up this irony by having Rip say to himself that "Surely . . . I have not slept here all night" (776). Calling for his dog, Rip is "only answered by the cawing of a flock of idle crows" (777)[4]; these crows are replaced in ***Vineland*** by the blue jays that, in Zoyd's dream, had been carrier pigeons, "each bearing a message for him" (3). The military formation of the blue jays, along with their arrogant "stomping," the "creeping" fig, and the profusion of "messages," evoke the many-tentacled military and government bureaucracies that shape so much of modern life—and their publicly accountable apex, the president and commander-in-chief.[5]

But the parallel does not end here. Both texts also include arrival scenes wherein the protagonists, oddly dressed, are attended by the heckling of children and by feelings of disorientation. As Rip approaches the village, he notes with surprise the costumes worn by its habitants, and when we find that "[t]hey all stared at him with equal marks of surprise," we must recall the outlandishness of Rip's own outmoded dress. As he enters the village itself, "[a] troop of strange children ran at his heels, hooting after him" (778). Similarly, Zoyd, wearing a colorful dress (bought at a discount shop specializing in large sizes, called, appropriately enough, "More Is Less"[6]), and en route to a bar known as the Log Jam, gets stuck in "a convoy of out-of-state Winnebagos . . . among whom . . . he was obliged to gear down and put up with a lot of attention, not all of it friendly" (5). One girl screams that Zoyd "ought to be locked up" (5).

Rip's feelings of disorientation ("The very village was altered—it was larger and more populous . . . his familiar haunts had disappeared . . . every thing was strange" [778]) are echoed by Zoyd's experience at the Log Jam, where "right away he noticed that everything, from the cooking to the clientele, smelled different" (5). The Log Jam has been recently renovated and is now outfitted with "designer barstools" and a "jukebox . . . reformatted to light classical and New Age music that gently peep[s] at the edges of audibility" (5, 6). "[A]bout the only thing that ha[s]n't been replaced [is] the original bar" (7).

Not only the architecture is different, however. On returning to the village, Rip discovers that "[t]he very character of the people seemed changed. There was a busy, bustling disputatious tone about it, instead of the accustomed phlegm and drowsy tranquility" (779). When a "short but busy little fellow . . . pull[s] him by the arm . . . and enquire[s] in his ear 'whether he was Federal or Democrat?'" (779), the uncomprehending Rip gets himself in a tight spot by crying, "Alas . . . I am a poor quiet man, a native of the place, and a loyal subject of the King—God bless him!" (780). Rip has slept through the change in governments; Zoyd and the contemporary American voter have done much the same.

Despite his somnolence, however, Zoyd recognizes that the Log Jam is only the latest in a long line of Vineland County bars to undergo gentrification and that the assiduous remodeling by so many bar owners has worked another kind of change in the "very character of the people." As Zoyd explains to Buster, the owner of the Log Jam: "[O]nly reason I'm up here is 'at the gentrification of South Spooner, Two Street, and other more familiar hellraisin' locales has upped the ante way outa my bracket, these are all folks *now* who like to sue, and for big bucks, with hotshot PI lawyers up from the City" (7, emphasis added). This new litigiousness[7] takes the place, in the late twentieth century, of the early republic's impassioned political discussion. The Vineland County locals are no less "busy" and "disputatious" than the citizenry that greeted Rip Van Winkle, but while that citizenry had fought and won a war for independence (and so cultivated an immediate interest in politics), the loggers that Zoyd meets, "sipping kiwi mimosas" and clad in "three-figure-price-tag jeans by Mme. Gris" (5, 6), are interested only in maintaining the feverish materialism of the 1980s.

Both Rip and Zoyd, then, wind up at drinking establishments, but even before entering both men experience a dislocation akin to finding themselves in foreign countries. For Rip, this dislocation is ironic and literal. He is, of course, in the same geographical area, but that area is now literally a new country:

> Instead of the great tree, that used to shelter the quiet little Dutch inn of yore, there now was reared a tall naked pole . . . and from it was fluttering a flag on

> which was a singular assemblage of stars and stripes—all this was strange and incomprehensible. He recognized on the sign, however, the ruby face of King George under which he had smoked so many a peaceful pipe, but even this was singularly metamorphosed. The red coat was changed for one of blue and buff; a sword was held in the hand instead of a sceptre; the head was decorated with a cocked hat, and underneath was printed in large characters GENERAL WASHINGTON.
>
> (779)

For Zoyd, the dislocation is ironic and metaphorical. The first of "several rude updates" he encounters at the Log Jam is the "collection of upscale machinery parked in the lot, itself newly blacktopped" (5). In response to Buster's claim that he and his clientele are "just country fellas," Zoyd says, "From the looks of your parking lot, the country must be Germany" (7). This metaphor ironically and humorously introduces what will become one of the novel's key themes, the movement in the United States in recent years away from democracy and toward dictatorship. Thus Pynchon's novel updates Irving's story, which marked the transition from monarchy to democracy.

The basis for another parallel is Rip's first view of his grown son. After asking about his old cronies, all apparently dead or gone away, the despairing Rip cries, "Does nobody here know Rip Van Winkle?" At this, two or three startled people exclaim:

> "[O]h to be sure!—that's Rip Van Winkle—yonder—leaning against the tree." Rip looked and beheld a precise counterpart of himself, as he went up the mountain: apparently as lazy, and certainly as ragged! The poor fellow was now completely confounded. He doubted his own identity, and whether he was himself or another man.
>
> (781)

The scene's corollary in ***Vineland*** comes when Zoyd takes his infant daughter north. After hitchhiking to San Francisco, they take the bus the rest of the way. Meanwhile, Zoyd's running buddy Van Meter has agreed to drive Zoyd's car:

> Zoyd caught up with Van Meter in Eureka, at the corner of 4th and H, as, suddenly disoriented, he observed his '64 Dodge Dart, unmistakably his own short, with the LSD paint job . . . and at the wheel a standard-issue Hippie Freak who looked *just like him.* Woo-oo! An unreal moment for everybody, with the driver staring twice as weirdly *right back at Zoyd!*
>
> (315)

In Irving's story, Rip's identity crisis is a synechdochic reproduction of the early republic's crisis of political identity. The question of Federal or Democrat, first foregrounded by Rip's arrival at the polling place on Election Day, is quickly overwhelmed by Rip's pledged allegiance to King George, reminding us of the more fundamental shift from monarchy to democracy. In ***Vineland,*** the shift in the political paradigm is similarly fundamental. Although Zoyd's moment of identity crisis occurs in a flashback to 1970 or '71, the zeitgeist to which the flashback refers sets up an implicit contrast between the mid-sixties and 1984, when he arrives at the Log Jam.

But rather than presenting the mid-sixties as the moment of ultimate freedom, Pynchon presents that time as the halfway point between a "green free America" and a "scabland garrison state" of the future (314). In San Francisco, the halfway point of his journey up the coast, Zoyd and Mucho Maas listen to and are comforted by *The Best of Sam Cooke,* "though outside spread the lampless wastes, the unseen paybacks, the heartless power of the scabland garrison state the green free America of their childhoods even then was turning into" (314). More is involved, however, than the simple modulation of a Democratic administration into a Republican one. Indeed, the fact that the Vietnam War was prosecuted by the administrations of both parties (and dramatically escalated by a Democratic one) suggests that party politics has little to do with the real change in America's political direction. As in Irving's story, then, Zoyd's identity crisis points to a shift from one political order to another—in this case, from democracy to dictatorship.

In addition to these parallels, Pynchon counters Rip's "naturally . . . thirsty soul" (776) with Zoyd's once-regular marijuana use and tubal intoxication, physiological manifestations of the political apathy displayed by the majority of Americans since the 1970s. That there are reasons for that apathy is beside the point: Pynchon is not interested in excuses, but effects. As Pynchon himself put it in **"Nearer, My Couch, to Thee"**:

> In this century we have come to think of Sloth as primarily political, a failure of public will allowing the introduction of evil policies and the rise of evil regimes, the worldwide fascist ascendancy of the 1920's and 30's being perhaps Sloth's finest hour, though the Vietnam era and the Reagan-Bush years are not far behind.
>
> (57)

Neither is Rip's invocation of the tyrant George III irrelevant, considering the Reagan administration's systematic attempts to extend its authority while avoiding accountability. The message sent to Zoyd "from forces unseen" is that Johnson is no longer in the White House, and it is time to start paying attention (3).[8]

Notes

1. The phrase is the title of Arthur M. Schlesinger, Jr.'s study of executive aggrandizement, first published in 1973, the same year as *Gravity's Rainbow,* a novel

that features a Nixon look-alike driving a "black Managerial Volkswagen" like a mad führer down the Los Angeles freeways (755).

2. For a concise history of executive aggrandizement, including an account of the judiciary branch's reluctance to hear cases involving such issues, see Jules Lobel's excellent discussion. For more detailed, although less contemporary discussions, see Rossiter and Schlesinger.
3. A more extensive discussion of the historical and thematic context surrounding this parallel appears in my article "The President's Emergency War Powers and the Erosion of Civil Liberties in Pynchon's *Vineland,*" *Oklahoma City University Law Review* 24 (1999): 761-98.
4. After Rip's twenty-year nap, his dog Wolf has "disappeared" (777). Similarly, Zoyd's dog Desmond disappears for much of *Vineland.* Rumored a ghost dog, "spotted out by *Shade Creek* . . . with a pack of dispossessed pot-planters' dogs . . . who were *haunting* the local pastures" (357, emphasis added), Desmond returns "home" only on the last page of the novel (385).
5. Readers of *Gravity's Rainbow* will also recall the intelligence messages delivered to Pirate Prentice via V-2 rockets and the grating high-ranking government voice that "tells Pirate now there's a message addressed to him, waiting at Greenwich" (11).
6. Pynchon's pun here also reverses the 1980s mantra of minimalist fiction.
7. We see another sign of the litigiousness that has come to dominate American life later in the novel when, in a burst of nostalgia for "the malls [she'd] grown up with," Zoyd's daughter Prairie recalls that "there even used to be ice rinks, back when insurance was affordable, she could remember days . . . where all they did for hours was watch kids skate" (326).
8. The Great Society and the Civil Rights movement notwithstanding, Johnson occupies no idealized (or even privileged) position in either Pynchon's political reckoning or in the history of executive aggrandizement. I invoke Johnson's administration not because he represents the high point of civil libertarianism in America but because Zoyd's lack of attention and political responsibility can be traced to Johnson's years in office. The earliest flashback dealing with Zoyd dramatizes his years in Gordita Beach, "shortly after Reagan was elected governor of California" (22), which would be 1966.

Works Cited

Irving, Washington. "Rip Van Winkle." *Washington Irving: History, Tales and Sketches.* Ed. James Tuttleton. New York: Library of America. 769-85.

Lobel, Jules. "Emergency Power and the Decline of Liberalism." *Yale Law Journal* 98 (1989): 1385-433.

Pynchon, Thomas. *Gravity's Rainbow.* New York: Viking, 1973.

———. "Nearer, My Couch, to Thee." *New York Times Book Review* 6 June 1993: 3+.

———. *V.* 1963. New York: Perennial-Harper, 1990.

———. *Vineland.* New York: Penguin, 1991.

Rossiter, Clinton L. *Constitutional Dictatorship: Crisis Government in the Modern Democracies.* Princeton: Princeton UP, 1948.

Schlesinger, Arthur M., Jr. *The Imperial Presidency.* Rev. ed. Boston: Houghton, 1989.

Matthew Eklund (essay date summer 2001)

SOURCE: Eklund, Matthew. "Pynchon's *The Crying of Lot 49.*" *Explicator* 59, no. 4 (summer 2001): 216-18.

[*In the following essay, Eklund considers the importance of musical signifiers in* The Crying of Lot 49.]

For Oedipa Maas in Thomas Pynchon's novel ***The Crying of Lot 49,*** the world of the sign is one that she would transcend to know the meaning behind the post horn and the reality of the Tristero. Such knowledge, though, must remain uncertain because she can only "recognize signals like that, as the epileptic is said to—an odor, color, pure piercing grace note announcing his seizure" (95). Indeed, Pynchon's metaphor of the epileptic attack is appropriate for a world where only signals or signifiers remain "but never the central truth itself," no remnant of the signified that may have existed before the onset of the seizure (95). It is within the context of this epileptic world where Oedipa must search for the meaning behind the "clues, announcements, imitations" that define her reality (95). The post horn and the organizations associated with it are the dominant signifiers in the novel, but another that is often in the background but important nevertheless is the representation of music. Music in ***The Crying of Lot 49*** is always in some way artificial, with the effect that real music—natural sounds produced by true musicians—has been replaced by musical signifiers that exist outside the original music that they signify. The musical signifiers include the Paranoids, Baby Igor's song, the Scope's "music policy," the Yoyodyne songfest, and finally, Muzak.

The first example of how musical signifiers have replaced their original is the teenage band that Oedipa meets early in the novel. This band is obviously an imitation of another—the lead singer, Miles, has a

"Beatle haircut," and Oedipa asks, "Why do you sing with an English accent?" (27). Of course, the band's manager says they "should sing like that," so they "watch English movies a lot, for the accent" (27). The Paranoids, then, are simply an image; their music is a representation of another band's music, perhaps the Beatles or possibly "Sick Dick and the Volkswagens," another English group whose song Oedipa hears Mucho, her husband, whistling (23). The fact is that nobody can tell what band the Paranoids stand for, only that they and their music are an image.

The meaning of musical signifiers sinks deeper into uncertainty when in Oedipa's motel room, Metzger hears Baby Igor's song on television. The song is part of Metzger's childhood movie, *Cashiered,* and the song itself is attached to an image on television, so it is not surprising that the narcissistic Metzger sings along. If Metzger's youthful image is what prompts him to sing, then the signifier, Baby Igor's song, is dictating the meaning of the signified, the real musical sounds coming from Metzger's vocal chords. And because Metzger does not exist outside his own youthful image on television, the musical signifier must lose any certain meaning.

Later Oedipa encounters the music scene in the Scope bar. "A sudden chorus of whoops and yibbles burst from a kind of jukebox," and Oedipa finds out that the Scope is "the only bar in the area [. . . with] a strictly electronic music policy" (48). Whether "whoops and yibbles" can be considered music is anyone's guess, but in this case it is how the music is produced that suggests that electronic or artificial sounds render the existence of real musicians uncertain. The bartender informs Oedipa and Metzger that in the live jam sessions held in the Scope "they put it on the tape live" (48). If electronic music was ever meant to signify the natural sounds of real music, then that possibility is blurred even more when musicians only appear live in order to encapsulate their music in yet another imitation, the tape. Therefore, the sound is removed from its source, and the original shrinks only further into the background.

Even traditional or sentimental music does not retain the meaning of its original sound, as in the Yoyodyne stockholders' meeting, where they hold a company songfest. A song that would in another setting have great emotional importance, "the tune of Cornell's alma mater," is butchered into a corporate hymn that contains none of the music's original meaning (83). The same goes for "the tune of 'Aura Lee,'" which in its original form would have had sentimental meaning, but in the world of mixed musical signifiers it can also be associated with a lifeless corporate entity (83).

The final but perhaps most telling of the musical signifiers is Muzak, which is music designed to imitate other well-known tunes. At the beginning of the novel, when Oedipa is at the market in Kinneret-Among-The-Pines, she hears "the Fort Wayne Settecento Ensemble's variorum recording of the Vivaldi Kazoo Concerto, Boyd Beaver, soloist" (10). The Muzak is supposed to be a representation of a Vivaldi concerto, and the link between the signifier and the signified seems clear enough. But also at the end of the novel, when Oedipa confronts Mucho at his radio station, Mucho suddenly begins talking about a passage of violin music, and "it dawned on her that he was talking about the Muzak." She does not notice it at first because it had "been seeping in, in its subliminal, unidentifiable way" (141). The sad truth behind this statement is that Muzak, even if it is designed to have sounds corresponding to a popular tune, has nothing to do with its original because the reality of Muzak is that it is not meant to be consciously heard or identified. Therefore, the signified original is inconsequential to the existence and pervasiveness of the signifier. Furthermore, if real music is meant to be heard and is meant to make us feel, then Muzak can only have the effect of making us feel nothing by taking the original's place. Indeed, the excess of musical signifiers in ***The Crying of Lot 49*** can only further distance Oedipa from the "epileptic Word" (118).

Work Cited

Pynchon, Thomas. *The Crying of Lot 49.* New York: Harper, 1966.

Samuel Cohen (essay date fall 2002)

SOURCE: Cohen, Samuel. "*Mason & Dixon* & the Ampersand." *Twentieth Century Literature* 48, no. 3 (fall 2002): 264-91.

[In the following essay, Cohen views the ampersand in the title of Mason & Dixon *as an important figure in the novel, corresponding with Pynchon's symbolic use of lines and a shift in the author's literary vision.]*

> "It goes back," he might have begun, "to the second Day of Creation, when 'G-d made the Firmament, from the waters which were under the Firmament,'—thus the first Boundary Line. All else after that, in all History, is but Sub-Division."
>
> —Mr. Edgewise (***Mason & Dixon*** 360-61)

> And wherever you may stand, given the Convexity, each of you is slightly *pointed away* from everybody else. . . . Here in the Earth Concave, everyone is pointed *at* everyone else,—ev'rybody's axes converge,—forc'd at least thus to acknowledge one another,—an entirely different set of rules for how to behave.
>
> —Resident of Terra Concava (***Mason & Dixon*** 741)

> for the Times are as impossible to calculate, this Advent, as the Distance to a Star.
>
> —Rev. Wicks Cherrycoke (***Mason & Dixon*** 6)

The story goes that Thomas Pynchon was heavily involved in the graphic design of his 1997 novel ***Mason & Dixon,*** inside and out. In particular, he is said to have been involved in the making of the novel's cover (Mxyzptlk). The dust jacket comes in two parts, a paper jacket and a transparent overlay. The paper jacket features the title, in an eighteenth-century-looking typeface, magnified and spread across the front and back. On the front of the transparent overlay are the more legibly sized author name and title running across the top and bottom. It is a distinctive design, but it may also serve a purpose other than marketing. Without making too much of something as (by definition) superficial as cover design, we are given space to think about its significance by the fact of Pynchon's attention to its details. One particular detail that I believe is significant results from the way in which the title is expanded and placed—the ampersand that fills the space between author name and title. In effect, the centrally placed ampersand is magnified to the point that it moves from the background to become the central element, more illustration than typography.

The emphasis on the ampersand is likely no accident, because it points to what I will argue is a central idea in the book, one that is essential to its vision and so, also, to its difference from its author's earlier works. ***Mason & Dixon***'s ampersand is more than historically accurate; it expresses the shift in Pynchon's thinking that the novel represents. As he spins a picaresque historical tale in ***Mason & Dixon,*** Pynchon also tells a new, more hopeful story about America, emphasizing relation, connection, and possibility. At the center of this new story is the ampersand.

* * *

Mason & Dixon is in many ways a novel about lines. It is the story of Charles Mason and Jeremiah Dixon, astronomer and surveyor, who from 1763 to 1767 were in charge of drawing and blazing the 233-mile latitudinal line dividing the Penns' Pennsylvania and Lord Calvert's Maryland, the line that later came to divide North from South, free states from slave. The novel follows them, in part 1, "Latitudes and Departures," from their meeting in 1760, when they travel to Cape Town to observe the Transit of Venus between the earth and the sun and help determine the Solar Parallax, to Mason's side trip to St. Helena for further measurement, to their return to London, and finally, in part 2, "America," to their acceptance and execution of a commission to chart the disputed southern border of Pennsylvania. The novel ends in part 3, "Last Transit," with their return to England, Dixon's death, and Mason's eventual relocation to America. The tale is told by the Rev. Wicks Cherrycoke, who was a member of the expedition and who has come to stay (and stay and stay) with family on the occasion of Mason's demise in 1786. Mason, as astronomer, and Dixon, as surveyor, are professionally dedicated to the measuring, charting, and drawing of lines. The task that occupies the majority of their time in the novel is to plot and cut an 8-yard-wide line.

But this is only the first and most obvious way in which ***Mason & Dixon*** is about lines. Pynchon's telling of their story and the story of pre-Revolutionary America contains many kinds of lines, as do the larger contexts within which the story is set. To argue for the ampersand's place as an important figure in the novel, I will first sketch the ways in which the novel is so marked, the ways in which Pynchon understands these stories and their contexts in terms of the metaphor of the line. This metaphor has thus far understandably dominated the novel's reception by reviewers and critics. It is, after all, the word most closely associated with the names of the title characters, in the name given the swath they cut (a name only given, interestingly, long after they created it, and never in the novel itself). I will first read ***Mason & Dixon*** in this way because it is has been the dominant reading in the few years since its publication, with good reason, and because it is in relation to Pynchon's use of the line that his use of the ampersand makes sense, and, ultimately, vice versa. The ways in which the ampersand responds to the line, the ways in which connection and possibility answer division and difference, make ***Mason & Dixon*** something truly new for Pynchon.

* * *

Even before the two title characters receive their assignment in the colonies, ***Mason & Dixon*** is filled with geometry. The first sentence of the novel begins: "Snow-Balls have flown their arcs" (5). The phrase seems a humorous allusion to the opening of ***Gravity's Rainbow*** (1973), "A screaming comes across the sky" (3). There is of course a bathetic drop from the latter to the former, or perhaps an ostensible lightening not just of mood but also of stakes. As becomes clear once the book gets rolling, though, Pynchon brings the reader past or more exactly through the playful and apparently (mostly) accurate eighteenth-century English of his narrator and other characters, and his almost compulsive punning, to arrive at the serious ideas he explores in the novel.[1] While he is clearly being playful—a mood hardly new for his work—and may be establishing a warmer tone than exists in his earlier work, Pynchon is certainly from the start creating a serious world. It is also, from the start, a geometrical world.

As has been noted by many readers, Pynchon's big novels have all had central geometric figures, which are even referred to in their titles: *V.* (1963) has the chevron,

Gravity's Rainbow has the parabola, and ***Mason & Dixon*** has the line. From the arc of the snowball to the Transit of Venus and the Solar Parallax to the equator Mason and Dixon cross in their travels to chart these celestial phenomena, the world of the novel is from its beginning crossed by these straight lines, curved along hemispheres or orbits.

An important aspect of this crisscrossing in the novel is that the lines do not in one sense exist independently of the astronomers and surveyors who chart them and so, in effect, create them. Geometry exists in the abstract, as do laws of gravity and movement; all are assumed to be independent in their own right. However, in their embodiment in concrete, particular instances, they depend on people believing in them, understanding them, and applying them. From particular positions and with precision instruments, Mason and Dixon are able not just to chart the movement of heavenly bodies but also to divide the earth by degrees, to establish where every part of the earth is in relation to every other part, but their ability depends in the end on their belief. Their ability, therefore, provides an apt metaphor for their times. In a nascent America, a creation of the Enlightenment, their applications of science to government, of rationality to the wilderness, embody the claims of the Age of Reason. While the drawing of the line is on a (literally) mundane level, mere surveying and cutting (as the unhappy, stargazing astronomer Mason sometimes sees it), it depends on a belief in the human ability to domesticate the natural.

One important context for the story of this line, then, is the story of the Enlightenment. Pynchon's telling of it is less celebratory than the traditional version and more nuanced than the usual revision. One way to think about Pynchon's version is, conveniently, in terms of lines. The understanding of the Enlightenment that in the twentieth century came under attack saw the eighteenth century as the time, in Kant's words, of "man's emergence from his self-imposed immaturity," as a time when reason reigned supreme, and when, as a result, civilization built up a great, improving head of steam called progress. Fundamental to this story are at least two kinds of lines. First is the line of progress, the inexorably upward-moving line charting intellectual, social, and material improvement. The second kind consists of the lines drawn between concrete things and people. There are the lines of classification and division with which Western science understands the world. These are the lines between the enlightened and the unenlightened, the civilized and the uncivilized, the included and the excluded—and those drawn between abstract ideas—the provable and the unprovable, the rational and the mystical, fact and fiction. The Enlightenment, not just in its intellectual projects—Diderot's *Encyclopédie,* Johnson's dictionary, Linnaeus's taxonomy—but also in its revolutions, French and American, and its imperial and colonial manifestations, depended on and in fact championed the drawing and maintaining of lines. The upward-tending line of progress, then, depended on the drawing of lines of division. As this kind of "progress" continues to be made, this story of the Enlightenment continues to be told.

Theodor Adorno and Max Horkheimer told a different story in the middle of the last century. In their *Dialectic of Enlightenment,* they argue that what has been called Enlightenment and hailed as progress in fact led to the gas chambers. With roots in Marx and Nietzsche, Adorno and Horkheimer and others in and outside of the Frankfurt School saw the belief in human mastery through reason and attempts to impose it on the universe, or "instrumental reason," as the root of the miseries of their contemporary world, miseries that they could not cite as evidence of progress. As Walter Benjamin (also associated with the Frankfurt School) wrote in his "Theses on the Philosophy of History," "There is no document of civilization which is not at the same time a document of barbarism" (*Illuminations* 256). Earlier, Max Weber had told his own version of this story, noting that the classification of the natural world and organization of the human world, what he called the "rationalization" of the world, in effect "disenchanted" it. By drawing lines across experience, Weber argued, the Enlightenment project of understanding and domesticating the world had the unfortunate effect of robbing it of its magic.

Both versions of this story, the traditional and the revised, are recognizable in ***Mason & Dixon.*** The question of what to think of these ideas follows closely behind, carried most prominently in the question of what to think of the line, or "visto," but present also in many of the novel's factual and fantastic, tangential and strangely germane subplots, incidents, and mysteries. However this question is raised, at stake ultimately is the value of the drawing of lines, and all that this action comes to symbolize in the novel, including not only division and classification of the natural and social worlds but also the rationalization of space and time. A focus on the line as the dominant figure in the novel can lead to a reading of Pynchon as squarely on the side of Adorno, Horkheimer, and others in condemning the Enlightenment as the cause of many modern ills. This condemnation would square with the readings many have made of ***V.*** and ***Gravity's Rainbow*** as depicting worlds disfigured by science and modernity. Reading ***Mason & Dixon*** only through the figure of the line yields this same reading, as I will show first. Reading it through both the line and the ampersand, however, complicates things. A thorough condemnation of the period in which he sets this novel is not, I will argue, what Pynchon is making.

As Mason and Dixon progress westward in their cutting of the visto, into the unsettled yet not unpopulated frontier and away from the fast-dividing East, the significance of the visto as embodiment of the Enlightenment is raised in stark relief. Among the more direct ways is the opposition of the Chinese *feng shui* expert Captain Zhang, who, upon learning of their project, asks Mason and Dixon, "you two crazy?" He continues:

> Ev'rywhere else on earth, Boundaries follow Nature,—coast-lines, ridge-tops, river-banks,—so honoring the Dragon or Shan within, from which Land-Scape ever takes its form. To mark a right Line upon the Earth is to inflict upon the Dragon's very Flesh, a sword-slash, a long, perfect scar, impossible for any who live out here the year 'round to see as other than hateful Assault.
>
> (542)

Zhang recognizes the brutal, incongruous regularity of the line as an attack on the very nature of things. The Dragon within the earth is dishonored and wounded by the incising of a right line into its flesh, into the living flesh of nature. The Enlightenment roots of the line are here expressly criticized from a non-Western perspective.

Zhang's criticisms go beyond the nature of the line itself to a more pointed indictment of its effects. He asks, "Shall wise Doctors one day write History's assessment of the Good resulting from this Line, vis-à-vis the not-so-good? I wonder which list would be longer" (666) and later characterizes the line as a "conduit for Evil" (701). The list enumerating the not-so-good effects of the visto—and of the other lines it comes to represent—can be drawn from many parts of the novel. Lines to which our attention is drawn include those between black and white, which we encounter early in Cape Town, later in the colonies, and in the backs of our minds whenever we remember what the Mason-Dixon line came to divide; the related line between Native Americans and the settlers and colonists who pushed them westward; that between Old World and New, between hoary, tradition-bound Europe and the New Eden of America, which the founding-fathers-to-be and would-be Adams into whom Mason and Dixon run are intent on fixing; the line between those included in this new paradise and those excluded; the line between Elect and Preterite, Saved and Damned; the line between the empirically known and the possible unknown, what the novel calls the indicative and the subjunctive, the former of which they set out from in the form of the governed, measured world of bureaucratic administration, and the latter of which they quickly emerge into in the form of talking dogs, amorous mechanical ducks, the 11 lost days created by the switch from the Julian to the Gregorian calendars, the race that lives on the inside of the earth, the ghost of Mason's wife, and many other fantastic yet plausibly presented phenomena; and the line between fact and fiction, history and romance in eighteenth-century terms, a line highlighted by the form of the novel itself, which takes the strands of actual historical events and weaves fiction from them.

Each of these lines can be read as Zhang reads the visto, as conduits for evil. The line between black and white is first examined during Mason and Dixon's stay in the Cape Town home of the Vrooms, where Mason is recruited to impregnate one of the family's slaves to help produce light-skinned stock. It reappears most plainly for them in America, prompting Dixon at one point to say:

> —and now here we are again, in another Colony, this time having drawn them a line between their Slave-Keepers, and their Wage-Payers, as if doom'd to re-encounter thro' the World this public Secret, this shameful Core. . . . Christ Mason. . . . Where does it end? No matter where in it we go, shall we find all the World Tyrants and Slaves? America was the one place we should not have found them.
>
> (692-93)

Finding all the world tyrants and slaves means uncovering a shameful secret, a concealed truth of the Enlightenment world, namely that freedom is reserved only for some. Even an incipient America, a land soon to proclaim all men equal, hides this truth, and not very well. Near the end of their time in America, Dixon tears the whip from the hand of a slave driver busy beating his property, whom Dixon frees. The act is clearly heroic, and a judgment of the place in which it occurs. This line between black and white is most clearly represented by one significance of the visto that, because of chronology, can never be made quite explicit within the novel: as the popularly designated divider of Union from Rebel states in the Civil War. The absence from the novel of the name by which the line came to be known underscores this implicit knowledge.

The ill effects of the line drawn between Native Americans and colonists become clear as Mason and Dixon and their party progress westward. But it is not just a phenomenon of the frontier. Long before they stop the line rather than cross the Great Warrior Path—the crossing of which, their new Mohawk companions inform them (through a translator), "would be like putting an earthen Dam across a River"—the presence of natives and the effects of contact are clear. The division of Indian from settler was enforced from the moment of settlement, a fact to which Mason and Dixon's visit to Lancaster alludes (647). They are there to inspect the site on which an Indian massacre occurred the year before; however, as Cherrycoke mentions when explaining why Mason did not go alone as originally intended, Lancaster, the location of more than one Indian fight, is "a Town notorious for Atrocity" (341). Among the more notorious is the 1676 Indian attack on Lancaster, which took place during Metacom's or King Philip's War. While the hanging of three Indians for the murder of another, converted Indian was the proximate cause of the war (still the most devastating, in terms of fatalities as percentage of population, in American history), the real cause was the encroachment of the settlers. The attack gained fame in America and especially in Britain from a book published as *The Sovereignty and Goodness of God* (in England, *A True History of the Captivity and Restoration of Mrs. Mary Rowlandson*). A first-person narrative of Rowlandson's captivity, it provides a historical record of Puritan attitudes toward the Indians, including both the missionaries' desire to convert them and the belief of Rowlandson and others that the natives were a race of unredeemable savages. Rowlandson's book helped win the day, and many subsequent years of American history, for her racial attitudes.

Pynchon's allusion, then, is to a long history of American attitudes toward its original inhabitants, attitudes that led to results such as those of Metacom's War, which killed 40 percent of the local Indian population. This line is related, like all the others in this book, to one that many Americans were intent on fixing: between themselves and Europe, the Old World and the New. This line appears behind much of the intrigue and paranoia Mason and Dixon encounter on their arrival on America's shores, in the street and in coffee houses, conspiracies and plots they first hear of from Benjamin Franklin, who they meet in a drugstore running a brisk trade in opium, and then from a Colonel George Washington, between puffs from his hemp pipe. Like the plotting they have encountered and imagined in their earlier travels, these plots depend on division, on nations and factions; this line in particular, though, is one many Americans are soon to draw in indelible ink. The line between America and not-America, that which it will leave behind and that which it will exclude, has, like the line drawn between slave states and free, old roots. Of these shared roots, Tony Tanner writes:

> "North and South" is just one more example of the pernicious binary habit of thought, which Pynchon sees as having been so disastrous for America. He traces it back to the Puritan division—or line of demarcation—between the Elect and the Preterite, the Saved and the Damned, Us and Them.
>
> (*American Mystery* 288-89)

The significance of the Revolutionary line, like that of the line between Pennsylvania and Maryland, is one more example of what Tanner rightly identifies as binary thought, a phenomenon Pynchon has spent much time anatomizing elsewhere. Here it is the delineation of a New Eden; everything else is without, unsaved. The line between the elect and the damned preoccupied the Calvinist-descended early settlers, whose anxiety led them in their lay doctrine to work around predestination by sneaking the doctrines of work and faith back in under cover of signs of election. Their profound anxiety found some release, then, in works, faith, close attention to who would receive grace, and attempts to define their earthly version of paradise as open to those who could call themselves the English, as they referred to themselves, as us versus the various thems outside. The scrutiny on identity defined by group membership and the defensive stance against the external continue, 100 years later, to shape attitudes about nation, religion, race, and countless other arenas in which lines of exclusion could be drawn.

The line Mason and Dixon draw, then, shares two things with the line America draws both around itself and against those within its borders it would rather were without: an inheritance and an essential structure. Also related to the line that defines America is a line that appears and reappears throughout ***Mason & Dixon,*** a line that also can claim a long descent: that between what Pynchon calls the indicative and the subjunctive. This line is not so much grammatical as metaphysical, though the deep connection of the former to the latter is noted in the borrowing of terms: it distinguishes between what we can say "is" and what "might be." The connection of the American line to this line between what is and what might be—of America's self-definition and differentiation to the line between the known and the possible—is best seen in a passage set, fittingly, during the visit to Lancaster:

> Does Britannia, when she sleeps, dream? Is America her dream?—in which all that cannot pass in the metropolitan Wakefulness is allow'd Expression away in the restless Slumber of those Provinces, and on Westward, wherever'tis not yet mapp'd, nor written down, nor ever, by the majority of Mankind, seen,—serving as a very Rubbish-Tip for subjunctive Hopes, for all that *may yet be true,*—Earthly Paradise, Fountain of Youth, Realms of Prester John, Christ's Kingdom, ever behind the sunset, safe till the next Territory to the West be seen and recorded, measur'd and tied in, back into the Net-Work of Points already known, that slowly triangulates its way into the continent, changing all from subjunctive to declarative, reducing Possibilities to Simplicities that serve the ends of Governments,—winning away from the realm of the Sacred, its Borderlands one by one, and assuming them unto the bare mortal World that is our home, and our Despair.
>
> (345)

America as possibility—as the New World, as the place that allows what Europe cannot—is the dream of the Old World, and like a dream it is not true, but might be. But although it is Britain's dream, America keeps awakening itself, as it turns frontier into settlement into colony, curtailing its possibility, consigning hopes to its rubbish heap. The western frontier was only seemingly boundless. As long as it seemed so, America could be the place where the West in the larger sense could escape the Enlightenment reduction of possibility. When the western frontier's apparent boundlessness was revealed as only ostensible—when lines were measured and laid down across it, disproving its infiniteness—this escape route was cut off. Mason and Dixon run into a number of examples of the subjunctive, both before they begin their line and as they blaze it across the frontier, discovering what would seem impossible and its near-simultaneous disappearance or destruction—its absorption into the bare, mortal world. When anything seems possible, the Enlightenment certainties, it seems, reassert themselves.

In their travels, Mason and Dixon come across, among many other unlikely phenomena, a talking dog, a flying mechanical duck with a crush on an unwilling French chef, a giant cheese, the ghost of Mason's late wife, and a race of people living inside the earth. Each of these exceeds the conditions of Enlightenment understanding, as does Mason's experience of the 11 days "lost" when the calendar was switched from the Julian to the Gregorian in the "Schizochronick" (192) year of 1752:

> 'Twas as if this Metropolis of British Reason had been abandon'd to the Occupancy of all that Reason would deny. Malevolent shapes flowing in the streets. Lanthorns spontaneously going out. Men roaring, as if chang'd to Beasts in the Dark. A Carnival of Fear. Shall I admit it? I thrill'd. I felt that if I ran fast enough, I could gain altitude, and fly.
>
> (559-60)

The occupancy of America by all that reason would deny dramatizes its status as the land of possibility. The loss of these phenomena, their eviction, dramatizes the loss of this possibility. Dixon's visit to Hollow Earth makes plain that it is eviction:

> "Once the solar parallax is known," they told me, "once the necessary Degrees are measur'd, and the size and weight and shape of the Earth are calculated inescapably at last, all this will vanish. We will have to seek another Space."
>
> (741)

Even though we know such a world could not exist, we still feel its impending loss; it as if the loss of possibility is doubled.

The line between subjunctive and indicative, then, is crucial both to the book's understanding of the Enlightenment—as the demarcation between what the Enlightenment can know and what it cannot, and so between what is and is not—and also to its understanding of America, as the demarcation between what America might be and what it can no longer be. The visto Mason and Dixon draw, as it cuts through America, is the vehicle through which the novel encounters the ways America is built on lines, and, more importantly, through which it—and we—are able to think about how America became marked by these old lines when at first it seemed open and unlimited. It was one place we should not have found them. The disenchantment of America, the turning of the New World into just another part of the Old, is the turning of subjunctive into indicative.

The fate of the Indians illustrates this aspect of the line. In the end, the mysteries of their world, while given a reprieve by Mason and Dixon's party, seem surely doomed. Mason and Dixon turn back East, giving up the visto, when they reach the Great Warrior Path, an ancient North-South road reported to have a power that science does not recognize. They learn of the Path from Hugh Crawfford, the white man who accompanies the band of Indians that joins them toward the end of their journey. He tells them that it is sacred, and that they will not be allowed to pass. At this point drawing the line becomes fraught with tension, as they do not want to stumble upon the Path and have only an inexact idea how far they are from it, because they do not know its precise location, and because, as Crawfford says, "Distance is not the same here, nor is Time" (647). Out in this still unmeasured wilderness, occupied by the Indians with their unenlightened worldview, the impossible is still possible, and the laws of Western science may not apply:

> We all feel it Looming, even when we're awake, out there ahead someplace, the way you come to feel a River or Creek ahead, before anything else,—sound, sky, vegetation,—may have announced it. Perhaps 'tis the very deep sub-audible Hum of its Traffic that we feel with an equally undiscover'd part of the Sensorium,—does it lie but over the next Ridge? the one after that? We have Mileage Estimates from Rangers and Runners, yet for as long as its Distance from the Post Mark'd West remains unmeasur'd, nor is yet recorded as Fact, may it remain, a-shimmer, among the few final Pages of its Life as Fiction.
>
> (650)

As Cherrycoke notes when they reach the Path, the frontier is "the Membrane that divides their [Indians'] Subjunctive World from our number'd and dreamless Indicative" (677). As soon as they come to the Path, as soon as they are able to fix it in latitude and longitude, the dream will be over, it will be Fact. Like the Hollow Earth, it will cease to exist. Again, applying geometry is, in Michael Wood's words, an "imperialist gesture, an administrative onslaught by the numbered on the unimagined" (128). The unimagined, when seen and counted, must by definition cease to exist as such.

As do the Indians, at least the way they were, untouched by the Old World. When the party finally reaches the line, Mason wants to continue, thinking that the Indians who travel the path and live beyond it will not threaten them once they see that they are harmless. Dixon, on the other hand, wants to stop:

> They don't want nay of thah'? They want to know how to stop this great invisible Thing that comes crawling straight over their Lands, devouring all in its Path. . . . A tree-slaughtering Animal, with no purpose but to continue creating forever a perfect Corridor over the Land. Its teeth of steel,—its Jaws, Axmen,—its Life's Blood, Disbursement. And what of its intentions, beyond killing ev'rything due west of it? do you know? I don't either.
>
> (678)

After some disagreement, the line is ended, and the party turns back, but the Indians by whose war parties they are surrounded at the end will not be able to turn back those who sent Mason and Dixon.

The unlimited possibility of America, of the New Eden, the land not just of the free but the equal, will not survive either. As is seen in the novel's frame, Wicks Cherrycoke's 1786 telling of the story of Mason and Dixon, its great promise will not be met. He says, "This Christmastide of 1786, with the War settl'd and the Nation bickering itself into Fragments, wounds bodily and ghostly, great and small, go aching on, not ev'ry one commemorated,—nor, too often, even recounted" (6). After the American Revolution, we see the failure of this promise, and this failure is seen specifically to take the shape of lines. The fragments into which the nation is dividing, the wounds that go aching on, existed long before the revolution, as Cherrycoke's story illustrates. Though he is not recounting the story of the contemporary wounds, the story Cherrycoke does tell clearly applies. The American mania for drawing lines, and for thinking them progress, is not specific to the 1760s.

Nor is it specific to the eighteenth century. Pynchon is reading not just a historical moment but also all of American history. The drawing of lines that characterizes the birth of the nation is explicitly linked to a more recent time, 100 years after the time of ***Mason & Dixon.*** The Civil War was another moment when the various lines dividing the country were contested. The racial lines drawn at America's birth remained, despite military, legal, and social efforts to erase them, and just as they persisted through Reconstruction and resurfaced in Jim Crow, Pynchon seems to believe, these lines are still evident today. His concern for racial prejudice and systemic discrimination can be seen in his novels, his early short fiction, such as **"The Secret Integration"** (1964), and even his non-fiction, such as his 1965 essay in the *New York Times Magazine,* **"A Journey into the Mind of Watts."** We are thus led to ask how the century of ***Mason & Dixon***'s writing fits into this pattern of Pynchon's, how in the second half of the twentieth century we see possibility raised and unrealized. How does the tendency to draw lines, the binary habit of thought seen as dominating American history, exist in our time? To address this question, we need to go beyond a reading of ***Mason & Dixon*** solely as a novel of lines, as a reckoning of the costs of America's addiction to binarism. To do this, to get at other ways of thinking and being that ***Mason & Dixon*** might entertain, we have to focus on the other figure that dominates the novel.

* * *

The ampersand is an ancient Roman symbol derived from the ligature or combination into one character of the *e* and *t* in the Latin *et,* meaning *and.* In modern English usage, it continues to serve as shorthand for *and.* Its English name is a corruption of the words English schoolchildren used to recite at the end of the alphabet: "X, Y, Zed, and per se and." The last phrase refers to the ampersand character, which is per se (by itself) the word *and,* and which came to be pronounced "ampersand." Modern typefaces have variations on the ampersand in which the original *e* and *t* have become lost. Eighteenth-century typefaces, such as William Caslon's, preserved the distinction between the two letters, linking them only at the end of the second, bottom stroke of the cursive capital *E* and the *t.* The ampersand on the cover of ***Mason & Dixon*** is Caslon's.

Pynchon's choice of this variation of the character is worth noting because of its symbolic importance to the novel. A character whose meaning is equal to *and,* it is not, however, *and* itself. It is a character that means "and" but which has a physical form and a name that can both be read to express certain ideas of and-ness. The ligature of the two letters expresses combination, connection, while the separate recognizability of the letters in the eighteenth-century version expresses the preservation of distinct identities, of difference. The name, which again literally means that the character itself means "and," conveys both by itselfness and its opposite—because the ampersand is not *and* itself but rather is joined to *and* as signifier to signified, so that when we see it we think "and." In other words, the name of the ampersand holds the same potentially paradoxical meaning as its form, namely, the simultaneous coexistence of the ideas of distinctness and unity, of difference and individual identity. This meaning is paradoxical, though, only if it is assumed that such a thing is impossible.

As I have tried to show, ***Mason & Dixon*** can be read as a book about the destructive prevalence of the setting up and maintaining of binary difference in American history. But from the choices made on its cover to the story told on its pages, it is also a book about the possibility of connection, relation, simultaneity, about possibility itself, about the ideas expressed in the character that dominates its cover. A good place to start examining these ideas would be this first expression of them, paying attention not just to the particulars of the character itself but also to the immediate context in which it appears, the title, between the names of the novel's heroes.

The binary created in the title could be said to capture the geometric form of the line, since what is emphasized is the line between the two names, the distinction between the characters. But by using the ampersand rather than the word *and,* Pynchon expresses something else: the connection between these two distinct characters, just like that between the *e* and *t* from which the ampersand derives. The differences between the two men are clear from the start. Mason is a top-flight astronomer from the south of England, a deistic Anglican. Dixon is a surveyor, a Geordie, a Quaker. Temperamentally, they are also quite different: one attuned to mystical possibility, the other a good Enlightenment rationalist; one reserved, one loud and convivial; one a wine man, the other fonder of beer. However, as many reviewers noted, these differences do not drive them apart. Joined by circumstance, they become an instance of "the classic comedy team of straight man and flake" (Boyle), and the novel becomes "a buddy story" (Menand 24) "like *Huckleberry Finn,* like *Ulysses* . . . one of the great novels about male friendship in anybody's literature" (Leonard 68).

The relationship between these two is one element of ***Mason & Dixon*** that makes it new in Pynchon's corpus. It is generally accepted that ***V., The Crying of Lot 49*** (1966), ***Gravity's Rainbow,*** and ***Vineland*** (1984) are not marked by the creation of and attention to fully rounded characters. As one review of ***Gravity's Rainbow*** put it, "Pynchon doesn't create characters so much as mechanical men to whom a manic comic impulse or vague free-floating anguish can attach itself, often in brilliant streams of consciousness" (Locke 12). This reviewer finds the absence of more typically novelistic characters appropriate to the worlds their author creates in his fiction, worlds in which only mechanical men have a place: "In Pynchon's world there is almost no trust, no human nurture, no mutual support, no family life" (12). This characterization of Pynchon's fictional worlds is also generally accepted: though there is much humor in the novels, and much attention to the prevalence of human indecency and unkindness, there is not much warmth. Though some demur, Pynchon's work up until ***Mason & Dixon*** has been largely seen as relatively cold; in its attention to large ideas, national and international histories of ideas and systems, and in its painting pictures of the world as a place riven by conspiracy or suspicions thereof, his work has had neither the time nor the inclination to present round, sympathetic, engaging characters.[2]

Mason & Dixon has been widely seen to have a warmth lacking in these earlier works, and this perception is due in large part to the way Pynchon draws these two men, separately and together. The stories of their lives before and after their partnership create sympathy for them as individuals, and their story together—stumbling across America, completing a task whose meaning dawns slowly upon them, and supporting each other as it does—creates sympathy for them as a pair. As Michael Wood writes, we see them

> arguing, Anglican against Quaker, mystic against rationalist, and finally discovering that their need and respect for each other, in spite of the frequent acidity of their exchanges and their constant mutual fending off of real intimacies, the drawing of a sort of line between Mason and Dixon, add up to a form of passion, indeed the central passion and care of their lives.
>
> (124)

The line between them, the binary expectation set up by the juxtaposition of their names and the difference in their characters, becomes instead a connection, a relationship between two men who still remain distinct.

The possibility of connection across difference, illustrated in the relationship between these two men, is an important subject of ***Mason & Dixon.*** It is a possibility that applies not just to the main characters but also to America, not just to the line drawn between these two people or any two people but also to the lines drawn between kinds of people, between aspects of experience, between times and places and ideas, between what is and what might be. What Pynchon sees in the relationship between Mason and Dixon, he sees in American history, and what he sees in American history, he sees in the American present: not just the age-old fact of division but also the possibility of something else.

The relationship between Mason and Dixon is important because they connect across their difference. Just as their differences make for the texture of their bickering and, in the end, their friendship, so the division, rather than deserving only condemnation, is valued positively for making the connection possible. For the novel as a whole, then, lines are not simply to be condemned. They make possible many things, including the existence of connections across them.

Without lines, we would have a world without difference. And in some ways we are moving closer to such a world all the time. Louis Menand sees ***Mason & Dixon*** as a novel about colonialism and an adaptation of Pynchon's favorite multidisciplinary metaphor, entropy. He calls the novel an American *Tristes Tropiques* because Pynchon seems to be practicing an anthropology like that of Levi-Strauss, which Menand says might as well be called "entropology" because it sees history as the process of increasing homogenization through contact (24). Homogenization—a world without lines—is not for Pynchon a victory over division but a defeat of energy, of motion, of change. It is also, in the process by which it occurs, a victory for cruelty.

Seeing the American frontier as Britannia's dream, as the place where it seemed that the impossible might be possible, Pynchon explores the simultaneous opening up and shutting down of possibility that America as frontier came to represent and that the Mason-Dixon line symbolizes. As they travel westward, Mason and Dixon encounter the fantastic possibility of America beyond the New Eden of the New American Adam, the mysterious, mystical world both excluded and in a way created by the Enlightenment. As they encounter it, though, the line they blaze into the heart of this frightening and wonderful darkness brings a harmful light. Thus the moment of expansion is at the same time the moment of contraction, when that not normally seen is glimpsed and quickly domesticated. When Pynchon entertains us with tales of the impossible, and in so doing laments its loss, he might seem to be resigned to this inevitable process, as we all must be resigned to the final loss of possibility that ends the book, the deaths of its heroes. What happens in the fantastic lives of Mason and Dixon and in the fantastic life of America might seem inevitable, as might the cruelty that sometimes results from America's old binarism.

This sense of the inevitable—that people die, that cultural entropy occurs, that bad things happen to good people for no good reason—is undeniably part of ***Mason & Dixon.*** And the movement in ***Mason & Dixon*** beyond what readers of Pynchon over the years have called paranoia or conspiracy certainly contributes to this sense of the inevitable. Rather than a grand conspiracy, there is simply history. Mason and Dixon are not pawns in some great game. Dixon does ask, "Are we being us'd, by Forces invisible?" and "Whom are we working for, Mason?" (347). But this is not a paranoid book. The Jesuits, the trading companies, Captain Zhang, Royalists, many different forces and causes and organizations try to influence history, and while there may be trends, no mysterious master plan is in evidence. As Menand writes of this sentiment in the novel, "This is just the direction human history happens to run" (25).

But Pynchon's paranoia has not been replaced by an equally unknowable, unalterable historical inevitability. In ***Mason & Dixon,*** Pynchon presents a different sense of history. The old search for the conspirators in Pynchon's work is here, at bottom, explicitly what it was sometimes only implicitly in its earlier incarnations: a search for the answer to the question of the impossible. As is made clear in ***V.,*** when Weissman deciphers an atmospheric message spelling out Wittgenstein's proposition, "the world is all that is the case," Pynchon is concerned with how we know, with the implications of whether we accept only what we see or are open to more. All the searches for transcendent patterns or forces or impossible things in Pynchon's work ask if indeed the world is all that is the case. This question is asked in ***Gravity's Rainbow***—where Roger Mexico sees no transcendent meaning, while Slothrop is open to anything, becomes Rocketman, and eventually fragments into many possibilities—and in ***The Crying of Lot 49,*** where Oedipa Maas must decide whether or not, beneath the surface of everyday life, there lives a great conspiracy. In the end the questions go unanswered: ***The Crying of Lot 49*** ends as the title event, which should reveal all to Oedipa, is about to happen. We cannot know if the world is all that is the case. The implication of this argument, which Pynchon seizes on in ***Mason & Dixon,*** is that we also cannot rule out other possibilities. And if we cannot rule out other possibilities, we cannot rule out different historical outcomes. Pynchon insists in ***Mason & Dixon*** on the possibility that other worlds might exist in order to ask if things might have turned out differently, or might still. If this is the way history has happened to run, it does not follow that it has had to. The cruelty that fills history does not always, in every instance, have to happen. Those who try to stop it—as Dixon does when he challenges the slave driver—are not fools. They are simply open to the possibility of what might seem historically impossible.[3]

This is openness not just to difference—to recognizing both the existence of difference and also the possibility of connecting across it—but also to a history that could have turned out differently and can still. Seeing this kind of history in ***Mason & Dixon*** requires seeing not just the line but what the line makes possible, seeing not just an anatomy of loss but also a celebration of continued possibility.

The course of history runs, in ***Mason & Dixon,*** up to a present that is multiple. There is the present of the novel's frame, that is, the 1786 from which Cherrycoke looks back and thinks about the lost promise of prerevolution America. There is also Pynchon's present, about 200 years later, the implicit frame around Cherrycoke's frame, which is all that has happened since. Thus the retrospective takes on a wider focus, including the Civil War and the postbellum years as well as the turmoil of the 1960s and the years between that turmoil and the time of the novel's publication. All of America's past between then and now, from Lancaster to Gettysburg to Kent State to Oliver North, is part of the story.

The structure of the novel, then, makes possible a way of thinking about America that crosses the lines between eras, making American history a single connected story.

It also makes possible a way of thinking about history itself, about its connections and cycles. The picture of history we see in ***Mason & Dixon,*** like the relation of all the pasts and presents in the line of the novel, is not linear, nor is it progressive. The literary-historical argument implicit in Pynchon's use of forms from the eighteenth-century novel is that the road the novel takes through literary history is not one of progressive innovation but of recyclings, repetitions, adaptations. It is itself ampersandic. The larger historical argument implicit in Pynchon's use of forms is the same. While it seems not to accept the traditional, Enlightenment, progressivist model of history, ***Mason & Dixon*** does not draw a downward line either. It does not tell a story of descent or degradation. The story this novel tells is one of repetition, of repeated moments of potential change, of utopian promise, followed by failures to fully realize that promise. Each of these moments is at bottom about changing the ways in which America wants to deal with the lines it has drawn down the middle of itself and around itself, about the promise of constructing difference less divisively. And each of these subsequent failures of possibility—of these moments when the subjunctive is reduced to the indicative—is about the failure to remain open to alternatives, particularly to the alternative of connection.

As Tony Tanner notes, ***Mason & Dixon***'s 1760s, the important moments in the Trystero's history in ***The Crying of Lot 49,*** and the moment in the German Zone in ***Gravity's Rainbow*** can all be seen as "explosions of change" (*American Mystery* 235).[4] All are times when much seemed possible, when barriers were down, boundaries fluid. The American 1860s and 1960s were also explosions of change. ***Mason & Dixon***'s interest in slavery and the Civil War is clear. And while Pynchon's concern with the issues debated in and now identified with the 1960s may not be as evident in ***Mason & Dixon*** as it is in his earlier works, it is nonetheless at the center of this novel.[5]

Mason & Dixon is the product of Pynchon's continued exploration of the drawing of lines, an exploration apparently motivated in large part by the hopes raised and disappointed by the 1960s. It asks us to see the persistence of this American way of thinking by linking the 1760s, 1860s, and 1960s. What ***Mason & Dixon*** does not ask us to see, I am arguing, is its inevitability. Unlike Pynchon's earlier works, it accepts neither paranoia nor hopelessness nor unknowability. It does not accept the failure of the 60s to fully realize its utopian visions. Lines will always be erased and drawn again, but the way America deals with them has changed many times, and can continue to do so. It changes when America remembers that history, its history in particular, is not finished. ***Mason & Dixon*** is the first novel in which Pynchon can look back historically on the decade that raised so many of the issues at the center of his work: the Cold War has ended, the century's end approaches, and the 60s appears as the decade at the chronological and ideological center of the Cold War era in a way it could not have appeared at the time he wrote ***Vineland.*** In retrospect, the 60s have stood as a kind of running historical Rorschach test, with successive decades and different political orientations rereading the 60s according to their needs.[6] The retrospective stance on the 60s and on American history as a whole in ***Mason & Dixon*** is not nostalgic, as in ***Vineland,*** nor merely allusive. This novel is a reminder, in a post-Cold War America grown complacent in its ostensible victory, that history is not over. In the face of the triumphalist 1990s—characterized by announcements of the end of ideological contest made by Francis Fukuyama and others, nostalgic World War II anniversary celebrations, and the end not just of a century but also of a millennium—***Mason & Dixon*** insists that history continues, that no telos has been reached, no real war won.[7] As America in the 90s experienced a national retrospective mood,[8] Pynchon's novel insisted that the past is still tied to the future, and utopias imagined and grasped for in the past can still be imagined and grasped for.

Michael Wood interprets the tension in the novel between indicative and subjunctive in this way: Pynchon is suggesting that what we "miss is not a mystical revelation or an ancient wisdom, and not the grand conspiracy underlying all things, but a sense of 'Human Incompletion'" (129). This incompletion, he argues, is what we need to remember if we wish to avoid the errors and cruelties of American history, the ways of dealing with division that have led to so much that is regrettable in our past. Perhaps we need to remember that there are things we don't know, that what lies on the other side of the line is not inherently worse than what is on our side, that we ought to see America always as frontier, in its most hopeful sense. America as frontier does not have to be the America that acts as if everything is new, and that what is previously established—ideas, communities—does not matter. America as frontier can simply be America as possibility. What America remembers, when it remembers that it is unfinished, is possibility; what it forgets, when it forgets to see its past and present as continuous and ongoing, is that whatever is, is not inevitable, that the world may not be all that is the case.

This sense of incompletion, of unfinishedness, can keep us open to possibility, a way of thinking represented in ***Mason & Dixon*** by the imagined world inside the earth. As one resident says:

> And wherever you may stand, given the Convexity, each of you is slightly *pointed away* from everybody else. . . . Here in the Earth Concave, everyone is pointed *at* everyone else,—ev'rybody's axes con-

> verge,—forc'd at least thus to acknowledge one another,—an entirely different set of rules for how to behave.
>
> (741)

This is also a set of rules for how to think, a way of seeing the world not just in terms of possibility but also in terms of relatedness. If each of us on the Earth Convex, in this Terra Concavan's terms, stands on the outside of an outwardly curving earth and so points slightly away from each other, then we can ignore each other and act accordingly; those on the inside of the inwardly curving Earth Concave are forced to act with others in mind. The former way of thinking and acting is presented in the novel as Mason and Dixon's: the line they draw ignores its effects on the lives they draw it through. By extension, it is an American way of being, an Enlightenment way of being, a Western way of being. The Earth Concave's alternative is thus presented not only as an alternative to American exceptionalism. Acknowledgment of the crossing of lines that is the world's reality, of the world's ampersandic actuality, is wanting everywhere. This acknowledgment is not an unfinished task only for America.

Just as the unending road of ***Mason & Dixon***'s picaresque form lends a sense of unfinishedness, so too do its other borrowings from the past. The novel's intentionally anachronistic references and language are crucial to its sense of history not as simply unfinished but also as recrossing itself, as cycling back and crossing over its own past like the line of our contemporary ampersand. This sense of history can be seen in two of Pynchon's anachronistic uses of caffeinated beverages and other addictive luxuries: the last name of the narrating Rev. Cherrycoke and the Starbucks-like All Nations coffeehouse with its half-caf ordering. The first anachronism alludes to Coca-Cola, of course, the caffeinated stuff that empire now spreads around the globe. The second anachronism links the eighteenth century to the contemporary corporate homogenization exemplified by Starbucks. These two moments are connected across time and space to a present concern when Mason and Dixon stand before a tableful of coffee and sweets that a Quaker gentleman reminds them is "bought . . . with the lives of African slaves, untallied black lives broken upon the greedy engines of the Barbadoes" (329). The Quaker's remark echoes the moment in *Candide* when Candide comes across a maimed slave lying at a crossroads, who says of the hand and leg he lost in the cane fields of Surinam, "this is the price of the sugar you eat in Europe" (40). When Candide breaks into tears and wonders for a moment if maybe this is not, as Pangloss has taught him, the best of all possible worlds, he cries not just for the slave (or for himself, finding another instance of Pangloss's error) but because he is confronted by this disturbing evidence of empire's effects. The eighteenth-century concern over the deleterious effects of globalism raised by Pynchon's allusion echoes our own contemporary concern over globalization and connects the substances that fueled empire and revolutionary thinkers like those in Pynchon's inn—the coffee, sugar, and tobacco firing their dreams of freedom, democracy, and untaxed profits—to the substances that fuel today's workers and their empire.

Pynchon's ampersandic history, connecting these different moments, enables further thought about how America has ended up where it has, and why, and whether it can go somewhere else. It asks whether the line of American history will endlessly recross itself as does the line that symbolizes the infinite, or whether the opening in one loop of our contemporary ampersand can be taken to signify the possibility of things taking off in another direction. The line of empire America has blazed across the North American continent and the world stage, according to ***Mason & Dixon,*** has not ended so much as paused, ready perhaps to loop back on itself once again and then continue on as before or, perhaps, head off on another path. Perhaps, this novel asks, the recognition in our post-Vietnam, post-Reagan, post-Cold War time that we have in many senses been here before will force the realization that we are more concave than convex, more pointed toward each other than away. Once that realization sets in, perhaps we will be forced not just to acknowledge each other, as the resident of Hollow Earth puts it, but to see that in our still divided yet ever more connected world, our axes converge.

Ultimately, if attention is paid only to the meanings of the line in ***Mason & Dixon,*** what is missed is the historical sense emblematized by the ampersand—awareness of the connections between disparate moments from across American history, the feeling that these explosions of change are repeated resurfacings of possibility, of alternative outcomes for an only seemingly inevitable future. These moments resurface in the midst of forgetting, a historical amnesia that results not only when America ignores its past entirely, or when it sees in that past only the glorious story of its founding followed by the upward path leading to its triumphant present, but also when it sees in its past only the inevitable cruelty attendant upon its persistent binarism. Rather than seeing our past as the story of failure to get this binary monkey off its back, ***Mason & Dixon*** wonders if we can learn to think in terms of possibility. Certainly, as Bernard Duyfhuizen writes, the book aims "to unravel the historical roots of the racial and social dislocations" of contemporary America. But its exploration of the past is more than a disinterment, an autopsy explaining the death of American promise. If a medical analogy is wanted, the psychotherapeutic might be more apt: Pynchon's talking cure aims to get America to realize the patterns of thought it learned in its youth, in order to get it to think differently in the future. Cherrycoke ends the paragraph in which he describes the America of 1786 as bickering itself into fragments: "for the Times are as impossible to calculate, this Advent, as the Distance to a Star" (6). Pynchon's contemporary America might also seem to be following an old pattern by bickering itself into fragments, and might seem as difficult to understand as Cherrycoke's times did to him. This phrase comes from the very beginning of the book; by the end, through telling his story, Cherrycoke may have figured a few things out. And they may be things Pynchon thinks applicable to our own era.

Mason & Dixon ends sadly, with Mason descending not just into senescence but also into paranoia. But he has, from his relationship with Dixon and his relation to the land through which they drew their line, learned some of the lessons I argue Pynchon is trying to teach. At the end of the American section of the book, they are both in flux, and have learned to like it:

> Betwixt themselves, neither feels British enough anymore, nor quite American, for either Side of the Ocean. They are content to reside like Ferrymen or Bridge-Keepers, ever in a Ubiquity of Flow, before a ceaseless spectacle of Transition.
>
> (713)

While Mason has learned a new way to think about division, to reside in transition, he cannot hold on to it forever. When he regresses to his previous way of seeing things, it is the last moment of the subjunctive: "the Event not yet 'reduc'd to Certainty' . . . [a] last moment of Immortality" (177). The inevitability of death, though, is accompanied by a reminder of the magical possibility inherent in and symbolized by America. In the words of Mason's once estranged children, words that close the novel,

> "The Stars are so close you won't need a Telescope."
>
> "The Fish jump into your Arms. The Indians know Magick."
>
> (773)

Any times, especially those times of retrenchment following explosions of change, can be as difficult to calculate as the distance to a star. ***Mason & Dixon*** reminds us that there have been times when we were closer to the stars, that they may come again, that in some ways our distance to them is always in flux. Impossibly far or unimaginably close, the stars will always be separate from us, but, like the residents of the Earth Concave, we can lean toward them, and each other.

Notes

1. For the accuracy of Pynchon's language, see Menand.
2. Some argue that *Vineland,* with its focus on family, is an exception; see Moody and Berger, who notes, "The novel ends with a family reunion; its final word is 'home'" (par. 3), though he gives more weight to the relationship between two other (unrelated) characters, Prairie and Weed (par. 45).
3. Ricciardi also sees a turn away from total resignation in *Mason & Dixon.* She cites Richard Rorty's argument in his recent essay "Achieving Our Country," in which he

    > argues that Pynchon's novels in general, and *Vineland* in particular, merely articulate a desperate pessimism unaccompanied by any impulse to outrage or protest and exemplify a "rueful acquiescence in the end of American hopes"

    and disagrees, arguing that "*Mason & Dixon* deviates from the sense of resignation that permeates Pynchon's earlier works insofar as the novel responds to an urgent consciousness of the need for historical witnessing" (1072). While failing to take issue with Rorty's overstatement or specify the content of this need, Ricciardi does identify the turn taken by Pynchon in *Mason & Dixon.*
4. For a description of a similar meaning in the representation of a single historical moment, the 1960s, in *Vineland,* see Berger, who likens Pynchon's understanding of later interpretations of the 60s to Walter Benjamin's *jeztzeit,* "the critical moment of historical, redemptive possibility which continues to erupt into the present even after many previous failures" (par 5).
5. As David Cowart has pointed out, the connections between the 1960s and Pynchon's work have not been much explored by critics, a failure only slightly redressed by reactions to *Vineland* ("Pynchon" 12).
6. See Miller for the ways in which the 1960s have been reimagined by subsequent decades.
7. For the way in which the dissolution of the Soviet Union was incorporated into the triumphalist reading of American history, see Engelhardt, *End* and "Victors."
8. The national mood of retrospection—which can be ascribed not just to the end-of-an-era sense imparted by the close of the century and the millennium but also to the end of the Cold War and the 50th anniversaries of World War II-era events—can be seen in a number of ways: the works of Ken Burns; the rise of the History Channel, which was launched in 1995; the growth of the *Biography* series in the mid-90s; the popularity of historian Stephen Ambrose; war movies such as *Saving Private Ryan* (1998), *The Thin Red Line* (1998), and *Pearl Harbor* (2001); CNN's 1998 24-part history of the Cold War; the 1998 miniseries *The Sixties*; and decade-specific revivals in popular music and television (*That Seventies Show,* 1998).

Works Cited

Adorno, Theodor, and Max Horkheimer. *Dialectic of Enlightenment.* Trans. John Cumming. New York: Continuum, 1995.

Benjamin, Walter. *Illuminations.* Trans. Harry Zohn. Ed. Hannah Arendt. New York: Schocken, 1968.

Berger, James. "Cultural Trauma and the 'Timeless Burst': Pynchon's Revision of Nostalgia in *Vineland.*" *Postmodern Culture* 5.3 (May 1995) http://www.iath.virginia.edu/pmc/text-only/issue,595berger.595.

Boyle, T. Coraghessan. "*Mason & Dixon,* by Thomas Pynchon." *New York Times Book Review* 18 May 1997:9.

CNN. *History of the Cold War,* 12 Feb. 2002 <http://www.cnn.com/SPECIALS/cold.war/guides/about.series/>.

Cowart, David. "Pynchon and the Sixties." *Critique* 41.1 (Fall 1999): 3-12.

———. *Thomas Pynchon: The Art of Allusion.* Carbondale: Southern Illinois UP, 1980.

Duyfhuizen, Bernard. Rev. of *Mason & Dixon,* by Thomas Pynchon. *The News and Observer* (Raleigh) 4 May 1997: G4.

Engelhardt, Tom. *The End of Victory Culture; Cold War America and the Disillusioning of a Generation.* New York: Basic, 1995.

———. "The Victors and the Vanquished." *History Wars: The Enola Gay and Other Battles for the American Past.* Ed. Tom Engelhardt and Edward T. Linenthal. New York, Holt, 1996. 210-49.

Hite, Molly. *Ideas of Order in the Novels of Thomas Pynchon.* Columbus: Ohio State UP, 1983.

Kundera, Milan. *Testaments Betrayed: An Essay in Nine Parts.* New York: Harper, 1996.

Leonard, John. "Crazy Age of Reason." *The Nation* (12 May 1997): 65-68.

Levine, George, and David Leverenz, eds. *Mindful Pleasures: Essays on Thomas Pynchon.* Boston: Little, 1976.

Locke, Richard. "One of the Longest, Most Difficult, Most Ambitious Novels in Years." *New York Times Book Review* 11 Mar. 1973: 1-2, 12, 14.

Menand, Louis. "Entropology." *New York Review of Books* 12 June 1997: 22-25.

Miller, Stephen Paul. *The Seventies Now: Culture as Surveillance.* Durham: Duke UP, 1999.

Moody, Rick. "Surveyors of the Enlightenment." *The Atlantic* July 1997 <http://www.atlantic.com/97jul/pynchon.htm>.

Mxyzptlk, Mr. "Great Expectations." *Suck* 28 July 1997 <http://www.suck.com/daily/97/07/28/daily.html>.

Pearl Harbor. Dir. Michael Bay. Touchstone, 2001.

Pynchon, Thomas. *The Crying of Lot 49.* New York: Harper, 1966.

———. *Gravity's Rainbow.* New York: Penguin, 1973.

———. "Is It O.K. to Be a Luddite?" *New York Times Book Review* 28 Oct. 1984: 1, 40-41.

———. "A Journey into the Mind of Watts." *New York Times Magazine* 12 June 1966: 34-35, 78, 80-82, 84.

———. *Mason & Dixon.* New York: Holt, 1997.

———. *V.* New York: Harper, 1963.

———. *Vineland.* New York: Penguin, 1990.

Ricciardi, Alessia. "Lightness and Gravity: Calvino, Pynchon, and Postmodernity." *MLN* 114 (1999), 1062-77.

Rowlandson, Mary. *The Sovereignty and Goodness of God.* Ed. Neal Salisbury. Boston: Bedford, 1997.

Sante, Luc. "Long and Winding Line." *New York* 19 May 1997: 65-66.

Saving Private Ryan. Dir. Steven Spielberg. Dreamworks, 1998.

Schaub, Thomas. *Pynchon: The Voice of Ambiguity.* Urbana: U of Illinois P, 1981.

Seed, David. *The Fictional Labyrinths of Thomas Pynchon.* Iowa City: U of Iowa P, 1988.

Sieber, Harry. *The Picaresque.* London: Methuen, 1977.

Tanner, Tony. *The American Mystery: American Literature from Emerson to DeLillo.* Cambridge: Cambridge UP, 2000.

———. *Thomas Pynchon.* London: Methuen, 1982.

The Thin Red Line. Dir. Terence Malick. Twentieth-Century Fox, 1998.

Voltaire. *Candide, or Optimism: A Fresh Translation, Backgrounds, Criticism,* 2nd ed. Trans. and ed. Robert M. Adams. New York: Norton, 1991.

Weber, Max. *The Protestant Ethic and the Spirit of Capitalism.* Trans. Talcott Parsons. New York: Scribner's, 1976.

Wicks, Ulrich. *Picaresque Narrative, Picaresque Fictions: A Theory and Research Guide.* New York: Greenwood, 1989.

Wood, Michael. "Pynchon's *Mason & Dixon.*" *Raritan* 17.4 (Spring 1998): 120-30.

Terry Caesar and Takashi Aso (essay date summer 2003)

SOURCE: Caesar, Terry and Takashi Aso. "Japan, Creative Masochism, and Transnationality in *Vineland.*" *Critique* 44, no. 4 (summer 2003): 371-87.

[*In the following essay, Caesar and Aso analyze the representation of Japan in* Vineland, *underscoring sa-*

domasochistic elements and the depiction of Japanese economic strength as a potential threat to American cultural superiority.]

How can the presence of Japan in ***Vineland*** be explained? Western critics have been content either to take its presence for granted or to comprehend Japan as part of the purely formal or structural dynamics of cyberpunk. Thus, Brian McHale insists on cyberpunk's "principle of incongruous juxtaposition"—including that of American culture with Japanese culture (226). His chapter on ***Vineland,*** which is a discussion of television in the novel, passes over the curiosity of why, in each of the two appearances of television in ***Gravity's Rainbow,*** Japan, of all countries, is chosen as the means for the representation. In this way, Japan lacks any sort of specificity in Pynchon criticism. Our discussion tries to establish the difference an attempt to restore that specificity makes to the understanding of ***Vineland,*** in particular.

We have no quarrel seeing ***Vineland*** within the project of cyberpunk. Indeed, following Larry McCaffery's formula of the "avant-pop" (a coinage for the literature of the hyper-real in which Pynchon is regarded as a father figure of second-generation postmodernist writers), Takayuki Tatsumi argues that the presentation of Japan in ***Vineland*** represents Pynchon's response to William Gibson or Bruce Sterling; it is a sort of "disdain for the new kids on the block," a mockery of "their high-tech-hyper Orientalist discourse" ("Comparative Metafiction" 2).[1] In another article, Tatsumi continues to develop a notion of "creative masochism" that is crucial to our discussion. Creative masochism is not only an umbrella term for power dynamics between Japan and the United States, or what Ian Buruma characterizes as the circumstance of "a resentful and mercantilist power locked into a state of infantile dependence on US security" (260). The term aims to stipulate a quite specific, recurrent dynamic between the two countries, whereby Japan is in a position of subservience to the United States, on the model, for example, of the musician who would imitate authentic American jazz.

In a recent discussion, E. Taylor Atkins explains how historically the consequence has been as follows: "Japanese were thus in the humiliating position of having their own artistic future mapped out by Americans" (38). The masochism, we might say, lies in the position itself, and the creativity consists in both accepting it and nonetheless trying to turn it into an enabling strategy, as Atkins explains successive generations of Japanese jazz musicians have tried to do. Or to take a related example, as Japanese rap music has developed under the strong influence of American rap throughout the '80s and '90s. Ben the Ace, a Japanese DJ, regards his music as "the real thing": "For us, raised in a different environment and different language, Japanese rap by rappers raised in the country is much more 'real' [*riaru*] than American rap," "Japanese rappers," Ian Condroy comments, "construct social boundaries through the decisions they make in appropriating hip-hop as their own" (166, 180).

How to describe the enduring international dynamic as well as the respective social boundaries in this state of affairs? Creative masochism. Tatsumi continues, "will lead us to reconsider the potential existence of S&M metaphorics which is always lurking within international politics generally—and especially within the Japan-U.S. relationship" ("Creative Masochism" 61-62). ***Vineland,*** we argue, is, precisely, at once a reflection of these "metaphorics" and a narrative in which they are played out. The subject of the novel is not merely America, either in terms of its mythic prehistory or its '60s revolutionary energies, coopted in the '80s. ***Vineland*** is also about an American who employs Japanese techniques to kill another American who turns out to be Japanese. That is, the narrative strives to include some consideration of America as a global power, in competition most particularly with Japan, and therefore in the thrall of a relationship on the model of the sadomasochistic one between Darrel Louis Chastain and Takeshi Fumimota. That relationship is customarily understood as merely a double of the central relationship between Frenesi Gates and Brock Vrond. (For a full reading, see Strehle.) But such an understanding fails to account for the reason that Japan is present initially.

According to Tatsumi, "cyberpunk was based on the perception of Japan as a semiotic ghost country liberated from the Hegelian metaphysical system of 'history'" ("Comparative Metafiction," 9). ***Vineland*** gives body to this perception, although now fraught with international politics as much as semiotics. A Western cultural history is inescapably part of the novel, whose Orientalist determinants cannot be easily undone. Or can they? In fact the relationship between DL and Takeshi stands in vivid contrast to that between Frenesi and Brock, which is at least equally sadomasochistic yet far more exploratory of what we read at one point as Frenesi's fear of "some Cosmic Fascist [. . .] spliced into a DNA sequence" (83). In such contrast, the relationship between DL and Takeshi is so provocative because it seems played out over a larger scale, more historically conditioned and open to more hybrid, and even emancipatory, energies. At one point at the highly international orgy aboard the *Anubis* in ***Gravity's Rainbow*** we read of "the Jap liaison man," Ensign Morituri, who as "the only person not connected" is merely sitting watching the river. "Well," comments the narrator, "they're pretty inscrutable, you know, those Japs" (467). In a quite emphatic sense, ***Vineland*** narrativizes this indulgent, (self) mocking comment, only now from a historical position in which Japan has become part of the action.

"Japan and the United States are *inter pares,*" states Gayatri Spivak, writing in the late '90s. "It looks like, in 1984, the buildings were Bank of New York and the merchandise Tokyo's Fuji Bank" (339). Although, in comparison to Spivak's utterance, Pynchon's novel is almost exclusively situated in one national space—that of the United States—what we ultimately find compelling about ***Vineland*** is how it is nonetheless marked by so much ambivalence about cultural translation. On the one hand, creative masochism is seen as the limit of how a narrative about the relation between Japan and the United States can proceed. On the other hand, transnationality is nonetheless representable in the novel as a possible basis for constructing another narrative, in which the relationship between Japan and the United States could be re-created as more fluid, discontinuous, and hybrid.

"[I]n what sense," Leo Ching asks in a recent essay, "can we speak of Coca-cola or the karaoke sing-along as examples of cultural products that merit evaluation on the basis of an American or a Japanese *national* identity" (191)? This is a troublesome question for the reader of ***Vineland*** today, when, a decade after the publication of the novel, we are accustomed to celebrations of the end of the nation-state and the rise of transnational visions of culture. Pynchon's novel is the product of a time when such celebrations were less common and fixations more intense about the structural grip any one country has on another. His narrative consistently evaluates DL and Takeshi precisely on the basis of their respective national identities. Before we dismiss these identities, we need to understand the peculiar torsions between them, particularly with respect to their unequal power and the creative strategies designed to be free of the inequality.

I

Sadomasochism, of course, has been an important subject throughout Pynchon's fiction. Hanjo Berressem states the matter succinctly: "As in ***Gravity's Rainbow,*** the most important hinge between power and the subject in ***Vineland*** is the economy of sadomasochism, the sexual machine in and by which power is produced. Although sadomasochism is the most common 'perversion' in Pynchon's work, because it mirrors the perversion of culture in general, in ***Vineland*** it becomes the *central* concern" (215). Berressem then gestures at Lacan. We, on the other hand, would gesture at the wonderfully named Eric von Lustbader. His best-selling Ninja novels of the 1980s, *The Ninja* and *The Miko,* not only typify American interest in Japan during the decade in which ***Vineland*** is set but represent something of American fears that Japan may now be in a strong enough position to reverse the economic terms by which cultural power is produced. In *The Ninja,* just as in ***Vineland,*** a Ninja assassin is employed to kill a powerful American.

Pynchon, of course, alters the terms of the assignment. His Ninja, DL, is an American as well as a woman. Moreover, her employer. Mafia don Ralph Wayvone, is also an American, not the Japanese businessmen of von Lustbader's novel. ***Vineland*** obviously parodies the knowing air of Ninja mystery and mystification common to both *The Ninja* and *The Miko.* In part, we need to see Pynchon's novel in the context of popular fiction about Japan, including such best-selling reactionary novels as Clive Cussler's *Dragon* (1990), in which villainous Japanese threaten the United States with their unique, microstructured organization, or Michael Crichton's *Rising Sun* (1992), in which the Japanese are presented as equally ruthless and, in addition, rife with what Scott Wright notes as "a supposed Japanese predilection for kinky sex" (177). More important, however, we need to understand why Pynchon is moved to parody von Lustbader in the first place, much less why he is interested in Ninja.

It will not do merely to invoke Frederic Jameson's well-known formulation of "blank parody" in postmodernism; the parody lies in its blankness rather than in its pointedness or adherence to some original. (See Jameson 114.) Pynchon's interest in Ninja tradition seems too careful, too invested in the original. For example, at one point van Lustbader's hero explains how Japanese businessmen employ a technique known as "To Move the Shade," which is lifted straight from a guide to martial arts strategy written by a warrior in 1645.[2] Compare the "grab bag of strategies" DL learns, such as the Nosepicking of Death or "the truly unspeakable *Gojira no Chimpira*" (127). Instead, we maintain that the parody permits the operation of a quite serious question in ***Vineland,*** one fully conversant with the political and economic tensions between Japan and the United States during the decade preceding the novel's publication.

DL's adoption of ninjutsu (the correct term for the technique, rather than "ninjitsu" as in the novel) effectively becomes a test case for how an American can employ a Japanese cultural and spiritual tradition. The power of this particular fantasy—indulged in *as* a fantasy through the medium of parody—should come as no surprise during a period in which the yen's value increased by over 50% against the dollar; Japan's trade deficit fell by nearly as much by the end of the '80s; and Japanese investors made such widely publicized purchases as Rockefeller Center and Columbia Pictures. In 1985, Lee Iacocca, the CEO of Chrysler, wrote a best-selling autobiography in which he compared the current trade war with Japan to World War II. (Cited in Johnson 122, which is valuable for a brief review of the economic and social tensions of this period.) In ***Vineland,*** however, Pynchon represses the tensions of the political realm to release them in the displaced form of personal, sexual conflict. In popular narratives, the question is, who will be the victor—Japan or the United States? In ***Vineland,*** the question becomes on whose terms will the battle be conducted?

Initially, the terms are purely Japanese. Recalling her mother, Noreen, victimized by her husband's domestic violence, DL reflects at one point on how first she tried to rescue her body from masculine appropriation through being enlightened by Inoshiro Sensei:

> The schoolroom line was, You'll never know enough about your body to take responsibility for it, so better just hand it over to those who are qualified, doctors and lab technicians and by extension coaches, employers, boys with hardons, so forth—alarmed, not to mention pissed off, DL reached the radical conclusion that her body belonged to herself. That was back when she was still thinking about ninjitsu.
>
> (128)

We would emphasize that DL's agency here is readable in respect to nation as well as gender. DL effectively becomes yet another American infatuated by the Wisdom of the East, albeit one who eventually learns that the alleged integration of mind and body of the ninjutsu tradition (which can be traced back to Chinese mysticism mixed up with medieval Japanese folkloric traditions of *yamabushi* [mountain warrior-priests] and *sen-nin* [ascetic recluses]) was in fact continually appropriated by the state. Shogun Yoshihisa Asikaga, for example, is said to have been one of the first rulers to employ the ninja, at the height of the civil wars in the mid-fifteenth century. (See Hayes.) As a result, the original purity of ninjutsu became contaminated, "made cruel and more worldly, bled of spirit," as the narrative voice of ***Vineland*** tells us (127).

Inoshiro Sensei explains to DL, therefore, that what he now has in his possession with which to instruct her is more like assassination machinery imbued with an inherited sense of spiritual corruption:

> "Sure," he told her, "this is for all the rest of us down here with the insects, the ones who don't quite get to make warrior, who with two tenths of a second to decide fail to get it right and live with it for the rest of our lives—it's for us drunks, and sneaks, and people who can't feel enough to kill if they have to, [. . .] this is our equalizer, our edge—all we have to share. Because we have ancestors and descendants too—our generations . . . our traditions."
>
> (127)

In short, the very subject that van Lustbader mystifies in *The Ninja* is finally the one Pynchon demystifies in ***Vineland.***[3] Why would he want to do so in the first place? Not only does ninjutsu thereby become another example of an exemplary Pynchonesque theme: the fallen world. (See Berressem 239.) Through a parodic critique of ninjutsu, we argue, Pynchon accomplishes two things simultaneously. First, ***Vineland*** exhibits itself as a text intricately aware of (if not—as we shall see—entirely free from) the moment of naïve idealism in a '60s version of Orientalism, whereby the Spirit of the East is posited as an alternative to what the novel characterizes as so many Western "karmic inbalances" (173). Second, and more to our interest here. DL herself becomes, in effect, a hybrid figure, at once American and Japanese. A corrupted ninjutsu tradition opens up the opportunity for an American to take possession of it, even if the fact that she has to learn to do so through a sensei testifies to the abiding cultural location of ninjutsu as distinctively Japanese.

At the end of his own contribution to his recent collection, *The Cultures of Globalization,* Fredric Jameson conjures up the full measure of Hegelian dialectic, whereby, after watching Identity and Difference turn into each other, "you find out that they are not in opposition to each other, but rather, in some sense, one and the same as each other" (76). Japan and the United States are not presented according to such logic in ***Vineland.*** The very subject of ninjutsu ensures that they are not. Furthermore, the whole conceptualization of globalization was not as current in 1990 as it is today when such developments as the international division of labor, the modulation of capital into the structures of transnational enterprise, and the internationalization of commodities and financial markets make it easier to see how Japan and the United States can be comprehended as most nondialectically one. (Hegelian logic—through which Contradiction ultimately returns—to the contrary notwithstanding.) And yet part of what had come to America by 1990 through pop versions of Ninja as well as cyberpunk was the spectacle of Japan and the United States already so mutually interpenetrated in cultural terms as to be inseparable from each other. Consequently, ***Vineland*** not only represents a political and economic struggle by other means. It embodies in DL a figure representing how this struggle need not necessarily be readable as a contradiction.

Homi Bhabha formulates the process of hybrid displacement and estrangement as follows: "Hybridity [always] represents that ambivalent 'turn' of the discriminated subject into the terrifying, exorbitant object of paranoid classification—a disturbing questioning of the images and presences of authority" (113). The question of what sort of authority ninjutsu still possesses is converted into its embodiment in the person of DL, whose agency, in turn, resides in the fact that she is not a Japanese woman. Traise Yamamoto is the latest of a number of critics to note that one of the inaugural strategies whereby the West has consistently "Japanized" Japan "has been to reduce Japan to a country of childlike women" (11).[4] ***Vineland*** may seek to refuse this Orientalist strategy and yet risks reinscribing it for the same reason: DL remains a woman, American or Japanese, and ninjutsu remains idealized, parodied or not.

"Gendering Japan as female," continues Yamamoto, "is central to the ease with which Western discourse, informed by both nationalism and misogyny, shifts between the romantic and the brutal, between structures of reciprocity and structures of mastery" (23). ***Vineland*** would disrupt this ease; even in her role as a prostitute, DL is no geisha. Yet in another sense, this novel restores, if not precisely the ease of Western discourse about Japan, at least its coordinates. Yamamoto effectively characterizes the tonal spectrum of the relationship between DL and Takeshi as well as the full range of its structuring principles. In addition, these structures can easily be transposed into those of masochism. Indeed, one of the reasons why such "metaphorics" are always most particularly "lurking" in the case of Japan and the United States is that the relationship is fated by Western discourse to be masochistic, whereby the United States always becomes triumphant while Japan always remains (until recently) in the position to suffer rather than produce power.[5]

How to escape this economy? In ***Vineland*** a powerful Japanese martial tradition operates, employed by a Western woman. DL's belief that she can kill Brock Vond may sound like a sort of female "revenge" upon the male hegemony that shattered the counterculture of the '60s. It also suggests a sort of Western "revenge" upon the Japanese economic success that shattered European and American hegemony in the '80s. In either case, though, we can easily see the extent to which DL herself is deeply immersed not only in the masculinist ideology represented by a Mafia don but in the political and cultural organization represented by the "cheapskates at the ol' Depaato" [whorehouse] who cause her to misrecognize her target because she has been given someone else's contact lenses (151).[6] Were the actual "cheapskates" Japanese or American? That question is not an insignificant one. Brock may insist on "an American girl [. . .] always the same," as DL has explained to her (140). Yet how precisely does a ninja-empowered American girl dressed up to resemble an American girl disrupt the circuit of power between the two nations more than a Japanese girl dressed up to resemble an American girl?

The narrative of Japan in ***Vineland*** appears to be established to do so by changing the content of the respective national identities and therefore the masochistic logic in place to define their interaction. Furthermore, in the most impeccable cyberpunk fashion, as well as in anticipation of today's much-theorized globalization, the world already appears to have changed. Fixed boundaries of all sorts are less relevant. The novel, although preeminently embodied in the nation of Japan, features a world of "flows" and "zones" rather than nations. International symposia are common now, such as the one for international prosecutors that initially brings Brock to Tokyo. And yet Brock insists on an American girl—everywhere—and DL remains an American girl, even if she cannot successfully hide from global plots in Columbus, Ohio. Whether as hapless signs or fateful origins, national categories continue to function in ***Vineland.*** Worse, insofar as it concerns Japan and the United States, they appear to function ultimately in the same masochistic ways as those national categories always have, despite the creative designs of the narrative, both with respect to DL's Ninja empowerment and her subsequent action toward Brock.

In the following section, we examine the relationship between DL and Takeshi as another attempt to represent creative masochism as a liberating strategy within Orientalist discourse. However, once again we find at the center of the relationship between DL and Takeshi another instance of a familiar narrative: American "masculine" hegemony "feminizing" Japan. In this particular narrative a woman acts as a man; however, what confers more authority on her action within the Orientalist framework is the fact that she is an American. Therefore, a Japanese man becomes all the more decisively positioned as a woman—especially, we might add, if allied with kamikaze activity in World War II. (See ***Vineland*** 175). He is also so positioned if otherwise figured according to an inescapable historical trace. Most striking in this last regard is the moment when, after his initial encounter with DL, Takeshi feels "like a toxic dump," and his body is reduced to the materiality of his suit, "full of holes, each five to ten centimeters across, in front of the jacket and at the top of the pants, the edges ragged and black, as if burned and rotted through at the same time" (156). In the charred ruins of his destruction by DL, Takeshi recalls the victims of Hiroshima, or, in Japanese, *Hibakusha.* Indeed, DL's "Ninja Death Touch" becomes what ***Gravity's Rainbow*** at one point refers to as "Miss Enola Gay's nuclear clit" (588).

II

In another essay that suggests something of a Japanese intellectual genealogy for the strategy of creative masochism, Tatsumi mentions a number of critics who helped establish "the econo-political principle of total destruction and radical reconstruction in postwar Japan" ("Full Metal" 40). Cyberpunk, of course, also has its place in this principle; so does "the Japanese representative monster," Godzilla. (The subject of Pynchon's next novel after ***Gravity's Rainbow,*** according to once widely reported rumors and eventually present in ***Vineland*** in the trace of the huge footprint in the stomped buildings of the Chapco company, 142.) Tatsumi sums up the matter as follows: "Japanese intellectual history has [. . .] radically transformed the humiliating experience of diaspora into the techno-utopian principle of construction" ("Full Metal" 41). If ***Vineland*** is, as we have been arguing, deeply informed by the principle of creative masochism, we must understand Takeshi's subsequent actions with respect to DL as an attempt to contest the terms of the power to which he has been made subject. How is creativity at all possible from a masochistic position?

The moment when Takeshi, after his arrival in San Francisco, first sees DL again is an interesting one: rather than anger or hatred at the woman who has murdered him, he feels sexual excitement. He remembers in some detail the night of their lovemaking, "killing him in the process. Terrific! The thought should have discouraged his erection but, strangely, didn't" (161). Takeshi has in fact fulfilled through this night a typical Japanese male fantasy: sex with a white woman. In one respect, DL's "assassination" of Takeshi at *Haru no Depaato* symbolically represents the Western despiritualization of the so-called *Yamato-Damashii* [Japanese masculine snobbery over others, both East and West] that continues to empower both the nation's corporate culture and its post-World War II economic surge. In another, more personal respect, a specific Japanese male fantasy for sexual domination continues to reside in Takeshi.[7]

Even more interesting, however, is that at one point during this first San Francisco meeting, he proceeds to reach into his bag, produce a ukulele, and sing "Just Like A William Powell." The lyrics at once express the hopelessness of his relation to DL—"Guess I'll just, throw in the towel, / Aw I'll never find the real McCoy"—and his hope that there could be a relationship. But why one on the model of that between Powell and Myrna Loy? Is it because the relationship will only be one in which he suffers the loss of his own power as a man? Or as a Japanese man? The parody allows us to secure only the most equivocal sense of Takeshi's authority here, Enmeshed as a Japanese male in a Hollywoodized cultural narrative (more accurately, a series of narratives) in which it is incumbent on him as a man to seek out a woman, however haplessly, he transforms himself into a Western "character."

Once more, we need to refer to ***Gravity's Rainbow.*** Brian McHale notes that in the episode of the Japanese kamikaze pilots in the remote Pacific, the scene "abruptly 'loses' its reality, undergoing a sudden demotion of ontological status" into a World War II situation comedy (133-34). One of these pilots is named Takeshi. Whether or not he is the same Takeshi, a Takeshi in ***Vineland*** functions once more as what McHale terms "a metonymic figure of ontological plurality" (134). We read this figure as the sign of "Japan" in the Western imaginary, registered in the Pynchon text. Like Japan, after either World War II or the Ninja Death Touch, Takeshi is effectively dead, killed each time by Americans. And yet, again like Japan, each time at the moment of death Takeshi suffers pluralization or reconstruction—and therefore is "creatively" reborn.

This is not the place to give a full reading of the presence of Japan in Western discourse. (For literature, see Miner's venerable study; for a recent political and philosophical critique, see Ivy.) We simply emphasize one thing about it: from the beginning of the modern period to the present, Japan has been characterized in the West by a certain chimerical representationalism, perfectly expressed in Oscar Wilde's famous line: "The actual people who live in Japan are not unlike the general run of English people; that is to say, they are extremely common-place, and have nothing curious or extraordinary about them. In fact the whole of Japan is a pure invention" (46-47). Such a witty dismissal is perfectly consonant with Roland Barthes's more recent treatment of Japan, a consciously "invented name" about which he writes: "to me the Orient is a matter of indifference, merely providing a reserve of features whose manipulation [. . .] allows me to 'entertain' the idea of an unheard-of symbolic system, one altogether detached from our own" (3). In each case, Japan does not have to exist to be represented. Indeed, the more its existence can be ignored, the better it can be represented.

In ***Vineland*** (as well as in ***Gravity's Rainbow***), Japan is accorded enough specific valence on its own terms—Japanese vocabulary, Tokyo place names—to enable it to suffer transformation into a markedly American theater of representation. (According to the Japanese translator of the novel, who corresponded with the author through his agent, Pynchon never came to Japan [Sato 601].) Pynchon, it appears, joins a long list of Western authors attracted to Japan for its existence as (to recall Tatsumi's words) a "semiotic ghost country." However, this is not because Japan is seen as liberated from history (Tatsumi's point) but because it never had any of its own. Flying to San Francisco, Takeshi thinks at one point that an American to whom he has been speaking might be referring to Takeshi's ex-wife, Michiko, an actress, currently starring in a Japanese import television series "blowing away all its U.S. rating competition" (159). It is as if she foreshadows his own fate: undeniably Japanese, but designed (if not conceived) for export, and comprehended wholly within American terms.

Much as Takeshi would reignite his male fantasies, much less contest the terms by which power has been exercised over his very life, he finally cannot succeed. The song he sings indicates that this power is not only something outside him but also within him. If an exclusively American theater of representation circumscribes his "ontological" being, the remorselessly Ninjette no-sex clause of Sister Rochelle's decree on both him and DL effectively disempowers Takeshi's sexual being. Most interesting from our point of view, DL's stipulation of no sex means that the "masochism" implicit in the continuing relation with her is fated to be, so to speak, merely masochistic, deprived of sexual force, and therefore bereft of any ground for creativity other than a lame parodic sort.[8] The Punctutron machine may be designed to bring Takeshi back to life, but it only enforces his subject, colonial status. Furthermore, if the machine addresses the sexual determinants of the relationship between DL and Takeski, it cannot rectify their culturally distorted coordinates; in this respect, politicosexual stereotypes between them will remain unchanged—not to say the economic and cultural forces that underlie those stereotypes.

Ultimately, the relationship between DL and Takeski becomes hard to read. The "karmic adjustment" consequent from their working through the death touch is stated rather than demonstrated. The sex that eventually takes place between them is referred to almost as an afterthought. "As their business dealings take them into the eschatological realm of 'karmic adjustment,'" writes Molly Hite, "their relationship evolves into an increasingly egalitarian and finally erotic partnership, of a sort as yet underrepresented inside the Tubal frame" (145). Of course we could recall the sexless relationship of William Powell and Myrna Loy. But another critic Hite cites makes perhaps a more searching point about representational horizons: not only is the "macabre coupling" of DL and Takeshi an "alternate take" on the "grim union" of Frenesi and Brock, but it seems "a vision preserved of the absurd comedy that this relationship, in a better world (or movie) would have remained" (152). In appearing to return at the novel's end to the original note of absurd comedy, we are simply given to understand that DL and Takeshi, in Sister Rochelle's words, "deserve each other" (163). But precisely why? According to what logic? It appears to be of the essence of the relationship between DL and Takeshi that it must not be represented. It may in fact be unrepresentable.[9] Notwithstanding the heavily "metaphysical" rhetoric of the couple's last characterization in the novel—celebrated by Susan Strehle as indicating "their resolute resistance to the authority of all downward drags" (113)—DL and Takeshi together suggest nothing so much as the emergent politicoeconomic reality of the relationship between the United States and Japan in 1990, when ***Vineland*** was published. That is, the two countries are rapidly entering into a common identity that is hybrid in nature, but only if the structuring principles are understood as partaking of a new global order that makes the very notion of hybridity available for all sorts of new connections and reconstitutions.

Some of these are able to be more careless of national identity or history than others. Introducing a recent collection of essays on millennial capitalism, Jean and John Comaroff state that at one point in "their capacity to regulate boundaries and to control flows—of capital and cultural property, communication and currencies, persons and informations"—nations were "invariably incomplete in the face of transnational pressures and incentives" (323). ***Vineland*** imagines this incompleteness very well; the whole relationship between DL and Takeshi is testimony. However, the novel does not wholly imagine either national identity or hegemony as incomplete because of transnational reasons; if that were the case, there would be no need to feel the "pressure" of creative masochism, which is dyadic rather than diffuse in nature. In our final section, we try to clarify the presence of transnationality in ***Vineland.***

III

Writing a few years after 1990, Tatsumi states not only that "the U.S. and Japan have recently exchanged their respective S & M roles," but that "exposure to hyperconsumerism" has variously led both nations to "opening up the possibility of becoming creative and masochistic at once" ("Creative Masochism" 65). In a more recent article, he warms to the same theme: not only has the ideology of both metafiction and cyberpunk become evident in consumer society, but "the more advanced the logic of consumer-capitalism becomes, the more difficult it is to distinguish its ideology from sexual masochism" ("Comparative Metafiction" 16). Perhaps so.[10] Certainly it has become an axiom of cultural studies that there now obtains what John Whittier Treat terms a "hegemonizing postmodernity," which he explains as, "an obsession that means the most basic structures of social existences, whether 'ours' or 'theirs,' have been reinterpreted against a 'cultural logic' locally modulated but universally applied" (11). In other words, consumer capitalism now constitutes a global system.

However, Tatsumi's idea of creative masochism has the virtue of restoring significance to national spaces that may have been discursively evacuated too hastily. His judgment in the latter article that Pax Japonica replaced Pax Americana has proved too ephemeral. But his conception that these two nations are inextricably entangled together—not to say structurally linked—in an unequal, eroticized relation of power is, we believe, an enduring one. In a sense, through the plot of DL and Takeshi, ***Vineland*** demonstrates one possibility of how this relation can be narrativized: in personal, explicitly sexual terms, according to protocols respective to each culture, and with due allowance being made for the fact that each culture is already constituted in part by the other.

In another sense, though, the plot of DL and Takeshi demonstrates the limits of such a narrative. Even in the postmodern world of flows and zones, Orientalist fantasies die as hard as the national or cultural locations that ground them. Treat himself has lately proposed a handy definition of Orientalism: "the Western study of everywhere else" (*Great Mirrors,* ix). In ***Vineland,*** Japan ultimately remains securely in place, narrated from a Western position, in which the creativity of the masochistic relationship with the United States has been—from the Japanese point of view—either elided or effaced. (Much in contrast to the Japanese fictions that Tatsumi studies; see in particular *Yappo the Human Cattle,* discussed at the end of "Comparative Metafiction.") At most, the relation between the two nations in the novel continues, marginally as well as indeterminately, if only because throughout there has been a larger, more exclusively American plot.

"Whether Japan should be bashed or not," remarks Tatsumi, "depends upon whether you accept its hyper-consumerist development or not." ("Creative Masochism" 65). In writing ***Vineland,*** Pynchon appears to have made up his mind that Japan should not be bashed—as it has been in the popular fiction of the time. Instead, the nation's hyperconsumerist development is provocative: fun, cyber-, post-, and much else besides. Yet what to do with the sheer power of the provocation? In addition, there are times, it seems, when it is best to draw a veil over the matter of who is producing whatever is being consumed. An especially interesting instance in that regard occurs on Takeshi's plane to San Francisco, when the American to whom he has been speaking returns to his computer game, "something called 'Nukey,' which included elements of sex and detonation" (160). Talk about creative masochism!

The sound chips are cheap, though, so the orgasm is whiny and the nuclear explosion is feeble. It is not clear if the game is the product of American or Japanese technology. In 1990, it cannot be both. However, the scene takes place in 1978. (See ***Vineland*** 147.) In historical fact, ten years would have to pass before Nintendo released the portable "Game Boy" (1989) on the market (Larimer 23). Yet early computer games provide an especially interesting example of near-aporetic moments of cultural translation. A Japanese video game manufacturer produced a game known as "Space Invaders" in 1978. Very popular in Japan, the game, once exported, eventually became the first overseas success for Japan in the video market. However, lest it seem now merely like another Japanese high-tech triumph, "Space Invaders" was actually based on an American product, "Break-Out."[11] Thus, once transmitted from the United States to Japan, the technology was modified to "invade" the American market.

At this point, though, the whole notion of the market needs to be mapped along permeable coordinates of international production and consumption rather than fixed national boundaries. The failure of ***Vineland***'s narrative to clarify the origin of "Nukey" (either at point of design or conception as well as production) may of course testify once more to Pynchon's ambivalence concerning Japan's economic development. Yet the momentary appearance of this game may just as well testify to his prescience—largely unnarrativized yet nonetheless present—about the East-West demarcation already becoming economically renegotiated. Consider Leo Chin's compelling essay on Japanese cultural influence in Taiwan, in which he sets the whole matter of the possible dominance of one country by another on a global scale:

> In an era of transnational capitalism, cultural convergence seems to be occurring at various levels. Foreign cultural products and their meanings are not only readily available but also easily transferable. Because no one can escape the continuous exposure to the enormous range of presentation and reference to the ever differentiating and changing commodified cultural practices, the attempt to locate identifiable and stable presentations and relations has become extremely difficult.
>
> (186)

"Nukey" marks the moment in ***Vineland*** of such a transfer. A cultural convergence has already occurred; and, in a more expansive sense, we might suggest that the whole idea of Japan occurs in Pynchon as the sign for such an occurrence. The space for it is already manifest in ***Gravity's Rainbow*** through the figure of Ensign Morituri, the "inscrutable" Japanese on the *Anubis,* whose identity—it develops—is already subject to some division. Granted, he is an exile from his family in Hiroshima after having washed out of "Kamikaze school" (473). (His wife's name, Michiko, is the same name as that of Takeshi's wife.) His very name, however, is, as Steven Weisenburger notes, of a Latin origin, as if to betray a certain constitutive Americanness that owes something to W. J. Lueddecke's 1964 spy thriller entitled *Morituri,* made into a 1965 movie starring Marlon Brando and Yul Brynner (Weisenburger, 217).[12] In—or rather, by—a word, Ensign Morituri thus becomes readable not only as an "exile" (the more explicit thematization emphasized by the text) but as a hybrid, in a more overarching sense as part of a whole vocabulary for global dispersal and reconfiguration.

Or is Ensign Morituri better comprehended in Bhabha's more special sense of the term, as a figure who blasphemes, that is, overwhelms or alienates "the subject-matter or the content of a cultural tradition in the act of translation" (225)? We argue that Takeshi, by contrast, abides in ***Vineland*** as a more protracted figure of this kind, who by virtue of his very relation to DL—whether or not their "karmic adjustments" are given more valence than we have here—ultimately challenges the Orientalist tradition in which it is embedded. Recall the carefully orchestrated opening of ***Vineland,*** in which Zoyd Wheeler's annual act of window-breaking is analyzed on TV in terms of "the useful distinction between the defenestrative personality, which prefers jumping *out of* windows, and the transfenestrative, which tends to jump *through,* each reflecting an entirely different psychic subtext" (15, our italics). It is important to note that, as he jumps, Zoyd himself is not quite aware of "a number of positions" that he is actually in, as he recognizes only later on TV when the videotape is "being repeated in slow motion" (15). Just so, we can suggest that the whole matter of Orientalism in ***Vineland*** consists in this "unconscious" subtext of border-passing.

And yet, as Bhabha reminds us, incommensurable elements remain the basis of cultural translations. If there were no national sites for culture, there would be no need for translations. Therefore, as far as national orthodoxies are concerned, "hybridity is heresy" (225)—as we see in Pynchon's outrageous characterization of Ensign Morituri. Nevertheless, Bhabha continues, "if hybridity is heresy, then to blaspheme is to dream." To dream of what, precisely? The end of the need for cultural translation? Or a creative celebration of its endurance? ***Vineland,*** finally, represents an example of a narrative where transcultural negotiations aim at recuperating the "untranslatable" elements on which the respective cultures have been founded, at least with respect to each other. "Creative masochism" has been the name we have used throughout to describe these elements. Takeshi is finally to be DL's real-life partner (cf. 381-84). His name is more properly Japanese but his look could be more properly American. Takeshi is not only a mirror figure of Brock Vond; Noreen exclaims, "he looks just like a Jap Robert Redford!"? (381).

How are we to understand a "Jap Robert Redford"? By the end, ***Vineland*** bids us to imagine such a figure but merely evokes rather than represents the world in which the imagining would be grounded. For such a world, we need to return to cyberpunk, which is where we began this discussion. Of course, in addition, such a world now actually exists. The union between Takeshi and DL anticipates a new, postbubble, Japanese generation called "Shin-Jinrui" [New People], which, as recently reported in *Face* magazine, for example, has emerged "through the cracks of corporate culture," thus: "They are as familiar with hamburgers as *onigiri* (rice balls), Guns 'N Roses as *ikebana* (flower arranging), and folding a paper packet of cocaine or heroin as folding an *origami* crane" (Greenfield 63). However, ***Vineland*** demonstrates to us through the narrative of Takeshi and DL that hybrids are never so easily glossed and the psychic accents of older, more enduring narratives not so confidently banished.

The cultural transaction between Japan and the United States is not free from the pressures of creative masochism simply because a transnational comprehension is now available, either to dispel or to diffuse those pressures. Indeed, ***Vineland*** is remarkable for registering them in nervous, ambivalent, varied ways. The narrative looks backward as well as forward, both to the specific history between Japan and the United States that seems impossible for each nation to forget as well as to global political and economic developments that would make the history between the two countries merely a thing of the past.

Notes

1. Tatsumi is a rare exception among Japanese critics. See Kamioka, Miyamoto, and Sato for representative views, all of which ignore the Japanese elements. McCaffery's term can be found in "Pynchon Ikou No Postmodern [Everything Is Permitted: New Cartographies for the Post-Pynchon, Post-modern American Fiction]." McHale's concluding two chapters, "POSTcyberMODERNpunkISM" and "Towards a poetics of cyberpunk," sketch Pynchon's influence and traces the genealogy and thematics of cyberpunk and its relationship to postmodernism. For a larger framework for cyberpunk, see Dery.

2. The passage is quoted in Johnson 119. For more on the influence of von Lustbader, see Olster. Pynchon's (or von Lustbader's) use of Ninja can of course be aligned with the attempt during the late '80s and early '90s by any number of American businesses to make use of Japanese business techniques and practices; see, for example, Vogel.

3. Ninjutsu was all the more dispirited by the American ban on the practice of all martial arts during the period of occupation after World War II, when most of the Japanese population was absorbed into the industrial and trading sectors, with few even remaining in ninja clans to inherit the ancient esoterics. Historically, as Hayes—himself the first foreigner admitted, in 1975, into the Togakure-ryu, one of the few remaining sects—states: "Ninjutsu was a profession inherited at birth" (25).

4. She continues: "The continual reification of Japan as absolute other must be understood within the context of its perceived threat to the West" (11). In recreating the threat as American ninja, Pynchon, of course, diminishes something of its "absoluteness." On Japan under the sign of the female, see also Littlewood, Part III. He notes, for example, at the outset of his discussion that of twelve countries represented in a new mail-order house advertising campaign, only one was represented by a human figure: Japan, in the person of a geisha.

5. Compare Marilyn Ivy: "In the American national rhetoric of deficit, Japan marks out a nation-space of excess operating as the nameable supplement of the

United States, the defeated term that comes both to add to and invasively supplant the victorious one (even American cars are made with Japanese parts) (7)."

6. Released into action yet from a masochistic (as well as partially blinded) position, DL at this moment resembles no one so much as Oedipa Maas. For another Japanese reading of masochism in Pynchon—albeit one that does not mention Tatsumi (or *Vineland*)—see Ishiwari.

7. In a series of essays on Japan, Angela Carter criticizes Japanese male desire for white women: "In Japan, I learned what it is to be a [white] woman and became radicalized" (28). See also Millie Creighton, who, analyzing the representation of Caucasians in Japanese advertising campaigns, finds "the allure of the occidental woman" as a typical articulation of "Japanese occidentalism" that reflects not only "attraction to and exoticization of the Western other" but, more important, "a need to assert control over the moral threat of an intruding outside world" (144). From this particular sexual dynamic, Tatsumi's notion of creative masochism becomes another representation of Japanese occidentalism, which negatively defines econocultural self-images of Japan in its relation to the United States.

   More positively, is this why Takeshi is introduced as no longer a member of a corporation? Even when a *sarariman* at Wawazume Life & Non-Life, Takeshi "had dreamed of disengagement and freedom, of working as a *ronin.* or samurai without a master, out free-lancing in a dangerous world" (143). Now a "nomad in the sky's desert"—precisely what he does is not entirely clear—Takeshi (even though still attached to his "former mentor," the "eccentric" CEO, Professor Wawazume) is to some measure effectively free from social, if not cultural, constraint.

8. Again, compare Ishiwara's reading of Oedipa Maas's relationship with Pierce Inverarity, in which masochism turns out to be in reality more reactionary than transgressive, "implicated in and part of the dominating and 'orthodox' patriarchal structure, with no possibility that the female slave will ever gain power over her master" (132). See also his final point about Oedipa "*not living capitalism enough*" (139; his emphasis). Can we say, by contrast, that Takeshi does not live Orientalism enough?

9. If the relationship between DL and Takeshi is unrepresentable in its essence, so is that between Michiko and Takeshi. Or, more precisely, although the DL-Takeshi relation as in some sense at least manifest, the Michiko-Takeshi relation is simply bracketed and cannot be imagined at all. In fact, no Japanese female character is represented in the novel. With respect to Western discourse on Japan. *Vineland* is not unique. See, for example, David Hwang's *M Butterfly,* in which even Madame Butterfly turns out to be a man in drag (and a spy).

10. For a short, most suggestive alternate reading—that compares the West's either "elderly" or "mature" capitalism to Japan's "infantile" brand—see Akira. See also Cheah, who characterizes hybridity theory in terms of "its predication of culture as the human realm of flux and freedom from the bondage of being-in-nature, and its understanding of national culture as an ideological or naturalized constraint to be overcome" (298). The "bondage," that is, lies in the fact of culture itself, rather than its economic pulsions.

11. "We wanted to make something better than 'Break-out,'" explains Tomohiro Nishikado, the creator of the new game, looking back on the '70s, "and so we did by making our product 'interactive.'" This meant that, although the player in "Space Invaders" "breaks out" a set of immovable blocks with a white ball, just as in "Break-Out," and he shoots the invaders, he also has to face invaders who shoot back at him as they descend from the sky. See Aida 129-33.

12. The Latin origin also recalls the well-known words of Roman gladiators to Caesar: "Morituri te salutamus" ("We who are about to die salute you."). A name with such a derivation would appear especially appropriate for a man whose family lives in Hiroshima at the end of World War II, and therefore is about to die—as he himself may be, if he returns home in time. We would like to thank an anonymous reader for pointing this out.

Works Cited

Aida, Yutaka, and Atsushi Ohgaki. *Shin-Denshi Rikkoku.* Vol. 4. Tokyo, NHK, 1997.

Akira, Asada. "Infantile Capitalism and Japan's Postmodernism: A Fairy Tale." *South Atlantic Quarterly* 87.3 (Summer 1988): 629-34.

Atkins, E. Taylor, "Can Japanese Sing the Blues? 'Japanese Jazz' and the Problem of Authenticity." *Japan Pop! Inside the World of Japanese Popular Culture.* Ed. Tim Craig. New York: M. E. Sharpe, 2000: 27-59.

Barthes, Roland. *Empire of Signs.* New York: Hill and Wang, 1982.

Berressem, Hanjo. *Pynchon's Poetics: Interfacing Theory and Text.* Urbana: U of Illinois P, 1993.

Bhabha, Homi. *The Location of Culture.* London: Routledge, 1994.

Buruma, Ian. *The Missionary and the Libertine.* London: Faber, 1996.

Carter, Angela. *Nothing Sacred: Selected Writings.* London: Virago, 1993.

Cheah, Peng. "Given Culture: Rethinking Cosmopolitical Freedom in Transnationalism." *Cosmopolitics: Thinking and Feeling Beyond the Nation.* Ed. Peng Cheah and Bruce Robbins. Minneapolis: U of Minnesota P, 1998: 290-328.

Ching, Leo, "Imaginings in the Empire of the Sun." *Contemporary Japan and Popular Culture.* Ed. John Whittier Treat. Honolulu: U of Hawaii P, 1995.

Comaroff, Jean, and John Comaroff. "Millennial Capitalism: First Thoughts on a Second Coming." *Public Culture* 12.2 (Spring 2000): 291-343.

Condroy, Ian. "The Social Production of Difference: Imitation and Authenticity in Japanese Rap Music." *Transactions, Transgressions, Transformations: American Culture in Western Europe and Japan.* Ed. Heide Fehrenbach and Uta Poiger, New York: Berghahn, 2000: 166-84.

Creighton, Millie. "Imaging the Other in Japanese Advertising Campaigns." *Occidentalism: Images of the West.* Ed. James G. Carrier. Oxford: Clarendon, 1996.

Derry, Mark, *Escape Velocity: Cyberculture at the End of the Century.* New York: Grove, 1996.

Fallows, James. *Looking at the Sun: The Rise of the New East Asian Economic and Political System.* New York: Vintage, 1995.

Green, Geoffrey. Donald Greiner, and Larry McCaffery, eds. *The* Vineland *Papers.* Normal, IL: Dalkey Archive, 1994.

Greenfield, Karl Taro. "The New People." *Face.* April 1993: 62-75.

Hayes, Stephen. *The Ninja and their Secret Fighting Art.* Tokyo: Tuttle, 1990.

Hite, Molly. "Feminist Theory and the Politics of *Vineland.*" Green, Greiner, and McCaffery 135-53.

Huang, David Henry. *M. Butterfly.* New York: Penguin, 1988.

Ishiwari, Takayoshi. "Anti-Oedipa: Masochism, Self-Portrait, and *The Crying of Lot 49.*" *Studies in English Literature* LXXVI, 2 (December 1999): 125-40.

Ivy, Marilyn. *Discourses of the Vanishing: Modernity, Phantasm, Japan.* Chicago: U of Chicago P, 1995.

Jameson, Fredric. "Notes on Globalization as a Philosophical Issue." *The Cultures of Globalization.* Durham: Duke UP. 1998: 54-77.

———. "Postmoderism and Consumer Society." *The Anti-Aesthetic: Essays on Postmodern Culture.* Ed. Hal Foster. Port Townsend, WA: Bay Press, 1983: 111-25.

Kamioka, Nobuo. *Virtual Fiction: Multi-Media Jidai no America Bungaku [Virtual Fiction: American Literature in the Age of the Multi-Media].* Tokyo: Kokushokankoukai, 1998.

Larimer, Tim. "Rage for the Machine." *Time.* 1-8 May, 2000: 18-23.

Littlewood, Ian. *The Idea of Japan: Western Myths.* Chicago: Ivan Dee. 1996.

Lustbader, Eric von. *The Miko.* New York: Fawcett Crest, 1985.

———. *The Ninja.* New York: Fawcett Crest. 1981.

McCaffery, Larry. "Pynchon Ikou No Postmodern" ["Everything is Permitted: New Cartographies for the Post-Pynchon, Postmodern American Fiction"]. Trans. Takayuki Yatsumi. *Avant-Pop.* Ed. Takayuki Tatsumi and Yoshiaki Koshikawa. Tokyo: Chikuma, 1995: 15-41.

McHale, Brian. *Constructing Postmodernism.* London: Routledge, 1992.

Miner, Earl. *The Japanese Tradition in British and American Literature.* Princeton: Princeton UP, 1958.

Miyamoto, Yoichiro. "Hyperreal Jidai no Bungaku: Wangan Sensou Ikou no Postmodernism" [Literature in the Age of the Hyperreal: Postmodernism after the Gulf War]. *Hermes* 36 (1992): 30-37.

Olster, Stacey. "When You're a (Nin)jette, You're a (Nin)jette All the Way—or Are You? Feminist Filmmaking in *Vineland.*" Green, Greiner, and McCaffery 119-34.

Pynchon, Thomas. *Gravity's Rainbow.* New York: Viking, 1973.

———. *Vineland.* Boston: Little, Brown. 1990.

Sato, Yoshiaki. "Toki no Nami, Katari no Nami: Pynchon no Shin-shousetsu" [A Wave of Time, a Wave of Narrative: Pynchon's New Novel]. *Hermes* 32 (1991): 22-28.

———. "Translator's Notes," *Vineland.* By Thomas Pynchon. Tokyo: Shinchou, 1998: 574-635.

Spivak, Gayatri Chakravorty. *A Critique of Postcolonial Reason: Toward a History of the Vanishing Present.* Cambridge: Harvard UP, 1999.

Strehle, Susan. "Pynchon's 'Elaborate Game of Doubles' in *Vineland*": Green, Greiner, and McCaffery 101-18.

Tatsumi, Takayuki. "Comparative Metafiction: Somewhere between Ideology and Rhetoric." *Critique* 39.1 (Fall 1997): 2-17.

———. "Creative Masochism as an Approach to Avant-Pop." *In Memoriam to Postmodernism.* Ed. Mark Amerika and Lance Olson. 57-69.

———. "Full Metal Apache: Shinya Tsukamoto's *Tetsuo* Diptych: The Impact of American Narratives upon the Japanese Representation of Cyborgian Identity." *Japanese Journal of American Studies* 7 (1996): 25-47.

Treat, John Whittier. "Introduction: Japanese Studies into Cultural Studies." *Contemporary Japan and Popular Culture.* Ed. John Whittier Treat. Honolulu: U of Hawaii P, 1996: 1-15.

———. *Great Mirrors Shattered: Homosexuality, Orientalism, and Japan.* New York: Oxford, 1999.

Vogel, Ezra. *Japan as Number 1: Lessons for America.* Cambridge: Harvard UP, 1979.

Weisenburger, Steven. *A* Gravity's Rainbow *Companion. Sources and Contexts for Pynchon's Novel.* Athens: U of Georgia P, 1988.

Wright, Scott. *Japan Encountered.* New York: UP of America, 1996.

Yamamoto, Traise. *Masking Selves, Making Subjects: Japanese American Women, Identity, and the Body.* Berkeley: U of California P, 1999.

Wilde, Oscar. *Intentions.* London: Methuen, 1905.

Bruno Arich-Gerz (essay date 2004)

SOURCE: Arich-Gerz, Bruno. "The Comet and the Rocket: Intertextual Constellations about Technological Progress in Bruno Schulz's 'Kometa' and Thomas Pynchon's *Gravity's Rainbow.*" *Comparative Literature Studies* 41, no. 2 (2004): 231-56.

[*In the following essay, Arich-Gerz traces parallels between* Gravity's Rainbow *and Polish modernist Bruno Schulz's "The Comet," linking them with the poetry of Rainer Maria Rilke and the nonfiction writing of German rocket scientist Wernher von Braun.*]

At one point in Thomas Pynchon's ***Gravity's Rainbow,*** the protagonist Tyrone Slothrop comes up with what he calls a "Partial List of Wishes on Evening Stars for This Period." The period is the summer of 1945, the setting is Germany, and in one of his wishes Slothrop implores: "Let that only be a meteor falling" (553).[1] Slothrop's anxiousness evidently roots in the existence of more dreadful alternatives to "only" a meteor, two of which will be dealt with in the following investigation. The falling object could of course be a supersonic rocket like the one that constitutes the thematic center of Pynchon's 1973 novel: a device, to be more precise, which figures as that technological means which preserves the power for a mysterious in-group of *illuminati* (whom Pynchon's book about paranoiacs calls in true paranoid fashion "They") over the out-group of so-called *preterites* (or "We-system"). The falling object might likewise be a celestial body, a larger and usually more destructive one than a mere meteor—a bolide, in other words, like the one described in the 1938 tale "Kometa" ("The Comet") by the Polish artist-writer Bruno Schulz.[2] The rocket and the comet have in common that Pynchon and Schulz ascribe a special significance to their respective flight curves and, more specifically, to the turning point of this parabola. Although this must be measured against the obvious differences of the two objects—the first a result of technological progress, the second a natural phenomenon—both are presented as immobile objects menacingly pending at the peak of the parabola. Pynchon furthermore associates the issue of immobility at the rocket's turning point with that of transformation. Bruno Schulz, one of the most influential representative of Polish literary modernism next to Witold Gombrowicz and Stanisław Ignacy Witkiewicz, likewise connects transformation and immobility; moreover (and not surprisingly for a writer whose special concern was with matters of symbolism) he does so with reference to cyclists transmogrified into frozen firmament riders.

The imagery of the celestial rider is similarly invoked by Pynchon. Obviously, the reason for this correspondence is that ***Gravity's Rainbow*** and Schulz's narrative share a common intertextual reference point in the poetry of Rainer Maria Rilke, the outstanding German lyricist of the 1910s and 1920s. In the *Duino Elegies* and the *Sonnets to Orpheus,* Rilke links one of the major topoi of his poetry, the yearning for transformation, with a constellation of new stars named "Rider." In ***Gravity's Rainbow,*** it is the sinister Nazi official Weissmann, a fervent Rilke reader, who seeks and in the end apparently indeed achieves this kind of transformation at the rocket's peak point. Metamorphosed into the supernumerary sky constellation, he comes to portend absolute oppression for those who stay behind. Schulz endows the Rilkean imagery with an altogether different significance, although he, like Pynchon, converts the poet's original rider—a celestial horse rider—into the rider of a bicycle. In "The Comet," the stellar cyclist is presented as a chiffre of ambivalence. At first, the bicycle stands for technical progress and, ultimately, for man's tendency for self-destruction when the cyclists seek to transmute the pending annihilation through the comet into a trick-cyclist's end of the world. The blind belief in progress emblematized in the bicycle is checked, however, by the quasi-divine intervention of the narrator's father. His realization that the only alternative to the apocalyptic threat is the relinquishment of technical progress results in a contrived (and phantasmagoric) salvation of the world. The celestial bicycle outruns and finally defeats the comet.

Pynchon's fiction describes technological progress as a means to divide the world into oppressors and oppressed, whereas Schulz champions the cause of relinquishment as the only way to prevent self-annihilation. The final section of the article will confront these conclusions from the Rilkean intertext with the distinctly non-fictional writings of the Germany-born rocket scientist Wernher von Braun. ***Gravity's Rainbow,*** whose central theme is after all rocket technology, explicitly mentions von Braun and establishes certain parallels between him and the oppressor figure of Weissmann. Pynchon's undoubtingly critical judgement of von Braun's role in Nazi-Germany, in the US spaceflight and military armament programs is however challenged by a seeming affinity, or complicity, with the German's frame of mind on the level of ***Gravity's Rainbow***'s fictional strategy. No such direct invocation of the historical figure of von Braun exists in the tale by Schulz, who died at approximately the same time when the rocketry specialists around von Braun launched their first supersonic missile in the fall of 1942. It is nevertheless insightful to conjecture and combine his "Kometa" tale with the German engineer, his concrete scientific projects and the moral attitudes they implictly betray. In 1946, von Braun was working on a project for a two-stage supersonic missile with an atomic warhead; the sketch was titled (and the missile was to be named) "Comet." As a result, therefore, the often noted "strange anticipatory intelligence" in Schulz's fiction—that, as one of his critics has noted, "subsequent events brought grotesque life to his feverish imagination"[3]—can finally be related to the moral implications of von Braun's research activities. Likewise, it can be reconciled to Pynchon's undeniable concern with the conditions of those who come to live under the threat of supersonic missiles.

Parabolas

"That year the end of the winter stood under the sign of particularly favorable astronomical aspects," Schulz announces at the beginning of his 15-page tale (97),[4] a slightly lesser-known narrative, compared to his master works *The Street of Crocodiles* and *Sanatorium Under the Sign of the Hourglass.*[5] The tale goes on to describe what looks like the onset of modernity in the small town of Drohobycz in Eastern Poland: "It was the age of electricity and mechanics and a whole swarm of inventions was showered on the world by the resourcefulness of human genius" (99). Electric lighters, bells and conductors fascinate the people: while some are at the beginning puzzled by "the mysterious life enclosed in an electric circuit" (100), the majority soon welcomes the new era and actively appropriates its gadgets. Hence "[i]t was not long before the city filled with velocipedes of various sizes and shapes. [. . .] Whoever admitted to a belief in progress had to draw the logical conclusion and ride a velocipede" (99-100). As Schulz's poetological writings indicate, these insignia of modernity and techn(olog)ical progress are however less "grounded in *res gestae,* bearing the stamp of history."[6] In other words, their invocation reflects less the historical situation in early 20th century Drohobycz than it figures as a symbolic act in its own right in which words have accordingly a value of their own. Words are capable, in their turn, to turn upside down the conventional relationship between reality and its representation: "We usually regard the word as the shadow of reality, its symbol. The reverse of the statement would be more correct," Schulz declares 1936 in one of his essays before he opines that instead, "reality is the shadow of the word."[7] Schulz's verbal art takes this proto-constructivist principle at face value when he *transmogrifies* the world into words[8] instead of merely *representing* the era of electricity in its historical reality. Inhering a mythopoeic quality, Schulz's fiction combines in a curious way a fascination with the pre-cultural age in which the word "was not yet a sign but myth, story, sense"[9] that partakes in "the mythological idiom"[10] on the one hand, with the notoriously modernist awareness of the sign as a cultural achievement on the other. Thus he reaffirms the prevalence of mythical Nature (over progressive Culture) precisely by describing it in the most advanced cultural terms which are, in their turn, capable of generating unexplored and unprecedented and therefore exciting revelations. Words must become "the conductor of new meanings" in order to be literally electrifying: "The poet," writes Schulz, "restores conductivity to words by new quasi-electric tensions that are produced by an accumulation of charges."[11]

A case in point for this are the experiments of the narrator's father in "The Comet," a character who is even more than any other inspired and fascinated by the new insights and inventions of modernity. "It was Nature that willed and worked," he at one point remarks, "man was nothing more than an oscillating arrow, the shuttle of a loom, darting here or there according to Nature's will. He was himself only a component, a part of Neeff's hammer [a device for interrupting electric circuits]." If words figure as transformers of this, the world they reflect is conspicuously different from ordinary reality. Instead they convey phantasmagorias in which "an electric bell, built on the principle of Neeff's hammer" (102) anthropomorphizes in the narrator's own uncle.[12] By the same token, the people of Drohobycz, "[l]ost in the infinite" of Nature and disoriented as they are, transgress those boundaries and laws (like that of gravity) which would otherwise tie them to their ordinary existence on earth:

> Thus we meandered in extended, disorderly, single file, [. . .] emigrants from the abandoned globe, plundering the immense antheap of stars. The last barriers fell, the cyclists rode into stellar space, rearing on their vehicles, and were perpetuated in an immobile flight in the interplanetary vacuum, which revealed ever new constellations.
>
> (107)

This purely phantasmagorical ascent of bicycle riders into stellar space happens in response to (and is duplicated in Schulz's description of) a comet which threatens to fall down on earth, and which a critic has identified as the 1910 re-appearance of Halley's comet.[13] Using the same words as in the description of the stellar cyclists, Schulz writes: "One saw already the astonishing action of the distant comet, whose parabolic summit remained in the sky in immobile flight, still pointing towards the earth, and approaching it at a speed of many miles per second" (107). Agitated by this, people begin to prepare for "the imminent end of the world"—not, however, as a "tragic finale as forecast long ago by the prophets" but in terms of an almost pagan ecstasy that welcomes the newness (or, literally, modernity) of this kind of apocalypse: "this was a simply incredible chance, the most progressive, freethinking end of the world imaginable, in line with the spirit of times, an honourable end, a credit to the Supreme Wisdom" (106-7).

The thrill of newness in techn(olog)ical progress as weighed against the anxiety about a falling object of immense destructive potential is also the major theme of ***Gravity's Rainbow.*** In Pynchon's novel, it is not some comet coming from outer space that threatens to annihilate the blue planet, but the technical device of a supersonic rocket: the German *Aggregat 4* or V-2 *Vergeltungswaffe* (retaliatory weapon), which ever since its first successful launching by a crew of engineers around Wernher von Braun and General Walter Dornberger on October 3, 1942, was held to be the most progressive ballistic missile of the time, and which later became the ur-model for U.S. and Soviet spaceflight and warfare rocket programs. Yet the similarities of Schulz's comet and the Nazi rocket as portrayed by Pynchon are as striking as their major difference—the first is a natural bolide, the second a product of engineering culture—is evident. Apart from the destructiveness ascribed to both, the passage of the rocket through space is like the comet's, parabolic in shape, a geometrical figure that pervades the whole of ***Gravity's Rainbow.***[14] Two of the curve's three distinctive phases are for example invoked in the subtitles of the novel's last two sections in which Pynchon portrays the flight of the notorious 00000 rocket, a special construction based on V-2 technology designed to launch SS officer Weissmann's lover Gottfried into space: "Ascent" (758), which ends with the sentences: "The first star hangs between his feet. *Now*—," and "Descent" (760). Most important, however, is the third (and in terms of duration, infinitely short) phase of the parabola: the turning point when the projectile reaches its peak of altitude, which Pynchon notably associates with a star hanging between Gottfried's feet. At the other end(ing) of the novel's own parabola,[15] in the first of its 73 chapters, this phase in the flight of "the new, and still Most Secret, German rocket bomb" is explained as "equaling the moment of [. . .] fuel cutoff, end of burning, what's their word [. . .] Brennschluss" (6). As on the last page of the book, the instant when ascent tips over into descent is indicated by one short, italicized word: "The missile, sixty miles high, must be coming up on the peak of its trajectory by now [. . .] beginning its fall [. . .] *now*" (7).

It is first and foremost this peak point of the rocket's flight that Pynchon subsequently (re-)charges with extra significance, exploiting it much like Schulz in terms of a "conductor of new meaning" or agent of transformation. But in the present case, the transmogrification operates less on the linguistic-semantic level. Instead Pynchon—known for his profound background knowledge of the technical and engineering sciences and famous for the complicated algebraic equations that pervade his fiction—provides a prime example of what Lance W. Ozier has called "[t]he Calculus of Transformation"[16] when he invokes the tip of the parabola. Halfway into the novel, Pynchon mentions the double integral, a preeminent feature in rocketry calculations conventionally symbolized with a double S, and goes on to associate it with the shape of the underground *Mittelwerke* rocket production plant ("Picture the letters SS each stretched lengthwise a bit. These are the two main tunnels, driven well over a mile into the mountain" (299)[17] and the portals of these tunnels ("The entrance to the tunnel is shaped like a parabola. The Albert Speer touch [. . .] of the New German Architecture then" (298)). Then, in a scientific tour de force, he conjoins the shapes and symbols of architecture and algebraic analysis in the disclosure that "in the dynamic space of the living Rocket, the double integral has a different meaning. To integrate here is to operate on a rate of change so that time falls away: change is stilled. [. . .] 'Meters per second' will integrate to 'meters.' The moving vehicle is frozen, in space, to become architecture, and timeless. It was never launched, it will never fall" (301). The mathematically accomplished freeze of a vehicle in mid-air (or mid-space) indicates two things at once. First, it designates the parabola as no longer a geometrical figure, but an algebraic one. Through the elimination of the perimeter of time, it secondly preserves the idea of the parabola (as well as, of course, the turning point itself, the determination of which is what the whole calculation is about), but double-integrates away both the seconds it takes to bring the rocket up high and the time-span of its descent. Taken together, this evokes the peak point of the parabola as an instance outside the phenomenological setup, i.e. that framework in which time is as much a constituent part of reality as ascent and descent are of the ordinary flight curve of a rocket, and where as a consequence any historical "ascent will be betrayed to Gravity" (758). The "paradoxical timelessness within time"[18] that Pynchon derives mathematically here has—technically somewhat inaccurately—*Brennschluß* as "a point in *space,* a point hung precise as the point where burning must end, never launched, never to fall" (302, emphasis added). Connoting moreover "an interface between one order of things and another" (302), the tip of this parabola figures as the mathematician's equivalent of Schulz's transformer-words, capable like these of evoking a scenario that contrasts with, goes beyond or even transcends the accepted standards of world-perception.[19]

As mentioned, transformer-words in "The Comet" are for example the "riders on their bicycles"—Schulz transmogrifies the ordinary world when he employs this signifier, "cyclists," to describe a wholly unrealistic and fantastic "ride in the sky." This allows in turn for the following interim conclusion: the rocket, the comet and the bicycles have been qualified in Pynchon's mathematical and Schulz's phantasmagorical depictions as stationary objects, "frozen" or caught in immobile flight. The use of that term—"immobile flight"—links the heavenly object and the bikes in Schulz's tale, the latter moreover standing in, much like Pynchon's rockets, for technical-cultural achievements of the present which leave the earth to "ride" the sky. And it is the imagery of the parabola—and in particular the tip of the curve—that completes the triangular interrelatedness between the two vehicles and the bolide, connecting as it does Schulz's comet with the V-2 rocket: "each night appeared that fatal comet, hanging aslant, at the apex of its parabola," Schulz notes, "perform[ing its] daily work with mathematical precision" according to "the fatal formula expressed in the logarithm of a multiple integer" (109).

Rilkean Riders

While the rocket at *Brennschluß* point, the comet at the cusp of its curve, and the bicycle riders all share the nominal characteristics of stationary celestial figures, only the rider and the rocket are at the same time associated with the issue of transformation. Much as the modes of invoking this issue differ—a verbally accomplished transformation in Schulz's phantasmagoria, a mathematically conceived transformation in the case of Pynchon's novel—the two writers nevertheless borrow the concept of transformation itself as well as the imagery used to illustrate its consequences from the same source. Their common intertextual frame of reference is Rainer Maria Rilke's poetry.[20]

Rilke directly connects the issue of transformation with the turning point (or point of inflection) that characterizes the parabolic curve. Moreover, and in line with his understanding of transformation as a state in which the "ordeals" of the ordinary world are ultimately "overcome," his poetry explicitly associates it with the sky as a location beyond the confines and limitations of earthly existence. Hence, the twelfth sonnet from the second cycle of the *Sonnets to Orpheus* begins with:

> Wolle die Wandlung. O sei für die Flamme begeistert,
> drin sich ein Ding dir entzieht, das mit Verwandlungen prunkt;
> jener entwerfende Geist, welcher das Irdische meistert,
> liebt in dem Schwung der Figur nicht wie den wendenden Punkt.

> [Will transformation. Oh be crazed for the fire
> in which something boasting with change is recalled
> from you; that designing spirit, the earthly's master,
> loves nothing as much as the turning point of the soaring symbol.][21]

Pynchon's novel has the beginning of the poem as one of its rare direct quotations (97) and recycles a large variety of themes and topoi from the sonnet such as the above described implications of transformation/turning point ("(Ver-)Wandlung/wendenden Punkt").[22] By the same token, the mention of fire/flame as well as the idea of its innermost that is mysteriously barred from sight point to the rocket and, more exactly, to the fuel burning inside its combustion chamber: for example when the narrator calls this burning oven a "mystical egg" in which "creation and destruction, fire and water, chemical plus and chemical minus" unite unseen (403). Another such instance is that of the genius overcoming earth's gravity: Rilke's "designing spirit" materializes in the rocket scientists and, most notably, in the "brand-new military type, part salesman, part scientist" (401) of Weissmann.[23]

A fervent reader of the German's poems, Weissmann systematically seeks the Rilkean transformation, or entrance into "another order of being" (239) in which death seems incorporated into a larger life. In order to bring this transformation about, he coerces a crew of engineering specialists into constructing a specially equipped V-2. In the spring of 1945, he uses this rocket, the so-called 00000, to launch young Gottfried up to the parabola's turning point, the "wendenden Punkt" at which transformation is consummated. Although Weissmann physically stays behind in order to supervise the rocket's ascent, Gottfried's unconditional love enables him to accompany the boy spiritually on his journey to death and beyond: "I want to break out—to leave this cycle of infection and death," he announces before the launching to his lover, "I want to be taken in love: so taken that you and I, and death, and life, will be gathered, inseparable, into the radiance of what we would become" (724). In the end, the Rilkean scheme of using the peak point of the 00000 parabola's flight curve for his personal transformation apparently comes off for Weissmann. He wanted the change ("Wolle die Wandlung"), and from what other figures report, there is reason to assume that his final disappearance can indeed be explained in these terms: that, as Judith Chambers puts it, the "'fair intellectual king Weissmann [. . .] sacrifices Gottfried for his own transcendence.'"[24] Shortly before the liftoff of the 00000, the actress Greta Erdmann had observed Weissmann murmur in Rilkean fashion of the imminent passage into his "Ur-Heimat" before she in an anticipatory manner concludes that "he was seeing the world now in *mythical regions.* [. . .] It was not Germany he moved through. It was his own space" (486). And after the launching another character, Weissmann's other lover boy Enzian, conspicuously speculates that "he may have changed now past our recognition. We could have driven under him in the sky today and never seen. Whatever happened at the end, he has transcended. Even if he's only dead" (660-1).

The combination of a mathematically derived timeless point in space with the Rilkean idea of transformation, enacted by Weissmann here, is admittedly a very particular—and particularly radical—interpretation of the German poet's oeuvre. ***Gravity's Rainbow*** functionalizes Rilke as an intertextual *advocatus diaboli,* it seems, whom and whose poetry Weissmann (mis)uses "on his way to achieving some infrahuman demonic status beyond the remotest extremes of natural existence."[25] Similarly noteworthy is the depiction of Weissmann as "him in the sky" or, for that matter, the narrator's appeal to "[l]ook high, not low". for him (749) because this reverberates, as mentioned, with Rilkean undertones too. Back in his youth, way before he severs all ties with humanity and nature, Weissmann experiences the intensive lure of Rilke's poetry in terms of a "Yearning" for transformation. Like the "newly-dead youth" from the *Tenth Elegy,* he seeks to "embrac[e] his Lament, his last link, leaving now her marginally human touch forever, climbing all alone, terminally alone, up and up into the mountains of primal Pain, with the wildly alien constellations overhead" (98). The subsequent step from a yearning *for* to the accomplishment *of* transformation apparently effects a radical repositioning of Weissmann: no longer an earthbound star gazer, he is now (being conceived of as) a celestial phenomenon himself—from now on he makes his appearance in the medium of the new, wildly alien constellation and its astrology. Concomitantly the signification of "pain" changes. In Rilke's original, it is for instance invoked in the passage "Und höher, die Sterne. Neue. Die Sterne des Leidlands" [And higher, the stars. New ones. Stars of the Land of Grief],[26] a line which Pynchon, focalized through young Weissmann, again repeats almost literally: "the constellations, like the new stars of Pain-land, had become all unfamiliar" (99). After the transformation, however, Weissmann is no longer subject to human perceptions like that of pain; as Enzian puts it, he has now "gone beyond *his* pain, *his* sin" (661). If pain as a category has for Weissmann been eliminated in the very moment of his entrance into the celestial "Painland," and if he now indeed figures as part and parcel of such a new constellation himself, it follows that those who come to live under these stars encounter them as similarly unfamiliar ones. In contrast to what the new stars had meant for Weissmann, however, for them they signify suffering, anxiety and terror. Pynchon illustrates this with another invocation of Rilke's poems, submitting these again to certain "interpretative liberties."[27]

In the *Tenth Elegy,* but also in the *Sonnets to Orpheus,* Rilke defines the new cluster of stars on the firmament with more precision. The eleventh sonnet of the first series thus begins with the musing: "Look at the sky. Is no constellation called 'Rider?'" ["Sieh den Himmel. Heisst kein Sternbild 'Reiter?'"].[28] Likewise, the elegy "slowly names" the new stars of Pain-Land: "Look, there: the *Rider,* the *Staff,* and they call that bigger constellation *Garland of Fruit.* Then farther toward the Pole: *Cradle, Road, The Burning Book, Doll, Window*" [Hier, siehe: den *Reiter,* den *Stab,* und das vollere Sternbild nennen sie: *Fruchtkranz.* Dann, weiter, dem Pol zu: *Wiege; Weg; Das Brennende Buch; Puppe, Fenster*].[29] Pynchon, in his turn, invokes the Rilkean Rider as symbolic of the ill-omened existence of those whom Weissmann's rocket-propelled passage into the other order of being leaves behind. In ***Gravity's Rainbow,*** Tyrone Slothrop is presumably the most prominent figure among these doomed "to stay down among the Preterite" (544), i.e., the counterparts of the Elect or illuminati à la Weissmann.[30] Hence in Peenemünde, where the historical V-2 missiles had been developed by von Braun, Dornberger and their crew of engineers (and where Weissmann had begun to gather experts for the construction of his 00000 rocket), he comes to look, in the summer of 1945, "into a sky flowing so even and yellowed a brown that the sun could be anywhere behind it, and the crosses of the turning windmills could be spoke-blurs of the terrible Rider himself, Slothrop's Rider, his two explosions up there, his celestial cyclist." For Slothrop, the unfamiliar apparition in the sky figures as the complete contrary of an accomplishable transformation in the sense of a fulfillment of one's yearning—the subsequent sentence makes that clear beyond all doubts: "No, but even *That* only flickers now briefly across a bit of Slothropian lobe-terrain, and melts into its surface, vanishing. So here passes for him one more negligence [. . .] and likewise groweth his Preterition sure" (509).[31] Rather, it seems to be Weissmann himself who, in the medium of the new stars of Pain-Land that Rilke's lament names "Rider," materializes here *as* Slothrop's rider, signifying terror for the latter, and assigning the power of executing this terror to the first. In thus summing up, Pynchon instrumentalizes Rilke's poetry and his imagery of the Rider in particular in order to describe, first, the transformation of Weissmann at the very moment when the rocket reaches the tip of its flight curve. Second, he presents the consequences of this in terms of a difference between what the rider signifies for him who has transcended earthly existence on the one hand and for those who stay behind on the other.[32]

At first sight, Bruno Schulz's invocation of the Rilkean Rider requires a less intricate reading. As mentioned, the celestial stage where the bike riders are frozen in immobile flight is at the same time described as revealing ever new constellations. According to Rilke, the new constellation *is* that of the rider, and Schulz thus continues:

> Oh, stellar arena of night, scarred by the evolutions, spirals and leaps of those nimble riders; oh, cycloids and epi-cycloids executed in inspiration along the diagonals of the sky, amid lost wire spokes, hoops shed with indifference, to reach the bright goal denuded, with nothing but the pure idea of cycling! From these days dates a new constellation, the thirteenth group of stars, included for ever in the zodiac and resplendent since then in the firmament of our nights: *The Cyclist.*
>
> (108)

Schulz's adaptation of the Rilkean Rider however lacks the allusive division into oppressor and oppressed from Pynchon's novel—last but not least because in "The Comet," it is not this rider but, if anything, the natural bolide at the peak of its flight curve that might take over the function of a new star symbolizing subjugation. Instead, the cyclist here is "forecasting a new happy era for mankind—salvation through the bicycle" (100), which at the very end of the tale seems to mean: salvation from the threat of the comet. Schulz releases the bicycle rider and the comet from their stasis again, transmogrifying both into competing mounts on a celestial racetrack:

> The comet proceeded bravely, rode fast like an ambitious horse in order to reach the finish line on time. The fashion of the season [i.e., the cyclist] ran with him. For a time, he took the lead of the era, to which he lent his shape and name. Then the two gallant mounts drew even and ran neck-to-neck in a strained gallop, our hearts beating in fellow feeling with them. Later on, fashion overtook by a nose and outstripped the indefatigable bolide. That millimetre decided the fate of the comet. It was doomed, it has been outdistanced forever. Our hearts now ran along with fashion, leaving the splendid comet behind. We looked on indifferently as he became paler, smaller, and finally sank resignedly to a point just above the horizon, leaned over to one side, trying in vain to take the last bend of its parabolic course, distant and blue, rendered harmless forever. He was unplaced in the race, the force of novelty was exhausted, nobody cared any more for a thing that had been outstripped so badly. Left to itself, it quietly withered away amid universal indifference.
>
> (111)

Schulz's phantasmagoric space race appears as irreconcilable with the wider thematic context of Rilke's elegies and sonnets as the (re-)interpretation of the rider imagery and its implications in ***Gravity's Rainbow*** was provocative. Nowhere in Rilke's poetry is there a suggestion that the constellation of the rider stands itself in a constellation, and a competitive one at that, with another heavenly object. Yet apart from the liberties that also Schulz takes in his intertextual reference to Rilke's cluster of new stars, the narrow escape from the world's annihilation through the comet reveals more than just the ultimate victory of man's culture (as the invention of bicycles) over nature and its destructive forces as emblematized in the comet. The happy outcome of the showdown in the sky after all eclipses the initial, strangely megalomaniac hopes of the Drohobycz citizens to appropriate the imminent apocalypse and endow it with a man-made air. Articulating a collective desire reminiscent of the Freudian death drive, the people had hoped to level the natural catastrophe with a "cultural" counterpart, and to celebrate it primarily as a technically conceived and therefore self-annihilative event: "It was to be a trick cyclist's, a prestidigitator's end of the world, splendidly hocus-pocus and bogus-experimental—accompanied by the plaudits of all the spirits of Progress" (106). The function they ascribe to the bicycle is clearly not the prevention of the disaster in the sense of a protection shield against falling meteors or, if one wishes, a before-the-letter SDI weapon; rather, the bicycles figure as reinforcements for the pending catastrophe and thus complement (and compete with) the fatal comet in terms of purpose. By the same token, the Drohobycz people are "richer by one more disappointment" (111) when the comet loses its force of novelty and the end of the world is foreclosed by, now, the bicycle's salvational intervention.

If the salvation therefore contradicts the people's (death-) wishful thinking because it happens in spite of man's profoundly narcissistic inclinations and self-destructive drives, Schulz resolves the dilemma with an artistic sleight-of-hand that discloses his terminal conclusion about the *conditio humana* in the era of advanced technological progress. The trick, which in turn outtricks the self-aggrandizing cyclist in the sky, consists of, first, framing the ecstatic star-flights of fantasy as dreamlike delusions of an unseeing crowd: "Thus circling on an endless track, they marked the paths of a sleepless cosmography, while in reality, black as soot, they succumbed to a planetary lethargy, as if they had put their heads into the fireplace, the final goal of all those blind flights" (107). Schulz then presents the father as the *deus ex machina* in whose supreme knowledge the salvation through the bicycle ultimately rests: "While the mob scattered in the open, losing itself under the starry lights and celestial phenomena, my father remained stealthily at home. He was the only one who knew a secret escape from our trap, the back door of cosmology" (109-10). Through another of his transmogrifications, Schulz then gathers the dream-riders in outer space and the father at home in the house's sooty fireplace. Putting "his head into the chimney shaft of the stove," the father discovers how "the frail light of a star" lights "a spark in the hearth, a tiny seed in the retort of the chimney." A process of growth sets in, supervised by the father and depicted by Schulz as a bewildering combination of the telescopic with the microscopic, in which the birth of a new star and universal cosmogony fuses with the phylogenetic-historical development of the human species in general, that of the Drohobycz people in particular, and with the prenatal ontogenesis of a human individual. Simultaneously visible in the sky (and through a telescope) and inside the stove (through a microscope), the "fatal creation" develops from a cheese-like object into a human brain covered with tiny letters and, finally, "an embryo in a characteristic head-over-heels position [. . .], sleeping upside-down its blissful sleep in the light waters of amnion." Before it can develop any further under the demiurgic manipulations of the father, he "left it in that position" (110), neutralizing thus its evolution toward a *homo faber* capable of self-extinction. The alternative to man's will of self-extinction epitomized in the bicycle, Schulz seems to say, is the relinquishment of man's will of progress, which is consequentially—and at the same time most ironically—accounted for by the salvation through the same bicycle.[33] But as Schulz's parabolic tale seems just as well to suggest, it takes a superhuman effort (or, as here, a quasi-divine intervention) to bring this relinquishment into effect.[34]

Pynchon's and Schulz's respective citations of Rilke's rider in the sky have in common that they take it as a cue to discuss the issues of progress and modernity, new technologies and their feasibility. For that purpose, both convert the horseman from Rilke's original into a cyclist, hence retain and in fact reinvigorate the idea of newness that Rilke had associated with this constellation, and link it with foreboding human ambitions, be these personally motivated as in the case of Weissmann, or collective as in that of the Drohobycz citizens. Much as these foci join their narratives in a position other than those inherent in Rilke's source text, they nevertheless draw different, almost diametrically opposed conclusions about the celestial rider as a token of the very consequences of these ambitions. In ***Gravity's Rainbow,*** the bicycle rider in the sky comes to represent the eager scientist Weissmann's unrestrained, yet ultimately successful plan of reaching personal transformation *qua* rocketry as bearing a dire portent for the multitude that stay behind. In "The Comet," the celestial cyclist stands in various respects for the exact inversion of this setup. Here, it is the multitude, in its zealousness comparable to Weissmann, that aspires to profane the modern version of the Rilkean rider by deliberately turning this constellation of new stars into a Slothropian Pain-Land for themselves. The "streets of the City of Pain" (as the *Tenth Elegy* has it elsewhere)[35] revolve into the mundane world of Drohobycz and other metropolises: "In illustrated journals whole-page pictures began to appear, drawings of the anticipated catastrophe" which "represented panic-stricken populous cities under a night sky resplendent with lights and astronomical phenomena" (107). And it is the scientist-father—Schulz's equivalent to Weissmann in terms of power and superiority, but his exact opposite in that of moral responsibility—whose conscious act of renunciation leads to the salvational intervention which finally (and through an ironic deployment of the same rider) forecloses this kind of apocalypse.

If Schulz centers his discussion of the modern mount derived from Rilke's poetry on the ethical aspects of modern science, this is embedded in a context that almost completely screens out phenomenological probability and historical reality (with the Drohobycz setting and the above-mentioned 1910 appearance of Halley's comet as a possible trigger for the tale as notable exceptions). Pynchon, in turn, apparently downplays the issue of the moral implications of scientific progress when he radicalizes Rilke's idea of transformation in the persona of Weissmann and the equally fictional 00000 rocket. On the other hand, his "historical novel of a whole new sort"[36] explicitly integrates the historically real forerunners of Weissmann and the quintuple zero missile. The leap back into concrete history, ventured in the following part, will therefore sustain the subtle critique that Schulz grafts onto Rilke's Rider by combining it with these precursors: the first, the model for Weissmann (at least one of them) is Wernher von Braun;[37] the second, the forerunner of his 00000 is primarily his standard V-2 rocket.

The attempt to constellate rider, rocket and comet anew on a non-fictional and historical background by conjoining the two prose writers, their respective intertextual references to Rilke's poetry and Wernher von Braun's engineering achievements quite obviously begs the question of the relatability of the latter with Schulz's fiction. Whereas the rider and the comet play a prominent role, the tale of the Pole conspicuously lacks the explicit mention of supersonic rockets.[38] Two ways exist to substantiate the connection nevertheless. The first is the detour via Pynchon's novel, whose linking up of rider and rocket as astrologically and historically new items indeed figures as the *tertium comparationis* between "Schulz" (rider and comet) and "von Braun" (rocket) here. For example, ***Gravity's Rainbow*** relocates the "Cyclist" and the criticism Schulz distilled from his phantasmagoria within the context of factual reality. The moments of fuel cutoff of the various V-2s deployed by the Nazis against their enemies create the same figuration: "There's a Brennschluss point for every firing site. They still hang up there, a constellation waiting to have a 13th sign of the Zodiac named for it" (302). The other way of establishing the connection between Schulz's fiction and von Braun's factual rocketry research hinges on a strange coincidence: one of the follow-up rocket projects that von Braun had worked on after the V-2 bore the same name as Schulz's natural bolide: "Comet."

Von Braun's "Comet"

Wernher von Braun pursued his scientific aims with extraordinary tenaciousness and persistence, regardless of the radically different tenets of those he had (or chose) to conduct his research for. A bit like the *A-9* rocket he had been devising for the Nazis, a missile nicknamed *Amerikarakete* ("America rocket") which remained unfinished business until the U.S. troops finally captured him, von Braun's career was a two-stage one—the first in Germany, the second in the United States, whose citizen he became in 1955—guided by the unshakable desire to advance the science of rocketry.

Surprisingly or not, the continuity of his research activities has, in the history of the numerous biographies about von Braun, led to a discontinuity of its own, taking a curious turn from approval and admiration to disapproval and criticism. If one ventures to describe this development from early hagiography to critical assessment in a rise-and-fall picture, publications of the 1960s like Ernst Klee and Otto Merk's or Bernd Ruland's mark the ascent with their—in a way very logical—focus on von Braun's leading role on the way up high to the stars.[39] The turning point was primarily effected by the memoirs of former concentration camp prisoner Jean Michel, who in 1975 pointed to the role of slave labor in the development and production of the Nazi rockets, and the writings of Linda Hunt and Tom Bower in the early and mid-eighties.[40] Pynchon critics like Inger Dalsgaard and Dale Carter moreover include ***Gravity's Rainbow*** itself;[41] hence, the moment when rise tipped over into fall may equally logically be dated around the time of von Braun's death in 1977. The descent, among whose most recent representatives are Michael J. Neufeld and Rainer Eisfeld,[42] logically shifts into focus what the earlier eulogistic biographies had downplayed, and what protest singer Tom Lehrer sardonically sums up like this: "'Once the rockets are up, / who cares where they come down? / That's not my department,' / Says Wernher von Braun."[43]

If the course of von Braun's career and the biographical criticism of that career until the late 1970s stood under the sign of a continuous ascent, later criticism developed an awareness for the collateral damage (to use the cynical military jargon) that has ever since the first successful launch of a von Braunian rocket been inseparable from this rise. The V-2s eventually came down, so would the *Amerikarakete* (which was planned to be targeted against *Amerika*) or, to anticipate its successor here, the hardware and payload of the missile that von Braun would in 1946 re-devise for *Amerika*'s defense. But at the time when such awareness began to gain ground, von Braun himself did not have to care any more indeed: in the zenith of his career and, simultaneously, at the turning point of his career's estimation, he passed away. As the beliefs of the man who brought the rockets and himself up show, this passing away possesses the same peculiarly Rilkean flavor as Weissmann's scheme of transcending his pain and sin. Pynchon seems to substantiate the resulting mini constellation of Rilke, Weissmann and von Braun when he chooses the following passage from von Braun's religious reasonings (which the engineer elaborated in a pamphlet for the magazine *Words to Live By*) for an epitaph of the first part of ***Gravity's Rainbow***: "Nature does not know extinction; all it knows is transformation. Everything science has taught me, and continues to teach me, strengthens my belief in the continuity of our spiritual existence after death."[44]

If, as Dalsgaard puts it, "von Braun seems to forget himself in his own idea of immortality, transcending not just gravity but history when he fantasizes about blasting into eternal space," and if this coincides with "the way Blicero [alias Weissmann] dreams his rocket's special payload will allow him to do"[45] as ***Gravity's Rainbow*** intimates, the conclusion that Pynchon draws from the Rilkean Rider likewise seems to include von Braun's historical person. Indeed, Pynchon allocates the new, extraordinary or supernumerary sign of the zodiac, an ill-starred constellation for those who come to stand beneath it, next to von Braun's birthday, and thus associates the two: "Wernher von Braun [. . .] was born close to the Spring Equinox," which allows him "to confront the world from that most singular of the Zodiac's singular points" (588). By the same token, ***Gravity's Rainbow*** mentions the frenzy of the people, reminiscent of the pagan ecstasy of the Drohobycz citizens in Schulz's tale and at the same time reverberating the attitude of von Braun's early biographers: "It's a Rocket-raising: a festival new to this country. Soon it will come to the folk-attention how close Wernher von Braun's birthday is to the Spring Equinox, and [people] will be erecting strange floral towers out in the clearings and meadows, and the young scientist-surrogate will be going round and round with old Gravity or some such buffoon" (361).

The novel is however conspicuously equivocal about the flip side of the blind worship of the surmounter of nature's obsolescent forces, even though it contains painfully detailed descriptions of the disastrous effect of V-2 attacks against London and thus challenges von Braun's notorious indifference about where his rockets come down. But these explicit descriptions are levelled by the book's notable silence when it comes to the consequences of the successors of the V-2s, i.e., the optimized versions in terms of range and destructive potential. As mentioned before, ***Gravity's Rainbow*** ends with an episode titled "Descent" in which the audience in a contemporary movie theater in L.A. impatiently waits for the film to begin. The strike of the Rocket itself is conspicuously suspended: "it is just here [. . .] that the pointed tip of the Rocket, falling nearly a mile per second, [because of its supersonic quality] absolutely and forever without sound, reaches its last unmeasurable gap above the roof of this old theatre" (760). While the novel remains absolutely and forever silent about the disastrous consequences of this particular strike at this (final) point, critics have responded to the open ending in mainly two ways: by identifying the Rocket with a nuclear missile because of the 1970s setting of the scene, and with a metaleptical interpretation of the film audience as the novel's preterite reader.[46] A radical conclusion from these two readings would however cast a dubious light on Pynchon and, more exactly, on the fictional strategies he employs. For if one interprets his last-page Rocket as, first, equipped with an atomic warhead that is, second, about to hit an audience reflecting, on a different level, the novel's own readership, this would by consequence endow its very author with Weissmannian features—as Leo Bersani concludes, it "would constitute Thomas Pynchon as the reader's They."[47] In short: Pynchon's concern and, as can be surmised, his criticism of von Braun's obliviousness about the descent-part of the V-2s' parabolas seems eclipsed by the function he attributes to (or derives from) the next generation of rockets as long as these were essentially based on the same von Braun's engineering activities: the "Amerikarakete" (and was not the Rocket on the novel's last page about to hit a *Californian* movie theater?), but just as well the development of a missile with an atomic warhead for the United States, a project which the *Beutedeutscher* ("booty German") began to outline in 1946.

When U.S. Intelligence squads discovered the whereabouts of Nazi-German rocket hardware in the spring of 1945, immediate action was taken to ship these—and the big names among their inventors—to the States. While many of the V-2s were subsequently used, in White Sands, for ionospheric and other outer space research, Wernher von Braun soon volunteered "to produce free rockets and controlled missiles that meet military requirements," as his new superior, Colonel Holger N. Toftoy, put it in a memorandum for the Pentagon.[48] In an undated *Beschreibung* (description), von Braun "presents a project outline for a missile of very wide range which consists of a combination of the German A 4-rocket (V-2) and a new device named 'Comet.'"[49] In a more detailed draft, he specifies on April 12, 1946 "that after completion of the development, either normal high explosives or atomic war heads can be used.[50] Equipped with this payload, the new device was planned to be launched, in the first of its two stages, to the turning point of the [. . .] only marginally modified V-2 rocket." At this point of the curve, "a special mechanism severs the front part (Comet) from the V-2 rocket," and it is here that for once, von Braun indeed seems to care where his V-2 comes down: "From this height, the empty V-2 itself begins to fall and can, if necessary, be blown up into small particles when it is still in the air in order to avoid collateral damage." Disconnected from the V-2 carrier rocket and lighter in weight than this, the "upper part" continues its ascent up to a height of "approximately 20 kilometers" before "two supersonic athodyde devices will be ignited" to propel the von Braunian "Comet" further:[51] "The fuel supply will provide for a range between 1000 and 2000 kilometers [1250 miles], depending on the payload weight, which may vary between 500 and 1000 kg (1110 or 2220 lbs)."[52]

Although the newly founded "V-2 Panel" in White Sands soon aborted the *Comet* project again in favor of more upper atmosphere research, Wernher von Braun's engagement here reveals a facet of his personality that remains for better or worse inexplicit in the plot and plottings (i.e., the fictional strategies) of Pynchon's novel: his uncompromising will to push progress further, regardless of moral considerations. This facet is all the more effectively put into perspective if one contrasts it with Schulz's fiction. The nightmarish vision of a comet threatening to annihilate the earth has its counterpart, no less nightmarish yet now man-made, in the projected atomic missile of the same name—a difference which by itself will make a difference, compared to the conscious decision of the father in Schulz's "Comet" tale to refrain from pushing progress over the edge. The contrast between von Braun and the father becomes palpable, however, if one takes into consideration the rocket engineer's attempt to involve other renowned scientists of the time into his *Comet* project. The above mentioned detailed description of the two-stage atomic missile was part of a letter of inquiry for the "Los Alamos Laboratory, Dr. J. R. Oppenheimer."[53] When the letter was drafted in early 1946, though, the addressee of the letter had freshly withdrawn from the director post at Los Alamos. After the so-called *Manhattan Project* had under his supervision produced the first U.S. atomic bomb in 1943, J. Robert Oppenheimer refused to partake in the development of the H Bomb. In the end, therefore, Oppenheimer followed precisely those qualms which von Braun obviously subordinated to his strivings for technological progress.

The mention of Oppenheimer, finally, helps to redirect the attention to the common denominator of Schulz's and Pynchon's analyses of 20th-century scientific progress. Notwithstanding the differences in the presentation of the genius figures—the father in "The Comet," Weissmann in ***Gravity's Rainbow***—and the diametrically opposed attitudes of these when it comes to the issue of responsibility in science, both betray a keen awareness of the equivalent, in terms of true affliction, of Rilke's celestial Pain-Land. Both, in other words, demonstrate a sensitivity for the literally down-to-earth "streets of the City of Pain." In Schulz's tale, this was for instance implied in the mention of "panic-stricken populous cities" (107) awaiting the apocalyptic strike of the comet. In an episode of the fourth part of ***Gravity's Rainbow*** subtitled "Streets," it is conveyed through the prime example of a city afflicted with nuclear destruction:

> "MB DRO
> ROSHI"

reads "a scrap of newspaper headline" (693), and the context of the passage makes it obvious that the whole headline must be "A BOMB DROPPED ON HIROSHIMA." The streets are those of unspecified towns in Northern Germany and the person who comes to read the news from Japan is the preterite figure par excellence, Tyrone Slothrop. Dark forebodings had overcome him even before he noticed the newspaper scrap, and on looking at the destroyed buildings he feels as if walking through a city that has itself been the target of some such bomb: "Perhaps there is a new bomb that can destroy only the *insides* of structures," he speculates about what would later be described the effect of the H Bomb. And although the towns could be Stralsund, Greifswald, Rostock or Lüneburg, but are definitely not Hiroshima, his anxiousness is symptomatic: "why was he looking *upward*?" (692).

If Slothrop had shortly before done the same when he looked up heavenward in order to produce his partial list of wishes on evening stars, it now turns out that this moment might coincide, temporally, with "the instant it happened" (694) in Japan: August 6, 1945, at 9:15 a.m. local time (which was indeed nighttime in Germany).[54] The events of that night in August would once and for all render another of Slothrop's evening wishes unfulfillable: "Let the peace of this day be here tomorrow when I wake up" (553). Instead, the night has a new, nightmarish threat in store for him and others: one that justifies the fright and alarm with which they would from now on look upward, one that von Braun's 1946 project intended to "optimize" when the engineer sought to combine his V-2 mastery with Oppenheimer's A Bomb expertise, and last but not least one that Bruno Schulz's fiction seems to have prophesied with disturbing precision.

Notes

1. Further citations in text. Quotations are from Thomas Pynchon, *Gravity's Rainbow* [1973] (London: Picador, 1975).
2. The Polish original, "Kometa," first appeared in *Wiadomości Literackie* 35 (1938), a literary journal edited by Mieczysław Grzydzewski.
3. Daniel R. Schwarz, *Imagining the Holocaust* (New York: St. Martin's Press, 1999) 317-8.
4. Bruno Schulz, "The Comet" in *The Fictions of Bruno Schulz: The Streets of Crocodiles & Sanatorium Under the Sign of the Hourglass,* trans. Celina Wieniewska (London: Picador, 1988) 97-111. Further citations in text.
5. *The Street of Crocodiles* was originally published as *Sklepy cinamonowe* (or Cinnamon Shops) in 1934; *Sanatorium pod Klepsydrą* appeared in 1937. In the American edition just mentioned, "The Comet" is included in the first-mentioned cycle of tales, whereas other translated editions such as the German keep it separate: see Mikolaj Dutsch and Jerzy Ficowski (eds.), *Bruno Schulz: Die Zimtläden und alle anderen Erzählungen* (Frankfurt: Fischer, 1994).
6. Bruno Schulz, "A Description of the Book *Cinnamon Shops*" in Jerzy Ficowski (ed.), *Letters and Drawings of Bruno Schulz with Selected Prose* (New York: Fromm, 1990) 153-5, 154.
7. Bruno Schulz, "The Mythologizing of Reality" in Ficowski (ed.), *Letters and Drawings of Bruno Schulz,* 115-7, 116-7.
8. See John Updike's introduction to the American edition of *Sanatorium Pod Klepsydrą*: "Bruno Schulz was one of the great writers, one of the great transmogrifiers of the world into words" ("Introduction," *The Fictions of Bruno Schulz* 117-22, 117).
9. Schulz, "Mythologizing," 116.
10. Schulz, "A Description," 154.
11. Schulz, "Mythologizing," 116.
12. "Uncle Edward had no objections at all to be physically reduced [by the father] to the bare principle of Neeff's hammer" (104). Once transmogrified, he then "was ringing to high heaven through all these bright and empty rooms" (109).
13. M. A. Nelson, "Bruno Schulz—parabola komety," trans. Anna Olszowy, *Kresy* 27/3 (1996): 121-7.
14. Indirectly, the parabolic shape is also invoked in the title-giving rainbow. And conspicuously, it reoccurs in the title of its German translation, *Die Enden der Parabel* ("The Endings of the Parabola"), trans. Elfriede Jelinek and Thomas Piltz (Reinbek: Rowohlt, 1981).
15. Pynchon criticism has repeatedly commented on the structural similarities between the novel and the rocket. For an early example see Lawrence C. Wolfley, "Repression's Rainbow: The Presence of Norman O. Brown in Pynchon's Big Novel," *PMLA* 92 (1977): 873-89, 883. For a more recent one see my own "Lesen-Beobachten: Modell einer Wirkungsästhetik mit Thomas Pynchon's *Gravity's Rainbow*" ["Reading-Observing: A Model of Reader Response Criticism Based on Thomas Pynchon's *Gravity's Rainbow*"] (Konstanz: UVK, 2001) 39-43 and 114-20.

16. Lance W. Ozier, "The Calculus of Transformation: More Mathematical Imagery in *Gravity's Rainbow,*" *TCL* 21 (1975): 193-210.

17. As maps from the underground *Mittelwerke* factory show, the plant indeed looked like an elongated double S. (See for example Michael J. Neufeld's "Introduction" in Yves Beón's *Planet Dora* (New York: HarperCollins, 1997) ix-xxviii, xiii.

18. Ozier, "Calculus," 200.

19. Strictly speaking, "Brennschluss Point" does not coincide with the peak point at which the rocket tips over into descent. Momentum will carry the missile still a bit further before it eventually starts to fall. There is reason to assume, however, that Pynchon "integrates" the two points as the full quotation intimates: "a point in space, a point hung precise as the point where burning must end, never launched, never to fall. And what is the specific shape whose center of gravity is Brennschluss Point? Don't jump at an infinite number of possible shapes. There's only one. It is most likely an interface between one order of things and another" (302). The (timeless) point in space, which the narrator here clearly identifies as that point "where burning must end," must be the one that separates—and at the same time negates the spatio-temporal dimension of—the launching (or ascent) and the fall (or descent).

20. It would go beyond the scope of this article to expand on Rilke's poetry and its intricate relationship of lament and praise, nor can a detailed analysis of the German poet's influence on Bruno Schulz and Thomas Pynchon be provided here. Schulz openly admitted his admiration for Rilke in his letters. They deserve to be quoted here as examples of how the typical flavor of Schulz's language and the leitmotifs of his fiction pervade also his private communication. "I am very glad you proved accessible to Rilke," he wrote in August 1940 to the painter Anna Plockier. "In time, as you familiarize yourself with his poetry, worlds of still more concentrated beauty will open up to you. May you often experience such revelations." Reading Rilke thus seems to Schulz an experience comparable to that of dwelling in inter-planetary space because it similarly reveals "ever new constellations" (to reinvoke the above-quoted passage from "The Comet"). This becomes all the more obvious in a 1936 letter to Romana Halpern: "From time to time I take a few moments to enter his [Rilke's] tense and difficult world, walk under the multiple vaultings of his skies, and then return home" (Ficowski (ed.), *Letters and Drawings of Bruno Schulz,* 199 and 135-6). For a critical assessment of Rilke's influence on Schulz see for example Jan Zielinski, "Schulz a Rilke. Hipotetyczna próba rekonstrukcji lektury," G. Matuszek, G. Ritz (eds.), *Recepcja literacka i proces literacki. O polsko-niemieckich kontaktach literackich od modernizmu po okres mildzywojenny* (Kraków: UP, 1999) 248-63. In the case of Thomas Pynchon, notably the great recluse of American literature, the private exchange of letters has indeed remained "private" so far. Regardless of this, Pynchon criticism has never ceased to elaborate on the Rilke connection in, first and foremost, *Gravity's Rainbow.* The most comprehensive study is without doubt Charles Hohmann's voluminous monograph *Thomas Pynchon's* Gravity's Rainbow*: A Study of Its Conceptual Structure and of Rilke's Influence* (New York: Peter Lang Publishers, 1986). Hohmann's theory-informed poststructuralist approach was later complemented by Dwight Eddins's analysis of Rilke's Orphic mysticism in the 1973 novel (Eddins, *The Gnostic Pynchon* [Bloomington: Indiana UP, 1990], 109-54, especially 116-46). The most recent contribution is Preben Jordal's "The Savage Flower: Reading Pynchon Reading Rilke," Anne Mangen, Rolf Gaasland eds., *Blissful Bewilderment: Studies in the Fiction of Thomas Pynchon* (Oslo: Novus, 2002) 103-23.

21. Rainer Maria Rilke, *Duino Elegies and The Sonnets to Orpheus,* trans. A. Poulin, Jr. (Boston: Houghton Mifflin, 1975), 160-1.

22. Notably, the German "wenden" not only equates with "to turn," but is also etymologically adjacent to "(ver)wandeln" ("to transform").

23. The sonnet contains two more phrases that similarly point to the supersonic V-2 rocket, especially its allegedly counter-chronological succession of first strike, then sound: "Imagine a missile one hears approaching only *after* it explodes. The reversal! [. . .] the blast of the rocket, fallen faster than sound—then growing *out of it* the roar of its fall, catching up to what's already death and burning" (48). Rilke invokes this reversal of the usual order of sequence—which was still valid in the case of the V-1 "buzzbombs"—when "the serene Creation" (or for that matter the technically achieved creation of the V-2) is presented as something "that often ends with beginning and begins with ending." Acoustically imperceptible for those it strikes and ultimately kills, the rocket resembles "the upswing of an absent hammer!" (Rilke, *Duino Elegies and The Sonnets to Orpheus,* 161). Dwight Eddins therefore concludes: "Similarly, the poem [. . .] applies easily to those who seek refuge from the V-2: 'Beware, from afar a hardest comes warning the hard. / Woe—, an absent hammer lifts!'" (Eddins, *The Gnostic Pynchon* 144). Eddins draws on a different translation of Rilke's poems here.

24. Judith Chambers, *Thomas Pynchon* (New York: Twayne Publishers, 1992), 149. The mention of the "fair intellectual-king" is taken from a sequence near the end of *Gravity's Rainbow* in which Weismann's Tarot is laid out (see also below, footnote 33). Based on the full passage given there, it might be contended that Weissmann has by no means vanished for good, but instead resides "among the successful academics,

the Presidential advisers, the token intellectuals who sit on boards of directors. He is almost surely there. Look high, not low" (749). There is however a catch, as the special context of the Tarot divination reveals. The third card (out of ten) which is at stake here—the King of Cups, conventionally depicted as a "[f]air man" with "creative intelligence"—stands for "that which has not yet been made actual." A. E. Waite, *The Pictorial Key to the Tarot* (1910; Stamford: United Games 2000) 198 and 301. The "not yet actual" or future boards of directors invoked here—"future" from the present of the fall of 1944, when the launching of the 00000 takes place—are elsewhere in the novel specified as belonging to corporations involved in "[a] Rocket-cartel," a structure of utmost complexity which "*begins* to take form in the stateless German night, a State that spans oceans and surface politics" (566, emphasis added). As Walter Rathenau, another presumable board member, suggests, the dwelling of these boards is not (going to be) located within the confines of the ordinary and secular any more, but likewise in a realm "on the other side" (165). To interpret Weissmann's final destiny in terms of an accomplished transformation could thus be maintained, notwithstanding the seemingly strong counter evidence that he has "almost surely" found entrance to the top echelons of the political-military-industrial complex. As often with Pynchon, textual evidence (such as here the clue of Weissmann's subsequent career as a board member) is challenged by contextual counter-evidence (such as the embedment of the clue in the special discourse of Tarot divination), and "words," to reapply a passage from *Gravity's Rainbow* in a self-referential way onto the novel itself, are often indeed "an eye-twitch away from the things they stand for" (100).

25. Eddins, *The Gnostic Pynchon* 144. Unlike other critics (e.g., Preben Jordal), Eddins is one of the few to acknowledge the dilemma that results from the instrumentalization of Rilke's literature for the purpose of explaining Weissmann's motives. For Eddins, Weissmann is "a figure of such portentous evil and insidious capacity that his creator Pynchon occasionally seems, like Milton, to be of the Devil's party without knowing it" (142).

26. Rilke, *Duino Elegies and The Sonnets to Orpheus* 74-5.

27. Hohmann, *Thomas Pynchon's* Gravity's Rainbow, 284.

28. Rilke, *Duino Elegies and The Sonnets to Orpheus,* 104-5. Rilke unmistakably means a horseman, as becomes clear when he speaks of "our sinewy way of being, to be whipped on, and then reined in," or when rider and horse are "divided by table and trough" (105).

29. Rilke, *Duino Elegies and The Sonnets to Orpheus,* 74-5.

30. The religious, and more specifically Puritan, differentiation of Elect and Preterite is one of many that Pynchon employs to suggest the above-mentioned impression of "[t]wo orders of being" (202). Others include They/We or, as an attempt to cope with the paranoia that results from the assumed, yet unverifiable omnipresence of "Them," the distinction of a "They-System" as opposed to a "We-System" (638) which is later in the novel drawn by the so-called "Counterforce" (617).

31. For a different view see Ozier, who "suggests that the dissolution of Slothrop's persona [later in the novel: 622-6] is not a diminution but part of a transformation into the timeless Being of Rilke's angels" (Ozier, "Calculus" 197).

32. The ambivalence in the significance of the celestial rider for Weissmann and Slothrop respectively—in the case of the first it is associated with domination, for the other it heralds oppression—is repeated in another "discourse" that Pynchon similarly makes use of: the arcane knowledge and art of divination symbolized in the Tarot cards. Toward the end of the novel, the Tarots of Slothrop and Weissmann are laid out and interpreted in the so-called "Celtic style [. . .] suggested by Mr. A. E. Waite" (738, cf. Waite's *Pictorial Key to the Tarot*). Slothrop's Tarot, though it remains incomplete, is determined by one of the Major Arcana cards, the "Fool," which notably figures as "a background for [him] in his role as 'holy Fool,' [. . .] and in his final 'invisible' preterition." Thomas Moore, *The Style of Connectedness:* Gravity's Rainbow *and Thomas Pynchon* (Columbia: Missouri UP, 1987) 240. By comparison, "Weissmann's Tarot is better than Slothrop's" (*Gravity's Rainbow* 746), as the first of Weissmann's ten cards already suggests. This card—the "Significator" which according to Waite is "to represent the person or matter about which inquiry is made" (Waite, *Pictorial Key* 299)—is the "Knight of Swords," a figure "riding in full course, as if scattering his enemies" (230, see also the illustration there). In the medium of his Tarot Weissmann thus "appears first with boots and insignia shining as the rider on a black horse," as Pynchon notes (747). In this assignation of a rider, Weissmann makes his appearance in yet another description of the sky over Peenemunde, as Steven Weisenburger intimates in *A* Gravity's Rainbow *Companion: Sources and Contexts for Pynchon's Novel* (Athens: Georgia UP, 1988, see the entries on 223-4 and 225). In a modernized version of the Tarot rider (as well as, again, that of Rilke's), Weissmann-as-Knight-of-Swords materializes as "the Bicycle Rider in the Sky, the black and fatal silhouette on the luminous breast of sky, of today's Rocket Noon, two circular explosions inside the rush hour, in the death-scene of the sky's light. How the rider twirls up there, terminal and serene" (501). For Slothrop who walks beneath the apparition, however, the Tarot provides a completely different interpretation of the celestial

rider than that of a Significator of "skill, bravery, capacity" (Waite, *Pictorial Key* 230). Accordingly, the phrase "How the rider twirls up there, terminal and serene" is followed by one assigned, now, to Slothrop: "In the Tarot he is known as The Fool" (501).

33. The ironic underpinnings of the rescue through the bicycle are multiple. Hence, as a *rescue,* it mocks the ecstatic death wish of the people; as a rescue *through the bicycle,* it employs the exemplary cultural accompaniment for the natural catastrophe to ward off precisely this end; as *trick* rescue through the bicycle, it parodizes the people's idea of a trick cyclist's end of the world; as a result of the father's machinations, of which the people remain utterly unaware, the rescue instantiates dramatic irony.

34. Accordingly, Schulz describes the father like a benevolent god who watches the people of his hometown in their state of dreamers partaking in mankind's nightmare of self-annihilation: "my father alone was awake, wandering silently through the rooms filled with the singsong of sleep. Sometimes he opened the door of the flue and looked grinning into its dark abyss, where a smiling homunculus slept for ever its luminous sleep, enclosed in a glass capsule, bathed in fluourescent light, already adjudged, erased, filed away, another record card in the immense archives of the sky" (111). While the idea of a homunculus in a glass capsule (or retort) is a common literary and filmic topos, that of the homunculus in the sky is lesser known. There exists, however, the "Homunculus Nebulae," a result of the 1841 eruption of the Eta Carinae star whose appearance strikingly matches Schulz's description of the brain-like embryo or homunculus.

35. Rilke, *Duino Elegies and Sonnets to Orpheus,* 69.

36. Inger Hunnerup Dalsgaard, "*Gravity's Rainbow*: An Historical Novel of a Whole New Sort," Anne Mangen and Rolf Gaasland eds., *Blissful Bewilderment: Studies in the Fiction of Thomas Pynchon* (Oslo: Novus, 2002) 81-102. Dalsgaard borrows the title of her essay from Tony Tanner (81).

37. Friedrich Kittler identifies the above-mentioned General Dornberger, director of the *Heeresversuchsanstalt Peenemünde* and von Braun's congenial counterpart there, and SS-*Obergruppenführer* (Chief Group Leader) Hans Kammler as possible other models. From of August, 1943, Kammler had organized the building of the underground *Mittelwerke* rocket factory. See Friedrich Kittler, "Media and Drugs in Pynchon's Second World War," Joe Tabbi, Michael Wutz eds., *Reading Matters: Narrative in the New Media Ecology* (Ithaca, London: Cornell UP, 1997) 157-72, 167-8.

38. At the time of Schulz's death, supersonic rockets had just taken the leap from the drawing boards and test stands of their engineers (and filmic fantasies like Fritz Lang's 1929 movie, *Die Frau im Mond*) to actual—and actually functioning—missiles. Interned until he died on November 18, 1942 in the ghetto of Drohobycz, it is most unlikely that Schulz had ever come to know about the first successful—and top secret—launching of the A-4, the later V-2, in Peenemünde on October 3 of that year.

39. Ernst Klee, Otto Merk, *The Birth of the Missile: The Secrets of Peenemünde* (London: E. P. Dutton & Co., 1965); the German original had been published two years before: *Damals in Peenemünde* (Oldenburg/Hamburg: Gerhard Stalling Verlag, 1963). Bernd Ruland, *Wernher von Braun-Mein Leben für die Raumfahrt* ["My Life for the Flight into Space"] (Offenburg: Burda, 1969).

40. Jean Michel, *Dora* (Paris: J. C. Lattès, 1975); Linda Hunt, "U.S. Cover-up of Nazi Scientists," *Bulletin of the Atomic Scientists* (April 1985) 16-24; Linda Hunt, *Secret Agenda: The United States Government, Nazi Scientists, and Project Paperclip, 1945-1990* (New York: St. Martin's Press, 1991); Tom Bower, *Blind Eye to Murder: Britain, America and the Purging of Nazi Germany* (London: Andre Deutsch, 1981); Tom Bower: *The Paperclip Conspiracy* (London and Glasgow: Michael Joseph, 1987).

41. "That von Braun's character [in *Gravity's Rainbow*] is grounded in history [. . .] does not, on closer inspection of the text, turn out to mark such an unbridgeable boundary between real life and inventions as might at first appear. Firstly, one may question whether *Gravity's Rainbow* is the boundless *fiction* it at first seems. Secondly, one may investigate and challenge the historical truth value of von Braun himself and discover the extent to which the 'von Braun' Americans recognized was a fictional product created by himself, the US Army, NASA and his autobiographers [sic] in the decades following World War Two" (Dalsgaard, "*Gravity's Rainbow*: 'An Historical Novel of a Whole New Sort'" 85). Dale Carter's study is *The Final Frontier: The Rise and Fall of the American Rocket State* (London: Verso, 1988).

42. Michael J. Neufeld, *The Rocket and the Reich: Peenemünde and the Coming of the Ballistic Missile Era* (Cambridge: Harvard UP, 1996); Rainer Eisfeld, *Mondsüchtig: Wernher von Braun und die Geburt der Raumfahrt aus dem Geist der Barbarei* ["Moonstruck: Wernher von Braun and the Birth of Spaceflight from the Spirit of Barbarism"] (Reinbek: Rowohlt, 1996).

43. Tom Lehrer, *Tom Lehrer's Second Song Book* (New York: Crown, 1968) 43.

44. The contribution is from William Nichols (ed.), *The Third Book of Words to Live By* (New York: Simon & Schuster, 1962); see also the reference in Terry

Caesar, "Texts of the Text: Citations in *Gravity's Rainbow*" (*Pynchon Notes* 40-41, 1997) 125-33, 132 (footnote 2). The motto in *Gravity's Rainbow* is on page 1.

Weissmann and von Braun share more than rocketry expertise or the preference of resp. belief in transformation. Thus, if Weissmann figures as "a brand-new military type, part salesman, part scientist" (401), Eisfeld and Neufeld describe von Braun as his non-fictional alter ego: according to the first, von Braun was a master in effectively selling his ideas ("Von Braun beherrschte die Kunst, Ideen zugkräftig 'an den Mann' zu bringen," Eisfeld, *Mondsüchtig* 235), and Neufeld similarly mentions his "charismatic and visionary personality combined with his excellent management skills" (Neufeld, *The Rocket and the Reich* 79; see also 101-2).

45. Dalsgaard, "*Gravity's Rainbow*: 'An Historical Novel of a Whole New Sort'" 98.

46. "This reading of the final page is so common in Pynchon criticism that it almost passes without notice, as an authoritative reading." Alec McHoul, David Wills, *Writing Pynchon: Strategies in Fictional Analysis* (London: Macmillan, 1990) 222, footnote 6. McHoul and Wills have provided a "post-apocalyptic" reading of the ending in the last chapter of their poststructuralist analysis ("Fall Out," 211-23); for another approach coupling Derrida's philosophy and Pynchon's fiction under the sign of the "post-apocalyptic" see Laurent Milesi, "Postmodern Ana-Apocalyptics: Pynchon's V-Effect and the End (of Our Century)," Luc Herman ed., *Approach and Avoid: Essays on* Gravity's Rainbow (special issue of *Pynchon Notes* 42-43 (1998) 213-43.

47. Leo Bersani, "Pynchon, Paranoia, and Literature," *Representations* 25 (1989) 99-118, 108. As mentioned in footnote 31, "They" figure here as a synonym of the Elect or Illuminati. For an analysis of *Gravity's Rainbow*'s reader subtext in general, and the book's biting remarks about the *conditio lectoris* in particular, see my *Lesen-Beobachten* 95-114, especially 111-2

48. The quotation is from a transcript, "Joint Army-Navy Meeting on Army Ordnance Research and Development, the Pentagon, 26 June 1946," p. 37. Box 767A, RG 156, *Records of the Office of the Chief of Ordnance, Department of the Army* (Records housed at the Washington National Records Center, Suitland, Maryland). David H. DeVorkin quotes the archival source in his extensive study about the American deployment of the booty weapons, *Science with a Vengeance: How the Military Created the US Space Sciences After World War II* (New York, Berlin, Heidelberg: Springer, 1992) 61.

49. "Beschreibung der Fernrakete 'Comet,'" *Wernher von Braun Papers* (archived in the U.S. Space & Rocket Center, Huntsville) 1. ["ein Projekt fuer eine Fernrakete sehr grosser Reichweite vorgelegt, das aus einer Kombination der deutschen A 4-Rakete (V-2) und einem neuen Geraet besteht, das den Namen 'Comet' traegt."] I am indebted to Rainer Eisfeld (University of Osnabrück, Germany) for providing me with Xerox copies of this and other documents. Eisfeld briefly comments on the archive: "Halfway in the Space & Rocket Center, two narrow side rooms stashed with books and papers contain von Braun's written heritage: unordered and with no assistant means for their exploration. Accordingly, the inspection of these documents proves to be difficult" (Eisfeld, *Mondsüchtig* 287-8). ["Zwei enge, mit Büchern und Papieren vollgestopfte Seitenräume auf halber Höhe des Space & Rocket Center bergen von Brauns schriftlichen Nachlaß, ungeordnet und ohne Hilfsmittel zur Erschließung. Entsprechend mühsam gestaltet sich die Sichtung der Unterlagen."]

50. "Use of Atomic Warheads in Projected Missiles. Letter to Office Chief of Ordnance, 12 April 1946," *Wernher von Braun Papers* (archived in the U.S. Space & Rocket Center, Huntsville) 1.

51. "Beschreibung der Fernrakete 'Comet'" ["Diese neue Fernrakete stellt ein zweistufiges Geraet dar, dessen unterer Teil eine nur unwesentlich abgeaenderte V-2 Rakete ist. [. . .] In Punkt A dieser Bahn, nach Erreichung der genannten Geschwindigkeit, wird durch einen besonderen Mechanismus der vordere Teil (Comet) von der V-2 Rakete getrennt. Die V-2 Rakete selbst stuerzt aus dieser Hoehe leer zur Erde ab und kann, um Schaden zu verhueten, noetigenfalls noch in der Luft durch Sprengung in kleine Splitter zerlegt werden. Das obere Teil fliegt zunaechst ohne Antrieb bis zu dem Punkt B weiter, der in etwa 20 km Hoehe liegt. [. . .] In Punkt B werden zwei Ueberschall-Athodyd-Anlagen gezuendet."]

52. "Beschreibung der Fernrakete 'Comet'" ["Der Treibstoffvorrat reicht [. . .] fuer eine Reichweite von etwa 1000 bis 2000 km aus. Die Nutzlast betraegt dabei wahlweise 500 oder 1000 kg (1110 bezw. 2220 lbs.)."]

53. "Briefentwurf an Los Alamos Laboratory, Dr. J. R. Oppenheimer," *Wernher von Braun Papers* 1 (see footnote 51). Again, I am indebted to Rainer Eisfeld for making a Xerox copy of the letter available to me. The German title of the letter is however crossed out; instead, a handwritten "SECRET" has been added. Eisfeld himself mentions the *Comet* project twice in *Mondsüchtig* (178-9, and in his "afterword" 287-8)

54. According to Steven Weisenburger, the 25th episode of part three of *Gravity's Rainbow* (which includes Slothrop's "Partial List of Wishes") is set "[s]ometime in early August." Slothrop's meandering through the streets of Northern German towns begins in the same episode; chronologically, therefore, his discovery of the Hiroshima bombing a couple of days later

can be reconstructed as well ("The time is therefore mid-August," as Weisenburger notes), although about 140 pages lie between the descriptions of the two incidents (Weisenburger, *A* Gravity's Rainbow *Companion* 236 and 282).

Stacey Olster (essay date summer 2004)

SOURCE: Olster, Stacey. "A 'Patch of England, at a Three-Thousand-Mile Off-Set'?: Representing America in *Mason & Dixon.*" *Modern Fiction Studies* 50, no. 2 (summer 2004): 283-302.

[*In the following essay, Olster investigates issues of American national identity as presented in* Mason & Dixon.]

Thomas Pynchon's ***Mason & Dixon*** ends with the death of Charles Mason in 1786 and the decision of his two eldest children to stay in Philadelphia and "be Americans" (772). As to just what constitutes that nationality, however, Pynchon remains silent. J. Hector St. John de Crèvecoeur, in contrast, had no such reticence. Addressing the question of "What is an American?" in those *Letters from an American Farmer* published four years before Mason's death, Crévecoeur defined America with respect to a litany of terms destructive of the past: "new laws, a new mode of living, a new social system," "new mode of life," "new government," "new rank," yielding, finally, "a new race of men" (38-39; letter 3). And yet, for all the emphasis on "newness" that his paean to American exceptionalism displayed, Crévecoeur remained acutely aware of the existence of a historical past: his views of America in "embryo" follow those of Italy in exhaustion and at the end of a cultural epoch (6; letter 1); frontiersmen free of past constraints live side-by-side with Indians whose past is seen as vanishing. In this understanding, Crévecoeur was not alone. Indeed, far from being dismissive of their own European past in particular, colonists in the seventeenth and eighteenth centuries often made a great point of the bond they retained to their British heritage. The Massachusetts Bay Puritans described their immigration as "a *Local Secession,* yet not a *Separation*" (Higginson 69-70). Virginia's colonists, in the words of Robert Carter Nicholas, professed "*sentiments of duty and affection*" as late as 1774 (qtd. in Bailyn 142). The dissidents of 1776 distinguished their acts as revolution and not rebellion, their original impulse being restorative in nature, namely, the return of those liberties traditionally granted all British subjects by England's constitution—liberties the colonists saw endangered by recent impositions of unfair taxation, plural officeholders, and standing armies. Viewed with respect to the historical context provided by earlier writings, one then may assume, as does Mason, that, far from being a nation distinct unto itself, America is but "a Patch of England, at a three-thousand-Mile Off-set" (248). If such is the case, and the New World is indistinguishable from the Old, its history of empire (past, present, and future) that the novel traces may simply confirm the view of history implied by the Indian lore of forestry in which, as Pynchon writes, "ev'ryone comes 'round in a Circle sooner or later" until "[o]ne day, your foot comes down in your own shit" (677).

I use the term "empire" deliberately here, for the critique of American exceptionalism that prompts Pynchon's return to the late-eighteenth-century period during which the modern nation-state was conceived reflects the late-twentieth-century period in which the end of the Cold War and emergence of a globalized economy have led critics to proclaim the entire era of the nation-state as over.[1] Recreating the eighteenth century in fiction as an "Era of fluid Identity" therefore concerns more than postmodern notions of individual selfhood (469). In terms of national identity, it concerns the relevance of individual nationhood within a world in which a shift from imperialist to imperial sovereignty has resulted in the decentered and deterritorialized apparatus that Michael Hardt and Antonio Negri call "Empire." As even Mason, more at home with stars than stocks, cannot help but notice, "Charter'd Companies may indeed be the form the World has now increasingly begun to take" (252). Establishing what is an American and, by extension, what is America under these circumstances thus becomes an act of representation, not simply a "making present again" as the word's etymological origins indicate, but, as Hanna Fenichel Pitkin recognizes, "the making present *in some sense* of something which is nevertheless *not* present literally or in fact" (8-9). Because that act, as Wolfgang Iser adds, is performative rather than mimetic, a function of the "active imaginings" through which "the intangible can become an image" (226), representing America in Pynchon's novel will turn out to be less a question of politics, as the colonists demanded, and more a question of aesthetics, as the mapping in which Pynchon's eponymous characters engage illustrates.

Separation, Consolidation, and East India Company Administration

The modern nation-state, most scholars agree, could not have emerged without the legacies of the American and French Revolutions, whose movements rapidly were turned into models and blueprints.[2] As those scholars also acknowledge, the political grounds upon which nations were first proposed had to be supplemented, in the absence of historical rootedness, by a cultural terrain on which nations were created discursively, through what Geoff Eley and Ronald Grigor Suny term "processes of imaginative ideological labor" ("From the Moment" 8). Central to those discursive processes were separation and consolidation. In the past, this meant defining, and hence distinguishing, the modern nation-state within a system of territorially-bound nation-states, on the one hand (Breuilly 355-56), and relativizing internal differences (and emphasizing as irreducible those that denoted foreign others), on the other hand, so as to constitute "the people" from whom sovereignty now emanated (Balibar 139). In ***Mason & Dixon,*** it means destabilizing the idea of nation-states by stressing the similarities that bind Americans to foreign others while showing the differences that prevent their provinces from truly merging in any way to become a United States.

Charles Mason and Jeremiah Dixon, in fact, suspect this to be the case from the start. As they come 'round the globe to America in 1763, they wonder whether, given the rumors they have heard, they will be stepping down in a land that is any different from those to which the Royal Society has previously sent them: "Another Slave-Colony," the melancholic Mason notes (248). Certainly, this is the way those who clamor for citizenship untinged by servitude, singing "Americans all, / Slaves ne'er again," currently see it (571). Having defined slavery as "a force put upon humane nature, by which a man is obliged to act, or not to act, according to the arbitrary will and pleasure of another," as one newspaper writer stated in 1747 (qtd. in Bailyn 233), regardless of whether that servitude was public or private, civil or political, eighteenth-century colonists viewed being taxed without consent as turning them from subjects into slaves. In Pynchon's novel, unfortunately, Mason's remark comes in response to Dixon's observation that it is the colonists themselves who are said to keep slaves, "as did our late Hosts" in Cape Town, that "they are likewise inclin'd to kill the People already living where they wish to settle" (248). And so they do, as is repeatedly confirmed by events either recalled for or witnessed at firsthand by the Englishmen: the massacre of Indians at Conestoga; the murder of twenty-six more men, women, and children taking refuge in Lancaster's jail; the whipping of Africans in chains by a slave-driver in Baltimore.

As readers of Pynchon's fiction are well aware, this is hardly the first time that Pynchon has portrayed America as a land to which the subjugation of others is fundamental—it is, after all, in Columbus, Ohio, that DL Chastain's efforts to start anew in ***Vineland*** are interrupted by kidnapping and subsequent white slavery (133-35). But to portray America as *another* slave colony in a novel in which its origins are specifically explored is to expose the vexing contradiction at the heart of revolutionary rhetoric, the fact that, as Jeff Baker points out, the very trade the colonists were attempting to protect from British interference had as its economic basis the enslavement of human beings (172)—a conceptual roadblock on the way to nationhood, to be sure. Even more important, it reduces to nil any differences by which the country coming into being can claim distinction, as the analogical rhetoric with which the surveyors' encounters are depicted makes clear. Edward Braddock shoots at American Indians, "treacherous Natives, disrespectful, rebellious, waiting in Ambuscado, behind ev'ry stone wall" (501), in the same spirit that James Wolfe shoots at British weavers, "Red Indians, spying upon them from the Woodlands they thought were theirs" (313).[3] Sterloop rifles with five-pointed stars abuse Africans in the Cape of Good Hope (101) just as Sterloops effect "the Catastrophick Resolution of Inter-Populational Cross-Purposes" in Pennsylvania (342-43) just as Sterloops drive Africans to labor in Lord and Lady Lepton's Chesapeake Iron-Plantation and to perform in their Ridotto's Slave Orchestra, prototype for the musical reception committee at Auschwitz (427-28). All of which makes moot all questions of whether the provenance of the gun is Dutch, as Mason insists, or American, as Dixon claims (428), or whether Americans are any more British than the Cape Dutch are Dutch (248).

Contributing further to this collapsing of national categories is the element of cultural hybridity that Pynchon introduces into the novel, which makes it difficult to ascertain if any uniquely Dutch or American or British identity even exists in the eighteenth century—the very period, ironically, in which the English were scrambling to expurgate all traces of their French-Norman past in order to emphasize their Germanic-Saxon origins (Doyle 39). The Virginian George Washington displays an old pitman's lilt to the British Dixon, and also sounds like an African to Pennsylvanians (276). His African-American servant Gershom is also a yarmulke-wearing Jew, as skilled at rustling up a mess of hog jowls as he is a batch of *kasha varnishkies* (279)—a perfect exemplar of those "hybrid hyphenations" in which incompatible traits provide the basis for cultural identification (Bhabha 219), since the protein source of his first dish is prohibited by the dietary laws that govern his second. ("Yet if a Jew cooking pork is a Marvel, what of a Negroe, working a Room?" asks the astounded colonel [279].) Unlike, then, the depiction of slavery in earlier works like ***Gravity's Rainbow,*** in which the slaughters of dodoes, Hereros, and Jews are all analogically related, and in which white/black and Elect/Preterite binaries are fairly stable, and ***Vineland,*** in which oppression is delineated with respect to clear gender divisions ("humans, usually male . . . committing these crimes, major and petty, one by one against other living humans" [80]), the depiction of slavery in ***Mason & Dixon*** makes slavery a function of cultural context. According to Stig the Axman, Swedes are just another tribe of Indians to the British William Penn, whose earlier settlement on his land he found irksome (611). Yet to Stig's own people, "Northern and very White," residing even farther north than Sweden, "you British to us appear as do Africans, to you" (612).

And because the economic cultural context that informs ***Mason & Dixon*** makes slavery a function of ownership more than oppression, "the one place we should *not* have found them" (693)—"place" meaning America, "them" meaning tyrants and slaves—is revealed to be a place as filled with slaves, whether denoted as hirelings, indentured servants, or contractual agents, as any Old World colonized territory. Captain Zhang reminds the surveyors that Pennsylvania is as much a slave-holding province as Maryland: "They are not all African, nor do some of them even yet know,—may never know,—that they are Slaves" (615). Captain Volcanoe reminds Mason that he is one such slave himself: "Someone owns you, Sir. He pays for your Meals and Lodging. He lends you out to others. What is that call'd, where you come from?" (406). By the time that Zsuzsa Szabó, entertainer extraordinaire, poses her version of the question in its broadest form, the answer is already self-evident: "Who is unique? Who is not own'd by someone?" (551). No one in ***Mason & Dixon,*** it would appear, not even the Learnèd English Dog, a.k.a. Fang, whose services Foretopman Bodine offers to buy after attempts at snatching him prove to be unsuccessful (21-23).

This is not to suggest, of course, that Pynchon is preaching an equivalency among the various forms of bondage that the novel depicts. Mason, caught in the hold of a meat ship while returning to his Royal Society employers, does not experience the horrors of the Middle Passage however many hundreds of lamb carcasses "slither'd lethally 'round him" (736)—sailors rescue him from an entrapment that does not last even one night. The life of "Drudging Captivity" that his rival Nevil Maskelyne claims for himself, working for a Society that "own[s] the products of [his] thinking" (727), cannot be equated with the lives of shackled Africans who do not even own their own bodies. But the similarities those forms exhibit jettison any attempt to represent America as emerging by way of contrast. If this be American exceptionalism, in other words, it is of the kind described by Michael Rogin, a function of reconnection to, not separation from, a European capitalist world system of which its settler society is a fragment (277-78).

Given this ongoing Old World connection, it is not surprising that the anthem to independence sung by voices that are "unmistakably, American" (571) is listened to by colonists still identified by way of regional origins—"New-Yorkers in Georgia, Pennsylvanians in the Carolinas, Virginians ev'rywhere" (570)—hardly an imagined community, to borrow Benedict Anderson's term, much less "Americans All," as the song proclaims. For, as scholars of the American Enlightenment have argued, colonists prior to the American Revolution had a very limited sense of national identity. According to Robert A. Ferguson, it was only after 1764 that the word "Americans" replaced "Englishmen" as the preferred term of self-reference in newspapers (436). And with no institutions around which to consolidate themselves prior to that time, politics in the colonies remained a "piecemeal" affair, as David S. Shields asserts, "a politics constituted more in the relations of individual provinces with the metropolis than in terms of British America" (223), as evidenced by the rejection of the plan of union for purposes of "Security and defense" that Benjamin Franklin proposed in 1754 to the Albany Congress (222). Because it also was the metropolis, or sovereign center, that produced the more valued manufactured goods that were exchanged for raw materials in outposts and colonies, it was in the best interests of the metropolis to keep the provinces separate, and it was the metropolis that restricted the colonies—in this case, through parliamentary Acts upon Trade and Navigation from 1651 onwards—from engaging in free trade and from developing manufacturing economies of their own.

In Pynchon's Maryland and Pennsylvania, as it turns out, there is no need for any sovereign center to prevent the provinces from uniting. The people living near the border are doing that all by themselves, as seen in the experiences of Thomas Cresap (638-41), Pynchon's version of one Mr. Crisep, who, with fourteen accomplices, defended his residence as being in Maryland while surrounding his house with fifty-five more men (Mason 67). By bringing astronomical tools to resolve formally that eighty-two-year-old disputed boundary (1681-1763), Mason and Dixon only formalize that separation, and, ironically, they do so with reference to the same discipline of science that colonists later would use to promote both federation among themselves (as illustrated by the flag whose design of thirteen white stars on a blue background was intended by Congress to "represent a new constellation") and separation from their mother country (as symbolized by the Declaration of Independence first being read to colonists from the Philadelphia Observatory platform built to observe the transit of Venus).[4] For all Mason's assumption that astronomy removes him from politics, as occurs when he leaves Stroud to work with Bradley the year of the 1756 riots, his application of astronomy in the colonies is very much a political activity, promoting as it does the interests of British colonial hegemony and thereby confirming—as Thomas H. Schaub astutely recognizes—his own interpellated subjectivity (198).[5] Dixon admits as much about their efforts when earlier distinguishing the practice of British astronomy from that of other nations:

> 'Tis said of the French Astronomers, that they never turn their Instruments, be it out of Pride or Insouciance or some French Sentiment we don't possess, whilst what seems to distinguish us out here, is that we do. We reverse our Sectors, we measure ev'rything in both Directions. . . . 'Tis the British Way, to take the extra

> step that may one day give us an Edge when we need one, probably against the French. Small Investment, large Reward. I regard myself as a practitioner of British Science now.
>
> (121)

But in a novel in which an earlier world of cores and peripheries is being replaced by "the world that is to come, [in which] all boundaries shall be eras'd" (406), the surveyors' work to prevent colonial consolidation is as compromised as the colonists' attempts to promote exceptionalist separation. This is not for lack of trying. As a glance at the historical Mason's *Journal* indicates, Mason practiced the fastidious extra steps his partner in fiction is shown to preach. A "disagreement" arises between a mark in one field and a mark by a road leading from Philadelphia to Nottingham, and the two "beg[in] again at the Mark in Mr. Wilson's field and measured in our return" (50). Chain carriers measure 22.51 chains between a point of intersection on the surveyors' Line and the tangent point in a circle around Newcastle, and Mason remeasures it himself a few days later to make sure that they have not made any errors (60). A 1766 figure regarding distance between the 39 mile post and the 41 mile post is found to be doubtful, and it is recalculated in 1768 to reveal that one chain too many has been used between the forty-second and forty-third mile posts (171). So precise does Mason try to be in his calculations that figures are determined to degrees of inches, and sometimes even less: the party crosses the Nanticoke River and finds it is five inches from where it should be (63); new directions taken from the stars verify the West Line to be within two inches (97); hail strikes and a piece is recorded as being one and six-tenth inches in length and one and two-tenths inches in breadth (100). Yet, as the *Journal* also shows, the exactitude of Mason's yearnings is repeatedly frustrated by the inexactitude of his findings, situations whose calculations are most often appended by the adjective "dubious": "By the Pole Star's transiting the Meridian we placed a mark in the Meridian northward, but it was rendered a little dubious on account of flying clouds" (45); "Made a few observations, but dubious" (74); "A little dubious on account of a screw not quite fast" (82); "the 1st Satellite of Jupiter Immerged, very dubious by its near approach to Jupiters Limb" (158); "In the afternoon Observations the Sun's Lower Limb was rendered dubious something, by the Moon's Body" (195).

Pynchon, as a historical novelist investigating the past, traces such uncertainty back to a number of earlier sources. One is the overlapping nature of the original land grants, "Geometrickally impossible territory" parceled out by Charles II and James II, "as if in playful refusal to admit that America, in any way, may be serious" (336, 337), "more like fantastickal Tales, drafted in the days of some Kings who were not altogether real themselves," as Washington's Jewish-African-American servant notes (282). Another is the shape of the earth itself, a planet, as the historical Mason writes the Commissioners for Dividing the Provinces of Maryland and Pennsylvania, "not known to be exactly a Spheroid, nor whether it is everywhere of equal Density" (194), about which all determinations must remain approximate at best and arbitrary at worst, as everyone concerned with geographical measurement since the time of Ptolemy understood. Together they make the surveyors' task to establish a definitive Maryland and Pennsylvania a venture that is doomed from the start:

> there exists no "Maryland" beyond an Abstraction, a Frame of right lines drawn to enclose and square off the great Bay in its unimagin'd Fecundity, its shoreline tending to Infinite Length, ultimately unmappable,—no more, to be fair, than there exists any "Pennsylvania" but a chronicle of Frauds committed serially against the Indians dwelling there, check'd only by the Ambitions of other Colonies to north and east.
>
> (354)

In the case of Maryland, in fact, there is not even very much land to circumscribe, since when "Maryland" is finally "reveal'd" by the surveyors, its area is found to consist mostly of water (616).

Were the matter left here, Pynchon could be viewed as simply rewriting John Barth's *The Sot-Weed Factor,* whose portrait of a tidewater province's uncertain topography and geography ***Mason & Dixon*** obviously calls to mind. Yet Pynchon, unlike Barth, repeatedly breaks his novel's early American temporal frame with anachronistic allusions—to coffee bars, split ends, and no-smoking taverns (276, 91, 365), to name but a few—that suggest that the desire that most informs his historical novel is what Georg Lukács called "bringing the past to life as the prehistory of the present" (53). This affects the presentations of space that each writer offers in two crucial ways. First, Pynchon attributes geography a moral component that Barth, more concerned with Heraclitean flux and the fears that living on the edge (both literally and figuratively) as "Chance's fool, the toy of aimless Nature," does not (372).[6] Heretical in mimicking the first boundary line by which God divided firmament from water (Pynchon 361), the Visto that Mason and Dixon carve out is presented as eventuating in an eighty-mile shopping mall, "lin'd with Inns and Shops, Stables, Games of Skill, Theatrickals, Pleasure-Gardens . . . a Promenade" (701).[7] The Delaware Triangle, or "Wedge," on whose latitude they later work as "an Atonement" (701), reflects "an emerging moral Geometry" (323) in being an area of "doubtful ownership" perhaps exempt from the book's delineation of slavery (469).[8] Second, and more relevant to my purposes, spatial indeterminacy for Barth remains a transhistorical phenomenon, its apocalyptic reverberations as relevant to colonial as contemporary times, whereas spatial indeterminacy for Pynchon, as that envisioned shopping mall implies, reflects the particularities of late capitalism in which globalization has shifted power from nation-states to huge conglomerates.

The most powerful of such conglomerates in ***Mason & Dixon,*** of course, is the East India Company. Located "ev'rywhere, and [in] Ev'rything" (69), with individual outposts that all perform "the Doings of Global Trade in miniature" (159), it embodies perfectly the concept of Empire that, according to Hardt and Negri, exists "everywhere and nowhere" while "progressively expand[ing] its boundaries to envelop the entire globe as its proper domain" (190, 189). Dixon repeatedly suspects it is the Company, and not the British government, that is the sovereign power from which the surveyors' mission to separate Maryland and Pennsylvania emanates (73, 252, 692-93), and the connections between the Company and their Royal Society employers corroborate his suspicions, portrayed, as they are by Pynchon, in terms of marriages no less dynastic than those between royal families.[9] Susannah Peach, daughter of a silk merchant who is "a growing Power within the East India Company" (169), marries astronomer James Bradley, and his observations buy her father a Directorship in the Company (189). Margaret Maskelyne marries Robert Clive, the "Clive of India" in Pynchon's novel, and her brother Nevil is made Astronomer Royal upon Bradley's death.

As those dynastic connections also imply, this deterritorialized organization possesses few of the more benign qualities by which scholars sometimes distinguish economic from political dealings, the kind that enables John Breuilly, when discussing nineteenth-century capitalism, to assert that "[w]hile political relationships internationally were seen as threatening relationships of power where individuals were represented through their state, economic relationships were regarded as non-coercive dealings between individuals which could operate across state boundaries" (358). Quite the contrary. Precisely because the "rule of Empire operates on all registers of the social order," the "object of its rule is social life in its entirety" (Hardt and Negri xv). So it is in ***Mason & Dixon,*** in which Pynchon attributes to the East India Company every abuse of power that he formerly had ascribed to the state. The V. O. C. "Searches in the middle of the Night, [and] property impounded" that force farmers in Cape Town to move north (154) are no different from the D. O. J. "search-and-destroy missions" that force pot growers in ***Vineland*** to move in that same direction (334); just as the Company that "desire[s] total Control over ev'ry moment of ev'ry Life" (154) is no different from the zero-tolerance state that seeks to police "anything that could remotely please any of your senses, because they need to control all that" (***Vineland*** 313). Only in ***Mason & Dixon,*** such intrusions into civil liberties can no longer be dismissed as the product of individual fantasy or an author's long-standing distrust of corporate villainy. The "stately Finger" in ***Gravity's Rainbow*** that points to a "city of the future where every soul is known, and there is no place to hide" may prefigure a world in which IG Farben is "*the very model of nations*" or reflect the paranoia of characters who think that Providence is always giving them the finger (566). The "Invisible Hand," in Pynchon's appropriation of Adam Smith, with whose workings one dare not interfere in ***Mason & Dixon,*** is indubitably "a superior Power,—not in this case, God, but rather, Business" (411).

And in ***Mason & Dixon,*** that superior power has the military power to enforce its will, for, by the time that Mason and Dixon make their 1760s expedition to America, the East India Company had shifted from a trading to an armed power, mirroring the British empire's own shift from the pacifist trade policies of Robert Walpole to the militaristic ones of William Pitt. Pynchon hints at this shift early in the novel when Mason stumbles into the Jenkin's (sic) Ear Museum (175-80), honoring the captain whose 1738 brandishing to Parliament of a mummified ear, severed by the cutlass of a Spanish *guarda costa,* led to war with Spain in Spanish America over who controlled the empire of the seas trade (1739-48). Even more important, he suggests the forcible interventions that followed when Mason and Maskelyne trace the doings of "the wealthy-without-limit Clive of India" (131), whose career embodied that of the Company in miniature: rising to fame after switching from its civil to military service; becoming a national hero during the period of the Seven Years' War (1756-63) by leading troops that recaptured Calcutta after the 1756 Black Hole outrage and, in 1757, defeating at Plassey the forces of the Nawab who had perpetrated it; and, finally, giving the Company, with the post of *diwan* accorded it in 1765, authority over all territorial revenues in the imperial provinces of Bengal, Bihar, and Orissa, thus nullifying the independence of their own mogul rulers (Lawson 85-106).

When Maskelyne, then, summarizes for Mason the situation in which they find themselves on St. Helena, the imperial power he holds accountable for their lot is characterized more by way of global pillage than global village, to borrow Anthony Giddens's phrasing (34). "We are quite the Pair, then," Maskelyne concludes,

> both Subjects of the same Invisible Power? . . . Something richer than many a Nation, yet with no Boundaries,—which, tho' never part of any Coalition, yet maintains its own great Army and Navy,—able to pay for the last War, as the next, with no more bother than finding the Key to a certain iron Box,—yet which allows the Brittannick Governance that gave it Charter, to sink beneath oceanick Waves of Ink incarnadine.
>
> (140)

No wonder Dixon feels discomfort with interstitial spaces in such an "all-business world" (164), in which Lord Pennycomequick reigns as "global-Communications Nabob" (721). Conceptually unable, in Fredric Jameson's terms, "to map the great global multinational and decentered communicational network" in which he feels himself ensnared (44), Dixon cannot locate himself, either perceptually or cognitively, in a mappable external world. The only question that remains is whether the "overhead view" of that world that Dixon must produce as part of his employment, the "Map entirely within his mind" that he begins to contrive before he even gets to America, will represent an alternative "World he could escape to, if he had to" (242), or remain a miniaturized version of the one in which he finds himself already embedded.

Representation and Mapping

Jameson proposes an aesthetic of "cognitive mapping" as a response to these conditions, which, in practical terms, takes the form of a "reconquest of a sense of place and the construction or reconstruction of an articulated ensemble which can be retained in memory and which the individual subject can map and remap along the moments of mobile, alternative trajectories" (51). Dixon's tutor, Emerson, advances a similar proposal in recommending maps as "*Aides-mémoires* of flight" (504), and early in their partnership the surveyors gain experience in following his prescription. Sumatra they turn into a game called "Sumatra," "their Board a sort of *spoken Map* of the island they have been kept from and will never see" (57), St. Helena "a Plantation, sent out years since by its metropolitan Planet, which will remain invisible for years indeterminate before revealing itself and acquiring a Name, this place till then serving as an *Aide-Mémoire,* a Representation of Home" (133). By the time the surveyors get to America, this idea of representation will be particularly important, not only because of the impossibility of establishing with any fixity the actuality of America, but also because one of the ways in which nationhood is constructed is through linguistic identification with kinship or home (Anderson 131).

Mason's brother-in-law, in fact, warns him of the importance that representation will have when Mason arrives in the New World. Broaching the future apprenticeship of Mason's sons to their grandfather in exchange for financial assistance in caring for them during Mason's absence, another trade of bodies for booty, Elroy informs Mason that he represents the elder Mason, although not a lawyer himself, because "ev'ryone needs Representation, from time to time. If you go to America, you'll be hearing all about that, I expect" (202). And so Mason does. But in America, Mason also learns that there are different forms that representation can take. Politically, he discovers this most clearly while listening to Captain Volcanoe's Sons of Liberty ferociously debate whether or not "America has long been perfectly and entirely represented in the House of Commons, thro' the principle of Virtual Representation" (404). England, of course, contended America was, having defined Parliament as, in the words of Edmund Burke, not "a *congress* of ambassadors from different and hostile interests, which interests each must maintain, as an agent and advocate, against other agents and advocates," but "a *deliberative* assembly of *one* nation, with *one* interest, that of the whole, where, not local purposes, not local prejudices ought to guide, but the general good, resulting from the general reason of the whole" (qtd. in Bailyn 163). The colonies, not surprisingly, alleged they were not, having defined representation, much like Mason's brother-in-law, more in terms of medieval attorneyship in which elected local men, acting on behalf of their constituents, were enabled, as attorneys for their electors, to seek redress from the royal court of Parliament (Bailyn 162).

The members of Volcanoe's crew quickly put an end to any British notion that virtual representation—which, in effect, dissolves the referent into its representations—has any credence: "Suggest you, Sir, even in Play, that this giggling Rout of poxy half-wits, *embody* us? Embody *us*? America but some fairy Emanation, without substance, that hath pass'd, by Miracle, into *them*?" (404). Yet in exposing the futility of Mason encountering his dead wife Rebekah in women whose resemblances constitute a "*Point-for-Point Representation*" (536), Pynchon also exposes the folly of Volcanoe's crew presuming its notion of proportional representation will "extend beyond simple Agentry . . . unto at least Mr. Garrick, who in 'representing' a rôle, becomes the character, as by some transfer of Soul," and thereby yield "something styling itself 'America'" (405). As Pitkin reminds us, accuracy of depiction does not define any kind of representation (66-68). Mason's wife learns this lesson the hard way: having assumed "*some* Honesty" from those who give her a sketch of the man she is told she must marry, and found "Picture and Man *quite* as different as they prov'd to be," she is told, in explanation, "'Twas but a Representation" (186). A disappointment. And to found proportional political representation on what Pitkin has called "the recurrent ideal of the perfect replica" is to assume an unchanging notion of what politically relevant features are meant to be represented (86-87). A danger.

The artistry that Garrick employs as an actor nonetheless does bear fruit in the form that ***Mason & Dixon*** finally presents America as being revealed: Dixon's "Pen-and-Paper Representation" (687), a method of artistic composition Dixon spends years studying, "grinding and mixing his own Inks," much like any painter working with easel and canvas, "siftings and splashes ev'rywhere of King's Yellow, Azure, red Orpiment, Indian lake, Verdigris, Indigo, and Umber," "[l]evigating, elutriating, mixing the gum-water, pouncing and rosining the Paper to prevent soak-through" (242), resulting in a picture that he appends by his signature fleur-de-lis hallmark (688). The text of America that emerges from his endeavors is, finally, the Text that the Kabbalists who gather in the Rabbi of Prague tavern have anticipated all along: "Forms of the Land, the flow of water, the occurrence of what us'd to be call'd Miracles, all are Text,—to be attended to, manipulated, read, remember'd" (487).

In emphasizing the pictorial nature of Dixon's endeavors in this way, Pynchon invokes the element of craftsmanship that had been a part of cartography since its inception. Medieval cartographers referred to a map as *orbis imago* (representation of the world), or *pictura* (picture), as Leo Bagrow has noted (215), and this view survived well after the close of the Middle Ages. Geographer Philipp Clüver, for instance, characterized a map as a picture "*qua situs terrae vel eius partes in plano artificiosè describitur*" [in which a place on earth or its parts on a flat surface is by art described] at the end of the seventeenth century (qtd. in Bagrow 215), the degree of artifice employed to depict those earthly places or borders extending from the mere use of color (the Red Sea almost invariably appearing as red) to the wholesale contrivance of people and places. Such latter flights of fancy generally depended upon the amount of blank space that needed to be filled, which, in turn, generally depended upon the degree of familiarity that the area to be mapped possessed. Thus, the late-thirteenth-century circular world map known as the Hereford map populated Africa with headless men and four-eyed Ethiopians consorting with mermaids, unicorns, and dragons. The 1492 terrestrial globe constructed by Martin Behaim, whose maps were first drawn on strips of parchment by an artist named Glockenthon and then pasted on a spheroid shell, situated mythical islands in the Atlantic, notably the island of "Antilia" or "Isle of the Seven Cities," beyond the already-charted Azores (Wilford 46-47, 60-61).[10]

Perhaps more important, in emphasizing the textual nature of Dixon's endeavors, Pynchon suggests how much a land's being "attended to, manipulated, read, [and] remember'd" depended upon its having been rendered as recorded document, since, as Norman J. W. Thrower has argued, "a place is not really discovered until it has been mapped so that it can be reached again" (64). During the age of explorations, such rendering was aided considerably by the invention of printing, which provided for the reproduction of more or less identical copies at reduced costs. Leif Eriksson may have reached the western hemisphere nearly five hundred years before Christopher Columbus, but credit for discovering a fourth continent was accorded Columbus because the Norse produced no maps that had an impact upon the European consciousness, and authenticity of the one fifteenth-century (1440s) map that surfaced in 1957, with its Latin inscription attributing discovery of the large "Vinlanda Insula" to the west of Greenland to Eriksson and Bjarni Herjolfsson, continues to be contested. And Columbus, in turn, may have reached that continent seven years before Amerigo Vespucci, but the maps derived from his voyages continued to refer to the land he discovered as "Asia," in accordance with Columbus's conviction that he had found the desired passage to the Indies. So it was the successor whose published letters proclaimed discovery of a New World who had his name immortalized in that of the continent after a German mapmaker, Martin Waldeseemüller, prepared a 1507 woodcut print and scrawled over the region of Brazil the word "America" in Vespucci's honor.[11]

One can argue, of course, that, having earlier been delineated in the utopian tracts of writers such as Thomas More and Francis Bacon, America as a geographical entity had been a text all along. But America as an nation could not be revealed until its colonists had composed texts of their own with which to construct it, since, as Anderson has argued, in a hemisphere in which "an almost perfect isomorphism" existed between "the stretch of the various empires and that of their vernaculars" (75), it was print-language that enabled colonists to envision a community of thousands like themselves—hence, the importance Anderson attaches to Benjamin Franklin's trade (62). In one sense, then, it is a relatively minor character, the masquerading fop Philip Dimdown, who does more to advance the cause of nationhood in Pynchon's book than any political pundit, since he is arrested while operating a clandestine printing press whose broadsides proclaim the word "LIBERTY" in large letters (390). In another sense, however, it is Dixon himself who assumes this role, since appreciation of the text of America that he composes in pictures, no more accurate than any two-dimensional rendering of a three-dimensional reality can be, is not restricted in any way by its audience's degree of literacy.

In assessing this seminal role that Pynchon portrays Dixon as, intentionally or not, enacting, it is worth remembering how many of those who later became known as Founding Fathers assumed similar roles over the course of their careers. George Washington chose surveying as his first profession and over one hundred maps either surveyed or annotated by him exist today. Benjamin Franklin produced his own map of the boundary between Maryland and Pennsylvania in 1733 and, in collaboration with his cousin Timothy Folger, later prepared the first accurate chart of the Gulf Stream, based on thermometer readings. Thomas Jefferson, whose father also was a surveyor, published his "Map of the Country between Albemarle Sound and Lake Erie, 1787" in England after the Revolutionary War.[12]

These imaginative efforts notwithstanding, the nation that they collectively helped to draft is presented by Pynchon as, ultimately, a tenuous and fragile creation, apt to deconstruct or even self-destruct with very little provocation—and not only because Pynchon writes from a contemporary perspective in which the idea of the nation-state has itself been shown to be tenuous and fragile. The "War" may be "settl'd" in Christmas of 1786, but "the Nation [is] bickering itself into Fragments" (6), and the historicist perspective from which Pynchon writes allows him to trace the measures that, over time, have been used to rebind it to its very inception. Indeed, in the same year that the nation was being brought into political being, John Adams was proposing a representative delegation of power as a substitute for Thomas Paine's idea of single democratic assembly, writing in his 1776 *Thoughts on Government* pamphlet that "[t]he first necessary step, then, is to depute power from the many to a few of the most wise and good" (183). Neither an aberration nor an anomaly, such a reaction was but an inevitable stage in the creation of what Anderson terms "official nationalism," in which "even the most determinedly radical revolutionaries always, to some degree, inherit the state from the fallen regime," and, much like the electrical system in any large mansion that the owner has abandoned, "the state awaits the new owner's hand at the switch to be very much its old brilliant self again" (145).

We forget (if we ever knew) how much the mapping of the Mason-Dixon line contributed to this last gasp at traditional empire, so much do we think of it as a dividing line between North and South, between free and slave states, that was made irrelevant after the Civil War. We forget that the Land Ordinance of 1785 that was meant to survey and auction off public lands in order to pay the national debt took as its starting point the Mason-Dixon line, which already had been extended to the southwest corner of Pennsylvania by David Rittenhouse and Andrew Ellicott, and would be extended still farther by Thomas Hutchins as the geographer in charge appointed by Congress. In other words, we forget how fundamental to westward expansion the Mason-Dixon line was, even though the evidence of all those right-angled boundaries that are superimposed upon the landscape today—framing Colorado, Wyoming, Utah, Arizona, and New Mexico—reminds us of how lasting the legacy of that eighteenth-century line is. If a surveying style exists that can be considered "peculiarly American," it is safe to say, as John Noble Wilford does, that it is that "vast checkerboard" of right angles that defines it (189).

With that point in mind, I would like to close with reference to another representation of American right angles, composed exactly two hundred years after the colonies first declared their intent to unite in federation, a world map, in this case, exhibiting all the artistry of the earlier *pictura,* which situates its focal checkerboard in the context of other territories that surround it. On this map, China, Russia, and Japan appear as faint slivers on the horizon, and Mexico and Canada as small triangles off to the sides. On this map, Los Angeles is denoted by a small (somewhat misplaced) butte and Las Vegas by an even smaller cactus. And on this map, the Hudson River is a minuscule band that runs parallel to the even more minuscule band that is New Jersey. On this map, in other words, there is no question about where the impulse to empire is located—it resides in that urban grid delineated by Ninth and Tenth Avenues, whose looming buildings take up four-fifths of Saul Steinberg's western hemisphere and two-thirds of his entire world's space.

Some might say that this map, which first appeared as the 29 March 1976 cover of the *New Yorker,* is an exaggerated if not—given the recent ceding of Ellis Island to New Jersey (New Jersey!) and even more recent exposure of the city's vulnerability—an outdated rendering. Others might say it reflects the privileged, but not preeminent, place that the United States still occupies within the global affairs of contemporary Empire.[13] People like myself just view it as an expression of our diehard residency. New York rules, an unwritten caption might proclaim, and for those of us who continue to live there, that's exactly the way things should be.

Notes

1. See, for instance, Giddens 24-37 and Held 407-16.

2. See, for instance, Anderson 78 and Guibernau 45.

3. For an account of the 1756 rural riots in England, which presents a more sympathetic view of Wolfe than Pynchon's novel, see Hayter 75-92.

4. See Ferguson 455, 439. As Ferguson also makes clear, however, physics and astronomy served as blank checks to foster sovereignty or separation depending upon the political inclinations of individual writers. Anticolonial writers invoked Newton's laws of revolving orbs and equal force to make Great Britain the center of attraction for its colonies (438-39). Thomas Paine invoked the same scientist to assert how "[i]n no instance hath nature made the satellite larger than its primary planet" (457). See, especially, Ferguson's discussion of astronomer David Rittenhouse's writings on separation (454-56).

5. For a discussion of Pynchon's earlier works that portray surveying and mapmaking as inherently political, commercial, and colonialist endeavors, see Seed 85, 93-94.

6. Barth's use of Maryland's uncertain geography to suggest a precarious state of the universe, in fact, more closely resembles Pynchon's delineation of

Cape Town, with its "precarious Hold upon the Continent" and apocalyptic "Daughters of the End of the World" (58, 155), and St. Helena's James's Town, which "clings to the edge of an interior that must be reckoned part of the Other World" (107).

7. Different interpretations of the Visto have turned it into a veritable Rorschach test for critics who view it as an American fault line (Greiner 78-79), a "symbolic sign of cartographic codification" (Seed 92), a symbol of "realism, and the rationalized narrative structures that derive from it" (Baker 180), and a "powerful symbol of rationalism's putting its mark on a land once consecrated to multiple perspectives" (Cowart 344), to give but a few examples. David Cowart is unique among these critics in adding the caveat that the Line is not "irredeemably evil," but the product of a "legitimate activity of human beings, who must pay attention to boundaries or lapse . . . into vastly more primitive forms of territorialism" (361).
8. See, in this regard, McHale's discussion of "subjunctive space" as a hypothetical alternative to the America that time has brought into being (43-49).
9. This is not to suggest that the British government and the East India Company were unconnected. The Company's 1709 monopoly charter was predicated upon the Company lending the state 3,200,000 pounds, for example, and by the 1760s twenty-eight percent of House of Commons MPs were Company stockholders, often large stockholders (Lawson 74, 80). It is, instead, to emphasize the large degree of sovereignty by which the colonial operations of these first capitalist companies were characterized. In the case of the East India Company, that sovereignty lasted until the East India Act of 1858 brought it under the rule of Queen Victoria. For an extended discussion of these connections between government and Company, see Sutherland 14-31.
10. Not until Guillaume Delisle (1675-1726) acknowledged the limits of contemporary geographical knowledge by including blank spaces on the maps that he drew did such imaginative contrivances end and the initiation of what has been called "the reformation of cartography" begin (Crone 132-33).
11. Not even Waldeseemüller was able to correct for this erroneous impression by crediting discovery of the New World to Columbus in an inscription on a plane chart drafted in 1513 (Thrower 71).
12. See Wilford 178-79; Bagrow 193; and Thrower 120.
13. See, especially, Hardt and Negri 384.

Works Cited

Adams, John. *Thoughts on Government: Applicable to the Present State of the American Colonies: In a Letter From a Gentleman to his Friend.* Philadelphia: Dunlap, 1776. Rpt. in *John Adams: A Biography in His Own Words.* Ed. James Bishop Peabody. New York: Harper, 1973. 182-88.

Anderson, Benedict. *Imagined Communities: Reflections on the Origin and Spread of Nationalism.* London: Verso, 1983.

Bagrow, Leo. *History of Cartography.* 1951. Trans. D. L. Paisey. Rev. R. A. Skelton. Cambridge: Harvard UP, 1966.

Bailyn, Bernard. *The Ideological Origins of the American Revolution.* Cambridge: Harvard UP, 1967.

Baker, Jeff. "Plucking the American Albatross: Pynchon's Irrealism in *Mason & Dixon.*" Horvath and Malin 167-88.

Balibar, Étienne. "The Nation Form: History and Ideology." Eley and Suny, *Becoming* 132-50.

Barth, John. *The Sot-Weed Factor.* 1960. New York: Bantam, 1969.

Bhabha, Homi K. *The Location of Culture.* London: Routledge, 1994.

Breuilly, John. *Nationalism and the State.* New York: St. Martin's, 1982.

Cowart, David. "The Luddite Vision: *Mason & Dixon.*" *American Literature* 71 (1999): 341-63.

Crèvecoeur, J. Hector St. John de. *Letters from an American Farmer.* 1782. New York: Everyman, 1957.

Crone, G. R. *Maps and Their Makers: An Introduction to the History of Cartography.* London: Hutchinson's Univ. Lib., 1953.

Doyle, Laura. *Bordering the Body: The Racial Matrix of Modern Fiction and Culture.* New York: Oxford UP, 1994.

Eley, Geoff, and Ronald Grigor Suny, eds. *Becoming National: A Reader.* New York: Oxford UP, 1996.

———. "From the Moment of Social History to the Work of Cultural Representation." Introduction. Eley and Suny, *Becoming* 3-37.

Ferguson, Robert A. "The American Enlightenment, 1750-1820." *The Cambridge History of American Literature, Vol. I: 1590-1820.* Ed. Sacvan Bercovitch. Cambridge: Cambridge UP, 1994. 345-537.

Giddens, Anthony. *Runaway World: How Globalization is Reshaping our Lives.* 1999. New York: Routledge, 2000.

Greiner, Donald J. "Thomas Pynchon and the Fault Lines of America." Horvath and Malin 73-83.

Guibernau, Montserrat. *Nationalisms: The Nation-State and Nationalism in the Twentieth Century.* Cambridge: Polity, 1996.

Hardt, Michael, and Antonio Negri. *Empire.* 2000. Cambridge: Harvard UP, 2001.

Hayter, Tony. *The Army and the Crown in Mid-Georgian England.* London: Roman, 1978.

Held, David. "The Decline of the Nation State." Eley and Suny, *Becoming* 407-16.

Higginson, John. "Attestation." 1697. *Magnalia Christi Americana: Books I and II.* By Cotton Mather. London, 1702. Ed. Kenneth B. Murdock and Elizabeth W. Miller. Cambridge: Harvard UP, 1977. 63-73.

Horvath, Brooke, and Irving Malin, eds. *Pynchon and* Mason & Dixon. Newark: U of Delaware P, 2000.

Iser, Wolfgang. "Representation: A Performative Act." *The Aims of Representation: Subject/Text/History.* Ed. Murray Krieger. New York: Columbia UP, 1987. 217-32.

Jameson, Fredric. *Postmodernism, or, the Cultural Logic of Late Capitalism.* Durham: Duke UP, 1991.

Lawson, Philip. *The East India Company: A History.* London: Longman, 1993.

Lukács, Georg. *The Historical Novel.* 1937. Trans. Hannah and Stanley Mitchell. Boston: Beacon, 1963.

Mason, Charles. *The Journal of Charles Mason and Jeremiah Dixon, 1763-1768.* Philadelphia: Amer. Philos. Soc., 1969.

McHale, Brian. "*Mason & Dixon* in the Zone, or, A Brief Poetics of Pynchon-Space." Horvath and Malin 43-62.

Pitkin, Hanna Fenichel. *The Concept of Representation.* Berkeley: U of California P, 1967.

Pynchon, Thomas. *Gravity's Rainbow.* New York: Viking, 1973.

———. *Mason & Dixon.* New York: Holt, 1997.

———. *Vineland.* Boston: Little, 1990.

Rogin, Michael Paul. *Ronald Reagan, the Movie and Other Episodes in Political Demonology.* Berkeley: U of California P, 1987.

Schaub, Thomas H. "Plot, Ideology, and Compassion in *Mason & Dixon.*" Horvath and Malin 189-202.

Seed, David. "Mapping the Course of Empire in the New World." Horvath and Malin 84-99.

Shields, David S. *Oracles of Empire: Poetry, Politics, and Commerce in British America, 1690-1750.* Chicago: U of Chicago P, 1990.

Steinberg, Saul. Cartoon. *New Yorker* 29 Mar. 1976: cover.

Sutherland, Lucy S. *The East India Company in Eighteenth-Century Politics.* Oxford: Clarendon, 1952.

Thrower, Norman J. W. *Maps and Civilization: Cartography in Culture and Society.* Chicago: U of Chicago P, 1996.

Wilford, John Noble. *The Mapmakers.* 1981. New York: Vintage, 1982.

Margaret Lynd (essay date fall 2004)

SOURCE: Lynd, Margaret. "Science, Narrative, and Agency in *Gravity's Rainbow.*" *Critique* 46, no. 1 (fall 2004): 63-80.

[*In the following essay, Lynd considers the relationship between agency, subject, and scientific discourse in* Gravity's Rainbow.]

> The current amazement that these things we are experiencing are "still" possible in the twentieth century is *not* philosophical. This amazement is not the beginning of knowledge—unless it is the knowledge that the view of history which gives rise to it is untenable.
>
> —Walter Benjamin, "Theses on the Philosophy of History"

> Every morning brings us the news of the globe, and yet we are poor in newsworthy stories.
>
> —Walter Benjamin, "The Storyteller"

The power that science has acquired over the past four centuries to determine the scope and parameters of human possibility dominates the multiple themes of ***Gravity's Rainbow.*** Pynchon's fictional account of that power closely parallels Michel Foucault's work on the power of discourse to regulate and prescribe behavior and sexual pleasure and provokes similar concerns about the question of agency and subjectivity. Foucault's analysis of power in *The History of Sexuality* leaves little room for agency in its characterization of power as an inevitable factor immanent in all human interactions, arising (at least since the beginnings of modernity) from institutional discourses and limiting the boundaries of the subject.[1] Pynchon's analysis of scientific discourse in ***Gravity's Rainbow*** echoes that argument, but, in the case of the novel, a space for agency is carved out by the function of narrative to represent action, change, even revelation. I focus here primarily on how agency and the subject are imagined in relation to scientific discourse in ***Gravity's Rainbow*** and on the role that narrative might usefully play as a significant and perhaps necessary component in theorizations of agency and subject relations. But I also show how the particular voices that dominate the novel deeply undercut Pynchon's otherwise powerful vision.

The grimly carnivalesque atmosphere of the novel, with its endless midway of unresolved subplots, peripheral excursions, and mutable characters, each trapped in one or another pattern of conditioned behavior—sadomasochism; paranoia; the seductive, heart-numbing abstractions of science—seems an unlikely ground on which to argue for agency. Even the erstwhile "protagonist," Tyrone Slothrop, is so deeply conditioned—"so well have They busted the sod prairies of his brain, tilled and sowed there, and subsidized him not to grow anything of his own . . ." (210)—that exposure to the anarchic environment of the Zone causes him finally to dissipate. Slothrop loses the capacity to narrate and his consciousness is reduced to a series of vaguely poignant but fleeting images cut loose from the contesting storylines that once had anchored them in time and space. Organized opposition to the nefarious power of global cartels and the nation-states that do their bidding hardly holds more promise for action or change, merely repeating and reifying the terms of engagement: The Counterforce is "as schizoid, as double-minded in the massive presence of money as any of the rest of us, and that's the hard fact. The Man has a branch office in each of our brains. [. . .] They will use us. We will help legitimize Them, though They don't need it really, it's another dividend for Them, nice but not critical . . ." (712-13). Scant room is there for agency, then, with colonized cortexes scattered through the Zone and with the political wing of the dispossessed, the Counterforce itself, the normalized (and loyal) opposition that merely reaffirms the validity of the Elect-Preterite binary. But if, as most critics agree, the book is neither despairing nor absurd, where is the room for agency?[2] Is this simply one more postmodern carnival of decentered subjects, interpellated subjects, fragmented selves? Or does Pynchon recuperate an essentialized humanistic self (Pökler, Seaman Bodine, Geli Tripping, Enzian) and set before us kindness and generosity as the transparent virtues that such a subject might display? Is ***Gravity's Rainbow*** after all a sly endorsement and remystification of individualism and its mythic powers of independent action? Certainly such a formulation would invite new and seductive possibilities for the very romanticism that Pynchon appears to make monstrous in the person of Blicero/Weissmann.

What the novel suggests instead is that an adequate theorization of the subject—or at least of the subject who is capable of agency—depends in part on the premise that the world is so complex that an element of randomness, uncertainty, or unpredictability is always present (one version of Gödel's theorem, as well as a tenet of chaos theory).[3] Randomness is a crucial element because it opens a space for agency—the random event creates a condition of possibility that the alert subject may seize on and turn to subversive purposes. But, the novel suggests, agency further requires an element of narrativity. The capacity to narrate allows the subject to place his or her own potentially subversive acts within the self- and world-constructing narratives through which consciousness emerges as both contingent and continuous. That is, narrative—structured by time, always constructed, and always incomplete—may be a useful discursive tool through which to represent the fluidity of the subject over time and within which to rethink the question of agency as a function of desire as it intersects with random events and opportunities.[4] If serious fiction can be said to "theorize" through the representation of concrete events that invite broader speculation, then narrative itself may open a space for thinking through a provisional and unfixed identity that is nonetheless continuous and capable of narrating more than one course of action. The trick that Pynchon accomplishes in the book is to create an anxious, unstable subject that hovers between an essentialized self and a purely contingent one, a subject buffeted and battered by texts, yet capable, maybe, of authoring one as well. The hopeless desire for narrative closure could then become not a closing off of possibilities but a spur to action.

Pynchon does not completely avoid the dangers of romanticization, but he does sidestep them in this complex weaving together of randomness, desire, and narrative possibility. A striking number of characters undergo revelatory moments of self-reflexivity just beyond the realm of paranoia and just, it seems, outside the clutches of discourse: Pökler acknowledges complicity in the Dora death camp; Seaman Bodine offers Slothrop John Dillinger's bloody T-shirt; Enzian reads the "real" Text; Tchitcherine abandons his mission of revenge; Katje Borgesian acknowledges her aversion to blackness; and so on. Through narrative, then, Pynchon deconstructs his own recuperation of the humanistic self. The subject that emerges is one with no fixed identity but, rather, with something like what Judith Butler theorizes as a provisional self with multiple connections and allegiances, one that is defined by the performance of those interrelations, not by a set of multiple identities that could only be produced by the rejection of others.[5] Colonized as all our brains may be by the onslaughts of discourse, the possibility of agency emerges for Pynchon and Butler alike through the inevitable gaps and aporias of those same discourses.

The case that Pynchon makes for such a contingent self depends on his unrelenting critique of science as a radically reductive enterprise that represents complexity as simplicity, diversity as uniformity, and multiplicity as (in practice, at least) a finite set of classifiable objects. The proclaimed "innocence" of science—its ungrounded positioning of the scientist as a disinterested seeker of knowledge; its claims of progressive, self-correcting mechanisms of "discovery"; its practice of quantifying and representing sensory data in highly abstract form; its insistence on a sharp and impermeable boundary between subject and object; its pretense that rhetorical strategy and emotional engagement are absent from scientific discourse; its ability to absorb and contain epistemological uncertainties about its knowledge claims—all of these factors, Pynchon's text suggests, contribute to the hegemonic tendencies of scientific discourse and provide a nearly impenetrable shield for the deep and illicit desires that drive it.[6] The movement toward death in the novel plays itself out for some in sadism—rape, torture, murder, genocide—and infects others with masochistic fantasies and realities of victimization.

For Pynchon, the discourses of science regulate pleasure and construct categories of difference, specifically black and female, which, in turn, lay the grounds of possibility on which the sadomasochistic desires of white men may be satisfied, certainly in the violent sexual encounters of torturer and victim, but more mundanely and more continuously in the requirements of technology—its care, its use, its promotion. Scientific enterprise and technological progress work to establish the Raketen-stadt to which, Walter Rathenau explains, the War itself is dedicated:

> The persistence, then, of structures favoring death. Death converted into more death. Perfecting its reign, just as the buried coal grows denser, and overlaid with more strata—epoch on top of epoch, city on top of ruined city. [. . .] All talk of cause and effect is secular history, and secular history is a diversionary tactic.
>
> (167)

Through the metaphor of the rocket and the emergent Raketen-stadt that produced it, Pynchon articulates not a cause-and-effect relationship between science and oppression but a dialectic in which sadomasochistic desire drives science, while scientific discourse, in turn, regulates sadomasochistic pleasure and pain. Science effects this regulatory power in part by incorporating into its methodology the processes of "naming," categorizing, quantifying so that the assumptions governing those processes recede to the realm of the ideological.[7] By constructing "essential" categories of difference, actual differences are elided and reduced to the familiar litany of binary oppositions, their middles excluded in a process Pynchon calls, quite simply, "bad shit": Self/Other, Black/White, Male/Female, Civilized/Savage, Man/Animal. In ***Gravity's Rainbow,*** each of these oppositions is subsumed by Pynchon's Elect-Preterite binary, based on distributions of power rather than on real or imaginary physical or cultural differences.[8] All Otherness is defined against self-perceived qualities of the Elect, measured both by concrete parameters (money, family, occupation) and purely imaginary ones (intelligence, racial purity, moral character).

For Pynchon, these rigid categories of difference not only collapse everyone (and everything) into the Elect-Preterite binary but are simultaneously a product of scientific discourse, a reification of scientific practice, and a hedge against subtextual eruptions. Potentially disruptive discourses that science itself generates, through both data-gathering and theoretical constructions, are invariably reinscribed as normative. To take a simple example from outside the novel, the statistics gathered by Charles Murray and Michael Herrnstein should make clear the pervasive facts of racism and economic oppression but are instead offered as proof that poverty is the consequence of inherited traits. It could be argued that *The Bell Curve* is bad science, but it is no different in kind from well-funded, less controversial projects linking, for example, a propensity for violence or "deviant" behavior to gene sequences or—believing their vocation immune to the bag of tricks the language demons never tire of deploying—physicists' search for the "theory of everything" (it should come as no surprise, incidentally, that the Bell Curve coincides with the Rocket's gray parabola).[9] Similarly, the theoretical uncertainties generated by twentieth-century scientists (Einstein, Gödel, Heisenberg) are reinscribed within scientific discourse as conundra or paradoxes or brain-teasers for dreamy theoretical physicists. Profound uncertainties become minor, forgotten Achilles' heels that bear no relation to scientific or technological progress and do nothing to temper sensational rhetorical devices depicting science as a pioneering expedition to conquer frontiers, a journey toward destiny, a promise to decode the body and colonize the stars.

Scientific discourse, according to Pynchon, attacks diversity and multiplicity by relegating all that is not self to the single category of Otherness, but it does so also by attending to and inscribing the most minute differences of motion as well as of bodies in the various texts of calculus, chemistry, biology, and physics. Imagined as inert, passive, and reactive, the Preterite offspring of Nature and the life processes they embody are disassembled and reassembled as representations. As Michael Bérubé has argued, Pynchon defines that process of transformation as pornography.[10] The real movement of the rocket in space and time and the consequences of that movement are reduced to the "bourgeois terms" of calculus, the "pornographies of flight." The Rocket (itself a pornographic representation of, say, the eagle) follows the prescribed and limiting rules of a pornographic script, but its short and parabolic life delivers real pain and real death. The Rocket, then, is pornography brought to life and, as the central metaphor of the novel, correlates the discourses of science with pornographic production. Much as pornography reduces the complexities of erotic pleasure to a dreary and predictable sameness, science disassembles the world and reassembles it in controllable, manageable forms—mathematical formulas and taxonomic systems, steel beams and concrete slabs, the disembodied simulacra of cyberspace.[11]

For Pynchon, this disjunction between the world itself and its representation produces the two-edged sword of paranoia, the capacity to find other orders beneath an only apparent reality. Paranoia has the potential to lead either to a resolute desire to "discover," contain, and transform that other order into fetish or, on the other hand, to piece together the scattered clues that reveal the many forms of power lending themselves to that process. This second notion, in turn, opens the further possibility of what Donna Haraway calls "situated knowledges." Haraway, in the full spirit of deconstructive play, posits a form of objectivity that incorporates assumptions about knowledge that science represses, specifically the impossibility of unsituated knowledge and dispassionate (nondesiring) discourse. Science's vision of Nature as inert and feminized matter, waiting—indeed, asking—to be ravaged is countered by Haraway's subject of science: Nature as trickster, the tenacious coyote who, despite his popular cartoon incarnation, is mighty tough to outsmart.[12] If ***Gravity's Rainbow*** is problematic in its own frequent association of Nature with conservative notions of "femininity," it nonetheless assigns power finally to whatever unpredictable forces (something like Nature) may lie beyond human control and attempts (unsuccessfully, a point I will revisit) to imagine an egalitarian subjectivized sexuality in the process: the wintry forces of death (read discourses of science) are powerful, Pynchon tells us, but only almost as powerful as the "revolutionaries of May" (281). This latter image, in contrast to that of the Counterforce (representing the active mechanisms of organized political opposition), suggests an alternate image of the forlorn stragglers who (may) manage to escape Their games: leaderless and without a political agenda or strategy, this refugee army of malcontents may be effective to the extent that it remains disorganized and anarchic, capable of sliding affiliations and random acts of subversion.[13] Such a position is small consolation and dangerously close to an endorsement of apathy; but it is designed, it seems, to preclude the seductions of power that merely reverse (temporarily) the roles of oppressor and victim or, more dangerously, that reproduce similar discourses that, in turn, produce new regulatory mechanisms and a new set of victims (new, but always the same Preterite crowd—the poor, the dispossessed, the marginalized, and, of course, the nonhuman world).

At issue in Pynchon's dance around the question of agency and subjectivity and in his refusal to endorse a political agenda is the capacity of scientific discourse to repress its own contradictions and aporias. This issue is explored most fully in the repeated interrogations of science that recur throughout the novel; particularly important is the case with which even potential disruptions generated by scientific discourses themselves are repressed and subverted to reinscribe the normative procedures of science. As Katherine Hayles points out, scientific language, like any other, relies heavily on metaphor and is inherently self-reflexive: Just as the distinction between discursive theory and discursive practice is never complete, the language of science necessarily produces science.[14] One possible restatement (among many) of Gödel's theorem undermining the validity of propositions is that all linguistic or discursive systems are self-reflexive. Gödel's work, like Heisenberg's, presents to science, and notably from within science, what Hayles (referring to Maxwell's demon) calls a "self-reflexive moment." a gap in the text that is laden with possibilities for change, redefinition, and reassessment. Yet, by acknowledging uncertainty, the discourses and practices of science barrel along unimpeded, accumulating and interpreting data and continuously reproducing themselves anew. In a reversal of its subversive potential, the problem of uncertainty is relegated to the realm of the purely theoretical where it cannot do any real harm.

Similarly, the aporias of normative science are incorporated to explain away alternative interpretive strategies. Of the several disciplines of science interrogated in ***Gravity's Rainbow,*** each reveals its particular strategies of self-containment and "deep conservatism." The frequently noted binary opposition between Roger Mexico's allegiance to the uncertainties of statistical probability and Edward Pointsman's to the certainties of causality is not an opposition but a demonstration of the role that internal squabbles among scientists play in repressing contradictions. Pointsman is excommunicated from the White Visitation not because of his outmoded positivism, but because he overreached his grasp (poor experimental design), let Slothrop slip through his fingers (fudged, then lost his data), and mistakenly castrated, in one of the few moments of justice in the entire novel, repulsive Major Marvy instead of Slothrop (became emotionally involved in his inquiry). That the stars of sexual conquest on Slothrop's map mapped only Slothrop's fantasies (just as the points on Pointsman's map of Dog Vanya's tortured brain map only Pointsman's) is not at issue. The sheer, inept lunacy of Pointsman's projects, like those detailed in *The Bell Curve,* are never an issue. In fact, the usefulness of behavioral conditioning is reaffirmed when Clive Mossmoon realizes that the dog packs at large in the Zone, conditioned to attack any creature other than their own individual trainers, are nicely poised to kill each other, thus dispensing with the need for costly canine hit men. Similarly, the distributions of Mexico's Poisson and his careful explanations of the unpredictability of the precise points where the rockets will fall blind him to the fact that the Poisson distribution can only measure that randomness already accounted for by the system itself. The real threat of the random event—sudden death, a looming Void, pain and loss—which Roger's statistics only serve to allay, is repressed along with any possibility of alternate interpretations of data, let alone an interrogation of the status of "data" as transparently factual. Thus, the discursive representations of science are reinscribed through the very process of accounting for randomness and the limits of predictability. Opportunities for change are lost, uncertainty is just another discourse, and the bodies and cortexes of Man's best friend and Man's closest relative continue to be mapped and mutilated as the Rocket makes its way across the sky.

The combinatory power of extradisciplinary discourses, when brought to bear on a new object of study, is similarly repressed, not through the evisceration of subversive discourses or the rationalization of normative ones but through reconception of the object of study. What if, Pynchon's narrator speculates, "Clerk Maxwell intended his Demon not so much as a convenience in discussing a thermodynamic idea as a parable about the *actual existence* of personnel like Liebig . . ." the scientist who had inspired Kekulé the architect to become Kekulé the biochemist (411, emphasis in original). When Kekulé's training in architecture is brought to bear on organic chemistry, the principles of polymerization are not far behind: the casual covalent bonds of life's molecules, indolent, erotic, magical—a "stringing of rings and chains in nets only God can tell the meshes of" (6), "flowery, permeating, surprising, more than the color of winter sunlight, [. . .] a spell, against falling objects" (10)—are jettisoned for the sturdy, no-nonsense ionic links of polyester chains, and plastics are born, their Whiteness, Strength, and Stability a tribute to and sign of Western ingenuity and Nazi dreaming.

Thus, the closed system of science, its own sorting demons kept busy policing potential troublemakers, confirms itself through the power of its own discourses.[15] The closed system of sadomasochism not only parallels that process but also is represented as both the repressed narrative and the locus of desire motivating science and the particular discourses proscribing sexual pleasure. The confluence of sexuality, technology, and power, and the intersections of these with race and gender, crescendo toward full expression in the drama staged by Blicero/Weissmann around the construction and launch of Rocket 00000. Here, the economies of race, sex, and gender are played out among Blicero, Katje, Enzian, and Gottfried. Notably missing from the cast is the doubly absent black woman, who, being neither male nor white, remains fully invisible, silenced and unaccounted for, a problem that undermines Pynchon's attack on univocality and binarism.

Gravity's Rainbow is not immune to deconstruction, however impressively it deconstructs itself in multiple ways. The premise that science is distinctively male and European leads to a romanticizing of the "feminine" and the "primitive" that Pynchon does not succeed in subverting. Because his critique of science posits white male desire as the central motivating factor in virtually every act of violence since the Renaissance, from schoolyard bullying to genocide, it is easy to imagine why this is so. The logic of the argument, however, is not the problem; Pynchon's critique is limited, rather, by its near exclusion of female and nonwhite voices. Even the heavy-handed but versatile narrator emerges as a consistent and distinctly male character. Critics often describe the narrator, despite his third-person, omniscient status, as unfixed, elusive, multivocal, calling on an enormous range of discourse genres, including pop music, street slang, ethnography, literature, technical papers, historical tracts, newspapers, film, and many others. Notwithstanding such eclecticism and fancy linguistic footwork, the narrator's outrage and frustration are obvious and consistent; throughout the text, he borders on cynicism or despair. Yet invariably he stops just short of either by noting a character's gesture of kindness or moment of vulnerability or by invoking the sweet nature of a lost dog or the resplendent beauty of a sunset, but always too briefly to allow for sentimentality or a parody of it. Thus, the act of narrating produces not a fragmented, unidentifiable character/narrator but a fully realized dialogic one, the Bakhtinian orchestrator of a multiplicity of white male voices.

Male characters, good and bad, dominate the novel; and focalizations are almost completely limited to them. The few nonmale characters are mostly negative: Jessica returns from the Zone to suburban housewifery; and Greta, when not swooning under the whip, murders children, including her own. Katje, the most complex of all of the characters, is a composite, unlike the most fully developed male characters, who are distinctively and individualistically drawn. Geli Tripping is positively, but also simplistically, characterized. Leni Pökler, in her political activism, perhaps comes closest to autonomy; but she disappears early in the text and reappears only as a fragment of the stitched-together character of Katje. In short, the novel both reinscribes and deconstructs a feminizing discourse: Geli Tripping emerges as the good witch, metaphor and synecdoche for "lovable but scatterbrained Mother Nature" (324); nevertheless, her sexuality is fully realized and subjectively wrought. Her magical ritual of celebratory masturbation gives her the power to bewitch Tchitcherine, releasing him from his homicidal-suicidal mission. More than any other character, Geli escapes the moribund cycle of sado-masochism, but Pynchon treads dangerous ground in feminizing the "Natural" and in reinscribing the brutalized Greta Erdmann as a devouring and craven female archetype. The problem of each of these characterizations reverts to voice. It is impossible to imagine Geli's magical powers outside male fantasies of them: "May he be blind now to all but me. May the burning sun of love shine in his eyes forever. [. . .] She fixes on Tchitcherine's memory and his wayward eyes and lets it build, pacing her orgasm to the incantation, so that, by the end, naming the last Names of Power, she's screaming, coming, without help from her fingers, which are raised to the sky" (734). Again, it is an unmistakably male voice that describes Greta's pleasure-pain: "She comes once, then perhaps again before Slothrop puts the whip down and climbs on top, [. . .] the old phony rack groaning beneath them, Margherita whispering *God how you hurt me* and *Ah, Max . . .*" (397). Descriptions of her, when not given by the narrator, are provided by such shaky sources as Slothrop and Thanatz. Women almost never interact with other women outside the presence of men, and the erotic responses of twelve-year-old Bianca, although ambiguously represented as Slothropean fantasy, nevertheless leave Bianca with no voice even of complicity, let alone of protest, confusion, or pain. And she ends up hanging dead from a meathook, presumably killed, not by any of the many men who rape her but by her own mother, Greta Erdmann.

Male characters are treated differently. Some sympathy is evoked for even repulsive Pointsman and more repulsive Major Marvy, not to mention arch-Nazi Blicero. The evil Blicero alone understands the depth of European depravity required to ravage most of the planet, and the knowledge tortures him to madness: "'In Africa, Asia, Amerindia, Oceania, Europe came and established its order of Analysis and Death. What it could not use, it killed or altered. [. . .] Now we are in the last phase. American Death has come to occupy Europe. It has learned Empire from its old metropolis'" (722). Blicero alone understands and articulates the narrator's complaint. The sheer honesty of his compulsion elevates his suffering; his peculiar madness is to play out all the implications of Europe's sadomasochism to their logical end, the launch of Rocket 00000. Meanwhile, the supposed sympathy for a fully active sexual, powerful, and compassionate femininity emerges, in the absence of either female voices or female brains, as little more than male fantasy. This is not to say that women characters are not given power. They are, but it is the perverse and reactive power of the victimized, though they are not held responsible for their own depravity. Indeed, child-killer Greta, double-agent Katje, or seductress Jessica become who they are in response to "Their" masculine games. White men hold all the cards, and women can stay at the table only by agreeing to play, even though they know the deck is stacked and the cards marked. Despite Pynchon's outrage at this state of affairs, no female character is comparable to the complex, conflicted males who most deeply engage the narrator's attention. Most characters are composites or chameleons (Slothrop appears as a lackadaisical research assistant, a bumbling private eye, a Zoot-suited hipster, Rocketman, a human-sized pig), but the narrator blurs the boundaries among individual female characters differently than he does for the males. The poignancy and depth of Pökler's despair as he wanders the Dora death camp, the tragic dimensions of Blicero's perverse romanticism, Enzian's hopeless compassion for the Zone-Hereros, even poor Slothrop's inability to prevent his own dissipation by linking the images of his battered memory into the simplest of storylines—such narrative moments, however fleeting, make male characters *matter* in ways that female characters do not. If Pynchon intends to foreground the willing complicity of women in masculinist discourses—no small problem, to be sure, whether in Nazi Germany or contemporary America—he certainly succeeds. But in ***Gravity's Rainbow,*** *everyone* is complicit, making a generous interpretation ring a bit hollow.

The racialization of sexuality invokes a somewhat different set of problems, but here, too, Pynchon both reinscribes and deconstructs the feminized black male.[16] Again, the invisibility and silence of black female characters are part of the problem. Black women are even less individualized than white women, who at least get to be villains (Greta, Katje), victimizers (Katje, Ilse), seductresses (Jessica, again Katje), even borderline goddesses (Geli). Black women, on the other hand, appear only briefly as silent companions of the Schwarzkommando or as mutilated victims of genocide, or, in two rare instances of individuation, as the three-day mistress of Enzian's German seaman father (the narrator tells us she enjoyed the brief affair) and as the Earth itself, an Erdschweinhohle woman buried to the neck to restore fertility. Herero culture is posed as neither male nor female, but as cyclic and egalitarian, organic, unified, and whole. Death for the African Hereros is neither the escape that burned out ex-warriors like Brigadier Pudding long for nor the transcendence that Blicero (and Werner von Braun) imagine, but a return to life, ancestral souls forever lodged in the living flesh of Herero worlds. Pynchon inverts the "heart of darkness" metaphor to invoke Africa not as the black origin of depraved sexuality and savagery but as the peaceful source of sunlight and sanity. If such a representation of the precolonial Hereros is overly simplistic—a new iteration of the noble savage it is nonetheless the white power of Europe that brings darkness to Africa and turns its lands into, in Pynchon's words, the "outhouses of the European soul" (317), where any sadomasochistic fantasy may be realized and acted on. Pynchon repeatedly identifies whiteness with forces of death and points to the European need to construct African depravity to define itself otherwise.

Pynchon's characterization of race depends most heavily on the representation of Enzian and, to a lesser degree, Ombindi, the two lone African voices in the novel. They are refugees in the Zone—both bent on suicide, one seduced by despair, the other by the romance of science and salvation—and their respective followers represent reactions to colonialism that recall Fanon's double consciousness and Bhabha's psychoanalytic rereading of colonizer-colonized relations.[17] To lead his followers to racial self-destruction Ombindi incorporates European discourses of death into his own culture's stories of return, whereas Enzian, absorbing those same discourses, turns to salvation Christian-style, through his own anticipated martyrdom and its promise of a new mythology to guide the Zone-Hereros. Taken together, they are the two components of the colonized's gaze: Ombindi obliging the colonizer's desire for his elimination in mass suicide, Enzian incorporating Blicero's mad desire for transcendence as his own, and, indeed, loving Blicero until the end. Enzian and Ombindi are represented with sympathy, with much insight into the psychology of the colonized and with the recognition that "blackness" is an overdetermined sign constructed by Europeans. Indeed, der Springer takes credit for constructing the Schwarzkommando in the film he had produced for the White Visitation, a fake documentary employing actors in blackface, designed to produce fear in white Europeans. But Pynchon's keen insight into the racial and sexual dynamics of colonialism is not sufficient. Apart from Enzian, the black male voice remains largely silent, and Enzian himself, though sympathetically drawn, comes perilously close to the idealized, exoticized Other that Pynchon surely cannot intend him to be.

Throughout the text, Blicero, like the Rocket and its parts, is a continual presence, but he does not appear until the final sections of "The Counterforce." Blicero designs the Rocket to reproduce himself in pornographic splendor, and he embodies the sadomasochistic desire that works to repress the contradictions and aporias of the culture of science. His three victims, Katje, Enzian, and Gottfried, all respond differently to victimization. Katje, the white woman, is a double agent and a composite character incorporating the victimized child Bianca/Ilse, the victimized and victimizing woman Greta Erdmann, and the hollow suburbanite Jessica Swanlake, but also the independent activist Leni Pökler and the sexual enchantress Geli Tripping. Katje's escape, first from Blicero and later from the bureaucratic entrapments of the White Visitation, suggests the possibility of disruption of a white female identity conditioned to victimization and complicity in the destructive and self-destructive system of the Raketenstadt. If, like Slothrop, Katje is able to shed her conditioning further to play out that possibility, she may be able to resist Them successfully and retrieve the storyless Slothrop from the Zone. Condemned, as Enzian tells her, to freedom, she is given the opportunity to narrate herself and even Slothrop into being. Her meeting with Enzian is an ambiguous point of departure for her. On the one hand, her self-reflection, "Understand it isn't *his* blackness, but her own—an inadmissible darkness she is making believe for the moment is Enzian's. [. . .] It is shaking itself into her consciousness" (661); on the other hand, the old, self-protective habits: "'You black bastard.' 'Exactly.' He has allowed her to speak the truth" (662-63). Her story, which Enzian has categorized as "the saddest of all" (661), precisely because it is potentially unscripted, is left unresolved, yet her chances to produce a story of her own are greater than zero. "There are," the narrator tells us at the end of this episode, "things to hold on to . . ." (663).

Similarly, Enzian leaves Blicero, but we are given to understand that Blicero had served as a kind of Great White Hope for Enzian, grooming him as the Schwarzgerät who would martyr himself to save Blicero or, perhaps, as the shadow Schwarzgerät who would martyr himself to save the Zone-Hereros (the reader finds Enzian pursuing the latter option in "The Counterforce"). Nor do we know whether he had escaped from Blicero or had been given (as Gottfried will be) the option to leave; in any case, he retains, as does Katje, a deep attachment, nostalgic and affectionate, for Blicero. Enzian, alone among the survivors of genocide, had been chosen by Blicero as the "passed over" Herero, either saved (From the genocide of his fellow tribesmen? For transcendence?) or damned (To survive alone the slaughter of his tribesmen? To be the sacrificial lamb and savior of his people amidst the horrors of the Zone?). Unlike Ombindi, with his suicidal plans, Enzian imagines himself as a Black Blicero, not the hero of his own story but the center and source of a new mythology for his people. His intent is to reproduce Blicero's transcendental act with a second, shadow copy of Blicero's Rocket. But, as with Katje, other possibilities emerge as he begins to recognize the possibility that the Rocket will not reorder the cosmos for the Zone-Hereros. The master narrative that he is eager to sacrifice himself to produce begins to deconstruct itself before his amphetamine-rattled eyes. It occurs to him that it may be the Zone itself—the context rather than the content (the Rocket)—that he and the Zone-Hereros will need to learn to read: "We have to look for power sources here, and distribution networks we were never taught, routes of power our teachers never imagined, or were encouraged to avoid . . ." (521). The Zone in this new perspective is both a carnival of anarchy and a crucial stage in the development of the Raketen-stadt. Enzian sees that searching out its weaknesses, its lapses, its anarchic possibilities may be more fruitful, if less dramatic, than attempting to transcend the cycle of death, disease, and destruction the Zone maintains and promotes. Blicero's sadomasochism had provided shelter and safety, a pornographic release from the real pain, loss, and random destructiveness of the colonial past, the War, the Zone, and the coming Raketenstadt; nonetheless, both Enzian and Katje were able to depart from it, however haltingly. Like Katje's story, Enzian's remains unfinished, but here, too, the *possibility* of emerging from years of training in the art of victimization is raised by their meeting together, when Katje both actively resists and reaffirms her conditioned response to hate blackness and Enzian offers her the promise of "something to hold on to." In that brief moment of reprieve from the gloomy shadow of the Rocket, black man and white woman connect, opening a small space within which they might seize the anarchic possibilities of the Zone and begin to decolonize their own brutalized minds and bodies. They might make of these elusive gleanings an event—a new narrative—that matters.

Unlike either Enzian or Katje, Gottfried remains fully enclosed within the sadomasochistic cycle. Blicero's prelaunch offer of release is not so much refused as uncomprehended. Gottfried—unflinching, obedient Brownshirt to the end—cannot fathom even the possibility of agency, at least not until he approaches Brennschluss. Gottfried is the embodiment of the Strength, Stability, and Whiteness of Blicero's own youth; and by sacrificing him, Blicero intends to transcend the prison-house of white male identity that constitutes his past and binds him to the present. Blicero, figured as the witch in Hansel and Gretel, perversely exploits his own misreading of Rilke ("Once, only once . . .") to inscribe his own narrative on the brutalized, plasticized body of Gottfried, whose presence transforms the Rocket into the perfect organism. At once shroud and womb, the mysterious polymer, Imipolex-G, extinguishes at last the boundary between body and machine, collapsing at Brennschluss the cruel and tedious stretch of time that separates birth and death into a single painful moment of orgasmic intensity. If Gottfried brings the Rocket to life, Gottfried can also be said truly to come alive only within the Rocket as he becomes conscious for the first time of real pain—pain not inscribed within the comfortable sadomasochistic cycle he inhabits. Blicero's offer to release Gottfried just before the launch ensures that Gottfried will, in fact, experience that pain as he finally realizes not only the value of the life he is losing but also his own failure to choose not to lose it. But Blicero's offer is also, as he says, his own last chance to be proven wrong: "'I want to break out—to leave this cycle of infection and death'" (724). Long since incapable of scripting a single moment of his own, Gottfried is launched, his perfect blond body and Aryan mind giving the Rocket life, reduced now to the simple capacity to feel pain and receiving it in return at Brennschluss: "[W]hen did the roaring stop? Brennschluss, when was Brennschluss *it can't be this soon* . . ." (759). The complex, nonlinear, multiple narrativity of real life is reduced to the single erotic trajectory of white male desire.

So conditioned are these characters to remaining within the limits of the discourses surrounding them that, Pynchon suggests, the only conceivable escape must begin, in effect, outside discourse—outside the rules of the game, to be found in a look or a gesture or the exchange of a few potatoes and a handful of cigarettes between two estranged half-brothers as they pass without recognition in the night. Here, too, is the space within which the contingent, postmodern, fragmented self might be glued together: in action and in the desire to narrate the self and the world into being. ***Gravity's Rainbow*** suggests the capacity of narrative to represent, but also to produce, an acting self, or at least to magnify certain crucial moments of awareness that disrupt the predictable and make action imaginable. Narrative then may work in opposition to science and its desire to define, dissect, and classify, to reduce complexity and diversity to the confining space of a Rocket going nowhere. Yet if Nature's complexity and its wanton acts of randomness are the saving grace of narrative production—a jumpstart to imagining a different story—the dangers of narrative closure are also fully explored. Of the entire motley, mutable cast of characters in ***Gravity's Rainbow,*** only Blicero, whom we last see entranced in self-arousal at the launching of Gottfried/00000, completes his own story.

A word in closing about the form of ***Gravity's Rainbow***: Displaying the excesses of a literary bacchanalia, ***Gravity's Rainbow*** is nonetheless a tightly structured novel. The relentlessly linear progression of the Rocket arches across the sky from the beginning to an ending that returns the reader to the novel's famous opening line (one that surely strikes a deeper chord after September 11, 2001): "A screaming comes across the sky." Catapulted from the Peenemunde launch site of Rocket 00000 in 1945 to a movie theater in 1970s Los Angeles, readers suddenly join an impatient audience clapping for the interrupted film to resume, to fill the apparently blank screen whose images we have not yet learned to see. We "old fans who've always been at the movies (haven't we?)" insist on getting back to the same familiar movie that will make us believe we are safe and happy, while "it is just here, just at this dark and silent frame, that the pointed tip of the Rocket, falling nearly a mile a second, absolutely and forever without sound, reaches its last unmeasurable gap above the roof of this old theatre, the last delta-t" (760). There is no screaming this time because there will be no lucky survivors to hear it. The screaming that comes across the sky at the beginning of the novel, then, makes the novel itself the unreadable blank movie screen, the warning we have not yet learned to read of the Rocket's immanent and imminent presence. This is a rereversal of the reversal of cause and effect frequently noted by the narrator, in which the Rocket's explosion precedes the sound of its arrival. Signifier and signified collapse in the Sign of the Rocket, but the Rocket is more than a sign—it is also the concrete manifestation and symbol of the perverse power of science and technology. It hovers above every word, every letter, every comma of the text. The novel is a kind of triple narrative comprising the predictable, linear plot of the Rocket's rise and fall; the multiple, disconnected, unfinished, fragmented narratives that constitute the narrator's tale; and finally the discourse of the novel, the deep connections and interplay between the characters' stories and the production and launch of the Rocket. ***Gravity's Rainbow*** in its structure and complexity both reaffirms the dangers of a narrative that is single, closed, and predictable and celebrates the power of narrative to reimagine a new self and a kinder world.

Walter Benjamin's assertion that the unspeakable violence of the twentieth century (and now the twenty-first)—far from surprising us—was predictable is underscored by the bleak assessment in ***Gravity's Rainbow*** of science as a set of destructive discourses permeating Western culture and dominating the world since the Renaissance. For Pynchon, it is neither accidental nor puzzling that the history of science should coincide with the history of the West at its global worst. If other discourses—political, psychological, economic, religious, aesthetic—are interwoven with the scientific, both in history and in the novel's narrative trajectory, the development of the V-2 rocket, a sign of things to come in the postwar period, marked the nearly—but only nearly—complete hegemony of science in a world bent on self-destruction. Yet however persistently the Rocket may hover. Nature the trickster just as persistently follows Gödel: there is always a little noise in the system, something forgotten, misplaced, unaccounted for—perhaps the never-quite-extinct desire for life (even dull-witted Gottfried finally remembers that). "We are poor," Benjamin tells us, "in newsworthy stories," and the ubiquitous sources of news and entertainment at our disposal, Pynchon suggests with Benjamin, are the last place on earth to look for one. ***Gravity's Rainbow,*** however glaring its consistent failure to lend credible voice to those of us who are not white or male, opens at least the possibility of rediscovering voice and agency by reaching through the gaps of discourse to reclaim the story and the self.

Notes

1. For Foucault, the "subject" is contingent and enmeshed in a web of power relations that are shifting but constantly at play. Any action that the subject might undertake is necessarily a negotiation of power and is therefore largely a reaction to existing power relations, which are themselves determined by discursive practices. The theoretical possibility of agency, then, would seem to be cut off. See Foucault, especially 92-98. Pynchon's representation of the power of scientific discourses of all kinds—from physics to behaviorism—to regulate and organize thought, behavior, and pleasure is similar to Foucault's critique of scientia sexualis. Moreover, Foucault's description of the immanence of power in human interaction could also describe the workings of power as Pynchon lays them out in *Gravity's Rainbow.* Unlike Foucault, however, Pynchon relies also on a psychoanalytic model derived largely, it would seem, from Norman O. Brown's *Life Against Death,* in which, simply put, Pynchon identifies the desire for absolute control that he ascribes to science as a primary symptom of the death wish. See Wolfley.

2. Even as some early critics deemed *Gravity's Rainbow* "unreadable" or "hopeless," others found it value laden. For example, Mendelson calls it "a tragic, not a pessimistic, novel" (17); Smith and Tololyan say it allows for the possibility of freedom within the "chronometric Now"; Levine finds the promise of freedom in the dissolution of self that the novel projects.

3. Chaos theory first began to take root among mathematicians and scientists from various disciplines in the early 1970s, about the time *Gravity's Rainbow* was published. Pynchon probably was not much aware of the emergence of this interesting and disruptive field, but he seems to have intuited not only its most revolutionary tenets but also to have found them applicable to human behavior. In the context of human subjectivity and behavior, chaos theory is relevant to *Gravity's Rainbow* in part because it supplies a theoretical basis for the possibility of choice and agency. Even though, statistically, human behavior falls within the limits of normative, predictable behavior, no individual case is ever precisely predictable. Choices may be limited, but they remain choices—forks in the road (like the one taken by Tyrone Slothrop's ancestor William, but not the United States). Moreover, the specific choices one makes matter, insofar as they have the power to alter succeeding events in unpredictable ways. See Gleick.

4. The literature on narrative desire is extensive, and the specter of Freud pervades much of it. Here I am suggesting that the (unfulfillable) desire for narrative closure is precisely what makes action possible as an imagined sequence of events.

5. In *Bodies That Matter,* Judith Butler attempts to find theoretical grounding for the "subject" as it emerges through and is founded by the constraints and restrictions of a constructed sexuality. Rather than reject competing theories of the subject (derived most importantly from Foucault, Derrida, Lacan, and Zizek), she adds to and expands on each of them to found a continuously emergent subject that can never be fully articulated. Her goal is to delineate a model of political agency that can work to effect a democratic community, that is, one in which power negotiations are performed on more egalitarian terms than is currently the case. See especially "Phantasmatic Identification and the Assumption of Sex," 93-119. Pynchon, as I discuss later, takes sexual difference as a biological given—precisely the contended point of departure for Butler. But his insistence on an unfixed subject with the potential to act not despite, but because of, its unfixedness, has much in common

with both the political goals and the performative element of Butler's work, if not with its theoretical foundations.

6. The psychoanalytic overlay in *Gravity's Rainbow* is everywhere, of course, from Slothrop's predictive penis to Blicero and Gottfried's sadomasochism. Pynchon's narrator comes closest to despair when he suggests that the desire for death is no quirk of modernity but a feature of human life since the beginning of time: "[H]uman consciousness, that poor cripple, that deformed and doomed thing is about to be born" (720), incapable of apprehending a living world, drawn always by the siren song of death. *Gravity's Rainbow* repeatedly draws on a wide range of discourses (religious, legal, political, philosophical, historical, as well as scientific) that have all, in their time, worked to contain and control the natural world and the human mind. Nevertheless, I argue that Pynchon employs a crude psychoanalysis, imagined rather simplistically, and effective aesthetically largely through the powerful and complex metaphor of the Rocket. The real story here is about science; the psychoanalytic model functions above all as a convenient way of unmasking the drive for absolute control that science disavows.

7. I use the word "ideological" in at least one of its Marxist senses: to characterize a system of thought that obfuscates rather than exposes true relations of power. Pynchon does not use the term, preferring psychoanalytic or psychiatric ones, but I know of no better word to describe his representation of the headlong rush of science toward power and control and the particularly efficient means it has developed for absorbing and enfeebling its own contradictions.

8. Pynchon's binary term Elect/Preterite is conceived as a power differential, as in Foucault's schema. The Elect are those already and irrevocably saved (as in the Puritan hierarchy of souls) but here transposed as a measure of power. Not all white males are among the Elect, but all of the Elect are white and male. Crudely put, the Preterite is everything else—women, non-European men, children, animals, plants, all of the natural world. The Elect generate power through the discourses of science (as the Puritans once did through religious tracts). The end toward which the Elect work is the obliteration of the Preterite—and, of course, of themselves, because the Elect requires the Preterite in order to exist as the Elect.

9. Murray and Herrnstein's *The Bell Curve* has spawned much contentious, impassioned, and very public debate, as well as nearly a dozen academic books, mainly anthologies, questioning their premises, conclusions, and motivations. However convincing its critics. I would nonetheless argue that the extraordinary attention paid to *The Bell Curve* serves primarily to legitimize the neoracist premises on which its argument is built.

10. See Bérubé's discussion of the various inflections of "pornography" in *Gravity's Rainbow* (239-66). I agree with his argument that Pynchon's use of the term is so far-reaching as to include "scientifically neutral" (263) descriptions in general, because they necessarily obscure interrelationships (between, for example, cybernetics and rocket science, blueprints and death camps). He also admits that Pynchon's own pornographic replays are themselves problematic, even though the text provides its own "autocritique." Bérubé cites the problem without seriously addressing either it or, more broadly, the absence of credible female characters in the novel. See also Chapman's discussion of Pynchon's antimasculinist discourse.

11. See Hayles's *How We Became Posthuman* for a discussion of the phenomenon of disembodiment in relation to computers, cybernetics, and contemporary theory. Written two decades before computers became ubiquitous among the Elite, *Gravity's Rainbow* locates disembodiment in the transformation of the material world and its processes to the intersecting symbol systems of calculus, physics, biochemistry, architecture, the phonetic alphabet, and, pursued more rigorously in *Mason & Dixon,* the latitude-longitude grid that traps the earth in its unyielding net. Like Benjamin's lack of surprise at the horrors of the twentieth century, the desire for disembodiment is the continuing subtext of *Gravity's Rainbow.* We have arrived, Pynchon tells us, at a world in which "the real and only fucking is done on paper . . ." (616).

12. Rethinking "nature" from a feminist perspective, Haraway remarks, "We need not lapse into an appeal to a primal mother resisting becoming resource. The Coyote or Trickster [. . .] suggests our situation when we give up mastery but keep searching for fidelity, knowing all the while we will be hoodwinked" ("Situated Knowledges" 199). Pynchon is no feminist, and it is surely a beleaguered coyote who wanders the Zone. The image is, nonetheless, apt for the novel.

13. Here again, Pynchon's political subject echoes Butler's performative self, although his vision is bleaker. His characters are capable of acts that affirm a connection between (or, rarely, among) human beings that is outside the constraints of sadomasochism and escapes the workings of power. Such acts are motiveless, except as confirmations of that momentary connection and hence, the mere possibility of some other mode of being, "something to hold on to," in Enzian's terms. The only plausible political consequence would necessarily depend on a kind of butterfly effect, the dust mote in the Rocket at Brennschluss, gumming up the works.

14. See Hayles, "Self-Reflexive Metaphors" 209-37.

15. Obviously, science confirms itself most spectacularly in the concrete productions of technology: nuclear bombs, heart transplants, computers, light bulbs,

vacuum cleaners. As Donna Haraway suggests (see *Modest Witness* 1-16), the point is not to embark on the fool's errand of pointing out the lack of theoretical grounding for scientific "objectivity" (long since accomplished by a string of philosophers from Hume to Wittgenstein and Derrida) or of dwelling solely on the accomplished and looming disasters that technology has spawned (drug-resistant bacteria, dying species, toxic waste, and so on) or even on the unsurprising fact that the rich get to replace their worn-out hearts whereas poor infants die of simple dehydration. Pynchon's point, rather, is that the scientific enterprise legitimates and promotes a public agenda that purports to be benevolent and progressive, although its repressed agenda works to promote death by climinating the unpredictability that makes life not only interesting, but also possible.

16. In his critique of *History of Sexuality,* Abdul JanMohamed takes Foucault to task for underestimating the institutional power that has been brought to bear legally, politically, socially, and economically on people of color. Racialized sexuality, he argues, unlike white sexuality, is repressed and silenced, precisely because the violation of the racial boundary (originally the white patriarch's habitual rape of the female slave) has to remain an open secret so that an impermeable border between the races can be maintained, ensuring stability in the distribution of power in a racist society. Pynchon's complete silencing of black women and virtual silencing of black men (only Enzian is allowed to speak, and rarely) unfortunately perpetuates the silence JanMohamed identifies as being at the heart of racialized sexuality, even though the narrator explains with considerable insight the necessity of an imaginary Africa and its central role in European constructions of self and sexuality.

17. Bhabha argues that the colonial fantasy closely parallels the primal sexual fantasy; the psychic processes by which sexual desire is repressed occur as the colonizer marks black skin as the sign of difference. The colonized as fetishized object of fear and desire and the many forms of violence that ambivalence generates are invoked repeatedly in *Gravity's Rainbow.* Rocket 00000, hovering above every page of the novel, could be read as a polymorphous and perverse sign of that ambivalence. Bhabha's psychoanalytic reading of the colonial situation is present throughout his work, but of particular relevance here are two essays revised for *The Location of Culture.* In both, Bhabha relies heavily on Fanon's groundbreaking psychoanalytic theorization of colonizer-colonized relations in Frantz Fanon's *Black Skin, White Masks.*

Works Cited

Benjamin, Walter. *Illuminations.* New York: Schocken, 1968.

———. "The Storyteller." Benjamin 83-110.

———. "Theses on the Philosophy of History." Benjamin 253-64.

Bérubé, Michael. *Marginal Forces/Cultural Centers: Tolson, Pynchon, and the Politics of the Canon.* Ithaca and London: Cornell UP, 1992.

Bhabha, Homi. *The Location of Culture.* London: Routledge, 1994.

———. "Interrogating Identity: Frantz Fanon and the Postcolonial Prerogative." Bhabha 40-65.

———. "The Other Question: Stereotype, Discrimination, and the Discourse of Colonialism." Bhabha 66-84.

Bloom, Harold, ed. *Modern Critical Views: Pynchon.* New York and Philadelphia: Chelsea House, 1986.

Brown, Norman O. *Life Against Death: The Psychoanalytic Meaning of History.* Middletown, CT: Wesleyan UP, 1959.

Butler, Judith. *Bodies That Matter.* London: Routledge, 1993.

Chapman, Wes. "Male Pro-Feminism and the Masculinist Gigantism of *Gravity's Rainbow.*" *Postmodern Culture* 6 (1996). http://muse.jhu.edu/journals/postmodern_culture/.

Fanon, Frantz. *Black Skin, White Masks.* New York: Grove, 1967.

Foucault, Michel. *The History of Sexuality: Volume I.* 1976. New York: Vintage, 1990.

Gleick, James. *Chaos: Making a New Science.* New York: Penguin, 1987.

Haraway, Donna. *Modest_WitnessSecond_Millennium: FemaleMan©_Meets_Oncomouse™.* London: Routledge, 1997.

———. "Situated Knowledges: The Science Question in Feminism and the Privilege of Partial Perspective." *Simians, Cyborgs, and Women: The Reinvention of Nature.* New York and London: Routledge, 1991, 183-202.

Hayles, N. Katherine. *How We Became Posthuman: Virtual Bodies in Cybernetics, Literature, and Informatics.* Chicago: U of Chicago P, 1999.

———. "Self-Reflexive Metaphors in Maxwell's Demon and Shannon's Choice: Finding the Passages." *Literature and Science: Theory and Practice.* Ed. Stuart Peterfreund. Boston: Northeastern UP, 1990. 209-37.

JanMohamed, Abdul. "Sexuality on/of the Racial Border: Foucault, Wright, and the Articulation of Racialized Sexuality." *Discourses of Sexuality: From Aristotle to AIDS.* Ed. Domna Stanton. Ann Arbor: U of Michigan P, 1992. 94-116.

Levine, George. "Risking the Moment: Anarchy and Possibility in Pynchon's Fiction." *Mindful Pleasures: Essays on Thomas Pynchon.* Ed. George Levine and David Leverenz. Boston: Little, Brown, 1976. 113-36.

Mendelson, Edward. "Pynchon's Gravity." Bloom 1-19.

Murray, Charles, and Michael Herrnstein. *The Bell Curve: Intelligence and Class Structure in American Life.* New York: Free Press, 1994.

Pynchon, Thomas. *Gravity's Rainbow*: New York: Vintage, 1973.

Smith, Marcus, and Khachig Tololyan. "The New Jeremiad: *Gravity's Rainbow.*" Bloom 139-56.

Wolfley, Lawrence C. "Repression's Rainbow: The Presence of Norman O. Brown in Pynchon's Big Novel." *PMLA* 92 (1977): 873-89.

Paul A. Bové (essay date fall 2004)

SOURCE: Bové, Paul A. "History and Fiction: The Narrative Voices of Pynchon's *Gravity's Rainbow.*" *Modern Fiction Studies* 50, no. 3 (fall 2004): 657-80.

[*In the following essay, Bové analyzes* Gravity's Rainbow *as a historical novel and contends that any reading of the novel must "proceed from a secure sense of Pynchon's aesthetic relation to history."*]

In 1982, Tony Tanner, probably the most sensitive and best-informed English critic of American fiction, published a small book on Thomas Pynchon in the Methuen Series on Contemporary Writers. Tanner had the unenviable task of introducing, evaluating, and clarifying Pynchon's fiction in fewer than one hundred pages. He succeeded so remarkably that a great deal of Pynchon criticism has, in the last fifteen years, merely elaborated on Tanner's readings.

When a critic of Tanner's sensitivity and knowledge judges a novel's worth, other readers should pay attention. In his chapter on ***Gravity's Rainbow,*** Tanner writes, "Pynchon has created a book that is both one of the great historical novels of our time and arguably the most important literary text since *Ulysses*" (75). As far as I can tell, no critic involved in the careful study and teaching of English language fiction has contested this judgment. Even Salman Rushdie, himself one of the most important and certainly most prolific of contemporary English-language storytellers—we should remember that the Booker Prize committee has judged *Midnight's Children* the best Booker Prize novel in twenty years[1]—publicly acknowledges his admiration for Pynchon's accomplishments as an historical and political writer (1).[2] As far as I can tell no one has dared to contradict either part of Tanner's judgment that ***Gravity's Rainbow*** is the most important literary work in English since *Ulysses* and also a great historical novel—that is, no one has dared until Pynchon's next major novel appeared.

In his review of ***Mason & Dixon,*** T. Coraghessan Boyle declared, "This is the old Pynchon, the true Pynchon, the best Pynchon of all. ***Mason & Dixon*** is a groundbreaking book, a book of heart and fire and genius, and there is nothing quite like it in our literature, except maybe ***V.*** and ***Gravity's Rainbow.***" Boyle then adds, "the book . . . evokes its time and place better than any historical novel I can recall." Boyle has, as we might say in America, upped the ante on Tanner; he has placed a very large bet: ***Mason & Dixon*** is a unique literary work and the best historical novel Boyle knows. Put aside theories of the European novel and comparisons with Walter Scott, Balzac, Dickens, and Tolstoy to understand what this means to the history of American writing. Suddenly, *Moby-Dick* has lost its place as the preeminent American literary-historical achievement. Critics have always placed Pynchon in the tradition of Melville, for they are encyclopedic writers, proliferating tales, characters, plots, subplots, displaying massive erudition, a familiarity with technology, industry, and arcane but important forms of knowledge.[3] Not since the rediscovery of Melville in the early decades of this century and especially not since F. O. Matthiessen's scholarly masterpiece, *The American Renaissance,* taught us to understand Melville's place in the construction of an American national literary tradition—not since those days has any critic dared propose the supersession of Melville's whale in art or in history.[4]

Critics of different generations facing different pressures of history and formed by different criteria of judgment not surprisingly often disagree. Most important, though, is the fact that from 1973, careful academic critics and respected writer-critics have recreated the tradition of US fiction and placed Pynchon in the first rank of American and world writers in English. Consequently, it is impossible to teach or study modern writing in English without taking Pynchon into account, indeed, without giving him a prominent place in our understanding of English language literature since Wordsworth and Byron.[5] Moreover, some critics claim an even grander genealogy for Pynchon. Edward Mendelson, for example, says of ***Gravity's Rainbow*** that it should be placed with six other books familiar to us from history: "Dante's *Commedia,* Rabelais' five books of Gargantua and Pantagruel, Cervantes' *Don Quixote,* Goethe's *Faust,* Melville's *Moby-Dick,* and . . . Joyce's *Ulysses*" (10).[6]

Critics rightly claim that Pynchon draws various elements of his novels from many different traditions: Menippean satire, the encyclopedic epic, the utopia, the dystopia, and so on. The most important critical perception is that ***Gravity's Rainbow*** is an historical novel and Pynchon an historical novelist. Richard Poirier puts the case most strongly when he notes that Pynchon's serious readers "eventually . . . get to wonder at almost every point if perhaps we are being given not fiction at all, but history" (53). Over and against this line of argument stands a minority, those who mistakenly think Pynchon is an antihistorical postmodern writer like Barth, Bartheleme, Kostelanetz, and so on—all writers either lost in the fun house or caught in the so-called prison-house of language.[7]

Any reading or teaching of Pynchon must begin with the recognition that his novels stand in complex relations to history. Unfortunately, though, scholarship does not make clear enough either the nature of those relations or the importance of history to Pynchon's poetics.[8] It is essential that any reading or teaching of ***Gravity's Rainbow*** proceed from a secure sense of Pynchon's aesthetic relation to history.

Throughout ***Gravity's Rainbow*** Pynchon develops the theme of history contrapuntally. The narrative sounds the main ideas on the opening page; as Pirate Prentice dreams the evacuation of London, he imagines a train's movement out of the city center as "not a disentanglement from, but a progressive *knotting into*" (3).[9] The counterpoint is simple: linear direction is set against folded return. A dilemma emerges: entanglement is the given state of things and human actions, even attempts to escape from, to clarify, or to untie these entanglements not only further the difficulty, but prove, in Pynchon's view, that reality is such that it can never be disentangled. Furthermore, it proves that ethically humankind should not even attempt it for only catastrophes result from the effort.[10]

Pynchon develops this dilemma as a conflict between two groups of people and two sets of ideas. His basic metaphors derive from the history of American Puritanism and revolve around the opposition between "the elect" and "the preterite." Pynchon's sympathies are always with the preterit, those who are not graced by God with the promise of salvation. Tyrone Slothrop, who is for a while "the main character," himself of New England Puritan descent, has an ancestor, William Slothrop, who wrote an heretical text defending the holiness, the value, the essential role of the preterit, of the passed-over to history. For his pains, the Puritan fathers banish William Slothrop.

As the novel develops, Pynchon increasingly identifies the elect as those who, careless of consequence but assuming their own state of grace, desire to disentangle themselves from fallen history and nature. They leave the preterit entangled not only in the immanent processes of nature—death, natural reproduction, disease, and so on—but in the webs of power and conflict produced by the elect in their struggles to transcend the fallen historical, natural world. For Pynchon, conflict results from a seeming choice between the human embrace of entanglement and the sociopathic attempt to transcend it, mostly in the forms of murder and suicide.

In ***Gravity's Rainbow,*** the symbol of elect ambition is the V-2 Rocket developed by Hitler in his war on England. But it is more than a symbol; it is the mechanic system in the service of which the elect reorganize society against the human, against nature, and against the entanglements of history.[11] Indeed, it is also the fulfillment of such a plan since it seems to promise the transcendence of Earth's gravity. Pynchon makes much of a grizzly character, Laslo Jamf, who floats through the novel and its many different time periods—from Slothrop's childhood when, as a Pavlovian, Jamf chemically conditioned the infant Tyrone's sexual reflexes, to his development of a substitute for living flesh, the plastic called Imipolex-G. Pynchon uses Jamf to figure the elect's ambition to develop productive forces in such a way that the elect can transcend the weight of earth and fallen human agency as the Rocket marks their ambition to escape the pull of gravity. The elect, the chosen of God, seize for themselves godlike powers to produce a substitute creation. Imipolex-G, emblematically made of silicon and nitrogen rather than carbon and oxygen, is a responsive and erectile material; it responds to touch and stimulates response when touched. It is like flesh and greater than flesh in its immunity to disease, death, and time. Along with the Rocket, it embodies the ambition of technologizing society to the end of overcoming natural and historical limitations upon the elect's freedom to act, upon their hyperbolic sense of their own status as the guiding agency of the universe.

We might say, then, that ***Gravity's Rainbow*** is an historical novel that stages the conflict between elect and preterit, between nature and technology, between historical human agency and grace by embedding its themes within the specificity in Central Europe at the end of World War II. Europe after the war is merely a special scene for Pynchon's vision of an almost Manichean conflict between good and evil that plays itself out within, or, indeed, constitutes history itself.

Critics, especially those following Lukács, believe historical novels are different than this. Lukács derives from Goethe the idea that historical novels always require a return to a past moment, a society that clearly is presented as an earlier stage of one's own. We might say, with Lukács, that Goethe allows us to see that all historical novels are anachronistic, able to reveal the past as the present's predecessor only by assuming a vantage point that lets us see what others who came before us must have missed.[12] In other words, historical novelists must see humanity as saturated with history, as taking form and shape in history which is progressive and developing. Historical novelists, in this sense, can only write retrospectively from a point farther along a linear continuum of time, progress, and identity; this means, for example, that Scott is an historical novelist of the eighteenth century in a fuller way than Fielding, who offers himself as the chronicler of his present. Of course, for Lukács and his followers, what is interesting about Scott as an historical novelist are the ideologemes that his historical reconstructions reflect. So the better historical novelist of the eighteenth century is a revelatory historical novelist of the nineteenth.

If Pynchon is an historical novelist then, on Pynchon's own terms, he does not fit this Lukácsian model. Indeed, after Pynchon, critics should be cautious in attempting to apply it or develop it since ***Gravity's Rainbow*** generates a serious critique of Lukács's basic worldview. In the novel, only the elect assume that history is linear, consistent, and progressive—or, if you prefer, dialectical, contradictory, and utopian. Indeed, the elect not only act on their assumption but use power to assure it. Pynchon's opening theme treats this ambition ironically and condemns its ethics: the progressive is not, as the technologists believe, an ahuman and utopian movement out of but a deepening into the entanglements that, with every effort at escape, simply become more human and historical in ways that are more harmful to the preterit and inescapable. In other words, the elect's utopian becomes the preterit's nightmare in a way that seems akin to such works as Philip K. Dick's 1968 novel, *Do Androids Dream of Electric Sheep?,* or Terry Gilliam's 1985 Reagan-era dystopian film, *Brazil.* As ***Gravity's Rainbow*** develops, Pynchon reveals that the elect's logic is a logic of death: not only must the preterit be left to die, or be used up in the elect's plans, but the elect finds that the only end of its ambition is suicide—the suicide of Nazi Germany, the suicide of those who adopt similar ambitions, and the figural suicide of all those who destroy their own humanity as the object of contemptuous self-abuse. In other words, the elect's logic is nihilism, and the preterit's powerless response has not yet risen, as in Vietnam, to the level of guerrilla resistance. Much of the novel's drama stems from the preterit's various efforts to recover agency, political power, and efficacy from those graced to destroy the merely human. Pynchon's suicide theme repeats throughout the novel as a variation and response on these questions of nihilism, resistance, agency, and survival.

An important variation brings history and science together in the novel with personal experience and memory. If the elect desire time to be integral as the calculus imagines, it is because history then best fits their instruments of control. Not surprisingly their favorite intellectual discipline is thermodynamics and its foci, the second law and Maxwell's Demon. At first this seems odd. The second law promises us only a dying universe, an increase of entropy, an irreversibility of time and action. Unlike chemistry, which has never lost sight of the reversibility of reactions even in a stable state, thermodynamics promises irreversible heat death. In fact, the elect, accepting the second law as inescapable, conclude that nature itself must be transcended and that their election by God entitles them to dispose all of nature's resources and human agency to the effort to escape entropy and gravity. Over and against this thermodynamic and gnostic compulsion, Pynchon places the human historical domain of life, earth, and generation—where the preterit indwells.

Pynchon's most intellectually and dramatically intense variation on this major theme is the novella involving the so-called Schwarzkommando or the Zone Hereros. Reading it clarifies a great deal about ***Gravity's Rainbow***'s status as an historical novel—and the essentially historical nature of Pynchon's poetics—and puts the book's narrative complexity in a context that graces the preterit domain and redeems it from the elect's nihilism.

In England during the war an exiled German film director makes a propaganda movie pretending that the Nazis have imported Africans into the fatherland for political control at home and into new German African colonies built upon the presumed ruins of the British and French empires. As it turns out, we might say, life imitates art. In the Zone, in the momentarily unregulated and ungoverned spaces of central Europe after the surrender, lives a developing nation, the Zone Hereros. These are people brought from the Südwest over a period of time beginning in 1904. During the war, they dedicate themselves to the Rocket, as if it were their new divinity, their salvation in exile, the center to their new nation's formation.

When the Hereros first appear, Pynchon treats them at chapter length—telling a story that develops his largest themes of preterition, regeneration, suicide, and memory—in such a way that readers must see history as the trope for human redemption of the earth as the place for the preterit's self-making in time.

Pynchon does not directly represent the Holocaust; nonetheless, extermination dominates the novel, which, after all, ends with the threatening image of immediate apocalypse. Three exterminations confront the reader: first and throughout the novel, the Euro-American slaughter of the misnamed American Indians; second, the Dutch extermination of the dodos on Mauritius in the seventeenth century; third, the genocidal war fought by the Germans in response to the Herero uprising of 1904—a subject treated at length in Pynchon's earlier novel, *V.* (And we should add as well the novel's constant attention to a related form of mass murder, the slave trade.)

The two-generation-long struggle between German and Herero, from Südwest to Berlin, becomes an internecine conflict between those Schwarzkommando committed to forming a new nation around the Rocket and those "Empty Ones" who continue the logic of genocidal resistance by practicing abortion and tribal suicide. One of the most important and persistent characters in the novel, Enzian, the leader of those with national ambitions, is called "Otyikondo, the Half-breed," because his father was European, a Russian sailor visiting Africa on his way around the horn to suffer defeat in the war with Japan. Enzian's half-brother, Tchitcherine, a Soviet intelligence operative also pursuing the remnants of the Rocket for his masters in Moscow, hopes to kill Enzian to wipe out the very threat blackness poses to his white ideals. Furthermore, while in Südwest, Enzian becomes the lover of a German officer named Weissmann who, back in Germany, also has the names Blicero and Bleicheröde: "And Enzian found the name Bleicheröde close enough to 'Blicker,' the nickname the early Germans gave to Death. They saw him white: bleaching and blankness. The name was later Latinized to 'Dominus Blicero.' Weissmann, enchanted, took it as his SS code name" (322).

With these lines, the novel appropriates a familiar image linking death to whiteness and the north; its counterpart is blackness, linked to life and the south. Yet the novel varies this thematic opposition in interesting ways. Blackness is no certain marker of life because of the effects of the elect's actions in history. In this case, that action goes under the names of imperialism and extermination.

The Zone Hereros, known as the "Empty Ones," call themselves the Otukungurua because this word refers to their status as "inanimate" (316). Having been brought to Germany after the 1904 uprising in Südwest, they see themselves as the elect see them; they understand themselves as inhuman, as without the capacity to act—except in one way. The narrator describes them in this fashion: "Revolutionaries of the Zero, they mean to carry on what began among the old Hereros after the 1904 rebellion failed. They want a negative birth rate. The program is racial suicide. They would finish the extermination the Germans began in 1904" (317). Blackness defeats attempts to preserve itself from further defeat by internalizing the enemy's goal, by making their own the enemy's desire: extermination and suicide become identical; the will to suicide is the reductive residue of human life usurped by the exterminating angel, by Weissmann.

Pynchon's treatment of this matter is very complex. The alternative to the suicidal Hereros—the Empty Ones, as they are called, for their women's wombs are always empty or emptied—the alternative seems, at first, to be Enzian's group of Hereros, those who attempt to form an identity for themselves, who hope to become, once more, a people with a history that has no obvious end: "Over the couple of generations, moved by accelerations unknown in the days before the Empire, they have been growing an identity that few can see as ever taking final shape" (316). The novel quickly moves to show that this is a false alternative to the fate of the Empty Ones, to show that it is in fact very much in keeping with the Rocket and its masters' plans for the preterit. Pynchon works this out meticulously.

The Empty Ones resent history as the domain of Weissmann's power, and they see suicide, the ironic embrace of imperial history's role for the black African, as not only their one remaining sphere of freedom, but also as a terrible salvation, as an acceptance of the fact that the "end of history," the Rocket's desire, is the only end that history itself can have. Pynchon insists that the end of history is the primary desire of the Euro-American ambition to see history as calculable, as amenable to the elect's constant and, if necessary, increasing application of power; it is the desire to transcend not only history through power but nature and, so, humanity as well. For the elect, the telos of history is its own transcendence and the transfiguration of the elect—a transfiguration achieved by turning humans and human institutions into transcendent, nonorganic, plastic death-dealing creatures.

Confronted with the overwhelming power of the elect—and we must remember that in this novel the elect, even though unelected, control the State's resources, as well as those of transnational corporations and technology—the preterit resists only with difficulty, if at all. Indeed, the preterit's fundamental weakness is an inability to see the threat confronting them. Like the Empty Ones, most humans willfully or accidentally assent to the elect's program: in the novel this is called worshipping the Rocket. The Empty Ones embrace suicide as an irreversible action, a choice that still belongs to them, guaranteeing their being as agents who can choose their own fate—or, perhaps better, choose to make their own a fate created for them by others. The novel, in essence, asks, "What is the ethical life of such assenters, of the preterit who embrace the fate the elect plans for them? How do they live, as it were, while on their way to death?"

When Enzian and Josef Ombindi, the leader of the Empty Ones, debate their competing tactics, Ombindi defends his chosen course as the most erotic of all actions: the most erotic act must be nonrepeatable. What might this be and why? Thinking his way to answers to these questions, Pynchon entwines ethics and history. The nonrepeatable act, Enzian knows, "embraces all the Deviations," but, Enzian, who is gay, does not choose to "call" Ombindi "on this use of 'Deviations.'" The verbal sparring between a tired and wise Enzian and a flippant, arrogant, and mordant Ombindi goes on. The only nonrepeatable act, they agree, must embrace all other eroticism: "Homosexuality, for example," offers

Enzian. "Sadism *and* masochism. Onanism? Necrophilia." The list continues: bestiality, pedophilia, lesbianism, "coprophilia and urolagnia," fetishism—"A wide choice of death-fetishes, naturally," concludes Ombindi, to which Enzian's only reply is the ironic repetition, "Naturally" (319).[13]

Gravity's Rainbow has a power to move its audiences emotionally and intellectually because Pynchon forces readers to think about, to imagine, and to understand American structures of power that a death-worshipping, death-dealing, and yet death-fearing culture establishes as its ethos. It would be wrong to think that Pynchon's world places these "Deviations" on the margins or merely in the interregna of liberal democratic systems, for these structures are neither nationalist nor liberal; in fact, although ubiquitous, they are paradoxically the reactionary norm. Death (and its willful variant, suicide) is the normal ethos, and its existence can be found everywhere, from Brigadier Pudding's coprophilia—of which he eventually dies despite large doses of penicillin—to the fact that, as Katje discovers, the elect has a mathematical formula for determining the relative market value of human life and information.

The Zone Hereros' peculiar position dramatizes the ethical and historical conundrum of a culture that believes mastery of death is its right, but within the conflicts between Enzian and Ombindi, the novel finds no solution, no convenient either/or that provides clear alternatives. Always the novel's themes and narratives insist upon a progressive knotting into rather than a disentanglement from as the inescapable consequence of a history that creates an elect self-destructively self-determined to master its creator. This elect is the opposite of an aesthetic or liberal elite; its style lacks the lightest touch of irony, wit, and complexity. It knows only bludgeoning to achieve itself in face of any resistant reality, the existence of which it almost always denies, even as it applies more power to overcome it.

So, conventionally we might expect that in opposition to Ombindi's suicidal embrace of all forms of sexuality that prevent reproduction, we would find in Enzian an embrace of generation, of institution building that would assure life through marriage, intercourse, and proper burial. The novel plays with ethical questions of a profoundly historical and even historicist kind: if the basic problem of forming human society requires the poetic construction of institutions to regulate sexuality and decay, to manage birth and death, to let new bodies emerge while discarding dead ones—and here, of course, I am only mildly alluding to a great humanistic tradition at least as old as Vico—then Ombindi, whose task is to improve the means of contraception and abortion, to persuade others that tribal suicide is the only way to escape the arrogant life-denying imprisonment of empire—then Ombindi must appear as just one of many individuals and groups in the novel whose embrace of suicide both helps explain part of the Nazis' appeal and places that appeal within a longer story of death-dealing, loving, and fearing. To put it simply, Ombindi is not a humanist and, as such, he embraces the logic of the end of history as the only logic history allows those who have neither power nor place; indeed, in embracing the end of history, he deviantly shadows and fulfills the logic of the elect: to end history in its overcoming, to commit suicide as historical beings, to transcend nature and history in a plasticity that aims to supplant the flawed organic world of earth and homo sapiens. To put it even more simply, in the character of Ombindi the novel presents a lucid reduction of the elect's logic and so of the civilization over which it rules. There are possibilities of resistance, forms and modes of resistance exist—these existences are real and everywhere in the novel's interregna, in characters like Pig Bodine; in practices such as the Pig Festival; and in certain intellectuals' reflections on the historical circumstances that seem to imprison them. Chief among these intellectuals, of course, are Roger Mexico, the statistician who can think the excluded middle; Pointsman, the Pavlovian who must push aside all his doubts about causality and reinforcement; Slothrop, of course; Katje, whose historical understanding comes from thinking about her own sexuality to her masters; and Enzian.

Enzian is a political leader whose complex history—especially as a gay man, a lover of Blicero/Weissmann, and "half-breed"—shapes his reflections upon his people's current position and fragile future. (Recall that as the novel goes on there are several references to "using the British army" to take care of the Schwarzkommando; in one of these mentions we hear that the US won't object to such military action because the Americans are trying to figure out how to deal with their own black forces.) Enzian's reflections are the novel's principle means to expose as false and unsatisfying any traditional humanistic alternative to the Empty Ones' program of *posthistoire.*[14]

This chapter presents, in the program of action Enzian urges upon his followers, precisely the traditional alternative that his own reflections upon historical circumstance lead us to abandon. Of course, other parts of the novel support Enzian's reasons for doubting his own plan, but his intellectual function is to state explicitly much of what elsewhere must be inferred about the dangers of certain ethical and political traditions.

This chapter opens with an epigraph from a fictional work edited by a Gnostic philosopher who is elsewhere a character in the novel. Steve Edelman is a kind of philologist who collects *The Tales of the Schwarzkommando.* The epigraphic citation from this mock text recounts a founding moment in the cultural history of an emerging people, a moment when a Moses-like wise man, Enzian, advises his priests, the white engineers of the Rocket, to treat the Rocket's own word, the experimental data it returns, as revelation, as logos.

With the fictional citation that opens this chapter, the narrator reenacts two typical moments in human history and knowledge, namely, both the founding moment of a culture and the Western anthro-philological project of historical humanism: the preservation, collection, editing, and circulation of foundational texts as an essential contribution to the life of nations and states. Having set the opening of the chapter, then, in a doubled time, a time of founding and a time of continuing (if you will, a time of action and a time of science), the narrative moves into history itself: the Hereros in the Zone and their struggles in 1945. Forcefully, it then moves back in time, to a recent past, into the events of memory, and the nature of empire in 1904.

Pynchon's narrative takes one word as the device for these complex time shifts: Erdschweinhöle. Under threat and living in not yet completely occupied Zones, the Schwarzkommando live an underground existence in all senses of the term; like the Rocket, they live in tunnels and caves. Like the other marginal social groups during the interregna of the postwar, they try to live out of sight and away from officialdom; they are a "black market," indeed. "Around here," says the narrator, "they are known collectively as the Erdschweinhöle. This is a Herero joke, a bitter one" (315). What has the narrator done with this joke that enables his temporal movements? The narrator has introduced an affective state that can only be understood from within the cultural memory of the Herero. Having begun the chapter with an epigraphic allusion to a mythical future that will not come to be—but one presented as if it were already in need of preservation—the narrator moves rapidly into the "real" history of the Hereros and the Germans, into the history and nature of European expansion and extermination.

The Erdschwein (aardvark) was the totem of the lowest of the Herero, the Ovatjimba, who, without village or farm, lived as outcasts on the veld: "They took their name from him, never ate his flesh, dug their food from the earth, just as he does" (315). Suddenly, the narrative swerves again, and once more around a single word; having opened with philological humanism, with the gnosis of chosen (not gentile) nation founding, having moved ethnographically to history, the narrative forcefully pulls away from the impersonality of such conventions and inserts the (Euro-American?) reader and the reader's history and memory openly into the text:

> You were likely to come across them at night, their fires flaring bravely against the wind, out of rifle range from the iron tracks: there seemed no other force than that to give them locus out in that emptiness. You knew what they feared—not what they wanted, or what moved them. And you had business upcountry, at the mines; so, presently, as the sputtering lights slipped behind, so did all the further need to think of them. . . .
>
> (315)

This introduction of the second-person pronoun shifts the narrative and the relations between audience and narrator. The reading "you" becomes one or all of those who travel the iron roads passing by the forgotten victims of the technological, capital forces that build the roads and mine the lands. Moreover, this "you" places the reader into two histories: the real history of German colonization of Südwest and the equally real but literary history of Conrad's *Heart of Darkness,* which text must be, in these lines, the object of an allusion. As Conrad's pilgrims travel into the heart of darkness, they shoot at the "natives" in the forest, in a game that reveals the death-dealing of Kurtz's whited sepulchers. In turn they echo one of the most famous scenes in modern English writing: "Once, I remember," Marlow recounts of his approach to West Africa,

> we came upon a [French] man-of-war anchored off the coast. There wasn't even a shed there, and she was shelling the bush. . . . In the empty immensity of earth, sky, and water, there she was, incomprehensible, firing into a continent. Pop, would go one of the six-inch guns . . .—and nothing happened. Nothing could happen. There was a touch of insanity in the proceeding, a sense of lugubrious drollery in the sight; and it was not dissipated by somebody on board assuring me earnestly there was a camp of natives—he called them enemies!—hidden out of sight somewhere.
>
> (14)

Not only does the imperialist shell from afar, but the narrator observes from a distance that permits him a touch of superiority in mocking the futility and clownishness of French military technology. Closer up, however, the elect's violence has more effect. Marlow comes to learn that one danger of distance is misperception, as Conrad's own style of immanent impressionism makes certain he must. For a moment, though, Marlow is like the "you" of Pynchon's narrator—or like all of us who as readers can remember this kind of moment. As literate heirs of writing in, for, and against imperial traditions—especially in English and French—how can any of us not remember?

When the narrator turns the tale to the second person, collapsing the distance implicit in the conventions of the third person and the practices of ethnography or philology, he also sounds again a variation on the opening theme: The white "you" rides a train, takes it toward an end, and moving linearly toward the goal—mining the earth—leaves behind, forgets, the tangled complexities of history and, in this case, imperial actions and reactions. Since the novel's narrative is contrapuntal, though, the seeming movement out of can only be a return, an inevitable knotting into.

Let us follow the movement closely for another moment. We remember that, riding the iron rails, "you" have turned away from the lights of the Erdschweinhöle:

> But as you swung away, who was the woman alone in the earth, planted up to her shoulders in the aardvark whole, a gazing head rooted to the desert plane, with an upsweep of mountains far behind her, darkly folded, far away in the evening? She can feel the incredible pressure, miles of horizontal sand and clay, against her belly. Down the trail wait the luminous ghosts of her four stillborn children, fat worms lying with no chances of comfort among the wild onions, one by one, crying for milk more sacred that what is tasted and blessed in the village calabashes. In preterite line they have pointed her here, to be in touch with Earth's gift for genesis. The woman feels power flood in through every gate: a river between her thighs, light leaping at the ends of fingers and toes. It is sure and nourishing as sleep. It is a warmth. The more the daylight fades, the further she submits—to the dark, to the descent of water from the air. She is a seed in the Earth. The holy aardvark has dug her bed.
>
> (315-16)

There are a great many interesting and relevant aspects to this passage not the least of which is, of course, that it represents the original relation of the Hereros to the earth, to nature and its fecundity, a relationship largely abrogated by imperial intrusion (we remember "you" are a miner) and, in the West itself, by the artifice of its elect culture—plastics that remake the molecules of fossils. As such, this passage—as an act of critical implicating memory—seems to offer the alternative path to that taken by the Empty Ones; but, despite the fact that the novel paints this scene with touches of nostalgia that usefully reminds us or "you" of the costs of modernization, it is not an alternative. At best, it is an impossible nostalgia, that is, etymologically a present pain caused by the desire for an impossible return home. As memory, it seemingly provides an ideal to guide the Herero to a new future as fulfilling as the old, but, as we soon learn from Enzian's thinking, because, taking the form of what the Kierkegaardian tradition might call a "repetition backward," it is a false guide. The narrator himself tells us that although the aardvark whole is a powerful symbol, "here in the Zone, its real status is not so clear" (316).

What should we find in it? Two words stand out sustaining the basic themes within the narrative time shifts: "fold" and "submit." They stand in strong contrast to the emblems of the elect: "line" and "dominate"—as in Dominus Blicero. The woman embedded in earth submits not merely to gain anew the power of fertilization, but she gains it in submission to an earth "folded" around her. The entire image is complex: the Herero submit to the gravity of earth as the source of life—the babies' dead bodies are near the buried woman; this kind of submission allows them to accept death and place it in a context that recognizes it as an unconditional part of humanity and life itself. The earth's power is the entangled fold of mountains, of shapes and forces, shifting and surrounding in which the human—life and death—is embedded as part. All the elements of this complex image stand importantly in opposition to the ethical horrors of the Empty Ones, to the nightmares of genocide, and, more profoundly, the civilizational impulse to overthrow the natural historical order for a world of silicon and nitrogen, as Jamf says, of a world of ionic rather than covalent bonds, a world of permanent capture rather than a system of sharing.

Why then is it not an acceptable alternative to the logic that results in the Empty Ones? In what way is its status not clear? Nostalgia always involves an act of return, and Enzian realizes that the literal return is impossible. He also knows that a return in the form of renewal of conditions—those that existed prior to the European intrusion and the insertion of Africans into the patterns of Eurocentric world history—is impossible unless some effective substitute, some new fetish can be found. Ironically and tragically the only available fetish object is the Rocket, but Enzian knows that if a new fetish is to be effective, it must not fail to protect. In this case, protection involves a form of return, a return not to a *status quo ante,* but to something better: a recovery of a nonhistoric state that can never again be overthrown, that can never again fail to protect the people from a violent tragic fall into time and history. With a memory of the Erdschwein as guide and lesson, Enzian leads his people in search of a fetish that will take them back to a future permanently out of time. Their fetish then must be the same as the elect's, namely, the Rocket itself: "What Enzian wants to create will have no history. It will never need a design change. Time, as time is known to the other nations, will wither away inside this new one." As the narrator goes on to say, "He has thus found himself in a strange rapprochement with the Empty Ones" (319).

Enzian mistakenly sees his choice as other than the Western time-bound aspirations of the Rocket; this is because he misunderstands the Rocket and the desires of the elect who also wish to have an experience of time different from those of the other or gentile nations. The Rocketmen worship the Rocket for its promised victory over disease and death, as Blicero tells his boy lover Gottfried, shooting him to his death, shrouded in Imipolex-G, in the mystical S-Gerat. Another subtheme—the history of the calculus and the elect's hope to achieve, not merely approach, the limit when delta-t vanishes—is a resonance of the elect's determination to develop knowledges that will put an end to time. Calculus presents an instant of time, the cusp of the Rocket's parabolic flight path, as the moment when the Rocket is free of gravity, transcending humanity and the Earth. (Of course, at the end of this rainbow lies death in the fall.) Enzian's plan, inspired by his memories and shaped by the impossibility of ending his pain by going home, needs to find another power and another form of return. "Once," the narrator says of Enzian, "he could not imagine a life without return" (322). His youthful consciousness was formed by tribal rituals of return.

After the events of 1904 to 1945, such ritual return has been made impossible. Innocence has been lost as a fall into time—one of the many instances wherein we see Pynchon's use of Eliot. Within history there is only time. Returns against time, out of time back to some moment before the fall into history, as we might say—such a return is also impossible. Confronted by these dead ends, Enzian makes a revealing intellectual and political error. He opts to affiliate his people to the Rocket in the hope that they can derive their own benefit from it rather than being mastered by it. Pynchon dramatizes the intellectual's difficulty in a time of interregnum but also shows how alluring is the logic of the elect—alluring because it resonates with the desires of the preterit seduced by the elect's projection of a fetish-object that apparently meets what seem to be universal desires: It is the desire to disinter oneself from folded pressures of history, to achieve a return that makes life something that must be mastered, disentangled, superseded, and unfolded. Enzian sees the danger, but he believes that it matters who seizes and uses the Rocket; he has a wrong sense of history, consequence, power, and agency. He does not realize that taking the Rocket as his fetish means, despite intent, accepting the ethics of the elect who have shaped history so narrowly that, in their attempts to become divine, they have made it, like energy, a one-way street. As the narrator tells us, "Captivity, sudden death, one-way departures were the ordinary things of every day" (323).[15] Once reversibility, the possibility of return has been destroyed, all that remains is the tragic repetition of a desire for return, a desire so strong that it mistakenly finds in technologized "solutions" a powerful and self-created substitute for the lost but given center.

To put the matter summarily, we would say that while the elect plan to end history and to transcend nature and humanity as the telos of time itself, Enzian embraces the plan in hopes that the Rocket can be made into a new religion that will send his people back to a moment outside of time and history from which they can never fall. He desires perfect cabalistic or Lurianic security.[16] The novel represents the continuity of these positions (Enzian's and the elect's) in two ways, first, as either end of the rainbow or parabola that is the flight path of the Rocket; second, as the ouroboros, the image of the snake closed round upon itself, the snake forming a circle biting its own tale. In the novel, the ouroboros is the fetish object of the plastic men: it is the mythic interpretation put by Jamf upon the ring structure of benzene.

Pynchon should be seen to reject the classic modernist aesthetic alternatives we find in Eliot, Yeats, and Joyce, and elaborated in the writings of Mircea Eliade, to the linearity of history dominant in modernized thought and cultural common sense. Seen more historically, Pynchon rejects international high modernism's formal solution to the problems of time, namely all attempts at circular or closed form. Put somewhat differently, Pynchon opens up the circular form of mythic consciousness in which so much primitivist modernism invests by dramatizing, after fascism and the rise of Americanism, that the ouroboros itself opens up to become the parabola of death and apocalypse.

English language modernism, voiced in Eliot's famous essay on "Tradition and the Individual Talent," identifies science and modernity with a fall into time that needs to be reversed by some aesthetic that would resacralize time. This story, of course, is well known. Pynchon determinedly explores the civilizational consequences of an established modernity and discounts modernism's aesthetic responses by collapsing the supposed distinctions between science and myth, art and technology, into unities of mastery, of coercive desire for election, for an end to history, a desecularization of the human. It is no accident that with Bergson and T. E. Hulme modernism offered itself as antihumanism.

Pynchon is deeply and profoundly humanistic, a fact that postmodern readings of ***Gravity's Rainbow*** do not register. Although ***Gravity's Rainbow*** is a novel of bleak circumstances and few alternatives, Pynchon's creation of the Zone Commandos perfectly dramatizes a profound analytic and imaginative sympathy for human beings entangled in the midst of human history and an equally profound repulsion at the modern aesthetic and technological attempts to evade or transcend that entanglement. Furthermore, Pynchon's humanism alone accounts for his obsessive interest in secular institutions of law, society, ritual, education, learning, mass culture, government, corporations, and so on. These matter as modes of human poetry and, at the same time, as ethically unsound modes of poetic corruption. It is fundamental that despite Pynchon's use of the figural devices of Gnosticism and the Kaballah, his historicism precludes religious solutions to the problems of human entanglement. In this, he is the ideal follower of Vico. Enzian once more helps us see this:

> Enzian has grown cold: not so much a fire dying away as a positive coming on of cold, a bitter taste growing across the palate of love's first hopes. . . . It began when Weissmann brought him to Europe: a discovery that love, among these men, once past the simple feel and orgasming of it, had to do with masculine technologies, with contracts, with winning and losing. Demanded, in his own case, that he enter the service of the Rocket. . . . Beyond simple steel erection, the Rocket was an entire system *won,* away from the feminine darkness, held against the entropies of lovable but scatterbrained Mother Nature: that was the first thing he was obliged by Weissmann to learn, his first step towards citizenship in the Zone. He was led to believe that by understanding the Rocket, he would come to understand truly his manhood. . . .
>
> (324)

This is what happens when modernity substitutes its plastic, mechanical, and cybernetic fetishes. The result, says Enzian, is "devotion to the Leader, political intrigue."

History does not give ***Gravity's Rainbow*** either a linear or circular form—or the form of a parabola, despite the appearance suggested by beginning and ending with a Rocket falling from the sky. At the end, even as the nuclear-tipped Rocket hurtles silently toward a movie theater in LA, the final image Pynchon gives us is of entanglement, of humans in need, trying to understand their needs behind the technological screen projected to them as their lives. As they wait, unknowingly, for silent apocalypse to wipe them out, they sing an old hymn of the preterit written long ago by the heretical William Slothrop. They do this together, in a last moment, putting hands between their own or others' legs.

This is not a scene of neat circular closure. To end on the heretical casts us back throughout the novel to the elect's obsession with bringing the heretical under control by power or exile. The list of heretics is long even if they are relatively impotent. As the novel's final section develops under the title, "Counterforce," two things happen: the narrative fragments into smaller and smaller shards that are not recuperated, kabbalistically, into some newly remade whole, some new Word. Pynchon is no Luria.[17] Each fragment contains characters and events that either stage acts of resistance to the elect's agents or dramatize ways of life, ethics that the elect degrades. These heretical ethics stand in close relation to what modernity destroys in its transcending efforts. The most impressive of these scenes involves a reformed Pirate Prentice and the ever liberated Pig Bodine in a Buñuelesque destruction of a very elect dinner party from which our heretics flee after sickening all the corporate and governmental diners with exotic foods named mostly for the body's excrements.

If history is to be neither linear nor circular/parabolic, then it must be folded and entangled and more like the "progressive knotting into," which the final teeming section of the narrative resembles. Critics repeatedly treat the final section as disintegration, a falling apart of an otherwise complex but coherent narrative. This is wrong. Only from the standpoint of the elect can the last section of the novel be seen as fallen and degraded. Taken in itself, it is enfolded, entangled, a Zone or interregnum in which we see just what the elect disdains as organic and diseased.

Most important, the novel dramatizes a mode of thinking that cannot proceed without first dramatizing the necessary embrace of human life, without which the very possibilities of thinking and imagination come to an end, yielding to the second law of thermodynamics' dreaded story of heat death. This mode of thinking, so perfect for the novelistic machine to think, requires an ethical attitude toward the natural that, in these passages, includes history as humans live it.[18] Pynchon envisions history as entanglement and makes that acceptance and that truth the ground of his poetics, of his narrative shifts, developments, and turns. Since it is a vision, the novel, not surprisingly, elaborates that vision in a complex image of Pan that moves the narrative into a "primitive" time out of which the world of nations appears.

Geli has a vision on the crest of a hill: "It is golden-dark, almost night. The region is lonely and Pan is very close." She feels herself waiting to go to a space literally beyond good and evil. Whatever will take her, she calls "Pan" but does not know what "it" is. Pynchon places her in a familiar position, waiting on a hill for visionary inspiration: "Have you ever waited for *it*? wondering whether it will come from outside or inside?" Geli is granted her vision and, most importantly, the narrator confirms its authenticity. Waiting is a form of purgation "re-erasing Brain to keep it clean for the Visit," which, when it comes, surpasses understanding: "What you felt stirring across the land . . . it was the equinox . . . green spring equal nights . . . canyons are opening up, at the bottom are steaming fumaroles, steaming the tropical life there like greens in a pot, rank, dope-perfume, a hood of smell . . . human consciousness, that poor cripple, that deformed and doomed thing, is about to be born" (720). The narrator affirms the importance of Geli's vision and generalizes its meaning into a cosmic story of the world before human time, of and at the moment when humanity comes to be homo sapiens and finds itself set against the very forces of nature that summon it into being:

> This is the World just before men. Too violently pitched alive in constant flow ever to be seen by men directly. They are meant only to look at it dead, in still strata,

> transputrefied to oil or coal. [Remember the miner in Südwest set over and against the woman in the hole.] Alive it was a threat: it was Titans, was an overpeaking of life so clangorous and mad, such a green corona about Earth's body that some spoiler *had* to be brought in before it blew the Creation apart. So we, crippled keepers, were sent out to multiply, to have dominion. God's spoilers. Us. Counter-revolutionaries. *It is our mission to promote death.* The way we kill, the way we die, being unique among the Creatures. It was something we had to work on, historically and personally. To build from scratch up to its present status as reaction, nearly as strong as life, holding down the green uprising. But only nearly as strong.
>
> (720)

Those who form the counterforce are not counter-revolutionaries. They have not gone over to death and the zero; they have not become reactionaries. The spoilers suffer defections and these few, against whom the elect wage war, join in the subcreation that is life itself.

What is this life and what evidence have we for its persistence? In short, it is beauty come as something like the sublime, rare and too much to behold so that it overwhelms the human. It does not call the defecting human into being as technocratic and masterful subject and spoiler; rather, it draws the human back into place in the service of what is not merely anthropocentric, and in this lies the strength of Pynchon's deepest secularism. The world and humankind must be saved from the "human, all too human," from the spoilers of life (Nietzsche). The resources lie in the world of Pan and can be seen by those who defect.

What do the defectors see? Why are theirs the ethics of the Titans? What are those ethics? The defectors go over to the Titans, "into the rests of the folk-song Death . . . out, and through, and down under the net, down to the uprising" (720). Defectors discover what the elect despoils: The Titans

> are all the presences we are not supposed to be seeing—wind gods, hilltop gods, sunset gods—that we train ourselves away from to keep from looking further even though enough of us do, leave Their electric voice behind in the twilight at the end of the town and move into the constantly parted cloak of out nightwalk till
>
> Suddenly, Pan—leaping—its face too beautiful to bear, beautiful Serpent, its coils in rainbow lashings in the sky—into the sure bones of fright—
>
> (720-21)

Electric men, Rocket men, human spoilers read the world only as energy deposits of coal and oil, and have no sense of how a nonhuman reading of the Earth's history might place the human in an even grander and more capacious narrative than any we offer as our own guides.[19] Of course, linearity and circularity close history into the coercive destruction of a creation that needs to counter life which, otherwise, unchecked threatens to overwhelm creation itself with its own excess and proliferation.

Death has become the fetish of the merely human, the misplaced and sole object of its being, a mark that it has forgotten its own place in creation; and it has also become the fetish, in the name of which, ironically, humanity will destroy itself and the biosphere by so deeply burying the Titans as to do in the planet itself. Pynchon's deepest humanism requires of humanity—if it wishes to remain itself—a constant vigilance, a steady stream of defectors who accept the necessary role of death not in the overcoming of life but in its maintenance, who see that life and death are enfolded.

Loving creation, remaining human, means struggling to set aside the masculinist games of erectile technocracy to assure the needed balance between death and life. Histories have become agencies of those who love and deal death. History, by contrast, is the entangled relation between the Titans and the human. The human effort to win the battle is not only murderous but suicidal. Moreover, it is a nihilistic ethics based on the arrogant anthropocentrism that a long historical view of history itself brings into critical judgment. That long view, in terms of ***Gravity's Rainbow,*** comes about only after a period of waiting in which the Brain, cleansed of the elect's seductions, sees what is unbearable to see and filled with that beauty joins the counterforce of life. Of course, tragically, the period of waiting has been the period of ongoing extermination.

Students and teachers, Pynchon clearly hopes, shall come to a similar understanding from reading ***Gravity's Rainbow.*** The novel cleanses the Brain, prepare its readers to wait, to recognize glimpses of a too terrible beauty left only to poets and the preterit. Reading it is a discipline that purges settled forms of anthropocentric historical narrative by working obsessively through its forms and their entangled consequences in the creation. The result is a terrible beauty that puts history in place to welcome its derivative and subaltern relation to the entanglements of life.

Gravity's Rainbow should be seen as a celebration of love, but not merely human love, which quickly becomes masculinist games, but of love of creation, a deeply ecological sense of the location of human fate in that of the universe. As such a celebration, it should be seen as a deeply historical text, one that troubles us with the tactile immediacy of our own lives as these confront us, throughout the novel, in terms of the simple but devastating question: do we defect or despoil? Do we love life or death? Are we willing to leave behind our electric lights and "move into the constantly parted cloak of our nightwalk"? History and narrative must be placed in the service of an ethics that Creation itself imposes as a duty upon a never innocent and never to be transcendent humanity. Pynchon teaches us that the poet still has an old function: to keep the Creation in view and sing the justice of humanity's role in sustaining it. The poet knows that humanity cannot maintain its own being alone. The people must hear that truth in the poet's song.

Notes

1. "In 1993 it even won a special Booker Prize as the best Commonwealth novel in English of the previous 20 years" (Crowell).
2. In Rushdie's review of *Vineland,* he notices how much dates matter, particularly "1984." In this context, see Pynchon's foreword to the centennial edition of George Orwell's *Nineteen Eighty-Four.* See also Bérubé, who has made a statistical study showing that, as of 1992, Pynchon is more often written about than any other contemporary writer in English and that, among twentieth-century Americans, only T. S. Eliot, Ezra Pound, and William Faulkner have been more frequently studied.
3. I say this in purposeful opposition to Steiner's opinion that Pynchon, like other "verbose metafictionists," does not reward the effort to read him (18). See Steiner's article for an example of an ahistorical criticism that does not reflect upon its own intellectual and political situation.
4. Matthiessen, we recall, introduces Melville by describing him as "The American with the richest natural gifts as a writer" (371). Bérubé's study shows that, since 1981, *Moby-Dick* has been the only work of American prose fiction more often written about than *Gravity's Rainbow* (323).
5. For some evidence that critics place Pynchon into relation with the great English Romantics, see Bloom's "Introduction," which is a careful study of "Byron the Lightbulb" in *Gravity's Rainbow.* See Eddins for evidence of Pynchon's relations to Wordsworth (137, 151, 157). Poirier also links Pynchon to Wordsworth (54).
6. I would need an essay to analyze the fit between Franco Moretti's *Modern Epic* (1996) and Pynchon, whose name nowhere appears in Moretti's book, despite the prominence of Pynchon's predecessor, Herman Melville.
7. Often these critics, such as Maltby, follow the work of Jameson on the reduction of history to pastiche in postmodern writing.
8. Bloom's long-standing critical aversion to Pynchon rests on at least two evident claims: that Pynchon is a poet of imagination's decline and that he narrates history as a broken and irreparable vessel. Bloom's frame of reference is useful for thinking about Pynchon, even if Bloom has the matter upside down.
9. An attentive reader knows that these lines trope on lines from William Carlos Williams's great poem of the city, *Paterson.*
10. During the 1990s, Said developed a theory of intellectuals as contrapuntal figures in relation to their societies and associations. The most important texts here are *Musical Elaborations* and *Representations of the Intellectual.* My use of counterpoint intersects with one important perception of Said regarding Glenn Gould's first performance of the *Goldberg Variations*: Gould "strictly delivered [the variations] in correctly realized contrapuntal style, but always phrased, shaped, and rendered into a completely integrated characterization" (*Musical Elaborations* 25). Not only is this similar to my judgment of Pynchon's formal aesthetic resolution in *Gravity's Rainbow,* but it approaches my reading of Pynchon's presentation of the world as American history.
11. De Landa offers one of the most important attempts to conceptualize the mechanic and its ontological ambition as essential elements of especially American imperialism and war-making.
12. In *The Historical Novel,* Lukács derives from Goethe the insight that historical writing requires not naturalistic faithfulness to the details of the past, but "necessary anachronism." Lukács finds this notion in Goethe's comments on Manzoni's historical tragedy, *Adelchi* (61).
13. Certain critics accuse Pynchon of homophobia. Without entering into that debate, in this scene, onanism figures an essential part of the play of intellect over the problems history poses human choice. Critics who take this novel into the critical politics of representation will, of course, find and stress other textual elements that appear as sexuality and subjectivity.
14. For more on the *posthistoire,* see Niethammer and Jung.
15. I would like to open another brief parenthesis here. The echoes of Primo Levi's *Se questo è un uomo* (published 1958 in Italian, 1961 in English) are, as de Man would say, too interesting to be accidental and form part of Pynchon's response to the Holocaust.
16. Despite his antipathy to Pynchon, Bloom's cabbalistic criticism forms an important context for reading Pynchon. Of course, Eddins has best and most

thoroughly developed this gnostic reading of Pynchon, and I do little more in these paragraphs than build on his fine book.

17. For an expansive treatment of this topic, see Eddins 146.

18. Another essay could consider Pynchon's sense of nature and natural law in contrast to that advocated by reactionaries among America's political and legal elites.

19. Heidegger elaborates a critique of technological anthropocentrism as a worldview holding nature and the human (*Dasein*) as "standing-reserve" for the elect's ambitions.

Works Cited

Bérubé, Michael. *Marginal Forces/Cultural Centers.* Ithaca: Cornell UP, 1992.

Bloom, Harold. Introduction. Bloom, *Thomas Pynchon* 1-10.

———, ed. *Thomas Pynchon: Modern Critical Views.* New York: Chelsea, 1986.

Boyle, T. Coraghessan. "The Great Divide." Rev. of *Mason & Dixon,* by Thomas Pynchon. *New York Times Book Review* 18 May 1997: 9.

Conrad, Joseph. *Heart of Darkness.* New York: Norton, 1963.

Crowell, Todd. "The Best Book." *Asia's Best.* 2000. *Asiaweek* 29 Apr. 2004 <http://www.asiaweek.com/asiaweek/features/asiabest2000/ann.arch.booksb1.html>.

De Landa, Manuel. *War in the Age of Intelligent Machines.* New York: Zone, 1991.

Eddins, Dwight. *The Gnostic Pynchon.* Bloomington: Indiana UP, 1990.

Heidegger, Martin. "The Question Concerning Technology." *Martin Heidegger: Basic Writings.* Ed. David Farrell Krell. New York: Harper, 1977. 283-318.

Jameson, Fredric. *Postmodernism; or, the Cultural Logic of Late Capitalism.* Durham: Duke UP, 1991.

Jung, Thomas. *Vom Ende der Geschichte: Rekonstruktionen zum Posthistoire in kritischer Absicht.* Münster: Waxmann, 1989.

Lukács, Georg. *The Historical Novel.* Trans. Hannah and Stanley Mitchell. Lincoln: U of Nebraska P, 1983.

Maltby, Paul. *Dissident Postmodernists.* Philadelphia: U of Pennsylvania P, 1991.

Matthiessen, F. O. *The American Renaissance.* New York: Oxford UP, 1941.

Mendelson, Edward. Introduction. *Pynchon: A Collection of Critical Essays.* Ed. Edward Mendelson. Englewood Cliffs, NJ: Prentice, 1978. 1-15.

Moretti, Franco. *Modern Epic: The World System from Goethe to García Márquez.* Trans. Quintin Hoare. London: Verso, 1996.

Niethammer, Lutz. *Posthistoire.* Trans. Patrick Camiller. London: Verso, 1992.

Nietzsche, Friedrich. *Human, All Too Human.* New York: Cambridge UP, 1996.

Poirier, Richard. "The Importance of Thomas Pynchon." Bloom, *Thomas Pynchon* 54-68.

Pynchon, Thomas. *Gravity's Rainbow.* New York: Penguin, 1973.

———. "New Foreword." *Nineteen Eighty-Four.* By George Orwell. New York: Harcourt, 2003. vii-xxvi.

Rushdie, Salman. "Still Crazy After All These Years." Rev. of *Vineland,* by Thomas Pynchon. *New York Times Book Review* 14 Jan. 1990: 1+.

Said, Edward W. *Musical Elaborations.* New York: Columbia UP, 1991.

———. *Representations of the Intellectual.* New York: Pantheon, 1994.

Steiner, Wendy. "Look Who's Modern Now." *New York Times Book Review* 10 Oct. 1999: 18-19.

Tanner, Tony. *Thomas Pynchon.* London: Methuen, 1982.

FURTHER READING

Criticism

Abbas, Niran, ed. *Thomas Pynchon: Reading from the Margins.* Madison, N.J.: Fairleigh Dickinson University Press, 2003, 256 p.

Collection of essays that focus on how identity is shaped, gendered, and contested throughout Pynchon's work.

Attewell, Nadine. "'Bouncy Little Tunes': Nostalgia, Sentimentality, and Narrative in *Gravity's Rainbow.*" *Contemporary Literature* 45, no. 1 (spring 2004): 22-48.

Addresses Pynchon's treatment of sentimentality and nostalgia for the past in *Gravity's Rainbow.*

Bloom, Harold. *Thomas Pynchon.* Philadelphia: Chelsea House Publishers, 2003, 160 p.

Critical essays on Pynchon's novels by prominent scholar.

Punday, Daniel. "Pynchon's Ghosts." *Contemporary Literature* 44, no. 2 (summer 2003): 250-74.

Analyzes the role of the past within Pynchon's novels.

Additional coverage of Pynchon's life and career is contained in the following sources published by Thomson Gale: *American Writers Supplement,* Vol. 2; *Beacham's Encyclopedia of Popular Fiction: Biography and Resources,* Vol. 3; *Bestsellers,* Vol. 90:2; *Contemporary Authors,* Vols. 17-20R; *Contemporary Authors New Revision Series,* Vols. 22, 46, 73, 142; *Contemporary Literary Criticism,* Vols. 2, 3, 6, 9, 11, 18, 33, 62, 72, 123, 192; *Contemporary Novelists,* Ed. 7; *Contemporary Popular Writers,* Ed. 1; *Dictionary of Literary Biography,* Vols. 2, 173; *DISCovering Authors*; *DISCovering Authors: British Edition*; *DISCovering Authors: Canadian Edition*; *DISCovering Authors Modules: Most-studied Authors, Novelists,* and *Popular Fiction and Genre Authors*; *DISCovering Authors 3.0*; *Encyclopedia of World Literature in the 20th Century,* Ed. 3; *Literature Resource Center*; *Major 20th-Century Writers,* Eds. 1, 2; *Major 21st-Century Writers,* (eBook) 2005; *Reference Guide to American Literature,* Ed. 4; *St. James Guide to Science Fiction Writers,* Ed. 4; *Short Story Criticism,* Vols. 14, 84; *Twayne's Companion to Contemporary Literature in English,* Ed. 1:2; *Twayne's United States Authors*; and *World Literature Criticism.*

How to Use This Index

The main references

Calvino, Italo 1923-1985 .... CLC 5, 8, 11, 22, 33, 39, 73; SSC 3, 48

list all author entries in the following Gale Literary Criticism series:

AAL = *Asian American Literature*
BG = *The Beat Generation: A Gale Critical Companion*
BLC = *Black Literature Criticism*
BLCS = *Black Literature Criticism Supplement*
CLC = *Contemporary Literary Criticism*
CLR = *Children's Literature Review*
CMLC = *Classical and Medieval Literature Criticism*
DC = *Drama Criticism*
HLC = *Hispanic Literature Criticism*
HLCS = *Hispanic Literature Criticism Supplement*
HR = *Harlem Renaissance: A Gale Critical Companion*
LC = *Literature Criticism from 1400 to 1800*
NCLC = *Nineteenth-Century Literature Criticism*
NNAL = *Native North American Literature*
PC = *Poetry Criticism*
SSC = *Short Story Criticism*
TCLC = *Twentieth-Century Literary Criticism*
WLC = *World Literature Criticism, 1500 to the Present*
WLCS = *World Literature Criticism Supplement*

The cross-references

See also CA 85-88, 116; CANR 23, 61; DAM NOV; DLB 196; EW 13; MTCW 1, 2; RGSF 2; RGWL 2; SFW 4; SSFS 12

list all author entries in the following Gale biographical and literary sources:

AAYA = *Authors & Artists for Young Adults*
AFAW = *African American Writers*
AFW = *African Writers*
AITN = *Authors in the News*
AMW = *American Writers*
AMWR = *American Writers Retrospective Supplement*
AMWS = *American Writers Supplement*
ANW = *American Nature Writers*
AW = *Ancient Writers*
BEST = *Bestsellers*
BPFB = *Beacham's Encyclopedia of Popular Fiction: Biography and Resources*
BRW = *British Writers*
BRWS = *British Writers Supplement*
BW = *Black Writers*
BYA = *Beacham's Guide to Literature for Young Adults*
CA = *Contemporary Authors*
CAAS = *Contemporary Authors Autobiography Series*
CABS = *Contemporary Authors Bibliographical Series*
CAD = *Contemporary American Dramatists*
CANR = *Contemporary Authors New Revision Series*
CAP = *Contemporary Authors Permanent Series*
CBD = *Contemporary British Dramatists*
CCA = *Contemporary Canadian Authors*
CD = *Contemporary Dramatists*
CDALB = *Concise Dictionary of American Literary Biography*
CDALBS = *Concise Dictionary of American Literary Biography Supplement*
CDBLB = *Concise Dictionary of British Literary Biography*

CMW = *St. James Guide to Crime & Mystery Writers*
CN = *Contemporary Novelists*
CP = *Contemporary Poets*
CPW = *Contemporary Popular Writers*
CSW = *Contemporary Southern Writers*
CWD = *Contemporary Women Dramatists*
CWP = *Contemporary Women Poets*
CWRI = *St. James Guide to Children's Writers*
CWW = *Contemporary World Writers*
DA = *DISCovering Authors*
DA3 = *DISCovering Authors 3.0*
DAB = *DISCovering Authors: British Edition*
DAC = *DISCovering Authors: Canadian Edition*
DAM = *DISCovering Authors: Modules*
DRAM: *Dramatists Module;* ***MST:*** *Most-studied Authors Module;*
MULT: *Multicultural Authors Module;* ***NOV:*** *Novelists Module;*
POET: *Poets Module;* ***POP:*** *Popular Fiction and Genre Authors Module*
DFS = *Drama for Students*
DLB = *Dictionary of Literary Biography*
DLBD = *Dictionary of Literary Biography Documentary Series*
DLBY = *Dictionary of Literary Biography Yearbook*
DNFS = *Literature of Developing Nations for Students*
EFS = *Epics for Students*
EXPN = *Exploring Novels*
EXPP = *Exploring Poetry*
EXPS = *Exploring Short Stories*
EW = *European Writers*
FANT = *St. James Guide to Fantasy Writers*
FW = *Feminist Writers*
GFL = *Guide to French Literature,* Beginnings to 1789, 1798 to the Present
GLL = *Gay and Lesbian Literature*
HGG = *St. James Guide to Horror, Ghost & Gothic Writers*
HW = *Hispanic Writers*
IDFW = *International Dictionary of Films and Filmmakers: Writers and Production Artists*
IDTP = *International Dictionary of Theatre: Playwrights*
LAIT = *Literature and Its Times*
LAW = *Latin American Writers*
JRDA = *Junior DISCovering Authors*
MAICYA = *Major Authors and Illustrators for Children and Young Adults*
MAICYAS = *Major Authors and Illustrators for Children and Young Adults Supplement*
MAWW = *Modern American Women Writers*
MJW = *Modern Japanese Writers*
MTCW = *Major 20th-Century Writers*
NCFS = *Nonfiction Classics for Students*
NFS = *Novels for Students*
PAB = *Poets: American and British*
PFS = *Poetry for Students*
RGAL = *Reference Guide to American Literature*
RGEL = *Reference Guide to English Literature*
RGSF = *Reference Guide to Short Fiction*
RGWL = *Reference Guide to World Literature*
RHW = *Twentieth-Century Romance and Historical Writers*
SAAS = *Something about the Author Autobiography Series*
SATA = *Something about the Author*
SFW = *St. James Guide to Science Fiction Writers*
SSFS = *Short Stories for Students*
TCWW = *Twentieth-Century Western Writers*
WLIT = *World Literature and Its Times*
WP = *World Poets*
YABC = *Yesterday's Authors of Books for Children*
YAW = *St. James Guide to Young Adult Writers*

Literary Criticism Series Cumulative Author Index

Andrade, Carlos Drummond de ..... **CLC 18**
See Drummond de Andrade, Carlos
See also EWL 3; RGWL 2, 3
Andrade, Mario de .... **TCLC 43**
See de Andrade, Mario
See also DLB 307; EWL 3; LAW; RGWL 2, 3; WLIT 1
Andreae, Johann V(alentin) 1586-1654 .... **LC 32**
See also DLB 164
Andreas Capellanus fl. c. 1185- .... **CMLC 45**
See also DLB 208
Andreas-Salome, Lou 1861-1937 ... **TCLC 56**
See also CA 178; DLB 66
Andreev, Leonid
See Andreyev, Leonid (Nikolaevich)
See also DLB 295; EWL 3
Andress, Lesley
See Sanders, Lawrence
Andrewes, Lancelot 1555-1626 .... **LC 5**
See also DLB 151, 172
Andrews, Cicily Fairfield
See West, Rebecca
Andrews, Elton V.
See Pohl, Frederik
Andreyev, Leonid (Nikolaevich) 1871-1919 .... **TCLC 3**
See Andreev, Leonid
See also CA 104; 185
Andric, Ivo 1892-1975 .... **CLC 8; SSC 36; TCLC 135**
See also CA 81-84; 57-60; CANR 43, 60; CDWLB 4; DLB 147; EW 11; EWL 3; MTCW 1; RGSF 2; RGWL 2, 3
Androvar
See Prado (Calvo), Pedro
Angela of Foligno 1248?-1309 .... **CMLC 76**
Angelique, Pierre
See Bataille, Georges
Angell, Roger 1920- .... **CLC 26**
See also CA 57-60; CANR 13, 44, 70; DLB 171, 185
Angelou, Maya 1928- ... **BLC 1; CLC 12, 35, 64, 77, 155; PC 32; WLCS**
See also AAYA 7, 20; AMWS 4; BPFB 1; BW 2, 3; BYA 2; CA 65-68; CANR 19, 42, 65, 111, 133; CDALBS; CLR 53; CP 7; CPW; CSW; CWP; DA; DA3; DAB; DAC; DAM MST, MULT, POET, POP; DLB 38; EWL 3; EXPN; EXPP; LAIT 4; MAICYA 2; MAICYAS 1; MAWW; MTCW 1, 2; NCFS 2; NFS 2; PFS 2, 3; RGAL 4; SATA 49, 136; WYA; YAW
Angouleme, Marguerite d'
See de Navarre, Marguerite
Anna Comnena 1083-1153 .... **CMLC 25**
Annensky, Innokentii Fedorovich
See Annensky, Innokenty (Fyodorovich)
See also DLB 295
Annensky, Innokenty (Fyodorovich) 1856-1909 .... **TCLC 14**
See also CA 110; 155; EWL 3
Annunzio, Gabriele d'
See D'Annunzio, Gabriele
Anodos
See Coleridge, Mary E(lizabeth)
Anon, Charles Robert
See Pessoa, Fernando (Antonio Nogueira)
Anouilh, Jean (Marie Lucien Pierre) 1910-1987 . **CLC 1, 3, 8, 13, 40, 50; DC 8, 21**
See also CA 17-20R; 123; CANR 32; DAM DRAM; DFS 9, 10, 19; EW 13; EWL 3; GFL 1789 to the Present; MTCW 1, 2; RGWL 2, 3; TWA
Anselm of Canterbury 1033(?)-1109 .... **CMLC 67**
See also DLB 115
Anthony, Florence
See Ai
Anthony, John
See Ciardi, John (Anthony)
Anthony, Peter
See Shaffer, Anthony (Joshua); Shaffer, Peter (Levin)
Anthony, Piers 1934- .... **CLC 35**
See also AAYA 11, 48; BYA 7; CA 200; CAAE 200; CANR 28, 56, 73, 102, 133; CPW; DAM POP; DLB 8; FANT; MAICYA 2; MAICYAS 1; MTCW 1, 2; SAAS 22; SATA 84, 129; SATA-Essay 129; SFW 4; SUFW 1, 2; YAW
Anthony, Susan B(rownell) 1820-1906 .... **TCLC 84**
See also CA 211; FW
Antiphon c. 480B.C.-c. 411B.C. .... **CMLC 55**
Antoine, Marc
See Proust, (Valentin-Louis-George-Eugene) Marcel
Antoninus, Brother
See Everson, William (Oliver)
Antonioni, Michelangelo 1912- .... **CLC 20, 144**
See also CA 73-76; CANR 45, 77
Antschel, Paul 1920-1970
See Celan, Paul
See also CA 85-88; CANR 33, 61; MTCW 1; PFS 21
Anwar, Chairil 1922-1949 .... **TCLC 22**
See Chairil Anwar
See also CA 121; 219; RGWL 3
Anzaldua, Gloria (Evanjelina) 1942-2004 .... **CLC 200, HLCS 1**
See also CA 175; 227; CSW; CWP; DLB 122; FW; LLW 1; RGAL 4; SATA-Obit 154
Apess, William 1798-1839(?) .... **NCLC 73; NNAL**
See also DAM MULT; DLB 175, 243
Apollinaire, Guillaume 1880-1918 .... **PC 7; TCLC 3, 8, 51**
See Kostrowitzki, Wilhelm Apollinaris de
See also CA 152; DAM POET; DLB 258; EW 9; EWL 3; GFL 1789 to the Present; MTCW 1; RGWL 2, 3; TWA; WP
Apollonius of Rhodes
See Apollonius Rhodius
See also AW 1; RGWL 2, 3
Apollonius Rhodius c. 300B.C.-c. 220B.C. .... **CMLC 28**
See Apollonius of Rhodes
See also DLB 176
Appelfeld, Aharon 1932- ... **CLC 23, 47; SSC 42**
See also CA 112; 133; CANR 86; CWW 2; DLB 299; EWL 3; RGSF 2
Apple, Max (Isaac) 1941- .... **CLC 9, 33; SSC 50**
See also CA 81-84; CANR 19, 54; DLB 130
Appleman, Philip (Dean) 1926- .... **CLC 51**
See also CA 13-16R; CAAS 18; CANR 6, 29, 56
Appleton, Lawrence
See Lovecraft, H(oward) P(hillips)
Apteryx
See Eliot, T(homas) S(tearns)
Apuleius, (Lucius Madaurensis) 125(?)-175(?) .... **CMLC 1**
See also AW 2; CDWLB 1; DLB 211; RGWL 2, 3; SUFW
Aquin, Hubert 1929-1977 .... **CLC 15**
See also CA 105; DLB 53; EWL 3
Aquinas, Thomas 1224(?)-1274 ..... **CMLC 33**
See also DLB 115; EW 1; TWA
Aragon, Louis 1897-1982 .... **CLC 3, 22; TCLC 123**
See also CA 69-72; 108; CANR 28, 71; DAM NOV, POET; DLB 72, 258; EW 11; EWL 3; GFL 1789 to the Present; GLL 2; LMFS 2; MTCW 1, 2; RGWL 2, 3
Arany, Janos 1817-1882 .... **NCLC 34**
Aranyos, Kakay 1847-1910
See Mikszath, Kalman
Aratus of Soli c. 315B.C.-c. 240B.C. .... **CMLC 64**
See also DLB 176
Arbuthnot, John 1667-1735 .... **LC 1**
See also DLB 101
Archer, Herbert Winslow
See Mencken, H(enry) L(ouis)
Archer, Jeffrey (Howard) 1940- .... **CLC 28**
See also AAYA 16; BEST 89:3; BPFB 1; CA 77-80; CANR 22, 52, 95; CPW; DA3; DAM POP; INT CANR-22
Archer, Jules 1915- .... **CLC 12**
See also CA 9-12R; CANR 6, 69; SAAS 5; SATA 4, 85
Archer, Lee
See Ellison, Harlan (Jay)
Archilochus c. 7th cent. B.C.- .... **CMLC 44**
See also DLB 176
Arden, John 1930- .... **CLC 6, 13, 15**
See also BRWS 2; CA 13-16R; CAAS 4; CANR 31, 65, 67, 124; CBD; CD 5; DAM DRAM; DFS 9; DLB 13, 245; EWL 3; MTCW 1
Arenas, Reinaldo 1943-1990 .. **CLC 41; HLC 1**
See also CA 124; 128; 133; CANR 73, 106; DAM MULT; DLB 145; EWL 3; GLL 2; HW 1; LAW; LAWS 1; MTCW 1; RGSF 2; RGWL 3; WLIT 1
Arendt, Hannah 1906-1975 .... **CLC 66, 98**
See also CA 17-20R; 61-64; CANR 26, 60; DLB 242; MTCW 1, 2
Aretino, Pietro 1492-1556 .... **LC 12**
See also RGWL 2, 3
Arghezi, Tudor .... **CLC 80**
See Theodorescu, Ion N.
See also CA 167; CDWLB 4; DLB 220; EWL 3
Arguedas, Jose Maria 1911-1969 .... **CLC 10, 18; HLCS 1; TCLC 147**
See also CA 89-92; CANR 73; DLB 113; EWL 3; HW 1; LAW; RGWL 2, 3; WLIT 1
Argueta, Manlio 1936- .... **CLC 31**
See also CA 131; CANR 73; CWW 2; DLB 145; EWL 3; HW 1; RGWL 3
Arias, Ron(ald Francis) 1941- .... **HLC 1**
See also CA 131; CANR 81; DAM MULT; DLB 82; HW 1, 2; MTCW 2
Ariosto, Ludovico 1474-1533 ... **LC 6, 87; PC 42**
See also EW 2; RGWL 2, 3
Aristides
See Epstein, Joseph
Aristophanes 450B.C.-385B.C. .... **CMLC 4, 51; DC 2; WLCS**
See also AW 1; CDWLB 1; DA; DA3; DAB; DAC; DAM DRAM, MST; DFS 10; DLB 176; LMFS 1; RGWL 2, 3; TWA
Aristotle 384B.C.-322B.C. .... **CMLC 31; WLCS**
See also AW 1; CDWLB 1; DA; DA3; DAB; DAC; DAM MST; DLB 176; RGWL 2, 3; TWA
Arlt, Roberto (Godofredo Christophersen) 1900-1942 .... **HLC 1; TCLC 29**
See also CA 123; 131; CANR 67; DAM MULT; DLB 305; EWL 3; HW 1, 2; LAW

Armah, Ayi Kwei 1939- . **BLC 1; CLC 5, 33, 136**
See also AFW; BRWS 10; BW 1; CA 61-64; CANR 21, 64; CDWLB 3; CN 7; DAM MULT, POET; DLB 117; EWL 3; MTCW 1; WLIT 2
Armatrading, Joan 1950- .... **CLC 17**
See also CA 114; 186
Armitage, Frank
See Carpenter, John (Howard)
Armstrong, Jeannette (C.) 1948- .... **NNAL**
See also CA 149; CCA 1; CN 7; DAC; SATA 102
Arnette, Robert
See Silverberg, Robert
Arnim, Achim von (Ludwig Joachim von Arnim) 1781-1831 .. **NCLC 5, 159; SSC 29**
See also DLB 90
Arnim, Bettina von 1785-1859 ...... **NCLC 38, 123**
See also DLB 90; RGWL 2, 3
Arnold, Matthew 1822-1888 ..... **NCLC 6, 29, 89, 126; PC 5; WLC**
See also BRW 5; CDBLB 1832-1890; DA; DAB; DAC; DAM MST, POET; DLB 32, 57; EXPP; PAB; PFS 2; TEA; WP
Arnold, Thomas 1795-1842 .... **NCLC 18**
See also DLB 55
Arnow, Harriette (Louisa) Simpson 1908-1986 .... **CLC 2, 7, 18**
See also BPFB 1; CA 9-12R; 118; CANR 14; DLB 6; FW; MTCW 1, 2; RHW; SATA 42; SATA-Obit 47
Arouet, Francois-Marie
See Voltaire
Arp, Hans
See Arp, Jean
Arp, Jean 1887-1966 .... **CLC 5; TCLC 115**
See also CA 81-84; 25-28R; CANR 42, 77; EW 10
Arrabal
See Arrabal, Fernando
Arrabal, Fernando 1932- ... **CLC 2, 9, 18, 58**
See Arrabal (Teran), Fernando
See also CA 9-12R; CANR 15; EWL 3; LMFS 2
Arrabal (Teran), Fernando 1932-
See Arrabal, Fernando
See also CWW 2
Arreola, Juan Jose 1918-2001 .... **CLC 147; HLC 1; SSC 38**
See also CA 113; 131; 200; CANR 81; CWW 2; DAM MULT; DLB 113; DNFS 2; EWL 3; HW 1, 2; LAW; RGSF 2
Arrian c. 89(?)-c. 155(?) .... **CMLC 43**
See also DLB 176
Arrick, Fran .... **CLC 30**
See Gaberman, Judie Angell
See also BYA 6
Arrley, Richmond
See Delany, Samuel R(ay), Jr.
Artaud, Antonin (Marie Joseph) 1896-1948 .... **DC 14; TCLC 3, 36**
See also CA 104; 149; DA3; DAM DRAM; DLB 258; EW 11; EWL 3; GFL 1789 to the Present; MTCW 1; RGWL 2, 3
Arthur, Ruth M(abel) 1905-1979 ..... **CLC 12**
See also CA 9-12R; 85-88; CANR 4; CWRI 5; SATA 7, 26
Artsybashev, Mikhail (Petrovich) 1878-1927 .... **TCLC 31**
See also CA 170; DLB 295
Arundel, Honor (Morfydd) 1919-1973 .... **CLC 17**
See also CA 21-22; 41-44R; CAP 2; CLR 35; CWRI 5; SATA 4; SATA-Obit 24
Arzner, Dorothy 1900-1979 .... **CLC 98**
Asch, Sholem 1880-1957 .... **TCLC 3**
See also CA 105; EWL 3; GLL 2
Ascham, Roger 1516(?)-1568 .... **LC 101**
See also DLB 236
Ash, Shalom
See Asch, Sholem
Ashbery, John (Lawrence) 1927- .. **CLC 2, 3, 4, 6, 9, 13, 15, 25, 41, 77, 125; PC 26**
See Berry, Jonas
See also AMWS 3; CA 5-8R; CANR 9, 37, 66, 102, 132; CP 7; DA3; DAM POET; DLB 5, 165; DLBY 1981; EWL 3; INT CANR-9; MTCW 1, 2; PAB; PFS 11; RGAL 4; WP
Ashdown, Clifford
See Freeman, R(ichard) Austin
Ashe, Gordon
See Creasey, John
Ashton-Warner, Sylvia (Constance) 1908-1984 .... **CLC 19**
See also CA 69-72; 112; CANR 29; MTCW 1, 2
Asimov, Isaac 1920-1992 ..... **CLC 1, 3, 9, 19, 26, 76, 92**
See also AAYA 13; BEST 90:2; BPFB 1; BYA 4, 6, 7, 9; CA 1-4R; 137; CANR 2, 19, 36, 60, 125; CLR 12, 79; CMW 4; CPW; DA3; DAM POP; DLB 8; DLBY 1992; INT CANR-19; JRDA; LAIT 5; LMFS 2; MAICYA 1, 2; MTCW 1, 2; RGAL 4; SATA 1, 26, 74; SCFW 2; SFW 4; SSFS 17; TUS; YAW
Askew, Anne 1521(?)-1546 .... **LC 81**
See also DLB 136
Assis, Joaquim Maria Machado de
See Machado de Assis, Joaquim Maria
Astell, Mary 1666-1731 .... **LC 68**
See also DLB 252; FW
Astley, Thea (Beatrice May) 1925-2004 .... **CLC 41**
See also CA 65-68; 229; CANR 11, 43, 78; CN 7; DLB 289; EWL 3
Astley, William 1855-1911
See Warung, Price
Aston, James
See White, T(erence) H(anbury)
Asturias, Miguel Angel 1899-1974 .... **CLC 3, 8, 13; HLC 1**
See also CA 25-28; 49-52; CANR 32; CAP 2; CDWLB 3; DA3; DAM MULT, NOV; DLB 113, 290; EWL 3; HW 1; LAW; LMFS 2; MTCW 1, 2; RGWL 2, 3; WLIT 1
Atares, Carlos Saura
See Saura (Atares), Carlos
Athanasius c. 295-c. 373 .... **CMLC 48**
Atheling, William
See Pound, Ezra (Weston Loomis)
Atheling, William, Jr.
See Blish, James (Benjamin)
Atherton, Gertrude (Franklin Horn) 1857-1948 .... **TCLC 2**
See also CA 104; 155; DLB 9, 78, 186; HGG; RGAL 4; SUFW 1; TCWW 2
Atherton, Lucius
See Masters, Edgar Lee
Atkins, Jack
See Harris, Mark
Atkinson, Kate 1951- .... **CLC 99**
See also CA 166; CANR 101; DLB 267
Attaway, William (Alexander) 1911-1986 .... **BLC 1; CLC 92**
See also BW 2, 3; CA 143; CANR 82; DAM MULT; DLB 76
Atticus
See Fleming, Ian (Lancaster); Wilson, (Thomas) Woodrow
Atwood, Margaret (Eleanor) 1939- ... **CLC 2, 3, 4, 8, 13, 15, 25, 44, 84, 135; PC 8; SSC 2, 46; WLC**
See also AAYA 12, 47; AMWS 13; BEST 89:2; BPFB 1; CA 49-52; CANR 3, 24, 33, 59, 95, 133; CN 7; CP 7; CPW; CWP; DA; DA3; DAB; DAC; DAM MST, NOV, POET; DLB 53, 251; EWL 3; EXPN; FW; INT CANR-24; LAIT 5; MTCW 1, 2; NFS 4, 12, 13, 14, 19; PFS 7; RGSF 2; SATA 50; SSFS 3, 13; TWA; WWE 1; YAW
Aubigny, Pierre d'
See Mencken, H(enry) L(ouis)
Aubin, Penelope 1685-1731(?) .... **LC 9**
See also DLB 39
Auchincloss, Louis (Stanton) 1917- .. **CLC 4, 6, 9, 18, 45; SSC 22**
See also AMWS 4; CA 1-4R; CANR 6, 29, 55, 87, 130; CN 7; DAM NOV; DLB 2, 244; DLBY 1980; EWL 3; INT CANR-29; MTCW 1; RGAL 4
Auden, W(ystan) H(ugh) 1907-1973 . **CLC 1, 2, 3, 4, 6, 9, 11, 14, 43, 123; PC 1; WLC**
See also AAYA 18; AMWS 2; BRW 7; BRWR 1; CA 9-12R; 45-48; CANR 5, 61, 105; CDBLB 1914-1945; DA; DA3; DAB; DAC; DAM DRAM, MST, POET; DLB 10, 20; EWL 3; EXPP; MTCW 1, 2; PAB; PFS 1, 3, 4, 10; TUS; WP
Audiberti, Jacques 1899-1965 .... **CLC 38**
See also CA 25-28R; DAM DRAM; EWL 3
Audubon, John James 1785-1851 . **NCLC 47**
See also ANW; DLB 248
Auel, Jean M(arie) 1936- .... **CLC 31, 107**
See also AAYA 7, 51; BEST 90:4; BPFB 1; CA 103; CANR 21, 64, 115; CPW; DA3; DAM POP; INT CANR-21; NFS 11; RHW; SATA 91
Auerbach, Erich 1892-1957 .... **TCLC 43**
See also CA 118; 155; EWL 3
Augier, Emile 1820-1889 .... **NCLC 31**
See also DLB 192; GFL 1789 to the Present
August, John
See De Voto, Bernard (Augustine)
Augustine, St. 354-430 .... **CMLC 6; WLCS**
See also DA; DA3; DAB; DAC; DAM MST; DLB 115; EW 1; RGWL 2, 3
Aunt Belinda
See Braddon, Mary Elizabeth
Aunt Weedy
See Alcott, Louisa May
Aurelius
See Bourne, Randolph S(illiman)
Aurelius, Marcus 121-180 .... **CMLC 45**
See Marcus Aurelius
See also RGWL 2, 3
Aurobindo, Sri
See Ghose, Aurabinda
Aurobindo Ghose
See Ghose, Aurabinda
Austen, Jane 1775-1817 ...... **NCLC 1, 13, 19, 33, 51, 81, 95, 119, 150; WLC**
See also AAYA 19; BRW 4; BRWC 1; BRWR 2; BYA 3; CDBLB 1789-1832; DA; DA3; DAB; DAC; DAM MST, NOV; DLB 116; EXPN; LAIT 2; LATS 1:1; LMFS 1; NFS 1, 14, 18, 20; TEA; WLIT 3; WYAS 1
Auster, Paul 1947- .... **CLC 47, 131**
See also AMWS 12; CA 69-72; CANR 23, 52, 75, 129; CMW 4; CN 7; DA3; DLB 227; MTCW 1; SUFW 2
Austin, Frank
See Faust, Frederick (Schiller)
See also TCWW 2

Baraka, Amiri 1934- .... **BLC 1; CLC 1, 2, 3, 5, 10, 14, 33, 115, 213; DC 6; PC 4; WLCS**
See Jones, LeRoi
See also AFAW 1, 2; AMWS 2; BW 2, 3; CA 21-24R; CABS 3; CAD; CANR 27, 38, 61, 133; CD 5; CDALB 1941-1968; CP 7; CPW; DA; DA3; DAC; DAM MST, MULT, POET, POP; DFS 3, 11, 16; DLB 5, 7, 16, 38; DLBD 8; EWL 3; MTCW 1, 2; PFS 9; RGAL 4; TUS; WP
Baratynsky, Evgenii Abramovich 1800-1844 .... **NCLC 103**
See also DLB 205
Barbauld, Anna Laetitia 1743-1825 .... **NCLC 50**
See also DLB 107, 109, 142, 158; RGEL 2
Barbellion, W. N. P. .... **TCLC 24**
See Cummings, Bruce F(rederick)
Barber, Benjamin R. 1939- .... **CLC 141**
See also CA 29-32R; CANR 12, 32, 64, 119
Barbera, Jack (Vincent) 1945- .... **CLC 44**
See also CA 110; CANR 45
Barbey d'Aurevilly, Jules-Amedee 1808-1889 .... **NCLC 1; SSC 17**
See also DLB 119; GFL 1789 to the Present
Barbour, John c. 1316-1395 .... **CMLC 33**
See also DLB 146
Barbusse, Henri 1873-1935 .... **TCLC 5**
See also CA 105; 154; DLB 65; EWL 3; RGWL 2, 3
Barclay, Alexander c. 1475-1552 .... **LC 109**
See also DLB 132
Barclay, Bill
See Moorcock, Michael (John)
Barclay, William Ewert
See Moorcock, Michael (John)
Barea, Arturo 1897-1957 .... **TCLC 14**
See also CA 111; 201
Barfoot, Joan 1946- .... **CLC 18**
See also CA 105
Barham, Richard Harris 1788-1845 .... **NCLC 77**
See also DLB 159
Baring, Maurice 1874-1945 .... **TCLC 8**
See also CA 105; 168; DLB 34; HGG
Baring-Gould, Sabine 1834-1924 ... **TCLC 88**
See also DLB 156, 190
Barker, Clive 1952- .... **CLC 52, 205; SSC 53**
See also AAYA 10, 54; BEST 90:3; BPFB 1; CA 121; 129; CANR 71, 111, 133; CPW; DA3; DAM POP; DLB 261; HGG; INT CA-129; MTCW 1, 2; SUFW 2
Barker, George Granville 1913-1991 .... **CLC 8, 48**
See also CA 9-12R; 135; CANR 7, 38; DAM POET; DLB 20; EWL 3; MTCW 1
Barker, Harley Granville
See Granville-Barker, Harley
See also DLB 10
Barker, Howard 1946- .... **CLC 37**
See also CA 102; CBD; CD 5; DLB 13, 233
Barker, Jane 1652-1732 .... **LC 42, 82**
See also DLB 39, 131
Barker, Pat(ricia) 1943- .... **CLC 32, 94, 146**
See also BRWS 4; CA 117; 122; CANR 50, 101; CN 7; DLB 271; INT CA-122
Barlach, Ernst (Heinrich) 1870-1938 .... **TCLC 84**
See also CA 178; DLB 56, 118; EWL 3
Barlow, Joel 1754-1812 .... **NCLC 23**
See also AMWS 2; DLB 37; RGAL 4
Barnard, Mary (Ethel) 1909- .... **CLC 48**
See also CA 21-22; CAP 2
Barnes, Djuna 1892-1982 .... **CLC 3, 4, 8, 11, 29, 127; SSC 3**
See Steptoe, Lydia
See also AMWS 3; CA 9-12R; 107; CAD; CANR 16, 55; CWD; DLB 4, 9, 45; EWL 3; GLL 1; MTCW 1, 2; RGAL 4; TUS
Barnes, Jim 1933- .... **NNAL**
See also CA 108, 175; CAAE 175; CAAS 28; DLB 175
Barnes, Julian (Patrick) 1946- . **CLC 42, 141**
See also BRWS 4; CA 102; CANR 19, 54, 115; CN 7; DAB; DLB 194; DLBY 1993; EWL 3; MTCW 1
Barnes, Peter 1931-2004 .... **CLC 5, 56**
See also CA 65-68; CAAS 12; CANR 33, 34, 64, 113; CBD; CD 5; DFS 6; DLB 13, 233; MTCW 1
Barnes, William 1801-1886 .... **NCLC 75**
See also DLB 32
Baroja (y Nessi), Pio 1872-1956 .... **HLC 1; TCLC 8**
See also CA 104; EW 9
Baron, David
See Pinter, Harold
Baron Corvo
See Rolfe, Frederick (William Serafino Austin Lewis Mary)
Barondess, Sue K(aufman) 1926-1977 .... **CLC 8**
See Kaufman, Sue
See also CA 1-4R; 69-72; CANR 1
Baron de Teive
See Pessoa, Fernando (Antonio Nogueira)
Baroness Von S.
See Zangwill, Israel
Barres, (Auguste-)Maurice 1862-1923 .... **TCLC 47**
See also CA 164; DLB 123; GFL 1789 to the Present
Barreto, Afonso Henrique de Lima
See Lima Barreto, Afonso Henrique de
Barrett, Andrea 1954- .... **CLC 150**
See also CA 156; CANR 92
Barrett, Michele .... **CLC 65**
Barrett, (Roger) Syd 1946- .... **CLC 35**
Barrett, William (Christopher) 1913-1992 .... **CLC 27**
See also CA 13-16R; 139; CANR 11, 67; INT CANR-11
Barrett Browning, Elizabeth 1806-1861 ... **NCLC 1, 16, 61, 66; PC 6, 62; WLC**
See also BRW 4; CDBLB 1832-1890; DA; DA3; DAB; DAC; DAM MST, POET; DLB 32, 199; EXPP; PAB; PFS 2, 16; TEA; WLIT 4; WP
Barrie, J(ames) M(atthew) 1860-1937 .... **TCLC 2, 164**
See also BRWS 3; BYA 4, 5; CA 104; 136; CANR 77; CDBLB 1890-1914; CLR 16; CWRI 5; DA3; DAB; DAM DRAM; DFS 7; DLB 10, 141, 156; EWL 3; FANT; MAICYA 1, 2; MTCW 1; SATA 100; SUFW; WCH; WLIT 4; YABC 1
Barrington, Michael
See Moorcock, Michael (John)
Barrol, Grady
See Bograd, Larry
Barry, Mike
See Malzberg, Barry N(athaniel)
Barry, Philip 1896-1949 .... **TCLC 11**
See also CA 109; 199; DFS 9; DLB 7, 228; RGAL 4
Bart, Andre Schwarz
See Schwarz-Bart, Andre
Barth, John (Simmons) 1930- ... **CLC 1, 2, 3, 5, 7, 9, 10, 14, 27, 51, 89; SSC 10**
See also AITN 1, 2; AMW; BPFB 1; CA 1-4R; CABS 1; CANR 5, 23, 49, 64, 113; CN 7; DAM NOV; DLB 2, 227; EWL 3; FANT; MTCW 1; RGAL 4; RGSF 2; RHW; SSFS 6; TUS
Barthelme, Donald 1931-1989 ... **CLC 1, 2, 3, 5, 6, 8, 13, 23, 46, 59, 115; SSC 2, 55**
See also AMWS 4; BPFB 1; CA 21-24R; 129; CANR 20, 58; DA3; DAM NOV; DLB 2, 234; DLBY 1980, 1989; EWL 3; FANT; LMFS 2; MTCW 1, 2; RGAL 4; RGSF 2; SATA 7; SATA-Obit 62; SSFS 17
Barthelme, Frederick 1943- .... **CLC 36, 117**
See also AMWS 11; CA 114; 122; CANR 77; CN 7; CSW; DLB 244; DLBY 1985; EWL 3; INT CA-122
Barthes, Roland (Gerard) 1915-1980 .... **CLC 24, 83; TCLC 135**
See also CA 130; 97-100; CANR 66; DLB 296; EW 13; EWL 3; GFL 1789 to the Present; MTCW 1, 2; TWA
Bartram, William 1739-1823 .... **NCLC 145**
See also ANW; DLB 37
Barzun, Jacques (Martin) 1907- .... **CLC 51, 145**
See also CA 61-64; CANR 22, 95
Bashevis, Isaac
See Singer, Isaac Bashevis
Bashkirtseff, Marie 1859-1884 .... **NCLC 27**
Basho, Matsuo
See Matsuo Basho
See also PFS 18; RGWL 2, 3; WP
Basil of Caesaria c. 330-379 .... **CMLC 35**
Basket, Raney
See Edgerton, Clyde (Carlyle)
Bass, Kingsley B., Jr.
See Bullins, Ed
Bass, Rick 1958- .... **CLC 79, 143; SSC 60**
See also ANW; CA 126; CANR 53, 93; CSW; DLB 212, 275
Bassani, Giorgio 1916-2000 .... **CLC 9**
See also CA 65-68; 190; CANR 33; CWW 2; DLB 128, 177, 299; EWL 3; MTCW 1; RGWL 2, 3
Bastian, Ann .... **CLC 70**
Bastos, Augusto (Antonio) Roa
See Roa Bastos, Augusto (Antonio)
Bataille, Georges 1897-1962 .... **CLC 29; TCLC 155**
See also CA 101; 89-92; EWL 3
Bates, H(erbert) E(rnest) 1905-1974 .... **CLC 46; SSC 10**
See also CA 93-96; 45-48; CANR 34; DA3; DAB; DAM POP; DLB 162, 191; EWL 3; EXPS; MTCW 1, 2; RGSF 2; SSFS 7
Bauchart
See Camus, Albert
Baudelaire, Charles 1821-1867 . **NCLC 6, 29, 55, 155; PC 1; SSC 18; WLC**
See also DA; DA3; DAB; DAC; DAM MST, POET; DLB 217; EW 7; GFL 1789 to the Present; LMFS 2; PFS 21; RGWL 2, 3; TWA
Baudouin, Marcel
See Peguy, Charles (Pierre)
Baudouin, Pierre
See Peguy, Charles (Pierre)
Baudrillard, Jean 1929- .... **CLC 60**
See also DLB 296
Baum, L(yman) Frank 1856-1919 .. **TCLC 7, 132**
See also AAYA 46; BYA 16; CA 108; 133; CLR 15; CWRI 5; DLB 22; FANT; JRDA; MAICYA 1, 2; MTCW 1, 2; NFS 13; RGAL 4; SATA 18, 100; WCH
Baum, Louis F.
See Baum, L(yman) Frank

Baumbach, Jonathan 1933- .... **CLC 6, 23**
See also CA 13-16R; CAAS 5; CANR 12, 66; CN 7; DLBY 1980; INT CANR-12; MTCW 1

Bausch, Richard (Carl) 1945- .... **CLC 51**
See also AMWS 7; CA 101; CAAS 14; CANR 43, 61, 87; CSW; DLB 130

Baxter, Charles (Morley) 1947- . **CLC 45, 78**
See also CA 57-60; CANR 40, 64, 104, 133; CPW; DAM POP; DLB 130; MTCW 2

Baxter, George Owen
See Faust, Frederick (Schiller)

Baxter, James K(eir) 1926-1972 .... **CLC 14**
See also CA 77-80; EWL 3

Baxter, John
See Hunt, E(verette) Howard, (Jr.)

Bayer, Sylvia
See Glassco, John

Baynton, Barbara 1857-1929 .... **TCLC 57**
See also DLB 230; RGSF 2

Beagle, Peter S(oyer) 1939- .... **CLC 7, 104**
See also AAYA 47; BPFB 1; BYA 9, 10, 16; CA 9-12R; CANR 4, 51, 73, 110; DA3; DLBY 1980; FANT; INT CANR-4; MTCW 1; SATA 60, 130; SUFW 1, 2; YAW

Bean, Normal
See Burroughs, Edgar Rice

Beard, Charles A(ustin)
1874-1948 .... **TCLC 15**
See also CA 115; 189; DLB 17; SATA 18

Beardsley, Aubrey 1872-1898 .... **NCLC 6**

Beattie, Ann 1947- ..... **CLC 8, 13, 18, 40, 63, 146; SSC 11**
See also AMWS 5; BEST 90:2; BPFB 1; CA 81-84; CANR 53, 73, 128; CN 7; CPW; DA3; DAM NOV, POP; DLB 218, 278; DLBY 1982; EWL 3; MTCW 1, 2; RGAL 4; RGSF 2; SSFS 9; TUS

Beattie, James 1735-1803 .... **NCLC 25**
See also DLB 109

Beauchamp, Kathleen Mansfield 1888-1923
See Mansfield, Katherine
See also CA 104; 134; DA; DA3; DAC; DAM MST; MTCW 2; TEA

Beaumarchais, Pierre-Augustin Caron de
1732-1799 .... **DC 4; LC 61**
See also DAM DRAM; DFS 14, 16; EW 4; GFL Beginnings to 1789; RGWL 2, 3

Beaumont, Francis 1584(?)-1616 .. **DC 6; LC 33**
See also BRW 2; CDBLB Before 1660; DLB 58; TEA

Beauvoir, Simone (Lucie Ernestine Marie Bertrand) de 1908-1986 .... **CLC 1, 2, 4, 8, 14, 31, 44, 50, 71, 124; SSC 35; WLC**
See also BPFB 1; CA 9-12R; 118; CANR 28, 61; DA; DA3; DAB; DAC; DAM MST, NOV; DLB 72; DLBY 1986; EW 12; EWL 3; FW; GFL 1789 to the Present; LMFS 2; MTCW 1, 2; RGSF 2; RGWL 2, 3; TWA

Becker, Carl (Lotus) 1873-1945 ..... **TCLC 63**
See also CA 157; DLB 17

Becker, Jurek 1937-1997 .... **CLC 7, 19**
See also CA 85-88; 157; CANR 60, 117; CWW 2; DLB 75, 299; EWL 3

Becker, Walter 1950- .... **CLC 26**

Beckett, Samuel (Barclay)
1906-1989 .. **CLC 1, 2, 3, 4, 6, 9, 10, 11, 14, 18, 29, 57, 59, 83; DC 22; SSC 16, 74; TCLC 145; WLC**
See also BRWC 2; BRWR 1; BRWS 1; CA 5-8R; 130; CANR 33, 61; CBD; CDBLB 1945-1960; DA; DA3; DAB; DAC; DAM DRAM, MST, NOV; DFS 2, 7, 18; DLB 13, 15, 233; DLBY 1990; EWL 3; GFL 1789 to the Present; LATS 1:2; LMFS 2; MTCW 1, 2; RGSF 2; RGWL 2, 3; SSFS 15; TEA; WLIT 4

Beckford, William 1760-1844 .... **NCLC 16**
See also BRW 3; DLB 39, 213; HGG; LMFS 1; SUFW

Beckham, Barry (Earl) 1944- .... **BLC 1**
See also BW 1; CA 29-32R; CANR 26, 62; CN 7; DAM MULT; DLB 33

Beckman, Gunnel 1910- .... **CLC 26**
See also CA 33-36R; CANR 15, 114; CLR 25; MAICYA 1, 2; SAAS 9; SATA 6

Becque, Henri 1837-1899 .... **DC 21; NCLC 3**
See also DLB 192; GFL 1789 to the Present

Becquer, Gustavo Adolfo
1836-1870 .... **HLCS 1; NCLC 106**
See also DAM MULT

Beddoes, Thomas Lovell 1803-1849 .. **DC 15; NCLC 3, 154**
See also DLB 96

Bede c. 673-735 .... **CMLC 20**
See also DLB 146; TEA

Bedford, Denton R. 1907-(?) .... **NNAL**

Bedford, Donald F.
See Fearing, Kenneth (Flexner)

Beecher, Catharine Esther
1800-1878 .... **NCLC 30**
See also DLB 1, 243

Beecher, John 1904-1980 .... **CLC 6**
See also AITN 1; CA 5-8R; 105; CANR 8

Beer, Johann 1655-1700 .... **LC 5**
See also DLB 168

Beer, Patricia 1924- .... **CLC 58**
See also CA 61-64; 183; CANR 13, 46; CP 7; CWP; DLB 40; FW

Beerbohm, Max
See Beerbohm, (Henry) Max(imilian)

Beerbohm, (Henry) Max(imilian)
1872-1956 .... **TCLC 1, 24**
See also BRWS 2; CA 104; 154; CANR 79; DLB 34, 100; FANT

Beer-Hofmann, Richard
1866-1945 .... **TCLC 60**
See also CA 160; DLB 81

Beg, Shemus
See Stephens, James

Begiebing, Robert J(ohn) 1946- .... **CLC 70**
See also CA 122; CANR 40, 88

Begley, Louis 1933- .... **CLC 197**
See also CA 140; CANR 98; DLB 299

Behan, Brendan (Francis)
1923-1964 .... **CLC 1, 8, 11, 15, 79**
See also BRWS 2; CA 73-76; CANR 33, 121; CBD; CDBLB 1945-1960; DAM DRAM; DFS 7; DLB 13, 233; EWL 3; MTCW 1, 2

Behn, Aphra 1640(?)-1689 .. **DC 4; LC 1, 30, 42; PC 13; WLC**
See also BRWS 3; DA; DA3; DAB; DAC; DAM DRAM, MST, NOV, POET; DFS 16; DLB 39, 80, 131; FW; TEA; WLIT 3

Behrman, S(amuel) N(athaniel)
1893-1973 .... **CLC 40**
See also CA 13-16; 45-48; CAD; CAP 1; DLB 7, 44; IDFW 3; RGAL 4

Belasco, David 1853-1931 .... **TCLC 3**
See also CA 104; 168; DLB 7; RGAL 4

Belcheva, Elisaveta Lyubomirova
1893-1991 .... **CLC 10**
See Bagryana, Elisaveta

Beldone, Phil ''Cheech''
See Ellison, Harlan (Jay)

Beleno
See Azuela, Mariano

Belinski, Vissarion Grigoryevich
1811-1848 .... **NCLC 5**
See also DLB 198

Belitt, Ben 1911- .... **CLC 22**
See also CA 13-16R; CAAS 4; CANR 7, 77; CP 7; DLB 5

Belknap, Jeremy 1744-1798 .... **LC 115**
See also DLB 30, 37

Bell, Gertrude (Margaret Lowthian)
1868-1926 .... **TCLC 67**
See also CA 167; CANR 110; DLB 174

Bell, J. Freeman
See Zangwill, Israel

Bell, James Madison 1826-1902 .... **BLC 1; TCLC 43**
See also BW 1; CA 122; 124; DAM MULT; DLB 50

Bell, Madison Smartt 1957- ...... **CLC 41, 102**
See also AMWS 10; BPFB 1; CA 111, 183; CAAE 183; CANR 28, 54, 73, 134; CN 7; CSW; DLB 218, 278; MTCW 1

Bell, Marvin (Hartley) 1937- .... **CLC 8, 31**
See also CA 21-24R; CAAS 14; CANR 59, 102; CP 7; DAM POET; DLB 5; MTCW 1

Bell, W. L. D.
See Mencken, H(enry) L(ouis)

Bellamy, Atwood C.
See Mencken, H(enry) L(ouis)

Bellamy, Edward 1850-1898 ..... **NCLC 4, 86, 147**
See also DLB 12; NFS 15; RGAL 4; SFW 4

Belli, Gioconda 1948- .... **HLCS 1**
See also CA 152; CWW 2; DLB 290; EWL 3; RGWL 3

Bellin, Edward J.
See Kuttner, Henry

Bello, Andres 1781-1865 .... **NCLC 131**
See also LAW

Belloc, (Joseph) Hilaire (Pierre Sebastien Rene Swanton) 1870-1953 .... **PC 24; TCLC 7, 18**
See also CA 106; 152; CLR 102; CWRI 5; DAM POET; DLB 19, 100, 141, 174; EWL 3; MTCW 1; SATA 112; WCH; YABC 1

Belloc, Joseph Peter Rene Hilaire
See Belloc, (Joseph) Hilaire (Pierre Sebastien Rene Swanton)

Belloc, Joseph Pierre Hilaire
See Belloc, (Joseph) Hilaire (Pierre Sebastien Rene Swanton)

Belloc, M. A.
See Lowndes, Marie Adelaide (Belloc)

Belloc-Lowndes, Mrs.
See Lowndes, Marie Adelaide (Belloc)

Bellow, Saul 1915- . **CLC 1, 2, 3, 6, 8, 10, 13, 15, 25, 33, 34, 63, 79, 190, 200; SSC 14; WLC**
See also AITN 2; AMW; AMWC 2; AMWR 2; BEST 89:3; BPFB 1; CA 5-8R; CABS 1; CANR 29, 53, 95, 132; CDALB 1941-1968; CN 7; DA; DA3; DAB; DAC; DAM MST, NOV, POP; DLB 2, 28, 299; DLBD 3; DLBY 1982; EWL 3; MTCW 1, 2; NFS 4, 14; RGAL 4; RGSF 2; SSFS 12; TUS

Belser, Reimond Karel Maria de 1929-
See Ruyslinck, Ward
See also CA 152

Bely, Andrey .... **PC 11; TCLC 7**
See Bugayev, Boris Nikolayevich
See also DLB 295; EW 9; EWL 3; MTCW 1

Belyi, Andrei
See Bugayev, Boris Nikolayevich
See also RGWL 2, 3

Bembo, Pietro 1470-1547 .... **LC 79**
See also RGWL 2, 3

Benary, Margot
See Benary-Isbert, Margot

Blom, Jan
See Breytenbach, Breyten

Bloom, Harold 1930- .... **CLC 24, 103**
See also CA 13-16R; CANR 39, 75, 92, 133; DLB 67; EWL 3; MTCW 1; RGAL 4

Bloomfield, Aurelius
See Bourne, Randolph S(illiman)

Bloomfield, Robert 1766-1823 ..... **NCLC 145**
See also DLB 93

Blount, Roy (Alton), Jr. 1941- .... **CLC 38**
See also CA 53-56; CANR 10, 28, 61, 125; CSW; INT CANR-28; MTCW 1, 2

Blowsnake, Sam 1875-(?) .... **NNAL**

Bloy, Leon 1846-1917 .... **TCLC 22**
See also CA 121; 183; DLB 123; GFL 1789 to the Present

Blue Cloud, Peter (Aroniawenrate)
1933- .... **NNAL**
See also CA 117; CANR 40; DAM MULT

Bluggage, Oranthy
See Alcott, Louisa May

Blume, Judy (Sussman) 1938- .... **CLC 12, 30**
See also AAYA 3, 26; BYA 1, 8, 12; CA 29-32R; CANR 13, 37, 66, 124; CLR 2, 15, 69; CPW; DA3; DAM NOV, POP; DLB 52; JRDA; MAICYA 1, 2; MAICYAS 1; MTCW 1, 2; SATA 2, 31, 79, 142; WYA; YAW

Blunden, Edmund (Charles)
1896-1974 .... **CLC 2, 56; PC 66**
See also BRW 6; CA 17-18; 45-48; CANR 54; CAP 2; DLB 20, 100, 155; MTCW 1; PAB

Bly, Robert (Elwood) 1926- .... **CLC 1, 2, 5, 10, 15, 38, 128; PC 39**
See also AMWS 4; CA 5-8R; CANR 41, 73, 125; CP 7; DA3; DAM POET; DLB 5; EWL 3; MTCW 1, 2; PFS 6, 17; RGAL 4

Boas, Franz 1858-1942 .... **TCLC 56**
See also CA 115; 181

Bobette
See Simenon, Georges (Jacques Christian)

Boccaccio, Giovanni 1313-1375 ... **CMLC 13, 57; SSC 10**
See also EW 2; RGSF 2; RGWL 2, 3; TWA

Bochco, Steven 1943- .... **CLC 35**
See also AAYA 11; CA 124; 138

Bode, Sigmund
See O'Doherty, Brian

Bodel, Jean 1167(?)-1210 .... **CMLC 28**

Bodenheim, Maxwell 1892-1954 .... **TCLC 44**
See also CA 110; 187; DLB 9, 45; RGAL 4

Bodenheimer, Maxwell
See Bodenheim, Maxwell

Bodker, Cecil 1927-
See Bodker, Cecil

Bodker, Cecil 1927- .... **CLC 21**
See also CA 73-76; CANR 13, 44, 111; CLR 23; MAICYA 1, 2; SATA 14, 133

Boell, Heinrich (Theodor)
1917-1985 ..... **CLC 2, 3, 6, 9, 11, 15, 27, 32, 72; SSC 23; WLC**
See Boll, Heinrich
See also CA 21-24R; 116; CANR 24; DA; DA3; DAB; DAC; DAM MST, NOV; DLB 69; DLBY 1985; MTCW 1, 2; SSFS 20; TWA

Boerne, Alfred
See Doeblin, Alfred

Boethius c. 480-c. 524 .... **CMLC 15**
See also DLB 115; RGWL 2, 3

Boff, Leonardo (Genezio Darci)
1938- .... **CLC 70; HLC 1**
See also CA 150; DAM MULT; HW 2

Bogan, Louise 1897-1970 .... **CLC 4, 39, 46, 93; PC 12**
See also AMWS 3; CA 73-76; 25-28R; CANR 33, 82; DAM POET; DLB 45, 169; EWL 3; MAWW; MTCW 1, 2; PFS 21; RGAL 4

Bogarde, Dirk
See Van Den Bogarde, Derek Jules Gaspard Ulric Niven
See also DLB 14

Bogosian, Eric 1953- .... **CLC 45, 141**
See also CA 138; CAD; CANR 102; CD 5

Bograd, Larry 1953- .... **CLC 35**
See also CA 93-96; CANR 57; SAAS 21; SATA 33, 89; WYA

Boiardo, Matteo Maria 1441-1494 .... **LC 6**

Boileau-Despreaux, Nicolas 1636-1711 . **LC 3**
See also DLB 268; EW 3; GFL Beginnings to 1789; RGWL 2, 3

Boissard, Maurice
See Leautaud, Paul

Bojer, Johan 1872-1959 .... **TCLC 64**
See also CA 189; EWL 3

Bok, Edward W(illiam)
1863-1930 .... **TCLC 101**
See also CA 217; DLB 91; DLBD 16

Boker, George Henry 1823-1890 . **NCLC 125**
See also RGAL 4

Boland, Eavan (Aisling) 1944- .. **CLC 40, 67, 113; PC 58**
See also BRWS 5; CA 143, 207; CAAE 207; CANR 61; CP 7; CWP; DAM POET; DLB 40; FW; MTCW 2; PFS 12

Boll, Heinrich
See Boell, Heinrich (Theodor)
See also BPFB 1; CDWLB 2; EW 13; EWL 3; RGSF 2; RGWL 2, 3

Bolt, Lee
See Faust, Frederick (Schiller)

Bolt, Robert (Oxton) 1924-1995 .... **CLC 14**
See also CA 17-20R; 147; CANR 35, 67; CBD; DAM DRAM; DFS 2; DLB 13, 233; EWL 3; LAIT 1; MTCW 1

Bombal, Maria Luisa 1910-1980 .... **HLCS 1; SSC 37**
See also CA 127; CANR 72; EWL 3; HW 1; LAW; RGSF 2

Bombet, Louis-Alexandre-Cesar
See Stendhal

Bomkauf
See Kaufman, Bob (Garnell)

Bonaventura .... **NCLC 35**
See also DLB 90

Bonaventure, Saint c. 1217-1274 .. **CMLC 79**
See also DLB 115

Bond, Edward 1934- .... **CLC 4, 6, 13, 23**
See also AAYA 50; BRWS 1; CA 25-28R; CANR 38, 67, 106; CBD; CD 5; DAM DRAM; DFS 3, 8; DLB 13; EWL 3; MTCW 1

Bonham, Frank 1914-1989 .... **CLC 12**
See also AAYA 1; BYA 1, 3; CA 9-12R; CANR 4, 36; JRDA; MAICYA 1, 2; SAAS 3; SATA 1, 49; SATA-Obit 62; TCWW 2; YAW

Bonnefoy, Yves 1923- . **CLC 9, 15, 58; PC 58**
See also CA 85-88; CANR 33, 75, 97; CWW 2; DAM MST, POET; DLB 258; EWL 3; GFL 1789 to the Present; MTCW 1, 2

Bonner, Marita .... **HR 2**
See Occomy, Marita (Odette) Bonner

Bonnin, Gertrude 1876-1938 .... **NNAL**
See Zitkala-Sa
See also CA 150; DAM MULT

Bontemps, Arna(ud Wendell)
1902-1973 ..... **BLC 1; CLC 1, 18; HR 2**
See also BW 1; CA 1-4R; 41-44R; CANR 4, 35; CLR 6; CWRI 5; DA3; DAM MULT, NOV, POET; DLB 48, 51; JRDA; MAICYA 1, 2; MTCW 1, 2; SATA 2, 44; SATA-Obit 24; WCH; WP

Boot, William
See Stoppard, Tom

Booth, Martin 1944-2004 .... **CLC 13**
See also CA 93-96, 188; 223; CAAE 188; CAAS 2; CANR 92

Booth, Philip 1925- .... **CLC 23**
See also CA 5-8R; CANR 5, 88; CP 7; DLBY 1982

Booth, Wayne C(layson) 1921- .... **CLC 24**
See also CA 1-4R; CAAS 5; CANR 3, 43, 117; DLB 67

Borchert, Wolfgang 1921-1947 .... **TCLC 5**
See also CA 104; 188; DLB 69, 124; EWL 3

Borel, Petrus 1809-1859 .... **NCLC 41**
See also DLB 119; GFL 1789 to the Present

Borges, Jorge Luis 1899-1986 ... **CLC 1, 2, 3, 4, 6, 8, 9, 10, 13, 19, 44, 48, 83; HLC 1; PC 22, 32; SSC 4, 41; TCLC 109; WLC**
See also AAYA 26; BPFB 1; CA 21-24R; CANR 19, 33, 75, 105, 133; CDWLB 3; DA; DA3; DAB; DAC; DAM MST, MULT; DLB 113, 283; DLBY 1986; DNFS 1, 2; EWL 3; HW 1, 2; LAW; LMFS 2; MSW; MTCW 1, 2; RGSF 2; RGWL 2, 3; SFW 4; SSFS 17; TWA; WLIT 1

Borowski, Tadeusz 1922-1951 .... **SSC 48; TCLC 9**
See also CA 106; 154; CDWLB 4; DLB 215; EWL 3; RGSF 2; RGWL 3; SSFS 13

Borrow, George (Henry)
1803-1881 .... **NCLC 9**
See also DLB 21, 55, 166

Bosch (Gavino), Juan 1909-2001 ..... **HLCS 1**
See also CA 151; 204; DAM MST, MULT; DLB 145; HW 1, 2

Bosman, Herman Charles
1905-1951 .... **TCLC 49**
See Malan, Herman
See also CA 160; DLB 225; RGSF 2

Bosschere, Jean de 1878(?)-1953 ... **TCLC 19**
See also CA 115; 186

Boswell, James 1740-1795 ... **LC 4, 50; WLC**
See also BRW 3; CDBLB 1660-1789; DA; DAB; DAC; DAM MST; DLB 104, 142; TEA; WLIT 3

Bottomley, Gordon 1874-1948 ..... **TCLC 107**
See also CA 120; 192; DLB 10

Bottoms, David 1949- .... **CLC 53**
See also CA 105; CANR 22; CSW; DLB 120; DLBY 1983

Boucicault, Dion 1820-1890 .... **NCLC 41**

Boucolon, Maryse
See Conde, Maryse

Bourdieu, Pierre 1930-2002 .... **CLC 198**
See also CA 130; 204

Bourget, Paul (Charles Joseph)
1852-1935 .... **TCLC 12**
See also CA 107; 196; DLB 123; GFL 1789 to the Present

Bourjaily, Vance (Nye) 1922- .... **CLC 8, 62**
See also CA 1-4R; CAAS 1; CANR 2, 72; CN 7; DLB 2, 143

Bourne, Randolph S(illiman)
1886-1918 .... **TCLC 16**
See also AMW; CA 117; 155; DLB 63

Bova, Ben(jamin William) 1932- ...... **CLC 45**
See also AAYA 16; CA 5-8R; CAAS 18; CANR 11, 56, 94, 111; CLR 3, 96; DLBY 1981; INT CANR-11; MAICYA 1, 2; MTCW 1; SATA 6, 68, 133; SFW 4

Bowen, Elizabeth (Dorothea Cole) 1899-1973 . **CLC 1, 3, 6, 11, 15, 22, 118; SSC 3, 28, 66; TCLC 148**
See also BRWS 2; CA 17-18; 41-44R; CANR 35, 105; CAP 2; CDBLB 1945-1960; DA3; DAM NOV; DLB 15, 162; EWL 3; EXPS; FW; HGG; MTCW 1, 2; NFS 13; RGSF 2; SSFS 5; SUFW 1; TEA; WLIT 4

Bowering, George 1935- .... **CLC 15, 47**
See also CA 21-24R; CAAS 16; CANR 10; CP 7; DLB 53

Bowering, Marilyn R(uthe) 1949- .... **CLC 32**
See also CA 101; CANR 49; CP 7; CWP

Bowers, Edgar 1924-2000 .... **CLC 9**
See also CA 5-8R; 188; CANR 24; CP 7; CSW; DLB 5

Bowers, Mrs. J. Milton 1842-1914
See Bierce, Ambrose (Gwinett)

Bowie, David .... **CLC 17**
See Jones, David Robert

Bowles, Jane (Sydney) 1917-1973 ..... **CLC 3, 68**
See Bowles, Jane Auer
See also CA 19-20; 41-44R; CAP 2

Bowles, Jane Auer
See Bowles, Jane (Sydney)
See also EWL 3

Bowles, Paul (Frederick) 1910-1999 . **CLC 1, 2, 19, 53; SSC 3**
See also AMWS 4; CA 1-4R; 186; CAAS 1; CANR 1, 19, 50, 75; CN 7; DA3; DLB 5, 6, 218; EWL 3; MTCW 1, 2; RGAL 4; SSFS 17

Bowles, William Lisle 1762-1850 . **NCLC 103**
See also DLB 93

Box, Edgar
See Vidal, (Eugene Luther) Gore
See also GLL 1

Boyd, James 1888-1944 .... **TCLC 115**
See also CA 186; DLB 9; DLBD 16; RGAL 4; RHW

Boyd, Nancy
See Millay, Edna St. Vincent
See also GLL 1

Boyd, Thomas (Alexander) 1898-1935 .... **TCLC 111**
See also CA 111; 183; DLB 9; DLBD 16

Boyd, William 1952- .... **CLC 28, 53, 70**
See also CA 114; 120; CANR 51, 71, 131; CN 7; DLB 231

Boyesen, Hjalmar Hjorth 1848-1895 .... **NCLC 135**
See also DLB 12, 71; DLBD 13; RGAL 4

Boyle, Kay 1902-1992 .... **CLC 1, 5, 19, 58, 121; SSC 5**
See also CA 13-16R; 140; CAAS 1; CANR 29, 61, 110; DLB 4, 9, 48, 86; DLBY 1993; EWL 3; MTCW 1, 2; RGAL 4; RGSF 2; SSFS 10, 13, 14

Boyle, Mark
See Kienzle, William X(avier)

Boyle, Patrick 1905-1982 .... **CLC 19**
See also CA 127

Boyle, T. C.
See Boyle, T(homas) Coraghessan
See also AMWS 8

Boyle, T(homas) Coraghessan 1948- .... **CLC 36, 55, 90; SSC 16**
See Boyle, T. C.
See also AAYA 47; BEST 90:4; BPFB 1; CA 120; CANR 44, 76, 89, 132; CN 7; CPW; DA3; DAM POP; DLB 218, 278; DLBY 1986; EWL 3; MTCW 2; SSFS 13, 19

Boz
See Dickens, Charles (John Huffam)

Brackenridge, Hugh Henry 1748-1816 .... **NCLC 7**
See also DLB 11, 37; RGAL 4

Bradbury, Edward P.
See Moorcock, Michael (John)
See also MTCW 2

Bradbury, Malcolm (Stanley) 1932-2000 .... **CLC 32, 61**
See also CA 1-4R; CANR 1, 33, 91, 98; CN 7; DA3; DAM NOV; DLB 14, 207; EWL 3; MTCW 1, 2

Bradbury, Ray (Douglas) 1920- .... **CLC 1, 3, 10, 15, 42, 98; SSC 29, 53; WLC**
See also AAYA 15; AITN 1, 2; AMWS 4; BPFB 1; BYA 4, 5, 11; CA 1-4R; CANR 2, 30, 75, 125; CDALB 1968-1988; CN 7; CPW; DA; DA3; DAB; DAC; DAM MST, NOV, POP; DLB 2, 8; EXPN; EXPS; HGG; LAIT 3, 5; LATS 1:2; LMFS 2; MTCW 1, 2; NFS 1; RGAL 4; RGSF 2; SATA 11, 64, 123; SCFW 2; SFW 4; SSFS 1, 20; SUFW 1, 2; TUS; YAW

Braddon, Mary Elizabeth 1837-1915 .... **TCLC 111**
See also BRWS 8; CA 108; 179; CMW 4; DLB 18, 70, 156; HGG

Bradfield, Scott (Michael) 1955- .... **SSC 65**
See also CA 147; CANR 90; HGG; SUFW 2

Bradford, Gamaliel 1863-1932 .... **TCLC 36**
See also CA 160; DLB 17

Bradford, William 1590-1657 .... **LC 64**
See also DLB 24, 30; RGAL 4

Bradley, David (Henry), Jr. 1950- .... **BLC 1; CLC 23, 118**
See also BW 1, 3; CA 104; CANR 26, 81; CN 7; DAM MULT; DLB 33

Bradley, John Ed(mund, Jr.) 1958- . **CLC 55**
See also CA 139; CANR 99; CN 7; CSW

Bradley, Marion Zimmer 1930-1999 .... **CLC 30**
See Chapman, Lee; Dexter, John; Gardner, Miriam; Ives, Morgan; Rivers, Elfrida
See also AAYA 40; BPFB 1; CA 57-60; 185; CAAS 10; CANR 7, 31, 51, 75, 107; CPW; DA3; DAM POP; DLB 8; FANT; FW; MTCW 1, 2; SATA 90, 139; SATA-Obit 116; SFW 4; SUFW 2; YAW

Bradshaw, John 1933- .... **CLC 70**
See also CA 138; CANR 61

Bradstreet, Anne 1612(?)-1672 ...... **LC 4, 30; PC 10**
See also AMWS 1; CDALB 1640-1865; DA; DA3; DAC; DAM MST, POET; DLB 24; EXPP; FW; PFS 6; RGAL 4; TUS; WP

Brady, Joan 1939- .... **CLC 86**
See also CA 141

Bragg, Melvyn 1939- .... **CLC 10**
See also BEST 89:3; CA 57-60; CANR 10, 48, 89; CN 7; DLB 14, 271; RHW

Brahe, Tycho 1546-1601 .... **LC 45**
See also DLB 300

Braine, John (Gerard) 1922-1986 . **CLC 1, 3, 41**
See also CA 1-4R; 120; CANR 1, 33; CDBLB 1945-1960; DLB 15; DLBY 1986; EWL 3; MTCW 1

Braithwaite, William Stanley (Beaumont) 1878-1962 .... **BLC 1; HR 2; PC 52**
See also BW 1; CA 125; DAM MULT; DLB 50, 54

Bramah, Ernest 1868-1942 .... **TCLC 72**
See also CA 156; CMW 4; DLB 70; FANT

Brammer, William 1930(?)-1978 ...... **CLC 31**
See also CA 77-80

Brancati, Vitaliano 1907-1954 .... **TCLC 12**
See also CA 109; DLB 264; EWL 3

Brancato, Robin F(idler) 1936- .... **CLC 35**
See also AAYA 9; BYA 6; CA 69-72; CANR 11, 45; CLR 32; JRDA; MAICYA 2; MAICYAS 1; SAAS 9; SATA 97; WYA; YAW

Brand, Dionne 1953- .... **CLC 192**
See also BW 2; CA 143; CWP

Brand, Max
See Faust, Frederick (Schiller)
See also BPFB 1; TCWW 2

Brand, Millen 1906-1980 .... **CLC 7**
See also CA 21-24R; 97-100; CANR 72

Branden, Barbara .... **CLC 44**
See also CA 148

Brandes, Georg (Morris Cohen) 1842-1927 .... **TCLC 10**
See also CA 105; 189; DLB 300

Brandys, Kazimierz 1916-2000 .... **CLC 62**
See also EWL 3

Branley, Franklyn M(ansfield) 1915-2002 .... **CLC 21**
See also CA 33-36R; 207; CANR 14, 39; CLR 13; MAICYA 1, 2; SAAS 16; SATA 4, 68, 136

Brant, Beth (E.) 1941- .... **NNAL**
See also CA 144; FW

Brant, Sebastian 1457-1521 .... **LC 112**
See also DLB 179; RGWL 2, 3

Brathwaite, Edward Kamau 1930- .... **BLCS; CLC 11; PC 56**
See also BW 2, 3; CA 25-28R; CANR 11, 26, 47, 107; CDWLB 3; CP 7; DAM POET; DLB 125; EWL 3

Brathwaite, Kamau
See Brathwaite, Edward Kamau

Brautigan, Richard (Gary) 1935-1984 .... **CLC 1, 3, 5, 9, 12, 34, 42; TCLC 133**
See also BPFB 1; CA 53-56; 113; CANR 34; DA3; DAM NOV; DLB 2, 5, 206; DLBY 1980, 1984; FANT; MTCW 1; RGAL 4; SATA 56

Brave Bird, Mary .... **NNAL**
See Crow Dog, Mary (Ellen)

Braverman, Kate 1950- .... **CLC 67**
See also CA 89-92

Brecht, (Eugen) Bertolt (Friedrich) 1898-1956 ..... **DC 3; TCLC 1, 6, 13, 35, 169; WLC**
See also CA 104; 133; CANR 62; CDWLB 2; DA; DA3; DAB; DAC; DAM DRAM, MST; DFS 4, 5, 9; DLB 56, 124; EW 11; EWL 3; IDTP; MTCW 1, 2; RGWL 2, 3; TWA

Brecht, Eugen Berthold Friedrich
See Brecht, (Eugen) Bertolt (Friedrich)

Bremer, Fredrika 1801-1865 .... **NCLC 11**
See also DLB 254

Brennan, Christopher John 1870-1932 .... **TCLC 17**
See also CA 117; 188; DLB 230; EWL 3

Brennan, Maeve 1917-1993 ... **CLC 5; TCLC 124**
See also CA 81-84; CANR 72, 100

Brent, Linda
See Jacobs, Harriet A(nn)

Brentano, Clemens (Maria) 1778-1842 .... **NCLC 1**
See also DLB 90; RGWL 2, 3

Brent of Bin Bin
See Franklin, (Stella Maria Sarah) Miles (Lampe)

Brenton, Howard 1942- .... **CLC 31**
See also CA 69-72; CANR 33, 67; CBD; CD 5; DLB 13; MTCW 1

Breslin, James 1930-
See Breslin, Jimmy
See also CA 73-76; CANR 31, 75; DAM NOV; MTCW 1, 2

Breslin, Jimmy .... **CLC 4, 43**
See Breslin, James
See also AITN 1; DLB 185; MTCW 2
Bresson, Robert 1901(?)-1999 .... **CLC 16**
See also CA 110; 187; CANR 49
Breton, Andre 1896-1966 .. **CLC 2, 9, 15, 54; PC 15**
See also CA 19-20; 25-28R; CANR 40, 60; CAP 2; DLB 65, 258; EW 11; EWL 3; GFL 1789 to the Present; LMFS 2; MTCW 1, 2; RGWL 2, 3; TWA; WP
Breytenbach, Breyten 1939(?)- .. **CLC 23, 37, 126**
See also CA 113; 129; CANR 61, 122; CWW 2; DAM POET; DLB 225; EWL 3
Bridgers, Sue Ellen 1942- .... **CLC 26**
See also AAYA 8, 49; BYA 7, 8; CA 65-68; CANR 11, 36; CLR 18; DLB 52; JRDA; MAICYA 1, 2; SAAS 1; SATA 22, 90; SATA-Essay 109; WYA; YAW
Bridges, Robert (Seymour) 1844-1930 .... **PC 28; TCLC 1**
See also BRW 6; CA 104; 152; CDBLB 1890-1914; DAM POET; DLB 19, 98
Bridie, James .... **TCLC 3**
See Mavor, Osborne Henry
See also DLB 10; EWL 3
Brin, David 1950- .... **CLC 34**
See also AAYA 21; CA 102; CANR 24, 70, 125, 127; INT CANR-24; SATA 65; SCFW 2; SFW 4
Brink, Andre (Philippus) 1935- . **CLC 18, 36, 106**
See also AFW; BRWS 6; CA 104; CANR 39, 62, 109, 133; CN 7; DLB 225; EWL 3; INT CA-103; LATS 1:2; MTCW 1, 2; WLIT 2
Brinsmead, H. F(ay)
See Brinsmead, H(esba) F(ay)
Brinsmead, H. F.
See Brinsmead, H(esba) F(ay)
Brinsmead, H(esba) F(ay) 1922- ...... **CLC 21**
See also CA 21-24R; CANR 10; CLR 47; CWRI 5; MAICYA 1, 2; SAAS 5; SATA 18, 78
Brittain, Vera (Mary) 1893(?)-1970 . **CLC 23**
See also BRWS 10; CA 13-16; 25-28R; CANR 58; CAP 1; DLB 191; FW; MTCW 1, 2
Broch, Hermann 1886-1951 .... **TCLC 20**
See also CA 117; 211; CDWLB 2; DLB 85, 124; EW 10; EWL 3; RGWL 2, 3
Brock, Rose
See Hansen, Joseph
See also GLL 1
Brod, Max 1884-1968 .... **TCLC 115**
See also CA 5-8R; 25-28R; CANR 7; DLB 81; EWL 3
Brodkey, Harold (Roy) 1930-1996 .. **CLC 56; TCLC 123**
See also CA 111; 151; CANR 71; CN 7; DLB 130
Brodsky, Iosif Alexandrovich 1940-1996
See Brodsky, Joseph
See also AITN 1; CA 41-44R; 151; CANR 37, 106; DA3; DAM POET; MTCW 1, 2; RGWL 2, 3
Brodsky, Joseph . **CLC 4, 6, 13, 36, 100; PC 9**
See Brodsky, Iosif Alexandrovich
See also AMWS 8; CWW 2; DLB 285; EWL 3; MTCW 1
Brodsky, Michael (Mark) 1948- .... **CLC 19**
See also CA 102; CANR 18, 41, 58; DLB 244
Brodzki, Bella ed. .... **CLC 65**
Brome, Richard 1590(?)-1652 .... **LC 61**
See also BRWS 10; DLB 58
Bromell, Henry 1947- .... **CLC 5**
See also CA 53-56; CANR 9, 115, 116
Bromfield, Louis (Brucker) 1896-1956 .... **TCLC 11**
See also CA 107; 155; DLB 4, 9, 86; RGAL 4; RHW
Broner, E(sther) M(asserman) 1930- .... **CLC 19**
See also CA 17-20R; CANR 8, 25, 72; CN 7; DLB 28
Bronk, William (M.) 1918-1999 .... **CLC 10**
See also CA 89-92; 177; CANR 23; CP 7; DLB 165
Bronstein, Lev Davidovich
See Trotsky, Leon
Bronte, Anne 1820-1849 ..... **NCLC 4, 71, 102**
See also BRW 5; BRWR 1; DA3; DLB 21, 199; TEA
Bronte, (Patrick) Branwell 1817-1848 .... **NCLC 109**
Bronte, Charlotte 1816-1855 ...... **NCLC 3, 8, 33, 58, 105, 155; WLC**
See also AAYA 17; BRW 5; BRWC 2; BRWR 1; BYA 2; CDBLB 1832-1890; DA; DA3; DAB; DAC; DAM MST, NOV; DLB 21, 159, 199; EXPN; LAIT 2; NFS 4; TEA; WLIT 4
Bronte, Emily (Jane) 1818-1848 ... **NCLC 16, 35; PC 8; WLC**
See also AAYA 17; BPFB 1; BRW 5; BRWC 1; BRWR 1; BYA 3; CDBLB 1832-1890; DA; DA3; DAB; DAC; DAM MST, NOV, POET; DLB 21, 32, 199; EXPN; LAIT 1; TEA; WLIT 3
Brontes
See Bronte, Anne; Bronte, Charlotte; Bronte, Emily (Jane)
Brooke, Frances 1724-1789 .... **LC 6, 48**
See also DLB 39, 99
Brooke, Henry 1703(?)-1783 .... **LC 1**
See also DLB 39
Brooke, Rupert (Chawner) 1887-1915 ..... **PC 24; TCLC 2, 7; WLC**
See also BRWS 3; CA 104; 132; CANR 61; CDBLB 1914-1945; DA; DAB; DAC; DAM MST, POET; DLB 19, 216; EXPP; GLL 2; MTCW 1, 2; PFS 7; TEA
Brooke-Haven, P.
See Wodehouse, P(elham) G(renville)
Brooke-Rose, Christine 1926(?)- ..... **CLC 40, 184**
See also BRWS 4; CA 13-16R; CANR 58, 118; CN 7; DLB 14, 231; EWL 3; SFW 4
Brookner, Anita 1928- .. **CLC 32, 34, 51, 136**
See also BRWS 4; CA 114; 120; CANR 37, 56, 87, 130; CN 7; CPW; DA3; DAB; DAM POP; DLB 194; DLBY 1987; EWL 3; MTCW 1, 2; TEA
Brooks, Cleanth 1906-1994 . **CLC 24, 86, 110**
See also AMWS 14; CA 17-20R; 145; CANR 33, 35; CSW; DLB 63; DLBY 1994; EWL 3; INT CANR-35; MTCW 1, 2
Brooks, George
See Baum, L(yman) Frank
Brooks, Gwendolyn (Elizabeth) 1917-2000 ... **BLC 1; CLC 1, 2, 4, 5, 15, 49, 125; PC 7; WLC**
See also AAYA 20; AFAW 1, 2; AITN 1; AMWS 3; BW 2, 3; CA 1-4R; 190; CANR 1, 27, 52, 75, 132; CDALB 1941-1968; CLR 27; CP 7; CWP; DA; DA3; DAC; DAM MST, MULT, POET; DLB 5, 76, 165; EWL 3; EXPP; MAWW; MTCW 1, 2; PFS 1, 2, 4, 6; RGAL 4; SATA 6; SATA-Obit 123; TUS; WP
Brooks, Mel .... **CLC 12**
See Kaminsky, Melvin
See also AAYA 13, 48; DLB 26
Brooks, Peter (Preston) 1938- .... **CLC 34**
See also CA 45-48; CANR 1, 107
Brooks, Van Wyck 1886-1963 .... **CLC 29**
See also AMW; CA 1-4R; CANR 6; DLB 45, 63, 103; TUS
Brophy, Brigid (Antonia) 1929-1995 .... **CLC 6, 11, 29, 105**
See also CA 5-8R; 149; CAAS 4; CANR 25, 53; CBD; CN 7; CWD; DA3; DLB 14, 271; EWL 3; MTCW 1, 2
Brosman, Catharine Savage 1934- ..... **CLC 9**
See also CA 61-64; CANR 21, 46
Brossard, Nicole 1943- .... **CLC 115, 169**
See also CA 122; CAAS 16; CCA 1; CWP; CWW 2; DLB 53; EWL 3; FW; GLL 2; RGWL 3
Brother Antoninus
See Everson, William (Oliver)
The Brothers Quay
See Quay, Stephen; Quay, Timothy
Broughton, T(homas) Alan 1936- ..... **CLC 19**
See also CA 45-48; CANR 2, 23, 48, 111
Broumas, Olga 1949- .... **CLC 10, 73**
See also CA 85-88; CANR 20, 69, 110; CP 7; CWP; GLL 2
Broun, Heywood 1888-1939 .... **TCLC 104**
See also DLB 29, 171
Brown, Alan 1950- .... **CLC 99**
See also CA 156
Brown, Charles Brockden 1771-1810 .... **NCLC 22, 74, 122**
See also AMWS 1; CDALB 1640-1865; DLB 37, 59, 73; FW; HGG; LMFS 1; RGAL 4; TUS
Brown, Christy 1932-1981 .... **CLC 63**
See also BYA 13; CA 105; 104; CANR 72; DLB 14
Brown, Claude 1937-2002 ... **BLC 1; CLC 30**
See also AAYA 7; BW 1, 3; CA 73-76; 205; CANR 81; DAM MULT
Brown, Dan .... **CLC 209**
See also AAYA 55; CA 217; MTFW
Brown, Dee (Alexander) 1908-2002 .... **CLC 18, 47**
See also AAYA 30; CA 13-16R; 212; CAAS 6; CANR 11, 45, 60; CPW; CSW; DA3; DAM POP; DLBY 1980; LAIT 2; MTCW 1, 2; NCFS 5; SATA 5, 110; SATA-Obit 141; TCWW 2
Brown, George
See Wertmueller, Lina
Brown, George Douglas 1869-1902 .... **TCLC 28**
See Douglas, George
See also CA 162
Brown, George Mackay 1921-1996 ... **CLC 5, 48, 100**
See also BRWS 6; CA 21-24R; 151; CAAS 6; CANR 12, 37, 67; CN 7; CP 7; DLB 14, 27, 139, 271; MTCW 1; RGSF 2; SATA 35
Brown, (William) Larry 1951-2004 . **CLC 73**
See also CA 130; 134; CANR 117; CSW; DLB 234; INT CA-134
Brown, Moses
See Barrett, William (Christopher)
Brown, Rita Mae 1944- .... **CLC 18, 43, 79**
See also BPFB 1; CA 45-48; CANR 2, 11, 35, 62, 95; CN 7; CPW; CSW; DA3; DAM NOV, POP; FW; INT CANR-11; MTCW 1, 2; NFS 9; RGAL 4; TUS
Brown, Roderick (Langmere) Haig-
See Haig-Brown, Roderick (Langmere)
Brown, Rosellen 1939- .... **CLC 32, 170**
See also CA 77-80; CAAS 10; CANR 14, 44, 98; CN 7

POET; DLB 5, 41; EXPP; MAICYA 1, 2; MTCW 1, 2; PFS 1, 14; SATA 20, 69, 128; WP

Clinton, Dirk
See Silverberg, Robert

Clough, Arthur Hugh 1819-1861 ... **NCLC 27**
See also BRW 5; DLB 32; RGEL 2

Clutha, Janet Paterson Frame 1924-2004
See Frame, Janet
See also CA 1-4R; 224; CANR 2, 36, 76, 135; MTCW 1, 2; SATA 119

Clyne, Terence
See Blatty, William Peter

Cobalt, Martin
See Mayne, William (James Carter)

Cobb, Irvin S(hrewsbury)
1876-1944 .... **TCLC 77**
See also CA 175; DLB 11, 25, 86

Cobbett, William 1763-1835 .... **NCLC 49**
See also DLB 43, 107, 158; RGEL 2

Coburn, D(onald) L(ee) 1938- .... **CLC 10**
See also CA 89-92

Cocteau, Jean (Maurice Eugene Clement)
1889-1963 ...... **CLC 1, 8, 15, 16, 43; DC 17; TCLC 119; WLC**
See also CA 25-28; CANR 40; CAP 2; DA; DA3; DAB; DAC; DAM DRAM, MST, NOV; DLB 65, 258; EW 10; EWL 3; GFL 1789 to the Present; MTCW 1, 2; RGWL 2, 3; TWA

Codrescu, Andrei 1946- .... **CLC 46, 121**
See also CA 33-36R; CAAS 19; CANR 13, 34, 53, 76, 125; DA3; DAM POET; MTCW 2

Coe, Max
See Bourne, Randolph S(illiman)

Coe, Tucker
See Westlake, Donald E(dwin)

Coen, Ethan 1958- .... **CLC 108**
See also AAYA 54; CA 126; CANR 85

Coen, Joel 1955- .... **CLC 108**
See also AAYA 54; CA 126; CANR 119

The Coen Brothers
See Coen, Ethan; Coen, Joel

Coetzee, J(ohn) M(axwell) 1940- ..... **CLC 23, 33, 66, 117, 161, 162**
See also AAYA 37; AFW; BRWS 6; CA 77-80; CANR 41, 54, 74, 114, 133; CN 7; DA3; DAM NOV; DLB 225; EWL 3; LMFS 2; MTCW 1, 2; WLIT 2; WWE 1

Coffey, Brian
See Koontz, Dean R(ay)

Coffin, Robert P(eter) Tristram
1892-1955 .... **TCLC 95**
See also CA 123; 169; DLB 45

Cohan, George M(ichael)
1878-1942 .... **TCLC 60**
See also CA 157; DLB 249; RGAL 4

Cohen, Arthur A(llen) 1928-1986 ...... **CLC 7, 31**
See also CA 1-4R; 120; CANR 1, 17, 42; DLB 28

Cohen, Leonard (Norman) 1934- ...... **CLC 3, 38**
See also CA 21-24R; CANR 14, 69; CN 7; CP 7; DAC; DAM MST; DLB 53; EWL 3; MTCW 1

Cohen, Matt(hew) 1942-1999 .... **CLC 19**
See also CA 61-64; 187; CAAS 18; CANR 40; CN 7; DAC; DLB 53

Cohen-Solal, Annie 19(?)- .... **CLC 50**

Colegate, Isabel 1931- .... **CLC 36**
See also CA 17-20R; CANR 8, 22, 74; CN 7; DLB 14, 231; INT CANR-22; MTCW 1

Coleman, Emmett
See Reed, Ishmael

Coleridge, Hartley 1796-1849 .... **NCLC 90**
See also DLB 96

Coleridge, M. E.
See Coleridge, Mary E(lizabeth)

Coleridge, Mary E(lizabeth)
1861-1907 .... **TCLC 73**
See also CA 116; 166; DLB 19, 98

Coleridge, Samuel Taylor
1772-1834 ...... **NCLC 9, 54, 99, 111; PC 11, 39, 67; WLC**
See also BRW 4; BRWR 2; BYA 4; CDBLB 1789-1832; DA; DA3; DAB; DAC; DAM MST, POET; DLB 93, 107; EXPP; LATS 1:1; LMFS 1; PAB; PFS 4, 5; RGEL 2; TEA; WLIT 3; WP

Coleridge, Sara 1802-1852 .... **NCLC 31**
See also DLB 199

Coles, Don 1928- .... **CLC 46**
See also CA 115; CANR 38; CP 7

Coles, Robert (Martin) 1929- .... **CLC 108**
See also CA 45-48; CANR 3, 32, 66, 70, 135; INT CANR-32; SATA 23

Colette, (Sidonie-Gabrielle)
1873-1954 .... **SSC 10; TCLC 1, 5, 16**
See Willy, Colette
See also CA 104; 131; DA3; DAM NOV; DLB 65; EW 9; EWL 3; GFL 1789 to the Present; MTCW 1, 2; RGWL 2, 3; TWA

Collett, (Jacobine) Camilla (Wergeland)
1813-1895 .... **NCLC 22**

Collier, Christopher 1930- .... **CLC 30**
See also AAYA 13; BYA 2; CA 33-36R; CANR 13, 33, 102; JRDA; MAICYA 1, 2; SATA 16, 70; WYA; YAW 1

Collier, James Lincoln 1928- .... **CLC 30**
See also AAYA 13; BYA 2; CA 9-12R; CANR 4, 33, 60, 102; CLR 3; DAM POP; JRDA; MAICYA 1, 2; SAAS 21; SATA 8, 70; WYA; YAW 1

Collier, Jeremy 1650-1726 .... **LC 6**

Collier, John 1901-1980 . **SSC 19; TCLC 127**
See also CA 65-68; 97-100; CANR 10; DLB 77, 255; FANT; SUFW 1

Collier, Mary 1690-1762 .... **LC 86**
See also DLB 95

Collingwood, R(obin) G(eorge)
1889(?)-1943 .... **TCLC 67**
See also CA 117; 155; DLB 262

Collins, Billy 1941- .... **PC 68**
See also CA 151; CANR 92; MTFW; PFS 18

Collins, Hunt
See Hunter, Evan

Collins, Linda 1931- .... **CLC 44**
See also CA 125

Collins, Tom
See Furphy, Joseph
See also RGEL 2

Collins, (William) Wilkie
1824-1889 .... **NCLC 1, 18, 93**
See also BRWS 6; CDBLB 1832-1890; CMW 4; DLB 18, 70, 159; MSW; RGEL 2; RGSF 2; SUFW 1; WLIT 4

Collins, William 1721-1759 .... **LC 4, 40**
See also BRW 3; DAM POET; DLB 109; RGEL 2

Collodi, Carlo .... **NCLC 54**
See Lorenzini, Carlo
See also CLR 5; WCH

Colman, George
See Glassco, John

Colman, George, the Elder
1732-1794 .... **LC 98**
See also RGEL 2

Colonna, Vittoria 1492-1547 .... **LC 71**
See also RGWL 2, 3

Colt, Winchester Remington
See Hubbard, L(afayette) Ron(ald)

Colter, Cyrus J. 1910-2002 .... **CLC 58**
See also BW 1; CA 65-68; 205; CANR 10, 66; CN 7; DLB 33

Colton, James
See Hansen, Joseph
See also GLL 1

Colum, Padraic 1881-1972 .... **CLC 28**
See also BYA 4; CA 73-76; 33-36R; CANR 35; CLR 36; CWRI 5; DLB 19; MAICYA 1, 2; MTCW 1; RGEL 2; SATA 15; WCH

Colvin, James
See Moorcock, Michael (John)

Colwin, Laurie (E.) 1944-1992 .... **CLC 5, 13, 23, 84**
See also CA 89-92; 139; CANR 20, 46; DLB 218; DLBY 1980; MTCW 1

Comfort, Alex(ander) 1920-2000 .... **CLC 7**
See also CA 1-4R; 190; CANR 1, 45; CP 7; DAM POP; MTCW 1

Comfort, Montgomery
See Campbell, (John) Ramsey

Compton-Burnett, I(vy)
1892(?)-1969 .... **CLC 1, 3, 10, 15, 34**
See also BRW 7; CA 1-4R; 25-28R; CANR 4; DAM NOV; DLB 36; EWL 3; MTCW 1; RGEL 2

Comstock, Anthony 1844-1915 ...... **TCLC 13**
See also CA 110; 169

Comte, Auguste 1798-1857 .... **NCLC 54**

Conan Doyle, Arthur
See Doyle, Sir Arthur Conan
See also BPFB 1; BYA 4, 5, 11

Conde (Abellan), Carmen
1901-1996 .... **HLCS 1**
See also CA 177; CWW 2; DLB 108; EWL 3; HW 2

Conde, Maryse 1937- ..... **BLCS; CLC 52, 92**
See also BW 2, 3; CA 110, 190; CAAE 190; CANR 30, 53, 76; CWW 2; DAM MULT; EWL 3; MTCW 1

Condillac, Etienne Bonnot de
1714-1780 .... **LC 26**

Condon, Richard (Thomas)
1915-1996 .... **CLC 4, 6, 8, 10, 45, 100**
See also BEST 90:3; BPFB 1; CA 1-4R; 151; CAAS 1; CANR 2, 23; CMW 4; CN 7; DAM NOV; INT CANR-23; MTCW 1, 2

Condorcet 1743-1794 .... **LC 104**
See also GFL Beginnings to 1789

Confucius 551B.C.-479B.C. .... **CMLC 19, 65; WLCS**
See also DA; DA3; DAB; DAC; DAM MST

Congreve, William 1670-1729 ... **DC 2; LC 5, 21; WLC**
See also BRW 2; CDBLB 1660-1789; DA; DAB; DAC; DAM DRAM, MST, POET; DFS 15; DLB 39, 84; RGEL 2; WLIT 3

Conley, Robert J(ackson) 1940- .... **NNAL**
See also CA 41-44R; CANR 15, 34, 45, 96; DAM MULT

Connell, Evan S(helby), Jr. 1924- . **CLC 4, 6, 45**
See also AAYA 7; AMWS 14; CA 1-4R; CAAS 2; CANR 2, 39, 76, 97; CN 7; DAM NOV; DLB 2; DLBY 1981; MTCW 1, 2

Connelly, Marc(us Cook) 1890-1980 . **CLC 7**
See also CA 85-88; 102; CANR 30; DFS 12; DLB 7; DLBY 1980; RGAL 4; SATA-Obit 25

Connor, Ralph .... **TCLC 31**
See Gordon, Charles William
See also DLB 92; TCWW 2

Conrad, Joseph 1857-1924 ..... **SSC 9, 67, 69, 71; TCLC 1, 6, 13, 25, 43, 57; WLC**
See also AAYA 26; BPFB 1; BRW 6; BRWC 1; BRWR 2; BYA 2; CA 104; 131; CANR 60; CDBLB 1890-1914; DA; DA3; DAB; DAC; DAM MST, NOV; DLB 10, 34, 98, 156; EWL 3; EXPN; EXPS; LAIT

Author Index

Author Index

Duns Scotus, John 1266(?)-1308 ... **CMLC 59**
See also DLB 115
du Perry, Jean
See Simenon, Georges (Jacques Christian)
Durang, Christopher (Ferdinand)
1949- .... **CLC 27, 38**
See also CA 105; CAD; CANR 50, 76, 130; CD 5; MTCW 1
Duras, Claire de 1777-1828 .... **NCLC 154**
Duras, Marguerite 1914-1996 . **CLC 3, 6, 11, 20, 34, 40, 68, 100; SSC 40**
See also BPFB 1; CA 25-28R; 151; CANR 50; CWW 2; DLB 83; EWL 3; GFL 1789 to the Present; IDFW 4; MTCW 1, 2; RGWL 2, 3; TWA
Durban, (Rosa) Pam 1947- .... **CLC 39**
See also CA 123; CANR 98; CSW
Durcan, Paul 1944- .... **CLC 43, 70**
See also CA 134; CANR 123; CP 7; DAM POET; EWL 3
Durfey, Thomas 1653-1723 .... **LC 94**
See also DLB 80; RGEL 2
Durkheim, Emile 1858-1917 .... **TCLC 55**
Durrell, Lawrence (George)
1912-1990 ..... **CLC 1, 4, 6, 8, 13, 27, 41**
See also BPFB 1; BRWS 1; CA 9-12R; 132; CANR 40, 77; CDBLB 1945-1960; DAM NOV; DLB 15, 27, 204; DLBY 1990; EWL 3; MTCW 1, 2; RGEL 2; SFW 4; TEA
Durrenmatt, Friedrich
See Duerrenmatt, Friedrich
See also CDWLB 2; EW 13; EWL 3; RGWL 2, 3
Dutt, Michael Madhusudan
1824-1873 .... **NCLC 118**
Dutt, Toru 1856-1877 .... **NCLC 29**
See also DLB 240
Dwight, Timothy 1752-1817 .... **NCLC 13**
See also DLB 37; RGAL 4
Dworkin, Andrea 1946- .... **CLC 43, 123**
See also CA 77-80; CAAS 21; CANR 16, 39, 76, 96; FW; GLL 1; INT CANR-16; MTCW 1, 2
Dwyer, Deanna
See Koontz, Dean R(ay)
Dwyer, K. R.
See Koontz, Dean R(ay)
Dybek, Stuart 1942- .... **CLC 114; SSC 55**
See also CA 97-100; CANR 39; DLB 130
Dye, Richard
See De Voto, Bernard (Augustine)
Dyer, Geoff 1958- .... **CLC 149**
See also CA 125; CANR 88
Dyer, George 1755-1841 .... **NCLC 129**
See also DLB 93
Dylan, Bob 1941- .... **CLC 3, 4, 6, 12, 77; PC 37**
See also CA 41-44R; CANR 108; CP 7; DLB 16
Dyson, John 1943- .... **CLC 70**
See also CA 144
Dzyubin, Eduard Georgievich 1895-1934
See Bagritsky, Eduard
See also CA 170
E. V. L.
See Lucas, E(dward) V(errall)
Eagleton, Terence (Francis) 1943- .. **CLC 63, 132**
See also CA 57-60; CANR 7, 23, 68, 115; DLB 242; LMFS 2; MTCW 1, 2
Eagleton, Terry
See Eagleton, Terence (Francis)
Early, Jack
See Scoppettone, Sandra
See also GLL 1
East, Michael
See West, Morris L(anglo)
Eastaway, Edward
See Thomas, (Philip) Edward
Eastlake, William (Derry)
1917-1997 .... **CLC 8**
See also CA 5-8R; 158; CAAS 1; CANR 5, 63; CN 7; DLB 6, 206; INT CANR-5; TCWW 2
Eastman, Charles A(lexander)
1858-1939 .... **NNAL; TCLC 55**
See also CA 179; CANR 91; DAM MULT; DLB 175; YABC 1
Eaton, Edith Maude 1865-1914 .... **AAL**
See Far, Sui Sin
See also CA 154; DLB 221; FW
Eaton, (Lillie) Winnifred 1875-1954 .... **AAL**
See also CA 217; DLB 221; RGAL 4
Eberhart, Richard (Ghormley)
1904- .... **CLC 3, 11, 19, 56**
See also AMW; CA 1-4R; CANR 2, 125; CDALB 1941-1968; CP 7; DAM POET; DLB 48; MTCW 1; RGAL 4
Eberstadt, Fernanda 1960- .... **CLC 39**
See also CA 136; CANR 69, 128
Echegaray (y Eizaguirre), Jose (Maria Waldo) 1832-1916 .... **HLCS 1; TCLC 4**
See also CA 104; CANR 32; EWL 3; HW 1; MTCW 1
Echeverria, (Jose) Esteban (Antonino)
1805-1851 .... **NCLC 18**
See also LAW
Echo
See Proust, (Valentin-Louis-George-Eugene) Marcel
Eckert, Allan W. 1931- .... **CLC 17**
See also AAYA 18; BYA 2; CA 13-16R; CANR 14, 45; INT CANR-14; MAICYA 2; MAICYAS 1; SAAS 21; SATA 29, 91; SATA-Brief 27
Eckhart, Meister 1260(?)-1327(?) ... **CMLC 9**
See also DLB 115; LMFS 1
Eckmar, F. R.
See de Hartog, Jan
Eco, Umberto 1932- .... **CLC 28, 60, 142**
See also BEST 90:1; BPFB 1; CA 77-80; CANR 12, 33, 55, 110, 131; CPW; CWW 2; DA3; DAM NOV, POP; DLB 196, 242; EWL 3; MSW; MTCW 1, 2; RGWL 3
Eddison, E(ric) R(ucker)
1882-1945 .... **TCLC 15**
See also CA 109; 156; DLB 255; FANT; SFW 4; SUFW 1
Eddy, Mary (Ann Morse) Baker
1821-1910 .... **TCLC 71**
See also CA 113; 174
Edel, (Joseph) Leon 1907-1997 .. **CLC 29, 34**
See also CA 1-4R; 161; CANR 1, 22, 112; DLB 103; INT CANR-22
Eden, Emily 1797-1869 .... **NCLC 10**
Edgar, David 1948- .... **CLC 42**
See also CA 57-60; CANR 12, 61, 112; CBD; CD 5; DAM DRAM; DFS 15; DLB 13, 233; MTCW 1
Edgerton, Clyde (Carlyle) 1944- ...... **CLC 39**
See also AAYA 17; CA 118; 134; CANR 64, 125; CSW; DLB 278; INT CA-134; YAW
Edgeworth, Maria 1768-1849 ... **NCLC 1, 51, 158**
See also BRWS 3; DLB 116, 159, 163; FW; RGEL 2; SATA 21; TEA; WLIT 3
Edmonds, Paul
See Kuttner, Henry
Edmonds, Walter D(umaux)
1903-1998 .... **CLC 35**
See also BYA 2; CA 5-8R; CANR 2; CWRI 5; DLB 9; LAIT 1; MAICYA 1, 2; RHW; SAAS 4; SATA 1, 27; SATA-Obit 99
Edmondson, Wallace
See Ellison, Harlan (Jay)
Edson, Margaret 1961- ...... **CLC 199; DC 24**
See also CA 190; DFS 13; DLB 266
Edson, Russell 1935- .... **CLC 13**
See also CA 33-36R; CANR 115; DLB 244; WP
Edwards, Bronwen Elizabeth
See Rose, Wendy
Edwards, G(erald) B(asil)
1899-1976 .... **CLC 25**
See also CA 201; 110
Edwards, Gus 1939- .... **CLC 43**
See also CA 108; INT CA-108
Edwards, Jonathan 1703-1758 .... **LC 7, 54**
See also AMW; DA; DAC; DAM MST; DLB 24, 270; RGAL 4; TUS
Edwards, Sarah Pierpont 1710-1758 .. **LC 87**
See also DLB 200
Efron, Marina Ivanovna Tsvetaeva
See Tsvetaeva (Efron), Marina (Ivanovna)
Egeria fl. 4th cent. - .... **CMLC 70**
Egoyan, Atom 1960- .... **CLC 151**
See also CA 157
Ehle, John (Marsden, Jr.) 1925- ...... **CLC 27**
See also CA 9-12R; CSW
Ehrenbourg, Ilya (Grigoryevich)
See Ehrenburg, Ilya (Grigoryevich)
Ehrenburg, Ilya (Grigoryevich)
1891-1967 .... **CLC 18, 34, 62**
See Erenburg, Il'ia Grigor'evich
See also CA 102; 25-28R; EWL 3
Ehrenburg, Ilyo (Grigoryevich)
See Ehrenburg, Ilya (Grigoryevich)
Ehrenreich, Barbara 1941- .... **CLC 110**
See also BEST 90:4; CA 73-76; CANR 16, 37, 62, 117; DLB 246; FW; MTCW 1, 2
Eich, Gunter
See Eich, Gunter
See also RGWL 2, 3
Eich, Gunter 1907-1972 .... **CLC 15**
See Eich, Gunter
See also CA 111; 93-96; DLB 69, 124; EWL 3
Eichendorff, Joseph 1788-1857 .... **NCLC 8**
See also DLB 90; RGWL 2, 3
Eigner, Larry .... **CLC 9**
See Eigner, Laurence (Joel)
See also CAAS 23; DLB 5; WP
Eigner, Laurence (Joel) 1927-1996
See Eigner, Larry
See also CA 9-12R; 151; CANR 6, 84; CP 7; DLB 193
Eilhart von Oberge c. 1140-c. 1195 .... **CMLC 67**
See also DLB 148
Einhard c. 770-840 .... **CMLC 50**
See also DLB 148
Einstein, Albert 1879-1955 .... **TCLC 65**
See also CA 121; 133; MTCW 1, 2
Eiseley, Loren
See Eiseley, Loren Corey
See also DLB 275
Eiseley, Loren Corey 1907-1977 .... **CLC 7**
See Eiseley, Loren
See also AAYA 5; ANW; CA 1-4R; 73-76; CANR 6; DLBD 17
Eisenstadt, Jill 1963- .... **CLC 50**
See also CA 140
Eisenstein, Sergei (Mikhailovich)
1898-1948 .... **TCLC 57**
See also CA 114; 149
Eisner, Simon
See Kornbluth, C(yril) M.
Ekeloef, (Bengt) Gunnar
1907-1968 .... **CLC 27; PC 23**
See Ekelof, (Bengt) Gunnar
See also CA 123; 25-28R; DAM POET

Ekelof, (Bengt) Gunnar 1907-1968
See Ekeloef, (Bengt) Gunnar
See also DLB 259; EW 12; EWL 3
Ekelund, Vilhelm 1880-1949 .... **TCLC 75**
See also CA 189; EWL 3
Ekwensi, C. O. D.
See Ekwensi, Cyprian (Odiatu Duaka)
Ekwensi, Cyprian (Odiatu Duaka) 1921- .... **BLC 1; CLC 4**
See also AFW; BW 2, 3; CA 29-32R; CANR 18, 42, 74, 125; CDWLB 3; CN 7; CWRI 5; DAM MULT; DLB 117; EWL 3; MTCW 1, 2; RGEL 2; SATA 66; WLIT 2
Elaine .... **TCLC 18**
See Leverson, Ada Esther
El Crummo
See Crumb, R(obert)
Elder, Lonne III 1931-1996 ..... **BLC 1; DC 8**
See also BW 1, 3; CA 81-84; 152; CAD; CANR 25; DAM MULT; DLB 7, 38, 44
Eleanor of Aquitaine 1122-1204 ... **CMLC 39**
Elia
See Lamb, Charles
Eliade, Mircea 1907-1986 .... **CLC 19**
See also CA 65-68; 119; CANR 30, 62; CDWLB 4; DLB 220; EWL 3; MTCW 1; RGWL 3; SFW 4
Eliot, A. D.
See Jewett, (Theodora) Sarah Orne
Eliot, Alice
See Jewett, (Theodora) Sarah Orne
Eliot, Dan
See Silverberg, Robert
Eliot, George 1819-1880 ...... **NCLC 4, 13, 23, 41, 49, 89, 118; PC 20; SSC 72; WLC**
See Evans, Mary Ann
See also BRW 5; BRWC 1, 2; BRWR 2; CDBLB 1832-1890; CN 7; CPW; DA; DA3; DAB; DAC; DAM MST, NOV; DLB 21, 35, 55; LATS 1:1; LMFS 1; NFS 17; RGEL 2; RGSF 2; SSFS 8; TEA; WLIT 3
Eliot, John 1604-1690 .... **LC 5**
See also DLB 24
Eliot, T(homas) S(tearns) 1888-1965 ...... **CLC 1, 2, 3, 6, 9, 10, 13, 15, 24, 34, 41, 55, 57, 113; PC 5, 31; WLC**
See also AAYA 28; AMW; AMWC 1; AMWR 1; BRW 7; BRWR 2; CA 5-8R; 25-28R; CANR 41; CDALB 1929-1941; DA; DA3; DAB; DAC; DAM DRAM, MST, POET; DFS 4, 13; DLB 7, 10, 45, 63, 245; DLBY 1988; EWL 3; EXPP; LAIT 3; LATS 1:1; LMFS 2; MTCW 1, 2; NCFS 5; PAB; PFS 1, 7, 20; RGAL 4; RGEL 2; TUS; WLIT 4; WP
Elizabeth 1866-1941 .... **TCLC 41**
Elizabeth I .... **LC 118**
See also DLB 136
Elkin, Stanley L(awrence) 1930-1995 .. **CLC 4, 6, 9, 14, 27, 51, 91; SSC 12**
See also AMWS 6; BPFB 1; CA 9-12R; 148; CANR 8, 46; CN 7; CPW; DAM NOV, POP; DLB 2, 28, 218, 278; DLBY 1980; EWL 3; INT CANR-8; MTCW 1, 2; RGAL 4
Elledge, Scott .... **CLC 34**
Elliott, Don
See Silverberg, Robert
Elliott, George P(aul) 1918-1980 .... **CLC 2**
See also CA 1-4R; 97-100; CANR 2; DLB 244
Elliott, Janice 1931-1995 .... **CLC 47**
See also CA 13-16R; CANR 8, 29, 84; CN 7; DLB 14; SATA 119
Elliott, Sumner Locke 1917-1991 ..... **CLC 38**
See also CA 5-8R; 134; CANR 2, 21; DLB 289
Elliott, William
See Bradbury, Ray (Douglas)
Ellis, A. E. .... **CLC 7**
Ellis, Alice Thomas .... **CLC 40**
See Haycraft, Anna (Margaret)
See also DLB 194; MTCW 1
Ellis, Bret Easton 1964- ...... **CLC 39, 71, 117**
See also AAYA 2, 43; CA 118; 123; CANR 51, 74, 126; CN 7; CPW; DA3; DAM POP; DLB 292; HGG; INT CA-123; MTCW 1; NFS 11
Ellis, (Henry) Havelock 1859-1939 .... **TCLC 14**
See also CA 109; 169; DLB 190
Ellis, Landon
See Ellison, Harlan (Jay)
Ellis, Trey 1962- .... **CLC 55**
See also CA 146; CANR 92
Ellison, Harlan (Jay) 1934- ... **CLC 1, 13, 42, 139; SSC 14**
See also AAYA 29; BPFB 1; BYA 14; CA 5-8R; CANR 5, 46, 115; CPW; DAM POP; DLB 8; HGG; INT CANR-5; MTCW 1, 2; SCFW 2; SFW 4; SSFS 13, 14, 15; SUFW 1, 2
Ellison, Ralph (Waldo) 1914-1994 .... **BLC 1; CLC 1, 3, 11, 54, 86, 114; SSC 26, 79; WLC**
See also AAYA 19; AFAW 1, 2; AMWC 2; AMWR 2; AMWS 2; BPFB 1; BW 1, 3; BYA 2; CA 9-12R; 145; CANR 24, 53; CDALB 1941-1968; CSW; DA; DA3; DAB; DAC; DAM MST, MULT, NOV; DLB 2, 76, 227; DLBY 1994; EWL 3; EXPN; EXPS; LAIT 4; MTCW 1, 2; NCFS 3; NFS 2; RGAL 4; RGSF 2; SSFS 1, 11; YAW
Ellmann, Lucy (Elizabeth) 1956- ..... **CLC 61**
See also CA 128
Ellmann, Richard (David) 1918-1987 .... **CLC 50**
See also BEST 89:2; CA 1-4R; 122; CANR 2, 28, 61; DLB 103; DLBY 1987; MTCW 1, 2
Elman, Richard (Martin) 1934-1997 .... **CLC 19**
See also CA 17-20R; 163; CAAS 3; CANR 47
Elron
See Hubbard, L(afayette) Ron(ald)
El Saadawi, Nawal 1931- .... **CLC 196**
See al'Sadaawi, Nawal; Sa'adawi, al-Nawal; Saadawi, Nawal El; Sa'dawi, Nawal al-
See also CA 118; CAAS 11; CANR 44, 92
Eluard, Paul .... **PC 38; TCLC 7, 41**
See Grindel, Eugene
See also EWL 3; GFL 1789 to the Present; RGWL 2, 3
Ensler, Eve 1953- .... **CLC 212**
See also CA 172; CANR 126
Elyot, Thomas 1490(?)-1546 .... **LC 11**
See also DLB 136; RGEL 2
Elytis, Odysseus 1911-1996 .... **CLC 15, 49, 100; PC 21**
See Alepoudelis, Odysseus
See also CA 102; 151; CANR 94; CWW 2; DAM POET; EW 13; EWL 3; MTCW 1, 2; RGWL 2, 3
Emecheta, (Florence Onye) Buchi 1944- .... **BLC 2; CLC 14, 48, 128**
See also AFW; BW 2, 3; CA 81-84; CANR 27, 81, 126; CDWLB 3; CN 7; CWRI 5; DA3; DAM MULT; DLB 117; EWL 3; FW; MTCW 1, 2; NFS 12, 14; SATA 66; WLIT 2
Emerson, Mary Moody 1774-1863 .... **NCLC 66**
Emerson, Ralph Waldo 1803-1882 . **NCLC 1, 38, 98; PC 18; WLC**
See also AAYA 60; AMW; ANW; CDALB 1640-1865; DA; DA3; DAB; DAC; DAM MST, POET; DLB 1, 59, 73, 183, 223, 270; EXPP; LAIT 2; LMFS 1; NCFS 3; PFS 4, 17; RGAL 4; TUS; WP
Eminescu, Mihail 1850-1889 .. **NCLC 33, 131**
Empedocles 5th cent. B.C.- .... **CMLC 50**
See also DLB 176
Empson, William 1906-1984 ... **CLC 3, 8, 19, 33, 34**
See also BRWS 2; CA 17-20R; 112; CANR 31, 61; DLB 20; EWL 3; MTCW 1, 2; RGEL 2
Enchi, Fumiko (Ueda) 1905-1986 ..... **CLC 31**
See Enchi Fumiko
See also CA 129; 121; FW; MJW
Enchi Fumiko
See Enchi, Fumiko (Ueda)
See also DLB 182; EWL 3
Ende, Michael (Andreas Helmuth) 1929-1995 .... **CLC 31**
See also BYA 5; CA 118; 124; 149; CANR 36, 110; CLR 14; DLB 75; MAICYA 1, 2; MAICYAS 1; SATA 61, 130; SATA-Brief 42; SATA-Obit 86
Endo, Shusaku 1923-1996 ..... **CLC 7, 14, 19, 54, 99; SSC 48; TCLC 152**
See Endo Shusaku
See also CA 29-32R; 153; CANR 21, 54, 131; DA3; DAM NOV; MTCW 1, 2; RGSF 2; RGWL 2, 3
Endo Shusaku
See Endo, Shusaku
See also CWW 2; DLB 182; EWL 3
Engel, Marian 1933-1985 .... **CLC 36; TCLC 137**
See also CA 25-28R; CANR 12; DLB 53; FW; INT CANR-12
Engelhardt, Frederick
See Hubbard, L(afayette) Ron(ald)
Engels, Friedrich 1820-1895 .. **NCLC 85, 114**
See also DLB 129; LATS 1:1
Enright, D(ennis) J(oseph) 1920-2002 .... **CLC 4, 8, 31**
See also CA 1-4R; 211; CANR 1, 42, 83; CP 7; DLB 27; EWL 3; SATA 25; SATA-Obit 140
Enzensberger, Hans Magnus 1929- .... **CLC 43; PC 28**
See also CA 116; 119; CANR 103; CWW 2; EWL 3
Ephron, Nora 1941- .... **CLC 17, 31**
See also AAYA 35; AITN 2; CA 65-68; CANR 12, 39, 83
Epicurus 341B.C.-270B.C. .... **CMLC 21**
See also DLB 176
Epsilon
See Betjeman, John
Epstein, Daniel Mark 1948- .... **CLC 7**
See also CA 49-52; CANR 2, 53, 90
Epstein, Jacob 1956- .... **CLC 19**
See also CA 114
Epstein, Jean 1897-1953 .... **TCLC 92**
Epstein, Joseph 1937- .... **CLC 39, 204**
See also AMWS 14; CA 112; 119; CANR 50, 65, 117
Epstein, Leslie 1938- .... **CLC 27**
See also AMWS 12; CA 73-76, 215; CAAE 215; CAAS 12; CANR 23, 69; DLB 299
Equiano, Olaudah 1745(?)-1797 . **BLC 2; LC 16**
See also AFAW 1, 2; CDWLB 3; DAM MULT; DLB 37, 50; WLIT 2

Author Index

Author Index

DA3; DAB; DAC; DAM MST, NOV; DLB 75, 124; EW 13; EWL 3; MTCW 1, 2; RGWL 2, 3; TWA
Gratton, Thomas
See Hulme, T(homas) E(rnest)
Grau, Shirley Ann 1929- .... **CLC 4, 9, 146; SSC 15**
See also CA 89-92; CANR 22, 69; CN 7; CSW; DLB 2, 218; INT CA-89-92, CANR-22; MTCW 1
Gravel, Fern
See Hall, James Norman
Graver, Elizabeth 1964- .... **CLC 70**
See also CA 135; CANR 71, 129
Graves, Richard Perceval
1895-1985 .... **CLC 44**
See also CA 65-68; CANR 9, 26, 51
Graves, Robert (von Ranke)
1895-1985 .. **CLC 1, 2, 6, 11, 39, 44, 45; PC 6**
See also BPFB 2; BRW 7; BYA 4; CA 5-8R; 117; CANR 5, 36; CDBLB 1914-1945; DA3; DAB; DAC; DAM MST, POET; DLB 20, 100, 191; DLBD 18; DLBY 1985; EWL 3; LATS 1:1; MTCW 1, 2; NCFS 2; RGEL 2; RHW; SATA 45; TEA
Graves, Valerie
See Bradley, Marion Zimmer
Gray, Alasdair (James) 1934- .... **CLC 41**
See also BRWS 9; CA 126; CANR 47, 69, 106; CN 7; DLB 194, 261; HGG; INT CA-126; MTCW 1, 2; RGSF 2; SUFW 2
Gray, Amlin 1946- .... **CLC 29**
See also CA 138
Gray, Francine du Plessix 1930- ..... **CLC 22, 153**
See also BEST 90:3; CA 61-64; CAAS 2; CANR 11, 33, 75, 81; DAM NOV; INT CANR-11; MTCW 1, 2
Gray, John (Henry) 1866-1934 ...... **TCLC 19**
See also CA 119; 162; RGEL 2
Gray, Simon (James Holliday)
1936- .... **CLC 9, 14, 36**
See also AITN 1; CA 21-24R; CAAS 3; CANR 32, 69; CD 5; DLB 13; EWL 3; MTCW 1; RGEL 2
Gray, Spalding 1941-2004 .... **CLC 49, 112; DC 7**
See also CA 128; 225; CAD; CANR 74; CD 5; CPW; DAM POP; MTCW 2
Gray, Thomas 1716-1771 .... **LC 4, 40; PC 2; WLC**
See also BRW 3; CDBLB 1660-1789; DA; DA3; DAB; DAC; DAM MST; DLB 109; EXPP; PAB; PFS 9; RGEL 2; TEA; WP
Grayson, David
See Baker, Ray Stannard
Grayson, Richard (A.) 1951- .... **CLC 38**
See also CA 85-88, 210; CAAE 210; CANR 14, 31, 57; DLB 234
Greeley, Andrew M(oran) 1928- ...... **CLC 28**
See also BPFB 2; CA 5-8R; CAAS 7; CANR 7, 43, 69, 104; CMW 4; CPW; DA3; DAM POP; MTCW 1, 2
Green, Anna Katharine
1846-1935 .... **TCLC 63**
See also CA 112; 159; CMW 4; DLB 202, 221; MSW
Green, Brian
See Card, Orson Scott
Green, Hannah
See Greenberg, Joanne (Goldenberg)
Green, Hannah 1927(?)-1996 .... **CLC 3**
See also CA 73-76; CANR 59, 93; NFS 10
Green, Henry .... **CLC 2, 13, 97**
See Yorke, Henry Vincent
See also BRWS 2; CA 175; DLB 15; EWL 3; RGEL 2
Green, Julien (Hartridge) 1900-1998
See Green, Julian
See also CA 21-24R; 169; CANR 33, 87; CWW 2; DLB 4, 72; MTCW 1
Green, Julian .... **CLC 3, 11, 77**
See Green, Julien (Hartridge)
See also EWL 3; GFL 1789 to the Present; MTCW 2
Green, Paul (Eliot) 1894-1981 .... **CLC 25**
See also AITN 1; CA 5-8R; 103; CANR 3; DAM DRAM; DLB 7, 9, 249; DLBY 1981; RGAL 4
Greenaway, Peter 1942- .... **CLC 159**
See also CA 127
Greenberg, Ivan 1908-1973
See Rahv, Philip
See also CA 85-88
Greenberg, Joanne (Goldenberg)
1932- .... **CLC 7, 30**
See also AAYA 12; CA 5-8R; CANR 14, 32, 69; CN 7; SATA 25; YAW
Greenberg, Richard 1959(?)- .... **CLC 57**
See also CA 138; CAD; CD 5
Greenblatt, Stephen J(ay) 1943- ...... **CLC 70**
See also CA 49-52; CANR 115
Greene, Bette 1934- .... **CLC 30**
See also AAYA 7; BYA 3; CA 53-56; CANR 4; CLR 2; CWRI 5; JRDA; LAIT 4; MAICYA 1, 2; NFS 10; SAAS 16; SATA 8, 102; WYA; YAW
Greene, Gael .... **CLC 8**
See also CA 13-16R; CANR 10
Greene, Graham (Henry)
1904-1991 .... **CLC 1, 3, 6, 9, 14, 18, 27, 37, 70, 72, 125; SSC 29; WLC**
See also AITN 2; BPFB 2; BRWR 2; BRWS 1; BYA 3; CA 13-16R; 133; CANR 35, 61, 131; CBD; CDBLB 1945-1960; CMW 4; DA; DA3; DAB; DAC; DAM MST, NOV; DLB 13, 15, 77, 100, 162, 201, 204; DLBY 1991; EWL 3; MSW; MTCW 1, 2; NFS 16; RGEL 2; SATA 20; SSFS 14; TEA; WLIT 4
Greene, Robert 1558-1592 .... **LC 41**
See also BRWS 8; DLB 62, 167; IDTP; RGEL 2; TEA
Greer, Germaine 1939- .... **CLC 131**
See also AITN 1; CA 81-84; CANR 33, 70, 115, 133; FW; MTCW 1, 2
Greer, Richard
See Silverberg, Robert
Gregor, Arthur 1923- .... **CLC 9**
See also CA 25-28R; CAAS 10; CANR 11; CP 7; SATA 36
Gregor, Lee
See Pohl, Frederik
Gregory, Lady Isabella Augusta (Persse)
1852-1932 .... **TCLC 1**
See also BRW 6; CA 104; 184; DLB 10; IDTP; RGEL 2
Gregory, J. Dennis
See Williams, John A(lfred)
Grekova, I. .... **CLC 59**
See Ventsel, Elena Sergeevna
See also CWW 2
Grendon, Stephen
See Derleth, August (William)
Grenville, Kate 1950- .... **CLC 61**
See also CA 118; CANR 53, 93
Grenville, Pelham
See Wodehouse, P(elham) G(renville)
Greve, Felix Paul (Berthold Friedrich)
1879-1948
See Grove, Frederick Philip
See also CA 104; 141, 175; CANR 79; DAC; DAM MST
Greville, Fulke 1554-1628 .... **LC 79**
See also DLB 62, 172; RGEL 2
Grey, Lady Jane 1537-1554 .... **LC 93**
See also DLB 132
Grey, Zane 1872-1939 .... **TCLC 6**
See also BPFB 2; CA 104; 132; DA3; DAM POP; DLB 9, 212; MTCW 1, 2; RGAL 4; TCWW 2; TUS
Griboedov, Aleksandr Sergeevich
1795(?)-1829 .... **NCLC 129**
See also DLB 205; RGWL 2, 3
Grieg, (Johan) Nordahl (Brun)
1902-1943 .... **TCLC 10**
See also CA 107; 189; EWL 3
Grieve, C(hristopher) M(urray)
1892-1978 .... **CLC 11, 19**
See MacDiarmid, Hugh; Pteleon
See also CA 5-8R; 85-88; CANR 33, 107; DAM POET; MTCW 1; RGEL 2
Griffin, Gerald 1803-1840 .... **NCLC 7**
See also DLB 159; RGEL 2
Griffin, John Howard 1920-1980 ..... **CLC 68**
See also AITN 1; CA 1-4R; 101; CANR 2
Griffin, Peter 1942- .... **CLC 39**
See also CA 136
Griffith, D(avid Lewelyn) W(ark)
1875(?)-1948 .... **TCLC 68**
See also CA 119; 150; CANR 80
Griffith, Lawrence
See Griffith, D(avid Lewelyn) W(ark)
Griffiths, Trevor 1935- .... **CLC 13, 52**
See also CA 97-100; CANR 45; CBD; CD 5; DLB 13, 245
Griggs, Sutton (Elbert)
1872-1930 .... **TCLC 77**
See also CA 123; 186; DLB 50
Grigson, Geoffrey (Edward Harvey)
1905-1985 .... **CLC 7, 39**
See also CA 25-28R; 118; CANR 20, 33; DLB 27; MTCW 1, 2
Grile, Dod
See Bierce, Ambrose (Gwinett)
Grillparzer, Franz 1791-1872 .... **DC 14; NCLC 1, 102; SSC 37**
See also CDWLB 2; DLB 133; EW 5; RGWL 2, 3; TWA
Grimble, Reverend Charles James
See Eliot, T(homas) S(tearns)
Grimke, Angelina (Emily) Weld
1880-1958 .... **HR 2**
See Weld, Angelina (Emily) Grimke
See also BW 1; CA 124; DAM POET; DLB 50, 54
Grimke, Charlotte L(ottie) Forten
1837(?)-1914
See Forten, Charlotte L.
See also BW 1; CA 117; 124; DAM MULT, POET
Grimm, Jacob Ludwig Karl
1785-1863 .... **NCLC 3, 77; SSC 36**
See also DLB 90; MAICYA 1, 2; RGSF 2; RGWL 2, 3; SATA 22; WCH
Grimm, Wilhelm Karl 1786-1859 .. **NCLC 3, 77; SSC 36**
See also CDWLB 2; DLB 90; MAICYA 1, 2; RGSF 2; RGWL 2, 3; SATA 22; WCH
Grimmelshausen, Hans Jakob Christoffel von
See Grimmelshausen, Johann Jakob Christoffel von
See also RGWL 2, 3
Grimmelshausen, Johann Jakob Christoffel von 1621-1676 .... **LC 6**
See Grimmelshausen, Hans Jakob Christoffel von
See also CDWLB 2; DLB 168
Grindel, Eugene 1895-1952
See Eluard, Paul
See also CA 104; 193; LMFS 2

Author Index

Author Index

Joyce, James (Augustine Aloysius) 1882-1941 .... **DC 16; PC 22; SSC 3, 26, 44, 64; TCLC 3, 8, 16, 35, 52, 159; WLC**
See also AAYA 42; BRW 7; BRWC 1; BRWR 1; BYA 11, 13; CA 104; 126; CDBLB 1914-1945; DA; DA3; DAB; DAC; DAM MST, NOV, POET; DLB 10, 19, 36, 162, 247; EWL 3; EXPN; EXPS; LAIT 3; LMFS 1, 2; MTCW 1, 2; NFS 7; RGSF 2; SSFS 1, 19; TEA; WLIT 4
Jozsef, Attila 1905-1937 .... **TCLC 22**
See also CA 116; CDWLB 4; DLB 215; EWL 3
Juana Ines de la Cruz, Sor 1651(?)-1695 ...... **HLCS 1; LC 5; PC 24**
See also DLB 305; FW; LAW; RGWL 2, 3; WLIT 1
Juana Inez de La Cruz, Sor
See Juana Ines de la Cruz, Sor
Judd, Cyril
See Kornbluth, C(yril) M.; Pohl, Frederik
Juenger, Ernst 1895-1998 .... **CLC 125**
See Junger, Ernst
See also CA 101; 167; CANR 21, 47, 106; DLB 56
Julian of Norwich 1342(?)-1416(?) . **LC 6, 52**
See also DLB 146; LMFS 1
Julius Caesar 100B.C.-44B.C.
See Caesar, Julius
See also CDWLB 1; DLB 211
Junger, Ernst
See Juenger, Ernst
See also CDWLB 2; EWL 3; RGWL 2, 3
Junger, Sebastian 1962- .... **CLC 109**
See also AAYA 28; CA 165; CANR 130
Juniper, Alex
See Hospital, Janette Turner
Junius
See Luxemburg, Rosa
Just, Ward (Swift) 1935- .... **CLC 4, 27**
See also CA 25-28R; CANR 32, 87; CN 7; INT CANR-32
Justice, Donald (Rodney) 1925-2004 .... **CLC 6, 19, 102; PC 64**
See also AMWS 7; CA 5-8R; CANR 26, 54, 74, 121, 122; CP 7; CSW; DAM POET; DLBY 1983; EWL 3; INT CANR-26; MTCW 2; PFS 14
Juvenal c. 60-c. 130 .... **CMLC 8**
See also AW 2; CDWLB 1; DLB 211; RGWL 2, 3
Juvenis
See Bourne, Randolph S(illiman)
K., Alice
See Knapp, Caroline
Kabakov, Sasha .... **CLC 59**
Kabir 1398(?)-1448(?) .... **LC 109; PC 56**
See also RGWL 2, 3
Kacew, Romain 1914-1980
See Gary, Romain
See also CA 108; 102
Kadare, Ismail 1936- .... **CLC 52, 190**
See also CA 161; EWL 3; RGWL 3
Kadohata, Cynthia 1956(?)- ..... **CLC 59, 122**
See also CA 140; CANR 124
Kafka, Franz 1883-1924 ... **SSC 5, 29, 35, 60; TCLC 2, 6, 13, 29, 47, 53, 112; WLC**
See also AAYA 31; BPFB 2; CA 105; 126; CDWLB 2; DA; DA3; DAB; DAC; DAM MST, NOV; DLB 81; EW 9; EWL 3; EXPS; LATS 1:1; LMFS 2; MTCW 1, 2; NFS 7; RGSF 2; RGWL 2, 3; SFW 4; SSFS 3, 7, 12; TWA
Kahanovitsch, Pinkhes
See Der Nister
Kahn, Roger 1927- .... **CLC 30**
See also CA 25-28R; CANR 44, 69; DLB 171; SATA 37
Kain, Saul
See Sassoon, Siegfried (Lorraine)
Kaiser, Georg 1878-1945 .... **TCLC 9**
See also CA 106; 190; CDWLB 2; DLB 124; EWL 3; LMFS 2; RGWL 2, 3
Kaledin, Sergei .... **CLC 59**
Kaletski, Alexander 1946- .... **CLC 39**
See also CA 118; 143
Kalidasa fl. c. 400-455 .... **CMLC 9; PC 22**
See also RGWL 2, 3
Kallman, Chester (Simon) 1921-1975 .... **CLC 2**
See also CA 45-48; 53-56; CANR 3
Kaminsky, Melvin 1926-
See Brooks, Mel
See also CA 65-68; CANR 16
Kaminsky, Stuart M(elvin) 1934- ..... **CLC 59**
See also CA 73-76; CANR 29, 53, 89; CMW 4
Kamo no Chomei 1153(?)-1216 .... **CMLC 66**
See also DLB 203
Kamo no Nagaakira
See Kamo no Chomei
Kandinsky, Wassily 1866-1944 .... **TCLC 92**
See also CA 118; 155
Kane, Francis
See Robbins, Harold
Kane, Henry 1918-
See Queen, Ellery
See also CA 156; CMW 4
Kane, Paul
See Simon, Paul (Frederick)
Kanin, Garson 1912-1999 .... **CLC 22**
See also AITN 1; CA 5-8R; 177; CAD; CANR 7, 78; DLB 7; IDFW 3, 4
Kaniuk, Yoram 1930- .... **CLC 19**
See also CA 134; DLB 299
Kant, Immanuel 1724-1804 ..... **NCLC 27, 67**
See also DLB 94
Kantor, MacKinlay 1904-1977 .... **CLC 7**
See also CA 61-64; 73-76; CANR 60, 63; DLB 9, 102; MTCW 2; RHW; TCWW 2
Kanze Motokiyo
See Zeami
Kaplan, David Michael 1946- .... **CLC 50**
See also CA 187
Kaplan, James 1951- .... **CLC 59**
See also CA 135; CANR 121
Karadzic, Vuk Stefanovic 1787-1864 .... **NCLC 115**
See also CDWLB 4; DLB 147
Karageorge, Michael
See Anderson, Poul (William)
Karamzin, Nikolai Mikhailovich 1766-1826 .... **NCLC 3**
See also DLB 150; RGSF 2
Karapanou, Margarita 1946- .... **CLC 13**
See also CA 101
Karinthy, Frigyes 1887-1938 .... **TCLC 47**
See also CA 170; DLB 215; EWL 3
Karl, Frederick R(obert) 1927-2004 .... **CLC 34**
See also CA 5-8R; 226; CANR 3, 44
Karr, Mary 1955- .... **CLC 188**
See also AMWS 11; CA 151; CANR 100; NCFS 5
Kastel, Warren
See Silverberg, Robert
Kataev, Evgeny Petrovich 1903-1942
See Petrov, Evgeny
See also CA 120
Kataphusin
See Ruskin, John
Katz, Steve 1935- .... **CLC 47**
See also CA 25-28R; CAAS 14, 64; CANR 12; CN 7; DLBY 1983
Kauffman, Janet 1945- .... **CLC 42**
See also CA 117; CANR 43, 84; DLB 218; DLBY 1986
Kaufman, Bob (Garnell) 1925-1986 . **CLC 49**
See also BG 3; BW 1; CA 41-44R; 118; CANR 22; DLB 16, 41
Kaufman, George S. 1889-1961 ...... **CLC 38; DC 17**
See also CA 108; 93-96; DAM DRAM; DFS 1, 10; DLB 7; INT CA-108; MTCW 2; RGAL 4; TUS
Kaufman, Moises 1964- .... **DC 26**
CA 211; MTFW
Kaufman, Sue .... **CLC 3, 8**
See Barondess, Sue K(aufman)
Kavafis, Konstantinos Petrou 1863-1933
See Cavafy, C(onstantine) P(eter)
See also CA 104
Kavan, Anna 1901-1968 .... **CLC 5, 13, 82**
See also BRWS 7; CA 5-8R; CANR 6, 57; DLB 255; MTCW 1; RGEL 2; SFW 4
Kavanagh, Dan
See Barnes, Julian (Patrick)
Kavanagh, Julie 1952- .... **CLC 119**
See also CA 163
Kavanagh, Patrick (Joseph) 1904-1967 .... **CLC 22; PC 33**
See also BRWS 7; CA 123; 25-28R; DLB 15, 20; EWL 3; MTCW 1; RGEL 2
Kawabata, Yasunari 1899-1972 ..... **CLC 2, 5, 9, 18, 107; SSC 17**
See Kawabata Yasunari
See also CA 93-96; 33-36R; CANR 88; DAM MULT; MJW; MTCW 2; RGSF 2; RGWL 2, 3
Kawabata Yasunari
See Kawabata, Yasunari
See also DLB 180; EWL 3
Kaye, M(ary) M(argaret) 1908-2004 .... **CLC 28**
See also CA 89-92; 223; CANR 24, 60, 102; MTCW 1, 2; RHW; SATA 62; SATA-Obit 152
Kaye, Mollie
See Kaye, M(ary) M(argaret)
Kaye-Smith, Sheila 1887-1956 .... **TCLC 20**
See also CA 118; 203; DLB 36
Kaymor, Patrice Maguilene
See Senghor, Leopold Sedar
Kazakov, Iurii Pavlovich
See Kazakov, Yuri Pavlovich
See also DLB 302
Kazakov, Yuri Pavlovich 1927-1982 . **SSC 43**
See Kazakov, Iurii Pavlovich; Kazakov, Yury
See also CA 5-8R; CANR 36; MTCW 1; RGSF 2
Kazakov, Yury
See Kazakov, Yuri Pavlovich
See also EWL 3
Kazan, Elia 1909-2003 .... **CLC 6, 16, 63**
See also CA 21-24R; 220; CANR 32, 78
Kazantzakis, Nikos 1883(?)-1957 .... **TCLC 2, 5, 33**
See also BPFB 2; CA 105; 132; DA3; EW 9; EWL 3; MTCW 1, 2; RGWL 2, 3
Kazin, Alfred 1915-1998 ..... **CLC 34, 38, 119**
See also AMWS 8; CA 1-4R; CAAS 7; CANR 1, 45, 79; DLB 67; EWL 3
Keane, Mary Nesta (Skrine) 1904-1996
See Keane, Molly
See also CA 108; 114; 151; CN 7; RHW
Keane, Molly .... **CLC 31**
See Keane, Mary Nesta (Skrine)
See also INT CA-114
Keates, Jonathan 1946(?)- .... **CLC 34**
See also CA 163; CANR 126
Keaton, Buster 1895-1966 .... **CLC 20**
See also CA 194

King, Francis (Henry) 1923- .... **CLC 8, 53, 145**
See also CA 1-4R; CANR 1, 33, 86; CN 7; DAM NOV; DLB 15, 139; MTCW 1
King, Kennedy
See Brown, George Douglas
King, Martin Luther, Jr. 1929-1968 . **BLC 2; CLC 83; WLCS**
See also BW 2, 3; CA 25-28; CANR 27, 44; CAP 2; DA; DA3; DAB; DAC; DAM MST, MULT; LAIT 5; LATS 1:2; MTCW 1, 2; SATA 14
King, Stephen (Edwin) 1947- .... **CLC 12, 26, 37, 61, 113; SSC 17, 55**
See also AAYA 1, 17; AMWS 5; BEST 90:1; BPFB 2; CA 61-64; CANR 1, 30, 52, 76, 119, 134; CPW; DA3; DAM NOV, POP; DLB 143; DLBY 1980; HGG; JRDA; LAIT 5; MTCW 1, 2; RGAL 4; SATA 9, 55; SUFW 1, 2; WYAS 1; YAW
King, Steve
See King, Stephen (Edwin)
King, Thomas 1943- .... **CLC 89, 171; NNAL**
See also CA 144; CANR 95; CCA 1; CN 7; DAC; DAM MULT; DLB 175; SATA 96
Kingman, Lee .... **CLC 17**
See Natti, (Mary) Lee
See also CWRI 5; SAAS 3; SATA 1, 67
Kingsley, Charles 1819-1875 .... **NCLC 35**
See also CLR 77; DLB 21, 32, 163, 178, 190; FANT; MAICYA 2; MAICYAS 1; RGEL 2; WCH; YABC 2
Kingsley, Henry 1830-1876 .... **NCLC 107**
See also DLB 21, 230; RGEL 2
Kingsley, Sidney 1906-1995 .... **CLC 44**
See also CA 85-88; 147; CAD; DFS 14, 19; DLB 7; RGAL 4
Kingsolver, Barbara 1955- . **CLC 55, 81, 130**
See also AAYA 15; AMWS 7; CA 129; 134; CANR 60, 96, 133; CDALBS; CPW; CSW; DA3; DAM POP; DLB 206; INT CA-134; LAIT 5; MTCW 2; NFS 5, 10, 12; RGAL 4
Kingston, Maxine (Ting Ting) Hong 1940- .... **AAL; CLC 12, 19, 58, 121; WLCS**
See also AAYA 8, 55; AMWS 5; BPFB 2; CA 69-72; CANR 13, 38, 74, 87, 128; CDALBS; CN 7; DA3; DAM MULT, NOV; DLB 173, 212; DLBY 1980; EWL 3; FW; INT CANR-13; LAIT 5; MAWW; MTCW 1, 2; NFS 6; RGAL 4; SATA 53; SSFS 3
Kinnell, Galway 1927- ..... **CLC 1, 2, 3, 5, 13, 29, 129; PC 26**
See also AMWS 3; CA 9-12R; CANR 10, 34, 66, 116; CP 7; DLB 5; DLBY 1987; EWL 3; INT CANR-34; MTCW 1, 2; PAB; PFS 9; RGAL 4; WP
Kinsella, Thomas 1928- .... **CLC 4, 19, 138**
See also BRWS 5; CA 17-20R; CANR 15, 122; CP 7; DLB 27; EWL 3; MTCW 1, 2; RGEL 2; TEA
Kinsella, W(illiam) P(atrick) 1935- . **CLC 27, 43, 166**
See also AAYA 7, 60; BPFB 2; CA 97-100, 222; CAAE 222; CAAS 7; CANR 21, 35, 66, 75, 129; CN 7; CPW; DAC; DAM NOV, POP; FANT; INT CANR-21; LAIT 5; MTCW 1, 2; NFS 15; RGSF 2
Kinsey, Alfred C(harles) 1894-1956 .... **TCLC 91**
See also CA 115; 170; MTCW 2
Kipling, (Joseph) Rudyard 1865-1936 . **PC 3; SSC 5, 54; TCLC 8, 17, 167; WLC**
See also AAYA 32; BRW 6; BRWC 1, 2; BYA 4; CA 105; 120; CANR 33; CDBLB 1890-1914; CLR 39, 65; CWRI 5; DA; DA3; DAB; DAC; DAM MST, POET; DLB 19, 34, 141, 156; EWL 3; EXPS; FANT; LAIT 3; LMFS 1; MAICYA 1, 2; MTCW 1, 2; RGEL 2; RGSF 2; SATA 100; SFW 4; SSFS 8; SUFW 1; TEA; WCH; WLIT 4; YABC 2
Kirk, Russell (Amos) 1918-1994 .. **TCLC 119**
See also AITN 1; CA 1-4R; 145; CAAS 9; CANR 1, 20, 60; HGG; INT CANR-20; MTCW 1, 2
Kirkham, Dinah
See Card, Orson Scott
Kirkland, Caroline M. 1801-1864 . **NCLC 85**
See also DLB 3, 73, 74, 250, 254; DLBD 13
Kirkup, James 1918- .... **CLC 1**
See also CA 1-4R; CAAS 4; CANR 2; CP 7; DLB 27; SATA 12
Kirkwood, James 1930(?)-1989 .... **CLC 9**
See also AITN 2; CA 1-4R; 128; CANR 6, 40; GLL 2
Kirsch, Sarah 1935- .... **CLC 176**
See also CA 178; CWW 2; DLB 75; EWL 3
Kirshner, Sidney
See Kingsley, Sidney
Kis, Danilo 1935-1989 .... **CLC 57**
See also CA 109; 118; 129; CANR 61; CDWLB 4; DLB 181; EWL 3; MTCW 1; RGSF 2; RGWL 2, 3
Kissinger, Henry A(lfred) 1923- ..... **CLC 137**
See also CA 1-4R; CANR 2, 33, 66, 109; MTCW 1
Kivi, Aleksis 1834-1872 .... **NCLC 30**
Kizer, Carolyn (Ashley) 1925- ... **CLC 15, 39, 80; PC 66**
See also CA 65-68; CAAS 5; CANR 24, 70, 134; CP 7; CWP; DAM POET; DLB 5, 169; EWL 3; MTCW 2; PFS 18
Klabund 1890-1928 .... **TCLC 44**
See also CA 162; DLB 66
Klappert, Peter 1942- .... **CLC 57**
See also CA 33-36R; CSW; DLB 5
Klein, A(braham) M(oses) 1909-1972 .... **CLC 19**
See also CA 101; 37-40R; DAB; DAC; DAM MST; DLB 68; EWL 3; RGEL 2
Klein, Joe
See Klein, Joseph
Klein, Joseph 1946- .... **CLC 154**
See also CA 85-88; CANR 55
Klein, Norma 1938-1989 .... **CLC 30**
See also AAYA 2, 35; BPFB 2; BYA 6, 7, 8; CA 41-44R; 128; CANR 15, 37; CLR 2, 19; INT CANR-15; JRDA; MAICYA 1, 2; SAAS 1; SATA 7, 57; WYA; YAW
Klein, T(heodore) E(ibon) D(onald) 1947- .... **CLC 34**
See also CA 119; CANR 44, 75; HGG
Kleist, Heinrich von 1777-1811 ...... **NCLC 2, 37; SSC 22**
See also CDWLB 2; DAM DRAM; DLB 90; EW 5; RGSF 2; RGWL 2, 3
Klima, Ivan 1931- .... **CLC 56, 172**
See also CA 25-28R; CANR 17, 50, 91; CDWLB 4; CWW 2; DAM NOV; DLB 232; EWL 3; RGWL 3
Klimentev, Andrei Platonovich
See Klimentov, Andrei Platonovich
Klimentov, Andrei Platonovich 1899-1951 .... **SSC 42; TCLC 14**
See Platonov, Andrei Platonovich; Platonov, Andrey Platonovich
See also CA 108
Klinger, Friedrich Maximilian von 1752-1831 .... **NCLC 1**
See also DLB 94
Klingsor the Magician
See Hartmann, Sadakichi
Klopstock, Friedrich Gottlieb 1724-1803 .... **NCLC 11**
See also DLB 97; EW 4; RGWL 2, 3
Kluge, Alexander 1932- .... **SSC 61**
See also CA 81-84; DLB 75
Knapp, Caroline 1959-2002 .... **CLC 99**
See also CA 154; 207
Knebel, Fletcher 1911-1993 .... **CLC 14**
See also AITN 1; CA 1-4R; 140; CAAS 3; CANR 1, 36; SATA 36; SATA-Obit 75
Knickerbocker, Diedrich
See Irving, Washington
Knight, Etheridge 1931-1991 ... **BLC 2; CLC 40; PC 14**
See also BW 1, 3; CA 21-24R; 133; CANR 23, 82; DAM POET; DLB 41; MTCW 2; RGAL 4
Knight, Sarah Kemble 1666-1727 .... **LC 7**
See also DLB 24, 200
Knister, Raymond 1899-1932 .... **TCLC 56**
See also CA 186; DLB 68; RGEL 2
Knowles, John 1926-2001 ... **CLC 1, 4, 10, 26**
See also AAYA 10; AMWS 12; BPFB 2; BYA 3; CA 17-20R; 203; CANR 40, 74, 76, 132; CDALB 1968-1988; CLR 98; CN 7; DA; DAC; DAM MST, NOV; DLB 6; EXPN; MTCW 1, 2; NFS 2; RGAL 4; SATA 8, 89; SATA-Obit 134; YAW
Knox, Calvin M.
See Silverberg, Robert
Knox, John c. 1505-1572 .... **LC 37**
See also DLB 132
Knye, Cassandra
See Disch, Thomas M(ichael)
Koch, C(hristopher) J(ohn) 1932- .... **CLC 42**
See also CA 127; CANR 84; CN 7; DLB 289
Koch, Christopher
See Koch, C(hristopher) J(ohn)
Koch, Kenneth (Jay) 1925-2002 .... **CLC 5, 8, 44**
See also CA 1-4R; 207; CAD; CANR 6, 36, 57, 97, 131; CD 5; CP 7; DAM POET; DLB 5; INT CANR-36; MTCW 2; PFS 20; SATA 65; WP
Kochanowski, Jan 1530-1584 .... **LC 10**
See also RGWL 2, 3
Kock, Charles Paul de 1794-1871 . **NCLC 16**
Koda Rohan
See Koda Shigeyuki
Koda Rohan
See Koda Shigeyuki
See also DLB 180
Koda Shigeyuki 1867-1947 .... **TCLC 22**
See Koda Rohan
See also CA 121; 183
Koestler, Arthur 1905-1983 ... **CLC 1, 3, 6, 8, 15, 33**
See also BRWS 1; CA 1-4R; 109; CANR 1, 33; CDBLB 1945-1960; DLBY 1983; EWL 3; MTCW 1, 2; NFS 19; RGEL 2
Kogawa, Joy Nozomi 1935- ...... **CLC 78, 129**
See also AAYA 47; CA 101; CANR 19, 62, 126; CN 7; CWP; DAC; DAM MST, MULT; FW; MTCW 2; NFS 3; SATA 99
Kohout, Pavel 1928- .... **CLC 13**
See also CA 45-48; CANR 3
Koizumi, Yakumo
See Hearn, (Patricio) Lafcadio (Tessima Carlos)
Kolmar, Gertrud 1894-1943 .... **TCLC 40**
See also CA 167; EWL 3
Komunyakaa, Yusef 1947- .. **BLCS; CLC 86, 94, 207; PC 51**
See also AFAW 2; AMWS 13; CA 147; CANR 83; CP 7; CSW; DLB 120; EWL 3; PFS 5, 20; RGAL 4
Konrad, George
See Konrad, Gyorgy

Merchant, Paul
See Ellison, Harlan (Jay)
Meredith, George 1828-1909 .. **PC 60; TCLC 17, 43**
See also CA 117; 153; CANR 80; CDBLB 1832-1890; DAM POET; DLB 18, 35, 57, 159; RGEL 2; TEA
Meredith, William (Morris) 1919- .... **CLC 4, 13, 22, 55; PC 28**
See also CA 9-12R; CAAS 14; CANR 6, 40, 129; CP 7; DAM POET; DLB 5
Merezhkovsky, Dmitrii Sergeevich
See Merezhkovsky, Dmitry Sergeyevich
See also DLB 295
Merezhkovsky, Dmitry Sergeevich
See Merezhkovsky, Dmitry Sergeyevich
See also EWL 3
Merezhkovsky, Dmitry Sergeyevich 1865-1941 .... **TCLC 29**
See Merezhkovsky, Dmitrii Sergeevich; Merezhkovsky, Dmitry Sergeevich
See also CA 169
Merimee, Prosper 1803-1870 ... **NCLC 6, 65; SSC 7, 77**
See also DLB 119, 192; EW 6; EXPS; GFL 1789 to the Present; RGSF 2; RGWL 2, 3; SSFS 8; SUFW
Merkin, Daphne 1954- .... **CLC 44**
See also CA 123
Merleau-Ponty, Maurice 1908-1961 .... **TCLC 156**
See also CA 114; 89-92; DLB 296; GFL 1789 to the Present
Merlin, Arthur
See Blish, James (Benjamin)
Mernissi, Fatima 1940- .... **CLC 171**
See also CA 152; FW
Merrill, James (Ingram) 1926-1995 .. **CLC 2, 3, 6, 8, 13, 18, 34, 91; PC 28**
See also AMWS 3; CA 13-16R; 147; CANR 10, 49, 63, 108; DA3; DAM POET; DLB 5, 165; DLBY 1985; EWL 3; INT CANR-10; MTCW 1, 2; PAB; RGAL 4
Merriman, Alex
See Silverberg, Robert
Merriman, Brian 1747-1805 .... **NCLC 70**
Merritt, E. B.
See Waddington, Miriam
Merton, Thomas (James) 1915-1968 . **CLC 1, 3, 11, 34, 83; PC 10**
See also AMWS 8; CA 5-8R; 25-28R; CANR 22, 53, 111, 131; DA3; DLB 48; DLBY 1981; MTCW 1, 2
Merwin, W(illiam) S(tanley) 1927- ... **CLC 1, 2, 3, 5, 8, 13, 18, 45, 88; PC 45**
See also AMWS 3; CA 13-16R; CANR 15, 51, 112; CP 7; DA3; DAM POET; DLB 5, 169; EWL 3; INT CANR-15; MTCW 1, 2; PAB; PFS 5, 15; RGAL 4
Metastasio, Pietro 1698-1782 .... **LC 115**
See also RGWL 2, 3
Metcalf, John 1938- .... **CLC 37; SSC 43**
See also CA 113; CN 7; DLB 60; RGSF 2; TWA
Metcalf, Suzanne
See Baum, L(yman) Frank
Mew, Charlotte (Mary) 1870-1928 .. **TCLC 8**
See also CA 105; 189; DLB 19, 135; RGEL 2
Mewshaw, Michael 1943- .... **CLC 9**
See also CA 53-56; CANR 7, 47; DLBY 1980
Meyer, Conrad Ferdinand 1825-1898 .... **NCLC 81; SSC 30**
See also DLB 129; EW; RGWL 2, 3
Meyer, Gustav 1868-1932
See Meyrink, Gustav
See also CA 117; 190
Meyer, June
See Jordan, June (Meyer)
Meyer, Lynn
See Slavitt, David R(ytman)
Meyers, Jeffrey 1939- .... **CLC 39**
See also CA 73-76, 186; CAAE 186; CANR 54, 102; DLB 111
Meynell, Alice (Christina Gertrude Thompson) 1847-1922 .... **TCLC 6**
See also CA 104; 177; DLB 19, 98; RGEL 2
Meyrink, Gustav .... **TCLC 21**
See Meyer, Gustav
See also DLB 81; EWL 3
Michaels, Leonard 1933-2003 ..... **CLC 6, 25; SSC 16**
See also CA 61-64; 216; CANR 21, 62, 119; CN 7; DLB 130; MTCW 1
Michaux, Henri 1899-1984 .... **CLC 8, 19**
See also CA 85-88; 114; DLB 258; EWL 3; GFL 1789 to the Present; RGWL 2, 3
Micheaux, Oscar (Devereaux) 1884-1951 .... **TCLC 76**
See also BW 3; CA 174; DLB 50; TCWW 2
Michelangelo 1475-1564 .... **LC 12**
See also AAYA 43
Michelet, Jules 1798-1874 .... **NCLC 31**
See also EW 5; GFL 1789 to the Present
Michels, Robert 1876-1936 .... **TCLC 88**
See also CA 212
Michener, James A(lbert) 1907(?)-1997 .. **CLC 1, 5, 11, 29, 60, 109**
See also AAYA 27; AITN 1; BEST 90:1; BPFB 2; CA 5-8R; 161; CANR 21, 45, 68; CN 7; CPW; DA3; DAM NOV, POP; DLB 6; MTCW 1, 2; RHW
Mickiewicz, Adam 1798-1855 . **NCLC 3, 101; PC 38**
See also EW 5; RGWL 2, 3
Middleton, (John) Christopher 1926- .... **CLC 13**
See also CA 13-16R; CANR 29, 54, 117; CP 7; DLB 40
Middleton, Richard (Barham) 1882-1911 .... **TCLC 56**
See also CA 187; DLB 156; HGG
Middleton, Stanley 1919- .... **CLC 7, 38**
See also CA 25-28R; CAAS 23; CANR 21, 46, 81; CN 7; DLB 14
Middleton, Thomas 1580-1627 ...... **DC 5; LC 33**
See also BRW 2; DAM DRAM, MST; DFS 18; DLB 58; RGEL 2
Migueis, Jose Rodrigues 1901-1980 . **CLC 10**
See also DLB 287
Mikszath, Kalman 1847-1910 .... **TCLC 31**
See also CA 170
Miles, Jack .... **CLC 100**
See also CA 200
Miles, John Russiano
See Miles, Jack
Miles, Josephine (Louise) 1911-1985 .... **CLC 1, 2, 14, 34, 39**
See also CA 1-4R; 116; CANR 2, 55; DAM POET; DLB 48
Militant
See Sandburg, Carl (August)
Mill, Harriet (Hardy) Taylor 1807-1858 .... **NCLC 102**
See also FW
Mill, John Stuart 1806-1873 .... **NCLC 11, 58**
See also CDBLB 1832-1890; DLB 55, 190, 262; FW 1; RGEL 2; TEA
Millar, Kenneth 1915-1983 .... **CLC 14**
See Macdonald, Ross
See also CA 9-12R; 110; CANR 16, 63, 107; CMW 4; CPW; DA3; DAM POP; DLB 2, 226; DLBD 6; DLBY 1983; MTCW 1, 2
Millay, E. Vincent
See Millay, Edna St. Vincent
Millay, Edna St. Vincent 1892-1950 ..... **PC 6, 61; TCLC 4, 49, 169; WLCS**
See Boyd, Nancy
See also AMW; CA 104; 130; CDALB 1917-1929; DA; DA3; DAB; DAC; DAM MST, POET; DLB 45, 249; EWL 3; EXPP; MAWW; MTCW 1, 2; PAB; PFS 3, 17; RGAL 4; TUS; WP
Miller, Arthur 1915- ...... **CLC 1, 2, 6, 10, 15, 26, 47, 78, 179; DC 1; WLC**
See also AAYA 15; AITN 1; AMW; AMWC 1; CA 1-4R; CABS 3; CAD; CANR 2, 30, 54, 76, 132; CD 5; CDALB 1941-1968; DA; DA3; DAB; DAC; DAM DRAM, MST; DFS 1, 3, 8; DLB 7, 266; EWL 3; LAIT 1, 4; LATS 1:2; MTCW 1, 2; RGAL 4; TUS; WYAS 1
Miller, Henry (Valentine) 1891-1980 .... **CLC 1, 2, 4, 9, 14, 43, 84; WLC**
See also AMW; BPFB 2; CA 9-12R; 97-100; CANR 33, 64; CDALB 1929-1941; DA; DA3; DAB; DAC; DAM MST, NOV; DLB 4, 9; DLBY 1980; EWL 3; MTCW 1, 2; RGAL 4; TUS
Miller, Hugh 1802-1856 .... **NCLC 143**
See also DLB 190
Miller, Jason 1939(?)-2001 .... **CLC 2**
See also AITN 1; CA 73-76; 197; CAD; CANR 130; DFS 12; DLB 7
Miller, Sue 1943- .... **CLC 44**
See also AMWS 12; BEST 90:3; CA 139; CANR 59, 91, 128; DA3; DAM POP; DLB 143
Miller, Walter M(ichael, Jr.) 1923-1996 .... **CLC 4, 30**
See also BPFB 2; CA 85-88; CANR 108; DLB 8; SCFW; SFW 4
Millett, Kate 1934- .... **CLC 67**
See also AITN 1; CA 73-76; CANR 32, 53, 76, 110; DA3; DLB 246; FW; GLL 1; MTCW 1, 2
Millhauser, Steven (Lewis) 1943- .... **CLC 21, 54, 109; SSC 57**
See also CA 110; 111; CANR 63, 114, 133; CN 7; DA3; DLB 2; FANT; INT CA-111; MTCW 2
Millin, Sarah Gertrude 1889-1968 ... **CLC 49**
See also CA 102; 93-96; DLB 225; EWL 3
Milne, A(lan) A(lexander) 1882-1956 .... **TCLC 6, 88**
See also BRWS 5; CA 104; 133; CLR 1, 26; CMW 4; CWRI 5; DA3; DAB; DAC; DAM MST; DLB 10, 77, 100, 160; FANT; MAICYA 1, 2; MTCW 1, 2; RGEL 2; SATA 100; WCH; YABC 1
Milner, Ron(ald) 1938-2004 ..... **BLC 3; CLC 56**
See also AITN 1; BW 1; CA 73-76; CAD; CANR 24, 81; CD 5; DAM MULT; DLB 38; MTCW 1
Milnes, Richard Monckton 1809-1885 .... **NCLC 61**
See also DLB 32, 184
Milosz, Czeslaw 1911- ...... **CLC 5, 11, 22, 31, 56, 82; PC 8; WLCS**
See also CA 81-84; CANR 23, 51, 91, 126; CDWLB 4; CWW 2; DA3; DAM MST, POET; DLB 215; EW 13; EWL 3; MTCW 1, 2; PFS 16; RGWL 2, 3

Moorcock, Michael (John) 1939- ...... **CLC 5, 27, 58**
See Bradbury, Edward P.
See also AAYA 26; CA 45-48; CAAS 5; CANR 2, 17, 38, 64, 122; CN 7; DLB 14, 231, 261; FANT; MTCW 1, 2; SATA 93; SCFW 2; SFW 4; SUFW 1, 2

Moore, Brian 1921-1999 ... **CLC 1, 3, 5, 7, 8, 19, 32, 90**
See Bryan, Michael
See also BRWS 9; CA 1-4R; 174; CANR 1, 25, 42, 63; CCA 1; CN 7; DAB; DAC; DAM MST; DLB 251; EWL 3; FANT; MTCW 1, 2; RGEL 2

Moore, Edward
See Muir, Edwin
See also RGEL 2

Moore, G. E. 1873-1958 .... **TCLC 89**
See also DLB 262

Moore, George Augustus 1852-1933 .... **SSC 19; TCLC 7**
See also BRW 6; CA 104; 177; DLB 10, 18, 57, 135; EWL 3; RGEL 2; RGSF 2

Moore, Lorrie .... **CLC 39, 45, 68**
See Moore, Marie Lorena
See also AMWS 10; DLB 234; SSFS 19

Moore, Marianne (Craig) 1887-1972 .... **CLC 1, 2, 4, 8, 10, 13, 19, 47; PC 4, 49; WLCS**
See also AMW; CA 1-4R; 33-36R; CANR 3, 61; CDALB 1929-1941; DA; DA3; DAB; DAC; DAM MST, POET; DLB 45; DLBD 7; EWL 3; EXPP; MAWW; MTCW 1, 2; PAB; PFS 14, 17; RGAL 4; SATA 20; TUS; WP

Moore, Marie Lorena 1957- .... **CLC 165**
See Moore, Lorrie
See also CA 116; CANR 39, 83; CN 7; DLB 234

Moore, Thomas 1779-1852 .... **NCLC 6, 110**
See also DLB 96, 144; RGEL 2

Moorhouse, Frank 1938- .... **SSC 40**
See also CA 118; CANR 92; CN 7; DLB 289; RGSF 2

Mora, Pat(ricia) 1942- .... **HLC 2**
See also AMWS 13; CA 129; CANR 57, 81, 112; CLR 58; DAM MULT; DLB 209; HW 1, 2; LLW 1; MAICYA 2; SATA 92, 134

Moraga, Cherrie 1952- ...... **CLC 126; DC 22**
See also CA 131; CANR 66; DAM MULT; DLB 82, 249; FW; GLL 1; HW 1, 2; LLW 1

Morand, Paul 1888-1976 .... **CLC 41; SSC 22**
See also CA 184; 69-72; DLB 65; EWL 3

Morante, Elsa 1918-1985 .... **CLC 8, 47**
See also CA 85-88; 117; CANR 35; DLB 177; EWL 3; MTCW 1, 2; RGWL 2, 3

Moravia, Alberto .... **CLC 2, 7, 11, 27, 46; SSC 26**
See Pincherle, Alberto
See also DLB 177; EW 12; EWL 3; MTCW 2; RGSF 2; RGWL 2, 3

More, Hannah 1745-1833 ...... **NCLC 27, 141**
See also DLB 107, 109, 116, 158; RGEL 2

More, Henry 1614-1687 .... **LC 9**
See also DLB 126, 252

More, Sir Thomas 1478(?)-1535 .... **LC 10, 32**
See also BRWC 1; BRWS 7; DLB 136, 281; LMFS 1; RGEL 2; TEA

Moreas, Jean .... **TCLC 18**
See Papadiamantopoulos, Johannes
See also GFL 1789 to the Present

Moreton, Andrew Esq.
See Defoe, Daniel

Morgan, Berry 1919-2002 .... **CLC 6**
See also CA 49-52; 208; DLB 6

Morgan, Claire
See Highsmith, (Mary) Patricia .
See also GLL 1

Morgan, Edwin (George) 1920- .... **CLC 31**
See also BRWS 9; CA 5-8R; CANR 3, 43, 90; CP 7; DLB 27

Morgan, (George) Frederick 1922-2004 .... **CLC 23**
See also CA 17-20R; 224; CANR 21; CP 7

Morgan, Harriet
See Mencken, H(enry) L(ouis)

Morgan, Jane
See Cooper, James Fenimore

Morgan, Janet 1945- .... **CLC 39**
See also CA 65-68

Morgan, Lady 1776(?)-1859 .... **NCLC 29**
See also DLB 116, 158; RGEL 2

Morgan, Robin (Evonne) 1941- .... **CLC 2**
See also CA 69-72; CANR 29, 68; FW; GLL 2; MTCW 1; SATA 80

Morgan, Scott
See Kuttner, Henry

Morgan, Seth 1949(?)-1990 .... **CLC 65**
See also CA 185; 132

Morgenstern, Christian (Otto Josef Wolfgang) 1871-1914 .... **TCLC 8**
See also CA 105; 191; EWL 3

Morgenstern, S.
See Goldman, William (W.)

Mori, Rintaro
See Mori Ogai
See also CA 110

Mori, Toshio 1910-1980 .... **SSC 83**
See also AAL; CA 116; DLB 312; RGSF 2

Moricz, Zsigmond 1879-1942 .... **TCLC 33**
See also CA 165; DLB 215; EWL 3

Morike, Eduard (Friedrich) 1804-1875 .... **NCLC 10**
See also DLB 133; RGWL 2, 3

Mori Ogai 1862-1922 .... **TCLC 14**
See Ogai
See also CA 164; DLB 180; EWL 3; RGWL 3; TWA

Moritz, Karl Philipp 1756-1793 .... **LC 2**
See also DLB 94

Morland, Peter Henry
See Faust, Frederick (Schiller)

Morley, Christopher (Darlington) 1890-1957 .... **TCLC 87**
See also CA 112; 213; DLB 9; RGAL 4

Morren, Theophil
See Hofmannsthal, Hugo von

Morris, Bill 1952- .... **CLC 76**
See also CA 225

Morris, Julian
See West, Morris L(anglo)

Morris, Steveland Judkins 1950(?)-
See Wonder, Stevie
See also CA 111

Morris, William 1834-1896 . **NCLC 4; PC 55**
See also BRW 5; CDBLB 1832-1890; DLB 18, 35, 57, 156, 178, 184; FANT; RGEL 2; SFW 4; SUFW

Morris, Wright 1910-1998 .. **CLC 1, 3, 7, 18, 37; TCLC 107**
See also AMW; CA 9-12R; 167; CANR 21, 81; CN 7; DLB 2, 206, 218; DLBY 1981; EWL 3; MTCW 1, 2; RGAL 4; TCWW 2

Morrison, Arthur 1863-1945 .... **SSC 40; TCLC 72**
See also CA 120; 157; CMW 4; DLB 70, 135, 197; RGEL 2

Morrison, Chloe Anthony Wofford
See Morrison, Toni

Morrison, James Douglas 1943-1971
See Morrison, Jim
See also CA 73-76; CANR 40

Morrison, Jim .... **CLC 17**
See Morrison, James Douglas

Morrison, Toni 1931- ..... **BLC 3; CLC 4, 10, 22, 55, 81, 87, 173, 194**
See also AAYA 1, 22; AFAW 1, 2; AMWC 1; AMWS 3; BPFB 2; BW 2, 3; CA 29-32R; CANR 27, 42, 67, 113, 124; CDALB 1968-1988; CLR 99; CN 7; CPW; DA; DA3; DAB; DAC; DAM MST, MULT, NOV, POP; DLB 6, 33, 143; DLBY 1981; EWL 3; EXPN; FW; LAIT 2, 4; LATS 1:2; LMFS 2; MAWW; MTCW 1, 2; NFS 1, 6, 8, 14; RGAL 4; RHW; SATA 57, 144; SSFS 5; TUS; YAW

Morrison, Van 1945- .... **CLC 21**
See also CA 116; 168

Morrissy, Mary 1957- .... **CLC 99**
See also CA 205; DLB 267

Mortimer, John (Clifford) 1923- ..... **CLC 28, 43**
See also CA 13-16R; CANR 21, 69, 109; CD 5; CDBLB 1960 to Present; CMW 4; CN 7; CPW; DA3; DAM DRAM, POP; DLB 13, 245, 271; INT CANR-21; MSW; MTCW 1, 2; RGEL 2

Mortimer, Penelope (Ruth) 1918-1999 .... **CLC 5**
See also CA 57-60; 187; CANR 45, 88; CN 7

Mortimer, Sir John
See Mortimer, John (Clifford)

Morton, Anthony
See Creasey, John

Morton, Thomas 1579(?)-1647(?) .... **LC 72**
See also DLB 24; RGEL 2

Mosca, Gaetano 1858-1941 .... **TCLC 75**

Moses, Daniel David 1952- .... **NNAL**
See also CA 186

Mosher, Howard Frank 1943- .... **CLC 62**
See also CA 139; CANR 65, 115

Mosley, Nicholas 1923- .... **CLC 43, 70**
See also CA 69-72; CANR 41, 60, 108; CN 7; DLB 14, 207

Mosley, Walter 1952- .... **BLCS; CLC 97, 184**
See also AAYA 57; AMWS 13; BPFB 2; BW 2; CA 142; CANR 57, 92; CMW 4; CPW; DA3; DAM MULT, POP; DLB 306; MSW; MTCW 2

Moss, Howard 1922-1987 . **CLC 7, 14, 45, 50**
See also CA 1-4R; 123; CANR 1, 44; DAM POET; DLB 5

Mossgiel, Rab
See Burns, Robert

Motion, Andrew (Peter) 1952- .... **CLC 47**
See also BRWS 7; CA 146; CANR 90; CP 7; DLB 40

Motley, Willard (Francis) 1909-1965 .... **CLC 18**
See also BW 1; CA 117; 106; CANR 88; DLB 76, 143

Motoori, Norinaga 1730-1801 .... **NCLC 45**

Mott, Michael (Charles Alston) 1930- .... **CLC 15, 34**
See also CA 5-8R; CAAS 7; CANR 7, 29

Mountain Wolf Woman 1884-1960 . **CLC 92; NNAL**
See also CA 144; CANR 90

Moure, Erin 1955- .... **CLC 88**
See also CA 113; CP 7; CWP; DLB 60

Mourning Dove 1885(?)-1936 .... **NNAL**
See also CA 144; CANR 90; DAM MULT; DLB 175, 221

Mowat, Farley (McGill) 1921- .... **CLC 26**
See also AAYA 1, 50; BYA 2; CA 1-4R; CANR 4, 24, 42, 68, 108; CLR 20; CPW; DAC; DAM MST; DLB 68; INT CANR-24; JRDA; MAICYA 1, 2; MTCW 1, 2; SATA 3, 55; YAW

Author Index

POET; DLB 20; EWL 3; EXPP; MTCW 2; PFS 10; RGEL 2; WLIT 4
Owens, Louis (Dean) 1948-2002 .... **NNAL**
See also CA 137, 179; 207; CAAE 179; CAAS 24; CANR 71
Owens, Rochelle 1936- .... **CLC 8**
See also CA 17-20R; CAAS 2; CAD; CANR 39; CD 5; CP 7; CWD; CWP
Oz, Amos 1939- ...... **CLC 5, 8, 11, 27, 33, 54; SSC 66**
See also CA 53-56; CANR 27, 47, 65, 113; CWW 2; DAM NOV; EWL 3; MTCW 1, 2; RGSF 2; RGWL 3
Ozick, Cynthia 1928- .... **CLC 3, 7, 28, 62, 155; SSC 15, 60**
See also AMWS 5; BEST 90:1; CA 17-20R; CANR 23, 58, 116; CN 7; CPW; DA3; DAM NOV, POP; DLB 28, 152, 299; DLBY 1982; EWL 3; EXPS; INT CANR-23; MTCW 1, 2; RGAL 4; RGSF 2; SSFS 3, 12
Ozu, Yasujiro 1903-1963 .... **CLC 16**
See also CA 112
Pabst, G. W. 1885-1967 .... **TCLC 127**
Pacheco, C.
See Pessoa, Fernando (Antonio Nogueira)
Pacheco, Jose Emilio 1939- .... **HLC 2**
See also CA 111; 131; CANR 65; CWW 2; DAM MULT; DLB 290; EWL 3; HW 1, 2; RGSF 2
Pa Chin .... **CLC 18**
See Li Fei-kan
See also EWL 3
Pack, Robert 1929- .... **CLC 13**
See also CA 1-4R; CANR 3, 44, 82; CP 7; DLB 5; SATA 118
Padgett, Lewis
See Kuttner, Henry
Padilla (Lorenzo), Heberto 1932-2000 .... **CLC 38**
See also AITN 1; CA 123; 131; 189; CWW 2; EWL 3; HW 1
Page, James Patrick 1944-
See Page, Jimmy
See also CA 204
Page, Jimmy 1944- .... **CLC 12**
See Page, James Patrick
Page, Louise 1955- .... **CLC 40**
See also CA 140; CANR 76; CBD; CD 5; CWD; DLB 233
Page, P(atricia) K(athleen) 1916- ...... **CLC 7, 18; PC 12**
See Cape, Judith
See also CA 53-56; CANR 4, 22, 65; CP 7; DAC; DAM MST; DLB 68; MTCW 1; RGEL 2
Page, Stanton
See Fuller, Henry Blake
Page, Stanton
See Fuller, Henry Blake
Page, Thomas Nelson 1853-1922 .... **SSC 23**
See also CA 118; 177; DLB 12, 78; DLBD 13; RGAL 4
Pagels, Elaine Hiesey 1943- .... **CLC 104**
See also CA 45-48; CANR 2, 24, 51; FW; NCFS 4
Paget, Violet 1856-1935
See Lee, Vernon
See also CA 104; 166; GLL 1; HGG
Paget-Lowe, Henry
See Lovecraft, H(oward) P(hillips)
Paglia, Camille (Anna) 1947- .... **CLC 68**
See also CA 140; CANR 72; CPW; FW; GLL 2; MTCW 2
Paige, Richard
See Koontz, Dean R(ay)
Paine, Thomas 1737-1809 .... **NCLC 62**
See also AMWS 1; CDALB 1640-1865; DLB 31, 43, 73, 158; LAIT 1; RGAL 4; RGEL 2; TUS
Pakenham, Antonia
See Fraser, Antonia (Pakenham)
Palamas, Costis
See Palamas, Kostes
Palamas, Kostes 1859-1943 .... **TCLC 5**
See Palamas, Kostis
See also CA 105; 190; RGWL 2, 3
Palamas, Kostis
See Palamas, Kostes
See also EWL 3
Palazzeschi, Aldo 1885-1974 .... **CLC 11**
See also CA 89-92; 53-56; DLB 114, 264; EWL 3
Pales Matos, Luis 1898-1959 .... **HLCS 2**
See Pales Matos, Luis
See also DLB 290; HW 1; LAW
Paley, Grace 1922- .. **CLC 4, 6, 37, 140; SSC 8**
See also AMWS 6; CA 25-28R; CANR 13, 46, 74, 118; CN 7; CPW; DA3; DAM POP; DLB 28, 218; EWL 3; EXPS; FW; INT CANR-13; MAWW; MTCW 1, 2; RGAL 4; RGSF 2; SSFS 3, 20
Palin, Michael (Edward) 1943- .... **CLC 21**
See Monty Python
See also CA 107; CANR 35, 109; SATA 67
Palliser, Charles 1947- .... **CLC 65**
See also CA 136; CANR 76; CN 7
Palma, Ricardo 1833-1919 .... **TCLC 29**
See also CA 168; LAW
Pamuk, Orhan 1952- .... **CLC 185**
See also CA 142; CANR 75, 127; CWW 2
Pancake, Breece Dexter 1952-1979
See Pancake, Breece D'J
See also CA 123; 109
Pancake, Breece D'J .... **CLC 29; SSC 61**
See Pancake, Breece Dexter
See also DLB 130
Panchenko, Nikolai .... **CLC 59**
Pankhurst, Emmeline (Goulden) 1858-1928 .... **TCLC 100**
See also CA 116; FW
Panko, Rudy
See Gogol, Nikolai (Vasilyevich)
Papadiamantis, Alexandros 1851-1911 .... **TCLC 29**
See also CA 168; EWL 3
Papadiamantopoulos, Johannes 1856-1910
See Moreas, Jean
See also CA 117
Papini, Giovanni 1881-1956 .... **TCLC 22**
See also CA 121; 180; DLB 264
Paracelsus 1493-1541 .... **LC 14**
See also DLB 179
Parasol, Peter
See Stevens, Wallace
Pardo Bazan, Emilia 1851-1921 .... **SSC 30**
See also EWL 3; FW; RGSF 2; RGWL 2, 3
Pareto, Vilfredo 1848-1923 .... **TCLC 69**
See also CA 175
Paretsky, Sara 1947- .... **CLC 135**
See also AAYA 30; BEST 90:3; CA 125; 129; CANR 59, 95; CMW 4; CPW; DA3; DAM POP; DLB 306; INT CA-129; MSW; RGAL 4
Parfenie, Maria
See Codrescu, Andrei
Parini, Jay (Lee) 1948- .... **CLC 54, 133**
See also CA 97-100, 229; CAAE 229; CAAS 16; CANR 32, 87
Park, Jordan
See Kornbluth, C(yril) M.; Pohl, Frederik
Park, Robert E(zra) 1864-1944 ..... **TCLC 73**
See also CA 122; 165
Parker, Bert
See Ellison, Harlan (Jay)
Parker, Dorothy (Rothschild) 1893-1967 . **CLC 15, 68; PC 28; SSC 2; TCLC 143**
See also AMWS 9; CA 19-20; 25-28R; CAP 2; DA3; DAM POET; DLB 11, 45, 86; EXPP; FW; MAWW; MTCW 1, 2; PFS 18; RGAL 4; RGSF 2; TUS
Parker, Robert B(rown) 1932- .... **CLC 27**
See also AAYA 28; BEST 89:4; BPFB 3; CA 49-52; CANR 1, 26, 52, 89, 128; CMW 4; CPW; DAM NOV, POP; DLB 306; INT CANR-26; MSW; MTCW 1
Parkin, Frank 1940- .... **CLC 43**
See also CA 147
Parkman, Francis, Jr. 1823-1893 .. **NCLC 12**
See also AMWS 2; DLB 1, 30, 183, 186, 235; RGAL 4
Parks, Gordon (Alexander Buchanan) 1912- .... **BLC 3; CLC 1, 16**
See also AAYA 36; AITN 2; BW 2, 3; CA 41-44R; CANR 26, 66; DA3; DAM MULT; DLB 33; MTCW 2; SATA 8, 108
Parks, Suzan-Lori 1964(?)- .... **DC 23**
See also AAYA 55; CA 201; CAD; CD 5; CWD; RGAL 4
Parks, Tim(othy Harold) 1954- ...... **CLC 147**
See also CA 126; 131; CANR 77; DLB 231; INT CA-131
Parmenides c. 515B.C.-c. 450B.C. .... **CMLC 22**
See also DLB 176
Parnell, Thomas 1679-1718 .... **LC 3**
See also DLB 95; RGEL 2
Parr, Catherine c. 1513(?)-1548 .... **LC 86**
See also DLB 136
Parra, Nicanor 1914- ... **CLC 2, 102; HLC 2; PC 39**
See also CA 85-88; CANR 32; CWW 2; DAM MULT; DLB 283; EWL 3; HW 1; LAW; MTCW 1
Parra Sanojo, Ana Teresa de la 1890-1936 .... **HLCS 2**
See de la Parra, (Ana) Teresa (Sonojo)
See also LAW
Parrish, Mary Frances
See Fisher, M(ary) F(rances) K(ennedy)
Parshchikov, Aleksei 1954- .... **CLC 59**
See Parshchikov, Aleksei Maksimovich
Parshchikov, Aleksei Maksimovich
See Parshchikov, Aleksei
See also DLB 285
Parson, Professor
See Coleridge, Samuel Taylor
Parson Lot
See Kingsley, Charles
Parton, Sara Payson Willis 1811-1872 .... **NCLC 86**
See also DLB 43, 74, 239
Partridge, Anthony
See Oppenheim, E(dward) Phillips
Pascal, Blaise 1623-1662 .... **LC 35**
See also DLB 268; EW 3; GFL Beginnings to 1789; RGWL 2, 3; TWA
Pascoli, Giovanni 1855-1912 .... **TCLC 45**
See also CA 170; EW 7; EWL 3
Pasolini, Pier Paolo 1922-1975 .. **CLC 20, 37, 106; PC 17**
See also CA 93-96; 61-64; CANR 63; DLB 128, 177; EWL 3; MTCW 1; RGWL 2, 3
Pasquini
See Silone, Ignazio
Pastan, Linda (Olenik) 1932- .... **CLC 27**
See also CA 61-64; CANR 18, 40, 61, 113; CP 7; CSW; CWP; DAM POET; DLB 5; PFS 8

Quasimodo, Salvatore 1901-1968 .... **CLC 10; PC 47**
See also CA 13-16; 25-28R; CAP 1; DLB 114; EW 12; EWL 3; MTCW 1; RGWL 2, 3
Quatermass, Martin
See Carpenter, John (Howard)
Quay, Stephen 1947- .... **CLC 95**
See also CA 189
Quay, Timothy 1947- .... **CLC 95**
See also CA 189
Queen, Ellery .... **CLC 3, 11**
See Dannay, Frederic; Davidson, Avram (James); Deming, Richard; Fairman, Paul W.; Flora, Fletcher; Hoch, Edward D(entinger); Kane, Henry; Lee, Manfred B(ennington); Marlowe, Stephen; Powell, (Oval) Talmage; Sheldon, Walter J(ames); Sturgeon, Theodore (Hamilton); Tracy, Don(ald Fiske); Vance, John Holbrook
See also BPFB 3; CMW 4; MSW; RGAL 4
Queen, Ellery, Jr.
See Dannay, Frederic; Lee, Manfred B(ennington)
Queneau, Raymond 1903-1976 ..... **CLC 2, 5, 10, 42**
See also CA 77-80; 69-72; CANR 32; DLB 72, 258; EW 12; EWL 3; GFL 1789 to the Present; MTCW 1, 2; RGWL 2, 3
Quevedo, Francisco de 1580-1645 .... **LC 23**
Quiller-Couch, Sir Arthur (Thomas) 1863-1944 .... **TCLC 53**
See also CA 118; 166; DLB 135, 153, 190; HGG; RGEL 2; SUFW 1
Quin, Ann (Marie) 1936-1973 .... **CLC 6**
See also CA 9-12R; 45-48; DLB 14, 231
Quincey, Thomas de
See De Quincey, Thomas
Quindlen, Anna 1953- .... **CLC 191**
See also AAYA 35; CA 138; CANR 73, 126; DA3; DLB 292; MTCW 2
Quinn, Martin
See Smith, Martin Cruz
Quinn, Peter 1947- .... **CLC 91**
See also CA 197
Quinn, Simon
See Smith, Martin Cruz
Quintana, Leroy V. 1944- ...... **HLC 2; PC 36**
See also CA 131; CANR 65; DAM MULT; DLB 82; HW 1, 2
Quintilian c. 35-40–c. 96. .... **CMLC 77**
See also AW 2; DLB 211; RGWL 2, 3
Quiroga, Horacio (Sylvestre) 1878-1937 .... **HLC 2; TCLC 20**
See also CA 117; 131; DAM MULT; EWL 3; HW 1; LAW; MTCW 1; RGSF 2; WLIT 1
Quoirez, Francoise 1935- .... **CLC 9**
See Sagan, Francoise
See also CA 49-52; CANR 6, 39, 73; MTCW 1, 2; TWA
Raabe, Wilhelm (Karl) 1831-1910 . **TCLC 45**
See also CA 167; DLB 129
Rabe, David (William) 1940- .. **CLC 4, 8, 33, 200; DC 16**
See also CA 85-88; CABS 3; CAD; CANR 59, 129; CD 5; DAM DRAM; DFS 3, 8, 13; DLB 7, 228; EWL 3
Rabelais, Francois 1494-1553 .... **LC 5, 60; WLC**
See also DA; DAB; DAC; DAM MST; EW 2; GFL Beginnings to 1789; LMFS 1; RGWL 2, 3; TWA
Rabinovitch, Sholem 1859-1916
See Aleichem, Sholom
See also CA 104
Rabinyan, Dorit 1972- .... **CLC 119**
See also CA 170
Rachilde
See Vallette, Marguerite Eymery; Vallette, Marguerite Eymery
See also EWL 3
Racine, Jean 1639-1699 .... **LC 28, 113**
See also DA3; DAB; DAM MST; DLB 268; EW 3; GFL Beginnings to 1789; LMFS 1; RGWL 2, 3; TWA
Radcliffe, Ann (Ward) 1764-1823 ... **NCLC 6, 55, 106**
See also DLB 39, 178; HGG; LMFS 1; RGEL 2; SUFW; WLIT 3
Radclyffe-Hall, Marguerite
See Hall, (Marguerite) Radclyffe
Radiguet, Raymond 1903-1923 ...... **TCLC 29**
See also CA 162; DLB 65; EWL 3; GFL 1789 to the Present; RGWL 2, 3
Radnoti, Miklos 1909-1944 .... **TCLC 16**
See also CA 118; 212; CDWLB 4; DLB 215; EWL 3; RGWL 2, 3
Rado, James 1939- .... **CLC 17**
See also CA 105
Radvanyi, Netty 1900-1983
See Seghers, Anna
See also CA 85-88; 110; CANR 82
Rae, Ben
See Griffiths, Trevor
Raeburn, John (Hay) 1941- .... **CLC 34**
See also CA 57-60
Ragni, Gerome 1942-1991 .... **CLC 17**
See also CA 105; 134
Rahv, Philip .... **CLC 24**
See Greenberg, Ivan
See also DLB 137
Raimund, Ferdinand Jakob 1790-1836 .... **NCLC 69**
See also DLB 90
Raine, Craig (Anthony) 1944- .. **CLC 32, 103**
See also CA 108; CANR 29, 51, 103; CP 7; DLB 40; PFS 7
Raine, Kathleen (Jessie) 1908-2003 .. **CLC 7, 45**
See also CA 85-88; 218; CANR 46, 109; CP 7; DLB 20; EWL 3; MTCW 1; RGEL 2
Rainis, Janis 1865-1929 .... **TCLC 29**
See also CA 170; CDWLB 4; DLB 220; EWL 3
Rakosi, Carl .... **CLC 47**
See Rawley, Callman
See also CA 228; CAAS 5; CP 7; DLB 193
Ralegh, Sir Walter
See Raleigh, Sir Walter
See also BRW 1; RGEL 2; WP
Raleigh, Richard
See Lovecraft, H(oward) P(hillips)
Raleigh, Sir Walter 1554(?)-1618 .... **LC 31, 39; PC 31**
See Ralegh, Sir Walter
See also CDBLB Before 1660; DLB 172; EXPP; PFS 14; TEA
Rallentando, H. P.
See Sayers, Dorothy L(eigh)
Ramal, Walter
See de la Mare, Walter (John)
Ramana Maharshi 1879-1950 .... **TCLC 84**
Ramoacn y Cajal, Santiago 1852-1934 .... **TCLC 93**
Ramon, Juan
See Jimenez (Mantecon), Juan Ramon
Ramos, Graciliano 1892-1953 .... **TCLC 32**
See also CA 167; DLB 307; EWL 3; HW 2; LAW; WLIT 1
Rampersad, Arnold 1941- .... **CLC 44**
See also BW 2, 3; CA 127; 133; CANR 81; DLB 111; INT CA-133
Rampling, Anne
See Rice, Anne
See also GLL 2
Ramsay, Allan 1686(?)-1758 .... **LC 29**
See also DLB 95; RGEL 2
Ramsay, Jay
See Campbell, (John) Ramsey
Ramuz, Charles-Ferdinand 1878-1947 .... **TCLC 33**
See also CA 165; EWL 3
Rand, Ayn 1905-1982 ...... **CLC 3, 30, 44, 79; WLC**
See also AAYA 10; AMWS 4; BPFB 3; BYA 12; CA 13-16R; 105; CANR 27, 73; CDALBS; CPW; DA; DA3; DAC; DAM MST, NOV, POP; DLB 227, 279; MTCW 1, 2; NFS 10, 16; RGAL 4; SFW 4; TUS; YAW
Randall, Dudley (Felker) 1914-2000 . **BLC 3; CLC 1, 135**
See also BW 1, 3; CA 25-28R; 189; CANR 23, 82; DAM MULT; DLB 41; PFS 5
Randall, Robert
See Silverberg, Robert
Ranger, Ken
See Creasey, John
Rank, Otto 1884-1939 .... **TCLC 115**
Ransom, John Crowe 1888-1974 .. **CLC 2, 4, 5, 11, 24; PC 61**
See also AMW; CA 5-8R; 49-52; CANR 6, 34; CDALBS; DA3; DAM POET; DLB 45, 63; EWL 3; EXPP; MTCW 1, 2; RGAL 4; TUS
Rao, Raja 1909- .... **CLC 25, 56**
See also CA 73-76; CANR 51; CN 7; DAM NOV; EWL 3; MTCW 1, 2; RGEL 2; RGSF 2
Raphael, Frederic (Michael) 1931- ... **CLC 2, 14**
See also CA 1-4R; CANR 1, 86; CN 7; DLB 14
Ratcliffe, James P.
See Mencken, H(enry) L(ouis)
Rathbone, Julian 1935- .... **CLC 41**
See also CA 101; CANR 34, 73
Rattigan, Terence (Mervyn) 1911-1977 .... **CLC 7; DC 18**
See also BRWS 7; CA 85-88; 73-76; CBD; CDBLB 1945-1960; DAM DRAM; DFS 8; DLB 13; IDFW 3, 4; MTCW 1, 2; RGEL 2
Ratushinskaya, Irina 1954- .... **CLC 54**
See also CA 129; CANR 68; CWW 2
Raven, Simon (Arthur Noel) 1927-2001 .... **CLC 14**
See also CA 81-84; 197; CANR 86; CN 7; DLB 271
Ravenna, Michael
See Welty, Eudora (Alice)
Rawley, Callman 1903-2004
See Rakosi, Carl
See also CA 21-24R; CANR 12, 32, 91
Rawlings, Marjorie Kinnan 1896-1953 .... **TCLC 4**
See also AAYA 20; AMWS 10; ANW; BPFB 3; BYA 3; CA 104; 137; CANR 74; CLR 63; DLB 9, 22, 102; DLBD 17; JRDA; MAICYA 1, 2; MTCW 2; RGAL 4; SATA 100; WCH; YABC 1; YAW
Ray, Satyajit 1921-1992 .... **CLC 16, 76**
See also CA 114; 137; DAM MULT
Read, Herbert Edward 1893-1968 ..... **CLC 4**
See also BRW 6; CA 85-88; 25-28R; DLB 20, 149; EWL 3; PAB; RGEL 2
Read, Piers Paul 1941- .... **CLC 4, 10, 25**
See also CA 21-24R; CANR 38, 86; CN 7; DLB 14; SATA 21
Reade, Charles 1814-1884 .... **NCLC 2, 74**
See also DLB 21; RGEL 2
Reade, Hamish
See Gray, Simon (James Holliday)

Scannell, Vernon 1922- .... **CLC 49**
See also CA 5-8R; CANR 8, 24, 57; CP 7; CWRI 5; DLB 27; SATA 59

Scarlett, Susan
See Streatfeild, (Mary) Noel

Scarron, Paul 1610-1660 .... **LC 116**
See also GFL Beginnings to 1789; RGWL 2, 3

Scarron 1847-1910
See Mikszath, Kalman

Schaeffer, Susan Fromberg 1941- ..... **CLC 6, 11, 22**
See also CA 49-52; CANR 18, 65; CN 7; DLB 28, 299; MTCW 1, 2; SATA 22

Schama, Simon (Michael) 1945- ..... **CLC 150**
See also BEST 89:4; CA 105; CANR 39, 91

Schary, Jill
See Robinson, Jill

Schell, Jonathan 1943- .... **CLC 35**
See also CA 73-76; CANR 12, 117

Schelling, Friedrich Wilhelm Joseph von 1775-1854 .... **NCLC 30**
See also DLB 90

Scherer, Jean-Marie Maurice 1920-
See Rohmer, Eric
See also CA 110

Schevill, James (Erwin) 1920- .... **CLC 7**
See also CA 5-8R; CAAS 12; CAD; CD 5

Schiller, Friedrich von 1759-1805 ...... **DC 12; NCLC 39, 69**
See also CDWLB 2; DAM DRAM; DLB 94; EW 5; RGWL 2, 3; TWA

Schisgal, Murray (Joseph) 1926- .... **CLC 6**
See also CA 21-24R; CAD; CANR 48, 86; CD 5

Schlee, Ann 1934- .... **CLC 35**
See also CA 101; CANR 29, 88; SATA 44; SATA-Brief 36

Schlegel, August Wilhelm von 1767-1845 .... **NCLC 15, 142**
See also DLB 94; RGWL 2, 3

Schlegel, Friedrich 1772-1829 .... **NCLC 45**
See also DLB 90; EW 5; RGWL 2, 3; TWA

Schlegel, Johann Elias (von) 1719(?)-1749 .... **LC 5**

Schleiermacher, Friedrich 1768-1834 .... **NCLC 107**
See also DLB 90

Schlesinger, Arthur M(eier), Jr. 1917- .... **CLC 84**
See also AITN 1; CA 1-4R; CANR 1, 28, 58, 105; DLB 17; INT CANR-28; MTCW 1, 2; SATA 61

Schlink, Bernhard 1944- .... **CLC 174**
See also CA 163; CANR 116

Schmidt, Arno (Otto) 1914-1979 ...... **CLC 56**
See also CA 128; 109; DLB 69; EWL 3

Schmitz, Aron Hector 1861-1928
See Svevo, Italo
See also CA 104; 122; MTCW 1

Schnackenberg, Gjertrud (Cecelia) 1953- .... **CLC 40; PC 45**
See also CA 116; CANR 100; CP 7; CWP; DLB 120, 282; PFS 13

Schneider, Leonard Alfred 1925-1966
See Bruce, Lenny
See also CA 89-92

Schnitzler, Arthur 1862-1931 ..... **DC 17; SSC 15, 61; TCLC 4**
See also CA 104; CDWLB 2; DLB 81, 118; EW 8; EWL 3; RGSF 2; RGWL 2, 3

Schoenberg, Arnold Franz Walter 1874-1951 .... **TCLC 75**
See also CA 109; 188

Schonberg, Arnold
See Schoenberg, Arnold Franz Walter

Schopenhauer, Arthur 1788-1860 . **NCLC 51, 157**
See also DLB 90; EW 5

Schor, Sandra (M.) 1932(?)-1990 ..... **CLC 65**
See also CA 132

Schorer, Mark 1908-1977 .... **CLC 9**
See also CA 5-8R; 73-76; CANR 7; DLB 103

Schrader, Paul (Joseph) 1946- . **CLC 26, 212**
See also CA 37-40R; CANR 41; DLB 44

Schreber, Daniel 1842-1911 .... **TCLC 123**

Schreiner, Olive (Emilie Albertina) 1855-1920 .... **TCLC 9**
See also AFW; BRWS 2; CA 105; 154; DLB 18, 156, 190, 225; EWL 3; FW; RGEL 2; TWA; WLIT 2; WWE 1

Schulberg, Budd (Wilson) 1914- .. **CLC 7, 48**
See also BPFB 3; CA 25-28R; CANR 19, 87; CN 7; DLB 6, 26, 28; DLBY 1981, 2001

Schulman, Arnold
See Trumbo, Dalton

Schulz, Bruno 1892-1942 .. **SSC 13; TCLC 5, 51**
See also CA 115; 123; CANR 86; CDWLB 4; DLB 215; EWL 3; MTCW 2; RGSF 2; RGWL 2, 3

Schulz, Charles M(onroe) 1922-2000 .... **CLC 12**
See also AAYA 39; CA 9-12R; 187; CANR 6, 132; INT CANR-6; SATA 10; SATA-Obit 118

Schumacher, E(rnst) F(riedrich) 1911-1977 .... **CLC 80**
See also CA 81-84; 73-76; CANR 34, 85

Schumann, Robert 1810-1856 ...... **NCLC 143**

Schuyler, George Samuel 1895-1977 .... **HR 3**
See also BW 2; CA 81-84; 73-76; CANR 42; DLB 29, 51

Schuyler, James Marcus 1923-1991 .. **CLC 5, 23**
See also CA 101; 134; DAM POET; DLB 5, 169; EWL 3; INT CA-101; WP

Schwartz, Delmore (David) 1913-1966 ... **CLC 2, 4, 10, 45, 87; PC 8**
See also AMWS 2; CA 17-18; 25-28R; CANR 35; CAP 2; DLB 28, 48; EWL 3; MTCW 1, 2; PAB; RGAL 4; TUS

Schwartz, Ernst
See Ozu, Yasujiro

Schwartz, John Burnham 1965- .... **CLC 59**
See also CA 132; CANR 116

Schwartz, Lynne Sharon 1939- .... **CLC 31**
See also CA 103; CANR 44, 89; DLB 218; MTCW 2

Schwartz, Muriel A.
See Eliot, T(homas) S(tearns)

Schwarz-Bart, Andre 1928- .... **CLC 2, 4**
See also CA 89-92; CANR 109; DLB 299

Schwarz-Bart, Simone 1938- . **BLCS; CLC 7**
See also BW 2; CA 97-100; CANR 117; EWL 3

Schwerner, Armand 1927-1999 .... **PC 42**
See also CA 9-12R; 179; CANR 50, 85; CP 7; DLB 165

Schwitters, Kurt (Hermann Edward Karl Julius) 1887-1948 .... **TCLC 95**
See also CA 158

Schwob, Marcel (Mayer Andre) 1867-1905 .... **TCLC 20**
See also CA 117; 168; DLB 123; GFL 1789 to the Present

Sciascia, Leonardo 1921-1989 .. **CLC 8, 9, 41**
See also CA 85-88; 130; CANR 35; DLB 177; EWL 3; MTCW 1; RGWL 2, 3

Scoppettone, Sandra 1936- .... **CLC 26**
See Early, Jack
See also AAYA 11; BYA 8; CA 5-8R; CANR 41, 73; GLL 1; MAICYA 2; MAICYAS 1; SATA 9, 92; WYA; YAW

Scorsese, Martin 1942- .... **CLC 20, 89, 207**
See also AAYA 38; CA 110, 114; CANR 46, 85

Scotland, Jay
See Jakes, John (William)

Scott, Duncan Campbell 1862-1947 .... **TCLC 6**
See also CA 104; 153; DAC; DLB 92; RGEL 2

Scott, Evelyn 1893-1963 .... **CLC 43**
See also CA 104; 112; CANR 64; DLB 9, 48; RHW

Scott, F(rancis) R(eginald) 1899-1985 .... **CLC 22**
See also CA 101; 114; CANR 87; DLB 88; INT CA-101; RGEL 2

Scott, Frank
See Scott, F(rancis) R(eginald)

Scott, Joan .... **CLC 65**

Scott, Joanna 1960- .... **CLC 50**
See also CA 126; CANR 53, 92

Scott, Paul (Mark) 1920-1978 ...... **CLC 9, 60**
See also BRWS 1; CA 81-84; 77-80; CANR 33; DLB 14, 207; EWL 3; MTCW 1; RGEL 2; RHW; WWE 1

Scott, Ridley 1937- .... **CLC 183**
See also AAYA 13, 43

Scott, Sarah 1723-1795 .... **LC 44**
See also DLB 39

Scott, Sir Walter 1771-1832 .... **NCLC 15, 69, 110; PC 13; SSC 32; WLC**
See also AAYA 22; BRW 4; BYA 2; CDBLB 1789-1832; DA; DAB; DAC; DAM MST, NOV, POET; DLB 93, 107, 116, 144, 159; HGG; LAIT 1; RGEL 2; RGSF 2; SSFS 10; SUFW 1; TEA; WLIT 3; YABC 2

Scribe, (Augustin) Eugene 1791-1861 . **DC 5; NCLC 16**
See also DAM DRAM; DLB 192; GFL 1789 to the Present; RGWL 2, 3

Scrum, R.
See Crumb, R(obert)

Scudery, Georges de 1601-1667 .... **LC 75**
See also GFL Beginnings to 1789

Scudery, Madeleine de 1607-1701 .. **LC 2, 58**
See also DLB 268; GFL Beginnings to 1789

Scum
See Crumb, R(obert)

Scumbag, Little Bobby
See Crumb, R(obert)

Seabrook, John
See Hubbard, L(afayette) Ron(ald)

Seacole, Mary Jane Grant 1805-1881 .... **NCLC 147**
See also DLB 166

Sealy, I(rwin) Allan 1951- .... **CLC 55**
See also CA 136; CN 7

Search, Alexander
See Pessoa, Fernando (Antonio Nogueira)

Sebald, W(infried) G(eorg) 1944-2001 .... **CLC 194**
See also BRWS 8; CA 159; 202; CANR 98

Sebastian, Lee
See Silverberg, Robert

Sebastian Owl
See Thompson, Hunter S(tockton)

Sebestyen, Igen
See Sebestyen, Ouida

Sebestyen, Ouida 1924- .... **CLC 30**
See also AAYA 8; BYA 7; CA 107; CANR 40, 114; CLR 17; JRDA; MAICYA 1, 2; SAAS 10; SATA 39, 140; WYA; YAW

Smith, Betty (Wehner) 1904-1972 .... **CLC 19**
See also BPFB 3; BYA 3; CA 5-8R; 33-36R; DLBY 1982; LAIT 3; RGAL 4; SATA 6
Smith, Charlotte (Turner) 1749-1806 .... **NCLC 23, 115**
See also DLB 39, 109; RGEL 2; TEA
Smith, Clark Ashton 1893-1961 .... **CLC 43**
See also CA 143; CANR 81; FANT; HGG; MTCW 2; SCFW 2; SFW 4; SUFW
Smith, Dave .... **CLC 22, 42**
See Smith, David (Jeddie)
See also CAAS 7; DLB 5
Smith, David (Jeddie) 1942-
See Smith, Dave
See also CA 49-52; CANR 1, 59, 120; CP 7; CSW; DAM POET
Smith, Florence Margaret 1902-1971
See Smith, Stevie
See also CA 17-18; 29-32R; CANR 35; CAP 2; DAM POET; MTCW 1, 2; TEA
Smith, Iain Crichton 1928-1998 .... **CLC 64**
See also BRWS 9; CA 21-24R; 171; CN 7; CP 7; DLB 40, 139; RGSF 2
Smith, John 1580(?)-1631 .... **LC 9**
See also DLB 24, 30; TUS
Smith, Johnston
See Crane, Stephen (Townley)
Smith, Joseph, Jr. 1805-1844 .... **NCLC 53**
Smith, Lee 1944- .... **CLC 25, 73**
See also CA 114; 119; CANR 46, 118; CSW; DLB 143; DLBY 1983; EWL 3; INT CA-119; RGAL 4
Smith, Martin
See Smith, Martin Cruz
Smith, Martin Cruz 1942- .. **CLC 25; NNAL**
See also BEST 89:4; BPFB 3; CA 85-88; CANR 6, 23, 43, 65, 119; CMW 4; CPW; DAM MULT, POP; HGG; INT CANR-23; MTCW 2; RGAL 4
Smith, Patti 1946- .... **CLC 12**
See also CA 93-96; CANR 63
Smith, Pauline (Urmson) 1882-1959 .... **TCLC 25**
See also DLB 225; EWL 3
Smith, Rosamond
See Oates, Joyce Carol
Smith, Sheila Kaye
See Kaye-Smith, Sheila
Smith, Stevie .... **CLC 3, 8, 25, 44; PC 12**
See Smith, Florence Margaret
See also BRWS 2; DLB 20; EWL 3; MTCW 2; PAB; PFS 3; RGEL 2
Smith, Wilbur (Addison) 1933- .... **CLC 33**
See also CA 13-16R; CANR 7, 46, 66, 134; CPW; MTCW 1, 2
Smith, William Jay 1918- .... **CLC 6**
See also AMWS 13; CA 5-8R; CANR 44, 106; CP 7; CSW; CWRI 5; DLB 5; MAICYA 1, 2; SAAS 22; SATA 2, 68, 154; SATA-Essay 154
Smith, Woodrow Wilson
See Kuttner, Henry
Smith, Zadie 1976- .... **CLC 158**
See also AAYA 50; CA 193
Smolenskin, Peretz 1842-1885 .... **NCLC 30**
Smollett, Tobias (George) 1721-1771 ... **LC 2, 46**
See also BRW 3; CDBLB 1660-1789; DLB 39, 104; RGEL 2; TEA
Snodgrass, W(illiam) D(e Witt) 1926- .... **CLC 2, 6, 10, 18, 68**
See also AMWS 6; CA 1-4R; CANR 6, 36, 65, 85; CP 7; DAM POET; DLB 5; MTCW 1, 2; RGAL 4
Snorri Sturluson 1179-1241 .... **CMLC 56**
See also RGWL 2, 3
Snow, C(harles) P(ercy) 1905-1980 ... **CLC 1, 4, 6, 9, 13, 19**
See also BRW 7; CA 5-8R; 101; CANR 28; CDBLB 1945-1960; DAM NOV; DLB 15, 77; DLBD 17; EWL 3; MTCW 1, 2; RGEL 2; TEA
Snow, Frances Compton
See Adams, Henry (Brooks)
Snyder, Gary (Sherman) 1930- . **CLC 1, 2, 5, 9, 32, 120; PC 21**
See also AMWS 8; ANW; BG 3; CA 17-20R; CANR 30, 60, 125; CP 7; DA3; DAM POET; DLB 5, 16, 165, 212, 237, 275; EWL 3; MTCW 2; PFS 9, 19; RGAL 4; WP
Snyder, Zilpha Keatley 1927- .... **CLC 17**
See also AAYA 15; BYA 1; CA 9-12R; CANR 38; CLR 31; JRDA; MAICYA 1, 2; SAAS 2; SATA 1, 28, 75, 110; SATA-Essay 112; YAW
Soares, Bernardo
See Pessoa, Fernando (Antonio Nogueira)
Sobh, A.
See Shamlu, Ahmad
Sobh, Alef
See Shamlu, Ahmad
Sobol, Joshua 1939- .... **CLC 60**
See Sobol, Yehoshua
See also CA 200
Sobol, Yehoshua 1939-
See Sobol, Joshua
See also CWW 2
Socrates 470B.C.-399B.C. .... **CMLC 27**
Soderberg, Hjalmar 1869-1941 ...... **TCLC 39**
See also DLB 259; EWL 3; RGSF 2
Soderbergh, Steven 1963- .... **CLC 154**
See also AAYA 43
Sodergran, Edith (Irene) 1892-1923
See Soedergran, Edith (Irene)
See also CA 202; DLB 259; EW 11; EWL 3; RGWL 2, 3
Soedergran, Edith (Irene) 1892-1923 .... **TCLC 31**
See Sodergran, Edith (Irene)
Softly, Edgar
See Lovecraft, H(oward) P(hillips)
Softly, Edward
See Lovecraft, H(oward) P(hillips)
Sokolov, Alexander V(sevolodovich) 1943-
See Sokolov, Sasha
See also CA 73-76
Sokolov, Raymond 1941- .... **CLC 7**
See also CA 85-88
Sokolov, Sasha .... **CLC 59**
See Sokolov, Alexander V(sevolodovich)
See also CWW 2; DLB 285; EWL 3; RGWL 2, 3
Solo, Jay
See Ellison, Harlan (Jay)
Sologub, Fyodor .... **TCLC 9**
See Teternikov, Fyodor Kuzmich
See also EWL 3
Solomons, Ikey Esquir
See Thackeray, William Makepeace
Solomos, Dionysios 1798-1857 .... **NCLC 15**
Solwoska, Mara
See French, Marilyn
Solzhenitsyn, Aleksandr I(sayevich) 1918- .. **CLC 1, 2, 4, 7, 9, 10, 18, 26, 34, 78, 134; SSC 32; WLC**
See Solzhenitsyn, Aleksandr Isaevich
See also AAYA 49; AITN 1; BPFB 3; CA 69-72; CANR 40, 65, 116; DA; DA3; DAB; DAC; DAM MST, NOV; DLB 302; EW 13; EXPS; LAIT 4; MTCW 1, 2; NFS 6; RGSF 2; RGWL 2, 3; SSFS 9; TWA
Solzhenitsyn, Aleksandr Isaevich
See Solzhenitsyn, Aleksandr I(sayevich)
See also CWW 2; EWL 3
Somers, Jane
See Lessing, Doris (May)
Somerville, Edith Oenone 1858-1949 .... **SSC 56; TCLC 51**
See also CA 196; DLB 135; RGEL 2; RGSF 2
Somerville & Ross
See Martin, Violet Florence; Somerville, Edith Oenone
Sommer, Scott 1951- .... **CLC 25**
See also CA 106
Sommers, Christina Hoff 1950- ...... **CLC 197**
See also CA 153; CANR 95
Sondheim, Stephen (Joshua) 1930- . **CLC 30, 39, 147; DC 22**
See also AAYA 11; CA 103; CANR 47, 67, 125; DAM DRAM; LAIT 4
Sone, Monica 1919- .... **AAL**
Song, Cathy 1955- .... **AAL; PC 21**
See also CA 154; CANR 118; CWP; DLB 169; EXPP; FW; PFS 5
Sontag, Susan 1933- .... **CLC 1, 2, 10, 13, 31, 105, 195**
See also AMWS 3; CA 17-20R; CANR 25, 51, 74, 97; CN 7; CPW; DA3; DAM POP; DLB 2, 67; EWL 3; MAWW; MTCW 1, 2; RGAL 4; RHW; SSFS 10
Sophocles 496(?)B.C.-406(?)B.C. .... **CMLC 2, 47, 51; DC 1; WLCS**
See also AW 1; CDWLB 1; DA; DA3; DAB; DAC; DAM DRAM, MST; DFS 1, 4, 8; DLB 176; LAIT 1; LATS 1:1; LMFS 1; RGWL 2, 3; TWA
Sordello 1189-1269 .... **CMLC 15**
Sorel, Georges 1847-1922 .... **TCLC 91**
See also CA 118; 188
Sorel, Julia
See Drexler, Rosalyn
Sorokin, Vladimir .... **CLC 59**
See Sorokin, Vladimir Georgievich
Sorokin, Vladimir Georgievich
See Sorokin, Vladimir
See also DLB 285
Sorrentino, Gilbert 1929- .. **CLC 3, 7, 14, 22, 40**
See also CA 77-80; CANR 14, 33, 115; CN 7; CP 7; DLB 5, 173; DLBY 1980; INT CANR-14
Soseki
See Natsume, Soseki
See also MJW
Soto, Gary 1952- ... **CLC 32, 80; HLC 2; PC 28**
See also AAYA 10, 37; BYA 11; CA 119; 125; CANR 50, 74, 107; CLR 38; CP 7; DAM MULT; DLB 82; EWL 3; EXPP; HW 1, 2; INT CA-125; JRDA; LLW 1; MAICYA 2; MAICYAS 1; MTCW 2; PFS 7; RGAL 4; SATA 80, 120; WYA; YAW
Soupault, Philippe 1897-1990 .... **CLC 68**
See also CA 116; 147; 131; EWL 3; GFL 1789 to the Present; LMFS 2
Souster, (Holmes) Raymond 1921- .... **CLC 5, 14**
See also CA 13-16R; CAAS 14; CANR 13, 29, 53; CP 7; DA3; DAC; DAM POET; DLB 88; RGEL 2; SATA 63
Southern, Terry 1924(?)-1995 .... **CLC 7**
See also AMWS 11; BPFB 3; CA 1-4R; 150; CANR 1, 55, 107; CN 7; DLB 2; IDFW 3, 4
Southerne, Thomas 1660-1746 .... **LC 99**
See also DLB 80; RGEL 2
Southey, Robert 1774-1843 .... **NCLC 8, 97**
See also BRW 4; DLB 93, 107, 142; RGEL 2; SATA 54
Southwell, Robert 1561(?)-1595 .... **LC 108**
See also DLB 167; RGEL 2; TEA

Steiner, K. Leslie
See Delany, Samuel R(ay), Jr.

Steiner, Rudolf 1861-1925 .... **TCLC 13**
See also CA 107

Stendhal 1783-1842 .. **NCLC 23, 46; SSC 27; WLC**
See also DA; DA3; DAB; DAC; DAM MST, NOV; DLB 119; EW 5; GFL 1789 to the Present; RGWL 2, 3; TWA

Stephen, Adeline Virginia
See Woolf, (Adeline) Virginia

Stephen, Sir Leslie 1832-1904 .... **TCLC 23**
See also BRW 5; CA 123; DLB 57, 144, 190

Stephen, Sir Leslie
See Stephen, Sir Leslie

Stephen, Virginia
See Woolf, (Adeline) Virginia

Stephens, James 1882(?)-1950 .... **SSC 50; TCLC 4**
See also CA 104; 192; DLB 19, 153, 162; EWL 3; FANT; RGEL 2; SUFW

Stephens, Reed
See Donaldson, Stephen R(eeder)

Steptoe, Lydia
See Barnes, Djuna
See also GLL 1

Sterchi, Beat 1949- .... **CLC 65**
See also CA 203

Sterling, Brett
See Bradbury, Ray (Douglas); Hamilton, Edmond

Sterling, Bruce 1954- .... **CLC 72**
See also CA 119; CANR 44, 135; SCFW 2; SFW 4

Sterling, George 1869-1926 .... **TCLC 20**
See also CA 117; 165; DLB 54

Stern, Gerald 1925- .... **CLC 40, 100**
See also AMWS 9; CA 81-84; CANR 28, 94; CP 7; DLB 105; RGAL 4

Stern, Richard (Gustave) 1928- ... **CLC 4, 39**
See also CA 1-4R; CANR 1, 25, 52, 120; CN 7; DLB 218; DLBY 1987; INT CANR-25

Sternberg, Josef von 1894-1969 .... **CLC 20**
See also CA 81-84

Sterne, Laurence 1713-1768 .... **LC 2, 48; WLC**
See also BRW 3; BRWC 1; CDBLB 1660-1789; DA; DAB; DAC; DAM MST, NOV; DLB 39; RGEL 2; TEA

Sternheim, (William Adolf) Carl
1878-1942 .... **TCLC 8**
See also CA 105; 193; DLB 56, 118; EWL 3; RGWL 2, 3

Stevens, Mark 1951- .... **CLC 34**
See also CA 122

Stevens, Wallace 1879-1955 . **PC 6; TCLC 3, 12, 45; WLC**
See also AMW; AMWR 1; CA 104; 124; CDALB 1929-1941; DA; DA3; DAB; DAC; DAM MST, POET; DLB 54; EWL 3; EXPP; MTCW 1, 2; PAB; PFS 13, 16; RGAL 4; TUS; WP

Stevenson, Anne (Katharine) 1933- .. **CLC 7, 33**
See also BRWS 6; CA 17-20R; CAAS 9; CANR 9, 33, 123; CP 7; CWP; DLB 40; MTCW 1; RHW

Stevenson, Robert Louis (Balfour)
1850-1894 ...... **NCLC 5, 14, 63; SSC 11, 51; WLC**
See also AAYA 24; BPFB 3; BRW 5; BRWC 1; BRWR 1; BYA 1, 2, 4, 13; CDBLB 1890-1914; CLR 10, 11; DA; DA3; DAB; DAC; DAM MST, NOV; DLB 18, 57, 141, 156, 174; DLBD 13; HGG; JRDA; LAIT 1, 3; MAICYA 1, 2; NFS 11, 20; RGEL 2; RGSF 2; SATA 100; SUFW; TEA; WCH; WLIT 4; WYA; YABC 2; YAW

Stewart, J(ohn) I(nnes) M(ackintosh)
1906-1994 .... **CLC 7, 14, 32**
See Innes, Michael
See also CA 85-88; 147; CAAS 3; CANR 47; CMW 4; MTCW 1, 2

Stewart, Mary (Florence Elinor)
1916- .... **CLC 7, 35, 117**
See also AAYA 29; BPFB 3; CA 1-4R; CANR 1, 59, 130; CMW 4; CPW; DAB; FANT; RHW; SATA 12; YAW

Stewart, Mary Rainbow
See Stewart, Mary (Florence Elinor)

Stifle, June
See Campbell, Maria

Stifter, Adalbert 1805-1868 .. **NCLC 41; SSC 28**
See also CDWLB 2; DLB 133; RGSF 2; RGWL 2, 3

Still, James 1906-2001 .... **CLC 49**
See also CA 65-68; 195; CAAS 17; CANR 10, 26; CSW; DLB 9; DLBY 01; SATA 29; SATA-Obit 127

Sting 1951-
See Sumner, Gordon Matthew
See also CA 167

Stirling, Arthur
See Sinclair, Upton (Beall)

Stitt, Milan 1941- .... **CLC 29**
See also CA 69-72

Stockton, Francis Richard 1834-1902
See Stockton, Frank R.
See also CA 108; 137; MAICYA 1, 2; SATA 44; SFW 4

Stockton, Frank R. .... **TCLC 47**
See Stockton, Francis Richard
See also BYA 4, 13; DLB 42, 74; DLBD 13; EXPS; SATA-Brief 32; SSFS 3; SUFW; WCH

Stoddard, Charles
See Kuttner, Henry

Stoker, Abraham 1847-1912
See Stoker, Bram
See also CA 105; 150; DA; DA3; DAC; DAM MST, NOV; HGG; SATA 29

Stoker, Bram . **SSC 62; TCLC 8, 144; WLC**
See Stoker, Abraham
See also AAYA 23; BPFB 3; BRWS 3; BYA 5; CDBLB 1890-1914; DAB; DLB 304; LATS 1:1; NFS 18; RGEL 2; SUFW; TEA; WLIT 4

Stolz, Mary (Slattery) 1920- .... **CLC 12**
See also AAYA 8; AITN 1; CA 5-8R; CANR 13, 41, 112; JRDA; MAICYA 1, 2; SAAS 3; SATA 10, 71, 133; YAW

Stone, Irving 1903-1989 .... **CLC 7**
See also AITN 1; BPFB 3; CA 1-4R; 129; CAAS 3; CANR 1, 23; CPW; DA3; DAM POP; INT CANR-23; MTCW 1, 2; RHW; SATA 3; SATA-Obit 64

Stone, Oliver (William) 1946- .... **CLC 73**
See also AAYA 15; CA 110; CANR 55, 125

Stone, Robert (Anthony) 1937- ... **CLC 5, 23, 42, 175**
See also AMWS 5; BPFB 3; CA 85-88; CANR 23, 66, 95; CN 7; DLB 152; EWL 3; INT CANR-23; MTCW 1

Stone, Ruth 1915- .... **PC 53**
See also CA 45-48; CANR 2, 91; CP 7; CSW; DLB 105; PFS 19

Stone, Zachary
See Follett, Ken(neth Martin)

Stoppard, Tom 1937- ... **CLC 1, 3, 4, 5, 8, 15, 29, 34, 63, 91; DC 6; WLC**
See also BRWC 1; BRWR 2; BRWS 1; CA 81-84; CANR 39, 67, 125; CBD; CD 5; CDBLB 1960 to Present; DA; DA3; DAB; DAC; DAM DRAM, MST; DFS 2, 5, 8, 11, 13, 16; DLB 13, 233; DLBY 1985; EWL 3; LATS 1:2; MTCW 1, 2; RGEL 2; TEA; WLIT 4

Storey, David (Malcolm) 1933- . **CLC 2, 4, 5, 8**
See also BRWS 1; CA 81-84; CANR 36; CBD; CD 5; CN 7; DAM DRAM; DLB 13, 14, 207, 245; EWL 3; MTCW 1; RGEL 2

Storm, Hyemeyohsts 1935- ... **CLC 3; NNAL**
See also CA 81-84; CANR 45; DAM MULT

Storm, (Hans) Theodor (Woldsen)
1817-1888 .... **NCLC 1; SSC 27**
See also CDWLB 2; DLB 129; EW; RGSF 2; RGWL 2, 3

Storni, Alfonsina 1892-1938 . **HLC 2; PC 33; TCLC 5**
See also CA 104; 131; DAM MULT; DLB 283; HW 1; LAW

Stoughton, William 1631-1701 .... **LC 38**
See also DLB 24

Stout, Rex (Todhunter) 1886-1975 ..... **CLC 3**
See also AITN 2; BPFB 3; CA 61-64; CANR 71; CMW 4; DLB 306; MSW; RGAL 4

Stow, (Julian) Randolph 1935- ... **CLC 23, 48**
See also CA 13-16R; CANR 33; CN 7; DLB 260; MTCW 1; RGEL 2

Stowe, Harriet (Elizabeth) Beecher
1811-1896 .... **NCLC 3, 50, 133; WLC**
See also AAYA 53; AMWS 1; CDALB 1865-1917; DA; DA3; DAB; DAC; DAM MST, NOV; DLB 1, 12, 42, 74, 189, 239, 243; EXPN; JRDA; LAIT 2; MAICYA 1, 2; NFS 6; RGAL 4; TUS; YABC 1

Strabo c. 64B.C.-c. 25 .... **CMLC 37**
See also DLB 176

Strachey, (Giles) Lytton
1880-1932 .... **TCLC 12**
See also BRWS 2; CA 110; 178; DLB 149; DLBD 10; EWL 3; MTCW 2; NCFS 4

Stramm, August 1874-1915 .... **PC 50**
See also CA 195; EWL 3

Strand, Mark 1934- .. **CLC 6, 18, 41, 71; PC 63**
See also AMWS 4; CA 21-24R; CANR 40, 65, 100; CP 7; DAM POET; DLB 5; EWL 3; PAB; PFS 9, 18; RGAL 4; SATA 41

Stratton-Porter, Gene(va Grace) 1863-1924
See Porter, Gene(va Grace) Stratton
See also ANW; CA 137; CLR 87; DLB 221; DLBD 14; MAICYA 1, 2; SATA 15

Straub, Peter (Francis) 1943- ... **CLC 28, 107**
See also BEST 89:1; BPFB 3; CA 85-88; CANR 28, 65, 109; CPW; DAM POP; DLBY 1984; HGG; MTCW 1, 2; SUFW 2

Strauss, Botho 1944- .... **CLC 22**
See also CA 157; CWW 2; DLB 124

Strauss, Leo 1899-1973 .... **TCLC 141**
See also CA 101; 45-48; CANR 122

Streatfeild, (Mary) Noel
1897(?)-1986 .... **CLC 21**
See also CA 81-84; 120; CANR 31; CLR 17, 83; CWRI 5; DLB 160; MAICYA 1, 2; SATA 20; SATA-Obit 48

Stribling, T(homas) S(igismund)
1881-1965 .... **CLC 23**
See also CA 189; 107; CMW 4; DLB 9; RGAL 4

Strindberg, (Johan) August
1849-1912 ... **DC 18; TCLC 1, 8, 21, 47; WLC**
See also CA 104; 135; DA; DA3; DAB; DAC; DAM DRAM, MST; DFS 4, 9; DLB 259; EW 7; EWL 3; IDTP; LMFS 2; MTCW 2; RGWL 2, 3; TWA

Stringer, Arthur 1874-1950 .... **TCLC 37**
See also CA 161; DLB 92

Tabori, George 1914- .... **CLC 19**
See also CA 49-52; CANR 4, 69; CBD; CD 5; DLB 245

Tacitus c. 55-c. 117 .... **CMLC 56**
See also AW 2; CDWLB 1; DLB 211; RGWL 2, 3

Tagore, Rabindranath 1861-1941 .... **PC 8; SSC 48; TCLC 3, 53**
See also CA 104; 120; DA3; DAM DRAM, POET; EWL 3; MTCW 1, 2; PFS 18; RGEL 2; RGSF 2; RGWL 2, 3; TWA

Taine, Hippolyte Adolphe 1828-1893 .... **NCLC 15**
See also EW 7; GFL 1789 to the Present

Talayesva, Don C. 1890-(?) .... **NNAL**

Talese, Gay 1932- .... **CLC 37**
See also AITN 1; CA 1-4R; CANR 9, 58; DLB 185; INT CANR-9; MTCW 1, 2

Tallent, Elizabeth (Ann) 1954- .... **CLC 45**
See also CA 117; CANR 72; DLB 130

Tallmountain, Mary 1918-1997 .... **NNAL**
See also CA 146; 161; DLB 193

Tally, Ted 1952- .... **CLC 42**
See also CA 120; 124; CAD; CANR 125; CD 5; INT CA-124

Talvik, Heiti 1904-1947 .... **TCLC 87**
See also EWL 3

Tamayo y Baus, Manuel 1829-1898 .... **NCLC 1**

Tammsaare, A(nton) H(ansen) 1878-1940 .... **TCLC 27**
See also CA 164; CDWLB 4; DLB 220; EWL 3

Tam'si, Tchicaya U
See Tchicaya, Gerald Felix

Tan, Amy (Ruth) 1952- . **AAL; CLC 59, 120, 151**
See also AAYA 9, 48; AMWS 10; BEST 89:3; BPFB 3; CA 136; CANR 54, 105, 132; CDALBS; CN 7; CPW 1; DA3; DAM MULT, NOV, POP; DLB 173; EXPN; FW; LAIT 3, 5; MTCW 2; NFS 1, 13, 16; RGAL 4; SATA 75; SSFS 9; YAW

Tandem, Felix
See Spitteler, Carl (Friedrich Georg)

Tanizaki, Jun'ichiro 1886-1965 ... **CLC 8, 14, 28; SSC 21**
See Tanizaki Jun'ichiro
See also CA 93-96; 25-28R; MJW; MTCW 2; RGSF 2; RGWL 2

Tanizaki Jun'ichiro
See Tanizaki, Jun'ichiro
See also DLB 180; EWL 3

Tannen, Deborah F. 1945- .... **CLC 206**
See also CA 118; CANR 95

Tanner, William
See Amis, Kingsley (William)

Tao Lao
See Storni, Alfonsina

Tapahonso, Luci 1953- .... **NNAL; PC 65**
See also CA 145; CANR 72, 127; DLB 175

Tarantino, Quentin (Jerome) 1963- .... **CLC 125**
See also AAYA 58; CA 171; CANR 125

Tarassoff, Lev
See Troyat, Henri

Tarbell, Ida M(inerva) 1857-1944 . **TCLC 40**
See also CA 122; 181; DLB 47

Tarkington, (Newton) Booth 1869-1946 .... **TCLC 9**
See also BPFB 3; BYA 3; CA 110; 143; CWRI 5; DLB 9, 102; MTCW 2; RGAL 4; SATA 17

Tarkovskii, Andrei Arsen'evich
See Tarkovsky, Andrei (Arsenyevich)

Tarkovsky, Andrei (Arsenyevich) 1932-1986 .... **CLC 75**
See also CA 127

Tartt, Donna 1963- .... **CLC 76**
See also AAYA 56; CA 142

Tasso, Torquato 1544-1595 .... **LC 5, 94**
See also EFS 2; EW 2; RGWL 2, 3

Tate, (John Orley) Allen 1899-1979 .. **CLC 2, 4, 6, 9, 11, 14, 24; PC 50**
See also AMW; CA 5-8R; 85-88; CANR 32, 108; DLB 4, 45, 63; DLBD 17; EWL 3; MTCW 1, 2; RGAL 4; RHW

Tate, Ellalice
See Hibbert, Eleanor Alice Burford

Tate, James (Vincent) 1943- ..... **CLC 2, 6, 25**
See also CA 21-24R; CANR 29, 57, 114; CP 7; DLB 5, 169; EWL 3; PFS 10, 15; RGAL 4; WP

Tate, Nahum 1652(?)-1715 .... **LC 109**
See also DLB 80; RGEL 2

Tauler, Johannes c. 1300-1361 ...... **CMLC 37**
See also DLB 179; LMFS 1

Tavel, Ronald 1940- .... **CLC 6**
See also CA 21-24R; CAD; CANR 33; CD 5

Taviani, Paolo 1931- .... **CLC 70**
See also CA 153

Taylor, Bayard 1825-1878 .... **NCLC 89**
See also DLB 3, 189, 250, 254; RGAL 4

Taylor, C(ecil) P(hilip) 1929-1981 .... **CLC 27**
See also CA 25-28R; 105; CANR 47; CBD

Taylor, Edward 1642(?)-1729 . **LC 11; PC 63**
See also AMW; DA; DAB; DAC; DAM MST, POET; DLB 24; EXPP; RGAL 4; TUS

Taylor, Eleanor Ross 1920- .... **CLC 5**
See also CA 81-84; CANR 70

Taylor, Elizabeth 1932-1975 ..... **CLC 2, 4, 29**
See also CA 13-16R; CANR 9, 70; DLB 139; MTCW 1; RGEL 2; SATA 13

Taylor, Frederick Winslow 1856-1915 .... **TCLC 76**
See also CA 188

Taylor, Henry (Splawn) 1942- .... **CLC 44**
See also CA 33-36R; CAAS 7; CANR 31; CP 7; DLB 5; PFS 10

Taylor, Kamala (Purnaiya) 1924-2004
See Markandaya, Kamala
See also CA 77-80; 227; NFS 13

Taylor, Mildred D(elois) 1943- .... **CLC 21**
See also AAYA 10, 47; BW 1; BYA 3, 8; CA 85-88; CANR 25, 115; CLR 9, 59, 90; CSW; DLB 52; JRDA; LAIT 3; MAICYA 1, 2; SAAS 5; SATA 135; WYA; YAW

Taylor, Peter (Hillsman) 1917-1994 .. **CLC 1, 4, 18, 37, 44, 50, 71; SSC 10, 84**
See also AMWS 5; BPFB 3; CA 13-16R; 147; CANR 9, 50; CSW; DLB 218, 278; DLBY 1981, 1994; EWL 3; EXPS; INT CANR-9; MTCW 1, 2; RGSF 2; SSFS 9; TUS

Taylor, Robert Lewis 1912-1998 .... **CLC 14**
See also CA 1-4R; 170; CANR 3, 64; SATA 10

Tchekhov, Anton
See Chekhov, Anton (Pavlovich)

Tchicaya, Gerald Felix 1931-1988 .. **CLC 101**
See Tchicaya U Tam'si
See also CA 129; 125; CANR 81

Tchicaya U Tam'si
See Tchicaya, Gerald Felix
See also EWL 3

Teasdale, Sara 1884-1933 .... **PC 31; TCLC 4**
See also CA 104; 163; DLB 45; GLL 1; PFS 14; RGAL 4; SATA 32; TUS

Tecumseh 1768-1813 .... **NNAL**
See also DAM MULT

Tegner, Esaias 1782-1846 .... **NCLC 2**

Fujiwara no Teika 1162-1241 .... **CMLC 73**
See also DLB 203

Teilhard de Chardin, (Marie Joseph) Pierre 1881-1955 .... **TCLC 9**
See also CA 105; 210; GFL 1789 to the Present

Temple, Ann
See Mortimer, Penelope (Ruth)

Tennant, Emma (Christina) 1937- .. **CLC 13, 52**
See also BRWS 9; CA 65-68; CAAS 9; CANR 10, 38, 59, 88; CN 7; DLB 14; EWL 3; SFW 4

Tenneshaw, S. M.
See Silverberg, Robert

Tenney, Tabitha Gilman 1762-1837 .... **NCLC 122**
See also DLB 37, 200

Tennyson, Alfred 1809-1892 ... **NCLC 30, 65, 115; PC 6; WLC**
See also AAYA 50; BRW 4; CDBLB 1832-1890; DA; DA3; DAB; DAC; DAM MST, POET; DLB 32; EXPP; PAB; PFS 1, 2, 4, 11, 15, 19; RGEL 2; TEA; WLIT 4; WP

Teran, Lisa St. Aubin de .... **CLC 36**
See St. Aubin de Teran, Lisa

Terence c. 184B.C.-c. 159B.C. ...... **CMLC 14; DC 7**
See also AW 1; CDWLB 1; DLB 211; RGWL 2, 3; TWA

Teresa de Jesus, St. 1515-1582 .... **LC 18**

Terkel, Louis 1912-
See Terkel, Studs
See also CA 57-60; CANR 18, 45, 67, 132; DA3; MTCW 1, 2

Terkel, Studs .... **CLC 38**
See Terkel, Louis
See also AAYA 32; AITN 1; MTCW 2; TUS

Terry, C. V.
See Slaughter, Frank G(ill)

Terry, Megan 1932- .... **CLC 19; DC 13**
See also CA 77-80; CABS 3; CAD; CANR 43; CD 5; CWD; DFS 18; DLB 7, 249; GLL 2

Tertullian c. 155-c. 245 .... **CMLC 29**

Tertz, Abram
See Sinyavsky, Andrei (Donatevich)
See also RGSF 2

Tesich, Steve 1943(?)-1996 .... **CLC 40, 69**
See also CA 105; 152; CAD; DLBY 1983

Tesla, Nikola 1856-1943 .... **TCLC 88**

Teternikov, Fyodor Kuzmich 1863-1927
See Sologub, Fyodor
See also CA 104

Tevis, Walter 1928-1984 .... **CLC 42**
See also CA 113; SFW 4

Tey, Josephine .... **TCLC 14**
See Mackintosh, Elizabeth
See also DLB 77; MSW

Thackeray, William Makepeace 1811-1863 .... **NCLC 5, 14, 22, 43; WLC**
See also BRW 5; BRWC 2; CDBLB 1832-1890; DA; DA3; DAB; DAC; DAM MST, NOV; DLB 21, 55, 159, 163; NFS 13; RGEL 2; SATA 23; TEA; WLIT 3

Thakura, Ravindranatha
See Tagore, Rabindranath

Thames, C. H.
See Marlowe, Stephen

Tharoor, Shashi 1956- .... **CLC 70**
See also CA 141; CANR 91; CN 7

Thelwell, Michael Miles 1939- .... **CLC 22**
See also BW 2; CA 101

Theobald, Lewis, Jr.
See Lovecraft, H(oward) P(hillips)

Theocritus c. 310B.C.- .... **CMLC 45**
See also AW 1; DLB 176; RGWL 2, 3

Theodorescu, Ion N. 1880-1967
See Arghezi, Tudor
See also CA 116

Tolstoy, Leo (Nikolaevich) 1828-1910 . **SSC 9, 30, 45, 54; TCLC 4, 11, 17, 28, 44, 79; WLC**
See Tolstoi, Lev
See also AAYA 56; CA 104; 123; DA; DA3; DAB; DAC; DAM MST, NOV; DLB 238; EFS 2; EW 7; EXPS; IDTP; LAIT 2; LATS 1:1; LMFS 1; NFS 10; SATA 26; SSFS 5; TWA
Tolstoy, Count Leo
See Tolstoy, Leo (Nikolaevich)
Tomalin, Claire 1933- .... **CLC 166**
See also CA 89-92; CANR 52, 88; DLB 155
Tomasi di Lampedusa, Giuseppe 1896-1957
See Lampedusa, Giuseppe (Tomasi) di
See also CA 111; DLB 177; EWL 3
Tomlin, Lily .... **CLC 17**
See Tomlin, Mary Jean
Tomlin, Mary Jean 1939(?)-
See Tomlin, Lily
See also CA 117
Tomline, F. Latour
See Gilbert, W(illiam) S(chwenck)
Tomlinson, (Alfred) Charles 1927- .... **CLC 2, 4, 6, 13, 45; PC 17**
See also CA 5-8R; CANR 33; CP 7; DAM POET; DLB 40
Tomlinson, H(enry) M(ajor) 1873-1958 .... **TCLC 71**
See also CA 118; 161; DLB 36, 100, 195
Tonna, Charlotte Elizabeth 1790-1846 .... **NCLC 135**
See also DLB 163
Tonson, Jacob fl. 1655(?)-1736 .... **LC 86**
See also DLB 170
Toole, John Kennedy 1937-1969 ..... **CLC 19, 64**
See also BPFB 3; CA 104; DLBY 1981; MTCW 2
Toomer, Eugene
See Toomer, Jean
Toomer, Eugene Pinchback
See Toomer, Jean
Toomer, Jean 1894-1967 .. **BLC 3; CLC 1, 4, 13, 22; HR 3; PC 7; SSC 1, 45; WLCS**
See also AFAW 1, 2; AMWS 3, 9; BW 1; CA 85-88; CDALB 1917-1929; DA3; DAM MULT; DLB 45, 51; EWL 3; EXPP; EXPS; LMFS 2; MTCW 1, 2; NFS 11; RGAL 4; RGSF 2; SSFS 5
Toomer, Nathan Jean
See Toomer, Jean
Toomer, Nathan Pinchback
See Toomer, Jean
Torley, Luke
See Blish, James (Benjamin)
Tornimparte, Alessandra
See Ginzburg, Natalia
Torre, Raoul della
See Mencken, H(enry) L(ouis)
Torrence, Ridgely 1874-1950 .... **TCLC 97**
See also DLB 54, 249
Torrey, E(dwin) Fuller 1937- .... **CLC 34**
See also CA 119; CANR 71
Torsvan, Ben Traven
See Traven, B.
Torsvan, Benno Traven
See Traven, B.
Torsvan, Berick Traven
See Traven, B.
Torsvan, Berwick Traven
See Traven, B.
Torsvan, Bruno Traven
See Traven, B.
Torsvan, Traven
See Traven, B.
Tourneur, Cyril 1575(?)-1626 .... **LC 66**
See also BRW 2; DAM DRAM; DLB 58; RGEL 2
Tournier, Michel (Edouard) 1924- .... **CLC 6, 23, 36, 95**
See also CA 49-52; CANR 3, 36, 74; CWW 2; DLB 83; EWL 3; GFL 1789 to the Present; MTCW 1, 2; SATA 23
Tournimparte, Alessandra
See Ginzburg, Natalia
Towers, Ivar
See Kornbluth, C(yril) M.
Towne, Robert (Burton) 1936(?)- ..... **CLC 87**
See also CA 108; DLB 44; IDFW 3, 4
Townsend, Sue .... **CLC 61**
See Townsend, Susan Lilian
See also AAYA 28; CA 119; 127; CANR 65, 107; CBD; CD 5; CPW; CWD; DAB; DAC; DAM MST; DLB 271; INT CA-127; SATA 55, 93; SATA-Brief 48; YAW
Townsend, Susan Lilian 1946-
See Townsend, Sue
Townshend, Pete
See Townshend, Peter (Dennis Blandford)
Townshend, Peter (Dennis Blandford) 1945- .... **CLC 17, 42**
See also CA 107
Tozzi, Federigo 1883-1920 .... **TCLC 31**
See also CA 160; CANR 110; DLB 264; EWL 3
Tracy, Don(ald Fiske) 1905-1970(?)
See Queen, Ellery
See also CA 1-4R; 176; CANR 2
Trafford, F. G.
See Riddell, Charlotte
Traherne, Thomas 1637(?)-1674 .... **LC 99**
See also BRW 2; DLB 131; PAB; RGEL 2
Traill, Catharine Parr 1802-1899 .. **NCLC 31**
See also DLB 99
Trakl, Georg 1887-1914 .... **PC 20; TCLC 5**
See also CA 104; 165; EW 10; EWL 3; LMFS 2; MTCW 2; RGWL 2, 3
Tranquilli, Secondino
See Silone, Ignazio
Transtroemer, Tomas Gosta
See Transtromer, Tomas (Goesta)
Transtromer, Tomas (Gosta)
See Transtromer, Tomas (Goesta)
See also CWW 2
Transtromer, Tomas (Goesta) 1931- .... **CLC 52, 65**
See Transtromer, Tomas (Gosta)
See also CA 117; 129; CAAS 17; CANR 115; DAM POET; DLB 257; EWL 3; PFS 21
Transtromer, Tomas Gosta
See Transtromer, Tomas (Goesta)
Traven, B. 1882(?)-1969 .... **CLC 8, 11**
See also CA 19-20; 25-28R; CAP 2; DLB 9, 56; EWL 3; MTCW 1; RGAL 4
Trediakovsky, Vasilii Kirillovich 1703-1769 .... **LC 68**
See also DLB 150
Treitel, Jonathan 1959- .... **CLC 70**
See also CA 210; DLB 267
Trelawny, Edward John 1792-1881 .... **NCLC 85**
See also DLB 110, 116, 144
Tremain, Rose 1943- .... **CLC 42**
See also CA 97-100; CANR 44, 95; CN 7; DLB 14, 271; RGSF 2; RHW
Tremblay, Michel 1942- .... **CLC 29, 102**
See also CA 116; 128; CCA 1; CWW 2; DAC; DAM MST; DLB 60; EWL 3; GLL 1; MTCW 1, 2
Trevanian .... **CLC 29**
See Whitaker, Rod(ney)
Trevor, Glen
See Hilton, James
Trevor, William .. **CLC 7, 9, 14, 25, 71, 116; SSC 21, 58**
See Cox, William Trevor
See also BRWS 4; CBD; CD 5; CN 7; DLB 14, 139; EWL 3; LATS 1:2; MTCW 2; RGEL 2; RGSF 2; SSFS 10
Trifonov, Iurii (Valentinovich)
See Trifonov, Yuri (Valentinovich)
See also DLB 302; RGWL 2, 3
Trifonov, Yuri (Valentinovich) 1925-1981 .... **CLC 45**
See Trifonov, Iurii (Valentinovich); Trifonov, Yury Valentinovich
See also CA 126; 103; MTCW 1
Trifonov, Yury Valentinovich
See Trifonov, Yuri (Valentinovich)
See also EWL 3
Trilling, Diana (Rubin) 1905-1996 . **CLC 129**
See also CA 5-8R; 154; CANR 10, 46; INT CANR-10; MTCW 1, 2
Trilling, Lionel 1905-1975 ..... **CLC 9, 11, 24; SSC 75**
See also AMWS 3; CA 9-12R; 61-64; CANR 10, 105; DLB 28, 63; EWL 3; INT CANR-10; MTCW 1, 2; RGAL 4; TUS
Trimball, W. H.
See Mencken, H(enry) L(ouis)
Tristan
See Gomez de la Serna, Ramon
Tristram
See Housman, A(lfred) E(dward)
Trogdon, William (Lewis) 1939-
See Heat-Moon, William Least
See also CA 115; 119; CANR 47, 89; CPW; INT CA-119
Trollope, Anthony 1815-1882 .... **NCLC 6, 33, 101; SSC 28; WLC**
See also BRW 5; CDBLB 1832-1890; DA; DA3; DAB; DAC; DAM MST, NOV; DLB 21, 57, 159; RGEL 2; RGSF 2; SATA 22
Trollope, Frances 1779-1863 .... **NCLC 30**
See also DLB 21, 166
Trollope, Joanna 1943- .... **CLC 186**
See also CA 101; CANR 58, 95; CPW; DLB 207; RHW
Trotsky, Leon 1879-1940 .... **TCLC 22**
See also CA 118; 167
Trotter (Cockburn), Catharine 1679-1749 .... **LC 8**
See also DLB 84, 252
Trotter, Wilfred 1872-1939 .... **TCLC 97**
Trout, Kilgore
See Farmer, Philip Jose
Trow, George W. S. 1943- .... **CLC 52**
See also CA 126; CANR 91
Troyat, Henri 1911- .... **CLC 23**
See also CA 45-48; CANR 2, 33, 67, 117; GFL 1789 to the Present; MTCW 1
Trudeau, G(arretson) B(eekman) 1948-
See Trudeau, Garry B.
See also AAYA 60; CA 81-84; CANR 31; SATA 35
Trudeau, Garry B. .... **CLC 12**
See Trudeau, G(arretson) B(eekman)
See also AAYA 10; AITN 2
Truffaut, Francois 1932-1984 ... **CLC 20, 101**
See also CA 81-84; 113; CANR 34
Trumbo, Dalton 1905-1976 .... **CLC 19**
See also CA 21-24R; 69-72; CANR 10; DLB 26; IDFW 3, 4; YAW
Trumbull, John 1750-1831 .... **NCLC 30**
See also DLB 31; RGAL 4
Trundlett, Helen B.
See Eliot, T(homas) S(tearns)
Truth, Sojourner 1797(?)-1883 ...... **NCLC 94**
See also DLB 239; FW; LAIT 2

Villa, Jose Garcia 1914-1997 .... **AAL; PC 22**
See also CA 25-28R; CANR 12, 118; EWL 3; EXPP

Wallace, David Foster 1962- ... **CLC 50, 114; SSC 68**
See also AAYA 50; AMWS 10; CA 132; CANR 59, 133; DA3; MTCW 2
Wallace, Dexter
See Masters, Edgar Lee
Wallace, (Richard Horatio) Edgar 1875-1932 .... **TCLC 57**
See also CA 115; 218; CMW 4; DLB 70; MSW; RGEL 2
Wallace, Irving 1916-1990 .... **CLC 7, 13**
See also AITN 1; BPFB 3; CA 1-4R; 132; CAAS 1; CANR 1, 27; CPW; DAM NOV, POP; INT CANR-27; MTCW 1, 2
Wallant, Edward Lewis 1926-1962 ... **CLC 5, 10**
See also CA 1-4R; CANR 22; DLB 2, 28, 143, 299; EWL 3; MTCW 1, 2; RGAL 4
Wallas, Graham 1858-1932 .... **TCLC 91**
Waller, Edmund 1606-1687 .... **LC 86**
See also BRW 2; DAM POET; DLB 126; PAB; RGEL 2
Walley, Byron
See Card, Orson Scott
Walpole, Horace 1717-1797 .... **LC 2, 49**
See also BRW 3; DLB 39, 104, 213; HGG; LMFS 1; RGEL 2; SUFW 1; TEA
Walpole, Hugh (Seymour) 1884-1941 .... **TCLC 5**
See also CA 104; 165; DLB 34; HGG; MTCW 2; RGEL 2; RHW
Walrond, Eric (Derwent) 1898-1966 .... **HR 3**
See also BW 1; CA 125; DLB 51
Walser, Martin 1927- .... **CLC 27, 183**
See also CA 57-60; CANR 8, 46; CWW 2; DLB 75, 124; EWL 3
Walser, Robert 1878-1956 ..... **SSC 20; TCLC 18**
See also CA 118; 165; CANR 100; DLB 66; EWL 3
Walsh, Gillian Paton
See Paton Walsh, Gillian
Walsh, Jill Paton .... **CLC 35**
See Paton Walsh, Gillian
See also CLR 2, 65; WYA
Walter, Villiam Christian
See Andersen, Hans Christian
Walters, Anna L(ee) 1946- .... **NNAL**
See also CA 73-76
Walther von der Vogelweide c. 1170-1228 .... **CMLC 56**
Walton, Izaak 1593-1683 .... **LC 72**
See also BRW 2; CDBLB Before 1660; DLB 151, 213; RGEL 2
Wambaugh, Joseph (Aloysius), Jr. 1937- .... **CLC 3, 18**
See also AITN 1; BEST 89:3; BPFB 3; CA 33-36R; CANR 42, 65, 115; CMW 4; CPW 1; DA3; DAM NOV, POP; DLB 6; DLBY 1983; MSW; MTCW 1, 2
Wang Wei 699(?)-761(?) .... **PC 18**
See also TWA
Warburton, William 1698-1779 .... **LC 97**
See also DLB 104
Ward, Arthur Henry Sarsfield 1883-1959
See Rohmer, Sax
See also CA 108; 173; CMW 4; HGG
Ward, Douglas Turner 1930- .... **CLC 19**
See also BW 1; CA 81-84; CAD; CANR 27; CD 5; DLB 7, 38
Ward, E. D.
See Lucas, E(dward) V(errall)
Ward, Mrs. Humphry 1851-1920
See Ward, Mary Augusta
See also RGEL 2
Ward, Mary Augusta 1851-1920 ... **TCLC 55**
See Ward, Mrs. Humphry
See also DLB 18
Ward, Nathaniel 1578(?)-1652 .... **LC 114**
See also DLB 24
Ward, Peter
See Faust, Frederick (Schiller)
Warhol, Andy 1928(?)-1987 .... **CLC 20**
See also AAYA 12; BEST 89:4; CA 89-92; 121; CANR 34
Warner, Francis (Robert le Plastrier) 1937- .... **CLC 14**
See also CA 53-56; CANR 11
Warner, Marina 1946- .... **CLC 59**
See also CA 65-68; CANR 21, 55, 118; CN 7; DLB 194
Warner, Rex (Ernest) 1905-1986 ...... **CLC 45**
See also CA 89-92; 119; DLB 15; RGEL 2; RHW
Warner, Susan (Bogert) 1819-1885 .... **NCLC 31, 146**
See also DLB 3, 42, 239, 250, 254
Warner, Sylvia (Constance) Ashton
See Ashton-Warner, Sylvia (Constance)
Warner, Sylvia Townsend 1893-1978 .. **CLC 7, 19; SSC 23; TCLC 131**
See also BRWS 7; CA 61-64; 77-80; CANR 16, 60, 104; DLB 34, 139; EWL 3; FANT; FW; MTCW 1, 2; RGEL 2; RGSF 2; RHW
Warren, Mercy Otis 1728-1814 ..... **NCLC 13**
See also DLB 31, 200; RGAL 4; TUS
Warren, Robert Penn 1905-1989 .. **CLC 1, 4, 6, 8, 10, 13, 18, 39, 53, 59; PC 37; SSC 4, 58; WLC**
See also AITN 1; AMW; AMWC 2; BPFB 3; BYA 1; CA 13-16R; 129; CANR 10, 47; CDALB 1968-1988; DA; DA3; DAB; DAC; DAM MST, NOV, POET; DLB 2, 48, 152; DLBY 1980, 1989; EWL 3; INT CANR-10; MTCW 1, 2; NFS 13; RGAL 4; RGSF 2; RHW; SATA 46; SATA-Obit 63; SSFS 8; TUS
Warrigal, Jack
See Furphy, Joseph
Warshofsky, Isaac
See Singer, Isaac Bashevis
Warton, Joseph 1722-1800 .... **NCLC 118**
See also DLB 104, 109; RGEL 2
Warton, Thomas 1728-1790 .... **LC 15, 82**
See also DAM POET; DLB 104, 109; RGEL 2
Waruk, Kona
See Harris, (Theodore) Wilson
Warung, Price .... **TCLC 45**
See Astley, William
See also DLB 230; RGEL 2
Warwick, Jarvis
See Garner, Hugh
See also CCA 1
Washington, Alex
See Harris, Mark
Washington, Booker T(aliaferro) 1856-1915 .... **BLC 3; TCLC 10**
See also BW 1; CA 114; 125; DA3; DAM MULT; LAIT 2; RGAL 4; SATA 28
Washington, George 1732-1799 .... **LC 25**
See also DLB 31
Wassermann, (Karl) Jakob 1873-1934 .... **TCLC 6**
See also CA 104; 163; DLB 66; EWL 3
Wasserstein, Wendy 1950- ... **CLC 32, 59, 90, 183; DC 4**
See also CA 121; 129; CABS 3; CAD; CANR 53, 75, 128; CD 5; CWD; DA3; DAM DRAM; DFS 5, 17; DLB 228; EWL 3; FW; INT CA-129; MTCW 2; SATA 94
Waterhouse, Keith (Spencer) 1929- . **CLC 47**
See also CA 5-8R; CANR 38, 67, 109; CBD; CN 7; DLB 13, 15; MTCW 1, 2
Waters, Frank (Joseph) 1902-1995 .. **CLC 88**
See also CA 5-8R; 149; CAAS 13; CANR 3, 18, 63, 121; DLB 212; DLBY 1986; RGAL 4; TCWW 2
Waters, Mary C. .... **CLC 70**
Waters, Roger 1944- .... **CLC 35**
Watkins, Frances Ellen
See Harper, Frances Ellen Watkins
Watkins, Gerrold
See Malzberg, Barry N(athaniel)
Watkins, Gloria Jean 1952(?)- .... **CLC 94**
See also BW 2; CA 143; CANR 87, 126; DLB 246; MTCW 2; SATA 115
Watkins, Paul 1964- .... **CLC 55**
See also CA 132; CANR 62, 98
Watkins, Vernon Phillips 1906-1967 .... **CLC 43**
See also CA 9-10; 25-28R; CAP 1; DLB 20; EWL 3; RGEL 2
Watson, Irving S.
See Mencken, H(enry) L(ouis)
Watson, John H.
See Farmer, Philip Jose
Watson, Richard F.
See Silverberg, Robert
Watts, Ephraim
See Horne, Richard Henry Hengist
Watts, Isaac 1674-1748 .... **LC 98**
See also DLB 95; RGEL 2; SATA 52
Waugh, Auberon (Alexander) 1939-2001 .... **CLC 7**
See also CA 45-48; 192; CANR 6, 22, 92; DLB 14, 194
Waugh, Evelyn (Arthur St. John) 1903-1966 .. **CLC 1, 3, 8, 13, 19, 27, 44, 107; SSC 41; WLC**
See also BPFB 3; BRW 7; CA 85-88; 25-28R; CANR 22; CDBLB 1914-1945; DA; DA3; DAB; DAC; DAM MST, NOV, POP; DLB 15, 162, 195; EWL 3; MTCW 1, 2; NFS 13, 17; RGEL 2; RGSF 2; TEA; WLIT 4
Waugh, Harriet 1944- .... **CLC 6**
See also CA 85-88; CANR 22
Ways, C. R.
See Blount, Roy (Alton), Jr.
Waystaff, Simon
See Swift, Jonathan
Webb, Beatrice (Martha Potter) 1858-1943 .... **TCLC 22**
See also CA 117; 162; DLB 190; FW
Webb, Charles (Richard) 1939- .... **CLC 7**
See also CA 25-28R; CANR 114
Webb, Frank J. .... **NCLC 143**
See also DLB 50
Webb, James H(enry), Jr. 1946- ...... **CLC 22**
See also CA 81-84
Webb, Mary Gladys (Meredith) 1881-1927 .... **TCLC 24**
See also CA 182; 123; DLB 34; FW
Webb, Mrs. Sidney
See Webb, Beatrice (Martha Potter)
Webb, Phyllis 1927- .... **CLC 18**
See also CA 104; CANR 23; CCA 1; CP 7; CWP; DLB 53
Webb, Sidney (James) 1859-1947 .. **TCLC 22**
See also CA 117; 163; DLB 190
Webber, Andrew Lloyd .... **CLC 21**
See Lloyd Webber, Andrew
See also DFS 7
Weber, Lenora Mattingly 1895-1971 .... **CLC 12**
See also CA 19-20; 29-32R; CAP 1; SATA 2; SATA-Obit 26
Weber, Max 1864-1920 .... **TCLC 69**
See also CA 109; 189; DLB 296

Williams, John A(lfred) 1925- . **BLC 3; CLC 5, 13**
See also AFAW 2; BW 2, 3; CA 53-56, 195; CAAE 195; CAAS 3; CANR 6, 26, 51, 118; CN 7; CSW; DAM MULT; DLB 2, 33; EWL 3; INT CANR-6; RGAL 4; SFW 4
Williams, Jonathan (Chamberlain) 1929- .... **CLC 13**
See also CA 9-12R; CAAS 12; CANR 8, 108; CP 7; DLB 5
Williams, Joy 1944- .... **CLC 31**
See also CA 41-44R; CANR 22, 48, 97
Williams, Norman 1952- .... **CLC 39**
See also CA 118
Williams, Sherley Anne 1944-1999 ... **BLC 3; CLC 89**
See also AFAW 2; BW 2, 3; CA 73-76; 185; CANR 25, 82; DAM MULT, POET; DLB 41; INT CANR-25; SATA 78; SATA-Obit 116
Williams, Shirley
See Williams, Sherley Anne
Williams, Tennessee 1911-1983 . **CLC 1, 2, 5, 7, 8, 11, 15, 19, 30, 39, 45, 71, 111; DC 4; SSC 81; WLC**
See also AAYA 31; AITN 1, 2; AMW; AMWC 1; CA 5-8R; 108; CABS 3; CAD; CANR 31, 132; CDALB 1941-1968; DA; DA3; DAB; DAC; DAM DRAM, MST; DFS 17; DLB 7; DLBD 4; DLBY 1983; EWL 3; GLL 1; LAIT 4; LATS 1:2; MTCW 1, 2; RGAL 4; TUS
Williams, Thomas (Alonzo) 1926-1990 .... **CLC 14**
See also CA 1-4R; 132; CANR 2
Williams, William C.
See Williams, William Carlos
Williams, William Carlos 1883-1963 .... **CLC 1, 2, 5, 9, 13, 22, 42, 67; PC 7; SSC 31**
See also AAYA 46; AMW; AMWR 1; CA 89-92; CANR 34; CDALB 1917-1929; DA; DA3; DAB; DAC; DAM MST, POET; DLB 4, 16, 54, 86; EWL 3; EXPP; MTCW 1, 2; NCFS 4; PAB; PFS 1, 6, 11; RGAL 4; RGSF 2; TUS; WP
Williamson, David (Keith) 1942- ..... **CLC 56**
See also CA 103; CANR 41; CD 5; DLB 289
Williamson, Ellen Douglas 1905-1984
See Douglas, Ellen
See also CA 17-20R; 114; CANR 39
Williamson, Jack .... **CLC 29**
See Williamson, John Stewart
See also CAAS 8; DLB 8; SCFW 2
Williamson, John Stewart 1908-
See Williamson, Jack
See also CA 17-20R; CANR 23, 70; SFW 4
Willie, Frederick
See Lovecraft, H(oward) P(hillips)
Willingham, Calder (Baynard, Jr.) 1922-1995 .... **CLC 5, 51**
See also CA 5-8R; 147; CANR 3; CSW; DLB 2, 44; IDFW 3, 4; MTCW 1
Willis, Charles
See Clarke, Arthur C(harles)
Willy
See Colette, (Sidonie-Gabrielle)
Willy, Colette
See Colette, (Sidonie-Gabrielle)
See also GLL 1
Wilmot, John 1647-1680 .... **LC 75; PC 66**
See Rochester
See also BRW 2; DLB 131; PAB
Wilson, A(ndrew) N(orman) 1950- .. **CLC 33**
See also BRWS 6; CA 112; 122; CN 7; DLB 14, 155, 194; MTCW 2
Wilson, Angus (Frank Johnstone) 1913-1991 . **CLC 2, 3, 5, 25, 34; SSC 21**
See also BRWS 1; CA 5-8R; 134; CANR 21; DLB 15, 139, 155; EWL 3; MTCW 1, 2; RGEL 2; RGSF 2
Wilson, August 1945- ... **BLC 3; CLC 39, 50, 63, 118; DC 2; WLCS**
See also AAYA 16; AFAW 2; AMWS 8; BW 2, 3; CA 115; 122; CAD; CANR 42, 54, 76, 128; CD 5; DA; DA3; DAB; DAC; DAM DRAM, MST, MULT; DFS 3, 7, 15, 17; DLB 228; EWL 3; LAIT 4; LATS 1:2; MTCW 1, 2; RGAL 4
Wilson, Brian 1942- .... **CLC 12**
Wilson, Colin 1931- .... **CLC 3, 14**
See also CA 1-4R; CAAS 5; CANR 1, 22, 33, 77; CMW 4; CN 7; DLB 14, 194; HGG; MTCW 1; SFW 4
Wilson, Dirk
See Pohl, Frederik
Wilson, Edmund 1895-1972 .. **CLC 1, 2, 3, 8, 24**
See also AMW; CA 1-4R; 37-40R; CANR 1, 46, 110; DLB 63; EWL 3; MTCW 1, 2; RGAL 4; TUS
Wilson, Ethel Davis (Bryant) 1888(?)-1980 .... **CLC 13**
See also CA 102; DAC; DAM POET; DLB 68; MTCW 1; RGEL 2
Wilson, Harriet
See Wilson, Harriet E. Adams
See also DLB 239
Wilson, Harriet E.
See Wilson, Harriet E. Adams
See also DLB 243
Wilson, Harriet E. Adams 1827(?)-1863(?) .... **BLC 3; NCLC 78**
See Wilson, Harriet; Wilson, Harriet E.
See also DAM MULT; DLB 50
Wilson, John 1785-1854 .... **NCLC 5**
Wilson, John (Anthony) Burgess 1917-1993
See Burgess, Anthony
See also CA 1-4R; 143; CANR 2, 46; DA3; DAC; DAM NOV; MTCW 1, 2; NFS 15; TEA
Wilson, Lanford 1937- .. **CLC 7, 14, 36, 197; DC 19**
See also CA 17-20R; CABS 3; CAD; CANR 45, 96; CD 5; DAM DRAM; DFS 4, 9, 12, 16, 20; DLB 7; EWL 3; TUS
Wilson, Robert M. 1941- .... **CLC 7, 9**
See also CA 49-52; CAD; CANR 2, 41; CD 5; MTCW 1
Wilson, Robert McLiam 1964- .... **CLC 59**
See also CA 132; DLB 267
Wilson, Sloan 1920-2003 .... **CLC 32**
See also CA 1-4R; 216; CANR 1, 44; CN 7
Wilson, Snoo 1948- .... **CLC 33**
See also CA 69-72; CBD; CD 5
Wilson, William S(mith) 1932- .... **CLC 49**
See also CA 81-84
Wilson, (Thomas) Woodrow 1856-1924 .... **TCLC 79**
See also CA 166; DLB 47
Wilson and Warnke eds. .... **CLC 65**
Winchilsea, Anne (Kingsmill) Finch 1661-1720
See Finch, Anne
See also RGEL 2
Windham, Basil
See Wodehouse, P(elham) G(renville)
Wingrove, David (John) 1954- .... **CLC 68**
See also CA 133; SFW 4
Winnemucca, Sarah 1844-1891 .... **NCLC 79; NNAL**
See also DAM MULT; DLB 175; RGAL 4
Winstanley, Gerrard 1609-1676 .... **LC 52**
Wintergreen, Jane
See Duncan, Sara Jeannette
Winters, Janet Lewis .... **CLC 41**
See Lewis, Janet
See also DLBY 1987
Winters, (Arthur) Yvor 1900-1968 .... **CLC 4, 8, 32**
See also AMWS 2; CA 11-12; 25-28R; CAP 1; DLB 48; EWL 3; MTCW 1; RGAL 4
Winterson, Jeanette 1959- .... **CLC 64, 158**
See also BRWS 4; CA 136; CANR 58, 116; CN 7; CPW; DA3; DAM POP; DLB 207, 261; FANT; FW; GLL 1; MTCW 2; RHW
Winthrop, John 1588-1649 .... **LC 31, 107**
See also DLB 24, 30
Wirth, Louis 1897-1952 .... **TCLC 92**
See also CA 210
Wiseman, Frederick 1930- .... **CLC 20**
See also CA 159
Wister, Owen 1860-1938 .... **TCLC 21**
See also BPFB 3; CA 108; 162; DLB 9, 78, 186; RGAL 4; SATA 62; TCWW 2
Wither, George 1588-1667 .... **LC 96**
See also DLB 121; RGEL 2
Witkacy
See Witkiewicz, Stanislaw Ignacy
Witkiewicz, Stanislaw Ignacy 1885-1939 .... **TCLC 8**
See also CA 105; 162; CDWLB 4; DLB 215; EW 10; EWL 3; RGWL 2, 3; SFW 4
Wittgenstein, Ludwig (Josef Johann) 1889-1951 .... **TCLC 59**
See also CA 113; 164; DLB 262; MTCW 2
Wittig, Monique 1935(?)-2003 .... **CLC 22**
See also CA 116; 135; 212; CWW 2; DLB 83; EWL 3; FW; GLL 1
Wittlin, Jozef 1896-1976 .... **CLC 25**
See also CA 49-52; 65-68; CANR 3; EWL 3
Wodehouse, P(elham) G(renville) 1881-1975 . **CLC 1, 2, 5, 10, 22; SSC 2; TCLC 108**
See also AITN 2; BRWS 3; CA 45-48; 57-60; CANR 3, 33; CDBLB 1914-1945; CPW 1; DA3; DAB; DAC; DAM NOV; DLB 34, 162; EWL 3; MTCW 1, 2; RGEL 2; RGSF 2; SATA 22; SSFS 10
Woiwode, L.
See Woiwode, Larry (Alfred)
Woiwode, Larry (Alfred) 1941- ... **CLC 6, 10**
See also CA 73-76; CANR 16, 94; CN 7; DLB 6; INT CANR-16
Wojciechowska, Maia (Teresa) 1927-2002 .... **CLC 26**
See also AAYA 8, 46; BYA 3; CA 9-12R, 183; 209; CAAE 183; CANR 4, 41; CLR 1; JRDA; MAICYA 1, 2; SAAS 1; SATA 1, 28, 83; SATA-Essay 104; SATA-Obit 134; YAW
Wojtyla, Karol
See John Paul II, Pope
Wolf, Christa 1929- .... **CLC 14, 29, 58, 150**
See also CA 85-88; CANR 45, 123; CDWLB 2; CWW 2; DLB 75; EWL 3; FW; MTCW 1; RGWL 2, 3; SSFS 14
Wolf, Naomi 1962- .... **CLC 157**
See also CA 141; CANR 110; FW
Wolfe, Gene (Rodman) 1931- .... **CLC 25**
See also AAYA 35; CA 57-60; CAAS 9; CANR 6, 32, 60; CPW; DAM POP; DLB 8; FANT; MTCW 2; SATA 118; SCFW 2; SFW 4; SUFW 2
Wolfe, George C. 1954- .... **BLCS; CLC 49**
See also CA 149; CAD; CD 5
Wolfe, Thomas (Clayton) 1900-1938 ...... **SSC 33; TCLC 4, 13, 29, 61; WLC**
See also AMW; BPFB 3; CA 104; 132; CANR 102; CDALB 1929-1941; DA; DA3; DAB; DAC; DAM MST, NOV;

Literary Criticism Series Cumulative Topic Index

This index lists all topic entries in Gale's *Children's Literature Review* (CLR), *Classical and Medieval Literature Criticism* (CMLC), *Contemporary Literary Criticism* (CLC), *Drama Criticism* (DC), *Literature Criticism from 1400 to 1800* (LC), *Nineteenth-Century Literature Criticism* (NCLC), *Short Story Criticism* (SSC), and *Twentieth-Century Literary Criticism* (TCLC). The index also lists topic entries in the Gale Critical Companion Collection, which includes the following publications: *The Beat Generation* (BG), and *Harlem Renaissance* (HR).

Topic Index

CLC Cumulative Nationality Index

Nationality Index

Nationality Index

Nationality Index

ESTONIAN

FIJI ISLANDER

FILIPINO

FINNISH

FRENCH

Nationality Index

SALVADORAN

SCOTTISH

SENEGALESE

SLOVENIAN

SOMALIAN

SOUTH AFRICAN

SPANISH

SRI LANKAN

ST. LUCIAN

SWEDISH

SWISS

TRINIDADIAN

TURKISH

UGANDAN

URUGUAYAN

WELSH

YUGOSLAVIAN

CLC-213 Title Index

ISBN 0-7876-7983-6
90000
9 780787 679835